Basic Statistical Ideas for Managers

SECOND EDITION

David K. Hildebrand
Late of Wharton School, University of Pennsylvania

R. Lyman Ott

J. Brian Gray
University of Alabama

With Cases by

J. Brian Gray

Lawrence H. Peters
Texas Christian University

Australia • Canada • Mexico • Singapore • Spain
United Kingdom • United States

THOMSON

BROOKS/COLE

Publisher: Curt Hinrichs

Developmental Editor: Cheryll Linthicum

Assistant Editor: Ann Day

Editorial Assistant: Katherine Brayton

Technology Project Manager: Burke Taft

Marketing Manager: Tom Ziolkowski

Marketing Assistant: Jessica Bothwell

Advertising Project Manager: Nathaniel Bergson-Michelson

Project Manager, Editorial Production: Sandra Craig

Creative Director: Rob Hugel

Print/Media Buyer: Barbara Britton

Permissions Editor: Sarah Harkrader

Production: Martha Emry Production Services

Text Designer: Lisa Devenish

Copy Editor: Pamela Rockwell

Illustrator: Atherton Customs

Cover Designer: Bill Stanton

Cover Image: Robert Daly/Getty Images

Cover Printer: Phoenix Color Corp

Compositor: ATLIS Graphics

Printer: Quebecor World/Taunton

Printed in the United States of America

1 2 3 4 5 6 7 08 07 06 05 04

For more information about our products, contact us at:
Thomson Learning Academic Resource Center
1-800-423-0563

For permission to use material from this text or prouduct, submit a request online at
http://www.thomsonrights.com.

Any additional questions about permissions can be submitted by email to **thomsonrights@thomson.com.**

Library of Congress Control Number: 2003113508

Student Edition: ISBN 0-534-37805-6

Instructor's Edition: ISBN 0-534-49188-X

Thomson Brooks/Cole
10 Davis Drive
Belmont, CA 94002
USA

Asia
Thomson Learning
5 Shenton Way #01-01
UIC Building
Singapore 068808

Australia/New Zealand
Thomson Learning
102 Dodds Street
Southbank, Victoria 3006
Australia

Canada
Nelson
1120 Birchmount Road
Toronto, Ontario M1K 5G4
Canada

Europe/Middle East/Africa
Thomson Learning
High Holborn House
50/51 Bedford Row
London WC1R 4LR
United Kingdom

Latin America
Thomson Learning
Seneca, 53
Colonia Polanco
11560 Mexico D.F.
Mexico

Spain/Portugal
Paraninfo
Calle Magallanes, 25
28015 Madrid, Spain

Dedication

David K. Hildebrand was a distinguished author and professor of statistics at the Wharton School of the University of Pennsylvania. Dave was a vital part of the community of business statistics educators and is sorely missed by those of us who knew him well. Dave was enormously committed to teaching, especially at the introductory level. He often said that many colleges and universities had the situation entirely backwards—newly minted teachers should be relegated to the easy, advanced courses for a while, until they learn to teach the difficult, introductory course. After being diagnosed with cancer, he continued to teach the introductory course in statistics to Wharton's MBA's, at a level which won him an award for "best teaching in the core curriculum."

The titles of Dave's books, *Statistical Thinking for Managers,* for example, were not chosen capriciously. Dave was a great believer in thinking and was particularly concerned with developing critical thinking in students—helping them to write and think clearly. In light of his long-term association with the Making Statistics More Effective in Schools of Business conferences (www.msmesb.org), Dave described three fundamental choices he made about teaching statistics:

1. **Students should think, computers should calculate.** An introductory statistics course should emphasize core ideas rather than computation; a computer package should take care of almost all substantial arithmetic.
2. **Graphical looks at data should precede formal analysis.** Dave's long-time motto for the introductory statistics course was DTDP: Draw The Doggone Picture. (In stressful moments, he replaced "Doggone" with an alternative.)
3. **A manager must be literate in the practice of data analysis.** The important statistical skills for a fledgling manager to learn are choice of method, intelligent interpretation of results, and critical thought about assumptions.

Since Dave's death I have heard from many colleagues that his sessions at national meetings were always engaging, informal, and vital. In the introductory classroom he was even better—regularly keeping 150 students at a time involved in the class laughing, learning, and questioning. He could always read the room and keep things fresh and engaging. His syllabi were written on a word processor, not stone, and he refused to be one of those instructors who pulls out their notes every year and blows the dust off them. Dave was committed to listening to students, always getting to the heart of the problem with elegant simplicity. When students complained about not seeing the big picture, he started writing his outline for the day on the blackboard before class. Problem solved.

I miss Dave for many reasons, but most of all because he was really, really funny. A quick example: Remembering his youth and college days in Minnesota, Dave used to tell his family that his dream was to create for his alma mater (Carleton College) a fund for the removal of snow and ice, giving new meaning to the term "slush fund." The fund exists now, in his memory.

Thomas E. Love
Case Western Reserve University

BRIEF CONTENTS

CONTENTS

This book was written for a one-semester course in statistics for management students. The time limitations of a one-semester course force authors and instructors to focus on the most essential ideas, the concepts with the greatest value added. We believe that such a course demands a focus on concepts, interpretation, and assumptions, and must rely on computer software to carry out computations.

Emphasis

The first edition of this book grew out of a need for modifying the traditional number-grinding undergraduate and MBA business statistics course, and specifically from the redesign of the Wharton School's MBA statistics course, as originally developed by the first author of the book. The course and the book pare the traditional probability and statistical inference content to a minimum in order to focus on issues of variability, data exploration, and regression. Almost all the exercises and a great many of the text examples rely on computer software to do the arithmetic.

The first edition of this text was an abridged and substantially revised version of *Statistical Thinking for Managers,* Third Edition, by David K. Hildebrand and R. Lyman Ott. This second edition is a substantive revision of the first edition. Again, much of the probability material has been omitted from this book, along with time series concepts and decision theory. Of course, we believe that those topics are valuable, but the limitations of a one-semester course require hard choices about content.

Both this book and its parent have benefited greatly from ideas raised in the annual conferences on Making Statistics More Effective in Schools of Business. These conferences have been a major force in altering and improving the curriculum of business statistics courses. Much of the emphasis on statistical thinking and quality stems directly from those conferences. In addition, a great many of the examples and exercises are based on situations and analyses described at those conferences.

Unifying Theme of This Edition: Business Decision-Making in Action

This second edition of the book integrates a business decision-making case into each chapter for motivational and illustration purposes and includes business case assignments at the end of each chapter. These cases revolve around realistic business settings with realistic data sets that put students in the role of managers who must make business decisions based on data. These cases were developed out of the authors' prior practical consulting and professional experiences. Many of the new cases in this second edition are taken from *Business Cases in Statistical Decision Making* by Peters and Gray.

Based on our many years of experience, we have found that cases provide student motivation and have a dramatic impact on the learning experience of students in business statistics classes at all levels, from undergraduate large lecture classes to MBA and executive MBA classes.

- The data analysis and decision-making experience gained from the new in-chapter business case studies and the end-of-chapter business case assignments will help future managers better recognize how to approach professional decision-making situations.

- Chapter Case Introductions provide student motivation by demonstrating the relevance of course material to real-world business problems.

- Chapter Case Analyses illustrate how to solve real business problems using the statistical methods discussed in the current and preceding chapters.

- Additional end-of-chapter Business Cases provide students with interesting, realistic business problems to solve on their own.

Other Important Features of This Second Edition

- Chapter 2, "Summarizing Data," has been expanded with additional coverage of graphics and descriptive statistics.

- Twenty percent of the exercises in this second edition are updated or new.

- Additional examples have been added to increase clarity, particularly for *p*-values and probability concepts.

- Microsoft Excel output has been added to the existing output from other popular software packages such as Minitab and JMP.

- All computer output has been updated to reflect the most current versions of these software packages.

Important Features Retained from the First Edition

- Statistical thinking and data analysis techniques for decision-making purposes are the primary focus of the text, rather than mechanical application of formulas and methods.

- Difficult statistical concepts are presented with clarity and technical precision.

- The text is not tied to any particular software package. Various computer packages are used to analyze data.

- Three full chapters covering regression methods give business students ample exposure to this important, practical topic.

- Quality and productivity concepts and techniques are integrated throughout the text.

■ Review exercises are placed after blocks of two or three chapters. These exercises are stated in no particular order, so that students can work without the artificial cues of chapter placement.

Computing

The book does not require that students have access to any particular computer software package. The book could even be used without any computer assignments at all. Obviously, if time and resources permit, it would be highly desirable to use a computer program in conjunction with the book. The data sets for the exercises, examples, and cases in the text are stored on a CD included with each new copy of the text. The data sets are provided in several different formats (including Excel, Minitab, JMP, and ASCII text) for ease in using any of several packages. Several exercises at the end of each chapter ask that students analyze data sets by computer; in these exercises, no output is shown. Additionally, the cases are best analyzed by computer. An instructor may, if desired, distribute output that is relevant to these exercises and cases, so that direct student computer work is not absolutely required.

Coverage

The basic organization of this book is reasonably standard. After an overview in Chapter 1, the two basic "legs" of the course—descriptive statistics and probability concepts—are presented in the next four chapters. The key theoretical ideas of sampling distributions and inference follow in the next three chapters. The remainder of the book covers a variety of basic methods, culminating in a thorough introduction to multiple regression.

Within the overall structure of the book, there is considerable flexibility. In particular, sections describing nonparametric methods and chi-squared procedures can be omitted if necessary, as can sections on normal probability plots and choice of estimators. If necessary, the discussion of analysis of variance can be skimped or eliminated. Although we think it would be undesirable to do so, it is possible to skip some of the material on control charts and quality.

Our experience in teaching with this book indicates that the emphasis on computer usage allows for coverage of more ideas than was possible with the traditional number-crunching format. Time that formerly was spent on computational details can now be spent on more interesting topics. Therefore, instructors may wish to attempt somewhat wider coverage than had previously been possible.

This book's approach allows instructors to increase the emphasis on critical understanding and decrease the amount of hand computation, allowing managers much greater involvement in the real uses of statistical ideas.

There are several teaching aids associated with the book, in addition to the enclosed CD. Some exercises have full solutions available in the Student's Solutions Manual. Others have short answers at the end of the text. Still others must be solved without crutches. An Instructor's Resource Manual including teaching suggestions, comments on cases, and solutions to all exercises is available from the publisher.

Any text serves several functions. It is a teaching tool, a reference, and a source of practice problems. We have attempted to make the book useful as a tool and reference by showing many of the calculations needed. The exercises should make clear our conviction that the calculations are a limited issue. The bigger issues, as indicated by much of the text and the exercises, are careful interpretation and serious attention to underlying assumptions.

Acknowledgments

Much of the evolution of the parent *(Statistical Thinking for Managers)* and this book has been influenced by the annual Making Statistics More Effective in Schools of Business conferences. And, although we have not adopted all the ideas presented, many will recognize the source of some of the ideas and examples presented in the text. We are also very appreciative of the not-to-tender readings given preliminary versions of the first edition by Wharton MBA students and many others. For their feedback to the first edition, we are thankful to Sal Agnitori, Binghampton University; Steve M. Bajgier, Drexel University; Delores Conway, University of Southern California; George T. Geis, University of California, Los Angeles; and Nancy C. Weida, Bucknell University.

For this second edition, we are grateful for the following people for their valuable suggestions: Jerrold May, University of Pittsburgh; Soumen Ghosh, Georgia Institute of Technology; Murat Tarimcilar, George Washington University; Joan Donohue, University of South Carolina; and Bruce Cooil, Vanderbilt University.

We are most grateful to Curt Hinrichs, our publisher, and Cheryll Linthicum, our development editor, for their guidance, support, and availability. We also greatly appreciate the invaluable support and assistance provided by numerous editorial, production, and marketing people within Duxbury.

Finally, special thanks go to our families for their support.

About the Authors

David K. Hildebrand, late of the Wharton School at the University of Pennsylvania, was a professor of statistics for 34 years, teaching undergraduates, regular and executive MBAs, and doctoral students. Dr. Hildebrand served as department chair and faculty senate chair at Penn, was an active member of the Wharton curriculum committee, and was honored by the Wharton Graduate Association for his "outstanding contributions and commitment to educational excellence" in the MBA core curriculum. He was an associate editor of the *Journal of the American Statistical Association,* and had a long affiliation with the Making Statistics More Effective in Schools of Business conferences. Dr. Hildebrand was also a respected author; in addition to this text, he wrote *Statistical Thinking for Managers* (with Lyman Ott) and *Statistical Thinking for Behavioral Scientists* for Duxbury. In addition, he is co-author of two monographs in statistics and is author of numerous articles in professional journals.

R. Lyman Ott, now retired from the pharmaceutical industry, was senior vice president at Hoechst Marion Roussel, responsible for business process improvement, global development information systems, and biometrics and data management. Previously, Dr. Ott was vice president of systems and quality improvement at Marion Merrell Dow. At Merrell Dow Research Institute he was responsible for biostatistics, computer services, clinical data processing, laboratory automation and scientific information services and an adjunct professor in the Division of Biostatistics at the University of Cincinnati. Prior to his career in the pharmaceutical industry, he was a faculty member in the Department of Statistics at the University of Florida, where he taught service courses and courses for statistics majors at both the undergraduate and graduate levels. He has published many research articles in various statistical journals and several textbooks for Duxbury Press, including *An Introduction to Statistical Methods and Data Analysis,* Fifth Edition (with Michael Longnecker), *Basic Statistical Ideas for Managers* (with Dave Hildebrand), *Understanding Statistics,* Sixth Edition, and *Elementary Survey Sampling,* Fifth Edition. He is a Fellow of the American Statistical Association and has served on the ASA board of directors.

J. Brian Gray is professor of statistics in the Applied Statistics Program and in the Department of Information Systems, Statistics, and Management Science at the University of Alabama, where he teaches a variety of statistics courses at the undergraduate, masters, and doctoral levels. Dr. Gray has taught MBA and Executive MBA statistics courses for the past 20 years and has received several teaching awards from the MBA and Executive MBA Associations of the University of Alabama and Texas Christian University. He co-authored the book, *Business Cases in Statistical Decision-Making: Computer Based Applications.* Dr. Gray is an active member of the American Statistical Association. He has published research articles in journals including *Technometrics, Journal of Computational and Graphical Statistics, The American Statistician, Computational Statistics and Data Analysis, Journal of Statistical Computation and Simulation, Statistics and Computing, Journal of Real Estate Research,* and *Journal of Business, Finance, & Accounting.* Dr. Gray received the Wilcoxon Prize for Best Practical Application Paper in *Technometrics* in 1984.

Making Sense of Data

CHAPTER CONTENTS

Statistical thinking will one day be as necessary for efficient citizenship as the ability to read and write. **H. G. Wells**

Not many executives are information-literate. They know how to get data. But most still have to learn how to use data. **Peter F. Drucker**

Well-managed organizations use data intelligently; poorly managed ones don't. Virtually every manager—corporate president, cabinet member, hospital director, junior assistant to the associate deputy vice comptroller—has the need and opportunity to deal with data. The need may be obvious, as it is to loan officers who check the performance of thousands of consumer loans or to hospital managers who track the daily occupancy of beds and operating rooms. The opportunity may be less obvious (and therefore even more valuable) to hotel managers, for example, who might not realize they could experiment with advance check-in to reduce lines at the registration desk, or to owners of a chain of sound equipment stores, who might not think to combine sales and inventory data to see that the rush to meet quarterly sales quotas is causing avoidable quarterly inventory problems. Statistical thinking is important for every manager in every organization, both in dealing with day-to-day operations and in finding opportunities for improvement.

This is a book about making sense of data. To begin it, we need to consider what we mean by data, where and how data should be collected, what to do with the collected data, and how to assess other people's data. That's the agenda for this chapter in particular, and really for the whole book.

1.1   What Do We Mean by "Data"?

Statistical thinking deals with *numerical* data. Certainly there are other kinds of data. Anecdotal data, for example—specific results that happen in particular situations—can also be useful in pointing out problems or a need for change. But casual and anecdotal information is not systematic and may well emphasize extremes or odd cases. Thinking about numerical data usually provides a more complete picture.

Numbers by themselves don't constitute data. There's a great line from an old movie, along the lines of "Today's baseball scores are 7 to 2, 6 to 3, and 8 to 1." We need more than numbers to have data. We need to know what is being measured or counted. If a test of the acidity of various brands of orange juice yields an average of 5.7, we need to know the scale. Is it chemical pH, where 7 is neutral and where the lower the score, the more intense the acidity? Is it a concentration measure? Or is it a rating by veteran orange juice drinkers? To have data, we must have a description of the variable that's being measured or counted, together with the numerical results of the measurement or count.

A full description of data requires answers to two questions: How are the quantities defined, and how are the measured entities chosen? Some variables, such as acidity, have well-defined measurement scales, such as pH. Other variables are not so clearly defined. As any accountant can tell you, for example, the annual net profit of a corporation can be measured in several ways. How is inventory valued? Are special one-time costs taken into account? Is the income from subsidiaries included? That's why there are notes to financial statements. As another example, customer satisfaction with repair work done under warranty by a car dealer might be measured by customer answers to a questionnaire, percentage of second attempts at repair, or number of complaints received by the manufacturer.

operational definition   Understanding data well requires knowledge of the **operational definition** of the variables. An operational definition specifies just how a variable is measured or counted. For example, the weekly hours worked by clerical staff is likely to be measured by the hours during which employees are expected to be present at the office, possibly excepting a lunch break. Note that this definition does not directly measure the time during which employees are actually performing tasks, because it includes whatever time is spent in breaks, tending to personal business, and so on. The daily number of customers in a supermarket is likely to be measured by the number of transactions made at checkout stands; this definition excludes those who enter the store but make no purchases and counts as one person those who shop—and pay—together. Understanding the operational definition of a variable can help you understand the uses and limitations of the data.

Understanding data well also requires information about the entities that were actually measured. For example, a magazine tests automobiles. Were those tested obtained from the manufacturers especially for that purpose (and therefore likely to be the best the manufacturer can provide) or were they purchased randomly from dealers? Were the participants in a taste test of two brands of cola selected from people who were in the act of purchasing brand A, or were they chosen on a more neutral basis? Asking how the individual measurements were obtained can sometimes uncover "loaded" data, designed for propaganda, not information.

There is a danger of becoming too cynical. If you think long enough, you can almost always come up with objections, however far-fetched, to almost any data-gathering method. Data that have been collected in obviously biased ways can be, and should be, discounted; that doesn't mean that data collected honestly but imperfectly should be ignored.

In summary, data are numerical results of measurements on specified variables. To begin to understand the data, learn the operational definitions of how the measurements or counts were made and how the entities in the data-gathering process were selected.

1.2   Data About What?

In order to use data, you first have to realize that you need them. How can a manager decide what data may be important?

Most business and management courses deal with data needs specific to that field. Accounting classes deal with several kinds of data: financial (how much money was taken in and spent in this month, for example), physical (how much product is for sale on the shelves, for example), and operating (how many worker hours were expended on this product this month, for example). Marketing courses work with the kinds of data that are needed to see if a business is providing desired products or services to customers, making customers aware of the products and services, and introducing new or better products and services. Finance courses deal with data on yields and interest rates and risks. Much of business training and education has to do with gathering and using various kinds of data.

processes   There are methods to help you think systematically about what data may be needed. A useful way to think about an organization is as a set of **processes**—systematic, repetitive actions whose purpose is to create something of value. These processes link to one another, as well as to the external customers and environment of the organization. For example, think about a college or university. Every college routinely carries out many different processes. Scheduling classes, securing instructors, enrolling students, providing textbooks, securing payments, and paying creditors are all repeated actions taken by someone at that college. Each of these actions requires a systematic process to make sure it's done—preferably, done well. The processes must be connected. The student-enrollment process at our college had better obtain information from the course scheduling process, or else students will be enrolled for nonexistent courses or courses that meet at unpredictable times. It would be better if there were a link from the enrollment process to the scheduling process so additional sections could be scheduled for courses with high demand and courses with low demand could be reduced.

Thinking in terms of processes and the links among processes is one good way to discover what data will be useful. For a specific process, good questions are: "Where in the process are decisions made?" and "What parts of the problem are most frustrating to the people in the process?" A flowchart helps to pinpoint answers to these questions. In ordering textbooks, for example, the key decisions are what text to use and how many copies to order. The decision about which book to use is made by the instructor or the department teaching the course and is really basic input to the process. For a bookstore, the decision about the number of copies to order requires data. In the past, how many students have bought texts for this course through this bookstore? The answer will not be the same as enrollment in the course because students in the course may buy the book through other stores or (as used copies) from previous students. Typical frustrations for a bookstore manager are either having large numbers of copies unsold or having to reorder and deal with unhappy customers until the new shipment arrives. By collecting data comparing past enrollments and past number of purchases, the bookstore's manager might well improve forecasts about demand. Or, a manager might just find a professor's handwriting illegible. (Unlikely, of course, but possible.) In this case, a little data about how often illegibility is a problem might lead to redesigning the order form with individual letter boxes, thus encouraging printing rather than handwriting.

rework
scrap

A flowchart can also help to identify steps in the process that cause **rework,** undoing and redoing actions taken previously, and **scrap,** complete abandonment of a partly completed task. For example, if the bookstore orders a text but is told that a new edition is available, the textbook manager must rework the order, going back to the department and finding out which edition is desired. If the book is out of print and unavailable, the order must be scrapped and the process begun all over again. Rework and scrap are often the causes of major costs. Obtaining data on where these costs occur may pinpoint where improvements in the process could be made most readily.

One of the important ideas of modern quality-improvement methods is that the people who actually operate the processes of an organization should have a large say in how to improve those processes. The person in charge of actually obtaining textbooks for a bookstore is likely to know a great deal more about how that process works than is the Executive Vice President of Everything and Director of University Business Services. Furthermore, most processes involve several people at different points. Therefore, a good way to find out where problems are occurring and where data are needed is to form teams that include people who work "in the trenches." Such teams are often a great help in getting started on data collection and on making improvements to processes in an organization.

1.3 Gathering Data

To be useful, data obviously must be collected and made available. Simply deciding to measure and record relevant data is the necessary beginning for using data to solve problems. But if a manufacturer of microwave ovens records the occurrence of warranty repairs, not the specific malfunction needing repair, then the data are of no help in improving the oven manufacturing process. As discussed previously, the first decision, then, concerns what to measure. Often, the variables that are most convenient to measure are not the variables that are most relevant to solving problems. For example, a candy company that must schedule production of its basic chocolate bar would like to know the monthly consumer demand for the bar. It would be relatively easy to record monthly orders from wholesalers and retail chains, but that's not the same as customer demand; some customers may wish to purchase the bar but find it out of stock when shopping. It would be better to obtain not only order data but also stockout data. Giving the problem some thought helps in collecting data on the most relevant variables, not necessarily the easiest variables to measure.

The second decision concerns how to obtain the data. Often data can simply be recorded in the ordinary process of business; with some planning, data on production, warranty, order, and cash flow (for example) can be recorded and made available as a matter of normal procedure. Other times, data must be deliberately sought.

sampling

One important approach to data gathering is **sampling.** A market research group testing consumer reaction to a new design of automobile seats can't possibly talk to every potential car buyer; inevitably, data must be taken from a limited sample of potential buyers. Auditors trying to verify credit card accounts receivable are not about to write to every single cardholder; instead, they will verify a sample of accounts. It's natural, but wrong, to think of statistical sampling only in terms of sampling people; we can equally well sample records or places or times. Generally, statistical sampling is a plausible approach any time potentially valuable data are to be gathered by complete data would be impossible or uneconomical to gather.

experimentation

Another approach to data gathering is **experimentation.** Rather than present only one proposed new automobile seat to (a sample of) potential buyers, a market research group could create several seats combining different features and find out which seat types were most preferred. An operations team seeking to reduce bottlenecks in manufacturing computer boards can experiment with different operating speeds, staffing levels, and flow patterns, measuring the rate of production and the quality of boards. Designed experiments are one of the key components of the recent drive to improve quality of products and processes. Experiments aren't restricted to the lab; virtually any product or process that's part of an organization's business is a potential topic for experimentation.

1.4 Summarizing Data

Raw data, long lists of numbers, aren't useful as such. They must be summarized in useful, understandable ways. Imagine, just for instance, facing a major national bank's computer printout of the current balances, credit limits, and most recent payments of every Visa cardholder. No one could make sense of that pile of data. Summarization is the first step of data analysis.

The first and most important step in summarizing data is to draw pictures. Relatively simple plots and graphs can make important features of the data obvious. For example, a plot showing what fraction of Visa cardholders had paid about 10% of their outstanding balances, what fraction had paid about 20%, and so on up to 100% would indicate a great deal about potential repayment problems. If there was a sudden shift toward lower payments from one month to the next, the plot would clearly signal that cardholders were changing their habits and possibly having trouble paying their debts. A chart showing how often various parts of a toaster oven were responsible for warranty repairs would indicate quality problems very clearly; if there were 20 problems with a timer for every 1 problem with the heating element, design and production managers would know that timers, not heating elements, most needed improvement. The process of making sense of data almost always begins with plotting the data.

The next obvious step in analyzing data usually is finding some sort of typical, average value. Most people, whether they have formal statistical training or not, have a reasonable idea of what "average" means. Yet some thought is needed even for this simple step. For example, the mean sales price of single-family homes in a suburb will differ from the median sales price. Mean and median are different concepts of "average," and the difference is important to both realtors and tax assessors. Furthermore, an average may not be the most relevant summary statistic for a variable.

We would rather not live next to a flood control system that had been designed to handle an *average* year's rainfall; the designers of such systems must consider such extreme values as the every-hundred-years rainfall. Averages are not the only relevant summary figures.

The idea of variability is at least as important in statistical thinking as the idea of average. In fact, understanding variability may be the most important benefit of a formal study of statistics. A city's sanitation department will have a budget for overtime pay, but each week's actual overtime will almost surely vary from the budgeted, weekly average amount. Is the variability this week within reasonable limits, or is the variation big enough to deserve special attention? What accounts for the variability? Can it be controlled or predicted? A large part of this book deals with methods for understanding variability—how to summarize it, explain it, reduce it.

A final step in summarizing data is to assess any unusual shapes or patterns in the data. We will want to look for skewness—asymmetry—in data and for outliers—unusual, "freak" values that are far from the bulk of the data. Skewness may make summary figures misleading. For example, a plot of family wealth (monetary value of all assets) will not be symmetric; most families will have small values, some will have moderately large values, and a few will have very large values indeed. If we looked uncritically at only average family wealth, we might be badly fooled. Outliers can also distort averages. Further, outliers can signal unusual cases from which managers can learn: If we saw a supermarket with an unusually low value of cost per dollar of sales, we'd want to know how that market worked.

1.5   The Role of Probability

The most basic idea of statistical reasoning is that almost all data are a sample from a much larger underlying population or process. No sample is exactly, perfectly representative. We must always allow for error, if only from randomness. Newspaper reporting on political polls is careful to note an allowance for error. Much of this book indicates what those allowances for error should be, in various situations. One of the questions you, as a consumer of statistical analysis, should routinely ask is what is the appropriate allowance for error. Instinctively, you already have some idea of what's important in allowing for error; in particular, you know that the allowance for error in a small sample is more than the allowance in a big one. Any sample is imperfectly representative of the underlying reality; small samples are more imperfect than big ones.

To go beyond these obvious ideas, we need some technical machinery. First, any summary information based on sample data is subject to random variation from sample to sample. The language and technical basis of random variation is probability theory. We will introduce basic probability ideas (though not the deepest theory) in Chapters 3 through 5.

Given the language and concepts of probability, we can then introduce the basic question of statistical inference: What can one say from a limited sample about the underlying population or process? That's the core question for Chapters 6 through 8.

Once we have the basic principles, we can talk about specific methods for specific questions. There are many statistical methods—just look at the manual for any statistical computer package. We can't explain all the methods, but we can explain some of the most important ones. That's what we plan to do for the rest of the book in Chapters 9 through 13.

What should you do with data? Understand that they represent only a sample, summarize them in ways that help illuminate the underlying management question, and allow for a sensible amount of random error and systematic bias. Do that, and you won't be fooled very often. All the technical ideas that follow in this book really elaborate on this basic theme.

1.6 Evaluating Other People's Data and Conclusions

Most managers, especially as they progress to senior positions, spend less time analyzing data themselves and more time evaluating others' analyses. Therefore, it's important to think about assessing statistical analyses. There are some key questions to ask.

First, how were the entities selected to be in the sample? Think about possible biases. Are there evident, clear distortions in the way the data were gathered? Particularly when sampling people, it's almost impossible to have a perfectly unbiased sample. Are the biases—distortions—minor or serious?

Second, exactly what is being measured? A statement that the study measures "customer satisfaction" isn't very meaningful. A statement that the study measures responses to the question "Will you recommend this product/service to your friends and relatives?" is much better defined, and more helpful. An experiment that is said to measure "product quality" is very vague; an experiment that is said to measure "variation in fat content of individual potato chips" is much better defined. It's worth a manager's time to understand the actual, operational definition of what's being measured.

Third, what does the conclusion mean, and what does it not mean? We will spend a lot of time and effort talking about the concept of statistical significance, beginning in Chapter 8. To say that a result is statistically significant sounds like it means "this is important." As we will see, that's not what it really means. In Chapter 7, we will encounter statements such as "a 95% confidence interval for the true mean answer ranges from 3.9 to 4.6." It turns out that that does not mean that 95% of the individuals in the sample gave answers in that range; it means that we are 95% sure that the average value in the whole population falls in that range. How widely the individual responses vary is a completely different issue. One of the most important things that a manager-to-be should learn from a statistics book like this one is what the technical language really means.

Fourth, are the assumptions underlying the analysis reasonable? We will consistently look at assumptions as we consider various statistical methods. We will also consider "diagnostics"—methods for checking the reasonableness of these assumptions. A good statistical analysis should be backed up by consideration of the assumptions and diagnostics. If the person presenting the analysis hasn't checked the assumptions, that's a bad sign; the analysis may well be casual or thoughtless. Some assumptions are more important than others; as we consider various statistical methods, we will try to indicate which assumptions are more crucial and which less so.

We can't guarantee that obtaining answers to these four questions will always protect a manager from being fooled by a bad statistical analysis, but we can say that getting answers to these questions will go a long way toward giving the manager a good idea of the value (or lack thereof) of such an analysis.

1.7 The Role of the Computer

Making sense of data has become a great deal easier with the advent of modern computers. Computer programs have been written to do even the most tedious calculations described in this book. Some of the methods require so much calculation that they would be utterly impossible without a computer. Perhaps even more important, computers can plot the data easily and clearly. Therefore, managers can explore data rather than rely on cut-and-dried formulas. The results can be communicated effectively and clearly using plots and graphics. In addition, any statistical method involves assumptions; with a decent computer program, it's possible to check the reasonableness of these assumptions. Computers both reduce the tedium of data analysis and make better analyses possible.

The mere fact that data analysis has been done by computer, however, doesn't guarantee that it's any good. The data may be bad, in that the variables aren't really relevant, the data collection is biased, or the assumptions are grossly violated. The choice of the data analysis method may have been a bad one. The results may be correctly calculated but wrongly interpreted. A human being must still decide what data to use, choose the method of analysis, check the assumptions, and interpret the results reasonably. Until artificial intelligence improves greatly, human intelligence will still be required.

Literally hundreds of computer software packages are available to analyze data. Some, such as Minitab, SAS, SPSS, and BMDP, were originally developed for mainframe computers and later adapted for personal computers. Others, such as DataDesk, Systat, and JMP, were originally developed for personal computers. These packages are so useful, both in doing computations and in plotting data, that the investment in learning to use one is most amply repaid.

One needn't learn everything about a package to use it effectively. To begin, you need only learn the steps necessary to obtain the particular results you need. Typically, you'll need to enter the data, assign labels so the output is readable, select those variables and observations you want to use in a particular analysis, and call the correct part of the program to carry out the desired step.

We will use output from several widely available packages throughout this book. Most of the methods we describe can be carried out with any of these packages. There are so many packages, and they change so quickly, that trying to describe how to use them all is futile. Instead, we'll concentrate on interpreting the output. *Don't try to interpret every number in the output.* The designers of most packages, particularly the older, mainframe-based packages, had to include in the output almost everything that a user could conceivably want to know. As a result, in any particular situation, some of the output is likely to be irrelevant. *Look for the specific results you need; don't worry about the rest.* As you learn more about statistical methods, you'll understand more of the output. In the meantime, select only the specific output you need.

SUMMARY

This chapter sets the agenda for the book. The essential steps in making sense of data are gathering the data, summarizing the data, using pictures and summary numbers, and making inferences and predictions from the limited available data to other data or to the future. The logical structure of the book involves two separate bases—methods for summarizing data (Chapter 2) and concepts of probability (Chapters 3 through 5). These bases are combined to produce the basic theoretical structure of statistical inference (Chapters 6 through 8). Once the basic theory is in place, we will apply it (Chapters 9 through 13) using many methods in many specific situations.

Summarizing Data

CHAPTER CONTENTS

This chapter describes some of the important ideas for summarizing data. The key ideas are these:

- Distinguish between qualitative variables, where numbers, if used, are merely codes, and quantitative variables, where numbers are actual measurements.

- Plots of the data are the most important step in understanding the basic pattern. There are several convenient plots. Histograms indicate the general shape of the data distribution of a quantitative variable. Using a smoother can sometimes clarify a histogram by smoothing off the arbitrary corners. Stem-and-leaf diagrams are a convenient way to get histogram-like plots. In these plots, look for the average value, the amount of variability, any skewness, any outliers, and possibly multiple peaks. Box plots are particularly convenient to check for outliers.

- The most widely used measures of the typical, average value of a variable are: the mode, the most common value, for qualitative variables; the median, the middle value, for quantitative and ordinal variables; and the mean, the arithmetic average, for quantitative variables. Skewness can pull the mean away from the median, in the direction of the long tail of the data.

- The most common measure of variability is the standard deviation. It is the square root of the average squared deviation of the data values from the mean. Because it is based on squared deviations, it can be seriously distorted by skewness or outliers. Interpret the numerical value of the standard deviation using the Empirical Rule.

- For data taken over time, a sequence plot of the data against time will reveal trends or cycles in the data. An especially important sequence plot is a control chart. An x-bar chart plots means for each time period and can show any drift in the average value. R charts of the ranges or S charts of standard deviations can show any problem of increasing variability.

- Control charts are a key tool for quality management. They can reveal when a process goes out of statistical control. When a process is in control—statistically stable—a manager can consider special causes of large variability and common causes of normal variability. In most cases, improving quality implies reducing variability.

An unorganized mass of numbers is virtually useless in understanding anything. The first task in making sense out of a data set is to summarize it. In this chapter we focus on three aspects of the data-summarization problem: finding and displaying the frequencies of various data values, calculating a typical value, and indicating the degree of variability around that typical value. We also consider displays for summarizing the relationship between two variables.

Summarizing data is one important part of the fundamental management problem of controlling and improving quality. Many of the ideas in this chapter are central to modern quality methods. The computations aren't hard, and a computer can do them; the major issue is understanding what the results mean.

Most statistical problems encountered in practice involve several key variables. But an important first step in making sense of such data is to summarize the variables one by one; methods for doing so are described in this chapter.

Glenco Manufacturing Company

Everybody at Glenco Manufacturing, a moderate-sized manufacturing company, is talking about the new incentive bonus program. Last August, John Marchant, CEO of Glenco, announced a new program designed to encourage production workers to make their best effort. While production employees could count on their usual regular pay raises, Glenco would now be offering a $1000 bonus to the top 20%. So of the 155 employees, about 31 could expect to get a nice surprise just in time for Christmas.

The reaction to Marchant's announcement was both immediate and mixed. A number of employees clearly liked the new bonus plan—a few even made bets on being in the top 20%. Sam Miller, Pete Cravens, Mike Sanders, and Tom Reeves decided to pool their bonuses to buy a new fishing boat, and they actually made a down payment on it in early November. Even "silent Harvey" Fried was heard to say, ". . . maybe I'll finally get some dough for all the sweat I've put in."

Not everyone, however, was upbeat—particularly those who knew that they would never receive a bonus. They complained loud and long about the proposed plan, claiming there were any number of "better" uses for the money. For example, Frank Phillips thought that the money was better spent on underwriting dental insurance for everybody, and Martha Renner thought the money would be better spent on day-care benefits. Other employees had still other suggestions for the money.

Even management reaction was split. Mark Brown, one of the senior foremen at Glenco, was the most outspoken. Mark said that he had seen incentive programs like this before on three previous jobs and that they never seemed to be fairly run and, as a result, always caused more problems than they seemed to solve. Mark said, "Programs like this never seem to run smoothly. Those who think they deserve the bonus and don't get it just get mad and make life miserable for the rest of us. It's a can of worms!"

In spite of the complaints, Glenco management went ahead with the plan. A new committee, the Employee Bonus Committee, was formed to choose the bonus recipients. Made up of five manufacturing managers, it was to choose based on supervisory ratings of employee performance, the normal way of evaluating employees.

Supervisors normally made their ratings in late November, using Glenco's standard performance appraisal form. Up to now this form had been reasonably satisfactory, although the evaluations had not been used as the basis for making salary adjustments or for distributing other types of rewards. In fact, the evaluations had been used as little more than formal documentation of poor performance of employees who were to be warned to shape up or face a pink slip. This year, the ratings will be turned in directly to the Employee Bonus Committee.

As a member of the Employee Bonus Committee, you have access to the Glenco personnel database containing the performance ratings and other employee data. The chairman has asked each committee member to come to the first meeting with a list of nominees for the $1000 bonus and to be prepared to defend the choices.

The personnel data for the Glenco Manufacturing case are contained in the file Glenco on the CD that came with your book. The file contains information on 155 employees. In addition to their ID number, the data file includes information on gender, race, age, tenure, and department for all employees as well as their hourly pay rate and performance rating. A partial listing of the data within Excel is shown in Figure 2.1.

FIGURE 2.1   Partial Listing of the Glenco Manufacturing Data

	A	B	C	D	E	F	G	H	I	J
1	ID	Last	First	Gender	Minority	Age	Department	Tenure	HourlyRate	Rating
2	4203	Alexander	Charles	M	0	35	1	10	18.00	4.5
3	1543	Ammann	Ray	M	0	60	1	37	23.75	4.8
4	1161	Anderson	James	M	1	61	2	41	24.63	4.1
5	5265	Babcock	Marilyn	F	1	36	2	0	15.55	5.0
6	4192	Bagley	Jan	F	0	40	5	11	17.90	7.5
7	2065	Baker	Lisa	F	0	59	3	32	22.88	5.9
8	4450	Baldwin	Lois	F	1	35	4	8	17.33	5.2
9	5055	Bartlett	Bill	M	1	26	4	2	16.46	4.4
10	4154	Blair	Elizabeth	F	0	41	6	11	18.27	4.6
11	4007	Bolden	Holly	F	0	50	6	12	18.21	4.0
12	5056	Bowling	Frances	F	0	22	7	2	16.01	8.3
13	4831	Brown	Charlotte	F	0	62	7	4	17.05	3.6
14	5221	Bruton	Penny	F	0	23	7	0	15.00	4.3
15	4258	Campbell	Delores	F	1	43	7	10	17.91	4.7
16	4215	Cash	Bill	M	1	35	7	10	17.52	6.7
17	4435	Chandler	Margo	F	0	42	4	8	16.96	7.0
18	4895	Chang	Sally	F	0	25	4	4	16.08	6.4

In the Glenco file, the variables are defined as follows:

ID: Employee identification number

Last: Last name

First: First name

Gender: M for male or F for female

Minority: 1, if minority; 0, if nonminority

Age: Age in years

Department: Department (1–7)

Tenure: Number of years with Glenco

HourlyRate: Hourly rate of pay (in dollars)

Rating: Employee performance rating (on a scale from 0 to 10 by tenths) as given by the departmental supervisor, with 10 as the highest rating and 0 as the lowest rating

At the end of this chapter, we will analyze these data in detail using graphical and numerical summaries of data covered in this chapter. After analyzing the data, we will be in a much better position to recommend a list of employees for the bonus. ∎

2.1   The Distribution of Values of a Variable

The single best summary of a set of data is a picture. Not only does a plot of the data help the manager who's analyzing the results, it also helps communicate the results to others. This section explains some standard, useful methods for plotting data on a single variable.

Many plots are based on simple counts, called *frequencies,* of how many times each possible data value occurs in a set of data. Either by hand or by computer, start

frequency table
distrbution
relative frequency

by finding the frequencies with which all the various values occur and displaying them in a **frequency table.** Such a table specifies the **distribution** of the data. A simple variation displays the **relative frequency** of each value, which is the frequency of that value divided by the total number of measurements.

EXAMPLE 2.1   A small printing firm has a total of 20 salespeople working in four offices. The downtown office is numbered 1, the western suburban office is 2, the northern office is 3, and the southern suburban office is 4. The firm's records show that the respective offices of the salespeople (when the names were listed in alphabetical order) are

1 4 1 3 3 2 1 1 1 3 4 4 2 2 1 1 2 4 4 1

Summarize the data by displaying the frequencies associated with the values 1, 2, 3, and 4 in a frequency table. Calculate the relative frequencies as well.

SOLUTION   The easiest way to obtain the frequencies is to list the values and count the frequencies. Then the frequency table is as follows:

Value (office number):	1	2	3	4
Frequency (number of salespeople):	8	4	3	5
Relative frequency:	$\frac{8}{20} = .40$	.20	.15	.25

qualitative

bar chart

Office number in Example 2.1 is a **qualitative** variable—a variable which merely defines categories, with no true numerical meaning. We could just as well have listed the names of the offices rather than the code numbers. A very simple, useful plot of qualitative, categorical data is a **bar chart.** Bar charts use rectangles to portray the data. The base of each rectangle indicates a value or a group (class) of values. The height of each rectangle represents the frequency or the relative frequency of each value or class. To create a bar chart, label the horizontal axis with values or categories of the variable, label the vertical axis with frequencies, and construct separate rectangles for each value with height corresponding to the frequency or relative frequency of that value. Figure 2.2 shows a bar chart of the data from Example 2.1.

A bar chart is an easy way to see whether the data are spread out more or less evenly among the possibilities or whether the data are concentrated at one or a few values.

FIGURE 2.2   **Bar Chart of Sales Office Data**

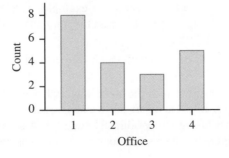

quantitative

grouped data

classes

Bar charts are used for qualitative (categorical) variables, where any numbers are arbitrary codes. Typically, such variables have only a few possible values. **Quantitative** variables, actual numerical measurements, typically have many possible values. With a variable that has many possible values, it's usually better to combine values into groups. The resulting data are referred to as **grouped data.** Suppose you had a list of the amounts paid by 850 customers at a supermarket's checkout counters in one day. If you listed the amounts to the penny and counted frequencies, you would probably list over 800 values with a frequency of 1 and a few values with frequencies of 2 or 3. That wouldn't be a very useful summary! In such a case you might want to round off the amounts to the nearest dollar or the nearest 5 dollars. This rounding-off process creates groups of similar checkout amounts.

The choice of groups (often called **classes**) for summarizing data from a single variable is somewhat arbitrary, but the selection of classes should conform to the requirement that each measurement falls into one and only one class. In addition, it is desirable to choose the classes so that (1) no gaps appear between the classes and (2) the classes have a common width. Typically, we want somewhere between 5 and 20 classes, relatively few for small data sets, relatively more for large ones. The midpoints of the classes should be convenient numbers. Most statistical computer programs do this reasonably well, so we needn't worry about specific rules for grouping.

EXAMPLE 2.2

Suppose that the 20 salespeople in Example 2.1 had the following commission incomes (excluding salaries) in a certain month:

| $850 | $1265 | $895 | $575 | $2410 | $470 | $660 | $1820 | $1510 | $1100 |
| $620 | $425 | $751 | $965 | $840 | $1505 | $1375 | $695 | $1125 | $1475 |

Use these data to construct a frequency table with suitable class intervals.

SOLUTION With only 20 observations, we want a small number of classes, such as 5. The incomes range from $425 to $2410; one convenient choice of classes groups incomes to the nearest $500. The results of one such grouping of the data are displayed here in a frequency table. We took the class midpoints at $500, $1000, and so on.

Class:	$250 to $749	$750 to $1249	$1250 to $1749	$1750 to $2249	$2250 to $2749
Frequency:	6	7	5	1	1
Relative frequency:	.30	.35	.25	.05	.05

Note that each measurement (recorded in dollars) falls into exactly one class; that's why we stated the first interval (for example) as $250 to $749 rather than as $250 to $750. There are no gaps between the intervals, and the classes have a common interval width of 500.

histograms

Histograms are constructed in the same way as bar charts. The only difference is that the rectangles in a bar chart are usually separated by some space, whereas the rectangles in a histogram are directly adjacent. A histogram is often used with grouped data. Figure 2.3 shows a histogram of commission income data grouped as in Example 2.2.

FIGURE 2.3   **Histogram of Grouped Commission Income Data**

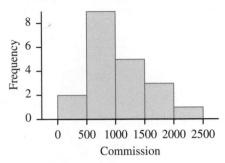

Bar charts are used with qualitative variables; the usual separation of rectangles suggests that each value of the variable represents a distinct category. Histograms are used with quantitative variables. The fact that rectangles in a histogram are adjacent (for intervals with nonzero frequencies) suggests that the variable's values are measured along a scale.

EXAMPLE 2.3   Quarterly percentage changes in the U.S. gross domestic product (GDP) from 1988 through the third quarter of 2002 are shown here. Construct a frequency histogram of these data.

GDP Change

2.7	4.8	2.1	5.3	5.0	2.2	1.9	1.4	5.1	0.9	−0.7
−3.2	−2.0	2.3	1.0	2.2	3.8	3.8	3.1	5.4	−0.1	2.5
1.8	6.2	3.4	5.7	2.2	5.0	1.5	0.8	3.1	3.2	2.9
6.8	2.0	4.6	4.4	5.9	4.2	2.8	6.1	2.2	4.1	6.7
3.0	2.0	5.2	7.1	2.6	4.8	0.6	1.1	−0.6	−1.6	−0.3
2.7	5.0	1.3	4.0							

SOLUTION   The data range from −3.2 to 7.1. If we define classes by rounding to the nearest unit, we will have 12 classes, which would be acceptable. A Minitab histogram based on this choice is shown in Figure 2.4 on the next page.

There are some minor variations in the presentation of histograms. The horizontal axis can be labeled with either class endpoints, as in Figure 2.3, or class midpoints. Thus, in Figure 2.3, we could have labeled the midpoints of the rectangles as $250, $750, . . . , rather than labeling the edges. The vertical axis of a histogram is labeled with frequencies or with relative frequencies. Because relative frequencies are proportional to frequencies, the frequency histogram and the relative frequency histogram have the same shape. The specific choice is mostly a matter of taste.

Recently, statisticians have developed improved versions of histograms by "smoothing off the corners." Smoothed histograms, also called *density estimates* or *kernel estimates,* avoid the arbitrary choice of class intervals in regular histograms and tend to show the important features of the distribution without the distraction of corners. To oversimplify, a smoothed histogram is constructed by selecting a point

FIGURE 2.4 **Histogram of GDP Change Data**

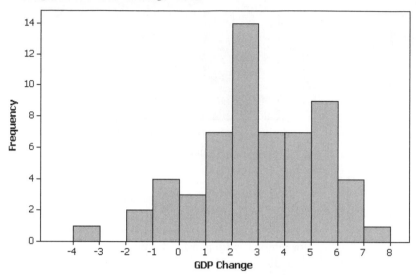

on the horizontal axis, finding the height of a rectangle centered at that point, moving right or left a little bit to another point, doing the same thing for that point, and so on. Then the heights are connected in a smooth curve. The width of the rectangle is called the *bandwidth* and can often be varied in a computer program. Wide bandwidths give very smooth curves at the cost of omitting details; narrow bandwidths reveal detail at the cost of a "wiggly" plot. Trial and error is the best way to pick a bandwidth. There are a number of variations, depending on the computer program used. The details aren't crucial. A smoothed histogram of the GDP change data of Example 2.3 drawn by Minitab is shown in Figure 2.5.

FIGURE 2.5 **Smoothed Histogram of GDP Change Data**

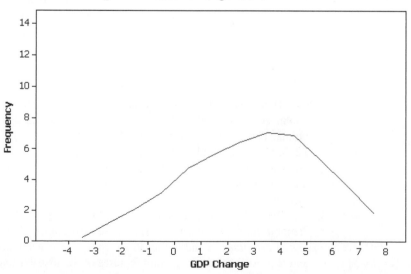

A histogram will reveal most of the important features of the distribution of data for a quantitative variable.

1. What is a typical, average value?

2. How much variability is there around the typical value? Are the data values all close, or do they spread out widely?

skewed

3. What is the general shape of the data? Are the data values distributed symmetrically around the middle or are they **skewed,** with a long tail in one direction or the other?

outliers

4. Are there **outliers**—"wild" values that are far from the bulk of the data?

bimodal

5. Does the distribution have a single peak or is it clearly **bimodal,** with two distinct peaks separated by a pronounced valley?

In the histogram of commission income, shown in Figure 2.3, an average value appears to be slightly above 1000. But there is substantial variability, with many values around 500 or so and a few around 2500. The data are skewed, with a long tail to the right. There don't seem to be any "wild" values, nor are there separate peaks.

stem-and-leaf diagram

A clever device that constructs a histogram-like picture is the **stem-and-leaf diagram.** It is best explained by an example.

EXAMPLE 2.4

Suppose that the grades of 40 job applicants on an aptitude test are as follows. Construct a stem-and-leaf diagram for these data.

42	21	46	71	87	29	34	59	81	97
64	60	87	81	69	77	75	47	73	82
91	74	70	65	86	87	67	69	49	57
55	68	74	66	81	90	75	82	37	94

SOLUTION The scores range from 21 to 97. The first digits, 2 through 9, are placed in a column—the stem—on the left of the diagram. The respective second digits are recorded in the appropriate rows—the leaves. The first three scores, 42, 21, and 46, would be represented as

```
2 | 1
3 |
4 | 2  6
```

The full stem-and-leaf diagram is shown next.

```
2 | 1  9
3 | 4  7
4 | 2  6  7  9
5 | 9  7  5
6 | 4  0  9  5  7  9  8  6
7 | 1  7  5  3  4  0  4  5
8 | 7  1  7  1  2  6  7  1  2
9 | 7  1  0  4
```

In general, data values are split into stem and leaf components as shown in Figure 2.6. First, we must decide where to split the data values. Most statistical software packages make this decision automatically. In Figure 2.6, the split is made between the hundreds and the tens positions. Everything to the left of the split (123) is called the *stem*. The first digit to the right of the split (4) is called the *leaf*. All digits to the right of the leaf (567) are discarded or truncated (without rounding the leaf). Note that stems can be any number of digits, but leaves must be only a single digit. Decimal points are not included in stems or leaves.

FIGURE 2.6   **How Stems and Leaves Are Determined**

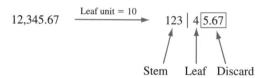

Stem   Leaf   Discard

To get a reasonable number of groups, we sometimes split up the stem. If the data values ranged between 20 and 43, we wouldn't want the stem to consist just of the numbers 2, 3, and 4; we could split the values in the 20s into low 20s (20 through 24) and high 20s (25 through 29) and the values in the 30s into low 30s and high 30s. If there were lots of values, we could even split the 20s into five groups (20 and 21, 22 and 23, 24 and 25, 26 and 27, 28 and 29) and similarly for the 30s and 40s. The aim is to have a reasonable number of categories, somewhere between 5 and 20.

The diagram is made a bit neater by ordering the data within a row, from lowest to highest score. The end result of a stem-and-leaf diagram looks much like a histogram turned sideways. The advantage of such a diagram is that it not only reflects frequencies but also contains the first digits of the actual values. Little or no information is lost.

There are many possible variations. A display (using Minitab) of the data from Example 2.4 with more classes is shown here.

```
Stem-and-leaf of Grades   N = 40
Leaf Unit = 1.0

     1      2 1
     2      2 9
     3      3 4
     4      3 7
     5      4 2
     8      4 679
     8      5
    11      5 579
    13      6 04
    19      6 567899
    (5)     7 01344
    16      7 557
    13      8 11122
     8      8 6777
     4      9 014
     1      9 7
```

This Minitab stem-and-leaf diagram splits each stem in two by placing placing observations with leaves of 0–4 in the first row of a split stem and observations with leaves of 5–9 in the second row of a split stem. For example, observations from the 90–94 range appear in the first 9 stem row and observations in the 95–99 range appear in the second 9 stem row.

The column to the left of the stem-and-leaf plot is called the *depth gauge*. The depth gauge is used for quickly locating important positions in the data. It gives a cumulative count of the data values from the top (or from the bottom, if closer) of the stem-and-leaf plot. A value on the depth gauge is a count of the number of data values on that row and all rows above (or below) that row. The depth gauge entry near the middle of the data values, (5), is in parentheses to indicate that the middle of the data set occurs on that row. The value in the parentheses reflects the number of data values on that row only.

The stem-and-leaf diagram, as well as many other innovative data summarization ideas, are described in Tukey (1977).

time series plot
sequence plot

A **time series plot** (also called a **sequence plot**) is a graph of the data values of a quantitative variable versus time (hour, day, week, month, year, etc.) or collection order. Time series plots often reveal patterns that cannot be discerned from a histogram of the same data.

EXAMPLE 2.5

At the beginning of each month, a liquor distributor has to purchase enough inventory of each item carried to satisfy demand for that month. The distributor has monthly champagne sales data for the past seven years (84 months). A partial listing of the data from Excel is shown in Figure 2.7. Use these data to project champagne sales for the next 12 months.

FIGURE 2.7

Partial Listing of the Champagne Sales Data in Excel

	A	B
	Month	Bottles
1	Month	Bottles
2	Jan-97	2815
3	Feb-97	2672
4	Mar-97	2755
5	Apr-97	2721
6	May-97	2946
7	Jun-97	3036
8	Jul-97	2282
9	Aug-97	2212
10	Sep-97	2922
11	Oct-97	4301
12	Nov-97	5764
13	Dec-97	7312
14	Jan-98	2541
15	Feb-98	2475
16	Mar-98	3031

SOLUTION The first step in our analysis is to graphically display the monthly sales data. Since this variable is quantitative, a histogram is appropriate. The Minitab histogram in Figure 2.8 shows the distribution of monthly champagne sales for the last 84 months.

FIGURE 2.8

Histogram of the Champagne Sales Data

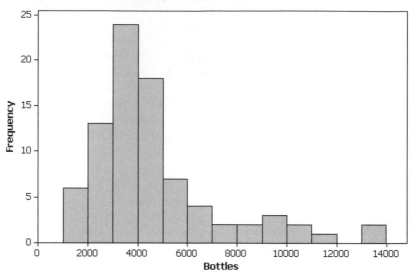

EXAMPLE 2.5
(continued)

Note the skewed nature of the data distribution. If the distributor stocks too little champagne, there is a high chance of running out of champagne too early in a month. If the distributor stocks too many bottles of champagne, he incurs higher inventory storage costs. If we knew the profit per bottle, cost of lost sales, and inventory carrying costs, we could determine an optimal number of bottles of champagne to stock.

By looking at a time series plot of these sales data, generated by Minitab and shown in Figure 2.9, we get a very different perspective on the data. First, we notice **seasonality** in the sales values, a recurring pattern in the data. The data also exhibit an increasing **trend,** a gradual increase in the mean level of monthly sales over time. There is also an increase in the variability of monthly sales over time.

seasonality
trend

FIGURE 2.9

Time Series Plot of the Champagne Sales Data

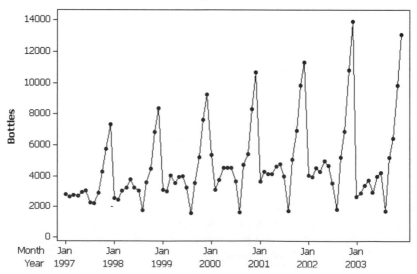

With regard to the seasonality, there is a large value or spike every December that can be explained by champagne purchases for New Year's Eve celebrations. There is also a minor increase in sales around June in time for weddings and graduation celebrations. Champagne sales appear to bottom out each year in August.

From the time series plot, it is clear that monthly champagne sales levels are a function of the month or time of year, so it would not make sense to recommend a single projected sales value for all 12 months. The forecast or projection should reflect the seasonality and trend of the time series pattern.

One additional feature of the time series that makes our task even more difficult is the noticeable decline in the final year of the data set. If this decline is due to a one-time occurrence (for example, a bad year for grape harvests and resulting decrease in supply), then we might expect the next 12 months to be back on the trend observed in the earlier years. On the other hand, if the decline is due to a change in the trend (for example, a decrease in demand due to raised health consciousness or the arrival of a competitor to our market), then we must decide whether the decline will continue at the same rate, at an increased rate, or at a decreased rate. Some investigation is obviously required into the reasons for the decline in sales over the last year of data before making any forecasts for next year.

Exercises

2.1 An automobile manufacturer routinely keeps records on the number of finished (passing all inspections) cars produced per eight-hour shift. The data for the last 28 shifts are

366	390	324	385	380	375	384	383	375	339
360	386	387	384	379	386	374	366	377	385
381	359	363	371	379	385	367	364		

a. Construct a histogram using convenient class intervals. Can you think of an explanation for the apparent shape of the histogram?
b. Construct a stem-and-leaf diagram of the data and compare it to the histogram. The left-hand "stem" should have an initial 3 in each value.

2.2 A city manager receives 17 bids for supplying new flat-screen computer displays. The dollar costs per unit are

847	849	838	841	852	846	812	838	850	836
871	849	824	846	864	843	839			

A histogram of the data was constructed using Minitab and is shown in Figure 2.10 (see next page). A smoothed histogram is superimposed on the graph.
a. According to the histogram, approximately what is the average bid? Is there much variability around that average? Is the histogram roughly symmetric or seriously skewed?

b. Does the smoothed histogram indicate skewness?
c. A stem-and-leaf diagram for these data is as follows.

```
Stem-and-leaf of Bids N = 17
Leaf Unit = 1.0

  1    81    2
  2    82    4
  6    83    6889
 (7)   84    1366799
  4    85    02
  2    86    4
  1    87    1
```

Are the classes defined by the stem-and-leaf display identical to those in the histogram? Do the two plots give the same general sense of the data?

2.3 Price-earnings ratios for a sample of 24 publicly owned companies involved in the sale of computer software used in manufacturing operations are given below:

7.7	8.5	9.6	10.3	13.6	14.5	19.5	10.1	9.7
11.4	17.8	15.9	14.2	13.7	20.7	22.1	25.9	29.1
32.6	36.7	32.4	35.9	40.1	45.9			

a. What sort of skewness is shown in the following stem-and-leaf display for these data?

FIGURE 2.10   **Histogram and Smoothed Histogram of Bid Data**

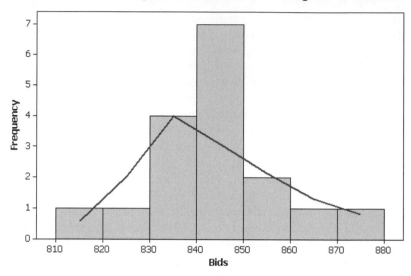

FIGURE 2.11   **Histogram of Hourly Pay Rates of Glenco Employees**

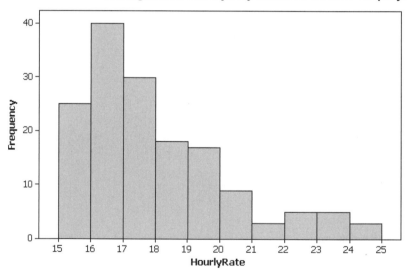

```
Stem-and-leaf of P/E Ratio   N = 24
Leaf Unit = 1.0

    4   0   7899
   11   1   0013344
  (3)   1   579
   10   2   02
    8   2   59
    6   3   22
    4   3   56
    2   4   0
    1   4   5
```

b. Use the same data to construct a histogram. Compare the histogram to the stem-and-leaf plot; which one do you find more informative?

2.4   A relative frequency histogram of hourly pay rates was constructed from the Glenco Manufacturing data using Minitab and is shown in Figure 2.11.

a. Describe the shape of the histogram.

b. Separate relative frequency histograms of hourly pay rates for male and female employees at Glenco are shown in Figure 2.12. (*Note:* The scales on both histograms were kept the same for comparison purposes.) Based on these histograms, is there any evidence that the hourly pay rate distributions for male and female employees at Glenco are substantially different?

c. Construct similar graphs of hourly pay rates for minority and nonminority employees at Glenco. (Be sure to keep the scales the same in all histograms for comparison purposes.) Based on these histograms, is there any evidence that the hourly pay rate distributions for minority and nonminority employees at Glenco are substantially different?

FIGURE 2.12 **Histograms of Hourly Pay Rates of Male and Female Glenco Employees**

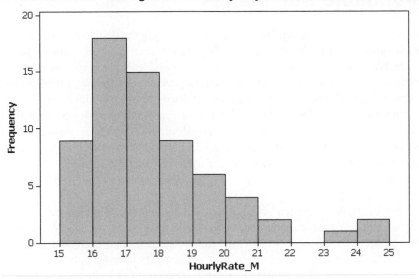

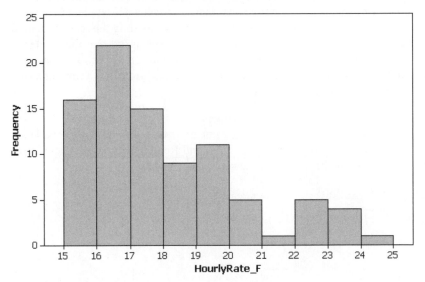

2.5 For each of the following variables in the Glenco Manufacturing data, construct a histogram, stem-and-leaf diagram, or a bar chart: Minority, Age, and Tenure. Use each type of graph once. Be sure that the type of graph used is appropriate for the variable. Comment on what you learn from each graph about its associated variable.

2.6 Cosp Industries produces custom-ordered specialty parts. Each order requires a new setup and training for the assembly workers. During a testing run, 50 parts are assembled and the assembly times are measured (in seconds) for the purpose of estimating the average assembly time. The assembly times for the most recent part produced are shown here.

AssemblyTime

40.0	36.5	38.5	34.9	36.7	33.4	31.8	33.7	29.8
32.8	31.1	29.1	27.5	29.9	27.4	27.2	25.5	27.1
27.9	25.6	25.6	25.0	23.8	24.8	23.7	24.8	23.6
23.0	24.0	23.8	22.6	24.4	24.2	23.3	23.2	23.7
24.1	23.3	24.2	23.3	24.5	23.4	23.2	24.0	22.9
24.4	24.5	23.5	23.1	23.6				

a. Construct a histogram of the assembly times. Based on this plot, estimate the average or typical time required to assemble this part.

b. Construct a time series plot of the assembly times. Do you learn anything from this plot that you did not observe in the histogram? Speculate as to the cause of this feature of the data. How does this finding change your estimate of the average time required to assemble this part?

2.2 Two-Variable Summaries

two-way frequency
table
cross-tabulation
stacked bar chart
100% stacked bar
chart

In the previous section, we described tools for summarizing the distribution of values for a single qualitative variable (frequency table and bar chart) and for a single quantitative variable (frequency table, histogram, and stem-and-leaf diagram). Often, a decision problem requires information about the relationship between two variables. In this section, we describe methods for summarizing two-variable relationships.

As with single variables, the type of table or graph required depends on the types of variables to be summarized. For two qualitative variables, a **two-way frequency table** or **cross-tabulation** is an appropriate tabular summary, and a **stacked bar chart** and a **100% stacked bar chart** are useful graphical displays.

EXAMPLE 2.6

A major university is concerned about recent declines in the retention rate of its freshman students. A significant number of freshmen drop out or transfer to another university before the sophomore year. One estimate suggests that each student generates approximately $100,000 in revenue for the university over the course of his or her undergraduate career. Knowing that it is likely to be less expensive to retain a student from the freshman to sophomore year than to attract a new student to the university, the administration is focusing its efforts on understanding the reasons behind the decline in the freshman retention rate. It has been suggested that the residency status of a student (in-state or out-of-state) may make a difference in the chances of a student remaining at the university. Data were collected from last year's entering freshman class for analysis.

SOLUTION The following two-way frequency table, based on last year's freshman enrollment data, shows the cross-classification of two variables, Residency (whether the student is in-state or out-of-state) and Retention (whether the student stayed or left before the beginning of the sophomore year).

```
Tabulated Statistics: Residency, Retention

Rows: Residency     Columns: Retention

                 Left    Stayed      All

In-State          400      1690      2090
Out-of-State      453       939      1392
All               853      2629      3482


 Cell Contents   --
                    Count
```

From the table, we see that there was a total of 3,482 students in the sample. Of those, 2090 were in-state students and 1392 were from out-of-state. We also observe that 853 students left before the sophomore year.

The stacked bar chart from Excel shown in Figure 2.13, a graphical representation of the two-way frequency table, is a bar chart of one of the variables (Residency in this case) where each bar is divided according to the frequencies of the second variable (Retention).

As an alternative, we can construct another two-way frequency table that displays percentages as well as the counts. For example, we see that 11.49% of the 3482 students were in-state residents and left before the sophomore year.

FIGURE 2.13

Stacked Bar Chart of Residency and Retention

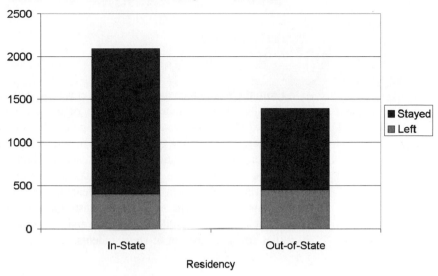

```
Tabulated Statistics: Residency, Retention

Rows: Residency     Columns: Retention

              Left     Stayed      All

In-State       400      1690      2090
             11.49     48.54     60.02

Out-of-State   453       939      1392
             13.01     26.97     39.98

All            853      2629      3482
             24.50     75.50    100.00

Cell Contents --
              Count
              % of Table
```

The main question of interest is: Are the two variables Retention and Residency related? In other words, is the retention rate for in-state students different from that for out-of-state students? To better answer this question, we can construct another version of this two-way table that shows row percentages.

```
Tabulated Statistics: Residency, Retention

Rows: Residency     Columns: Retention

              Left     Stayed      All

In-State       400      1690      2090
             19.14     80.86    100.00

Out-of-State   453       939      1392
             32.54     67.46    100.00
```

```
All                853       2629      3482
                  24.50      75.50    100.00

Cell Contents --
              Count
              % of Row
```

From the row percentages in this table, we see that 19.14% of in-state students and 32.54% of out-of-state students left before the sophomore year. The 100% stacked bar chart from Excel shown in Figure 2.14 is a graphical representation of the row percentages in the two-way frequency table that allows us to judge whether or not there is an association between Residency and Retention. In this case, we clearly see that the retention rates for in-state and out-of-state students are different.

On average, about 1 in 5 in-state students leaves early compared to about 1 in 3 out-of-state students. The evidence suggests that the retention problem is greater among the out-of-state students. The university administration might want to focus its initial efforts on the out-of-state students.

FIGURE 2.14   **100% Stacked Bar Chart of Residency and Retention**

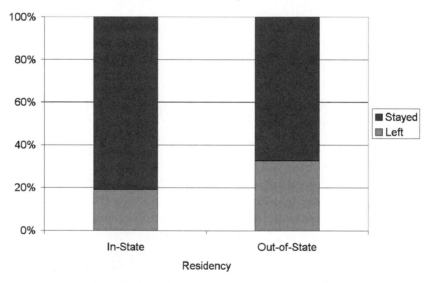

scatterplot   A **scatterplot** is the best tool for visualizing the relationship between two quantitative variables. For example, a realtor may be interested in the relationship between the selling price (as measured in dollars) of houses in her market and the size of these houses (as measured in square feet of heated/cooled floor space). Figure 2.15 is a scatterplot of selling price versus size for 50 recently sold homes in the realtor's area.

What can be learned from the scatterplot in Figure 2.15? As might be expected, we see that larger homes tend to sell for higher prices than smaller homes. Although the plotted points do not follow an exact mathematical relationship, there is a positive linear pattern in the graph suggesting that as square footage increases, selling prices tend to increase. We also observe some outliers, or unusual houses, for which the selling price was much lower or higher than expected based on the size of the

FIGURE 2.15   **Scatterplot of Selling Price Versus Size for 50 Houses**

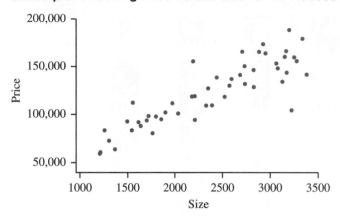

house. These differences might be explained by other factors, such as the condition or the location of the house.

The graphical tools presented in the last two sections are valuable for visualizing and summarizing data. Numerical summaries, such as averages, provide additional insights about data and are the subject of the next two sections of this chapter.

Exercises

2.7   Construct a two-way frequency table for the Department and Minority variables in the Glenco Manufacturing data. Include the percentage of minority and percentage of nonminority employees within each department in the cells of the table. What conclusion(s) can you draw from this table?

2.8   Construct a 100% stacked bar chart using the Glenco data with departments as the bars and the minority/nonminority percentages reflected within each bar. Interpret what you see in this data display.

2.9   Explain the advantage(s) of the stacked bar chart over the 100% stacked bar chart and the advantage(s) of the 100% stacked bar chart over the stacked bar chart.

2.10   Which is more useful for determining if there is an association between two categorical variables: stacked bar chart or 100% stacked bar chart? If two categorical variables are unrelated (that is, independent), what would you see in the chart?

2.11   University administrators who were studying the retention problem discussed in this section collected additional data on the entering freshmen from last year including Gender (M or F) and Major (Business, Education, Engineering, Arts & Sciences, Other).

a. Figure 2.16 is an Excel pivot table (two-way table) of Retention and Major and Figure 2.17 (see next page) is a 100% stacked bar chart of Retention and Major. Based on this output, is there an association between Retention and Major? Explain why or why not.

b. Construct an appropriate table and graph of the relationship between Retention and Gender. What conclusion can you draw from this analysis?

FIGURE 2.16   **Excel Pivot Table for Freshmen Retention Data**

Count of Retention	Major					
Residency	Arts&Sciences	Business	Education	Engineering	Other	Grand Total
In-State	717	543	371	284	175	2090
Out-of-State	441	403	241	208	99	1392
Grand Total	1158	946	612	492	274	3482

FIGURE 2.17 100% Stacked Bar Chart for Freshmen Retention Data

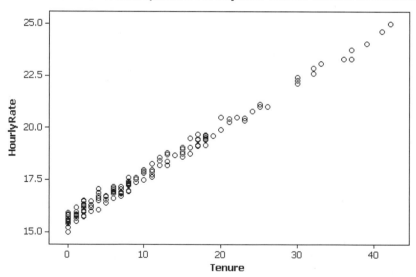

2.12 Figure 2.18 is a Minitab scatterplot of HourlyRate versus Tenure from the Glenco Manufacturing data. What do you learn from this plot about the relationship between these two variables?

2.13 Construct a scatterplot of Tenure versus Age from the Glenco Manufacturing data. Explain the reason behind the unusual pattern in this plot.

FIGURE 2.18 Scatterplot for HourlyRate versus Tenure in Glenco Data

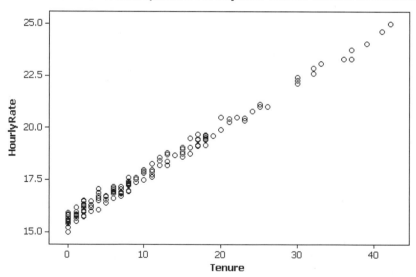

2.3 On the Average: Typical Values

Frequency tables, bar charts, histograms, and stem-and-leaf displays all give a general sense of the pattern or distribution of values in a data set. They do not indicate a typical, middle, or average value explicitly. A great many management decisions are based on what a typical result is. For example, the formulation of a particular frozen dinner may well be based on comparing the typical favorability ratings of three possible formulations. The choice of an investment advisor for a pension fund will be based largely on comparing the typical performance over time (relative to market averages) of each of several candidates. Many quality-improvement measures attempt to reduce the typical number of improperly made items per thousand. In this section we define some standard measures of the typical or average value.

The word *average* has at least three meanings. It can mean the most common value, the mode; it can mean the middle value, the median; or it can mean the arithmetic average, the mean. This section contains more careful definitions of these three basic concepts of typical values.

DEFINITION 2.1

Mode   The mode of a variable is the value or category with the highest frequency in the data. It is most commonly used with qualitative data.

In Example 2.1 the frequencies (counts) for offices 1, 2, 3, and 4 were 8, 4, 3, and 5, respectively. Therefore, the modal category for the qualitative variable "office number" is 1, because that office has the largest number of salespeople.

Because we do not usually have the original measurements that have been used to form a frequency table, the mode for grouped data is defined as the midpoint of the class with the highest frequency. This value approximates the mode of the actual (ungrouped) data.

In Example 2.2 the modal commission income is $1000, the midpoint of the class with endpoints of $750 and $1249. Unfortunately, the modal value is very sensitive to small changes in data values or class definitions. Had we defined the classes as $252 to $751, $752 to $1251, and so on in Example 2.2, the frequency table would change slightly, as shown here:

Class	Frequency
252–751	7
752–1251	6
1252–1751	5
1752–2251	1
2252–2751	1

The mode for these grouped data would be 501, the midpoint of the first interval, rather than 1000 as we found previously.

As we have illustrated, a mode calculated from a small amount of data or based on arbitrary class definitions is not too reliable and shouldn't be taken too seriously.

DEFINITION 2.2

Median   The median of a set of data is the middle value when the data are arranged from lowest to highest. It is meaningful only if there is a natural ordering of the values from lowest to highest. If n, the sample size, is odd, the median is the $(n + 1)/2$th value; if n is even, the median is the average of the $n/2$th and $(n + 2)/2$th values.

EXAMPLE 2.7

Suppose that the number of units per day of whole blood used in transfusions at a hospital over the previous 11 days is

25   16   61   12   18   15   20   24   17   19   28

Find the median.

SOLUTION   Arranged in increasing order, the values are

12   15   16   17   18   19   20   24   25   28   61

The sample size, n, is 11, so the median value is the $(11 + 1)/2$th, or sixth, value, 19.

If n, the number of measurements, is odd, there is no problem in finding the middle value. However, where n is even, there is no value exactly in the middle; for this situation, the median is conventionally defined as the average of the middle two values when the data are ordered from smallest to largest. If in Example 2.7 there had been a twelfth value of 72, the median would be the average of the sixth and seventh values $(19 + 20)/2 = 19.5$. Whether n is odd or even, there are equal numbers of observations above and below the median.

DEFINITION 2.3

> **Mean**   The mean of a variable is the sum of the measurements taken on that variable divided by the number of measurements. It is meaningful only for quantitative data.

The mean is simply the average of all the data values. It is the point at which a histogram of the data balances. Think of each point as a weight along a line. If a fulcrum (like the pivot point on a child's seesaw) is placed at the mean, the weights below the mean will exactly balance those above the mean. This is a good way to visualize the mean in a histogram or stem-and-leaf diagram.

In Example 2.2 the mean commission income was ($850 + $1265 + $\cdots$ + $1475)/20$, or $1066.55. We use two different symbols for the mean, depending on whether we want to regard the data as the entire population of interest or as a sample of measurements from the population of interest.

As we indicated in Chapter 1, a population of measurements is the complete set of measurements of interest to a manager; a sample of measurements is a subset of measurements selected from the population of interest. If we let $y_1, y_2, \ldots, y_n$ represent a sample of n measurements selected from a population, the sample mean is denoted by the symbol $\bar{y}$:

$$\bar{y} = \frac{\sum_i y_i}{n}$$

The corresponding mean of the population from which the sample was drawn is denoted by the Greek letter μ.

In most situations we do not know the population mean; the sample mean is used to make inferences about the corresponding unknown population mean. This is discussed in greater detail beginning in Chapter 7.

The mean is the most useful and convenient measure of the average value; however, any user of statistics should be alert to the possibility of distortions due to skewness or outliers. An extreme value can pull the mean in its direction and cause the mean to appear atypical of the values in the set. For this reason, statisticians have

trimmed means

outliers

developed the idea of **trimmed means.** To find a 40% trimmed mean, for instance, drop the highest 20% and lowest 20% of the values and average the remaining values. This trimming process eliminates the effect of **outliers,** data values that lie far above or below the preponderance of the data. Trimmed means are particularly useful in estimation of a population mean based on sample data because they reduce the impact of possible "freak" values.

FIGURE 2.19   **Measures of Location for Skewed Distribution**

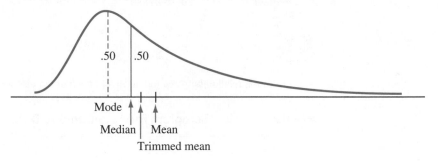

measures of location
measures of central
    tendency

The mode, median, mean, and trimmed means are called **measures of location** or **measures of central tendency;** they indicate the center or general location of data values. The relation among these measures depends on the skewness of the data. If the distribution is mound shaped—symmetric around a single peak—the mode, median, mean, and trimmed means are all equal. For a skewed distribution, one having a long tail in one direction and a single peak, the mean is pulled out toward the long tail; usually the median falls between the mode and the mean, and a trimmed mean between the median and the mean (see Figure 2.19).

Statistical thinking focuses very heavily on typical, average values. In many situations, inferences related to average or typical values will suffice, but there is a limit to such thinking. Sometimes the average value isn't important. A single, dramatically effective drug can propel a small pharmaceutical firm's ledger from the red to the black very quickly; a single disaster can propel an insurance firm into bankruptcy court. But it would be foolish to ignore statistical thinking on these grounds. Most products will not be overwhelming successes; most accidents will not be bankruptcy-causing disasters. Managers who assume that their results will always be better than average are in grave danger of becoming ex-managers. Measures of variability provide another dimension to our thinking; they are discussed in the next section.

Exercises

2.14   Compute the mean, median, and mode for the following data:

11   17   18   10   22   23   15   17   14   13   10   12   18   18   11   14

2.15   The Insurance Institute for Highway Safety published data on the total damage suffered by compact automobiles in a series of controlled, low-speed collisions. The data, in dollars, with brand names removed, are

| 361 | 393 | 430 | 543 | 566 | 610 | 763 | 851 | 886 | 887 | 976 | 1039 |
| 1124 | 1267 | 1328 | 1415 | 1425 | 1444 | 1476 | 1542 | 1544 | 2048 | 2197 | |

A histogram is shown in Figure 2.20 on the next page. A summary from Excel is given here.

```
    Damage
Mean                1090.6522
Standard Error      105.83343
Median              1039
Mode                #N/A
Standard Deviation  507.55928
Sample Variance     257616.42
```

```
Kurtosis          -0.363327
Skewness           0.4189689
Range                   1836
Minimum                  361
Maximum                 2197
Sum                    25085
Count                     23
```

What does the relation between the mean and median indicate about the shape of the data?

FIGURE 2.20   Histogram for Auto Damage Data

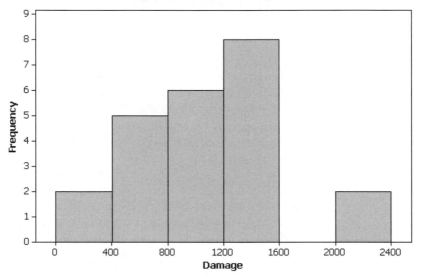

2.16 Production records for an automobile manufacturer show the following figures for production per shift (maximum production is 720 cars per shift):

688 711 625 701 688 667 694 630 547 703 688 697 703 656 677
700 702 688 691 664 688 679 708 699 667 703

a. Would the mode be a useful summary statistic for these data? Why?
b. Find the median.
c. Find the mean.
d. What does the relation between the mean and median indicate about the shape of the data?

2.17 Draw a stem-and-leaf plot of the data in Exercise 2.16. The "stem" should include (from highest to lowest) 71, 70, 69, ... Does the shape of the stem-and-leaf display confirm your judgment in part (d) of Exercise 2.16?

2.18 Many popular cellular phone plans have a fixed charge per month that provides a fixed number of usage minutes, referred to as "free minutes." Additional charges accrue to the customer for exceeding the "free minutes" and for "roaming" (that is, making calls from outside the customer's local calling area). Data were collected on the additional charges accrued by 100 randomly selected customers.
a. Consider the following descriptive statistics provided by Minitab.

```
Descriptive Statistics: CellCharges

Variable         N     Mean    Median    TrMean      StDev    SE Mean
CellCharges    100    33.87     36.71     32.12      33.93       3.39

Variable    Minimum    Maximum       Q1        Q3
CellCharges    0.00     106.60     0.00     63.26
```

Of the mean, median, and trimmed mean, which do you believe best represents the data as a measure of central tendency? Do you notice any unusual or surprising values in the output?

b. Consider the Minitab histogram of the cell phone charges data shown in Figure 2.21. Of the mean, median, and trimmed mean, which do you now believe best represents the data as a measure of central tendency?

c. Explain why the mean, median, and trimmed mean are not good summary statistics for the central tendency of the cell phone charges data. Write one or two sentences that correctly summarize the central tendency of the cell phone charges data.

FIGURE 2.21 Histogram of Cell Phone Additional Charges Data

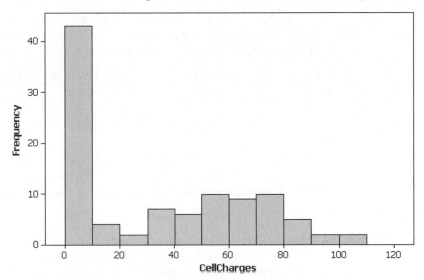

2.4 Measuring Variability

One of the most important unifying ideas in statistics is the notion of variability. Customers vary in time taken to pay bills. Caplets of a particular drug vary in their potency but had better not vary too much. Overtime payments to a city police force vary sharply from week to week. Variability in return on investment is the key to the idea of risk in finance. Variability is an absolutely fundamental idea in quality control; in many situations, such as caplets' varying in potency, variability is a major enemy of quality. One of the major themes of statistics and statistical quality control is accounting for sources of variability.

The first task in dealing with variability is summarizing it. In this section, we'll define several measures of variability and discuss strengths and weaknesses of each. The simplest measure of variability is the **range**—the difference between the largest and smallest values. It's easy to compute, so it is widely used to measure variability.

range

There are at least two problems with using the range as a measure of variability, however. First, the range is very sensitive to outliers—"wild" values far from the rest of the data. Second, as the sample size increases, the range tends to increase as well.

deviations from the mean

More useful measures of variability are based on **deviations from the mean.** The deviation of a sample measurement y_i from its mean $\bar{y}$ is defined as $(y_i - \bar{y})$. Some of these deviations are positive, others negative; their algebraic sum is always zero. Thus, the positive and negative deviations exactly balance. To measure variability, we must look at the magnitudes (ignoring the positive or negative sign) of the deviations; large positive and negative deviations indicate large variability.

mean absolute deviation

The simplest measure of the magnitudes of the deviations is the **mean absolute deviation** (MAD), defined as the average of the absolute values of the deviations:

$$\text{MAD} = \frac{\sum_i |y_i - \bar{y}|}{n}$$

Regard the data values 11, 12, 13, 14, and 30 as a sample of five measurements selected from a population of interest. Compute the average absolute deviation for the sample data. It is easy to show that $\bar{y} = 80/5 = 16$, so

$$\text{MAD} = \frac{|11 - 16| + |12 - 16| + |13 - 16| + |14 - 16| + |30 - 16|}{5}$$

$$= \frac{5 + 4 + 3 + 2 + 14}{5} = 5.6$$

Thus, on the average, an individual measurement deviates 5.6 units from the mean.

The mean absolute deviation is easy to compute and to interpret. However, it is difficult to deal mathematically with absolute values. Most statistical methods deal with squared deviations instead.

variance
standard deviation

The most useful statistical measures of variability are the **variance** and the **standard deviation.** The variance of a sample of n measurements $y_1, y_2, \ldots, y_n$ is often called the *mean squared error*. It is the average squared deviation, defined as the sum of the squared deviations divided by $(n - 1)$. We denote the sample variance by s^2.

The sample standard deviation s of the measurements is the (positive) square root of the variance. The corresponding population variance and standard deviation are denoted by σ^2 and σ, respectively.

DEFINITION 2.4

Variance and Standard Deviation

$$s^2 = \frac{\sum_i (y_i - \bar{y})^2}{n - 1}$$

$$s = \sqrt{s^2}$$

EXAMPLE 2.8

Compute the sample variance and sample standard deviation for the values 11, 12, 13, 14, and 30 (which have a mean of 16).

SOLUTION   With $\bar{y} = 16$, we can substitute into the formula for s^2 to obtain

$$s^2 = \frac{(11 - 16)^2 + (12 - 16)^2 + (13 - 16)^2 + (14 - 16)^2 + (30 - 16)^2}{5 - 1}$$

$$= \frac{250}{4} = 62.5$$

and thus

$$s = \sqrt{62.5} \approx 7.906$$

The use of $(n - 1)$ as the denominator of s^2 is not arbitrary. This definition of the sample variance makes it an "unbiased estimator" of the population variance σ^2. This roughly means that if we were to draw a very large number of samples each of size n from the population and if we computed s^2 for each sample, the average sample variance would equal the population variance σ^2. Had we divided by n in the definition of s^2, the average sample variance would be slightly less than the population variance, and hence s^2 would tend to slightly underestimate σ^2. The use of $n - 1$ rather than n is standard in most computer packages. Unless the sample size is very small, the effect of using $n - 1$ instead of n is numerically quite small, and not crucial.

The definitions of variance and standard deviation depend on whether the data are regarded as a population or as a sample. In practice, the available data are almost always a sample. Unless specifically indicated otherwise, we regard all data sets as samples and consider population means and variances as conceptual quantities to be estimated from the samples. Virtually all statistical computer programs also make this assumption.*

We have defined the variance and standard deviation but have not yet indicated how to interpret them. What does a standard deviation of, say, $552.51 mean? One reasonably good approximation assumes that the measurements have roughly a mound-shaped histogram—that is, a symmetric, single-peaked histogram that tapers off smoothly from the peak toward the tails. We call the approximation the Empirical Rule.

DEFINITION 2.5

Empirical Rule   For a set of measurements having a mound-shaped histogram, the interval

$\bar{y} \pm 1s$ contains approximately 68% of the measurements;

$\bar{y} \pm 2s$ contains approximately 95% of the measurements;

$\bar{y} \pm 3s$ contains approximately all of the measurements.

The approximation may be poor if the data are severely skewed or bimodal, or contain outliers.

EXAMPLE 2.9

A sample of prices for 20 days throughout the previous year indicates that the average wholesale price per pound for steers at a particular stockyard was $.61 and that the standard deviation was $.07. If the histogram for the measurements is mound-shaped, describe the variability of the data using the Empirical Rule.

---

*When a set of data is regarded as a population, the population variance is defined as the sum of squared deviations from the population mean μ, all divided by N, the population size—not by $(N - 1)$.

SOLUTION   Applying the Empirical Rule, we conclude that:

the interval .61 ± .07, or $.54 to $.68, contains approximately 68% of the measurements;

the interval .61 ± .14, or $.47 to $.75, contains approximately 95% of the measurements;

the interval .61 ± .21, or $.40 to $.82, contains approximately all of the measurements.

Because the standard deviation is based on *squared* deviations from the mean, it is more sensitive to outliers than the mean is. For example, suppose that the 10 salespeople at a new car dealership have monthly sales of 16, 18, 19, 20, 20, 22, 24, 26, 28, and 80 vehicles. (The 80 figure includes a very large fleet sale.) Taking all 10 scores into account, the mean is 27.30 and the standard deviation is 18.88. If the 80 score is omitted because it was obtained under different conditions—a fleet sale rather than individual sales—the mean drops to 21.44, but the standard deviation falls way down to only 3.91. Squaring the extremely large deviation yielded by an outlier blows up the variance; even taking the square root to get the standard deviation still results in a very large standard deviation.

interquartile range   An alternative way to approach variability is the **interquartile range** (IQR). The quartiles of a data distribution are the 25th and 75th percentiles—the values that mark the bottom one-fourth and top one-fourth of the data. Tukey (1977) calls these values "hinges" and notes that they can be found by taking medians of each half of the data. The median of the bottom half of the data is the 25th percentile, simply because half of one-half is one-fourth; similarly, the median of the top half of the data is the 75th percentile. The interquartile range is the difference between the two quartiles.

DEFINITION 2.6

Interquartile Range   To find the quartiles of a set of data on a variable,

1.   Sort the data and find the median.

2.   Divide the data into top and bottom halves (above and below the median). If the sample size n is odd, arbitrarily include the median in both halves.

3.   Find the medians of both halves. These are the 25th and 75th percentiles, or "hinges."

4.   IQR = 75th percentile − 25th percentile.

EXAMPLE 2.10   Find the interquartile range for the following data:

24   26   26   28   29   29   29   30   30   31   32   33   33   34   35
35   35   36   36   37   37   38   39   40   40   41   42   44   45   49

SOLUTION   The data are already sorted, lowest to highest. Because $n = 30$, the median is the average of the 15th and 16th values (both of which are 35), namely, 35. The bottom half of the data is the lowest 15 values; the top half is the highest 15 values. The median of the bottom half (that is, the 25th percentile) is the eighth value, 30. The 75th percentile is the eighth value from the top, 39. The IQR is 39 − 30 = 9.

The IQR is most commonly used in checking for outliers. Tukey (1977) defines the inner fences as follows:

lower inner fence = 25th percentile − 1.5 IQR

upper inner fence = 75th percentile + 1.5 IQR

Any value outside the inner fences is an outlier candidate. The choice of the number 1.5 is arbitrary, but it seems to work decently. Similarly, the outer fences are defined as 3 times the IQR from the "hinges."

lower outer fence = 25th percentile − 3.0 IQR

upper outer fence = 75th percentile + 3.0 IQR

Any data value outside the outer fences is a serious outlier.

EXAMPLE 2.11 Calculate the various fences for the data of Example 2.10. Does the fence test identify any outliers? Do there appear to be outliers on visual inspection?

SOLUTION A plot of the data, or merely a scan by eye, does not indicate that any value should be regarded as an outlier. The closest thing to an outlier is the value 49, but it is close to several other values. The 25th percentile and 75th percentile were found in Example 2.10 to be 30 and 39, so the IQR is 9. The inner fences are 30 − 1.5(9) = 16.5 and 39 + 1.5(9) = 52.5. No data value even comes close to the inner fences, so the fence test identifies no outliers.

The interquartile range is the basis for still another Tukey (1977) idea, the box plot, sometimes called the "box-and-whiskers plot."

DEFINITION 2.7 Box Plot

1. Draw the edges of a box at the 25th and 75th percentiles. Draw a vertical bar through the box at the median.

2. Draw lines ("whiskers") from the edges of the box to the adjacent values—the smallest and largest nonoutliers.

3. Plot each outlier candidate separately, conventionally using a * symbol. Plot each serious outlier, conventionally using a 0 symbol.

EXAMPLE 2.12 Suppose that the return on investments for 21 companies in a certain industry for a certain year is

−24.6 −2.6 2.4 2.7 3.8 5.6 5.9 6.7 7.0 7.2 7.5
8.0 8.2 8.5 8.6 8.8 9.0 9.2 9.7 10.0 20.5

Draw a box plot of these data.

SOLUTION   With $n = 21$, the median is the 11th score, 7.5. The 25th percentile is the median of the bottom 11 scores, namely 5.6. (Note that, because n is an odd number, we include the median in both halves of the data. Thus, the bottom half of the data comprises 11 scores, not 10.) The 75th percentile is the median of the top 11 scores, namely, 8.8. Thus, IQR $= 8.8 - 5.6 = 3.2$. The fences are

$$\text{lower outer fence} = 5.6 - 3.0(3.2) = -4.0$$

$$\text{lower inner fence} = 5.6 - 1.5(3.2) = 0.8$$

$$\text{upper inner fence} = 8.8 + 1.5(3.2) = 13.6$$

$$\text{upper outer fence} = 8.8 + 3.0(3.2) = 18.4$$

The fence test identifies two serious outliers, -24.6 and 20.5, and one outlier candidate, -2.6. (A plot of the data indicates that the serious outliers are obviously extreme and that the outlier candidate is debatably out.) The adjacent values are the smallest and largest nonoutliers, 2.4 and 10.0. The resulting box plot is shown in Figure 2.22.

FIGURE 2.22   Box Plot of Investment Returns

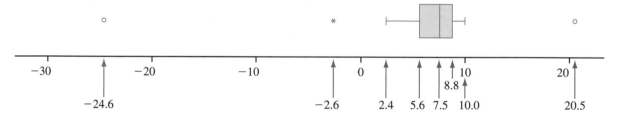

Apart from its use in box plots, the IQR is not as widely reported as the standard deviation. For most of our purposes, the standard deviation will be the most important measure of variability.

In Section 2.2, we discussed two-variable displays, including scatterplots for two quantitative variables and two-way frequency tables for two categorical variables. The real value of box plots is their ability to graphically summarize the relationship between two variables when one is quantitative and the other is categorical. In particular, box plots are a great alternative to side-by-side histograms for comparing distributions (of a quantitative variable) across groups (levels of a categorical variable).

EXAMPLE 2.13   A credit union is interested in comparing the efficiency of its three full-time tellers in serving their customers. For each teller, the required service times for 20 randomly selected customers were measured and recorded. The data are shown below. Construct a graphical display to compare the three tellers.

ServiceTime

Teller A:	2.5	1.8	1.5	1.6	1.3	1.6	2.8	2.5	0.2	7.3	4.5
6.5	5.5	2.6	1.6	2.6	4.3	0.9	2.8	5.4			

Teller B:	2.8	2.6	3.9	5.7	3.2	6.8	3.1	3.1	0.4	2.0	6.8
6.0	4.6	1.8	0.4	2.5	0.4	0.8	12.6	2.4			

Teller C:	3.5	10.4	2.7	4.6	1.9	12.6	4.6	3.2	6.9	14.0	4.9
2.4	1.5	18.6	2.7	8.2	7.0	1.6	3.4	10.1			

SOLUTION   We could create three separate histograms, one for each teller, and place them side-by-side (or stack them) for comparison. We would have to be careful to use the same scales for all three histograms to make the histograms comparable. The display would also take up a great deal of space. A better solution is to use box plots as shown in Figure 2.23. From this Minitab display, we see that two of the tellers (A and B) have roughly the same service time distribution, while the other teller (C) tends to have longer service times on average as well as more variation in service times.

FIGURE 2.23   **Box Plots of Teller Service Times**

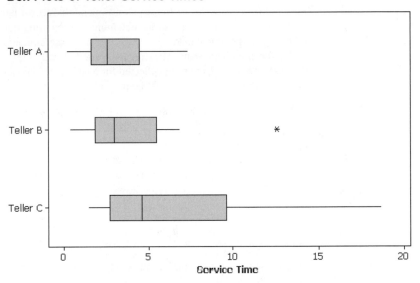

Exercises

2.19   Suppose that the data from two samples are

Sample 1:   15   19   21   25
Sample 2:   14   17   18   19   19   20   20   20   21   21   22   23   26

a. Find the range for each sample.
b. Find the standard deviation for each sample.
c. Which sample shows more variability? Construct histograms or box plots to support your opinion.

2.20   Data for car production per shift given in Exercise 2.16 are reproduced here, along with selected Excel output:

688   711   625   701   688   667   694   630   547   703   688   697   703
656   677   700   702   688   691   664   688   679   708   699   667   703

Production	
Mean	679.38
Median	688
Mode	688
Standard Deviation	34.83
Sample Variance	1213.13

```
Range                     164
Minimum                   547
Maximum                   711
Count                      26
```

a. Locate the mean and standard deviation.
b. How well does the Empirical Rule work for the fraction of data falling within 1 standard deviation of the mean?

2.21 Refer to Exercise 2.20.
a. Locate the median and IQR for the data shown.
b. Find the inner and outer fences. Are there outliers?
c. Draw a box plot of the data.

2.22 Directory assistance (information) operators receive requests for telephone numbers from customers. The procedure for obtaining and reporting numbers is highly computerized so that each operator should be able to handle a large number of calls in a workday. At one office, the minimum standard is regarded as 780 calls cleared per day—roughly, 2 calls cleared per minute. Data were collected for a day on 60 day-shift operators. What sources of variability among operators might be present?

2.23 Data on the 60 operators of Exercise 2.22 were analyzed using Minitab.

```
Descriptive Statistics: Cleared

Variable    N     Mean   SE Mean   StDev   Minimum       Q1   Median       Q3   Maximum
Cleared    60   794.23      4.42   34.25    601.00   789.00   799.00   807.75    844.00

Data Display

Cleared
    797    794    817    813    817    793    762    719    804    811    837    804    790
    796    807    801    805    811    835    787    800    771    794    805    797    724
    820    601    817    801    798    797    788    802    792    779    803    807    789
    787    794    792    786    808    808    844    790    763    784    739    805    817
    804    807    800    785    796    789    842    829
```

a. Calculate the "mean plus-or-minus 1 standard deviation" interval used in the Empirical Rule.
b. Of the 60 scores in "cleared," 51 fall within the 1 standard deviation interval. How does this result compare with the theoretical value of the Empirical Rule? What might explain the discrepancy?

2.24 A box plot of the data in Exercise 2.23 using Minitab is shown in Figure 2.24. How does the plot explain the failure of the Empirical Rule?

2.25 Operator 28 (the one with the 601 score in the data for Exercise 2.23) was a trainee who wasn't expected to perform to the standard of long-term operators. The data were reanalyzed omitting this operator.
a. How would you expect omitting the 601 score to affect the mean? The standard deviation?
b. Minitab output is shown here. How much were the mean and standard deviation affected?

```
Descriptive Statistics: Longterm

Variable     N     Mean   SE Mean   StDev   Minimum       Q1   Median       Q3   Maximum
Longterm    59   797.51      3.02   23.21    719.00   789.00   800.00   808.00    844.00
```

2.26 Scheduling the duration of airplane flights is critical to an airline's service, particularly at "hub" centers. At such centers, flights arrive in groups, passengers transfer to other flights, and these flights depart. If incoming flights require longer-than-scheduled times, passengers

FIGURE 2.24 **Box Plot of Calls Cleared Data**

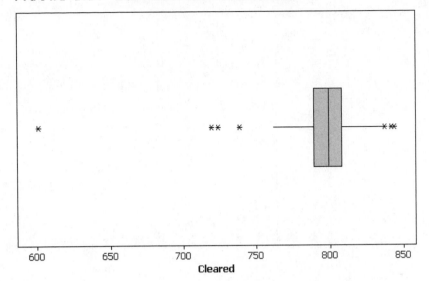

Cleared

may miss connecting flights, or the outgoing flights may have to be delayed. If, however, most flights require less-than-scheduled times, passengers will have to wait a long time for their connecting flights. An operations manager routinely records the actual times taken by 38 flights scheduled to arrive between 4:30 and 5:00 P.M. at a hub. The times are converted to percentage of scheduled time, so a "late percentage" of 100 indicates that a flight is exactly on time. Computer output of the 38 percentages is shown here.

```
Descriptive Statistics: Late%

Variable    N    Mean   StDev  Minimum     Q1  Median       Q3  Maximum
Late%      38  101.58    6.48    91.00  97.00  100.00   104.25   125.00
```

a. On average, how well did the flights do in meeting their schedules?
b. What sources of variability can you think of?
c. Find Empirical Rule limits that should include 95% of the flights.

2.27 A stem-and-leaf display of the data for Exercise 2.26 is shown here.

```
Stem-and-leaf of Late%   N = 38
Leaf Unit = 1.0

    3      9   123
   14      9   55677778999
  (15)    10   000000222223334
    9     10   556789
    3     11   1
    2     11   6
    1     12
    1     12   5
```

a. Do the data appear bell-shaped, so that the Empirical Rule should work reasonably well?
b. What percentage of the 38 scores fall within the limits calculated in part (c) of Exercise 2.26?

2.28 The late percentage data of Exercise 2.26 were plotted by Minitab in Figure 2.25, in order of scheduled arrival. Is there any indication of a trend?

FIGURE 2.25 **Sequence Plot of Lateness Data**

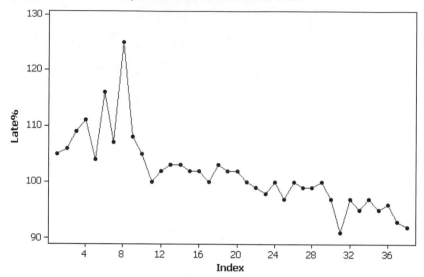

2.29 The operations manager of Exercise 2.26 also kept track of the lateness percentage of each flight over time. The results for flight 483 for 40 consecutive weekdays were analyzed by Minitab, as shown here.

```
Data Display

Late%
   100   107    97   101   103   101    95    92    96    93
   104   109   106   107   112   102   101    99    99    98
   104   109   116   118   104   106    99   105   104   107
    97    94   100   101   102   105   109    99   105    99

Descriptive Statistics: Late%

Variable    N    Mean   StDev  Minimum     Q1  Median      Q3  Maximum
Late%      40  102.63    5.75    92.00  99.00  102.00  106.00   118.00
```

a. Should one expect essentially the same variability in these time series numbers as we found for the cross-section data of Exercise 2.26?

b. Which standard deviation turned out smaller?

2.30 The lateness percentage data of Exercise 2.29 were plotted against day number, as shown in Figure 2.26. Is there any evidence of a time trend?

2.31 Typical advertisements for mutual funds report the average performance of funds over various time periods. Suppose that you are considering purchasing shares of one of three funds, the Alpha Fund, the Beta Fund, and the Gamma Fund. Over the past 30 years, the annual rates of return for the Alpha, Beta, and Gamma funds have been 10%, 14%, and 12%, respectively.

a. Which of these three funds would you choose for investment? What additional information, if any, about their performances over the past 30 years would you like to have before making your decision?

b. The annual returns for each of these three funds over the past 30 years are shown here. Analyze these data with appropriate statistical tools to compare the three funds.

FIGURE 2.26 **Sequence Plot for Exercise 2.30**

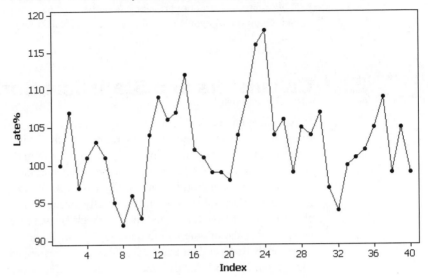

AnnualReturn

Alpha Fund: 9.67 11.26 11.17 8.86 10.69 7.59 13.10 9.13 6.10 11.52
11.21 5.06 9.48 12.67 11.40 9.78 9.62 13.21 9.47 8.47 12.11 7.29
12.05 9.31 11.37 8.12 12.10 8.46 10.31 9.42

Beta Fund: 10.21 9.14 24.47 6.06 35.34 9.01 20.67 −13.07 16.20
47.92 49.69 −21.91 3.21 7.55 −4.08 19.50 12.18 36.42 3.33 11.07
16.88 31.85 26.51 17.92 0.12 5.59 13.35 20.27 5.39 −0.76

Gamma Fund: 8.34 3.62 9.43 3.45 6.64 3.08 3.95 1.04 −4.03
1.55 2.82 5.66 6.26 8.39 8.13 9.74 3.30 10.64 11.58 11.14
3.08 6.91 12.28 10.90 3.36 −0.47 4.63 68.58 65.06 70.94

c. Which mutual fund would you now choose based on your analysis? Explain your reasoning.

2.32 The company golf tournament is next month and you have to pick a partner for your two-person team. The team with the *lowest total score* will win the tournament. Sam, Jack, and Bill have all offered to be your partner. Figure 2.27 contains box plots of their golf scores based on the last 50 rounds that each has played.

FIGURE 2.27 **Box Plots of Golf Scores**

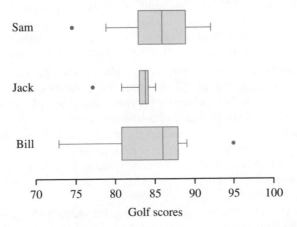

a. What statistical term or phrase best describes the shape of Sam's distribution?
b. What statistical term or phrase best describes the shape of Bill's distribution?
c. Which player will you choose for your team? Explain why.

2.5   Calculators and Statistical Software

Inexpensive hand calculators can be quite useful in performing many of the calculations in this chapter, especially for relatively small amounts of data. For example, many calculators have keys for obtaining the mean and standard deviation directly once the data have been entered. Some have special keys or programmable routines that will do more elaborate computations as well. When using a hand calculator, one must be very careful to enter data correctly, because the entries are usually unavailable for later review. It's a good idea to check answers for reasonableness. The mean should be in the middle of the data; if the calculated result is near one end or the other of the data, a data-entry error should be suspected. The Empirical Rule provides a useful check for the size of a standard deviation. If the one standard deviation interval around the mean includes virtually all the data, rather than about 68%, one again suspects a data-entry error.

For larger amounts of data, a computer is extremely useful. There are literally hundreds of programs available for doing statistical analyses by computer. Many are special-purpose programs for statistical analysis. Some spreadsheet programs, such as Excel, have limited statistical capabilities. Naturally, the special-purpose programs have more capability, but if you already are familiar with a spreadsheet, you may wish to try that first. Most of the programs will carry out virtually all the computations in this book and many more besides. Even more important, the good ones will do data plots very quickly and conveniently.

In general, these packages carry out several steps. First, one must make the data available to the package, either by entry from a keyboard or by importing a data file from a disk, database, or the Internet. Usually, to make eventual output more readable, a package will have some ability to name variables in a data set. There should be a facility to review the data set and edit it to remove errors. Once the data set is ready for analysis, any package can do plots and computations very quickly and make the results available in a variety of ways.

E notation
Some computer output states results in **E notation.** Rather than reporting a mean as 15,326, for example, a particular package may report the mean as 1.5326E04. The E (exponent) part of the expression tells you how many places to the right to move the decimal point. For instance, E04 indicates move the decimal point four places to the right, so that 1.5326E04 = 15,326. Similarly, a negative exponent corresponds to moving the decimal place to the *left:* 1.5326E−04 = 0.00015326.

We think that the data-plotting ability of computer packages, in particular the ones developed especially for statistical analysis, is their most crucial feature. It's so easy to obtain histograms, stem-and-leaf displays, box plots, and other data displays discussed in later chapters that there's little excuse for doing computations before looking at the data. In fact, it is good data-analysis practice to graphically display data before computing any numerical summaries. Any good display should alert you to skewness, outliers, or bimodality that distort the meaning of a mean or standard deviation.

It is perfectly possible to use any computer package badly. If you insist on entering "continent" as a numerical variable, with 1 meaning Africa; 2, Asia; 3, Australia; 4, Europe; 5, North America; and 6, South America; and if you ask for the mean continent, any package we know of will calculate it, to lots of decimal places. A good package will have a method for distinguishing qualitative from quantitative variables, but you have to use it. Further, if you ask for a standard deviation from wildly outlier-prone data, any package we know of will give it to you. You must take responsibility for looking at the data and doing sensible things with it.

We will use output from many statistical packages in this book. Remember that not all the output provided by a package will be relevant to a particular problem; rather than trying to interpret every number, find the relevant numbers. Used with thought, these packages can be immensely convenient and useful.

2.6 Statistical Methods and Quality Improvement

Statistical tools are a major contributor to quality control and process improvement in both the manufacturing and the service sectors. Examples of quality in the service sector include the monitoring of customer complaints about a product for quality and safety reasons, assessment of the accuracy of patient records within a hospital, and the monitoring of claims for fraud by insurance companies. Thinking statistically about averages and especially about variability is crucially important in thinking about quality and its improvement.

In this section, we illustrate the application of numerical and graphical summary tools, discussed in earlier sections of this chapter, in the context of quality.

Pareto chart

An important use of bar charts in statistical quality control is the **Pareto** (pronounced "pah-RAY-toe") **chart.** Alternative reasons for inadequate quality are specified, the number of occurrences are counted, and the frequencies are displayed in a bar chart. Usually, the reasons are displayed in order of frequency from highest to lowest. A Pareto chart is an effective way to highlight quality problems. For example, a mail-order firm analyzing reasons for returns of men's sport coats might find that among the 54 returned coats in the most recent month, there had been 4 returns for poor fit, 22 for disliking the color, 30 for disliking the fabric, 1 for poorly finished sleeves, 2 for improper installation of buttons, and 1 for poor attachment of the lining. Note that there are 60 reasons for 54 returned coats, implying that some coats were returned for multiple reasons; because we're more interested in quality issues than in accounting, we'll count each reason separately. A Pareto chart from Minitab for these returns is shown in Figure 2.28. That figure illustrates the point that we should look for the relevant parts of computer output and ignore what is not needed. The line at the top of the plot (which happens to be based on the cumulative total frequency) is not important for our purposes, so we ignore it. The chart makes it clear that color and fabric are major quality concerns *and* that finish (aspects of sewing the sport coats) is *not* such a major concern until the color and fabric problems are resolved.

means chart

In statistical quality control, a remarkably simple, remarkably useful device is a **means chart,** often called an x-bar chart. (Because we usually use y to denote the variable of interest, we'd call it a y-bar chart, but someone else got there first.) A simplified means chart is simply a plot of times (hours, days, weeks, or months) versus means of observations taken at those times. A process that is operating consistently will be in **statistical control.** The means will vary randomly, but won't show

statistical control

FIGURE 2.28 **Pareto Chart of Reasons for Returning Sports Coat**

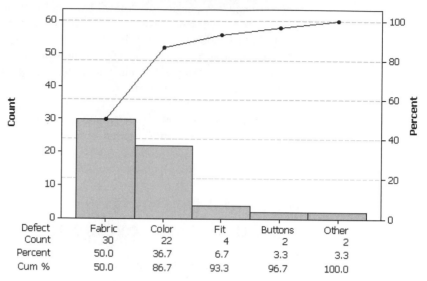

Defect	Fabric	Color	Fit	Buttons	Other
Count	30	22	4	2	2
Percent	50.0	36.7	6.7	3.3	3.3
Cum %	50.0	86.7	93.3	96.7	100.0

any systematic changes. A careful look will show any patterns indicating a process that is out of statistical control—a slow increasing or decreasing trend in the means, a sudden jump or drop, or a cyclic pattern.

EXAMPLE 2.14 A critical aspect of automatic transmissions for cars is the internal fluid pressure of the transmission. The ideal value is 35, in appropriate units. Too low a pressure results in sluggish performance; anything under 32 can be detected and any pressure under 30 results in bad performance. Too high a pressure results in jumpy overperformance; 38 is detectable and 40 is bad. A manufacturer of transmissions randomly samples five units from each day's production and measures the internal pressure on each. A list of the pressures for 40 days is shown here. The initial 3 has been dropped, so 6.01 represents 36.01.

Day	item1	item2	item3	item4	item5	mean
1	6.01	4.46	4.90	3.83	4.61	4.762
2	6.06	6.26	5.44	3.86	5.88	5.500
3	4.46	6.17	4.07	4.29	4.29	4.656
4	5.08	4.68	4.37	4.50	4.40	4.606
5	4.11	5.84	5.67	4.55	5.62	5.158
6	4.58	5.90	4.35	5.25	4.18	4.852
7	6.04	4.45	4.22	5.09	4.68	4.896
8	4.98	5.19	5.70	4.91	2.97	4.750
9	6.48	5.95	4.53	6.25	6.08	5.858
10	5.30	5.98	5.36	3.83	4.56	5.006
11	3.56	3.95	6.38	4.90	4.86	4.730
12	4.96	6.78	6.56	4.32	5.25	5.574
13	4.39	3.16	4.31	4.43	6.33	4.524
14	2.88	4.62	5.70	5.77	3.83	4.560

Day	item1	item2	item3	item4	item5	mean
15	2.81	4.27	3.19	6.02	5.94	4.446
16	2.77	3.20	3.60	5.75	4.57	3.978
17	4.88	3.37	4.69	4.02	3.30	4.052
18	6.06	4.49	3.40	5.03	6.63	5.122
19	6.17	2.64	5.90	4.75	5.22	4.936
20	5.85	5.00	3.31	4.58	7.37	5.222
21	5.10	5.39	5.37	4.33	7.28	5.494
22	7.29	2.77	3.54	7.45	5.14	5.238
23	4.44	5.87	5.52	5.03	4.13	4.998
24	4.94	5.97	6.30	8.22	4.72	6.030
25	5.56	5.59	4.63	3.56	6.84	5.236
26	5.48	4.74	6.51	6.76	4.13	5.524
27	5.31	6.87	2.82	3.55	3.47	4.404
28	3.69	4.01	5.16	3.87	4.93	4.332
29	3.32	6.22	2.12	6.01	5.60	4.654
30	5.14	6.57	6.37	6.98	6.66	6.344
31	4.93	6.02	5.10	5.58	6.62	5.650
32	4.93	5.45	2.16	6.25	5.05	4.768
33	6.64	7.00	5.39	4.87	6.76	6.132
34	7.85	4.97	4.68	5.48	4.07	5.410
35	4.02	6.64	7.62	5.91	4.15	5.668
36	4.51	5.42	4.81	5.00	3.74	4.696
37	3.62	5.41	4.78	1.78	3.88	3.894
38	3.06	5.90	6.96	4.96	2.72	4.720
39	2.04	3.22	3.76	3.44	6.76	3.844
40	4.99	6.20	4.73	3.87	3.79	4.716

SOLUTION A simplified *x*-bar chart from Minitab is shown in Figure 2.29. There are no obvious trends up or down, nor are there jumps to new plateaus. The means

FIGURE 2.29   **Simplified Means Chart for Transmissions Data**

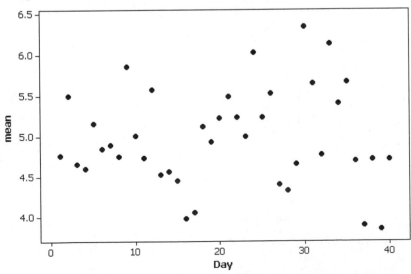

EXAMPLE 2.14
(continued)

mostly stay in the 4.00 to 6.00 range, corresponding to mean pressures of 34 to 36 units. Perhaps there are some cycles of a few days' length, but nothing huge. One troubling feature is that the mean in days 31–40 seem to "jump around" a little more. Several of the largest and smallest means occur during these days. We will need to consider this more when we measure variability in the next section.

EXAMPLE 2.15

A nationwide chain of motels has a national reservation center. Customers phone in reservations to an 800 number. One key measure of the quality of the center's service is the amount of "dead time"—waiting for the phone to be answered, being on hold, waiting for a response once a request has been made—endured by a customer. The chain's four regular inspectors record the dead time (in units of minutes) for their one reservation call each day. The results are averaged over each five-day work-week. A separate analysis is done for weekends and holiday weeks. Means are shown here. A simplified x-bar chart created in Minitab is shown in Figure 2.30. Is there any clear evidence of a problem?

Mean

0.765	0.775	1.025	0.910	0.665	0.825	0.720	0.720	0.795
0.845	0.645	0.905	0.845	0.790	0.950	0.735	0.765	0.710
1.045	1.215	1.085	0.925	1.075	1.100	1.330	1.215	0.996
1.185	1.115	1.110						

SOLUTION   For the first 18 weeks, except for week 3, the means are relatively low. Beginning at week 19, the means suddenly increase. The chart clearly signals that we should look for a cause for an increase in dead time around week 19.

FIGURE 2.30

Simplified Means Plot for Dead Time Data

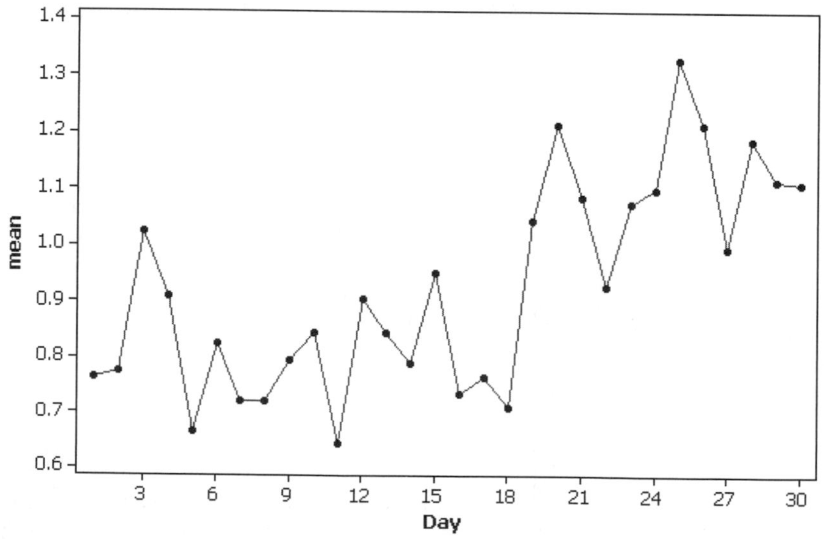

R chart

When data are taken over time and the range is plotted against time, the result is an **R chart.** For example, in the automatic transmission example, ranges were also computed as follows:

Day	Range	Day	Range	Day	Range	Day	Range
1	2.18	11	2.82	21	2.95	31	1.69
2	2.40	12	2.46	22	4.68	32	4.09
3	2.10	13	3.17	23	1.74	33	2.13
4	0.71	14	2.89	24	3.50	34	3.78
5	1.73	15	3.21	25	3.28	35	3.60
6	1.72	16	2.98	26	2.63	36	1.68
7	1.82	17	1.58	27	4.05	37	3.63
8	2.73	18	3.23	28	1.47	38	4.24
9	1.95	19	3.53	29	4.10	39	4.72
10	2.15	20	4.06	30	1.84	40	2.41

The automatic transmission data indicate that the largest value in day 1 is 6.01 (item 1) and the smallest value in day 1 is 3.83 (item 4). The range for day 1 is therefore $6.01 - 3.83 = 2.18$, as shown. Note that the actual pressures were 36.01 and 33.83; adding 30 to all the data doesn't change the range, because the 30s cancel. A Minitab R chart of range plotted against day is shown in Figure 2.31.

This chart shows that a problem is developing over time. Notice that in the first 10 days or so, the ranges are always lower than the average range for the entire period, shown as the center line of the graph. In the last 10 days, the ranges sometimes (not always) are above average. It appears that the ranges generally are increasing over time, so there's more and more variability as time goes by. The process is not in statistical control, not stable. Higher variability means that more transmissions will be either too high or too low in pressure. In seeking the cause, we should notice that there's no sudden jump upward but rather a gradual increase; we should look for a gradual factor such as machine wearout or worker complacency.

FIGURE 2.31   **Range Chart of Automatic Transmission Data**

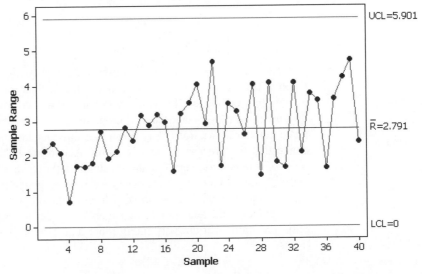

S chart

The standard deviation is less outlier-sensitive than the range. Thus an **S chart,** a plot of standard deviations against time, is also a useful quality-control tool in assessing whether there has been a change in variability.

EXAMPLE 2.16

Standard deviations for the automatic transmission data were plotted in Figure 2.32 against day number to make an S chart in Minitab. Is there evidence of a trend?

SOLUTION There is somewhat of an increasing trend in the standard deviations. Notice that the standard deviations up through week 10 are all lower than the average standard deviation, shown as the center line on the S chart. In later periods, the standard deviations often, though not always, are larger, indicating that variability is increasing with time.

FIGURE 2.32

S Chart of Automatic Transmission Data

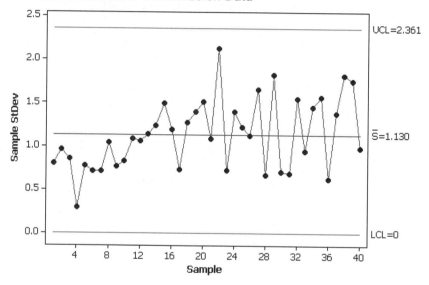

The standard deviation is also useful in *x*-bar quality control charts. From data taken when a process is in control, one can calculate the standard deviation of the means. In a complete *x*-bar chart, upper and lower **control limits** are drawn at the desired mean plus 3 standard deviations (of the mean) and at the desired mean minus 3 standard deviations. Any mean that falls outside these limits is taken as evidence that the process is out of control. According to the Empirical Rule, if the process is in control, very few means should fall outside the control limits, so "false alarms" should be rare. If and when the process goes seriously out of control, the means should go outside one control limit or the other. Control limits are very useful in reducing the tendency of managers to go chasing after every minor variation; only deviations that are very likely more than random will fall outside the control limits.

control limits

EXAMPLE 2.17   A Minitab control chart for the transmission data is shown in Figure 2.33. How, if at all, does it indicate that there is trouble brewing?

SOLUTION   At first glance, the chart doesn't indicate trouble. Every mean is within the control limits. Therefore, any problem doesn't seem to reside with the average value. The next thing to consider is variability. The best way to do that would be to look at an R or S chart. We can get some indirect evidence from the x-bar chart. Near the right-hand side of the chart, the means seem to jump around, suggesting that the process is not under control. Because there is no pattern of consistently high or consistently low readings, it seems reasonable to think that the problem is excessive variability. To confirm that variability is the problem, we should check an R or S chart. Results for previous examples confirm our idea. Management's task seems to be to find out why there is such variation in the transmission data.

FIGURE 2.33   **Control Chart for Automatic Transmission Data**

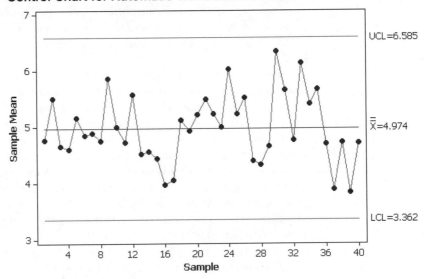

There are several kinds of control charts. We have described the most common ones—means (x-bar) charts, range charts, and standard deviation charts. These charts apply to measured, quantitative characteristics such as the strength of seat belt materials, the time required for a telephone to be answered, or the internal pressure of an automatic transmission. Another form of chart that is useful for quantitative **cusum chart**   characteristics is the **cusum chart,** which keeps track of the cumulative sum of a series of measurements. It is best suited for detecting a drift upward or downward in average level; it's not intended to detect a change in variability.

There are also control charts for tracking qualitative characteristics. The simplest chart applies to counting the number of defective items in a sample, where each item is categorized as either good or defective. For this situation, p charts and np charts are useful.

statistical control

The same basic ideas apply with all control charts. The first concern is whether an ongoing process is in **statistical control.** A process is said to be in statistical control if it is statistically stable—that is, if both the mean value and the amount of variability are staying constant over time. Sudden jumps or clear trends in either average values or amount of variability are indications that the process is changing and that the process needs to be corrected.

common causes
special causes

Assuming that the process is in control, the next concern is the degree of variability. In many cases, variability is an enemy of quality. There are exceptions: we wouldn't want all sports events to come out exactly the same, nor would we want every diamond ring to be identical to every other one. But in most cases, the less variability there is, the better. A useful way to think about causes of variability is to divide them into **common causes** and **special causes.** Common causes are the continuing sources of variability that affect a process. For example, a bakery tries to control the height of loaves of bread. Common causes of variation would include the amounts of flour, shortening, salt, and water put into the bread dough, the length of time allowed for the loaves to rise, and the temperature of the baking oven. Typically, common causes are small and yield results that stay within control limits; they are the reasons why the process varies, within control limits. Special causes, in contrast, are large, "one-time" causes that often take the process beyond control limits, temporarily. For a bread bakery, special causes of variation might include a contaminated batch of yeast that didn't allow the dough to rise or an accidental loss of heat in an oven.

Special causes are usually evident to the people running the process; common causes require systematic searching. When a control chart indicates a sudden failure in the process, typically the reason is obvious or relatively easy to figure out. If somebody left the oven partly open during the bread-baking process (which we would hope was a special situation, not a common one), one look at the oven door will indicate why the bread isn't coming out well. However, if the amount of flour measured for a loaf varies somewhat because of humidity variation or moisture differences in the flour, it won't be so easy to detect. As long as the people running the process are committed to quality, they should be able to deal with special causes. Managers can be more helpful by investigating the subtler, common causes of variation and finding ways to reduce them.

Statistical methods alone aren't enough. Control charts have been known in American industry for 60 years. If they cured all quality problems by themselves, American products would universally be the highest quality in the world; however, there are some individuals who assert that American quality is not absolutely the best.

Almost all the people who have studied good-quality and poor-quality operations agree that improving quality requires sustained, long-term, patient commitment by managers and workers at all levels. The best-known quality expert was probably W. Edwards Deming, a professional statistician who introduced statistical quality control and improvement methods in postwar Japan. Deming (1986) formulated a 14-point program for quality improvement. An interesting outsider's view is given in Walton (1986). Deming insisted on the absolute necessity of *sustained* management commitment; he abhorred short-term sloganeering ("zero defects") as a substitute for real effort.

Almost all quality experts concentrate on improving processes, as opposed to exhorting people. At bottom, most of the fundamental tasks of organizations are repetitive processes conducted under similar conditions. Most people tend to think of processes and quality control in the context of manufacturing, but the same ideas apply just as well to granting loans, servicing automobiles, handling airline reservations, and many other service-sector activities. One of the key messages to managers from modern quality-improvement experts is to think more about long-run improvements in processes and less about short-run "fire fighting." If managers modify a process in response to every short-term, random variation, that just adds another source of variation, without accomplishing anything systematic. Managers should identify the goals of the process, consider what aspects of the process can be varied, and carry out well-considered experiments to find the best possible design for the process.

Major process redesign initiatives can bring about quantum leaps foward in quality, but these initiatives are expensive to execute and offer no guarantees that the projected dramatic improvements in quality will be achieved. The more usual situation is where quality inches upward in small increments. An improved product design here, a modification of a service process there, improved cooperation with a supplier, a tailoring of a product to better fit customers' needs—all are small steps that must be taken repeatedly to improve quality; the common, small gains have a greater cumulative effect. It takes a patient, persevering management to press on for quality improvement without immediate, dramatic payoffs.

One key to improving process quality is intelligent experimentation. Almost any task can be accomplished in many ways, some good, some bad. A remarkably effective method for avoiding quality improvement is to insist on doing a task one way "because we've always done it that way." A not-much-better approach to quality improvement is casual, unplanned experimentation—manipulating one aspect of a process, then another, without pattern or planning. A far more productive approach is planned experimentation, systematically thinking about all the key aspects of a process and deliberately, systematically seeking improvements in all of them. Here's one place where statistical thinking becomes vital. One of the great success stories of recent years in quality improvement has been the effective use of statistically controlled experiments.

Statistical thinking is crucial in considering processes, particularly in dealing with variation within a process. Most accounting systems are designed to deal with averages and totals. Statistical thinking adds the key idea of variability. Any manufacturing or service process will have some degree of natural variability in results. The proverbial widgets will vary from one another because of differences in raw materials, wear on machine parts, changes in temperature and humidity, and many other reasons. Adjustable-rate mortgage loans will sometimes be in default because of a mortgage holder's losing a job, a sharp decline in value of the property, or a change in interest rates. The key question is whether recent variations in process results are within the normal range (and therefore not worth worrying much about) or into the "out-of-control" range (and therefore a cause for concern). One of the important functions of control charts is to indicate what is *not* worth management attention.

The statistical ideas of variation and experimentation often come together. In many quality-improvement problems, reducing variability is at least as important as improving average quality. A motel chain might institute a change in its reservations process that cuts the average time per reservation by 10%; if that change increased variability in times by 100%, the chain could expect to reduce the demand for its reservations considerably. A manager who uses statistical experiments and thinks about both averages and variability should be able to make a real difference in quality, given patience and sustained effort.

Exercises

2.33 A hotel kept records over time of the reasons why guests requested room changes. The frequencies were as follows:

Reason	Frequency
Room not cleaned	2
Plumbing not working	1
Wrong type of bed	13
Noisy location	4
Wanted nonsmoking room	18
Didn't like view	1
Room not properly equipped	8
Other, not coded	6

a. Construct a Pareto chart.

b. The hotel management had expected that the primary problems would be connected with maintenance and housekeeping. Does the chart confirm that such reasons were the primary complaints?

2.34 A manufacturer of tools for homeowners and contractors produces a line of masonry bits for drills. One of the critical qualities of these bits is hardness, measured on a standard scale. If the bits are not hard enough, they wear out rapidly. If the bits are too hard, they may be brittle and break; because the bits are used to drill holes in concrete and brick, it can be extremely dangerous to have a bit break. The scale used to measure hardness is quite sensitive; what would seem to an outsider to be small changes in hardness lead to fairly large changes on the scale. The target value on this scale is 16.0. Even when the production process is working well, there is some variability in bit hardness, mostly because of imperfect mixing of metals in the alloy and variation in heating during the tempering process. The target standard deviation is 0.5.

The tool manufacturer instituted a quality-improvement approach involving, among many other actions, use of control charts. Each production day, a sample of five bits was selected randomly from the day's production. The hardness of each bit was measured carefully (by a destructive process, which necessitates using a sample) and recorded. Data for the first 30 days following overhaul of the production process were used in a control chart for the mean and the range, shown in Figure 2.34.

F I G U R E 2 . 3 4 Control Charts for Bit Hardness Data

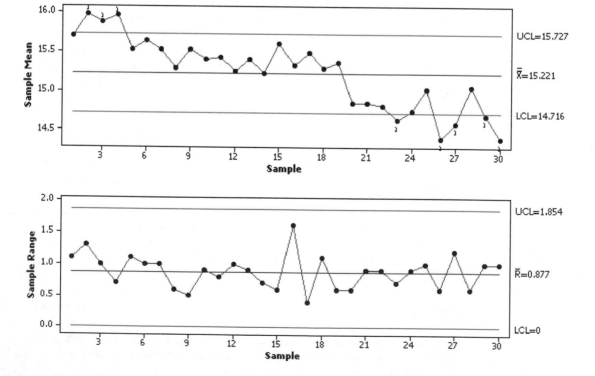

a. Does the chart indicate that there is a problem with the mean? If so, does it appear that there was a sudden jump or a gradual trend?

b. Does the chart indicate that there is a problem of excessive variability? If so, was there a jump or a trend?

2.35 The tool manufacturer in Exercise 2.34 believed there were two major explanations for unsatisfactory bit hardness. One potential problem would be bad lots of metal. Each lot is used for about six days of production; each lot is completely used up before another lot is begun. A second potential problem is the heating system used to temper the bits. Over time, this system can drift to higher or lower temperatures. Based on the Minitab control charts in Figure 2.34, which seems to be the more plausible culprit for any problems you identified in Exercise 2.34?

BUSINESS DECISION-MAKING IN ACTION

CHAPTER CASE

ANALYSIS

Glenco Manufacturing Company

Recall that your committee's charge in the Glenco Manufacturing Company case is to determine which of the 155 hourly workers at Glenco should receive a $1000 bonus. Figure 2.35 is a partial listing of the personnel data file you are to use to make the decision.

FIGURE 2.35 Partial Listing of the Glenco Manufacturing Company Data

	A	B	C	D	E	F	G	H	I	J
1	ID	Last	First	Gender	Minority	Age	Department	Tenure	HourlyRate	Rating
2	4203	Alexander	Charles	M	0	35	1	10	18.00	4.5
3	1543	Ammann	Ray	M	0	60	1	37	23.75	4.8
4	1161	Anderson	James	M	1	01	2	11	24.63	4.1
5	5265	Babcock	Marilyn	F	1	36	2	0	15.55	5.0
6	4192	Bagley	Jan	F	0	40	5	11	17.90	7.5
7	2065	Baker	Lisa	F	0	59	3	32	22.88	5.9
8	4450	Baldwin	Lois	F	1	35	4	8	17.33	5.2
9	5055	Bartlett	Bill	M	1	26	4	2	16.46	4.4
10	4154	Blair	Elizabeth	F	0	41	6	11	18.27	4.6
11	4007	Bolden	Holly	F	0	50	6	12	18.21	4.0
12	5056	Bowling	Frances	F	0	22	7	2	16.01	8.3
13	4831	Brown	Charlotte	F	0	62	7	4	17.05	3.6
14	5221	Bruton	Penny	F	0	23	7	0	15.00	4.3
15	4258	Campbell	Delores	F	1	43	7	10	17.91	4.7
16	4215	Cash	Bill	M	1	35	7	10	17.52	6.7
17	4435	Chandler	Margo	F	0	42	4	8	16.96	7.0
18	4895	Chang	Sally	F	0	25	4	4	16.08	6.4

The first step in any data analysis is to become familiar with the data by summarizing each of the variables with graphical displays. As we learned in Section 2.1, the type of variable, whether qualitative or quantitative, determines which graphical displays are appropriate.

At Glenco Manufacturing, each of the hourly employees works in one of seven departments (conveniently labeled 1 through 7). We can summarize the Department variable by displaying the frequencies (that is, number of employees) and relative frequencies associated with the departments in a frequency table as follows:

```
Tally for Discrete Variables: Dept

Dept  Count   Percent
   1     25    16.13
   2     25    16.13
   3     26    16.77
   4     17    10.97
   5     25    16.13
   6     19    12.26
   7     18    11.61

 N=     155
```

Figure 2.36 is a Minitab bar chart of the Department variable. From the frequency table and the bar chart, we can see that four of the seven departments have roughly 25 employees each, while three smaller departments have 17–19 employees each.

FIGURE 2.36

Bar Chart of Department

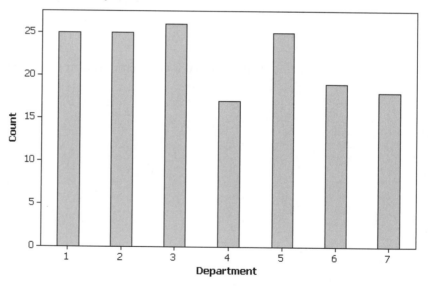

Figure 2.37 is a histogram of the quantitative variable HourlyRate, created in Minitab, which measures the hourly rate of pay for each of the 155 Glenco hourly employees. From this graph, we learn that all employees earn between $15 and $25 per hour, but the vast majority earn less than $20 per hour. Note the long right tail of the HourlyRate distribution indicating skewness in these data.

A stem-and-leaf diagram of the quantitative Rating variable is shown next. Recall that the Rating variable represents the performance rating of an hourly employee from his or her last evaluation review. From this graph, we observe that while the lowest possible ratings, say from 0.0 to 3.0, were not given out, earning a performance rating above 9.0 was very difficult!

FIGURE 2.37   **Histogram of Hourly Pay Rates for Glenco Employees**

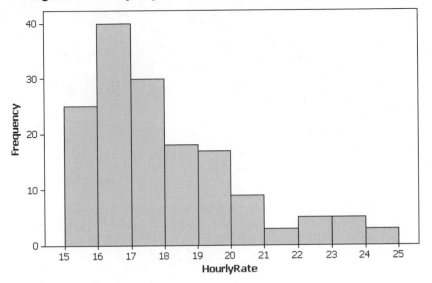

```
Stem-and-leaf of Rating       N = 155
Leaf Unit = 0.10

    1      3  3
   11      3  5556788889
   22      4  01111223344
   43      4  5555556666667777788999
   63      5  00000001111122222344
   76      5  5566667888899
  (16)     6  0000111222234444
   63      6  5567778899999
   50      7  000111222333334444
   32      7  5566677889
   22      8  001123334444
   10      8  5568
    6      9  2234
    2      9  6
    1     10  0
```

A simple, and seemingly justifiable, solution to our bonus decision problem
would be to award bonuses to the 20% of employees with the highest performance
ratings. Since there are 155 hourly employees, this would mean that approximately
31 employees would receive the $1000 bonus. From the depth gauge on the stem-
and-leaf diagram of the Rating variable, we see that 32 employees had performance
ratings of 7.5 or higher. It is relatively simple to sort the 155 employee records by
Rating (in descending order) in Excel and print out the top 32 recipients of the $1000
bonus. Figure 2.38 shows the results from Excel. Do you see any potential problems
with this decision?

So far, we used graphical summaries of individual variables to learn more about
the data. Now, we'll apply some of the two-variable displays discussed in Section
2.2 to the Glenco data to see if there are any interesting relationships between variables that might help in our bonus decision-making process.

A two-way table of Gender by Department showing the column percents as well
as frequencies in each cell of the table is shown here.

FIGURE 2.38 **Top 20% of Glenco Employees in Performance Ratings**

	A	B	C	D	E	F	G	H	I	J
	ID	Last	First	Gender	Minority	Age	Department	Tenure	HourlyRate	Rating
1										
2	5271	Gregory	Debbie	F	1	23	5	0	15.23	10.0
3	3409	Miller	Sam	M	0	48	5	18	19.66	9.6
4	3126	Ward	Ron	M	1	55	5	21	20.28	9.4
5	5041	Sanders	Mike	M	0	32	5	2	16.17	9.3
6	3644	Tucker	Kay	F	0	45	4	16	19.05	9.2
7	4425	Reeves	Tom	M	0	36	5	8	17.44	9.2
8	1506	Gebhardt	Virginia	F	0	57	6	37	23.30	8.8
9	4803	Schmidt	Carrie	F	1	24	3	4	16.51	8.6
10	3526	Rose	Debbie	F	0	46	5	17	19.14	8.5
11	4040	Robinson	Harvey	M	0	31	4	12	18.42	8.5
12	5021	Simmons	Alex	M	0	28	3	2	16.16	8.4
13	4917	Wadley	Carla	F	0	22	3	3	16.17	8.4
14	5180	Williams	Claudia	F	0	24	2	1	15.97	8.4
15	4246	Watson	Karen	F	0	43	6	10	17.93	8.4
16	4863	Jackson	Charlie	M	0	27	5	4	16.60	8.3
17	5056	Bowling	Frances	F	0	22	7	2	16.01	8.3
18	4960	Esterline	Laura	F	0	39	5	3	16.29	8.3
19	4481	Miller	Diane	F	0	31	5	8	17.24	8.2
20	3637	Horn	Ernest	M	0	57	7	16	18.76	8.1
21	3163	Cunningham	Sherry	F	0	48	3	21	20.44	8.1
22	3782	Thompson	Lori	F	1	51	3	15	18.97	8.0
23	4921	Dorsey	Patricia	F	0	44	3	3	16.17	8.0
24	4344	Ferguson	Sylvia	F	0	31	5	9	17.39	7.9
25	4641	Vandell	Debbie	F	0	45	3	6	16.63	7.8
26	4726	Tobias	Ron	M	0	41	5	5	16.73	7.8
27	5214	Sharpe	Alice	M	0	23	3	0	15.80	7.7
28	3434	Fried	Harvey	M	0	58	5	18	19.17	7.7
29	4348	Powell	Angie	F	1	27	5	9	17.41	7.6
30	4624	Tupper	Jean	F	1	34	4	6	17.16	7.6
31	4327	Cravens	Pete	M	1	55	5	9	17.55	7.6
32	4192	Bagley	Jan	F	0	40	5	11	17.90	7.5
33	5026	Welch	Jeffrey	M	0	36	3	2	16.33	7.5

```
Tabulated Statistics: Gender, Department
Rows: Gender      Columns: Department
            1         2         3         4         5         6         7       All

F          11        14        16        11        12        13        12        89
        44.00     56.00     61.54     64.71     48.00     68.42     66.67     57.42

M          14        11        10         6        13         6         6        66
        56.00     44.00     38.46     35.29     52.00     31.58     33.33     42.58

All        25        25        26        17        25        19        18       155
       100.00    100.00    100.00    100.00    100.00    100.00    100.00    100.00

Cell Contents --
                Count
                % of Col
```

From this table, we learn that the majority of Glenco employees are female (57.42%), but that the proportion of female employees varies across departments. In fact, Departments 1 and 5 actually have a majority of male employees (56% and 52%, respectively). Figure 2.39 is a 100% stacked bar chart of Gender and Department that depicts the tabled information in a graphical form. Based on the evidence, we would conclude that the two variables Gender and Department are related.

FIGURE 2.39   **100% Stacked Bar Chart of Gender and Department**

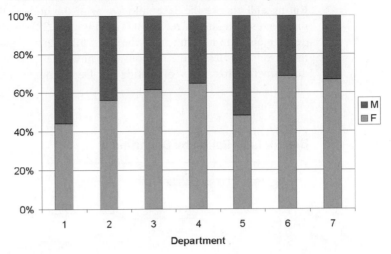

A scatterplot of Rating versus Tenure from Minitab is shown in Figure 2.40. For employees with fewer than 25 years with Glenco, the random pattern suggests that there is no relationship between these two variables. The average Rating appears to be fairly constant across all levels of Tenure less than 25 years, suggesting that there is no performance rating bias with regard to Tenure; that is, performance ratings are not tied to how long an employee has been with the company. However, the average Rating for employees who have been with Glenco longer than 25 years is much lower than for the other employees. This could be an indication that some of the long-time Glenco employees have "retired on the job." If this is the case, Glenco management may need to investigate ways to help keep these long-term employees engaged and motivated.

FIGURE 2.40   **Scatterplot of Rating Versus Tenure for Glenco Data**

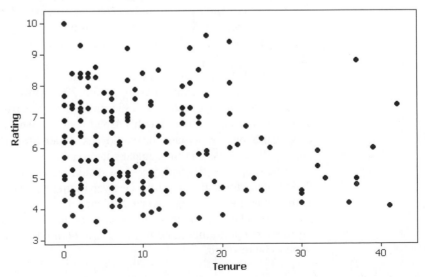

As already mentioned, one possible solution is to simply sort the data by the Rating and choose the 31 employees with the highest Rating values. In examining the resulting list of recipients (see Figure 2.38), however, we notice that some departments are missing from the list while other departments tend to dominate the list. This leads us to consider how the performance ratings differ by department. Box plots of Rating by Department from Minitab are shown in Figure 2.41.

FIGURE 2.41

Box Plots of Rating by Department

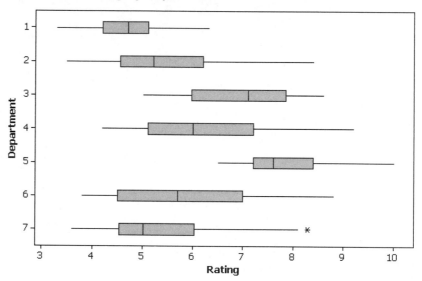

From the box plots, we see that the seven departmental supervisors use the 0–10 point Rating scale differently. The distribution of ratings for Department 1 has the smallest median and lowest variability of all the departments, which explains why no employees from Department 1 made the top 20% list. At the other extreme, the Rating distribution for Department 5 is highest on the 0–10 scale, explaining the overwhelming presence of employees from this department on the top 20% list.

So what should your committee do about the bonuses? One solution would be to award bonuses to employees in the top 20% within each department. This approach is not without problems. If the supervisor of Department 1 was correct in his assessment of the employees in his department, perhaps none of them should be receiving a bonus; or perhaps the employees in Department 5 were truly outstanding among all employees in the company last year.

The Employee Bonus Committee should recommend to company management that the departmental supervisors be given training in performance evaluation so that in the future these evaluations will be done fairly and will be comparable across departments. The committee should also recommend an evaluation of Department 1 given its low performance ratings to determine if there is an employee or supervisor issue to be resolved.

SUMMARY

Here are some suggestions for summarizing data.

1. Decide whether the variable being summarized should be regarded as quantitative (so that means and standard deviations make sense) or categorical (so that modes and proportions make sense).

2. For data for a single quantitative variable, obtain one or more plots of the distribution of the variable. Histograms, stem-and-leaf displays, box plots, and normal probability plots all help to indicate typical values, the degree of variability, the amount of skewness, and the presence of outliers.

3. For data for a single categorical variable, obtain one or more plots of the distribution of the variable. Bar charts and pie charts indicate the distribution of values across the various categories of the variable.

4. If the data for a variable were collected in time or sequence order, the first step is to plot the data in a time series plot. If the data show a trend in either average or variability, overall summary figures that ignore the trend can be misleading.

5. Control charts are a form of time series plot. An x-bar chart for means and either an S chart or an R chart for variability will indicate whether the process is in statistical control (statistically stable) or not.

6. If understanding the relationship between two variables is important, construct an appropriate two-variable display of the data. If both variables are quantitative, use a scatterplot. If both variables are categorical, use a two-way frequency table, a stacked bar chart, or a 100% stacked bar chart. If one variable is quantitative and the other variable is categorical, use box plots.

7. The mean and median are the most common measures of the typical average value of quantitative variables. A large difference between these two numbers suggests severe skewness or outliers.

8. The standard deviation is the most useful measure of variability for quantitative variables. Its numerical value may be interpreted by the Empirical Rule, provided that the distribution is not grossly skewed or outlier-prone.

In addition, you may want to reread the summary of key ideas in the Executive Overview at the beginning of this chapter.

Supplementary Exercises

2.36 A study of sick-leave days over one year for a sample of 20 workers in a company yields the following numbers, arranged in increasing order:

0 0 0 0 0 0 1 1 1 1 2 2 2 3 3 4 6 9 14 31

a. Verify that the sample mean is 4.0 and the sample standard deviation is 7.27.
b. What fraction of the observations actually falls within 1 standard deviation of the mean? What aspect of the data explains the discrepancy between this fraction and the Empirical Rule approximation?

2.37 If a computer package is available to you, use it to find the mean, median, and standard deviation for the data of Exercise 2.36. Is the standard deviation calculated with a denominator of $(n - 1)$ or n? Compare your results with these results from Excel:

```
LeaveDays

Mean                    4
Standard Error          1.625
Median                  1.5
Mode                    0
Standard Deviation      7.269
Sample Variance         52.84
```

2.38 Consider the following artificial data:

8   9   10   10   10   10   10   10   11   12   19   20   20   20   21   28   29   30   30
30   30   30   30   31   32

a. Plot the data using five classes. What pattern of skewness and modality do you see?
b. The mean of these values is 20. How can this result be obtained without computation? How about the median?
c. Calculate the standard deviation.
d. What fraction of the values falls within 1 standard deviation of the mean? How does this compare with the Empirical Rule fraction? Explain the discrepancy.
e. What fraction of the values falls within 2 standard deviations of the mean? How does this fraction compare with the Empirical Rule fraction?

2.39 Here is another artificial data set:

−36   −1   −1   −1   −1   0   0   1   1   2   3   4   6   9   14

a. Verify that the mean is 0 and that the standard deviation is 10.84.
b. Calculate the skewness coefficient $(\bar{y} - \text{median})/s$.
c. Plot the data. Can you identify an obvious skewness?

2.40 Assembling a circuit board requires several dozen soldering connections. The main soldering operation is automated. However, the process can yield defective connections, usually caused by poor penetration of a flux material used to prepare the connections. Each soldered board must be inspected visually and each defective soldering connection repaired by a relatively expensive hand touchup. The number of defects on each board is recorded. There are 20 boards produced each hour; an average of 2 defects per board is considered in control. The following means were obtained for a 30-hour production week. From the numbers, is there indication of an upward or downward trend?

Mean
1.45	1.65	1.50	2.25	1.65	1.60	2.30	2.20	2.70
1.70	2.35	1.70	1.90	1.45	1.40	2.60	2.05	1.70
1.05	2.35	1.90	1.55	1.95	1.60	2.05	2.05	1.70
2.30	1.30	2.35						

2.41 A simplified x-bar chart of the means in the previous exercise is shown in Figure 2.42. Does the chart indicate a trend?

2.42 Experience with the soldering process indicates that the standard deviation applicable to the average number of defectives among 20 boards is 0.38. Recall that the in-control mean is regarded as 2.0.
a. Calculate upper and lower control limits. Are there any means falling outside these limits?
b. If a mean fell below the lower control limit, would this indicate a problem?

FIGURE 2.42 **Simplified *x*-bar Chart**

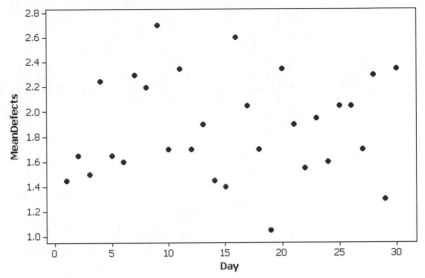

2.43 The individual board data underlying the mean number of soldering defects were not shown. Obviously, there can't be a negative number of defects; theoretically, there might be dozens of defects on a single board. Assuming that the process is in control (mean number of defects equals 2), what might be expected about the shape of the data? In particular, what kind of skewness might be expected?

2.44 A regional public transit agency runs a fleet of buses from suburban areas to the western terminal of a subway line. One important measure of service quality is how late buses are in arriving at the terminal; typically, riders will not be concerned about a minute or two of lateness, but longer delays indicate a deterioration in service. Each weekday morning, a dispatcher records the number of minutes late for a random sample of eight buses scheduled to arrive at the terminal between 7:30 and 8:30 A.M. The means over a 58-day period are shown here:

Mean

1.1250	1.3125	1.5000	1.6875	1.6250	1.9375	1.6250
1.6875	1.9375	1.8750	2.0625	1.5000	1.4375	1.3750
1.5000	1.5625	2.2500	1.1875	1.1250	1.8125	2.0000
2.6250	1.5000	1.8125	1.1875	1.7500	2.3750	2.0000
2.0000	2.4375	1.8125	2.4375	1.7500	1.5625	1.7500
2.2500	1.4375	1.6250	2.0625	2.3750	1.7500	1.6875
1.4375	1.6875	2.1250	1.5625	1.8750	1.6875	1.3750
1.6250	1.6875	1.5000	1.3750	4.0000	4.0000	2.0625
4.7500	3.1250					

By looking at the numbers, is it possible to detect where a lateness problem has occurred?

2.45 A simplified *x*-bar chart for the means in Exercise 2.44 is shown in Figure 2.43. Where were there lateness problems?

2.46 The standard deviation for the mean lateness of the eight buses in Exercise 2.44 and 2.45 is about 0.30 minute.
a. Construct control limits assuming that the target mean is 1.5 minutes.
b. On which days did the arrival process appear out of control?

FIGURE 2.43 Simplified *x*-bar Chart for Bus Lateness

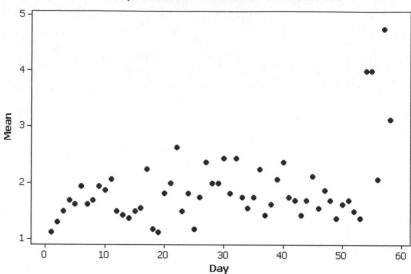

2.47 An S chart for the bus arrival process is shown in Figure 2.44. Do the high-variability days essentially coincide with the high-mean days?

FIGURE 2.44 Simplified S Chart for Bus Lateness

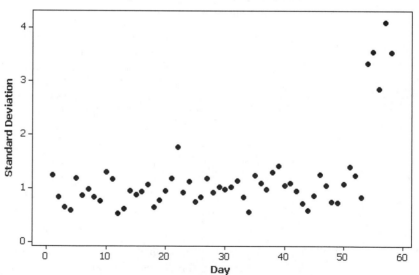

2.48 A major food products company uses sales representatives to work with wholesalers and supermarket chains. The representatives' chief tasks are to sell new products, secure adequate display space in stores, and coordinate promotions. Each representative is solely responsible for a district. Yearly volume of sales in the district is the primary measure of the representative's effectiveness. The results for the last year (in thousands of dollars) are analyzed in the following Minitab output.

```
Descriptive Statistics: Volume

Variable     N    Mean  StDev  Minimum      Q1  Median      Q3  Maximum
Volume     118  4336.2  401.4   3058.0  4154.3  4334.0  4551.8   5301.0
```

a. The company had attempted with only partial success to set up the districts to have equal sales volume potential. What other sources of variability can you think of?

b. What does the box plot in Figure 2.45 indicate about the overall shape of the data—in particular, the skewness and outlier-proneness?

FIGURE 2.45   Box Plot of Sales Volume Data

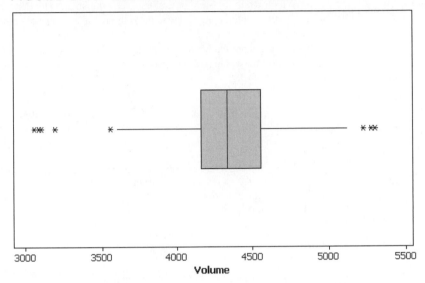

2.49   The data underlying Exercise 2.48 were plotted in Minitab against the identification number of each sales representative in Figure 2.46. The numbers are in order of seniority, with 1 being the most senior representative. Is there an evident trend in the plot?

FIGURE 2.46   Sequence Plot of Sales Volume Data

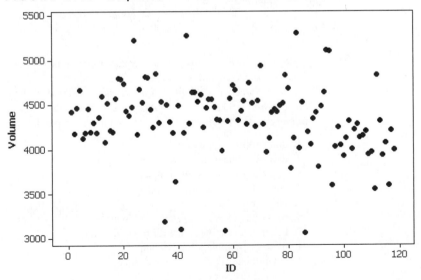

2.50   A junior manager, examining the data of Exercise 2.48, noticed that half the sales representatives were performing below average. The manager felt that this fact indicated deficiencies in the company's training or in the representatives' motivation. Is the manager's reasoning valid?

2.51   A publisher of computer science books needs fast action in handling page proofs of forthcoming books. These proofs must be delivered to the authors for a final check of layout, typographical errors, and other features. Because speed is essential in tight publication schedules, the publisher is considering using express delivery services. The last 90 sets of proofs have been randomly allocated to three different services. The number of hours required for delivery of each set has been recorded.

a. Which would be more desirable to the publisher, a smaller mean or a larger one?

b. Which would be more desirable to the publisher, a smaller standard deviation or a larger one?

c. Judging from the Minitab box plots in Figure 2.47, which server has the smallest mean? The smallest standard deviation?

FIGURE 2.47   Box Plots of Delivery Time Data

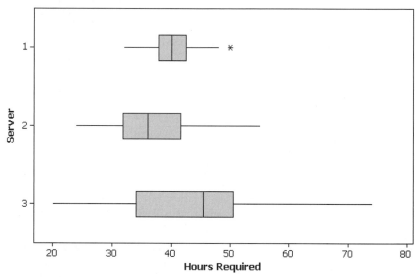

2.52   Most fast-food restaurants have a continuing problem with employee turnover. As a result, they must expend a great deal of time and effort hiring and training new workers. The franchise owner of 13 outlets of a hamburger chain conducted exit interviews with all employees who left any outlet voluntarily, as opposed to being fired. The interviewer judged the primary reason for leaving according to a list of 12 possibilities:

1. don't like the type of work
2. don't like the hours of work
3. don't like the work environment
4. conflict with other employees
5. conflict with managers
6. better pay elsewhere in the food industry
7. better pay elsewhere in a different industry
8. more responsible job elsewhere
9. pay not enough for loss of free time
10. leaving to enter college
11. moving to different geographical area
12. promotion within the franchise outlets

The interviewer obtained summary statistics from Minitab as follows:

```
Descriptive Statistics: Reason

Variable    N     Mean    StDev   Median
Reason     101   6.9703  2.3767  6.0000
```

The interviewer noted that the mean (average) was quite a bit larger than the median. What does this fact indicate about the data?

2.53   A Pareto chart of the reasons for leaving the hamburger outlet of Exercise 2.52, generated by Minitab, is shown in Figure 2.48.
a. Which codes account for the great majority of the reasons for leaving? Exactly what constitutes the "great majority" is up to you.
b. Are these codes related in any way?

FIGURE 2.48   Reasons for Leaving Employment—Interview Codes

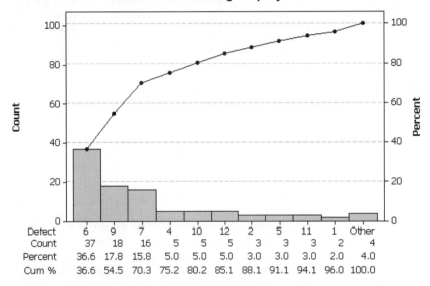

Detect	6	9	7	4	10	12	2	5	11	1	Other
Count	37	18	16	5	5	5	3	3	3	2	4
Percent	36.6	17.8	15.8	5.0	5.0	5.0	3.0	3.0	3.0	2.0	4.0
Cum %	36.6	54.5	70.3	75.2	80.2	85.1	88.1	91.1	94.1	96.0	100.0

2.54   The manager combined codes from Exercise 2.52 into four basic categories: Conditions (codes 1, 2, 3, 4, and 5); Improvement (codes 8 and 12); Pay (codes 6, 7, and 9); and Personal (codes 10 and 11). A Pareto chart by categories is shown in Figure 2.49 (see next page). Does the combining process reveal the essential reason for turnover more clearly?

2.55   One of the important factors in a customer's perception of food quality is the age of the product. Even with good, airtight packaging, a food product loses some of its appeal as it gets older. This problem is particularly acute for snack products, various chips and crackers intended for casual munching. A local manufacturer of one such snack visited 63 convenience stores that were outlets for the product. In each store, the age of the frontmost package was determined from the data code stamped on the package. The data were as follows:

Snack Age

1	29.000	7	17.000	13	19.000
2	16.000	8	27.000	14	25.000
3	47.000	9	16.000	15	27.000
4	49.000	10	19.000	16	12.000
5	26.000	11	22.000	17	18.000
6	18.000	12	16.000	18	10.000

FIGURE 2.49 **Reasons for Leaving Employment—Combined Categories**

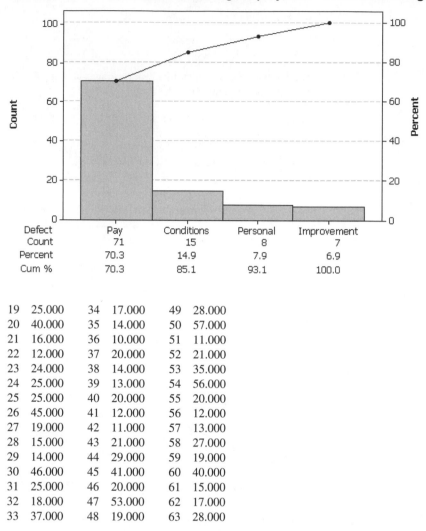

Defect	Pay	Conditions	Personal	Improvement
Count	71	15	8	7
Percent	70.3	14.9	7.9	6.9
Cum %	70.3	85.1	93.1	100.0

19	25.000	34	17.000	49	28.000
20	40.000	35	14.000	50	57.000
21	16.000	36	10.000	51	11.000
22	12.000	37	20.000	52	21.000
23	24.000	38	14.000	53	35.000
24	25.000	39	13.000	54	56.000
25	25.000	40	20.000	55	20.000
26	45.000	41	12.000	56	12.000
27	19.000	42	11.000	57	13.000
28	15.000	43	21.000	58	27.000
29	14.000	44	29.000	59	19.000
30	46.000	45	41.000	60	40.000
31	25.000	46	20.000	61	15.000
32	18.000	47	53.000	62	17.000
33	37.000	48	19.000	63	28.000

a. Construct a stem-and-leaf display of the data using intervals with a leaf unit = 1.
b. Redo the stem-and-leaf using intervals with a leaf unit = 1, and split stems in two.
c. Describe the general shape of the data. How much difference does it make which stem-and-leaf you look at?

2.56 A smoothed histogram of the snack age data of Exercise 2.55 was constructed using Minitab, as shown in Figure 2.50.
a. Does the histogram indicate the same general shape as the stem-and-leaf displays constructed in Exercise 2.55?
b. Why isn't the histogram shape exactly like either stem-and-leaf shape?

2.57 Summary statistics for the data of Exercise 2.55 were obtained using Excel, as follows:

```
        SnackAge

Mean                    24
Standard Error       1.516
Median                  20
Mode                    19
```

FIGURE 2.50   **Smoothed Histogram of Snack Age Data**

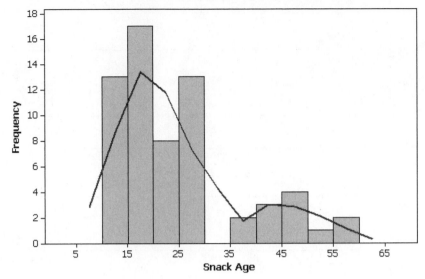

Standard Deviation	12.031
Sample Variance	144.742
Kurtosis	0.769
Skewness	1.237
Range	47
Minimum	10
Maximum	57
Sum	1512
Count	63

How is the right-skewness of the data reflected in the mean (average) and median?

2.58   A manufacturer of seat belts must be concerned about the breaking strengths of the belts. If a particular belt strength is lower than the design specification, the belt can give way too easily in a crash, causing injury to the wearer. As one part of its quality-control program, the manufacturer finds the breaking strength of five belts each day. (The test involves literally tearing the belt apart, so the manufacturer is less than eager to test all belts.) Design specifications are for a mean strength of 30.0 (in the appropriate units) and a standard deviation of 0.2 units. Minitab control charts for the sample mean and standard deviation for each of the most recent 30 days are shown in Figure 2.51 on the next page.

a. Does it appear that the mean strength is consistently within the control limits?

b. Does there appear to be a trend in the means or a sudden jump to a new level?

2.59   Refer to the standard deviation portion of the Minitab control chart in Figure 2.51.

a. Does it appear that the sample standard deviations are consistently within control limits? If not, are they too big or too small, generally?

b. What appears to be the primary quality problem for the manufacturer—average level or variability around average?

2.60   An office supply company does a third of its business supplying local governments and school districts. This business is done by competitive bids. Each potential sale requires a clerk to prepare a bid form. The firm had no real idea of how much effort the bid preparation required, so the bid clerk was asked to record the start and stop times for a sample of 65 bids. The data were recorded two ways: minutes spent per bid (MINPRBID in the output below) and bids per hour BIDPERHR = 60/MINPRBID.

FIGURE 2.51 **Control Charts for Seat Belt Strength**

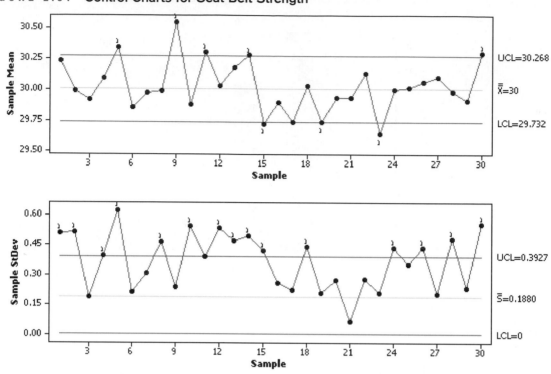

CASE	MINPRBID	BIDPERHR	CASE	MINPRBID	BIDPERHR
1	155.000	0.387	33	30.000	2.000
2	66.000	0.909	34	76.000	0.789
3	134.000	0.448	35	103.000	0.583
4	39.000	1.538	36	48.000	1.250
5	61.000	0.984	37	29.000	2.069
6	46.000	1.304	38	29.000	2.069
7	23.000	2.609	39	46.000	1.304
8	21.000	2.857	40	26.000	2.308
9	54.000	1.111	41	27.000	2.222
10	31.000	1.935	42	24.000	2.500
11	30.000	2.000	43	41.000	1.463
12	149.000	0.403	44	50.000	1.200
13	51.000	1.176	45	82.000	0.732
14	120.000	0.500	46	114.000	0.526
15	23.000	2.609	47	23.000	2.609
16	41.000	1.463	48	49.000	1.224
17	56.000	1.071	49	65.000	0.923
18	38.000	1.579	50	20.000	3.000
19	25.000	2.400	51	22.000	2.727
20	42.000	1.429	52	100.000	0.600
21	35.000	1.714	53	62.000	0.968
22	28.000	2.143	54	24.000	2.500
23	80.000	0.750	55	200.000	0.300
24	46.000	1.304	56	65.000	0.923
25	24.000	2.500	57	50.000	1.200
26	46.000	1.304	58	42.000	1.429
27	47.000	1.277	59	29.000	2.069
28	73.000	0.822	60	145.000	0.414
29	220.000	0.273	61	110.000	0.545
30	80.000	0.750	62	43.000	1.395
31	25.000	2.400	63	40.000	1.500
32	20.000	3.000	64	191.000	0.314
			65	126.000	0.476

a. Scan the MINPRBID columns and give a rough guess as to the mean.

b. Do the same for the BIDPERHR columns.

2.61 Histograms from Minitab for the data of Exercise 2.60 are shown in Figure 2.52.

a. Use these histograms to check the guesses for the mean that you made in Exercise 2.60.

b. Are the two variables skewed in about the same way?

2.62 Summary statistics for the data of Exercise 2.60 follow:

```
TOTAL OBSERVATIONS:      65
                     MINPRBID BIDPERHR
N OF CASES                 65       65
MINIMUM                20.000    0.273
MAXIMUM               220.000    3.000
MEAN                   62.462    1.432
VARIANCE             2199.971    0.610
STANDARD DEV           46.904    0.781
SKEWNESS(G1)            1.618    0.356
```

FIGURE 2.52 **Histograms for Exercise 2.61**

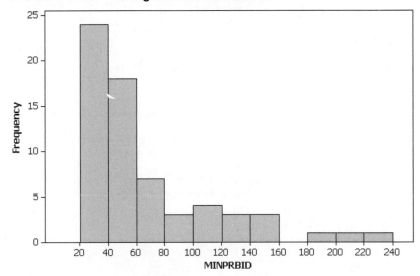

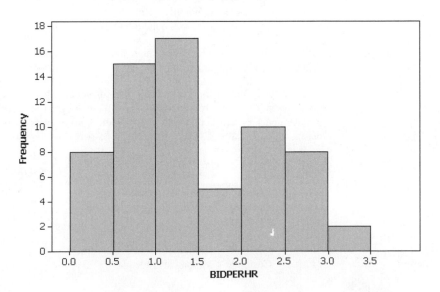

a. Locate the means.

b. Is it true that the mean for BIDPERHR is 60 divided by the mean for MINPRBID?

2.63   An automobile insurance company was considering expanding its sales effort in a midwestern city. As one part of its study, the claims department collected data on the size of claims for collision damage over the past year. Would you expect the data to be roughly symmetric around the mean?

2.64   A stem-and-leaf display of the collision claims data is as follows:

```
Stem-and-leaf of ClaimSize  N = 187
Leaf Unit = 0.10

  27    0   777777777777888888899999999
  61    1   0011111122222333334466667888899999
  79    2   000112335556677799
 (21)   3   000012333455555666778
  87    4   0122223344466666777899
  65    5   023377889
  56    6   0112557
  49    7   11123344467779
  35    8   2335567889
  25    9   7
  24   10   11
  22   11   0345
  18   12   99
  16   13   123
  13   14   24
  11   15   2

HI 168, 174, 190, 194, 205, 207, 209, 226, 266, 337
```

a. Does the stem-and-leaf display appear roughly symmetric?

b. Can you guess why some of the numbers are displayed in the HI leaf?

2.65   The data on collision insurance claims (in thousands of dollars) from Exercise 2.64 were summarized as follows:

```
Descriptive Statistics: ClaimSize

Variable    N   Mean  StDev  Minimum    Q1  Median    Q3  Maximum
ClaimSize  187  5.178  5.284    0.700  1.400   3.500  7.100   33.700
```

a. One standard deviation below the mean is about -0.1, which is an impossible value for an insurance claim. The Empirical Rule doesn't seem to work at all for these data. Why?

b. The mean (average) value is quite a bit larger than the median. Why did that happen?

2.66   A Minitab box plot of the claim size data for Exercise 2.64 is shown in Figure 2.53. What does this plot indicate about the shape of the claim size data?

2.67   The customer support service of a word-processing software company must call a customer back if it can't provide a problem-solving suggestion immediately. Callbacks are expensive and less satisfactory for the customer. A set of codes was developed to indicate the reason for each callback. The frequencies for a period of time were

Code	Explanation	Frequency
01	Problem not covered in manuals	27
02	Operator could not find correct section	56
03	Manual incorrect	3
04	Manual ambiguous	5
11	Customer's problem misstated	42
12	Customer's equipment inadequate	19

FIGURE 2.53   Box Plot of Collision Claims Data

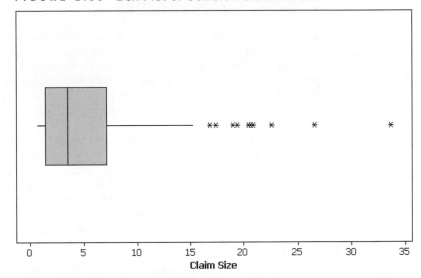

Claim Size

Code	Explanation	Frequency
13	Task not achievable in customer's version	5
21	Operator's suggestion failed	11
22	Operator answered for wrong version	8
99	All others	17

a. According to the Pareto chart in Figure 2.54, what are the most commonly occurring problems?

b. The company could do little about customer-related errors (codes 11–13). What do the results for other codes suggest about the most important possible improvements to the service?

FIGURE 2.54   Pareto Chart for Service Problems

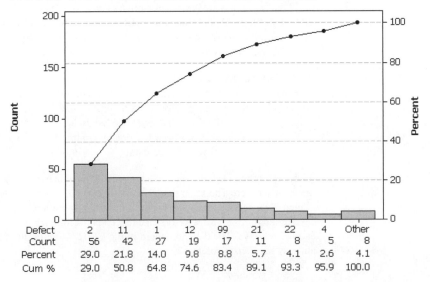

Defect	2	11	1	12	99	21	22	4	Other
Count	56	42	27	19	17	11	8	5	8
Percent	29.0	21.8	14.0	9.8	8.8	5.7	4.1	2.6	4.1
Cum %	29.0	50.8	64.8	74.6	83.4	89.1	93.3	95.9	100.0

2.68   The customer service manager for the software company in Exercise 2.67 asked what the average reason for a callback was. How would you answer this question?

2.69   The editor of a metropolitan newspaper's food section constructed a market basket of 30 items to reflect the "typical" family of four's basic food needs for a week. The editor also put together another list of nonfood items such as cleaning supplies and paper goods typically purchased at supermarkets. Reporters obtained prices for all items on both lists at 53 markets in the metropolitan area. The total cost of the food basket at each market is stored in column 1 of the EX0269 file on the CD that accompanies this book. The total cost of the nonfood list is stored in column 2.
a. Use any computer package that is available to you to load the data.
b. Obtain a histogram of the food cost data. How would you describe the general shape of the data?
c. From the histogram, make a rough guess of what the mean is.
d. Use the Empirical Rule idea that about 95% of the data should be within 2 standard deviations of the mean to guess the value of the standard deviation.
e. Have the computer package calculate the mean and standard deviation.

2.70   Refer to Exercise 2.69.
a. Obtain a stem-and-leaf display of the nonfood cost data shown. Describe the general shape.
b. Obtain the mean, median, and standard deviation of the nonfood cost.

2.71   Refer to Exercise 2.69.
a. Have your computer package calculate the ratio of food cost to the sum of food and nonfood costs for the data set. Obtain a box plot of the ratio data.
b. Does the box plot indicate any outliers?
c. Is the mean of the ratio data the same as the ratio of the mean food cost to the sum of the means of the two costs?

2.72   A copy center located near a university campus offers self-service copying. The daily number of copies made on self-service machines varies, depending on weather, number of assignments due at the university, number of machines under repair, and many other factors. The copy center recorded the number of copies made each day for 44 days. The data are stored in the EX0272 file on the CD; column 1 is number of copies, column 2 is day number.
a. Use a computer package to read in the data. Obtain a box plot of the number of copies available.
b. Identify any days that yielded outlier values.
c. Obtain the mean and standard deviation of the number of copies.
d. Delete all outliers from the data and recompute the mean and standard deviation. Which number changes more?

2.73   Refer to Exercise 2.72.
a. Have a computer package plot the data for number of copies against day number. The package should have a "plot" or "scatterplot" capability; if it has a special capability for plotting time series data, that would be handy here.
b. Can you see an evident upward or downward trend in the plot?
c. Are there evident cycles in the data?

2.74   An office-cleaning service has developed a numerical scale to assess the general cleanliness of an area. The scale ranges from 0 at worst to 100 at best. The target value is 80 or higher. (The service managers believe that shooting for a perfect 100 score would require excessive labor costs.) Supervisors calculated scores for each of four randomly chosen areas on each of 60 days. The data are stored in the EX0274 file on the CD, with scores in column 1 and day number in column 2.

a. Read the data into a computer package and obtain a stem-and-leaf display of the cleanliness scores.

b. Identify any evident departures from a normal distribution.

c. The president of the service suspected that supervisors might make a fast guess at the cleanliness score, rather than going through the details. If so, many scores would be likely to end in 0 or 5. Is there evidence of that phenomenon in the stem-and-leaf display?

2.75 Refer to Exercise 2.74.

a. Obtain the mean and standard deviation of the cleanliness scores.

b. Have the computer package obtain the mean score for each day and compute the standard deviation of those means.

c. If your computer package has the capability, obtain a control chart of the daily means. Use a target mean of 80 and the standard deviation of the means found in part (b) of this exercise.

d. Were there any days when the cleanliness was "out of control"?

BUSINESS CASES

Production Line Quality

A meat packer sells portion-controlled sirloin steaks to restaurant chains. The meat is cut, frozen, and packaged on two production lines called (not too imaginatively) the Left and Right lines. The target size for each steak is 12 ounces, but there is variability because of differences in meat density, slight differences in cut, slight differences in fat content, and several other factors. Each steak is visually inspected and also weighed by a rough scale along the production line; the scale is supposed to reject any steak that weighs less than 11.5 ounces and set aside any steak that weighs more than 12.6 ounces.

The production managers have noticed an increase in the number of 24-steak packages being rejected by customers for inadequate average weight. The managers traced the source of each rejected package and found that most had come from the Right line. They have written to you for help. "As you know, quality control picks 10 steaks each week from each line for careful testing. Before they're cooked, they're all weighed carefully. We've got weights for each line for the last 25 weeks. During the first 10 weeks, we were running at speeds well below capacity to make sure that our cutting was OK. The last 15 weeks, we've been running at nearly full capacity. What we can't figure out is that the average weights from the two lines are practically identical; if anything, the Right line averages a little heavier. So why are so many more of the Right line packages coming up short?" They enclosed the weights for each week's sample of 10 steaks.

```
Left Line

week                                                              Average
  1   12.32 12.16 12.34 12.03 11.95 12.05 11.78 12.01 11.95 12.39  12.098
  2   12.04 11.98 12.06 11.95 12.12 11.84 12.29 12.10 11.92 12.07  12.037
  3   11.78 12.07 12.11 11.71 11.87 11.88 11.61 11.93 12.08 12.01  11.905
  4   12.37 11.98 11.94 12.06 11.88 12.24 12.05 12.10 12.32 11.82  12.076
  5   12.08 11.95 11.82 11.86 12.51 12.07 12.07 12.25 11.98 12.28  12.087
  6   12.12 11.62 12.01 12.04 11.86 12.05 11.80 12.05 12.17 12.20  11.992
  7   12.49 12.12 11.92 11.76 11.97 11.78 11.80 11.69 12.04 12.01  11.958
  8   11.78 12.29 12.52 12.23 12.32 12.14 11.64 12.12 12.24 12.08  12.136
  9   12.00 11.95 12.05 12.15 11.89 12.27 12.23 12.00 12.01 12.22  12.077
 10   11.95 11.81 11.99 12.00 11.93 12.01 12.01 11.74 12.50 11.77  11.971
```

```
11  11.85 12.13 12.55 12.09 12.28 12.43 11.92 11.96 11.95 12.19 12.135
12  11.81 11.86 11.75 11.86 12.13 12.43 12.14 11.81 12.21 12.19 12.019
13  12.15 11.87 12.36 12.29 12.13 11.82 12.30 11.76 11.88 11.90 12.046
14  12.10 11.82 11.94 12.22 11.61 12.15 11.92 12.06 12.08 12.06 11.996
15  12.19 11.77 11.89 11.96 11.97 11.93 12.18 12.12 12.37 12.27 12.065
16  11.84 12.03 12.07 11.91 11.90 11.86 11.98 12.25 11.96 12.05 11.985
17  12.24 11.80 12.03 12.13 11.88 12.52 12.06 11.90 12.01 11.91 12.048
18  12.08 12.02 11.87 11.89 12.06 12.19 11.91 12.06 11.91 11.85 11.984
19  12.18 12.17 12.03 11.74 11.65 12.01 12.45 11.84 11.88 12.00 11.995
20  12.42 12.00 11.89 11.92 12.06 12.00 11.63 12.12 12.02 12.28 12.034
21  11.60 11.85 12.08 11.68 12.28 12.12 11.96 12.16 11.81 11.93 11.947
22  12.01 11.68 11.96 11.88 11.62 11.82 11.77 12.17 11.78 12.07 11.876
23  12.54 12.35 11.96 12.11 11.94 12.11 11.98 12.16 12.28 11.80 12.123
24  12.25 11.97 12.21 12.03 12.01 11.94 11.76 12.15 11.71 12.07 12.010
25  11.63 12.10 12.14 12.19 11.74 12.19 11.88 12.11 11.76 11.88 11.962
```

```
Right Line

week                                                          Average
 1  12.07 11.88 11.89 12.21 11.93 11.94 11.99 12.21 11.90 12.20 12.022
 2  11.82 11.83 12.22 12.06 11.96 12.11 11.52 11.96 12.11 11.93 11.952
 3  12.34 12.02 12.08 12.33 12.07 12.38 12.06 11.97 11.81 11.97 12.103
 4  11.87 12.17 12.01 12.02 12.21 12.33 11.98 12.04 11.80 12.33 12.076
 5  12.17 11.60 12.22 12.06 11.70 12.12 11.90 12.13 12.08 11.83 11.981
 6  12.00 12.05 11.91 12.24 11.99 12.00 12.21 12.15 11.98 11.73 12.026
 7  12.40 11.90 11.72 12.57 11.60 12.20 12.02 12.31 11.82 12.25 12.079
 8  11.99 11.95 12.19 12.24 12.19 12.08 12.27 12.15 12.43 12.14 12.163
 9  11.83 12.19 11.40 11.69 11.99 11.85 12.14 12.17 12.10 12.04 11.940
10  11.82 12.00 11.89 12.07 11.70 11.67 12.07 11.95 12.06 11.86 11.909
11  11.83 12.04 12.35 12.40 11.82 12.28 11.94 12.21 12.34 12.23 12.144
12  11.81 11.71 11.60 12.03 11.91 11.93 12.10 12.51 12.09 11.86 11.955
13  11.99 12.12 11.67 11.88 12.27 11.50 12.18 12.25 11.71 12.23 11.980
14  12.78 11.34 11.58 12.82 11.40 13.10 11.55 12.70 12.44 12.22 12.193
15  11.59 12.13 11.94 12.45 12.55 11.23 11.52 12.48 12.74 11.07 11.970
16  12.20 12.36 12.00 12.30 11.08 12.21 12.16 12.04 12.50 11.65 12.050
17  12.18 11.70 11.96 12.71 12.07 12.06 11.64 12.78 12.03 11.57 12.070
18  11.96 12.43 11.37 12.54 12.32 12.67 12.21 12.32 12.64 11.90 12.236
19  12.31 12.37 11.74 11.56 11.94 12.24 11.93 11.93 12.74 12.06 12.082
20  11.58 12.06 12.13 12.16 11.94 11.90 11.89 12.33 12.28 12.46 12.073
21  11.90 12.27 11.94 12.37 12.13 11.47 12.26 11.33 11.49 11.63 11.879
22  11.64 11.41 11.90 12.24 11.66 12.23 12.34 12.43 11.57 11.41 11.883
23  11.73 11.34 11.81 12.62 11.43 12.14 12.41 12.46 12.57 11.64 12.015
24  12.15 12.29 12.64 12.40 12.62 12.43 12.47 12.50 11.28 12.08 12.286
25  12.25 12.28 11.94 11.88 12.09 12.24 11.91 11.80 11.62 10.98 11.899
```

Assignment: Can you identify any difference between the Left and Right data that might explain the problem? Does the difference show up after the initial 10 weeks or during that period? You may want to use a computer program to do the arithmetic. Write a memorandum to the managers; they don't know any technical terms, so try to use ordinary English as much as possible.

Fastest Courier in the West

The law firm of Adams, Babcock, and Connors is located in the Dallas–Fort Worth metroplex. Randall Adams is the senior and founding partner in the firm. John Babcock has been a partner in the firm for the past eight years, and Blake Connors became a partner just last year. The firm employs two paralegals and three administrative assistants. In addition, Bill Davis, the newly hired office manager, is in charge of day-to-day operations and manages the financial affairs of the law firm.

The law firm prepares contracts and other legal documents and uses a courier service to deliver the documents to its many clients, who are scattered throughout the metroplex. Because the centers of Dallas and Fort Worth are separated by approximately 30 miles and the traffic is heavy, a trip from the southwest side of Fort Worth to the northeast side of Dallas can easily take longer than an hour. The importance of the legal documents involved makes their timely delivery a high priority. At a recent partner's meeting, the topic of courier delivery came up.

Adams: I got a couple of complaints recently from some of our best clients about delayed contract deliveries. It took the better part of an hour yesterday afternoon to calm down old man Dixon. He claims that if those contracts had arrived any later, his deal with the Taguchi Group would've fallen through.

Connors: Not our fault—Anne had the contracts all typed and proofread before nine in the morning.

Adams: No, no—everything was okay on our end. The delay was the courier's fault—something about a delay in the delivery. . . .

Babcock: Metro Delivery has always done a good job for us in the past. I'm sure that these are just a few unusual incidents.

Connors: On the other hand, their service could be slipping.

Adams: Anyway, we can't afford to make clients unhappy. No one's perfect, but only one or two bad incidents and we lose important clients. At least two new courier services have opened here during the last two years and I hear good things about them from some of my friends. The question is, should we keep using Metro or consider using one of these other services?

Connors: How should we decide?

Babcock: Give each one a trial period and choose the best performer?

Adams: Good idea! But how do we figure out who's best?

Babcock: Well, obviously that boils down to picking the fastest service. Given our recent problem, we also don't want delayed deliveries, even though they don't happen often. Cost is also important, of course.

Connors: Why not let our new office manager run this little "contest" for a few weeks? Bill normally keeps fairly detailed information about contract deliveries anyway. As the need arises, he can rotate through all three couriers.

Adams: Let's be sure not to let any of the couriers know about the contest; otherwise, we may not see their typical performance. We'll take this up again after Bill has collected and analyzed some data and is ready to make a presentation.

During the past month, Bill Davis has kept detailed records of the deliveries made by each of three courier services: DFW Express, Carborne Carrier, and Metro Delivery (the courier presently used by the law firm). Due to the importance of the documents delivered, a courier is required to phone the law office as soon as a delivery has been made. For each delivery, Bill's data set contains: the courier used, the pickup time, the delivery time, the mileage of the delivery, and the cost of the delivery. Each of the courier services charges a flat fee plus mileage for each delivery. These charges vary from courier to courier.

Assignment: As office manager, Bill Davis is responsible for deciding which courier service will be given the exclusive contract. You have been hired by the law firm as a consultant. Assist Bill in choosing among the three courier services and defending his choice to the partners of the firm by performing a statistical analysis of the data.

Write a short report to the partners giving your analysis of the data and final recommendation. The report should consist of two parts: (1) a one-page memo to the partners that briefly summarizes the results of your analysis and your recommendations and (2) a detailed analysis of the data that describes your analysis and interpretations. Incorporate important details, graphs, and tables from your analysis into your report to support your recommendation. Blend output, tables, and graphs with your written text. (Do not put all of the output and graphs in an appendix.) You may assume that the law partners are reasonably familiar with basic statistical techniques but make your written presentation as clear as possible to any other interested readers.

The courier data are contained in the file Courier on the CD that came with your book. The file contains information on 182 courier deliveries. For each delivery, the courier, the pickup time, the delivery time, the mileage, and the cost of the delivery are given. A partial listing of the data within Excel is shown in Figure 2.55.

FIGURE 2.55

Partial Listing of the Fastest Courier in the West Data

	A	B	C	D	E
1	Courier	Pickup Time	Delivery Time	Mileage	Cost
2	1	13	14	7	16.55
3	3	20	51	20	26.50
4	2	22	33	12	19.00
5	3	11	47	19	25.60
6	3	17	18	8	15.70
7	1	15	88	17	23.05
8	3	17	20	11	18.40
9	3	17	39	11	18.40
10	3	19	23	10	17.50
11	1	25	20	8	17.20
12	3	19	32	10	17.50
13	3	9	35	16	22.90
14	3	13	23	9	16.60
15	2	17	21	10	17.50
16	1	14	37	16	22.40

In the Courier file, the variables are defined as follows:

Courier:	1 = DFW Express,
	2 = Carborne Carrier,
	3 = Metro Delivery
Pickup Time:	Time in minutes from when the order is phoned in until a courier agent arrives at the law firm to pick up the package for delivery
Delivery Time:	Time in minutes that it takes for the documents to be delivered from the law firm to the destination
Mileage:	Distance in miles from the law firm to the destination
Cost:	Charge for the delivery (in dollars). Each of the courier services charges a flat fee plus a mileage charge. These charges vary from courier to courier.

A First Look at Probability

CHAPTER CONTENTS

Probability is the basic mathematical language of uncertainty. It gives us a way to deal with variability. This chapter presents a very basic introduction to that language. The key ideas are:

- Probability may be interpreted as classical probability if we can count equally likely outcomes, as long-run relative frequency probability if we can conceptually repeat the experiment many times, or as subjective probability if we are stating a personal opinion.

- There are three basic principles of probability: addition, to find the probability of one event *or* another; complements, to calculate the probability that an event does *not* happen; multiplication, to find the probability of one event *and* another.

- Probabilities may be conditional (given that another event has happened) or unconditional. The conditional probability of one event given another is the unconditional probability of both events, divided by the probability of the given event.

- Statistical independence of two events means that the occurrence of one event does not change the probability of the other. Sometimes, statistical independence is an empirical question. Often, independence is an assumption in solving probability problems. Because it *is* an assumption, it should be checked for reasonableness.

- Probability tables and trees are useful devices for clarifying probability reasoning. To make these devices work properly, we must define mutually exclusive categories—for the rows and columns of a table or for the branches of a tree.

- The addition (for mutually exclusive events), complements, and multiplication principles all are used to complete probability tables and trees. Conditional probabilities may be calculated by using the definition.

Probability theory is the basis of statistical inference; it is also fundamental in analyzing variability. In this chapter we sketch the basic concepts and principles of probability theory, beginning with some alternative interpretations of probability statements. Then we introduce the basic mathematical principles that underlie the more complex computations, and the important idea of statistical independence. Finally, we describe some techniques that can be used to combine the basic mathematical principles in the solution of more complicated problems.

This is an important foundation chapter for our later discussion of statistical inference. Probability theory is a major branch of pure and applied mathematics, and this chapter barely touches the basics. The illustrations and examples that we use are relatively simple but will suggest the wide variety of managerial applications.

Discount World, Inc.

Robert Wilton was facing a serious legal issue in his first month as the new Eastern Regional Vice President of Discount World, Inc. He received word that the management of the Discount World store in Taylorsville, Maryland, is being sued by two customers who are claiming racial discrimination.

Discount World is a national chain of retail stores selling a wide variety of products at sharply discounted prices. Although the corporation has existed for only five years, its number of stores nationwide has grown quickly. Discount World has become a serious competitor to Wal-Mart, Target, and Kmart in the markets it serves.

Like any large retailer, Discount World faces a serious shoplifting problem. Plainclothes security officers in each store are constantly on the watch and take any suspected shoplifter to the store manager's office. The store manager considers the evidence and the shoplifter is given a chance to explain. It's up to the store manager to decide if the suspected shoplifter should be released or turned over to the local authorities for prosecution.

Recently, an African-American man and woman were accused of shoplifting in the Discount World store in Taylorsville. Based on the convincing evidence of the security officer, the couple was turned over to the local police. Even though the case against the couple was very strong, the judge ruled in their favor and released them. Just one week later, the couple initiated a class action lawsuit against the manager of Discount World in Taylorsville. They complained that the manager and other employees discriminated against minority customers accused of shoplifting. Specifically, the lawsuit claimed that the store manager was racially biased in that he prosecuted minority suspects more frequently than nonminority suspects and was therefore more likely to release a nonminority suspect than a minority suspect.

Even though he had been in his new position only a short time, Robert Wilton was inclined to believe that the managers in Discount World stores behave in an ethical manner. However, Robert knew that a negative outcome in this case could lead to a string of additional class action suits against other stores and, eventually, corporate headquarters.

Lawyers for the presentation had requested and received the Taylorsville store records kept on all shoplifting incidents over the course of the past three years. The legal counsel for Discount World has received word that the statistical expert witness hired by the prosecution had analyzed the data and written a report that concluded there is sufficient evidence in the shoplifting records to indicate racial discrimination exists.

As the head of customer relations for Discount World, you have been asked by Robert Wilton to examine the shoplifting data analyzed by the prosecution's expert witness and to provide your own analysis, interpretations, and recommendations.

The shoplifting log data from the Discount World store in Taylorsville are contained in the file DiscountWorld on the CD that came with your book. The file contains information on the 486 shoplifting incidents handled at the Taylorsville store over the past three years. The data file includes the age, race, and gender of the accused, the total dollar amount stolen, and the decision by the store manager to release or prosecute the shoplifting suspect. A partial listing of the data within Excel is shown in Figure 3.1.

FIGURE 3.1

Partial Listing of the Discount World Shoplifting Data

	A	B	C	D	E	F
1	Age	AgeClass	Minority	Gender	Amount	Prosecuted
2	38	A	N	M	29.58	Y
3	20	A	N	F	13.91	N
4	18	J	N	M	12.34	Y
5	14	J	N	M	10.11	N
6	25	A	N	F	61.12	Y
7	16	J	N	M	8.29	N
8	40	A	N	M	118.02	Y
9	19	A	N	F	96.42	Y
10	19	A	N	F	116.25	Y
11	16	J	N	M	12.82	N
12	17	J	N	M	21.52	N
13	27	A	N	F	214.93	Y
14	18	A	N	M	12.34	N
15	18	A	N	M	22.50	Y

In the DiscountWorld file, the variables are defined as follows:

Age: Age of the accused shoplifter (in years)

Age Class: Age class of the accused shoplifter (J for juvenile, A for Adult)

Minority: Y (for Yes) if the accused shoplifter is a minority; N (for No), otherwise

Gender: Gender of the accused shoplifter (M for male, F for female)

Amount: Total dollar amount of the shoplifted items

Prosecuted: Store manager's decision (N for No or Released, Y for Yes or Prosecuted)

The numerical and graphical tools described in this chapter for summarizing data will be very helpful in our analysis of the Discount World case at the end of this chapter. ■

3.1 Basic Principles of Probability

The theory of probability is the basic language of uncertainty and also forms the basis for statistical inference. If 20% of the workforce at a textile company have signed union election cards, and if 8 randomly chosen workers are to be fired, then the probability of choosing 8 workers who have signed the cards is very small. Thus, if it turns out that all 8 workers fired by the company had signed union election cards, then we can make the inference that the firings were related to union activity.

The first step in the study of probability is understanding the possible interpretations of probability statements. The earliest mathematics, and the first interpretation, of probability theory arose from various games of chance. "The probability that a flip of a balanced coin will show heads is 1/2" and "the probability that a card selected at random from a standard deck of 52 cards will be a king is 4/52" are typical examples of this kind of probability statement. The numerical probability values arise from the physical nature of the experiment. A coin flip has only two possible outcomes: heads or tails; the probability that a head occurs should therefore be 1 out of 2. In a standard deck of 52 cards, 4 are kings, so the probability of drawing a king should be 4 out of 52.

classical interpretation

These probability calculations are based on the **classical interpretation** of probability. In this interpretation each distinct possible result of an experiment is called an **outcome;** an **event** is identified with certain of these outcomes. In the card-drawing illustration there are 52 possible outcomes, 4 of which are identified with the event drawing a king. According to the classical interpretation, the probability of an event E is taken to be the ratio of the number of outcomes favorable to an event, N_E, to the total number of possible outcomes, N, or symbolically,

outcome

event

$$P(\text{event E}) = \frac{N_E}{N}$$

The usefulness of this interpretation depends completely on the assumption that all possible outcomes are *equally likely*. If that assumption is false—if the coin is loaded or the deck marked, for instance—the classical interpretation does not apply.

EXAMPLE 3.1 An ordinary thumbtack is dropped on a hard surface. It can come to rest point up or on its side. Are the two outcomes equally likely?

SOLUTION There is no reason to assume so. There is no symmetry to the two possibilities.

random sample

The classical interpretation has many uses, even outside the gambling casino. A **random sample,** by definition, is taken in such a way that any possible sample (of a specific size) has the same probability as any other of being selected. Therefore the outcomes (possible samples) are equally likely, and probabilities can be found by counting favorable outcomes. We use this idea extensively throughout this book.

long-run relative frequency

Situations that do not readily allow a classical interpretation sometimes can be given a **long-run relative frequency** interpretation. If an experiment has been repeated over a huge number of trials, and if 24% of these trials have resulted in a particular event E, then the probability of the event E should be .24, at least to a very good approximation. Symbolically, if an experiment is repeated over n trials and the event E occurs in n_E trials, the probability of an event E is approximately n_E divided by n.

$$P(\text{event E}) \approx \frac{n_E}{n}$$

This definition looks very much like the definition of classical probability, but the meaning is different. In the relative frequency interpretation, n is the (very large) number of trials and n_E is the number of trials where event E occurs. In the classical interpretation, N is the number of possible, equally likely, outcomes and N_E is the number of outcomes in event E.

EXAMPLE 3.2 Suppose that in the thumbtack-tossing experiment of Example 3.1, it is claimed that the probability of the tack landing point up is .70. Give a long-run relative frequency interpretation that would justify the claim.

SOLUTION The claim could be justified on the grounds of long-run relative frequency if a tack had been tossed many times with 70% of the results being point up.

computer simulation

The relative frequency interpretation is often convenient. We use it whenever it seems sensible to imagine a large number of repeated trials of an experiment. This interpretation is also the basis for **computer simulation** of probabilities. As we will see, it is possible to program a computer to imitate a random, probabilistic situation a large number of times. Assuming that the program accurately reflects the reality of the situation, we can use computer simulation to find probabilities that are difficult to calculate mathematically.

Sometimes neither the classical nor the relative frequency interpretation is sensible. There are many applications of probability, particularly in management problems, that seem to be "one-shot" situations, those in which it's hard to imagine repeated trials. A product manager who estimates the probability that a new item will receive adequate shelf space is not imagining a long series of trials with this item; it can be introduced as a new product only once. The director of a state welfare agency who estimates the probability that a proposed revision in eligibility rules will pass the state legislature is not imagining a long series of identical proposals; the proposal will be considered only once in the particular legislative session. What then is the meaning of, say, a .6 probability of adequate shelf space or a .3 probability of legislative approval? Such probabilities are **subjective** or **personal probabilities.** One interpretation of such probabilities is that they represent willingness to make certain bets. If someone states that the probability of a certain event is .5, that person regards an even-money bet on the occurrence of that event as a fair bet (and is willing to take either side of the gamble). A subjective probability of .6 for an event means that "lose $6 if the event doesn't occur, win $4 if it does" is assumed to be a fair bet. This subjective, betting interpretation of probability is natural in describing the risk-taking questions that confront most managers.

subjective probabilities
personal probabilities

The mathematical laws of probability can help one make logically consistent probability estimates, but they cannot guarantee that those estimates are correct. A good manager will take better risks than a bad one and should do better in the long run. But there is no way to guarantee that one assessment of a particular subjective probability is correct and another incorrect. That, as they say, is what makes horse races!

EXAMPLE 3.3

Give a subjective probability interpretation of the statement "the probability that a thumbtack will land point up is .5."

SOLUTION If you made such a statement, you would be saying that you would take either side of a bet of $1 that the tack would land point up against $1 that it would not. As we suggested in Example 3.1, we would not agree with you. We believe that the tack is more likely to land point up and would prefer that side of the "even-money" bet.

The classical interpretation of probability gives us a good way to think about basic probability principles. All the basic probability ideas may be derived from the random drawing of individuals from a population. For example, suppose that a tasting panel of 200 men, who vary in marital status, test a potential new frozen dinner. Table 3.1 shows their opinions, broken down by marital status. For now, we'll regard the panelists as the entire population; in practice, we'd want to regard them as a sample from the much larger pool of potential male customers.

TABLE 3.1

Tasting Panelists' Opinions, by Marital Status

		Opinion				
		Poor	Fair	Good	Excellent	Total
	Never married	5	9	26	10	50
Marital	Divorced	1	4	16	9	30
Status	Married	12	23	37	32	104
	Widowed	2	8	5	1	16
	Total	20	44	84	52	200

Suppose that a panelist is drawn at random. What is the probability that he rates the dinner as poor? Using the classical interpretation, we have 20 poor opinion outcomes and 200 possible outcomes; the probability of poor opinion is $20/200 = .1$. Other probabilities can be found the same way.

addition law
mutually exclusive

The first probability principle is the **addition law.** It has two forms, depending on whether or not events are **mutually exclusive.** Events are mutually exclusive if they have no outcomes in common. The events poor opinion and fair opinion are mutually exclusive in drawing a panelist at random; the events poor opinion and widowed are not mutually exclusive. The addition law applies to finding "or" probabilities. What is the probability that a randomly chosen panelist has a poor opinion or a fair opinion? There are $20 + 44 = 64$ such panelists, so P(poor opinion or fair opinion) $= 64/200 = .32$. P(poor opinion) $= 20/200 = .10$, and P(fair opinion) $= 44/200 = .22$, so P(poor opinion or fair opinion) $= P$(poor opinion) $+ P$(fair opinion).

DEFINITION 3.1

Addition Law for Mutually Exclusive Events   If events A and B are mutually exclusive, then

$$P(A \text{ or } B) = P(A) + P(B)$$

If events are not mutually exclusive, then adding probabilities double-counts the outcomes that belong to both events. If we pick a panelist at random, the events poor opinion and widowed are not mutually exclusive; there are two panelists who are both. To find P(poor opinion or widowed), we must correct for the double counting. P(poor opinion or widowed) $= P$(poor opinion) $+ P$(widowed) $- P$(poor opinion and widowed) $= 20/200 + 16/200 - 2/200 = .10 + .08 - .01 = .17$. Alternatively, we can count the panelists who either have a poor opinion or are widowed, or both; there are $5 + 1 + 12 + 2 + 8 + 5 + 1 = 34$ such. So P(poor opinion or widowed) $= 34/200 = .17$, once again.

DEFINITION 3.2

General Addition Law   For any events A and B, not necessarily mutually exclusive,

$$P(A \text{ or } B) = P(A) + P(B) - P(A \text{ and } B)$$

We will sometimes use the symbol ∪ for "or" and the symbol ∩ for "and." If you happen to know some set theory, you'll recognize these as the symbols for union and intersection of sets. However, we needn't use formal set theory. Just read ∪ as "or" and ∩ as "and." In this notation, the general addition law is

$$P(A \cup B) = P(A) + P(B) - P(A \cap B)$$

EXAMPLE 3.4 A direct retailer receives orders from its catalog order forms, from the use of repeat-customer order forms, and by phone. The orders are classified as small (under $25.00), medium ($25.00–$99.99), large ($100.00–$299.99), or major ($300.00 and up). An analysis of the retailer's last 4000 orders yields Table 3.2.

a. Catalog and repeat-customer forms must go through an initial entry step. What is the probability that a randomly chosen order went through this step? That is, what is the probability that an order is either a catalog or a repeat-customer order?

b. Major orders and phone orders are held for verification of credit. What is the probability that a randomly chosen order is held?

SOLUTION

a. $P(\text{entry step}) = P(\text{catalog or repeat})$

$$= P(\text{catalog}) + P(\text{repeat}) = \frac{1360}{4000} + \frac{814}{4000}$$

$$= .3400 + .2035 = .5435$$

We needn't worry about double counting, because catalog and repeat are mutually exclusive categories.

b. There are orders that are both major and phone orders. We must use the general addition principle.

$$P(\text{held}) = P(\text{major or phone})$$

$$= P(\text{major}) + P(\text{phone}) - P(\text{major and phone})$$

$$= \frac{76}{4000} + \frac{1826}{4000} - \frac{13}{4000}$$

$$= .01900 + .45650 - .00325 = .47225$$

TABLE 3.2   **Sources and Sizes of Orders**

	Size				
	Small	**Medium**	**Large**	**Major**	**Total**
Catalog	1021	216	109	14	1360
Repeat	86	371	308	49	814
Phone	1497	230	86	13	1826
Total	2604	817	503	76	4000

complements law   A second probability principle is the **complements law.** It is often easier to find the probability that an event *doesn't* happen than the probability that it does. Because the total probability must equal 1, the complements principle is easy.

DEFINITION 3.3   Complements Law   If $\overline{A}$ is the event "not A,"

$$P(A) = 1 - P(\overline{A})$$

The tasting panel results in Table 3.1 can be used to illustrate the complements law. To find the probability that a randomly chosen rater gives a poor opinion or fair opinion or good opinion rating, we could note that the complementary event is excellent. So

$$P(\text{poor opinion or fair opinion or good opinion}) = 1 - P(\text{excellent})$$

$$= 1 - \frac{52}{200} = .74$$

Of course, we could also have used the addition law and added the probabilities of poor opinion, fair opinion, and good opinion. Very often, there are several ways to solve a probability problem.

EXAMPLE 3.5   As a quality-control measure, the direct retailer in Example 3.4 does an order verification check on all large and major orders, as well as on all catalog and repeat orders. Use the complements law to find the probability that a randomly chosen order will be checked.

SOLUTION   The only orders that are *not* checked are small or medium phone orders.

$$P(\text{checked}) = 1 - P(\text{small or medium phone order})$$
$$= 1 - [P(\text{small and phone}) + P(\text{medium and phone})]$$
$$= 1 - \left(\frac{1497}{4000} + \frac{230}{4000}\right) = .56825$$

Without the complements law, we would have had to add 10 different probabilities, corresponding to the 10 types of orders that are checked.

conditional probability   The concept of **conditional probability** is important in its own right; and it is also the key to another probability principle, the multiplication law. Many probability questions involve some restriction or condition on randomness. For example, in the tasting panel results of Table 3.1, we might ask for the probability that a randomly chosen married man would rate the product excellent. The condition—that the panelist be married—restricts the random choice to a subgroup, the 104 married men, of the population. Of this group, 32 rated the product excellent, so we should have $P(\text{excellent opinion}|\text{married}) = 32/104 = .308$. In the notation $P(B|A)$, the conditioning event is placed after the vertical bar. The bar should be read as "given," so $P(\text{excellent opinion}|\text{married})$ should be read as "the probability that a panelist will rate the product excellent given that the panelist is married."

A conditional probability such as $P(\text{excellent opinion}|\text{married})$ differs from a joint probability such as $P(\text{excellent opinion and married}) = 32/200$ in that the conditioning event has already occurred, or is assumed to occur. In the joint probability, the event (such as married) is random, and might or might not occur. The following definition of conditional probability indicates that there is a close relationship between conditional and joint probabilities.

DEFINITION 3.4

> **Conditional Probability** $P(\text{B}|\text{A})$
>
> $$P(\text{B}|\text{A}) = \frac{P(\text{A and B})}{P(\text{A})}$$

According to this definition,

$$P(\text{excellent opinion}|\text{married}) = \frac{P(\text{married and excellent opinion})}{P(\text{married})}$$

$$= \frac{32/200}{104/200} = \frac{32}{104}$$

as we found before.

EXAMPLE 3.6

For the direct retailer of Example 3.4, what is the probability that a written (non-phone) order is a repeat order?

SOLUTION First of all, we're looking for a conditional probability. We're assuming that the order is written. There are $1360 + 814 = 2174$ written orders, of which 814 are repeat. So $P(\text{repeat}|\text{written}) = 814/2174 = .374$. Alternatively, we may use the definition of conditional probability. Note that all repeat orders are written orders, so $P(\text{written and repeat}) = P(\text{repeat}) = 814/4000$.

$$P(\text{repeat}|\text{written}) = \frac{P(\text{written and repeat})}{P(\text{written})} = \frac{814/4000}{2174/4000}$$

$$= \frac{814}{2174} = .374 \quad \text{once again.}$$

multiplication law

The **multiplication law** of probability is simply a rewrite of the definition of conditional probability. The multiplication law is used to evaluate "and" probabilities, just as the addition law is used to evaluate "or" probabilities.

DEFINITION 3.5

> **Multiplication Law for Joint Probabilities** For any events A and B,
>
> $$P(\text{A and B}) = P(\text{A})P(\text{B}|\text{A})$$
> $$= P(\text{B})P(\text{A}|\text{B})$$

In the tasting panelists example of Table 3.1, we could find $P(\text{married and excellent opinion}) = 32/200 = .160$ directly. Alternatively, we could use the multiplication principle. We previously found that $P(\text{excellent opinion}|\text{married}) = 32/104 = .308$;

also, $P(\text{married}) = 104/200 = .520$. Therefore, $P(\text{married and excellent opinion}) = P(\text{married})P(\text{excellent opinion}|\text{married}) = (.520)(.308) = .160$, once again.

EXAMPLE 3.7

Table 3.2 in Example 3.4 can be converted to conditional and unconditional probabilities by appropriate division, as shown in Table 3.3.

a. How were the .751 and .3400 probabilities obtained?

b. Use the multiplication law to find $P(\text{catalog and small})$.

SOLUTION

a. The .751 probability is $P(\text{small}|\text{catalog})$. It was obtained by dividing the number of small catalog orders (1021) by the total number of catalog orders (1360); $1021/1360 = .751$. The .3400 is the unconditional probability of a catalog order. It is the number of catalog orders divided by the total number of all orders (4000); $1360/4000 = .3400$.

b. $P(\text{catalog and small}) = P(\text{catalog})P(\text{small}|\text{catalog})$

$$= (.3400)(.751) = .255$$

This could also have been obtained by dividing the 1021 small catalog orders by the 4000 total orders: $1021/4000 = .255$.

TABLE 3.3

Conditional Probabilities for Size Given Type of Order, and Unconditional Probabilities for Type of Order

	Size				
Type of order	**Small**	**Medium**	**Large**	**Major**	**Total**
Catalog	.751	.159	.080	.010	1.000
Repeat	.106	.456	.378	.060	1.000
Phone	.820	.126	.047	.007	1.000

	Type of Order			
	Catalog	**Repeat**	**Phone**	**Total**
Unconditional Probability	.3400	.2035	.4565	1.000

Exercises

3.1 For each of the following situations, indicate which interpretation of the probability statement seems most appropriate. (In many situations, it is arguable which is the best interpretation.)

a. A new statistics textbook for managers is about to be published. The editor states that the probability that at least enough copies will sell to break even is .8.

b. A small manufacturing firm produces a certain kind of dial for various electrical devices. A critical component of the dial assembly is a certain gear. The probability that a particular gear fails to satisfy tolerances is .002.

c. A random sample of 100 employees is to be taken from the 13,000 employees of a firm. It is known that 55% of the employees are men. As a check on the sampling process, the number of men in the sample will be counted. The probability that there will be 42 or fewer men in the sample is .0061.

d. The probability that the German inflation rate next year will exceed 6% is .3.

e. The probability that on a given day the demand for coronary-care beds at a local hospital exceeds the normal capacity is .004.

3.2   Give your own subjective probability for each of the following statements. If an entire class does this problem, it might be interesting to tabulate the various probabilities.

a. Russia will purchase wheat from the United States next year.

b. The next elected president of the United States will be a Democrat.

c. The increase in tuition costs for the major state university in your state will exceed 5% next year.

d. It will rain at some time next week.

3.3   An automobile dealer sells two brands of new cars. One, C, is primarily American in origin; the other, G, is primarily Japanese. The dealer performs repair work under warranty for both brands. Each warranty job is classified according to the primary problem to be fixed. If there is more than one problem in a given job, all problems are listed separately. Records for the past year indicate the following numbers of problems:

		Problem Area					
		Engine	**Transmission**	**Exhaust**	**Fit/Finish**	**Other**	**Total**
Brand	C	106	211	67	133	24	541
	G	21	115	16	24	6	182
	Total	127	326	83	157	30	723

a. What is the probability that a randomly chosen problem comes from brand C?

b. Serious problems are those involving the engine or transmission. What is the probability that a randomly chosen problem is serious?

c. The dealer is fully reimbursed for all brand C problems and all brand G engine, transmission, and fit/finish problems. What is the probability that a randomly chosen problem is *not* fully reimbursed?

3.4   Refer to Exercise 3.3.

a. For the automobile dealer's data provided, what is the probability that a randomly chosen problem is an engine problem, given that it comes from brand C?

b. Construct a table of conditional probabilities of problem areas, given the brand. Are the probability distributions similar for the two brands?

3.5   The automobile dealer's warranty repair data from Exercise 3.3 were reanalyzed to take into account multiple problems on a particular repair job.

		Number of Problems			
		1	**2**	**3**	**Total**
Brand	C	382	54	17	453
	G	135	16	5	156
	Total	517	70	22	609

a. What is the probability that a randomly chosen job involves more than one problem?
b. What is the probability that a randomly chosen brand C job involves more than one problem?

3.6 Use the data of Exercise 3.5 to construct a table of the conditional probabilities of the number of problems, given the brand. Would you say that the conditional probabilities are similar?

3.7 In both Exercises 3.3 and 3.5 the number of brand C entries is much higher than the number for brand G. Does this fact indicate that brand C is of poorer quality than brand G?

3.8 On a typical day a convenience store recorded 186 sales of gas, 207 sales of dairy products, 188 sales of sodas, 339 sales of packaged foods, and 316 sales of nonfood products, for a total of 1236 sales.
a. What is the probability that a randomly chosen sale is gas?
b. What is the probability that a randomly chosen sale is of some food product (including dairy and, by courtesy, soda)?

3.9 In Exercise 3.8 what is the probability that a randomly chosen food sale is a dairy product sale?

3.10 A market research firm regularly assembles panels of consumers to test new television commercials for effectiveness. The consumers are told that they are evaluating a pilot TV program. After viewing the hour-long program, complete with commercials, they are asked many questions about the program and some about the commercial—the actual object of research. A tabulation of results from one panel counted the number of panelists who recalled the product incorrectly, the number who recalled the product correctly and had a favorable opinion, and the number who recalled the product correctly and had an unfavorable opinion.

	Incorrect	Favorable	Unfavorable	Total
Men	42	38	20	100
Women	63	37	30	150
Total	105	95	50	250

a. Use the addition law to find the probability that a randomly chosen consumer recalled the commercial.
b. Use the complements principle to find the same probability.

3.11 In Exercise 3.10 what is the probability that a randomly chosen consumer is either a man or someone who recalled the product favorably?

3.12 Refer to Exercise 3.10.
a. Use the data to calculate the conditional probabilities of incorrect, favorable, and unfavorable responses among men. Do the same for women.
b. Are there gender differences in response to the commercial?

3.2 Statistical Independence

The concept of statistical independence is fundamental in probability theory and particularly in its statistical applications. Suppose that an auditor is auditing the receivables of a small company. There are 216 accounts, of which 24 contain errors; 36 of the 216 accounts are "foreign" and 4 of the 36 foreign accounts are in error. Does the probability of error given a foreign account differ from the overall (unconditional) probability of error? There were 24 erroneous accounts in the group of 216, so $P(\text{error}) = 24/216 = 1/9$. The conditional probability of error given a foreign account is $P(\text{error}|\text{foreign}) = P(\text{foreign and error})/P(\text{foreign}) = (4/216)/(36/216) = 4/36 = 1/9$, also. Because the conditional probability of error is exactly the same as the unconditional probability, the events, observing a foreign account and observing an account in error, are said to be **statistically independent.**

statistically independent

The idea of statistical independence is that the occurrence of event A does not change the probability that event B occurs. For the auditing example, the probability of error is the same when dealing with a foreign account as it is in the whole population, so it doesn't matter whether we're talking about a foreign account, an account generally, or a nonforeign account. In other words, the conditional probability $P(B|A)$ is the same as the unconditional probability $P(B)$.

DEFINITION 3.6

Definition of Independent Events   Events A and B are statistically independent if and only if $P(B|A) = P(B)$. Otherwise, they are dependent. Note: If A and B are independent, it also follows that $P(A|B) = P(A)$.

Hereafter, we simply say *independent events* and omit the word *statistically*.

EXAMPLE 3.8

Suppose two different accounts are drawn at random (not replacing the first before drawing the second) in the receivables auditing situation. Determine whether the events "first account erroneous" and "second account erroneous" are independent.

SOLUTION   Because the receivables sampling is done without replacement, the occurrence of an erroneous account on the first draw (slightly) reduces the probability of an erroneous account on the second. Therefore, the events are not independent. If the first account drawn is erroneous, there are 215 accounts remaining, of which 23 are erroneous. Therefore, $P(\text{second is erroneous}|\text{first is erroneous}) = 23/215 = .107$. If we are not given the result of the first draw, there is no difference between the first and second draws, so the unconditional probability $P(\text{second is erroneous}) = 24/216 = .111$. The numerical difference in probabilities is very small, so the events are nearly, but not quite, independent.

EXAMPLE 3.9

Suppose that in a university computing center 192 of 960 jobs are high-priority jobs: 128 of these are submitted by students and 64 by faculty. Of all jobs, 640 are from students and 320 from faculty. If one job is selected at random, are the events "high-priority job" and "student job" independent?

SOLUTION   Let A be the event that the job is submitted by a student and B the event that the job is a high-priority job. In order for events A and B to be independent, we must show

$$P(A|B) = P(A)$$

or

$$P(B|A) = P(B)$$

For this example we can compute $P(B|A)$ using the definition of conditional probability:

$$P(B|A) = \frac{P(A \cap B)}{P(A)}$$

$$= \frac{128/960}{640/960} = \frac{128}{640} = .200$$

Also, $P(B) = 192/960 = .200$, so the events A and B are independent.

The concepts of mutually exclusive events and independent events are *not* the same. "Mutually exclusive" is a logical concept; two events are mutually exclusive if one event logically can't happen when the other one does. "Statistically independent" is a probability concept; two events are independent if the occurrence of one doesn't change the probability of the other. Mutually exclusive events can't be independent. For mutually exclusive events, the occurrence of one event changes the probability of the other to zero!

The definition of independent events leads to a special case of the multiplication law that applies to independent events.

DEFINITION 3.7

Multiplication Law for Independent Events   If events A and B are independent,

$$P(A \cap B) = P(A \text{ and } B) = P(A)P(B)$$

This result is an alternate definition of independence.

EXAMPLE 3.10

Use the multiplication law for independent events to verify that the two events of Example 3.9 are independent.

SOLUTION   We showed previously that $P(A \cap B) = 128/960 = .133$. Similarly, $P(A)P(B) = (640/960) \times (192/960) = .133$. Because $P(A \cap B) = P(A)P(B)$, events A and B are independent.

The definition of independence suggests that we should find $P(A \text{ and } B)$, $P(A)$, and $P(B)$ and then check to determine if the events are independent. Sometimes this is in fact the procedure. More often, independence is a natural *assumption*. For example, sampling with replacement leads naturally to assumed independence. The multiplication principle is then used to calculate joint probabilities such as $P(A \text{ and } B)$.

EXAMPLE 3.11

Suppose that 70% of the teachers in a school district are rated as satisfactory, that 59% are age 40 or more, and that rating and age are assumed to be independent. What is the probability that a randomly chosen teacher is (a) rated satisfactory and over 40; (b) not rated satisfactory and not over 40; (c) not rated satisfactory, given under 40?

SOLUTION

a. Because the events "rated satisfactory" and "over 40 years of age" are independent, it follows that

$$P(\text{satisfactory and over 40}) = P(\text{satisfactory})P(\text{over 40})$$
$$= (.70)(.59) = .413$$

b. Because the events "rated satisfactory" and "over 40 years of age" are independent, their complements ("not rated satisfactory" and "not over 40") are also independent. Hence,

$$P(\text{not satisfactory and not over 40}) = (1 - .70)(1 - .59)$$
$$= .123$$

c. $P(\text{not satisfactory}|\text{not over 40}) = \dfrac{P(\text{not satisfactory and not over 40})}{P(\text{not over 40})}$

$$= \frac{.123}{.41} = .30$$

This is exactly the probability of the event "not rated satisfactory."

The multiplication law can be extended to more than two independent events, but to do so, we need the idea of independent processes. Processes are independent if *any* event from one process is independent of events from all other processes. If, for instance, there are four independent processes and events A, B, C, and D, then the probability of all four events occurring is

$$P(\text{A and B and C and D}) = P(\text{A})P(\text{B})P(\text{C})P(\text{D})$$

EXAMPLE 3.12

Assume that the probability that a buyer of a new automobile orders factory-installed air-conditioning is .6 and that the various buyers' decisions are independent processes. What is the probability that the next five buyers all order factory air-conditioning?

SOLUTION Let A_1, A_2, A_3, A_4, A_5 be the events that buyers 1, 2, 3, 4, 5 order factory air-conditioning. Then,

$$P(\text{all five order factory air-conditioning}) = P(A_1 \cap A_2 \cap A_3 \cap A_4 \cap A_5)$$
$$= P(A_1)P(A_2)P(A_3)P(A_4)P(A_5)$$
$$= (.6)(.6)(.6)(.6)(.6)$$
$$= .07776$$

Remember that the $\cap$ sign should be read as "and."

Exercises

3.13 A personnel officer for a firm that employs many part-time salespeople tries out a sales-aptitude test on several hundred applicants. Because the test is unproven, results are not used in hiring. Forty percent of applicants show high aptitude on the test and 12% of those hired both show high aptitude and achieve good sales records. The firm's experience shows that 30% of all salespeople achieve good sales. Let A be the event "shows high aptitude" and let B be the event "achieves good sales."
a. Find $P(A)$, $P(A$ and $B)$, and $P(B|A)$.
b. Are A and B independent?
c. How useful is the test in predicting good sales achievement?
d. Find $P(A$ and not $B)$ and $P(\text{not } B|A)$.
e. Are A and not B independent?

3.14 A survey of workers in two plants of a manufacturing firm includes the question, "How effective is management in responding to legitimate grievances of workers?" In plant 1, 48 of 192 workers respond "poor"; in plant 2, 80 of 248 workers respond "poor." An employee of the manufacturing firm is to be selected randomly. Let A be the event "worker comes from plant 1" and let B be the event "response is poor."
a. Find $P(A)$, $P(B)$, and $P(A$ and $B)$.
b. Are the events A and B independent?
c. Find $P(B|A)$ and $P(B|\text{not } A)$. Are they equal?

3.15 Show that $P(\text{not } B) \neq P(\text{not } B|\text{not } A)$ in Exercise 3.14.

3.16 A school district must staff two primary schools and one high school. On any particular day, the probability that no substitute for an absent teacher is needed at primary school 1 is .60; the same probability holds for primary school 2. At the high school, the probability that no substitute is needed is .50. Assume that absenteeism at the three schools defines three independent processes. Find the probability that no substitute is needed at any of the schools on a particular day.

3.17 Do you believe that the assumption of independent processes in Exercise 3.16 is realistic?

3.18 A computer manufacturer's sales data indicated that the probability that a randomly chosen computer had standard memory was .84, and the probability that it had both CD and DVD disk drives was .40. The probability that it had both types of disk drives and also had standard memory was .24.

a. Find the probability that a computer has both types of drives, given that it has standard memory.
b. Find the probability that a computer has standard memory, given that it has both types of drives.
c. Are the events "standard memory" and "both types of drives" independent?

3.19 In addition to the probabilities given in the previous exercise, the probability that a computer has a 180 GB hard disk is .45. The probability that a computer has both types of disk drives and also a 180 GB hard disk is .18. Are the events "both types of disk drives" and "180 GB hard disk" independent?

3.20 An airline keeps track of adjustment problems faced by airport attendants. It finds that 40% of all problems involve a missed connection; 10% of all problems involve mishandled baggage. Is it plausible to assume that 4% of all problems will involve both mishandled baggage and a missed connection?

3.21 A direct-order retailer finds that 40% of all orders arrive by telephone (and the remainder by mail). A partial or complete merchandise return is made in 10% of all orders. Is it reasonable to assume that 4% of all orders will arrive by telephone and involve a merchandise return?

3.22 Examine other two-variable relationships in the Discount World shoplifting case using the data in the file DiscountWorld on the CD that came with this book. Do you find anything interesting that might impact the discrimination case against Discount World?

3.23 For the past year, the credit card manager for a major bank in the Southeast has been conducting an experiment to compare the predictive ability of two credit scoring methods in identifying credit card customers who are at risk of defaulting on their payments. At the beginning of this year, the first 500 credit card applicants were each given a credit card with a $3000 credit limit without any consideration given to the information provided in their application. At the end of the year, data were collected to find out which customers paid their bills on time ("good" customers) and which were either behind in payments or had stopped making payments ("default" customers). The credit card manager also then applied each of the two credit scoring methods to each of the 500 customers' original credit application information. Both tests award either a "pass" or a "fail" to each application based on the information supplied by the customer. The following tables summarize the results of the experiment.

Customer Payment Record

Test A Result	Good (G)	Default (D)	Total
Passed (P)	350	20	370
Failed (F)	50	80	130
Total	400	100	500

Customer Payment Record

Test B Result	Good (G)	Default (D)	Total
Passed (P)	340	85	425
Failed (F)	60	15	75
Total	400	100	500

For each of the following questions, assume that the sample of data collected is representative of the population of all credit card customers of the bank. Also, express the answers using the $P(\bullet)$ probability notation as well as providing numerical values.

a. What is the probability of a customer defaulting on his or her credit card?

b. What is the probability that a customer application will fail test A?

c. What is the probability that a customer will default and pass test B?

d. Compute the conditional probability of a customer defaulting if he or she fails test A.

e. Are the events "defaulting" and "fail test A" independent or dependent?

f. Which of the two tests, A or B, would you recommend to the credit card manager?

3.3 Probability Tables, Trees, and Simulations

Many probability problems require the successive use of several of the basic principles to obtain a solution. These problems can be solved algebraically, but it is helpful to have some devices to keep the logic straight.

EXAMPLE 3.13

A firm has found that 46% of its junior executives have two-career marriages, 37% have single-career marriages, and 17% are unmarried. The firm estimates that 40% of the two-career marriage executives would refuse a transfer to another office, as would 15% of the single-career-marriage executives and 10% of the unmarried executives. If a transfer offer is made to a randomly selected executive, what is the probability that it will be refused?

SOLUTION First, the event "refused" can be thought of as "(refused and two-career) or (refused and single-career) or (refused and unmarried)." The three possibilities are mutually exclusive, so the addition law yields

$$P(\text{refused}) = P(\text{refused and two-career}) + P(\text{refused and single-career})$$
$$+ P(\text{refused and unmarried})$$

Second, each of the three joint probabilities can be evaluated by the multiplication law. For instance,

$$P(\text{refused and two-career}) = P(\text{two-career})\, P(\text{refused}|\text{two-career})$$
$$= (.46)(.40)$$

Putting the two ideas together, we have

$$P(\text{refused}) = P(\text{two-career})P(\text{refused}|\text{two-career})$$
$$+ P(\text{single-career})P(\text{refused}|\text{single-career})$$
$$+ P(\text{unmarried})P(\text{refused}|\text{unmarried})$$
$$= (.46)(.40) + (.37)(.15) + (.17)(.10) = .2565$$

EXAMPLE 3.14 Investments of $100 each are made in two projects. Project A is assumed to yield a net return of $8, $10, or $12, with respective probabilities .2, .6, and .2. Project B is assumed to yield a net return of $8, $10, or $12, with respective probabilities .3, .4, and .3. The returns from the two projects are assumed to be independent. What is the probability that the total of the two returns is exactly $20?

SOLUTION By the addition law,

$$P(\text{total} = \$20) = P(\text{A yields \$8 and B yields \$12})$$
$$+ P(\text{A yields \$10 and B yields \$10})$$
$$+ P(\text{A yields \$12 and B yields \$8})$$

The multiplication law for independent events may be applied to each joint probability to obtain

$$P(\text{total} = \$20) = P(\text{A yields \$8})P(\text{B yields \$12})$$
$$+ P(\text{A yields \$10})P(\text{B yields \$10})$$
$$+ P(\text{A yields \$12})P(\text{B yields \$8})$$
$$= (.2)(.3) + (.6)(.4) + (.2)(.3) = .36$$

There are no new ideas involved in the solution of such problems, but it is sometimes tricky to find the right order in which to apply the basic principles. With larger, more complicated problems, the difficulty is increased. Several methods have been invented to help clarify the reasoning involved in solving a problem.

One useful approach is to construct a table of joint probabilities. The desired answer can sometimes be found by adding the appropriate table entries.

EXAMPLE 3.15 Construct a joint probability table for marital status versus action on transfer offers for the data of Example 3.13. Use it to find $P(\text{refused})$.

SOLUTION First, put any known marginal probabilities on the appropriate margins of the table.

	Two-career	Single-career	Unmarried
Refused			
Accepted			
	.46	.37	.17

Now the body of the table can be filled in using the multiplication law. The remaining marginals can be found by addition.

	Two-career	Single-career	Unmarried	
Refused	(.46)(.40)=.1840	(.37)(.15)=.0555	(.17)(.10)=.0170	.2565
Accepted	(.46)(.60)=.2760	(.37)(.85)=.3145	(.17)(.90)=.1530	.7435
	.46	.37	.17	

$P(\text{Refused})$ is shown, in the right margin, to be .2565, as in Example 3.13.

EXAMPLE 3.16   Construct a joint probability table and find P(total return $= \$20$) for the data of Example 3.14.

SOLUTION   In this case, both sets of marginal probabilities have been specified.

		Return from A			
		$8	$10	$12	
Return	$8				.3
from	$10				.4
B	$12				.3
		.2	.6	.2	

The multiplication law for independent events can be used to fill in the body of the table.

		Return from A			
		$8	$10	$12	
Return	$8	.06	.18	.06*	.3
from	$10	.08	.24*	.08	.4
B	$12	.06*	.18	.06	.3
		.2	.6	.2	

The entries that correspond to a total return of $20 are marked with an asterisk. The addition law yields

$$P(\text{total return} = \$20) = .06 + .24 + .06 = .36$$

as in Example 3.14.

Probability tables are a convenient, compact way of solving many problems. As a by-product, they often yield the solution to related problems as well. You should have no difficulty, for instance, in finding P(total return $= \$22$) or P(total return $= \$16$) using the table in Example 3.16. For problems involving more than two categories of events, probability tables are at best awkward to use. If there had also been a project C in Example 3.14, some sort of three-dimensional table would have been necessary.

probability tree   Another device that often can be used is a **probability tree.** This method is best introduced by an illustration.

EXAMPLE 3.17   Use a probability tree to solve Example 3.13.

SOLUTION   First, construct branches for a set of events with known marginal probabilities. In this example we start with type of marriage, as in Figure 3.2.

Then, at the tip of each of these branches, construct branches for another set of events, using conditional probabilities (given the appropriate first branch). In this case, the second set of branches is based on whether the transfer offer is refused or accepted, as in Figure 3.3. Had there been another set of relevant events, we would have added another set of branches.

The probability for each specific path (sequence of branches) is found by multiplying the probabilities along that path. The probability of an event can be found by adding the probabilities of all paths that satisfy that event. The paths corresponding to "refused" are marked with an asterisk: $P(\text{refused}) = .1840 + .0555 + .0170 = .2565$, once again.

FIGURE 3.2   **Beginning of a Probability Tree**

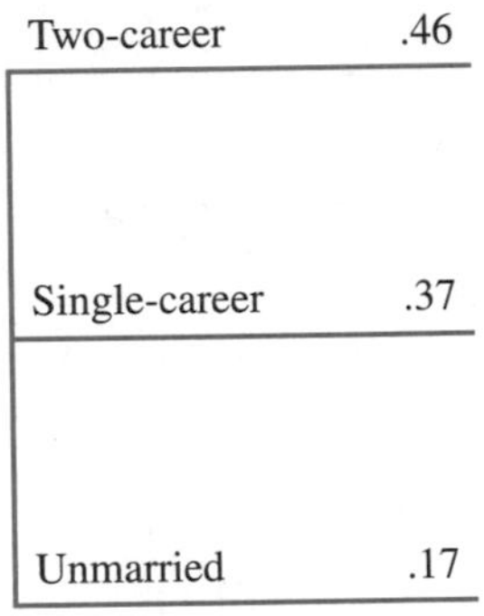

FIGURE 3.3   **Completion of a Probability Tree**

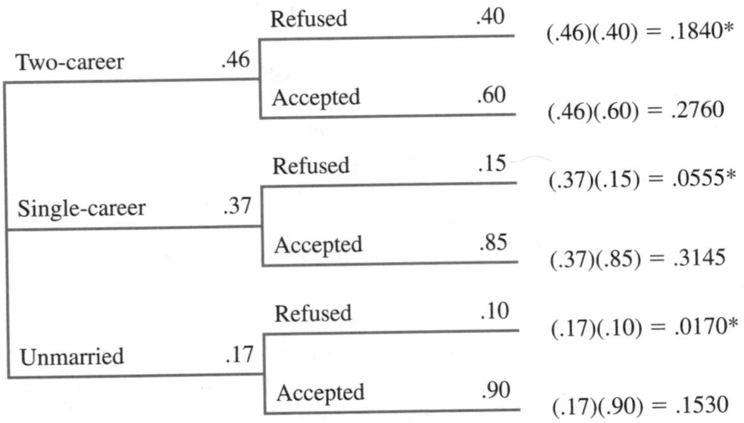

EXAMPLE 3.18   Use a probability tree to solve Example 3.14.

SOLUTION   Marginal probabilities are specified for both project A and project B, so we may use the returns to either project for the first set of branches. Out of sheer perversity, we begin by branching on project B in Figure 3.4.

In this case, because of assumed independence, the conditional probabilities of A returns given particular B returns are unnecessary. The path probabilities for a total return of $20 are marked with an asterisk: $P(\text{total return} = \$20) = .06 + .24 + .06 = .36$.

FIGURE 3.4

Probability Tree for Example 3.14

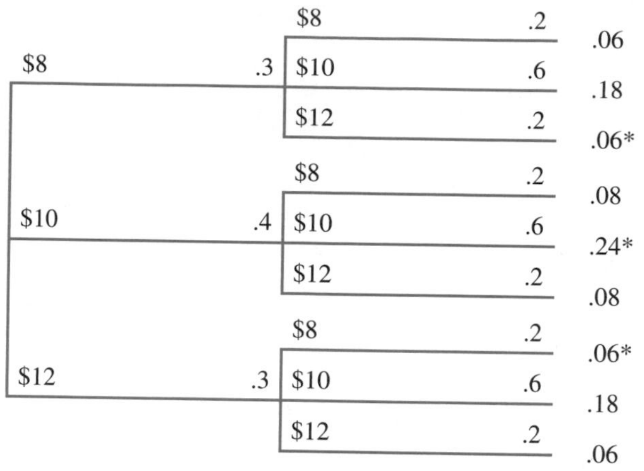

		$8	.2		.06	
$8	.3	$10	.6		.18	
		$12	.2		.06*	
		$8	.2		.08	
$10	.4	$10	.6		.24*	
		$12	.2		.08	
		$8	.2		.06*	
$12	.3	$10	.6		.18	
		$12	.2		.06	

To give correct answers, a probability tree must be constructed according to some simple rules.

Rules for Constructing a Probability Tree

1. Events forming the first set of branches must have known marginal probabilities, must be mutually exclusive, and should exhaust all possibilities (so that the sum of the branch probabilities is 1).
2. Events forming the second set of branches must be entered at the tip of each of the sets of first branches. Conditional probabilities, given the relevant first branch, must be entered, unless assumed independence allows the use of unconditional probabilities. Again, the branches must be mutually exclusive and exhaustive (so that the sum of the probabilities branching from any one tip is 1).
3. If there are further sets of branches, the probabilities must be conditional on all preceding events. As always, the branches must be mutually exclusive and exhaustive.
4. The sum of path probabilities must be taken over all paths included in the relevant event.

With a little practice, most people find probability trees quite easy to use. Trees and tables are both very useful in clarifying the logic of a solution. Both methods in effect construct a set of outcomes; a particular outcome corresponds to a path in a probability tree or an entry in a probability table. Trees can be used in a wider variety of problems. The only difficulty with using a tree for a large, complicated problem is that the tree can become impractically large. As long as one is willing to use a lot of paper, it is possible to solve some rather nasty problems surprisingly quickly.

EXAMPLE 3.19

In a certain television game show, a valuable prize is hidden behind one of three doors. You, the contestant, pick one of the three doors. Before opening it, the announcer opens one of the other two doors and you see that the prize isn't behind that door. The announcer offers you the chance to switch to the remaining door. Should you switch, or doesn't it matter?

SOLUTION   Let's make a tree.

Call the door that you select A, the others B and C. Assuming that the prize is distributed randomly among the doors, the probability that it's behind each of the doors is 1/3. If you picked a wrong door in door A, the announcer has no choice. If B contains the prize, the announcer must open C; if C has the prize, he must open B. But if you picked correctly and A has the prize, the announcer does have a choice. Let's assume that the announcer picks B or C randomly, each with probability 1/2 in this situation. We can construct the tree in Figure 3.5.

Suppose that the announcer has chosen B (and you chose A initially). What is the probability that the prize is behind door C?

$$P(\text{behind C}|\text{chose B}) = \frac{P(\text{behind C and chose B})}{P(\text{chose B})}$$

$$= \frac{1/3}{1/6 + 1/3} = \frac{1/3}{1/2} = \frac{2}{3}$$

so $P(\text{behind A}|\text{chose B}) = 1 - 2/3 = 1/3$. You have a better chance of winning if you switch to door C!

FIGURE 3.5   **Probability Tree for Three Doors**

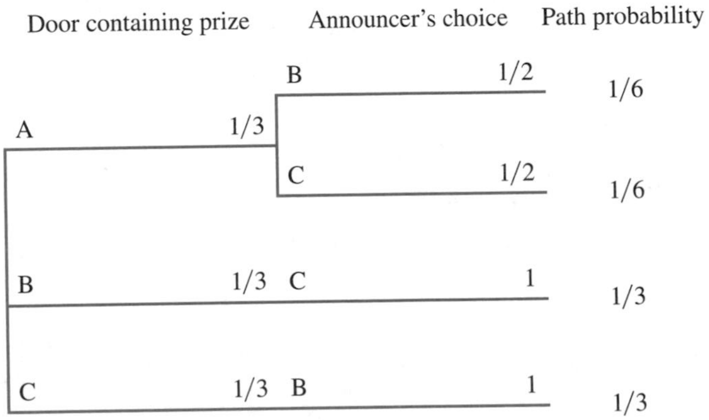

Door containing prize   Announcer's choice   Path probability

EXAMPLE 3.20   Suppose that 40% of all theoretically plausible pharmaceutical drug concepts are biologically active. Of the active drugs, 70% show serious side effects. Of those drugs that prove to be inactive, 20% can be reformulated to be active, and among these reformulated drugs, 80% show serious side effects. All drugs that are to be marketed must be approved by a government agency. The probability that a drug will be approved, given that it is biologically active and shows no side effects, is .90. Of drugs that are biologically active but show side effects, 5% will be approved. If a drug is not biologically active, it will not be approved.

a.   What is the probability that a new drug concept will result in an approved drug?

b.   What is the probability that a new drug concept will lead to a drug with side effects?

c.   If a drug is approved, what is the probability that it will lead to side effects?

SOLUTION   We can construct a moderately large probability tree, something like Figure 3.6. In this case, as often happens, the natural sequence of branches is chronological. The natural first branch reflects whether or not the drug is active. Whether the drug can be reformulated, whether it shows side effects, and finally whether it is approved are then considered.

a. To find the probability that a drug is approved, simply add the probabilities for all paths corresponding to a "yes" branch on the "approved" question:

$$P(\text{approved}) = .0140 + .1080 + .0048 + .0216 = .1484$$

b. Again, we must add the appropriate path probabilities. The paths corresponding to existence of side effects are the first, second, fifth, and sixth paths:

$$P(\text{side effects}) = .0140 + .2660 + .0048 + .0912 = .3760$$

Alternatively, we can draw the tree without the "approved" branches and obtain

$$P(\text{side effects}) = .40(.70) + .60(.20)(.80) = .280 + .096 = .376$$

once again.

c. To find a conditional probability like this one, we use the definition of conditional probability:

$$P(\text{side effects} | \text{approved}) = \frac{P(\text{side effects and approved})}{P(\text{approved})}$$

FIGURE 3.6   **Probability Tree for New Drug Example**

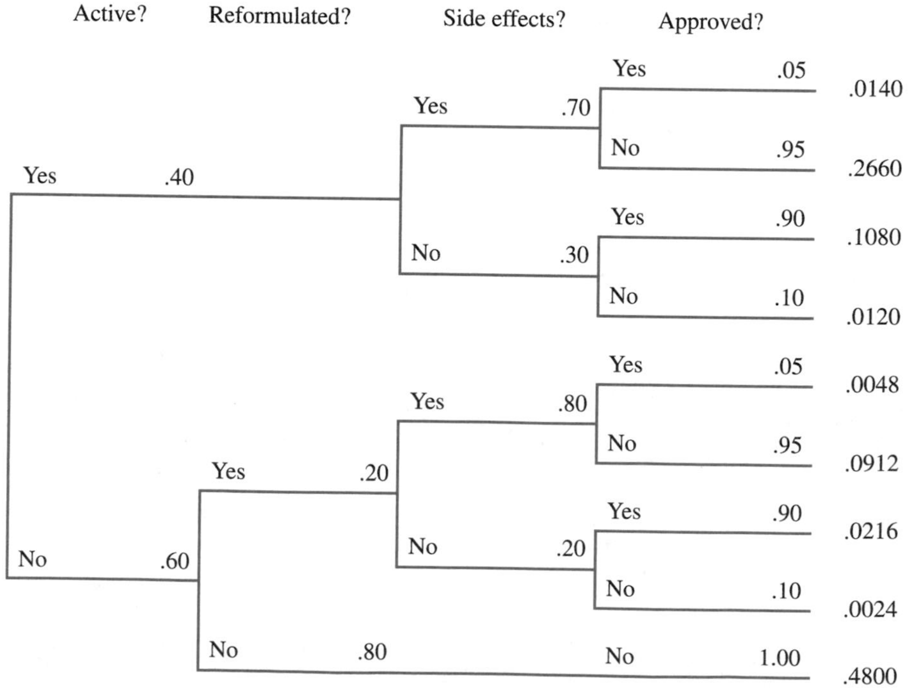

In part (a) we found P(approved) $= .1484$. Note that the first and fifth branches, with respective probabilities .0140 and .0048, are the only ones corresponding to "side effects and approved." Thus,

$$P(\text{side effects} | \text{approved}) = (.0140 + .0048)/(.1484) = .1267$$

There is another approach to finding approximate answers to probability problems. We can simulate the events using a computer program. Applying the long-run relative frequency idea of probability, if we run a large number of trials and find the fraction of cases in which an event occurs, we have a close approximation to the correct probability. We can't get an exact answer without an infinite number of trials, but usually we can get close enough for most purposes.

EXAMPLE 3.21   A Web-based catalog retailer uses three servers to support its on-line retail business. All three servers run independently and handle transactions from Web customers. If one of the servers fails, the remaining two servers handle all transactions without any problems or noticeable delays. However, if two servers fail and only one server is operating, the transaction system still works but is unacceptably slow from the customer's perspective. When a server "crashes," a technical support member can usually have the server back on-line within an hour. On weekends, however, there are no technical support workers on duty. The probability of any one of the servers crashing over a weekend period is .15. Compute the probability that the on-line retail business will experience unacceptably slow response times (only one server running) or total failure (none of the servers running) over a weekend.

SOLUTION   We could actually solve this problem using the rules of probability discussed in this chapter, but we will use a simulation approach instead. Figure 3.7 is a portion of an Excel worksheet showing the outcomes from a simulation of 1000 weekends. We created three columns in Excel (Server 1, Server 2, and Server 3) to indicate the status of the three servers at the end of a weekend. Each row represents a single weekend's outcome for the three servers. A "1" in a cell indicates that the

FIGURE 3.7   **Portion of Excel Spreadsheet Used in Three-Server Simulation**

	A	B	C	D	E	F	G	H
1	Weekend	Server 1	Server 2	Server 3	Running	Slow or Failure		Total
2	1	1	1	1	3	0		58
3	2	1	1	1	3	0		
4	3	1	1	0	2	0		
5	4	0	0	1	1	1		
6	5	0	0	1	1	1		
7	6	1	1	1	3	0		
8	7	1	1	1	3	0		
9	8	1	1	1	3	0		
10	9	1	1	1	3	0		
11	10	1	1	1	3	0		
12	11	1	1	1	3	0		
13	12	1	1	1	3	0		
14	13	1	0	1	2	0		
15	14	0	1	1	2	0		

FIGURE 3.8   **Same Portion of Excel Spreadsheet Showing Cell Formulas**

	A	B	C	D	E	F	G	H
1	Weekend	Server 1	Server 2	Server 3	Running	Slow or Failure		Total
2	1	=IF(RAND() <= 0.15, 0, 1)	=IF(RAND() <= 0.15, 0, 1)	=IF(RAND() <= 0.15, 0, 1)	=SUM(B2:D2)	=IF(E2 <= 1, 1, 0)		**=SUM(F2:F1001)**
3	2	=IF(RAND() <= 0.15, 0, 1)	=IF(RAND() <= 0.15, 0, 1)	=IF(RAND() <= 0.15, 0, 1)	=SUM(B3:D3)	=IF(E3 <= 1, 1, 0)		
4	3	=IF(RAND() <= 0.15, 0, 1)	=IF(RAND() <= 0.15, 0, 1)	=IF(RAND() <= 0.15, 0, 1)	=SUM(B4:D4)	=IF(E4 <= 1, 1, 0)		
5	4	=IF(RAND() <= 0.15, 0, 1)	=IF(RAND() <= 0.15, 0, 1)	=IF(RAND() <= 0.15, 0, 1)	=SUM(B5:D5)	=IF(E5 <= 1, 1, 0)		
6	5	=IF(RAND() <= 0.15, 0, 1)	=IF(RAND() <= 0.15, 0, 1)	=IF(RAND() <= 0.15, 0, 1)	=SUM(B6:D6)	=IF(E6 <= 1, 1, 0)		
7	6	=IF(RAND() <= 0.15, 0, 1)	=IF(RAND() <= 0.15, 0, 1)	=IF(RAND() <= 0.15, 0, 1)	=SUM(B7:D7)	=IF(E7 <= 1, 1, 0)		
8	7	=IF(RAND() <= 0.15, 0, 1)	=IF(RAND() <= 0.15, 0, 1)	=IF(RAND() <= 0.15, 0, 1)	=SUM(B8:D8)	=IF(E8 <= 1, 1, 0)		
9	8	=IF(RAND() <= 0.15, 0, 1)	=IF(RAND() <= 0.15, 0, 1)	=IF(RAND() <= 0.15, 0, 1)	=SUM(B9:D9)	=IF(E9 <= 1, 1, 0)		
10	9	=IF(RAND() <= 0.15, 0, 1)	=IF(RAND() <= 0.15, 0, 1)	=IF(RAND() <= 0.15, 0, 1)	=SUM(B10:D10)	=IF(E10 <= 1, 1, 0)		
11	10	=IF(RAND() <= 0.15, 0, 1)	=IF(RAND() <= 0.15, 0, 1)	=IF(RAND() <= 0.15, 0, 1)	=SUM(B11:D11)	=IF(E11 <= 1, 1, 0)		
12	11	=IF(RAND() <= 0.15, 0, 1)	=IF(RAND() <= 0.15, 0, 1)	=IF(RAND() <= 0.15, 0, 1)	=SUM(B12:D12)	=IF(E12 <= 1, 1, 0)		
13	12	=IF(RAND() <= 0.15, 0, 1)	=IF(RAND() <= 0.15, 0, 1)	=IF(RAND() <= 0.15, 0, 1)	=SUM(B13:D13)	=IF(E13 <= 1, 1, 0)		
14	13	=IF(RAND() <= 0.15, 0, 1)	=IF(RAND() <= 0.15, 0, 1)	=IF(RAND() <= 0.15, 0, 1)	=SUM(B14:D14)	=IF(E14 <= 1, 1, 0)		
15	14	=IF(RAND() <= 0.15, 0, 1)	=IF(RAND() <= 0.15, 0, 1)	=IF(RAND() <= 0.15, 0, 1)	=SUM(B15:D15)	=IF(E15 <= 1, 1, 0)		

EXAMPLE 3.21
(continued)

corresponding server survived the weekend without crashing, while a "0" in a cell indicates that the corresponding server failed at some point over the weekend. The Running column is the sum of the three server columns, which indicates how many of the three servers are running at the end of the weekend. The Slow or Failure column indicates whether the on-line system was unacceptably slow or failed (indicated by 1) over the weekend or not (indicated by 0). Finally, the Total column shows the number of weekends out of 1000 weekends experiencing slowness or total failure.

Figure 3.8 shows the same portion of the Excel worksheet, but this time with the cell formulas underlying the values shown in Figure 3.7. In each of the server outcome cells, a random number between 0 and 1 is generated using the Excel rand( ) function. If the random number is less than .15, a "0" is placed in the cell to indicate server failure; otherwise, a "1" is placed in the cell to indicate that the server survived that weekend. In this way, we allow for a .15 failure probability for each server and independence among the server outcomes.

In the total of 1000 weekends simulated, the Total of 58 slow and failure outcomes shown in Figure 3.7 provides an estimate of 58/1000 = .058 for the probability of the on-line catalog service experiencing slow service or failure over the weekend. This is very close to the actual value of .06075 that can be computed from the rules of probability.

Exercises

3.24 The experience of a data-processing firm has shown that the first time a new program is tested there is a .6 probability of finding one or more major "bugs"—flaws in the program that cause the program to fail completely. There is a .3 chance of detecting minor bugs—flaws that allow the program to run but produce erroneous results in certain situations—and a .1 chance that no bugs are detected. In each case, an attempt is made to correct all detected programming errors. Then the program is retested on a more extensive basis. The likely results of the retest are summarized in the following table of conditional probabilities:

		Retest		
		Major	Minor	None
	Major	.3	.5	.2
First test	Minor	.1	.3	.6
	None	0	.2	.8

a. Construct a table giving the joint probabilities of all the possible combinations of first test and retest results.

b. Find the probability that major bugs are still found at the retest.

c. Find the probabilities of minor bugs at retest and of no bugs at retest.

3.25 Construct a probability tree to answer Exercise 3.24.

3.26 In the data-processing firm of Exercise 3.24, programs that still show major or minor bugs on retesting are sent through one more round of correction. Programs that had major bugs in retest have a .1 probability of retaining major bugs in the third test (regardless of the result of the initial test) and a .2 probability of showing minor bugs. Those that showed only minor bugs at retesting have essentially no chance of showing major bugs at third test but a .1 chance of showing minor bugs (again regardless of the result of the first test). It is assumed that programs showing no bugs at retesting need not go through a third round.
a. Construct a probability tree for this situation.
b. Find the probability that a program will show major bugs at all three tests.
c. Find the probability that a program will show major bugs at the third test. Why is this answer different from that of part (b)?
d. Find the probability that a program will achieve no-bug status (whether after two or three tests).

3.27 A purchasing unit for a state government has found that 60% of the winning bids for office-cleaning contracts come from regular bidders, 30% from occasional bidders, and 10% from first-time bidders. The services provided by successful bidders are rated satisfactory or unsatisfactory after one year on the job. Experience indicates that 90% of the jobs done by regular bidders are satisfactory, as are 80% of the jobs done by occasional bidders and 60% of the jobs done by first-time bidders.
a. What is the probability that a job will be done by a first-time bidder and will be satisfactory?
b. What is the probability that a job will be satisfactory?
c. Given that a job is satisfactory, what is the probability that it was done by a first-time bidder?

3.28 A manufacturer of snack crackers introduces several new products each year. About 60% of the introductions are failures, 30% are moderate successes, and 10% are major successes. To try to improve the odds, the manufacturer tests new products in a customer tasting panel. Of the failures, 50% receive a poor rating in the panel, 30% a fair rating, and 20% a good rating. For the moderate successes, 20% receive a poor rating, 40% a fair rating, and 40% a good rating. For major successes, the percentages are 10% poor, 30% fair, and 60% good.
a. Find the joint probability of a new product being a failure and receiving a poor rating.
b. Construct a probability table of all possible joint probabilities of new product results and panel ratings.
c. If a new product receives a good rating, what is the probability that the product will be a failure?

3.29 Create a probability tree using the probabilities in Exercise 3.28. Use the tree to find the probability that a new product will be a major success, given that it gets a poor rating.

3.30 A trucking company specializing in bulk cargos has contract customers and occasional customers. Company policy dictates that contract customers' calls receive priority; contract calls are 40% of the total. The first four calls each day are assigned immediately to trucks; if at least three of these calls are from contract customers, the dispatcher must decline any further calls that day from occasional customers.
a. Construct a probability tree for the first four calls. The first branch should be for contract or occasional customer on the first call.
b. What is the probability that the dispatcher must decline any further calls from occasional customers?

3.31 In Exercise 3.30 suppose that the dispatcher must decline further calls from occasional customers. What is the probability that all four of the first four calls were from contract customers?

3.32 Screening people for the presence of a disease is not perfectly exact. One test has a 5% chance of a "false positive"—saying that someone has the disease who in fact doesn't. It also has a 2% chance of a "false negative"—saying that someone doesn't have the disease who in fact does. Suppose that one-tenth of 1% of the people in the screened population have the disease. If a randomly chosen person has a positive test result, what is the probability that the person actually does have it? Create an Excel simulation to estimate this probability.

3.33 Construct a probability table to find the probability of having the disease, given a positive diagnosis, as in the previous exercise.

3.34 Some people who use control charts say that eight or more consecutive values on the same side of the target mean indicate an out-of-control process. Assuming that the distribution of values is symmetric around the target mean, there is a 50–50 chance that a value will fall above the target. Create an Excel simulation to determine the probability of exactly eight consecutive values above the target mean or below the target mean.

3.35 Compute the probability of the preceding problem mathematically using the rules of probability discussed in this chapter.

3.36 Refer back to Example 3.21 in which an Excel simulation was used to estimate the probability of a three-server customer-transaction Web site experiencing either slow service or failure over a weekend period.

a. Compute the actual probability of .06075 mathematically using the rules of probability discussed in this chapter.

b. Repeat the Excel simulation, but this time assuming a 25% chance of an individual server failing. What is your estimate of the probability of either slow service or failure over a weekend period? How close is your simulation result to the true value?

c. Repeat the Excel simulation, but this time assuming there are only two servers. What is your estimate of the probability of either slow service or failure over a weekend period? How close is your simulation result to the true value?

BUSINESS DECISION-MAKING IN ACTION

CHAPTER CASE

ANALYSIS

Discount World, Inc.

Recall that you have been asked by Robert Wilton of Discount World, Inc. to examine the shoplifting log from the Taylorsville store and analyze the situation. A statistical expert witness for the prosecution has determined that there is sufficient evidence of racial discrimination by the store's management in deciding which shoplifting suspects are released and which are prosecuted. Figure 3.9 is a partial listing of the shoplifting log data.

FIGURE 3.9

Partial Listing of the Discount World Shoplifting Data

	A	B	C	D	E	F
1	Age	AgeClass	Minority	Gender	Amount	Prosecuted
2	38	A	N	M	29.58	Y
3	20	A	N	F	13.91	N
4	18	J	N	M	12.34	Y
5	14	J	N	M	10.11	N
6	25	A	N	F	61.12	Y
7	16	J	N	M	8.29	N
8	40	A	N	M	118.02	Y
9	19	A	N	F	96.42	Y
10	19	A	N	F	116.25	Y
11	16	J	N	M	12.82	N
12	17	J	N	M	21.52	N
13	27	A	N	F	214.93	Y
14	18	A	N	M	12.34	N
15	18	A	N	M	22.50	Y

The first step in any data analysis is to become familiar with the data by summarizing each of the variables with graphical or tabular displays. As we learned in Chapter 2, the type of variable, whether qualitative or quantitative, determines which graphical displays are appropriate. The Age and Amount variables are quantitative and can be summarized with histograms, while the AgeClass, Minority, Gender, and Prosecuted variables are categorical (binary) and can be summarized with frequency tables or bar charts.

Histograms for Age and Amount are shown in Figures 3.10 and 3.11, respectively. The distribution of Age is clearly skewed to the right. The majority of the shoplifting suspects are young, under the age of 30, but some of them are over the age of 50. The distribution of the amount shoplifting is also skewed to the right. Most shoplifted amounts are under $50, but they range as high as $650.

FIGURE 3.10   **Histogram of Age in the Shoplifting Data**

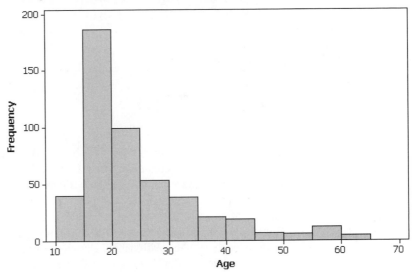

FIGURE 3.11   **Histogram of Amount in the Shoplifting Data**

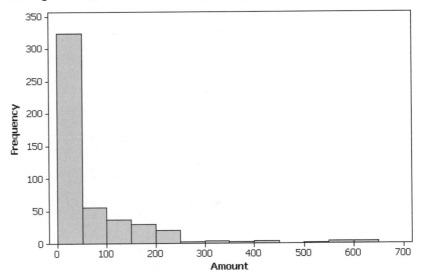

We can conveniently summarize the categorical variables with frequency tables from Minitab as follows:

```
Tally for Discrete Variables: AgeClass

AgeClass  Count Percent
       A    309   63.58
       J    177   36.42
      N=    486

Tally for Discrete Variables: Minority

Minority  Count  Percent
       N    371    76.34
       Y    115    23.66
      N=    486
```

```
Tally for Discrete Variables: Gender

Gender   Count    Percent
     F    236      48.56
     M    250      51.44
    N=    486


Tally for Discrete Variables: Prosecuted

Prosecuted   Count    Percent
        N     230      47.33
        Y     256      52.67
       N=     486
```

Even though the Age distribution was highly skewed right, the majority (64%) of suspected shoplifters were adults. Also, note that only about one-quarter of those apprehended were minority and that slightly more than half (51%) were male. Based on the last frequency table, we see that a little more than half (53%) of those apprehended are subsequently prosecuted.

While these single-variable displays are helpful in understanding the data, they do not allow us to see the relationships among the variables. One very important relationship of interest is that between the Prosecuted and Minority variables. Excel pivot tables (two-way cross-tabulations) of the relationship between Prosecuted and Minority are shown in Figure 3.12.

FIGURE 3.12   **Excel Pivot Tables for Prosecuted and Minority**

Frequency	Prosecuted		
Minority	N	Y	Grand Total
N	186	185	371
Y	44	71	115
Grand Total	230	256	486

% of Total	Prosecuted		
Minority	N	Y	Grand Total
N	38.27%	38.07%	76.34%
Y	9.05%	14.61%	23.66%
Grand Total	47.33%	52.67%	100.00%

% of Row	Prosecuted		
Minority	N	Y	Grand Total
N	50.13%	49.87%	100.00%
Y	38.26%	61.74%	100.00%
Grand Total	47.33%	52.67%	100.00%

The first of these three tables shows how the 486 suspected shoplifters break out jointly by Prosecuted and Race. For example, we see that 115 of the 486 suspects were minority and that 71 of the 486 suspects were minority and prosecuted. The second table gives the same information, but in percentage form. For example, 23.7% of those apprehended were minority (that is, $P(M) = .237$) and 14.6% of the suspects were minority and prosecuted (that is, $P(M \cap P) = .146$).

The third table in Figure 3.12 provides the information that we are after. This table shows the table entries of the first table as a percentage of each row, that is, conditional probabilities. If we assume that these 486 suspected shoplifters are a representative sample, we would estimate the conditional probability of a suspect being prosecuted given that he or she is a minority as $P(P|M) = .617$. On the other hand, for nonminority suspects, the probability is only $P(P|\overline{M}) = .499$. Compare these to the unconditional probability of a suspect being prosecuted, $P(P) = .527$. Figure 3.13 is a 100% stacked bar chart that graphically displays the same data.

FIGURE 3.13   **100% Stacked Bar Chart for Prosecuted and Minority**

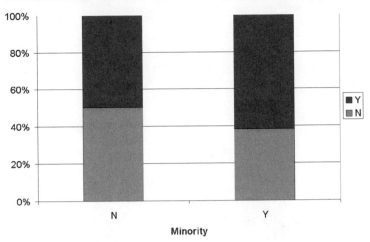

Based on this evidence, it appears that a minority shoplifting suspect is much more likely to be prosecuted than a nonminority suspect. At this point, things do not look good for Robert Wilton and Discount World!

Let's now dig a little deeper into the data to better our understanding of the relationships. Figure 3.14 shows a box plot of Amount by Prosecuted from which we can see that the amounts stolen by those suspects who are prosecuted tend to be much greater than for those who are released.

FIGURE 3.14   **Box Plot of Amount by Prosecuted in Shoplifting Data**

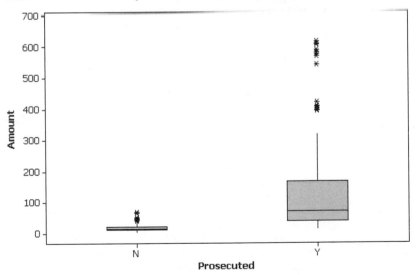

Figure 3.15 is a box plot of Age by Prosecuted that suggests the store manager is more lenient toward younger shoplifters. However, the box plot of Amount by AgeClass in Figure 3.16 shows the reason for this lenience: Juvenile shoplifters are stealing merchandise of lesser value than the adult shoplifters.

FIGURE 3.15

Box Plot of Age by Prosecuted in Shoplifting Data

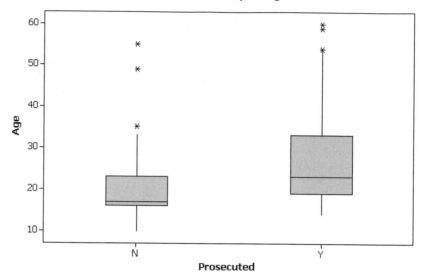

FIGURE 3.16

Box Plot of Amount by AgeClass in Shoplifting Data

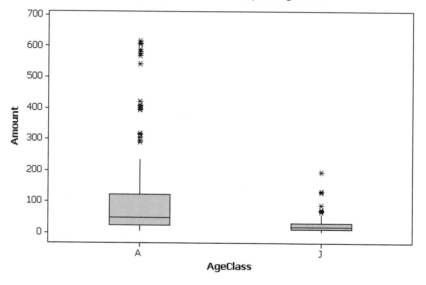

The box plot of Amount by Minority and AgeClass in Figure 3.17 contains an interesting discovery: Nonminority juveniles who are caught shoplifting typically steal merchandise of low value, perhaps music CDs or other such small items. The distribution of Amount for minority juveniles has a slightly larger median and more spread than for nonminority juveniles. The distributions of Amount for both minority and nonminority adults appear to be fairly similar.

The following descriptive statistics for Amount broken out by Minority and AgeClass provides a numerical summary version of Figure 3.17.

FIGURE 3.17   **Box Plot of Amount by Minority and AgeClass in Shoplifting Data**

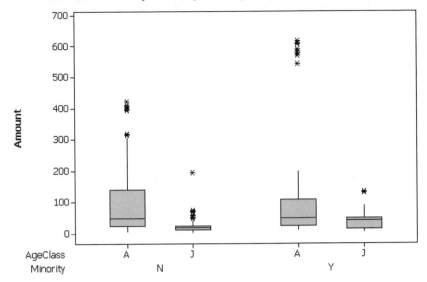

```
Descriptive Statistics: Amount

Results for Minority = N

Variable  AgeClass   N    Mean   StDev  Minimum     Q1  Median      Q3  Maximum
Amount    A        229   90.28  93.10     4.82  23.60   48.56  139.50   419.52
          J        142   20.89  20.41     2.96  10.13   17.39   23.10   192.65


Results for Minority = Y

Variable  AgeClass   N    Mean   StDev  Minimum     Q1  Median      Q3  Maximum
Amount    A         80   111.1  166.4     9.62   22.4    47.5   108.0    616.0
          J         35   41.61  32.49     6.93  13.23   40.19   48.03   132.45
```

The following two-way frequency table is for Minority and Prosecuted. As seen earlier, the evidence from this table suggests that minority suspected shoplifters are prosecuted more frequently than nonminority suspected shoplifters.

```
Tabulated Statistics: Minority, Prosecuted

Rows: Minority    Columns: Prosecuted

              N       Y      All
     N      186     185      371
          50.13   49.87   100.00

     Y       44      71      115
          38.26   61.74   100.00

    All     230     256      486
          47.33   52.67   100.00

    Cell Contents --
                  Count
                  % of Row
```

Given that prosecuted suspects tend to shoplift larger amounts and that the distributions of amounts are very different among the various minority and AgeClass combinations, it makes sense to consider the following three-way table of Prosecuted by Minority and AgeClass, which shows the percentage of suspects in each

Minority and AgeClass combination who are prosecuted. Figure 3.18 is a 100% stacked bar chart display from Excel of the two-way table.

```
Tabulated statistics: Minority, Prosecuted, AgeClass

Results for AgeClass = A

Rows: Minority   Columns: Prosecuted

            N       Y      All
N          80     149      229
        34.93   65.07   100.00

Y          27      53       80
        33.75   66.25   100.00

All       107     202      309
        34.63   65.37   100.00

Cell Contents:       Count
                     % of Row


Results for AgeClass = J

Rows: Minority   Columns: Prosecuted

            N       Y      All
N         106      36      142
        74.65   25.35   100.00

Y          17      18       35
        48.57   51.43   100.00

All       123      54      177
        69.49   30.51   100.00

Cell Contents:       Count
                     % of Row
```

FIGURE 3.18   **100% Stacked Bar Chart of Prosecuted by Minority and AgeClass**

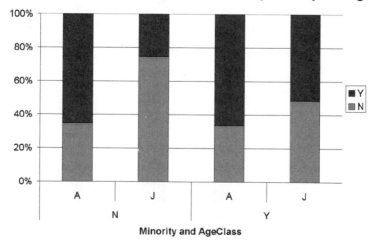

From this table and Figure 3.18, we see that minority and nonminority adults have roughly the same chance of prosecution (66.25% to 65.07%). For juveniles, it's a different story: While only one-quarter (23.35%) of nonminority juvenile suspects are prosecuted, a little over half (51.43%) of minority juvenile suspects are prosecuted. Figure 3.17 (and the corresponding table of summary statistics) suggests why: Minority juvenile suspects tend to shoplift items of higher dollar value than nonminority juvenile suspects.

After further discussion with the store manager, you learn that store policy has been to not prosecute cases in which the value of the shoplifted items is small. The store manager is also aware of a new "rite of passage" among nonminority teenagers in his store's local area. In these "shoplifting on a dare" cases, the teens take items such as cosmetics, music CDs, and other small, easily concealed items of relatively low value to impress their friends. These two new pieces of information would certainly explain the higher rate of releases among nonminority shoplifters.

Based on your analysis of the data and the discussion with the store manager, it is clear that the differences observed in the proportions of minority and nonminority shoplifters who are prosecuted are not due to racial discrimination. Shortly after your analysis and report are sent to the lawyers for the prosecution, Robert Wilton and Discount World are notified that the class action lawsuit has been dropped by the plaintiffs.

SUMMARY

Here are some suggestions for dealing with basic probability problems.

1. First, determine what probabilities are specified. In each case, is the probability conditional on something else or unconditional?

2. Next, determine what probabilities must be calculated. Are we trying to find a conditional or an unconditional probability?

3. Try using one of the reasoning devices—tables or trees—to help you work through the logic. Tables are often helpful if joint ("and" type) probabilities are specified. Trees are often helpful if conditional probabilities have been specified.

4. Be alert to any assumption of statistical independence of events. To assume that the probability of one event does not change when another event occurs *is* an assumption. Is it reasonable?

5. Use simulation to estimate a probability in complex situations in which it is too difficult to apply the basic rules of probability to determine an answer.

In addition, you may want to reread the summary of key ideas in the Executive Overview at the beginning of this chapter.

Supplementary Exercises

3.37 Airlines often accept tickets bought for other airlines' flights to the same destination. Suppose that final accounting and settlement of all such tickets is made yearly and that approximate monthly settlements are made on the basis of random samples of the month's accumulated tickets. Airline A draws a monthly sample of 60 tickets, which may have been bought from airlines B, C, or D. Indicate what a typical outcome of this experiment would be. Should all the outcomes be assumed to be equally likely?

3.38 Suppose that in the packaged-cereals industry, 29% of all vice presidents hold MBA degrees, 24% hold undergraduate business degrees, and 8% hold both. A vice president is to be selected at random.
  a. What is the probability that the vice president holds either an MBA or an undergraduate business degree (or both)?
  b. What is the probability that the vice president holds neither degree?

3.39   In Exercise 3.38 what is the probability that the vice president holds one degree or the other, but not both?

3.40   Suppose that the records of an automobile maker show that, for a certain compact car model, 50% of all customers order air-conditioning, 49% order power steering, and 26% order both. An order is selected randomly.
a. Construct a probability table.
b. What is the probability that air-conditioning is ordered but power steering is not?
c. What is the probability that neither option is ordered?

3.41   In Exercise 3.40 suppose that 68% of all customers order automatic transmissions, 19% order automatic transmissions and power steering without air-conditioning, 13% order automatic transmissions and air-conditioning without power steering, and 21% order all three options.
a. Construct a probability table for this situation. Use the results of the previous exercise to construct four rows of the table—respectively, both A and P, A but not P, P but not A, neither A nor P.
b. What is the probability that at least one of the options is ordered?
c. What is the probability that exactly one option is ordered?

3.42   Use the data of Exercises 3.40 and 3.41 to find P(automatic transmission and air-conditioning). Are these events independent?

3.43   Proponents of the random walk theory of stock prices hold that predictions of whether a particular stock will do better or worse than the market in the short run (say, over a one-month period) are no better than what could be obtained by flipping a fair coin. Suppose that a securities analyst selects eight stocks that are predicted to beat the market in the next month.
a. What is the probability that all eight stocks do beat the market, assuming the validity of the random walk theory?
b. State the assumptions you made in answering part (a).

3.44   Refer to Exercise 3.43 and assume that the random walk theory of stock behavior is valid. Suppose that each of 100 different analysts selects eight stocks.
a. What is the probability that no analyst gets eight winners?
b. What is the probability that at least one analyst gets eight winners?

3.45   A paperback book seller estimates the following probabilities for the weekly sales of a particular historical romance:

Sales: 10   20   30   40
Probability: .40   .30   .20   .10

Assume independence of sales from week to week.
a. Construct a probability table for the joint probabilities of various sales levels in week 1 and week 2.
b. Find the probability that the average sales level per week (over a two-week period) is 25.

3.46   Do you believe that the independence assumption made in Exercise 3.45 is reasonable?

3.47   A purchasing department finds that 75% of its special orders are received on time. Of those orders that are on time, 80% meet specifications completely; of those orders that are late, 60% meet specifications.
a. Find the probability that an order is on time and meets specifications.
b. Construct a probability table or tree for this situation.
c. Find the probability that an order meets specifications.

3.48   For the situation of Exercise 3.47, suppose that four orders are placed.
a. Find the probability that all four orders meet specifications.
b. State what assumptions you made in answering part (a).

3.49   A large credit card company finds that 50% of all cardholders pay a given monthly bill in full.
a. Suppose two cardholders are chosen at random. What is the probability that both pay a monthly bill in full? (The number of cardholders is so large that you need not worry about whether or not the first cardholder is replaced before the second draw.)
b. Suppose a cardholder is chosen at random. What is the probability that the holder pays both of two consecutive monthly bills in full?
c. What did you assume in answering parts (a) and (b)? Does the assumption seem unreasonable in either case?

3.50   A more detailed examination of the records of the credit card company in Exercise 3.49 shows that 90% of the customers who pay one monthly bill in full also pay the next monthly bill in full; only 10% of the customers who pay less than the full amount of one monthly bill pay the next monthly bill in full.
a. Find the probability that a randomly chosen customer pays two consecutive monthly bills in full.
b. Find the probability that a randomly chosen customer pays neither of two consecutive monthly bills in full.
c. Find the probability that a randomly chosen customer pays exactly one of two consecutive monthly bills in full.

3.51   In the previous exercise, if a randomly chosen customer pays the second monthly bill in full, what is the probability that that customer also pays the first monthly bill in full?

3.52   Records of a men's clothing shop show that alterations are required for 40% of the suit jackets that are bought and for 30% of the suit trousers. Alterations are required for both jacket and trousers in 22% of the purchases.
a. Find the probability that no alterations are required in a randomly chosen purchase. You may want to construct a table.
b. Find the probability that alterations are required for either the jacket or the trousers, but not for both.

3.53   Are the events in Exercise 3.52, "alteration to jacket" and "alteration to trousers," independent?

3.54   Suppose that in Exercise 3.52 a customer purchases two suits made by different manufacturers.
a. What is the probability that both suit jackets require alterations?
b. What did you assume in answering part (a)? Is the assumption reasonable?

3.55   A computer-supply retailer selected one batch of 10,000 disks and attempted to format them all for a particular machine. There were 8847 perfect disks, 1128 disks that were usable but had bad sectors, and 25 disks that couldn't be used at all.
a. What is the probability that a randomly chosen disk is not perfect?
b. If the disk is not perfect, what is the probability that it is not usable at all?

3.56   A simple piece of electronic equipment has 50 components. Each component must work for the equipment to work properly. Component quality isn't perfect; 99% of the components work, but 1% fail. The following Minitab output simulates the working of the equipment. What does it indicate about the probability that a randomly chosen item will work properly?

```
MTB > note Generate 1000 trials.  Each trial is 50 components (c1-c50)
MTB > note A 1 means that the component works; 0 means it fails.
MTB > Random 1000 c1-c50;
SUBC>   Bernoulli .99.
MTB > note If the minimum across a row is 1, the equipment works.
MTB > note If the minimum is 0, the equipment contains a failing component.
MTB > rmin c1-c50 put in c51
MTB > table c51
```

Tabulated Statistics

ROWS: C51

	COUNT
0	390
1	610
ALL	1000

3.57 Calculate the probability of the previous exercise. You might start a probability tree with the first component (work or fail), then the second (work or fail), and so on, until you see a pattern.

3.58 Suppose that the piece of equipment contains 100 components, each with probability .005 of failing. Is the probability that the equipment works much different from what was found in the two previous exercises?

```
MTB > note 100 components each with prob .995 of working
MTB > note C101 contains the minimum of 100 components
MTB > table c101
```
Tabulated Statistics

ROWS: C101

	COUNT
0	396
1	604
ALL	1000

3.59 A famous problem in the history of probability theory (which started with the analysis of games of chance) goes like this: In one game, a player rolls 6 fair, six-sided dice, and wins if one or more 6s appear. In a second game, the player rolls 12 fair dice and wins if at least two 6s appear. In a third game, the player rolls 18 fair dice and wins if at least three 6s appear. It was argued that a 6 would appear, on average, one-sixth of the time, so that the three games should have an equal chance of winning. Is this argument correct? Create an Excel simulation to help you decide.

BUSINESS CASES

Banking Customer Survey

The president of a small market research firm faced a problem with the data from a recent survey ordered by a major bank. The bank was considering a shift to consolidated billing of its revolving credit accounts (typically credit cards and equity loans). The change would have the most impact on customers who had multiple accounts with the bank, so the bank was most interested in the opinions of multiple-account customers.

The bank had provided the market research firm with random samples of essentially equal size from three lists of customers. The "pink" list (provided on pink index cards) was a sample from 190,878 customers and supposedly contained customers with no revolving accounts; the "yellow" list, a sample from 48,328 customers supposedly with exactly one such account; and the "blue" list, a sample from 21,539 customers supposedly with two or more accounts. The market researchers conducted phone interviews with all the customers; they asked each customer for an opinion on the proposed billing change and they also asked how many accounts the customer had. Tabulation of the responses showed that the customers disagreed with the bank on how many accounts they had.

		Reported Number of Accounts			
		0	**1**	**2+**	**Total**
	Pink	66	56	28	150
Sample	Yellow	24	90	36	150
	Blue	46	16	89	151
	Total	136	162	153	451

A check with the bank indicated that the lists were several months old, so that many customers had, in the meantime, changed the number of accounts they had with the bank. The market researchers also tabulated opinions on the proposed consolidated billing method.

Plnk Sample		Reported Number of Accounts		
		0	**1**	**2+**
	Favor	31	32	16
Opinion	Neutral	20	18	8
	Oppose	15	6	4

Yellow Sample		Reported Number of Accounts		
		0	**1**	**2+**
	Favor	9	41	19
Opinion	Neutral	7	30	9
	Oppose	8	19	8

Blue Sample		Reported Number of Accounts		
		0	**1**	**2+**
	Favor	18	6	44
Opinion	Neutral	21	5	20
	Oppose	7	5	25

Assignment: The president has asked you for help in estimating the proportions of people in each account group having each opinion. For example, what proportion of those who have two or more accounts favors the change? The president understands that the data are subject to sampling variation but mostly wants help in obtaining logical estimates of these proportions. In addition, the president is concerned whether these estimates would depend heavily on the numbers of customers from which the lists were drawn; everyone was suspicious of the accuracy of those numbers. Prepare a report; the justification for your answer will be an important part of the firm's report to the bank, so you should explain your logic as clearly as possible.

Amtech, Inc.

Amtech, Inc. sells sophisticated, computerized, point-of-sale cash registers, cash register printers, printer software and interfaces, printer supplies, and hands-on training to commercial accounts. Amtech targets smaller companies that appear ready for a large-scale expansion, with the idea that smaller companies need, and are willing to pay for, the personal attention and customization of the hardware, software, and training that Amtech offers. Small clients often blossom into larger businesses, and their growth typically signals the expansion of Amtech's sales as well, for once committed to a particular configuration of hardware and software, these clients seldom reconsider their alternatives when they expand.

The typical marketing plan is centered on identifying customer needs and then developing a plan to satisfy those needs. Amtech account executives emphasize their capability to customize both the software and training as what distinguishes Amtech from its competitors. They then ask permission to have key personnel fill out a questionnaire in order to develop a customization plan that "fits" the client's needs and to develop a presentation to the client based on the findings.

The questionnaire asks about important business issues and the backgrounds of those who will use the high-tech equipment. Part I deals with technical issues that reflect the nature of the client's business and business plan. These business functions, among others, are discussed with management and are part of designing the software to meet client's business needs. All senior-level management and headquarters' professional staff (for example, accountants) complete this part of the questionnaire.

The second part of the questionnaire is aimed at understanding the backgrounds of those who will use the equipment. This is important information, since the training program will have to be designed to meet their needs. If the typical employee has limited computer background, then a longer, more costly training program will be needed. On the other hand, if the background is substantial, then a mere orientation to the equipment might be enough. This is an important consideration for more than the training costs, since a great deal of evidence suggests that poorly trained employees either become frustrated and quit, or if they stay, never help the company reap the full benefit of the technology it has purchased.

Wendy Cambridge began her career at Amtech less than two years ago and has risen quickly from marketing assistant to assistant account manager for some of Amtech's larger clients. She was recently given her first opportunity to co-lead a sales team for a new potential client, Grass-Roots, Inc. Grass-Roots fits the profile of an ideal customer. It is setting up an additional chain of plant and garden stores in a large Southern city and has plans to expand to 10 additional cities over the next five years.

The Amtech sales team has made its initial presentation to Grass-Roots, which has agreed to allow Amtech to do a follow-up survey to see exactly how it can help. Amtech knows it has a "foot in the door" and can make a potentially lucrative sale depending on how good a job the sales team does from this point on.

Wendy was put in charge of administering the questionnaire and preparing a presentation on Grass-Roots' training needs. This is her first time to head any part of a sales effort and she wants to do it well. While she has never interpreted survey results, written a proposal, or made a sales presentation on her own, she has worked directly for Mary Gordon, Amtech's corporate sales manager, on these assignments and feels confident in her ability to take them on.

Wendy administered the Amtech questionnaire to all current management and operations employees at headquarters and at three retail store locations—in total, 6 corporate management and professional staff, 9 store management, and 33 operations staff. Only headquarters' managers and professional staff were given Part I of the questionnaire; everybody was asked to complete Part II. From a computerized file Wendy analyzed the data regarding employee background using a common PC statistical software package. Then, based on the results from Part II, she developed a training proposal. In preparation for her presentation to Grass-Roots, she also prepared charts (shown in Figures 3.19–3.21) that summarized her findings.

FIGURE 3.19   **Survey Results for Grass-Roots Employees**

	Responses	Mean	Std. Dev.
Age	48	29.5	10.4
Computer knowledge	27	3.0	1.3

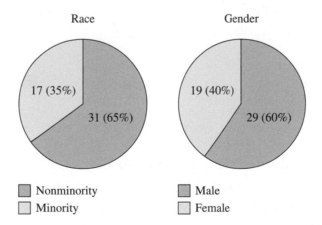

Race

17 (35%)   31 (65%)

Gender

19 (40%)   29 (60%)

■ Nonminority   ■ Male
□ Minority   □ Female

Briefly, Wendy suggested that Grass-Roots employees were reasonably computer literate and, as a result, would need only minimal training—possibly little more than an orientation program, a brief tutorial on the use of the cash registers, and a question-and-answer session. She based her conclusion on survey results that she interpreted as follows.

FIGURE 3.20   **Survey Results for Grass-Roots Employees**

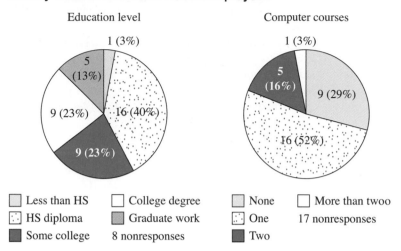

☐ Less than HS	☐ College degree	
⬚ HS diploma	■ Graduate work	
■ Some college	8 nonresponses	

☐ None	☐ More than twoo	
⬚ One	17 nonresponses	
■ Two		

FIGURE 3.21   **Survey Results for Grass-Roots Employees**

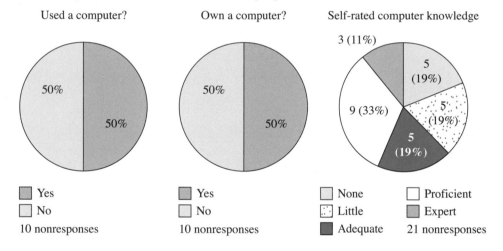

■ Yes	
☐ No	
10 nonresponses	

■ Yes	
☐ No	
10 nonresponses	

☐ None	☐ Proficient
⬚ Little	■ Expert
■ Adequate	21 nonresponses

1. Employees have a relatively high level of education.

2. More than half of the employees have taken at least one computer course.

3. More than half of the employees use or have used a computer on their present or prior jobs.

4. Half of the employees own a PC.

5. The average level of self-rated computer sophistication is at the adequate level of understanding.

Wendy's background is not in business, but she has a track record of doing good work and of growing as her responsibilities grow. But like most people, Wendy makes mistakes early on in new projects. With feedback, she quickly "catches on" and can be counted on to learn well from experience. For this reason, Mary Gordon has decided to give Wendy some backup help to ensure that she has the necessary "safety net" on her new assignment. Mary thinks a lot of Wendy's potential and knows that a little help early in her career will help make her a successful contributor for years to come.

Assignment: You have been assigned by Mary Gordon to be Wendy's "safety net." Look over the survey results and judge whether or not Wendy has correctly analyzed and interpreted the results. Prepare a brief report for Mary Gordon that reflects your interpretation of the survey's results and that makes a recommendation about Wendy's training proposal. Explain the business implications of your recommendation versus that of Wendy's. Finally, prepare charts that reflect the computer literacy levels of the relevant Grass-Roots personnel. Use important details from your analysis to support your recommendation.

You'll find the data in the file Amtech on the CD that came with your book. A partial listing of the data within Excel is shown in Figure 3.22. An asterisk indicates nonresponse or missing information.

FIGURE 3.22   Partial Listing of the Amtech, Inc. Survey Data

	A	B	C	D	E	F	G	H	I	J
1	ID	Position	Minority	Age	Gender	Education	Courses	UsedComp	OwnComp	CompKnow
2	1	3	Y	24	F	3	1	Y	Y	2
3	2	1	N	42	M	5	1	Y	Y	4
4	3	3	Y	19	F	*	*	*	*	*
5	4	3	N	22	M	2	*	N	N	*
6	5	3	Y	24	F	3	0	Y	N	*
7	6	1	N	47	M	5	3	Y	Y	5
8	7	1	N	43	F	4	1	Y	Y	3
9	8	2	N	36	M	4	1	Y	N	3
10	9	3	Y	22	M	*	*	N	N	*
11	10	3	Y	28	F	2	0	N	N	2
12	11	2	Y	29	M	4	1	Y	Y	4
13	12	3	N	26	F	2	0	N	N	1
14	13	3	Y	18	M	1	*	*	*	*
15	14	1	N	57	M	4	1	Y	Y	4
16	15	3	N	22	F	2	*	*	*	*
17	16	3	N	33	M	3	1	Y	Y	2
18	17	3	N	24	M	2	*	N	N	*

The variables in the file Amtech are defined as follows:

ID: Survey identification number of the employee

Position: Job position of the employee, where
             1 = Headquarters Management and Professional Staff,
             2 = Store Management,
             3 = Store Operations Staff

Minority: Race of the employee, where
             Y = minority,
             N = nonminority

Age: Age of the employee on his or her last birthday

Gender:	Gender of the employee (M or F)
Education:	Highest education level attained by the employee, where 1 = less than a high school diploma, 2 = high school diploma, 3 = some college work, 4 = college degree, 5 = graduate work or degree
Courses:	Number of computer courses taken by the employee
UsedComp:	Has the employee used a computer? (Y or N)
OwnComp:	Does the employee own a computer? (Y or N)
CompKnow:	Self-evaluation of computer knowledge using a rating scale, where 1 = no knowledge, 2 = little knowledge, 3 = adequate knowledge, 4 = better than adequate knowledge, 5 = expert level of knowledge

Review Exercises—Chapters 2–3

These exercises are intended to help you check your understanding of the topics in the chapters just completed. The problems are *not* in any particular order, so you can't tell how to do a problem by its location.

3.60 Samples of car door locks from four different suppliers are tested under high-stress conditions to determine the number of times that the locks can be operated before they fail. The data, in thousands, are

Supplier	Operations Before Failure									
A	24.7	19.8	22.0	37.6	21.8	25.4	20.6	48.7	23.9	22.6
B	26.8	25.7	39.7	25.8	28.0	52.4	29.4	31.1	26.0	28.4
C	15.3	35.7	18.2	15.3	21.0	19.9	42.6	21.1	18.9	19.7
D	31.4	21.2	24.5	22.0	26.7	61.0	22.6	23.5	25.0	22.6

The following summary statistics are obtained from Minitab:

```
Descriptive Statistics: Operations

Variable    Supplier   N    Mean   StDev  Minimum     Q1  Median     Q3  Maximum
Operations  A         10   26.71   9.21    19.80   21.50   23.25  28.45    48.70
            B         10   31.33   8.49    25.70   25.95   28.20  33.25    52.40
            C         10   22.77   9.02    15.30   17.48   19.80  24.75    42.60
            D         10   28.05  11.95    21.20   22.45   24.00  27.88    61.00
```

a. Summarize the data separately for each supplier. Be sure to discuss average, variability, and skewness.

b. Can the Empirical Rule be expected to work well for these data? Why or why not? You may want to construct stem-and-leaf displays for each supplier.

3.61   Prices posted on the shelves of a supermarket do not always match the correct current price of the item because of errors in posting price changes. Suppose that over time 60% of the price changes are increases and 40% are decreases. Also suppose that 93% of the price increases are posted correctly, as are 98% of the price decreases. If a price change is not posted correctly, what is the probability that the change is a decrease?

3.62   A study of small savings and loan associations yielded the following financial information:

Deposits ($000,000)	Capital ($000,000)	Reserves ($000,000)	Bad Debts (Percent of Portfolio)	Type of Bank (1 = Savings, 2 = Joint S & L, 3 = Stocks S & L)
3.68	1.14	0.97	1.62	2
11.64	4.03	3.28	0.97	1
31.62	10.63	9.22	2.00	3
2.62	0.85	0.53	3.97	2
1.97	0.61	0.79	0.75	1
15.21	5.21	3.77	1.11	3
3.88	0.65	1.10	1.77	2
5.01	1.00	1.15	0.32	1
7.53	1.16	3.02	4.31	3
3.67	0.89	0.92	1.12	2

a. Construct a stem-and-leaf plot for each quantitative variable.

b. Calculate the mean and standard deviation for the Bad Debts variable. Assuming that this sample is representative of all S & L's, within what range should most of the bad debt values fall for the general population of S & L's?

c. Are there any outliers in any of the variables?

3.63   A coal-burning electric generator occasionally is improperly stoked and emits unacceptable amounts of various gases. In the long run, this problem occurs in 1% of the generator's operating time. An air sample is taken and analyzed every hour. The analysis is not a perfect indicator of gas emissions. Calibration tests indicate that if the generator is emitting acceptable levels of the gases, the test shows excess emissions 4% of the time, borderline emissions 5% of the time, and acceptable emissions 91% of the time. If the generator is emitting excessive amounts of the gases, the test shows excess emissions 92% of the time, borderline emissions 5% of the time, and acceptable emissions 3% of the time. If the test indicates excess emissions, what is the probability that the generator is in fact emitting unacceptable amounts of the gases?

3.64   Show that "borderline emissions in the test" and "unacceptable emissions by the generator" are independent events in the preceding exercise.

3.65   A supermarket chain does a study of the effectiveness of its own coupons in inducing additional cereal sales. The data from the preliminary pilot study were as follows.

X_1 Cents Off	X_2 Current Price (Cents)	X_3 Type of Cereal	X_4 Normal Sales	X_5 Sales in Coupon Week
29	379	1	37,000	42,000
19	109	2	67,200	79,900
50	399	1	21,200	32,500
25	199	5	11,600	12,900
59	209	4	18,800	22,800
100	379	1	37,000	51,300
20	109	2	67,200	83,100
40	229	3	12,000	13,200
79	399	1	21,200	36,000
50	209	4	18,800	20,100
29	109	2	67,200	83,900
30	379	1	37,000	40,900
50	229	3	12,000	14,100

One part of the Excel output for these data follows:

```
                 CentsOff    Price      Type      Normal     CouponWeek
Sample size      13          13         13        13         13
Mean             44.6154     256.692    2.30769   32938.5    40976.9
Median           40          229        2         21200      36000
Std. deviation   24.0019     115.553    1.37747   21561.1    26433.1
```

a. Locate the mean and standard deviation of X_3.

b. What is the interpretation of the numbers determined in (a)?

3.66   Experience indicates that about 10% of new television shows place in the top third of all shows in audience ratings during the first year. About 40% place in the middle third and about 50% place in the bottom third. Of new shows placing in the top third, only 2% are canceled; 40% of shows placing in the middle third are canceled, as are 85% of shows placing in the bottom third. What fraction of new shows are in the bottom third and are not canceled?

3.67   In the previous exercise are rating and cancellation assumed to be independent? What would independence mean in this context?

3.68   Junior managers in a firm are rated by their bosses in terms of current performance and managerial potential. The current performance ratings are 18% excellent, 71% satisfactory, and 11% unsatisfactory. The managerial potential ratings are 24% definite, 40% possible, and 36% unlikely.

a. Using this information and any additional assumptions you must make, find the probability that a randomly selected junior manager will be rated "excellent" on the performance scale and "definite" on the potential scale.

b. What did you assume in answering part (a)? Are the assumptions reasonable? If not, is the probability you calculated likely to be too low or too high?

3.69   Records for a sample of employees in a large firm indicate the following distribution of claimed deductions on W-4 tax withholding forms:

Deductions:	0	1	2	3	4	5	6
Frequency:	201	287	364	332	151	97	52

Deductions:	7	8	9	10	11	12
Frequency:	28	11	5	2	0	3

a. Find the mean number of deductions.
b. Find the standard deviation. Does it make much difference if the data are regarded as a sample rather than a population?
c. How well does the Empirical Rule work for data within 1 standard deviation of the mean?

3.70   A W-4 form is drawn at random from the data of the previous exercise.
a. What is the probability that it claims at least one deduction?
b. If the form claims at least one deduction, what is the probability that it claims at most three?

3.71   Data are collected on the total compensation (salary plus bonuses) of samples of men and women junior managers in a firm. The data (in thousands of dollars per year) were

Men: 69.6 58.9 65.4 66.8 63.7 62.8 65.1 66.7 68.4 65.7 63.1
             61.6 64.7 63.8 66.2 64.9 65.7 70.2 66.5 67.4 65.2 66.6

Women: 64.2 61.8 62.7 57.6 63.0 68.1 63.0 61.5 59.8 61.8 74.7
          52.5 60.0 64.3 61.0 62.5

Excel output included the following:

```
Men:                          Women:

Mean         65.41            Mean       62.41
Median       65.55            Median     62.15
Mode         65.7             Mode       61.8
Standard Deviation   2.54     Standard Deviation   4.68
Sample Variance      6.469    Sample Variance      21.901
```

a. From the looks of the data, should the mean and median compensation for men be similar? Verify your answer from the Excel output.
b. Show that the smaller group (women) has a larger range than the other group (men). Explain what causes this phenomenon.

3.72   Construct box plots for both sets of data in the previous exercise. Include a check for outliers.

3.73   Calculate the mean and median compensation for the combined sample of managers in the preceding exercise. How do these values relate to the means and medians of the two groups separately?

3.74   Data from an automobile manufacturer indicate that, of all cars repaired under warranty, 57% require engine work, 47% require interior work, and 30% require exterior work. Also, 23% require both engine and interior work, 7% both engine and exterior work, and 13% both interior and exterior work; 5% require all three types of work. There are some cars that require other types of work.
a. Find the probability that a car repaired under warranty requires engine work but no interior or exterior work.
b. Find the probability that a car requires exactly one of the three types of work.
c. Are the events "engine work" and "interior work" independent?

3.75   A cereal manufacturer collects samples of the time required for workers to clean out the manufacturing line when switching from production of one cereal to production of another. The data, in actual worker-hours expended, are shown on the next page.

Previous Flour Base	Time									
Corn	10.0	11.0	11.5	9.5	10.0	12.5	8.5	9.0	10.0	10.5
	11.5	13.0	9.5	16.5	14.5	11.0	10.5	10.0	11.0	15.0
Oats	13.5	11.0	10.0	11.5	12.0	10.5	11.0	16.5	13.0	19.0
	12.5	17.0	11.0	13.5	12.0	11.0	13.5	15.0	.	.
Wheat	28.0	31.0	33.0	35.0	30.0	28.5	27.5	26.5	32.0	24.0
	30.5	32.0	31.5	40.5	31.0	33.0	30.5	33.0	28.5	47.5
	31.0	33.5	35.0	33.5	30.0	36.5	39.5	29.0	30.5	

Minitab output included box plots and histograms shown in Figures 3.23 and 3.24 and the summary statistics.

```
Descriptive Statistics

Variable    Code    N     Mean    Median    TrMean    StDev    SEMean
Time         1     20   11.250   10.750    11.111    2.093    0.468
             2     18   12.972   12.250    12.781    2.482    0.585
             3     29   32.138   31.000    31.870    4.613    0.857

Variable    Code    Min      Max       Q1        Q3
Time         1     8.500   16.500   10.000    12.250
             2    10.000   19.000   11.000    13.875
             3    24.000   47.500   29.500    33.500
```

FIGURE 3.23 **Box Plots of Worker-Hours Data by Grain Type**

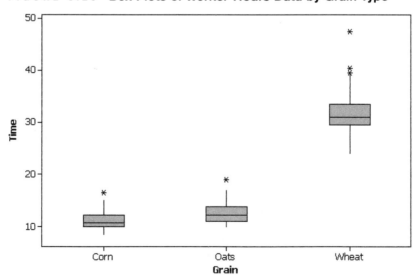

a. Based on the box plots, what is the general shape of the data?
b. Locate the means and medians for the three sets of times. Does the relation between the resulting means and medians confirm your judgment about the shapes?

3.76 Calculate the mean and median for the combined samples in the previous exercise. Is either of them a reasonable summary figure for a typical cleaning time?

3.77 Administrators at a rural regional hospital tracked the occupancy of beds in the surgical ward. Keeping these beds reasonably full was important to the financial stability of the hospital, but it was always preferable to have a few beds available for emergency cases. Careful scheduling of elective surgery was useful in reducing variability in bed usage. Occupancy

FIGURE 3.24   **Histogram of Combined Worker-Hours Data**

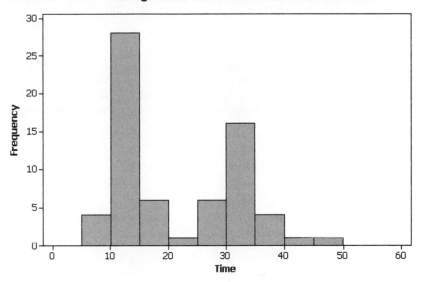

had been fairly stable around 78%, but administrators were concerned to detect any trend downward. The number of beds occupied at 6:00 each evening was recorded. Occupancy always was lower on weekends, so the weekly average was recorded on a control chart. X-bar and S charts are shown in Figure 3.25.

FIGURE 3.25   **Control Charts for Bed-Occupancy Data**

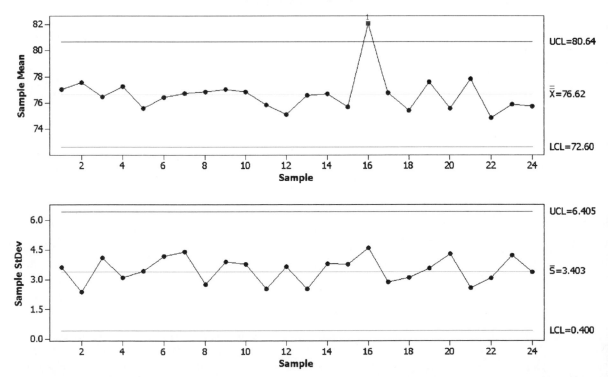

a. Is there any indication of a trend in means?

b. Is there any indication of a trend in variability?

c. Would you consider the process under statistical control?

3.78 Hospital administrators from the preceding exercise investigated the unusually high occupancy number in week 16. They found that the number of patients hadn't changed much. The head nurse in the surgical unit reminded them that several beds had been removed from service to allow for renovations. Should this result be regarded as a common cause or a special cause of variation? Does the value at week 16 indicate an improvement in performance?

CHAPTER 4

Random Variables and

Probability Distributions

CHAPTER CONTENTS

Random variables and probability distributions provide the language for quantitative variables that have a random component. They give us a way to tie together data summarization ideas like histograms, means, and standard deviations with probability ideas like addition and multiplication principles and independence. The fundamental concepts of this chapter are

- A probability distribution is specified by stating the possible values for the random quantity and calculating the probability of each value. The probability principles of the previous chapter apply here as well. Probabilities may be specified directly as a probability distribution or in terms of the cumulative distribution function.

- The expected value (mean) of a random variable is the probability-weighted average of its possible values. It is the point at which a probability histogram balances. It is the long-run average value of the random quantity, averaged over many repetitions of the experiment.

- The standard deviation of a random variable is the square root of the variance, which in turn is the probability-weighted average of squared deviations from the mean. The standard deviation may be interpreted according to the Empirical Rule, but this rule doesn't work very well for discrete random variables with very few possible values.

- Two random variables may be treated together by specifying the joint probability distribution, which gives the probability of each pair of possible values. From the joint distribution, the marginal probability distribution of each random variable may be found by addition.

- Two random variables are (statistically) independent if the probabilities for one random variable do not change, regardless of the value taken by the other one. Independence is often an assumption that should be checked for reasonableness.

- The correlation of two random variables measures the strength of the linear relation between the two. It is calculated using the standard deviations of both random variables and their covariance, the probability-weighted product of deviations from the respective means.

The probability ideas and laws developed in Chapter 3 apply to any kind of experiment, whether it yields qualitative or quantitative results. We will use these probability ideas mostly with numerical, quantitative variables. Ideas like averaging apply only to quantitative results. To make connections between ideas like mean and standard deviation from Chapter 2 with the probability concepts from Chapter 3, we need some additional probability language. The key ideas are the notions of a random variable (Section 4.1) and probability distribution (Section 4.2). Once we have these ideas, we can link probability concepts such as independence and correlation with the ideas of mean and standard deviation in the following sections of this chapter.

CHAPTER CASE

INTRODUCTION

Baldwin Computer Sales

Jonathan Baldwin, the founder of Baldwin Computer Sales, a small company located in Oldenburg, Washington, began the business by selling personal computers through mail order at discount prices—a first in the industry. Baldwin was also one of the first computer mail-order companies to offer a toll-free customer support phone number. While the company has grown over time, many new competitors have entered the marketplace and caused Baldwin's share of this market to decline.

Five years ago, Bob Gravenstein, a marketing consultant, was contracted by Baldwin to develop long-term marketing plans and strategies for the company. He recommended that Baldwin branch out to a new and growing segment of the computer sales market: college students. Many colleges and universities were beginning to require students to purchase their own computers and printers. After graduation, students could use their computers at their new jobs or at home. The percentage of college students owning a computer was increasing rapidly and Bob Gravenstein recommended that Baldwin Computer Sales take advantage of this marketing opportunity.

The marketing plan developed by Bob Gravenstein worked this way. Any student at one of a select number of universities was eligible to purchase a discounted NBD-3000 microcomputer system with printer from Baldwin Computer Sales. The NBD-3000 is a private-label, fully compatible system with all of the features of brand-name models. The student makes a small payment each semester at the same time regular tuition payments are due. When the student graduates and finds a job, the payments are increased so that the computer will be paid for within two years after graduation. If the student fails to make payments at any time, Baldwin can repossess the computer system.

The prospect of future sales of computer equipment to these students was also part of the marketing strategy. Many students who purchased the NBD-3000, an entry-level computer system adequate for most academic and professional uses, would eventually outgrow it and require an upgrade to a more powerful machine with more features. Bob Gravenstein argued that after their good experience with the NBD-3000, these customers would make their future purchases from Baldwin Computer Company.

Today, five years later, Baldwin Computer Sales is still operating the student purchase program and has expanded it to many other universities. There is currently enough data available from the early days of the program for Baldwin to determine whether or not the program has been successful and whether or not it should be continued. To discuss the future of the program, Jonathan Baldwin has called a meeting with Ben Davis, who has been in charge of the program since it began, and you, the new vice president of marketing.

Baldwin: As you know, the student purchase program has been in place for about five years—we need to decide where to go from here. Ben, weren't you telling me last week that we now have enough data to evaluate the program?

Davis: Yes, sir. Any student who began the program five years ago should have graduated and been employed for at least two years.

Baldwin: Well, based on your information, would you say the program has been a success or a failure?

Davis: That's a tough call, sir. While most of them eventually pay their account in full, we have had a high default rate—some while students were still in school, but mostly after they graduated.

Baldwin: How much are we losing to defaults?

Davis: Each case is different. As I said, some default early and others after they graduate. Repossession and repair to bring the product back up to resale quality also cost a lot, and a lot of times we weren't able to retrieve the systems. Our data suggest that our loss on each default is about $1200. On the other hand, our profit from those who pay their accounts in full is about $750. Overall, we are close to just breaking even.

You: What about "qualifying" students for the program—like a loan officer qualifies someone for a loan?

Davis: We thought about that, but we didn't think there was much information out there, if any, about the credit history of most college students. Oh, we still ask applicants for as much information as possible, including their class, grade point average, work experience, scholarships, and how much of their college expenses they earned through work. But we weren't sure that this was particularly useful in screening.

You: To get ready for this discussion, I had one of my assistants look over some of those data last week, and she developed a "screening test" based only on the information we've been collecting from student applicants. By being more selective about who we let in, we might increase our profit from the program.

Davis: It's easy enough to check out her screening test by trying it out on our early data from the program—in those cases, we actually know whether or not the student defaulted.

Baldwin: Why don't the two of you get back to me next week on this? Recommend to me to either discontinue the program, continue it as is, or continue it using this "screening test" idea. But make sure you have the evidence to back up what you recommend.

The data from the first five years of the Baldwin student purchase program are contained in the file Baldwin on the CD that came with your book. The file contains information on the 342 students who participated in the program over the past five years. A partial listing of the data is shown in Figure 4.1.

In the Baldwin file, the variables are defined as follows:

Student: Student transaction number (for identification purposes)

Outcome: Default, in the event of default;
Paid, if account was paid in full on time

When: Before, if default occurred or account paid in full before graduation;
After, if default occurred or account paid in full after graduation

Score: Score on the screening test based on student applicant information such as his or her class, grade point average, work experience, scholarships, and how much of his or her college expenses were earned through work

FIGURE 4.1   **Partial Listing of the Baldwin Computer Sales Data**

	A	B	C	D
1	Student	Outcome	When	Score
2	6547	Default	Before	64
3	4503	Paid	After	58
4	1219	Paid	After	52
5	9843	Default	After	56
6	6807	Paid	After	47
7	6386	Paid	After	58
8	4427	Paid	After	50
9	9668	Default	After	63
10	3697	Paid	After	71
11	6456	Default	Before	61
12	4838	Paid	After	72
13	7833	Paid	After	64
14	4698	Paid	Before	68
15	6496	Paid	After	85
16	1035	Paid	After	61

Using this data set and other information provided, evaluate the student purchase program and recommend any necessary changes in the program. In particular, you need to evaluate the profitability of the program as it is currently administered and to evaluate the usefulness of the screening test developed by your assistant. You will find the material covered in this chapter and in the previous chapters to be extremely helpful in the analysis and decision-making process outlined in the Chapter Case Analysis section at the end of this chapter. ■

4.1   Random Variables: Basic Ideas

Many of the probability issues most relevant to managers involve random, numerical outcomes. For example, the number of no-shows on a particular flight (people holding reservations for the flight who don't actually take it) is critically important in establishing an airline's reservation policy. The number of no-shows is random, varying from one flight to another and from day to day on the same flight. Certainly, the number of no-shows is a numerical variable. It makes perfectly good sense to talk about the average number of no-shows. The concept of random variable is the central idea in understanding random, numerical outcomes.

random variable   Informally, a **random variable** is a quantitative (numerical) result from a random experiment. For instance, consider the experiment of selecting a manager randomly from the middle management of an automobile manufacturer. Define the random variable Y to be number of years of formal schooling the manager has had. First of all, Y is numerical; the result will be a number like 12 or 16, not a category like "private college." Secondly, Y is subject to random variation. If the experiment is repeated with a new random selection, the result very likely will change. These two features—numerical result, subject to randomness—are the key aspects of the definition of a random variable.

To specify a random variable, we need to know its possible values and their respective probabilities. For the years of formal schooling example, the possible values could be 0, 1, 2, . . . , up to some maximum number, perhaps 20. Probabilities could be obtained from company personnel records; for example, if 284 of the 500 managers had completed exactly 4 years of college (after 12 years of elementary and high school), the probability that $Y = 16$ would be $284/500 = .568$. Probabilities for other values could be filled in similarly.

DEFINITION 4.1

Random Variable: Informal Definition A random variable is any quantitative result from an experiment that is subject to random variability. It is determined by specifying its possible values and the probability associated with each value.

The probability associated with each value of a random variable is found by adding the probabilities for all outcomes that are assigned that value. Suppose that a plant produces cellular telephones in equal numbers on two production lines. Three phones are selected at random each day for destructive testing. Call the lines H and T; this experiment is just like flipping a fair coin three times. Find the probability distribution of Y, the number of sampled phones produced on line H. There are eight possible outcomes:

Outcome	HHH	HHT	HTH	THH	HTT	THT	TTH	TTT
Probability	1/8	1/8	1/8	1/8	1/8	1/8	1/8	1/8
Value assigned by Y	3	2	2	2	1	1	1	0

Then, for instance,

$$P(Y = 2) = P(\text{HHT}) + P(\text{HTH}) + P(\text{THH}) = \frac{1}{8} + \frac{1}{8} + \frac{1}{8} = \frac{3}{8}$$

The custom is to denote random variables by capital letters at the end of the alphabet; thus we might define X = number of heads observed in three flips of a coin and Y = number of Theater Guild subscribers in a random sample of 200 persons. Possible values of a random variable are usually denoted by the corresponding lowercase letter; we would say that x could be 0, 1, 2, or 3 and y could be 0, 1, 2, . . . , 200. The subtle distinction between Y, the random variable itself, and y, one of its possible values, is the distinction between a process and one particular result of that process; it becomes clear with practice.

EXAMPLE 4.1

Suppose that a random sample of two persons is to be selected from a large population consisting of 30% Theater Guild subscribers and 70% nonsubscribers.

a. List the possible outcomes.

b. Assign probabilities.

c. Define the quantitative random variable Y as the number of Theater Guild subscribers in the sample. Specify the possible values that the random variable may assume and determine the probability of each.

SOLUTION

a. If we let S designate a subscriber and N a nonsubscriber, then the possible outcomes for the two persons sampled are

$$\{(S, S); (S, N); (N, S); \text{and } (N, N)\}$$

b. From the statement of the problem, we know that $P(S) = .3$ and $P(N) = .7$. Under the assumption that the outcomes for the two persons sampled are independent, we have the following probabilities associated with the four outcomes:

$$P(S, S) = (.3)^2 = .09$$
$$P(S, N) = (.3)(.7) = .21$$
$$P(N, S) = (.7)(.3) = .21$$
$$P(N, N) = (.7)^2 = \underline{.49}$$
$$1.00$$

c. If the random variable Y is the number of subscribers in a sample of two from the population of interest, then the possible values for Y are 0, 1, and 2. The probabilities associated with these values can be determined from probabilities for the outcomes that make up each numerical event.

Outcome	Probability	y	$P(y)$
(N, N)	.49	0	.49
(N, S)	.21	1 ⎤	
(S, N)	.21	1 ⎦	.42
(S, S)	.09	2	.09

discrete

continuous

    The random variables we have considered so far have been **discrete;** their possible values have been distinct and separate, like 0 or 1 or 2 or 3. Other random variables are most usefully considered to be **continuous:** Their possible values form a whole interval (or range, or continuum). For instance, the one-year return per dollar invested in a common stock could range from 0 to something quite large. In practice, virtually all random variables assume a discrete set of values; the return per dollar of a million-dollar common-stock investment could be 1.06219423 or 1.06219424 or 1.06219425 or . . .. But, when there are many, many possible values for a random variable, it is sometimes mathematically useful to treat that random variable as continuous. In fact, one of the most important theoretical probability specifications—the bell-shaped normal distribution—formally applies only to continuous random variables. In this chapter we define some language and notation for discrete random variables. Because the corresponding methods for continuous random variables require some knowledge of calculus, we only sketch them.

4.2 Probability Distributions: Discrete Random Variables

probability distribution

    The **probability distribution** $P_Y(y)$ for a discrete random variable Y assigns a probability to each value y of the random variable Y. The probability distribution for Y can be expressed as a formula, a graph, or a table.

DEFINITION 4.2

Properties of a Discrete Probability Distribution

1.   The probability $P_Y(y)$ associated with each value of Y must lie in the interval

$$0 \le P_Y(y) \le 1$$

2.   The sum of the probabilities for all values of Y equals 1.

$$\sum_{\text{all } y} P_Y(y) = 1$$

3.   Because different values of Y are mutually exclusive events, their probabilities are additive. Thus,

$$P(Y = a \text{ or } Y = b) = P_Y(a) + P_Y(b)$$

For the random variable $Y =$ number of line H phones in a sample of three, we might define $P_Y(y)$ by a table, as follows:

$$
\begin{array}{c|cccc}
y: & 0 & 1 & 2 & 3 \\
P_Y(y): & 1/8 & 3/8 & 3/8 & 1/8
\end{array}
$$

Or we might use the formula

$$P_Y(y) = \frac{3!}{y!(3-y)!}\left(\frac{1}{8}\right)$$

where, in general, $k! = k(k-1)(k-2)\cdots(1)$ and $0! = 1$ by convention. Substituting $y = 0, 1, 2,$ and 3 into the formula yields the same probabilities as those listed in the previous table:

$$
\begin{array}{c|cccc}
y: & 0 & 1 & 2 & 3 \\
P_Y(y): & \dfrac{3\cdot2\cdot1}{(1)(3\cdot2\cdot1)}\dfrac{1}{8}=\dfrac{1}{8} & \dfrac{3\cdot2\cdot1}{(1)(2\cdot1)}\dfrac{1}{8}=\dfrac{3}{8} & \dfrac{3\cdot2\cdot1}{(2\cdot1)(1)}\dfrac{1}{8}=\dfrac{3}{8} & \dfrac{3\cdot2\cdot1}{(3\cdot2\cdot1)(1)}\dfrac{1}{8}=\dfrac{1}{8}
\end{array}
$$

probability histogram

A graph of this probability distribution, called a **probability histogram,** is shown in Figure 4.2. The discrete random variable Y is the number of line H phones in a sample of three.

cumulative distribution function

The **cumulative distribution function** is another function that is particularly appropriate when calculating probabilities and has applications in computer simulation methods. In general, the cumulative distribution function $F_Y(y)$ for a dis-

FIGURE 4.2

Graph of $P_Y(y)$ for the Phone-Sampling Experiment

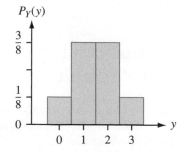

crete random variable Y is a function that specifies the probability that $Y \leq y$ for all values of y. By the addition law for probabilities, all we must do is add the individual probabilities for values less than or equal to the specified y. Thus,

$$F_Y(y) = P(Y \leq y) = P_Y(0) + P_Y(1) + \cdots + P_Y(y)$$

This can be illustrated for the phone-sampling example discussed previously:

y:	0	1	2	3
$P_Y(y)$:	1/8	3/8	3/8	1/8
$F_Y(y)$:	1/8	4/8	7/8	8/8

As the name suggests and the example illustrates, the cumulative distribution function at a particular value y sums all probabilities for $Y \leq y$. For example,

$$F_Y(2) = P(Y \leq 2) = \frac{1}{8} + \frac{3}{8} + \frac{3}{8} = \frac{7}{8}$$

and

$$F_Y(3) = P(Y \leq 3) = 1$$

The cumulative distribution function (abbreviated cdf) is often used in constructing probability tables so the table user does not have to add up many table entries to find a certain probability. As an illustration, suppose that a large metropolitan teaching hospital has data on the number of acute coronary cases Y arriving at the hospital in a given day. The cdf is tabulated as follows:

y:	0	1	2	3	4	5	6	7	8
$F_Y(y)$:	.001	.003	.006	.011	.024	.061	.139	.224	.336

y:	9	10	11	12	13	14	15	16	17
$F_Y(y)$:	.510	.672	.782	.870	.925	.964	.988	.997	1.000

Suppose that the hospital has 14 coronary-care beds available at the beginning of a particular day. The probability that the number of new cases Y is less than or equal to 14 can be read directly from the table as .964. It's almost as easy to find the probability that Y is 15 or more; $P(Y \geq 15) = 1 - P(Y \leq 14) = 1 - .964 = .036$. Had the table been stated in terms of individual probabilities $P(y)$, it would have been necessary to add up many entries to find these probabilities.

General use of cdf tables is easy enough if you draw a probability histogram. A probability histogram for the coronary-care illustration is shown in Figure 4.3; the probability $P_Y(y)$ of each particular value y is indicated by the height of the rectangle erected atop that y value.

For example, suppose we want $P(7 \leq Y \leq 12)$. We want the total area of the rectangles above $y = 7, 8, 9, 10, 11$, and 12, which are shaded in Figure 4.3. $F_Y(12)$ is the total area of all the rectangles above $y = 0, 1, \ldots, 12$; to find $P(7 \leq Y \leq 12)$ we must subtract the combined probabilities for $y = 0, 1, \ldots, 6$, namely, $F_Y(6)$, from $F_Y(12)$:

$$P(7 \leq Y \leq 12) = F_Y(12) - F_Y(6) = .870 - .139 = .731$$

Generally, it's useful to draw a probability histogram whenever you want to use tables to calculate probabilities.

FIGURE 4.3   **Probability Histogram for the Coronary-Care Illustration**

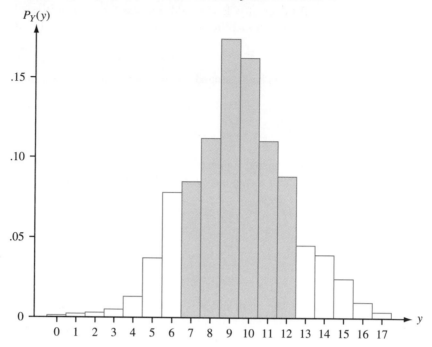

EXAMPLE 4.2   Suppose that a cosmetic company plans to market a new perfume. The product manager has assessed the following subjective cumulative probabilities for the first-year sales (denoted by X) in millions of bottles:

x:	0	1	2	3	4	5	6	7	8
$F_X(x)$:	.05	.20	.40	.60	.75	.85	.90	.95	1.00

Find the following probabilities, as assessed by the product manager:

a. $P(X \geq 5)$

b. $P(2 \leq X \leq 4)$

c. $P(X \leq 1)$

SOLUTION   A probability histogram for this example is shown in Figure 4.4. Areas relevant to each problem are indicated by a, b, or c.

a. $P(X \geq 5) = 1 - P(X \leq 4) = 1.00 - .75 = .25$

The area of all the rectangles is 1.00. We must subtract the areas of all rectangles through $x = 4$.

b. Subtract the areas of the rectangles for $x = 0, 1$ from the areas of the rectangles for $x = 0, 1, 2, 3, 4$, to get $P(2 \leq X \leq 4)$:

$$P(2 \leq X \leq 4) = F_X(4) - F_X(1) = .75 - .20 = .55$$

c. By definition, $P(X \leq 1) = F_X(1) = .20$; no subtraction is needed.

FIGURE 4.4 **Probability Histogram for Example 4.2**

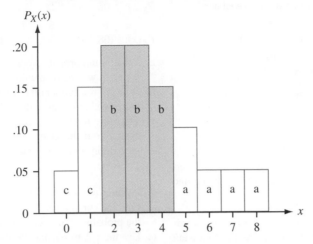

Continuous random variables, those which take all values in an interval, also have probability histograms. The technical problem is that continuous random variables take on so many values—mathematically, infinitely many—that the rectangles in the histogram are very, very thin—mathematically, infinitely thin. Rather than adding the areas in a discrete histogram, we must use calculus methods to integrate the area under a smooth curve. The basic ideas for continuous random variables are the same as for discrete ones, but the required math can get in the way. Those who know calculus can obtain the basic results for continuous random variables from those for discrete random variables by replacing summation by integration.

Exercises

4.1 Among its various routes, a transit agency operates a trolley line. The line has a total of 18 trolley cars. Some of these cars are unavailable because they are being maintained or repaired. The probability distribution of Y = number of cars out of service on a randomly chosen day is given by the Excel spreadsheet in Figure 4.5.

FIGURE 4.5 **Probability Distribution of Y in Exercise 4.1**

	A	B
1	y	P(y)
2	0	0.28
3	1	0.16
4	2	0.11
5	3	0.10
6	4	0.08
7	5	0.07
8	6	0.05
9	7	0.04
10	8	0.04
11	9	0.03
12	10	0.02
13	11	0.01
14	12	0.01

a. What is the probability that all the trolleys are operating?
b. The agency needs at least 14 cars available for normal operation of the line. What is the probability that the operation will not be normal?

4.2 Calculate the cdf for Y in the previous exercise. Use it to recalculate the probabilities for that exercise.

4.3 The personnel department of a large firm employs five men and three women as college recruiters. For visits to certain large campuses, a team of two people is sent. Suppose that two of the eight recruiters are chosen at random. Let Y = number of women selected.
a. Construct the sample space; call the recruiters A, B, . . . , H.
b. Find the value of Y for each outcome in the sample space.
c. Find $P_Y(y)$ by counting. Construct a probability histogram.
d. Find the cdf of Y. Plot $F_Y(y)$ against y.

4.4 An appliance store has the following probabilities for Y = number of major appliances sold on a given day:

y:	0	1	2	3	4	5
$P_Y(y)$:	.100	.150	.250	.140	.090	.080

y:	6	7	8	9	10
$P_Y(y)$:	.060	.050	.040	.025	.015

a. Construct a probability histogram.
b. Find $P(Y \le 2)$.
c. Find $P(Y \ge 7)$.
d. Find $P(1 \le Y \le 5)$.

4.5 Calculate the cdf corresponding to $P_Y(y)$ in Exercise 4.4. Use this cdf to find $P(Y \le 2)$, $P(Y \ge 7)$, and $P(1 \le Y \le 5)$.

4.6 The weekly demand X for copies of a popular word-processing program at a computer store has the following probability distribution shown here.

x:	0	1	2	3	4	5
$P_X(x)$:	.06	.14	.16	.14	.12	.10

x:	6	7	8	9	10
$P_X(x)$:	.08	.07	.06	.04	.03

a. What is the probability that three or more copies of the program will be demanded in a particular week?
b. What is the probability that the demand will be for at least two but no more than six?
c. The store policy is to have eight copies of the program available at the beginning of every week. What is the probability that the demand will exceed the supply in a given week?

4.7 Refer to Exercise 4.6.
a. Find the cumulative distribution function (cdf) $F_X(x)$ for the probability distribution shown.
b. Use the cdf to recalculate the probabilities requested in Exercise 4.6.

4.3 Expected Value, Variance, and Standard Deviation

In the previous section we introduced the language of random variables. Because random variables have numerical values, it makes sense to talk about averages and variability. In this section we'll define the mean (or expected value) and variance of a random quantity.

expected value

The average value of a random variable must take into account the possible values of that variable and also the respective probabilities. The **expected value** of a discrete random variable Y with probability distribution $P_Y(y)$ is the probability-weighted average of its possible values. Recall that a weighted average is the sum of weights times values, divided by the sum of the weights. If the relatively heavy weights are toward one end of the range of values, a weighted average is pulled in that direction, as compared to an unweighted average. The expected value is also called the mean of Y and is denoted by $E(Y)$ or μ_Y. Multiply each possible value by its probability and sum. The sum of the probability weights is always 1; we needn't worry about dividing by 1.

DEFINITION 4.3

Expected Value of a Discrete Random Variable For a discrete random variable Y with probability distribution $P_Y(y)$, the expected value of Y is

$$\mu_Y = E(Y) = \sum_{\text{all } y} y P_Y(y)$$

To find $E(Y)$, take each possible value y, multiply (weight) it by the associated probability $P_Y(y)$, and add the results.

EXAMPLE 4.3 A firm is considering two possible investments. As a rough approximation, the firm assigns (subjective) probabilities of losing 20% per dollar invested, losing 10%, breaking even, gaining 10%, and gaining 20%. Let Y be the return per dollar invested in the first project and Z the return per dollar invested in the second. The firm's probabilities are

$$
\begin{array}{lccccc}
y: & -.20 & -.10 & 0 & +.10 & +.20 \\
P_Y(y): & .1 & .2 & .4 & .2 & .1
\end{array}
$$

$$
\begin{array}{lccccc}
z: & -.20 & -.10 & 0 & +.10 & +.20 \\
P_Z(z): & .01 & .04 & .10 & .50 & .35
\end{array}
$$

Calculate expected returns per dollar invested in each project. Which project appears to be the more attractive investment?

SOLUTION   Project Y, by any reasonable standard, appears less attractive. It is thought to be as likely to lose 20% as to gain 20%, and as likely to lose 10% as to gain 10%. Project Z is thought to be very likely to gain 10% or 20% and relatively unlikely to lose.
Calculations:

y	$P_Y(y)$	$yP_Y(y)$	z	$P_Z(z)$	$zP_Z(z)$
$-.20$	.1	$-.02$	$-.20$	.01	$-.002$
$-.10$	.2	$-.02$	$-.10$	.04	$-.004$
0	.4	0	0	10	0
$+.10$	.2	$+.02$	$+.10$	.50	$+.050$
$+.20$	.1	$+.02$	$+.20$	.35	$+.070$
		$E(Y) = 0$			$E(Z) = .114$

The expected Y return is (as anticipated) less than the expected Z return.

These calculations can be done easily with a spreadsheet or a statistical package. List the possible values in one column, the corresponding probabilities in another column, multiply the corresponding values, and sum.

interpretations of $E(Y)$

The expected value (mean) of a random variable Y can be interpreted in several ways. First, it is simply a probability-weighted average, a summary figure that takes into account the relative probabilities of different values of Y. Second, it can be thought of as a **long-run average** of Y. For example, suppose that the firm of Example 4.3 could invest in a very large number of projects with the same return probabilities as Project Z. The average return per dollar invested would be .114 or 11.4%. (This fact follows because about 1 of 100 such projects would lose 20%, 4 of 100 would lose 10%, 10 of 100 would break even, 50 of 100 would earn 10%, and 35 of 100 would earn 20%.) Third, the expected value defines, in a certain sense,* the **fair value** of a gamble. Suppose that a casino gambling game pays $3 with probability 12/38 and nothing with probability 26/38. If we let $Y =$ the return on one play of the game, $E(Y) = 3(12/38) + 0(26/38) = 36/38$, or about .947. In a fair game, the casino ought to charge the player 36/38 of a dollar, or about 94.7 cents, to play. (Devotees of the American form of the game of roulette will recognize the nature of

long-run average

fair value

---

*This interpretation ignores the risk factor.

the game, the fact that the actual charge is $1, and the long-run effect of the 2/38 increment on casino profitability.) Fourth, the expected value is a balance point for a probability histogram. Think of probabilities as weights along a line. A fulcrum (like the pivot point on a child's seesaw) placed at the expected value will make these probabilities balance exactly. In particular, if the probabilities are exactly symmetric around a specific value, that value must be the expected value. And finally, the expected value of Y represents a generalization of the concept of a population mean μ. If Y is a discrete random variable corresponding to a value drawn at random from a discrete population of values, then $E(Y) = \mu$, the mean of the population.

EXAMPLE 4.4   Suppose that a population consists of the following values and associated frequencies:

$$
\begin{array}{lcccc}
\text{Value:} & 1000 & 2000 & 3000 & 4000 \\
\text{Frequency:} & 80 & 60 & 40 & 20 \\
(N = 200) & & & & \\
\end{array}
$$

The population mean is 2000. Let Y denote a single value drawn at random from the population. Find $P_Y(y)$ and $E(Y)$.

SOLUTION   The possible values and their probabilities are

$$
\begin{array}{lcccc}
y: & 1000 & 2000 & 3000 & 4000 \\
P_Y(y): & 80/200 = .4 & 60/200 = .3 & 40/200 = .2 & 20/200 = .1 \\
\end{array}
$$

The expected value is

$$
\begin{aligned}
E(Y) &= 1000(.4) + 2000(.3) + 3000(.2) + 4000(.1) \\
&= 400 + 600 + 600 + 400 = 2000
\end{aligned}
$$

$E(Y)$ is exactly equal to the population mean.

EXAMPLE 4.5   Another way to approximate an expected value is by computer simulation. We took the values and probabilities for the random variable Z of Example 4.3 and entered them into the Excel spreadsheet package. Using Excel's random number generator and LOOKUP function (with cumulative probabilities), we drew 1000 observations (which is a reasonably long run) from the Z distribution. We obtained the following results:

```
Z Value Frequency
   -0.2       11
   -0.1       44
      0       91
    0.1      501
    0.2      353

        ZValue
Mean                0.1141
Median                 0.1
Mode                   0.1
Standard Deviation  0.0837
Sample Variance   0.006998
```

How do the simulation approximations compare to the exact frequencies and expected value?

SOLUTION The frequencies in the simulation are very close to correct. For example, $Z = -.2$ occurred in $11/1000 = .011$ of the trials, compared to the correct .010. The mean of the 1000 trials should be, and is, very close to the expected value (long-run average), 0.114.

variance of a discrete random variable

We have discussed the different interpretations associated with the expected value of a discrete random variable. Equally important characteristics of a discrete random variable are the **variance** and standard deviation, which measure the probability dispersion or variability of a random variable. Recall from Chapter 2 that the variance of a set of data is the average squared deviation from the mean. Similarly, the variance of a random variable Y, $\text{Var}(Y)$, is the probability-weighted average of squared deviations from the mean (expected value).

DEFINITION 4.4

Variance and Standard Deviation: Discrete Random Variable If Y is a discrete random variable,

$$\sigma_Y^2 = \text{Var}(Y) = \sum_{\text{all } y} (y - \mu_Y)^2 \, P_Y(y), \qquad \text{where } \mu_Y = E(Y)$$

The standard deviation of Y, denoted σ_Y, is (as for other standard deviations) the positive square root of the variance:

$$\sigma_Y = \sqrt{\text{Var}(Y)}$$

To calculate $\text{Var}(Y)$, take each value y, subtract the expected value $\mu_Y = E(Y)$, square the result, multiply by the probability $P_Y(y)$, and sum.

EXAMPLE 4.6

Find the variance and standard deviation for Y and Z in Example 4.3.

SOLUTION In Example 4.3 we found $\mu_Y = E(Y) = 0$ and $\mu_Z = E(Z) = .114$. A worksheet shows the computations required.

y	$P_Y(y)$	$(y - \mu_Y)$	$(y - \mu_Y)^2$	$(y - \mu_Y)^2 P_Y(y)$
$-.20$	.1	$-.20$	.04	.004
$-.10$	.2	$-.10$	.01	.002
0	.4	0	0	0
.10	.2	.10	.01	.002
.20	.1	.20	.04	.004

$$\sigma_Y^2 = .012$$
$$\sigma_Y = \sqrt{.012} = .110$$

z	$P_Z(z)$	$(z - \mu_Z)$	$(z - \mu_Z)^2$	$(z - \mu_Z)^2 P_Z(z)$
$-.20$	.01	$-.314$	.098596	.00098596
$-.10$	.04	$-.214$	.045796	.00183184
0	.10	$-.114$	.012996	.00129960
.10	.50	$-.014$	.000196	.00009800
.20	.35	.086	.007396	.00258860

$$\sigma_Z^2 = .00680400$$
$$\sigma_Z = .082$$

The Y distribution has greater variability. The bulk of the Z distribution is concentrated on the larger values .10 and .20, whereas the Y probabilities are somewhat more spread out over all possible values. The variance for a return on investment is often taken as a measure of risk, with larger variances indicating greater risk. In this example, the Z investment has both a higher expected return and a lower risk.

Variance and standard deviation computations are easy with a spreadsheet or statistical package. List values and probabilities in two rows (or two columns), as we did to compute the expected value. Calculate a new row or column by subtracting the mean from each value and squaring the result. Multiply the values in the new row or column by the corresponding probabilities and sum to get the variance. Then take the square root to get the standard deviation. Using a feature such as Excel's "array" calculation (check the manual or help files) makes the computation even easier. The Excel output in Figure 4.6 shows the array formulas needed to calculate the expected value, variance, and standard deviation for Y = number of checkout lanes open at a supermarket at 8 P.M; the last part of the output is the result of the array calculations.

FIGURE 4.6

Expected Value, Variance, and Standard Deviation Calculations in Excel

	A	B	C	D	E	L
1	y	0	1	2	...	10
2	P(y)	0.1	0.15	0.25	...	0.015
3						
4	Exp. Value	=SUM(B1:L1*B2:L2)				
5	Variance	=SUM((B1:L1-B4)^2*B2:L2)				
6	Std. Dev.	=SQRT(B5)				
7						
8	Exp. Value	3.235				
9						
10	Variance	6.079				
11						
12	Std. Dev.	2.466				

The variance and standard deviation of a random variable can't be negative. They are 0 only if all the probability is concentrated at one value. The more the probability is spread out toward the extremes of the possible values, the larger the variance and standard deviation will be. This fact follows because the variance is a probability-weighted average of squared deviations. If the large squared deviations, corresponding to values at the extremes, have large probabilities, the variance and standard deviation will be large. The computation of a variance by hand can be clumsy, involving lots of many-digit numbers, as in Var(Z) in the previous example. Most statistical computer packages can be used to do the arithmetic, as can a spreadsheet. If you must do the computations by hand, there is a shortcut formula for variance computations that can be of help.

DEFINITION 4.5

Shortcut Method for Var(Y) If Y is a discrete random variable,

$$\text{Var}(Y) = \sum_{\text{all } y} y^2 P_Y(y) - \mu_Y^2, \qquad \text{where } \mu_Y = E(Y)$$

We square the original values, weight by $P_Y(y)$, and add. At the end of that computation, we subtract the square of the mean (expected value) to get the variance.

EXAMPLE 4.7   Use the shortcut formula to repeat the variance calculations of Example 4.6.

SOLUTION   For Y it is the same calculation, because $\mu_Y = E(Y) = 0$. It doesn't matter when we subtract 0, or even 0^2. For Z, with $\mu_Z = E(Z) = .114$, we have $\text{Var}(Z) = .0198 - (.114)^2 = .006804$, as in Example 4.6.

z	$P_Z(z)$	z^2	$z^2P_Z(z)$
$-.20$	.01	.04	.0004
$-.10$	.04	.01	.0004
0	.10	0	0
.10	.50	.01	.0050
.20	.35	.04	.0140
			.0198

EXAMPLE 4.8   Computer simulation can also be used to approximate the variance and standard deviation of a random variable. The Excel output of Example 4.5 yielded these results:

```
                    ZValue
Mean                0.1141
Median              0.1
Mode                0.1
Standard Deviation  0.0837
Sample Variance     0.006998
```

How closely does the simulation variance compare to the correct variance of Z, .006804?

SOLUTION   The variance is shown as .006998, only slightly larger than the correct value.

The Empirical Rule, introduced for samples and populations in Chapter 2, applies to random variables as well. It works less well when there are very few possible values for the random variable.

DEFINITION 4.6

> **Empirical Rule for Random Variables**   If the random variable Y has roughly a mound-shaped probability histogram,
>
> $$P(Y \text{ falls within one } \sigma_Y \text{ of its mean } \mu_Y) \approx .68$$
>
> and
>
> $$P(Y \text{ falls within two } \sigma_Y \text{ of its mean } \mu_Y) \approx .95$$

For the random variable Y of Examples 4.5 and 4.7, $E(Y) = 0$ and $\sigma_Y = .110$. The actual probabilities are

$$P(Y \text{ falls within } \sigma_Y \text{ of its mean}) = P(-.110 \leq Y \leq .110)$$
$$= P(Y = -.10) + P(Y = 0) + P(Y = .10)$$
$$= .80$$

and

$$P(Y \text{ falls within two } \sigma_Y \text{ of its mean}) = P(-.220 \leq Y \leq .220) = 1.00$$

The Empirical Rule approximation is mediocre in this case, in part because Y takes on a small number of values. Had the firm assessed subjective probabilities for returns of, say, $-.25, -.20, -.15, \ldots, +.15, +.20, +.25$, the Empirical Rule would most likely have been a somewhat better approximation, although the distribution might not be exactly mound shaped.

Just as the mean of a random variable is a generalization of the idea of a population mean, so the variance of a random variable Y is a generalization of a population variance. If Y is a random variable corresponding to a value drawn randomly from a population, $\sigma_Y^2 = $ the population variance.

We have defined the expected value, variance, and standard deviation for discrete random variables. The mathematical definitions of their counterparts for continuous random variables necessarily involve calculus. Again, those who know calculus may obtain these definitions by replacing sums by integrals.

Exercises

4.8   The product development laboratory of a paint manufacturer is asked to develop a modified paint for automobiles. The director of the laboratory estimates the following probabilities for the required development time (in months):

y:	2	3	4	5	6	7	8	9	10	11	12
$P_Y(y)$:	.20	.30	.15	.10	.08	.06	.04	.03	.02	.01	.01

a. Construct a probability histogram.
b. Calculate the expected value of Y.
c. Mark $E(Y)$ on the histogram. How does the shape of the histogram affect $E(Y)$?

4.9   Refer to Exercise 4.8.
a. Calculate the standard deviation of Y. Use the definition.
b. Use the shortcut method to calculate σ_Y.

4.10   Refer to Exercise 4.8. What is the actual probability that Y differs from μ_Y by less than 1 standard deviation? Why does this probability differ from the Empirical Rule estimate?

4.11   An investment syndicate is trying to decide which of two \$200,000 apartment houses to buy. An advisor estimates the following probabilities for the five-year net returns (in thousands of dollars):

Return:	-50	0	50	100	150	200	250
Probability for house 1:	.02	.03	.20	.50	.20	.03	.02
Probability for house 2:	.15	.10	.10	.10	.30	.20	.05

a. Calculate the expected net return for house 1 and for house 2.
b. Calculate the respective variances and standard deviations.

4.12   Refer to Exercise 4.11.
a. Is one investment better than the other in terms of both expected return and risk?
b. If you had a spare \$200,000 to invest, which investment would you prefer?

4.13   In Exercise 4.6 we considered the probability distribution

x:	0	1	2	3	4	5	6	7	8	9	10
$P_X(x)$:	.06	.14	.16	.14	.12	.10	.08	.07	.06	.04	.03

a. Find the mean of X.

b. Use the definition to calculate the variance of X.

c. Use the shortcut method to recalculate the variance of X.

4.14   Calculate the probability that X in Exercise 4.13 is within 2 standard deviations of its mean. How does this probability compare to the theoretical values given by the Empirical Rule?

4.15   The number of cars sold each day at a small used car lot (X) follows the following discrete probability distribution:

x	$P_X(x)$
0	.15
1	.40
2	.25
3	.15
4	.05

a. Compute the expected value and standard deviation of X and interpret their meanings.

b. Assume the profit per car is $500 and the fixed costs of running the business total $800 per day, that is, the daily profit when X cars are sold is $Y = 500X - 800$. Write the probability distribution of Y in tabular form.

c. Compute the expected daily profit and the standard deviation of the daily profit.

4.16   Bill is a 35-year-old male who has recently purchased a five-year, $100,000 term life policy. Assume that mortality tables show that there is a .012 probability for a randomly selected 35-year-old male to die within five years.

a. Which of the three methods for assessing probability (classical, relative frequency, or subjective) was used to obtain the .012 probability found in the mortality tables?

b. If Bill dies sometime in the next five years, the policy will pay $100,000 to his survivors; otherwise, the policy will pay nothing. Let X be the random variable representing the payoff from the policy at the end of the five-year period. Write the probability distribution of X in tabular form.

c. Compute the expected value of X.

d. Briefly interpret the expected value of X *from the insurance company's perspective*.

e. Compute the variance of X.

f. The insurance company charged Bill $200 more than the expected value for the policy. Assuming Bill is rational, why was he willing to pay more?

4.17   Hal recently accepted a sales position with International Business Machines (IBM) selling "big iron" (mainframe computers). He has to decide between taking a salary only or taking a smaller salary plus commissions on sales. As part of his decision-making process, he has collected historical data from previous years on the number of mainframe sales made by individual salespeople at IBM. Following is the probability distribution for $X =$ number of mainframes sold in one year by a single salesperson:

x	$P_X(x)$
0	.38
1	.30
2	.15
3	.10
4	.05
5	.02

a. Compute the expected number of mainframes that Hal will sell in one year.
b. Compute the standard deviation of X.
c. Under the "salary plus commission" option, Hal will receive a base salary of $30,000 and earn $20,000 in commission from each mainframe sale. Compute Hal's expected annual salary and the standard deviation in annual salary.
d. If he takes the "salary only" option, Hal will be paid $52,000 annually. Which of the two options would you recommend that he take? Explain your answer.

4.18   An office supply company currently holds 30% of the market for supplying suburban governments. This share has been quite stable and there is no reason to think it will change. The company has three bids outstanding, prepared by its standard procedure. Let Y be the number of the company's bids that are accepted.
a. Find the probability distribution of Y.
b. What assumptions did you make in answering part (a)? Are any of the assumptions clearly unreasonable?

4.19   Find the expected value and variance of Y in Exercise 4.18.

4.20   It could be argued that if the company in Exercise 4.18 loses on the first bid, that signals that a competitor is cutting prices and the company is more likely to lose the other bids also. Similarly, if the company wins on the first bid, that signals that competitors are trying to improve profit margins and the company is more likely to win the other bids also. If this argument is correct, and the two sides of the argument balance out to a 30% market share for the company, will the expected value of Y be increased or decreased compared to the value found in Exercise 4.19? Will the variance be increased or decreased? That is, will there be more variability in results, or less?

4.4   Joint Probability Distributions and Independence

We have developed some basic language for dealing with one random variable. In this section we extend that language to deal with joint probability distributions for two random variables, X and Y. We define everything in terms of discrete random variables. Those who are tolerably comfortable with calculus should be able to supply the analogues for continuous random variables.

joint probability

joint probability distribution

When we deal with two random variables, X and Y, it is convenient to work with joint probabilities. The **joint probability** of events A and B is the probability of both events, $P(A$ and $B)$. Let A be the event $X = x$, and B, the event $Y = y$. Define the **joint probability distribution,** $P_{XY}(x, y)$ to be a function that supplies the joint probability for each pair of values, x and y.

EXAMPLE 4.9

Suppose that, in the emergency room of a small hospital, the most serious cases involve coronary attack and trauma (injury by violence or severe accident). Define X = number of coronary cases and Y = number of trauma cases arriving on a particular weekday night. It is assumed that the joint probability distribution $P_{XY}(x, y)$ is given by

x	0	1	2	3
			y	
0	2/84	3/84	4/84	5/84
1	4/84	6/84	8/84	10/84
2	6/84	9/84	12/84	15/84

Interpret the value 10/84 shown in the table.

SOLUTION   The value 10/84 is the joint probability $P_{XY}(1, 3)$, that is, the probability of $X = 1$ coronary case *and* $Y = 3$ trauma cases on a weekday night. Other probabilities in the joint probability distribution table are interpreted in a similar way.

marginal probabilities

Once a joint probability distribution has been specified, **marginal probabilities** can be calculated by summation. In Chapter 3, when we dealt with joint probabilities like $P(A$ and $B)$, $P(A$ and not $B)$, and so on, the term *marginal probability* referred to the probability of one event alone, like $P(A)$. We calculated marginal probabilities by the additive law. Because this section is different only notationally from the basic principles of probability, the same principle can be used here.

EXAMPLE 4.10

Find the marginal probability distribution of X and the marginal probability distribution of Y in Example 4.9.

SOLUTION   Sum across rows to get X probabilities and down columns to get Y probabilities.

x	0	1	2	3	$P_X(x)$
			y		
0	2/84	3/84	4/84	5/84	14/84
1	4/84	6/84	8/84	10/84	28/84
2	6/84	9/84	12/84	15/84	42/84
$P_Y(y)$	12/84	18/84	24/84	30/84	

This idea can be expressed in a formula. To find the probability $P_X(x)$, add the joint probabilities of that x value and each possible y value:

$$P_X(x) = \sum_{\text{all } y} P_{XY}(x, y)$$

In this example

$$P(X = 1) = \sum_{\text{all } y} P_{XY}(1, y)$$
$$= P_{XY}(1, 0) + P_{XY}(1, 1) + P_{XY}(1, 2) + P_{XY}(1, 3)$$
$$= \frac{4}{84} + \frac{6}{84} + \frac{8}{84} + \frac{10}{84} = \frac{28}{84}$$

In the same way, the marginal probabilities for Y can be computed as

$$P_Y(y) = \sum_{\text{all } x} P_{XY}(x, y)$$

In this example

$$P(Y = 1) = \sum_{\text{all } x} P_{XY}(x, 1)$$

$$= P_{XY}(0, 1) + P_{XY}(1, 1) + P_{XY}(2, 1)$$

$$= \frac{3}{84} + \frac{6}{84} + \frac{9}{84} = \frac{18}{84}$$

The idea is simply a translation of the addition principle.*

A spreadsheet program can do these calculations very easily. For example, suppose that an automobile loan company, as part of its credit scoring system, collects information on $X =$ number of mortgages held and $Y =$ number of unpaid credit card balances outstanding for a randomly chosen applicant. The Excel output in Figure 4.7 shows how to calculate marginal probabilities and the result.

FIGURE 4.7 **Excel Calculation of Marginal Probabilities**

	A	B	C	D	E	F	G
1	Joint Probabilities				y		
2			0	1	2	3	
3		0	0.06	0.11	0.16	0.03	=SUM(C3:F3)
4	x	1	0.13	0.24	0.09	0.02	=SUM(C4:F4)
5		2	0.08	0.04	0.03	0.01	=SUM(C5:F5)
6			=SUM(C3:C5)	=SUM(D3:D5)	=SUM(E3:E5)	=SUM(F3:F5)	=SUM(C3:F5)

	A	B	C	D	E	F	G
1	Joint Probabilities			y			
2			0	1	2	3	
3		0	0.06	0.11	0.16	0.03	0.36
4	x	1	0.13	0.24	0.09	0.02	0.48
5		2	0.08	0.04	0.03	0.01	0.16
6			0.27	0.39	0.28	0.06	1.00

The "=SUM" formulas calculate the marginal probabilities immediately.

We can extend basic probability notation to conditional probabilities. Just as we defined the conditional probability of B given A as

$$P(B|A) = \frac{P(A \cap B)}{P(A)}$$

conditional distribution   we can define the **conditional distribution** of Y given $X = x$ as

$$P_{Y|X}(y|x)$$

---

*Now we can explain why we use the apparently redundant notation $P_X(x)$, $P_Y(y)$. If we merely wrote $P(x)$ or $P(y)$, we would not know whether $P(1)$ meant $P(X = 1) = P_X(1)$ or $P(Y = 1) = P_Y(1)$.

Thus for any value of Y,

$$P(Y = y | X = x) = \frac{P(X = x \cap Y = y)}{P(X = x)}$$

$$= \frac{P_{XY}(x, y)}{P_X(x)}$$

The need for this notation arises from the idea of independence. Remember that we had two equivalent definitions of independence for events A and B:

$$P(B|A) = P(B)$$
$$P(A \cap B) = P(A)P(B)$$

equivalent definitions of statistical independence

We also have two **equivalent definitions of statistical independence** for random variables X and Y:

$$P_{Y|X}(y|x) = P_Y(y), \qquad \text{for all } x, y$$
$$P_{XY}(x, y) = P_X(x)P_Y(y), \qquad \text{for all } x, y$$

We usually use the second form of the independence definition in this text.

EXAMPLE 4.11   Show that X and Y of Examples 4.9 and 4.10 are independent.

SOLUTION   In Example 4.10 we found $P_X(x)$ and $P_Y(y)$. When we multiply the appropriate $P_X(x)$ and $P_Y(y)$, we get the following table

			y		
x	0	1	2	3	$P_X(x)$
0	(12/84)(14/84)	(18/84)(14/84)	(24/84)(14/84)	(30/84)(14/84)	14/84
1	(12/84)(28/84)	(18/84)(28/84)	(24/84)(28/84)	(30/84)(28/84)	28/84
2	(12/84)(42/84)	(18/84)(42/84)	(24/84)(42/84)	(30/84)(42/84)	42/84
$P_X(x)$	12/84	18/84	24/84	30/84	

When we reduce the fractions in this table, we find that every table entry equals the $P_{XY}(x, y)$ entry in Example 4.9. Therefore, $P_{XY}(x, y) = P_X(x)P_Y(y)$ for all x and y; that is, X and Y are independent.

The assumption of independence was built into the mathematical form of this particular $P_{XY}(x, y)$. In practice, we often assume that X and Y are independent; once we specify $P_X(x)$ and $P_Y(y)$, this assumption lets us calculate $P_{XY}(x, y)$ as the product $P_X(x)P_Y(y)$. Example 4.9 is one situation in which the independence assumption seems reasonable. The number of coronary cases arriving at an emergency room should have no relevance to predictions of the number of trauma cases.

Exercises

4.21   A manufacturer of television sets sells two principal models. Define X = sales of model A next December (nearest 100,000) and Y = sales of model B next December. The marketing staff estimates that the joint probabilities $P_{XY}(x, y)$ are

		y		
x	1	2	3	4
1	.030	.055	.070	.075
2	.055	.070	.075	.070
3	.070	.075	.070	.055
4	.075	.070	.055	.030

a. Find $P(X = 1, Y = 2)$.
b. Find $P(X \le 2, Y \le 2)$.
c. Find $P_X(x)$ and $P_Y(y)$.
d. Are X and Y independent?

4.22   The owner of a small sound-system store determines the following probabilities for X = number of amplifiers sold during a weekday and for Y = number of speaker systems sold during the same day:

x:	0	1	2	3	4	
$P_X(x)$:	.10	.40	.25	.20	.05	

y:	0	1	2	3	4	5
$P_Y(y)$:	.10	.30	.25	.20	.10	.05

a. Assuming that X and Y are independent, calculate the joint probability distribution $P_{XY}(x, y)$.
b. Check your work by finding the marginal probabilities $P_X(x)$ and $P_Y(y)$.

4.23   Do you believe that independence is a reasonable assumption for Exercise 4.22? Should it be true that the sales of amplifiers will be irrelevant to the sales of speakers?

4.24   A small management consulting firm presents both written and oral proposals in an effort to get new consulting contracts. Records indicate that the probability distribution $P_{XY}(x, y)$ of X = number of oral proposals in a week and Y = number of written proposals in that week is given by the following table:

			y		
x	0	1	2	3	4
0	.010	.015	.030	.075	.050
1	.020	.030	.045	.060	.040
2	.030	.045	.100	.045	.030
3	.040	.060	.045	.030	.020
4	.050	.075	.030	.015	.010

a. Find the probability that there are two oral proposals and two written proposals in a particular week.
b. Find the probability that there are exactly two oral proposals and two or fewer written proposals in a particular week.
c. Find the probability that there are two or fewer oral proposals and two or fewer written proposals in a particular week.

4.25   Refer to Exercise 4.24.
a. Use the probability distribution to calculate the marginal probability distributions of X and of Y.
b. Assuming these probabilities, are X and Y independent?

4.26   Calculate the conditional distribution of Y given each possible value of X using the probability distribution of Exercise 4.24. Do these conditional probability distributions indicate that X and Y are independent?

4.5 Covariance and Correlation of Random Variables

In the previous section, we defined the *independence* of two random variables. Now we consider how to measure the degree of *dependence* between two random variables. There are many measures of dependence that one might use. Two measures, covariance and correlation, are particularly important because they are closely related to the concept of variance of a random variable. Correlation, in particular, is a way to measure how closely two random quantities vary together.

Again we begin with an example. A trust officer of a bank assumes the following (subjective) joint probabilities for the percentage return (interest plus change in market value) of two utility bonds. The returns are labeled X and Y.

			y			
x	8	9	10	11	12	$P_X(x)$
8	.03	.04	.03	.00	.00	.10
9	.04	.06	.06	.04	.00	.20
10	.02	.08	.20	.08	.02	.40
11	.00	.04	.06	.06	.04	.20
12	.00	.00	.03	.04	.03	.10
$P_Y(y)$	.09	.22	.38	.22	.09	1.00

There is a relation between X and Y. For example, given $x = 8$, the Y probabilities are concentrated on the smaller values $y = 8, 9$, and 10. At the other extreme, given $x = 12$, the Y probabilities are concentrated on the larger values $y = 10, 11$, and 12. In general, there is a tendency for the X and Y outcomes to vary together. The covariance and correlation of two random variables measure the *strength* of that tendency.

The covariance of two random variables is based on products of deviations from means, weighted by joint probabilities. If a particular x value is below μ_X and a y value is below μ_Y, both deviations will be negative numbers and their product will be positive. Similarly, if both values are above their expected values, both deviations will be positive and their product will be positive. Negative products result for one value above its mean and the other below its mean. If most of the probability is associated with (low, low) and (high, high) pairs of (x, y) values, as in the bond-return example, then most of the weight will go to positive products and the covariance will be positive. If most of the probability is associated with (low, high) and (high, low) values, the covariance will be negative.

DEFINITION 4.7

Covariance of Random Variables X and Y   If X and Y are discrete random variables with respective expected values μ_X and μ_Y, and with joint probability distribution $P_{XY}(x, y)$, the **covariance** of X and Y, denoted by Cov(X, Y) is defined as

$$\text{Cov}(X, Y) = \sum_x \sum_y (x - \mu_X)(y - \mu_Y)P_{XY}(x, y)$$

A shortcut method for computing the covariance is

$$\text{Cov}(X, Y) = \left[\sum_x \sum_y xy P_{XY}(x, y) \right] - \mu_X \mu_Y$$

EXAMPLE 4.12   Compute Cov(X, Y) for the joint distribution of bond yields given in the preceding discussion. Use the definition first and check to see that the shortcut method gives the same answer.

SOLUTION From the marginal probabilities $P_X(x)$ and $P_Y(y)$, we get the expected values:

$$\mu_X = 8(.10) + 9(.20) + 10(.40) + 11(.20) + 12(.10) = 10$$
$$\mu_Y = 8(.09) + 9(.22) + 10(.38) + 11(.22) + 12(.09) = 10$$

In fact, we could have noted that the marginal probability distribution for X is symmetric around 10, so μ_X must equal 10; the same holds for μ_Y.

The covariance can be computed using the definition as follows:

$$\begin{aligned}
\text{Cov}(X, Y) &= \sum_x \sum_y (x - \mu_X)(y - \mu_Y)\, P_{XY}(x, y) \\
&= (8 - 10)(8 - 10)(.03) + (8 - 10)(9 - 10)(.04) \\
&\quad + (8 - 10)(10 - 10)(.03) + \cdots + (12 - 10)(12 - 10)(.03) \\
&= .60
\end{aligned}$$

Similarly, using the shortcut method,

$$\begin{aligned}
\text{Cov}(X, Y) &= \sum \sum xy P_{XY}(x, y) - \mu_X \mu_Y \\
&= 8(8)(.03) + 8(9)(.04) + 8(10)(.03) + \cdots + 12(12)(.03) - 10(10) \\
&= 100.60 - 100 = .60
\end{aligned}$$

A spreadsheet program will do the computations readily. In the Excel output of Figure 4.8, the bottom table contains computed values of $(x - \mu_X)(y - \mu_Y)$ $P_{XY}(x, y)$ for each (x, y) combination. The total of these values, shown at the bottom right of the output, is the covariance.

Note that most of the terms in the bottom table are positive numbers in this example. Also, the positive numbers are larger in magnitude than the negative numbers, because of the relatively high probability in the "northwest" and "southeast" parts of the table. That's why the covariance comes out positive in this case.

FIGURE 4.8   **Excel Calculation of Covariance in Example 4.12**

	A	B	C	D	E	F	G	H	I
1	Joint Probabilities				y				
2			8	9	10	11	12	Total	
3		8	0.03	0.04	0.03	0.00	0.00	0.10	
4		9	0.04	0.06	0.06	0.04	0.00	0.20	
5	x	10	0.02	0.08	0.20	0.08	0.02	0.40	
6		11	0.00	0.04	0.06	0.06	0.04	0.20	
7		12	0.00	0.00	0.03	0.04	0.03	0.10	
8	Total		0.09	0.22	0.38	0.22	0.09	1.00	
9									
10	(x-10)*(y-10)*P(x,y)								
11			0.12	0.08	0.00	0.00	0.00		
12			0.08	0.06	0.00	-0.04	0.00		
13			0.00	0.00	0.00	0.00	0.00		
14			0.00	-0.04	0.00	0.06	0.08		
15			0.00	0.00	0.00	0.08	0.12		
16								0.60	cov(X,Y)

The covariance of two random variables is closely related to their correlation.

DEFINITION 4.8

Correlation of Random Variables X and Y   If X and Y are discrete random variables with respective standard deviations σ_X and σ_Y, their correlation ρ_{XY} is defined as

$$\rho_{XY} = \frac{\text{Cov}(X, Y)}{\sigma_X \sigma_Y}$$

It follows that

$$\text{Cov}(X, Y) = \rho_{XY}\sigma_X\sigma_Y$$

The correlation between X and Y ranges between -1.00 and $+1.00$. A value of -1.00 or $+1.00$ indicates perfect *linear* prediction in the population, whereas a value of 0 indicates no linear predictive value.

EXAMPLE 4.13

Find ρ_{XY} for the bond-yield distribution discussed earlier in this section.

SOLUTION   In Example 4.12 we found $\text{Cov}(X, Y) = .60$. To get ρ_{XY} we need the standard deviations of X and Y, which can be computed from the respective marginal probabilities. The shortcut formula for a variance can be used to compute σ_X^2 and σ_Y^2.

$$\sigma_X^2 = \sum_x x^2 P_X(x) - \mu_X^2$$

$$= 8^2(.10) + 9^2(.20) + 10^2(.40) + 11^2(.20) + 12^2(.10) - (10)^2$$

$$= 101.20 - 100 = 1.20$$

and hence $\sigma_X = \sqrt{1.20} = 1.095$. Similarly, we have

$$\sigma_Y^2 = \sum_Y y^2 P_Y(y) - \mu_Y^2 = 1.16$$

and $\sigma_Y = \sqrt{1.16} = 1.077$.

Substituting into the definition for ρ_{XY}, we find

$$\rho_{XY} = \frac{\text{Cov}(X, Y)}{\sigma_X \sigma_Y} = \frac{.60}{1.095(1.077)} = .509$$

EXAMPLE 4.14

Covariance and correlation may also be approximated by computer simulation. We used Excel's random number generation and LOOKUP function (in a cumulative probability list) to draw 1000 pairs of x and y values in the previous example. Then Excel's built-in covariance and correlation functions were applied to these simulated values, with the following results:

```
Variances,Covariance      X          Y
            X           1.2208
            Y           0.5877    1.0974

        Correlations        X          Y
            X                      1
            Y           0.5060              1
```

How closely do the covariance and correlation compare to the exact values, .600 and .509, respectively?

SOLUTION The covariance is shown as .5877 and the correlation as .5060, both slightly less than the correct values. Presumably, if we had taken some enormous number of pairs, the simulation values would be very close to the correct ones; even with 1000 pairs, the values are close enough for most purposes.

Covariance and correlation are immensely important ideas in managing portfolios of investments. The main reason why someone invests in a portfolio of several different assets is to reduce risk. Suppose that the returns to two assets are strongly negatively correlated. If one return happens to come out low, the other will tend to come out high, thus reducing the overall risk of variability in returns. On the other hand, suppose that the returns are highly positively correlated. Then if one return happens to be low, the other will also tend to be low; investing in such a portfolio won't reduce the risk much. Mathematically, risk can be measured by variance. If we denote the returns on two investments as R_1 and R_2,

$$\text{Var}(R_1 + R_2) = \text{Var}(R_1) + \text{Var}(R_2) + 2\,\text{Cov}(R_1, R_2)$$

This follows from the algebraic fact that $(a + b)^2 = a^2 + b^2 + 2ab$. The risk (variance) of the total return depends not only on the risk of each return separately but also on the covariance between them. All else being equal, if the correlation between the returns is low or, even better, negative, the covariance will also be low or negative and the variance of the total return will be relatively low. This idea is elaborated in most finance books.

If the random variables X and Y are independent, there should be no relation (linear or otherwise) between them. Reasonably enough, when X and Y are independent, $\text{Cov}(X, Y) = 0$ and therefore $\rho_{XY} = 0$ also.

EXAMPLE 4.15   An assembly line can be stopped temporarily to adjust for either bad parts alignment or bad welds. Production records indicate the following joint distribution for $X =$ number of stops for bad alignment in a production shift and $Y =$ number of stops for bad welds in a production shift.

			y			
x	0	1	2	3	4	$P_X(x)$
0	.03	.06	.12	.06	.03	.30
1	.04	.08	.16	.08	.04	.40
2	.03	.06	.12	.06	.03	.30
$P_Y(y)$	.10	.20	.40	.20	.10	1.00

a. What should $\text{Cov}(X, Y)$ equal for these probabilities?

b. Verify your answer numerically.

SOLUTION

a. In every case $P_{XY}(x, y) = P_X(x)P_Y(y)$. For example, $P_{XY}(2, 4) = .03$ and $P_X(2) \times P_Y(4) = (.30)(.10) = .03$ also. Therefore, X and Y are independent and $\text{Cov}(X, Y)$ should equal zero.

b. By the symmetry of the marginal probabilities for X and for Y, it follows that $\mu_X = 1$ and $\mu_Y = 2$. So

$$\text{Cov}(X, Y) = [0(0)(.03) + 0(1)(.06) + \cdots + 2(4)(.03)] - 1(2)$$
$$= 2.00 - 2 = 0$$

as it should be.

It is mathematically possible to have $\text{Cov}(X, Y) = 0$ even though X and Y are dependent. The reason is that covariance and correlation measure only the strength of *linear* relation. If there is a relation between X and Y but that relation cannot be approximated by a linear relation, the covariance can be zero.

EXAMPLE 4.16   Suppose that in Example 4.15 the following probabilities are obtained:

			y			
x	0	1	2	3	4	$P_X(x)$
0	.03	.06	.12	.06	.03	.30
1	.04	.08	.16	.08	.04	.40
2	.03	.06	.12	.06	.03	.30
$P_Y(y)$	.10	.20	.40	.20	.10	1.00

Are X and Y independent? What is the covariance between X and Y?

SOLUTION   No, there is dependence. For example, $P_{XY}(0, 0) = .01$, but $P_X(0)P_Y(0) = (.10)(.30) = .03$. However,

$$\text{Cov}(X, Y) = [0(0)(.01) + 0(1)(.05) + \cdots + 2(4)(.06)] - 1(2)$$
$$= 2.00 - 2 = 0$$

(Note that $\mu_X = 1$ and $\mu_Y = 2$, as in Example 4.15.) The reason that the covariance is 0 is that there is no linear relation. Note that when y is either 0 or 4, the most likely x value is 2; when y is either 1 or 3, the most likely x value is 1; and when y is 2, the most likely x value is 2. Computation of expected X values given each value y also shows a completely nonlinear pattern. Given $y = 0$, the probabilities for $x = 0, 1, 2$ are $1/10$, $3/10$, $6/10$, respectively, so the expected value of X given $Y = 0$ is $0(1/10) + 1(3/10) + 2(6/10) = 1.5$. Similar computations yield the following table.

y:	0	1	2	3	4
$E(X|Y = y)$:	1.50	1.00	0.75	1.00	1.50

As y increases from 0 to 2, the expected value of X given $Y = y$ decreases; but then, as y increases from 2 to 4, the expected value of X given $Y = y$ increases right back. There is no straight-line relation at all.

Exercises

4.27 In Exercise 4.24 we considered the following joint distribution $P_{XY}(x, y)$ of X = number of oral proposals in a week and Y = number of written proposals in that week as given by the following table:

			y			
x	0	1	2	3	4	$P_X(x)$
0	.010	.015	.030	.075	.050	.180
1	.020	.030	.045	.060	.040	.195
2	.030	.045	.100	.045	.030	.250
3	.040	.060	.045	.030	.020	.195
4	.050	.075	.030	.015	.010	.180
$P_Y(y)$	.150	.225	.250	.225	.150	1.000

a. What are the means of X and Y? (Think, don't calculate.)
b. Calculate the standard deviations of X and Y.

4.28 Refer to Exercise 4.27.
a. Find the covariance of X and Y.
b. Find the correlation of X and Y. What does it indicate about the relation between X and Y? In particular, could X and Y be independent?

4.29 Find the conditional expectation of Y, given $X = 0$, for the probability distribution of Exercise 4.27. That is, calculate conditional probabilities given $X = 0$ and use these probabilities to calculate an expected value. Do the same for other x values. Does the conditional expectation change with x?

4.30 Define $T = X + Y$ to be the total number of proposals made by the firm in Exercises 4.24 and 4.27 in a particular week.
a. Calculate the probability distribution of T, using the probability table.
b. Calculate the expected value and variance of T directly from this probability distribution.
c. Use the facts that $E(X + Y) = E(X) + E(Y)$ and $\text{Var}(X + Y) = \text{Var}(X) + \text{Var}(Y) + 2\,\text{Cov}(X, Y)$ to recalculate the mean and variance of T.

4.31 A quality issue concerns a manufacturing process in which holes are drilled in blocks. The probability that a hole is defectively drilled is .10. Let X = number of defects in a sample of two blocks (there is only one hole per block).
a. Find the probability distribution of X. You may wish to draw a tree.
b. Find the expected value and variance of X.
c. What have you assumed in answering parts (a) and (b)? Under what conditions might the assumption be unreasonable?

4.32 Assume that an inspector in the process of the previous exercise fails to detect a defect with probability .10; im-

plicitly, we assume that the inspector does not "detect" defects when in fact there are none. Let Y = number of detected defects. Use a probability tree to derive the joint distribution of X (from Exercise 4.31) and Y. Note that Y cannot be larger than X.

4.33 Refer to Exercise 4.32.
a. Find the mean and standard deviation of Y.
b. Use the joint distribution of X and Y to find the correlation of X and Y.
c. Explain why the correlation should naturally be positive. Remember, X is the actual number of defects and Y is the detected number of defects in the same, randomly chosen, item.

4.34 Earlier in this section we considered the joint probability distribution for the annual percentage returns (interest plus change in market value), X and Y, of two utility bonds. The joint and marginal distributions are repeated here. Assume that an investor has a fixed amount of money to be invested during the coming year.

			y			
x	8	9	10	11	12	$P_X(x)$
8	.03	.04	.03	.00	.00	.10
9	.04	.06	.06	.04	.00	.20
10	.02	.08	.20	.08	.02	.40
11	.00	.04	.06	.06	.04	.20
12	.00	.00	.03	.04	.03	.10
$P_Y(y)$	.09	.22	.38	.22	.09	1.00

a. Compute the expected value and standard deviation of the percentage return earned by the investor if she puts all of her money into the first utility bond (whose return is denoted by X).
b. Compute the expected value and standard deviation of the percentage return earned by the investor if she puts all of her money into the second utility bond (whose return is denoted by Y).
c. Compute the expected value and standard deviation of the percentage return earned by the investor if she puts half of her money into each of the two utility bonds.
d. Which of these three strategies would you recommend? Explain your answer.
e. Suppose that information was available that could correctly predict in advance which of the two utility bonds would have the higher percentage return over the course of the coming year. Compute the expected value and standard deviation of the percentage return given this information.

BUSINESS DECISION-MAKING IN ACTION

CHAPTER CASE

ANALYSIS

Baldwin Computer Sales

In the computer purchase program Baldwin Computer Sales began five years ago at several universities on the advice of a marketing strategist, students could purchase a computer system and make small payments while still in school. After leaving school and finding a job, their payments were increased so that the computer would be paid for within two years. The promotion has been profitable in most cases, but many students default on their payments and Baldwin loses money.

In the Baldwin Computer Sales case, the random variable of interest is the profit or loss realized from the sale of a computer to a single student. We are told that for each student who defaults, the loss to Baldwin is $1200, and the profit is $750 from each student who pays his or her account in full. Among the 342 students who have participated in the program, there are 137 students who defaulted and 205 who paid in full. If we define X to be the profit (loss) from any one student, the estimated probability distribution for X is

x	$P_X(x)$
-1200	$137/342 = 0.4006$
750	$205/342 = 0.5994$

Although the amount for a loss is larger in magnitude than the amount for a profit, there is a higher probability of a profit than a loss, but is it enough to break even "in the long run"?

The probability distribution shows that approximately 60% of the former participants in the program eventually paid in full, and the other 40% defaulted at some point on their payments, resulting in a loss for Baldwin. Since the profit for accounts paid in full is $750 and the loss on accounts in default is $1200, the expected profit per student in the program, $E(X)$, is

$$E(X) = \sum x \cdot P_X(x) = 750(.5994) + (-1200)(.4006) = -\$31.17$$

that is, an average *loss* of $31.17 per student in the program. Although this may suggest discontinuing the program, we might argue that it could be worth the cost because of the future business that might be generated from students who are satisfied with their first computer system from Baldwin and make later purchases.

Your assistant has developed a screening test for being more selective in who is allowed to participate in the purchase program. The value of the test, based on student background information, is reported as the variable Score for each of the 342 students in the data set. Box plots of Score for those who defaulted and those who paid in full are shown in Figure 4.9.

The difference in the distribution of screening test scores of the "defaulters" and "payers" suggests that the test may be useful in screening out high-risk students. For example, suppose we consider that 70 is the minimum score for eligibility. An indicator variable can be created in Minitab with a value of 1 for applicants who score at least 70 and a value of 0 otherwise. The cross-tabulation of this new variable, SCORE>=70, with DEFAULT is shown on the next page.

FIGURE 4.9   **Box Plots of Score by Outcome for the Baldwin Data**

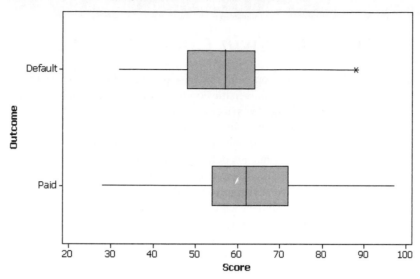

```
MTB > let 'SCORE>=70' = ('SCORE' >= 70)

MTB > table 'DEFAULT' by 'SCORE>=70';
SUBC> counts;
SUBC> colpercents.

 ROWS: DEFAULT      COLUMNS: SCORE>=70
             0         1      ALL
    0      142        63      205
           55.47     73.26    59.94

    1      114        23      137
           44.53     26.74    40.06

  ALL      256        86      342
          100.00    100.00   100.00

 CELL CONTENTS --
                  COUNT
                  % OF COL
```

From the table, we see that the conditional probability of defaulting given that an applicant scored at least 70 on the screening test is .2674 as compared to the unconditional default probability of .4006. If we allow only students scoring at least 70 to participate in the program, then the expected profit becomes

$$E(X|\text{Score} \geq 70) = 750(.7326) + (-1200)(.2674) = \$228.57$$

that is, an average profit of \$228.57 per student. By varying the minimum required screening test score, we can determine the score that will result in the highest expected profit per student. Figure 4.10 is an Excel worksheet summarizing quantities of interest for various choices of the minimum screening test score.

The variable MINSCORE is the arbitrarily chosen minimum required score on the screening test to qualify for the program. The variables N_PASS, N_DEFAULT, and N_PAID give the number of applicants who passed the test at the MINSCORE level, the number of those who eventually default, and the number who eventually paid their account in full, respectively. EXP_PROFIT is the expected profit for the given value of MINSCORE based on the assumption of \$750 profit from those who pay in full and \$1200 in losses from those who default. Note that the expected profit generally increases as MINSCORE increases, up to the maximum value of \$750. Of

FIGURE 4.10   **Calculation of Total Profit by Minimum Test Score for the Baldwin Data**

	A	B	C	D	E	F
1	MINSCORE	N_PASS	N_DEFAULT	N_PAID	EXP_PROFIT	TOT_PROFIT
2	5	342	137	205	-31.14	-10650
3	10	342	137	205	-31.14	-10650
4	15	342	137	205	-31.14	-10650
5	20	342	137	205	-31.14	-10650
6	25	342	137	205	-31.14	-10650
7	30	341	137	204	-33.43	-11400
8	35	340	136	204	-30.00	-10200
9	40	324	122	202	15.74	5100
10	45	311	112	199	47.75	14850
11	50	274	92	182	95.26	26100
12	55	229	76	153	102.84	23550
13	60	177	58	119	111.02	19650
14	65	126	33	93	239.29	30150
15	70	86	23	63	228.49	19650
16	75	58	12	46	346.55	20100
17	80	23	5	18	326.09	7500
18	85	10	1	9	555.00	5550
19	90	2	0	2	750.00	1500
20	95	1	0	1	750.00	750

course, at this level of MINSCORE, very few people are allowed to participate in the program and these people are highly unlikely to default. However, Baldwin is more concerned with the total profit, shown in the column labeled TOT_PROFIT. The total profit starts at a $10,650 loss, the amount the company actually lost on the 342 students in this data set, because every applicant is passing the test at these lowest minimum values. The profit begins increasing as MINSCORE increases, to a maximum of $30,150, and then decreases due to fewer people passing the test and participating in the program at the higher levels of MINSCORE. A finer grid of MINSCORE values can be generated to produce a plot of TOT_PROFIT versus MINSCORE as shown in Figure 4.11.

From the plot, it appears that setting the minimum required score on the screening test to some value between 50 and 70 will produce the desired results. (Realize that the TOT_PROFIT figures are based on sample data and hence subject to random

FIGURE 4.11   **Scatterplot of Total Profit by Minimum Test Score for the Baldwin Data**

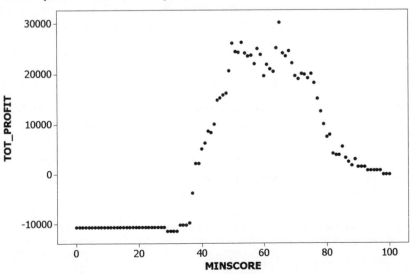

fluctuation, that is, setting the cutoff at 65 does not guarantee $30,150 in profit.) As more data are collected over time, this analysis should be updated and the minimum required score adjusted on the basis of the updated results.

SUMMARY

Here are some suggestions for dealing with random variables and probability distributions. The ideas in this chapter combine the probability ideas from Chapter 3 and the data summarization ideas from Chapter 2.

1. Decide whether the random variables are discrete—with distinct, separate possible values—or continuous—with an entire interval or range of possible values. Discrete random variables require addition in expected value and standard deviation calculations; continuous random variables require integration.

2. A random variable is determined by its possible values and their associated probabilities. Probabilities may be specified directly or calculated using the methods of Chapter 3.

3. The cumulative distribution function (cdf) is convenient for tables and is often used in software packages. Probabilities can be found from cdf's by subtraction (in both discrete and continuous cases).

4. The expected value of a random variable is a generalization of the concept of a mean. It is found by weighting each value by its probability (or probability density) and summing (or integrating) over all possible values.

5. The variance and standard deviation of a random variable are also generalizations of concepts from Chapter 2 and also require the same weighting by probabilities.

6. Joint probabilities may be defined for two (or more) random variables. Marginal probabilities may be found for each variable separately by summing (or integrating) over the values of the other variable or variables.

7. Covariance and correlation measure the extent to which random variables tend to vary together. They only reflect the degree of linear relation; if the relation is nonlinear, they understate the closeness of the relationship.

8. Covariances enter the calculation of risk (variance) of a portfolio of investments and consideration of the trade-off of risk and return (expected profit). The smaller the correlation between investments, the more benefit there is in reducing risk.

In addition, you may want to reread the summary of key ideas in the Executive Overview at the beginning of this chapter.

Supplementary Exercises

4.35 A new-car dealer offers three packages of optional equipment for a particular model. There is an automatic transmission package, with a profit of $200 to the dealer, an air-conditioning package, with a profit of $150, and an interior decor package, with a profit of $100. Data indicate that 80% of customers order the automatic transmission package; 60% of these and 50% of those who don't order automatic transmissions also order the air-conditioning package. Of those who order both of these packages, 40% order the interior decor package, as do 30% of those who order exactly one of the transmission and air-conditioning packages and 20% of those who order neither of the other packages. Let Y = the number of packages ordered on a randomly chosen new car.

a. Find the probability distribution of Y.

b. Find $P(Y \geq 2)$.

c. Find the cumulative distribution function of Y; use it to recalculate $P(Y \geq 2)$.

4.36 Find the mean and standard deviation of Y in Exercise 4.35.

4.37 Let X = the profit from sales of optional packages for the dealer in Exercise 4.35. Note that X is not directly a function of Y, because the profit depends not only on how many but also on which packages are sold.

a. Find the probability distribution of X.

b. Find the mean and standard deviation of X.

4.38 The sales force of a small firm consists of four field engineers (three of whom are over 40 years old) and six sales representatives (two of whom are over 40 years old). One field engineer and two sales representatives are chosen, supposedly at random, to receive special training.

a. Construct outcomes for this experiment. Number the field engineers $1, \ldots, 4$ and the sales representatives $5, \ldots, 10$.

b. Let Y = number of persons selected who are over 40 years old. Find $P_Y(y)$ and $F_Y(y)$ by counting.

4.39 In Exercise 4.38 find $E(Y)$ and σ_X.

4.40 A state public health agency investigates reported unhealthful practices in restaurants, food stores, and the like. The number of cases varies week to week. The data indicate the following:

Number of cases/week:	0	1	2	3	4	5	6
Probability:	.02	.13	.20	.30	.19	.15	.01

a. For Y = number of cases in a specified week, find $F_Y(y)$.

b. Find $E(Y)$ and σ_Y.

c. Find $P(\mu_Y - \sigma_Y \leq Y \leq \mu_Y + \sigma_Y)$. Compare to the Empirical Rule approximation.

4.41 The records of a small autobody repair shop indicate the following relative frequencies for the number of customers per day:

Number of customers:	0	1	2	3	4	5	6
Relative frequency:	.21	.38	.20	.11	.06	.03	.01

Let Y = number of customers on one particular day.

a. Calculate $F_Y(y)$.

b. Find $E(Y)$ and σ_Y.

4.42 Assume that the numbers of customers on successive days in Exercise 4.41 are independent. Let Y_1 and Y_2 be the respective numbers of customers on two consecutive days.

a. Construct a table for $P_{Y_1 Y_2}(y_1, y_2)$.

b. Define $S = Y_1 + Y_2$, the two-day total number of customers. Find $P_S(s)$.

c. Calculate $E(S)$ and σ_S.

4.43 Two radar stations are positioned at a country's eastern border to detect incoming attacks from enemy aircraft. Each of these radar stations has a .90 probability of detecting an enemy aircraft attack. Let X be the number of radar stations detecting an attack.

a. Construct the probability distribution of X in tabular form. What assumption did you have to make in order to answer this question? (Use this same assumption in all of the following questions.)

b. What is the probability that an attack is detected by *both* radar stations?

c. What is the probability that the attack is detected by *at least one* of the two radar stations?

d. The enemy has recently developed a new stealth aircraft that is detected by a radar station with only .50 probability. What is the minimum number of radar stations needed so that the probability of at least one radar station detecting an attack from the stealth aircraft is greater than .95? Use trial and error, if necessary, but show your work. (*Hint:* What is the complement of "at least one"?)

4.44 A roulette wheel has 38 slots. Each slot has a number and a color associated with it. The numbers are 0, 00, and 1–36; the colors are red, black, and green. 0 and 00 are the only green. To make things easy, assume that the even numbers $(2, 4, 6, \ldots, 36)$ are red and the odd numbers $(1, 3, 5, \ldots, 35)$ are black.

a. Suppose that you place a $10 bet on black ("even odds"). If a black number comes up, you win $10; otherwise, you lose $10. Find the probability distribution of X = amount won betting black on one spin of the roulette wheel. (*Hint:* A loss is a "negative win.")

b. Compute the expected value and variance of X. Interpret the expected value.

c. Now suppose that you place a $10 bet on "12 red" ("35 to 1 odds"). If "12 red" comes up, you win $350; otherwise, you lose your $10. Find the probability distribution of Y = amount won betting on "12 red" on one spin of the roulette wheel. (*Hint:* Again, a loss is a "negative win.")

d. Compute the expected value and variance of Y and compare to the expected value and variance of X. What can you conclude from this comparison?

e. Suppose you place a $10 bet on black for each of three separate spins of the roulette wheel. Compute the expected value and variance of the random variable $W = $ total amount won from the three separate bets of $10 on black.

f. Suppose you place a $30 bet on black for one spin of the roulette wheel. Compute the expected value and variance of the random variable $Z = $ total amount won from the $30 bet on black. How does this bet compare to that of part (e)?

4.45 Based on historical records, a rental company has determined that the probability distribution of $X = $ the number of daily rentals of a certain piece of equipment is as follows:

x	$P_X(x)$
0	.10
1	.25
2	.40
3	.20
4	.05

a. Compute the expected value *and* variance of X.

b. Assuming the rental company charges $25 per rental, compute the expected value *and* variance of the daily income from renting this equipment.

4.46 The director of publications for the University of Alabama is in charge of deciding how many programs to print for football games. Based on past data, the director has estimated the following probability distribution for the random variable $X = $ number of programs sold at an Alabama football game:

x	$P_X(x)$
25,000	.10
40,000	.30
55,000	.45
70,000	.15

a. Compute the expected number of programs sold at Alabama football games.

b. Compute the variance of the number of programs sold at Alabama football games.

c. Each program costs $1.25 to print and sells for $3.25. Any programs left unsold at the end of the game are discarded. The director has decided to print either 55,000 or

70,000 copies. Which of these two options maximizes the expected profit from program sales?

4.47 A book club announces a sweepstakes to attract new subscribers. The prizes and the chances of winning each are

Prize	Chance of Winning
$50,000	1 in 1,000,000
$5,000	1 in 250,000
$100	1 in 5,000
$20	1 in 500

Suppose you have just mailed in your sweepstakes ticket. Let X represent your winnings in the sweepstakes.

a. List the probability distribution of the random variable X in tabular form.

b. Calculate your expected winnings from the sweepstakes. Interpret this value.

c. Calculate the variance of the random variable X.

4.48 Insurance companies rely on probability theory when they compute the premiums to charge for various lift insurance and annuity products. Suppose a 40-year-old male purchases a $100,000 10-year term life policy from an insurance company. The insurance company must pay out $100,000 if the insured male dies within the next 10 years. Consider the following table in answering the questions:

Number of Deaths at Various Ages Out of 100,000 American Males Born Alive

Age Interval	Number of Deaths
0–1	1,527
1–9	495
10–19	927
20–29	1,901
30–39	2,105
40–49	4,502
50–59	10,330
60–69	19,954
70–79	28,538
80 and over	29,721
Total	100,000

a. Let X represent the insurance company's payout on a policy sold to a randomly selected 40-year-old male. Write the probability distribution for X (in table form).

b. Compute the expected value and standard deviation of X.

c. What is the "fair" premium for this policy (that is, the amount the insurance company should charge just in order to break even)? Don't factor in any other profits or costs.

4.49 You are the owner of the Trapper's Crossing apartment complex, which has 80 two-bedroom apartments. The number of apartment air-conditioner units that must be replaced during the summer season has the following probability distribution:

Air Conditioners Replaced	Probability
0	.30
1	.35
2	.20
3	.10
4	.05

a. Which of the three methods of assessing probability (classical, relative frequency, or subjective) was most likely used to create this probability distribution?

b. What is the long-run average number of air-conditioner units that will be replaced during a summer season?

c. What is the variance of the number of air-conditioner units replaced in a summer season?

d. If it costs $850 to replace an air conditioner, what is the expected total cost and the variance of the total cost during a summer season?

e. Compute the expected total cost and the variance of the total cost for *two* summer seasons. What assumption did you make to solve the problem?

4.50 Suppose that a real estate agent has the following probability distribution for the number of residential homes sold each month:

X = Homes Sold	Probability
0	.20
1	.60
2	.18
3	.02

a. Which of the three methods of assessing probability was most likely used to create this probability distribution?

b. Compute the long-run average number of homes sold per month by the agent.

c. Compute the standard deviation of the random variable X.

d. If the real estate agent earns a commission of $5000 per home sold plus a monthly salary of $1000, what is his expected monthly income and the variance of his monthly income?

4.51 A lottery is to be conducted in which 10,000 tickets are to be sold for $1 each. Six winning tickets are to be randomly selected: one grand-prize winner of $5000, one second-prize winner of $2000, one third-prize winner of $1000, and three other winners of $500 each.

a. Let X represent the net winnings of a person who purchases one ticket in the lottery. Construct the probability distribution of X in table format.

b. Compute the expected net winnings from buying a ticket in the lottery.

c. Should the sponsor conduct this lottery if its cost to administer the lottery is $0.15 per ticket? Explain why or why not.

BUSINESS CASES

Debit Cards

A regional bank was interested in new products and services to expand its customer base. One suggested product was a "debit card." This card works like a credit card in that a cardholder presents it to a merchant as payment. The difference is that the cardholder keeps a balance in an account, from which payments are deducted, rather than effectively borrowing from a bank, which is the case with credit cards. The cardholder does not pay interest on a loan when using a debit card, but the holder must have sufficient funds in the bank to use the card. The bank usually does not charge fees for a debit card; it makes its profit on the difference between interest earned on the cardholder's funds and the costs of servicing the account.

A product manager for the bank carried out a survey of 2150 current bank customers. You are assigned to do a careful analysis of three items from the survey: the reported number of cards in active use by the customer, the reported number that usually have some unpaid balance after a payment, and the reported number of debit cards that the customer would like to have. If we call these items X, Y, and Z, respectively, the survey data yield the following frequencies:

x:	0	0	0	1	1	1	1	1	1	2	2	2	2	2	2
y:	0	0	0	0	0	0	1	1	1	0	0	0	1	1	1
z:	0	1	2	0	1	2	0	1	2	0	1	2	0	1	2
Freq.:	98	45	10	125	110	28	171	203	38	96	87	18	150	228	66

x:	2	2	2	3	3	3	3	3	3	3	3	3	3	3	3
y:	2	2	2	0	0	0	1	1	1	2	2	2	3	3	3
z:	0	1	2	0	1	2	0	1	2	0	1	2	0	1	2
Freq.:	43	160	51	11	15	10	37	78	29	13	51	22	10	23	34

Assignment: The product manager had a hunch that customers with few cards in active use and customers who had few cards with unpaid balances would be more likely to desire debit cards than those with many cards or with many unpaid balances. Use the survey results as if they perfectly represented the entire population of the bank's current customers (thereby ignoring all variation due to sampling) to investigate this hunch. Write a brief report to the product manager explaining your findings; you should prepare a one-paragraph summary, followed by supporting evidence. The product manager doesn't remember probability theory, so be careful with your use of technical language.

A Safe and Secure Retirement

After a satisfying and successful 40-year management consulting career, you are now in a position to retire, travel with your spouse, play a little golf, and spend time with your grandchildren. Your investments have done well, resulting in a balance of $3,000,000 in your S&P 500 Index mutual fund account.

You expect to spend 25 years in retirement, so you have decided to keep your investment funds in the S&P 500 Index mutual fund to provide additional growth and sufficient income during the retirement years. Of course, this strategy exposes your savings to market risk, but you need to offset the impact of inflation on your later retirement years. At the historical inflation rate of 3–4%, the cost of living will more than double over your retirement years.

The difficult decision you face now is determining how much you can safely withdraw each month from your retirement savings to avoid running out of money in less than 25 years. You also want to allow for the effects of inflation by increasing your monthly withdrawal by 4% at the beginning of each year.

Note: Mathematical and financial formulas exist for solving this problem under the assumption of a fixed interest (or growth) rate, but the monthly returns of the S&P 500 Index are random. Assuming a fixed growth rate, such as the historical average return from the S&P 500 Index, would certainly not capture the market risk involved.

Assignment: Determine the schedule of monthly withdrawals (at the first of each month) from your retirement account that maximizes your monthly income while providing a high probability of not running out of money in 25 years of retirement. Assume that today is January 1 and that you will make the first withdrawal today. The schedule of withdrawals must allow for a 4% increase in the withdrawal amount at the beginning of each year (starting with January 1 of the second year).

There are many random variables in this problem, including the actual value of the S&P 500 Index at the beginning of each month. The main random variable of interest is X = the number of months that your investment funds will last for a given schedule of withdrawals. We would like for X to be 300 (that is, the money runs out in exactly 25 years, also known as the "die broke" strategy), but X is random. If you choose your withdrawal amounts in such a way that $E(X) = 300$, there would be a significant probability of running the balance down to zero before the end of 300 months (25 years). Instead, you need to maximize your withdrawal amounts in such a way that $P(X < 300)$ is very small, say less than 5%.

Important note: The withdrawal amounts are not random variables; they are decision variables that you have control over. Once you specify the value of the initial withdrawal amount (that is to be taken out today), the others are automatically determined by the 4% "raise" that you give yourself each year.

Given the mathematical difficulty in solving such a program by computing the probability distribution of X for a sequence of withdrawal amounts, you will have to use simulation. Using Minitab, Excel, or another software package, you need to construct a simulation that allows you to specify a starting monthly withdrawal amount and then determines the value of X, that is, in which month you run out of money.

The value of your mutual fund account will vary each month due to changes in the value of the S&P 500 Index. To incorporate these random fluctuations in your model, you will need to construct the probability distribution of *price relatives* from the S&P 500 Index. The price relative for month t is given by

$$R_t = \frac{P_t}{P_{t-1}}$$

where P_t is the value of the S&P 500 Index at the beginning of month t and P_{t-1} is the value of the S&P 500 Index at the beginning of the previous month, $t-1$. If B_{t-1} represents the balance of your retirement account at the beginning of month $t-1$, then the total value of your retirement account at the beginning of month t is given by

$$B_t = \frac{P_t}{P_{t-1}} B_{t-1} = R_t B_{t-1}$$

before taking your monthly withdrawal. You can find and download the monthly price levels of the S&P 500 Index on the Internet. From this data, you can compute values of R_t over the past 50 or more years and use them in the simulation. Your computer software package can randomly draw R_t values from the historical data values for 300 future months (25 years) for each run (retirement scenario) in your simulation. You can use these to compute the balance at the beginning of each month and to estimate the probability of running out of money before the end of 300 months.

Your simulation model should allow for a 4% increase in the monthly withdrawal amount at the end of each 12-month period and a .25% expense ratio charged by the mutual fund at the beginning of each year.

CHAPTER 5

Some Special

Probability Distributions

CHAPTER CONTENTS

This chapter introduces three special probability distributions that apply to many managerial situations. There are, of course, many more, but these distributions do cover a wide range of applications. The key concepts are:

- We have methods for counting the number of sequences (order matters) and subsets (order doesn't matter) of a specified number of items, chosen from a larger set. These methods allow us to determine probabilities, assuming equally likely outcomes.

- When an experiment consists of a specified number of distinct success/failure trials, binomial probabilities may apply. Two assumptions that must be checked for reasonableness are constant probability of success over trials and independence of the results from one trial to the next. The independence assumption is numerically more crucial. Positive dependence from one trial to the next yields more variability than that given by the binomial model.

- When an experiment consists of counting the number of randomly occurring events over a specified length of time, Poisson probabilities may apply. Two assumptions that must be checked for reasonableness are "nonclumping"—that events do not occur together—and independence over time. Violation of either assumption tends to yield more variability than that given by the Poisson model.

- Many measurements yield approximately a bell-shaped, normal probability distribution. This distribution arises whenever the random variable is a sum or average of many measurements, as well as by construction. Whether it in fact is a good approximation should be checked by a histogram or other data plot.

- Probability tables or computer programs may be used to calculate probabilities for these distributions. Expected values and standard deviations can be found using shortcut formulas for the binomial and Poisson models.

The ideas, notations, and results of the previous chapter apply to any random variables and any probability distributions. Now we identify and present formulas for some particular probability distributions that arise very often in practice. In particular, we describe the kind of situation and the critically important assumptions that justify the use of each distribution.

CHAPTER CASE

INTRODUCTION

Kilgore Manufacturing, Inc.

Kilgore Manufacturing, Inc. (KMI), a small manufacturing company in the St. Louis area, produces components used in the aerospace industry. James Kilgore, the president and owner, started the company five years ago. Although business has been reasonably steady for the last two years, KMI has yet to establish any long-term relationships with major aerospace contractors. This is important, because small companies like KMI only get business from subcontractors to the large aerospace manufacturing companies that win major contracts, many of which are with the federal government.

Jim has just learned that a new defense contract has been awarded to one of the major aerospace contractors. A certain system in the project requires one of the components produced by KMI, a relay switch manufactured by only three other companies in the United States. After finding out about the new contract, Jim held a strategy meeting with Tim Reynolds, vice president of manufacturing, and Bill Shelton, plant manager.

Jim: I don't know if you've heard yet, but Avionics just got a new government contract. The good news is that our R-7 relay switch plays a big role in the project. I think this is the opportunity we've been waiting for.

Tim: How many units will Avionics need?

Jim: One of my Washington contacts gave me enough information to think that they'll need at least 600 R-7 switches per day. My guess is that the subcontract will go to the company that can provide the largest number of switches per day at the lowest cost to the government. It's lucky that our current contracts for the R-7 are about to run out, so we could devote that entire production line to the new Avionics subcontract. What do you think, Bill?

Bill: Meeting the 600-per-day quota is easy. Our production data for the past two years show an average daily run of around 635 relay switches when we're running at full capacity.

Jim: All well and good, Bill, but we really need to know something about the amount of variability in daily production. The new subcontract requires a guaranteed minimum level of daily production in addition to an average or typical daily level. The government is really serious about contractors and subcontractors meeting their obligations—if we fall short of the guaranteed minimum, we get socked with a $5000 penalty.

Tim: $5000! Ouch! Isn't that a little much?

Jim: Washington's making the rules, not us, but we do want to play the game. Now, look, I want this contract; it's the break we've been looking for to get in solid with one of the key manufacturers. But we can't afford to lose money.

Bill: Well, let's see what we know. Over the past two years, our lowest daily production run was 494 units and the highest was 768. In fact, if I remember right, the actual distribution of daily production levels is described fairly well by a normal distribution with a mean of about 635 and a standard deviation of about 40.

Tim: So there are definitely days when we can't make 600 units. If we were to bid 600 units, we would be hit with the $5000 penalty from time to time. What sort of profit margin can we expect from Avionics, Jim?

Jim: I don't think that's going to be a problem. As best we can tell, our competitors are pretty close to us in terms of their production capabilities and costs, so I think we can maintain our usual profit margin of $3.80 per switch. It really boils down to who can produce the most switches daily. But we have to be very careful—bid too low on the guaranteed daily minimum and we lose the contract to one of our competitors; bid too high and we get the contract but lose our shirts in penalties.

Tim: So if I understand correctly, if we were to guarantee a minimum daily production level of 600 units but fell short, say, 5% of the time, then by my calculations we would net an average daily profit of $2163.

Jim: Whoa! Slow down! How did you come up with that figure?

Tim: Well, each day's production level will be different and there's no way we can predict when we'll fall short of the guaranteed bid level, but we can still talk in terms of averages. Using my example, suppose we fall short 5% of the time. We would get slapped with the $5,000 penalty about once in every 20 days, which averages out to $250 per day. If we actually average 635 switches per day, then over a typical 20-day period we would produce about 12,700 switches. At a $3.80 profit margin per switch, the average profit for a 20-day period would be $48,260, which comes to $2,413 per day. After subtracting the $5,000 penalty for 1 day out of the 20, our average net daily profit over the 20 days drops to $2,163.

Bill: Where did the 5% figure come from?

Tim: I just made it up for the example. It should be pretty close to correct, but I'm not sure.

Jim: Great! That's how to think this problem through! Of course, everything depends on how often we fall short, and our guaranteed bid level determines that.

Tim: You know, one way we could cut out some of the penalty costs would be to stockpile switches on those days that we produce more than the guaranteed level.

Jim: Good idea, Tim. I'd thought of that already but then found out from Avionics that we have to turn over our entire production to them each day.

Bill: And we can't use any overtime to meet the minimum when we are just short because we'll be operating 24 hours a day with our three shifts. If we borrow a little from the next day's production to meet the minimum, we stand a higher chance of not meeting the minimum the next day.

Jim: Right, so to come up with a guaranteed minimum daily production level, we need to assume we'll sell everything we produce each day, we can't stockpile or create a standby inventory, and we can't use any overtime or borrow from later production to avoid a penalty.

Bill: When is the bid due?

Jim: That's the good news. The deadline is about three months from now.

Bill: Great! Here's why I ask. A new worker suggested some changes to the R-7 production process during one of our quality circle meetings last week. I think the idea is a winner. These changes would make production more complicated and put the workers on a steep learning curve, but it could eventually lead to higher production levels. Here's the best part— we can do it with only minor equipment modifications and it will cost practically nothing to make the changes! We could start using the new procedure in less than a week.

Jim: This could be what we need to pull off this deal. Bill, start making the necessary changes. We'll monitor production levels for the next 60 production days. If the new process works as you suggest, we'll make our bid based on the new process; otherwise, we'll switch back to the old procedure and base our bid on the data from the past two years.

Tim: Getting back to profits again, how much profit do we really need to make in order to go after this contract?

Jim: I can't tell you enough about how important this contract is. If we get it and do a good job, it could lead to a long-term relationship with Avionics and would certainly make our name with the other major companies. We can't afford to lose money on this contract—I'd be willing to break even just to get the nonmonetary benefits, but we can't. Listen, if we could make just $1000 per day on this contract, the accountants and I would be happy. Bill, report back in 60 days to let us know how the new production plan is working. The three of us will take a look at the situation at that time and then work out the bid proposal.

We will check back later in this chapter with the management team at Kilgore Manufacturing to see how their experiment with the new production process turns out and to provide some statistical analysis to help them in their bid decision. You will find the material covered in this chapter and in the previous chapters to be extremely helpful in the analysis and decision-making process. ■

5.1 Counting Possible Outcomes

This chapter contains a discussion of the probability distributions that apply to several commonly occurring situations. Among the most common is taking a random sample. As we suggested when we discussed the classical interpretation of probability, we have considerable use for the idea that

$$P(\text{event}) = \frac{\text{number of outcomes favoring event}}{\text{total number of outcomes}}$$

To use this idea, we need a method for counting possible outcomes without the labor of actually listing the outcomes. This section contains a brief discussion of counting formulas. These formulas are also needed for the development of the binomial probability distribution of the next section. The counting methods arise as answers to the following two questions:

sequences   1. How many **sequences** of k symbols can be formed from a set of r distinct symbols, using each symbol no more than once?

subsets   2. How many **subsets** of k symbols can be formed from a set of r distinct symbols, using each symbol no more than once?

The only difference between a sequence and a subset is that order matters for sequences and not for subsets. The sequence ABC is not the same as the sequence CAB, but the subset {A, B, C} is the same as the subset {C, A, B}. As an example, consider sequences and subsets consisting of three of the first five letters. There are 60 sequences but only 10 subsets (Table 5.1).

TABLE 5.1

Subsets and Sequences of the Five Letters A, B, C, D, and E

Subsets	Sequences					
{A,B,C}	ABC	ACB	BAC	CAB	BCA	CBA
{A,B,D}	ABD	ADB	BAD	DAB	BDA	DBA
{A,B,E}	ABE	AEB	BAE	EAB	BEA	EBA
{A,C,D}	ACD	ADC	CAD	DAC	CDA	DCA
{A,C,E}	ACE	AEC	CAE	EAC	CEA	ECA
{A,D,E}	ADE	AED	DAE	EAD	DEA	EDA
{B,C,D}	BCD	BDC	CBD	DBC	CDB	DCB
{B,C,E}	BCE	BEC	CBE	EBC	CEB	ECB
{B,D,E}	BDE	BED	DBE	EBD	DEB	EDB
{C,D,E}	CDE	CED	DCE	ECD	DEC	EDC

$$\text{number of sequences} = r(r-1)\cdots(r-k+1)$$

For example, to choose a sequence of $k = 3$ letters from $r = 5$ letters, as in Table 5.1, we have 5 choices for the first letter, 4 for the second, and 3 for the third. There are $5 \times 4 \times 3 = 60$ different sequences.

The sequences formula looks like a factorial ($r!$) except that it is truncated at $r - k + 1$ instead of continuing down to 1. The number of sequences is often called the number of **permutations** of r symbols taken k at a time, and we denote it as $_rP_k$ or r_k. It can be expressed via factorials as

permutations

$$_rP_k = \frac{r!}{(r-k)!} = r(r-1)\cdots(r-k+1)$$

combinations

The number of subsets is called the number of **combinations** of r symbols taken k at a time and is denoted as $_rC_k$ or $\binom{r}{k}$.

$$\binom{r}{k} = \frac{r!}{k!(r-k)!}$$

For example, to choose a subset of $k = 3$ letters from $r = 5$ letters, as in Table 5.1, we have $\binom{5}{3} = \frac{5!}{3!(5-3)!} = \frac{5 \times 4 \times 3 \times 2 \times 1}{(3 \times 2 \times 1)(2 \times 1)} = 10$. The symbol $\binom{r}{k}$ is read "r choose k," suggesting a choice of a subset of k things from a set of r things.

The combinations formula is particularly useful in random sampling, because choosing a sample of size k without replacement from a population of size r is exactly the same as choosing a subset of k things from a set of r things. We do not typically care about the ordering of items during sampling, so the permutation formula is somewhat less central. There are many uses for these ideas in probability theory; games of chance in particular can often be figured out with these formulas. However, we won't go deeply into such applications.

Very often, we must count the number of ways that we can obtain *two* subsets. For example, if we have a total of 920 good items and 80 bad items, how many ways are there to choose 12 good and 4 bad items? Order doesn't matter, so we're considering subsets. We can choose the good items in $\binom{920}{12}$ ways and the bad items in $\binom{80}{4}$ ways. Any choice of good items can be put together with any choice of bad ones; to find the number of ways of choosing 12 good items *and* 4 bad ones, multiply. There are $\binom{920}{12}\binom{80}{4}$ ways of making the choices.

EXAMPLE 5.1

In auditing the 87 accounts payable of a small firm, a sample of 10 account balances is checked. How many possible samples are there? Assuming that 13 of the accounts contain errors, how many samples contain exactly 2 erroneous accounts?

SOLUTION There is no need to consider the sequence (order) in which the 10 accounts are drawn because all 10 are checked. Therefore, we can count the number of combinations. There are $\binom{87}{10} = \frac{87!}{10!77!} \approx 4,000,000,000,000$ possible samples. To obtain all samples with two erroneous accounts, we can combine any of the $\binom{13}{2}$ choices of two from the 13 erroneous accounts with any of the $\binom{74}{8}$ choices of eight from the 74 correct accounts. Because any choice of two erroneous accounts can be matched with any choice of eight correct ones, we must multiply these numbers together. There are $\binom{13}{2}\binom{74}{8} \approx 1,200,000,000,000$ samples with two erroneous and eight correct accounts.

EXAMPLE 5.2

In a sales contest, the 10 top performers out of 612 salespeople receive prizes ranging from a free vacation for the overall winner to \$50 for the tenth-place finisher. How many different prize lists are possible?

SOLUTION Here the ordering is certainly relevant, so the permutation formula applies. There are $_{612}P_{10} = 612!/602! \approx 6,800,000,000,000,000,000,000,000,000$ possibilities.

Exercises

5.1 In a certain state, an appeals court consists of seven judges. For a routine case, three judges are chosen at random as a panel to hear a case and render a decision. How many distinct panels can be formed?

5.2 Suppose that five of the seven judges on the appeals court in Exercise 5.1 are considered potentially sympathetic to a particular legal argument. How many panels can be formed having exactly two potentially sympathetic judges? How many panels have at least two such judges?

5.3 A grocery chain wants to taste-test a private-label cola drink. A tester is given eight unmarked glasses, four containing the private-label drink and four containing a nationally advertised cola. The tester is asked to identify the four glasses containing the private-label drink. How many different choices of four glasses can the taster make?

5.4 How many of the choices in Exercise 5.3 include three correct glasses and one incorrect glass?

5.2   Bernoulli Trials and the Binomial Distribution

The simplest data-gathering process is counting the number of times a certain event occurs. When taking a random sample of registered voters, we can count the number who prefer the incumbent to the challenger. When sampling pistons for an auto engine assembly, we can count the number that fail to meet tolerances. When examining hiring practices, we can count the number of minority workers hired by a firm. When examining credit policies, we can count the number of bad debt accounts. We can reduce an almost endless variety of situations to this simple yes/no process.

trial

These examples, and many others, share certain common features. First, the overall process can be thought of as a series of **trials,** each trial yielding exactly one of two possible outcomes. In sampling registered voters, each person constitutes a trial. The incumbent is either preferred or not preferred. In sampling pistons, each trial yields a defective piston or a piston within tolerances. Each person hired is or is not a minority member, and each credit account is or is not a bad debt. The standard language is to call one outcome "success" and the other "failure." Which outcome is called success does not matter—a bad debt account could be called a success.

Second, in each of these situations, it is reasonable to assume that the probability of success is constant over trials. The probability of finding a registered voter who favors the incumbent does not change in midsample (unless the sample is conducted over an extended period of time), nor does the probability of a defective piston, nor does the probability of a bad debt. If relative unemployment rates and the firm's hiring practices do not change, the probability that a given new employee is a minority worker does not change. We denote the probability of success on any one trial as π (not to be confused with $\pi = 3.14159$ from geometry).

And finally, in each situation, the results of the various trials can be assumed to be independent. The preference of one voter for the incumbent should not affect the preference of another voter; at least that shouldn't occur in a carefully designed study. If one account happens to be a bad debt, that fact doesn't change the likelihood that the next account sampled will be good.

Bernoulli trials

These three assumptions—each trial results in either a success or failure, constant probability π of success, and independence of trials—define a series of **Bernoulli trials.** The assumptions *are* assumptions; not every counting process can reasonably be modeled as Bernoulli trials. Whether these assumptions are reasonable depends on the situation. Success–failure trials are not always independent and identical. But in many cases these assumptions hold to a good approximation, which makes Bernoulli trials a useful model.

EXAMPLE 5.3

Discuss whether or not a series of Bernoulli trials provides a reasonable model for each of the following situations.

a.   A telephone researcher involved in a television-viewing survey calls different homes (selected at random), one each 15 minutes between 5:30 P.M. and 10:00 P.M. Each person contacted is asked if anyone in the household is watching the ABC network program. A trial consists of contacting a household to determine whether or not someone in the house is watching an ABC network program.

b. A trust officer examines a sample of stock listings from those on the New York Stock Exchange to determine whether or not each stock has risen in price during the past week. Here a trial consists of selecting a stock and determining whether or not the price has risen during the past week.

c. Each of 50 newly hired management trainees is rated outstanding, acceptable, or unsatisfactory at the conclusion of a training program. Determining the rating for a newly hired management trainee constitutes a trial.

SOLUTION

a. The assumption of constant probability from trial to trial is not plausible in this survey, because the level of television watching in general is relatively lower early in the evening. Hence, the probability of finding someone watching the ABC network program may vary depending on the time of the call.

b. The independence assumption is very dubious. During any particular time period, there's a moderately strong tendency for stock prices to move up or down together, because of interest rate changes, political news, or the herd instinct of investors. So for the stocks listed in the sample, the outcome on any one trial would depend heavily on price changes for the other stocks.

c. For this problem there are three possible outcomes on each trial, not two. However, if we define a success to be a rating of outstanding and a failure to be the complement (not rated outstanding), Bernoulli trials may be a good model. The key question is whether the trial outcomes are independent. If there is an effective ceiling or quota for the number (or proportion) of outstanding ratings (for instance, a restriction that the supervisor can rate no more than 10% of the group as outstanding), then the independence assumption is violated. But if each trainee is rated according to established, reasonably objective criteria, independence of trials (ratings) should be a reasonable assumption.

There is one additional feature common to all the situations in Example 5.3. We are counting the number of successes that occur in a fixed number n of trials, without regard to the particular order in which successes and failures occur. This would not be true if, for instance, an interviewer called homes at random until 24 television-watching homes had been obtained. In this situation, n is not fixed and the order of successes and failures *is* relevant; the last trial (call) is guaranteed to be a success.

A collection of a fixed number n of Bernoulli trials in which the researcher is **binomial experiment** interested in the total number of successes defines a **binomial experiment.** The properties of a binomial experiment are repeated here.

DEFINITION 5.1

Properties of a Binomial Experiment

1. There are n Bernoulli trials; each one results in either a success (S) or a failure (F).

2. The probability of a success on any individual trial, $\pi = P(S)$, remains constant over trials [$P(F) = 1 - \pi$].

3. The trials are independent. (Assumptions 1–3 define Bernoulli trials.)

4. The random variable of interest is Y, which is the number of successes in n trials. The ordering of successes is not important.

FIGURE 5.1   **Probability Tree for Binomial Distribution with *n* = 3**

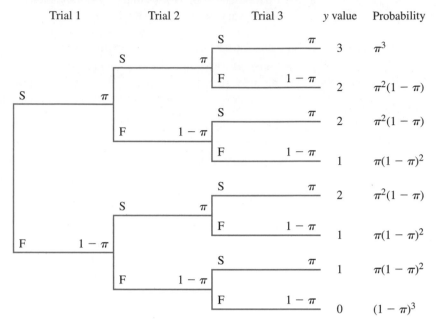

A **binomial random variable** is a discrete random variable that can assume any one of the values 0, 1, 2, . . . , *n*. The **binomial probability distribution** $P_Y(y)$, which assigns probabilities to each value of *Y*, is best understood by considering a simple example.

Suppose we take a random sample of three individuals from a population with a proportion π of successes. Figure 5.1 shows a probability tree for calculating the distribution of *Y*. By adding up the probabilities of appropriate paths, we can find the binomial probability distribution for *n* = 3. For instance, the second, third, and fifth paths (counting from the top) give *y* = 2; each of these paths has probability $\pi^2(1 - \pi)$. We add the path probabilities to get $P(Y = 2)$; $P_Y(2) = \pi^2(1 - \pi) + \pi^2(1 - \pi) + \pi^2(1 - \pi) = 3\pi^2(1 - \pi)$. The complete probability distribution is

$$y: \quad 0 \qquad 1 \qquad\qquad 2 \qquad\quad 3$$
$$P_Y(y): \quad (1 - \pi)^3 \quad 3\pi(1 - \pi)^2 \quad 3\pi^2(1 - \pi) \quad \pi^3$$

EXAMPLE 5.4   Find the binomial distribution for *n* = 4.

SOLUTION   To save space, we have listed the paths instead of drawing the tree. You may wish to construct the probability tree that gives rise to these paths.

Path Number	Path Sequence	*y*	Probability
1	SSSS	4	π^4
2	SSSF	3	$\pi^3(1 - \pi)$
3	SSFS	3	$\pi^3(1 - \pi)$
4	SSFF	2	$\pi^2(1 - \pi)^2$
5	SFSS	3	$\pi^3(1 - \pi)$

Path Number	Path Sequence	y	Probability
6	SFSF	2	$\pi^2(1 - \pi)^2$
7	SFFS	2	$\pi^2(1 - \pi)^2$
8	SFFF	1	$\pi(1 - \pi)^3$
9	FSSS	3	$\pi^3(1 - \pi)$
10	FSSF	2	$\pi^2(1 - \pi)^2$
11	FSFS	2	$\pi^2(1 - \pi)^2$
12	FSFF	1	$\pi(1 - \pi)^3$
13	FFSS	2	$\pi^2(1 - \pi)^2$
14	FFSF	1	$\pi(1 - \pi)^3$
15	FFFS	1	$\pi(1 - \pi)^3$
16	FFFF	0	$(1 - \pi)^4$

All the paths corresponding to a particular y value have the same probability; for instance, each of the six paths that yield $y = 2$ has probability $\pi^2(1 - \pi)^2$. So adding up the path probabilities for a particular y value amounts to multiplying the number of paths by the appropriate probability.

$$
\begin{array}{cccccc}
y: & 0 & 1 & 2 & 3 & 4 \\
P_Y(y): & (1 - \pi)^4 & 4\pi(1 - \pi)^3 & 6\pi^2(1 - \pi)^2 & 4\pi^3(1 - \pi) & \pi^4
\end{array}
$$

We need a formula to save the labor of actually counting paths. We can use the methods of Section 5.1. One way to specify a path in a binomial experiment is to state the trials on which a success occurs. For example, if $n = 5$, to say that the successes occur only at trials 1 and 4—for short, S at (1,4)—specifies the path SFFSF. The ordering of the trial numbers is irrelevant; S at (4,1) also specifies the path SFFSF. Therefore, in n trials, the number of paths containing y successes is the same as the number of subsets of size y out of the first n integers. From Section 5.1 this number is

$$
\binom{n}{y} = \frac{(n!)}{y!(n - y)!}
$$

Using this expression for the relevant number of paths in a binomial probability tree, we obtain a general expression for the binomial probability distribution.

DEFINITION 5.2

Binomial Probability Distribution

$$
P_Y(y) = \frac{n!}{y!(n - y)!} \pi^y(1 - \pi)^{n-y}, \qquad \text{for } y = 0, 1, \ldots, n
$$

Appendix Table 1 (at the end of the book) contains numerical values of binomial probabilities. Each value of n determines a block of probabilities. For values of π below .5, values of π are read at the top of the block and values of y are read on the left. For values of π above .5, values of π are read at the bottom and values of y on the right. Many computer programs will also calculate these probabilities.

EXAMPLE 5.5

In Appendix Table 1 of binomial probabilities, find the probability distribution of a binomial random variable for $n = 5$ and (a) $\pi = .2$, (b) $\pi = .5$, and (c) $\pi = .7$.

SOLUTION We look in the $n = 5$ block of Appendix Table 1. For $\pi = .2$, we read *down* the .20 column; for $\pi = .5$, we use the $\pi = .50$ column; for $\pi = .7$, we read *up* the $\pi = .70$ column. The resulting distribution is

y	0	1	2	3	4	5
$P_Y(y)$ for $\pi = .20$	.3277	.4096	.2048	.0512	.0064	.0003
$P_Y(y)$ for $\pi = .50$	.0313	.1563	.3125	.3125	.1563	.0313
$P_Y(y)$ for $\pi = .70$	.0024	.0284	.1323	.3087	.3602	.1681

EXAMPLE 5.6

In the long run, 20% of all management trainees are rated outstanding, 50% acceptable, and 30% unsatisfactory. In a sample of 20 randomly selected trainees, find the following probabilities:

a. Exactly 4 trainees are rated outstanding.

b. At least 4 trainees are rated outstanding.

c. Exactly 15 trainees are rated outstanding or acceptable.

d. At least 15 trainees are rated outstanding or acceptable.

Assume that we have a set of Bernoulli trials.

SOLUTION

a. Find the entry for $n = 20$, $\pi = .20$ (on top of the block), and $y = 4$ (to the left). The probability is .2182.

b. Add the entries for $n = 20$, $\pi = .20$, $y = 4, 5, 6, \ldots, 20$, and get .5886.

c. The probability that a rating is outstanding or acceptable is $.20 + .50 = .70$. Find the entry for $n = 20$, $\pi = .70$ (below the block), and $y = 15$ (to the right): .1789. Alternatively, this probability must equal the probability of exactly five unsatisfactory ratings, which has $\pi = .30$ and $y = 5$. This reasoning yields the same table entry: .1789.

d. Add the entries for $n = 20$, $\pi = .70$, $y = 15, 16, \ldots, 20$ to get .4163. Or add the entries for $n = 20$, $\pi = .30$, and $y = 5, 4, \ldots, 0$ to get the equivalent probability of five or fewer unsatisfactory ratings.

EXAMPLE 5.7

Use the following Minitab output to find the probabilities of the preceding example. In the output, PDF is the probability of the specified value and CDF is the cumulative probability up through the specified value.

```
MTB > PDF 4;
SUBC> Binomial 20 .20.
         x       P( X = x )
      4.00         0.2182

MTB > CDF 3;
SUBC> Binomial 20 .20.
         x      P( X <= x )
      3.00         0.4114
```

```
MTB > PDF 15;
SUBC> Binomial 20 .70.
        x       P( X = x )
     15.00         0.1789

MTB > CDF 14;
SUBC> Binomial 20 .70.
        x       P( X <= x )
     14.00         0.5836
```

SOLUTION

a. As in the table, the probability of exactly 4 successes is shown as .2182.

b. $P(Y \geq 4) = 1 - P(Y \leq 3) = 1 - .4114 = .5886$.

c. Once again, the probability of exactly 4 successes is shown directly as .1789.

d. $P(Y \geq 15) = 1 - P(Y \leq 14) = 1 - .5836 = .4164$. There is a tiny discrepancy from the part (d) answer of the previous example because of round-off error.

The expected value and variance of a binomial random variable Y depend, of course, on the values of n and π.

DEFINITION 5.3

Mean and Variance of a Binomial Random Variable

$$\mu_Y = E(Y) = n\pi$$

$$\sigma_Y^2 = \text{Var}(Y) = n\pi(1 - \pi), \qquad \sigma_Y = \sqrt{n\pi(1 - \pi)}$$

The resulting expected value for a binomial random variable seems intuitively reasonable. If, on average, 30% of all trainees are rated outstanding, then in a sample of 20 trainees we would expect to find $20(.3) = 6$ who are rated outstanding. The variance and standard deviation expressions aren't particularly intuitive. Notice that the standard deviation increases like the square root of n, the number of trials. The variance and standard deviation are largest (for a specified n) when $\pi = .50$. This makes sense; there is the most random variability in results when there is a 50–50 chance of a success on any trial.

The effect of violation of assumptions can be understood in terms of these formulas. The two assumptions of interest here are constant probability and independence. (If there are more than two outcomes on a given trial, or if the experiment doesn't count the number of successes in a fixed number of trials, then binomial probabilities are simply irrelevant.) There is a difference between constant probability and independence. The constant probability assumption is violated if the probability of success changes *regardless* of the results of past trials; the independence assumption is violated if the probability of success changes *depending* on the results of past trials. For example, suppose a house inspector checks 20 houses to see whether or not each house's roof is sound. Ten of the houses are in a relatively new subdivision, about 10 years old; the remaining 10 are in a much older subdivision. Whether or not any particular house happens to have a sound roof, the probability that a house in the new subdivision will have a sound roof will be higher than the probability that a house in the older subdivision will have one. The constant probability assumption would almost certainly be violated. For another example, suppose a sales representative checks 20 boxes of snack crackers to see if the boxes have been bent or cut by rough handling. If one box has been marred, the probability that other boxes also are marred will go up, because all the boxes have been handled (or perhaps place-kicked) in about the same way. Notice the condition: *If* one box has been marred, the probability for others will go up. Here, the independence assumption would almost certainly be violated.

Violation of the independence assumption usually has more numerical effect on binomial probabilities. In particular, if there is positive dependence (a success tends to be followed by other successes, a failure by other failures), the binomial variance and standard deviation expressions will be too small. There will be more random variation than indicated by those formulas; there will be more cases of very large numbers of successes and of very small numbers of successes. In contrast (and perhaps oddly), if the probability of success changes at a fixed point during the trials, the violation of the constant probability assumption actually reduces the amount of random variation. Consider the extreme case of 20 trials, where the first 10 have probability 0 of success and the last 10 have probability 1 of success. The 20 trials are guaranteed to yield 10 successes, with no random variation at all. In most reasonable situations, the numerical effect of dependence is greater than that of nonconstant probability.

EXAMPLE 5.8   Minitab was used to simulate 1000 samples of data, each sample consisting of 100 Bernoulli trials. The first 50 trials had a probability of success equal to .30 and the remaining 50 had a probability of success equal to .70. Let Y represent the sum of the 100 values in a sample. The Minitab output is shown next. What binomial assumption is violated in these samples? What is the anticipated effect of this violation? Where does the simulation show this effect?

```
MTB > Random 1000 c1-c50;
SUBC>    Bernoulli .3.

MTB > Random 1000 c51-c100;
SUBC>    Bernoulli .7.

MTB > RSum c1-c100 c101
MTB > Name c101 'Y'
MTB > Describe 'Y'

Descriptive Statistics: Y

Variable      N        Mean      Median      TrMean      StDev    SE Mean
Y          1000      49.921      50.000      49.880      4.764      0.151

Variable    Minimum     Maximum          Q1          Q3
Y            32.000      64.000      47.000      53.000
```

SOLUTION   The probability of success is not constant; it changes from .3 to .7 halfway through the series of trials. The "average π" is .5. If binomial assumptions are met, the expected value will be $\mu_Y = n\pi = 100(.5) = 50$. The violation of assumptions should reduce the variance (and standard deviation). If the probability of success had been constant at .5, the variance would be $\sigma_Y^2 = n\pi(1 - \pi) = 100(.5)(1 - .5) = 25.0$. The simulation shows that the mean value is almost exactly 50.0, but the variance is $(4.764)^2 = 22.696$, smaller than the binomial value of 25.0.

EXAMPLE 5.9   Excel was used to simulate 1000 samples of data, each sample consisting of 100 Bernoulli trials. The probability on the first trial was .5. If a trial is a success, the probability of success on the next trial is .7; otherwise, the probability of success on the next trial is .3. Let Y represent the sum of the 100 values in a sample. The Excel

FIGURE 5.2   **Excel Spreadsheet for the Simulation in Example 5.9**

	A	B	C	CU	CV	CW	CX	CY	CZ	DA
1	0	0	0	0	1		55		Average =	49.664
2	1	1	0	0	0		50		StdDev =	7.456
3	0	0	1	0	0		50		Var =	55.593
4	0	0	1	1	1		50			
5	1	0	0	0	0		30			
6	0	0	0	0	1		38			
7	1	1	1	1	1		67			
8	1	0	0	1	0		54			
9	1	1	1	1	1		62			
10	1	1	0	0	0		45			
11	0	0	0	1	0		57			
12	0	1	1	1	1		46			
997	1	1	1	0	0		54			
998	0	0	0	1	1		47			
999	1	1	1	1	1		63			
1000	0	0	0	0	0		37			

spreadsheet, with most of the rows and columns hidden, is shown in Figure 5.2. (The Excel spreadsheet is in the file XM0509 on the CD.) What binomial assumption is violated in these samples? What is the anticipated effect of this violation? Where does the simulation show this effect? Is the effect smaller or larger than in the previous example?

SOLUTION   Again, the "average π" is .5. (Draw a tree if that's not clear.) This time, the independence assumption is violated. The binomial variance equals 25.0 once again. In this simulation, however, the variance is much larger than the theoretical value. The simulation variance is 55.593. The discrepancy between the theoretical variance and the simulation variance is much larger in this simulation than in the previous example, indicating that violation of the independence assumption has a greater numerical effect than violation of the constant probability assumption.

Probability calculations, such as those based on the binomial distribution, are used in statistical inference to assess the strength of the evidence in sample data against (or in favor of) a claim made about the population from which the sample is collected.

EXAMPLE 5.10   Historically, 5% of all claims filed with the Beta Insurance Company are fraudulent. The manager of the Claims Division at Beta has reason to believe that the percentage of fraudulent claims may have risen recently. To test his theory, a random sample of 15 recently filed claims was selected. After extensive, careful investigation of each of these 15 claims, it is discovered that 4 are fraudulent. Is there sufficient evidence in this outcome to conclude that the percentage of fraudulent claims has actually risen at Beta Insurance Company?

SOLUTION   The basic question to be addressed is this: Is it unreasonable to observe 4 fraudulent claims in a random sample of 15 filed claims, assuming that the true percentage of fraudulent claims is actually 5%? The sample proportion of $4/15 = .266$ or 26.6% is certainly larger than the historical value of 5%, but could this difference be accounted for by random sampling variation? We can answer this question using the binomial distribution.

Let Y represent the number of fraudulent claims found in a random sample of 15 Beta Insurance claims. Assuming that the filed claims are independent and that the true probability of a fraudulent claim has remained constant, the variable Y follows a binomial distribution with $n = 15$. What about the value of the second parameter, π? π represents the probability that a single filed claim is fraudulent. Although we don't know the true value of π, the historical evidence suggests that $\pi = .05$. If we assume that the actual fraudulent rate has not increased, then $Y \sim B(n = 15, \pi = .05)$.

Figure 5.3 shows the $B(n = 15, \pi = .05)$ distribution as computed from Minitab. If the historical fraudulent claim rate of $\pi = .05$ is correct, then this distribution reflects what we would observe in a large number of samples of 15 claims. For example, roughly 46% of samples of 15 claims would contain no fraudulent claims and approximately 37% would contain exactly 1 fraudulent claim.

In the actual sample of 15 claims collected, we observed $Y = 4$ fraudulent claims. According to the probability distribution in Figure 5.3, which assumes the true fraudulent rate is $\pi = .05$, the chance of observing 4 or more fraudulent claims is .005468, that is, roughly a 1-in-200 event. There are two possible explanations: either (1) we have witnessed a rare event, or (2) the historical rate of fraudulent claims has increased, and the true value of π is much higher than 5%. Most reasonable people would conclude that there is sufficient evidence to conclude that the rate of fraudulent claims has risen above 5%.

FIGURE 5.3   **The $B(n = 15, \pi = .05)$ Distribution**

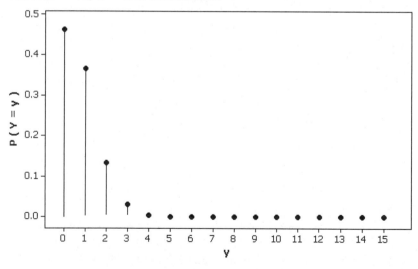

y	$P(Y = y)$	y	$P(Y = y)$
0	0.463291	8	0.000000
1	0.365756	9	0.000000
2	0.134752	10	0.000000
3	0.030733	11	0.000000
4	0.004853	12	0.000000
5	0.000562	13	0.000000
6	0.000049	14	0.000000
7	0.000003	15	0.000000

p-value

In hypothesis testing, to be covered in Chapter 8, the calculated probability of .005468 is referred to as a **p-value**. P-values provide a way to measure the strength of the evidence contained in a random sample of data against a hypothesis or assumption made about the population. In the previous example, the p-value of .005468 is the probability of observing an outcome as contradictory or more contradictory than what we actually observed in our sample (that is, 4 or more fraudulent claims in a random sample of 15 claims), under the assumption of no change in the fraudulent claim rate (that is, $\pi = .05$). The small p-value indicates that we have observed a rare event if the assumption of no change in the fraudulent claim rate is correct. We take this as sufficient evidence to conclude that the assumption is false and that the fraudulent claim rate has increased.

Exercises

5.5 Let Y be a binomial random variable. Compute $P_Y(y)$ for each of the following situations:
a. $n = 10$, $\pi = .2$, $y = 3$
b. $n = 4$, $\pi = .4$, $y = 2$
c. $n = 16$, $\pi = .7$, $y = 12$

5.6 Let Y have a binomial probability distribution with $n = 6$ and $\pi = .25$.
a. Calculate $P_Y(y)$ by hand for $y = 1, 2,$ and 3. Compare your results to those listed in Appendix Table 1.
b. Draw a probability histogram of $P_Y(y)$.
c. Find the mean and standard deviation of Y.

5.7 Let $Y = $ the number of successes in 20 independent trials, where the probability of success on any one trial is .4. Find
a. $P(Y \geq 4)$
b. $P(Y > 4)$
c. $P(Y \leq 10)$
d. $P(Y > 16)$

5.8 Let Y be a binomial random variable with $n = 20$ and $\pi = .6$. Find $P(Y \leq 16)$ and $P(Y < 16)$. Compare these probabilities to the ones found in parts (a) and (b) of Exercise 5.7.

5.9 A chain of motels has adopted a policy of giving a 3% discount to customers who pay in cash rather than by credit cards. Its experience is that 30% of all customers take the discount. Let $Y = $ number of discount takers among the next 20 customers.
a. Do you think the binomial assumptions are reasonable in this situation?
b. Assuming that binomial probabilities apply, find the probability that exactly 5 of the next 20 customers take the discount.
c. Find $P(5$ or fewer customers take the discount).

d. What is the most probable number of discount takers in the next 20 customers?

5.10 Find the expected value and standard deviation of the number of discount takers in Exercise 5.9.

5.11 Use the Empirical Rule to approximate the probability that Y in Exercise 5.9 falls within 1 standard deviation of its expected value. Use binomial tables to find the exact probability. How good is the Empirical Rule approximation?

5.12 A small company uses a parcel service to ship packages of special cheeses ordered as gifts. The company has found that 90% of all orders are delivered on time. A batch of 100 packages is sent out. Let $Y = $ number of packages delivered on time.
a. Do the binomial assumptions seem reasonable in this situation?
b. Assuming that binomial probabilities apply, find $P(Y \geq 85)$.

5.13 Find μ_Y and σ_Y in Exercise 5.12, assuming binomial probabilities.

5.14 A prescription drug manufacturer claims that only 10% of all new drugs that are shown to be effective in animal tests ever pass through all the additional testing required to be marketed. The manufacturer currently has eight new drugs that have been shown to be effective in animal tests, and they await further testing and approval.
a. Find the probability that none of the eight drugs is marketed.
b. Find the probability that at least two are marketed.
c. Find the expected number of marketed drugs among the eight.

5.15 Plot a probability histogram of $P_Y(y)$ in Exercise 5.14.

5.16 Suppose that 5% of all items produced by a manufacturing company are defective. To check the quality of production, you are assigned to take a sample of eight items each hour. Let Y = the number of defective items in a sample of eight items.
a. What values of Y are possible? most likely? least likely?
b. What is the population distribution of Y if 5% of all items are defective?
c. Graph the population distribution of Y.
d. If you were to find five defective items in your sample of eight items in the next hour, what conclusion would you reach about the production process?

5.17 City Bank has recently begun a new credit program. Customers meeting certain credit requirements can obtain a credit card accepted by participating area merchants that carries a discount. Past numbers show that 25% of all applicants for this card are rejected. Out of the next 10 people who apply for the credit card, what is the probability that exactly 4 will be rejected?

5.18 A direct-mail advertiser has a continuing problem with mailing lists. Historically, about 18% of the addresses on mailing lists have been bad, so that the intended recipient never gets the mail. The advertiser has the opportunity to buy a new list, which claims to have a lower percentage of bad addresses. As a test before purchasing the new list, the advertiser takes a random sample of 200 addresses and sends catalogs by first-class mail. For this class of mail, undeliverable catalogs are returned to the sender, giving a count of the number of bad addresses in the sample of 200. After sufficient time has passed, the advertiser finds that 32 of the 200 addresses were bad.
a. Compute the probability of 32 or fewer bad addresses in a random sample of 200 addresses from the new list under the assumption that the percentage of bad addresses in the new list is the same as the historical rate of 18%.
b. Based on this probability calculation, do you believe there is sufficient evidence to conclude that the new list has a lower percentage of bad addresses than the historical rate of 18%?
c. Someone comments that 32 bad addresses is certainly fewer than the expected value of 36 bad addresses, based on the historical rate of 18%, and recommends that the advertiser purchase the new list. How would you respond?

5.19 A company has decided to conduct random drug testing of its employees. To set an example, 15 departmental managers have volunteered to be tested for drug use. The drug test used has been extensively tested. In trials with people known to be drug users, the test was positive for drug use

98% of the time. In trials with people known not to use drugs, the test was negative 95% of the time.
a. Assume that none of the 15 managers is a drug user. Let X be the number of managers in the 15 who test positive for drug use. Does X have a binomial distribution?
b. Assume that none of the 15 managers is a drug user. Compute the probability that exactly 4 managers test positive for drug use ("false positives").
c. Again, assume that none of the 15 managers is a drug user. Compute the probability that at least 1 manager will test positive for drug use.
d. Compute the average number of false positives in testing 15 people who do not use drugs and interpret this value.
e. Construct a two-way table to show the outcome of testing the entire company of 10,000 employees. Assume 8% of all employees are drug users.

5.20 Historically, 8% of all claims filed with the Alpha Insurance Company are fraudulent. The manager of the Claims Division at Alpha suspects that the percentage of fraudulent claims may have decreased after the recent implementation of new customer filing procedures that discourage fraud. To test his theory, a random sample of 120 recently filed claims was selected. After careful investigation of each of these 120 claims, only 2 are found to be fraudulent.
a. Assume the true fraudulent claim rate has remained at 8%. Compute the probability of *2 or fewer* fraudulent claims in a random sample of 120 claims.
b. Based on your answer in part (a), what do you conclude about the possible decrease in the fraudulent claim percentage?

5.21 As the vice president of marketing for Sparkling Clean dishwasher detergent, you have recently become concerned by a new marketing campaign of one of your competitors. Historically, Sparkling Clean has held a 30% share of the dishwasher detergent market. In order to see if the competitor's marketing campaign has reduced your market share, you charge your marketing team with taking a survey based on a random sample of 25 consumers to determine their dishwasher detergent preferences.
a. Assuming Sparkling Clean still maintains its 30% market share, what is the probability that *exactly* 5 respondents in the survey will say they prefer Sparkling Clean over other brands of dishwashing detergent?
b. In the actual survey of 25 consumers, only 2 consumers indicated a preference for Sparkling Clean. Is there sufficient evidence to conclude that there has been a loss of market share for Sparkling Clean? (*Hint:* Compute the probability of 2 or fewer consumers indicating a preference for Sparkling Clean in the sample of 25 consumers under the assumption that Sparkling Clean has a 30% market share. Work this calculated figure into your response.)

5.3   **The Poisson Distribution**

A different sort of probability situation occurs when a succession of events seems to happen at random over time. An electrical utility faces occasional thunderstorms that down power lines or damage transformers. Although the long-run probability of occurrence of such storms can be determined quite accurately, the timing of the next storm is rather unpredictable. A company that insures oil tankers cannot predict the time of the next sinking. The manager of a university computer center faces random variation in the timing of job submissions. It's important to be able to protect against probable variation in such situations.

Poisson probability distribution

The **Poisson probability distribution*** is the simplest and most widely used model of events occurring randomly in time. This distribution is the mathematical result of certain assumptions. If the assumptions are not correct, at least approximately, for a particular situation, then the Poisson distribution may be a bad model in that situation. The two crucial assumptions can be translated (without doing much violence to the mathematical niceties) as follows:

1. Events occur one at a time. Two or more events do not occur at precisely the same time.

2. The occurrence of the event of interest in a given period is independent of the occurrence of the event in a nonoverlapping period; that is, the occurrence (or nonoccurrence) of an event during one period does not change the probability of an event occurring in some later period.

In many discussions on this topic, a third assumption is added: That the expected number of events in a period of specified length stays constant, so that the expected number of events during any one period is the same as during any other period. This third assumption makes the math easier, but it has been proven to be essentially irrelevant. As long as the first two assumptions hold, the Poisson distribution results.

There are two approaches to assessing whether or not a Poisson distribution is a reasonable model in a given situation. One is to see if the assumptions seem reasonable in a given context; the other is to see if the actual data histogram looks like a Poisson probability histogram. Of course, the ideal is to have both.

EXAMPLE 5.11   In the three situations described at the beginning of this section, should the Poisson assumptions hold?

SOLUTION   We would expect that the assumption of independence would be shaky for the electrical utility example. It seems to us that if lightning from one storm knocks out some equipment, it is quite likely that lightning from the same storm or another in the vicinity will knock out other equipment. For the oil tanker example, one could argue that since one large tanker might collide with another,

---

*Named for Simeon Poisson, the mathematician who first derived it.

sinking both, the assumption that events happen one at a time doesn't hold. Although this is certainly possible, we would guess that such flukes are sufficiently rare that the Poisson distribution is a decent model for the probability of a tanker sinking in a given period. In the computer center, much depends on the situation. If there are only a few terminals, which are tied up during the processing of a job, then the submission of a job now reduces the probability of submission of another job (from the same terminal) a bit later, which violates the assumption of independence. But if there are many terminals or if a terminal is not tied up during processing, the Poisson assumptions look good to us. We would like to see some data!

DEFINITION 5.4

Poisson Probability Distribution

$$P_Y(y) = \frac{e^{-\mu}\mu^y}{y!}, \qquad y = 0, 1, 2, \ldots$$

where μ is the expected number of events occurring in a given period and $e = 2.71828\ldots$.

A Poisson random variable Y is the number of random events that occur in a fixed period; in principle, there's no upper limit to the values of y. In practice, very large values of y are extremely unlikely. Probabilities for the Poisson probability distribution are shown in Appendix Table 2 and can also be calculated by many computer packages. To find μ, it is often necessary to multiply the expected rate for one time unit (e.g., one hour) times the number of time units per period (e.g., hours per shift).

EXAMPLE 5.12

On Saturday mornings, customers enter a boutique at a suburban shopping mall at an average rate of .50 per minute. Let Y = number of customers arriving in a specified 10-minute interval of time. Find the following probabilities:

a. $P(Y = 3)$

b. $P(Y \leq 3)$

c. $P(Y \geq 4)$

d. $P(4 \leq Y \leq 10)$

SOLUTION The Poisson assumptions seem fairly reasonable in this context. We assume that customers don't arrive in groups (or else count the entire group as one arrival) and that the arrival of one customer neither decreases nor increases the probability of other arrivals.

To obtain μ, we note that at an average rate of .50 per minute over a 10-minute time span, we would expect $\mu = (.50)(10) = 5.0$ arrivals. To find the probabilities, we consult Appendix Table 2.

a. $P(Y = 3)$ is read directly from Appendix Table 2 with $\mu = 5$ and $y = 3$:
$P(Y = 3) = .1404$.

b. $P(Y \leq 3) = P(Y = 0) + P(Y = 1) + P(Y = 2) + P(Y = 3) = .0067 + .0337 + .0842 + .1404 = .2650$

c. $P(Y \geq 4) = 1 - P(Y \leq 3) = 1 - .2650 = .7350$

d. $P(4 \leq Y \leq 10) = P(Y = 4) + P(Y = 5) + \cdots + P(Y = 10) = .1755 + .1755 + \cdots + .0181 = .7213$

EXAMPLE 5.13

Use the following Minitab output to obtain the probabilities found in the previous example. Once again, PDF is the probability of the indicated value; CDF, the cumulative probability up through the indicated value.

```
MTB > PDF 3;
SUBC> Poisson 5.
        x       P( X = x )
       3.00         0.1404

MTB > CDF 3;
SUBC> Poisson 5.
        x       P( X <= x )
       3.00         0.2650

MTB > CDF 10;
SUBC> Poisson 5.
        x       P( X <= x )
      10.00         0.9863
```

SOLUTION   The probability shown for $y = 3$, .1404, is what we found in part (a) of the previous example. The cumulative probability $F_Y(3) = .2650$ is the answer to part (b) of the previous exercise, and its complement, .7350, is the answer to part (c). To find $P(4 \leq Y \leq 10)$, take $F_Y(10) - F_Y(3) = .9863 - .2650 = .7213$, as before.

As indicated in the definition of the Poisson probability distribution, the expected value is $E(Y) = \mu$. Coincidentally, the variance of a Poisson random variable is also μ.

DEFINITION 5.5

Mean and Variance for a Poisson Random Variable   If Y has a Poisson probability distribution, then

$$\mu_Y = E(Y) = \mu$$
$$\sigma_Y^2 = \text{Var}(Y) = \mu$$

EXAMPLE 5.14

Find the standard deviation of Y in Example 5.12.

SOLUTION   We noted in Example 5.12 that $\mu = 5.0$. Thus,

$$\sigma_Y = \sqrt{\text{Var}(Y)} = \sqrt{5.0} = 2.24$$

The most important assumptions underlying the Poisson probability model are "nonclumping" (events don't occur together) and independence (the occurrence of one event doesn't change the probability of another). If events do, in fact, occur together, or if there is positive dependence—that is, if the occurrence of one event increases the probability of another event happening soon—there will be more random variation than the Poisson model states. In this case, the standard deviation of the number of events will be larger than the square root of the mean, which is what the Poisson model specifies.

EXAMPLE 5.15   The emergency telephone (911) center in a suburban county receives an average of 42 calls per hour during the busiest period, weekend evenings between 7 and 11 o'clock. Each call requires about 2 minutes for a dispatcher to receive the emergency call, determine the nature and location of the problem, and send the required individuals (police, fire, or ambulance) to the scene. The center must have an adequate number of dispatchers on duty; it has asked a consultant to determine the proper staffing level. The consultant assumes that calls come in completely at random over time, so that Poisson probabilities apply. However, the current dispatchers point out that many times, several calls are received at nearly the same time, reporting on the same emergency. What does this fact imply about the use of Poisson probabilities?

SOLUTION   The fact that multiple calls are received at virtually the same time indicates a violation of the "nonclumping" assumption. Therefore, there will be more variability than would occur if Poisson probabilities applied. There will be more time periods with very few calls and more periods with very large numbers of calls. To deal with the bursts of multiple calls will most likely require more dispatchers than would be needed if the Poisson model applied.

EXAMPLE 5.16   Historically, Gosler Tool and Die Corporation has experienced an average of .85 work-related injuries per month on the plant floor. One year ago, the plant manager instituted new safety regulations in order to reduce the number of work-related injuries. Over the course of this past year, there were seven work-related injuries at Gosler Corporation. Is there sufficient evidence to conclude that the average number of work-related injuries has decreased after implementing the new safety regulations?

SOLUTION   What do you think? Is observing seven work-related injuries in one year convincing evidence that the rate of work-related injuries has decreased? Or is it an ordinary occurrence?

Once again, statistics and probability can help us to answer this question. The Poisson distribution should be a reasonably accurate description of the random variable Y = the number of work-related injuries occurring in one year under the new safety regulations. If we assume that the average number of work-related injuries has not changed after implementing the new safety regulations, then $Y \sim$ Poisson ($\mu = 12 \times .85 = 10.2$), since an average of .85 injuries per month is equivalent to an average of $12 \times .85 = 10.2$ injuries per year.

Last year, there were seven work-related injuries, certainly fewer than the assumed average of 10.2 injuries per year, but is it enough to convince us that the true average has decreased? Figure 5.4 shows the Poisson distribution with $\mu = 10.2$. If the average number of work-related injuries has not changed after implementing the new safety regulations, then this distribution reflects the annual injury counts we could expect to see for a large number of years. For example, we expect to have exactly ten work-related injuries in 12.5% of all years, or in one out of every eight years on average.

From the table in Figure 5.4, we see that there is an 8.5% chance of experiencing exactly seven work-related injuries in one year and a 20.3% chance of experiencing seven or fewer injuries in one year. If the average number of injuries has not changed, then on average about one out of every five years would experience seven or fewer work-related injuries. This suggests that the seven injuries observed last year is reasonably consistent with the assumption of a Poisson distribution with a mean of $\mu = 10.2$ and should not lead us to conclude that the work-related injury rate decreased after instituting the new safety regulations. Gosler should certainly monitor the situation over the next few months, but there is insufficient evidence in last year's outcome to indicate a decreased risk of injuries to workers as a result of the new safety regulations.

FIGURE 5.4   **The Poisson Distribution with $\mu = 10.2$**

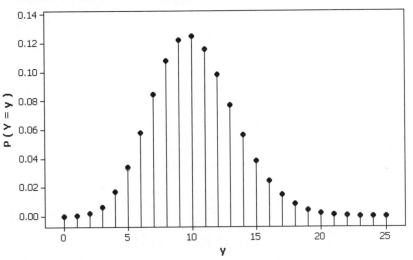

y	$P(Y = y)$	y	$P(Y = y)$
0	0.000037	13	0.077218
1	0.000379	14	0.056259
2	0.001934	15	0.038256
3	0.006574	16	0.024388
4	0.016764	17	0.014633
5	0.034199	18	0.008292
6	0.058139	19	0.004451
7	0.084716	20	0.002270
8	0.108013	21	0.001103
9	0.122415	22	0.000511
10	0.124863	23	0.000227
11	0.115782	24	0.000096
12	0.098415	25	0.000039

Exercises

5.22 Let Y denote a random variable with a Poisson distribution. Use Appendix Table 2 to calculate
a. $P_Y(1)$ for $\mu = .4$, $\mu = .7$, and $\mu = 4.8$
b. $P(Y \leq 3)$ for $\mu = 1.6$ and $\mu = 7.0$
c. $P(Y \leq 10)$ for $\mu = 2.1$ and $\mu = 10.0$

5.23 Graph the Poisson probability distribution for $\mu = .5$. Is the distribution roughly symmetric?

5.24 A firm that insures homes against fire assumes that claims arise according to a Poisson distribution at an average rate of 2.25 per week. Let Y be the number of claims arising in a four-week period. Find
a. $P(Y \leq 10)$
b. $P(Y \geq 7)$
c. $P(7 \leq Y \leq 11)$
d. Find the expected value and standard deviation of Y.

5.25 Can you think of insurance situations that would make the Poisson assumption in Exercise 5.24 unreasonable?

5.26 Logging trucks have a particular problem with tire failures due to blowouts, cuts, and large punctures; these trucks are driven fast over very rough, temporary roads. Assume that such failures occur according to a Poisson distribution at a mean rate of 4.0 per 10,000 miles.
a. If a truck drives 1000 miles in a given week, what is the probability that it does not have any tire failures?
b. What is the probability that it has at least two failures?

c. What is the expected value and standard deviation of the number of tire failures per 1000 miles driven?

5.27 The Poisson distribution also applies to events occurring randomly over an area or in a volume. Chocolate chips spread through well-mixed cookie dough tend to follow a Poisson distribution. A commercial baker produces cookies with an average of eight chips per cookie.
a. What is the probability of (horrors!) a chipless cookie?
b. A cookie is considered acceptable only if it has at least five chips. What fraction of the cookies are acceptable?

5.28 Phone calls for information arrive at an operator switchboard at an average rate of two calls per minute. Assume that the number of calls in any time interval is a Poisson random variable.
a. What is the probability of exactly five calls in the next three minutes?
b. What is the probability that the operator will receive at least one phone call for information in the next three minutes?

5.29 Suppose that the number of defaults on home mortgage loans at National Mortgage Company follows a Poisson distribution with an average of 8.2 defaults per month.
a. Compute the probability of exactly 12 defaults at NMC next month.
b. What is the chance of *at least* one default *next week*?

5.4 The Normal Distribution

Now we turn to the most fundamental distribution used in statistical theory, the normal distribution. The normal distribution is a bell-shaped curve that appears in a very wide variety of settings. Standardized test scores are often constructed to yield normal distributions. (In fact, a recent and very controversial book on intelligence tests is titled *The Bell Curve.*)

Services that rate mutual funds publish data on the yields of various funds with a specified objective; these yields appear nearly normally distributed. Yields of lumber from trees in a mature forest appear normally distributed. There are theoretical reasons why the normal distribution occurs so often. In particular, the Central Limit Theorem that we consider in the next chapter says that any random quantity that is a sum or average of many components will have a nearly normal distribution. Even in situations that don't seem to have a theoretical reason for a normal distribution, that distribution "just happens" very often.

Many standard statistical procedures that we discuss in later chapters are based on the formal mathematical assumption that the underlying population has a normal distribution. Many methods that are widely used in economics, finance, and marketing are based on an assumption of a normal population. This section is therefore important in understanding many later sections of the text.

A normally distributed random variable is continuous, as opposed to the discrete binomial and Poisson probabilities. Therefore, it has a probability density, a smooth curve that may be thought of as an idealized histogram. Probabilities are not found by simply adding numbers in a table; instead, they must be found by calculating areas under the curve. We won't need to do a lot of math with the normal distribution equation, but it's worth presenting.

DEFINITION 5.6

Normal Probability Density

$$f_Y(y) = \frac{1}{\sqrt{2\pi}\sigma} \, e^{-.5((y-\mu)/\sigma)^2}$$

Notice that the value of y appears in this equation only in the term $((y - \mu)/\sigma)$. The values μ and σ in the normal density function are in fact the mean and standard deviation of Y (though we don't prove it). A probability histogram, called the **normal curve,** for a normal random variable is bell-shaped and symmetric around the mean μ, as shown in Figure 5.5.

normal curve

FIGURE 5.5

Normal Probability Distribution

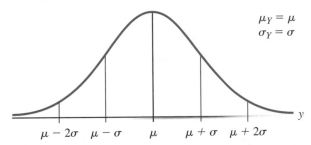

$$\mu_Y = \mu$$
$$\sigma_Y = \sigma$$

$\mu - 2\sigma \quad \mu - \sigma \quad \mu \quad \mu + \sigma \quad \mu + 2\sigma$

Because the math of the normal curve is a little too much like hard work, we will use normal distribution tables. Tables of normal curve areas (probabilities) are always given for the **standard normal distribution,** which has mean 0 and standard deviation 1. This distribution is universally called the Z distribution. Appendix Table 3 gives areas between 0 and a positive number z. For instance, the entry for $z = 1.00$ is .3413; if Z is the standard normal random variable, then $P(0 \leq Z \leq 1.00) = .3413$, as in Figure 5.6.

standard normal distribution

FIGURE 5.6

Standard Normal Probability Distribution

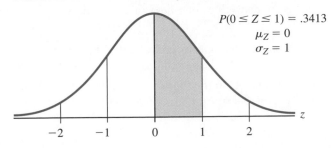

$$P(0 \leq Z \leq 1) = .3413$$
$$\mu_Z = 0$$
$$\sigma_Z = 1$$

$-2 \quad -1 \quad 0 \quad 1 \quad 2$

EXAMPLE 5.17   Let Z be a standard normal random variable. Find

a. $P(0 \leq Z \leq 1.96)$

b. $P(Z > 1.96)$

c. $P(-1.96 \leq Z \leq 1.96)$

d. $P(-1.00 \leq Z \leq 1.96)$

SOLUTION An illustration like Figure 5.7 makes it much easier to use normal tables. The entry for $z = 1.96$ (found by looking in the 1.9 row and .06 column) is .4750.

a. $P(0 \leq Z \leq 1.96) = .4750$

b. Because the area to the right of 0 must be .5000 (the normal curve is symmetric and the total area beneath the curve is 1), $P(Z > 1.96) = .5000 - .4750 = .0250$.

c. By symmetry, the area between -1.96 and 0 must also be equal to .4750. So $P(-1.96 \leq Z \leq 1.96) = .4750 + .4750 = .9500$.

d. $P(-1.00 \leq Z \leq 1.96) = .3413 + .4750 = .8163$. (Draw a picture.)

FIGURE 5.7   **Solution to Example 5.17**

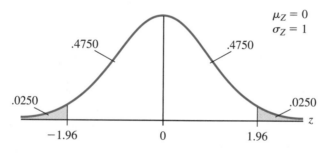

EXAMPLE 5.18   Find k_1 such that $P(0 \leq Z \leq k_1) = .40$ and k_2 such that $P(-k_2 \leq Z \leq k_2) = .60$.

SOLUTION This problem is in a sense the opposite of Example 5.17, in that problem values of z are given and probabilities have to be found. Here probabilities are given and values of z have to be found. Again, a picture is helpful (see Figure 5.8).

a. Looking through Appendix Table 3 for an area of .40, we find that the closest z value is 1.28. Therefore, $P(0 \leq Z \leq 1.28) = .40$; that is, $k_1 = 1.28$.

b. An area of .30 (half the desired probability as shown in Figure 5.8) corresponds to $z \approx .84$, so $P(-.84 \leq Z \leq .84) = .60$; that is, $k_2 = .84$.

FIGURE 5.8

Solution to Example 5.18

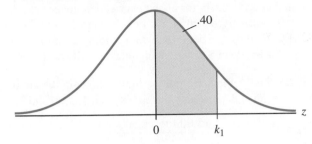

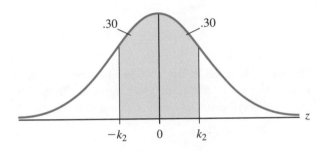

Any normal random variable Y can be transformed to a standard normal random variable Z by subtracting the expected value μ and dividing the result by the standard deviation σ:

$$Z = \frac{Y - \mu}{\sigma}$$

z-score

For a given value of y, the corresponding value of z, sometimes called a **z-score,** is the number of standard deviations that y lies away from μ. If $\mu = 100$ and $\sigma = 20$, a y value of 130 is 1.5 standard deviations above (to the right of) the mean μ, and the corresponding z-score is $z = (130 - 100)/20 = 1.50$. A y value of 85 is .75 standard deviations below (to the left of) the mean μ and

$$z = \frac{85 - 100}{20} = -.75$$

The relation between specific values of a normal random variable Y and corresponding z-scores is shown in Figure 5.9. [Note that $z = (y - \mu)/\sigma$.]

FIGURE 5.9

Relation Between Specific Values of Y and z-Scores

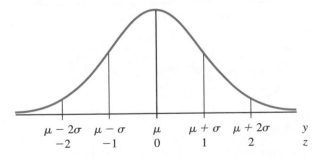

EXAMPLE 5.19

Annual benefits costs for career service employees at a large university are approximately normally distributed with a mean of $18,600 and a standard deviation of $2,700. Find the probability that an employee chosen at random has an annual benefits cost less than $15,000; an annual benefits cost greater than $21,000.

SOLUTION   First, we draw a figure showing the areas in question (Figure 5.10). Now we must determine the area between 15,000 and 18,600.

$$z = \frac{y - \mu}{\sigma} = \frac{15,000 - 18,600}{2700}$$

$$= \frac{-3600}{2700}$$

$$= -1.33$$

The area between the mean of a normal distribution and a value 1.33 standard deviations to the left of the mean, from Appendix Table 3, is .4082. Hence, the probability of observing annual benefits of less than $15,000 is

$$.5 - .4082 = .0918$$

Similarly, to compute the probability of observing benefits over $21,000, we determine the area between 18,600 and 21,000:

$$z = \frac{y - \mu}{\sigma} = \frac{21,000 - 18,600}{2700} = .89$$

The area corresponding to $z = .89$ is .3133. Hence the desired probability is

$$.5 - .3133 = .1867$$

FIGURE 5.10

Area Greater Than 21,000 and Smaller Than 15,000 for $\mu = 18,600$ and $\sigma = 2,700$

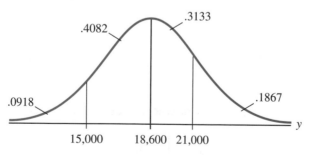

EXAMPLE 5.20

If Y has a normal distribution with mean 500 and standard deviation 100, find

a. $P(500 \leq Y \leq 696)$

b. $P(Y \geq 696)$

c. $P(304 \leq Y \leq 696)$

d. k such that $P(500 - k \leq Y \leq 500 + k) = .60$

SOLUTION

a. A y value of 696 is 1.96 standard deviations above the mean; $z = (696 - 500)/100 = 1.96$. Of course, 500 is 0 standard deviations above the mean, so $z = (500 - 500)/100 = 0.00$. Thus, $P(500 \leq Y \leq 696) = P(0 \leq Z \leq 1.96) = .4750$.

b. $P(Y \geq 696) = P(Z \geq 1.96) = .0250$.

c. $P(304 \leq Y \leq 696) = P(-1.96 \leq Z \leq 1.96) = .9500$, because 304 corresponds to a z of $(304 - 500)/100 = -1.96$.

d. As in Example 5.18, $P(-.84 \leq Z \leq .84) = .60$, so we want a range for Y from .84 standard deviation below the mean $\mu = 500$ to .84 standard deviation above the mean: $P[500 - .84(100) \leq Y \leq 500 + .84(100)] = P(416 \leq Y \leq 584) = .60$ (see Figure 5.11).

FIGURE 5.11   **Solution to Example 5.20**

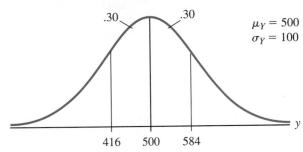

A little practice with such problems and a habit of drawing pictures makes normal probability calculations fairly easy.

As we've indicated previously, the concept of a continuous random variable is really an abstraction, because most variables of interest do have a finite number of possible values. But for many situations it is convenient to assume that the random variable of interest has a continuous distribution. In the same way, the normal random variable is an abstraction, because in theory any numerical value, negative as well as positive, is possible, and the probability histogram is a smooth, symmetric, bell-shaped curve. In practice, negative values or positive values such as $612.3142769 may be impossible. Such issues often don't really matter. If a random variable Y is assumed normal with mean 500 and standard deviation 100, the probability that $Y < 0$ is (by assumption) $P(Z < -5)$, which is effectively zero. Whether or not Y can actually assume negative values hardly matters. Similarly, the errors incurred by rounding off $612.3142769 to $612.31 or to $612 are tiny. If a population histogram for a random variable is generally bell shaped, the normal probability distribution usually provides an excellent model for the actual probability distribution.

Exercises

5.30 Suppose that Z represents a standard (tabled) normal random variable. Find the following probabilities:

a. $P(0 \leq Z \leq 1.00)$

b. $P(0 \leq Z \leq 1.65)$

c. $P(-1.00 \leq Z \leq 0)$

d. $P(-1.28 \leq Z \leq 0)$

e. $P(-1.65 \leq Z \leq 1.65)$

f. $P(-1.28 \leq Z \leq 1.28)$

g. $P(-1.07 \le Z \le 2.33)$

h. $P(Z \ge 2.65)$

i. $P(Z \le -2.42)$

j. $P(Z \ge 1.39 \text{ or } Z \le -1.39)$

Draw pictures.

5.31 For the standard normal random variable Z, solve the following equations for k:

a. $P(Z \ge k) = .01$

b. $P(-k \le Z \le k) = .98$

c. $P(Z \le -k) = .01$

d. $P(-k \le Z \le k) = .6826$

e. $P(-k \le Z \le k) = .9544$

f. $P(Z \ge k) = .95$

Again, draw pictures.

5.32 Refer to the answers to Exercise 5.31, parts (d) and (e). How do these answers relate to the Empirical Rule?

5.33 Suppose that Y represents a normally distributed random variable with expected value (mean) equal to 100 and standard deviation 15.

a. Show that the event $(Y \le 130)$ is equivalent to $(Z \le 2)$.

b. Convert the event $(Y \ge 82.5)$ to z-score form.

c. Find $P(Y \le 130)$ and $P(Y \ge 82.5)$.

d. Find $P(Y > 106)$, $P(Y < 94)$, and $P(94 \le Y \le 106)$.

e. Find $P(Y \le 70)$, $P(Y \ge 130)$, and $P(70 < Y < 130)$.

5.34 Consider the random variable Y of Exercise 5.33. Find the value of k satisfying

a. $P(100 \le Y \le 100 + k) = .45$

b. $P(100 - k \le Y \le 100 + k) = .90$

c. $P(Y \ge k) = .20$

d. $P(Y \le k) = .30$

e. $P(Y \le k) = .80$

f. $P(Y \ge k) = .70$

Draw appropriate pictures for each part.

5.35 A financial analyst states that the (subjective probability) price Y of a long-term $1000 government bond one year later is normally distributed with expected value $980 and standard deviation $40.

a. Find $P(Y \ge 1000)$.

b. Find $P(Y \le 940)$.

c. Find $P(960 \le Y \le 1060)$.

5.36 Refer to the random variable Y of Exercise 5.35.

a. Find the value of k satisfying $P(Y \ge k) = .90$.

b. Find the value k such that the probability that the price of the bond (one year later) exceeds k is .60.

5.37 Assume that the hourly wage rate earned by a worker in a clothing factory (based on a piecework pay system) is normally distributed with expected value $7.10 and standard deviation $0.40.

a. Find the probability that a worker's hourly rate exceeds $7.40.

b. Find the probability that a worker's hourly rate is between $6.70 and $7.50.

c. Find the probability that a worker's hourly rate exceeds a contractual minimum of $5.90.

5.38 The personnel director for ExxonMobil has observed that starting salaries for recent MBA graduates who get jobs in the oil industry tend to follow a normal distribution with a mean of $87,000 and a standard deviation of $6,000. They have a policy of paying recent MBA graduates a starting salary that is in the top 20% of comparable salaries in the oil industry. What is the minimum salary that ExxonMobil should offer?

5.39 The time required for a student to complete an Economics 101 exam is normally distributed with a mean of 55 minutes and a standard deviation of 12 minutes.

a. What percentage of students take between 40 and 60 minutes to complete an Economics 101 exam?

b. If 400 students take an Economics 101 exam, roughly how many students will *not* complete the exam in the allotted time of 75 minutes?

c. At what point in time (that is, how long after the exam starts) will the first one-fourth of the students have completed the exam?

5.40 Checking account balances at the Second National Bank follow a normal distribution with a mean of $700 and a standard deviation of $275.

a. What percentage of account balances fall between $500 and $1000?

b. Second National Bank has decided to give free checking to its best customers (that is, those with the highest checking account balances). If the bank decides to limit free checking to one-third of all customers, what is the minimum checking account balance required to qualify for free checking?

5.41 A potato chip packaging plant has a process line that fills 12-ounce bags of potato chips. At the current setting of the machine, the quality control engineer knows that the actual distribution of weights in the bags follows a normal distribution with a mean of 12.0 ounces and a standard deviation of .18 ounces.

a. What percentage of all bags filled contain exactly 12 ounces?

b. What percentage of all bags filled contain more than 12.4 ounces?

c. Find the 60th percentile of the actual weights of 12-ounce bags of potato chips.

d. Management is concerned when 12-ounce bags of potato chip contain less than 11.75 ounces. The quality control engineer can set the filling machine so that the actual mean filling weight is whatever he chooses, but the standard deviation always remains at .18 ounces. What mean filling weight should he set the machine to if he wants only 1% of all bags to contain less than 11.75 ounces? (*Hint:* Draw a picture.)

5.42 A person's cholesterol level is measured by taking a blood sample. If the cholesterol level is above 230, the person is said to have high cholesterol. Due to measurement error and daily fluctuations, there is variability in an individual's readings. Suppose that Judy's blood cholesterol readings follow a normal distribution with a mean of 200 and a standard deviation of 14.

a. What is the probability that Judy's next cholesterol reading will be high (above 230)?

b. Find the 15th percentile of Judy's cholesterol readings.

c. If Judy takes a cholesterol test each day for the next 10 days, what is the probability that at least one of those tests will indicate high cholesterol (that is, above 230)?

5.43 A new investor is considering making an investment of $100,000 in one of two stocks. Historically, the annual returns from ABC Corporation stock have averaged 12% with a standard deviation of 9%, and the annual returns from XYZ Corporation stock have averaged 10% with a standard deviation of 6%. Assume that annual returns are normally distributed for both stocks.

a. Compute the probability that an investment in ABC Corporation will have an annual return less than 14% next year.

b. Determine *k* such that there is a 70% probability that XYZ Corporation will earn at least *k*% in one year.

c. Which of these two investment options would you recommend to the investor if his primary investment objective is to avoid losing any of his original investment in the first year?

5.44 The owners of Spiffy Lube want to offer their customers a 10-minute guarantee on their standard oil change service. If the oil change takes longer than 10 minutes to complete, the customer is given a coupon for a free oil change at the next visit. Based on past history, the owners believe that the time required to complete an oil change has a normal distribution with a mean of 8.6 minutes and a standard deviation of 1.2 minutes.

a. What percentage of customers will receive a free oil change coupon?

b. If management wants to limit the percentage of customers receiving a coupon to no more than 1 out of every 25 customers on average, what should they change the guaranteed time to?

c. Suppose management could improve the process by reducing the mean time required for an oil change (but keeping the standard deviation the same). How much change in the mean service time would be required to allow for a 10-minute guarantee that gives a coupon to no more than 1 out of every 25 customers on average?

5.5 Checking Normality

The normal distribution of data occurs quite frequently. There are theoretical reasons for this occurrence, including the Central Limit Theorem, which will be explained in Chapter 6. Sometimes, data just happen to fit this distribution well. It certainly is *not* true that every distribution should look normal, or that other distributions are somehow "abnormal." But the distribution occurs often enough—and is the basis for enough statistical methods—that special tools have been developed to assess whether data fit a normal distribution.

Many statistical packages superimpose a plot of a normal curve over a histogram. For example, a manufacturer of plastic sheeting used as a protective cover while painting walls and ceilings sells one grade that is stated to be 2 mils thick. If the sheeting is not thick enough, it is likely to tear and fail in its job of protection. If it's too thick, the manufacturer is wasting money on the extra material. The manufacturer can measure the thickness quite closely using material trimmed off in the process of cutting the material for packaging. Suppose that a sample of 400 measurements is obtained. A histogram and normal curve, produced by JMP, are shown in Figure 5.12.

The data appear to be quite close to a normal distribution. The normal curve appears to be a good approximation to the histogram. Notice that the mean is 2.017, just above the stated value of 2 mils; the standard deviation is .0381. Because the data appear quite close to normally distributed, we can expect that the Empirical Rule will be a good approximation for these data. In fact, it is excellent; 290 of the 400 values (72.5%) are within 1 standard deviation of the mean, and 379 of the 400 values (94.8%) are within 2 standard deviations of the mean. Incidentally, rather than counting by hand, we had the program create a new variable that equaled 1 for each value within 1 standard deviation of the mean, and 0 for all other values. The sum of these 1s and 0s is simply the number of values within 1 standard deviation of the mean. A similar process gave us the count of values within 2 standard deviations of the mean.

FIGURE 5.12
Histogram and Normal Curve for Thickness Data

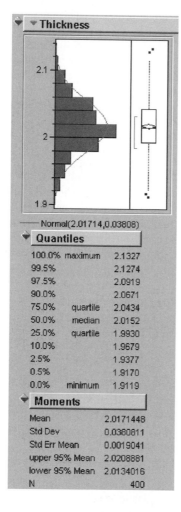

— Normal(2.01714,0.03808)

Quantiles

100.0%	maximum	2.1327
99.5%		2.1274
97.5%		2.0919
90.0%		2.0671
75.0%	quartile	2.0434
50.0%	median	2.0152
25.0%	quartile	1.9930
10.0%		1.9679
2.5%		1.9377
0.5%		1.9170
0.0%	minimum	1.9119

Moments

Mean	2.0171448
Std Dev	0.0380811
Std Err Mean	0.0019041
upper 95% Mean	2.0208881
lower 95% Mean	2.0134016
N	400

FIGURE 5.13
Plots for Cable Data

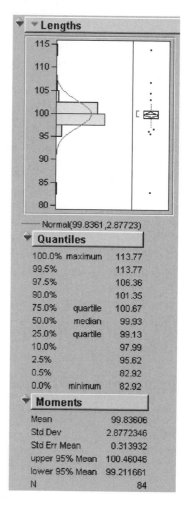

— Normal(99.8361,2.87723)

Quantiles

100.0%	maximum	113.77
99.5%		113.77
97.5%		106.36
90.0%		101.35
75.0%	quartile	100.67
50.0%	median	99.93
25.0%	quartile	99.13
10.0%		97.99
2.5%		95.62
0.5%		82.92
0.0%	minimum	82.92

Moments

Mean	99.83606
Std Dev	2.8772346
Std Err Mean	0.313932
upper 95% Mean	100.46046
lower 95% Mean	99.211661
N	84

EXAMPLE 5.21   A manufacturer of telephone cable cuts the cable into lengths that are sent to field engineers. The engineers use the cable to connect new installations to phone lines and to replace broken or defective cable. The cutting process is done at high speed, and the production manager was concerned that the cuts were not accurate. A sample of 84 sections of wire, each supposedly 100 meters long, was measured for actual length. The data were plotted by JMP, with a normal curve superimposed on the histogram, as shown in Figure 5.13. Does it appear that the Empirical Rule will work well for the length data?

SOLUTION   The histogram does not match the normal curve at all well. The sharp peak in the middle is much higher than the curve, and several values in the histogram are beyond the range shown for the normal curve. These values appear to be outliers. Notice that there are several outliers. In fact, we counted 75 of the 84 values within 1 standard deviation of the mean; that's about 90%, a very bad approximation to 68%.

normal probability plot

Another graphical method that is useful in checking whether data follow a normal distribution is a **normal probability plot,** sometimes called a *normal quantile plot.* We don't yet have all the ideas needed to describe how such a plot is constructed. For now, we simply state that (nearly) normally distributed data should appear as a (nearly) straight line in this plot. For example, we noted that the data on thickness of plastic sheeting appeared nearly normal. A normal probability plot of the data, constructed by JMP, is shown in Figure 5.14. The points in the plot are, indeed, quite close to a line, confirming that the data are nearly normally distributed.

FIGURE 5.14   **Normal Probability Plot for Thickness Data**

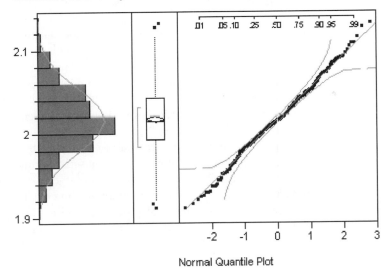

Normal Quantile Plot

EXAMPLE 5.22   A normal probability plot for the cable length data of the previous example is shown in Figure 5.15. How does the plot indicate that the data are not normally distributed?

SOLUTION   The plot doesn't look like a straight line. Instead, it has something of an inverted S shape. Note the point in the lower left corner, which is far away from the reference line.

FIGURE 5.15

Normal Probability Plot for Cable Lengths

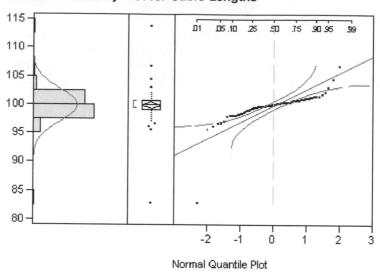

Normal Quantile Plot

capability

The normal distribution and Empirical Rule are useful tools in assessing the **capability** of a manufacturing process. Capability refers to the ability of a process to produce products that meet specifications. For example, suppose that external specifications for the thickness of 2-mil plastic sheeting call for actual thicknesses between 1.85 and 2.15 mils. Our sample of 400 thicknesses had a mean of 2.017 and a standard deviation of .0381. If we assume that these values represent the actual mean and standard deviation of all the sheeting that's produced, we can calculate that virtually all the values will be within 3 standard deviations of the mean. The range $2.017 \pm 3(.0381)$ is from 1.9027 to 2.1313, so practically all thicknesses should be in the specified range: 1.85 to 2.15.

A process can be incapable—fail to meet specifications—for several reasons. The process may be "off target," having a seriously incorrect average value. Or it may yield too much variation, having too large a standard deviation. Or it may produce outlying values that prevent application of the Empirical Rule. There are a number of special indices of process capability; we won't go into them here, except to note that several of them assume a roughly normal distribution of measurements.

EXAMPLE 5.23

The cable-cutting process in the previous two examples is intended to produce cables that are between 97 and 103 meters long. Based on the sample data, is the process capable?

SOLUTION   No. Assuming that 97 to 103 is intended to be the mean ± 3 standard deviations, we would need a mean of 100 and a standard deviation of 1. The standard deviation in the data is much larger than 1, so there is too much variability. Also, we saw that the data contained several outlying values; these values are well outside the desired range.

Exercises

5.45 In Exercises 2.22–2.25, we considered the number of calls cleared by operators in a directory assistance center. The data were somewhat skewed, with an outlier. A normal probability plot, produced using Minitab, is shown in Figure 5.16.
a. How does the normal probability plot reveal the skewness?
b. How does the plot show the outlier?

5.46 In the calls-cleared data, how will the outlier affect the standard deviation and the quality of the Empirical Rule approximation?

5.47 A Minitab normal probability plot of changes in the Consumer Price Index (CPI) for the Philadelphia region is shown in Figure 5.17 (see next page). What does the plot indicate about the shape of the distribution?

5.48 A supplier of lumber for home building sells construction-grade 2-by-4 lumber in 8-foot lengths. Because of irregularities in the wood and shrinkage caused by drying, there is some variation in actual length. Lumber is acceptable if it is between 95.5 and 96.5 inches. The current process produces lengths that are normally distributed with a mean of 96.04 inches and a standard deviation of .52 inch. Is this process capable of meeting standards of acceptability?

5.49 Lumber that is too long (over 96.5 inches) can be cut by the home builder. Lumber that is too short must be discarded. The supplier can increase the mean length to 96.54 inches without changing the standard deviation. What would this change do to the proportion of lumber that is too short?

FIGURE 5.16 **Normal Probability Plot for Calls-Cleared Data**

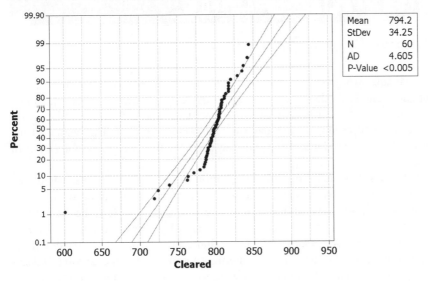

Mean	794.2
StDev	34.25
N	60
AD	4.605
P-Value	<0.005

FIGURE 5.17 **Normal Probability Plot for Change in CPI Data**

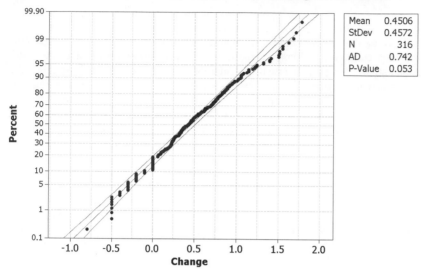

Mean	0.4506
StDev	0.4572
N	316
AD	0.742
P-Value	0.053

BUSINESS DECISION-MAKING IN ACTION

CHAPTER CASE

ANALYSIS

Kilgore Manufacturing, Inc.

Kilgore Manufacturing has an opportunity to bid on a defense contract that requires a component, the R-7 relay switch, produced by KMI and three of its competitors. Bidders must submit their bids in the form of a guaranteed minimum number of relay switches to be produced each day over the contract period. The winner of the contract will be assessed a $5000 penalty on each day that production falls short of the guaranteed number of units.

Bill Shelton has stated that the distribution of daily production levels of the R-7 relay switch at Kilgore is described well by a normal distribution with a mean of 635 units and a standard deviation of 40 units; that is, if we let Y be the random variable that represents the number of relay switches produced in one day by Kilgore, then $Y \sim N(635,40)$. Our problem is to find a value of Y, say y, such that if the guaranteed minimum bid level is y, then Kilgore will average the $1000 profit per day set by Kilgore management after allowing for penalties on those days when production falls short of y.

Following the example outlined by Tim Reynolds, the average daily profit without consideration of the penalty is 635 units times Kilgore's $3.80 profit margin per relay switch, which gives $2413. Tim used a 5% figure for the percentage of days on which production would fall short. For our yet-to-be-determined bid value of y, the true percentage of days on which production falls short of y and a penalty is incurred is given by $P(Y < y)$. In the long run, the average daily loss due to penalties will be $5000 \cdot P(Y < y)$.

Therefore, we need to find a value of y such that

$$\$2413 - \$5000 \cdot P(Y < y) = \$1000$$

in order for Kilgore to average the required $1000 profit per day. Solving this equation gives

$$P(Y < y) = .2826$$

which yields $y = 635 - .575(40) = 612$ units for the guaranteed minimum bid level. (The z-score of $-.575$ corresponds to the cumulative probability of .2826 and can be found from the standard normal distribution table.) Figure 5.18 illustrates this calculation.

FIGURE 5.18   **Calculation of the Optimum Bid Under the Current Production Process**

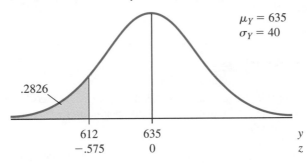

So, if Kilgore decides to stay with the original production process, it can afford to bid 612 R-7 relay units per day. Will that be enough to be competitive in the bid for the contract when the bidding is likely to start at 600 units?

As another important consideration, note that Kilgore's daily production of R-7 relay switches falls below 612 units on a little more than 28% of all production days. Falling short of the promised bid amount on such a high percentage of days will probably not help Kilgore achieve its goal of establishing a long term relationship with Avionics.

Kilgore will soon have the data from the 60-day production run under the new production process. In the case at the end of this chapter, those data are provided and you are asked to complete the strategic analysis for the Kilgore Manufacturing bidding decision.

SUMMARY

Here are some issues to consider when deciding whether a particular probability distribution applies to a problem.

1. The binomial distribution may apply when there is a fixed number of distinct, separate trials. In contrast, Poisson probabilities may apply when there is a fixed period of time and the interest is in the number of occurrences of some event over that time period.

2. Think about the reasonableness of assumptions. For binomial probabilities, the key assumptions are a fixed probability of success and independent trials. For Poisson probabilities, the key assumptions are nonclumping, a constant rate of occurrence, and independence.

3. For the normal distribution, a histogram of the data with a superimposed normal curve or a normal probability plot can be used to assess whether the data came from a normal distribution.

4. All these models apply only in special situations. If none of them are applicable, the general methods of Chapter 3 can still be used to find probabilities.

5. The shortcut formulas for expected values and variances also apply only to the special situations. If underlying assumptions aren't reasonable, the shortcut formulas don't apply and the general definitions in Chapter 4 must be used.

In addition, you may want to reread the Executive Overview at the beginning of this chapter.

Supplementary Exercises

5.50   A telephone-sales firm is considering purchasing a machine that randomly selects and automatically dials telephone numbers. The firm would be using the machine to call residences during the evening; calls to business phones would be wasted. The manufacturer of the machine claims that its programming reduces the business-phone rate to 15%. As a test, 100 phone numbers are to be selected at random from a very large set of possible numbers.
a. Are the binomial assumptions satisfied in this situation?
b. Find the probability that at least 24 of the numbers belong to business phones.
c. If in fact 24 of the 100 numbers turn out to be business phones, does this cast serious doubt on the manufacturer's claim? Explain.

5.51   Refer to Exercise 5.50. Find the expected value and variance of Y, the number of business-phone numbers in the sample.

5.52   It is estimated that 5% of all Medicaid claims in a particular city are fraudulent. A random sample of 50 claims is taken.
a. What is the probability that at most one claim in the sample is fraudulent?
b. What is the probability that at least four are fraudulent?

5.53   Some people claim that female managers tend to be placed in fringe areas, such as public relations or personnel management, as opposed to the central areas of production, marketing, and finance. Suppose that a firm has 24 male and 6 female managers at the assistant vice president level. Of these positions, 14 are regarded as fringe positions.
a. In how many distinct ways can the 14 fringe managers be selected?
b. In how many ways can the fringe managers be selected such that 5 of the 6 women are included?

c. If the fringe managers had been randomly selected, what is the probability that at least 5 would be women?

5.54   Assume that lost-time industrial accidents occur in a plant according to a Poisson distribution with mean .12 per day. Let Y = number of such accidents in a 10-day period.
a. Find $P(Y = 1)$ and $P(Y \le 1)$.
b. Find μ_Y and σ_Y.

5.55   The weekly demand for 5-pound sacks of flour at a particular supermarket is assumed to be approximately normal with mean 72.0 cases and standard deviation 1.6 cases. Let Y = demand in a particular week.
a. Find $P(Y \le 72.8)$ and $P(71.2 \le Y \le 72.8)$.
b. Find $P(Y \ge 74.0)$.
c. The ordering policy of the market is that there be a 1% chance of stockout (demand exceeding supply) in any particular week. How much flour must be stocked to achieve this goal?

5.56   Refer to Exercise 5.55.
a. What is the probability that demand exceeds 73.0 cases in a particular week?
b. What is the probability that demand exceeds 73.0 cases in exactly three of four consecutive weeks? Assume independence from week to week.

5.57   A certain amount of material is wasted in cutting patterns for garments. A producer of army uniforms has found that the wastage is normally distributed with mean 4.1% and standard deviation .6% from lot to lot.
a. In a particular lot, what is the probability that the wastage exceeds 5%?
b. If the actual amount of material required for a lot is 4700 yards, and 5000 yards of material are available, what is the probability that the supply of material is adequate?

5.58 Suppose that in Exercise 5.57 the wastage of a particular cutter is measured for 10 lots.
a. What is the probability of exceeding 5% in at least 8 of 10 lots?
b. Would such a result conclusively indicate that the cutter was inefficient?

5.59 A modem is an electronic device used in communication between computers. The specifications for a particular modem demand that the mean number of errors in transmitting through the device be one per 5000 words (or better). A particular modem is to be tested on a 25,000-word transmission. If eight or more errors occur in transmission, the device will not be accepted. Assume that Poisson probabilities apply and that the modem just meets the 1 per 5000 standard.
a. What is the probability that the device will be accepted?
b. Can you think of a reason why the Poisson assumptions may not hold?

5.60 Assume that the Poisson distribution applies in Exercise 5.59 but also that the modem has a mean error rate of one per 2500 words, thus not meeting specifications. What is the probability that the device will be accepted?

5.61 Executives at a soft drink company wish to test a new formulation of their chief product. The new drink is tested in comparison to the current one. Each of 1000 potential customers is given a cup of the current formulation and a cup of the new one. The cups are labeled H and K to avoid bias. Each customer indicates a preference. Assume that, in fact, the customers can't detect a difference and are, in effect, guessing. Define Y to be the number (out of 1000) indicating preference for the new formulation.
a. What probability distribution should apply to Y? Do the assumptions underlying that distribution seem plausible in this context?
b. Find the mean and standard deviation of Y.

5.62 A firm is considering using telemarketing techniques to supplement traditional marketing methods. It's estimated that 1 of every 100 calls results in a sale. Suppose that 250 calls are made in a single day.
a. Write an expression for the probability that there are five or fewer sales. Don't carry out any arithmetic.
b. What did you assume in answering part (a)? Are any of these assumptions grossly unreasonable?

5.63 The chief executive officer (CEO) of a medium-size corporation must select three individuals to head the firm's annual drive for community charities. There are three divisions (A, B, and C) within the firm and five, six, and four individuals, respectively, within the divisions who could be chosen.

a. How many combinations of three individuals can be chosen such that one individual comes from each of the three divisions?
b. Suppose that the CEO chooses the individuals at random. What is the probability that at least two of them come from division A?

5.64 Refer to Exercise 5.63, part (b). Let Y = number of individuals chosen from division A. Find the expected value and variance of Y.

5.65 Brand managers at a consumer-products company regard an introductory advertising campaign for a new product as successful if at least 20% of the target group are made aware of the product. After one such campaign, a market research study finds that 56 of 400 individuals sampled are aware of the product. The target group is all adults who possess driver's licenses in the United States.
a. Write an expression for the exact probability that 56 or fewer people in the sample are aware of the product, assuming that 20% of the target group is aware of the product. What probability distribution applies? What assumptions have you made?
b. Find the expected value and standard deviation for the number of people in the sample who are aware of the product.
c. Use the normal distribution with the mean and standard deviation just found to find a numerical value for this probability.
d. If you were the brand manager, would you believe that the advertising campaign had been successful?

5.66 A certain birth defect occurs with probability .0001; that is, 1 of every 10,000 babies has this defect. If 5,000 babies are born at a particular hospital in a given year, what is the probability that there is at least one baby with the defect? If you have access to a computer package that calculates probabilities, use it to find a numerical answer.

5.67 Several states now have a Lotto lottery game. A player chooses six distinct integers in the range 1 to 40. If exactly those six numbers are selected as the winning numbers, the player receives a very large prize. What is the probability that a particular set of six numbers will be drawn? You may wish to think of the six numbers drawn as "success" numbers.

5.68 In the Lotto game described in Exercise 5.67, there are smaller prizes for selecting exactly five of the six winning numbers and even smaller prizes for selecting exactly four of the six winning numbers.
a. What is the probability of selecting exactly four of the six winning numbers?
b. What is the probability of selecting at least four of the six winning numbers?

5.69 Suppose that the Lotto game in Exercise 5.67 is changed such that six numbers were chosen in the range 1 to 42, rather than 1 to 40.

a. Without doing any arithmetic, determine if the probability of selecting all six winning numbers should be larger or smaller than it was in Exercise 5.67. Will the change be small or large?

b. Now compute the probability of selecting all six winning numbers, chosen from the numbers 1 to 42.

c. Compare your answer to part (b) with the answer to Exercise 5.67. Did the probability change as you expected in part (a) of this exercise?

5.70 Suppose that, in the Lotto game of Exercise 5.67, 1,000,000 players make independent choices of the six numbers.

a. What probability distribution applies to the random variable Y = number of players selecting all six numbers?

b. Find an expression for $P(Y = 0)$. Don't carry out the arithmetic.

c. Write an expression for $P(Y \geq 2)$.

5.71 Refer to Exercise 5.70.

a. Find the expected value and variance of the random variable Y.

b. If you have a suitable computer program, use it to calculate a numerical value for the exact probability.

5.72 Fires in occupied homes in a particular city occur at a rate of one every two days.

a. What is the expected number of fires in homes over a seven-day week?

b. Find the probability that there are at least four fires in a particular week.

c. What are you assuming about the occurrence of fires in your answer to part (b)? Do any of the assumptions seem grossly unreasonable?

5.73 The operator of a mainframe computer system receives unscheduled requests to mount tapes. By policy, these requests must be answered as quickly as possible; therefore, they interrupt scheduled workflow. Data indicate that the rate of such requests during the 9 A.M.–5 P.M. shift is about 1.5 per hour. Let Y = number of requests received in a particular 9 A.M.–5 P.M. shift.

a. Find the mean and standard deviation of Y.

b. Find $P(Y > 8)$.

5.74 Refer to Exercise 5.73. Find the probability that the time between successive requests is at least two hours.

5.75 The computer system manager in Exercise 5.73 notes that the demand for unscheduled tape mounts varies during the typical workday. Between 9 A.M. and 1 P.M. there is an average of 1 request per hour; between 1 P.M. and 5 P.M. there is an average of 2 requests per hour.

a. Does this fact change your answers to part (a)?

b. Does this fact affect your answer to part (b)?

5.76 A manufacturing plant uses 2000 light bulbs on its floor. Suppose that light bulb lives are normally distributed with a mean of 500 hours and a standard deviation of 50 hours. Management wants to use a fixed replacement policy to minimize disruptions during plant operation. Every bulb, burning or not, will be replaced after a fixed interval of time has passed since the last replacement. OSHA regulations require that lighting in the plant must be at least 99% of capacity on the average. How often must the light bulbs be replaced so that on average at most 1% of the bulbs burn out between replacements?

5.77 Your stock broker has recommended the Mayflower Mutual Fund as an investment. Past data show that the annual rate of return for this fund follows a normal distribution with a mean of 15.2% and a standard deviation of 6.4%.

a. What is the probability that the Mayflower Fund will lose money next year?

b. Last year's rate of return on the Mayflower Fund was at the first quartile (25th percentile) of all its past performances. What was the actual rate of return for Mayflower last year?

c. Your stockbroker has also recommended another mutual fund, the Liberty Fund, which has annual returns that have historically followed a normal distribution with a mean of 14.5% and a standard deviation of 9.8%. Which of these funds is the better choice if your objective is to achieve a return of at least 20% next year? Explain this somewhat surprising answer.

d. A mutual fund specialist tells you that he can predict at the beginning of each year whether the Mayflower Fund or the Liberty Fund will have the higher annual return. Create a Minitab or Excel simulation to determine the expected value of this information; that is, how much you could increase your expected annual return by switching between the two funds based on the specialist's predictions over following a strategy of simply investing in the Mayflower Fund each year? Assume that the Mayflower and Liberty returns are independent.

5.78 Gil Bates of MicroGates Software claims that 75% of their registered Windoze 2000 customers have already upgraded to Windoze XP. In a random sample of 20 registered Windoze 2000 customers, 10 customers had upgraded to Windoze XP.

a. Before taking the sample, what was the probability of observing *exactly* 10 customers who upgraded to Windoze XP in a random sample of 20 Windoze 2000 users?

b. From Minitab, it can be determined that the probability of 10 or fewer upgraded customers in a random sample of 20 customers is .0139. What conclusion would you draw based on this information? Explain.

5.79 A snack food corporation produces granola bars. Although the packaging indicates a net weight of 58 grams, the actual weights of the granola bars follow a normal distribution with a mean of 64.0 grams and a standard deviation of 3.2 grams.

a. What percentage of granola bars have weights below the advertised weight?

b. The company can purchase some new production equipment that will improve the process by cutting the standard deviation in half (that is, from 3.2 to 1.6 grams). If the new equipment is installed, the company will change the mean of the process (from its current level of 64.0 grams) in such a way as to maintain the current level of "underweight" granola bars. Compute the value of the new mean.

c. Assuming that production remains at the current level of 50,000 granola bars per day and that each granola bar currently costs the company $0.392 (in ingredients) to produce, how much can the company expect to save (in ingredient costs) per day by purchasing the new equipment?

5.80 Lone Star Air is a small business-commuter air service in Crowley, Texas, with a single passenger jet that can carry up to 16 passengers. The practice at LSA is to overbook a flight by selling more tickets than there are seats available. Past experience suggests that, on average, about 1 in 12 passengers does not show up for a flight. On their next flight, LSA has booked 18 passengers. Compute the probability that at least 1 passenger will not have a seat due to overbooking.

5.81 The number of claims for missing baggage for a well-known airline in a small city averages nine per day. What is the probability that, on a given day, there will be *fewer than three* claims made?

Determining Workforce Size

A copy machine provider is about to undergo a major expansion. The company leases and services copiers for businesses and institutions. It is about to absorb another firm in the same business. One major question facing the company is: How many service technicians are required for the combined load of the two firms?

The company distinguishes two categories of copier. Office-use copiers are typically used for small numbers of copies and they are operated by secretaries and casual users. Production-use copiers are typically used for major jobs. They are operated by specialists. The company leases different styles of copiers for the two uses. It maintains separate staffs of service technicians for the two. Because the copiers are standard brands, service is the main area of competition with other providers. The company wants to have an adequate staff of technicians, but it doesn't want to have so many that they are idle a large fraction of the time.

Currently, before absorbing the other firm, the company has 2105 office-use copiers and 386 production-use copiers under lease. Requests for service are treated basically on a first-called, first-served basis. The service dispatcher logs requests and assigns technicians to them in order of request. Office-use technicians normally can service a maximum of eight requests per day; production-use technicians typically work on more complex problems and can service a maximum of four requests per day. If a sudden burst of requests overloads the supply of technicians, jobs are "bumped" to the next day. The company's president feels that bumped customers are likely to go elsewhere when their contracts expire. The company currently employs eight technicians for office-use copiers and seven technicians for production-use copiers. The company uses a guideline that office-use copiers will need service once every 50 workdays (though some think it's once every 40 or once every 60 days) and production-use copiers once every 20 workdays (possibly once every 16 or once every 24 days).

When the company absorbs the other firm, it will have 3185 office-use copiers and 596 production-use copiers under lease. The company president has heard two arguments about the required number of technicians. First, the absorption represents basically a 50% increase in leases, so an increase of 50% in technicians is necessary. The counterargument is that the company maintains an excess of technicians to protect against exceptionally heavy bursts of requests. The law of averages says that the bigger pool of copiers under lease should tend to even out these bursts, so a proportionate increase in technicians isn't necessary.

Assignment: The president has asked you to examine the question, particularly the risk of "bumping" requests to the next workday. You might reasonably assume that service calls occur essentially randomly. The president is willing to read technical material, but has had no formal training in statistics, so you'll have to explain your ideas clearly.

Kilgore Manufacturing, Inc. Revisited

Sixty production days have passed since Kilgore Manufacturing changed over to the new R-7 relay switch production process. Bill Shelton has kept careful track of the daily production levels over those 60 days.

The production data are contained in the file Kilgore on the CD that came with your book. The file contains information on the first 60 days of production under the new process. A partial listing of the data within Excel is shown in Figure 5.19.

FIGURE 5.19

Partial Listing of the Kilgore Manufacturing Data

	A	B	C	D
1	Month	Date	Day	Units
2	June	3	M	524
3	June	4	T	559
4	June	5	W	557
5	June	6	R	549
6	June	7	F	598
7	June	10	M	568
8	June	11	T	572
9	June	12	W	538
10	June	13	R	617
11	June	14	F	509
12	June	17	M	623
13	June	18	T	670
14	June	19	W	586
15	June	20	R	590
16	June	21	F	566
17	June	24	M	623
18	June	25	T	665

In the Kilgore file, the variables are defined as follows:

Month: Month of production for that production day (June, July, and August)

Date: Date of the month for that production day

Day: Day of the week for that production day (M, T, W, R, F)

Units: Number of units produced on that production day

Assignment: Assume that you have been hired as a statistical consultant to help Kilgore make the bidding decision for the Avionics contract. Using this data set and other information given in the case earlier in this chapter, help Jim Kilgore determine how to bid for the R-7 relay switch contract with Avionics. In particular, you need to decide whether Kilgore should go with the old or the new R-7 production process and then determine the optimal guaranteed minimum daily production level. Use important details from your analysis to support your recommendation.

Write a report to Jim Kilgore providing your analysis of the data and final recommendation. The report should consist of two parts: (1) a one-page executive memo that briefly summarizes the main findings of your analysis and your recommendation, and (2) a detailed analysis of the data that describes your analysis and interpretations. Incorporate important details, graphs, and tables from your analysis into the second part of your report to support your recommendation. Blend output, tables, and graphs with your written text. (Do not put all of the output and graphs in an appendix.) You may assume that Jim Kilgore is reasonably familiar with basic statistical techniques, but make your written presentation as clear as possible to any other interested readers.

CHAPTER 6

Random Sampling

and Sampling Distributions

CHAPTER CONTENTS

Any summary statistic will vary from one sample to another and from the true population or process value. We can determine the pattern of that variation. Using probability theory or computer simulation, we can determine the theoretical (sampling) distribution of a statistic, given certain assumptions. There are several important ideas in this chapter that will be used heavily later on:

- Any statistical study can be seriously distorted by bias—systematic distortions in the collection of data. There are several sources of bias, including selection bias, in which some subgroups are systematically over- or underrepresented in the data. One of the important steps in considering any statistical study is consideration of how serious the bias problem is.

- If a sample is genuinely random, we can derive the theoretical distribution of any summary statistic, given limited assumptions about the population. This theoretical distribution is different from the population distribution.

- In particular, the sample mean has expected value equal to the population or process mean. The standard deviation of its theoretical distribution, called the standard error of the mean, is the population standard deviation divided by the square root of the sample size.

- The sample mean (and sample sum) have approximately a normal distribution. The distribution is exactly normal if the population distribution is exactly normal. Otherwise, the Central Limit Theorem indicates that the distribution is approximately normal for a large enough sample size. The quality of the approximation depends most importantly on the skewness of the population or process distribution.

- A normal probability plot is useful for checking whether a distribution is nearly normal. It can be applied either to sample data or to a summary statistic such as a mean or median in a simulation study.

Now we can combine the ideas of summarizing data from Chapter 2 and the probability concepts from Chapters 3 to 5 into a central notion of statistics, which is the idea of the sampling distribution of a statistic.

Summary statistics—means, medians, standard deviations, anything—vary from one sample to another. Samples from populations are taken randomly, so the means (for example) of two samples from the same population will differ to some degree. Samples from ongoing processes like production or sales are affected by uncontrolled, random influences, so two sample means from the same process will differ randomly. The sampling distribution of a summary statistic is a way to describe the variability of that statistic from one sample to another.

Probability theory can be used to obtain a sampling distribution, given certain assumptions. Such probability concepts as expected value and standard deviation of a random variable will be used repeatedly in this chapter.

DataStor Company

"Another rejected shipment! That makes four in the past 20 days!" Tony Escalera knew that his boss, Bill Roberts, wouldn't be happy. Something was wrong, and things were going to be uncomfortable for everybody at DataStor until the problem was solved.

A few years ago, DataStor, a producer of magnetic data storage devices and media for the computer industry, began selling its new DataStor DS100, a compact hard drive, exclusively to Four-D Office Products, a national retailer. This arrangement with Four-D has been very profitable for DataStor.

Bill Roberts, vice president in charge of Sales at DataStor, rose rapidly up the management ladder due in large part to his role in developing the account with Four-D. Four-D had been impressed with Roberts and DataStor's commitment to quality.

In the manufacturing process, each of the three 8-hour shifts produces approximately 1200 DS100 drives per day. Once an hour as part of the quality inspection process, one drive is subjected to the PDQ (Performance and Drive Quality) test, originally developed by DataStor. The PDQ, a stiff test, measures the performance of the drive in a variety of conditions, checks accuracy and speed, and tests for defects in the drive's mechanism and storage media. The PDQ, a relatively expensive test that takes up to 20 minutes to do, computes an overall test score. The scores have historically followed a normal distribution with a mean value of 7.0 and a standard deviation of .30 when the process has been in control. Each hour, the new PDQ value is added to a control chart. Test scores below the lower control limit (LCL) may indicate a drop in quality, while scores above the upper control limit (UCL) may indicate a potential improvement in the process.

Shipments are made to Four-D once each day. Before Four-D accepts a shipment, it runs a random sample of 10 drives through the PDQ test as a final inspection. At Four-D, a drive is judged to be nonconforming if its score falls below 6.2. If one or more drives in the sample of 10 are found to be nonconforming, the entire shipment is judged to be "unacceptable" and returned to DataStor, which must pay a penalty to Four-D and replace the unacceptable shipment within 24 hours. Further penalties are assessed for each additional day that passes before the shipment is replaced.

The production engineers at DataStor have told Bill Roberts that "zero-defect" production is just about impossible, but that the percentage of defects has been reduced to the point that only rarely will a shipment be judged unacceptable. But in recent weeks, the frequency of returned shipments has noticeably increased. It was Tony's job as chief production engineer to bring the bad news of the latest returned shipment to Bill Roberts.

Roberts: Another rejected shipment! That makes four in the past 20 days! What's going on, Tony?

Escalera: Right now, I don't know any more than you do, Mr. Roberts. To borrow some statistical terminology, it's possible that we've just got a few "false rejections." After all, there's variability in any process. Even if the actual quality levels are on target, we expect a few inspections to indicate otherwise.

Roberts: But the number of rejections seems much higher than usual. Has Four-D changed their quality standards?

Escalera: Possibly, but I'm sure they would have told us about it. Maybe they're making mistakes when they do the PDQ tests or interpret the results.

Roberts: Or maybe we're the ones making the mistakes. Is there any sign of quality problems here?

Escalera: You know we sample one drive each hour in each shift and run the test. We used to plot the PDQ value on the control chart each hour, too, but the new quality-control guy told us to plot the average of the eight values at the end of each shift.

Roberts: So what are the control charts saying?

Escalera: No signs of trouble on the latest two-sigma control chart—no out-of-control signals in the past 150 shifts. That's actually a surprise—normally we'd expect about 7 or 8 values out of 150 to fall outside the two-sigma limits. If anything, it looks like the variability in process quality is much lower now than in the past.

FIGURE 6.1   **Two-Sigma Control Chart for 150 Shift PDQ Averages at DataStor**

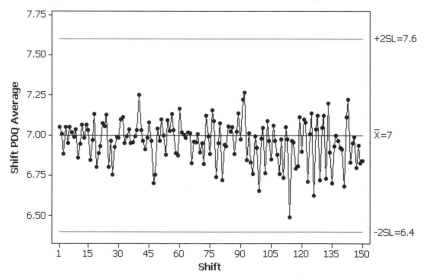

Roberts: But if the variability has actually gone down, why haven't we seen *fewer* returned shipments? Are we interpreting these charts correctly?

Escalera: I think so. I'll go back and check with the quality-control engineer.

Roberts: Maybe the problem really is at Four-D. Wait a minute! We're forgetting something. If everything looks good on our end, but Four-D is finding nonconformances, could damage in shipment be it?

Escalera: Someone else came up with that, but it's pretty unlikely given our protective packaging.

Roberts: We need to get to the bottom of this, Tony—and I mean ASAP! Check out our side first. If you can't turn up anything here, ask around at Four-D.

Tony collected the data from the tests over the past 150 shifts, which are contained in the file DataStor on the CD that came with your book. A partial listing of the data is shown in Figure 6.2.

FIGURE 6.2

Partial Listing of the DataStor Company Data

	A	B	C	D	E	F
1	Week	Day	Shift	WorkerHours	Drives	Shift PDQ
2	1	M	1	91.75	1115	7.052
3	1	M	2	91.25	1154	7.010
4	1	M	3	103.75	1275	6.884
5	1	T	1	96.75	1231	7.051
6	1	T	2	103.25	1280	6.952
7	1	T	3	91.50	1141	7.049
8	1	W	1	97.00	1173	7.018
9	1	W	2	99.25	1217	6.991
10	1	W	3	98.00	1148	7.035
11	1	R	1	95.50	1224	6.858
12	1	R	2	90.25	1156	6.944
13	1	R	3	89.75	1167	7.066
14	1	F	1	102.75	1285	6.984
15	1	F	2	91.25	1116	7.065

These data are coded as follows:

Week: Week (1–10)

Day: Day of the week (M, T, W, R, F)

Shift: Shift (1, 2, 3)

WorkerHours: Total number of hours worked by production employees during the shift

Drives: Number of DataStor DS100 hard drives produced during the shift

Shift PDQ: The average PDQ test score recorded for the eight drives tested during the shift. One randomly selected drive is tested each hour of every shift.

At the end of this chapter, we will help Bill Roberts and Tony Escalera solve the quality problem they are experiencing at DataStor by analyzing these data using statistical tools learned in this and earlier chapters of this book. ■

cross-sectional

time series
enumerative studies
analytic studies

IT'S USEFUL TO DISTINGUISH two kinds of samples. **Cross-sectional** samples are taken from an underlying population at a particular time. As the name implies, the idea is to obtain a reasonably accurate cross section of the relevant population at a particular time. **Time series** samples are taken over time from a random process. A closely related distinction is between **enumerative studies** and **analytic studies.** Enumerative studies involve sampling from a reasonably well-defined population; the purpose is usually to describe the nature of the population. Enumerative studies usually use cross-sectional samples. Analytic studies typically look at the results of a random process; the purpose is often to predict the future behavior of the process. Analytic studies usually involve time series samples.

In this chapter we usually think in terms of cross-sectional samples and enumerative studies. The basic ideas are easier to grasp in this context. The same principles apply to time series samples and analytic studies. Sample statistics will vary from one sample to another, whether the sample is cross-sectional or time series. The reason for the random variation is different in the two kinds of studies. In cross-sectional samples, the variation arises from the random sampling process. In time series samples, the variation is part of the random process itself, rather than being introduced by sampling. Time series samples require some extra care in analysis. The random variation may be more complicated than simply random sampling. In particular, there may well be statistical dependence in the series over time. This dependence violates one key assumption underlying many statistical procedures.

One way that randomness and probability relate to summary statistics is by way of random sampling. In Section 6.1 we consider why we want to sample randomly and how to do it. Then we turn to the basic definition of a sampling distribution and the use of expected value and standard deviation in that context in Section 6.2. In Section 6.3 we apply the basic ideas to the most important special case, namely, the sample mean. In this section we first encounter a critical mathematical result, the Central Limit Theorem, which we'll use heavily thereafter.

This is necessarily a theoretical chapter. The results of this chapter will be used over and over again in the methods of the following chapters.

6.1   Random Sampling

Sampling to obtain data is an important managerial role. Customers need to be sampled to find out what they like and don't like about the manager's business. The very definition of quality in a service business is customer satisfaction. One of the best ways of finding out if customers are satisfied is to ask them. Also, it's too expensive to check every part in a supplier's shipment to see if it meets the manager's specification; if testing the part is destructive, checking every part is *really* expensive. Further, auditing records is time-consuming and costly; almost all audits are based on sampling rather than a complete census.

Statistics books, including this one, urge you to use random sampling to collect data. A basic reason for using random sampling is to ensure that the inferences made from the sample data are not distorted by a **selection bias.** A selection bias exists whenever there is a systematic tendency to overrepresent or underrepresent some part of the population. For example, a telephone sample of households in a region, conducted entirely between the hours of 9 A.M. and 5 P.M., would be severely biased toward households with at least one nonworking member. Hence, any inferences made from the sample data would be biased toward the attitudes or opinions of nonworking members and might not be truly representative of households in the region. Similarly, a sample of charge accounts taken by selecting a set of transactions would be biased toward active, many-transaction accounts and away from inactive ones. Inferences from these data might not reflect the characteristics of the set of all accounts. A random sampling plan, by definition, avoids this kind of bias.

There are several other potential sources of bias. In general, a manager evaluating a statistical study should consider what possible systematic distortions there are

selection bias

in the way the data were gathered. Selection bias is one possibility. Another is *non-response,* or refusal, bias. Even though potential sample members have been chosen at random, not all of them will be willing to participate. It's a rather heroic assumption to believe that nonrespondents behave and believe the same way as respondents. This bias is a severe problem for market research studies. To the extent that repeated studies are done and sample results are compared to actual outcomes (such as the market share of new products), a manager can get some handle on this problem. It is always a concern.

Still another distortion can arise from the way questions are phrased. Many public opinion polls seem to swing wildly in assessing voters' beliefs about various issues. If you look carefully at the way questions are worded, very often you will see that the question is encouraging a particular response. One of the important steps in any sample survey of people is pretesting the questions to assure that they are neutral and allow the respondent to make a response without artificial pressure.

operational definitions

The bias in phrasing questions is one example of the need for **operational definitions.** Consider, for example, an opinion poll that reports on "attitudes toward unions." If this is defined as the answer to a question such as "Do you agree that unions can cause inconvenience and bad labor–management relations?," you will get one kind of answer. If the finding is defined as the answer to a question such as "Do you agree that unions have been important in securing employee rights and decent pay?," you will very likely get quite a different answer. Before taking a result at face value, ask exactly how the variables have been measured. A little detective work can often reveal which studies are propaganda and which are serious. An excellent question to ask of any statistical study is "just how did you define what you're measuring?" David Levine of Baruch College has a nice example. "How many doors are there in your home?" Does that include only the doors that people can walk through? The door to your refrigerator? The little trapdoor to pour water into your coffee maker? Obviously, the definition matters a lot.

target population

Simple random sampling is a process whereby each possible sample of a given size has the same probability of being selected. Obtaining a truly, or even approximately, random sample requires some thought and effort. A random sample is not a casual or haphazard sample. The **target population** must be identified. In principle, a list of all elements (possible individual values) in the population ought to be constructed with elements to be included in the sample selected randomly from the list, using a table of random numbers.

EXAMPLE 6.1

Suppose that the research staff of a Federal Reserve bank wishes to take a random sample of checks written on individual (nonbusiness) checking accounts to determine average amount, time to clearance, and insufficient-funds rates. How might they do so?

SOLUTION   First, the target population must be defined. Is it all individual checks written in a given period, or is it all checks processed by the Federal Reserve clearing house during that time? There's a difference, because a check that is cashed at the bank on which it was originally drawn never gets to the clearing house. Assume that the clearing-house definition is chosen. The next step is to establish a random sampling method. One could, in principle, put a numerical tag on every one of the 326,274 (or whatever number) checks processed by the center on a particular day.

Then a random sample of 1000 could be drawn by selecting six-digit random numbers and the checks with corresponding tags (passing over 000000 and anything larger than 326274). Obviously, this would be a very impractical and expensive way to obtain a random sample. Such a method serves only as an idealization against which a more practical method can be measured.

Another possibility is to sample every 326th check processed. This method is not literally random sampling, because, for instance, two successive checks couldn't be included in the sample. No doubt one could dream up some situations for which sampling every 326th check would introduce some kind of selection bias; however, this process should yield a fairly good approximation to random sampling, at a manageable cost.

The applicability of sampling methods is much broader than just the familiar political polls and market research studies. Sampling should be considered whenever information is desired and the cost (in dollars, in labor, or in time) of obtaining complete information is excessive. For example, suppose that a processor of potato chips sells the product through 1943 retail outlets. A critical variable for the success of the product is the average amount of shelf space devoted to the product per outlet. It would be absurd for the processor to visit every outlet and measure the shelf space devoted to that product. Assuming that the potato-chip processor had a list of the retail outlets, it would be relatively easy to obtain a random sample of, say, 100 outlets and to measure the average shelf space in that sample.

sampling frame

Ideally, one has a list of the elements of the target population. More often, one has a list that almost, but not quite, equals the target population. The almost-right list is called the **sampling frame,** to indicate that it is not exactly the same as the target population. A good sampling frame is sometimes fairly easy to obtain, as it would be in the case of the potato-chip processor, who most likely knows almost all, but not quite all, retail outlets. When sampling human populations, a good sampling frame is harder to develop. People move; a directory or a mailing list can become outdated quickly. Telephone directories are not a completely reliable source for developing a sampling frame; there are unlisted phone numbers and multiple phone numbers. Perhaps the most serious problem is that people without phones tend strongly to be poor people. This problem was a major cause of one of the most notorious failures in sampling, the *Literary Digest* poll before the 1936 U.S. presidential election. The *Literary Digest,* a popular magazine of the time, took a huge survey (2.4 million responses), based in large part on telephone books. In 1936, during the Great Depression, this procedure introduced a substantial bias. The magazine forecast that the Republican candidate would win the election; he won only two states. Much of the effort in conducting a good sampling study should go into developing the sampling frame.

Given a decent sampling frame, random sampling can be done with a computer program that generates random numbers or with a table of random numbers. Most statistical packages can be used to generate random numbers.

Careful planning and a certain amount of ingenuity are required to have even a decent approximation to a random sample. This is especially true when the elements in the target population are people. People throw away mail questionnaires, they are not home to answer telephone surveys, and they modify answers to conform to social norms. Too often, surveys of people are done in a haphazard way, using a hastily composed questionnaire mailed (often addressed to "occupant") according to a conveniently chosen mailing list, with no provisions for following up on those who do not respond. The result is bad data, riddled with biases that have unknowable effects. Lots of statistical methods can be applied to such data, but the well-known adage applies: Garbage in, garbage out. Getting reasonable samples of human populations is a considerable art (and a fairly substantial industry); we will not try to capture the essence of that art in a couple of pages.

There are other valid and useful sampling methods, such as stratified sampling. Most uses of probability theory in the remaining chapters are based on simple random sampling. The basic ideas remain the same when other sampling methods are used; the formulas just get a little more complicated.

Exercises

6.1   Suppose that we want to select a random sample of $n = 10$ entities from a population of 800 individuals. Use a computer package to identify the individuals to be sampled.

6.2   City officials sample the opinions of homeowners in a community about the possibility of raising taxes to improve the quality of local schools. A directory of all homes in the city is used; a computer generates random numbers to identify the addresses to be sampled. An interviewer visits each home between the hours of 3 P.M. and 6 P.M. If no one is home, the address is eliminated from the sample and replaced by another randomly chosen address. Does this process approximate random sampling?

6.3   A university bookstore manager is mildly concerned about the number of textbooks that were underordered and thus unavailable two days after the beginning of classes. The manager instructs an employee to pick a random number, go to the place where that number book is shelved, examine the next 50 titles, and record how many titles are unavailable.
a. Technically, this process doesn't yield a random sample of the books in the store. Why not?
b. How could a truly random sample be obtained?

6.4   A professional baseball team has a 20-game ticket plan and a 40-game ticket plan. The sales director wants to assess fan interest in a combination plan by which two separate purchasers of 20-game plans to pool their money and buy a 40-game plan at a modest discount. The target population to be sampled is all current 20-game plan purchasers. An up-to-date list of the 4256 current purchasers is available. Explain how to obtain a random sample of the current purchasers.

6.5   One way to sample the purchasers in Exercise 6.4 is to develop a list of the seat numbers held by purchasers and to take a random sample of seat numbers. Most likely this will not yield a random sample of purchasers. Explain why not.

6.6   A building manager for a 2526-office complex hires a new cleaning contractor. The manager wants to get a rough idea of how satisfactory the contractor's weekend cleaning efforts are. One possible strategy is to select 3 offices on the first three floors and to examine those offices and the 10 offices on either side. Another strategy, which requires roughly the same time, is to select 15 offices completely at random. It is argued that the first strategy is better because it allows for inspection of more offices. Is the argument valid?

6.2 Sample Statistics and Sampling Distributions

Once a sample has been selected and numerical data obtained, the first task is to summarize the data. In Chapter 2 we defined several summary measures, such as the sample mean and the sample standard deviation. Each of these is an example of a

sample statistic   **sample statistic.**

The value of any summary statistic will vary from one sample to another. The numerical value that a sample statistic will have cannot be exactly predicted in advance. Even if we know that a population mean μ is $216.37 and that the population standard deviation σ is $32.90—even if we know the complete population distribution—we cannot say that the sample mean $\bar{Y}$ will be exactly $216.37. A sample statistic is a random variable; it is subject to random variation because it is based on a random sample of measurements selected from the population or process of interest. Like any other random variable, a sample statistic has a probability distribution. We

sampling distribution   call the theoretical probability distribution of a sample statistic the **sampling distribution** of that statistic.

One useful way to think of a sampling distribution is to have a computer program draw many random samples from a specified population, compute the statistic for each sample, and construct a histogram of the results. Minitab drew 1000 samples, each of size $n = 4$, from an exponential population with mean $\mu = 1.0$ and standard deviation $\sigma = 1.0$. The exponential distribution is very skewed, as shown in Figure 6.3.

FIGURE 6.3   **Exponential Distribution**

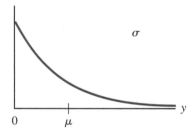

Minitab yielded the following summary statistics about the 1000 sample means. A histogram of the 1000 sample means is shown in Figure 6.4.

```
Variable        N    Mean  SE Mean   StDev  Minimum      Q1  Median      Q3
ybar(n=4)    1000  1.0019   0.0155  0.4892   0.1091  0.6489  0.9145  1.2830

Variable    Maximum
ybar(n=4)    3.1404
```

Notice that the histogram of the sampling distribution of means does *not* have the same shape as the population, but instead is less skewed to the right. The average of the sample means is (nearly) the same as the population mean $\mu = 1.0$, but the standard deviation of the sample means is *not* the same as the population standard deviation $\sigma = 1.0$.

The sampling distribution of a sample statistic is a probability distribution. Its exact form depends on the population distribution being sampled. Fortunately, we can derive the basic properties of the most important sampling distributions, those of sample means, from minimal assumptions about the population. In this section we find expected values and variances for these distributions. In the next section we show that the normal distribution is often a good approximation to the exact shapes of these sampling distributions.

The sample mean is the most widely used of all statistics, so its sampling distribution is most important. The expected value, variance, and standard deviation of this sampling distribution can be found using basic probability theory.

FIGURE 6.4

Histogram of Sample Means from 1000 Samples of Size $n = 4$ from an Exponential Distribution with $\mu = 1.0$ and $\sigma = 1.0$

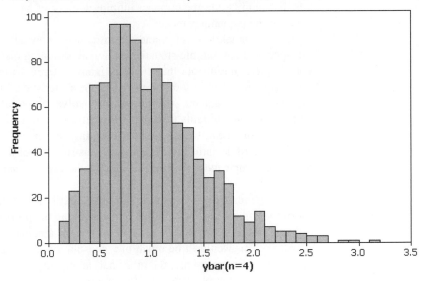

DEFINITION 6.1

Expected Value and Standard Deviation of $\bar{Y}$ If a random sample of size n is drawn from a population of Y values with mean μ and standard deviation σ, the expected value and standard deviation of $\bar{Y}$ are

$$\mu_{\bar{Y}} = E(\bar{Y}) = \mu$$

$$\sigma_{\bar{Y}} = \frac{\sigma}{\sqrt{n}}$$

EXAMPLE 6.2

Suppose that the long-run average of the number of Medicare claims submitted per week to a regional office is 62,000 and that the standard deviation is 7000. If we assume that the weekly claims submissions during a four-week period constitute a random sample of size 4, what are the expected value and standard error of the average weekly number of claims over a four-week period?

SOLUTION We have $\mu = 62{,}000$, $\sigma = 7000$, and $n = 4$. If Y is the four-week average of the weekly number of claims, then

$$\mu_{\bar{Y}} = \mu = 62{,}000$$

$$\sigma_{\bar{Y}} = \frac{\sigma}{\sqrt{n}} = 7000/\sqrt{4} = 3500$$

The fact that $\mu_{\bar{Y}} = \mu$ means that the sample mean estimates the population mean correctly on average. In one particular sample, the sample mean may overestimate the population mean. In another, the sample mean may underestimate. But in the long run there is no *systematic tendency* for a sample mean to overestimate or underestimate the population mean. This is true regardless of the sample size.

Remember, when the computer drew 1000 samples of 4 from an exponential population, the mean of the 1000 sample means (an approximation to the expected value, which would be the mean of an infinite number of sample means) was just about equal to the population mean.

At this point, it is very handy to introduce a new name for an existing concept. We specify many sample statistics and many sampling distributions in the next several chapters; it turns out that there are many different formulas for the standard deviations of the sampling distributions of these statistics. Most of the formulas (like the one for the standard deviation of $\bar{Y}$) involve the population standard deviation, and it becomes difficult to distinguish between the different standard deviations.

standard error

From here on, then, we use the term **standard error** to denote the theoretically derived standard deviation of the sampling distribution of a statistic. The standard error of the sample mean $\bar{Y}$ is the standard deviation of its sampling distribution; $\sigma_{\bar{Y}} = \sigma/\sqrt{n}$.

The standard deviation of the sampling distribution of the mean (the standard error of the sample mean) is crucial in determining the probable amount of error in an estimate. We just said that there is no systematic tendency to over- or underestimate μ with $\bar{Y}$. This wouldn't be much of a consolation if we knew that half the time we made a huge overestimate, the other half an equally huge underestimate! The standard error of a sample mean $\sigma_{\bar{Y}}$, in conjunction with the Empirical Rule of Chapter 2, can be used to give a good indication of the probable deviation of a particular sample mean from the population mean.

EXAMPLE 6.3

Suppose that a supermarket manager is interested in estimating the mean checkout time for the nonexpress checkout lanes. An assistant manager obtains a random sample of 25 checkout times. If previous data suggest that the population standard deviation is 1.10 minutes, describe the probable deviation of $\bar{Y}$ from the unknown population mean μ.

SOLUTION The Empirical Rule indicates that approximately 95% of the time $\bar{Y}$ is within 2 standard errors ($2\sigma_{\bar{Y}}$) of the population mean μ. For $n = 25$,

$$2\sigma_{\bar{Y}} = \frac{2\sigma}{\sqrt{n}} = \frac{2(1.10)}{5} = .44$$

The probable error for $\bar{Y}$ is no more than .44 minute.

The probable accuracy of a sample mean, as measured by its standard error, is affected by the sample size. Because the standard error of the sample mean is the population standard deviation divided by the square root of the sample size, the standard error decreases as the sample size increases. For example, if the sample size had been either 50 or 100 instead of 25 in the previous example, the probable errors ($2\sigma_{\bar{Y}}$) would have been, respectively, .31 or .22.

EXAMPLE 6.4

Minitab was used to draw 1000 samples of sizes 10, 30, and 60 from an exponential population having mean and standard deviation both 1.0. The averages of the 1000 means in each situation were, respectively, 1.0109, 1.0047, and 1.0025. The standard deviations of the 1000 means were, respectively, .31815, .17943, and .12662. Show that these values are close approximations to the theoretical expected value and standard error.

SOLUTION The average of the sample means should and does approximate the expected value, $\mu_{\bar{Y}} = 1.0000$. The standard deviation of the means should approximate the standard error of the sample mean, $\sigma/\sqrt{n} = 1.0/\sqrt{n}$. For $n = 10, 30,$ and 60, the theoretical standard errors are $1.0/\sqrt{10} = .31623$, $1.0/\sqrt{30} = .18257$, and $1.0/\sqrt{60} = .12910$. The approximations are quite close in all cases.

As the sample size increases to infinity, the standard error of the sample mean decreases toward zero. For a very large sample size, the standard error of the mean is very small, and the sample mean based on a huge, genuinely unbiased sample is very close to the true population mean, with very high probability. The condition that the sample be unbiased would be crucial in such a situation; a huge sample would reduce random variation to near zero but would *not* eliminate any data-gathering bias.

In Section 2.6 we defined control limits by adding and subtracting 3 standard deviations from the desired target value. The standard deviation in question is the standard error of the sample mean, based on the sample size used. For example, we discussed an automatic transmission in which the desired internal pressure was 35. The standard deviation of pressures of individual transmissions was about 1.2, and five transmissions were sampled each day. Thus, the standard deviation of the sample mean (standard error) should theoretically be 1.2 divided by the square root of 5, or .54.

In quality-control practice, there is an additional source of variability that's not found in sampling from fixed populations. Even if a process is in control, it will vary somewhat over time; for example, the true mean pressure for all transmissions may vary somewhat (over time) around 35, even though the process is basically satisfactory. This additional variation often makes the actual standard deviation of sample means slightly higher than the theoretical value. In the transmission example, the actual standard deviation of the means was .60.

Exercises

6.7 A random sample of size 8 is to be taken with replacement from a population with the following probability distribution:

Value:	4	8	12	16
Probability:	.50	.30	.15	.05

The exact sampling distributions of $\bar{Y}$, the sample mean, can be shown to be (to four decimal places):

$\bar{y}$:	4.0	4.5	5.0	5.5	6.0
$P_{\bar{Y}}(\bar{y})$:	.0039	.0188	.0488	.0898	.1293

$\bar{y}$:	6.5	7.0	7.5	8.0	8.5
$P_{\bar{Y}}(\bar{y})$:	.1535	.1550	.1359	.1048	.0718

$\bar{y}$:	9.0	9.5	10.0	10.5	11.0
$P_{\bar{Y}}(\bar{y})$:	.0718	.0439	.0119	.0053	.0021

$\bar{y}$:	11.5	12.0	12.5	13.0	13.5
$P_{\bar{Y}}(\bar{y})$:	.0008	.0002	.0001	.0000	.0000

$\bar{y}$:	14.0	14.5	15.0	15.5	16.0
$P_{\bar{Y}}(\bar{y})$:	.0000	.0000	.0000	.0000	.0000

Find the expected value and standard deviation of the *population* and the expected value and standard deviation of $\bar{Y}$. Show that these results agree with the theoretical results of this section.

6.8 An automobile insurer has found that repair claims have an average of $927 and a standard deviation of $871. Suppose that the next 50 claims can be regarded as a random sample from the long-run claims process. Find the expected value and standard error of the average of the next 50 claims.

6.9 A computer simulation can itself be regarded as a sampling process. Suppose that a simulation study is done concerning the time required to complete a research and de-

velopment project. There is considerable uncertainty in the times required to complete the various pieces of the project, so the overall completion time has considerable variability. Assume that the time to completion has a mean of 28.2 months and a standard deviation of 6.9 months.

a. If the simulation involves 1000 independent trials of the project, find the expected value and standard error of the simulation (sample) mean.

b. Find the expected value and standard error if 4000 trials are simulated.

6.3 Sampling Distributions for Means and Sums

In the last section we stated the appropriate expected values and standard errors for the sample mean $\bar{Y}$. In this section we show that in most situations a normal distribution provides a good approximation to the sampling distribution for $\bar{Y}$. According to a theorem of mathematical statistics, if a population distribution is (exactly) normal, then the sampling distribution for the sample mean $\bar{Y}$ is also (exactly) normal. The relevant expected value and standard error are given in the previous section.

Suppose that a meat packer provides "12-ounce" steaks that, in fact, have a mean weight of 12.10 ounces and a standard deviation of .20 ounce. Also, the individual weights have a normal distribution. Assume that a package of 25 steaks constitutes a random sample from the population (which might also be thought of as a long-run process) of steaks. What is the probability that the mean weight in the package exceeds 12.00 ounces? According to the theorem we just mentioned, if the population distribution is normal, the sampling distribution of sample means is also normal. The expected value for the sample mean will be 12.10, equal to the population mean. The standard deviation for the sample mean will *not* equal the population standard deviation; sample means are less variable than individual scores. The relevant standard deviation for the sample mean is the standard error; $\sigma_{\bar{Y}} = \sigma/\sqrt{n} = 0.20/\sqrt{25} = .040$. To find the probability that the sample mean will exceed 12.00 ounces, we go through the familiar z calculation, and we make sure that we use the standard error of the sample mean, not the population standard deviation.

$$P(\bar{Y} > 12.00) = P(z > (12.00 - 12.10)/.040) = P(z > -2.50)$$
$$= .5000 + .4938 = .9938 \quad \text{(from Appendix Table 3)}$$

EXAMPLE 6.5   A timber company is planning to harvest 400 trees from a very large 50-year-old stand. The yield of lumber from each tree is largely determined by its diameter. Assume that the distribution of diameters in the stand is normal with mean 44 inches and standard deviation 4 inches. Also assume (perhaps unrealistically) that the selection of the 400 trees is effectively random. Find the probability that the average diameter of the harvested trees is between 43.5 and 44.5 inches.

SOLUTION   The population distribution (of the diameters of all trees in the stand) is assumed to be normal. It follows from the previous result that the sampling distribution of $\bar{Y}$ is also normal. The appropriate expected value and standard error are

$$\mu_{\bar{Y}} = \mu = 44$$

$$\sigma_{\bar{Y}} = \frac{\sigma}{\sqrt{n}} = \frac{4}{\sqrt{400}} = .20$$

As usual, we calculate normal probabilities by calculating z-scores (see Figure 6.5):

$$P(43.5 \le \bar{Y} \le 44.5) = P\left(\frac{43.5 - 44}{.20} \le Z \le \frac{44.5 - 44}{.20}\right)$$

$$= P(-2.50 \le Z \le 2.50)$$

$$= 2(.4938) = .9876$$

FIGURE 6.5

Probability Calculation for Example 6.5

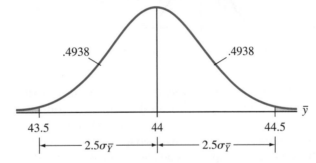

Use of this theorem, as stated, requires the assumption that the population distribution is exactly normal. In practice, no distribution is exactly normal. Another theorem, called the **Central Limit Theorem,** implies that the assumption of a normal population is not crucial.

Central Limit Theorem

DEFINITION 6.2

Central Limit Theorem for Sums and Means   For *any* population (with finite mean μ and standard deviation σ), the sampling distribution of the sample mean is approximately normal if the sample size n is sufficiently large.

This is a rather remarkable theorem. Regardless of the nature of the population distribution—discrete or continuous, symmetric or skewed, unimodal or multimodal—the sampling distribution of $\bar{Y}$ is always nearly normal as long as the sample size is large enough. This is illustrated in Figure 6.6 for the sample mean. The condition that the population mean and standard deviation must be finite is almost always satisfied.*

---

*The only exception we know of is the case of so-called stable law distributions, which are sometimes used as models in finance.

FIGURE 6.6   **An Illustration of the Central Limit Theorem**

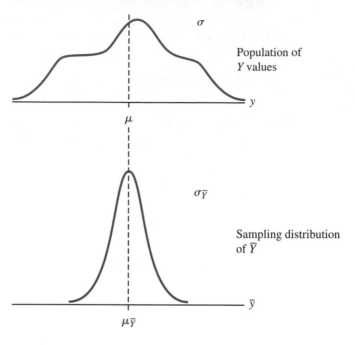

An obvious question is: How large a sample is sufficiently large? The Central Limit Theorem is a mathematical theorem—"n sufficiently large" is translated into "as n goes to infinity"—so it does not contain the answer to this question. An enormous number of studies have tried to answer the question, using other mathematical theorems and computer simulations. Many textbooks give a blanket rule: Use the normal approximation anytime n exceeds 30.

This rule is a good basic guide for using the Central Limit Theorem. A better rule would consider the effect of skewness. If the population distribution is very skewed, the actual sampling distribution for $n = 20$ or for $n = 40$ is also somewhat skewed, less so than the population distribution, but enough to make the normal approximation mediocre. If the population distribution is symmetric, the sampling distribution even with $n = 10$ or so is remarkably close to normal. A better rule would be based on a histogram or normal probability plot of the sample data. If a plot of the sample data shows obvious skewness (and hence suggests skewness for the population distribution), a normal approximation should be used skeptically unless n is up around 100. If the plot has little skewness, the normal approximation may be used confidently, even with an n of 15 or 20.*

---

*The quality of a normal approximation is also slightly affected by how heavy the tails are in the population. Even if a population is nearly symmetric, it may contain many more extremely large and extremely small values than would a near-normal distribution. A heavy-tailed population in a sample is suggested by the presence of outliers—a few individual values that fall very far from the bulk of the data. We discuss the treatment of outliers in later chapters.

EXAMPLE 6.6   A computer program was used to draw 1000 samples each, with sample sizes 4, 10, 30, and 60, from a highly right-skewed exponential population having mean and standard deviation both equal to 1. Histograms of the sample means are shown in Figure 6.7. As the sample size increases, how does the shape of the theoretical (sampling) distribution of means change? How does the variability of sample means change?

FIGURE 6.7   **Histograms of Sample Means: (a) Samples of Size 4; (b) Samples of Size 10; (c) Samples of Size 30; (d) Samples of Size 60**

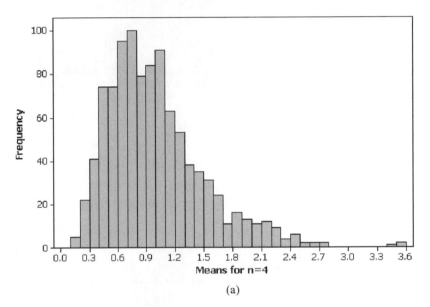

(a)

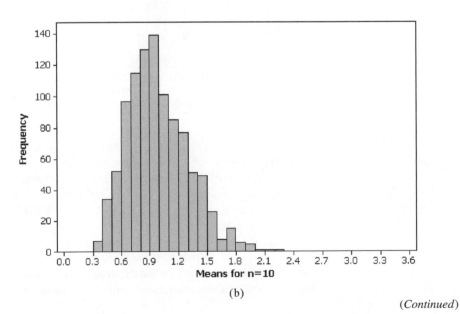

(b)

(*Continued*)

FIGURE 6.7   **(continued)**

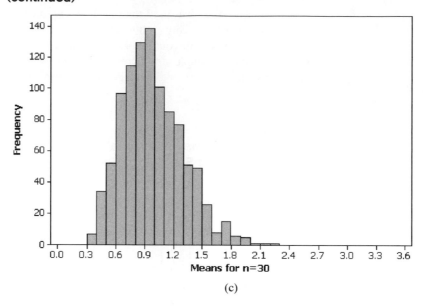

(c)

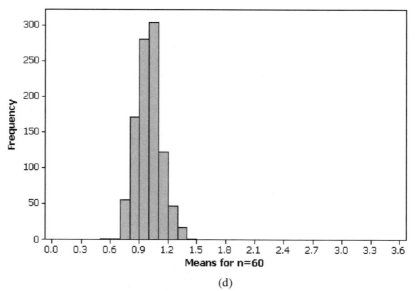

(d)

EXAMPLE 6.6
(continued)

SOLUTION   For $n = 4$, the distribution of means is clearly right-skewed, although not as skewed as the exponential distribution itself. As the sample size increases, the skewness decreases. For a sample of size 60, the distribution of means appears to be very close to normal. The Central Limit Theorem indicates that the theoretical distribution of sample means should, indeed, approach a normal distribution as the sample size increases.

From the scale at the bottom of each histogram, we can assess the variability of sample means. As n increases, the range of sample means decreases, indicating that variability decreases. The fact that the standard error of the sample mean decreases as n increases indicates that the variability of sample means should decrease as n increases.

Remember that you usually can't plot the sampling distribution itself. That is the theoretical, long-run distribution arising from repeated sampling; in practice, you take only one sample. The data plot that we refer to is the sample histogram. The sample histogram is useful as a rough indicator of the population shape, which is known to have an effect on the quality of the Central Limit Theorem normal approximation.

EXAMPLE 6.7   In the supermarket checkout time situation of Example 6.3, the following actual times in minutes were observed ($n = 25$): .4, .4, .5, .5, .5, .6, .6, .7, .8, .9, 1.1, 1.2, 1.4, 1.5, 1.8, 2.0, 2.3, 2.6, 2.9, 3.4, 4.2, 5.0, 6.6, 9.2, 16.3 ($\bar{y} = 2.70$). Does it appear that a normal approximation to the sampling distribution of $\bar{Y}$ (for future samples of size $n = 25$, for instance) would be satisfactory?

```
Data Display

Checkout
    0.40     0.40     0.50     0.55     0.50     0.60     0.60     0.70     0.80
    0.90     1.10     1.20     1.40     1.50     1.80     2.00     2.30     2.60
    2.90     3.40     4.20     5.00     6.60     9.20    16.30

Descriptive Statistics: Checkout

Variable   N    Mean   StDev  Minimum      Q1  Median      Q3  Maximum
Checkout  25   2.698   3.562    0.400   0.600   1.400   3.150   16.300
```

SOLUTION   The sample data suggest that the population distribution of checkout times is likely to be highly skewed. See the histogram in Figure 6.8. Most times are quite brief, but there are a few people who really slow things up. A sample of 25 is not enough to *deskew* the sampling distribution. Even a sample of 50 isn't really enough in this situation. Therefore, the Empirical Rule probabilities (which are based on the normal distribution) in Example 6.3 are most likely inaccurate for $n = 25$ and perhaps for $n = 50$. For $n = 100$, the probabilities should be fairly close.

FIGURE 6.8   **Histogram for Checkout Time Data**

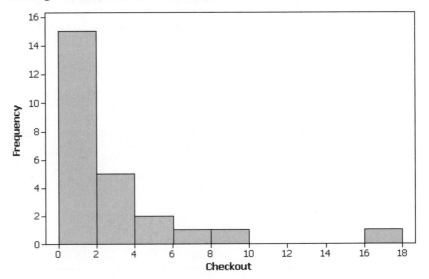

EXAMPLE 6.8

A firm that sells frozen 9-ounce steaks to restaurants is concerned about the fat content of individual steaks. It has claimed that the fat content has mean 8.1% and standard deviation 1.0%. Use a normal approximation to find the probability that the mean fat content in a random sample of 25 steaks exceeds 8.5%. Would you expect the normal approximation to be accurate?

SOLUTION   The appropriate expected value and standard error are

$$\mu_{\bar{Y}} = \mu = 8.1\%$$

$$\sigma_{\bar{Y}} = \frac{\sigma}{\sqrt{n}} = \frac{1.0}{\sqrt{25}} = 0.2\%$$

The normal approximation yields

$$P(\bar{Y} > 8.5) = P\left(Z > \frac{8.5 - 8.1}{0.2}\right) = P(Z > 2.00) \approx .0228$$

In this situation, we would expect the distribution to be fairly symmetric; we would not expect to see fat contents of (say) 15% or more (at least for a firm that stays in business) nor fat contents of practically 0%. (Of course, a plot of actual data would be useful in checking our guesses.) If our expectation is correct, the normal approximation should be quite good for $n = 25$.

Exercises

6.10   The number of column-inches of classified advertisements appearing on Mondays in a certain daily newspaper is roughly normally distributed with mean 327 inches and standard deviation 34 inches. Assume that the results for 10 consecutive Mondays can be regarded as a random sample.
a. Find the expected value and standard error of the average number of column-inches of classified advertisements for 10 Mondays.
b. Find the probability that the mean is between 315.0 and 339.0 inches.

6.11   Refer to Exercise 6.10. Find a range of the form $327 - k$ to $327 + k$ such that

$$P(327 - k \leq \bar{Y} \leq 327 + k) \approx .95$$

6.12   Suppose that a certain population has the following distribution:

Value:	200	300	400	500	600
Relative frequency:	.60	.20	.12	.06	.02

The population mean is 270, and the population standard deviation is 102.470. Exact probability computations show the following:

n	$\sigma_{\bar{Y}}$	$P(\bar{Y} < \mu - 2\sigma_{\bar{Y}})$	$P(\bar{Y} < \mu - \sigma_{\bar{Y}})$	$P(\bar{Y} > \mu + \sigma_{\bar{Y}})$	$P(\bar{Y} > \mu + 2\sigma_{\bar{Y}})$
2	72.46	0	0	.2160	.0336
4	51.23	0	.1296	.1965	.0521
8	36.23	0	.1460	.1594	.0319
16	25.62	.0173	.1876	.1486	.0295
32	18.11	.0127	.1543	.1473	.0340

a. Draw a histogram of the population distribution. What is the obvious feature of this histogram?

b. For each sample size, compute the exact probability that $\bar{Y}$ falls within 2 standard errors of μ. How good is the normal approximation for various values of n?

c. Repeat part (b) for $\bar{Y}$ within 1 standard error of μ.

6.13 In Exercise 6.8 we considered an automobile insurer whose repair claims averaged $927 over the past with a standard deviation of $871. A random sample of 50 new claims is taken.

a. Describe the sampling distribution for $\bar{Y}$.

b. Use a normal approximation to calculate $P(\bar{Y} > 1100)$.

6.14 How good would you expect the normal approximation in Exercise 6.13 to be? (Would you expect individual claims data to be something close to bell shaped?)

6.15 Refer to Exercise 6.13. Suppose $\bar{y} = \$1100$ is observed for the 50 new claims. What do you conclude about repair claims for this year? Would your conclusions change if $\bar{y} = \$1000$?

6.16 The average demand for rental skis on winter Saturdays at a particular area is 148 pairs, which has been quite stable over time. There is variation due to weather conditions and competing areas; the standard deviation is 21 pairs. The demand distribution seems to be roughly normal.

a. The rental shop stocks 170 pairs of skis. What is the probability that demand will exceed this supply on any one winter Saturday?

b. The shop manager will change the stock of skis for the next year if the average demand over the 12 winter Saturdays in a season (considered as a random sample) is over 155 or under 135. These limits aren't equidistant from the long-run process mean of 148 because the costs of oversupply and undersupply are different. If the population mean stays at 148, what is the probability that the manager will change the stock?

6.17 In Exercise 6.16 one could argue that the demand will not be normal. Instead, most Saturdays' demand will be around the mean, but on those few days when skiing conditions are poor, the demand will fall well below the mean.

a. According to this argument, what will be the shape (skewness) of the demand distribution?

b. Will the two answers in Exercise 6.16 be made equally wrong if this argument is correct? Why?

6.18 Computer chips have pins to connect them into sockets on computer boards. The thickness of the pins is important in determining the quality of the connection to the board. When the production process is running properly, the mean diameter of pins (relative to the design specification) is 1.000. There is some inevitable variation in diameters; the standard deviation is .006 unit. The distribution of diameters is normal.

a. A pin will make a highest-quality connection only if its diameter is between .997 and 1.003 units. What is the probability that an individual pin will make such a connection?

b. As part of its ongoing quality monitoring, the chip manufacturer takes samples of 20 pins from each lot of 25,000 pins. Assuming that the process is running properly, what is the probability that the mean diameter in the sample will be between .997 and 1.003 units?

c. Suppose that the process mean remains at 1.000 unit, but the variability increases greatly, so that the standard deviation is .020 unit. Without doing any arithmetic, what should this change do to the probability that an individual pin will make a highest-quality connection? Verify your answer by computing a revised probability and comparing it to your answer in part (a).

d. If the standard deviation is .020, what is the probability that a mean of a sample of 20 pins will be between .997 and 1.003 units?

6.19 In Exercise 6.18 suppose that the mean diameter of the population of pins is 1.000, but that the distribution is not normal. Instead, the standard deviation of .006 is the result of most pin diameters being extremely close to 1.000 and a few pin diameters being extremely far from that value. Does this mean that your answer to part (b) of Exercise 6.18 is seriously incorrect? Explain why or why not.

6.20 A downtown hotel runs a special promotion to try to fill rooms that aren't usually occupied on weekends. The long-run average response is 71 rooms per weekend. There is considerable variation due to weather, competing attractions, and other unknown causes. The standard deviation of responses is about 15 rooms. Suppose that the distribution of responses is normal.

a. The hotel schedules adequate staff to handle a response of 80 rooms. If more guests arrive, additional staff must be brought in at overtime rates. What is the probability that additional staff will be needed on one particular weekend?

b. The promotion manager reviews response rates for blocks of 10 weekends, which is regarded as a random sample. If the average demand over the 10-week sample exceeds 80, the manager will increase the scheduled staff. If the long-run mean stays at 71, what is the probability that a 10-week sample mean will exceed 80?

6.21 In Exercise 6.20 we assumed a normal distribution of responses. In fact, the distribution is skewed by a few weekends with extremely heavy demand. Can you assume that your answer to part (b) of that exercise is still correct because of the Central Limit Theorem effect?

6.22 Give the symbol used for the "standard error of the mean" and explain, in layman's terms, what it measures.

6.23 The distribution of starting salaries for recent MBA graduates is known to have a mean of $72,000 and a standard deviation of $14,000. The distribution is also known to be skewed to the right.

a. Is it possible to calculate the probability that an MBA graduate will receive a starting salary higher than $84,000? Explain.

b. Suppose that we consider taking a sample of $n = 5$ recent MBA graduates. What can be said about the sampling distribution of the average starting salary of $n = 5$ randomly selected MBA graduates? Can you calculate the probability that their average starting salary will be higher than $84,000?

c. Suppose that we consider taking a sample of $n = 40$ recent MBA graduates. What can be said about the sampling distribution of the average starting salary of $n = 40$ randomly selected MBA graduates? Can you calculate the probability that their average starting salary will be higher than $84,000?

6.24 In the population of all credit card sales today, suppose the actual mean charge amount is $48 and the standard deviation is $122.

a. The shape of the population distribution is (circle one):

symmetric   normal   skewed left   skewed right

b. What is the probability that the average amount charged in a random sample of 64 purchases will be higher than $70? Justify any necessary assumptions for your calculation.

c. After collecting a sample of 64 credit card purchases, we find that the average amount is $82 and the standard deviation is $140 in the sample. Choose the *correct notation* from the following list to label each of the following numbers *as they were used in the problem:*

μ $\bar{Y}$ $\mu_{\bar{Y}}$ σ s $\sigma_{\bar{Y}}$ n N λ

$64 = \underline{\hspace{1cm}}$ $48 = \underline{\hspace{1cm}}$ $82 = \underline{\hspace{1cm}}$

$140 = \underline{\hspace{1cm}}$ $122 = \underline{\hspace{1cm}}$

6.25   As a real estate agent, one of your career goals is to make the Five-Million Dollar Club by selling at least $5,000,000 of residential properties within a one-year time period. From recent data, it is known that the average residential sales price in your area is $104,000 and the standard deviation is $25,000. If you sell 45 residential properties next year, what is the probability that you will make the Five-Million Dollar Club?

BUSINESS DECISION-MAKING IN ACTION

CHAPTER CASE

ANALYSIS

DataStor Company

Recall that DataStor Company produces the DataStor DS100, a compact hard drive, and DataStor's main customer is the national retailer Four-D Office Products.

As part of DataStor's quality inspection process, one drive is subjected to the PDQ (Performance and Drive Quality) test hourly. The scores have historically followed a normal distribution with a mean value of 7.0 and a standard deviation of .30 when the process has been in control.

Before Four-D accepts a DS100 shipment, it subjects a random sample of 10 drives to the PDQ test as a final inspection. If one or more drives in the sample are found to be nonconforming (that is, PDQ < 6.2), the entire shipment is judged to be "unacceptable" and returned to DataStor.

The two-sigma control chart for the past 150 shifts, shown in Figure 6.1, does not indicate any problems to DataStor management that would explain the recent noticeable increase in the frequency of returned shipments from Four-D (4 out of the past 20 daily shipments). If anything, it appears that the variation in PDQ scores is actually lower than in the past, indicating higher consistency in drive quality.

We've been asked to examine the situation, using the data from the past 150 shifts recorded in the file DataStor on the CD that came with your book, to determine whether there's a problem and to find its source, if possible. The data for each of the past 150 shifts includes the week (1–10), the day of the week (M, T, W, R, F), the shift number (1, 2, or 3), the number of worker-hours recorded during the shift, the number of hard drives produced during the shift, and the average PDQ test score for the eight drives sampled and tested during the shift.

As a first step in the analysis, we can summarize the individual variables with the graphical and numerical tools described in Chapter 2.

Variable	N	Mean	SE Mean	StDev	Minimum	Q1	Median
WorkerHours	150	96.187	0.396	4.852	83.000	93.000	96.250
Drives	150	1204.0	4.2	51.1	1081.0	1171.5	1207.0
Shift PDQ	150	6.9614	0.0109	0.1334	6.4900	6.8840	6.9745

Variable	Q3	Maximum
WorkerHours	98.813	110.499
Drives	1237.3	1339.0
Shift PDQ	7.0492	7.2670

Figures 6.9, 6.10, and 6.11 are histograms of the WorkerHours, Drives, and Shift PDQ variables, respectively. The summary statistics and the histograms do not contain any serious outliers or unusual features that would suggest a quality problem at DataStor.

FIGURE 6.9

Histogram of WorkerHours in the DataStor Case

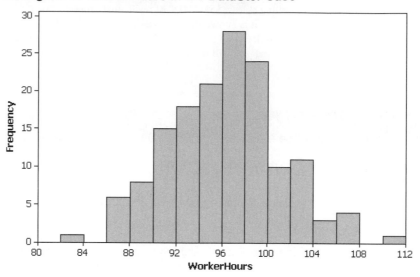

FIGURE 6.10

Histogram of Drives in the DataStor Case

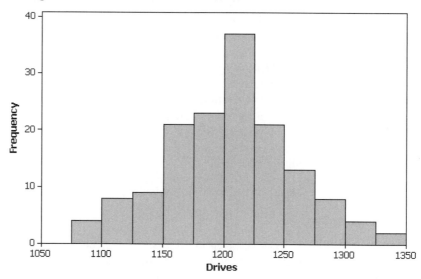

We next check to see if the number of rejected shipments seen recently could have been due to chance. Four-D declares a drive defective if its PDQ test score falls below 6.2. Let's first determine the probability of an individual drive having a score below 6.2. Recall that when the production process is in control, the distribution of scores follows a normal distribution with a mean of 7.0 and a standard deviation of .30, based on historical data. If we let Y denote the score of an individual drive, the probability of its having a score below 6.2 is given by

$$P(Y < 6.2) = P\left(\frac{Y - \mu}{\sigma} < \frac{6.2 - 7.0}{.30}\right) = P(Z < -2.67) = .0038$$

Therefore, Four-D would consider approximately 4 in every 1000 drives to be non-conforming when the production process is in control.

FIGURE 6.11   **Histogram of Shift PDQ Averages in the DataStor Case**

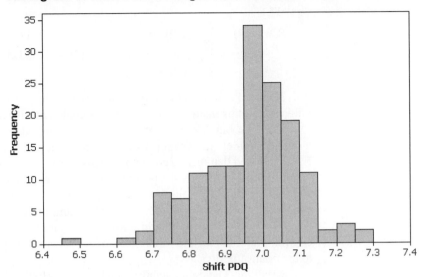

Assuming the PDQ scores in Four-D's daily sample of the 10 drives are independent and the process is in control, the number of drives in the 10 that fail the test, denoted X, follows a binomial distribution with parameters $n = 10$ and $\pi = .0038$. The probability that one or more drives in the sample of 10 fail the test and the shipment is returned to DataStor is given by

$$P(X \geq 1) = 1 - P(X = 0) = 1 - (1 - .0038)^{10} = .0374$$

If the production process is in control with respect to drive performance and quality, we expect Four-D to reject approximately 1 shipment in 27 (since $1/27 \approx .0374$).

What about the chance of 4 or more rejected shipments in the past 20 days? Is this an unusual event as Bill Roberts suggests? If we let W represent the number of rejected shipments in the past 20 days, then W follows a binomial distribution with $n = 20$ and $\pi = .0374$. The probability distribution for W is easily calculated in Minitab or Excel. (*Note:* Minitab does not show values of W for which the probability is .0000 to four decimals.)

```
MTB > PDF;
SUBC> Binomial 20 .0374.

    Binomial with n = 20 and p = 0.0374

        w           P( W = w )
        0             0.4666
        1             0.3626
        2             0.1338
        3             0.0312
        4             0.0052
        5             0.0006
        6             0.0001
        7             0.0000

MTB > CDF 3;
SUBC> Binomial 20 .0374.

    Binomial with n = 20 and p = 0.0374000

        w           P( W <= w )
     3.00             0.9941
```

From this table, we see that the chance of 4 or more rejected shipments in the past 20 days is

$$P(W \geq 4) = 1 - [P(W = 0) + P(W = 1) + P(W = 2) + P(W = 3)]$$
$$= 1 - [.4666 + .3626 + .1338 + .0312]$$
$$= 1 - .9942 = .0058$$

This is indeed unusual under our assumption that the process is in control. It is highly unlikely that this many rejected shipments could have been due to chance alone.

Since we can rule out chance variation, we might next check the possibility of a quality problem at DataStor by reexamining the control chart in Figure 6.1. Tony Escalera noted that there were no out-of-control signals from the process in the two-sigma control chart over the past 150 shifts and took this as a sign of less variation and improved quality. This is a clue to the problem. In a two-sigma control chart, we expect to have a 5% false alarm rate. Assuming the process is in control, over the course of 150 shifts, we should have seen about seven or eight values beyond the control limits! In fact, the variation of the points in the plot does not even come close to the control limits.

Recall that DataStor recently switched from plotting individual PDQ test scores to plotting shift average PDQ test scores based on eight individual test scores. It simply forgot to adjust the control limits to account for this change. (Obviously, averages have less variation than individual values, so DataStor should have tightened up the control limits on its chart.) Figure 6.12 shows a correct control chart for the 150 shift averages.

FIGURE 6.12   **Correct Three-Sigma Control Chart for Shift PDQ Averages**

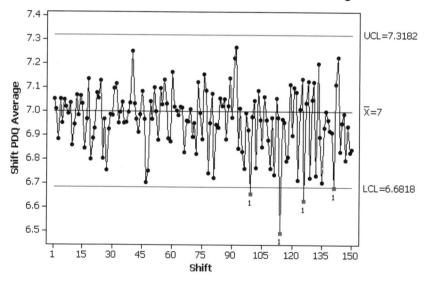

In this control chart, the three-sigma upper and lower control limits are shown instead of two-sigma control limits. We used the historical mean of 7.0 and the standard error of the sample mean, $\sigma/\sqrt{n} = .30/\sqrt{8} = .106$, based on the historical standard deviation of .30 for individual PDQ test values. Several of the plotted values fall below the lower control limit in the most recent 60 shifts.

We are now fairly certain that there is a recent quality problem at DataStor, but what is the source of the problem? We can examine the relationship between the shift average PDQ variable and each of the other variables in the data set for clues.

Figure 6.13 is a box plot of the shift PDQ average versus day of the week. Although some variation exists among the days of the week, there's no strong evidence that the problem is linked to day of the week.

FIGURE 6.13

Box Plots of Shift PDQ Averages by Day of the Week

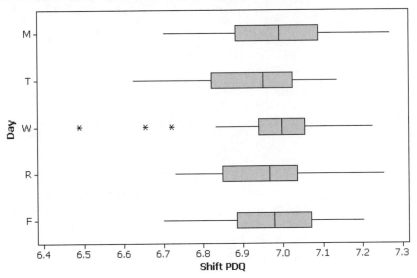

Figures and 6.14 and 6.15 are scatterplots of the shift PDQ average versus the WorkerHours and Drives variables, respectively. If production levels had been increased recently, that might account for a decrease in quality. For example, at higher levels of WorkerHours (or Drives), we might have seen an overall decrease in the shift PDQ averages. The lack of an unusual pattern in these scatterplots, however, suggests that DataStor has been operating well within its range of production capability.

FIGURE 6.14

Scatterplot of Shift PDQ Average Versus WorkersHours

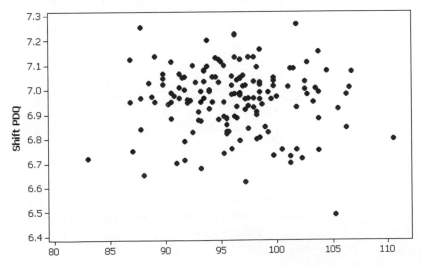

FIGURE 6.15

Scatterplot of Shift PDQ Average Versus Drives

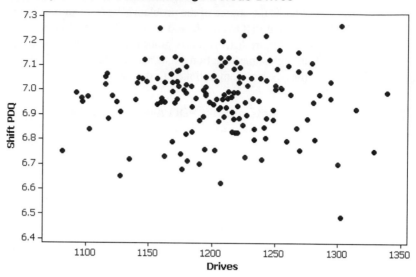

Figure 6.16 is a box plot of the shift PDQ average versus Shift. The graph shows clearly that the quality of drives produced in Shift 3 is worse on average and exhibits higher variation. Control charts for the three shifts, shown in Figure 6.17, indicate that Shifts 1 and 2 have not had any problems, but that Shift 3 has had declining quality in its drives over the past 60 days.

FIGURE 6.16

Box Plots of Shift PDQ Averages by Shift

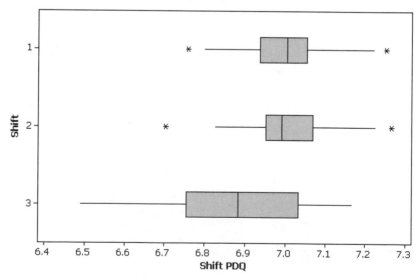

The quality problem is therefore real and the source is the third shift at DataStor. Further investigation by DataStor is needed to pin down the actual source of the problem, but we can say that the problem seems to have started roughly 20–30 days ago based on our analysis of the data.

FIGURE 6.17

Three-Sigma Control Charts of Shift PDQ Averages for Each Shift

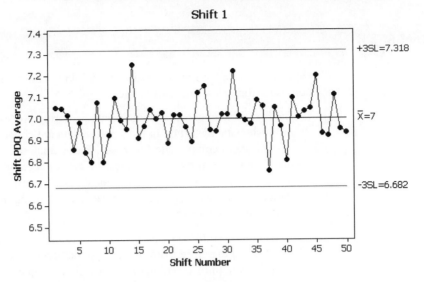

Shift 1

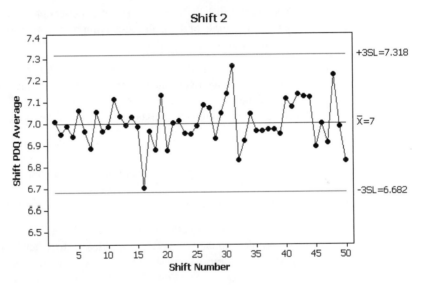

Shift 2

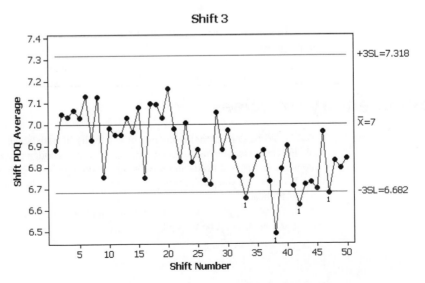

Shift 3

SUMMARY

Here are some of the important ideas for thinking about sampling and about the random variation in a summary statistic.

1. The first thing to consider about a data-gathering process is possible bias. Bias is any systematic distortion in the way the data are collected. In general, statistical methods can't compensate for biases. Biases may occur in the selection of individual items because of refusal to participate or because the measurement process doesn't yield correct answers. The ideal is that every individual item in the population or process has the same chance of being measured, and measured accurately.

2. A sampling distribution measures how a summary statistic varies from sample to sample (and therefore from the true population or process value). It is different from the pattern of variation of data within a sample.

3. A sampling distribution is a theoretical concept. It cannot be seen directly in a particular sample of data, although computer simulations that draw many samples can illustrate sampling distributions.

4. Two key theoretical results for any sample statistic are the expected value (the long-run average over many samples) and the standard error (the standard deviation of the statistic over many samples). The mathematical form of these quantities depends on which statistic is being considered and on the sampling method.

5. The Central Limit Theorem says that sample means (and sums) will follow approximately a normal distribution. The approximation gets better and better as the sample size gets larger. This theorem, as stated, applies only to sample means and sums; without further evidence, we can't assume that other statistics also follow a normal distribution.

6. The distribution of data within a sample, insofar as it indicates the distribution in the whole population, gives some idea as to whether key assumptions hold. In particular, extreme skewness in a sample indicates population skewness, which in turn indicates that the Central Limit Theorem effect will require a relatively large sample size.

   In addition, you may want to reread the Executive Overview at the beginning of the chapter.

Supplementary Exercises

6.26 While demonstrating the role of variability in statistical quality control, the statistician W. Edwards Deming had seminar participants dip a wooden paddle with 50 holes into a bowl containing 20% red beads and 80% white beads. The beads had been thoroughly mixed.
a. What would you think the expected number of red beads would be in the "paddle sample" of 50 beads?
b. In answering part (a), you made an assumption about the sampling method. What was it, and how might it be wrong?

6.27 In thousands of repetitions of the bead experiment of Exercise 6.26, Deming reported that the average number of red beads is approximately 9.4. What does this fact indicate about the assumption you made in answering Exercise 6.26?

6.28 One important application of sampling ideas in quality control is the inspection of incoming components from suppliers. In the assembly of an automobile door, suppliers must provide window glass, window-lowering mechanisms, door handles, door-lock mechanisms, and trim parts. All of these components can be tested to see if they meet initial fitness and long-term reliability specifications. In particular, suppose that the auto manufacturer specifies that door-lock mechanisms should work smoothly through 50,000 lock–unlock cycles.
a. Why would it be absolutely necessary to use sampling in testing the door-lock mechanisms?
b. One possible sampling method would be to test the first 5 door-lock mechanisms in each 1000-item shipment. Why would this method be unwise?

6.29 One way to specify inspection sampling of the auto door parts in Exercise 6.28 would be to demand that half of 1% of each shipment of each component be randomly sampled and tested. Shipment sizes range from 1000 door handles (from a new supplier of unknown quality) to 50,000 trim parts (from a long-time supplier with an established reputation for high quality). Would the "half a percent" rule yield a reasonable inspection approach?

6.30 Suppose that a random sample of 20 power window mechanisms is taken from each lot of 5000 supplied to the auto manufacturer in Exercise 6.28. Each sampled mechanism is tested by putting it through continuous up–down cycles until it fails. Suppose that in the entire lot, the mean time to failure (under these high-stress conditions) is 4200 cycles and that the standard deviation is 3400. The mean failure time for the sample is recorded.
a. What is the expected value of the sample mean?
b. What is the standard deviation of the sample mean? How much would it matter if the sample of 20 had been taken from a lot of 10,000 rather than a lot of 5,000 mechanisms?
c. Would it be reasonable to assume that the distribution of individual failure times should be roughly normal? Should the Empirical Rule apply?
d. Would it be reasonable to assume that the distribution of the sample mean should be roughly normal?

6.31 Assume that the testing method of Exercise 6.30 is modified by testing 40 mechanisms per lot rather than 20. Would this modification result in doubling the accuracy of estimation of the mean failure time?

6.32 Bad sectors on a microcomputer floppy disk cannot be used for data storage. Suppose that in a very large supply of floppy disks the mean bad-sector volume is 2.13 K (kilobytes) per disk, and that the standard deviation is .83 K. A retailer assembles packs of 100 floppy disks from the supply.
a. What is the expected average bad-sector volume in a pack?
b. What is the standard deviation of average bad-sector volume in a pack?

6.33 What did you assume about the assembly process of the retailer in Exercise 6.32? If the assumption is wrong, which part of your answer would be affected?

6.34 A purchaser of floppy disks assembles many 100-disk packs, laboriously finds the average bad-sector volume in each pack, and draws a histogram of the data. What would you expect the shape of the histogram to be? Why?

6.35 A newspaper columnist asserts that directors of Fortune 1000 firms paid, on the average, only 19.1% of their gross income in federal income tax the previous year. From the published column, it can be inferred that the claimed standard deviation is 6.8%. Suppose that you, as an Internal Revenue Service officer, are charged with taking a sample of 200 such executives to test this claim.

a. The names of all Fortune 1000 firm directors are publicly available. How can you use such a list to select a random sample? What problems might you encounter?

b. Can you assume that because $n = 200$ is a fairly large sample, the distribution of percentage of gross income paid by individuals in income tax in the sample is approximately normal? Explain.

6.36 Assume that the weekly demand for 5-pound sacks of flour at a particular supermarket is normally distributed with mean 72.0 cases and standard deviation 1.6 cases.

a. Do you think that a normal distribution might be a decent model?

b. How could you take a reasonable random sample of size 15 from this population?

6.37 Assume that a random sample of size 15 has been taken in Exercise 6.36.

a. What is $P(\bar{Y} \geq 73.0)$?

b. Find a 95% range for $\bar{Y}$; that is, find a value k such that $P(72.0 - k \leq \bar{Y} \leq 72.0 + k) = .95$.

6.38 A department store expects the average "inventory shrinkage" (a euphemism for theft by employees and customers) to be 2.2%. The standard deviation from one sale category to another is assumed to be 1.6%. The store has 2571 sales categories, from which a sample of 100 categories is to be selected for detailed inventory checking.

a. How would you select such a random sample?

b. Is a simple random sample desirable here? Granted that you don't know about fancier sampling methods, can you think of other considerations for sampling?

6.39 Suppose that a random sample of 100 categories is chosen in Exercise 6.38.

a. Find the expected value and standard error of the sample average shrinkage.

b. Use a normal approximation to calculate $P(\bar{Y} \geq 2.4\%)$.

6.40 How good do you expect the normal approximation in Exercise 6.39 to be? How would you use the sample data to help indicate how much faith you have in the approximation?

6.41 Suppose that a population has the following distribution:

Values: 10   80   90   100   110   120   190
Relative frequency: .02   .10   .20   .36   .20   .10   .02

a. Verify that the population mean is 100 and the population standard deviation is 21.07.

b. Draw a histogram of this distribution. What is the obvious feature?

6.42 Refer to Exercise 6.41. The exact sampling distribution of the sample mean (for sample sizes 2, 4, and 8) has the following properties:

Sample Size	Standard Error	$P(\bar{Y} < \mu - 2\sigma_{\bar{Y}})$	$P(\bar{Y} < \mu - \sigma_{\bar{Y}})$	$P(\bar{Y} > \mu + \sigma_{\bar{Y}})$	$P(\bar{Y} > \mu + 2\sigma_{\bar{Y}})$
2	14.90	.0388	.0888	.0888	.0388
4	10.54	.0488	.0899	.0899	.0488
8	7.45	.0333	.1456	.1456	.0333

a. For each sample size, compute the exact probability that $\bar{Y}$ is within 1 standard error of μ.

b. How good is the normal approximation for each n?

c. Repeat parts (a) and (b) for $\bar{Y}$ within 2 standard errors of μ.

6.43   The personnel records of an insurance firm's main office contain data on the number of leave days (for illness or personal reasons) taken in a year by each of 533 employees. The numbers are stored in column 1 of the EX0643 data set on the CD for this book.

a. Obtain a histogram or stem-and-leaf display of the data. Would you say that the population data were roughly normally distributed?

b. Obtain the mean and standard deviation. A computer program will probably regard the data as a sample, not a population. What difference will that make in the calculations? How important, numerically, will the difference be?

c. Have the computer program draw 25 random samples from the population, each of size 20, and compute the mean for each sample.

d. Obtain a histogram or stem-and-leaf display of the 25 sample means. Does this picture have the same shape as the population distribution? What explains the difference?

6.44   Have a computer program calculate the standard deviation of the sample means obtained in Exercise 6.43. What theoretical quantity is being approximated by this standard deviation? Does the numerical value you obtained come close to the theoretical value?

6.45   Many computer programs will choose random numbers that are uniformly distributed between 0 and 1. This distribution has a flat histogram over the range 0 to 1 and no probability outside this range.

a. Have the program take 100 such samples, each of size 12. Obtain the means of the 100 samples. Have the program draw a histogram of these means.

b. Should the histogram of means be approximately uniformly distributed between 0 and 1? Theoretically, why? Does the histogram you obtained roughly correspond to the theoretical result?

c. The variance of a uniform distribution (between 0 and 1) is $1/12 = .0833333$. What is the theoretical standard deviation of the means obtained in part (a)? Have the program compute this standard deviation. How well does it approximate the theoretical value?

d. What should be the mean (expected value) for a uniform distribution between 0 and 1? How does the average of the 100 sample means compare to this theoretical value?

BUSINESS CASES

Credit Risk Assessment

Your employer, a long-distance telephone company, issues charge cards to any customers who request them. Most customers are sales employees and executives of small or medium-sized firms. For such firms, telephone bill payments do not take highest priority, and your employer has difficulty collecting payment on about 8% of its charge cards. Therefore, the company is considering a credit-worthiness scoring system (available from a consulting firm) to decide whether or not to issue charge cards to employees of a particular firm. To try and decide whether to use the system in the future, the company plans to sample its current card users to estimate the average score on the system. Some of the variables in the scoring system are not available on the company's computer, so each firm in the sample requires about an hour of a clerk's time to find and enter the required information. The company can't decide how to take the sample: Some people want to sample individual card users; others want to sample the firms responsible for paying the phone bills. Some people want to sample about 200 accounts; others argue that such a sample would be too small a fraction of the (approximately) 80,000 accounts the company currently has.

No one seems to have thought much about how to take the sample, though the information systems group has available an up-to-date listing of all accounts, classified virtually in any desired way. The consultants aren't willing to specify what the average should be, though they have said that, in other applications of the system, a clear majority of firms tend to score between 75 and 85, and scores between 65 and 75 or between 85 and 95 aren't terribly unusual.

Assignment: Write a brief position paper on these problems, and focus on how the sample might be taken. Give your recommendations on choosing a sample size of 200 or some other sample size. You can assume that your readers will know what an average is, but don't assume that they know much more about technicial statistical issues. You can also figure that your readers have a one-page attention span.

Carson Cake and Cookie Company

The Carson Cake and Cookie Company produces a variety of packaged cookies and snack cakes that are sold in grocery and convenience stores. One of their top sellers is Devil's Delight, a dark chocolate snack cake with a milk chocolate creme filling. The cakes are individually wrapped and sold in boxes of one dozen cakes.

The machinery used in the Devil's Delight production process is about 15 years old. Over time, the variation in the weights of the cakes produced has gradually increased. While the weight of an individual cake is listed as 60 grams, the actual weights follow a normal distribution with a mean of 64 grams and a standard deviation of 1.8 grams. The production process is set at a mean of 64 grams in order to limit the percentage of cakes that are underweight (that is, weigh less than the advertised 60 grams). Of course, increased variation leads to increased waste. The ingredients cost about $0.0024 per gram of cake. The company currently produces 12,000 Devil's Delight cakes (that is, 1000 boxes of one dozen cakes) each day and makes a profit of $0.48 per box sold.

One possibility being considered is replacing the production machinery. The production supervisor has found some replacement equipment for Devil's Delight that will cut the variation in cake weights, as measured by the standard deviation, in half. The new equipment will also increase the daily production rate by 25%. Marketing is convinced that the strong temptation of Devil's Delight will easily absorb the anticipated increase in production, so that there will be no problem in selling the additional units. The cost of the new machinery, including installation, is $600,000.

Assignment: As the CFO of CCCC, you are in charge of deciding whether to buy the new equipment. The president of the company is expecting you to compare two options: (1) staying with the old equipment, or (2) buying the new equipment. Assume that the company wants to maintain the same percentage of underweight individual cakes if it decides on the new equipment. At a minimum, you should perform the following calculations: (1) percentage of underweight boxes of 12 cakes for both the new and old equipment, (2) dollar savings per day using the new equipment instead of staying with the old equipment, and (3) the payback period if the new equipment is purchased. Write a report to the president comparing the two options. Provide sufficient details and explanations of your calculations in the report.

Appendix: Standard Error of a Mean

Some students want to understand *why* the formula for the standard error of $\bar{Y}$ comes out as it does. For their benefit, this appendix contains a sketchy proof. There are two key ideas; each is stated in terms of variance. First, multiplying a random variable by a constant multiplies its variance by the *square* of the constant. Second, the variance of a sum of *independent* random variables is the sum of the component variances. Therefore,

$$\text{Var}(\bar{Y}) = \text{Var}\left(\frac{\sum Y_i}{n}\right)$$

$$= 1/n^2\,\text{Var}(\sum Y_i) \quad \text{because dividing by } n \text{ is equivalent to multiplying by } 1/n$$

$$= 1/n^2 \sum \text{Var}(Y_i) \quad \text{because the individual variables are, by assumption, independent}$$

$$= 1/n^2(\sigma^2 + \sigma^2 + \cdots + \sigma^2) \quad \text{because the variables are drawn from a population with variance } \sigma^2$$

$$= n\sigma^2/n^2 = \sigma^2/n$$

Taking a square root yields the standard error of $\bar{Y}$:

$$\sigma_{\bar{Y}} = \sqrt{\text{Var}(\bar{Y})}$$

$$= \frac{\sigma}{\sqrt{n}}$$

Review Exercises—Chapters 4–6

6.46   Consider a $B(n = 5, \pi = .75)$ distribution. What is the *median* of this distribution?

6.47   In a soft drink bottling process, the actual amount poured into a 20-ounce bottle follows a normal distribution with a mean of 20.0 ounces and a standard deviation of .18 ounces. The bottle can hold up to 20.25 ounces.
a. What percentage of bottles overflow when filled?
b. In the next three bottles filled, what is the probability that *all* will overflow?
c. In the next three bottles filled, what is the probability that the average amount per bottle is less than 19.8 ounces?

6.48   MicroGates claims that its Windoze NT operating system is so stable that a typical office environment should experience an average of .8 total system failures or fewer per day.
a. Today, in your typical office environment, you experienced 2 total system failures on your Windoze NT OS. Assuming that the claimed average of .8 failures per day is true, what is the probability of experiencing *2 or more* failures in one day?
b. What can you conclude about the company's claim based on this evidence? Explain.

6.49   Scores on an aptitude test for assembly workers are roughly normally distributed with a mean of 200 and a standard deviation of 40.
a. Find the probability that a randomly chosen individual scores above 210.
b. Find the probability that the mean of a random sample of 25 individuals is larger than 210.

6.50   If the distribution of scores in Exercise 6.49 is not exactly normal, which answer is a poorer approximation? Why?

6.51   A supermarket makes errors in posting 5% of the price changes it makes, in the long run. Suppose that a random sample of 50 price changes is selected The number of changes made during the period is so large that it doesn't matter whether the sample is taken with or without replacement.
a. Write an expression for the probability that three or fewer changes are posted incorrectly.
b. Find a numerical value for the probability in part (a).
c. What assumptions were made in answering part (a)? From what you know about supermarkets, under what conditions might any of these assumptions be in error?

6.52   A certain part is kept in inventory at an automobile dealership; the parts manager wants a maximum of 10 on hand. The number in stock at a given time follows the probability distribution

$$P_Y(y) = \frac{(y + 1)}{66}, \qquad y = 0, 1, \ldots, 10$$

a. Write out a table of numerical probabilities.
b. Find the mean and standard deviation of the number in stock at a given time.
c. If the dealer requires 3 of this part on a given day, what is the probability that there are enough in stock?

6.53   Suppose that the auto dealer in the previous exercise has 4 separate parts in stock and that the probability distribution for the number of each in stock is the distribution specified there.
a. Find the mean and variance of the average stock of the 4 parts.
b. What additional assumptions, if any, did you make in answering part (a)? For each assumption, is the assumption more critical in determining the mean or in determining the variance?

6.54   Now suppose that the dealer in the preceding exercises has 200 separate parts and that the availability of each part is given by the same probability distribution. Find the approximate probability that the average number in stock (averaged over the 200 parts) is greater than 7. Should the approximation be a good one?

6.55   The manufacturing process for glass wire used in fiber-optic transmission cables introduces impurities at an average rate of .0002 impurity per foot of wire. The wire is cut into 1000-foot sections; if any impurity is found in a section, that section is recycled. What is the probability that a randomly chosen section contains no impurities?

6.56   What additional assumptions beyond the stated ones did you make in answering the previous exercise?

6.57   A certain radio show has a catalog from which fans of the show may order compact discs or tapes as well as souvenir items. Suppose that 40% of the orders involve no CDs or tapes, 30% involve 1 CD or tape, 15% involve 2, 10% involve 3, and 5% involve 4. For each possible number of CDs or tapes ordered, the percentage of orders of 0, 1, 2, 3, 4, or 5 souvenir items is given in the following table:

Discs/Tapes Ordered	Souvenirs Ordered (%)					
	0	1	2	3	4	5
0	0	60	30	5	3	2
1	10	40	25	15	5	5
2	5	30	40	10	8	7
3	3	15	22	30	20	10
4	1	4	15	30	40	10

Calculate the joint probability distribution of X = number of records or tapes ordered and Y = number of souvenirs ordered, in table form. Are the two types of orders independent?

6.58 Find the expected number of souvenirs ordered, assuming the probabilities shown in the previous exercise. Also, find the standard deviation of the number of souvenirs ordered.

6.59 A manufacturing process that is working properly produces 5% defective items because of impurities in materials or other random factors. Suppose that 20 items are selected from the output of the process and inspected. Assume that the process is working properly.
a. Find the probability that 2 or more of the selected items are defective.
b. What did you assume in answering part (a)?

6.60 An alternative inspection method for the process in the previous exercise is to inspect every item and stop the process whenever 2 defectives have been found within the most recent 10 inspected. Does this inspection method satisfy the assumptions of a binomial random variable?

6.61 Suppose that it has been established that the number of program lines per week produced by computer programmers using a commercially available toolbox has a mean of 250 and a standard deviation of 70. Suppose that a random sample of 40 programmers is taken. What is the approximate probability that the average lines produced is greater than 265?

6.62 What did you assume in answering the previous exercise? Under what circumstances might the answer to that exercise be a poor approximation?

6.63 A realtor believes that under current conditions, 45% of walk-in customers eventually purchase a home through that realtor. In a random sample of 16 walk-in customers, what is the probability that 3 or fewer eventually purchase a home through the realtor? Provide a numerical answer.

6.64 Specify all assumptions you made in answering the previous exercise. Are there any assumptions that appear grossly unreasonable to you?

6.65 A bond broker occasionally calls clients to try to place tax-exempt bonds. Define X = number of calls made to a particular client in a three-month period and Y = number of orders made in that period by the client. Assume that

$$P_{XY}(x, y) = \frac{(4 - x)(xy + 1)}{30(1 + 2x)}, \qquad x = 1, 2, 3, \quad y = 0, 1, 2, 3, 4$$

The Excel spreadsheet program was used to create the following table of probabilities:

		0	1	2	y 3	4	Total
x	1	0.0333	0.0667	0.1	0.1333	0.1667	0.5
	2	0.0133	0.04	0.0667	0.0933	0.12	0.3333
	3	0.0048	0.0190	0.0333	0.0476	0.0619	0.1667
Total		0.0514	0.1257	0.2	0.2743	0.3486	1

a. Verify the calculation for $x = 1$, $y = 0$.
b. Find the conditional distribution of Y given X, in either mathematical or tabular form.
c. Are X and Y independent? In context, should they be?

6.66   Find the mean and variance of Y in the previous exercise.

6.67   In the preceding exercises would the bond broker expect a positive or a negative correlation between X, the number of calls made, and Y, the number of orders received?

6.68   The Excel program calculated each value of $(x - \mu_X)(y - \mu_Y)P_{XY}(x, y)$, as shown in the following output. The sum of these values is shown in the lower right, followed by this sum divided by the product of the X and Y standard deviations.

		0	1	2	y 3	4
x	1	0.0609	0.0775	0.0495	-0.0229	-0.1397
	2	-0.0122	-0.0232	-0.0165	0.008	0.0503
	3	-0.0174	-0.0443	-0.0330	0.0163	0.1038

$$0.0571$$
$$0.0637$$

a. What is the technical name for the sum, .0571?
b. Does the output show the sign (positive or negative) of the correlation that you would expect in this situation? Does the correlation seem strong, moderate, or weak?

6.69   A computer software wholesaler occasionally gets special-handling orders that must be shipped by air. Such orders are expensive and unprofitable. Records indicate that such orders occur at an average rate of 1.6 per workday. In a week with five workdays, what is the probability that there are 10 or more special-handling orders? Provide a numerical answer.

6.70   Carefully specify the assumptions you made in answering the previous exercise. Are any of these assumptions obviously wrong?

CHAPTER 7

Point and Interval Estimation

CHAPTER CONTENTS

The basic problem of statistical theory is how to infer a population or process value, given only sample data. Because any sample statistic will vary from the population value, we must consider random error in estimation. This chapter presents methods that make an explicit allowance for random error, but not systematic bias, in summary numbers. The key ideas in the chapter are the following:

- The first issue in dealing with sample data is how to summarize it. An important issue when estimating a population or process parameter is the choice of an estimator. A good estimation method is (close to) unbiased in that its average (expected) value over all samples equals the parameter value. Given that condition, the best method has the smallest possible standard error and therefore is efficient.

- A confidence interval is a process that has a specified chance of including the true population or process value over the long run of multiple samples. Often, this interval can be constructed as the sample estimate plus or minus a table value times a standard error. If the population/process standard deviation is somehow known, the standard error is the population standard deviation divided by the square root of n, and the table value comes from the z table.

- As a related method, a confidence interval for the proportion of "successes" can be calculated as the sample proportion plus or minus a z table value times a standard error. The standard error is the square root of the proportion times 1 minus the proportion divided by the sample size. This interval follows by regarding successes as 1s in data and failures as 0s. The same principles and interpretations apply.

- Confidence interval methods provide a way to decide how large a sample is needed. Given a desired confidence level and allowance for error, the confidence interval may be solved to find how large n must be. In the case of a proportion, an additional step is necessary, indicating whether the population proportion is assumed to be near .5 (the worst case) or can be bounded away from that value.

- In the realistic case that the population/process standard deviation is not known, the sample standard deviation must be used. When the sample standard deviation and estimated standard error are used, t tables rather than z tables must be used. In such a case, one must specify the degrees of freedom, equal to the sample size minus 1 in a random sample. Otherwise, the same confidence interval method applies.

- The key assumptions underlying confidence interval methods are lack of bias and independence of sample observations. Violation of either assumption can distort results seriously. Further, standard methods assume that the underlying population/process distribution is nearly normal. Violation of this assumption can make standard methods incorrect or, more likely with large n, inefficient.

Pronto Pizza

Antonio Scapelli started Antonio's Restaurant in the small, upstate New York city of Vinemont 30 years ago with just a few thousand dollars. Antonio, his wife, and their children, most now grown, operate the business. One of Antonio's sons, Tony, Jr., graduated from NYU with an undergraduate degree in business administration and came back to manage the family business. The restaurant was one of the first to offer home pizza delivery. Tony had the foresight to make this business decision a few years ago, and he also changed the restaurant's name from Antonio's to Pronto Pizza to emphasize the pizza delivery service. The restaurant has been successful since then and has become one of the leading businesses in the area. Many customers still "dine-in" at the restaurant, but nearly 90% of Pronto's current business comes from the pizza delivery service.

Recently, one of the national-chain fast-food pizza delivery services found its way to Vinemont. To attract business, this new competitor has guaranteed delivery of its pizzas within 30 minutes after the order is placed. If the delivery is not made within 30 minutes, the customer is not charged. It wasn't too long before the new pizza restaurant was taking business away from Pronto. Tony believed that Pronto would have to do the same to remain competitive.

After a careful cost analysis, Tony figured out that to offer a guarantee of 29 minutes or less, Pronto's average delivery time would have to be 25 minutes or less. Tony thought that this would limit the percentage of "free pizzas" under the guarantee to about 5% of all deliveries, which he figured to be the break-even point for such a promotion. To be sure of Pronto's ability to deliver on a promise of 29 minutes or less, Tony knew that he needed to collect data on Pronto's pizza deliveries.

Pronto Pizza's delivery service operates from 4:00 P.M. to midnight every day of the week. One of the two cooks prepares the order after it is phoned in. When the crust and the ingredients are ready, the pizza is put on an oven conveyor belt set so that pizzas come out perfectly, time after time. Then one of the available drivers, mostly juniors and seniors at the local high school, takes the pizza in a heat-insulated bag to the customer. Pronto uses approximately five to six drivers each night for deliveries.

Given the large number of deliveries made each night, Tony knew that he could not possibly monitor every single delivery. He had thought of having someone else collect the data, but given the importance of accurate data, he decided to make all of the measurements himself. This, of course, meant taking a random sample of some, rather than all, deliveries over some time period. Tony decided to check deliveries over the course of a full month. During each hour of delivery service, he randomly selected a phoned-in order and then carefully measured the time required to prepare the order and the time that the order had to wait for an available delivery person. Tony would then go on the delivery to accurately measure the delivery time. After returning, Tony randomly selected an order placed during the next hour and went through the process again. At the end of the month, Tony had collected data on 240 deliveries.

Once he had the data, Tony knew he had to deal with several issues. He was committed to the 29-minute delivery guarantee unless the data strongly indicated that the true average delivery time was more than 25 minutes. How would he decide?

FIGURE 7.1   **Partial Listing of the Pronto Pizza Case Data**

	A	B	C	D	E	F
1	Day	Hour	PrepTime	WaitTime	TravelTime	Distance
2	Fri	4	14.86	3.08	6.02	2.5
3	Fri	5	14.84	13.81	5.47	3.3
4	Fri	6	15.41	9.91	8.99	4.9
5	Fri	7	16.34	2.08	7.98	3.8
6	Fri	8	15.19	2.69	9.01	4.9
7	Fri	9	16.32	0.29	10.86	5.3
8	Fri	10	15.32	4.12	6.31	2.9
9	Fri	11	14.06	0.27	7.87	3.5
10	Sat	4	15.60	11.35	12.47	6.4
11	Sat	5	15.16	11.98	7.58	3.5
12	Sat	6	14.37	0.36	10.65	5.1
13	Sat	7	14.24	1.21	7.83	3.7
14	Sat	8	16.17	4.32	6.75	3.6
15	Sat	9	15.48	1.54	9.59	5.2

Tony also realized that there were three things that could affect pizza delivery times: preparation time, waiting time for an available driver, and travel time to deliver the pizza. Tony hoped that he had collected enough data to figure out how he might improve the delivery operation by reducing the overall delivery time.

What would you do if you were Tony? The data are in the file Pronto on the CD that came with your book. A partial listing of the data is shown in Figure 7.1. These data are coded as follows:

Day:	Day of the week (Mon, Tue, Wed, Thur, Fri, Sat, Sun)
Hour:	Hour of the day (4–11 P.M.)
PrepTime:	Time required (in minutes) to prepare the order
WaitTime:	Time (in minutes) from completing preparation of the order until a delivery person was available to deliver the order
TravelTime:	Time (in minutes) it took the car to reach the delivery location
Distance:	Distance (in miles) from Pronto Pizza to the delivery location

At the conclusion of this chapter, we will help Tony decide whether or not to offer the 29-minute guarantee to his customers by analyzing his collected data using statistical tools learned in this and earlier chapters of this book. ■

NOW WE ARE READY to discuss the basic problems of statistical inference. The problem of inferential statistics is to make inferences about one or more population parameters based on observable sample data. These inferences take several related forms. Conceptually, the simplest inference method is point estimation: What is the best single guess one can give for the value of the population parameter? Other related inference procedures are interval estimation, in which one specifies a reasonable range for the value of a parameter, and hypothesis testing, in which one isolates a particular possible value for the parameter and asks if this value is plausible, given the data. Interval estimation is a main topic of this chapter; hypothesis testing is the topic of the next chapter. Later chapters extend the basic principles stated in these two chapters to a number of commonly occurring situations.

7.1 Point Estimators

point estimation

The simplest statistical inference is **point estimation,** where we compute a single value (statistic) from the sample data to estimate a population parameter. How do we decide which sample statistic to compute to give a single, numerical estimate for a population parameter? Suppose that we are trying to estimate a population mean and that we are willing to assume that the population distribution is normal. One natural summary statistic that can be used to estimate the population mean is the sample mean. Because the population mean for a normal distribution is also the population median, the sample median is also a plausible estimating statistic. So is a 20% trimmed mean, the average of the middle 80% of the values. Even if the population is symmetric, the sample is almost sure to be somewhat asymmetric, because of random variation. Thus, for any particular sample, the three methods will yield somewhat different estimates. The mean is heavily influenced by outliers. A trimmed mean is less influenced by outliers, but it wastes data by ignoring (for instance) 20% of the data. We can think of the median as an extremely trimmed mean, where one discards all but the middle one or two data points. Which method should we use?

To begin the discussion, we need a technical definition. We use θ as the generic symbol for a population parameter. We use $\hat{\theta}$ to indicate an estimate of θ based on sample data.

DEFINITION 7.1

Estimator   An **estimator** $\hat{\theta}$ of a parameter θ is a function of random sample values $Y_1, Y_2, \ldots, Y_n$ that yields a point estimate of θ. An estimator is itself a random variable and therefore it has a theoretical (sampling) distribution.

There is a small technical distinction between an *estimator* as a function of random variables and an *estimate* as a single number. It is the distinction between a process (the estimator) and the result of that process (the estimate). The important aspect of this definition is that we can only define good processes (estimators), not guarantee good results (estimates). We will show, for example, that when one samples from a normal population, the sample mean is the best estimator of the population mean. However, we cannot guarantee that the result is always optimal—that is, we cannot guarantee that, in every single sample, the sample mean is always closer to the population mean than, say, the sample median. The best we can do is to find estimators that give good results in the long run.

An estimator (and its sampling distribution) should estimate the population parameter correctly on the average. For example, it seems wrong to use the sample 90th percentile to estimate the median (50th percentile) of a population as opposed to using the sample median. Although it is conceivable that, in a particular sample, the 90th percentile is closer to the population median than is the sample median, generally the sample 90th percentile is too large; that is, the 90th percentile of the sample tends to overestimate the median of the population. We want to use an estimating statistic that does not systematically overestimate or underestimate the desired population parameter.

DEFINITION 7.2

Unbiased Estimator   An estimator $\hat{\theta}$ that is a function of the sample data $Y_1, Y_2, \ldots, Y_n$ is called unbiased for the population parameter θ if its expected value equals θ; that is, $\hat{\theta}$ is an unbiased estimator of the parameter θ if $\mu_{\hat{\theta}} = E(\hat{\theta}) = \theta$.

An unbiased estimator is correct on the average. We can think of the expected value of $\hat{\theta}$ as the average of $\hat{\theta}$ values for all possible samples, or alternatively, as the long-run average of $\hat{\theta}$ values for repeated samples. The condition that the estimator $\hat{\theta}$ should be unbiased says that the *average* $\hat{\theta}$ value is exactly correct. It does not say that a *particular* $\hat{\theta}$ value is exactly correct (see Figure 7.2). If the estimator is biased, the amount of bias is $\text{Bias}(\hat{\theta}) = \mu_{\hat{\theta}} - \theta$.

FIGURE 7.2

Illustration of (a) Unbiased and (b) Biased Estimators

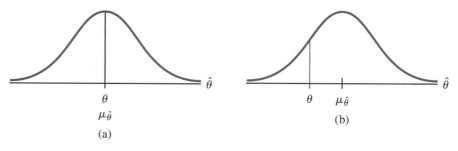

EXAMPLE 7.1

Suppose that $Y_1, Y_2, \ldots, Y_n$ represent the values obtained by a simple random sample from a population having mean μ and variance σ^2. Verify that $\overline{Y}$, the sample mean, is an unbiased estimator of μ.

SOLUTION   In Chapter 6 we showed that $\mu_{\overline{Y}} = E(\overline{Y}) = \mu$. Thus, by definition, the sample mean is an unbiased estimator of the population mean.

The requirement that an estimator be unbiased is not very restrictive. Usually there are many unbiased estimators of any population parameter. For example, when sampling from a normal population, the sample mean, median, and trimmed mean are all unbiased estimators of the population mean μ.

Lack of bias is not the only property that we want an estimator to possess. An estimator that is unbiased but grossly overestimates the parameter of interest half the time and grossly underestimates it the other half isn't a very good estimator. A second property that we require of an estimator is that it have a sampling distribution with most of its probability concentrated near the parameter to be estimated. One measure of this concentration of the sampling distribution of an estimator is given by its standard error: The smaller the standard error, the more concentration of probability there is near the parameter of interest. Figure 7.3 shows the sampling distributions for two hypothetical unbiased estimators of a population parameter θ. It is obvious that $\sigma_{\hat{\theta}_1} > \sigma_{\hat{\theta}_2}$ and hence that $\hat{\theta}_2$ is a more desirable estimator than is $\hat{\theta}_1$.

The standard error of an estimator is also related to the probable degree of error of an estimator: The smaller the standard error, the smaller the probable degree of error. Therefore, we would like to find an unbiased estimator with the smallest possible standard error, or equivalently, the smallest probable error.

DEFINITION 7.3

Efficient Estimator   An estimator is called most efficient for a particular problem if it has the smallest standard error of all possible unbiased estimators.

FIGURE 7.3   **Sampling Distributions of $\hat{\theta}_1$ and $\hat{\theta}_2$**

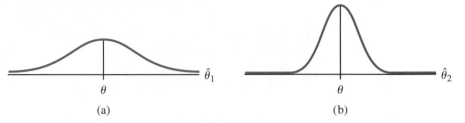

The word *efficient* is used because the estimator makes the best possible use of the sample data in a given situation. A most efficient unbiased estimator is usually preferred to any other, according to standard statistical theory. Given some very specific assumptions, it is possible to find most efficient estimators. For example, if the population from which the sample measurements are drawn is normal, the sample mean has a smaller standard error than the sample median, any sample trimmed mean, or any other unbiased estimator. Therefore, if there is good reason to assume a normal population, the sample mean is the best estimator of the population mean.

EXAMPLE 7.2   A computer program draws 1000 samples, each of size 30, from a normally distributed population having mean 50 and standard deviation 10. For each sample, the mean, median, and trimmed mean (average of the middle 80% of the sample data) are computed. The average value and standard deviation of each set of estimates for the 1000 samples are as follows:

Statistic	Average Value	Standard Deviation
Mean	50.1254	1.8373
Median	50.1696	2.2607
Trimmed mean	50.1196	1.8947

Do the three statistics appear to be unbiased? Which one appears to be most efficient?

SOLUTION The average value of each estimator is (a simulation approximation to) its expected value. The average value of each estimator is very close to the population mean, 50, so all three estimators appear to be unbiased, at least in this situation. The standard deviation of each estimator is (a simulation approximation to) its standard error. The sample mean has the smallest standard error, so it seems to be most efficient in this situation.

Unfortunately, efficiency claims are heavily dependent on assumptions. The sample mean is not always most efficient when the population distribution is not normal. In particular, when the population distribution has heavy tails, the sample mean is less efficient than a trimmed mean (though it still is unbiased). Heavy-tailed distributions tend to yield lots of extreme, "oddball" values that influence a mean more than a trimmed mean. A great deal of research is being conducted to find

robust estimators

so-called **robust estimators:** statistics that are nearly unbiased and nearly efficient for a wide variety of possible population distributions. There is not yet any general agreement on ideal robust estimators, but it's reasonable to assume that such methods will be used increasingly in the near future. We do not spend much space on these methods despite their potential usefulness. The formulas involved in robust estimation are more complicated than those we present, but the basic principles for using the formulas are the same.

EXAMPLE 7.3

A computer is programmed to draw 1000 samples, each of size 30, from an extremely heavy-tailed, outlier-prone population having mean 0 and standard deviation 9.95. Sample means, medians, and trimmed means are computed for each sample. The average values and standard deviations of the estimates are shown here:

Statistic	Average Value	Standard Deviation
Mean	.0228	1.8757
Median	.0148	.4510
Trimmed mean	.0081	.5667

What do these results indicate about the bias and efficiency of the three estimators when sampling from this population?

SOLUTION   All three averages, approximations to the expected values, are close to 0, so all three estimators seem to be unbiased. In this case the standard error of the median appears to be much smaller than the standard error of the mean and somewhat smaller than that of the trimmed mean. Thus, for this outlier-prone population, the sample median appears to be somewhat more efficient than the trimmed mean and much more efficient than the sample mean.

Exercises

7.1   A random sample of 20 vice presidents of Fortune 500 firms is taken. The amount each vice president paid in federal income taxes as a percentage of gross income is determined. The data are

16.0   18.1   18.6   20.2   21.7   22.4   22.4   23.1   23.2   23.5
24.1   24.3   24.7   25.2   25.9   26.3   27.9   28.0   30.4   33.7

a. Compute the sample mean and median.
a. Compute the 20% trimmed mean; that is, delete the lowest 10% and the highest 10% of the data and find the mean of the remainder.

7.2   Refer to the data of Exercise 7.1.
a. Construct a histogram using about six classes.
b. Is there evidence of nonnormality in the data?
c. Which of the sample statistics computed in Exercise 7.1 would you select to estimate the population mean?

7.3 A Monte Carlo study involves 10,000 random samples of size 16 from a normal population with $\mu = 100$ and $\sigma = 20$. For each sample, the mean, the median, and the 20% trimmed mean are calculated, with the following results:

Estimator	Mean	Median	Trimmed Mean
Average	100.23	99.96	99.98
Variance	26.52	40.61	27.49

a. What does the study suggest about the bias of the three estimators in this situation?
b. Which of the three estimators appears most efficient?

7.4 Box plots of means, trimmed means (with the top 10% and bottom 10% of the data deleted), and medians for samples of size 10 from a Laplace (mildly outlier-prone) population are shown in Figure 7.4. The mean of this population is 0.
a. Do the three estimators appear to be unbiased?
b. Which estimator appears to be most efficient?

FIGURE 7.4 **Box Plots for Three Estimators; Laplace Population, $n = 10$**

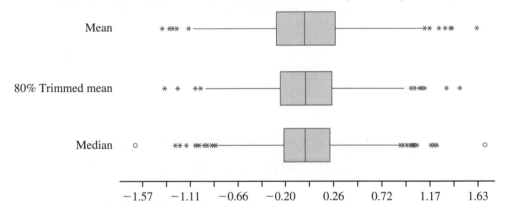

7.5 The averages and standard deviations for the three estimators in Exercise 7.4 are as follows:

Estimator	Average	Standard Deviation
Mean	.0100	.4366
Trimmed mean	.0040	.3899
Median	.0032	.3704

Are these results consistent with your answers to Exercise 7.4?

7.6 Samples of size 30 are chosen from a "uniform" population. The population mean is .500 and the population variance is .08333. The population shape is symmetric and absolutely flat; there are no values less than 0 or greater than 1, so there is no possibility of outliers. The following averages and standard deviations are obtained:

Estimator	Average	Standard Deviation
Mean	.5015	.0504
Trimmed mean	.5017	.0611
Median	.5043	.0644

a. Should the estimators be unbiased, given the nature of the population? Do they appear to be?

b. Which of the three estimators appears to be most efficient?

7.7   The operations manager for the automatic transmission department of an automobile maker obtains data on the operating pressure of a sample of 50 transmissions each week. One of the concerns is the mean for the entire weekly production, which is about 2200 transmissions. (Another concern is the variability around that mean.) Typically, the pressure for most transmissions is very slightly below or above the nominal level of 35 pounds per square inch. A few transmissions can have pressure readings quite far below or above the nominal level. One way to estimate the average for the entire production is to use the midrange of the sample data—the average of the largest and smallest of the 50 data values.

a. From the (admittedly limited) information that you have, is there reason to believe that this method will systematically underestimate the mean? Systematically overestimate it? What technical statistical concept is in question here?

b. Even if there is no systematic under- or overestimate, the midrange method may not be an effective use of the data. Explain why not.

7.8   Explain why the operations manager in Exercise 7.7 might not want to use the mean of the 50 sampled pressures as the estimator of the average for the entire weekly production.

7.2 Interval Estimation of a Mean, Known Standard Deviation

Any sample statistic we choose to use will vary from one sample to another. This fact is recognized in your daily newspaper, where the results of political polls indicate an allowance for sampling error. Whether we estimate using a mean, a median, a trimmed mean, a sample correlation, or whatever, the estimate will vary from one sample to another, and therefore from the true population or process value. In this section we begin to consider how to allow for random error in estimating a population or process number.

The ideas discussed in the previous section dealt with point estimation—finding a best guess for a population parameter. Such point estimates are almost inevitably **probable range** in error to some degree. Specification of a **probable range** for the parameter—a plus-or-minus range for error—is crucial in indicating the reliability of estimates. A statement like "the estimated response rate is 28%" is less useful than one like "the estimated response rate is 28% ± 2%." And 28% ± 2% indicates a much more reliable estimate than 28% ± 15%. In this section we use the idea of a sampling distribution **interval estimate** to construct an **interval estimate** for a population mean. We discuss confidence intervals for proportions in the next section.

The idea is best introduced by an example. Suppose that a random sample of size 36 is to be taken and that the sampling distribution of $\bar{Y}$ is normal. (If the population can be assumed to be reasonably close to symmetric, the Central Limit

Theorem should apply.) Somewhat artificially, we assume that the population standard deviation is known to be 18.0. The expected value of $\overline{Y}$ is the population mean μ, the parameter being estimated, and the standard error of $\overline{Y}$ is $\sigma_{\overline{Y}} = \sigma/\sqrt{n} = 18/\sqrt{36} = 3.0$. From the properties of a normal distribution, there is a 95% chance that $\overline{Y}$ is within 1.96 standard errors of μ (see Figure 7.5):

$$P[\mu - 1.96(3.0) \leq \overline{Y} \leq \mu + 1.96(3.0)] = .95$$

FIGURE 7.5

Sampling Distribution of $\overline{Y}$

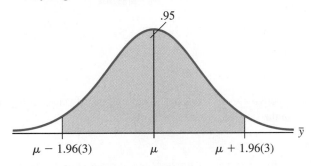

Look at it another way: Any time the observed sample mean $\overline{y}$ lies in the interval $\mu \pm 1.96(3)$, the interval $\overline{y} \pm 1.96(3)$ encloses μ. This is shown in Figure 7.6. Because there is a 95% chance that $\overline{Y}$ lies in the interval $\mu \pm 1.96(3)$, there is a 95% chance that the interval $\overline{Y} \pm 1.96(3)$ encloses μ. The interval $\overline{y} \pm 1.96(3)$ that we construct using the observed sample mean is called a **95% confidence interval for μ**.

95% confidence interval for μ

FIGURE 7.6

Sampling Distribution of $\overline{Y}$

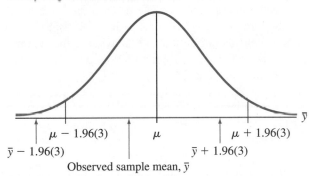

We derive the general formula for a confidence interval for a population mean in the same way. The result is exactly correct only when the population distribution is normal and the population standard deviation is known. Because of the Central Limit Theorem, it provides an excellent approximation when the population distribution is symmetric or only modestly skewed, for sample sizes of, say, 30 or more.

To state confidence intervals (and other statistical methods) generally, we need a bit of notation for probability table values. When we write z with a subscript, we mean "the z table value that cuts off a right-tail area specified by the subscript." Therefore, $z_{.025}$ means the z table (Appendix Table 3) value cutting off a right tail equal to .025. The area to the right of 0 is .5000, so the area between 0 and $z_{.025}$ must be .5000 − .025 = .4750. The required value is $z_{.025}$ = 1.96. Similarly, $z_{.05}$ = 1.645.

DEFINITION 7.4

100(1 − α)% Confidence Interval for μ with σ Known   Using the sample mean as an estimate of the population or process mean, allow for sampling error with a plus-or-minus term equal to a z table value times the standard error of the sample mean.

$$\bar{y} - z_{\alpha/2}\sigma_{\bar{Y}} \le \mu \le \bar{y} + z_{\alpha/2}\sigma_{\bar{Y}}$$

or

$$[\bar{y} - z_{\alpha/2}\sigma_{\bar{Y}}, \bar{y} + z_{\alpha/2}\sigma_{\bar{Y}}]$$

or

$$\bar{y} \pm z_{\alpha/2}\sigma_{\bar{Y}}$$

where $\sigma_{\bar{Y}} = \sigma/\sqrt{n}$ and $z_{\alpha/2}$ is the tabulated value cutting off a right-tail area of $\alpha/2$ in the standard normal (z) distribution.

EXAMPLE 7.4

An airline needs an estimate of the average number of passengers on a newly scheduled flight. Its experience is that data for the first month of flights are unreliable, but that thereafter the passenger load settles down. Therefore, the mean passenger load is calculated for the first 20 weekdays of the second month (regarded as a random sample of 20 days from a hypothetical population of weekdays) after initiation of this particular new flight. If the sample mean is 112.0 and the population standard deviation is assumed to be 25, find a 90% confidence interval for the true, long-run average number of passengers on this flight.

SOLUTION   We assume that the hypothetical population of daily passenger loads for weekdays is not badly skewed. Then the sampling distribution of $\bar{Y}$ is approximately normal and the confidence interval results are approximately correct, even for a sample size of only 20 weekdays. For this example, $\bar{y}$ = 112.0, σ = 25, and $\sigma_{\bar{Y}} = \sigma/\sqrt{20} = 5.59$. Then for a 90% confidence interval, we use $z_{.05}$ = 1.645 in the formula to obtain

$$112 \pm 1.645(5.59) \qquad \text{or} \qquad 102.80 \text{ to } 121.20$$

We are 90% confident that the long-run mean μ lies in this interval.

This confidence interval states an explicit allowance for random sampling error. It does not, and cannot, allow for other kinds of error, such as bias in selecting the data.

The "90%" in a 90% confidence interval refers to the *process* of constructing confidence intervals. Each particular confidence interval either does or does not include the true value of the parameter being estimated. We can't say that this particular estimate is correct to within the error. In the long run, 90% of the intervals so constructed include the population value. So, in the preceding example, as the **interpretation of the confidence interval,** we say that we have 90% confidence that $102.80 \le \mu \le 121.20$. This is shorthand for "the interval $102.80 \le \mu \le 121.20$ is the result of a process that in the long run has 90% probability of being correct."

interpretation of the
confidence interval

EXAMPLE 7.5   A Monte Carlo study considers 5000 samples, each of size 40, from a near-normal population. For each sample, 90% and 95% confidence intervals for the population mean are calculated. A count is made of those samples for which the true mean falls below, within, and above the confidence interval:

	Below	Within	Above
90% interval	236	4513	251
95% interval	129	4753	118

What are the expected frequencies? Compare the theoretical (expected) and the observed frequencies.

SOLUTION   The expected frequencies can be found by multiplying the theoretical probabilities by 5000:

	Below	Within	Above
90% interval	250	4500	250
95% interval	125	4750	125

The simulation frequencies are all quite close to the expected frequencies.

The discussion in this section has included one rather unrealistic assumption—namely, that the population standard deviation is known. Usually both the mean and the standard deviation must be estimated from the sample. Because σ is estimated by the sample standard deviation s, the actual standard error of the mean, $\sigma/\sqrt{n}$, is naturally estimated by $s/\sqrt{n}$. This estimation introduces another source of random error (s varies randomly, from sample to sample, around σ). The logically correct way to handle this problem is to use the t distribution introduced later in this chapter. If the sample size is quite large, say 100 or more, using the z confidence interval of this section with the sample standard deviation s substituted for the population **substituting s for σ**   standard deviation σ—in short, **substituting s for σ**—is a very good approximation. A better approximation uses the sample standard deviation and the t distribution, discussed later in this chapter.

EXAMPLE 7.6   Suppose that the airline in Example 7.4 takes a sample of 40 days and finds a sample mean of 112.0 and a sample standard deviation of 25. Find a 95% confidence interval for the true mean.

SOLUTION   We do not know the correct population standard deviation σ and must estimate it by the sample standard deviation $s = 25$. For $\bar{y} = 112$, $s = 25$, and $n = 40$, $\sigma_{\bar{Y}} \approx 25/\sqrt{40} = 3.95$. Then using $z_{.025} = 1.96$, the 95% confidence interval for μ is

$$112 \pm 1.96(3.95) \qquad \text{or} \qquad 104.26 \text{ to } 119.74$$

Because n is only 40, this confidence interval is not as appropriate as the correct t method introduced later in this chapter.

Exercises

7.9   The data from Exercise 7.1, specifying how much a sample of 20 executives paid in federal income taxes, as a percentage of gross income, are reproduced here.

16.0   18.1   18.6   20.2   21.7   22.4   22.4   23.1   23.2   23.5
24.1   24.3   24.7   25.2   25.9   26.3   27.9   28.0   30.4   33.7

Assume that the standard deviation for the underlying population is 4.0.
a. Calculate a 95% confidence interval for the population mean.
b. Calculate a 99% confidence interval for the population mean.

7.10   Give a careful verbal interpretation of the confidence interval in part (a) of Exercise 7.9.

7.11   From the appearance of the data in Exercise 7.9, is it reasonable to assume that the sampling distribution of the mean is nearly normal?

7.12   A business magazine samples 90 individuals responsible for economic forecasting for regional banks. The population is large enough that the with/without replacement distinction doesn't matter. Suppose that the sample of 90 forecasts yields an average prediction of a 2.7% growth in real disposable income. Assume that the population standard deviation is .4%. Calculate a 90% confidence interval for the population mean forecast.

7.13   In an audit of inventories, an internal auditor takes a sample of 36 items and determines the "shrinkage" (loss due to shoplifting or employee theft) for each item in percentage terms. The sample mean is 5.8% and the standard deviation is 4.2%. Calculate a 95% confidence interval for the true mean shrinkage.

7.14   Do you believe that the sampling distribution of $\bar{Y}$ in Exercise 7.13 would be approximately normal?

7.15   A chain of "quick lube" shops has a standard service for performing oil changes and basic checkups on automobiles. The chain has a standard that says that the average time per car for this service should be 12.5 minutes. There is considerable variability in times, due to differences in layout of engines, degree of time pressure from other jobs, and many other sources. The standard deviation for the chain has been 2.4 minutes. The manager of one shop picked 48 random times (four per day for 12 days) and timed the next job after each random time. The data were analyzed using Minitab, which gave the following results:

```
One-Sample Z: TimeUsed

The assumed standard deviation = 2.4

Variable    N    Mean    StDev   SE Mean        95% CI
TimeUsed   48  13.1041   2.4166   0.3464   (12.4251, 13.7830)
```

a. Write out the 95% confidence interval for the mean. State what the 95% figure means.
b. Does this interval indicate that the mean for this shop differs from the 12.5-minute standard?

7.16 Minitab also calculated a 90% confidence interval for the mean using the same data as in Exercise 7.15.

```
One-Sample Z: TimeUsed

The assumed standard deviation = 2.4

Variable   N    Mean    StDev  SE Mean        90% CI
TimeUsed   48   13.1041  2.4166  0.3464  (12.5343, 13.6739)
```

Does this interval indicate that the mean for this shop differs from the 12.5-minute standard? Why is the answer here different from the answer in part (b) of Exercise 7.15?

7.17 A box plot of the data in Exercise 7.15 is shown in Figure 7.7.

FIGURE 7.7   Box Plot of Job Time Data

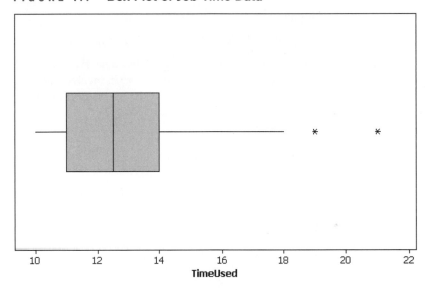

a. What form of nonnormality is indicated by the box plot?
b. Does this nonnormality invalidate the claimed confidence levels in Exercises 7.15 and 7.16?

7.3   Confidence Intervals for a Proportion

The proportion of successes—whether "success" means a likely voter favoring a particular candidate, a process yielding an unacceptable part, or a motel customer indicating a willingness to return on another trip—is another summary statistic from a random sample. It is therefore subject to random error just like any other summary number. We need to allow for random error in a sample proportion as well as in a mean or any other summary statistic from a sample. The confidence interval method in Section 7.2 can be adapted quite directly to give a confidence interval for a population proportion. Once again, we allow a plus-or-minus amount to deal with sampling error (but not with bias). The method is based on a normal approximation to the sampling distribution of a sample proportion. As such, it is an approximation, and some guidelines are needed for its use.

The sample proportion of successes, denoted $\hat{\pi}$, is just the number Y of successes divided by the sample size. If we think of a sample of 1s (successes) and 0s (failures), then $\hat{\pi}$ is the sample mean of these 1s and 0s. The **expected value and standard error of $\hat{\pi}$** are, respectively,

expected value and
standard error of $\hat{\pi}$

$$\mu_{\hat{\pi}} = E(\hat{\pi}) = \pi \quad \text{and} \quad \sigma_{\hat{\pi}} = \sqrt{\pi(1-\pi)/n}$$

where π is the population proportion.

For sufficiently large n, $\hat{\pi}$ has an approximately normal distribution; so, for instance,

$$P\left(-1.96 \leq \frac{\hat{\pi} - \pi}{\sigma_{\hat{\pi}}} \leq 1.96\right) \approx .95$$

Equivalently,

$$P(\hat{\pi} - 1.96\sigma_{\hat{\pi}} \leq \pi \leq \hat{\pi} + 1.96\sigma_{\hat{\pi}}) \approx .95$$

This looks very much like a confidence interval formula, but there is the problem that the standard error $\sigma_{\hat{\pi}} = \sqrt{\pi(1-\pi)/n}$ involves the unknown population parameter π. Just as we can replace σ by s in $\sigma_{\bar{Y}}$ when n is large, so can we replace $\pi(1-\pi)$ by $\hat{\pi}(1-\hat{\pi})$ in $\sigma_{\hat{\pi}}$. This yields a usable confidence interval formula for the population proportion:

DEFINITION 7.5

$100(1-\alpha)$% Confidence Interval for a Proportion

$$\hat{\pi} - z_{\alpha/2}\sqrt{\frac{\hat{\pi}(1-\hat{\pi})}{n}} \leq \pi \leq \hat{\pi} + z_{\alpha/2}\sqrt{\frac{\hat{\pi}(1-\hat{\pi})}{n}}$$

or

$$\hat{\pi} \pm z_{\alpha/2}\sqrt{\frac{\hat{\pi}(1-\hat{\pi})}{n}}$$

This is the same "sample statistic $\pm$ table value times standard error" that occurs in the confidence interval for a mean. The sample mean $\bar{y}$ is replaced by the sample proportion $\hat{\pi}$. Similarly, $\sigma_{\bar{Y}}$ is replaced by $\sigma_{\hat{\pi}}$.

EXAMPLE 7.7

Suppose that in a sample of 2200 households with one or more television sets, 471 watch a particular network's show at a given time. Find a 95% confidence interval for the population proportion of households watching this show.

SOLUTION The sample proportion is $\hat{\pi} = 471/2200 = .214$, and $\sqrt{\hat{\pi}(1-\hat{\pi})/n} = .00875$. The z table value that cuts off a right-tail area of .025 is 1.96. The confidence interval is

$$.214 - 1.96(.00875) \leq \pi \leq .214 + 1.96(.00875)$$

or

$$.197 \leq \pi \leq .231$$

You might check the rankings of current television shows to see how much the difference between a 19.7% share and a 23.1% share would make in a show's ranking.

normal approximation to a binomial distribution

This confidence interval method is based on a **normal approximation to a binomial distribution** that is appropriate for sufficiently large n. The rule is that both $n\pi$ and $n(1 - \pi)$ should be at least 5, but, because π is the unknown population proportion, the rule has to be based on $n\hat{\pi}$ and $n(1 - \hat{\pi})$ instead. Usually a sample size that violates this rule (or even comes close) yields a confidence interval that is too wide to be informative. For example, if $n = 20$ and $\hat{\pi} = .20$, then $n\hat{\pi} = 4$ and the 95% confidence interval for π is $.025 \le \pi \le .375$. This confidence interval is practically useless; we know of few product managers who would consider "your product's market share is between 2.5% and 37.5%" to be very informative. However, even if a sample size satisfies the rule, we are not assured that the interval is informative. The rule judges only the adequacy of the sample size and the accuracy of the confidence interval based on the normal approximation. It is possible to use binomial probabilities to develop exact, if very wide, 90% or 95% confidence intervals.

Simply stating whether or not a result is a success is not very informative. Each trial of a binomial (yes/no) experiment yields very limited information. As a consequence, confidence intervals for modest samples in the hundreds tend to be very wide. Typically, actual measurements yield greater information per trial than simple yes/no categorization. However, sometimes all that can be measured is a yes or no value. In such a case, larger sample sizes are needed to get results that "feel" adequate for managerial purposes. In the next section we'll consider how big a sample size must be to obtain a given degree of uncertainty.

Exercises

7.18 The sales manager for a hardware wholesaler finds that 229 of the previous 500 calls to hardware store owners resulted in new product placements. Assuming that the 500 calls represent a random sample, find a 95% confidence interval for the long-run proportion of new product placements.

7.19 Give a careful verbal interpretation of the confidence interval found in Exercise 7.18.

7.20 As part of a market research study, 84 individuals in a sample of 125 are aware of a certain product. Calculate a 90% confidence interval for the proportion of individuals in the population who are aware of the product.

7.21 Should the normal approximation underlying the confidence interval of Exercise 7.20 be adequate?

7.22 In a sample of 40 middle managers of a large firm, it is found that 8 are actively involved in local civic or charitable organizations. Calculate a 90% confidence interval for the proportion of all middle managers who are so involved.

7.4 How Large a Sample Is Needed?

Information is expensive. Gathering it is costly in terms of salaries, expenses, and time (and profits) lost. Obviously, some information is crucial for making management decisions. So the question of how much information (how large a sample) to gather is basic. The confidence interval provides a convenient method for answering this question.

Suppose that an operations officer of a large multibranch bank is concerned about the daily average level of checks left at branches on weeknights. Each day, armored cars take each branch's receipts to a processing center, where checks are recorded and sent to a clearinghouse. The cars must visit some of the branches before the end of banking hours, so a substantial volume of checks can remain un-collected until the next day. The lost interest can be costly. For how many days must the volume of uncollected checks be calculated to get a reasonable idea of the true daily average?

There are two related aspects of the phrase *reasonable idea* to consider in the context of a confidence interval. First, what confidence level should be selected? Second, how wide a confidence interval can be tolerated? The confidence level is often set at 95% or 90%. In part this is a primitive tribal custom, passed on by generations of statistics textbooks. In part it's a decent translation of reasonable certainty. It's fairly easy to understand 90 (or 95) chances in 100, but hard to comprehend 999,999 chances in 1,000,000.

tolerable width

The **tolerable width** depends heavily on the context of the problem. Plus or minus $80,000 (or a width of $160,000) is moderately large for the nightly idle-check volume of an entire bank, enormous for the nightly idle volume of one branch, and tiny for the average daily amount cleared by all U.S. banks. The tolerance must be determined by a manager who knows the situation.

When considering a confidence interval for a population mean μ, the plus-or-minus term of a confidence interval is $z_{\alpha/2}\sigma_{\bar{Y}}$, where $\sigma_{\bar{Y}} = \sigma/\sqrt{n}$. Three quantities determine the value of the plus-or-minus term: the desired confidence level (which determines the z table value used), the standard deviation σ, and the sample size (which together with σ determines the standard error $\sigma_{\bar{Y}}$). Usually a guess must be made about the size of the population standard deviation. (Sometimes an initial sample is taken to estimate the standard deviation; this estimate provides a basis for determining the additional sample size that is needed.) For a given tolerable width, once the confidence level is specified and an estimate of σ supplied, the required sample size can be calculated by trial and error or by a formula.

The trial-and-error approach can be illustrated with the idle check example. Suppose that a 95% confidence interval is desired with a width of no more than $5,000 (a plus-or-minus range no greater than $2,500) and that the long-run standard deviation is assumed to be $10,000. Suppose we first try $n = 16$. The confidence interval is $\bar{y} \pm 1.96(10,000/\sqrt{16})$ or $\bar{y} \pm 4,900$. This interval is about twice as wide as desired; to halve the width of the confidence interval, we must quadruple the sample size because the sample size appears in the standard error formula as $\sqrt{n}$. With $n = 64$, the 95% confidence interval is $\bar{y} \pm 1.96(10,000/\sqrt{64})$ or $\bar{y} \pm 2,450$, which is about what we want. Because the assumption that the standard deviation is $10,000 is just a guess, there's not much point in arguing over whether n should be 64 or 63 or 65; a "ballpark" value for n serves the purpose.

We can calculate the required sample size by formula. Set $z_{\alpha/2}\sigma/\sqrt{n}$ equal to the specified plus-or-minus tolerance E and solve for n.

DEFINITION 7.6

Sample Size for Interval of Given Width for μ   The sample size required to obtain a $100(1 - \alpha)\%$ confidence interval for a population mean μ of the form $\bar{y} \pm E$, where $E = z_{\alpha/2}\sigma/\sqrt{n}$, is

$$n = \frac{z_{\alpha/2}^2\sigma^2}{E^2}$$

The width of the confidence interval is $2E$. E is called the *margin of error*.

EXAMPLE 7.8

Union officials are concerned about reports of inferior wages being paid to employees of a company under its jurisdiction. How large a sample is needed to obtain a

90% confidence interval for the population mean hourly wage μ with width equal to $1.00? Assume that $\sigma = 4.00.

SOLUTION The desired width is $2E = 1.00$ (so $E = 0.50$) and $\sigma = 4.00$. Substituting into the sample size formula with $z_{\alpha/2} = 1.645$, we obtain

$$n = \frac{(1.645)^2(4^2)}{(.5)^2} \approx 173$$

EXAMPLE 7.9

How large a sample is needed to obtain a 95% confidence interval for μ with a width of two-tenths of a (population) standard deviation?

SOLUTION The desired width $2E = .2\sigma$, so $E = .1\sigma$. Therefore,

$$n = \frac{(1.96)^2\sigma^2}{(.1\sigma)^2} = \frac{(1.96)^2}{(.1)^2} \approx 384$$

Determining sample size for a confidence interval for a proportion is a similar process. The corresponding equation is

$$n = \frac{z_{\alpha/2}^2 \hat{\pi}(1 - \hat{\pi})}{E^2}$$

The only problem is that the sample size depends on $\hat{\pi}$. Until the sample size is determined and the sample taken, we do not know $\hat{\pi}$. There are several possible solutions to our problem. We can substitute $\hat{\pi} = .5$ into the sample-size formula, which results in a conservative sample size that is usually larger than is actually required. Another possibility is to substitute a value of $\hat{\pi}$ obtained from either a previous study or a pilot study. The sample-size formula for estimating a binomial proportion is shown next.

DEFINITION 7.7

Sample Size for Interval of Given Width for π The sample size required to obtain a $100(1 - \alpha)\%$ confidence interval for π of the form $\hat{\pi} \pm E$, where

$$E = z_{\alpha/2}\sqrt{\frac{\hat{\pi}(1 - \hat{\pi})}{n}}$$

is

$$n = \frac{z_{\alpha/2}^2 \hat{\pi}(1 - \hat{\pi})}{E^2}$$

Note: Use $\hat{\pi} = .5$ for a conservative (large) sample size or use the value of $\hat{\pi}$ from a previous (or pilot) study.

EXAMPLE 7.10

A direct-mail sales company must determine its credit policies quite carefully. Suppose that the firm suspects that advertisements in a certain magazine have led to an excessively high rate of write-offs (accounts regarded as uncollectible). The firm wants to establish a 90% confidence interval for this magazine's write-off proportion that is accurate to a margin of error of $\pm.02$.

a. How many accounts must be sampled to guarantee this goal?

b. If this many accounts are sampled and 10% of the sampled accounts are determined to be write-offs, what is the resulting 90% confidence interval?

SOLUTION

a. The sample size formula is

$$n = \frac{z_{\alpha/2}^2 \hat{\pi}(1 - \hat{\pi})}{E^2}$$

Using the conservative estimate $\hat{\pi} = .5$ and substituting $E = .02$ with $z_{\alpha/2} = 1.645$, the required sample size is

$$n = \frac{(1.645)^2(.5)^2}{(.02)^2} \approx 1691$$

b. If a sample of 1691 accounts shows 169 (essentially 10%) write-offs, the 90% confidence interval for the true write-off proportion is

$$.10 \pm 1.645\sqrt{(.10)(.90)/1691} = .10 \pm .012$$

The conservative nature of the confidence interval that results from a sample size determined by setting $\hat{\pi} = .5$ in the formula is indicated here. The actual confidence interval has $E = .012$, whereas the target was $E = .02$. Had the firm been willing to make an initial guess that $\hat{\pi}$ would be about .10, it could have used a smaller sample size.

$$n = \frac{(1.645)^2(.1)(.9)}{(.02)^2} \approx 609$$

As Example 7.10 indicates, basing a sample-size determination on the assumption that $\hat{\pi}$ is .5 can be excessively conservative. Whenever there is information to suggest that the sample proportion differs from .5, the substitution $\hat{\pi} = .5$ results in a large (conservative) sample size. The corresponding confidence interval has a smaller width than the target width.

Exercises

7.23 Refer to Example 7.8.

a. In the example σ was assumed to be $4.00. How large a sample is needed to obtain a 90% confidence interval with width $0.50? With width $0.25? With width $0.125?

b. In general, how much must one increase a sample size to cut the width of a confidence interval in half (using a specific confidence level)?

7.24 How large a sample is needed to obtain a 95% confidence interval with a width of three-tenths of a standard deviation? Four-tenths?

7.25 An automobile insurance firm wants to find the average amount per claim for autobody repairs. Its summary records combine amounts for body repair with all other amounts, so a sample of individual claims must be taken. A 95% confidence interval with a width no greater than $50 is wanted. A "horseback guess" says that the standard deviation is about $400. How large a sample is needed?

7.26 Suppose that the guess of the standard deviation in Exercise 7.25 is somewhere between $300 and $450.

a. Compute the required sample sizes for $\sigma = 300$ and for $\sigma = 450$.

b. What would happen to the width of the confidence interval if the *n* corresponding to $\sigma = 450$ was used but in fact the standard deviation came out to be $300?

7.27 Do you think that the sample size used in Exercise 7.25 would be adequate to assume the $\bar{Y}$ had approximately a normal sampling distribution?

7.28 A manufacturer of boxes of candy is concerned about the proportion of imperfect boxes—those containing cracked, broken, or otherwise unappetizing candies.

a. How large a sample is needed to get a 95% confidence interval for this proportion with a width no greater than .02? Use the conservative substitution.

b. How does the answer to part (a) change if we assume that the proportion of imperfect boxes is at least .005 and no more than .08?

7.5 The *t* Distribution

The confidence interval procedure for a population mean μ presented in Section 7.2 is based on the assumption that either σ, the standard deviation in the entire population, is known (even though the population mean isn't known and is being estimated) or that there is a large enough number of measurements (e.g., 100 or more) so that the sample standard deviation s can replace σ in the standard error for $\bar{y}$, $\sigma/\sqrt{n}$. Sometimes it is impossible or uneconomical to obtain a large sample when making an inference about a population mean. For example, in a study of rush-hour traffic patterns around a bridge on Friday evenings, it would take more than six months to generate 30 observations on the total Friday evening rush-hour traffic volume. This may be too long before some corrective remedies are proposed.

Thus far, the confidence interval has been based on the *z* statistic

$$\frac{\bar{Y} - \mu}{\sigma/\sqrt{n}}$$

When the population standard deviation σ is unknown (and it usually is unknown), it must be replaced by s, the sample standard deviation. This yields a summary statistic universally denoted as *t*.

$$t = \frac{\bar{Y} - \mu}{s/\sqrt{n}}$$

The theoretical distribution of this statistic was first investigated by W. S. Gosset in the 1900s. He was employed by the Guinness brewery, which didn't allow him to publish his results under his own name. Instead, he published his results under the pseudonym "Student." The statistic and its distribution have become known as Student's *t*.

When we substitute the sample standard deviation *s* for the population standard deviation σ, we introduce a second source of variability. Now, as we go from sample to sample, not only the sample mean will vary but also the sample standard deviation. Thus, the variance of the *t* statistic will be larger, reflecting the extra variability. We can summarize the properties of a *t* distribution by comparing it to a standard normal (*z*) distribution.

DEFINITION 7.8

Properties of Student's *t* Distribution

1. The *t* distribution, like the *z* distribution, is symmetric about the mean $\mu = 0$.

2. The *t* distribution is more variable than the *z* distribution (see Figure 7.8).

3. There are many different *t* distributions. We specify a particular one by its "degrees of freedom," d.f. If a random sample is taken from a normal population, then the statistic

$$t = \frac{\bar{Y} - \mu}{s/\sqrt{n}}$$

    has a *t* distribution with d.f. $= n - 1$.

4. As *n* increases (or equivalently, as the d.f. increases), the distribution of *t* approaches the distribution of *z*.

FIGURE 7.8

A *t* Distribution with a Normal Distribution Superimposed

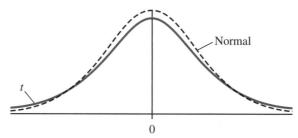

0

degrees of freedom

A general definition of the term **degrees of freedom** requires *n*-dimensional geometry and an understanding of linear algebra. We don't go into such detail; rather we try to give an intuitive idea of what the term means. The d.f. refers to the estimated standard deviation and is used to indicate the number of pieces of information available for that estimate. The standard deviation is based on *n* deviations from the mean; but the deviations must sum to 0, so only $n - 1$ deviations are free to vary. The last (*n*th) deviation is determined by the other $n - 1$ and conveys no new information. Therefore, the *t* statistic is said to have $n - 1$ degrees of freedom.

Although a mathematical formula can be given for the probability density function of the *t* distribution, we don't need it in this book. There are tables to evaluate *t* probabilities, and most statistical computer packages can do the same. Because of the symmetry of *t*, only upper-tail percentage points (probabilities or areas) of the distribution of *t* have been tabulated. These appear in Appendix Table 4. The degrees of freedom (d.f.) are listed along the left-hand column of the page. An entry in the table specifies a value of *t*, say, t_a, such that an area *a* lies to its *right* (see Figure 7.9). Various values of *a* appear across the top of the page. Thus, for example, with d.f. = 7, the value of *t* with an area .05 to its right is 1.895 (found in the $a = .05$ column and d.f. = 7 row).

FIGURE 7.9   **Illustration of Area Tabulated in Appendix Table 4 for the *t* Distribution**

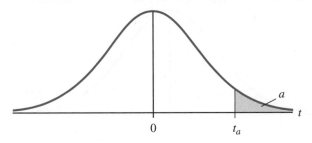

EXAMPLE 7.11   If a random sample of size $n = 15$ is taken from a normally distributed population, use the *t* table to find

$$P\left(\frac{\bar{Y} - \mu}{s/\sqrt{n}} > 2.145\right)$$

and

$$P\left(-2.145 \leq \frac{\bar{Y} - \mu}{s/\sqrt{n}} \leq 2.145\right)$$

Compare your result to the following Minitab output:

```
MTB > CDF 2.145;
SUBC> t 14.

Cumulative Distribution Function

Student's t distribution with 14 d.f.

          x        P( X <= x)
     2.1450           0.9750

MTB > InvCDF .9750;
SUBC> t 14.

Inverse Cumulative Distribution Function

Student's t distribution with 14 d.f.

P(X <=  x)              x
   0.9750          2.1448
```

SOLUTION   We must use the *t* table, provided in the Appendix as Table 4, with $n - 1 = 14$ d.f. The table indicates values that cut off specific right-tail areas. In particular, $P(t_{14\text{d.f.}} > 2.145)$ is shown to be .025, so

$$P\left(\frac{\bar{Y} - \mu}{s/\sqrt{n}} > 2.145\right) = .025$$

FIGURE 7.10   ***t* Distribution with 14 d.f.**

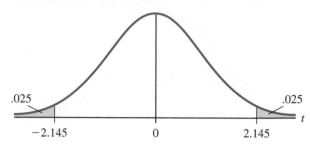

.025   .025

$$-2.145 \qquad\qquad 0 \qquad\qquad 2.145$$

EXAMPLE 7.11   (see Figure 7.10). The *t* distribution is symmetric around 0, so the left-tail area
(continued) $P(t_{14\text{d.f.}} < -2.145) = .025$ also. The remaining area after both tails are cut off is .95, so

$$P\left(-2.145 \le \frac{\bar{Y} - \mu}{s/\sqrt{n}} \le 2.145\right) = .95$$

The first part of the Minitab output specified the value 2.145 and finds the cumulative probability (CDF) up to 2.145 as .975. Therefore, the probability that *t* will be greater than 2.145 is the complement, $1 - .975 = .025$. The second part of the Minitab output reverses the procedure. In this "inverse" procedure, we state the desired probability as .975 and the program returns the table value 2.1448 (2.145 rounded to three decimal places).

An examination of the *t* table indicates the effect of changing from

$$z = \frac{\bar{Y} - \mu}{\sigma/\sqrt{n}}$$

to

$$t = \frac{\bar{Y} - \mu}{s/\sqrt{n}}$$

For very small *n*, *t* table values are quite large. For d.f. = 2, the right-tail area of .025 is cut off at 4.303, as compared to the *z* table value 1.96. As the d.f. increase, the *t* table values for a given tail area decrease. At the bottom line, which has infinite degrees of freedom, the *t* table contains the normal distribution (*z*) values.

This phenomenon can be explained by considering how the *t* distribution arises. We get a *t* statistic by replacing the true standard deviation σ by the sample standard deviation *s*, thus introducing an additional source of random variation. When *n* is small, the value of *s* can vary widely from the value of σ, and the *t* distribution must have quite a large variance. As *n* gets larger, there is less random variation of *s* from σ, and the *t* distribution's variance gets smaller. As *n* approaches infinity, *s* approaches σ, and the only important source of randomness is $\bar{Y}$; the *z* distribution accounts for the variation of $\bar{Y}$ around μ.

When we first discussed replacing σ by *s*, we used a rule that we could use the *z* tables if *n* was greater than or equal to 100. The *t* table values for large d.f. are fairly close to normal table values, except for very small tail areas. But there's no need to preserve this rule any longer. We may as well use the *t* tables routinely for all *t* statistics. If the actual d.f. are not shown in the table, a conservative approach is to use the next lower d.f. that appears in the table.

Exercises

7.29 A random sample of size 4 is to be taken from a normal population with mean $\mu = 100$. Let

$$t = \frac{\bar{Y} - 100}{s/\sqrt{4}}$$

Evaluate the following probabilities using Appendix Table 4 or a computer package:

a. $P(t > 1.638)$
b. $P(t > 5.841)$
c. $P(t < -2.353)$
d. $P(-2.353 < t < 2.353)$
e. $P(|t| > 3.182)$
f. $P(|t| > 4.541)$

Draw pictures.

7.30 Suppose that the *t* statistic in Exercise 7.29 is mistakenly assumed to have a normal (z) distribution. Evaluate $P(t > 1.64)$ and $P(|t| > 1.64)$ under this erroneous assumption. Does this assumption cause an overstatement or an understatement of the probabilities?

7.31 A Monte Carlo study is made by taking 1100 samples, each of size 4, from the normal population of Exercise 7.29. The *t* statistic is defined in that exercise. The results of the study are summarized as follows:

Event	Frequency
$t < -2.353$	44
$-2.353 < t < -1.638$	59
$-1.638 < t < 1.638$	896
$1.638 < t < 2.353$	47
$t > 2.353$	54

a. What are the theoretical relative frequencies?
b. Is there any evidence of a systematic departure from these theoretical relative frequencies?

7.6 Confidence Intervals with the *t* Distribution

The mathematical development of the previous section can be used to state inference procedures for a mean, used in the (typical) case that the population standard deviation is not known. This section is devoted to confidence intervals.

Remember that a confidence interval is designed to allow for some degree of sampling (random) error in estimating a population quantity. Remember also that a confidence interval does *not* allow for systematic biases in data collection. The *z* confidence interval for a population mean is calculated as the sample mean plus or minus a *z* table value times the true standard error, $\sigma/\sqrt{n}$. The changes in the confidence interval procedure when σ is unknown are easy enough. Replace the unknown σ by s to get an estimated standard error $s/\sqrt{n}$; use *t* tables instead of *z* tables.

EXAMPLE 7.12   Calculate a 95% confidence interval for the population mean if a sample of size $n = 25$ from a nearly normal population yields a sample mean of 96.2; assume that the population standard deviation is 15.0. Recalculate the interval, assuming that the population standard deviation is unknown and the sample standard deviation is 16.2.

SOLUTION   We may use the procedures of Section 7.2 for the first problem:

$$\bar{y} - z_{\alpha/2}\frac{\sigma}{\sqrt{n}} \le \mu \le \bar{y} + z_{\alpha/2}\frac{\sigma}{\sqrt{n}}$$

$$96.2 - 1.96\,\frac{(15.0)}{\sqrt{25}} \le \mu \le 96.2 + 1.96\,\frac{(15.0)}{\sqrt{25}}$$

$$90.32 \le \mu \le 102.08$$

In the second problem we need the t table value for $n - 1 = 24$ d.f. This value must cut off combined left- and right-tail areas of .05, so the desired right-tail area is .025. The t table value is 2.064. Replace $\sigma = 15.0$ by $s = 16.2$ and $z_{.025} = 1.96$ by $t_{.025} = 2.064$.

$$96.2 - 2.064\,\frac{(16.2)}{\sqrt{25}} \le \mu \le 96.2 + 2.064\,\frac{(16.2)}{\sqrt{25}}$$

$$89.51 \le \mu \le 102.89$$

This interval is wider than the previous one because $t_{.025} > z_{.025}$ and also because in this case $s = 16.2$ happens to be greater than the assumed $\sigma = 15.0$.

The general t confidence interval for μ based on a t distribution with d.f. $= n - 1$ is stated in the following definition.

DEFINITION 7.9

$100(1 - \alpha)\%$ Confidence Interval for μ, σ Unknown

$$\bar{y} - t_{\alpha/2}\frac{s}{\sqrt{n}} \le \mu \le \bar{y} + t_{\alpha/2}\frac{s}{\sqrt{n}}$$

or

$$\bar{y} \pm t_{\alpha/2}\frac{s}{\sqrt{n}}$$

where $t_{\alpha/2}$ is the tabulated t value cutting off a right-tail area of $\alpha/2$, with $n - 1$ d.f.

small-sample

This formula is often called a **small-sample** confidence interval for the mean, but it is valid for *any* sample size. For a large sample size, the difference between using t tables and z tables is negligible, so the importance of the t versus z distinction is greatest for small sample sizes. The assumption of a normal population is most crucial for small sample sizes, where the Central Limit Theorem has relatively little effect. Even with a larger sample, a confidence interval based on a mean may be inefficient (unnecessarily wide).

EXAMPLE 7.13

An airline has four ticket counter positions at a particular airport. In an attempt to reduce waiting lines for customers, the airline introduces the "snake system." Under this system, all customers enter a single waiting line that winds back and forth in front of the counter. A customer who reaches the front of the line proceeds to the first free position.

Each weekday for three weeks, the airline customer-relations manager charts the waiting time in minutes for the first customer entering after 4 P.M. One observation is excluded because of an unusual condition: The airport was fogged in and many flight plans had to be changed. The data are

4.3　5.2　2.1　6.2　5.8　4.7　3.8　9.3　5.0　4.1　6.0　8.7　0.5　4.9

Find a 95% confidence interval for the long-run mean waiting time on weekdays at 4 P.M. under normal conditions.

SOLUTION　First, calculate $n = 14$, $\bar{y} = 5.043$, and $s = 2.266$. The *t* table value (13 d.f., one-tail area .025) is 2.160. The interval is

$$5.043 - 2.160\frac{(2.266)}{\sqrt{14}} \leq \mu \leq 5.043 + 2.160\frac{(2.266)}{\sqrt{14}}$$

or

$$3.735 \leq \mu \leq 6.351$$

It would be better to report this, rounded off to roughly the accuracy of the data, as $3.7 \leq \mu \leq 6.4$.

A confidence interval is a useful way to present information to managers. Most people are familiar with the idea that political polls have an "allowance for error" of about three percentage points. Confidence intervals simply express that allowance for error (although, once again, they don't allow for bias). There are many other confidence intervals, for other population quantities. Many, but not all, of them have the same "estimate plus-or-minus table value times standard error" form. The *t* table is often, but not always, the useful table in these confidence intervals.

One of the important uses of confidence intervals is determining the sample size required to yield a desired degree of statistical accuracy. Accuracy is defined by the level of confidence and the width of the interval. Recall that when we assume σ is known and specify the degree of confidence $100(1 - \alpha)\%$ and the desired confidence interval width $2E$ (or margin of error equal to E), we find the desired **sample size required for estimating μ** by solving the equation

sample size required for estimating μ

$$\frac{z_{\alpha/2}\sigma}{\sqrt{n}} = E$$

for *n*. Now we would like to find *n* by solving $t_{\alpha/2}s/\sqrt{n} = E$, but there are two difficulties. First, *s* is not known until the sample is taken, and second, we do not have the d.f. for $t_{\alpha/2}$ until *n* is specified. The first problem can be handled either by using a rough, ballpark guess for *s* or by specifying the desired width as some fraction of a standard deviation. (An error in estimating a mean to within .01 standard deviation would be dwarfed by the variation of individual values from the mean, while an error of 1.00 standard deviation would be pretty substantial.) The second problem can be solved by making a preliminary assumption that *n* is large enough that *z* can be substituted for *t*. If the resulting *n* turns out to be too small, trial and error (in the direction of increasing *n* a little bit) usually gets an answer quickly.

EXAMPLE 7.14

Suppose that a 95% confidence interval with a plus-or-minus tolerance of half a standard deviation is desired. What sample size is needed?

SOLUTION E is to be $.5s$. For the moment, assume that we can use the z table value 1.96 as an approximation to $t_{.025}$. Solving the equation

$$\frac{1.96s}{\sqrt{n}} = .5s$$

for n, we get

$$n = \frac{(1.96s)^2}{(.5s)^2} = 15.4$$

For $n = 16$ (15 d.f.) we would use $t_{.025} = 2.131$ instead of 1.96 and get an actual value of E equal to

$$\frac{2.131s}{\sqrt{16}} \approx .533(s)$$

which is a bit too large an error. We need to increase n a little bit. Try $n = 18$ (17 d.f.); $t_{.025} = 2.110$, and

$$\frac{2.110s}{\sqrt{18}} \approx .497(s)$$

so $n = 18$ will do.

Exercises

7.32 A manufacturer of cookies and crackers does a small survey of the age at sale of one of its brands. A random sample of 23 retail markets in a particular region is chosen. In each store, the number of days since manufacture of the frontmost box of crackers is determined by a date code on the box.

The data (age in days, arranged from lowest to highest) are

27 34 36 36 38 39 39 39 40 40 42 45 47 51 52 57 63 71 75
84 96 110 147

Output from the Minitab package follows. A box plot is shown in Figure 7.11.

```
One-Sample T: Days

Variable    N      Mean     StDev   SE Mean        99% CI
Days        23   56.8695   28.9722   6.0411   (39.8410, 73.8979)
```

a. Locate the 99% confidence interval for the true mean age.
b. Is there any indication of a nonnormal population?
c. Do you think that the manufacturer would find the interval narrow enough to be useful?

7.33 Suppose that the manufacturer in Exercise 7.32 wants to obtain a 90% confidence interval with a width of no more than six days. Assuming that the sample standard deviation does not change, how large a sample is needed?

FIGURE 7.11   **Box Plot for Cracker Age Data**

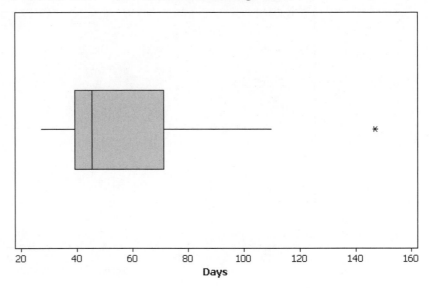

7.34   A consumer group wants to estimate the average delivered price of a certain model of refrigerator in the New York metropolitan area. Prices are determined by comparison shoppers at 14 randomly selected stores in the area. The following Minitab output was obtained:

```
Data Display

Price
 841   847   819   831   826   798   835   851   816   807   835   820   829   846

One-Sample T: Price

Variable    N     Mean     StDev    SE Mean          95% CI
Price      14   828.642   15.490    4.140    (819.698, 837.586)

Stem-and-Leaf Display: Price

Stem-and-leaf of Price   N  = 14
Leaf Unit = 1.0

   1   79   8
   2   80   7
   4   81   69
   7   82   069
   7   83   155
   4   84   167
   1   85   1
```

Locate the 95% confidence interval for the true mean.

7.35   In the previous exercise is there a clear indication that the underlying population of prices does not have a normal distribution?

7.36   A random sample of 20 taste-testers rate the quality of a proposed new product on a 0–100 scale. The ordered scores are

16 20 31 50 50 50 51 53 53 55 57 59 60 60 61 65 67 67 81 92

Minitab output follows. A box plot is shown in Figure 7.12.

FIGURE 7.12 **Box Plot for Taste-Test Data**

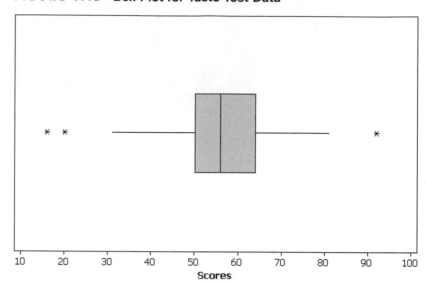

```
One-Sample T: Scores

Variable    N     Mean     StDev   SE Mean        95% CI
Scores     20   54.8999   17.7107   3.9603   (46.6110, 63.1888)
```

a. Locate the 95% confidence interval for the population mean score. Were *t* tables or *z* tables used?

b. Is there any reason to think that the use of a mean-based confidence interval is a poor idea?

7.37 A furniture mover calculates the actual weight as a proportion of estimated weight for a sample of 31 recent jobs. The sample mean is 1.13 and the sample standard deviation is .16.

a. Calculate a 95% confidence interval for the population mean using *t* tables.

b. Assume that the population standard deviation is .16. Calculate a 95% confidence interval for the population mean using *z* tables.

c. Are the intervals calculated in parts (a) and (b) of roughly similar size?

7.38 When the data underlying Exercise 7.37 are plotted, the plot shows a strong skewness to the right. Does this indicate that the nominal 95% confidence level may be in error?

7.39 A university must decide between two health plans for its faculty and staff. An important piece of information in making this decision is the average annual medical expenses of their individual employees. A random sample of 150 employees was surveyed. In this group, the average annual medical expense was $1782 and the standard deviation was $850.

a. Construct a 90% confidence interval for the true average annual medical expense of the university employees.

b. What assumption is necessary for this confidence interval to be valid? Do you know if this requirement is met? If so, state how.

c. Data from last year suggests that the average annual medical expense for university employees was $1700. Is there evidence that the true average has changed? Base your answer on the confidence interval in part (a) and explain your conclusion.

d. If it were important to estimate the average annual medical expense for university employees to within $50 of the true mean with 90% confidence, how many employees should be surveyed?

7.40 A corporation maintains a large fleet of company cars for its salespeople. To check the average number of miles driven per month per car, the mileage records for a random sample of 50 cars are examined. The mean and standard deviation in the sample are 2752 miles and 350 miles, respectively.

a. Construct a 95% confidence interval for the true average number of miles driven per month per car in the entire fleet of company cars.

b. What assumption is necessary for the confidence interval to be valid? Do you know if this requirement is met? If so, state how.

c. Records for previous years indicate that the average number of miles driven per car per month has been 2600 miles. Is there evidence that the true average has changed? Base your answer on the confidence interval in part (a) and explain your conclusion.

7.41 Mark Johnson is the administrator of Hugeley Hospital in Fort Worth, Texas. The board of trustees has approved Johnson's recent proposal for a new wing to be added to the hospital. One of the planning factors of concern is the capacity of the new wing, as measured by the number of beds. As a preliminary to projecting the number of beds, Johnson needs to estimate the average length of patient stays in days. Unfortunately, this information is not available from his computer database. He plans to estimate the average length of stay by taking a random sample of previous patient records.

a. Although Mark does not have an estimate of the standard deviation of hospital stays, he is reasonably certain that it does not exceed 7.5 days. What sample size is required if Mark wants to have a .95 probability that the resulting sample average will be within .5 days of the true average length of stay in the hospital?

b. Mark collected patient records for the sample size determined above and found an average stay of 8.7 days and a standard deviation of 5.4 days within the sample. Construct a 95% confidence interval for the true average hospital stay of patients at Hugeley Hospital.

c. After constructing the confidence interval, Mark examined a normal probability plot of the data and concluded that the distribution of lengths of hospital stays is highly skewed to the right. What does this imply about the confidence interval that he constructed?

7.42 Keely Temp Services Agency finds it difficult to retain its employees because most of them are looking for full-time positions and will leave the Keely Agency when a good opportunity comes along. For the 60 most recent Keely employees who terminated, the average time of employment was 7.2 months and the standard deviation was 10.5 months. Treat this as a random sample of Keely employees.

a. Compute a 95% confidence interval for the true average employment time of Keely Agency employees.

b. If an individual employee stayed with Keely for 18 months, would that be considered "unusually long"? Why or why not?

c. Data on how many terminated employees should be collected to estimate the average employment time to within .5 months with 95% probability?

7.43 A bottling process fills 16-ounce bottles. It is important that the average volume placed in each container is 16.0 ounces, that is, overfilling or underfilling is a problem. The quality-control inspector selects 20 bottles from the filling process and measures the volume of liquid each contains. The volumes in ounces are

16.37 16.13 16.54 16.31 15.63 16.31 16.10 16.37 16.03 16.00
15.67 16.20 15.96 16.13 16.41 16.55 16.27 15.89 16.36 16.33

a. Assume that the population standard deviation $\sigma = .3$. Use a statistical package to construct a 95% confidence interval for the true mean filling volume of the machine at its current settings. What do you conclude from your answer? What additional assumption is necessary for the confidence interval to be valid? Check this assumption using the appropriate tool or technique.

b. Repeat part (a) under the assumption that the population standard deviation is unknown.

7.44 A debt counselor works with families who have gotten themselves into financial trouble. To better understand family debt, he decides to collect data from 100 randomly selected families living in the region he serves. For each family, he measures several variables, including the total debt of the family (excluding home mortgage debt). The following Minitab output summarizes the data collected on the Debt variable.

```
Descriptive Statistics: Debt

Variable      N     Mean    Median   TrMean   StDev   SE Mean
Debt        100    21770    22077    21883    4063       406
```

a. Compute a 95% confidence interval for the average debt of all families in the region.
b. Provide an interval that contains approximately 95% of all family debt values in this region.

7.7 Assumptions for Interval Estimation

Any statistical method involves assumptions. Some assumptions are general and apply to a wide variety of methods; others are specific to a particular method. We'll have a lot to say about assumptions in future chapters. Because interval estimation of a single parameter (whether it be a mean, a proportion, or a median) is a relatively simple concept, we can deal with the issues of assumptions and assumption violation most clearly in this context.

First, we should emphasize that the methods in this chapter apply only to random samples. The allowance for error inherent in confidence intervals is an allowance only for *random* error; no allowance is made for any biases in data collection. If the data underlying a confidence interval have been collected in a lazy, convenient sample, the confidence interval is very likely to be wrong simply because of the biases in data collection. There are no known methods to compensate for the biases in badly chosen samples.

independence within samples

Within the context of legitimate random samples, there are some specific assumptions that can be problematic. One key assumption is **independence within samples.** All the methods described in this chapter assume that the observations are independent of each other. Not all random sampling methods yield independent observations. For example, suppose that a real estate assessor chooses 22 city blocks of homes to evaluate from the tax lists of a city and then assesses the market value of all homes in each block. Assuming that the assessor does, in fact, choose the blocks randomly, there is no systematic bias in favor of low-value homes or high-value homes. But there is a dependence problem. Given the well-established tendency of high-value homes to cluster together (and low-value homes to occur in bunches), if one home in the sample has higher-than-average values, so do adjacent homes. The assessment may involve, say, 300 homes; however, the method does not give 300 separate, independent measurements of home values. In fact, the data arising from the assessor's evaluations would be more appropriately evaluated by what are known as cluster-sampling methods.

time series

The most common source of problems with the assumption of independence occur in **time series** data, data collected in a well-defined chronological order. Suppose, for example, that we measure the dollar volume of back orders for a particular manufacturer on 20 consecutive Friday afternoons. It's reasonable to suppose that a high back-order volume on one Friday is likely to be followed by high back-order volumes on succeeding Fridays, and the same for low volumes. The standard error formulas that we use in confidence intervals depend very heavily on the assumption of independence of observations. When there is dependence, the standard error formulas may underestimate the actual uncertainty in an estimate. Even for modest dependencies, the degree of underestimation may be serious.

In effect, dependence means that we don't have as much information as the value of n indicates. Consider the extreme dependence that would arise in a sample of 25 observations if the first observation was genuinely random but every succeeding observation had to equal the first one. The confidence interval formula would be based on a sample of 25, but in fact we'd have a sample of only 1.

Whenever the data are taken in time order, it's a good idea to plot the observations against time. If the observations are really independent, there should be no pattern in the plot; the data should look random. Any clear pattern—cycles or trends—in this plot is reason for concern about independence. For example, look for a pattern in the Minitab plot of weekly worker absences in Figure 7.13. There is a clear up-down-up cyclic pattern in the data. We wouldn't be at all happy with an assumption of independence.

Beyond the assumption of independence, methods for means involve an assumption that the underlying population is normally distributed. *In practice, no population is exactly normal.* When we use t-distribution methods for a mean, we are assuming that the underlying population is normal, and this assumption is guaranteed to be more or less wrong.

FIGURE 7.13   **Plot of Absences by Week**

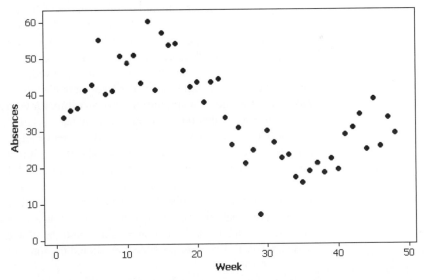

There are two types of issues to consider when populations are assumed to be nonnormal. First, what kind of nonnormality is assumed, and second, what possible effects do these specific forms of nonnormality have on the t-distribution procedures? The most important deviations from normality are skewed distributions and heavy-tailed distributions. (Heavy-tailed distributions show up in otherwise roughly symmetric data by the occurrence of outliers.)

In order to evaluate the effect of nonnormality as exhibited by skewness or heavy tails, we consider whether the t-distribution procedures are still approximately correct for these forms of nonnormality and whether there are other, more efficient procedures. Even if a confidence interval for μ based on t gives nearly correct results for, say, a heavy-tailed population distribution, there may be a more efficient procedure (which gives a smaller confidence interval width) based on a median, for example.

The question of approximate correctness of t procedures has been studied for quite a long time. The general conclusion of these studies is that the probabilities specified by the t procedures, particularly the confidence level, are fairly accurate even when the population distribution is heavy-tailed (or light-tailed). In contrast, skewness, particularly with small sample sizes, can have some effect on these probabilities, particularly in one-tailed procedures. A t distribution is symmetric, of course. When the population distribution is skewed, the actual sampling distribution of a t statistic is skewed. The skewness decreases as the sample size increases, but there is no magic sample size that completely deskews the actual sampling distribution.

The second question, that of the efficiency of t procedures, has only recently been studied seriously. There has been a near-unanimous conclusion from these studies. When the population distribution is symmetric but heavy-tailed, various **robust procedures** are more efficient than the standard t procedures. Virtually all robust procedures eliminate or give low weight to the few largest and smallest observations in the sample. The ordinary sample mean gives equal weight to all observations and is sensitive to extreme sample values. Therefore, when the population distribution is heavy-tailed, robust procedures tend to give more accurate estimates and have smaller standard errors than the ordinary sample mean.

Unfortunately, less work has been done on the effectiveness of these robust procedures when the population distribution is skewed. A 20% trimmed mean, which averages the middle 80% of the data values, is unquestionably a biased estimator of the population mean when the population is skewed. Whether this bias is compensated for by a lower standard error is an open mathematical and conceptual question. However, it would be worrisome to have an estimator with a small standard error that always overestimated the population parameter.

So what is a nonexpert manager to do? First of all, *look at the data.* One of the serious dangers of using available statistical software is that statistical analyses may be done untouched by human minds. A simple histogram of the data, or some other plotting device, reveals any gross skewness or extreme outliers. If there's no blatant nonnormality, the nominal t-distribution probabilities should be reasonably correct and the t procedure should be reasonably efficient. If the data values are obviously skewed or heavy-tailed, the t-distribution probabilities and the efficiency of the t procedure are highly suspect. Whenever possible, you should try something else in these situations.

robust procedures

EXAMPLE 7.15   A supermarket chain is considering reformulating its store brand of diet cola. Marketing managers for the store arranged for a sample of diet cola buyers to taste-test the new formulation. Each panelist was actually given three diet colas to taste. The first was identified as the current brand; this was the reference standard, assigned a rating of 50. The other two colas were the reformulation and a competitor brand. Each panelist assigned a preference rating to the other two colas, on a 0–100 scale. Higher scores indicated greater preference. The marketing manager took the data for the reformulation and analyzed it using Minitab. The "tinterval" in the following output is the *t* confidence interval for the mean. The "sinterval" is a confidence interval for the population median, obtained by a method we haven't discussed. What data problem is shown in Figure 7.14? How is this problem reflected in the confidence intervals? Is there a concern about dependence in the data?

```
One-Sample T: Ratings

Variable     N     Mean     StDev  SE Mean          95% CI
Ratings    263  53.5018    8.4179   0.5191  (52.4797, 54.5239)

Sign CI: Ratings

Sign confidence interval for median
                                     Confidence
                           Achieved   Interval
            N   Median    Confidence  Lower  Upper  Position
Ratings   263    53.00      0.9357    53.00  54.00     117
                            0.9500    53.00  54.00     NLI
                            0.9515    53.00  54.00     116
```

SOLUTION The normal plot has data on the horizontal axis and theoretical values on the vertical axis. There is a clear *S* shape in the plot, indicating that the data are outlier-prone (heavy-tailed). The sample size of 263 is certainly large enough that there is no need to worry about the correctness of the claimed 95% confidence. Outlying data tend to make mean-based methods inefficient. In this case, the confidence interval for the mean is more than twice as wide as any of the intervals for the median.

There shouldn't be a problem of dependence in the data if the study is done sensibly. The data are cross-sectional, not time series. About the only reason we can think of for dependence is if the raters could influence each other's decisions. So long as the raters were working separately, we do not believe that dependence would be a problem.

FIGURE 7.14   **Normal Probability Plot for the Diet Cola Ratings Data**

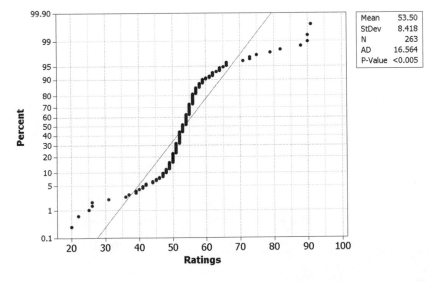

BUSINESS DECISION-MAKING IN ACTION

CHAPTER CASE

ANALYSIS

Pronto Pizza

Pronto Pizza is facing stiff competition from the new competing pizza restaurant guaranteeing pizza deliveries within 30 minutes or the pizza is free. To answer this challenge, Tony Scapelli wants to offer a 29-minute guarantee. After a careful cost analysis, Tony decided that such a guarantee would require an average delivery time of 25 minutes or less. Tony thought that this would limit the percentage of "free pizzas" under the guarantee to about 5% of all deliveries, which he had figured to be the break-even point for such a promotion.

To find out if Pronto can meet these requirements, Tony collected data for a month. He randomly selected a pizza order and clocked its preparation time, its waiting time for an available delivery person, and its actual travel time to the customer. These data are recorded in the file Pronto on the CD that came with your book.

What would you do if you were in Tony's position of having to decide if the average delivery time is greater than 25 minutes and if the percentage of free pizzas under a 29-minute guarantee will exceed 5%? What analyses of the data might you use and what other clues in the data might lead to improving Pronto Pizza's operations?

As a first step, we compute the TotalTime variable as the sum of PrepTime, WaitTime, and TravelTime. Descriptive statistics for TotalTime from Minitab follow and a histogram of the TotalTime variable is shown in Figure 7.15.

```
Descriptive Statistics: TotalTime

Variable     N    Mean  SE Mean  StDev  Minimum      Q1  Median      Q3
TotalTime  240  25.320    0.253  3.925   16.900  22.853  24.700  26.788

Variable   Maximum
TotalTime   46.000
```

FIGURE 7.15

Histogram of TotalTime

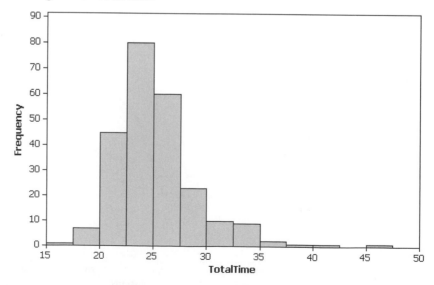

Tony Scapelli had figured out that if the true average delivery time (TotalTime) was 25 minutes or less, Pronto Pizza would break even. From the output, we note that the sample average TotalTime is 25.32 minutes, just above 25 minutes. However, as the following confidence interval output shows, the value of 25 minutes is contained in the interval, suggesting that there is insufficient evidence to conclude that the true average time is different from 25 minutes.

```
One-Sample T: TotalTime

Variable     N     Mean    StDev  SE Mean      95% CI
TotalTime  240  25.3204   3.9249   0.2534  (24.8213, 25.8194)
```

At this point, Tony might decide that Pronto Pizza should go ahead with its 29-minute guarantee. However, as seen in the following printout, the sample percentage of deliveries that did not meet the guarantee (33 out of 240 deliveries, or 13.75%) is almost 3 times higher than the 5% break-even point. A 95% confidence interval for the true proportion of free pizzas due to late deliveries, as shown in the Minitab output, does not contain the 5% target. From this it is clear that the actual proportion of late deliveries is higher than 5% and above Pronto Pizza's break-even point.

```
Test and CI for One Proportion: Late

Test of p = 0.05 vs p > 0.05

Event = 1
                                        95%
                                       Lower
Variable    X    N   Sample p          Bound   Z-Value  P-Value
Late       33  240   0.137500       0.100936      6.22    0.000
```

Could we have assumed that TotalTime is normally distributed and calculated the probability of a late delivery (that is, TotalTime above 29 minutes)? The normal probability plot of TotalTime in Figure 7.16 confirms that the TotalTime distribution is skewed, so a normal probability calculation would be incorrect in this case.

FIGURE 7.16

Normal Probability Plot of TotalTime

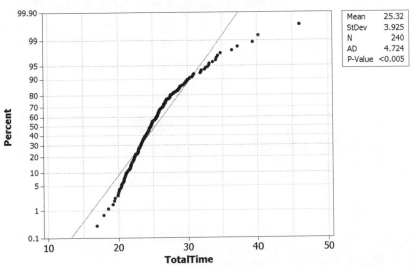

Based on what we've seen so far, Tony would be ill-advised to establish the 29-minute guarantee. But the data analysis shouldn't end here. Are there any other analyses of the data that would provide useful information to help Tony improve his pizza delivery business?

First, let's consider the effects of Day and Hour on TotalTime. Box plots of TotalTime versus Day, shown in Figure 7.17, indicate an effect due to day of the week. In particular, it appears that Saturdays, and possibly Fridays, have longer average delivery times.

FIGURE 7.17 **Box Plots of TotalTime by Day of the Week**

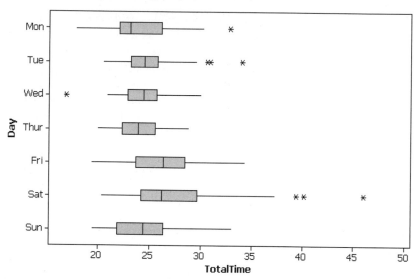

Figure 7.18 contains box plots of TotalTime by Hour that suggest the hour of the day is not a critical factor in delivery time. But note that from 5:00 to 8:00 P.M. there were slightly longer delivery times in the sample.

FIGURE 7.18 **Box Plots of TotalTime by Hour of the Day**

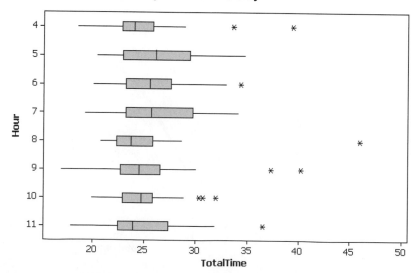

One option available to Tony is to offer the 29-minute guarantee on all nights except Friday and Saturday. But let's investigate the source of the longer delivery times on Fridays and Saturdays first. We might expect more orders to be placed on Fridays and Saturdays, which could overload the system and lead to longer preparation times. It could also lead to longer waiting times for available delivery people since there are more pizzas to be delivered. Finally, increased traffic on Friday and Saturday nights might increase the travel times for deliveries. The solution to reducing TotalTime on Fridays and Saturdays depends on which of these sources contribute to the increased times. The following table can be used to examine each of these possibilities:

```
Tabulated Statistics:  Day

  ROWS: Day

          PrepTime  WaitTime   TravelTime   TotalTime
            Mean      Mean        Mean         Mean

  Mon      14.712    2.1178      7.0563       23.886
  Tue      14.820    1.9856      8.2484       25.054
  Wed      14.898    1.4647      8.0900       24.453
  Thur     15.191    1.0178      7.7197       23.928
  Fri      14.921    3.6577      7.9615       26.541
  Sat      15.047    4.6842      8.0848       27.816
  Sun      15.068    1.9306      7.6388       24.637


  ALL      14.953    2.5259      7.8415       25.320
```

Based on this summary, it appears that PrepTime and TravelTime are not affected by Day. However, the WaitTime averages on Fridays and Saturdays are much higher than for other days of the week. Figure 7.19 shows box plots of WaitTime by Day and indicates that not only is the average waiting time higher on Fridays and Saturdays, the standard deviation is also higher on those days.

FIGURE 7.19   **Box Plots of WaitTime by Day of the Week**

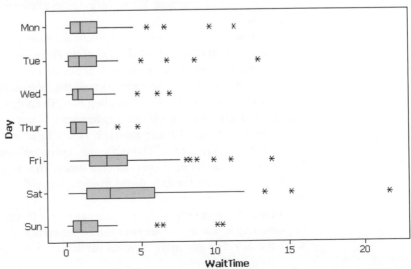

So the root problem appears to be longer WaitTimes on Fridays and Saturdays. It may be that because most teens want to date rather than work on Fridays and Saturdays, Pronto can't get enough delivery help on these nights. Pronto should consider adding more (older) drivers on weekends to decrease the WaitTime and speed up the delivery process.

Assuming that WaitTime can be shortened on Fridays and Saturdays to the same level as for other days of the week, we can turn to the data for the other five days of the week to get some idea of how much this improvement will help. The following Minitab output shows that the TotalTime average drops well below 25 minutes and that the percentage of "free pizzas" has been cut nearly in half and is close to the projected value of 5%.

```
Results for: Not(Fri or Sat)

Descriptive Statistics: TotalTime

Variable      N     Mean   SE Mean   StDev   Minimum      Q1   Median       Q3
TotalTime   160   24.391     0.238   3.005    16.900   22.365   24.170   25.783

Variable   Maximum
TotalTime   34.040

One-Sample T: TotalTime

Variable      N     Mean    StDev   SE Mean          95% CI
TotalTime   160   24.3914  3.0053    0.2376   (23.9222, 24.8606)

Test and CI for One Proportion: Late

Test of p = 0.05 vs p > 0.05

Event = 1

                                      95%
                                    Lower
Variable    X     N   Sample p     Bound   Z-Value   P-Value
Late       12   160   0.075000   0.040749      1.45     0.073
```

This analysis suggests that Tony's problems can be solved by simply adding drivers on Fridays and Saturdays, but remember that our analysis assumes there is no sampling bias in the data. Is this assumption reasonable for Tony's data? The answer is no.

There are at least two sources of potential bias in the data. First, Tony rode along with the driver on each of the sampled pizza deliveries. Riding with the boss could certainly have an effect on the driver's performance, a form of bias called *response bias*. Second, and perhaps more important, the method of sampling one pizza from each hour of operation leads to sampling bias. Even though this approach results in a random sample, it is not a simple random sample in which every pizza delivery has the same probability of being selected. Hours in which the volume of business is higher were undersampled. These are the deliveries that are likely to have longer WaitTimes and therefore longer delivery times. The net effect of this sampling bias would be to underestimate both the average TravelTime and the proportion of free pizzas.

In the case at the end of this chapter, we revisit Pronto Pizza after Tony has taken our sampling concerns into account and collected new data. You will be asked to analyze the new data and make a recommendation on the 29-minute guarantee.

SUMMARY

Here are some basic principles for estimating population or process parameters based on sample data:

1. Plot the data first, before doing arithmetic. Histograms, stem-and-leaf displays, box plots, and normal probability plots are all useful in indicating the shape of the sample data (and therefore roughly indicating the shape of the population).

2. Methods based on sample means are best suited to data that are at least roughly normally distributed. Severe skewness can make normal and t distributions poor approximations, especially for small sample sizes. Outliers make sample means an inefficient way to use the data.

3. A confidence interval provides an indication of how accurately the sample statistic estimates a population or process parameter. It allows for random sampling error, but not for systematic bias.

4. In most practical situations, a population standard deviation is not known, so t-distribution methods should be applied.

5. A confidence interval for a proportion based on a normal approximation is almost identical to a t confidence interval for a mean of a set of 1s and 0s.

6. The assumption of statistical independence is important for the correctness of confidence interval methods (and indeed of most other statistical methods). Dependence among measurements can reduce the effective sample size, thus making confidence intervals too optimistic (too narrow).

In addition, you may want to reread the summary of key ideas in the Executive Overview at the beginning of the chapter.

Supplementary Exercises

7.45   A research project for an insurance company wishes to investigate the mean value of the personal property held by urban apartment renters. A previous study suggested that the population standard deviation should be roughly $10,000. A 95% confidence interval with a width of $1,000 (a plus or minus of $500) is desired. How large a sample must be taken to obtain such a confidence interval?

7.46   It could be argued that the data of Exercise 7.45 would be quite skewed, with a few individuals having very large personal-property values. Therefore (the argument goes), the confidence interval would be completely invalid. Is the argument correct?

7.47   Many individuals over the age of 40 develop an intolerance for milk and milk-based products. A dairy has developed a line of lactose-free products that are more tolerable to such individuals. To assess the potential market for these products, the dairy commissions a market research study of individuals over age 40 in its sales area. A random sample of 250 individuals shows that 86 of them suffer from milk intolerance. Calculate a 90% confidence interval for the population proportion that suffers milk intolerance based on the sample results.

7.48 A follow-up study to the survey of Exercise 7.47 is planned. A 90% confidence interval is to be constructed. What sample size is needed to estimate the population proportion with an error of no more than .02 under the following conditions?

a. Assume that the sample proportion is approximately the same as that found in Exercise 7.47.

b. Now assume that the population proportion may be anything.

7.49 Shortly before April 15 of a particular year, a team of sociologists conducts a survey to study their theory that tax cheaters tend to allay their guilt by holding certain beliefs. A total of 500 adults are interviewed and asked under what situations they think cheating on an income tax return is justified. The responses include these:

56% agree that "other people don't report all their income."
50% agree that "the government is often careless with tax dollars."
46% agree that "cheating can be overlooked if one is generally law-abiding."

Assuming that the data are a simple random sample of the population of taxpayers (or nontaxpayers), calculate 95% confidence intervals for the population proportion that agrees with each statement.

7.50 An editorial writer, commenting on the study of Exercise 7.49, claims that the opinion of 500 individuals out of the total number of taxpayers in the United States is virtually worthless; these might be the "cheatingest" 500 people in the entire country. Criticize this editorial stand.

7.51 The caffeine content (in milligrams) of a random sample of 50 cups of black coffee dispensed by a new machine is measured. The mean and standard deviation are 100 milligrams and 7.1 milligrams, respectively. Construct a 98% confidence interval for the true (population) mean caffeine content per cup dispensed by the machine.

7.52 The machine in Exercise 7.51 is capable of dispensing 3000 cups per day. The caffeine content varies because of variation in caffeine content of the ground coffee beans and because of variation in brewing time.

a. Is the study in Exercise 7.51 questionable because such a small fraction of the machine's output is analyzed?

b. The 50 cups sampled are taken consecutively from the machine. Does this make the study questionable?

7.53 The police department of a medium-sized city recorded the response time to nonemergency crime calls, usually ones involving burglary or car theft. The times in minutes for 29 calls recorded during one week were thought of as a random sample from the ongoing process. The output from Minitab is shown here.

```
Data Display

RespTime
  24   25   18   25   15   11   11   19   36   29   13   21   12   12   26
  16   19   12   21   12   12   18   11   19   16   24   14   23   17

Descriptive Statistics: RespTime

Variable    N    Mean   SE Mean   StDev   Minimum     Q1   Median     Q3   Maximum
RespTime    29   18.31     1.17    6.29     11.00   12.00    18.00  23.50     36.00

One-Sample Z: RespTime

The assumed standard deviation = 6

Variable    N     Mean    StDev   SE Mean        90% CI
RespTime    29   18.3102  6.2912   1.1142   (16.4776, 20.1429)
```

```
One-Sample T: RespTime

Variable   N     Mean    StDev   SE Mean       90% CI
RespTime   29  18.3102   6.2912  1.1682   (16.3229, 20.2976)
```

a. Locate a 90% confidence interval for the process (long-run) mean time, assuming that the long-run process standard deviation is 6.0 minutes.

b. Locate the confidence interval done without assuming that the long-run standard deviation is known.

c. Why did the second interval come out wider than the first?

7.54   The data of Exercise 7.53 were plotted in a histogram (Figure 7.20). Does it appear that the distribution of response times is approximately normal?

FIGURE 7.20   Histogram of Response Times

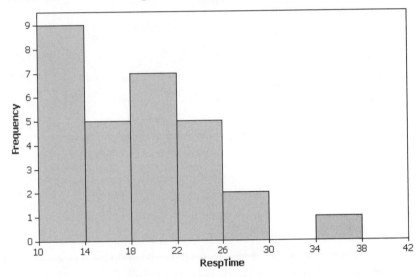

7.55   A state fish hatchery raises trout for stocking streams and lakes. The size of the fish at release time can be controlled to a fair degree by varying the rate of feeding. The target is a mean of 10 ounces; if the fish are too small, those who catch the fish aren't happy, but if the fish are too large, those who buy the feed aren't happy. A sample of 61 fish are weighed at release time. The weights, to the nearest tenth of an ounce, are as follows:

9.3	11.7	11.0	9.8	10.1	8.9	8.7	9.5	10.8	8.7	7.6
10.0	8.8	9.3	9.2	8.1	9.9	9.4	8.3	10.3	9.8	9.5
9.8	9.0	10.7	9.3	9.6	10.4	9.4	9.8	9.8	9.2	11.0
10.2	9.1	11.0	9.4	9.7	12.1	9.8	7.1	8.3	10.3	10.6
10.1	10.2	8.8	9.3	10.3	10.7	10.8	7.5	9.0	10.1	9.2
9.7	10.4	9.1	9.7	10.7	10.6					

a. Use a computer package to calculate a 95% confidence interval for the mean weight of the entire group of many, many thousands of fish. Should the standard deviation in the output be regarded as a population or a sample standard deviation?

b. Does the confidence interval indicate that the hatchery is clearly not meeting its 10-ounce goal?

7.56   Obtain a stem-and-leaf display of the data of Exercise 7.55. Does the plot indicate that the distribution of weights is roughly normal? If not, would that invalidate the confidence interval that we calculated in Exercise 7.55?

7.57 The data for Exercise 7.55 were obtained by dividing the fish randomly into batches intended for different destinations. Then some fish within each batch were taken out (as randomly as possible). One might suspect that larger fish would be netted first and put into the first few batches. A plot of fish weights against batch numbers is shown in Figure 7.21. Is there a clear indication that the weights are decreasing as batch number increases?

FIGURE 7.21 Plot of Fish Weights by Batch

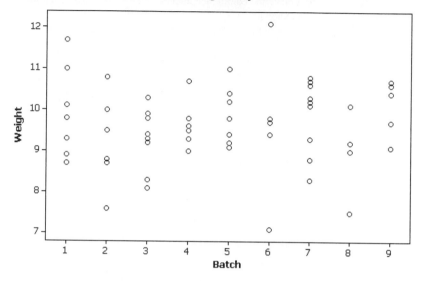

7.58 A manufacturer of mesh screening tries to limit the number of defects per thousand feet to no more than 5. The defects usually are broken wires in the mesh or "blobs" of paint. Each day, 24 sample sections of mesh screening, each 500 feet long, are inspected for defects. The following data are the numbers of defects found in the sampled sections:

3 4 3 0 6 1 0 2 1 3 4 4 3 6 4 4 3 4 5 2 1 0 5 2

a. Locate a 99% confidence interval for the mean number of defects in the entire day's production of many thousands of 500-foot sections.

b. According to the manufacturer's goal, what should the mean number of defects in 500-foot sections equal? Does the confidence interval indicate that this value is not plausible?

7.59 The data of Exercise 7.58 were collected by visual inspection of the screen for defects. Suppose that the inspection on this particular day was not as thorough as it should have been. What bias would this introduce? Would the confidence interval be too low or too high as a result?

7.60 Refer to Exercise 7.58.

a. The mean-minus-2-standard-deviations value is a negative number of defects. What does this fact suggest about the shape of the data?

b. Consider the following stem-and-leaf display. Does the picture confirm your answer in part (a)?

```
Stem-and-leaf of Defects   N  = 24
Leaf Unit = 0.10

    3    0    000
    6    1    000
    9    2    000
  (5)    3    00000
   10    4    000000
    4    5    00
    2    6    00
```

7.61 A manufacturer of floppy disks for personal computers is concerned about the reported number of bad sectors when a disk is formatted for a particular computer. A sample of 36 disks is selected from each day's production and it is formatted. The reported size of the bad sectors on each disk, in thousands of bytes, is recorded. Output from one day's data is shown here.

```
Data Display

BadSectors
     4.92   10.20   12.88    1.05   12.09    4.54    5.96    7.36   17.21
     6.97    4.69   14.79   15.53   12.43    8.00    7.97    4.85    0.94
     3.91    0.49    7.57    1.03    6.02   26.43    4.19    7.07   48.93
     5.47   26.03    0.63    5.77    1.68    3.68   31.68    3.21    5.43

Stem-and-leaf of BadSectors   N = 36
Leaf Unit = 1.0

   14    0   00011133344444
  (11)   0   55556677778
   11    1   02224
    6    1   57
    4    2
    4    2   66
    2    3   1
    1    3
    1    4
    1    4   8


One-Sample T: BadSectors

Variable     N     Mean     StDev   SE Mean         95% CI
BadSectors  36   9.48888  10.02104  1.67016   (6.09825, 12.87952)
```

a. Locate the confidence interval (for the mean) based on t-distribution methods.

b. Can this interval be interpreted to mean that 95% of the individual disks have between 6.10 and 12.88 thousand bytes of bad sectors?

7.62 The bad-sector data in Exercise 7.61 was obtained by taking samples from each of several lots. A plot of the data against the lot number is shown in Figure 7.22. Does it indicate that there is either an evident trend or an evident cycle in the data? Does any other aspect of the data show up clearly in the plot?

FIGURE 7.22 **Plot of Bad-Sector Data Versus Lot Number**

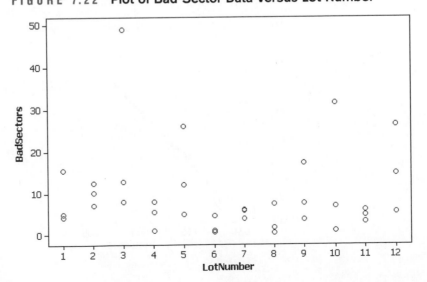

7.63 An automobile rental firm buys new cars and uses them for about six months, then resells them at auction. In effect, the firm is in the used-car futures business. Therefore, the firm wants accurate estimates of the future value of its current fleet of cars. A consultant proposes a new method of estimating future value. This method is tried on a sample of cars. The estimates are made initially, the cars are used in the business, and then the actual auction price for each car is obtained. The data are the ratio of actual to estimated values for each of 121 cars that had not been damaged during rental use. The computer output is shown here.

```
Data Display

RatioAtoE
    1.06198    1.05229    1.04322    0.98811    1.01540    1.01622    0.99736
    1.02993    1.03397    0.98592    0.98642    0.94018    1.00332    1.02558
    1.01684    1.04796    0.97700    1.01924    1.02072    0.99958    0.99779
    0.99455    0.97476    0.97945    1.00930    0.99424    0.94579    1.02618
    0.97248    0.95919    1.01083    0.97966    1.01627    0.98761    1.00587
    1.02350    1.01008    0.97001    0.97367    0.94322    0.99646    1.03997
    0.96854    0.95150    1.05237    1.07504    0.92022    0.96771    1.00414
    0.95360    1.00935    0.97817    1.01593    0.97268    1.07155    0.99601
    1.02528    0.95619    0.94588    1.00715    0.96353    0.99700    1.02567
    0.93217    1.02151    0.99164    1.05977    0.95503    0.94531    0.99293
    0.95890    0.99543    0.99503    1.07675    1.02706    1.02377    1.00244
    1.03938    1.00176    1.06579    1.01531    1.01127    1.05526    0.92391
    1.02163    0.98288    1.02443    0.97749    1.00131    0.99923    0.95374
    1.01263    0.99743    0.98494    1.01042    0.97302    1.06746    1.02829
    0.99937    1.02561    0.99079    0.99700    0.97111    0.99858    0.96359
    0.99122    0.96083    0.98466    0.99818    1.00697    0.93735    0.98747
    1.06841    1.01447    0.98473    1.02191    1.02079    0.98382    1.03723
    1.03125    0.94911
```

```
One-Sample T: RatioAtoE

Variable      N      Mean      StDev    SE Mean         95% CI
RatioAtoE   121   0.999840   0.034040   0.003095   (0.993713, 1.005967)
```

a. Locate the value of the 95% confidence interval for the mean, based on *t* methods.

b. Can the interval be interpreted to mean that the actual price is between 99.371% and 100.597% of estimate for 95% of the cars?

7.64 The data for Exercise 7.63 were plotted in Figure 7.23. Any evidence of nonnormality?

FIGURE 7.23 **Normal Probability Plot of Ratio of Actual Price to Estimate**

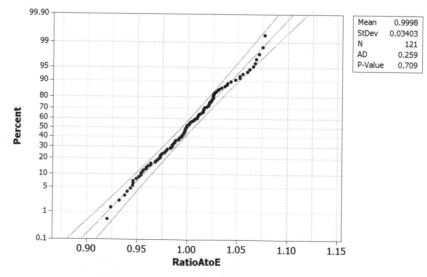

7.65 A restaurant tried to increase business on Monday nights, traditionally the slowest night of the week, by featuring a special $1.00 "Oh, Go Ahead!" dessert menu. The number of diners on each of 12 Mondays was recorded while the special menu was in effect. The data were

119   139   112   126   121   128   108   63   118   105   131   142

a. Calculate a 95% confidence interval for the long-run mean number of diners.
b. Before the special menu, the restaurant averaged 105.2 diners per Monday night. Is it reasonable to interpret the confidence interval from part (a) as indicating that the special menu did not increase the average number of diners?

7.66 A retail lumberyard routinely inspects incoming shipments of lumber from suppliers. For select grade 8-foot 2-by-4 pine shipments, the lumberyard supervisor chooses one gross (144 boards) randomly from a shipment of several tens of thousands of boards. In the sample, 18 boards are not salable as select grade.

a. Calculate a 95% confidence interval for the proportion of boards in the entire shipment that are not salable as select grade.
b. If 20% or more of the shipment is not salable as select grade lumber, the shipment is unprofitable. Does the confidence interval indicate that there is reason for concern about possible unprofitability of this shipment?

7.67 Refer to Exercise 7.66.
a. The lumberyard must decide how many boards per shipment will be inspected. What sample size is needed to obtain a 95% confidence interval for the proportion of unsalable boards with a width of .04? Assume that somewhere between 10% and 20% of a shipment is unsalable.
b. In this situation, would it be sensible to calculate a sample size based on the worst-case assumption that 50% of the shipment is unsalable?

7.68 Refer to Exercise 7.66.
a. The sample is always obtained from the pallet at the right rear of the truckload shipment. A pallet contains 4 gross (576 boards), so the lumberyard selects the 144 gross to sample by rotation—the first shipment, sample upper left; next shipment, sample upper right; and so on. Why isn't this a random sample of the boards? Wouldn't an unethical supplier take advantage of this process?
b. Do you think it would be feasible to take a simple random sample in this situation? How would you sample to make it more diffcult for an unethical supplier to cheat? Of course, there is no single correct answer here.

7.69 An electrical utility offers reduced rates to homeowners who have installed "peak hours" meters. These meters effectively shut off high-consumption electrical appliances (primarily dishwashers and clothes dryers) during the peak electrical usage hours between 3 P.M. and 9 P.M. daily. The utility wants to inspect a sample of these meters to determine the proportion that are not working, either because they were bypassed or because of equipment failure. There are 45,300 meters in use and the utility isn't about to inspect them all.
a. The utility wants a 90% confidence interval for the proportion with a width of no more than .04. How many meters must be sampled, if one makes no particular assumption about the correct proportion?
b. How many meters must be sampled if the utility assumes that the true population proportion is between .05 and .15?
c. Does the assumption in part (b) lead to a substantial reduction in the required sample size?

7.70 The electrical utility in Exercise 7.69 samples 640 meters and finds that 61 are not working, 28 because of bypass and 33 because of equipment failure. Calculate 90% confidence intervals for the population proportions of bypassed meters, equipment-failure meters, and nonworking meters.

7.71 The sample in Exercise 7.70 was obtained by randomly selecting 16 of the 1062 service sectors in the utility's area and inspecting all the meters in each selected sector. Each sector contains 30 to 50 meters. Why isn't this procedure a simple random sample?

7.72 In Chapter 2 we considered claims (in thousands of dollars) for automobile collision damage from a particular insurance company. A box plot of data is shown in Figure 7.24. Data analysis using the Minitab package is shown next. Interpret the confidence interval for the mean. How critical is it whether the interval is based on *t* tables or *z* tables?

```
One-Sample T: ClaimSize

Variable      N      Mean      StDev    SE Mean         95% CI
ClaimSize   187    5.17753   5.28387   0.38639   (4.41525, 5.93981)
```

FIGURE 7.24 Box Plot of Claim Size Data

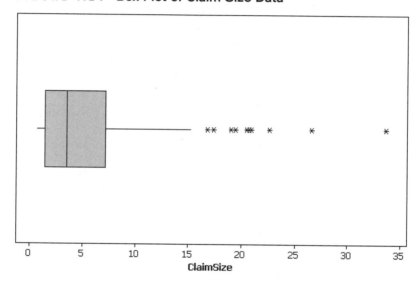

7.73 The box plot in Figure 7.24 indicates that the underlying population distribution is right-skewed. How does this fact affect the credibility of the confidence intervals in Exercise 7.72?

7.74 Many newspapers, when reporting results of political polls, say that "with 95% confidence, the results are in error by no more than ±3 percentage points." The typical sample size is about 1500. The allowance for error is intended to cover both sampling variability and the effect of small biases.
a. Assume that the poll (sample) indicates that just about 50% of likely voters favor a particular candidate. How large a ± term is required for a 95% confidence interval for the population proportion?
b. Would the ± term be much different if 40% of likely voters in the sample favored the candidate?
c. Why is the quoted ±.03 larger than the ± term you calculated in part (a)?

7.75 Consider political polls again, as in Exercise 7.74. When there are many political candidates, as in the early stages of a presidential primary, a particular candidate may be favored by only 2% of the poll participants. Given the quoted ±3 percentage points, the standard joke is that such a candidate may have a negative preference. What ± term should apply, with 95% confidence, if a candidate is favored by 30 of 1500 likely voters in a sample?

7.76 The marketing division of an automobile manufacturer wants to estimate customer satisfaction with a particular new-car dealer six months after purchase of a car. The marketing managers don't want to use mail surveys because they believe that nonresponse would lead to major biases. Sampling by telephone is feasible because customers' phone numbers are on warranty records. One key question would be, "Would you recommend this dealer to your friends and neighbors?" The marketing managers want to estimate the proportion of all customers that would answer "yes," based on a telephone sample.

a. How large a sample must be taken to obtain a 90% confidence interval for this proportion with a width of .10 (a ± term of .05)? Use the conservative, worst-case estimate.

b. Would doubling the sample size cut the width to .05?

7.77 Refer to Exercise 7.76.

a. By using the worst-case estimate, what are you assuming about customer satisfaction with the dealer? Do you think this would be a sensible assumption in practice?

b. How would the required sample size in part (a) of Exercise 7.76 change if you assumed that the "yes" proportion would be somewhere between .80 and .95?

7.78 A magazine for attorneys took a sample of 147 law firms to determine the rental cost (in dollars per square foot per year) each law firm is paying for its offices. The data were analyzed using Minitab, with the following results:

```
One-Sample T: Rentals

Variable    N     Mean    StDev   SE Mean         95% CI
Rentals    147   14.3655  2.9495   0.2433   (13.8848, 14.8463)
```

What is the meaning of the indicated 95% confidence interval?

7.79 A sample of 215 urban residents between the ages of 22 and 35 kept diaries for a month recording all expenses on entertainment. The total expenditure for each individual, expressed as a percentage of monthly take-home income, is stored in column 1 of the EX0779 file on the CD. (The number of the individual is stored in column 2.) Load the data into a computer program that is available to you.

a. Obtain the mean and standard deviation of the expenditure sample.

b. Calculate (either by computer or by hand) a 95% confidence interval for the population mean.

c. Interpret the confidence interval carefully.

7.80 Refer to Exercise 7.79.

a. Obtain a stem-and-leaf display or a box plot of the expenditure data.

b. On the basis of this plot of the data, is there reason to be concerned that the claimed 95% confidence level is incorrect?

7.81 An office equipment dealer provides service for leased copiers. All calls for service are logged with the time of request and the time of completion of service. The elapsed times (in minutes) between request and completion for the most recent 61 calls are stored in column 1 of the EX0781 file on the CD; column 2 contains the call number, in order from 1 to 61. Load the data into a computer program.

a. Obtain the mean and standard deviation of the elapsed time data.

b. Calculate a 90% confidence interval for the long-run process mean by the program or by hand.

7.82 Refer to Exercise 7.81.

a. Obtain a normal plot of the elapsed time data. (If the program won't provide that, get a stem-and-leaf display instead.) Does it appear that the data are roughly normally distributed?

b. Have the program plot the elapsed time data against the call number. (The call numbers are the time order of the requests.) Is there an indication of a pattern in this plot? If so, what is indicated about the assumption of independent observations?

7.83 An investment banking firm was considering two spreadsheet programs for possible use in its analysis. A sample of 20 typical analysis problems were carried out using both programs on the firm's standard personal computer. The time in minutes needed to load the data, program the spreadsheet calculations, carry them out, and print the results was recorded for each problem and each program. The data for spreadsheet A is stored in column 1 of the EX0783 file on the CD; the corresponding data for spreadsheet B is stored in column 2. Each row of the data corresponds to one of the 20 problems. Load the data into a computer program.
a. Have the program compute the differences of the 20 pairs of scores.
b. Obtain a 95% confidence interval for the mean of the differences.
c. Does this confidence interval clearly indicate that either spreadsheet program is better (requires less time on average)?

7.84 Refer to Exercise 7.83.
a. Obtain a box plot of the difference data. Are there any outliers?
b. Does it appear that the differences are seriously skewed?

BUSINESS CASES

Employee Benefits Plan

The benefits manager of a large university was asked to evaluate the costs of a proposed flexible benefits system. Under such a plan, individuals choose a "basket" of benefits best suited to their needs. The most important choices, in terms of cost to the university, are amount of life insurance, amount of medical insurance, and amount of retirement contribution. The benefits manager needed information about the average amounts of each of these choices to assess the university's cost per employee. Each employee would pay part of the cost (above a university-paid minimum), but the university's cost would also increase somewhat with increased benefits.

The manager did not want to survey the entire faculty and staff of the university. First, there were about 17,000 eligible employees, so such a survey would be too large a task. Second, the "flex" plan had not yet been approved, so there was a real danger that a campuswide survey could be interpreted as a promise that the plan would be available soon. The manager chose to take a sample of eligible employees from the current benefits file. Each employee was interviewed in person, partly to explain the choices and partly to stress the tentative nature of the plan. Data were obtained for 61 employees. The yearly costs, in current dollars, of each employee's choices were calculated. They are the following:

Employee	Life	Medical	Retirement	Employee	Life	Medical	Retirement
1	759	1184	915	32	585	740	646
2	424	239	538	33	472	847	637
3	157	630	639	34	535	1287	783
4	616	868	862	35	174	465	481
5	655	867	752	36	751	1143	794
6	559	945	613	37	579	751	700
7	651	1248	722	38	666	1098	770
8	519	648	750	39	596	729	571
9	358	361	670	40	251	1024	690
10	456	581	502	41	341	862	409
11	97	391	590	42	77	398	718
12	478	837	788	43	225	388	387
13	129	395	546	44	590	1262	851
14	661	535	633	45	330	609	742
15	245	472	597	46	736	1194	667
16	602	492	767	47	601	713	715
17	557	382	706	48	555	921	778
18	245	672	602	49	775	644	519
19	331	245	546	50	745	1183	868
20	545	1126	690	51	630	670	715
21	395	605	748	52	169	790	730
22	577	435	701	53	521	701	688
23	345	645	683	54	647	839	683
24	367	365	540	55	543	529	676
25	189	181	655	56	699	598	613
26	716	775	717	57	602	825	759
27	238	572	507	58	493	1120	882
28	867	776	799	59	731	481	761
29	475	1123	646	60	267	390	624
30	369	921	857	61	689	1179	629
31	245	881	724				

The benefits manager wants to know a reasonable range for the average cost to the university of each type of contribution, as well as the average total cost per employee. In addition, the manager's boss wants an idea of how large a survey must be done to estimate that total cost per employee to within plus-or-minus $50. They have asked you to work with the available data and to send them a brief memo answering their questions. Both of them studied statistics some time ago, but they've forgotten most of the concepts, so your report will have to explain any technical terms.

Pronto Pizza Revisited

After receiving your report, Tony Scapelli decided to delay the 29-minute guarantee program until after collecting additional data based on your recommendations. Tony also decided to hire two additional drivers for Friday and Saturday deliveries.

Over a period of five weeks, Tony monitored deliveries and collected data on the same variables as in his first data collection. To avoid the sampling bias of the earlier data, Tony sampled every 10th pizza delivery order. He carefully measured the time required to prepare the order and the amount of time it had to wait for a driver to become available. Instead of going on the delivery to measure the travel time, Tony phoned ahead to the waiting customer and offered a discount coupon if the customer would call back with the exact time the pizza arrived. In this way, Tony hoped to avoid the potential for response bias with the delivery person. At the end of the five-week period, Tony had collected data on 324 deliveries.

Assignment: Once again, Tony is relying on you to provide an analysis of the new data that he has collected and to recommend whether or not he should offer the 29-minute guarantee on Pronto Pizza deliveries. He is committed to going with the 29-minute delivery guarantee unless the data strongly indicate that the percentage of free pizzas given away due to late deliveries exceeds the 5% break-even point.

Thoroughly analyze the new data collected by Tony contained in the file ProntoRevisited on the CD that came with your book. Write a statistical consulting report detailing your analysis and your recommendation on the 29-minute guarantee. Be sure to discuss any other innovative things that Tony might do in order to improve his pizza delivery process and compete with his new rival.

Hypothesis Testing

Hypothesis testing, or significance testing, is a method for checking whether an apparent result from a sample could possibly be due to randomness. It serves to check on how strong the evidence is. Are sample data reflecting a real change or effect rather than a random fluke? This is a legitimate and useful task, but you shouldn't read more into the results than can be justified. The results of a test indicate how good the evidence is, not how important the result is. The key ideas include the following:

- A research hypothesis typically states that there is a real change, a real difference, or a real effect in the underlying population or process. The opposite, null hypothesis then states that there is no real change, difference, or effect.

- The basic strategy of hypothesis testing is to try to support a research hypothesis by showing that the sample results are highly unlikely, assuming the null hypothesis, and more likely, assuming the research hypothesis.

- The strategy can be implemented in equivalent ways by creating a formal rejection region, by obtaining a p-value, or by seeing whether the null-hypothesis value falls within a confidence interval.

- There are risks of both false positive (Type I) and false negative (Type II) errors. The basic strategy controls the probability α of a false positive error in setting up a rejection region, as a comparison standard for a p-value, or in setting a confidence level. The β probability of a false negative error depends on the choice of α, the sample size, and the hypothesized value of a mean or other parameter within the research hypothesis.

- Tests of a mean usually are based on the t distribution unless somehow the population or process standard deviation is known.

- Tests of a proportion can be done by using a normal (z) approximation to binomial probabilities or by using a t test with data 1s for successes and 0s for failures.

CHAPTER CASE

INTRODUCTION

Galarris Marketing Research Company

The Galarris Marketing Research Company conducts marketing research to help consumer products companies learn more about consumers' preferences for their own and competing products. A typical project for Galarris involves creating a marketing survey instrument, collecting data from a large random sample of consumers, analyzing the data using statistical techniques, and making recommendations to the corporate client based on analysis and interpretations of the survey results.

Recently, TopBrands Corporation, a major conglomerate and a former client of Galarris, announced that it was requesting bids from marketing research organizations, including Galarris, to conduct a large-scale telephone survey of consumers to learn more about their buying patterns and preferences for TopBrands products. Top-Brands' in-house marketing research group has already developed the questionnaire but was planning to outsource the actual data collection and analysis to the lowest bidder.

When conducting telephone surveys for clients, Galarris charges one of two rates: basic or premium. The basic rate is applied when the average time required by an associate to complete a survey is 15 minutes or less. The premium rate is charged if the average time to complete a survey is more than that.

Typically, Galarris waits until after a project is completed to determine which of the two rates to charge based on the actual average time required. However, in bidding for the TopBrands contract, Galarris must provide an estimate of the total cost of the survey before the data are collected.

TopBrands gave a copy of the survey instrument to all parties interested in bidding on the contract. To estimate the average time required to complete the telephone survey, six members of the Galarris telephone survey team performed a trial run for 25 randomly dialed numbers and recorded the time required for each survey.

After this trial run, the management team assigned to develop the bid proposal met with the president of Galarris to discuss their findings. Although you were not involved in these early stages of the bid analysis, the president of the company has asked you to attend the meeting because of your background and experience. The team reports that in the sample of 150, the average time to complete a survey was 15.66 minutes. Based on this, the bid proposal team has recommended the use of the premium rate in putting together the bid for the contract.

After the meeting, the president tells you that he is uneasy. If he follows the team's recommendation, Gallaris may lose the contract. On the other hand, if he goes against their recommendation, bases the bid on the lower basic rate, and wins the TopBrands contract, Galarris will lose money if the actual average survey time exceeds 15 minutes. The president asks you to take another look at the collected data to see if you agree with the bid analysis team.

The data are in the file Galarris on the CD that came with your book. The data file contains six columns, one for each of the six telephone survey associates. For each associate (column), there are 25 recorded survey times in the order collected.

At the end of this chapter, we will use the statistical tools learned in this and earlier chapters of this book to analyze the survey time data and help the president of Galarris decide whether to base the bid for the contract on the basic or premium rate for conducting the telephone surveys. ■

VERY OFTEN SAMPLE DATA will suggest that something relevant is happening in the underlying population or process. A sample of potential customers may show that a higher proportion prefer a new brand to the existing one. A sampling of telephone response time by reservation clerks may show an increase in mean customer waiting time. A sample of crankshafts produced with a new alloy composition may show a decrease in the standard deviation of metal hardness. In each case, the data are from only a limited sample and therefore they are subject to some degree of random variation.

The question is whether the apparent effect or result in the sample is an indication of something happening in the underlying population (or process) or if the apparent effect is possibly a mere fluke—a result of random variation alone. Statistical hypothesis testing is a means of assessing whether apparent results in a sample conclusively indicate that something is really happening. This chapter is devoted to the basic concepts of hypothesis testing.

Hypothesis testing involves quite a few new concepts and definitions, plus a number of formulas for carrying out computations. While working on these, try not to lose sight of the basic idea. Sample data are subject to random variation, so apparent results from the sample may be misleading. How conclusive is the evidence that sample results indicate a real, more-than-random effect in the underlying population or process?

There are almost always several ways to carry out a hypothesis test. We'll describe them all in this chapter. One can carry out a formal test using a five-step procedure described in this chapter, or one can compute a p-value to do the test, or one can use a confidence interval as a hypothesis test. These methods are equivalent; they will all lead to the same conclusion. The formal, five-step method is easiest to grasp initially, the p-value method is commonly used by computer packages, and the confidence interval approach is easy to interpret (and hard to misinterpret). They are all useful, equivalent ways to solve the problem.

8.1 A Test for a Mean, Known Standard Deviation

We'll start to explain basic hypothesis-testing concepts in the context of a statistical test for a single population mean. There are many other statistical tests discussed later in this chapter and beyond, but a test for a single mean is very simple. In addition, to keep things simple, we'll make the assumption—which is *not* usually valid in practice—that the population standard deviation is known.

As usual, we work by example. A manufacturer of frozen dinners must spend money every time it changes from one product to another on its production line, to clean out leftovers from the previously produced dinner and to set up production for the next one. Past practice has been to minimize this cost by scheduling very long production runs of a single product, but this practice led to large inventories, slow response to changing tastes, and frozen dinners being sold many weeks after they were produced. A worker team has suggested an alternate changeover procedure that it hopes will reduce the changeover cost. The current procedure requires an average of 16.2 worker-hours, with a standard deviation of 2.40 hours per changeover. The manufacturer decides to test the new procedure on the next 16 changeovers, which can be regarded as a random sample. How should the results of this test be used to see whether there is evidence that the new procedure really reduces changeover cost?

We can formulate this problem in terms of a statistical test about the population

research hypothesis

mean cost μ for all changeovers. There is a **research hypothesis,** also called an *alternative* hypothesis, that the long-run mean changeover time μ is less than 16.2 worker-hours. This is a statement about the long-run, population or process mean, *not* merely a statement about the mean in the sample of 16 changeovers. We write the research hypothesis as H_a; this notation comes from the name, alternative hypothesis. Here H_a: $\mu < 16.2$ worker-hours.

null hypothesis

The **null hypothesis,** denoted H_0, is the denial of the research hypothesis H_a. As the name suggests, the null hypothesis often has a negative quality. For the changeover-time example, the corresponding null hypothesis is H_0: $\mu \geq 16.2$ worker-hours. The primary concern is with the boundary value of the null hypothesis, so in this case we will take H_0: $\mu = 16.2$. (If we have clear evidence that the mean is less than 16.2, we have even clearer evidence that it is less than 16.3 or 17.1 or some other number larger than 16.2.) We denote the boundary value of the hypothesized mean by μ_0; here $\mu_0 = 16.2$.

one-sided
two-sided

The research hypothesis may be either **one-sided** (directional) or **two-sided.** In the example, we specify a particular direction for H_a relative to H_0. H_a: $\mu < 16.2$ is a one-sided hypothesis. In contrast, had we specified H_a: $\mu \neq 16.2$, we would have had a two-sided, nondirectional research hypothesis. The purpose of the study determines the choice of one-sided or two-sided research hypotheses. In comparing the new changeover process to the old one, we want to see if the new process is better, so we use a one-sided research hypothesis. If we were comparing two versions of a new process, we would want to test whether either version is clearly superior to the other and would use a two-sided, nondirectional research hypothesis.

basic strategy

The **basic strategy** in hypothesis testing is to attempt to support the research hypothesis by "contradicting" the null hypothesis. The null hypothesis is "contradicted" if the sample data are highly unlikely given H_0 and more likely given H_a. Thus, to support H_a: $\mu < 16.2$, we would need to find that the sample results are highly improbable assuming that H_0: $\mu = 16.2$ is true.

test statistic

The data must be summarized in a **test statistic** (T.S.). We calculate this statistic to see if it is reasonably compatible with the null hypothesis. When we are testing a population mean, the most plausible test statistic is the sample mean changeover time $\overline{Y}$ of the 16 trials. Sample means much less than μ_0 are unlikely under H_0 and relatively more likely if H_a: $\mu < 16.2$ is true. Therefore, the rejection region is "reject H_0 if $\overline{Y}$ is smaller than could reasonably occur by chance," when H_0 is true.

To repeat, the basic logic is as follows:

1. Assume that H_0: $\mu = 16.2$ is true.

2. Calculate the value of the T.S.: $\overline{y}$ = mean of the sample of 16 trials.

3. If this value is highly unlikely (which, in this case, means clearly smaller than 16.2), reject H_0 and support H_a.

It's necessary in hypothesis testing to draw the line between values of the test statistic that are relatively likely given the null hypothesis and values that are relatively unlikely. At what value of the test statistic do we start to say that the data support the research hypothesis? Knowledge of the sampling distribution of the test statistic is used to answer this question. Values of the test statistic that are sufficiently

rejection region

unlikely given the null hypothesis (as determined by the sampling distribution) form a **rejection region** (R.R.) for the statistical test.

Specification of a rejection region must recognize the possibility of error. Suppose that, for a sample of 16 trials, we set the rejection region at $\bar{Y} < 10.0$ worker-hours. Even if the null hypothesis H_0: $\mu = 16.2$ is true, there is a small probability of observing $\bar{Y} < 10.0$. If such a situation were to occur, the manufacturer would erroneously think that the new process was superior to the old one. This error—re-

Type I error

jecting a null hypothesis that is, in fact, true—is called a **Type I error.** In establishing a rejection region, an investigator must specify the maximum tolerable probability of a Type I error; this maximum probability is denoted by α.

To determine the exact rejection region, we need to know the sampling distribution of $\bar{Y}$. Recall from Chapter 6 that if the population distribution is normal with mean μ and standard deviation σ, then the sampling distribution of the sample mean is also normal with expected value equal to the population mean ($\mu_{\bar{Y}} = \mu$) and with standard error equal to $\sigma_{\bar{Y}} = \sigma/\sqrt{n}$.

Even if the population distribution is mildly nonnormal, the Central Limit Theorem helps to make this distribution a good approximation. For the changeover-time problem, $\sigma = 2.40$ (assuming that the new procedure has the same standard deviation as the current one), $n = 16$, and the crucial value for μ is the boundary null hypothesis value $\mu_0 = 16.2$. Thus, if the null hypothesis is true, the sample mean $\bar{Y}$ is normally distributed with $\mu = 16.2$ and standard error $\sigma_{\bar{Y}} = 2.40/\sqrt{16} = .60$. We can use this information about the sampling distribution of the test statistic $\bar{Y}$ to determine a rejection region.

Remember that we want to reject H_0 if the value of the test statistic is highly unlikely assuming that H_0 is true and more likely assuming that H_a is true. In this example, H_a specifies that the population mean is less than the null hypothesis mean. If so, only sample means clearly lower than 16.2 should lead us to reject H_0. In this case, we should use a one-tailed rejection region. The entire rejection region for testing H_0: $\mu = 16.2$ against H_a: $\mu < 16.2$ is in the lower tail of the distribution of $\bar{Y}$. In particular, from our knowledge of the properties of a normal distribution we know that the boundary of the rejection region is located at a distance of 1.645 standard errors ($1.645\sigma_{\bar{Y}}$) below $\mu = 16.2$ if α is taken to be .05 (see Figure 8.1).

To determine whether or not to reject the null hypothesis, we can also compute the number of standard errors $\bar{Y}$ lies below $\mu = 16.2$. This is done by computing a

z statistic

z **statistic** for the sample mean $\bar{y}$.

$$z = \frac{\bar{y} - \mu_0}{\sigma/\sqrt{n}} = \frac{\bar{y} - 16.2}{.60}$$

FIGURE 8.1 **Rejection Region for the Test Statistic $\bar{y}$ ($\alpha = .05$, one-tailed)**

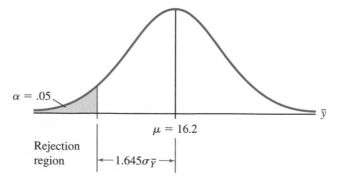

$\alpha = .05$

Rejection region

$\mu = 16.2$

$1.645\sigma_{\bar{y}}$

$\bar{y}$

rejection region
using ȳ

This suggests two ways to state the rejection region for a statistical test about μ. First, in terms of the test statistic $\bar{y}$, the rejection region is

R.R.: For $\alpha = .05$, reject H_0: $\mu = 16.2$ if $\bar{y}$ is more than $1.645\sigma_{\bar{Y}}$ below $\mu = 16.2$ (see Figure 8.1).

rejection region using z

An equivalent way to state the rejection region is in terms of the test statistic $z = (\bar{y} - \mu_0)/\sigma_{\bar{Y}}$, also called the z statistic:

R.R.: For $\alpha = .05$, reject H_0: $\mu = 16.2$ if z is less than -1.645 (see Figure 8.2).

Because the latter approach is shorter, simpler, and used by virtually all statistical computer programs, we use it throughout this text.

FIGURE 8.2

Rejection Region for the Test Statistic z ($\alpha = .05$, one-tailed)

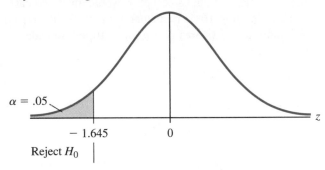

$\alpha = .05$

-1.645 0 z

Reject H_0

Finally, suppose that the sample mean changeover time for a sample of $n = 16$ trials is $\bar{y} = 14.4$ worker-hours. What can the manufacturer conclude concerning the population mean time? The z statistic has the value

$$z = \frac{14.4 - 16.2}{2.40/\sqrt{16}} = -3.00$$

which indicates that the sample mean lies 3 standard errors below the hypothesized mean $\mu = 16.2$. Because the computed value of the z statistic lies in the rejection region well beyond the critical value -1.645, the manufacturer can reject the null hypothesis and claim that the new process leads to lower changeover times. A five-step summary list displays the full process.

DEFINITION 8.1

Summary of One-tailed Test of μ, σ Known

H_0: $\mu = \mu_0$ ($\mu_0 = 16.2$ worker-hours)

H_a: $\mu < \mu_0$

T.S.: $z = \dfrac{\bar{y} - \mu_0}{\sigma_{\bar{Y}}}$, $\sigma_{\bar{Y}} = \dfrac{\sigma}{\sqrt{n}}$

R.R.: For $\alpha = .05$, reject H_0 if $z < -1.645$

Conclusion: $z = \dfrac{14.4 - 16.2}{2.40/\sqrt{16}} = -3.00$; reject H_0

Note: For H_0: $\mu = \mu_0$ and H_a: $\mu > \mu_0$, the R.R. for $\alpha = .05$ is $z > 1.645$.

We have noted that the boundary value of the null hypothesis is the important value. In the changeover-time example, suppose that we had taken some other value within H_0 as our hypothesized mean, such as $\mu = 16.3$ worker-hours. The resulting z statistic would fall even farther into the rejection region:

$$z = \frac{14.4 - 16.3}{2.40/\sqrt{16}} = -3.17$$

If the test statistic based on the boundary value leads to rejection of H_0, a test statistic based on any other value in H_0 also leads to rejection of H_0. Hereafter, we worry about the critical boundary value.

This test procedure for μ can easily be modified to handle other research hypotheses. For example, if a cereal company wants to establish beyond a reasonable doubt that the true mean weight of its nominal 16-ounce packages is in fact more than 16 ounces, it could start with the one-sided research hypothesis H_a: $\mu > 16$. Large values of $\bar{y}$ would then indicate rejection of the null hypothesis H_0: $\mu = 16$. In particular, for $\alpha = .05$, the rejection region would be values of $\bar{y}$ more than $1.645\sigma_{\bar{y}}$ *above* $\mu_0 = 16$, or equivalently, values of $z > 1.645$ (see Figure 8.3).

FIGURE 8.3   **Rejection Region for H_0: $\mu = 16$, H_a: $\mu > 16$, with $\bar{y}$ as Test Statistic**

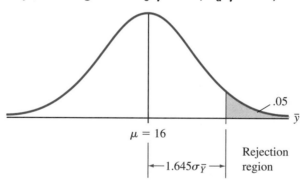

EXAMPLE 8.1   A researcher claims that the amount of time urban preschool children ages 3–5 watch television per week has a mean of 22.6 hours and a standard deviation of 6.1 hours. A market research firm believes that the claimed mean is too low. The television-watching habits of a random sample of 60 urban preschool children are measured, with a parent of each child keeping a daily log of television watching. If the mean weekly amount of time spent watching television is 25.2 hours and if the population standard deviation σ is assumed to be 6.1 hours, should the researcher's claim be rejected at an α value of .01?

SOLUTION   The marketing firm's research hypothesis is that 22.6 is too small a value for the population mean. Thus, the research hypothesis of interest is H_a: $\mu > 22.6$, and the null hypothesis is H_0: $\mu = 22.6$. We summarize the elements of the statistical test for $\alpha = .01$ as follows:

H_0: $\mu = 22.6$

H_a: $\mu > 22.6$

T.S.: $z = \dfrac{\bar{y} - \mu_0}{\sigma_{\bar{y}}} = \dfrac{25.2 - 22.6}{6.1/\sqrt{60}} = 3.30$

R.R.: For $\alpha = .01$, reject H_0 if $z > 2.33$

Conclusion: Because $z = 3.30$ is well within the rejection region, we reject H_0: $\mu = 22.6$, which was the researcher's claim. There is sufficient evidence to conclude the mean μ is greater than 22.6.

A two-tailed test for the research hypothesis H_a: $\mu \neq \mu_0$ follows directly from our discussion of one-tailed tests. For example, the manager of a cereal company who is concerned about possible overfilling or underfilling might well take as a research hypothesis that $\mu \neq 16$. Both large and small values of $\bar{y}$ would indicate rejection of H_0: $\mu = 16$. Assume $\sigma = .1$ and $n = 25$, so that $\sigma_{\bar{y}} = .1/\sqrt{25} = .02$. If we split the rejection region evenly in the tails, the rejection region for $\alpha = .05$ is as shown in Figure 8.4. Note that $z_{\alpha/2}\sigma_{\bar{y}} = 1.96(0.02) = .039$.

FIGURE 8.4

Rejection Region for H_0: $\mu = 16$, with $\bar{y}$ as Test Statistic

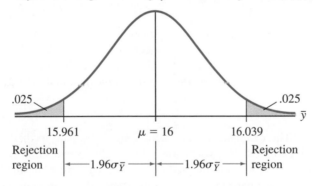

The summary chart for the z test can be written to cover all three forms for the research hypothesis. Recall that z_α is the z value that cuts off an area a in the right-hand tail of the z curve; thus $z_{.05} = 1.645$ and $z_{.025} = 1.96$. For a two-tailed test and a given α, the desired cutoff points are $\pm z_{\alpha/2}$. For $\alpha = .05$, we use $z_{.025} = 1.96$ and $-z_{.025} = -1.96$. The first four steps of the statistical test for μ (σ known) are shown here. These steps formulate the problem and establish the rejection region; the last step simply involves drawing a conclusion based on the computed value of the z test statistic. If the computed z value falls within the rejection region, we reject the null hypothesis in favor of the research hypothesis. If the z value does not fall within the rejection region, we don't have enough evidence to support our research hypothesis.

DEFINITION 8.2

Summary for z Test, with σ Known

H_0: $\mu = \mu_0$

H_a: 1. $\mu > \mu_0$
  2. $\mu < \mu_0$
  3. $\mu \neq \mu_0$

T.S.: $z = \dfrac{\bar{y} - \mu_0}{\sigma/\sqrt{n}}$

R.R.: For the probability of a Type I error α, reject H_0 if
  1. $z > z_\alpha$
  2. $z < -z_\alpha$
  3. $z > z_{\alpha/2}$ or $z < -z_{\alpha/2}$

EXAMPLE 8.2

Refer to the television-watching data of Example 8.1. Test the research hypothesis H_a: $\mu \neq 22.6$ using $\alpha = .01$.

SOLUTION The five steps of the solution are summarized here:

H_0: $\mu = 22.6$

H_a: $\mu \neq 22.6$

T.S.: $z = \dfrac{\bar{y} - \mu_0}{\sigma_{\bar{Y}}} = 3.30$

R.R.: For $\alpha = .01$, reject H_0 if $z > 2.58$ or if $z < -2.58$

Conclusion: Because the computed value of z (3.30) falls within the rejection region, we reject H_0: $\mu = 22.6$. Practically speaking, because the sample mean is greater than 22.6 and because we reject H_0: $\mu = 22.6$, we can safely conclude that $\mu > 22.6$.

The examples in this section are unrealistic in that we assumed a population standard deviation was known. In the changeover-time example, we had to assume that the new procedure had exactly the same standard deviation as the current one. Population parameters such as the standard deviation usually have unknown values. We managed the problem of unknown standard deviations in Chapter 7 by using the t distribution. Hypothesis-testing methods using the t distribution are discussed in Section 8.4. It is convenient to use z tests in our examples for a bit longer, only to avoid minor complications. Recall that for large samples, the difference between t and z tables is minor.

8.2 Type II Error, β Probability, and Power of a Test

Up to this point, we have been concerned about only one kind of error in hypothesis testing: Type I error, which rejects the null hypothesis when it is true. In the changeover-time example of the previous section, a Type I error would be a claim that the new process is better than the old one when, in fact, it is the same (or worse). But there is a second possibility for error in hypothesis testing. This error, a **Type II error,** is the failure to reject the null hypothesis when the research hypothesis is true. In the changeover-time example, a Type II error would be a claim that the new process is the same (or worse) than the old one when, in fact, it is better. This error would lead the manufacturer to overlook a chance to improve operations; often a Type II error is a missed opportunity.

Type II error

When the null hypothesis is negative, as it often is, a Type I error can be called a *false positive* error; by coming to the erroneous conclusion that a positive hypothesis H_a is true, we commit a false positive, Type I error. Similarly, a Type II error can be called a *false negative* error—an erroneous conclusion that a negative hypothesis H_0 is true.

EXAMPLE 8.3   A private-label bottler of soft drinks asks each of 100 members of a tasting panel (who are regarded as a sample from the millions of potential customers) to rate each of two possible formulations of a cola drink on a 100-point scale; higher scores are desirable. Formulation G is less expensive and will be used unless there is clear evidence that formulation R is preferred. From the data, the bottler obtains the difference (R − G) in ratings for each panelist. State the null hypothesis that the two formulations are equally good on average and an appropriate research hypothesis, based on the difference data. What are the consequences of false positive and false negative errors?

SOLUTION   If the two formulations are equally preferred, the mean of the differences will be 0. Therefore, we take H_0: $\mu = 0$. The bottler wants to see if there is evidence that R is preferred, in which case the average difference will be positive; H_a: $\mu > 0$. A false positive error would be to conclude that R is preferred even though, in fact, it is not. If this error happens, the bottler will waste money by using a more expensive formulation when the market can't detect the difference. A false negative (Type II) error would be to conclude that the two formulations are equally preferred even though, in fact, R is preferred. If a false negative error occurs, the bottler will use the less expensive G formulation even though the market would prefer R.

The two types of errors may be understood in the context of control charts. A false positive, Type I, error corresponds to saying that the process is out of control when, in fact, it's fine. In effect, this error is a false alarm. A false negative, Type II, error corresponds to saying that the process is in control when, in fact, there's a problem. In effect, this error is failure to sound an alarm when we should. By setting control limits at 3 standard errors from the nominal value, we guarantee a low "false alarm" rate at any given time but leave open the probability that we will not detect a problem quickly.

The probability that a Type II error will be committed, given that the research hypothesis is true, is denoted by β. The quantity $1 - \beta$ is called the **power** of the test; power is the probability that the test will support the research hypothesis, given that it is in fact true. The possible outcomes of a statistical test and the associated probabilities are summarized in Table 8.1.

power

TABLE 8.1 **Possible Outcomes and Probabilities for a Hypothesis Test**

	Condition	
Conclusion	H_0 **Is True**	H_a **Is True**
Accept H_0	Correct conclusion probability $1 - \alpha$	Type II error probability β
Reject H_0	Type I error probability α	Correct conclusion probability $1 - \beta$ (= power)

EXAMPLE 8.4   Refer to Example 8.3. Under certain conditions, the power of the test is .60. What does this mean?

SOLUTION   Power refers to the probability that a research hypothesis will be correctly supported. The sentence thus means that if the research hypothesis is true, there is a 60% chance that the test will discover that fact.

One problem with calculating β is that H_a usually doesn't specify one particular value for the population parameter. To calculate the risk of a Type II error (the probability of incorrectly accepting H_0), we must assume a hypothetical value for μ under H_a. The value of β depends on the assumed value of μ in H_a. Specifically, in the changeover-time example of the previous section (H_0: $\mu = 16.2$, $\alpha = .05$, with $\sigma = 2.40$ and $n = 16$), what if $\mu = 14.6$? This means that the new process, in the long run (not just in the short-run sample), would result in about a 10% decrease in the average number of worker-hours per changeover. What is the probability that the manager will retain the null hypothesis that the new process is no better than the old?

We will work through the logic of the calculation of β, then present a shortcut computation. The calculation is easier to understand if the rejection region is stated in terms of the sample mean $\bar{y}$ rather than the z statistic. The rejection region is $z < -1.645$, corresponding to a one-tailed α of .05; we therefore reject H_0: $\mu = 16.2$ for values of $\bar{y}$ at 1.645 standard errors below $\mu = 16.2$; that is, we reject H_0 if $\bar{y} < 16.2 - 1.645(2.40)/\sqrt{16} = 15.213$. If the true mean is $\mu = 14.6$, the probability β that the sample mean does *not* fall within the rejection region is

$$\beta = P(\bar{Y} \geq 15.213 \mid \mu = 14.6) = P\left(\frac{\bar{Y} - 14.6}{2.40/\sqrt{16}} \geq \frac{15.213 - 14.6}{2.40/\sqrt{16}}\right)$$

$$= P(z \geq 1.02) \approx .15.$$

β for a one-tailed test

The calculation is illustrated in Figure 8.5. Such calculations can be carried out for any test situation, and they can be summarized in a general formula. If μ_0 is the boundary value of μ under H_0 and μ_a is the selected research hypothesis mean, for a one-tailed test

$$\beta = P\left(z \geq -z_\alpha + \frac{|\mu_a - \mu_0|}{\sigma/\sqrt{n}}\right)$$

In our changeover-time example, $-z_\alpha = -z_{.05} = -1.645$, while

$$\frac{|\mu_a - \mu_0|}{\sigma/\sqrt{n}} = \frac{|14.6 - 16.2|}{2.40/\sqrt{16}} = \frac{1.6}{.60} = 2.667$$

FIGURE 8.5   **Calculation of β for One-Tailed z Test**

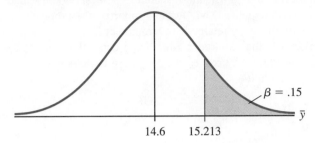

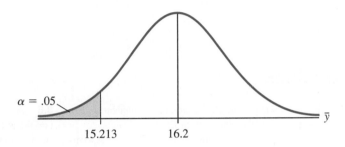

(Recall that "| |" indicates absolute value, or magnitude of a number without regard to sign.) Hence,

$$\beta = P(z \geq -1.645 + 2.667) = P(z \geq 1.022) \approx .15$$

Therefore, the manufacturer has a moderately small probability ($\beta = .15$) of failing to reject H_0 if the long-run improvement is about 10%. In other words, with this test procedure there is a fairly high power ($1 - \beta \approx .85$) for detecting a 10% improvement if it exists.

A similar calculation can be made for a two-tailed test. The only change is that z_α is replaced by $z_{\alpha/2}$. For $\alpha = .05$, replace 1.645 by 1.96.

DEFINITION 8.3

Calculation of β for a z Test

One-tailed test: $\beta = P\left(z \geq -z_\alpha + \dfrac{|\mu_a - \mu_0|}{\sigma/\sqrt{n}}\right)$

Two-tailed test: Replace $-z_\alpha$ in the one-tailed test by $-z_{\alpha/2}$

The numerical value of β depends on the value chosen for μ_a, the hypothesized value within the research hypothesis. One can calculate β for different values of μ_a and draw a curve with β on the vertical axis and μ_a on the horizontal axis. This curve will indicate how likely we are to get a false negative conclusion, depending on "how true" the research hypothesis is.

EXAMPLE 8.5

In Example 8.1 we planned to carry out a test of the research hypothesis that mean television-watching time per week was greater than 22.6 hours. The assumed standard deviation was 6.1, the sample size was 60, and α was .01. Suppose that the mean for the entire population (not merely the sample of 60) is 25.0. Find the probability that the research hypothesis will *not* be supported.

SOLUTION First, the research hypothesis is one-sided. The probability that the research hypothesis will not be supported, assuming a true mean of 25.0, is the probability that H_0 is retained, assuming that H_a is true. That is the β probability. Because $\alpha = .01$, the required z table value cuts off a right tail equal to .01; that value is $z_{.01} = 2.33$. We take $\mu_a = 25.0$, $\mu_0 = 22.6$, $\sigma = 6.1$, and $n = 60$. Using the short-cut calculation,

$$\beta = P\left(z \geq -2.326 + \frac{|25.0 - 22.6|}{6.1/\sqrt{60}}\right)$$

$$= P(z \geq .72) = .2358$$

Exercises

8.1 The manager of a health maintenance organization has set as a target that the mean waiting time of nonemergency patients will not exceed 30 minutes. In spot checks, the manager finds the waiting times for 22 patients; the patients are selected randomly on different days. Assume that the population standard deviation of waiting times is 10 minutes.
a. What is the relevant parameter to be tested?
b. Formulate null and research hypotheses.
c. State the test statistic and the rejection region corresponding to $\alpha = .05$.

8.2 Suppose that the mean waiting time for the 22 patients in Exercise 8.1 is 38.1 minutes. Can H_0 be rejected?

8.3 For the test procedure of Exercise 8.1, find the probability that H_0 will not be rejected, assuming a true mean waiting time of 34 minutes. Do the same for other values of μ, and sketch a β curve.

8.4 We stated in Exercise 8.1 that the 22 patients were selected on different days. Why would one not want to select 22 patients on one randomly chosen day?

8.5 A radio station wants to control the time allotted to unpaid public service commercials. If there are too many such commercials, the station loses revenue; if there are too few, the station loses points with the Federal Communications Commission. The target figure is an average of 1.5 commercial minutes per hour. A sample of 18 hours gives the following times (in minutes) allotted to public-service commercials:

.0   .0   .0   .0   .0   .0   .5   .5   .5   1.0   1.5   1.5
1.5   2.0   2.0   2.5   3.0   6.5   (mean = 1.278)

Assume that the population standard deviation is 1.60. State all parts of a z test of H_0: $\mu = 1.5$. Should H_a be one- or two-tailed? Use $\alpha = .05$.

8.6 Refer to Exercise 8.5. Calculate β probabilities for $\mu = 1.0, 1.2, 1.4, 1.6, 1.8$, and 2.0. Sketch a β curve.

8.7 The theory underlying the test in Exercise 8.5 assumes that $\bar{Y}$ has an approximately normal distribution. From the appearance of the data, do you believe that the approximation is a good one for this problem?

8.3 The *p*-Value for a Hypothesis Test

In the hypothesis-testing problems we've considered so far, we always come to a reject–don't reject decision, without regard to the conclusiveness of the decision. In practice, this is often an oversimplification. Evidently, the farther the value of the test statistic extends into the rejection region, the more conclusive is the rejection of the null hypothesis. How can we measure the weight of the sample evidence for rejecting a null hypothesis in favor of a research hypothesis?

p-value

The weight of evidence, or conclusiveness index, for rejecting a null hypothesis is called the **p-value** or attained-significance level.*The p-value is the probability (assuming H_0) of a test statistic value equal to or more extreme than the actually observed value.* Recall the basic strategy of hypothesis testing. We hope to support the research hypothesis and reject the null hypothesis by showing that the data are highly unlikely, assuming that H_0 is true. As the test statistic gets farther into the rejection region, the data become more unlikely, assuming H_0, the weight of the evidence for rejecting the null hypothesis gets more conclusive, and the *p*-value gets smaller. The farther within the rejection region the test statistic falls, the smaller the *p*-value is, and the stronger evidence we have to reject the null hypothesis and support the research hypothesis.

Very small *p*-values are strong, conclusive evidence for rejecting the null hypothesis. The reason is that a small *p*-value indicates that the actually observed data are very unlikely, assuming that the null hypothesis is true. Although no null hypothesis can ever be absolutely disproven, a very small *p*-value leads to its rejection and to support of the research hypothesis beyond a reasonable doubt.

The computation of *p*-values is straightforward for a *z* test. In Section 8.1, we discussed a test of H_0: $\mu = 16.2$ versus H_a: $\mu < 16.2$ with $\sigma = 2.40$ and $n = 16$. The sample mean was $\bar{y} = 14.4$, leading to a *z* statistic of

$$z = \frac{14.4 - 16.2}{2.40/\sqrt{16}} = -3.00$$

The *p*-value is the probability of at least as extreme a value as $z = -3.00$; in this case "more extreme" means less than (more negative than) -3.00. The one-tailed *p*-value is $P(z \leq -3.00) = .5 - .4987 = .0013$. See Figure 8.6.

FIGURE 8.6   **One-Tailed *p*-Value**

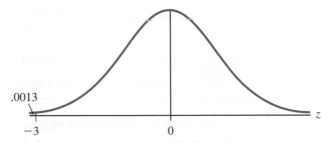

This figure looks very much like the calculation of a rejection region, but the calculation of a *p*-value goes in the opposite direction. To find a rejection region, we specify α and look up the appropriate *z* value. To find a *p*-value, we specify a *z* value—namely, the observed *z* test statistic—and look up the appropriate tail probability. Note also that α is a long-run probability (of a false positive error), whereas a *p*-value is a property of one particular sample. If we redid a hypothesis test using a new sample, α would not change, but we would get a different value for the test statistic and a different *p*-value.

For a two-tailed test, such as that for H_0: $\mu = 16.2$, H_a: $\mu \neq 16.2$ in the preceding example, the *p*-value, $P(z \leq -3.00 \text{ or } z \geq 3.00) = .0026$, is twice the one-tailed *p*-value, by symmetry. See Figure 8.7.

FIGURE 8.7   **Two-Tailed _p_-Value**

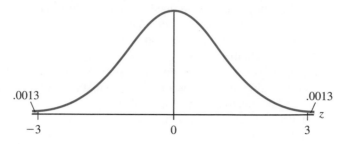

.0013   .0013

−3   0   3

In general, the computation of _p_-values based on the _z_ statistic proceeds as follows.

DEFINITION 8.4   **_p_-Value for a _z_ Test**   The _p_-value is the probability, assuming that the null hypothesis is true, of obtaining a test statistic at least as extreme as the observed value.

1.   If H_a: $\mu > \mu_0$, _p_-value = $P(z > z_{actual})$

2.   If H_a: $\mu < \mu_0$, _p_-value = $P(z < z_{actual})$

3.   If H_a: $\mu \neq \mu_0$, _p_-value = $2P(z > |z_{actual}|)$

Most computer programs automatically compute _p_-values. A very small _p_-value indicates that the null hypothesis may be rejected at any plausible α value; a large _p_-value, such as .4 or .6, indicates that the null hypothesis should not be rejected at plausible α values. A very general principle relates _p_-values to α; the principle is so general that it deserves to be called the Universal Rejection Region.

DEFINITION 8.5   **Universal Rejection Region**   If α has been specified, reject the null hypothesis if and only if the _p_-value is less than the specified α.

EXAMPLE 8.6   Many computer software programs for statistical analyses routinely compute _p_-values, usually in two-tailed form.

a.   For the following Minitab output, find the appropriate one-tailed _p_-value.

b.   Verify the _p_-value computation using _z_ tables.

c.   Can the null hypothesis be rejected at $\alpha = .05$ for a two-tailed test?

```
One-Sample Z: Data

Test of mu = 150 vs > 150
The assumed standard deviation = 20

                                         95%
                                        Lower
Variable    N     Mean    StDev  SE Mean   Bound    Z      P
Data        25  156.479  22.554    4.000  149.900  1.62  0.053

One-Sample Z: Data
```

```
Test of mu = 150 vs not = 150
The assumed standard deviation = 20

Variable    N     Mean    StDev   SE Mean      95% CI        Z      P
Data       25   156.479   22.554    4.000  (148.639, 164.319)  1.62  0.105
```

SOLUTION

a. The first part of the output indicates a "Test of mu = 150.00 vs mu > 150.00." This is a one-sided research hypothesis and should indicate a one-tailed *p*-value. The *p*-value is shown as .053.

b. The *z* statistic is shown as 1.62. From the normal tables, the area to the right of 1.62 is $.5000 - .4474 = .0526$.

c. Because the *p*-value is not less than .05, we cannot reject H_0 at $\alpha = .05$, although we can come close. Note also that the test statistic, $z = 1.62$, is not greater than the *z* table value for $\alpha = .05$, namely 1.645, although it also is close. Thus, we barely retain the null hypothesis; there is not quite enough evidence to support the research hypothesis.

statistically significant

The *p*-value is sometimes called the attained significance level of a statistical test. The results of a statistical test are often summarized by stating that the result is **statistically significant** at the specified *p*-value. In the changeover-time example, $z = -3.00$ is statistically significant at $p = .0013$. The smaller the *p*-value, the more conclusive the rejection of the null hypothesis.

The phrase *statistically significant* is unfortunate. The word *significant* suggests "important," "interesting," and "large." Statistical significance does not necessarily imply importance, relevance, or practical significance. Statistical significance implies only that a null hypothesis can be rejected with a specified low risk of error. A better phrase would be *statistically detectable*. To say that a difference is statistically significant or statistically detectable is to say that the observed result cannot reasonably be attributed to random variation alone.

The *p*-value is an indication of the amount of evidence supporting a research hypothesis. It is not a measure of how large the apparent deviation is from the null hypothesis. A test statistic and therefore a *p*-value are affected by two factors: the amount of deviation from the null hypothesis value, and the sample size. The *z* statistic can be rewritten as

$$z = \frac{\bar{y} - \mu_0}{\sigma} \sqrt{n}$$

The first part of this expression is the deviation of the sample mean from the H_0 value, expressed as a fraction of the standard deviation. The second part is a function only of the sample size. A large deviation of $\bar{y}$ from the null hypothesis, together with a modest *n*, will produce a fairly large *z* statistic and therefore a fairly small *p*-value. But so will a modest deviation and a large *n*. In either case, there will be fairly conclusive evidence to support a research hypothesis. That is the only role for a *p*-value.

One should recognize that rarely is any null hypothesis exactly true. For this reason, with a large enough sample size, almost any null hypothesis can be rejected. What does this mean? If the null hypothesis is rejected, it means that a difference has been established fairly conclusively, but no judgment has been made as to the importance or practical significance of the apparent difference.

Conversely, a sample result with associated p-value $> .05$ (and considered by some to indicate "not statistically significant") could, but may not, have been the result of random fluctuation; that is, even though the p-value is greater than .05, there still may be an underlying effect. The problem is that we have not established it beyond a reasonable doubt. A large p-value does not necessarily mean that nothing is happening; it means that we don't have enough evidence to say that the apparent change is more than random. All in all, you should be careful not to read too much into statistical significance. The p-value gives the weight of the sample evidence for rejection of the null hypothesis. A manager must still judge the practical significance of observed results that are declared statistically significant.

Exercises

8.8   A sales manager believes that a firm's sales representatives should spend about 40% of their working days traveling. If they are on the road for much less, new orders decline and the service and news-gathering functions of the representatives are not adequately met. If they travel much more than 40% of the time, expense accounts eat up any incremental profit. A study of the previous five months (110 working days) shows the following data (number of traveling days by each representative):

32   36   41   45   48   48   51   54   57   64   ($\overline{y} = 47.6$, $s = 9.65$, $n = 10$)

Minitab computer output for these data is shown next (based on an assumed population standard deviation of 10.0).

```
One-Sample Z: TravelDays

Test of mu = 44 vs not = 44
The assumed standard deviation = 10

Variable     N   Mean   StDev   SE Mean        95% CI          Z      P
TravelDays   10  47.6   9.6517  3.1623  (41.4019, 53.7979)   1.14  0.255
```

a. Identify the value of the z statistic.
b. Identify the p-value.
c. Is a one-tailed or a two-tailed p-value more appropriate for this problem?

8.9   The sales manager of Exercise 8.8 concludes that the discrepancy between the observed average of 47.6 and the desired average of 44.0 is not statistically significant and therefore the study proves that the travel-days situation is under control.
a. Do you agree that the result is not statistically significant (at the usual α levels)?
b. Do you agree that the study proves that the travel-days situation is under control?

8.10   The battery pack of a hand calculator is supposed to perform 20,000 calculations before needing recharging. The quality-control manager for the manufacturer is concerned that the pack may not be working for as long as the specifications state. A test of 114 battery packs gives an average of 19,695 calculations and a standard deviation of 1,103.
a. Formulate null and research hypotheses.
b. Calculate the appropriate test statistic and p-value.

8.11   Is the result in Exercise 8.10 statistically significant at the usual α levels? Would you call the result practically significant?

8.12 A major insurance company is in the process of deciding whether or not to raise its base rate on automobile insurance policies. A premium analyst has determined that the base rate must be increased if the average claim amount over the past year was greater than $1400. A random sample of 60 claims from last year will be collected to help make the decision.

a. Set up an appropriate one-sided hypothesis test to determine if there is sufficient evidence in the sample to conclude that the base rate should be increased. Use a 5% level of significance and a nonstandardized test statistic. Assume that the population standard deviation in claim amounts is $800. Stop after stating the rejection rule.
b. In business terms, what is a Type II error in this situation?
c. What is the probability of a Type II error if the true average claim amount is $1700?
d. In a random sample of 60 recent claims, the average claim amount was $1542. What is the appropriate statistical decision based on your test from part (a)?
e. Compute the *p*-value for the data.

8.4 Hypothesis Testing with the *t* Distribution

Now we get rid of the usually false assumption that a population standard deviation is known in hypothesis testing. The changes we make will be technical; the basic ideas of hypothesis testing aren't affected. We still hope to support a research hypothesis by rejecting the null hypothesis. H_0 still is rejected if the data are highly unlikely given that hypothesis and relatively more likely given the research hypothesis. The *p*-value still measures the degree of evidence supporting the research hypothesis.

The modifications of normal (*z*) procedures to get *t*-distribution confidence intervals also apply to hypothesis tests. Once again, we replace σ by *s* and use *t* tables instead of *z* tables. In this section we summarize the procedure and take care of some other small differences in mechanics.

The basic procedure for any hypothesis-testing method requires formulating null and research hypotheses (H_0 and H_a), choosing a test statistic (T.S.), defining a rejection region (R.R.), calculating the T.S. value, and finally stating a conclusion. Here we are concerned with testing hypotheses about a population mean; we are still making the formal mathematical assumption that the sampling distribution of $\bar{y}$ is exactly normal.

DEFINITION 8.6

t Test of Hypotheses about μ

$H_0: \mu = \mu_0$

$H_a:$ 1. $\mu > \mu_0$
    2. $\mu < \mu_0$
    3. $\mu \neq \mu_0$

T.S.: $t = \dfrac{\bar{y} - \mu_0}{s/\sqrt{n}}$

R.R.: For a given probability α of a Type I error, reject H_0 if
    1. $t > t_\alpha$
    2. $t < -t_\alpha$
    3. $|t| \geq t_{\alpha/2}$
    where t_α cuts off a right-tail area of α in a *t* distribution with $n - 1$ d.f.

EXAMPLE 8.7

An airline institutes a "snake system" waiting line at its counters to try to reduce the average waiting time. The mean waiting time under specific conditions with the previous system was 6.1 minutes. A sample of 14 waiting times is taken; the times are measured at widely separated intervals to eliminate the possibility of dependent observations. The resulting sample mean is 5.043 and the standard deviation is 2.266. Test the null hypothesis of no change against an appropriate research hypothesis, using $\alpha = .10$. Assume that the population of waiting times is approximately normal.

SOLUTION The population parameter of interest is μ, the long-run mean waiting time under normal conditions using the snake system. The research hypothesis is that the mean is lower than the previous mean, 6.1, so H_a: $\mu < 6.1$. We may take the null hypothesis to be H_0: $\mu = 6.1$ (no change). As usual, we need worry only about the boundary value of the null hypothesis.

H_0: $\mu = 6.1$

H_a: $\mu < 6.1$

T.S.: $t = \dfrac{5.043 - 6.1}{2.266/\sqrt{14}} = -1.75$

R.R.: For $\alpha = .10$ and d.f. $= 13$, reject H_0 for $t < -1.350$

Because the observed value of t, -1.75, is less than -1.350, we reject H_0 and conclude that the apparent reduction in mean waiting time (from 6.1 to about 5 minutes) is not merely a random, statistical fluke.

Earlier in this chapter we introduced the p-value as an index of the degree of support for a research hypothesis from a given data set. There we were able to use z tables to compute p-values. Now we must use t tables, which are much less extensive; for given degrees of freedom, a t table gives only a few values. Most computer packages will compute exact **p-values for a t test,** so the problem is not too serious.

p-value for a t test

EXAMPLE 8.8

The data for Example 8.6 were used to test H_a: $\mu > 150$ under the assumption that σ was somehow known to be 20.0. The following Minitab output carries out a t test for this research hypothesis, without assuming that σ is known. Locate the p-value. What does it indicate?

```
One-Sample T: Data

Test of mu = 150 vs > 150
```

Variable	N	Mean	StDev	SE Mean	95% Lower Bound	T	P
Data	25	156.479	22.554	4.511	148.762	1.44	0.082

SOLUTION The output indicates that a one-sided research hypothesis is being used. The p-value is shown as .082. That indicates that the evidence in support of the research hypothesis is modest, at best. The difference between the sample mean and the null hypothesis value could possibly have arisen by chance.

With tables we can get only approximate *p*-values. The key to the approximation is the fact that the *p*-value is the smallest α value that allows rejection of the null hypothesis. Remember the Universal Rejection Region: Reject the null hypothesis if and only if the *p*-value is less than α. If the null hypothesis can be rejected at a particular α level, the *p*-value must be less than that α. Therefore, we can often bracket the *p*-value between two numbers. All that is needed is to locate the actually observed *t* statistic between two *t* table values. The bounds on the *p*-value can be read directly.

EXAMPLE 8.9

Find the bounds on the *p*-value in Example 8.7.

SOLUTION In Example 8.7 we found that we could reject H_0 at $\alpha = .10$ because $t = -1.75$ was below $-t_{.10, 13 \text{ d.f.}} = -1.350$. Therefore, $p < .10$. When we try $\alpha = .05$, we find that we cannot quite reject H_0; the tabulated *t* value is $-t_{.05, 13 \text{ d.f.}} = -1.771$. Therefore, $p > .05$. We can summarize the approximate *p*-value as $.05 < p < .10$.

EXAMPLE 8.10

An insurance adjuster in a small city uses two different garages to handle repairs to foreign cars damaged in collisions. To test whether the garages are competitive in cost, the adjuster obtains estimates from both garages for repair costs on each of 15 such cars. The data are shown in the following table. Test the null hypothesis that the mean difference is zero against an appropriate research hypothesis. What can be said about a *p*-value?

Repair Estimates (in hundreds of dollars)

Car	1	2	3	4	5	6	7
Garage 1	7.6	10.2	9.5	1.3	3.0	6.3	5.3
Garage 2	7.3	9.1	8.4	1.5	2.7	5.8	4.9
Difference, *d*	.3	1.1	1.1	−.2	.3	.5	.4

Repair Estimates (in hundreds of dollars)

Car	8	9	10	11	12	13	14	15
Garage 1	6.2	2.2	4.8	11.3	12.1	6.9	7.6	8.4
Garage 2	5.3	2.0	4.2	11.0	11.0	6.1	6.7	7.5
Difference, *d*	.9	.2	.6	.3	1.1	.8	.9	.9

SOLUTION The null hypothesis is that the true mean difference $\mu_d = 0$. As no particular direction has been specified for the research hypothesis, take $H_a: \mu_d \neq 0$. We base the test on the differences (which are designated by *d* rather than *y* here). The test statistic is

$$t = \frac{\bar{d} - 0}{s_d / \sqrt{n}}$$

and is based on $n - 1 = 14$ d.f. Routine calculations give $\bar{d} = .613$ and $s_d = .394$, so

$$t = \frac{.613 - 0}{.394/\sqrt{15}} = 6.03$$

The largest tabled t value for 14 d.f. is 2.977, corresponding to a one-tailed area of .005. Thus, even for a (two-tailed) α of .01, H_0 could easily be rejected. The p-value must be less than .01; in fact, we suspect that the p-value is much smaller than .01. Formally, we conclude that the two garages have different average estimates. Practically, it is clear that garage 1 has higher average estimates than garage 2.

Evaluation of β and power is a bit more difficult for t tests than for z tests. The method for calculating β stated in Section 8.2 is strictly valid only for z tests, but it can be used as an approximation for t tests. Because a t statistic is more variable than a z statistic, the formula tends to underestimate β and therefore to overestimate power. The easiest way to use the method is to specify a value for

$$\frac{\mu_a - \mu_0}{\sigma}$$

and a value for α. For example, suppose that a t test is run using $n = 25$ and $\alpha = .05$ (two-tailed) and that we hypothesize that the true population mean is .8 standard deviation above the null hypothesis mean:

$$\frac{\mu_a - \mu_0}{\sigma} = .8$$

Then, approximately,

$$\beta = P\left(z > -z_{\alpha/2} + \frac{|\mu_a - \mu_0|}{\sigma/\sqrt{n}}\right)$$

$$= P\left(z > -1.96 + \frac{.8}{1/\sqrt{25}}\right)$$

$$= P(z > 2.04) = .0207$$

It follows that power is approximately $1 - .0207 = .9793$ under these conditions. As we indicated, the calculation underestimates β and overestimates power. Thus, the power is not quite as good as the calculation indicates.

EXAMPLE 8.11 In a computer simulation, 1000 samples of size 30 are drawn from a normal population having mean 55 and standard deviation 10. The null hypothesis that the population mean is 50 is tested, based on each sample. For a test of H_a: $\mu > 50$, using $\alpha = .10$, the null hypothesis is rejected 919 times out of the 1000 samples. What probability is being approximated by the fraction 919/1000? How close is this approximation to the theoretical probability calculated by formula?

SOLUTION   In this simulation, the null hypothesis is false; μ is 55, not 50. The fraction 919/1000 approximates the probability that the test will reject the null hypothesis when it is false; by definition, that probability is $1 - \beta$, the power of the test. We can calculate the theoretical β by formula. For a one-tailed test with $\alpha = .10$, the required table value is $z_{.10} = 1.28$: $\mu_0 = 50$, $\mu_a = 55$, $\sigma = 10$, and $n = 30$. Therefore,

$$\beta = P\left(z > -1.28 + \frac{|55 - 50|}{10/\sqrt{30}}\right) = P(z > 1.46)$$

$$= .0721$$

So power $= 1 - .0721 = .9279$. The simulation value, .919, is quite close to the calculated power.

Exercises

8.13   A dealer in recycled paper places empty trailers at various sites; these are gradually filled by individuals who bring in old newspapers and the like. The trailers are picked up (and replaced by empties) on several schedules. One such schedule involves pickup every second week. This schedule is desirable if the average amount of recycled paper is more than 1600 cubic feet per two-week period. The dealer's records for 18 two-week periods show the following volumes (in cubic feet) at a particular site:

1660 1820 1590 1440 1730 1680 1750 1720 1900
1570 1700 1900 1800 1770 2010 1580 1620 1690
($\bar{y} = 1718.3$, $s = 137.8$)

a. Assume that these figures represent the results of a random sample. Do they support the research hypothesis that $\mu > 1600$, using $\alpha = .10$? Write out all parts of the hypothesis-testing procedure.
b. Place an upper bound on the p-value that is, state "p-value less than number." Would you say that $\mu > 1600$ is strongly supported?

8.14   A federal regulatory agency is investigating an advertised claim that a certain device can increase the gasoline mileage of cars. Seven such devices are purchased and installed in seven cars belonging to the agency. Gasoline mileage for each of the cars under standard conditions is recorded both before and after installation.

	Car						
	1	**2**	**3**	**4**	**5**	**6**	**7**
Mpg before	19.1	19.9	17.6	20.2	23.5	26.8	21.7
Mpg after	20.0	23.7	18.7	22.3	23.8	19.2	24.6
Change	.9	3.8	1.1	2.1	.3	−7.6	2.9

The Minitab package gave the following results:

```
Test of mu = 0 vs mu not = 0

Variable        N      Mean      StDev    SE Mean
Change          7      0.50      3.77        1.43
```

```
Variable                 90.0% CI          T      P
Change                (-2.27,  3.27)      0.35   0.738
```

a. Formulate appropriate null and research hypotheses.
b. Is the advertised claim supported at $\alpha = .05$? What is the two-tailed p-value? How could we find a one-tailed p-value?

8.15 Use the output of Exercise 8.14 to find a 90% confidence interval for the mean change. On the basis of this interval, can one reject the hypothesis of no mean change?

8.16 Would you say that the agency of Exercises 8.14 and 8.15 has conclusively established that the device has no effect on the average mileage of cars? What does the width of the interval in Exercise 8.15 have to do with your answer?

8.17 A small manufacturer has a choice between shipping via the postal service and shipping via a private shipper. As a test, 10 destinations are chosen and packages are shipped to each by both routes. The delivery times in days are shown in the table and followed by Minitab output.

	Destination									
	1	**2**	**3**	**4**	**5**	**6**	**7**	**8**	**9**	**10**
Postal service	3	4	5	4	8	9	7	10	9	9
Private shipper	2	2	3	5	4	6	9	6	7	6
Difference	1	2	2	−1	4	3	−2	4	2	3

Minitab output:

```
Test of mu = 0 vs mu > 0

Variable         N       Mean      StDev    SE Mean
Difference      10      1.800      1.989     0.629

Variable      99.0% Lower Bound       T       P
Difference              0.024       2.86   0.009
```

a. Locate the mean and standard deviation of the differences.
b. Test the null hypothesis of no mean difference in delivery times against the research hypothesis that the private shipper has a shorter average delivery time. Use $\alpha = .01$.

8.18 MCI is offering a new savings plan on long-distance phone calls that it claims will result in an average savings of 20% for its customers who go on the plan. To check out MCI's claim, a consumer watchdog organization contacted 35 MCI customers who enrolled in the new plan and computed their individual savings in long-distance calls. The Minitab output is

```
Test of mu = 20 vs mu not = 20

Variable         N       Mean      StDev    SE Mean
Savings         35     18.630      5.833     0.986

Variable           95.0% CI           T       P
Savings        (16.626,  20.634)    -1.39   0.174
```

a. One person who saw these results said, "The average savings of 18.63% are clearly less than the 20% claimed by MCI. MCI's claim is obviously incorrect." How would you respond to this statement?
b. Using a 5% level of significance, should the null hypothesis be rejected or not? Interpret this result in terms of the problem.

8.5 Assumptions for *t* Tests

Like any other statistical procedures, hypothesis tests rely on assumptions. The assumptions underlying *t* tests are exactly the same as those underlying *t* confidence intervals. In fact, in the next section we will show that hypothesis tests and confidence intervals are equivalent.

Hypothesis tests allow for random variation, but not for bias. A bias in selecting the sample may cause either kind of error, false positive or false negative. It is always worth considering how the data were obtained to see if there are serious, evident biases.

In addition, the *t* test of a mean, and most other statistical tests, assume that the measurements in the sample are statistically independent. The most likely source of dependence arises in time series data, where values of a variable are measured at successive times. If there are carryover effects from one time to the next, the values will be dependent. Just as in the confidence-interval case, statistical dependence causes a change in the "effective *n*." Positive correlation of successive values means that the effective sample size is less than it appears. This fact makes the apparent result of the test too strong, too conclusive. The stated *p*-value will be less than it should be. When the data arise from a time series, it's always useful to plot the data in time order, looking for cycles and trends.

We discussed the effect of population nonnormality on *t* confidence intervals in Section 7.7. The same conclusions apply to *t* tests. If the underlying population is skewed and the sample size is fairly small, the claimed α and *p*-value probabilities may be in error. This is particularly a problem for one-tailed probabilities. If there is skewness, typically one tail is too large but the other is too small; when the probabilities are combined in a two-tailed test, the effect of skewness tends to cancel out. The nominal α value and *p*-value are reasonably accurate if the population is symmetric but heavy- or light-tailed relative to the normal distribution. In this case, a *t* test may be inefficient. Inefficiency, in hypothesis-testing terms, means that some other test—such as a median test—has better power at the same α level. We illustrate these effects of nonnormality with computer simulation studies.

EXAMPLE 8.12   A simulation study takes 1000 samples of size 30 from a Laplace population, a symmetric, moderately outlier-prone population. The population mean is 50 and the population standard deviation is 10. For $\alpha = .025$, the null hypothesis H_0: $\mu = 50$ is rejected 28 times in favor of H_a: $\mu > 50$; similarly, for $\alpha = .025$, the null hypothesis H_0: $\mu = 50$ is rejected 24 times in favor of H_a: $\mu < 50$.

Which hypothesis is true in the simulation? Does the outlier-proneness of the Laplace population have a serious effect?

SOLUTION   Here H_0 is $\mu = 50$, and indeed the population mean is 50. The null hypothesis is true, so rejecting it constitutes a false positive (Type I) error. Therefore, fractions such as 28/1000 are approximating α, the probability of Type I error. The fractions are approximations because they are based on 1000 samples, not an infinite number. The fractions 28/1000 and 24/1000 are very close to the nominal α value, .025.

EXAMPLE 8.13   Another simulation study involves samples of size 30 from a Laplace population. In this study, the mean is 55, so H_0: $\mu = 50$ is false. A t test and also a sign test (a test for the median, which is also 55 by the symmetry of the Laplace population) were performed for each sample. Using $\alpha = .05$, H_a: $\mu > 50$ was supported in 831 of the samples and H_a: median > 50 was supported (by the sign test) in 905 of the samples. Which test appears to have better power?

SOLUTION   Recall that power is the probability that the null hypothesis will be rejected, assuming that it is false. The sign test rejects the (false) null hypothesis more frequently than does the t test. Therefore, the sign test appears generally more powerful for this moderately outlier-prone population.

8.6   Testing a Proportion: Normal Approximation

Thus far in this chapter, we have concentrated on testing hypotheses about means. We can equally well test hypotheses about proportions. Recall that defining successes to be 1s and failures to be 0s allows us to regard a proportion as a mean. In this section, we will sketch how such tests are done.

For example, suppose that we wish to compare two versions of a product. We ask a panel of 100 customers (which we hope is an unbiased random sample of potential customers) to choose between a new version of the product and the existing version. We will adopt the new product only if there is clear evidence that more than half the customers prefer it. Thus we take the null hypothesis as H_0: $\pi = .50$, and the research hypothesis is H_a: $\pi > .50$. Hence, we want a one-tailed test. If n is large and π is not too close to 0 or 1, the z statistic for the standardized binomial random variable Y,

$$z = \frac{Y - n\pi}{\sqrt{n\pi(1 - \pi)}}$$

is approximately standard (tabled) normal. This z can be used as the test statistic instead of Y, the number of successes; the relevant value for π is the (boundary) null hypothesis value, $\pi_0 = .50$. As with a statistical test for μ, the one-tailed rejection region for $\alpha = .05$ is $z > 1.645$. In fact, 68 of the 100 panelists preferred the new version. The observed y value of 68 corresponds to a z score of 3.6:

$$z = \frac{y - n\pi_0}{\sqrt{n\pi_0(1 - \pi_0)}} = \frac{68 - 50}{\sqrt{100(.5)(.5)}} = 3.6$$

Hence, we reject H_0: $\pi = .05$ for $\alpha = .05$ (and in fact for $\alpha = .01$). The approximate procedure for testing a population proportion using a z statistic is summarized in Definition 8.7.

DEFINITION 8.7

Test of a Population Proportion, Normal Approximation

H_0: $\pi = \pi_0$

H_a: 1. $\pi > \pi_0$

2. $\pi < \pi_0$

3. $\pi \neq \pi_0$

T.S.: $z = \dfrac{y - n\pi_0}{\sqrt{n\pi_0(1 - \pi_0)}}$

R.R.: For the probability of a Type I error α, reject H_0 if

1. $z > z_\alpha$

2. $z < -z_\alpha$

3. $z > z_{\alpha/2}$ or $z < -z_{\alpha/2}$

Note: π_0 is the (boundary) null-hypothesis value of the population proportion π.

There's another way to write the test statistic z. If $\hat{\pi}$ is the sample proportion (so $\hat{\pi} = Y/n$), then z can be written

$$z = \frac{\hat{\pi} - \pi_0}{\sqrt{\pi_0(1 - \pi_0)/n}}$$

For the product-comparison example, $\hat{\pi} = 68/100 = .68$ and again $z = 3.6$. The two forms of z are algebraically equal, so they always give the same answer.

Most computer packages do not include this test. However, by coding successes as 1s and failures as 0s, we can approximate this test. This trick works exactly if the package includes a z test. Specify σ as $\sqrt{(\pi_0)(1 - \pi_0)}$. If the package includes a one-sample t test, the result will be slightly different, but often close enough. For example, in the product-comparison example, we input as data 68 1s and 32 0s in a column labeled "Yes_No." We obtained the following Minitab results; note that we specified σ as $\sqrt{(\pi_0)(1 - \pi_0)} = \sqrt{(.5)(1 - .5)} = .5$,

```
One-Sample Z: Yes_No

Test of mu = 0.5 vs not = 0.5
The assumed standard deviation = 0.5

Variable    N    Mean    StDev  SE Mean      95% CI          Z      P
Yes_No    100  0.6800  0.4688   0.0500  (0.5820, 0.7780)  3.60  0.000

One-Sample T: Yes_No

Test of mu = 0.5 vs not = 0.5

Variable    N    Mean    StDev  SE Mean      95% CI          T      P
Yes_No    100  0.6800  0.4688   0.0469  (0.5870, 0.7730)  3.84  0.000
```

The results of the ZTest procedure are exactly what we obtained by hand. The results of the TTest procedure are not quite the same, basically because that procedure used a sample standard deviation instead of $\sqrt{(\pi_0)(1 - \pi_0)}$. The conclusion is the same; the research hypothesis of a difference in preferences is strongly supported, with a very low p-value. Though the t test based on 1s and 0s is not exactly the same as the z test, usually the results are so similar that we needn't worry too much about the difference.

**sample-size
requirement**

We said that the z test for π is approximate and works best if n is large and π_0 is not too near 0 or 1. A natural next question is, When can we use it? There are several rules to answer the question; none of them should be considered sacred. Our sense of the many studies that have been done is this: If either $n\pi_0$ or $n(1 - \pi_0)$ is less than about 2, treat the results of a z test very skeptically. If $n\pi_0$ and $n(1 - \pi_0)$ are at least 5, the z test should be reasonably accurate. For the same sample size, tests based on extreme values of π_0 (for example, .001) are less accurate than tests for values of π_0 such as .05 or .10. For example, a test of H_0: $\pi = .0001$ with $n\pi_0 = 1.2$ is much more suspect than one for H_0: $\pi = .10$ with $n\pi_0 = 50$. If the issue becomes crucial, it's best to interpret the results skeptically.

Exercises

8.19 A market research firm interviewed a large number of potential automobile buyers by phone. One of the several questions asked was whether the customer would prefer 0% financing or a $2000 rebate on the price of the car. In the following Minitab output, the variable PrefZero is 1 for customers indicating a preference for the 0% financing, 0 for customers indicating a preference for the rebate.

```
One-Sample Z: PrefZero

Test of mu = 0.5 vs not = 0.5
The assumed standard deviation = 0.5

Variable     N    Mean    StDev  SE Mean      95% CI          Z      P
PrefZero   1586  0.5340  0.4990  0.0126  (0.5094, 0.5587)   2.71  0.007

One-Sample T: PrefZero

Test of mu = 0.5 vs not = 0.5

Variable     N    Mean    StDev  SE Mean      95% CI          T      P
PrefZero   1586  0.5340  0.4990  0.0125  (0.5095, 0.5586)   2.72  0.007
```

a. Formulate the null hypothesis that customers are equally divided in preferring the 0% financing or the discount.
b. Before taking such a survey, would you use a one-sided or two-sided research hypothesis? Which was used in the output?
c. Is there a statistically significant difference in preference shown in the data, using $\alpha = .01$?
d. Can the market researcher claim there is a dramatic preference for 0% financing, because the p-value is so low?

8.20 In Exercise 8.19 should the normal approximation used to compute the p-value be reasonably accurate?

8.21 A team of builders has surveyed buyers of their new homes for years. Consistently, only 41% of the buyers have indicated they were "quite satisfied" or "very satisfied" with the construction quality of their homes. The builders have adopted a revised quality-inspection system to try to improve customer satisfaction. They have surveyed 104 buyers since then; these buyers seem representative, with no systematic changes from past purchasers. Of the 104 buyers, 51 indicated they were quite or very satisfied.
a. Formulate the null hypothesis that there has been no real change in customer satisfaction from the past rate.
b. Before taking such a survey, would you use a one-sided or two-sided research hypothesis?
c. Calculate a z statistic for testing the null hypothesis.
d. Show that the null hypothesis cannot be rejected, using $\alpha = .05$.

8.22 Can the builders in Exercise 8.21 interpret the results as showing that the new inspection system has proved *not* to increase satisfaction?

8.23 In Exercise 8.21 is the normal approximation reasonably accurate?

8.24 A bakery produces bread for specialty stores. It wants to provide enough bread to meet the demand, but not so much that it has lots of unsold bread. Balancing the costs of lost sales and unsold bread, it wants 10% of stores to be sold out each day. The bakery's delivery people reported on one particular day that 27 of 137 stores were sold out. Coding the sold-out stores as 1, the others as 0, the bakery owner obtained the following Minitab output:

```
Test of p = 0.1 vs p not = 0.1

Variable   X    N  Sample p      95.0% CI      Z-Value  P-Value
SoldOut   27  137   0.1971   (0.1305, 0.2637)    3.79    0.000
```

a. Is there a statistically detectable deviation from the desired 10% sold-out rate? Use $\alpha = .05$.
b. Find a two-tailed p-value.

8.25 The delivery people in Exercise 8.24 reported that several stores in one area had had unusually high demand because of a rumor of heavy snow. Show that this fact violates an assumption underlying the test.

8.7 Hypothesis Tests and Confidence Intervals

We now have two forms of inference: Confidence intervals and hypothesis tests. Both can be performed on the same data. How are they related? For the changeover-time example we used in previous sections, a 95% confidence interval for the true mean time is $\bar{y} \pm 1.96\sigma_{\bar{y}}$; the sample mean was $\bar{y} = 14.4$, with $\sigma = 2.40$ and $n = 16$. Substituting $\bar{y} = 14.4$, $n = 16$, and $\sigma = 2.40$, we have

$$14.4 - 1.96\frac{(2.40)}{\sqrt{16}} \le \mu \le 14.4 + 1.96\frac{(2.40)}{\sqrt{16}} \quad \text{or} \quad 13.22 \le \mu \le 15.58$$

In our statistical test of H_0: $\mu < 16.2$, the boundary value $\mu_0 = 16.2$ does not fall within the 95% confidence interval, so it seems plausible to reject H_0. The probability of a Type I error for a statistical test based on a 95% confidence interval is just $\alpha = .05$.

DEFINITION 8.8

Use of Confidence Interval for Testing In general, a particular null-hypothesis value, say, θ_0, of any population parameter θ may be rejected with the probability of a Type I error α if and only if θ_0 does not fall in a $(1 - \alpha) \times 100\%$ confidence interval for θ.

For example, because the 95% confidence interval $13.22 \le \mu \le 15.58$ does not include $\mu_0 = 16.2$, we can reject H_0: $\mu = 16.2$, based on $\alpha = .05$. In fact, this is a general method for constructing confidence intervals; a 95% confidence interval can be defined as the set of nonrejectable ($\alpha = .05$) null hypothesis values. In a two-tailed test, a particular μ value is not rejected using $\alpha = .05$ if the z statistic lies in the interval

$$-1.96 \le \frac{\bar{y} - \mu}{\sigma/\sqrt{n}} \le 1.96$$

A little algebra shows that this is equivalent to

$$\bar{y} - 1.96 \frac{\sigma}{\sqrt{n}} \le \mu \le \bar{y} + 1.96 \frac{\sigma}{\sqrt{n}}$$

which is the 95% confidence interval for μ. In this sense, confidence intervals and hypothesis tests give equivalent results.

The usual confidence interval is two-sided. As above, such confidence intervals correspond to two-tailed tests. There is such a thing as a one-sided confidence interval. The nonrejection region for a left-tailed test at $\alpha = .05$ is

$$\frac{\bar{y} - \mu}{\sigma/\sqrt{n}} \ge -1.645$$

When solved for μ, this is

$$\mu \le \bar{y} + 1.645 \frac{\sigma}{\sqrt{n}}$$

one-sided confidence interval

which is a **one-sided confidence interval.** In the changeover-time example, this becomes $\mu \le 15.39$; because the boundary value $\mu_0 = 16.2$ does not fall within this interval, $H_0: \mu = 16.2$ may be rejected using $\alpha = .05$, one-tailed. For the remainder of this text, we use two-sided confidence intervals, which can be used to test two-sided research hypotheses.

EXAMPLE 8.14

For the television-watching data of Example 8.1, use a 99% confidence interval to test $H_0: \mu = 22.6$ versus $H_a: \mu \ne 22.6$ at $\alpha = .01$.

SOLUTION The two-sided research hypothesis implies that a two-sided confidence interval may be used to test the null hypothesis. In Example 8.1 $\bar{y} = 25.2$, σ is assumed to be 6.1, and $n = 60$. The 99% confidence interval is

$$25.2 - 2.576 \frac{6.1}{\sqrt{60}} \le \mu \le 25.2 + 2.576 \frac{6.1}{\sqrt{60}} \qquad \text{or} \qquad 23.2 \le \mu \le 27.2$$

Because the value of μ under H_0, 22.6, does not fall within the interval, we reject H_0 using $\alpha = .01$. Of course, the same conclusion was obtained in Example 8.1.

confidence intervals as β indicators

When the null hypothesis is not rejected, **confidence intervals** are useful in giving a crude measure of the risk of a Type II error. Roughly speaking, a wide 95% confidence interval indicates a high degree of uncertainty and therefore a high probability β of a Type II error. (Of course, 95% confidence fixes α at .05.) For example, if a seller of high-intensity lights for portable television cameras claims a mean life of 40 hours, and a sample of 10 lights yields a 95% confidence interval of $28.0 \le \mu \le 44.0$, the seller's claim cannot be rejected using an $\alpha = .05$ level. Note, too, that the interval is very wide; the lower limit of 28.0 is 30% below the claimed value. If the difference between a mean life of 40 hours and, say, a mean life of 30 hours was crucial in deciding whether to buy, the buyer would not be comfortable in accepting $\mu = 40$. The probability of a Type II error corresponding to $\mu = 30$ would undoubtedly be quite large.

The equivalence of hypothesis tests and confidence intervals works for any sort of statistical test. Whether we're doing a z test of a mean, a z test of a proportion, a t test of a mean, or any of the other procedures we will discuss in later chapters, we can reject a null hypothesis at a specified α (and have a p-value $< \alpha$) if and only if a $100(1 - \alpha)\%$ confidence interval does not include the H_0 value. The five-step formal test method, the p-value method, and the confidence-interval method are equivalent.

Exercises

8.26 In Chapter 2 we considered claims (in thousands of dollars) for automobile collision damage from a particular insurance company. A box plot of data is shown in Figure 8.8. Data analysis using the Minitab package follows:

```
Variable      N    Mean   StDev   SE Mean      95.0% CI
ClaimSize   187   5.178   5.284    0.386    (4.415,  5.940)
```

a. The company's national mean claim size is 4.62 thousand dollars. The data come from a particular midwestern city. Does the confidence interval for the mean indicate that the city's mean claim size might be the same?

b. One claims department staff member said that the deviation from 4.62 was not statistically significant, so the company could safely assume that the mean for this city was also 4.62. Is this a valid interpretation of the results?

FIGURE 8.8   **Box Plot of Collision Claims Data**

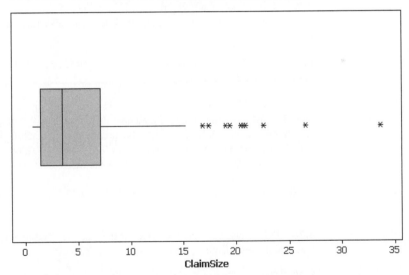

8.27 The boxplot of claims in Figure 8.8 shows some skewness. Does that mean that the claimed probabilities for the test of the mean are wrong?

8.28 In Exercise 8.5 we tested the null hypothesis that the long-run mean number of public-service commercials was 1.50. The test was based on a sample of 18 observations with a sample mean of 1.278; the assumed population standard deviation was 1.60. The null hypothesis was retained, using $\alpha = .05$.

a. Calculate a 95% confidence interval for the population (long-run) mean. Because we're assuming that σ is known, use the z table.

b. Show that this confidence interval is consistent with the conclusion of Exercise 8.5.

8.29 The null hypothesis in Exercise 8.8, that the mean number of travel days of a population of sales representatives was 44, was barely retained, using $\alpha = .20$. The sample mean was 47.6, the sample size was 10, and the assumed σ was 10.0.

a. Calculate an 80% confidence interval for the population mean; the required $z_{.10}$ value is 1.28.

b. How does this confidence interval indicate that the null hypothesis must be retained?

c. How does it indicate that H_0 is barely retained?

8.30 In Exercise 8.10 we tested a claim that the mean life of a battery for a calculator was 20,000 calculations. In a sample of 114 batteries, the mean was 19,695 and the standard deviation was 1,103.

a. Calculate a 99% confidence interval for the population mean lifetime.

b. Show that the null hypothesis that the mean is 20,000 must be rejected at $\alpha = .01$.

c. Would it be reasonable to say that because H_0 is rejected so emphatically, the mean lifetime must be much lower than 20,000?

8.31 The main access road to a suburban shopping mall sometimes becomes severely congested. On weekdays, excluding holidays, the average number of vehicles going toward the mall between 9 A.M. and 7 P.M. that pass a counter is 11,260. The highway department tried to improve traffic flow by changing stoplight cycles and improving turn lanes. For the first five nonholiday weekdays after the changes, the volumes were 10,690, 11,452, 12,316, 12,297, and 12,647. The mean for this sample is 11,880.4 and the standard deviation is 798.68.

a. Calculate a 95% confidence interval for the long-run (population) mean.

b. Show that the null hypothesis that the mean is still 11,260 must be retained at $\alpha = .05$.

8.32 A local politician who reviewed the results of Exercise 8.31 said that the data proved there had been no improvement in traffic volume. Is this a reasonable interpretation of the confidence interval?

8.33 The data for Exercise 8.31 are listed in time order. Is there any suggestion of dependence or a trend over time?

8.34 A clothing manufacturer cuts fabric from bolts. In the process, a certain amount of cloth is wasted. Using standard methods, the wastage is 9.26%. The maker of a computer-controlled machine allowed the manufacturer to test the machine on a sample of 762 different cuts. In the sample, the mean wastage was 9.11% and the standard deviation was 1.07%.

a. Calculate a 99% confidence interval for the mean wastage using the computer-controlled machine.

b. Show that there has been a statistically detectable (significant) change in the mean, using $\alpha = .01$.

8.35 In Exercise 8.34 can the maker of the machine legitimately say that statistics show the machine makes a large improvement in wastage?

8.36 The data underlying Exercise 8.34 were skewed by a few cases with large wastage numbers. Does this invalidate the confidence interval and test in Exercise 8.34?

BUSINESS DECISION-MAKING IN ACTION

CHAPTER CASE
ANALYSIS

Galarris Marketing Research Company

The president of Galarris Marketing Research Company has asked you to make a recommendation for the TopBrands survey bid. The bid preparation team collected sample data that it says indicates Galarris should use the higher premium rate because the average survey time will exceed 15 minutes. The president wants to know if you agree that the data support this recommendation.

Galarris is assuming that the average survey time will be 15 minutes or less and will apply the basic charge, unless the data indicate that the time will be longer, in which case it will use the higher premium charge. Given this, the appropriate null hypothesis is $H_0: \mu = 15$ and the one-sided alternative is $H_a: \mu > 15$, where μ is the true average time required to conduct the TopBrands survey.

FIGURE 8.9

Partial Listing of the Galarris Marketing Research Company Data

	A	B	C	D	E	F
1	A	B	C	D	E	F
2	27.2	24.3	23.1	25.1	26.2	26.4
3	22.8	23.7	21.8	21.4	22.2	20.0
4	19.1	18.7	18.8	23.4	19.2	22.3
5	21.3	19.8	21.0	22.3	18.7	19.0
6	18.6	20.0	18.7	18.4	19.2	17.8

Figure 8.9 gives a partial listing of the data. Since the data are in six separate columns, one for each of the data collectors, we should first combine the data into a single column for the purposes of the hypothesis test. Minitab output for this step and for the hypothesis test follow:

```
MTB > Stack  'A'-'F' 'Time';
SUBC>    Subscripts 'Surveyor';
SUBC>    UseNames.

MTB > OneT 'Time';
SUBC>    Test 15;
SUBC>    Alternative 1.

One-Sample T: Time

Test of mu = 15 vs > 15
                                         95%
                                        Lower
Variable    N     Mean    StDev   SE Mean   Bound     T      P
Time       150  15.6612  3.6076   0.2946  15.1737  2.25  0.013
```

With a *p*-value of .013, the hypothesis test suggests that there is sufficient evidence to conclude that the true average survey time will be more than 15 minutes. But as we have learned in previous data analyses, it is always a good idea to examine the data graphically to make sure we haven't missed anything.

One possible concern is differences in (or variation due to) the different survey associates. Figure 8.10 is a box plot of survey times by associate. Overall, the individual distributions appear to be very similar, skewed right with a few outlying values. The variation among survey associates seems to be small.

FIGURE 8.10

Box Plots of Survey Times by Surveyor

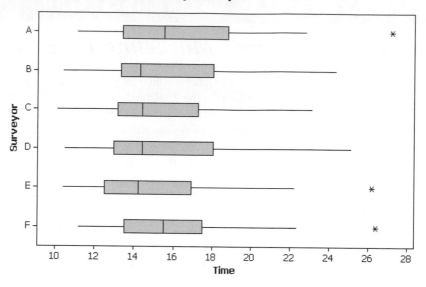

Because the data were collected in time order, we should examine a time series plot of the data to see if there are any unusual patterns. With six different time series, we can either plot them separately or together in a multiple time series plot, such as the one from Excel shown in Figure 8.11.

FIGURE 8.11

Multiple Time Series Plot of Survey Times by Surveyor

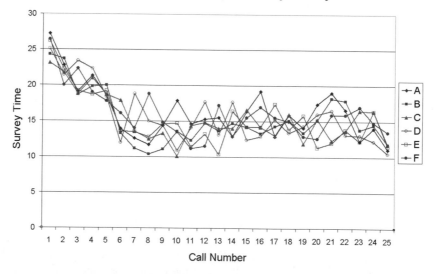

The left-hand side of the plot reveals an unexpected pattern: For each survey associate, there are several long survey times (18–28 minutes) in the beginning followed by random variation in survey times within a horizontal band around the 15-minute mark. As they became more experienced with the survey, the associates took less time to complete it. After five or six surveys, the average time appears to become more consistent.

Clearly, the first few times reflect a "learning phase" and inflate the sample average time. The 6th through 25th observations for each associate are more typical of the distribution of survey times likely in conducting the actual survey for Top-Brands.

Figure 8.12 is a normal probability plot of the 120 observations remaining after deleting the first five observations for each survey associate. The plot and associated p-value suggest that the individual survey times are approximately normally distributed. That fact, the relatively large sample size, and the Central Limit Theorem support the use of a normal-theory hypothesis test based on these data. The box plots of survey times by survey associate in Figure 8.13 indicate that it is reasonable to combine the data from the associates, as their individual survey time distributions are reasonably similar.

FIGURE 8.12 **Normal Probability Plot of Survey Times (6 through 25)**

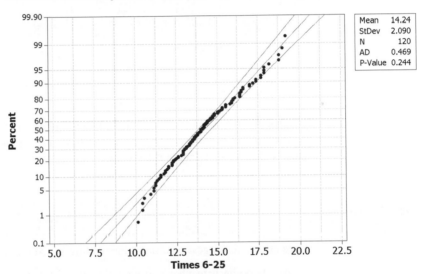

FIGURE 8.13 **Box Plots of Survey Times (6 through 25) by Telephone Survey Associate**

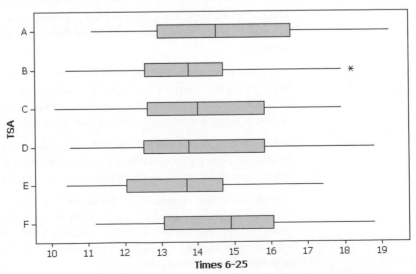

Minitab output is shown for the hypothesis test after eliminating the "start-up" data. The sample average survey time is now 14.24 minutes and, with a *p*-value of 1.000, the hypothesis test indicates that there is insufficient evidence in the data to conclude the true average survey time is greater than 15 minutes. In fact, there is sufficient evidence to conclude that the true mean is less than 15 minutes, since the observed sample mean is nearly 4 standard errors ($t = -3.99$) below 15 minutes.

```
MTB > Copy 'A'-'F' c11-c16;
SUBC>    Omit 1:5.

MTB > Stack  C11-C16 'Times 6-25';
SUBC>    Subscripts 'TSA';
SUBC>    UseNames.

MTB > OneT  'Times 6-25';
SUBC>    Test 15;
SUBC>    Alternative 1.

One-Sample T: Times 6-25

Test of mu = 15 vs > 15
                                              95%
                                            Lower
Variable       N    Mean    StDev  SE Mean  Bound      T      P
Times 6-25   120  14.2391  2.0896   0.1908  13.9228  -3.99  1.000
```

Based on this analysis, you should recommend to the president of Galarris that he prepare the bid proposal based on the basic rate. This should improve the company's chances of winning the contract bid.

SUMMARY

Here are some suggestions for understanding statistical hypothesis-testing methods.

1. Any hypothesis test has a limited, though useful, purpose: to assess whether a deviation of a sample result from a theoretical population or process value might possibly have occurred by chance, merely by sampling variation.

2. The result of a hypothesis test can't tell you directly whether the deviation is large or small. The test is affected not only by the size of the deviation but also by the sample size.

3. A *p*-value is a convenient way to summarize a test, especially because it is so often reported by computer packages. A *p*-value is an index of how conclusive the evidence is of a real, more than random, deviation from the hypothetical value. Again, it is not a direct indication of how large that deviation is.

4. A confidence interval can indicate not only whether a deviation is statistically detectable (significant) but also how large the deviation might reasonably be. A confidence interval is often easier to interpret correctly than a hypothesis test.

5. The choice of test method is similar to the choice of an estimation method. Tests based on means are most effective when the underlying population or process generates approximately normally distributed data. Other methods are more powerful (have a higher probability of detecting a real change) for seriously skewed or outlier-prone populations.

6. A result that is not statistically significant does *not* prove that there is no difference in the hypothesized and true values of the parameter. Such a result only says that the discrepancy in the sample statistic and the hypothesized population parameter *might* have occurred by chance. If the power of the test is low or the associated confidence interval is very wide, a nonsignificant result means very little.

In addition, you may want to reread the summary of key ideas in the Executive Overview at the beginning of this chapter.

Supplementary Exercises

8.37   EPA miles-per-gallon ratings are obtained for all models of cars sold in the United States. One of these figures purports to represent mileage in combined city–country driving. Suppose a consumer group test-drives eight cars of a model with an EPA rating of 28.2 miles per gallon. If H_0 is $\mu = 28.2$, what argument would lead to a one-sided research hypothesis?

8.38   Assume that the population standard deviation is 2.1 and that the mean gas mileage for the eight cars is 26.7 in Exercise 8.37. Can a two-sided research hypothesis be supported at $\alpha = .01$?

8.39   Find the *p*-value in Exercise 8.37.

8.40   An official of the consumer group interprets the result of Exercise 8.37 as being not statistically significant. The official concludes that therefore it can reliably be assumed that the true mean is 28.2. Do you agree?

8.41   Compute a 99% confidence interval for the true mean mileage in Exercise 8.37. Use this interval to confirm the result of that exercise. What can we "reliably assume" about the true mean mileage?

8.42   In a nationwide opinion poll based on a random sample of 2417 people, one question is: "How do you rate the ethics of business executives of large companies?" A rating of 3 means "no better or worse than most people," a rating of 1 is "much better than most people," and 5 is "much worse than most people." The mean rating is 3.05 and the standard deviation is .62.
a. Calculate a 95% confidence interval for the population mean rating.
b. Can H_0: $\mu = 3.00$ be rejected (against a two-sided alternative) at $\alpha = .05$?

8.43   A newspaper reporting on the poll of Exercise 8.42 reports that "respondents rated the ethics of big business significantly worse than average."
a. Is this statement true in the statistical sense?
b. Do you think it might mislead the general public?

8.44   What can be said about the *p*-value of Exercise 8.42?

8.45   In Exercise 7.53, a police department obtained data on response times to nonemergency crime calls. The data and Minitab output are reproduced here:

```
Data Display

RespTime
   24  25  18  25  15  11  11  19  36  29  13  21  12  12  26
   16  19  12  21  12  12  18  11  19  16  24  14  23  17

Descriptive Statistics: RespTime

Variable   N   Mean  SE Mean  StDev  Minimum    Q1 Median    Q3  Maximum
RespTime  29  18.31    1.17   6.29    11.00  12.00  18.00  23.50    36.00
```

```
One-Sample Z: RespTime

Test of mu = 20 vs < 20
The assumed standard deviation = 6
                                         95%
                                        Upper
Variable    N    Mean    StDev  SE Mean   Bound      Z      P
RespTime   29  18.3102  6.2912  1.1142  20.1429  -1.52  0.065
```

a. The department wants to have conclusive evidence that the mean is less than 20 minutes. Formulate this goal as a research hypothesis. What is the corresponding null hypothesis?

b. Assume that the distribution of response times is roughly normal and that the true (population or process) standard deviation is 6.0 minutes. What is the appropriate test statistic?

c. Write out the five parts of a formal hypothesis test, using $\alpha = .05$. The preceding Minitab output may be helpful.

8.46 What is the p-value for the data in Exercise 8.45?

8.47 The data in Exercise 8.45 were plotted as a stem-and-leaf display. Is there a clear indication of a nonnormal distribution? If so, does this completely invalidate your answers in Exercise 8.45?

```
Stem-and-Leaf Display: RespTime

Stem-and-leaf of RespTime  N  = 29
Leaf Unit = 1.0

    3    1   111
    9    1   222223
   11    1   45
   14    1   667
   (5)   1   88999
   10    2   11
    8    2   3
    7    2   4455
    3    2   6
    2    2   9
    1    3
    1    3
    1    3
    1    3   6
```

8.48 In Exercise 8.45 we assumed a population standard deviation of 6.0 minutes. Test the research hypothesis that the population mean is less than 20 minutes, using $\alpha = .05$, without making this assumption. The following Minitab output may be of use:

```
One-Sample T: RespTime

Test of mu = 20 vs < 20
                                         95%
                                        Upper
Variable    N    Mean    StDev  SE Mean   Bound      T      P
RespTime   29  18.3102  6.2912  1.1682  20.2976  -1.45  0.080
```

8.49 A fish hatchery was concerned that the (population) mean weight of released fish might differ from 10.0 ounces. Differences in either direction were undesirable. The data are reproduced here.

9.3	11.7	11.0	9.8	10.1	8.9	8.7	9.5	10.8	8.7	7.6
10.0	8.8	9.3	9.2	8.1	9.9	9.4	8.3	10.3	9.8	9.5
9.8	9.0	10.7	9.3	9.6	10.4	9.4	9.8	9.8	9.2	11.0
10.2	9.1	11.0	9.4	9.7	12.1	9.8	7.1	8.3	10.3	10.6
10.1	10.2	8.8	9.3	10.3	10.7	10.8	7.5	9.0	10.1	9.2
9.7	10.4	9.1	9.7	10.7	10.6	(mean = 9.6803, standard deviation = .95983)

a. Formulate a research hypothesis and a null hypothesis.
b. Assume that the population standard deviation is 1.0 ounce. Write down a test statistic.
c. Carry out the five parts of a statistical test with $\alpha = .10$. State the conclusion carefully.

8.50 State a p-value for Exercise 8.49. Should it be one-tailed or two-tailed?

8.51 We obtained the following Minitab output from the sample of 61 fish. Use these results to test the research hypothesis that the population mean weight is not equal to 10.0 ounces. Make no assumption about the population standard deviation.

```
Variable     N     Mean    StDev   SE Mean       90.0% CI
Weights     61    9.680    0.960     0.123   (9.475, 9.886)
```

8.52 What can be said about a two-tailed p-value in Exercise 8.51?

8.53 A consulting firm often submits health care management proposals for projects in competition with one particular firm of very similar capabilities. A relatively new vice president in charge of the health care division has submitted 16 proposals against the competitor. The firm has won contracts in only 5 of these cases, with the competitor winning the other 11. The president of the firm, noting this fact, concludes that the data prove that the v.p. can't win half the time against the competitor.
a. Formulate the null hypothesis that the firm will win half the time in the long run.
b. Show that the research hypothesis that the firm will win less than half the time can't be rejected at $\alpha = .05$.
c. Does this fact prove that the firm will, in fact, win half the time?

8.54 In Exercise 8.53 will a normal approximation be reasonably accurate?

8.55 As cable television availability has increased, broadcast television networks and advertisers have become increasingly concerned with the amount of time that their target audiences spend watching conventional broadcast television. A sampling of one particular target group recorded the hours of conventional TV watched in one week to the nearest half hour. A Minitab stem-and-leaf display is as follows:

```
Stem and leaf of HrsWatched  N  = 44
Leaf Unit = 1.0
   1    2  1
   2    2  2
   5    2  445
  21    2  6666777777777777
 (14)   2  88888888999999
   9    3  0
   8    3  33333
   3    3
   3    3
   3    3  9
   2    4  1
   1    4  3
```

Is it fair to say that the data appear close to normally distributed?

8.56 A normal probability plot of the data of Exercise 8.55 is shown in Figure 8.14. Would you judge that the data fell close to the indicated straight line? If not, what sort of nonnormality seems to be present?

8.57 For the target population of Exercise 8.55, the mean (and median) hours watched was 30.4, according to a very extensive survey made two years previously. The data of Exercise 8.55 were analyzed by the Minitab package, with the following results:

```
One-Sample T: HrsWatched

Variable      N      Mean    StDev   SE Mean         90% CI
HrsWatched   44   28.8976   4.2952    0.6475   (27.8091, 29.9862)
```

FIGURE 8.14   **Normal Plot for Hours-Watched Data**

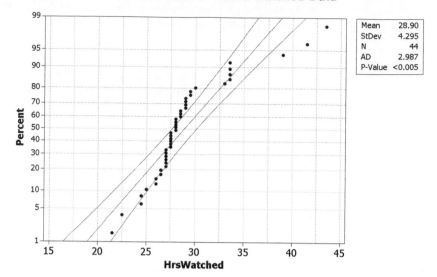

a. According to the confidence interval for the mean, is there conclusive evidence that the mean hours watched has changed since the previous survey?
b. The plots of Exercises 8.55 and 8.56 indicated that the data are not normally distributed. Does that fact indicate that the claimed confidence of the interval for the mean is seriously incorrect?

8.58   The Minitab output from Exercise 8.57 also included the result of a formal hypothesis test, as follows:

```
One-Sample T: HrsWatched

Test of mu = 30.4 vs not = 30.4

Variable      N     Mean    StDev   SE Mean       90% CI          T      P
HrsWatched   44   28.8976   4.2952   0.6475   (27.8091, 29.9862)  -2.32  0.025
```

a. According to the computed t statistic, can the null hypothesis be rejected using $\alpha = .10$ and a two-tailed test? The output indicated 43 d.f.
b. Is your answer consistent with the answer to part (a) of Exercise 8.57?
c. How is the p-value shown in the output? Does this p-value indicate that the null hypothesis should be rejected using $\alpha = .10$?

8.59   A mortgage service company processes a large volume of transactions every day. Because many of the transactions involve depositing funds, it's important for the company to complete processing and not leave unprocessed items for the following day. The operations manager has a target that processing will be complete in 96% of all workdays. Records for the last 212 days have been kept. In the following Minitab output, an AllDone value of 1 indicates complete processing and a 0 indicates that unprocessed items were left for the next day. Does the output indicate there has been a statistically significant departure from the 96% target, using reasonable α levels?

```
Test and CI for One Proportion: AllDone

Test of p = 0.96 vs p not = 0.96

                                                          Exact
Variable    X     N   Sample p          95% CI           P-Value
AllDone    194   212  0.915094   (0.869132, 0.948903)    0.004
```

8.60 Examination of the data in Exercise 8.59 shows that the incomplete-processing days occurred in "streaks." On one occasion, there was incomplete processing for 8 consecutive days; on others, 4 consecutive days. This fact suggests that one of the assumptions underlying hypothesis tests was violated. Which one? What is the consequence of the violation?

8.61 A package delivery service adopted a new dispatching system to try to reduce the total mileage required by its truck fleet to make deliveries. The new system would be worth the cost if it reduced the fleet mileage by more than 5% from its current level of 2420 miles per day (that is, decrease it to less than 2299 miles per day). The miles required for each of 49 days under a trial of the new system are recorded in column 1 of the EX0861 file on the CD; day number is recorded in column 2. Load the data into a computer package.
a. Obtain the mean and standard deviation of the miles data.
b. Using the computer package, if possible, test the research hypothesis that the long-run mean will be less than 2299. Obtain a *p*-value.

8.62 Refer to Exercise 8.61.
a. Obtain a stem-and-leaf display of the miles data. Is there reason to think there is a problem of nonnormality?
b. The data are a time series. Obtain a plot of miles against day number. Is there evidence of a trend? Of cycles, indicating day-to-day dependence in the data?

8.63 An inexpensive restaurant featuring steak dinners makes most of its profits from side orders suggested to diners by the staff. As an experiment, the restaurant owner rewarded each server with 10% of the price of all side orders made through that server. After 10 days, the owner computed the side-order volume per customer for each of 41 servers. The data are stored in column 1 of the EX0863 file on the CD; server number is stored in column 2. Load the data into a computer package.
a. Obtain the mean and standard deviation of the volume data.
b. The reward policy will be profitable if the mean volume is more than $2.40 per customer. Is there strong evidence in the data that the policy will, in fact, be profitable?

8.64 Refer to Exercise 8.63.
a. Obtain a box plot of the volume data. Are there any outliers?
b. Obtain a normal plot of the data. What nonnormality, if any, appears to be present?

8.65 The human resources director for a large corporation tested an incentive policy to try to reduce the number of personal leave days taken by employees. A sample of 50 employees (out of several hundred in the company) was offered bonuses if the average number of leave days taken could be reduced from the current level of 5.7 per employee per year. After a year, the number of leave days was computed for each employee. The data are stored in column 1 of the EX0865 file on the CD; employee ID number is in column 2. Load the data into whatever statistical computer package you can use.
a. Obtain the mean, median, and standard deviation of the leave-days data. What does this information suggest about the skewness of the data?
b. Get a stem-and-leaf display or histogram of the data. Does the plot confirm your impression about the skewness in the data?

8.66 Refer to Exercise 8.65.
a. Have the computer package used for Exercise 8.65 test the null hypothesis that the mean leave days is still 5.7. You may have to subtract 5.7 from all the data to be able to test the hypothesis that the mean is 0.
b. Obtain a *p*-value for the test. Is it one-sided or two-sided in the computer output? Do you think a one-sided test or a two-sided test is more appropriate in this situation?

BUSINESS CASES

Truck Springs Quality

A manufacturer of heavy-duty leaf springs for trucks begins by making basic castings. The most important factor in the quality of a casting is its length. Ideally, the casting should be 8.05 inches. (The basic casting is finished to a specification length of 8.00 inches.) There is substantial variation of casting lengths, even if the process is working properly, because of variation in outside temperature and humidity and variations in the quality of the steel raw material. Experience has indicated that the standard deviation of lengths of basic castings is about .180 inch, when the casting process is working well.

Systematic problems with the process tend to show up mostly in incorrect mean lengths, rather than in increased variability. Therefore, the length of each casting is measured. After each set of 16 castings, the average length is found. If the mean for any sample of 16 castings is too far away from the desired mean, 8.05 inches, the casting process is halted and a lengthy (and moderately expensive) reset procedure is carried out to bring the process back to standard. One major problem is the definition of "too far away" from 8.05 inches. The casting-process manager wants to establish limits of 7.915 inches and 8.185 inches, but the finishing-process manager favors limits of 8.000 inches and 8.100 inches. Both of them agree with an official target that says that the long-run mean (over many thousands of castings) must be kept within the range of 7.95 to 8.15 inches; they disagree over the implications of this target for the samples of 16 castings.

Assignment: Write a report to both managers and explain the implications of their choice of limits. Indicate what seem to be the important issues and what other facts may need to be found to come to a reasonable conclusion. Neither manager knows much statistical theory, so try to explain any technical ideas carefully.

The Five-Star Corporation

The Five-Star Corporation is a large U.S. company with 8000 employees in 40 corporate locations scattered around the continental United States. As the vice president of human resources, you are currently considering a new optional vision plan benefit for employees. After a long search, you have trimmed potential providers down to one company, VisionOne. VisionOne's plan requires monthly premiums from the participating employees with a matching contribution from the employer.

In order for the vision plan to be financially feasible for both Five-Star and VisionOne, at least 25% of all Five-Star employees must participate. Unfortunately, Five-Star doesn't have the data that would allow it to determine the actual percentage of employees who would enroll in the plan.

VisionOne has found in the past that individual presentations to employees have worked best in explaining the benefits of the vision plan and identifying which employees will actually participate, so VisionOne has agreed to make individual presentations. But given the large employee base of Five-Star, it was impossible to do this for every employee or at all 40 Five-Star corporate locations.

After several discussions with VisionOne representatives, you developed a multistage random sample of offices and employees within offices for VisionOne's presentations. The data collected are contained in the file FiveStar on the CD that came with your book. The file contains information on the sampled employees who were given the presentation by a VisionOne representative. Figure 8.15 contains a partial listing of the data.

FIGURE 8.15

Partial Listing of the Five-Star Corporation Data

	A	B	C	D	E	F	G
1	Employee	Office	Sex	MaritalStatus	Salary	SpousePlan	Intention
2	5429	3	M	M	56578	N	N
3	8232	3	M	S	46302	N	N
4	2473	3	F	M	65418	N	N
5	4973	3	M	M	42154	N	Y
6	3943	3	F	S	46632	N	Y
7	4729	3	M	M	60716	Y	N
8	8721	3	M	S	40225	N	Y
9	3239	3	M	S	43809	N	Y
10	5788	3	M	S	52824	N	N
11	3297	3	M	S	48167	N	N
12	5408	3	F	M	49181	Y	N

In the FiveStar file, the variables are defined as follows:

Employee: Employee ID number

Office: Office location (1–40)

Sex: Male (M) or female (F)

MaritalStatus: Single (S) or married (M)

Salary: Annual salary in dollars

SpousePlan: Currently covered by spouse's vision plan (Y or N)

Intention: Intends to enroll in VisionOne (Y) or does not intend to enroll (N)

Assignment: As the vice president for human resources, you must decide to offer or not offer the VisionOne plan. Using the data provided, determine whether or not the plan should be offered, that is, whether or not it is financially feasible for the company. Write a report to the CEO of Five-Star Corporation that contains a brief description of the vision plan (which will be provided by VisionOne), a detailed statistical analysis of the data, and your decision.

Review Exercises—Chapters 7–8

8.67   A larger computer software firm installs a new editor for use by a random sample of its programmers. After the programmers have learned to use the editor comfortably, the firm measures the number of lines of debugged code produced by each programmer. (The programming tasks are of comparable difficulty.) The data are

```
178  183  199  201  204  210  218  218  219  220  225  227  231
232  232  233  233  235  238  239  241  243  244  246  247  249
250  251  264  266  270  271  271  283  275  276  277  279  283
284  285  286  289  289  298  303  306  315  315  345
```

For these data, the sample size is 50, the sample mean is 253.32, and the sample standard deviation is 36.1.

a. The population standard deviation using the previous editor was 35.4. Assume that this population standard deviation applies to the new editor as well. Calculate a 99% confidence interval for the population mean using the new editor. Compare to the following Minitab results:

```
One-Sample Z: CodeDone

The assumed standard deviation = 35.4

Variable    N     Mean     StDev   SE Mean         99% CI
CodeDone   50   253.319   36.095     5.006   (240.424, 266.214)
```

b. Is there clear evidence in the normal plot shown in Figure 8.16 that the sample mean is likely to be an inefficient estimator of the population mean?

FIGURE 8.16   Normal Plot for Programmer Data

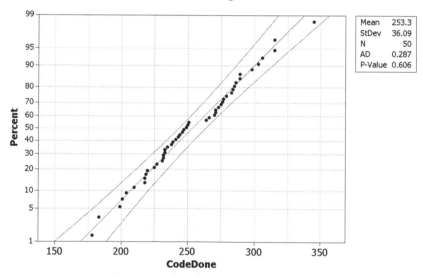

8.68   Refer to the confidence interval calculated in part (a) of the previous exercise. The population mean using the old editor was 230.2. Can we reject the null hypothesis that the mean for the new editor is 230.2, using $\alpha = .01$, based on the confidence interval?

8.69   Carry out a formal hypothesis test of the null hypothesis that the population mean in Exercise 8.67 remains 230.2 against the research hypothesis that it is not equal to 230.2 for the data of the previous exercise. Use $\alpha = .01$ and assume that the population standard deviation is 35.4.

8.70 For the hypothesis test of Exercise 8.69, state a p-value. Compare to the following Minitab results:

```
One-Sample Z: CodeDone

Test of mu = 230.2 vs not = 230.2
The assumed standard deviation = 35.4

Variable   N    Mean    StDev   SE Mean       99% CI          Z      P
CodeDone   50  253.319  36.095   5.006  (240.424, 266.214)  4.62  0.000
```

8.71 Redo the preceding exercises without making the assumption that the population standard deviation is 35.4. Compare your results to the following Minitab output. Do any of your conclusions change substantially?

```
One-Sample T: CodeDone

Test of mu = 230.2 vs not = 230.2

Variable   N    Mean    StDev   SE Mean       99% CI          T      P
CodeDone   50  253.319  36.095   5.105  (239.639, 266.999)  4.53  0.000
```

8.72 Minitab calculated a 99% confidence interval for the population median in the preceding exercises by a method not discussed in this book. On the basis of this interval, can one reject the null hypothesis that the population median is 230, using $\alpha = .01$?

```
Sign confidence interval for median

                       Achieved
          N  Median  Confidence  Confidence Interval  Position
CodeDone  50  248.0    0.9847      ( 233.0,  273.0)       17
                       0.9900      ( 233.0,  273.9)      NLI
                       0.9934      ( 233.0,  275.0)       16
```

8.73 Which 99% confidence interval in the preceding exercises is wider, the t interval or the interval for the median? What does your answer suggest about the efficiency of the sample mean as compared to the sample median in this particular case?

8.74 It is claimed that 45% of all walk-in customers at a particular real estate office eventually buy a home through that office. To test the claim, it plans to regard the next 100 customers as a random sample. Set up a formal test of the research hypothesis that the population proportion is less than .45, using $\alpha = .05$.

8.75 How does the rejection region in the previous exercise change if the maximum allowable α is set at .01?

8.76 Suppose that the head of the real estate office in the previous exercises determines that 32 of the 100 walk-in customers eventually buy homes through the office. Does this fact support H_a if α is set at .05?

8.77 Does the result in Exercise 8.76 lead to rejection of H_0 if α is set at .01? What does your answer indicate about the p-value for the data?

8.78 A forester needs to test a new method for growing pine trees for lumber, one designed to minimize the loss to browsing deer. A five-year trial is needed. A sample of 25 stands is to be planted and tended using the new method. The current yield has a mean of 272.6 and a standard deviation of 67.3, in appropriate units of measurement.
a. Formulate reasonable null and research hypotheses. In particular, should the research hypotheses be one-sided or two-sided?
b. Set up the first four parts of a formal test of the null hypothesis. Assume that the population standard deviation remains unchanged. The desired α value is .05.

8.79   Suppose that the population mean yield under the new growing method in Exercise 8.78 is 305. Calculate the probability that the test will not reject the null hypothesis. What is the technical name for this probability?

8.80   Assume that the population mean yield is 295 rather than the 305 assumed previously. Should the probability that the null hypothesis will not be rejected be larger or smaller than the probability calculated in the previous exercise?

8.81   Assume that the experiment of the previous three exercises results in the following yield data:

135 185 231 247 262 285 300 304 310 312 313 319 322
322 324 328 335 362 366 368 370 384 384 385 401
($\bar{y} = 314.16$, $s = 64.0$)

The following Minitab output was obtained:

```
Descriptive Statistics: Yield

Variable    N    Mean SE Mean   StDev  Minimum      Q1  Median      Q3  Maximum
Yield      25   314.2    12.8    64.0    135.0   292.5   322.0   367.0    401.0

Stem-and-Leaf Display: Yield

Stem-and-leaf of Yield  N  = 25
Leaf Unit = 10

   1    1  3
   2    1  8
   4    2  34
   6    2  68
 (11)   3  00111122223
   8    3  6667888
   1    4  0


One-Sample T: Yield

Test of mu = 272.6 vs > 272.6

                                          95%
                                        Lower
Variable    N     Mean   StDev  SE Mean  Bound     T      P
Yield      25  314.159  63.993   12.799  292.262  3.25  0.002
```

What is the conclusion of the *t* test? Is there clear evidence that the mean has increased?

8.82   In the previous output, locate the probability that a sample mean is equal to or larger than 314.16, given a population mean of 272.6. What is the technical name for this probability?

8.83   The Minitab output in Exercise 8.81 contains a stem-and-leaf plot of the yield data. Is there any reason to believe that the sample mean is not the best estimator of the population mean?

8.84   A computer center that serves, among other clients, small savings and loan associations needs to know the proportion of jobs from these businesses that requires intervention by the computer operator. In a random sample of 133 such jobs, 22 require operator intervention. Calculate a 95% confidence interval for the population proportion of jobs requiring intervention.

8.85   Suppose that the confidence interval in Exercise 8.84 is felt to be too wide. Calculate the sample size required to obtain a 95% confidence interval with a width of .06 (a plus or minus of .03) under each of two assumptions:
a. Assume that the sample proportion will continue to be roughly 22/133.
b. Assume that the sample proportion can take any value.

8.86   A normal approximation is used in the confidence intervals of the preceding two exercises. Can we be confident that the approximation is a good one?

8.87   An auditor wishes to verify transaction records of a firm. The transactions are placed in random order. An auditor trainee keeps a cumulative total of the dollar amounts of the transactions; every time the total moves over a $100,000 increment (that is, when the total passes $100,000, $200,000, $300,000, etc.), the transaction is set aside for verification. Show that this process does not yield a random sample of the transactions.

8.88   The process of the previous exercise yields 241 transactions. The mean size of the transactions is $5381 and the standard deviation is $2271. The amounts, when plotted, show substantial right-skewness.
a. Calculate a supposed 95% confidence interval for the population mean transaction size.
b. This interval is in fact quite likely *not* to include the actual mean transaction size of the population. Explain why.

8.89   A chemical manufacturer doing a pilot study of yields obtains a sample of 26 small batches. The yields, expressed as percentages of the theoretical maximum, are

67.6   68.5   74.7   77.6   78.4   79.3   79.5   80.3   80.3   80.7   80.8   80.8   80.9
81.2   81.4   81.4   81.5   82.5   82.5   82.9   82.9   83.8   84.4   84.4   85.4   86.0
$(\bar{y} = 80.37, s = 4.37)$

The following Minitab output was obtained:

```
One-Sample T: Yield

Variable    N      Mean    StDev    SE Mean      90.0% CI
Yield       26    80.373   4.371     0.857    (78.909, 81.837)
```

State a 90% confidence interval for the population mean yield.

8.90   Use the confidence interval of Exercise 8.89 to test the null hypothesis that the population mean is 82.0 against a two-sided research hypothesis. What does the conclusion indicate about the p-value according to the Universal Rejection Region?

8.91   The complete pilot study for the preceding exercises eventually involves a sample of 150 batches. Assuming that the population standard deviation is about 4.4 and that the population mean is 80.4, find the probability that H_0: population mean = 82.0 will be rejected. Assume an α of .05.

8.92   The probability calculated in the preceding exercise is *not* a p-value. Explain why not.

8.93   The Litchfield Company owns and operates movie theaters in the Southeast. The manager of one theater is concerned that DVDs are hurting his business because people can simply rent a movie and watch it at home. He conducts a quick phone survey of 15 homes in the surrounding area, asking how many movies were rented and watched on a DVD at each home during the previous month. The sample average and standard deviation for the 15 homes were 3.4 and 1.6 movies, respectively.
a. Calculate a 90% confidence interval for the true average number of movies rented last month by households in the surrounding area.
b. What assumption are you making in answering part (a)?

8.94   First State National Bank is concerned that its per check charge to customers is insufficient. Management decides to conduct a survey of customers to estimate the average number of checks written in a month. Based on a small pilot sample of customers, management determines that the population standard deviation of the number of checks written in a month by customers cannot exceed 20. How many customers should be sampled to ensure with .92 probability that the sample mean will be within 1.0 check of the true average?

8.95 At a certain manufacturing company, a 95% confidence interval for the true average daily production based on a sample of 30 days of production is computed to be (651,669).
a. Label each statement below as true (T), false (F), or cannot be determined (C).

____ The sample mean production level for the 30 days lies between 651 and 669 units.
____ The true mean production level of the new process lies between 651 and 669 units.
____ Approximately 95% of daily production values under the new process will be between 651 and 669 units.
____ A 90% confidence interval using the same data will be narrower than (651,669).

b. True or False (if false, explain why): Assuming the confidence level of 95% is fixed in part (a), in order to cut the margin of error in half, we would need to double the sample size.

8.96 The manufacturer of Died-Hard automobile batteries claims that its batteries last at least 48 months on average. A consumers' advocate group has received many complaints and decides to conduct an experiment to evaluate the longevity claim. Data were collected and analyzed in Minitab. Output from the analysis follows:

Descriptive Statistics

Variable	N	Mean	Median	TrMean	StDev	SEMean
BAT_LIFE	28	43.33	42.35	43.38	8.54	1.61

Variable	Min	Max	Q1	Q3
BAT_LIFE	25.00	60.10	38.98	48.60

a. Construct a 95% confidence interval for the true average life of Died-Hard batteries.
b. Based on your confidence interval in part (a), what can you conclude about the 48-month claim of Died-Hard batteries? Explain why.
c. How many observations should have been collected if the consumers' advocacy group wanted the margin of error on the sample average life to be 1 month?

8.97 Based on a large marketing survey conducted last year, it was determined that 15% of consumers could not identify your product. A recent survey of 702 consumers revealed that 86 could not identify your product. Based on a 90% confidence interval, has there been any change in consumer knowledge about your product?

8.98 A hospital is negotiating with medical insurance providers who would like to reduce the amount they pay as reimbursement for hospital stays. For a particular procedure, they would like to reduce payment by $300 and have patients go home one day earlier. To see what effect this would have on hospital costs, a random sample of 50 patients who were recently admitted for this procedure was analyzed. The savings for each patient were calculated under the assumption that he or she had left the hospital one day earlier. Minitab output is shown next.

Descriptive Statistics

Variable	N	Mean	Median	TrMean	StDev	SE Mean
Savings	50	322.44	315.60	320.55	21.71	3.07

Variable	Minimum	Maximum	Q1	Q3
Savings	294.78	378.10	306.12	333.00

a. Compute a 95% confidence interval for the true average savings from sending patients having this procedure home one day earlier.
b. Can it be concluded that the true average savings are above the $300 reduction recommended by the provider? Explain why or why not.

Comparing Two Samples

This chapter applies the basic ideas of statistical inference—confidence intervals and hypothesis tests—to problems of comparison. The choice of method depends on the nature of the problem and the apparent shape of the data distribution. The key ideas are:

- Samples may be paired or independent. In paired (matched) samples, each value in one sample is linked to a specific value in the other sample; in independent samples, there is no logical connection between items. Paired samples may be analyzed by considering the differences between paired values.

- The most efficient, effective way to analyze data that appear nearly normally distributed is by t-distribution methods. For paired samples, a test or confidence interval based on the single sample of differences may be used. For independent samples, either a pooled-variance procedure (which assumes equal population variances) or a separate-variance (t') method may be used. The two methods give substantially different answers only when the sample sizes are quite different; if the population variances are also different, the pooled-variance method is not reliable.

- If the data in independent samples are skewed or outlier-prone, a rank sum test is more efficient, better able to detect a real difference than a t method. The rank-sum method is based on ranking the data from smallest to largest and thus is less affected by skewness or outliers.

- If the difference data from paired samples is outlier-prone, a signed-rank test is more effective than a t test. The signed-rank test, however, is not reliable if the underlying population of differences is badly skewed.

- A comparison of proportions can be done with either a normal (z) approximation or with a t test on 1s and 0s. The two methods are virtually identical.

- Deviations of a set of proportions from a set of theoretical probabilities may be done using a χ^2 goodness-of-fit test. This test compares observed counts to expected counts, assuming the theoretical probabilities.

- Possible dependence between two qualitative variables may be tested using a χ^2 independence test, also called a test of homogeneity of proportions.

- Dependence within samples can make any of these procedures erroneous. This problem is particularly likely with time series data.

Comparing sets of data is basic to using statistical ideas in management. To decide which of two formulations of a cereal to introduce, a market researcher needs to compare consumer reactions to the two. To decide which parts supplier will receive a contract, a manufacturer needs to compare the quality of samples of the suppliers' goods. To decide which of two telephone systems to purchase, an office manager needs to compare rates for calls to a sample of places. Until now we have discussed basic principles of statistical inference in the context of a single sample. The basic ideas of estimation, confidence intervals, and hypothesis tests have much wider applications. In this chapter, we extend them to deal with comparisons of two samples.

CHAPTER CASE

INTRODUCTION

Circuit Systems, Inc.

Circuit Systems, Inc., located in Northern California, produces integrated circuit boards for the microcomputer industry. In addition to salaried management and office staff, Circuit Systems currently employs about 250 hourly production workers in the actual assembly of the circuit boards. These hourly employees typically work 8 hours per day for 5 days per week and earn an average of $11.00 per hour.

The biggest headache Thomas Nelson, the director of human resources at Circuit Systems, has is hourly employee absenteeism. Each hourly employee is eligible for up to 18 days of paid sick leave per year, but Tom has found that many use most or all of their sick leave well before the year is over. After an informal survey of employee records, Tom is convinced that while most hourly employees make legitimate use of their sick leave, many view paid sick leave as "extra" vacation time and "call in sick" when they want to take off from work. This has been a source of labor–management conflict. In part, the problem is caused by the company's restrictive vacation policy—hourly employees get only 5 days of paid vacation per year in addition to a few paid holidays. With only 5 days of paid vacation and a few paid holidays, employees work a 50-week year, not counting paid sick leave.

To save money and increase productivity, Tom has developed a two-point plan that was recently approved by the president of Circuit Systems. To combat paid sick leave abuse, hourly workers will now be allowed to convert unused paid sick leave to cash on a "three-for-one" basis, that is, each unused sick leave day can be converted into an additional one-third of a day's pay. An hourly employee could earn up to an additional six days of pay each year if no paid sick leave is taken during the year. Even though a worker could gain more time off by dishonestly "phoning in sick," Tom hopes that the majority will view this conversion of sick leave into extra pay as a better alternative. In the second part of his plan, Tom is setting up a voluntary exercise program to improve employees' overall health. At an annual company expense of $200 for each hourly employee who participates, Circuit Systems will pay for membership in a local health club. In return, the participating employee is required to exercise at least three times per week outside of regular working hours. At no cost to Circuit Systems, the company's health insurance carrier has also agreed to reduce the monthly premiums of those who participate in the exercise program and are nonsmokers (or have quit smoking). In fact, in the long term, an investment in employees' physical well-being is expected to substantially reduce the company's contribution to health insurance premiums. In talking with hourly employees, Tom has found that many of them are interested and willing to join.

Many of the supervisors have told Tom that the paid sick leave conversion and the exercise program may help to curb absenteeism, but others did not think so and thought the cost would outweigh any benefits. The president of Circuit Systems agreed to give the proposal a one-year trial. At the end of this period, Tom must evaluate the new antiabsenteeism plan, present the results, and recommend whether to continue or discontinue the plan.

Over the next year, during which time the sick-leave conversion and exercise program are in place, Tom Nelson maintains data on employee absences, use of the sick-leave conversion privilege, participation in the exercise program, and other pertinent information. He has also gone back to collect data from the year prior to starting the new program in order to evaluate the new program.

The collected data are contained in the file Circuit on the CD that came with your book. The file contains data for the past two years on hourly production employees in the company who were with the company for that entire period of time. Figure 9.1 is a partial listing of the data within Excel.

FIGURE 9.1

Partial Listing of the Circuit Systems Data

	A	B	C	D	E
1	Employee	HourlyPay	SickLeaveBefore	SickLeaveAfter	Exercise
2	6631	10.97	3.50	2.00	0
3	7179	11.35	24.00	12.50	0
4	2304	10.75	18.00	12.75	0
5	9819	10.96	21.25	14.00	0
6	4479	10.59	16.50	11.75	0
7	1484	11.41	16.50	9.75	1
8	4203	11.01	10.50	7.00	0
9	2547	10.98	11.50	10.75	0
10	8953	11.98	18.00	12.50	0
11	3953	11.25	6.50	3.25	0
12	9196	11.11	4.50	0.50	1

In the Circuit file, the variables are defined as follows:

Employee: Employee identification number

HourlyPay: Hourly pay of the employee in both years. Unfortunately, due to economic conditions, there were no pay raises last year.

SickLeaveBefore: Actual number of days of sick leave taken by the employee last year before the new program started

SickLeaveAfter: Actual number of days of sick leave taken by the employee this year after the new program started

Exercise: 1, if participating in the exercise program,

0, if not participating

Tom has asked you, the assistant director of human resources, to perform an analysis of the data and recommend whether to continue or discontinue the new absenteeism program. Using the collected data and other information presented in the case, determine if the program is effective in reducing the average cost of absenteeism by hourly employees, thereby increasing worker productivity. In particular, you need to compare this year's data to last year's data. You will find the material covered in this chapter and in the previous chapters to be extremely helpful in your analysis and decision-making process. At the end of this chapter, we will analyze the data to evaluate the effectiveness of the new program. ■

WE DEVELOP METHODS FOR comparison in this chapter. The first section contains confidence intervals and hypothesis tests for comparing two means from independent samples. Then we describe an alternative approach to inference based on ranking data from lowest to highest. Sections 9.3 and 9.4 describe methods for comparison when two samples are based on paired or matched individuals. Sections 9.5 deals with methods for comparing proportions; these methods are extended to tests of proportions from several samples in Section 9.6.

This chapter is an extension of the basic principles we discussed in the last two chapters. The formulas get a little longer, but the basic principles are those we've already described. All the methods discussed in this chapter are carried out by almost every statistical computer package. The key issues for a manager are what method to use and what the results mean.

9.1 Comparing the Means of Two Populations

Comparison is a fundamental component of a manager's job. If we want to ask how much a market research panel likes a new product, we need to compare that product to another one. If we want to assess the effect of production speed on variability of the resulting products, we should compare two (or more) speeds. If we want to look at the effect of tax-auditing procedures for state income taxes, we can compare the results for states with two different auditing methods. Therefore, we begin by considering methods for comparing two samples.

independent versus paired samples

A key distinction for comparing two samples is **independent versus paired samples.** Two samples are paired if each data value in one sample is naturally linked to a specific data value in the other sample by the way the data are gathered. For example, if a panelist rates product A and product B, the A and B samples are paired by rater. If worker output is measured before and after a new computer program is installed, the before and after samples are paired by worker. If there is no pairing, the samples are independent. You can usually sense when samples are paired because it's natural to write down the paired measurements side by side in entering the data. With independent samples, there's no particular reason to write a value from one sample next to a particular value for the other. In this section and the next we deal with independent samples.

The basic principles underlying the statistical methods for two-sample inferences are the same as those developed in the preceding chapters for single-sample inferences. For example, suppose a chain of coffee houses is trying to decide which of two bakers should supply pastries for sale in the chain's outlets. The managers of the chain decide to test the sales appeal of both by putting pastries from baker 1 into some coffee houses and those from baker 2 in others, randomly. They obtain total dollar sales over a two-week period for each outlet. Box plots of the sales data, shown in Figure 9.2, appear reasonably normal.

The following computer output indicates that there are two different confidence intervals for the difference of mean sales. The difference is whether or not the underlying population variances are assumed to be equal. Similarly, there are two different forms of the hypothesis test.

```
              Two-Sample Analysis for Sales by Baker

                        1                2

Sample size            14               23
Mean                   243              259.913       diff. = -16.913
Variance               934.615          258.628       ratio = 3.61374
Std. deviation          30.5715          16.0819
```

FIGURE 9.2   **Pastry Sales for Two Bakers**

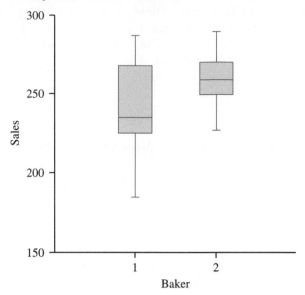

```
95% confidence intervals
mu1 - mu2:(-32.4496,-1.37651) assuming equal variances
mu1 - mu2:(-35.5098,1.68376) not assuming equal variances

                    Hypothesis Test - Difference of Means

Null hypothesis: difference of means = 0
Alternative: not equal
Equal variances assumed: yes

Computed t statistic = -2.20998
            P value = 0.0337

                    Hypothesis Test - Difference of Means

Null hypothesis: difference of means = 0
Alternative: not equal
Equal variances assumed: no

Computed t statistic = -1.91499
            P value = 0.0720
```

The methods are based on assumptions much like those in the previous chapters. We assume that the samples are not biased, that the underlying populations are (more or less) normally distributed, and that the observations are all independent. Because each sample mean is an unbiased estimator of the corresponding population mean, $\bar{Y}_1 - \bar{Y}_2$ is an **unbiased estimator of $\mu_1 - \mu_2$.**

unbiased estimator of $\mu_1 - \mu_2$

$$E(\bar{Y}_1 - \bar{Y}_2) = E(\bar{Y}_1) - E(\bar{Y}_2) = \mu_1 - \mu_2$$

The key to inference problems related to $\mu_1 - \mu_2$ is that the variances (not the standard errors) of $\bar{Y}_1$ and $\bar{Y}_2$ can be added, because the random variables $\bar{Y}_1$ and $\bar{Y}_2$ are independent.

DEFINITION 9.1

Variance of $\bar{Y}_1 - \bar{Y}_2$ for Independent Samples

$$\text{Var}(\bar{Y}_1 - \bar{Y}_2) = \text{Var}(\bar{Y}_1) + \text{Var}(\bar{Y}_2) = \frac{\sigma_1^2}{n_1} + \frac{\sigma_2^2}{n_2}$$

standard error of
$\bar{Y}_1 - \bar{Y}_2$

The true **standard error of $\bar{Y}_1 - \bar{Y}_2$** is

$$\sigma_{\bar{Y}_1 - \bar{Y}_2} = \sqrt{\frac{\sigma_1^2}{n_1} + \frac{\sigma_2^2}{n_2}}$$

assumption of equal
variances

Technically, when the standard deviations are unknown, exact t inferences about $\mu_1 - \mu_2$ based on independent random samples require an additional assumption besides unbiased sampling, independence, and population normality. We also assume that the two unknown population variances are equal: $\sigma_1^2 = \sigma_2^2$. The common unknown variance resulting from this **assumption of equal variances** is designated σ^2. The *sample* variances will not be equal, if only because of random variation. Given the assumption of equal population variances, we must combine the sample variances to estimate the common population variance. Then the confidence interval has the usual form—estimate plus or minus a table value times a standard error. Most computer packages will do the arithmetic.

DEFINITION 9.2

Confidence Interval for $\mu_1 - \mu_2$, σ's Equal

$$\bar{y}_1 - \bar{y}_2 - t_{\alpha/2}s_p\sqrt{\frac{1}{n_1} + \frac{1}{n_2}} \leq \mu_1 - \mu_2 \leq \bar{y}_1 - \bar{y}_2 + t_{\alpha/2}s_p\sqrt{\frac{1}{n_1} + \frac{1}{n_2}}$$

where

$$s_p = \sqrt{\frac{(n_1 - 1)s_1^2 + (n_2 - 1)s_2^2}{n_1 + n_2 - 2}}$$

and

$$\text{d.f.} = n_1 + n_2 - 2$$

Note: This procedure can be used for all sample sizes.

pooled variance

The pooled standard deviation, s_p, in the confidence interval for $\mu_1 - \mu_2$ is an estimate of the common population standard deviation σ and is formed by combining information from the two independent samples. The two estimates s_1^2 and s_2^2 are weighted by their respective degrees of freedom to form the **pooled variance, s_p^2**. For the special case in which the sample sizes are the same ($n_1 = n_2$), the formula for s_p^2 reduces to $s_p^2 = (s_1^2 + s_2^2)/2$, the average of the two sample variances. The degrees of freedom for s_p^2 combine the degrees of freedom for s_1^2 and s_2^2; d.f. $= (n_1 - 1) + (n_2 - 1) = n_1 + n_2 - 2$.

EXAMPLE 9.1

A taxicab company wants to test two programs for improving the gasoline mileage of its drivers. Under program A, drivers are assigned a target mileage and receive modest bonuses for better performance. Under program B, drivers are allowed a maximum monthly quota of gasoline; if it runs out, a driver has to pay for extra gasoline out of pocket. All taxis used are standard models and they are given standard maintenance. After three months, each driver's mileage per gallon is calculated. The data are as follows:

A: 15.9   17.5   19.1   16.9   18.3   17.3   17.0   16.2   16.8   17.1
B: 16.1   15.8   15.3   16.5   14.9   15.5   16.4   16.0   16.7   17.2

Minitab output yielded the following results:

```
Two-sample T for Mileage

Program     N      Mean      StDev   SE Mean
A          10    17.210     0.937     0.30
B          10    16.040     0.693     0.22


Difference = mu (A) - mu (B)
Estimate for difference:  1.170
95% CI for difference: (0.40, 1.94)
T-Test of difference = 0 (vs not =): T-Value = 3.17   P-Value = 0.0053   DF = 18
Both use Pooled StDev = 0.824
```

Locate the 95% confidence interval for the difference in mean gasoline mileage. Verify the calculation.

SOLUTION   The confidence interval is shown as (0.40, 1.94).

Program	Mean	Variance	Standard Deviation	Sample Size
A	17.21	.8788	.9374	10
B	16.04	.4804	.6931	10

The required table value for a 95% confidence interval with $10 + 10 - 2 = 18$ d.f. is $t_{.025}$; from Appendix Table 4, $t_{.025} = 2.101$. The pooled sample variance is

$$s_p^2 = \frac{9(.8788) + 9(.4804)}{18} = .6796$$

so

$$s_p = \sqrt{.6796} = .8244$$

The confidence interval is

$$(17.21 - 16.04) - 2.101(.8244)\sqrt{\frac{1}{10} + \frac{1}{10}}$$

$$\le \mu_A - \mu_B \le (17.21 - 16.04) + 2.101(.8244)\sqrt{\frac{1}{10} + \frac{1}{10}}$$

or

$$.40 \le \mu_A - \mu_B \le 1.94$$

The corresponding t test for comparing μ_1 and μ_2, based on independent samples with the standard deviations unknown, is summarized here.

DEFINITION 9.3

Hypothesis Test for $\mu_1 - \mu_2$, σ's Equal

H_0: $\mu_1 - \mu_2 = D_0$ (D_0 is specified; often $D_0 = 0$)

H_a: 1. $\mu_1 - \mu_2 > D_0$
 2. $\mu_1 - \mu_2 < D_0$
 3. $\mu_1 - \mu_2 \neq D_0$

T.S.: $t = \dfrac{(\bar{y}_1 - \bar{y}_2) - D_0}{s_p\sqrt{\dfrac{1}{n_1} + \dfrac{1}{n_2}}}$

R.R.: 1. $t > t_\alpha$
 2. $t < -t_\alpha$
 3. $|t| > t_{\alpha/2}$

where t_a cuts off a right-tail area a for the t distribution with $n_1 + n_2 - 2$ d.f.

Note: This method can be used for all sample sizes.

EXAMPLE 9.2

Refer to Example 9.1 and the Minitab output shown there. Verify the calculations to test the research hypothesis that program A yields a higher mean mileage than program B. Use $\alpha = .10$.

SOLUTION   The output shows a t statistic equal to 3.17 and a two-tailed p-value of .0053. The one-tailed p-value should be about .0027; thus the research hypothesis is supported.

H_0: $\mu_A - \mu_B = 0$

H_a: $\mu_A - \mu_B > 0$

T.S.: $t = \dfrac{(\bar{y}_A - \bar{y}_B) - 0}{s_p\sqrt{\dfrac{1}{n_1} + \dfrac{1}{n_2}}} = \dfrac{(17.21 - 16.04)}{.8244\sqrt{\dfrac{1}{10} + \dfrac{1}{10}}} = 3.17$

R.R.: Reject H_0 if $t > t_{.10,\,18\,\text{d.f.}} = 1.330$

Conclusion: Because $t = 3.17 > 1.33$, the mean mileage under A is significantly greater than under B based on $\alpha = .10$. In fact, because H_0 can be rejected at $\alpha = .01(t_{.01,18} = 2.552)$, the p-value is less than .01.

The two-sample t test and confidence interval are based on several mathematical assumptions. Once again, these assumptions are not exactly satisfied in practice. We assume that the samples are taken without bias. Sometimes, managers note that a bias in taking one sample will also be present when taking the other sample, and the biases will cancel out. That's a legitimate hope, but it would certainly be better to take both samples without bias in the first place. Consider whether the biases built into taking the data favor one situation over the other.

Assuming no serious bias, the most crucial assumption is the independence of the two samples, both within samples and between samples. Once again, dependence within samples will result in a smaller effective sample size than is indicated in the output. Now we must also be concerned with dependence between the two samples.

The assumption is that the two samples were taken completely at random. If this assumption is not valid, the procedures can be grossly erroneous. If the samples are taken randomly from different populations, and if there is no connection between the elements of one sample and those of the other, the **independence assumption** should be valid. But if the two measurements are taken on the same elements at different times or if there is any connection between elements of the samples, the two-sample t test is not appropriate and other methods of analysis must be used. For example, if one sample represents measurements on product awareness for individuals before an advertising campaign and the second sample represents measurements of product awareness on these same individuals after advertising exposure, the two-sample t test is not appropriate. The paired-sample procedures of Sections 9.3 and 9.4 should be used to compare the difference in mean awareness before and after.

independence assumption

normality assumption

The **normality assumption**—that both populations are normally distributed—is less crucial because of the Central Limit Theorem. Even if the populations are not normal, the sampling distributions of $\bar{Y}_1$ and $\bar{Y}_2$ are approximately normal for modestly large sample sizes. Moderate population skewness is not a serious problem. If both populations are skewed in the same direction, the fact that we are dealing with a difference in means tends to make the sampling distribution of $\bar{Y}_1 - \bar{Y}_2$ more symmetric. In effect, the skewness will cancel when we take the difference. Generally, if $n_1 + n_2$ is at least 30 or so, we are confident of the t probabilities. Of course, with small samples, confidence intervals are wide and β probabilities high. The point is that the t probabilities are reasonably accurate. A nonparametric alternative to the two-sample t test (called Wilcoxon's rank sum test) that does not require normality of the two populations is discussed in Section 9.2.

equal variance assumption

The new **equal variance assumption** is that of equal population variances; even though two *population* variances are equal, the *sample* variances differ because of random variation. Many studies have been made of the effect of unequal population variances. The universal conclusion is that for *equal* sample sizes, even substantial differences in variances (such as $\sigma_1^2 = 3\sigma_2^2$) have remarkably little effect. The most dangerous situation is one in which a larger population variance is associated with a smaller sample size. If n_1 is only half the size of n_2 but σ_1^2 is, say, twice σ_2^2, the usual t probabilities may be seriously in error. The best cure for this problem is to take equal sample sizes. When the sample variances (s_1^2 and s_2^2) suggest that there may be a problem in assuming that the two population variances are equal, we can modify the usual t statistic to obtain an approximate t test or t confidence interval. Welch (1938) showed that the distribution of the statistic

$$t' = \frac{\bar{y}_1 - \bar{y}_2}{\sqrt{\dfrac{s_1^2}{n_1} + \dfrac{s_2^2}{n_2}}}$$

can be approximated by a t distribution using approximate degrees of freedom.

DEFINITION 9.4

t' Statistic; Independent Samples

1. $H_0: \mu_1 - \mu_2 = 0$
2. The test statistic is

$$t' = \frac{\bar{y}_1 - \bar{y}_2}{\sqrt{(s_1^2/n_1) + (s_2^2/n_2)}}$$

3. The rejection region for t' can be obtained from Appendix Table 4 for

$$\text{d.f.} = \frac{(n_1 - 1)(n_2 - 1)}{(n_2 - 1)c^2 + (1 - c)^2(n_1 - 1)}$$

where

$$c = \frac{s_1^2/n_1}{(s_1^2/n_1) + (s_2^2/n_2)}$$

separate variance *t* test

unequal variance *t* test

The test based on the t' statistic is sometimes referred to as the **separate variance *t* test** or the **unequal variance *t* test.** The statistic replaces each population variance (σ_1^2 and σ_2^2) with the separate sample variances s_1^2 and s_2^2.

EXAMPLE 9.3

A firm has a generous but rather complicated policy concerning end-of-year bonuses for its lower-level managerial personnel. The policy's key factor is a subjective judgment of "contribution to corporate goals." A personnel officer takes samples of 24 female and 36 male managers to see if there is evidence of any differences in average bonuses, expressed as a percentage of yearly salary. The data are listed next.

Gender	Bonus Percentage								
F	9.2	7.7	11.9	6.2	9.0	8.4	6.9	7.6	7.4
	8.0	9.9	6.7	8.4	9.3	9.1	8.7	9.2	9.1
	8.4	9.6	7.7	9.0	9.0	8.4			
M	10.4	8.9	11.7	12.0	8.7	9.4	9.8	9.0	9.2
	9.7	9.1	8.8	7.9	9.9	10.0	10.1	9.0	11.4
	8.7	9.6	9.2	9.7	8.9	9.2	9.4	9.7	8.9
	9.3	10.4	11.9	9.0	12.0	9.6	9.2	9.9	9.0

The Excel spreadsheet program yields the following output:

```
t-Test: Two-Sample Assuming Equal Variances

                                  Female      Male
Mean                            8.533333   9.683333
Variance                        1.413623   1.007714
Observations                          24         36
Pooled Variance                 1.168678
Hypothesized Mean Difference           0
df                                    58
t Stat                          -4.03675
P(T<=t) one-tail                8.04E-05
t Critical one-tail             1.671553
P(T<=t) two-tail                0.000161
t Critical two-tail             2.001716


t-Test: Two-Sample Assuming Unequal Variances

                                  Female      Male
Mean                            8.533333   9.683333
Variance                        1.413623   1.007714
Observations                          24         36
```

```
Hypothesized Mean Difference        0
df                                  44
t Stat                        -3.90126
P(T<=t) one-tail              0.000162
t Critical one-tail            1.68023
P(T<=t) two-tail              0.000324
t Critical two-tail           2.015367
```

a. Identify the value of the pooled-variance t statistic.

b. Identify the value of the t' statistic.

c. Use both statistics to test the research hypothesis of unequal means at $\alpha = .05$ and at $\alpha = .01$. Does the conclusion depend on which statistic is used?

SOLUTION

a. The pooled-variance statistic is shown under "Assuming Equal Variances" as $t = -4.03675$.

b. The "Assuming Unequal Variances" t statistic is $t' = -3.90126$.

c. In both cases, the p-value is much smaller than α, so the null hyptheses is conclusively rejected.

   Alternatively, we can construct a rejection region. The t statistic based on the pooled variance has d.f. $= 24 + 36 - 2 = 58$. For a two-sided H_a, we reject H_0 at $\alpha = .05$ if $|t| > t_{.025} \approx 2.00$ (as shown in the output); with $\alpha = .01$, reject if $|t| > t_{.005} \approx 2.66$. Because $|t| = 4.037$, we can easily reject H_0 even at $\alpha = .01$. For the t' statistic based on separate variances the degrees of freedom can be computed using the formula

$$\text{d.f.} = \frac{(n_1 - 1)(n_2 - 1)}{(n_2 - 1)c^2 + (1 - c)^2(n_1 - 1)}, \qquad \text{with } c = \frac{s_1^2/n_1}{(s_1^2/n_1) + (s_2^2/n_2)}$$

For these data,

$$c = \frac{1.4136/24}{1.4136/24 + 1.0077/36} = \frac{.0589}{.0589 + .0280} = .6778$$

and

$$c^2 = .4594, \qquad (1 - c)^2 = .1038$$

Then,

$$\text{d.f.} = \frac{23(35)}{35(.4594) + .1038(23)}$$

$$= \frac{805}{16.0790 + 2.3876}$$

$$= \frac{805}{18.4671} = 43.59$$

Rounding down to the nearest integer, d.f. $= 43$. (The output shows 44 d.f.; the difference isn't important.) For a two-sided research hypothesis and $\alpha = .05$, we reject H_0 if $|t'| > t_{.025,43} \approx 2.02$. For $\alpha = .01$ we reject H_0 if $|t'| > t_{.005,43} =$

2.70. Because $|t'| = 3.90$, we can easily reject H_0 even at $\alpha = .01$. The conclusions from the t and t' tests are essentially the same and the research hypothesis is quite conclusively supported.

We have presented two slightly different approaches. In this section we developed pooled-variance t methods based on an assumption of equal population variances. In addition, we introduced the t' statistic for an approximate t test when the variances are not equal. Confidence intervals and hypothesis tests based on these different procedures (t or t') need not give identical results. Standard computer packages often report the results of both the pooled-variance and separate-variance t tests. Which should a manager believe?

The choice depends on the evidence about underlying assumptions. If plots of each sample appear roughly normal, and if the sample variances are roughly equal, the pooled-variance t test should be valid and most efficient. If plots of each sample are normal but the sample variances are clearly different (especially if the sample sizes differ), the separate-variance t' test is more believable. If the sample sizes are equal, the pooled-variance and separate-variance t tests will usually give the same results; in fact, the test statistics are algebraically equal for equal sample sizes. But if the data in one or both samples are obviously nonnormal, the rank sum approach discussed in the next section is preferred. As usual, a little thought and some careful looks at the data will let a manager make a reasonable choice.

EXAMPLE 9.4   A simulation study involves 1000 samples taken from two independent, normal populations. Both population means equalled 50. The first population has $\sigma = 14.1421$; the second, $\sigma = 10$. The sample sizes are $n_1 = 10$ and $n_2 = 20$. At $\alpha = .10$, two-tailed, using the pooled-variance t test, H_0 was rejected 70 times, indicating that the first mean was higher, and an additional 71 times, indicating the second mean was higher. For the t' test, the corresponding numbers were 44 and 41. What do these results indicate about the choice of pooled-variance t versus t'?

SOLUTION   One of the assumptions underlying the pooled-variance t test has been violated; the population variances aren't equal. In addition, the sample sizes aren't equal, and the larger sample size is associated with the smaller variance. The null hypothesis is true because the population means are equal. The pooled-variance t test rejects the null hypothesis more frequently than the nominal α value would indicate. For example, for a nominal $\alpha/2$ of .05, we would expect 50 and 50 rejections, but we get 70 and 71 rejections. The t' test rejects the null hypothesis just about as often as α indicates, or perhaps slightly less often. If anything, the t' method is conservative in making too few false positive errors.

Exercises

9.1   A processor of recycled aluminum cans is concerned about the levels of impurities (principally other metals) contained in lots from two sources. Laboratory analysis of sample lots yields the following data (kilograms of impurities per hundred kilograms of product):

Source I: 3.8   3.5   4.1   2.5   3.6   4.3   2.1   2.9   3.2   3.7   2.8   2.7
(mean = 3.267, standard deviation = .676)

Source II: 1.8   2.2   1.3   5.1   4.0   4.7   3.3   4.3   4.2   2.5   5.4   4.6
(mean = 3.617, standard deviation = 1.365)

Minitab output follows:

```
Two-sample T for Impurity

Source       N       Mean      StDev    SE Mean
I           12       3.267     0.676      0.20
II          12       3.62      1.37       0.39


Difference = mu (I)  - mu (II)
Estimate for difference:  -0.350
95% CI for difference: (-1.262, 0.562)
T-Test of difference = 0 (vs not =): T-Value = -0.80   P-Value = 0.435   DF = 22
Both use Pooled StDev = 1.08

Two-sample T for Impurity

Source       N       Mean      StDev    SE Mean
I           12       3.267     0.676      0.20
II          12       3.62      1.37       0.39


Difference = mu (I )  - mu (II)
Estimate for difference:  -0.350
95% CI for difference: (-1.282, 0.582)
T-Test of difference = 0 (vs not =): T-Value = -0.80   P-Value = 0.438   DF = 16
```

a. Locate a 95% confidence interval for the difference in mean impurity levels, assuming equal variances. Do the same without assuming equal variances. How much of a difference does it make which interval is used?

b. Can the processor conclude, using $\alpha = .05$, that there is a nonzero difference in means?

9.2   Examine the plots of the impurities data in Figure 9.3. Which of the assumptions (if any) of the t test seem suspect? Do you think there is serious reason to doubt the conclusion?

9.3   A large insurance company wants to estimate the difference between the average amount of term life insurance and the average amount of whole life insurance purchased by families. One of the company's actuaries randomly selected 27 families who have term life insurance only and 22 families who have whole life policies only. Each sample is taken from families in which the head of household is less than 45 years old. For the whole-life families, the average amount was $145,000 and the standard deviation was $15,500. For the term-life families, the average amount was $175,000 and the standard deviation was $22,000. Assuming that life insurance amounts are normally distributed for both whole and term life families, construct a 95% confidence interval for the true difference in the mean insurance amounts of the two populations. What conclusion can you reach based on your confidence interval?

9.4   In a computer simulation study, 1000 samples were taken from each of two populations. Both populations were normal, and both populations had means equal to 50. The first population had a standard deviation of 20; the second had a standard deviation of 10. The first sample size was 5; the second sample size was 20. The null hypothesis of equal means was

FIGURE 9.3 **Box Plots for Impurities Data**

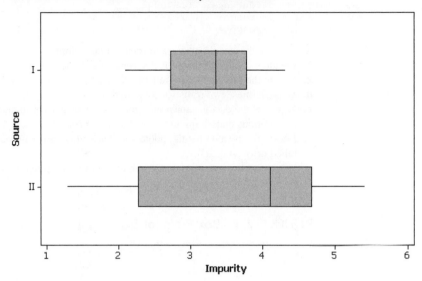

rejected at $\alpha = .05$ in 203 of the samples, using the pooled-variance t test; this hypothesis was rejected, again at $\alpha = .05$, in 48 samples using the t' test.

a. Should the pooled-variance t test or the t' test be better in this situation? What does "better" mean?

b. Does the computer simulation result confirm your judgment in part (a)?

9.5 Company officials are concerned about the length of time a particular drug retains its potency. A random sample (sample 1) of 10 bottles of the product is drawn from current production and analyzed for potency. A second sample (sample 2) is obtained, stored for one year, and then analyzed. The readings obtained are

Sample 1: 10.2 10.5 10.3 10.8 9.8 10.6 10.7 10.2 10.0 10.6
Sample 2:   9.8   9.6 10.1 10.2 10.1 9.7   9.5   9.6   9.8   9.9

The relevant Minitab output follows:

```
Two-Sample T-Test and CI: Potency, Sample

Two-sample T for Potency

Sample   N    Mean   StDev   SE Mean
1        10   10.370  0.323    0.10
2        10    9.830  0.241    0.076


Difference = mu (1) - mu (2)
Estimate for difference:  0.540000
95% CI for difference:  (0.272230, 0.807770)
T-Test of difference = 0 (vs not =): T-Value = 4.24   P-Value = 0.000   DF = 18
Both use Pooled StDev = 0.2850

Two-Sample T-Test and CI: Potency, Sample

Two-sample T for Potency

Sample   N    Mean   StDev   SE Mean
1        10   10.370  0.323    0.10
2        10    9.830  0.241    0.076
```

```
Difference = mu (1) - mu (2)
Estimate for difference:  0.540000
95% CI for difference:  (0.269810, 0.810190)
T-Test of difference = 0 (vs not =): T-Value = 4.24  P-Value = 0.001  DF = 16
```

a. Identify the sample means and standard deviations.
b. Locate the value of the pooled-variance t statistic.
c. Locate the value of the t' statistic.
d. Why are these two statistics equal in this case?
e. A plot of the data is shown in Figure 9.4. Does it seem there are serious violations of the assumptions underlying the pooled-variance test?
f. Locate the p-value for the pooled-variance t test in the output of this exercise. Is it one-tailed or two-tailed?
g. What conclusion would you reach concerning the possibility of a decrease in mean potency over one year?

FIGURE 9.4 **Box Plots for Exercise 9.5**

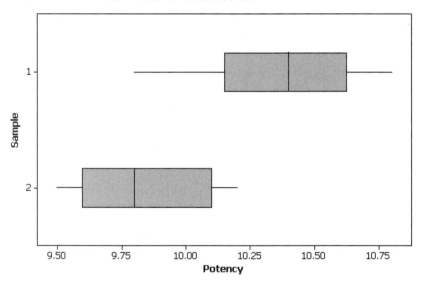

9.6 To compare the performance of two spreadsheet programs, teams of three students each choose whatever spreadsheet program they wish. Each team is given the same set of standard accounting and finance problems to solve. The time (minutes) required for each team to solve the set of problems is recorded. The following data and Minitab output are obtained for the two most widely used programs:

Program	Time										$\bar{y}$	s	n
A	39	57	42	53	41	44	71	56	49	63	51.50	10.46	10
B	43	38	35	45	40	28	50	54	37	29			
	36	27	52	33	31	30					38.00	8.67	16

```
Two-sample T for Time

Program     N      Mean     StDev    SE Mean
A          10      51.5      10.5        3.3
B          16     38.00      8.67        2.2
```

```
Difference = mu (A) - mu (B)
Estimate for difference:  13.50
95% CI for difference: (5.69, 21.31)
T-Test of difference = 0 (vs not =): T-Value = 3.57  P-Value = 0.002  DF = 24
Both use Pooled StDev = 9.38

Two-sample T for Time

Program     N      Mean     StDev   SE Mean
A          10      51.5      10.5      3.3
B          16     38.00      8.67      2.2


Difference = mu (A) - mu (B)
Estimate for difference:  13.50
95% CI for difference: (5.12, 21.88)
T-Test of difference = 0 (vs not =): T-Value = 3.41  P-Value = 0.004  DF = 16
```

a. Locate the pooled standard deviation.
b. Find a 95% confidence interval for the difference of population means, assuming equal variances.
c. According to this interval, can the null hypothesis of equal means be rejected at $\alpha = .01$?
d. Redo parts (b) and (c) using a separate-variance (t') method. Which method is more appropriate in this case? How critical is it which method is used?

9.7 A market research firm supplies manufacturers with estimates of the retail sales of their products based on samples of retail stores. A simple random sample of 75 stores this month shows mean sales of 52.1 units of a small appliance and a standard deviation of 13.2 units. During the same month last year, a simple random sample of 58 stores gave mean sales of 48.9 units and a standard deviation of 11.1 units.

a. Compute a 95% confidence interval for the increase in the average number of units sold at all retail stores from last year to this year.
b. The marketing manager is happy because the data indicate that sales are up 6.5% over last year. Briefly explain in language the manager can understand why he can or cannot be confident that the actual average sales of the small appliance rose by 6.5%.

9.8 A computer manufacturer uses microcomputer chips from two different sources. As part of quality-control testing, the manufacturer obtains data on the rate of defective chips per thousand for each lot of chips. The following results and Excel output are obtained; note that the rate is not necessarily an integer number because the lot sizes are not exactly 1000 chips per lot.

Source	Number of Defectives/1000									
I	9.8	9.9	10.2	10.5	10.7	10.8	11.7	13.9	19.2	27.6
II	10.6	11.0	11.5	11.8	11.9	12.7	14.2	16.8	21.7	29.9

```
t-Test: Two-Sample Assuming Equal Variances

                              Source_I Source_II
Mean                            13.43     15.21
Variance                      32.92456   38.121
Observations                       10        10
Pooled Variance               35.52278
Hypothesized Mean Difference        0
df                                 18
t Stat                       -0.66781
P(T<=t) one-tail              0.256364
t Critical one-tail          1.734063
P(T<=t) two-tail             0.512728
t Critical two-tail          2.100924
```

```
t-Test: Two-Sample Assuming Unequal Variances

                                Source_I  Source_II
Mean                              13.43     15.21
Variance                         32.92456  38.121
Observations                        10        10
Hypothesized Mean Difference         0
df                                  18
t Stat                           -0.66781
P(T<=t) one-tail                  0.256364
t Critical one-tail               1.734063
P(T<=t) two-tail                  0.512728
t Critical two-tail               2.100924
```

a. What are the means and standard deviations for each source? Which source appears to be better?

b. Locate the pooled-variance t statistic for testing the null hypothesis of equal means.

c. Explain why t and t' are equal for these data.

d. Can the null hypothesis in Exercise 9.8 be rejected at $\alpha = .05$ in favor of a two-sided research hypothesis? Use the pooled-variance t statistic. State the p-value.

e. Based on this output, is there clear evidence that one source is better than the other? Explain your answer.

9.9 A television manufacturer is currently dual-sourcing its supply of a certain component from suppliers A and B. Management has decided to go with a single source if either A or B is more efficient in delivering the components. Over a period of four months, each supplier is given 30 orders to fill and the delivery times are recorded. Supplier A responded with an average delivery time of 4.2 days and a standard deviation of 1.3 days. Supplier B had an average of 5.8 days and a standard deviation of 1.7 days. Construct a 99% confidence interval for the true average difference in delivery times for the two suppliers. Which supplier should the manufacturer choose? Why?

9.2 A Nonparametric Test: The Wilcoxon Rank Sum Test

The two-sample t test we described in the previous section is based on several mathematical assumptions. In particular, we assume that both populations have normal distributions with equal variances. When the assumptions are not satisfied, the t test may still be valid, in the sense that the nominal probabilities are approximately correct, particularly if the sample sizes are large and equal. Even so, there is another hypothesis-testing method that requires weaker mathematical assumptions, is almost as powerful when the t assumptions are satisfied, and is more powerful in other situations. We describe this test, called the *Wilcoxon rank sum test,* in this section.

The mathematical assumption for this test is that independent random samples are taken from two populations; the null hypothesis is that the two population distributions are identical (but not necessarily normal). The Wilcoxon rank sum test probabilities are exactly correct for any two populations with identical continuous distributions and are generally slightly conservative (committing slightly fewer false positive errors than the claimed α would indicate) for two populations with identical discrete distributions.

The test is based on the ranks of the sample data values. The rank of an individual observation is its position in the combined sample: Rank 1 indicates the smallest value, rank 2 indicates the next smallest value, and so on. As the phrase *rank sum test* indicates, the Wilcoxon rank sum test is based on the sum of the ranks in either sample. Under the null hypothesis of identical population distributions, the sum of the ranks in one sample is proportional to the sample size. If one population is shifted to the right of another, that is, if the first population tends to yield larger observations, the rank sum for the first sample tends to be large. Of course, a small rank sum for the first sample indicates that the first population is shifted to the left of the second. Define T to be the sum of the ranks in the first sample. Under the null hypothesis, the expected value and variance of T have been determined:

$$\mu_T = \frac{n_1(n_1 + n_2 + 1)}{2}, \qquad \sigma_T^2 = \frac{n_1 n_2}{12}(n_1 + n_2 + 1)$$

If both n_1 and n_2 are 10 or larger, the sampling distribution of T is approximately normal. This allows use of a z statistic in testing the hypothesis of equal distributions.

DEFINITION 9.5

Wilcoxon Rank Sum Test

H_0: The two populations are identical

H_a: 1. Population 1 is shifted to the right of population 2
2. Population 1 is shifted to the left of population 2
3. Population 1 is shifted to the right or left of population 2

T.S.: $z = \dfrac{T - \mu_T}{\sigma_T}$

where T denotes the rank sum for sample 1

R.R.: 1. $z > z_\alpha$
2. $z < -z_\alpha$
3. $|z| > z_{\alpha/2}$

Note: The normal approximation is reasonably accurate if $n_1 \geq 10$ and $n_2 \geq 10$. Special tables are available for smaller values of n_1 and n_2 (for example, Hollander and Wolfe, 1999).

EXAMPLE 9.5

Perform a rank sum test for Example 9.1. Compare to the following Minitab output:*

```
MTB > Mann-Whitney 95.0 'Program1' 'Program2'.

Mann-Whitney Confidence Interval and Test

Program1   N =  10    Median =      17.050
Program2   N =  10    Median =      16.050
Point estimate for ETA1-ETA2 is     1.050
95.5 Percent C.I. for ETA1-ETA2 is (0.399,1.900)
W = 141.0
Test of ETA1 = ETA2  vs.  ETA1 not = ETA2 is significant at 0.0073
```

*The Wilcoxon rank sum test is equivalent to the Mann–Whitney test procedure used in Minitab. Minitab reports the value of the rank sum statistic as W along with a *p*-value.

SOLUTION Minitab shows the rank sum as W = 141.0 and the *p*-value as 0.0073.

To do the analysis by hand, the first step is to rank the observations. It helps in doing the ranking to order the values in each sample from lowest to highest.

					Program A					
Value:	15.9	16.2	16.8	16.9	17.0	17.1	17.3	17.5	18.3	19.1
Rank:	5	8	12	13	14	15	17	18	19	20

					Program B					
Value:	14.9	15.3	15.5	15.8	16.0	16.1	16.4	16.5	16.7	17.2
Rank:	1	2	3	4	6	7	9	10	11	16

The sum of the ranks in the A sample is

$$T = 5 + 8 + \cdots + 20 = 141$$

Under the null hypothesis

$$\mu_T = \frac{10(10 + 10 + 1)}{2} = 105$$

$$\sigma_T^2 = \frac{(10)(10)}{12}(10 + 10 + 1) = 175$$

$$\sigma_T = \sqrt{175} = 13.23$$

So

$$z = \frac{T - \mu_T}{\sigma_T} = \frac{141 - 105}{13.23} = 2.72$$

In Example 9.1, the research hypothesis H_a was that the mean for program A was larger than the mean for program B. The corresponding research hypothesis for the rank sum test is that the program A distribution is shifted to the right of the program B distribution. This research hypothesis is supported and the null hypothesis is rejected if T (and therefore z) is too large to be attributed to chance. The one-tailed *p*-value for $z = 2.72$ is .0033, so the null hypothesis is rejected for $\alpha = .10, .05, .01$, or even .005. The calculated *p*-value differs from the one shown in the output, which corrects for the fact that the rank sum is a discrete quantity that doesn't take on fractional values. As $n_1 = n_2 = 10$, we are barely within the adequacy range of the normal approximation. It is conceivable that the real *p*-value is a bit larger than .0033, but still the null hypothesis should be rejected at any conventional α level.

EXAMPLE 9.6

Refer to the following computer output for Example 9.3.

```
Mann-Whitney Test and CI: Bonus_F, Bonus_M

          N   Median
Bonus_F   24  8.5500
Bonus_M   36  9.4000
```

```
Point estimate for ETA1-ETA2 is -1.0000
95.1 Percent CI for ETA1-ETA2 is (-1.6002,-0.5001)
W = 481.0
Test of ETA1 = ETA2 vs ETA1 not = ETA2 is significant at 0.0002
The test is significant at 0.0002 (adjusted for ties)
```

a. Identify the value of the rank sum statistic.

b. State an approximate two-tailed p-value for the test in part (b).

c. How does the conclusion of this test compare with that found in Example 9.3?

SOLUTION

a. The sum is 481.0.

b. The p-value is shown as 0.0002.

c. As in Example 9.3, we have conclusive support for the research hypothesis.

ties

The theory behind the rank sum test assumes that the population distributions are continuous, so there is zero probability that two observations are exactly equal. In practice, there are often **ties**—two or more equal observations. Each observation in a set of tied values is assigned the average of the ranks for the set. If two observations are tied for ranks 2 and 3, each is given rank 2.5; the next larger value gets rank 4, and so on. There is a correction to the variance formula for the case of tied ranks (see Ott and Longnecker, 2001). The preceding variance formula is generally conservative and usually very close, unless there are many, many ties.

The Wilcoxon rank sum test is a direct competitor of the two-sample t test. Both tests are sensitive to differences in location (mean or median) as opposed to dispersion or spread. In most situations, the two tests give the same basic conclusion, so it doesn't matter which test is used. The rank sum test requires fewer assumptions than the t test (in particular, it does not assume population normality), but it uses less information from the data; only ordering information is relevant to the rank sum test.* When the assumptions underlying the t test are close to correct, the t test is better. Both theoretical results and simulations clearly indicate that a t test (using the pooled variance if the sample variances are roughly equal or if the sample sizes are roughly equal, but separate variances if neither variances nor sample sizes are equal) will have correct α values and optimal power for normal populations. For obviously nonnormal data, the rank sum test has a more believable α value (especially for small samples) and it usually has better power.

EXAMPLE 9.7

To investigate the effect of skewness on the pooled-variance t test as well as the rank sum test, 1000 samples are drawn from two squared-exponential populations; this type of population is extremely right-skewed. Both population means are 50; both standard deviations were 10. The sample sizes were 5 and 25, respectively. At a nominal $\alpha = .05$, one-tailed, the pooled-variance t test rejects the null hypothesis of

---

*Therefore, the rank sum test can be used when the observations are qualitative and ordinal, as when 1 = strongly opposed, 2 = opposed, 3 = neutral, and so on.

equal means in favor of H_a: $\mu_1 > \mu_2$ 95 times. The rank sum test rejected the null hypothesis of identical distributions in favor of H_a: first population tends to be larger than the second, 37 times. What do the results indicate about the effect of skewness on the two tests?

SOLUTION   The null hypothesis is true in this simulation; both means are 50. The actual number of rejections of the null hypothesis by the t test is far from what is indicated by the nominal α value for one-tailed probabilities. The rank sum test, which doesn't assume normal populations, appears to be rejecting the null hypothesis the correct number of times (or even less).

EXAMPLE 9.8

A simulation study investigating the effect of outliers on the t and rank sum tests involves independent samples from Laplace (mildly outlier-prone) populations. One part of the study has both population means equal; a second part involves different means. When the means (and variances) are equal, both the pooled-variance t and the rank sum test rejected the null hypothesis (at $\alpha = .05$, one-tailed) 47 times out of 1000. When the first mean was 50, the second mean was 60, and both standard deviations were 10, the pooled-variance t test rejected H_0: $\mu_1 = \mu_2$ 986 times, and the rank sum test rejected it 998 times. What do these results indicate about the choice of the t or rank sum test when the populations are outlier-prone?

SOLUTION   The results for both tests when the null hypothesis is true indicate that the nominal α is (very close to) correct. The simulation obtained just about the expected number of false rejections. When the research hypothesis is true, as in the second part of the study, we want to reject the null hypothesis. The rank sum test yielded more rejections than did the t test. The rank sum test is more powerful in this situation.

Exercises

9.10   The computer package used in Exercise 9.5 also calculated rank sums. The relevant output follows:

```
Mann-Whitney Test and CI: Potency_1, Potency_2

            N  Median
Potency_1  10  10.400
Potency_2  10   9.800

Point estimate for ETA1-ETA2 is 0.550
95.5 Percent CI for ETA1-ETA2 is (0.200,0.900)
W = 146.0
Test of ETA1 = ETA2 vs ETA1 not = ETA2 is significant at 0.0022
The test is significant at 0.0021 (adjusted for ties)
```

a. Identify the rank sum statistic.
b. Formulate appropriate null and research hypotheses.
c. Is H_a supported at $\alpha = .01$?

9.11   Refer to Exercise 9.10.

a. Locate the p-value in the output. Is it one-tailed or two-tailed? What p-value should be reported in Exercise 9.10?

b. What conclusion would be reached in using the rank sum test? How does it compare to the conclusion of the t test ($t = 4.24$, p-value .0005)? Does it matter much which test is used?

9.12   The data for Exercise 9.6 are reproduced here:

Program	Time										$\bar{y}$	s	n
A	39	57	42	53	41	44	71	56	49	63	51.50	10.46	10
B	43	38	35	45	40	28	50	54	37	29			
	36	27	52	33	31	30					38.00	8.67	16

```
Two-sample T for Time

Program     N       Mean      StDev    SE Mean
A          10       51.5       10.5        3.3
B          16      38.00       8.67        2.2

Difference = mu (A) - mu (B)
Estimate for difference:  13.50
99% CI for difference: (2.92, 24.08)
T-Test of difference = 0 (vs not =): T-Value = 3.57   P-Value = 0.002   DF = 24
Both use Pooled StDev = 9.38

Mann-Whitney Test and CI: Time_A, Time_B

Time_A    N =  10     Median =       51.00
Time_B    N =  16     Median =       36.50
Point estimate for ETA1-ETA2 is       13.00
99.1 Percent CI for ETA1-ETA2 is (2.00,26.00)
W = 191.0
Test of ETA1 = ETA2  vs  ETA1 not = ETA2 is significant at 0.0034
```

a. Find the ranks of the combined data. It's much easier if you sort the data in each sample first.

b. Verify that the sum of ranks in the first sample is 191.

c. Is there a statistically significant difference ($\alpha = .01$) between programs according to the rank sum test?

9.13   Do the data of Exercise 9.6 (and 9.12) indicate that the rank sum test is preferable to a t test? Explain, preferably with pictures.

9.14   The data of Exercise 9.8 are as follows:

Source	Number of Defectives/1000									
I	9.8	9.9	10.2	10.5	10.7	10.8	11.7	13.9	19.2	27.6
II	10.6	11.0	11.5	11.8	11.9	12.7	14.2	16.8	21.7	29.9

a. Use a rank test to test the null hypothesis that both sources have the same distribution of defectives per 1000. Use $\alpha = .05$ and a two-sided research hypothesis.

b. Find the two-tailed p-value.

9.15   Is there reason to think that a rank test is more appropriate than a t test for the data of Exercise 9.8 (and 9.14)?

9.3 Paired-Sample Methods

The methods of the preceding two sections are appropriate for the analysis of two independent samples. We have emphasized that those methods are not appropriate for situations in which each measurement in one sample is matched or paired with a corresponding measurement in the other. In this section we discuss methods for paired-sample data.

control of variability

The advantage of pairing observations is the **control of variability** that would otherwise obscure a real difference in means. For example, suppose that an office manager wants to test two new word processors to find which one yields greater average speed. One test procedure would be to assign 10 secretaries randomly to one model and another 10 secretaries to the other. This procedure would yield two independent samples. Another procedure would be to have 10 randomly chosen secretaries type on both models; the 10 typing speeds on each model would constitute paired or matched samples. Of course, there are large differences in speed among secretaries. These differences would cause large variability in the independent-samples experiment and would tend to conceal any real differences between the two models. In the paired-sample experiment, the manager can calculate the difference in the two models' speeds for the same secretaries; individual variability in speed cancels out of the difference. The individual-variability factor does not cause random variability in the paired-sample experiment.

As indicated in the secretary example, statistical methods for working with paired samples are all based on the same idea. Calculate all differences of matched scores and apply single-sample methods to the resulting sample of differences. In particular, the t distribution methods for confidence intervals and hypothesis tests described in Chapters 7 and 8 may be used.

EXAMPLE 9.9   Insurance adjusters investigate the relative automobile repair costs at two garages. Each of 15 cars recently involved in accidents is taken to both garages 1 and 2 for separate estimates of repair costs. The resulting data are analyzed incorrectly as coming from two independent samples and correctly as coming from paired samples. Use the following computer printouts to compare the resulting t statistics. What accounts for the difference in these statistics? (Costs are entered in hundreds of dollars.)

```
Two-sample T for Garage1 vs Garage2

          N      Mean     StDev    SE Mean
Garage1   15     7.68     2.72     0.70
Garage2   15     6.64     3.05     0.79

Difference = mu Garage1 - mu Garage2
Estimate for difference:  1.04
95% CI for difference: (-1.12, 3.21)
T-Test of difference = 0 (vs not =): T-Value = 0.989  P-Value = 0.331  DF = 28
Both use Pooled StDev = 2.89

Two-sample T for Garage1 vs Garage2

          N      Mean     StDev    SE Mean
Garage1   15     7.68     2.72     0.70
Garage2   15     6.64     3.05     0.79
```

```
Difference = mu Garage1 - mu Garage2
Estimate for difference:  1.04
95% CI for difference: (-1.12, 3.21)
T-Test of difference = 0 (vs not =): T-Value = 0.989  P-Value = 0.331  DF = 27


Paired T for Garage1 - Garage2

                 N      Mean     StDev    SE Mean
Garage1         15     7.680     2.725     0.704
Garage2         15     6.636     3.048     0.787
Difference      15     1.044     1.087     0.281

95% CI for mean difference: (0.442, 1.646)
T-Test of mean difference = 0 (vs not = 0): T-Value = 3.72  P-Value = 0.0023
```

SOLUTION The pooled-sample and separate-sample (t') statistics are equal because $n_1 = n_2$; the value is only .989. The *p*-value is about .33, so there isn't enough evidence to say that the garages differ in their average estimates. The difference *t* statistic equals 3.72, and the *p*-value is .0023, statistically significant at all reasonable α levels. The reason for the difference in conclusions is that there is huge variability in the severity of damage to the 15 cars. This source of variability makes the standard error very large and therefore t_{pooled} and t' quite small. Because the difference *t* is based on differences between the two garages' estimates on the same cars, it is not affected by the variability among cars.

EXAMPLE 9.10 A tasting panel of 15 people is asked to rate two new kinds of tea on a scale ranging from 0 to 100; 25 means "I would try to finish it only to be polite," 50 means "I would drink it but not buy it," 75 means "it's about as good as any tea I know," and 100 means "it's superb; I would drink nothing else." (What 0 means is left to your imagination.) The ratings are as follows:

	Person							
	1	**2**	**3**	**4**	**5**	**6**	**7**	**8**
Tea S	85	40	75	81	42	50	60	15
Tea J	65	50	43	65	20	65	35	38
Difference	+20	−10	+32	+16	+22	−15	+25	−23

	Person						
	9	**10**	**11**	**12**	**13**	**14**	**15**
Tea S	65	40	60	40	65	75	80
Tea J	60	47	60	43	53	61	63
Difference	+5	−7	0	−3	+12	+14	+17

a. Calculate a 95% confidence interval for the population difference in mean ratings.

b. Test the null hypothesis of no difference against a two-sided alternative using $\alpha = .05$.

c. What advantage does matching have in this situation?

SOLUTION

a. If we call the differences d_i, then $\bar{d} = 7.00$ and $s_d = 16.08$. Of course,

$$\bar{d} = \frac{\sum d_i}{15} \quad \text{and} \quad s_d^2 = \frac{\sum (d_i - \bar{d})^2}{14}$$

The population mean of the differences is the same as the difference in means, so $\mu_d = \mu_S - \mu_J$. Because our calculations are based on 15 differences, there are 14 d.f., and the required t table value is 2.145. The confidence interval is

$$7.00 - 2.145 \frac{16.08}{\sqrt{15}} \le \mu_S - \mu_J \le 7.00 + 2.145 \frac{16.08}{\sqrt{15}}$$

or

$$-1.9 \le \mu_S - \mu_J \le 15.9$$

b. Because the value 0 is included in this 95% confidence interval, it follows that $H_0: \mu_S - \mu_J = 0$ cannot be rejected at $\alpha = .05$ using a two-tailed test. The t statistic is

$$t = \frac{7.00 - 0}{16.08/\sqrt{15}} = 1.69$$

which has a two-tailed p-value a little larger than .10.

c. The matching is somewhat useful in accounting for individual differences in taste. There is some tendency for those who give high scores to S to also give high scores to J, and for those who give low S scores to also give low J scores. Had we erroneously used the two-sample formula, we would have had a larger standard error

$$s_p \sqrt{\frac{1}{15} + \frac{1}{15}} = 6.21$$

rather than the correct standard error

$$s_d/\sqrt{15} = 4.15$$

The formal statement of these matched-pairs procedures merely requires replacing y's by d's in the one sample t-distribution procedures. These are summarized here:

DEFINITION 9.6

Confidence Interval for μ_d, Matched Samples

$$\bar{d} - t_{\alpha/2} s_d / \sqrt{n} \le \mu_d \le \bar{d} + t_{\alpha/2} s_d \sqrt{n}$$

where n is the number of pairs of observations (and therefore the number of differences) and $t_{\alpha/2}$ cuts off a right-tail area of $\alpha/2$ for the t distribution with $n - 1$ d.f.

DEFINITION 9.7

Hypothesis Test for Matched Samples

H_0: $\mu_d = D_0$ (D_0 is specified; often $D_0 = 0$)

H_a: 1. $\mu_d > D_0$
2. $\mu_d < D_0$
3. $\mu_d \neq D_0$

T.S.: $t = \dfrac{\bar{d} - D_0}{s_d/\sqrt{n}}$

R.R.: 1. $t > t_\alpha$
2. $t < -t_\alpha$
3. $|t| > t_{\alpha/2}$

Most computer packages will carry out these calculations. For example, the tea-tasting experiment data of Example 9.10 were analyzed using Minitab, with the following results:

```
Paired T for Tea_S - Tea_J

                 N      Mean     StDev   SE Mean
Tea_S           15     58.20     19.94      5.15
Tea_J           15     51.20     13.44      3.47
Difference      15      7.00     16.08      4.15

95% CI for mean difference: (-1.90, 15.90)

T-Test of mean difference = 0 (vs not = 0): T-Value = 1.69   P-Value = 0.114
```

The results are the same as we calculated in the example.

9.4 The Signed-Rank Method

In the previous section we considered a *t* test for paired samples. Like any *t* test, it is based on an assumption that the underlying population (or process) has something reasonably close to a normal distribution. But what if a histogram, stem-and-leaf display, or box plot of the differences—which are the data we're analyzing—clearly indicates a nonnormal distribution? There are alternatives to the *t* test that are more effective in clear nonnormal cases. One could test the null hypothesis that the *median* difference is 0. In this context, a median test is usually called a **sign test;** it counts the number of successes (values above the hypothesized median, zero), which is the same as counting the number of plus signs in the data. The sign test, or equivalently, a median confidence interval, is often a good choice in the case of a highly skewed distribution, especially if the sample size is too small to place much reliance on the Central Limit Theorem.

sign test

An alternative test, designed for data that are basically symmetric but outlier-prone, is the **Wilcoxon signed-rank test.** The formal null hypothesis for this test is that the true distribution of differences is symmetric around a specified number D_0; almost always D_0 is taken to be zero. The test is primarily sensitive to the distribution being shifted to the right or left of D_0; one- or two-sided research hypotheses

Wilcoxon signed-rank test

may be tested. Again the test works with differences (if D_0 is not zero, D_0 is subtracted from each difference). Discard all differences that are exactly zero and reduce n accordingly. Then the differences are ranked in order of absolute value, smallest to largest. The appropriate sign is attached to each rank. Define

T_+ = the sum of the positive ranks; if there are no positive ranks, $T_+ = 0$

T_- = the sum of the negative ranks; if there are no negative ranks, $T_- = 0$

and

n = the number of nonzero differences

The Wilcoxon signed-rank test is presented next.

DEFINITION 9.8

Wilcoxon Signed-Rank Test

H_0: The distribution of differences is symmetric around D_0 (usually D_0 is zero)

H_a: 1. The differences tend to be larger than D_0
2. The differences tend to be smaller than D_0
3. The differences tend to be shifted away from D_0

T.S.: 1. $T = |T_-|$
2. $T = T_+$
3. T = smaller of $|T_-|$, T_+

R.R.: ($n \le 50$): For a specified value of α (one-tailed .05, .025, .01, or .005; two-tailed .10, .05, .02, .01) and fixed number of nonzero differences n, reject H_0 if the value of T is less than or equal to the appropriate entry in Appendix Table 7.

($n > 50$): Compute the test statistic

$$z = \frac{T - \dfrac{n(n+1)}{4}}{\sqrt{\dfrac{n(n+1)(2n+1)}{24}}}$$

For cases 1 and 2, reject H_0 if $z < -z_\alpha$; for case 3, reject H_0 if $z < -z_{\alpha/2}$.

EXAMPLE 9.11

Refer to the data of Example 9.10. Use the signed-rank test to test the null hypothesis of symmetry around $D_0 = 0$ against a two-sided alternative. Use $\alpha = .05$. Compare your results to the following Minitab output:

```
Wilcoxon Signed Rank Test: Difference

Test of median = 0.000000 versus median not = 0.000000

                        N
                      for   Wilcoxon              Estimated
              N    Test   Statistic       P       Median
Difference   15     14       78.0     0.117       7.250
```

SOLUTION The differences and their signed ranks are as follows:

	Person							
	1	2	3	4	5	6	7	8
Difference	+20	−10	+32	+16	+22	−15	+25	−23
Signed rank	+10	−4	+14	+8	+11	−7	+13	−12

	Person						
	9	10	11	12	13	14	15
Difference	+5	−7	0	−3	+12	+14	+17
Signed rank	+2	−3	X	−1	+5	+6	+9

The 0 difference (person 11) is discarded, so $n = 14$.

$$T_+ = 10 + 14 + 8 + 11 + 13 + 2 + 5 + 6 + 9 = 78$$
$$T_- = -4 - 7 - 12 - 3 - 1 = -27$$

(A good check is that $T_+ - T_-$ must always equal $n(n + 1)/2$, which equals 105 here.) For a two-sided research hypothesis, $T = \{$smaller of $|-27|$ and $78\} = 27$. Note that the Minitab output selects the value 78 for the test statistic. So long as the program has tables that are consistent with the choice, it doesn't matter; if we know the sample size and the sum of the positive ranks, we also know the sum of the negative ranks and can use either one.

As $n = 14 < 50$, we find the $\alpha = .05$ (two-sided) entry in Appendix Table 7; it is 21. Because $T = 27 > 21$, we cannot reject H_0 at $\alpha = .05$. We cannot reject at $\alpha = .10$ either; the table value is 25. Although we do not need the large-sample ($n > 50$) approximation in this problem, it can be computed:

$$z = \frac{27 - (14)(15)/4}{\sqrt{\dfrac{(14)(15)(29)}{24}}} = -1.60$$

For $\alpha = .10$ (two-tailed), we reject if $z < -z_{.05} = -1.645$; if we had used the z approximation, we would not have rejected H_0 at $\alpha = .10$. Note that the output shows a p-value slightly larger than .10, which is consistent with our calculations. However we carry out the test, we can't reject the null hypothesis, even at $\alpha = .10$. There isn't much evidence that customers can detect the difference in the two teas, based on our data.

EXAMPLE 9.12 Use the signed-rank information in the following computer printout for the data of Example 9.9 to test the research hypothesis that garage 1's estimates tend to be higher than garage 2's. How does the result of the signed-rank test compare with the result of the t test of Example 9.9?

```
Paired T-Test and CI: Garage 1, Garage 2

Paired T for Garage 1 - Garage 2

                 N     Mean    StDev   SE Mean
Garage 1     15   7.67999   2.72479   0.70353
Garage 2     15   6.63599   3.04816   0.78702
Difference   15   1.04399   1.08748   0.28078

95% CI for mean difference: (0.44176, 1.64622)
T-Test of mean difference = 0 (vs not = 0): T-Value = 3.72  P-Value = 0.002

Wilcoxon Signed Rank Test: Diff

Test of median = 0.000000 versus median not = 0.000000

                  N
                for   Wilcoxon            Estimated
          N    Test   Statistic     P      Median
Diff   15      15       111.0    0.004     1.100
```

SOLUTION The output shows the signed-rank results as a test of median (ranks method). The *p*-value is shown as .004, compared to the *p*-value of .002 shown for the *t* test. The *t* test is slightly more conclusive, but whichever test is used, there is fairly clear evidence that the first garage has higher estimates than the second.

choice of method   The **choice** of the appropriate paired-sample test from this section follows the guidelines of Chapter 8. If the assumptions of the *t* test are satisfied—in particular, if the distribution of differences is roughly normal—the *t* test is more powerful. If the distribution of differences is grossly skewed, the nominal *t* and signed-rank probabilities may be misleading. If the distribution is roughly symmetric but has heavy tails (as indicated by the presence of outliers), the signed-rank test may be more powerful. Often, as in Examples 9.11 and 9.12, the tests yield essentially the same conclusion.

Unless there are very obvious features (such as severe skewness or major outliers) in the data, these three methods will often give very similar conclusions. With a computer package, it's not difficult to obtain tests or confidence intervals using all three methods. If the results are similar, you can report them with comfort. If the results are clearly different, you should be able to find the "data gremlin" that is causing the difference; in such a case, use the analysis that is least sensitive to the particular problem you found.

EXAMPLE 9.13   A normal probability plot of the differences for the tea-tasting example is shown in Figure 9.5. Does this plot indicate that the signed-rank test should definitely be used instead of the *t* test of differences?

SOLUTION The plot is pretty much a straight line. There is no evident reason to think that the differences are nonnormal and therefore no evident reason to prefer a signed-rank test.

FIGURE 9.5   **Normal Probability Plot—Tea-Tasting Experiment**

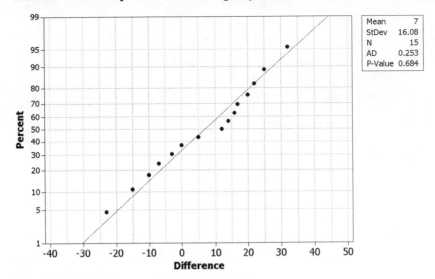

Exercises

9.16 A manufacturer of an air compressor and tire pump wants to test two possible point-of-purchase displays. The product is sold through independent auto parts stores, which vary greatly in sales volume. A total of 30 stores agree to feature the display for one month. The stores are matched on the basis of annual sales volume. One of the two largest stores is randomly chosen to receive display A, while the other receives B. The same thing is done for the third- and fourth-largest stores, and so on down to the two smallest. Sales for the one-month period are recorded, along with Minitab output:

							Pairing								
Display	**1**	**2**	**3**	**4**	**5**	**6**	**7**	**8**	**9**	**10**	**11**	**12**	**13**	**14**	**15**
A	46	39	40	37	32	26	21	23	20	17	13	15	11	8	9
B	37	42	37	38	27	19	20	17	20	12	12	9	7	2	6
Difference	+9	−3	+3	−1	+5	+7	+1	+6	0	+5	+1	+6	+4	+6	+3

```
Paired T for DisplayA - DisplayB

               N       Mean     StDev    SE Mean
DisplayA       15      23.80    12.33     3.18
DisplayB       15      20.33    13.04     3.37
Difference     15      3.467     3.314    0.856

90% CI for mean difference: (1.960, 4.974)
T-Test of mean difference = 0 (vs not = 0): T-Value = 4.05   P-Value = 0.001

Wilcoxon Signed Rank Test: Diff

Test of median = 0.000000 versus median not = 0.000000
```

```
                           N for    Wilcoxon              Estimated
                    N      Test    Statistic        P      Median
Diff               15      14         98.0       0.005     3.500

Sign Test for Median: Diff

Sign test of median = 0.00000 versus  not =  0.00000

                    N    Below  Equal  Above         P      Median
Diff               15     2      1      12        0.0129    4.000

Stem-and-Leaf Display: Diff

Stem-and-leaf of Diff      N  = 15
Leaf Unit = 1.0

     1     -0 3
     2     -0 1
     5      0 011
     7      0 33
    (3)     0 455
     5      0 6667
     1      0 9
```

a. Use a paired-sample t test to test the research hypothesis of unequal means. Use $\alpha = .10$.

b. Locate the 90% confidence interval for the true mean difference. Show that it gives the same conclusion as the t test.

c. The signed-rank test for the data is shown in the output. Perform a two-tailed test of the null hypothesis that the median is 0, with $\alpha = .10$.

d. How does the conclusion of this test compare with that of the t test?

e. Does the stem-and-leaf display indicate that either test should not be believed?

9.17 Consider the situation of Exercise 9.16. An alternative approach would be to assign display A to 15 randomly chosen stores and display B to the rest. Assuming that the data were collected in that way, consider the following Minitab output:

```
Two-sample T for DisplayA vs DisplayB

               N      Mean     StDev    SE Mean
DisplayA   15        23.8      12.3       3.2
DisplayB   15        20.3      13.0       3.4

Difference = mu DisplayA - mu DisplayB
Estimate for difference:  3.47

95% CI for difference: (-6.04, 12.98)

T-Test of difference = 0 (vs not =): T-Value = 0.75   P-Value = 0.461   DF = 27
```

a. Does the t test support the research hypothesis of unequal means, at usual α values?

b. Does there seem to be any advantage to the pairing process actually used?

9.18 Carry out a binomial (sign) test—using the Minitab output of Exercise 9.16—of the null hypothesis that the proportion of positive differences equals the proportion of negative differences.

9.19 A long-distance telephone company claims that by switching to its services, long-distance telephone costs for your department would decrease. To evaluate this claim, you sample the last eight monthly long-distance phone bills for your department. The estimated bill based on the new company's pricing structure is computed for each actual monthly bill from your current phone company. The data are listed here:

Month	1	2	3	4	5	6	7	8
Current	420	493	234	334	216	149	337	209
New	336	421	298	314	228	151	329	177

Is there sufficient evidence at the 5% level of significance to conclude that the average cost of long-distance service is lower with the new company? Use an appropriate statistical technique and explain your answer.

9.20 The owners of Luigi's Pizza have decided to offer a new deep-dish crust pizza. Unfortunately, there is disagreement over whether to use Luigi's recipe or his wife Maria's recipe. To decide the issue, a group of 10 customers was randomly selected and asked to rate the two recipes. Each of the 10 customers tried both types of crust and assigned each a rating from 0–100. (The order of taste-testing was randomized to prevent bias.) The ratings data are shown here:

Customer	1	2	3	4	5	6	7	8	9	10
Luigi's	78	85	73	80	94	92	64	82	78	84
Maria's	70	86	62	76	82	94	68	70	72	82

Is there sufficient evidence to conclude that customers prefer Luigi's recipe over Maria's? Use a 10% level of significance.

9.21 A maker of over-the-counter pain relief products feels ethically bound to put its products in child-resistant packages. However, many of its sales were to older people who might also have problems opening the packages. Two package designs were proposed. A sample of 40 older customers opened both packages; the time required (in seconds) was recorded. The data were input to the Minitab computer package, with the following results:

```
Paired T for Package1 - Package2

               N      Mean    StDev   SE Mean
Package1      40     36.95    24.35     3.85
Package2      40     40.80    21.90     3.46
Difference    40     -3.85    13.48     2.13

99% CI for mean difference: (-9.62, 1.92)
T-Test of mean difference = 0 (vs not = 0): T-Value = -1.81   P-Value = 0.079

Sign Test for Median: Diff

Sign test of median = 0.00000 versus  not =  0.00000

          N  Below  Equal  Above        P    Median
Diff     40     30      0     10   0.0022    -4.000

Wilcoxon Signed Rank Test: Diff

Test of median = 0.000000 versus median not = 0.000000

             N for  Wilcoxon             Estimated
         N   Test   Statistic      P      Median
Diff    40     40     209.0    0.007     -4.500
```

Does the *t* test indicate a statistically detectable difference, say at $\alpha = .01$?

9.22 A normal probability plot of the data from Exercise 9.21 is shown in Figure 9.6. Does this plot show that the data aren't normally distributed?

FIGURE 9.6 **Normal Plot of Package-Opening Time Differences**

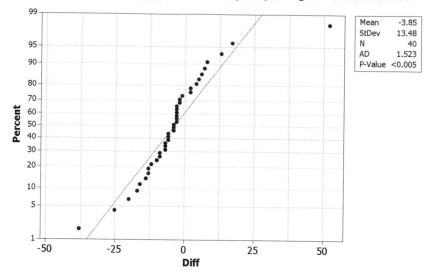

9.23 Minitab also performed sign and signed-rank tests of the null hypothesis that the median difference is 0, using the data of Exercise 9.21.
a. Does the sign test indicate that the null hypothesis should be rejected at $\alpha = .01$?
b. Does the signed-rank test indicate that the null hypothesis should be rejected at $\alpha = .01$?
c. How do the results of these tests compare to the results of the t test in Exercise 9.21? If there is a difference in the conclusion of the tests, what accounts for it?

9.5 Two-Sample Procedures for Proportions

So far in this chapter we have concentrated entirely on tests and confidence intervals for means. In this section we consider procedures for proportions. The methods are based on the normal approximation to the binomial distribution, so some consideration of required sample size is necessary.

We assume that two *independent* random samples of sizes n_1 and n_2 are taken. The respective sample proportions are denoted as $\hat{\pi}_1$ and $\hat{\pi}_2$, and the (unknown) population proportions are called π_1 and π_2. Our goal is to make inferences about the difference, if any, in the population proportions. The natural estimator is the difference in sample proportions $\hat{\pi}_1 - \hat{\pi}_2$. It is unbiased: $E(\hat{\pi}_1 - \hat{\pi}_2) = \pi_1 - \pi_2$. To calculate confidence intervals and perform hypothesis tests, we need a standard error formula. Recall from Chapter 8 that the variance of a sample proportion $\hat{\pi}$ is $\pi(1 - \pi)/n$. By the assumed independence of the two samples, we may add the variances of $\hat{\pi}_1$ and $\hat{\pi}_2$ to obtain

$$\mathrm{Var}(\hat{\pi}_1 - \hat{\pi}_2) = \frac{\pi_1(1 - \pi_1)}{n_1} + \frac{\pi_2(1 - \pi_2)}{n_2}$$

$$\sigma_{\hat{\pi}_1 - \hat{\pi}_2} = \sqrt{\frac{\pi_1(1 - \pi_1)}{n_1} + \frac{\pi_2(1 - \pi_2)}{n_2}}$$

The confidence interval for $\pi_1 - \pi_2$ follows the familiar form estimate $\pm$ a table value times a standard error. Now the estimate is the difference of sample proportions of successes, $\hat{\pi}_1 - \hat{\pi}_2$, and $\sigma_{\hat{\theta}}$ is $\sigma_{\hat{\pi}_1 - \hat{\pi}_2}$. Because the **standard error of $\hat{\pi}_1 - \hat{\pi}_2$** ($\sigma_{\hat{\pi}_1 - \hat{\pi}_2}$) depends on the unknown population proportions π_1 and π_2, in practice we must substitute the sample proportions $\hat{\pi}_1$ and $\hat{\pi}_2$ into the standard-error formula. If both sample sizes are sufficiently large (say, at least 30), this substitution can be made without affecting the normal approximation.

standard error of $\hat{\pi}_1 - \hat{\pi}_2$

DEFINITION 9.9

100$(1 - \alpha)$% Confidence Interval for $\pi_1 - \pi_2$

$$(\hat{\pi}_1 - \hat{\pi}_2) - z_{\alpha/2}\sigma_{\hat{\pi}_1 - \hat{\pi}_2} \leq \pi_1 - \pi_2 \leq (\hat{\pi}_1 - \hat{\pi}_2) + z_{\alpha/2}\sigma_{\hat{\pi}_1 - \hat{\pi}_2}$$

where

$$\sigma_{\hat{\pi}_1 - \hat{\pi}_2} \approx \sqrt{\frac{\hat{\pi}_1(1 - \hat{\pi}_1)}{n_1} + \frac{\hat{\pi}_2(1 - \hat{\pi}_2)}{n_2}}$$

EXAMPLE 9.14

A new product is test-marketed in the Grand Rapids, Michigan, and Wichita, Kansas, metropolitan areas. Advertising in the Grand Rapids area is based almost entirely on television commercials. In Wichita, a roughly equal dollar amount is spent on a balanced mix of television, radio, newspaper, and magazine ads. Two months after the ad campaign begins, surveys are taken to determine consumer awareness of the product.

	Grand Rapids	Wichita
Number interviewed	608	527
Number aware	392	413

Calculate a 95% confidence interval for the regional difference in the proportion of all consumers who are aware of the product.

SOLUTION The sample awareness proportion is higher in Wichita, so make Wichita region 1.

$$\hat{\pi}_1 = 413/527 = .784, \qquad \hat{\pi}_2 = 392/608 = .645$$

The estimated standard error is

$$\sqrt{\frac{(.784)(.216)}{527} + \frac{(.645)(.355)}{608}} = .0264$$

Therefore, the 95% confidence interval is

$$(.784 - .645) - 1.96(.0264) \leq \pi_1 - \pi_2 \leq (.784 - .645) + 1.96(.0264)$$

or

$$.087 \leq \pi_1 - \pi_2 \leq 1.91$$

which indicates that somewhere between 8.7% and 19.1% more Wichita consumers than Grand Rapids consumers are aware of the product.

This confidence interval method is based on the normal approximation to the binomial distribution. In Chapter 8 we indicated as a general rule that $n\hat{\pi}$ and $n(1 - \hat{\pi})$ should both be at least 5 to use this normal approximation. For this confidence interval to be used, the **rule for sample sizes** should hold for each sample. In practice, sample sizes that come even close to violating this rule aren't very useful, because they lead to excessively wide confidence intervals. For instance, even though $n\hat{\pi}$ and $n(1 - \hat{\pi})$ are greater than 5 for both samples when $n_1 = 30$, $\hat{\pi}_1 = .20$ and $n_2 = 60$, $\hat{\pi}_2 = .10$, the 95% confidence interval is $-.06 \le \pi_1 - \pi_2 < .26$; π_1 could be anything from 6 percentage points lower than π_2 to 26 percentage points higher.

rule for sample sizes

Hypothesis testing about the difference between two population proportions is based on the z statistic from a normal approximation. The typical null hypothesis is that there is no difference between the population proportions, though any specified value for $\pi_1 - \pi_2$ may be hypothesized. The procedure is summarized in the following definition.

DEFINITION 9.10

> **Hypothesis Test for $\pi_1 - \pi_2$**
>
> H_0: $\pi_1 - \pi_2 = D_0$ (D_0 is specified; often $D_0 = 0$)
>
> H_a: 1. $\pi_1 - \pi_2 > D_0$
> 2. $\pi_1 - \pi_2 < D_0$
> 3. $\pi_1 - \pi_2 \ne D_0$
>
> T.S.: $z = \dfrac{(\hat{\pi}_1 - \hat{\pi}_2) - D_0}{\sqrt{\dfrac{\hat{\pi}_1(1 - \hat{\pi}_1)}{n_1} + \dfrac{\hat{\pi}_2(1 - \hat{\pi}_2)}{n_2}}}$
>
> R.R.: 1. $z > z_\alpha$
> 2. $z < -z_\alpha$
> 3. $|z| > z_{\alpha/2}$
>
> *Note:* This test should be used only if $n_1\hat{\pi}_1$, $n_1(1 - \hat{\pi}_1)$, $n_2\hat{\pi}_2$, and $n_2(1 - \hat{\pi}_2)$ are all at least 5.

EXAMPLE 9.15

Refer to Example 9.14. Test the hypothesis of equal population-awareness proportions against a two-sided alternative. State a p-value.

SOLUTION $\hat{\pi}_1 = .784$, $n_1 = 527$, $\hat{\pi}_2 = .645$, and $n_2 = 608$. This general rule for using a z test is amply met; the smallest of the four indicators is $n_1(1 - \hat{\pi}_1) = 114$.

$$z = \frac{(.784 - .645) - 0}{\sqrt{\dfrac{(.784)(.216)}{527} + \dfrac{(.645)(.355)}{608}}}$$

$$= \frac{.139}{.0264} = 5.26$$

A z value of 5.26 is far beyond the range of our z table. The p-value is some very small number.

As in the one-sample situation, tests for a proportion can be approximated by t tests of means, using 1s and 0s for data. For example, the data of the previous examples, as a set of 392 1s and 216 0s for Grand Rapids and 413 1s and 114 0s for Wichita, yielded the following Minitab output:

```
Two-sample T for Aware

City              N     Mean    StDev   SE Mean
GrandRapids     608    0.645    0.479    0.019
Wichita         527    0.784    0.412    0.018

Difference = mu (GrandRapids) - mu (Wichita)
Estimate for difference:   -0.1389

95% CI for difference: (-0.1908, -0.0870)

T-Test of difference = 0 (vs not =): T-Value = -5.25   P-Value = 0.000   DF = 1132
```

The confidence interval and test are very close to the results we obtained with hand calculation. For all practical purposes, the 1s and 0s method is as good as the hand calculation method.

Exercises

9.24 A consumer finance company considers its bad-debt experience for married and unmarried couples. A sample of 3200 loans yields the following data:

Status	Number of Loans	Bad Debts
Married	2128	102
Unmarried	1072	31

Calculate a 90% confidence interval for the true difference in proportions of bad debts.

9.25 Refer to the preceding exercise. Test the null hypothesis of equal proportions. Let H_a be two-sided. Use $\alpha = .10$.

9.26 Find p-values for the z statistic in Exercise 9.25.

9.27 In a survey, it is found that 1697 of 2961 urban-area residents regularly watch a network television news program, whereas 674 of 983 rural or small-town residents are regular watchers.
a. Calculate a 95% confidence interval for the difference in proportions.
b. Test the research hypothesis that a higher percentage of rural (small-town) residents are regular watchers. Use $\alpha = .05$.

9.28 Find the p-value in Exercise 9.27. How conclusive is the evidence favoring the research hypothesis?

9.29 A retail computer dealer is trying to decide between two methods for servicing customers' equipment. The first method emphasizes preventive maintenance; the second emphasizes quick response to problems. Samples of customers are each served by one of the two methods. After six months, it is found that 171 of 200 customers served by the first method are very satisfied with the service, as compared to 153 of 200 customers served by the second method. Computer output, based on 1s and 0s for data, follows:

```
Test and CI for Two Proportions

Sample    X      N    Sample p
1        171    200   0.855000
2        153    200   0.765000

Difference = p (1) - p (2)
Estimate for difference:  0.09
95% CI for difference:  (0.0136180, 0.166382)
Test for difference = 0 (vs not = 0):  Z = 2.31  P-Value = 0.021
```

Test the research hypothesis that the population proportions are different. Use $\alpha = .05$. State your conclusion carefully.

9.30   Locate a confidence interval for the difference of proportions in Exercise 9.29. Show that it reaches the same conclusion as the formal test about the research hypothesis.

9.31   The media-selection manager for an advertising agency inserts the same advertisement for a client bank in two magazines. The ads are similarly placed in each magazine. One month later, a market research study finds that 226 of 473 readers of the first magazine are aware of the banking services offered in the ad, as are 165 of 439 readers of the second magazine (readers of both magazines are excluded). The following Minitab output was based on the appropriate number of 1s and 0s as data:

```
Two-sample T for Aware?

Magazine    N      Mean    StDev   SE Mean
1          473    0.478    0.500    0.023
2          439    0.376    0.485    0.023

Difference = mu (1) - mu (2)
Estimate for difference:  0.1019

95% CI for difference: (0.0379, 0.1660)

T-Test of difference = 0 (vs not =): T-Value = 3.13  P-Value = 0.002  DF = 908
```

    a. Calculate by hand a 95% confidence interval for the difference of proportions of readers who are aware of the advertised services. Compare your answer to the interval given by Minitab.

    b. Are the sample sizes adequate to use the normal approximation?

    c. Does the confidence interval indicate that there is a statistically significant difference using $\alpha = .05$?

9.32   Using the output of Exercise 9.31, perform a formal test of the null hypothesis of equal populations. Use $\alpha = .05$.

9.33   Samples of 30 electric motors for inkjet printers are subjected to severe testing for reliability. Of the motors from supplier 1, 22 pass the test; of the motors from supplier 2, only 16 pass.

    a. Show that the difference is not statistically significant at $\alpha = .05$ (two-tailed).

    b. Can we claim to have shown that the two suppliers provide equally reliable motors?

9.34   Use the data of Exercise 9.33 to calculate a 95% confidence interval for the difference of proportions. Interpret the result carefully in terms of the relative reliability of the two suppliers.

9.6   Chi-Squared Tests for Count Data

In the previous section we showed a test for comparing two proportions. The data were simply counts of how many times we got a particular result in two samples. In this section we'll extend that test. First, we present a single test statistic for testing whether several deviations of sample data from theoretical proportions could plausibly have occurred by chance. The test uses a new distribution, the χ^2 distribution. The χ^2 table (Appendix Table 5) gives critical values that cut off a specified right-tail area a for given degrees of freedom (d.f.). In this respect, the χ^2 table is similar to the t table we used in the past few chapters. The χ^2 distribution is not symmetric; in this section we need be concerned only about values in the upper tail of the distribution, so the asymmetry won't be crucial. Any statistical computer package we know of can also be used to find χ^2 probabilities.

goodness-of-fit test

The χ^2 **goodness-of-fit test** is used to test the hypothesis that several proportions have specified numerical values. For instance, suppose that a life insurance company has a mix of 40% whole life policies, 25% level term policies, 15% decreasing term policies, and 20% other types. A change in this mix could signal a need to change commission, reserve, or investment practices, but the company does not want to react to random short-term fluctuation. If the company does a study of the last 1200 policies issued (regarded as a random sample), the χ^2 goodness-of-fit test can be used to test the statistical significance of deviations from the historical percentages.

In Chapter 8 we developed a test for a single binomial proportion; we often used a z approximation. We could run a separate test on the proportion for each policy type. The trouble with such a procedure is that although the Type I error is controlled at some level α for each test, the overall probability of error (incorrectly rejecting the null hypothesis in at least one test) may be much larger than α. If four separate tests are run at $\alpha = .05$, what is the probability of at least one Type I error? The tests are not independent. (If one sample proportion is too high, the others tend to be too low, because the sample proportions must add to 1.) But there is no way to get an accurate assessment of the overall probability of error from combining several z tests. The goodness-of-fit method yields a combined test of all proportions with a specified overall α level.

multinomial sampling

The χ^2 procedure assumes **multinomial sampling.** This is the extension of binomial sampling to more than two categories. Now we have k categories, and in each of n independent trials, the probability of observing a member of category i is π_i. This probability is assumed to be constant over trials.

expected number

The procedure works by comparing the observed number in each category to the **expected number** in that category. If there are n items in a sample and the probability of any item falling in category i is π_i, then, by the binomial distribution, the expected number in category i is

$$E_i = n\pi_i$$

The test procedure is summarized next.

DEFINITION 9.11

Goodness-of-Fit Test for Several Proportions

H_0: $\pi_i = \pi_{i,0}$ for categories $i = 1, \ldots, k$; $\pi_{i,0}$ are specified probabilities or proportions

H_a: H_0 is not true

T.S.: $\chi^2 = \sum_i \dfrac{(n_i - E_i)^2}{E_i}$ where n_i is the observed number in category i and

$E_i = n\pi_{i,0}$ is the expected number under H_0.

R.R.: Reject H_0 if $\chi^2 > \chi_\alpha^2$, the right-tail α percentage point of a χ^2 distribution with d.f. $= k - 1$. Note that the d.f. depends on k, the number of categories, not on n, the number of observations.

EXAMPLE 9.16

Suppose that, in the insurance company illustration at the beginning of this section, the previous 1200 policies issued consist of 439 whole life policies, 323 level term policies, 197 decreasing term policies, and 241 others. Assess the statistical significance (at $\alpha = .10$) of any shift from the historical policy mix.

SOLUTION   The following table summarizes the calculations:

Category, i	Whole Life	Level Term	Decreasing Term	Other	Total
Historical proportions, $\pi_{i,0}$	.40	.25	.15	.20	1.00
Observed number, n_i	439	323	197	241	1200
Expected number, $E_i = 1200\pi_{i,0}$	480	300	180	240	1200
$n_i - E_i$	−41	+23	+17	+1	0
$\dfrac{(n_i - E_i)^2}{E_i}$	3.502	1.763	1.606	.004	6.875

The number of categories is $k = 4$, so there are $k - 1 = 3$ d.f.; $\chi_{.10}^2 = 6.25$ for 3 d.f. Because $\chi^2 = 6.875 > 6.25$, H_0 is rejected, and the shift from the historical mix is statistically significant at $\alpha = .10$. It appears that term policies are becoming more popular and whole life policies less so. (*Note:* The $\alpha = .05$ percentage point is 7.81. H_0 could not be rejected at $\alpha = .05$; therefore, the p-value is somewhere between .05 and .10.)

multinomial assumptions

As with the binomial distribution, the key **multinomial assumptions** are independence of trials and constant probabilities over trials. Independence would be violated if several of the policies were sold to the same person or within the same family. Constant probability would be violated if the 1200 policies were sold over a long enough period that a time trend could matter. The most serious possible violation would occur if the policies were sold by relatively few agents and if there were major differences in product mix among agents.

The statistic for the χ^2 goodness-of-fit test is the sum of k terms, which is why d.f. depends on k, not n. There are $k - 1$ d.f. instead of k because the sum of the $n_i - E_i$ terms must always equal $n - n = 0$; $k - 1$ of these terms are free to vary but the kth is determined by this requirement.

The mathematics underlying this test is based on an approximation that is a lineal descendant of the normal approximation to the binomial distribution. The quality of this approximation has been extensively studied. A very conservative general rule is that the approximation is adequate if all E_i are at least 5.0.

The goodness-of-fit test is used extensively to test the adequacy of various scientific theories. One problem of such applications is that the hypothesis of interest is formulated as the null hypothesis, not the research hypothesis. If a scientist has a pet theory and wants to show that it gives a good fit to the data, the scientist wants to accept the null hypothesis. But the potential error in accepting it is Type II, and β probabilities of Type II errors are hard to calculate. In general, the null hypothesis tends to be accepted (the β probability is high) if n is small, or if there are many categories. Even if the general rule that all E_i are at least 5.0 is satisfied, the β risk can be large. **A "good fit" conclusion** is always a suspect. Perhaps the best procedure for a manager is to look at deviations of sample proportions from theoretical proportions and to use the χ^2 test results as an indicator of the degree of potential random variation.

a "good fit" conclusion

EXAMPLE 9.17

Suppose that in a test of a random walk theory of stock price changes, 125 security analysts are each asked to select four stocks listed on the New York Stock Exchange that are expected to outperform the S&P 500 Index over a 90-day period. According to one random walk theory of stock price changes, the analysts should do no better than coin flipping; the number of correct guesses by any particular analyst should follow a binomial distribution with $n = 4$ and probability of success .50. The data are

Number correct:	0	1	2	3	4
Frequency:	3	23	51	39	9

Test the random walk hypothesis at $\alpha = .05$ and at $\alpha = .10$.

SOLUTION

Number correct	0	1	2	3	4
Theoretical proportion (based on binomial probability)	.0625	.2500	.3750	.2500	.0625
Observed proportion	.0240	.1840	.4080	.3120	.0720
n_i	3	23	51	39	9
E_i	7.8125	31.250	46.875	31.250	7.8125
$\dfrac{(n_i - E_i)^2}{E_i}$	2.9645	2.1780	.3630	1.922	.1805

$$\chi^2 = \sum \frac{(n_i - E_i)^2}{E_i} = 7.608$$

An Excel worksheet can be used to do the calculations, as follows. The observed counts and the hypothesized probabilities are entered as data. The spreadsheet program then is used to calculate expected counts and each term of the χ^2 statistic. Finally, the terms are summed. The last entry is a p-value.

The tabled .05 and .10 points for χ^2 with $5 - 1 = 4$ .d.f. are 9.49 and 7.78, respectively. Thus, H_0 cannot be rejected at $\alpha = .05$ or even at $\alpha = .10$. The p-value is just slightly above .10. The data might be declared "a good fit" to the random walk theory. But the actual proportions of analysts who are correct for two, three, or four stocks are larger than those predicted by the theory.

```
        Observed  Probs     Expected  (O-E)sq/E
              3    0.0625    7.8125    2.9645
             23    0.25      31.25     2.178
             51    0.375     46.875    0.363
             39    0.25      31.25     1.922
              9    0.0625    7.8125    0.1805

            125                        7.608
                                       0.10704
```

The result of the χ^2 test indicates that this fact could conceivably have been a collective lucky break for the analysts. We would say that such data would suggest, though by no means conclusively prove, that analysts can do somewhat better than the random walk theory would indicate.

cross-tabulations
contingency tables

dependence

When we first introduced probability ideas in Chapter 3, we started by using tables of frequencies (counts). At the time, we treated these counts as if they represented the whole population. In practice, we'll hardly ever know the complete population data; we'll usually have only a sample. When we have counts from a sample, they're usually arranged in **cross-tabulations** or **contingency tables** such as those in Chapter 3. In this section we'll describe one particular test that is often used for such tables, a chi-squared *test of independence*.

In Chapter 3 we introduced the idea of independence. In particular, we discussed the idea that **dependence** of variables means that one variable has some value for predicting the other. With sample data there usually appears to be some degree of dependence. In this section we develop a χ^2 test that assesses whether the perceived dependence in sample data may be a fluke—the result of random variability rather than real dependence.

First, the frequency data are to be arranged in a cross-tabulation with r rows and c columns. The possible values of one variable determine the rows of the table and the possible values of the other determine the columns. We denote the population proportion (or probability) falling in row i, column j as π_{ij}. The total proportion for row i is $\pi_{i.}$, and the total proportion for column j is $\pi_{.j}$. If the row and column proportions (probabilities) are independent, then $\pi_{ij} = \pi_{i.}\pi_{.j}$. For instance, suppose that a personnel manager for a large firm wants to assess the popularity of three alternative flexible time-scheduling (flextime) plans among clerical workers in four different offices. The following indicates a set of proportions (π_{ij}) that exhibit independence. The proportion of all clerical workers who favor plan 2 and work in office 1 is $\pi_{21} = .03$; the proportion of all workers favoring plan 2 is $\pi_{2.} = .30$ and the proportion working in office 1 is $\pi_{.1} = .10$. Independence holds for that cell because $\pi_{21} = .03 = (\pi_{2.})(\pi_{.1}) = (.30)(.10)$. Independence also holds for all other cells.

| | *Office* | | | | |
Favored Plan	1	2	3	4	Total
1	.05	.20	.15	.10	.50
2	.03	.12	.09	.06	.30
3	.02	.08	.06	.04	.20
Total	.10	.40	.30	.20	1.00

The null hypothesis for this χ^2 test is independence. The research hypothesis specifies only that there is some form of dependence, that is, that it is not true that $\pi_{ij} = \pi_{i.}\pi_{.j}$ in every cell of the table. The test statistic is once again the sum over all cells of

(observed value − expected value)^2/expected value

The computation of expected values E_{ij} under the null hypothesis is different for the independence test than for the goodness-of-fit test. The null hypothesis of independence does not specify numerical values for the row probabilities $\pi_{i.}$ and column probabilities $\pi_{.j}$, so these probabilities must be estimated by the row and column relative frequencies. If $n_{i.}$ is the actual frequency in row i, estimate $\pi_{i.}$ by $\hat{\pi}_{i.} = n_{i.}/n$; similarly, $\hat{\pi}_{.j} = n_{.j}/n$. Assuming the null hypothesis of independence is true, it follows that $\hat{\pi}_{ij} = \hat{\pi}_{i.}\hat{\pi}_{.j} = (n_{i.}/n)(n_{.j}/n)$.

DEFINITION 9.12

Estimated Expected Values $\hat{E}_{ij}$ Under the hypothesis of independence the estimated expected value in row i, column j is

$$\hat{E}_{ij} = n\hat{\pi}_{ij} = n\,\frac{(n_{i.})}{n}\,\frac{(n_{.j})}{n} = \frac{(n_{i.})(n_{.j})}{n}$$

the row total multiplied by the column total divided by the grand total.

EXAMPLE 9.18

Suppose that in the flexible time-scheduling illustration a random sample of 216 workers yields the following frequencies:

	Office				
Favored Plan	**1**	**2**	**3**	**4**	**Total**
1	15	32	18	5	70
2	8	29	23	18	78
3	1	20	25	22	68
Total	24	81	66	45	216

Calculate a table of $\hat{E}_{ij}$ values.

SOLUTION   For row 1, column 1 the estimated expected number is

$$\hat{E}_{11} = \frac{(\text{row 1 total})(\text{column 1 total})}{\text{grand total}} = \frac{(70)(24)}{216} = 7.78$$

Similar calculations for all cells yield the following table:

	Office				
Plan	**1**	**2**	**3**	**4**	**Total**
1	7.78	26.25	21.39	14.58	70.00
2	8.67	29.25	23.83	16.25	78.00
3	7.56	25.50	20.78	14.17	68.01
Total	24.01	81.00	66.00	45.00	216.01

Note that the row and column totals in the $\hat{E}_{ij}$ table equal (except for round-off error) the corresponding totals in the observed (n_{ij}) table.

DEFINITION 9.13

χ^2 Test of Independence

H_0: The row and column variables are independent

H_a: The row and column variables are dependent (associated)

T.S.: $\chi^2 = \sum_{i,j}(n_{ij} - \hat{E}_{ij})^2/\hat{E}_{ij}$

R.R.: Reject H_0 if $\chi^2 > \chi_\alpha^2$, where χ_α^2 cuts off area α in the upper tail of a χ^2 distribution with $(r-1)(c-1)$ d.f.; $r =$ number of rows, $c =$ number of columns

EXAMPLE 9.19

Carry out the χ^2 test of independence for the data of Example 9.18. First use $\alpha = .05$, then obtain a bound for the p-value.

SOLUTION   The term for cell (1,1) is $(n_{11} - \hat{E}_{11})^2/\hat{E}_{11} = (15 - 7.78)^2/7.78 = 6.70$. Similar calculations are made for each cell. Substituting into the test statistic, we find $\chi^2 = 6.70 + \cdots + 4.33 = 27.12$. For $(3-1)(4-1) = 6$ d.f., the tabled χ^2 value (6 d.f., $\alpha = .05$) is 12.59. The observed χ^2 value of 27.12 far exceeds 12.59, so H_0 is rejected at $\alpha = .05$. In fact, 27.12 exceeds the tabled value even for $\alpha = .001$ (the smallest α in the table), namely, 21.46. Therefore, H_0 is rejected even for $\alpha = .001$ and p-value $<.001$.

d.f. for table

The **degrees of freedom** for the χ^2 test of independence relate to the number of cells in the two-way table that are free to vary while the marginal totals remain fixed. For example, in a 2×2 table (2 rows, 2 columns) only one cell entry is free to vary. Once that entry is fixed, we can determine the remaining cell entries by subtracting from the corresponding row or column total. In Table 9.1a we have indicated some (arbitrary) totals. The cell indicated by * could take any value (within the limits implied by the totals), but then all remaining cells would be determined by the totals. Similarly, with a 2×3 table (2 rows, 3 columns), two of the cell entries as indicated by *, are free to vary. Once these entries are set, the remaining cell entries are determined by subtracting from the appropriate row or column total (see Table 9.1b). In general, for a table with r rows and c columns, $(r-1)(c-1)$ of the cell entries are free to vary. This number represents the degrees of freedom for the χ^2 test of independence.

TABLE 9.1

(a) One d.f. in a 2 × 2 Table; (b) Two d.f. in a 2 × 3 Table

	Category B		Total			Category B			Total
Category A	*		16		Category A	*	*		51
			34						40
Total	21	29	50		Total	28	41	22	91
		(a)					(b)		

This χ^2 test of independence is also based on an approximation. A conservative rule is that each $\hat{E}_{ij}$ must be at least 5 to use the approximation comfortably. Standard practice if some $\hat{E}_{ij}$'s are too small is to lump together those rows (or columns) with small totals until the rule is satisfied.

The only function of this χ^2 test is to determine whether apparent dependence in sample data may be a fluke, plausibly a result of random variation. Rejection of the null hypothesis indicates only that the apparent association is not reasonably at-

strength of association

tributable to chance. It does not indicate anything about the **strength** or type **of association**.

The same χ^2 test statistic applies to a slightly different sampling procedure. An implicit assumption of our discussion surrounding the χ^2 test of independence is that the data result from a single random sample from the whole population. Often, separate random samples are taken from the subpopulations defined by the column (or row) variable. In the flextime example (9.18) the data might well have resulted from separate samples (of respective sizes 24, 81, 66, and 45) from the four offices rather than from a single random sample of 216 workers. The null hypothesis of independence is then stated (in an equivalent form) as H_0: The conditional probability of row

test of homogeneity

i given column j is the same for all columns j. The test is called a **test of homogeneity** of distributions (that is, that the probabilities or proportions by column are equal). The mechanics and conclusions of the test are identical, so the distinction is minor.

EXAMPLE 9.20

A poll of attitudes toward five possible energy policies is taken. Random samples of 200 individuals from major oil- and natural-gas-producing states, 200 from coal states, and 400 from other states are drawn. Each respondent indicates the most preferred alternative from among the following:

1. primarily emphasize conservation

2. primarily emphasize domestic oil and gas exploration

3. primarily emphasize investment in solar-related energy

4. primarily emphasize nuclear-energy development and safety

5. primarily reduce environmental restrictions and emphasize coal-burning activities

The results are as follows:

Policy Choice	Oil/Gas States	Coal States	Other States	Total
1	50	59	161	270
2	88	20	40	148
3	56	52	188	296
4	4	3	5	12
5	2	66	6	74
Total	200	200	400	800

Minitab output also carries out the calculations. The second entry in each cell is a percentage in the column.

```
        Tabulated Statistics: Policy, State

    Rows: Policy      Columns: State

            Coal    OilGas    Other      All

      1       59        50      161      270
            29.50     24.63    40.25    33.62

      2       20        88       40      148
            10.00     43.35    10.00    18.43

      3       52        56      188      296
            26.00     27.59    47.00    36.86

      4        3         8        5       16
             1.50      3.94     1.25     1.99

      5       66         1        6       73
            33.00      0.49     1.50     9.09

    All      200       203      400      803
           100.00    100.00   100.00   100.00

    Cell Contents --
                    Count
                    % of Col

    Chi-Square = 297.784, DF = 8, P-Value = 0.000
    2 cells with expected counts less than 5.0
```

Conduct a χ^2 test of homogeneity of distributions for the three groups of states. Give the p-value for this test.

SOLUTION A test that the corresponding population distributions are different makes use of the following table of expected values:

Policy Choice	Oil/Gas States	Coal States	Other States
1	67.5	67.5	135
2	37	37	74
3	74	74	148
4	3	3	6
5	18.5	18.5	37

The table violates our general rule that all $\hat{E}_{ij}$'s be at least 5. There is no obvious choice for combining policy 4 with some other. Therefore, we leave the table as is, but we realize that the nominal χ^2 probabilities are slightly suspect. The test procedure is outlined here:

H_0: The column distributions are homogeneous

H_a: The column distributions are not homogeneous

T.S.: $\chi^2 = \sum(n_{ij} - \hat{E}_{ij})^2/\hat{E}_{ij} = (50 - 67.5)^2/67.5 + (88 - 37)^2/37 + \cdots + (6 - 37)^2/37$

R.R. and Conclusion: Because the tabled value of χ^2 for d.f. $= 8$ and $\alpha = .001$ is 26.12, p-value is $< .001$.

Even recognizing the limited accuracy of the χ^2 approximations, we can reject the hypothesis of homogeneity at some very small p-value. Percentage analysis, particularly of state type for a given policy choice, shows dramatic differences; for instance, 1% of those living in oil/gas states favor policy 5, compared to 33% of those in coal states who favor policy 5.

The χ^2 test described in this section has a limited, but important, purpose. This test only assesses whether the data indicate a statistically detectable (significant) relation among various categories. It doesn't measure how strong the apparent relation might be. A weak relation in a large data set may be detectable (significant); a strong relation in a small data set may be nonsignificant.

Exercises

9.35 The director of a data-processing center wants to test the Poisson distribution model for arrivals of jobs to a central computer. The mean arrival rate during the relevant period is 3.8 jobs per minute. Records are kept on the number of arrivals in each of 2000 1-minute periods. The results are

Arrivals:	0	1	2	3	4	5	6	7	8	9+
Frequency:	38	155	328	392	415	399	170	61	27	15

a. Use Poisson tables ($\mu = 3.8$) to calculate probabilities for each category of number of arrivals.
b. Calculate expected frequencies.
c. Is the Poisson model a good fit to the data? Use $\alpha = .01$.

9.36 Can you detect any systematic discrepancy between the observed frequencies and the expected (Poisson model) frequencies in the data of Exercise 9.35?

9.37 A gift shop owner believes that 30% of the customers who enter the shop buy no items, 45% buy 1 item, and 25% buy 2 or more items. Observation of 25 customers yields the following data:

Number of purchases:	0	1	2+
Frequency:	10	6	9

a. Calculate the expected frequencies, assuming that the owner's hypothesis is valid.
b. Test the owner's hypothesis using $\alpha = .05$. Can the owner claim a good fit based on these data?

9.38 Suppose that the data in Exercise 9.37 are based on 250 customers, with respective frequencies 100, 60, and 90.
a. Test the owner's hypothesis at $\alpha = .05$.
b. Explain the discrepancy in the conclusion between this exercise and Exercise 9.37.

9.39   A personnel director for a large, research-oriented firm categorizes colleges and universities as most desirable, good, adequate, and undesirable for purposes of hiring their graduates. Data are collected on 156 recent graduates, and each is rated by a supervisor.

School	*Rating* Outstanding	Average	Poor
Most desirable	21	25	2
Good	20	36	10
Adequate	4	14	7
Undesirable	3	8	6

Output from the Minitab computer package is shown next.

```
Tabulated Statistics: School, Rating

Rows: School     Columns: Rating

                 Average Outstanding     Poor       All

MostDesirable        25          21         2        48
                  52.08       43.75      4.17    100.00

Good                 36          20        10        66
                  54.55       30.30     15.15    100.00

Adequate             14           4         7        25
                  56.00       16.00     28.00    100.00

Undesirable           8           3         6        17
                  47.06       17.65     35.29    100.00

All                  83          48        25       156
                  53.21       30.77     16.03    100.00

  Cell Contents --
                  Count
                  % of Row

Chi-Square = 15.967, DF = 6, P-Value = 0.014
2 cells with expected counts less than 5.0
```

a. Locate the value of the χ^2 statistic.
b. Locate the *p*-value.
c. Can the director safely conclude that there is a relation between school type and rating?
d. Is there any problem in using the χ^2 approximation?

9.40   Do the row percentages (the second entry in each cell of the output) reflect the existence of the relation we found in Exercise 9.39?

9.41   A study of potential age discrimination considers promotions among middle managers in a large company. The data are

	Age Under 30	30–39	40–49	50 or Over	Total
Promoted	9	29	32	10	80
Not promoted	41	41	48	40	170
Total	50	70	80	50	

Minitab output follows:

```
Tabulated Statistics: Promoted, Age

Rows: Promoted     Columns: Age

              Under 30    30-39     40-49   50 or Over      All

Promoted            9        29        32           10       80
                18.00     41.43     40.00        20.00    32.00

NotPromoted        41        41        48           40      170
                82.00     58.57     60.00        80.00    68.00

All                50        70        80           50      250
               100.00    100.00    100.00       100.00   100.00


  Cell Contents --
                Count
                % of Col

Chi-Square = 13.025, DF = 3, P-Value = 0.005
```

a. Find the expected numbers under the hypothesis of independence.
b. Justify the indicated degrees of freedom.
c. Is there a statistically significant relation between age and promotions, using $\alpha = .05$?

9.42 Place bounds on the *p*-value in Exercise 9.41.

9.43 The data of Exercise 9.41 are combined as follows:

	Age		
	Up to 39	**40 or Over**	**Total**
Promoted	38	42	80
Not promoted	82	88	170
Total	120	130	250

Minitab results:

```
Tabulated Statistics: Promoted, Age

Rows: Promoted     Columns: Age

              39 or Less   40 or Over       All

Promoted             38           42        80
                  31.67        32.31     32.00

NotPromoted          82           88       170
                  68.33        67.69     68.00

All                 120          130       250
                 100.00       100.00    100.00


  Cell Contents --
                Count
                % of Col

Chi-Square = 0.012, DF = 1, P-Value = 0.914
```

a. Can the hypothesis of independence be rejected using a reasonable α?
b. What is the effect of combining age categories? Compare the answers to Exercise 9.41 and 9.43.

BUSINESS DECISION-MAKING IN ACTION

CHAPTER CASE
ANALYSIS

Circuit Systems, Inc.

Tom Nelson, director of human resources at Circuit Systems, believed that hourly employees were using paid sick leave as "extra" paid vacation because of Circuit System's limited vacation policy. Trying to reduce the costs of paid sick leave, he instituted a new policy that allows employees to convert unused sick leave to extra pay on a "three sick days for one day of pay" basis. He also started a voluntary exercise program to improve employees' overall health. Circuit Systems expects its investment in employees' well-being to substantially reduce the company's contribution to health insurance premiums in the long term. Data have been collected for the past two years—the year before the policy went into effect and the first year under the new policy. Tom has asked you, the assistant director of human resources, to evaluate the cost-effectiveness of the new policy and its effect on paid sick leave.

The data on each hourly employee include hourly pay, the amount of sick leave taken last year before the new policy went into effect, the amount of sick leave taken this year after the new policy went into effect, and whether or not the employee participates in the exercise program. Only those employees who have been with the company over the entire two-year period are included in the data set, hence there are only 233 records in the data set even though the company regularly employs approximately 250 hourly workers.

In order to assess the effectiveness of the new policy, you must first decide what to measure and compare between the two years. Obviously, a comparison of paid sick leave between the two years might be misleading, because employees are converting unused sick leave into extra pay in the second year. Also, each employee participating in the exercise program costs the company $200 per year. It would seem more reasonable to compare the average cost of paid sick leave per employee before the antiabsenteeism program to the average cost of paid sick leave per employee after the new program was begun.

As a first step, we compute summary statistics for the variables. Minitab output is as follows:

```
Descriptive Statistics: HourlyPay, SickLeaveBefore, SickLeaveAfter

Variable              N      Mean    Median    TrMean     StDev   SE Mean
HourlyPay           233    10.959    11.010    10.963     0.697     0.046
SickLeaveBefore     233    13.161    13.250    13.176     5.018     0.329
SickLeaveAfter      233     8.683     9.250     8.854     3.420     0.224

Variable         Minimum   Maximum        Q1        Q3
HourlyPay          8.900    13.230    10.520    11.410
SickLeaveBefore    2.250    29.500     9.500    17.500
SickLeaveAfter     0.500    15.750     7.000    11.000

Tally for Discrete Variables: Exercise

Exercise   Count   Percent
       0     161     69.10
       1      72     30.90
      N=     233
```

Histograms of the variable SickLeaveBefore (days of sick leave taken last year before the new policy started) and SickLeaveAfter (days of sick leave taken this year under the new policy) are shown in Figure 9.7.

FIGURE 9.7   **Histograms of SickLeaveBefore and SickLeaveAfter**

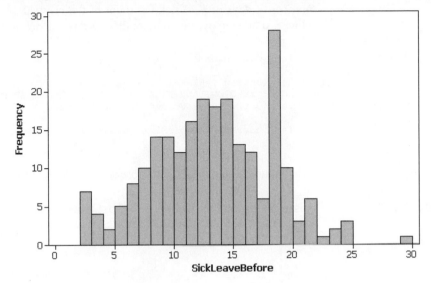

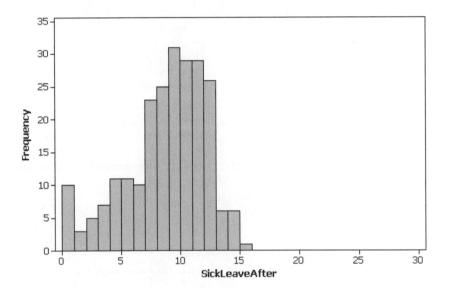

The summary statistics and the histograms show that there is a dramatic difference between SickLeaveBefore and SickLeaveAfter. (Note the excessive number of
values piled up at the "maximum allowable" 18 paid sick-leave days in the Sick-
LeaveBefore plot.) However, this difference is incomplete for determining the effectiveness of the new policy because the employees are converting their unused sick
leave into extra pay, which represents a cost to the company. Also, the company is
paying $200 for each of those employees participating in the exercise program (Ex-
ercise = 1). The costs of implementing the new policy must be included in the comparison to evaluate the effects of the sick-leave conversion and the exercise program.
Before the new policy went into effect, the cost related to absenteeism (CostBefore)
was simply the sick pay. Under the new policy, the costs (CostAfter) include sick
pay, the extra pay for unused sick leave, and the cost of the health club membership
for those employees participating in the exercise program. The Minitab calculations

of these two comparable cost figures follow. (The Unused variable represents the number of days of paid sick leave out of the original 18 days not used by an employee. If an employee used more than 18 days of sick leave, Unused is set to zero.)

```
MTB > let 'CostBefore' = 'SickLeaveBefore' * 'HourlyPay' * 8

MTB > let 'Unused' = 18 - 'SickLeaveAfter'
MTB > NOTE: ZERO OUT ANY NEGATIVE VALUES OF UNUSED SICK LEAVE.
MTB > let 'Unused' = ('Unused' >= 0) * 'Unused'

MTB > let 'CostAfter' = ('SickLeaveAfter' + 'Unused'/3) * 'HourlyPay' * 8
                        + 200 * 'Exercise'
```

Summary output for CostBefore and CostAfter are shown next and in Figure 9.8.

FIGURE 9.8 **Histograms of CostBefore and CostAfter**

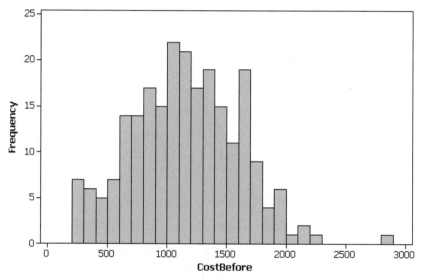

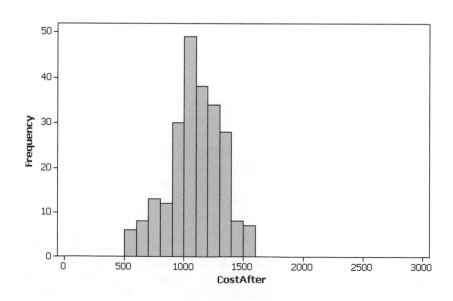

```
Descriptive Statistics: CostBefore, CostAfter

Variable          N        Mean      Median      TrMean       StDev    SE Mean
CostBefore      233      1153.6      1129.4      1151.2       452.3       29.6
CostAfter       233      1095.3      1094.4      1099.2       220.5       14.4

Variable    Minimum     Maximum          Q1          Q3
CostBefore    209.0      2817.8       830.9      1472.9
CostAfter     559.4      1595.0       966.0      1255.5
```

The data suggest that there has been a slight reduction in the average cost of paid sick leave since the new policy was begun (and a large reduction in the variation of paid sick-leave costs). To perform a statistical test of the effectiveness of the new policy, we could use a means comparison test. Incorrectly treating the data as two independent samples results in a failure to reject the null hypothesis of no difference at the 5% level of significance ($p = .078$). (A two-sided test should be used because it is possible that the new policy has resulted in an increase in the cost of paid sick leave.)

```
Two-sample T for CostBefore vs CostAfter

             N      Mean     StDev    SE Mean
CostBefore  233     1154       452        30
CostAfter   233     1095       220        14

Difference = mu CostBefore - mu CostAfter
Estimate for difference:  58.2
95% CI for difference: (-6.6, 123.1)
T-Test of difference = 0 (vs not =): T-Value = 1.77   P-Value = 0.078   DF = 336
```

The appropriate test, of course, is a paired-difference test because the two sets of measurements come from the same set of individuals. Minitab output is shown here for the paired test. The test shows that there is strong evidence ($p = .004$) to conclude a difference exists, in particular that there has been a significant reduction in the costs associated with paid sick leave under the new policy.

```
Paired T for CostBefore - CostAfter

              N      Mean     StDev    SE Mean
CostBefore   233    1153.6     452.3      29.6
CostAfter    233    1095.3     220.5      14.4
Difference   233      58.2     306.4      20.1

95% CI for mean difference: (18.7, 97.8)
T-Test of mean difference = 0 (vs not = 0): T-Value = 2.90   P-Value = 0.004
```

This example provides an excellent illustration of the difference between *statistical significance* and *practical significance*. When testing a hypothesis on a relatively large sample of data, such as we have here, it is possible to detect fairly small differences in the true means since the standard error of our test statistic is small. At issue is whether or not the *statistically* significant result we have observed is *practically* significant. (For example, in testing a null hypothesis that a certain car model obtains at least 35 mpg on average, when in fact the true mean is 34.9, we can always collect a large-enough sample to detect this difference statistically, but it is doubtful that anyone would consider this statistically significant result to be practically important.) Although the observed difference is statistically significant (those who don't agree should review *p*-values again!), you may conclude that the observed difference of $58.20 is not practically important. On an individual employee basis, this may be true, but in a company that employs approximately 250 hourly production workers, such as Circuit Systems, the annual savings amounts to $14,550. (For the 233 hourly workers in the data set, the actual total cost in the year before the new program was $268,780, and the total cost in the year under the new program was $255,209, for a savings of $13,571, or 5%.)

We should also note the increased production from reducing the amount of paid sick leave taken. As an example, consider a worker making the average $11.00 per hour who cashes in three unused paid sick-leave days. The sick leave would have cost the company $264 for no work. When the employee cashes in those three days of sick leave instead, the company pays only $88 but receives three full days of work from that employee. Since the difference in the average number of sick days before and after implementation is $(13.161 - 8.683) = 4.478$ days, the company received an additional $4.478 \times 233 = 1043.4$ days of work from the 233 hourly workers last year in addition to the cost savings of $13,571 under the new program. Assuming 250 working days in a year, that is equivalent to having 4.17 extra hourly production employees at no additional cost!

Now let's turn our attention to determining the value of the voluntary exercise program in the new antiabsenteeism program. Originally Tom hoped that the exercise program would reduce the cost of paid sick leave by improving the overall health of employees. However, it costs the company $200 per year for each employee taking advantage of this benefit. Approximately 31% of the employees accepted the subsidized health club membership in the first year of the program. Figure 9.9 shows box plots of SickLeaveBefore for the exercise group (Exercise = 1) and the nonexercise group (Exercise = 0), and a test of the difference in average paid sick leave taken by these groups before the new antiabsenteeism program was implemented is shown next.

```
Two-sample T for SickLeaveBefore

Exercise       N     Mean     StDev    SE Mean
0            161    13.15     5.08      0.40
1             72    13.18     4.91      0.58


Difference = mu (0) - mu (1)
Estimate for difference:  -0.028
95% CI for difference: (-1.420, 1.363)
T-Test of difference = 0 (vs not =): T-Value = -0.04  P-Value = 0.968  DF = 140
```

This evidence suggests that there was no difference between the two groups before the new program took effect. A similar analysis of SickLeaveAfter in the following Minitab output and in Figure 9.10 shows a difference of approximately one day in the average paid sick leave taken by the two groups.

```
Two-sample T for SickLeaveAfter

Exercise       N     Mean     StDev    SE Mean
0            161     8.97     3.43      0.27
1             72     8.03     3.33      0.39


Difference = mu (0) - mu (1)
Estimate for difference:  0.939
95% CI for difference: (-0.004, 1.882)
T-Test of difference = 0 (vs not =): T-Value = 1.97  P-Value = 0.051  DF = 140
```

FIGURE 9.9   **Box Plots of SickLeaveBefore by Exercise**

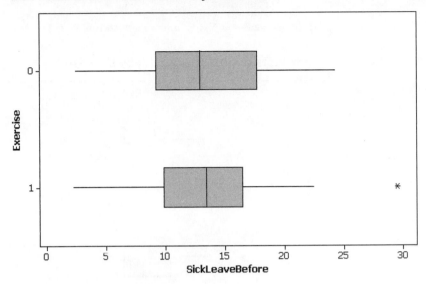

FIGURE 9.10   **Box Plots of SickLeaveAfter by Exercise**

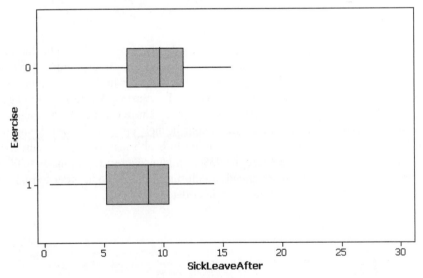

In the final analysis, however, cost is the most important factor in evaluating the worth of the exercise program. Box plots of the paired-difference cost variable Cost-Bef-CostAft for the exercise and nonexercise groups are shown in Figure 9.11 and a two-independent-samples test of the difference in average cost is shown next.

```
Two-sample T for CostBef-CostAft

Exercise      N       Mean      StDev    SE Mean
0            161       102        301        24
1             72       -40        297        35
```

```
Difference = mu (0) - mu (1)
Estimate for difference:  142.7
95% CI for difference: (59.0, 226.4)
T-Test of difference = 0 (vs not =): T-Value = 3.37  P-Value = 0.001  DF = 138
```

FIGURE 9.11   **Box Plots of CostBef-CostAft by Exercise**

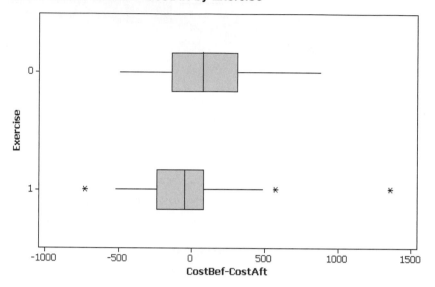

The analysis shows that the exercise group has an average paid sick-leave cost that is $142 less than that of the nonexercise group. However, remember that it costs the company $200 for each worker in the exercise program for membership in the local health club. After this adjustment, you might suggest discontinuing the exercise portion of the new program in order to save money. However, Circuit Systems expects this investment in their employees' well-being to substantially reduce the company's contribution to health insurance premiums in the long term. You might also point to the 95% confidence interval, noting that 200 is included in the interval, and recommend monitoring further data in order to make a decision about the exercise program at a later date.

SUMMARY

Here are some suggestions for making comparisons between two samples.

1. As usual, consider possible biases in the samples. Equivalent biases may more or less cancel each other out in making the comparison, but that's a risky assumption.

2. In analyzing the results, the first consideration is whether the samples are independent or paired. If there is a link between specific items in the two samples, they are paired.

3. For independent samples, plot the two samples separately in histograms and in side-by-side box plots. As usual, tests based on means (the pooled-variance t and the t' tests) are most effective for populations or processes that generate roughly

normally distributed data. A rank sum test is more powerful for highly skewed or outlier-prone data.

4. The choice between the pooled-variance t and the t' tests depends on whether the sample sizes are roughly equal. If they aren't, the pooled-variance t method can give badly incorrect probability statements. If the sample sizes are balanced, the pooled-variance t method will give correct probabilities unless there is extreme skewness.

5. For paired samples, the relevant plot is a histogram or stem-and-leaf plot of differences. If the differences appear roughly normally distributed, it doesn't matter what the two sample distributions look like. Again, the t methods work best for roughly normally distributed data. The signed-rank approach works well for symmetric but outlier-prone differences, but can give incorrect probabilities if the differences are clearly skewed. In the skewed-data case, a median (sign) procedure is the safest choice unless the sample size is large enough that the Central Limit Theorem effect can work.

6. A chi-square goodness-of-fit test compares counts to theoretical probabilities that are specified outside the data. In contrast, a chi-square independence test compares counts in one subset (one row, for example) to counts in other subsets (rows, for example) within the data. One way to decide which test is needed is to ask whether there is an externally stated set of theoretical probabilities. If so, the goodness-of-fit test is in order.

7. As is true with any significance test, the only purpose of a chi-square test is to see whether differences in sample data might reasonably have arisen by chance alone. A test cannot tell you directly how large or important the difference is. In particular, a statistically detectable (significant) chi-square independence test does not necessarily imply a strong relation, nor does a nonsignificant goodness-of-fit test necessarily imply that the sample percentages are very close to the theoretical probabilities.

8. Looking thoughtfully at the sample percentages is crucial in deciding whether the results show practical importance.

    In addition, you may want to reread the summary of key ideas in the Executive Overview at the beginning of this chapter.

Supplementary Exercises

9.44 An auditor for a national bank credit card samples the accounts of two local banks that process cardholders' accounts. The results are

Bank	Accounts Audited	Accounts in Error	Mean Error	Standard Deviation
A	475	41	$41.27	$19.42
B	384	39	$60.38	$31.68

The mean and standard deviations are based on only those accounts that are in error.

  a. Calculate a 95% confidence interval for the difference in true error proportions.
  b. Can the research hypothesis of unequal proportions be supported using $\alpha = .05$?

9.45   Find the p-value for the test in Exercise 9.44.

9.46   Refer to the data of Exercise 9.44.
  a. Calculate a 90% confidence interval for the difference in means.
  b. Give a careful interpretation of this confidence interval. To what population(s) does it apply?
  c. Test the research hypothesis of unequal means. Use $\alpha = .05$.
  d. Find the p-value for the test.

9.47   A small manufacturer has a choice between shipping via the postal service and via a private shipper. To compare the alternatives, 45 packages were shipped using the postal service and 35 packages were shipped via the private shipper. The postal service delivered its 45 packages in an average of 5.8 days while the private shipper delivered its 35 packages in an average of 5.2 days. The delivery times for the postal service had a standard deviation of 1.2 days and the delivery times for the private shipper had a standard deviation of 1.8 days. Construct a 95% confidence interval for the true difference in shipping times. Based on your interval, which of the two shipping methods, if either, is better? Explain why.

9.48   A fruit grower plants 12 stands of each of two varieties of apple tree. At maturity, the following yields are observed (in bushels per 100 trees):

Variety R: 64.2   71.1   59.8   74.6   37.1   58.7   61.6   54.0   47.3   53.2   68.0   61.1
Variety K: 59.9   72.0   62.1   66.7   32.4   49.0   57.4   50.8   49.0   48.6   61.9   60.0

Assume that the 24 stands are randomly selected from the grower's available acreage and that the yields are listed in an arbitrary order. Minitab output follows:

```
Two-sample T for VarietyR vs VarietyK

             N      Mean     StDev    SE Mean
VarietyR    12      59.2     10.4       3.0
VarietyK    12      55.8     10.5       3.0

Difference = mu VarietyR - mu VarietyK
Estimate for difference:  3.41

95% CI for difference: (-5.43, 12.24)

T-Test of difference = 0 (vs not =): T-Value = 0.80   P-Value = 0.432   DF = 22

Both use Pooled StDev = 10.4
```

  a. Use the t test to test the research hypothesis that the mean yield of variety R exceeds that of variety K. Use $\alpha = .10$.
  b. Use an appropriate rank test for the same hypothesis. Again use $\alpha = .10$.

9.49   Histograms of the data of Exercise 9.48 are shown in Figure 9.12. Which of the tests in that exercise seems more appropriate? Does it matter (to the conclusion) which test is used?

9.50   Find p-values for the tests of Exercise 9.48.

9.51   Refer to the data of Exercise 9.48. Now assume that the grower plants the two varieties side by side on 12 plots and that the data are presented by plot number, as analyzed in the following Minitab output:

FIGURE 9.12   **Histograms for Exercise 9.48**

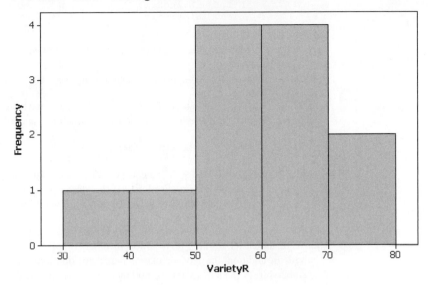

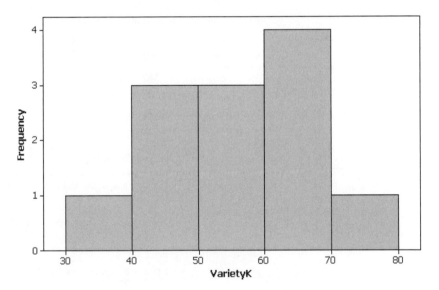

```
Paired T for VarietyR - VarietyK

              N      Mean     StDev    SE Mean
VarietyR      12     59.23    10.38    3.00
VarietyK      12     55.82    10.50    3.03
Difference    12      3.41     3.74    1.08

95% CI for mean difference: (1.03, 5.79)

T-Test of mean difference = 0 (vs not = 0): T-Value = 3.15   P-Value = 0.009

Wilcoxon Signed Rank Test: R-K

Test of median = 0.000000 versus median not = 0.000000
```

```
              N for   Wilcoxon            Estimated
         N    Test   Statistic      P      Median
R-K      12    12      70.0      0.017     3.700
```

a. Use a *t* test for the research hypothesis that the mean yield of variety R exceeds that of variety K. Use $\alpha = .10$.

b. Use a rank test for this hypothesis, again using $\alpha = .10$.

9.52 Plot the relevant data for Exercise 9.51. Which of the tests in that exercise seems more appropriate? Does it matter (to the conclusion) which test is used?

9.53 Find *p*-values for the tests of Exercise 9.51.

9.54 Exercises 9.48 and 9.51 indicate two alternative experimental designs. What is the advantage of the design in Exercise 9.51? If this design is adopted, how would you select the plots to ensure that the yield ratings were reasonably valid for the grower's entire farm?

9.55 A speaker who advises managers on how to avoid being unionized claims that only 25% of industrial workers favor union membership, 40% are indifferent, and 35% are opposed. In addition, the advisor claims that these opinions are independent of actual union membership. A random sample of 600 industrial workers yields the following data:

	Favor	**Indifferent**	**Opposed**	**Total**
Members	140	42	18	200
Nonmembers	70	198	132	400
Total	210	240	150	600

a. What part of the data is relevant to the 25%, 40%, 35% claim?

b. Test this hypothesis using $\alpha = .01$.

9.56 What can be said about the *p*-value in Exercise 9.55?

9.57 Test the hypothesis of independence in the data of Exercise 9.55, using the following output. How conclusively is it rejected?

```
Tabulated statistics: Membership, Opinion

Rows: Membership   Columns: Opinion

              Favor  Indifferent  Opposed  All

Member          140           42       18  200
                 70           80       50  200
              70.00        18.05    20.48    *

NonMember        70          198      132  400
                140          160      100  400
              35.00         9.02    10.24    *

All             210          240      150  600
                210          240      150  600
                  *            *        *    *

Cell Contents:       Count
                     Expected count
                     Contribution to Chi-square

Pearson Chi-Square = 162.794, DF = 2, P-Value = 0.000
Likelihood Ratio Chi-Square = 163.814, DF = 2, P-Value = 0.000
```

9.58 Calculate (for the data of Exercise 9.55) percentages of workers in favor of unionization, indifferent, and opposed; separately for members and for nonmembers. Do the percentages suggest that there is a strong relation between membership and opinion?

9.59 A coffee company wished to test its current method for grinding premium coffee against an experimental "coarse grind." The market research staff assembled 80 coffee drinkers as a test panel. Each panelist was present when pots of both grinds were brewed (because aroma during brewing was thought to be a cause of customer preference) and each tasted cups of coffee made from both grinds. The panelists evaluated taste and aroma on a 10-point scale where 1 was worst, 10 was best.

a. Why might the research staff want to make the study "blind," so that the panelists didn't know which coffee was which? How could blinding be arranged?

b. Why might the staff want to present the coffees in random order? How could that be done?

9.60 The panelists' ratings in Exercise 9.59 were entered into Minitab and analyzed.

a. Why should we regard the study as a paired-sample experiment?

b. One part of the Minitab output is the following:

```
Paired T-Test and CI: Original, Coarse

Paired T for Original - Coarse

               N       Mean     StDev     SE Mean
Original      80    4.76249   1.48616     0.16615
Coarse        80    5.66249   1.51735     0.16964
Difference    80   -0.900000  1.062598    0.118802

95% CI for mean difference: (-1.136470, -0.663530)
T-Test of mean difference = 0 (vs not = 0): T-Value = -7.58   P-Value = 0.000
```

The differences were taken as "original"–"coarse." What does the interval indicate about the null hypothesis that $\mu_d = 0.00$?

c. Calculate a 99% confidence interval for the mean difference. What does this interval indicate about the null hypothesis that $\mu_d = 0$?

9.61 Further output for Exercise 9.59, this time from Excel, is the following:

```
t-Test: Paired Two Sample for Means

                              Original    Coarse
Mean                            4.7625    5.6625
Variance                      2.208703  2.302373
Observations                        80        80
Pearson Correlation           0.749864
Hypothesized Mean Difference         0
df                                  79
t Stat                        -7.57563
P(T<=t) one-tail              2.91E-11
t Critical one-tail           1.664371
P(T<=t) two-tail              5.82E-11
t Critical two-tail           1.990452
```

Explain why the two-tailed p-value shown in the output is compatible with your answers in parts (b) and (c) of Exercise 9.59.

9.62 The data from Exercise 9.59 are also analyzed using a pooled-variance t method.

a. Explain why this method should *not* be used in this situation.

b. The Minitab results are as follows:

```
Two-sample T for Original vs Coarse

             N     Mean    StDev    SE Mean
Original    80     4.76     1.49       0.17
Coarse      80     5.66     1.52       0.17
```

```
Difference = mu Original - mu Coarse
Estimate for difference:  -0.900

95% CI for difference: (-1.369, -0.431)

T-Test of difference = 0 (vs not =): T-Value = -3.79  P-Value = 0.000  DF = 158

Both use Pooled StDev = 1.50
```

What do the confidence interval and *p*-value in the output indicate about the null hypothesis of equal means?

c. How does the width of this confidence interval compare to the width of the interval based on differences? What does the comparison indicate about the effectiveness of the pairing of observations?

9.63 A confidence interval and test based on the signed-rank method was also obtained for the data of Exercise 9.59.

```
Wilcoxon Signed Rank CI: Diff

                 Estimated    Achieved
            N     Median    Confidence  Confidence Interval
Diff        80    -1.000       95.0      ( -1.000,  -0.500)

Wilcoxon Signed Rank Test: Diff

Test of median = 0.000000 versus median not = 0.000000

                N for    Wilcoxon             Estimated
            N    Test    Statistic      P      Median
Diff        80    60       160.5     0.000     -1.000
```

Would you call these results substantially different from those we obtained in Exercises 9.59 and 9.60?

9.64 A stem-and-leaf display of the differences in Exercise 9.59 was obtained from Minitab.

```
Stem-and-leaf of Diff      N  = 80
Leaf Unit = 0.10

     1    -1 9
     7    -0 999999
    17    -0 0000000000
    27     0 0000000000
   (31)    1 0000000000000000000000000000000
    22     2 00000000000000000
     5     3 00000
```

Are the data so nonnormal that a *t* method should not be used?

9.65 Three different television commercials are advertising an established product. The commercials are shown separately to theater panels of consumers; each consumer views only one of the possible commercials and then states an opinion of the product. Opinions range from 1 (very favorable) to 5 (very unfavorable). The data are

	Opinion					
Commercial	1	2	3	4	5	Total
A	32	87	91	46	44	300
B	53	141	76	20	10	300
C	41	93	67	36	63	300
Total	126	321	234	102	117	900

Minitab output follows:

Tabulated Statistics: Commercial, Opinion

Rows: Commercial   Columns: Opinion

	1	2	3	4	5	All
A	32	87	91	46	44	300
	10.67	29.00	30.33	15.33	14.67	100.00
B	53	141	76	20	10	300
	17.67	47.00	25.33	6.67	3.33	100.00
C	41	93	67	36	63	300
	13.67	31.00	22.33	12.00	21.00	100.00
All	126	321	234	102	117	900
	14.00	35.67	26.00	11.33	13.00	100.00

Cell Contents --
                Count
                % of Row

Chi-Square = 72.521, DF = 8, P-Value = 0.000

Is there evidence that the opinion distributions are different for the various commercials? Use $\alpha = .01$.

9.66 A machine shop has changed some of its welders from a straight salary to a piece rate. To see if this resulted in a change in worker productivity, the foreman was asked to keep a record of one day's output (number of pieces completed) for each employee. The 12 salaried workers completed an average of 118.3 pieces per employee and had a standard deviation of 5.4 pieces. The 15 piece-rate workers completed an average of 124.1 pieces per employee and had a standard deviation of 8.2 pieces.

a. Construct a 90% confidence interval for the true difference in the average number of pieces completed per day by the two groups.

b. Based on your confidence interval, what can be concluded about the production levels of salaried versus piece-rate welders in this company?

9.67 Recently, a number of opticians established on-site laboratories for preparing prescription eyeglasses. These labs provide much more rapid service than conventional off-premises labs. Conventional opticians have questioned the accuracy of on-site labs. As a test, eyeglasses prescribed for nearsightedness were prepared by both types of labs. The glasses were evaluated by very accurate devices that determine the percentage deviation from the prescribed correction. A minus sign indicates that the actual correction was less than prescribed; a plus sign, more than prescribed. Computer output is shown below; source 1 is conventional labs, source 2 is on-site labs.

Two-Sample T-Test and CI: Deviation, Source

Two-sample T for Deviation

Source	N	Mean	StDev	SE Mean
1	43	-0.24	3.57	0.54
2	26	-0.37	7.09	1.4

Difference = mu (1) - mu (2)
Estimate for difference: 0.120349
95% CI for difference: (-2.920170, 3.160867)
T-Test of difference = 0 (vs not =): T-Value = 0.08 P-Value = 0.936 DF = 32

```
Test for Equal Variances: Deviation versus Source

95% Bonferroni confidence intervals for standard deviations

Source   N    Lower     StDev    Upper
     1  43  2.86745   3.57164   4.7072
     2  26  5.37559   7.08647  10.2795

F-Test (normal distribution)
Test statistic = 0.25, p-value = 0.000

Levene's Test (any continuous distribution)
Test statistic = 7.32, p-value = 0.009
```

    a. Is there a statistically detectable (significant) difference of means, according to the output?
    b. Can the result be interpreted that there is no evidence of a difference between conventional and on-site labs?

9.68 Refer to Exercise 9.67.
    a. Use the computer output to test the null hypothesis of equal standard deviations, using a two-sided research hypothesis. Find bounds on the p-value. Note that we have not described this test, but the p-value may be interpreted as usual.
    b. What does the result of this test indicate about the relative quality of the two sources?

9.69 An accountant decided to test whether submitting federal income tax forms electronically will speed the delivery of refunds. The accountant submitted one sample of forms electronically and sent another sample by mail. The number of business days until a refund was received was recorded in column 1 of the EX0969 file on the CD. Column 2 contains a code for the type of submission; a 1 indicates electronic submission, a 2 indicates mail submission. Load the data into the statistical computer package you use.
    a. Obtain means, standard deviations, and sample sizes for the two samples.
    b. Obtain separate plots of the two samples (histograms, stem-and-leaf displays, or normal plots, as you prefer).
    c. Based on this information, which of the several possible methods for comparing the average values in the samples seems most appropriate to you? Why?
    d. Carry out a formal test of the null hypothesis of equal means using the method you selected in part (c). Locate the p-value.

9.70 Refer to Exercise 9.69.
    a. Obtain a 99% confidence interval for the difference of means. Use the method you selected in that exercise.
    b. How does the interval confirm the result of the test in part (d) of Exercise 9.69?

9.71 A magazine conducted an experiment concerning investment advisers. The editors prepared 50 descriptions of the financial positions of hypothetical families with the husband earning a larger share of the income; they prepared an additional 50 descriptions that were identical, except that the wife earned the larger share of the income. Each description was sent to one of 100 advisers, who recommended a portfolio of investments. The editors calculated the previous year's yield on each investment. The yields are stored in the EX0971 file on the CD, with the husband-larger-income descriptions in column 1 and the matching wife-larger-income descriptions in column 2. Load the data into a statistical computer package that you can use.
    a. Explain why the data should *not* be analyzed using pooled-variance t methods.
    b. Have the package compute differences. Obtain a normal plot of the differences. Is there a clear indication of nonnormality?
    c. Obtain a t statistic for the null hypothesis that the mean of the differences is 0. Obtain a p-value.
    d. Should a one-sided or two-sided test be used here? (This question might just possibly provoke some gender-based disagreement.)

9.72   Refer to Exercise 9.71.

a. Have the computer package perform a signed-rank test of the null hypothesis that the differences are symmetric around 0, using the difference data. Which result is more conclusive, the signed-rank or the t test of Exercise 9.71?

b. Test the null hypothesis that the *median* difference is 0 using the same data. Is this test more or less conclusive than the other two, or do they all give about the same conclusion?

9.73   Refer to Exercise 9.71.

a. Ignore the fact that the pooled-variance t test isn't appropriate for the data of the exercise and have the computer package use that method to test the null hypothesis of equal means. Locate the p-value.

b. Is the pooled-variance t result more conclusive (that there is a detectable difference) than the t test on differences, or less so? What does the comparison of results indicate about the usefulness of matching descriptions?

9.74   A supermarket mailed coupons good for 25 cents off the price of cleaning products. At random, either product 1 or product 2 received the cents-off promotion. The supermarket wanted to find out which product would attract better-spending shoppers. The amount spent by each shopper who redeemed a coupon is recorded in column 1 of the EX0974 file on the CD; the product receiving the cents off for that coupon is shown in column 2. Load the data into your computer package.

a. Obtain histograms or stem-and-leaf displays of the purchase amounts separately for the two products. Do the plots appear roughly normal?

b. Obtain a 95% confidence interval for the difference of means using the pooled-variance t method. Also, obtain a similar interval using the separate-variance (t') method. For each interval, can we reject the null hypothesis of equal means using $\alpha = .05$?

c. Are the two intervals we obtain in part (b) essentially identical? If not, which one should be believed?

9.75   Refer to Exercise 9.74.

a. Carry out formal t tests (both pooled-variance and t') of the null hypothesis of equal means for the spending data. Obtain two-tailed p-values for both tests.

b. Carry out a test of the null hypothesis of equal distributions using a rank sum test. Again, obtain a two-tailed p-value.

c. Which of the three test results appears to be most conclusive? Can the p-value for this test be believed?

BUSINESS CASES

Snack Food Market Testing

A maker of crackers and other snack food was market-testing two versions of a microwaved snack. A total of 200 adult volunteers were recruited to appear at a suburban shopping mall one evening. Each person filled out a brief questionnaire concerning age, education, income, and similar facts. From these facts, each person received a Target Customer Score (TCS) based on how desirable the person would be as a customer. Then the questionnaires were sorted from lowest to highest TCS score. Customers with TCS scores 1, 4, 5, 8, 9, 12, and so on were assigned to Group K; TCS scores 2, 3, 6, 7, 10, 11, and so on went to Group S. (The letters meant nothing, deliberately.) Customers in both groups evaluated several other products and a number of possible television commercials. The important data were approval ratings of two versions (also labeled K and S) of the microwaved snack product. The ratings were based on a bidding system that the company believed gave accurate readings of actual preferences. The company thought that each additional bidding point, on average, would result in about three-tenths of a point of additional market share for the selected version of the product.

```
Group K
   33   67   39   48   69   55   66   52   58   43   57   77   58   58   71   40   54
   52   60   69   70   76   62   73   69   72   56   54   68   55   45   82   82   66
   63   67   59   69   65   73   65   66   62   83   59   77   62   68   67   71   75
   74   59   65   59   73   71   75   59   76   72   61   79   63   58   64   68   77
   85   68   58   88   65   74   60   62   59   58   66   77   65   60   68   73   74
   78   68   60   71   67   75   71   84   65   63   57   83   75   72   67

Group S
   27   64   48   43   66   45   64   52   45   35   62   69   70   55   66   52   48
   45   61   72   64   57   61   60   63   85   55   51   76   68   48   81   80   67
   70   68   68   63   63   76   67   66   62   76   67   73   59   66   61   66   85
   65   60   78   56   78   74   76   72   78   62   72   76   64   66   70   72   73
   86   84   60   87   78   82   73   61   59   68   73   81   69   66   84   82   75
   78   69   67   80   72   86   74   78   67   62   71   86   79   82   70
```

```
                 N      MEAN    MEDIAN    TRMEAN    STDEV    SEMEAN
Group K         100     65.76    66.50     66.14    10.15     1.01
Group S         100     67.42    68.00     67.97    11.65     1.16

                MIN      MAX       Q1        Q3
Group K       33.00    88.00     59.00     73.00
Group S       27.00    87.00     61.25     76.00
```

Assignment: The data, in order from lowest to highest TCS score, and some very preliminary analyses have been supplied to you. You have been selected as a consultant to determine whether the study has provided adequate information to decide which microwaved snack is better and by how much. Perform whatever additional analyses you feel are necessary and prepare a consultant's report to the company.

ServPro, Inc.

It all started out peaceably enough. Tom Johnson, one of the new service reps, asked Al Washington and Michael Post about their salaries. The question was innocent enough and the answers suggested that all three were making about the same money. Nobody seemed concerned. Then Michael Post said that he had seen a memo on his boss's desk that listed salaries for the entire department and noticed something "funny"—all three of them were near the bottom. In fact, he said, "Just about every other minority in the department was in the bottom half of the list."

Well, this started the three of them wondering out loud about whether their company, ServPro, Inc., was discriminating against minorities. They kicked it around all through lunch and then talked about it again each day for the next week. And each day, somebody would come in with scuttlebutt from one of the other national offices that suggested minorities were not being paid the same as nonminorities. They had "rough" information from four additional offices that, on average, suggested minorities were making about $250 a month less than nonminorities.

Tom Johnson got mad. He told the others, "When Al Miller recruited me here last year, he told me that ServPro's management believed in affirmative action. He promised that I would go as far in this company as my effort and good work would take me. I'm not saying that this past year has been bad, but this salary stuff makes me wonder about whether I should stay or start looking for a place where minorities are treated the same as nonminorities!" Al and Michael agreed.

The more they talked, the more they felt let down by a company that at first had looked like a place that would ignore race. They had all been impressed with the company's strong affirmative action stance. They were told that advancement, and salary, would depend on how well they did their jobs—that they could expect to move from an assistant service rep (grade 1) to service rep (grade 2) in two to three years and then move to senior service rep (grade 3) somewhere from three to four years later. They were led to expect annual performance reviews, with pay raises determined by their performance during the previous year. They liked the developmental program ServPro had to offer and looked forward to more responsibility as they moved up the career ladder. It was disappointing to think that ServPro might turn out to be the kind of place where racial discrimination would limit their opportunities.

For several weeks Tom Johnson didn't say anything about the salary incident. On his own, though, he started reading about fair employment law and his options if he believed that his civil liberties were being violated. He even called the local office of the Equal Employment Opportunity Commission (EEOC) and spoke with a field agent, Mark Malone, about his situation, who suggested he bring the matter up with his supervisor. Malone told him that in his experience, appearances were not always what they seemed and that usually matters such as this are easily explained by the company. He did, however, clarify that a $250 per month salary difference between minorities and nonminorities was not trivial and would indeed get EEOC's attention if Tom were still concerned after going through official company channels.

Escorted by his two friends, Tom Johnson went to see Howard Kirk, his department manager. Kirk seemed somewhat agitated when Johnson confronted him with the "facts" and simply dismissed their protest as "complete nonsense." He told the three of them to leave the management work to managers and to get back to work so they could learn their jobs well enough to earn a good evaluation and a good pay raise next year. When Tom Johnson "wondered out loud" about whether their performance evaluations were chosen to justify lowered pay raises to minorities, Kirk blew up. He told them bluntly to quit trying to cause trouble. He informed them, in no uncertain terms and very loudly, that ". . . salary is based on performance and loyalty to the company. The single best way you can improve your salaries is to pay as much attention to your jobs as apparently you're paying to information that is none of your business." He then "dismissed" them.

Predictably, Tom Johnson found the content and tone of Kirk's remarks offensive. Together with Al and Michael, he organized a small group of minority peers and threatened to visit the EEOC claims office to pursue their conviction that ServPro practices discriminatory pay practices.

As president of ServPro, you heard about the problem almost immediately through the grapevine and called a meeting with Johnson, Washington, and Post that afternoon. It was a more relaxed conversation. You began by asking them to explain their concerns. Tom Johnson went through the "facts," this time describing how they were treated by Howard Kirk.

You assured the three of them that ServPro did not discriminate against anybody. You repeated Kirk's message about how pay is determined, but without the offensive tone. You outlined the voluntary affirmative action program initiated by ServPro over two years ago as being just an example of the philosophy that ServPro values what people do on the job over their race or gender. Johnson was willing to listen to the pay policy and talk about the affirmative hiring program but continued to focus on the apparent salary differences despite such policies. He insisted that salary equity be achieved and so would not relinquish his claim of discrimination. But because he was impressed by your statements regarding the company's affirmative stance in hiring, Johnson expressed a willingness to meet with you again, once you had more information.

You promised you would report back to the three employees personally at the second meeting, based on having looked into this matter and into the data relevant to it. Johnson and the others seemed willing for you to gather and organize that information and said they looked forward to meeting with you again.

Assignment: The director of human resources has provided you with employment information for all 140 service representatives within the company. You need to examine the data contained in this file and attempt to resolve the issues brought forth by Tom Johnson.

Based on your understanding of the issues and your interpretation of the employment and salary data, write a brief report summarizing your beliefs about the presence or absence of salary discrimination at ServPro. Use important details from your data analysis to support your findings.

The personnel data for ServPro, Inc. are contained in the file ServPro on the CD that came with your book. The file contains employment and salary data for ServPro's 140 employees. Figure 9.13 shows a partial listing of the data within Excel.

FIGURE 9.13 | **Partial Listing of the ServPro Data**

	A	B	C	D	E	F	G	H	I
1	ID	PayGrade	Gender	Minority	Married	Age	Tenure	Rating	Salary
2	1	1	M	1	0	18	0.5	2	2390
3	2	1	M	0	0	25	2.4	3	2860
4	3	2	M	0	0	23	3.6	7	3570
5	4	1	F	1	0	26	1.9	3	2690
6	5	2	M	0	1	22	3.4	6	2790
7	6	1	M	1	1	23	2.8	4	2510
8	7	1	F	0	1	31	2.3	3	2590
9	8	1	M	0	1	21	0.4	2	2380
10	9	2	F	0	0	31	3.0	5	3020
11	10	1	M	1	1	38	1.4	3	2790
12	11	2	M	0	1	32	3.8	7	2690
13	12	3	M	0	0	24	4.6	10	3750
14	13	1	F	0	1	20	1.8	3	2630
15	14	1	F	1	1	23	3.4	4	2690
16	15	3	F	1	1	32	3.8	9	3480

In the ServPro file, the variables are defined as follows:

ID:	Sequential ID number assigned to all employees
Pay Grade:	Pay grade (= 1, 2, or 3)
Gender:	F, for female; M, for male
Minority:	1, if minority; 0, otherwise
Married:	1, if married; 0, if not married
Age:	Age in years at last birthday
Tenure:	Number of years employed as a service representative at ServPro
Rating:	Employee performance rating, on a 10-point scale, where 1 = poor performance and 10 = excellent performance
Salary:	Current monthly salary, expressed in dollars

CHAPTER 10

Analysis of Variance

and Designed Experiments

This chapter introduces some of the basic ideas of designing and analyzing statistical experiments. Careful experimentation is one key to improving the quality of goods and services. Analysis of variance (ANOVA) methods can deal with a wide variety of experimental situations. The key ideas are

- The first step in analyzing an experiment is to determine what are the factors (variables that are deliberately varied in carrying out the experiment) and what is the response or dependent variable.

- The analysis of variance is based on taking apart the total sum of squared deviations from the grand mean. In a one-factor experiment, the total sum of squares is analyzed into sums of squares between groups (reflecting differences in mean values for the levels of the factor) and within groups (reflecting random variation or error).

- An F test is an overall test to determine whether there is a more-than-random difference somewhere among the means.

- If the underlying populations are highly skewed or outlier-prone, a Kruskal–Wallis rank test usually is more effective in detecting any real differences.

- The Tukey method for comparing pairs of means controls the overall risk of false positive errors. Each pair of means is compared to a critical value determined by a table value times a standard error.

- When there are two or more factors, there is the possibility of interaction. Interaction is an "it depends" concept. Two factors interact if the effect on the response variable of varying one factor depends on the level of the other factor.

- Interaction can be detected graphically by using a profile (interaction) plot. Profiles that are nearly parallel indicate little interaction. Interaction can be detected numerically by comparing cell means to the results predicted by simply adding the effects of each factor. The ANOVA table for a two-factor experiment with multiple measurements in each cell includes sums of squares for each factor separately, for interaction, and for random error.

- When interaction is large, the separate effect of one factor (averaged over levels of the other) is usually not very relevant. What is more interesting is finding the best combination of factor levels.

- A randomized block experiment is an extension of the idea of paired samples. In such an experiment, the factor of interest is randomized within levels of another, nuisance factor which is thought to affect the response. The purpose is to avoid confounding (mixing together) the effects of the two factors and to control for an important source of variability. When there is only one observation per cell, as is usually true in randomized block experiments, it isn't possible to separate interaction from random error.

CHAPTER CASE
INTRODUCTION

Checker's Pizza

Checker's Pizza is a chain of 40 pizza restaurants in the New England area. Started in 1985, Checker's specialized in pizzas "from scratch" with a special sauce made from a "secret" family recipe that kept customers coming back for more. But Checker's, like other pizza restaurants in the 1980s and 1990s, had to respond to the new wave of fast-food pizza restaurants and delivery services that seemed to corner the market.

Checker's changed the way it did business. Not only did it expand the product line and start delivering pizzas like its competitors, it also started making pizza using the same "fast-food" techniques as they did. Old customers were very aware that the pizzas were different. But while the pizzas were now baked in a conveyer oven and made from frozen dough prepared in a central kitchen, the sauce had not changed at all. And that was the key to the business. Old customers knew that the pizzas were not as good, but new customers knew only that the pizzas were better.

Still, the pizza business had fallen on hard times by the late 1990s. Competition for customers in the fast-food business was fierce and the weak economy at that time had reduced everybody's business. It was in this business climate that Terri Chester was hired as general manager of the Checker's Pizza chain. Her job was to restore market share and profits.

Terri went about her mission systematically. She worked with her executive team to identify and prioritize key issues and then set up a series of task forces to deal with those problems that needed immediate attention. Among the key problems was employee turnover, which was considered extremely high. Terri knew that the high turnover rate not only raised expenses due to the cost of replacing personnel but also affected customer service. It's hard to serve customers well when you have a continual stream of new staff who don't yet know their jobs.

Checker's Pizza, like all fast-food restaurants, employs teenagers in most positions. They work on the counter and as wait staff, cooks, and delivery drivers. As is typical with this group, turnover tends to be high. In fact, in the fast-food industry, annual turnover for younger employees typically ranges from 200 to 600%! So a lot of money is spent on recruitment, interviewing, hiring, and training, as well as on the intangible costs associated with staff who haven't climbed the learning curve far enough to fully pull their own weight. The employee turnover task force estimated that it costs Checker's about $500 to replace someone who quits.

Over the past three years, Checker's Pizza has had an average annual turnover rate of 400% across all of its restaurants. This translates into an average stay of 90 days for newly hired personnel. In turn, this means that on average each store replaces 48 employees over the course of a year since each store has 12 employees. At a $500 replacement cost, it all adds up to $24,000 in annual replacement costs per store and $960,000 per year across the chain!

Terri Chester hired a consultant, Dr. Shannon Train, from a local university to study why people were leaving. The consultant conducted a brief telephone interview with a sample of former employees. While a large list of specific reasons was put together, the one theme that came up time and again was the treatment employees received from store management. Leavers said they were often treated "like children" by their managers. Store managers reacted quickly and harshly toward employees whenever they did anything that did not reflect store policy, even toward newly hired people who didn't fully understand what store policy actually was. Also, managers seldom involved staff in any discussion of problems.

Dr. Train suggested that Terri focus on store management's treatment of staff, particularly newly hired staff. Out of the several approaches commonly used to deal with this problem, he recommended two in particular. First, he suggested that store managers receive a two-day human relations training program designed not only to impress upon them the importance of interpersonal relations but to help managers develop the important interpersonal skills that help establish good working relationships. The second alternative was to give store managers an incentive for keeping staff from quitting. He had heard that other companies in the fast-food industry had some success with this approach. He suggested that managers be given $200 (40% of the replacement costs that would have been spent) for keeping employees twice as long as they currently stayed. So store managers would receive a $200 bonus for each new hire who stayed at least six months (180 days). The cost of the two-day interpersonal skills workshop would be $500 per manager, or $20,000 for all 40 store managers.

Dr. Train suggested doing both the training and the bonus and undertaking a less-expensive pilot study instead of a full-scale program. As Dr. Train put it, "If you really hope to put a dent in the retention problem, you might need to do both training and the bonus. Think of it this way: To get managers to change their behavior, you need to give them not only a reason to change but the skills to do so. As I tell my students, empowerment requires enablement. Now, managers may know perfectly well how to treat their people to keep them from leaving in droves. If true, you only need to give them some incentive. On the other hand, your managers may have good interpersonal skills in general but may not have the interpersonal skills needed to work with teenagers. So, maybe all that's needed is the skills training. It's hard to say, without looking into it more carefully, whether either one or the other approach will be enough to do the trick or whether both might be necessary."

While Terri liked both ideas, she wasn't ready to proceed with both at the same time. That would take a substantial commitment of money at a time when the budget was tight. Dr. Train suggested running an experiment to see if either, or both, approaches worked before Terri committed funds company-wide to either, and she bought the idea.

In the experiment Dr. Train designed, 40 store managers were randomly assigned to one of four "experimental" conditions that reflected all combinations of the training and bonus conditions: (1) no training–no bonus, (2) no training–bonus, (3) training–no bonus, and (4) training–bonus. Ten store managers were assigned to each condition.

The training and a presentation of the bonus program were done by the end of the month and the actual experiment began the following month. All restaurant staff hired during the month were included in the study, and their length of stay was followed for 12 months. Tenure was recorded in days, from the date of hire until the date of termination or until the date the study ended. Thus, tenure could range from 1 day up to 365 days for those who were still employed when the study ended.

All data for this staff retention study are contained in the file Checkers on the CD that came with your book. A partial listing of the data within Excel is shown in Figure 10.1.

FIGURE 10.1   **Partial Listing of the Checker's Pizza Data**

	A	B	C	D
1	ID	Training	Bonus	Tenure
2	1	0	0	14
3	2	0	1	178
4	3	1	1	164
5	4	0	1	97
6	5	0	1	116
7	6	1	0	231
8	7	1	0	108
9	8	0	1	55
10	9	1	0	102
11	10	0	1	85
12	11	1	0	91

In the Checkers file, the variables are defined as follows:

ID: Sequential identification number assigned to an employee included in the study

Training: 1 = training given to employee's store manager,

           0 = no training given

Bonus: 1 = bonus given to employee's store manager,

           0 = no bonus given

Tenure: Number of days the person was employed, from date of hire to the date of termination or the date the study ended

As a member of the retention task force, you have been asked by Terri Chester to examine these data. Based on your analysis and other information presented in this case, you are to make a recommendation whether or not to use either, or both, of the training and bonus interventions to reduce turnover among restaurant staff. Use important details from your analysis to support your recommendation. You will find the material covered in this chapter and in the previous chapters to be extremely helpful in your analysis and decision-making process. ■

ONE OF THE MOST notable trends in management during the past decade has been the use of scientifically controlled, carefully designed experiments. Controlled experiments are especially useful to managers in the assessment of the likely effect of changes. To assess the probable results of a change in product, process, or policy, one can perform an experiment on carefully chosen samples, make the change, and measure the results. Well-designed experiments convert a discussion from speculative opinion to the assessment of actual data. That's an improvement.

This chapter is devoted to analysis of variance (ANOVA) methods that were specifically developed to analyze experimental data. These methods are also useful in certain nonexperimental situations. Typically, the data resulting from an experiment consist of multiple samples, so we must extend the two-sample methods from Chapter 9 to apply to many samples. In Section 10.1 we discuss ANOVA methods for one-factor experiments in which the multiple samples are obtained by changing the values of a single experimental variable. We explore a rank-based alternative method in Section 10.2. We list some more detailed methods for exploring specific parts of the data when we discuss the topic of multiple comparisons in Section 10.3. The recent realization of the value of experiments has led to much more interest in more complex multifactor experiments, which we discuss in Sections 10.4 and 10.5.

10.1 Testing the Equality of Several Population Means

factor
dependent variable

The simplest experiments vary only one variable and measure the results on another, response variable. The experimental variable, which often is qualitative, is called a **factor.** The response variable, which is quantitative, is called a **dependent variable,** or simply the response. For example, suppose that a manufacturing firm is considering possible policies for selecting supervisors for work areas. Three possible policies are A, to promote from within the work force, using in-house training; B, to promote from within, using a local community college for supervisory training; and C, to hire only experienced supervisors from outside. The firm wants to see if the effectiveness rating varies by selection policy. The response of interest is the rating. The factor being varied is the selection policy.

This is not a true designed experiment. The firm has supervisors hired under each of the three conditions. Ideally, these supervisors would be assigned completely at random to work areas to avoid any biases caused by the assignment process. This is an idealization; without randomization, we may have to make an unverified assumption that there are no biases. Assume that no evident source of bias can be identified, so that we're willing to use the data, which are effectiveness ratings on the firm's standard 100-point scale. The data are

								Mean	Variance	n
Policy A	39	51	58	61	65	72	86	61.71	225.24	7
Policy B	22	38	43	47	49	54	72	46.43	232.95	7
Policy C	18	31	41	43	44	54	65	42.29	229.24	7

It appears that the policy A supervisors have substantially higher average ratings, but there is a great deal of variability within each group and the sample sizes are very small. Is it plausible to assume that the apparent differences in average ratings are merely the result of random variation?

overall risk

We might be tempted to run a two-sample t test on all pairs of means, using the methods of Chapter 9. Resist the temptation. If we ran many t tests, each at a given α level, we wouldn't know what the **overall risk** of a Type I (false positive) error is. Certainly, the more tests one runs, the greater the risk of a false positive conclusion somewhere among the tests. The analysis of variance (ANOVA) method leads to a single test statistic for comparing all the means, so the overall risk of Type I error can be controlled. Therefore, ANOVA is preferable to multiple t tests.

sums of squares

The analysis of variance is based on "taking apart" the variability in the data into (1) a part attributable to variation between groups, and (2) another remaining part attributable to variation within groups. Variation is assessed by **sums of squares** (SS). The calculations can be done by most statistical packages. For example, here is part of the output analyzing the ratings data using the Minitab package.

```
One-way ANOVA: Rating versus Policy

Source   DF    SS    MS      F      P
Policy    2   1466   733   3.20   0.065
Error    18   4125   229
Total    20   5591
```

To begin with, we (or the computer program) calculate the total sum of squares as the sum of squared deviations of individual values around the grand mean of all scores. For the example, we can calculate the grand mean by averaging all 21 values or by averaging the 3 group means:

$$\bar{y} = \frac{39 + 51 + 58 + \cdots + 44 + 54 + 65}{21}$$

$$= (61.71 + 46.43 + 42.29)/3 = 50.142$$

SS(Total)

Then **SS(Total)** is by definition the sum of all squared deviations around this mean.

$$SS(Total) = (39 - 50.142)^2 + (51 - 50.142)^2 + (58 - 50.142)^2 + \cdots$$
$$+ (44 - 50.142)^2 + (54 - 50.142)^2 + (65 - 50.142)^2$$
$$= 5590.57$$

variability between groups

Variability between groups is denoted SS(Between) or SS(Factor). It is the sum of squared deviations of each group mean from the grand mean, multiplied by the sample size for the group.

$$SS(Between) = 7(61.71 - 50.142)^2 + 7(46.43 - 50.142)^2 + 7(42.29 - 50.142)^2$$
$$= 1466.00$$

If the means for the various groups (the various levels of the experimental factor) are nearly the same, there is little variability attributed to the factor and SS(Between) will be small. But if the means differ greatly, there will be large variability attributed to the factor and a large SS(Between) value.

variability within groups

To evaluate **variability within groups,** we look at deviations within each group from the mean *for that group.* The calculation can be done either from the raw data or from the group variances multiplied by the respective degrees of freedom.

$$SS(Within) = (39 - 61.714)^2 + (51 - 61.714)^2 + \cdots + (22 - 46.428)^2$$
$$+ (38 - 46.428)^2 + \cdots + (18 - 42.285)^2 + \cdots + (65 - 42.285)^2$$
$$= (7 - 1)225.24 + (7 - 1)232.95 + (7 - 1)229.24$$
$$= 4124.57$$

If all the data in each group are close together and therefore close to the group mean, the variances and SS(Within) will be small. If the data in each group vary considerably, the variances and SS(Within) will be large.

ANOVA calculations are based on the following notation; they can be done by most statistical packages. See Table 10.1.

$y_{ij} = j$th sample measurement in group i

$\quad i = 1, 2, \ldots, I; \qquad j = 1, 2, \ldots, n_i$

$n_i = $ sample size for group i

$\bar{y}_i = $ sample mean for group i

$\bar{y} = $ average of all the sample measurements

$n = $ the total sample size. For the preceding data, $n = n_1 + n_2 + \cdots + n_I$

With this notation it is possible to express the variability of the n sample measurements about $\bar{y}$ as

$$SS(\text{Total}) = \sum_{i,j} (y_{ij} - \bar{y})^2$$

and to partition this quantity into two components, SS(Between) and SS(Within).

$$\sum_{i,j} (y_{ij} - \bar{y})^2 = \sum_i n_i(\bar{y}_i - \bar{y})^2 + \sum_{i,j} (y_{ij} - \bar{y}_i)^2$$

$$SS(\text{Total}) = SS(\text{Between}) + SS(\text{Within})$$

SS(Within)

Because **SS(Within)** is based on deviations from specific group means, it is not affected by possible deviations of these sample means from each other; SS(Within) reflects only random variation within the samples. In contrast, SS(Between) is strongly affected by discrepancies among group means. If the true group means μ_i are equal, the sample means $\bar{y}_i$ are close to each other and therefore close to the grand mean $\bar{y}$, and SS(Between) tends to be small. But if the true group means are different, the sample means tend to be far apart and **SS(Between)** tends to be large. If SS(Between) is large relative to SS(Within), the null hypothesis that the true group means are equal should be rejected.

SS(Between)

TABLE 10.1

Notation for Sample Data in an ANOVA

Group	Sample Data	Sample Mean	Unknown Group Mean
1	$y_{11}y_{12} \cdots y_{1n_1}$	$\bar{y}_1$	μ_1
2	$y_{21}y_{22} \cdots y_{2n_2}$	$\bar{y}_2$	μ_2
$\vdots$	$\vdots \quad \vdots \qquad \vdots$	$\vdots$	$\vdots$
I	$y_{I1}y_{I2} \cdots y_{In_i}$	$\bar{y}_I$	μ_I

We make the following formal mathematical assumptions:

DEFINITION 10.1

Assumptions for an ANOVA

1. The sample measurements $y_{i1}, y_{i2}, \ldots, y_{in_i}$ are selected from a normal population ($i = 1, 2, \ldots, I$).

2. The samples are independent.

3. The unknown population mean and variance for the measurements from sample i are μ_i and σ^2, respectively.

Note that we assume the population variances are equal, but the means may differ. These assumptions are direct extensions of those made for the pooled-variance t test in Chapter 9.

d.f. for SS(Within)

The **degrees of freedom for SS(Within)** can be found by realizing that there are $n_i - 1$ d.f. for squared deviations within group i and that d.f.'s can be added across the groups. Therefore, there are $(n_1 - 1) + (n_2 - 1) + \cdots + (n_I - 1) = n - I$ d.f. for SS(Within). The quantity $SS(\text{Between}) = \sum_i n_i(\bar{y}_i - \bar{y})^2$ has I terms, but because the constraint $\sum_i n_i(\bar{y}_i - \bar{y}) = 0$ determines one term (once the remaining $I - 1$ have been found), there are $I - 1$ **d.f. for SS(Between).** The term **mean square (MS)** is given to any sum of squares divided by its degrees of freedom.

d.f. for SS(Between)
mean square (MS)

With this terminology, the test statistic for our analysis of variance is

$$F = \frac{MS(\text{Between})}{MS(\text{Within})}$$

Large positive values of MS(Between) relative to MS(Within) indicate differences among the population means and lead to the rejection of the null hypothesis.

The F statistic has another tabulated distribution, found in Appendix Table 6. This distribution has two d.f. numbers, $I - 1$ for the numerator and $n - I$ for the denominator. For example, if we had $I = 3$ groups and a total of $n = 21$ measurements, we would have $3 - 1 = 2$ d.f. in the numerator (shown along the top of the table) and $21 - 3 = 18$ d.f. in the denominator (shown on the side of the F table). The table value corresponding to $\alpha = .05$ for these d.f. is 3.55. The tables are rather large; they are effectively built into software packages such as Minitab and Excel.

DEFINITION 10.2

ANOVA for Testing the Equality of I Group Means

H_0: $\mu_1 = \mu_2 = \cdots = \mu_I$

H_a: Not all μ_i are equal

$$\text{T.S.: } F = \frac{MS(\text{Between})}{MS(\text{Within})} = \frac{\sum_i n_i(\bar{y}_i - \bar{y})^2/(I - 1)}{\sum_{ij} (y_{ij} - \bar{y}_i)^2/(n - I)}$$

R.R.: For a specified α, reject H_0 if $F > F_\alpha$, where F_α cuts off a right-tail area of α in the F distribution with $I - 1$ numerator and $n - 1$ denominator d.f.

We calculated the necessary sums of squares for the supervisor-effectiveness data given near the beginning of this section. The results are usually organized in an ANOVA table, as shown here:

Source	SS	d.f.	MS	F
Between	1466.00	2	733.00	3.20
Within	4124.57	18	229.14	
Total	5590.57	20		

For a test at $\alpha = .05$, we compare the F value of 3.20 to the tabled .05 point (2 and 18 d.f.), namely 3.55. Because $3.20 < 3.55$, we would retain the null hypothesis. It is possible that the apparent differences among the sample means are the result of chance variation. It is also possible that they reflect real differences; we can't say which is the case.

EXAMPLE 10.1

An investor is interested in comparing the annual returns of three mutual funds: Alpha, Beta, and Gamma. The annual returns of each fund over a 12-year period are shown next.

Fund	Annual Returns											
Alpha	1.1	2.1	−1.7	18.3	14.2	4.2	10.5	2.8	7.6	9.8	0.3	6.9
Beta	14.9	11.7	7.2	18.2	11.5	12.4	16.8	20.3	1.7	21.6	16.9	8.4
Gamma	17.9	10.5	12.1	8.4	18.1	7.5	−5.2	3.5	5.4	−1.4	8.7	15.6

An ANOVA is performed on the data; Excel output is shown in Figure 10.2. Identify the following: the sample means, the mean squares MS(Between) and MS(Within), the value of the F statistic, and the p-value for H_0: $\mu_{\text{Alpha}} = \mu_{\text{Beta}} = \mu_{\text{Gamma}}$.

SOLUTION The sample means are shown under the heading Average; they are, respectively, 6.342, 13.467, and 8.425. The mean square for Fund in this case is MS(Between), namely 161.049. MS(Within) is 40.6236, F is 3.964, and the p-value is .0286. Thus the evidence for differences in mean annual return for the three funds is conclusive. As yet, we can't formally say which funds differ in their average returns.

FIGURE 10.2

ANOVA of Mutual Fund Data from Excel

	A	B	C	D	E	F	G
1	Anova: Single Factor						
2							
3	SUMMARY						
4	*Groups*	*Count*	*Sum*	*Average*	*Variance*		
5	Alpha	12	76.1	6.34167	36.3336		
6	Beta	12	161.6	13.4667	33.7933		
7	Gamma	12	101.1	8.425	51.7439		
8							
9							
10	ANOVA						
11	*Source of Variation*	*SS*	*df*	*MS*	*F*	*P-value*	*F crit*
12	Between Groups	322.097	2	161.049	3.96441	0.02864	3.28492
13	Within Groups	1340.58	33	40.6236			
14							
15	Total	1662.68	35				

Like all statistical inference procedures, this F test is based on certain assumptions. These are the same assumptions that we made for the pooled-variance t test of the previous chapter. Besides the fundamental assumption that the data aren't biased, the three basic assumptions are population normality, equal group variances, and independence of observations. The **normality assumption** is perhaps the least crucial. The ANOVA test is a test on means (despite its name); the Central Limit Theorem has its effect. If the populations are badly skewed and if the sample sizes are small (such as 10 each), the Central Limit Theorem effect doesn't take over and the nominal F probabilities may be in error. However, barring severe skewness and quite small samples, this shouldn't be a major problem. But if the population distributions are seriously skewed or roughly symmetric with heavy tails (as indicated by outliers in the sample data), the F probabilities are reasonably accurate, but alternative procedures may be more efficient (make better use of the data). One particular alternative, the Kruskal–Wallis rank test, is discussed in the next section.

normality assumption

The **assumption of equal variances** for each group is important if the sample sizes are substantially different. Many studies have indicated that when all n_i's are equal, in what is called a **balanced design,** the effect of even grossly unequal variances is minimal. However, if the n_i's are substantially different—say, if the largest n_i is at least twice the smallest—then unequal variances can cause major distortions in the nominal F probabilities. The worst case is when large variances occur in groups with small sample sizes. The best way to avoid problems is to strive for equal n_i's.

assumption of equal variances

balanced design

assumption of
independence

Once again, violation of the **assumption of independence** can cause a great deal of trouble. Dependence within the sample means that the effective n differs from the apparent sample size, just as was the case for t tests. (For example, suppose that all the supervisors in policy A were in one department, all those in policy B were in another, and all those in policy C were in a third; also, suppose that the ratings largely reflected department performance, not individual work. Then the scores within each policy would be highly correlated, and we would basically have one rating within a policy, not the apparent 7.) When the data arise from a cross-sectional random sample taken at a specific time, independence should hold unless there is some other connection than the experimental factor among the scores. If the data arise by measurements taken repeatedly over time, there is a possibility of dependence from one measurement to the next. In such situations, nominal F probabilities are very suspect. Any procedure that assumes independence will be unbelievable when that assumption is wrong.

EXAMPLE 10.2   Refer to the data of Example 10.1, the box plots in Figure 10.3, and the time series plots in Figure 10.4. Is there any indication of trouble because of violation of assumptions?

SOLUTION   Although the data were collected over time, there is no indication of a connection among the returns, so independence is not a problem. The data don't appear to be particularly skewed. The variances appear very similar, and the n's are equal. The F test was quite conclusive, and there's no reason to question its correctness.

FIGURE 10.3   **Box Plots of Mutual Fund Data**

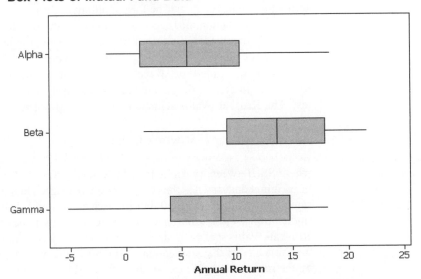

FIGURE 10.4

Time Series Plot of Mutual Fund Data

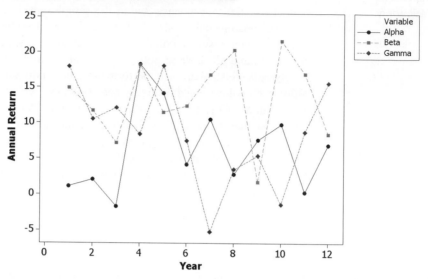

10.2 Comparing Several Distributions by a Rank Test

In Section 10.1 we noted that one assumption underlying the ANOVA F test was that all populations were normal. If that assumption is incorrect, as evidenced by substantial skewness or outliers in the samples, the nominal probabilities given by the F table may be slightly in error. More importantly, the F test may not be the most effective way to analyze the data. In this section we introduce the Kruskal–Wallis rank sum test, which doesn't require the normal-population assumption. This test is not terribly sensitive to the equal-variance assumption, but it does depend heavily on the independence assumption.

The Kruskal–Wallis test is an extension of the Wilcoxon rank sum test we described in the last chapter. The formal null hypothesis is that all the populations have the same distribution, not necessarily a normal distribution. The formal research hypothesis is that the populations differ in some way; the test is primarily sensitive to differences of location (means or medians), rather than differences of variances.

To carry out the test, all the data values are combined and ranked from lowest to highest. In case of ties, average ranks are assigned, as in the Wilcoxon rank sum test. The Kruskal–Wallis statistic may be thought of as

$$H = \frac{12}{n(n+1)} \text{ SS(Between, ranks)}$$

where SS(Between, ranks) is the SS(Between) obtained for the rankings rather than the original data and n is the combined sample size. Thus if the average rank in every sample is equal, H will be 0, but if the average ranks differ greatly among samples (indicating a clear difference in locations), H will be large. Conventionally, the Kruskal–Wallis statistic is stated in terms of T_i, the sum of the ranks in group i, rather than in terms of the average rank. Of course, the average is simply the sum divided by the relevant sample size, so the test could be stated either way.

DEFINITION 10.3

Kruskal–Wallis Test

H_0: The distributions are identical (effectively, have equal means)

H_a: The distributions differ in location

T.S.: $H = \left\{ \dfrac{12}{n(n+1)} \sum_i \dfrac{T_i^2}{n_i} \right\} - 3(n+1)$

where n_i = sample size in sample i, $(i = 1, 2, \ldots, I)$, n = total sample size, and T_i = sum of combined-sample ranks for measurements in sample i.

R.R.: For specified α, reject H_0 if $H > \chi_\alpha^2$ where χ_α^2 cuts off a right-tail area α for the χ^2 distribution with $I - 1$ d.f.

EXAMPLE 10.3

Use the following Minitab output to perform a Kruskal–Wallis test for the data of Example 10.1. First use $\alpha = .05$, then find a p-value.

```
Kruskal-Wallis Test: Return versus Fund

Fund      N   Median   Ave Rank      Z
Alpha    12    5.550       13.5   -2.00
Beta     12   13.650       24.6    2.47
Gamma    12    8.550       17.3   -0.47
Overall  36               18.5

H = 6.86   DF = 2   P = 0.032
H = 6.86   DF = 2   P = 0.032   (adjusted for ties)
```

SOLUTION The required χ^2 table value for $\alpha = .05$ and 2 d.f. is 5.99 from Appendix Table 5. The actual test statistic is 6.86, which is greater than 5.99, so we reject the null hypothesis that the three funds have the same distribution of annual returns.

The p-value is shown as .032, much smaller than $\alpha = .05$. This also indicates that we reject the null hypothesis.

Exercises

10.1 A test is made of five different incentive-pay schemes for piece workers. Eight workers are assigned randomly to each plan. The total number of items produced by each worker over a 20-day period is recorded.

	Plan				
	A	**B**	**C**	**D**	**E**
Production	1106	1214	1010	1054	1210
	1203	1186	1069	1101	1193
	1064	1165	1047	1029	1169
	1119	1177	1120	1066	1223
	1087	1146	1084	1082	1161
	1106	1099	1062	1067	1200
	1101	1161	1051	1109	1189
	1049	1153	1029	1083	1197
Mean	1104.38	1162.62	1059.00	1073.88	1192.75
Variance	2136.55	1116.84	1137.71	662.41	409.93

```
One-way ANOVA: Production versus Plan

Source  DF     SS      MS      F      P
Plan     4  105529   26382   24.14  0.000
Error   35   38244    1093
Total   39  143773

S = 33.06   R-Sq = 73.40%   R-Sq(adj) = 70.36%


                              Individual 95% CIs For Mean Based on
                              Pooled StDev
Level  N    Mean   StDev   ---+---------+---------+---------+------
1      8   1104.4   46.2                 (----*----)
2      8   1162.6   33.4                           (----*---)
3      8   1059.0   33.7   (----*----)
4      8   1073.9   25.7         (----*----)
5      8   1192.8   20.2                                 (----*---)
                           ---+---------+---------+---------+------
                           1050      1100      1150      1200


Pooled StDev = 33.1

Kruskal-Wallis Test: Production versus Plan

Plan    N  Median  Ave Rank      Z
1       8   1104     18.7     -0.49
2       8   1163     28.3      2.11
3       8   1057      9.1     -3.09
4       8   1075     12.3     -2.23
5       8   1195     34.2      3.70
Overall 40             20.5

H = 26.37   DF = 4   P = 0.000
H = 26.38   DF = 4   P = 0.000   (adjusted for ties)
```

a. Locate the grand mean.
b. Locate SS(Between) and SS(Within).
c. Explain the indicated degrees of freedom for these sums of squares.

10.2 Locate the ANOVA F test for the data of Exercise 10.1, and the p-value. What would you conclude?

10.3 Minitab constructed box plots of the data of Exercise 10.1 by plan, as shown in Figure 10.5. Do there appear to be any blatant violations of assumptions?

10.4 Locate the Kruskal–Wallis test in the output of Exercise 10.1. Find the p-value.

10.5 How do the results of the F test and Kruskal–Wallis test on the data of Exercise 10.1 compare? Does it matter much which test is used?

10.6 A supermarket experimented with three different staffing policies to try to determine when to open new cash registers or add more staff in service areas (such as the deli section). The time of most concern is weekdays between 5 and 6 P.M. when the store is crowded with impatient shoppers. The manager of the store was told to vary the three different staffing policies in a random way. A hired shopper came in each weekday shortly after 5 P.M. and measured the waiting time (in minutes) needed to obtain a standard set of items. The output from JMP is shown in Figure 10.6.
a. Find mean and standard deviation of times for each policy. Find the grand mean.
b. Locate d.f. and MS values, between and within groups.
c. Find the F statistic for testing the null hypothesis of equal means.
d. Can this null hypothesis be rejected at $\alpha = .01$?
e. Locate the p-value.

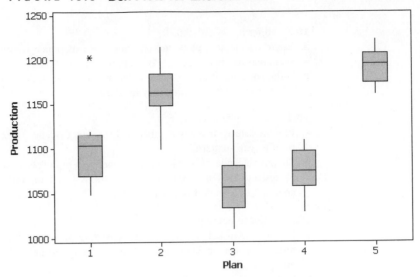

FIGURE 10.5 Box Plots for Exercise 10.1

FIGURE 10.6 JMP Output for Exercise 10.6

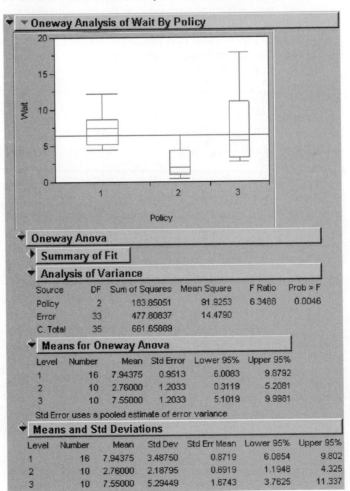

10.7 Refer to Figure 10.6.

a. Based on the data plots and on your own experience waiting in supermarkets, would it seem reasonable to you to assume normal populations?

b. If the populations are, in fact, moderately nonnormal, does that mean that the conclusions of Exercise 10.6 are completely invalid?

10.8 Refer to Exercise 10.6.

a. Plot the data against day number. Is there clear evidence of an upward or downward trend, or of a cyclic pattern?

b. Suppose a cyclic pattern had been found, with high values usually followed by other high values, and lows usually followed by lows. Which assumption underlying analysis of variance would be called into question?

10.9 Refer to Exercise 10.6.

a. Perform a Kruskal–Wallis test for the waiting-time data. According to the Kruskal–Wallis results, is there a statistically detectable (significant) difference in times among the groups?

b. Is the result we found here greatly different from the result we found by an F test in Exercise 10.6?

10.10 A nationwide chain of automobile repair shops had a standard procedure for dealing with complaints of improper work. As part of a systematic practice of checking customer satisfaction, regional managers reviewed records of all complaints; one particular concern was the number of business days required before each complaint was resolved. A regional manager obtained samples of records from each of the districts in the region. Computer output of the results is shown here.

```
One-way ANOVA: Delay versus District

Source     DF      SS      MS      F      P
District    3   1774.5   591.5   7.52   0.000
Error      36   2831.3    78.6
Total      39   4605.8

S = 8.868    R-Sq = 38.53%    R-Sq(adj) = 33.40%

                              Individual 95% CIs For Mean Based on
                              Pooled StDev
Level   N    Mean   StDev   -------+---------+---------+---------+--
1       10  38.000  9.933                         (-------*-------)
2       10  33.100  4.954                     (-------*-------)
3       10  24.000  8.756           (-------*-------)
4       10  21.600 10.710   (-------*-------)
                            -------+---------+---------+---------+--
                              21.0      28.0      35.0      42.0
```

a. Is the value of F statistically significant at $\alpha = .05$?

b. What is the meaning of the indicated p-value?

10.11 According to the box plots shown in Figure 10.7, is there strong evidence that the data are not coming from normal populations? If so, does that mean that the conclusions drawn in Exercise 10.10 are likely to be wrong?

10.12 A Kruskal–Wallis test of the delay-time data for the repair chain was also performed in the following computer output:

FIGURE 10.7   Box Plots for Delay Data by District

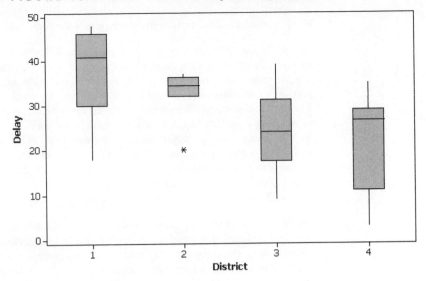

```
Kruskal-Wallis Test: Delay versus District

District   N   Median   Ave Rank      Z
1         10    41.00      29.8     2.90
2         10    34.50      25.7     1.61
3         10    24.00      14.1    -2.00
4         10    26.50      12.4    -2.51
Overall   40               20.5

H = 16.01   DF = 3   P = 0.001
H = 16.05   DF = 3   P = 0.001   (adjusted for ties)
```

Is there a statistically significant difference among the four levels (which were the four districts in a particular region), say using $\alpha = .01$? Locate the p-value. Is there a radical difference between this p-value and the one from the F test of Exercise 10.11?

10.13   A direct-mail retailer used three different ways of incorporating an order form into the catalog. A relevant question for the retailer is the dollar amount of each order using the different forms. The total sale and type of form were recorded for each order received; the data were analyzed by Excel. The results are shown in Figure 10.8.

FIGURE 10.8   ANOVA for Exercise 10.13

	A	B	C	D	E	F	G
1	Anova: Single Factor						
2							
3	SUMMARY						
4	*Groups*	*Count*	*Sum*	*Average*	*Variance*		
5	FormType1	56	3562.16	63.61	3328.67		
6	FormType2	39	2068.01	53.0259	4736.88		
7	FormType3	85	5570.39	65.534	3474.18		
8							
9							
10	ANOVA						
11	*Source of Variation*	*SS*	*df*	*MS*	*F*	*P-value*	*F crit*
12	Between Groups	4338.44	2	2169.22	0.58627	0.55748	3.04701
13	Within Groups	654909	177	3700.05			
14							
15	Total	659247	179				

a. Are there statistically detectable differences among the means, using any reasonable α value?

b. How much evidence is there that the type of order form influences the amount of sale?

10.14 In the output of Exercise 10.13, the standard deviations (found by taking the square root of each variance) are about as big as the means, so a value that is 1 standard deviation below the mean would be essentially $0. The Empirical Rule indicates that a substantial proportion of individual scores should be even less than 1 standard deviation below the mean, but a negative order amount is impossible (the retailer fervently hopes).

a. What do these facts suggest about the shape of the data?

b. What assumption of analysis of variance seems likely to be violated in this situation?

c. Further output for the data of Exercise 10.13 was obtained from Minitab and showed a Kruskal–Wallis statistic equal to 3.12 and a p-value of .210. Does the Kruskal–Wallis result conclusively indicate that there is a difference in the average SalesTotal for the three FormType groups?

10.15 A manufacturer of wooden moldings takes "blanks" of pine wood and converts them into floor and ceiling decorative molding for sale in lumberyards. The important step in the manufacturing process involves a router, a tool for carving decorative shapes into wood. The router bit is a metal attachment that carries out this task. It is subject to wear just as any other manufacturing part. The wear, and the resulting production level, depends on the speed set for routing the wood. Too slow, and production quantities are too low; too fast, and the bit wears so fast that production time is lost changing bits. The manufacturer tested various speeds and measured the yield, in board feet per hour, of salable molding that resulted. The data were analyzed using JMP, with output shown in Figure 10.9.

FIGURE 10.9 **Plot of Router Yield Data**

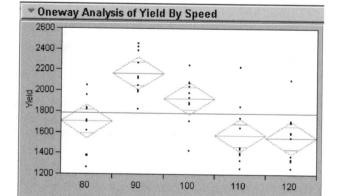

a. Which speed appears to be best, without doing any formal test?

b. Is there any indication of a problem such as skewness, unequal variances, or outliers?

c. Additional JMP output, showing an ANOVA table, for the router yield data is shown in Figure 10.10. Is there a statistically significant difference somewhere among the five means at usual α levels?

d. Still more JMP output, showing results of a Kruskal–Wallis test, is shown in Figure 10.11. According to this test, is there a statistically significant difference in yield distribution among the five speeds?

e. How important is it to the conclusion whether an F test or a Kruskal–Wallis test is used?

FIGURE 10.10   ANOVA Table for Router Yield Data

Oneway Anova

Summary of Fit

Rsquare	0.495387
Adj Rsquare	0.450533
Root Mean Square Error	246.5867
Mean of Response	1782.58
Observations (or Sum Wgts)	50

Analysis of Variance

Source	DF	Sum of Squares	Mean Square	F Ratio	Prob > F
Speed	4	2686200.1	671550	11.0443	<.0001
Error	45	2736226.1	60805		
C. Total	49	5422426.2			

Means for Oneway Anova

Level	Number	Mean	Std Error	Lower 95%	Upper 95%
80	10	1703.00	77.978	1545.9	1860.1
90	10	2162.80	77.978	2005.7	2319.9
100	10	1923.70	77.978	1766.6	2080.8
110	10	1572.40	77.978	1415.3	1729.5
120	10	1551.00	77.978	1393.9	1708.1

Std Error uses a pooled estimate of error variance

FIGURE 10.11   Kruskal–Wallis Test for Router Yield Data

Wilcoxon / Kruskal-Wallis Tests (Rank Sums)

Level	Count	Score Sum	Score Mean	(Mean-Mean0)/Std0
80	10	220	22.0000	-0.837
90	10	418	41.8000	3.941
100	10	324	32.4000	1.661
110	10	168	16.8000	-2.098
120	10	145	14.5000	-2.656

1-way Test, ChiSquare Approximation

ChiSquare	DF	Prob>ChiSq
24.5760	4	<.0001

10.3 Specific Comparisons Among Means

The ANOVA F test and the Kruskal–Wallis test developed in this chapter test for an overall pattern of discrepancies among the group means. Rejection of the hypothesis that all population (group) means are equal does not indicate specifically which means are not equal. In this section we outline one of many possible methods for assessing differences among specified means. Several other methods are discussed in Ott and Longnecker (2001), and there are other minor variations available. We state this method in terms of confidence intervals. As usual, we can use the resulting intervals to perform hypothesis tests.

One approach would be to use the t methods of Chapter 9 to construct t-type confidence intervals for all possible pairs of means. The objection to this is essentially the same as our objection to multiple t tests in Section 10.1. While the confidence level for each interval separately may be 95%, there is no way to measure the overall confidence that all the intervals are correct. We use the Tukey method in this section to yield a desired overall confidence level.

The assumptions are the same as those underlying the F test. The data constitute independent random samples from I groups or subpopulations. The groups are labeled by the index i, where $i = 1, 2, \ldots I$, and the sample size for group i is n_i. We assume that the population distribution in group i is normal with mean μ_i and variance σ^2. There is no subscript on σ^2 because we assume that the population variances for all groups are identical. The estimate $\hat{\sigma}^2$ is MS(Within), a generalization of the pooled variance we defined in Chapter 9.

Tukey method

The **Tukey method** is designed specifically to compare any two means, say, $\bar{y}_i$ and $\bar{y}_{i*}$. The underlying mathematical theory assumes that all sample sizes are equal: $n_1 = n_2 = \cdots = n_I$. The common sample size is usually denoted n. Note that here n means the individual sample size, *not* the overall sample size.

DEFINITION 10.4

Confidence Intervals for Pairs of Means, Tukey Method

$$(\bar{y}_i - \bar{y}_{i*}) - q_\alpha(I, \text{d.f.}_2)\sqrt{\text{MS(Within)}/n} \le \mu_i - \mu_{i*}$$
$$\le (\bar{y}_i - \bar{y}_{i*}) + q_\alpha(I, \text{d.f.}_2)\sqrt{\text{MS(Within)}/n}$$

where n is the sample size for each sample, I is the number of samples, d.f.$_2$ is the degrees of freedom for MS(Within), and $q_\alpha(I, \text{d.f.}_2)$ is found in Appendix Table 8. There is $100(1 - \alpha)\%$ confidence that *all possible* intervals comparing two means are correct.

EXAMPLE 10.4

Construct (overall) 95% confidence intervals for the differences in mean annual returns for the three mutual funds of Example 10.1.

SOLUTION The relevant summary statistics are

Fund i	Alpha	Beta	Gamma
$\bar{y}_i$	6.34	13.47	8.43
n_i	12	12	12
MS(Within) = 40.624			

The desired $q_\alpha(I, \text{d.f.}_2)$ value has $\alpha = .05$, $I = 3$, and d.f.$_2 = 33$. There is no d.f.$_2 = 33$ entry in Appendix Table 8, so we use d.f.$_2 = 30$, $q_\alpha(3,30) = 3.49$. It's clear from the table that $q_\alpha(3,30)$ is just a little larger than the desired $q_\alpha(3,33)$, so we err slightly on the conservative (wider-interval) side. The desired 95% confidence intervals are

$$(6.34 - 13.47) - 3.49\sqrt{40.624/12} \le \mu_{\text{Alpha}} - \mu_{\text{Beta}}$$
$$\le (6.34 - 13.47) + 3.49\sqrt{40.624/12}$$
$$(13.47 - 8.43) - 3.49\sqrt{40.624/12} \le \mu_{\text{Beta}} - \mu_{\text{Gamma}}$$
$$\le (13.47 - 8.43) + 3.49\sqrt{40.624/12}$$
$$(6.43 - 8.43) - 3.49\sqrt{40.624/12} \le \mu_{\text{Alpha}} - \mu_{\text{Gamma}}$$
$$\le (6.34 - 8.43) + 3.49\sqrt{40.624/12}$$

or

$$-13.55 \le \mu_{\text{Alpha}} - \mu_{\text{Beta}} \le -0.71$$
$$-1.38 \le \mu_{\text{Beta}} - \mu_{\text{Gamma}} \le 11.46$$
$$-8.51 \le \mu_{\text{Alpha}} - \mu_{\text{Gamma}} \le 4.33$$

Compare these results to the following Minitab output:

```
Tukey 95% Simultaneous Confidence Intervals
All Pairwise Comparisons among Levels of Fund

Individual confidence level = 98.04%

Fund = Alpha subtracted from:

Fund    Lower  Center   Upper  ------+---------+---------+---------+---
Beta    0.740   7.125  13.510                      (--------*--------)
Gamma  -4.301   2.083   8.468            (--------*--------)
                               ------+---------+---------+---------+---
                                  -7.0       0.0       7.0      14.0


Fund = Beta subtracted from:

Fund     Lower  Center   Upper  ------+---------+---------+---------+---
Gamma  -11.426  -5.042   1.343  (--------*--------)
                                ------+---------+---------+---------+---
                                   -7.0       0.0       7.0      14.0
```

Recall that confidence intervals may be used to conduct (two-sided) hypothesis tests. The natural null hypothesis, H_0: $\mu_i - \mu_j = 0$, is rejected if zero does not fall in the interval. The 95% confidence intervals indicate that at $\alpha = .05$ we can reject $\mu_{\text{Alpha}} - \mu_{\text{Beta}} = 0$, but must retain $\mu_{\text{Alpha}} - \mu_{\text{Gamma}} = 0$ and $\mu_{\text{Beta}} - \mu_{\text{Gamma}} = 0$. We conclude that the mean annual return of the Beta Fund is higher than the mean annual return of the Alpha Fund. The other two pairwise mean differences could be the result of random variation.

The formal assumption in the Tukey method that $n_1 = n_2 = \cdots = n_I$ may be relaxed. A modification for unequal sample sizes is built into most computer programs that calculate Tukey tests or intervals.

Exercises

10.16 Here is Minitab output for the data of Exercise 10.1, comparing production levels under five different plans.

```
One-way ANOVA: Production versus Plan

Source  DF      SS     MS      F      P
Plan     4  105529  26382  24.14  0.000
Error   35   38244   1093
Total   39  143773

S = 33.06   R-Sq = 73.40%   R-Sq(adj) = 70.36%

                        Individual 95% CIs For Mean Based on
                        Pooled StDev
Level  N    Mean  StDev  ---+---------+---------+---------+------
1      8  1104.4   46.2             (----*----)
2      8  1162.6   33.4                        (----*---)
3      8  1059.0   33.7  (----*----)
4      8  1073.9   25.7      (----*----)
5      8  1192.8   20.2                            (----*---)
                        ---+---------+---------+---------+------
                        1050      1100      1150      1200
```

```
Pooled StDev = 33.1

Tukey 95% Simultaneous Confidence Intervals
All Pairwise Comparisons among Levels of Plan

Individual confidence level = 99.32%

Plan = 1 subtracted from:

Plan    Lower   Center   Upper   ---------+---------+---------+---------+-
2       10.68    58.25  105.82                      (----*----)
3      -92.94   -45.38    2.19          (---*----)
4      -78.07   -30.50   17.07          (----*----)
5       40.81    88.38  135.94                   (----*----)
                                --------+---------+---------+---------+-
                                     -100        0       100      200

Plan = 2 subtracted from:

Plan    Lower   Center   Upper   --------+---------+---------+---------+-
3     -151.19  -103.63  -56.06    (----*---)
4     -136.32   -88.75  -41.18    (----*----)
5      -17.44    30.12   77.69              (----*----)
                                --------+---------+---------+---------+-
                                     -100        0       100      200

Plan = 3 subtracted from:

Plan    Lower   Center   Upper   --------+---------+---------+---------+-
4      -32.69    14.88   62.44               (---*----)
5       86.18   133.75  181.32                       (---*----)
                                --------+---------+---------+---------+-
                                     -100        0       100      200

Plan = 4 subtracted from:

Plan  Lower  Center   Upper   --------+---------+---------+---------+-
5     71.31  118.88  166.44                       (----*----)
                              --------+---------+---------+---------+-
                                   -100        0       100      200
```

a. Write out overall 95% confidence intervals for all possible differences of means.
b. Which differences can be declared significant at $\alpha = .05$?

10.17 The means, standard deviations, sample sizes, and MS(Within) for the supermarket waiting times in Exercise 10.6 are shown here along with additional Minitab output.

   MS(Within) = 14.479, with 33 degrees of freedom

Policy	n	Mean	St. Dev.
1	16	7.944	3.487
2	10	2.760	2.188
3	10	7.550	5.294

```
Tukey 95% Simultaneous Confidence Intervals
All Pairwise Comparisons among Levels of Policy

Individual confidence level = 98.04%

Policy = 1 subtracted from:
```

```
Policy   Lower   Center  Upper   --------+---------+---------+---------+-
2        -8.947  -5.184  -1.420  (-------*------)
3        -4.157  -0.394   3.370           (------*-------)
                                 --------+---------+---------+---------+-
                                       -5.0      0.0       5.0      10.0


Policy = 2 subtracted from:

Policy   Lower   Center  Upper   --------+---------+---------+---------+-
3        0.615   4.790   8.965                    (--------*------)
                                 --------+---------+---------+---------+-
                                       -5.0      0.0       5.0      10.0
```

Which means, if any, are detectably (significantly) different?

10.18 The data in Exercise 10.6 were collected by asking the store manager to specify a policy for the day haphazardly. What would be a better way to obtain the data?

10.19 The relevant computer output for the delay-time data for Exercise 10.10 is reproduced here.

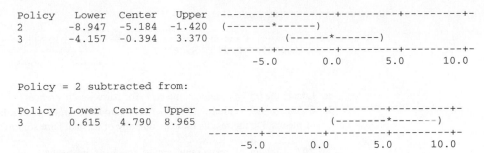

```
One-way ANOVA: Delay versus District

Source     DF     SS      MS     F      P
District    3   1774.5  591.5  7.52  0.000
Error      36   2831.3   78.6
Total      39   4605.8

S = 8.868   R-Sq = 38.53%   R-Sq(adj) = 33.40%

                              Individual 95% CIs For Mean Based on
                              Pooled StDev
Level   N   Mean    StDev   -------+---------+---------+---------+--
1      10   38.000  9.933                         (-------*-------)
2      10   33.100  4.954                 (-------*-------)
3      10   24.000  8.756       (-------*-------)
4      10   21.600  10.710  (-------*-------)
                            -------+---------+---------+---------+--
                                 21.0      28.0      35.0      42.0


Pooled StDev = 8.868

Tukey 95% Simultaneous Confidence Intervals
All Pairwise Comparisons among Levels of District

Individual confidence level = 98.93%

District = 1 subtracted from:

District   Lower    Center   Upper   --------+---------+---------+---------+-
2         -15.585   -4.900    5.785              (------*------)
3         -24.685  -14.000   -3.315       (------*------)
4         -27.085  -16.400   -5.715   (------*------)
                                      --------+---------+---------+---------+-
                                            -15        0        15        30


District = 2 subtracted from:

District   Lower    Center   Upper   --------+---------+---------+---------+-
3         -19.785   -9.100    1.585        (------*------)
4         -22.185  -11.500   -0.815     (------*------)
                                      --------+---------+---------+---------+-
                                            -15        0        15        30
```

```
District = 3 subtracted from:

District    Lower  Center  Upper    --------+---------+---------+---------+-
4          -13.085  -2.400  8.285          (------*------)
                                     --------+---------+---------+---------+-
                                        -15        0       15       30
```

a. Locate the 95% confidence intervals for pairwise differences.

b. Calculate 99% (rather than 95%) Tukey confidence intervals for the differences of all pairs of means. Do the results indicate that any of the pairs are significantly different?

10.20 A chain of restaurants makes much of its profit from "add-ons," items such as desserts or beverages ordered at extra cost by customers. Servers taking the orders are instructed to suggest such items to diners. At one restaurant in the chain, the manager took samples of orders taken by each of seven servers to see if there were evident differences in the servers' success at obtaining add-on orders. The data were analyzed using JMP, with results shown in Figure 10.12.

FIGURE 10.12 **Plot and ANOVA Table for Add-On Data**

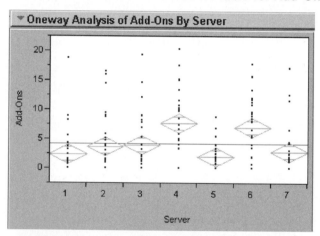

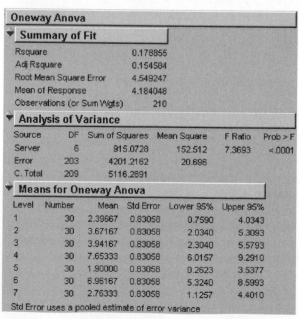

Oneway Anova

Summary of Fit

Rsquare	0.178855
Adj Rsquare	0.154584
Root Mean Square Error	4.549247
Mean of Response	4.184048
Observations (or Sum Wgts)	210

Analysis of Variance

Source	DF	Sum of Squares	Mean Square	F Ratio	Prob > F
Server	6	915.0728	152.512	7.3693	<.0001
Error	203	4201.2162	20.696		
C. Total	209	5116.2891			

Means for Oneway Anova

Level	Number	Mean	Std Error	Lower 95%	Upper 95%
1	30	2.39667	0.83058	0.7590	4.0343
2	30	3.67167	0.83058	2.0340	5.3093
3	30	3.94167	0.83058	2.3040	5.5793
4	30	7.65333	0.83058	6.0157	9.2910
5	30	1.90000	0.83058	0.2623	3.5377
6	30	6.96167	0.83058	5.3240	8.5993
7	30	2.76333	0.83058	1.1257	4.4010

Std Error uses a pooled estimate of error variance

a. Is there a statistically detectable difference among the servers in the mean add-on per order?

b. Is any major violation of assumptions apparent in the data?

JMP also performed Tukey comparisons of means, with results shown in Figure 10.13. The value 3.4982 shown along the diagonal of the second table in the figure is the plus or minus required for 95% confidence.

c. Which pairs of means show a statistically detectable difference?

d. Find a 95% confidence interval for the difference of means for servers 4 and 5. Does this interval confirm your judgment of whether these means are statistically significantly different?

FIGURE 10.13 **Tukey Comparisons for Add-On Data**

Means Comparisons

Dif=Mean[i]-Mean[j]

	4	6	3	2	7	1	5
4	0.0000	0.6917	3.7117	3.9817	4.8900	5.2567	5.7533
6	-0.6917	0.0000	3.0200	3.2900	4.1983	4.5650	5.0617
3	-3.7117	-3.0200	0.0000	0.2700	1.1783	1.5450	2.0417
2	-3.9817	-3.2900	-0.2700	0.0000	0.9083	1.2750	1.7717
7	-4.8900	-4.1983	-1.1783	-0.9083	0.0000	0.3667	0.8633
1	-5.2567	-4.5650	-1.5450	-1.2750	-0.3667	0.0000	0.4967
5	-5.7533	-5.0617	-2.0417	-1.7717	-0.8633	-0.4967	0.0000

Alpha= 0.05

Comparisons for all pairs using Tukey-Kramer HSD

q*

2.97815

Abs(Dif)-LSD

	4	6	3	2	7	1	5
4	-3.4982	-2.8065	0.2135	0.4835	1.3918	1.7585	2.2552
6	-2.8065	-3.4982	-0.4782	-0.2082	0.7002	1.0668	1.5635
3	0.2135	-0.4782	-3.4982	-3.2282	-2.3198	-1.9532	-1.4565
2	0.4835	-0.2082	-3.2282	-3.4982	-2.5898	-2.2232	-1.7265
7	1.3918	0.7002	-2.3198	-2.5898	-3.4982	-3.1315	-2.6348
1	1.7585	1.0668	-1.9532	-2.2232	-3.1315	-3.4982	-3.0015
5	2.2552	1.5635	-1.4565	-1.7265	-2.6348	-3.0015	-3.4982

Positive values show pairs of means that are significantly different.

10.4 Two-Factor Experiments

Until now, we have considered only single-factor experiments in which one variable is manipulated. Often managers can learn more with more complex experiments. It is perfectly possible to vary several experimental factors in the same experiment. In this section we describe the basic ideas and computations that arise when there are two factors being varied. In this context, we will describe a fundamental statistical idea, interaction.

For example, a clothing contractor who supplies military uniforms must cut fabric for coats, shirts, and pants (in many different sizes) from layers of fabric. The fabric is expensive, so wastage has a big effect on profitability. The contractor has a choice among three computer-aided cutting machines, A, B, and C. Rather than guessing which machine would give the least wastage, the contractor can experiment by having each machine cut several lots for coats, several more for shirts, and several more for pants. This experiment has two factors—the machine and the type of garment. One possible set of mean wastage percentages is shown in the next table.

Factor 1 (Machine)	Factor 2 (Type of Garment)			Average
	Coats	Shirts	Pants	
A	7.6	9.1	7.3	8.0
B	6.5	8.0	6.2	6.9
C	5.1	6.6	4.8	5.5
Average	6.4	7.9	6.1	6.8

In this table, there's a consistent pattern. Machine A is consistently 1.1 percentage points higher (poorer) in wastage than machine B, whether we consider coats, shirts, or pants. In turn, machine B is consistently 1.4 percentage points higher than machine C. The consistency goes in the other direction, too: Shirts have a 1.5 percentage points higher wastage than coats and a 1.8 percentage points higher wastage than pants, consistently in all three machines.

Alternatively, the means might look like the following table:

Factor 1 (Machine)	Factor 2 (Type of Garment)			Average
	Coats	Shirts	Pants	
A	5.1	11.1	7.8	8.0
B	8.1	8.5	4.1	6.9
C	6.0	4.1	6.4	5.5
Average	6.4	7.9	6.1	6.8

In this second table, the averages across rows or down columns are exactly the same as in the first table, but the pattern is *not* consistent. For example, machine A is 3.0 percentage points lower than B for coats but 2.6 points *higher* for shirts and 3.7 points higher for pants. The second table shows an **interaction** between machine and garment-type factors; there is no such interaction in the first table.

interaction

Interaction can be described in several equivalent ways. **Two experimental factors interact in their effect on a response variable if the effect of changing one factor depends on the level of the other factor.** In the second table, changing from machine A to machine B increases the wastage by 3.0 points for coats, decreases it 2.6 points for shirts, and decreases it 3.7 points for pants. Which machine is better? It depends on what type of garment we're cutting. This "it depends" answer is characteristic of interaction. What type of garment has the lowest wastage in the second table? It depends on which machine we're using.

Another way to say the same thing is that when interaction is present, differences for one factor themselves differ as we change the other factor. The difference between A and B changes as we change type of garment in the second table.

effect

A more mathematical description of interaction depends on the idea of effect of a factor. The (main) **effect** of one level of a factor is the difference between its mean response and the grand mean. In either of the preceding tables, the effect of machine

A is $8.0 - 6.8 = 1.2$, the effect of B is $6.9 - 6.8 = 0.1$, and the effect of C is $5.5 - 6.8 = -1.3$. (In passing, note that the effects must sum to 0, because they are deviations from a mean. With three levels of a factor, only two of the effects are free to vary, so there are two degrees of freedom, as we saw in Section 10.1.) Similarly, the garment type effects are $-.4$ for coats, 1.1 for shirts, and $-.7$ for pants.

Effects are used to define models for cell means, where a cell is a particular combination of a row and a column (just like spreadsheet computer programs). The **additive model** is

additive model

cell mean = grand mean + row effect + column effect

For example, for machine A working on coats the additive model would predict a mean of $6.8 + (1.2) + (-.4) = 7.6$; for machine C working on pants, the model predicts a mean of $6.8 + (-1.3) + (-.7) = 4.8$. These predictions for the additive model are exactly correct for the first table. *When there is no interaction, the additive model is exactly correct. When there is interaction, effects are not additive and the additive model is incorrect.* Another way to define interaction is that there is a "combination effect" for the levels of the two factors that cannot be predicted by adding the separate effects of the levels. For example, in the second table, adding the effects of machine A and of coats to the grand mean yields a predicted mean of 7.6; but this particular combination actually yields a mean of 5.1, substantially lower than we would predict from the separate effects of machine A and of coats.

EXAMPLE 10.5

A company is interested in the percentage of salary that its employees contribute to their 401(k) retirement savings plans. A table of means by department and gender is shown here. Assume for the purposes of this example that the sample sizes are large enough to ignore sampling error.

	Gender		
Dept.	Female	Male	Average
A	10.8	12.8	11.8
B	9.8	10.4	10.1
C	8.2	9.2	8.7
Average	9.6	10.8	10.2

a. Is there some degree of interaction between the department and gender factors?

b. Construct a table of predicted means based on the additive model. Does a comparison of actual means with additive model values indicate the presence of an interaction?

SOLUTION

a. There are several ways to check for interaction. We could compare department A to department B; the difference is $10.8 - 9.8 = 1.0$ for females and $12.8 - 10.4 = 2.4$ for males. The difference between mean percentage 401(k) contributions for departments A and B depends on the gender of the employee, so there is interaction. Also, the B $-$ C difference is 1.6 for females and 1.2 for males, so again interaction is shown. In this case, the interaction is not extremely large. Department A shows the highest mean percentage 401(k) contributions for both female and male employees, and department C shows the lowest for both.

b. It's convenient to put the effects (mean − grand mean) in the rows and columns of the table. For example, the effect for department A is $11.8 − 10.2 = 1.6$; the effect for females is $9.6 − 10.2 = −.6$. Then we can fill in the cells for an additive model. We show the computations for female employees; the ones for male employees are similar.

Depart.	*Gender* Female	Male	Average
A	$10.2 + 1.6 − 0.6 = 11.2$	12.4	$(+1.6)$
B	$10.2 − 0.1 − 0.6 = \ 9.5$	10.7	$(−0.1)$
C	$10.2 − 1.5 − 0.6 = \ 8.1$	9.3	$(−1.5)$
Effect	$(−0.6)$	$(+0.6)$	Gr. mean 10.2

The results for the additive model do not equal the actual means, so again we see interaction. The actual mean for (A, Female) is 10.8; the additive model for this cell is 11.2, a slightly different number. Note that the additive model values are close to the actual means, though not identical; again, the interaction seems to be small.

profile plot

A very convenient check for interaction is a **profile plot.** Label the horizontal axis with levels of one factor—it doesn't matter which one—and the vertical axis for means. Plot each mean as a point, and connect the points corresponding to a level of the other factor. For example, Figure 10.14 shows profile plots for the two tables of wastage means for the military clothing contractor example at the beginning of this section. The first table showed no interaction at all. Notice that the profile lines are exactly parallel. When there's no interaction, the differences between means for lev-

FIGURE 10.14

Profile Plots for Wastage Means: (a) No Interaction; (b) Interaction

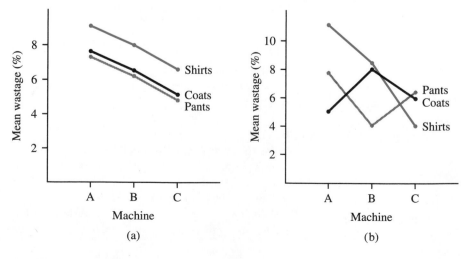

els of one factor are equal over all levels of the other factor; that's why the no-interaction profiles are parallel. The second table had large interaction and the profile plot shows the interaction by definite nonparallel profiles.

EXAMPLE 10.6 In Example 10.5 we noted that the means exhibited interaction, but the interaction didn't seem large. Construct a profile plot. How does it display the small interaction?

SOLUTION Several computer packages can produce plots with labels on each point. The following plot (Figure 10.15) is from Minitab. The lines connecting the two A's, the two B's, and the two C's aren't parallel. Therefore, the profile plot shows interaction. The lines are not far from parallel though, which indicates that the interaction is small.

FIGURE 10.15 **Profile Plot for 401(k) Contribution Means**

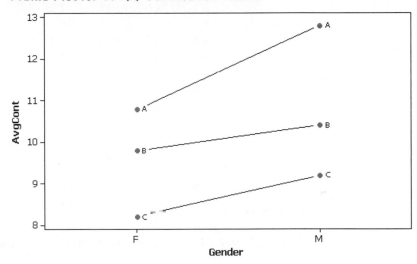

general model

A full model for a two-factor experiment allows for possible interaction of the factors. The **general model** is

individual score = grand mean + row factor effect

$$+ \text{ column factor effect } + \text{ interaction } + \text{ random error}$$

The additive model assumes that the interaction term is 0. An analysis of variance (ANOVA) for a two-factor experiment will take apart SS(Total), which is the total squared variation (of individual scores around the grand mean) into components that correspond to terms in the model:

SS(Row effect) + SS(Column effect) + SS(Interaction) + SS(Error)

There's enough arithmetic involved to make a computer package very useful. We will discuss how to use computer output for two-factor experiments first, before we consider how the arithmetic is done.

balanced design

One key to computer analysis is that most packages assume **balanced design**—equal numbers of observations in all cells. The analysis for unbalanced designs is possible but more subtle. Whenever possible, multiple-factor experiments should have balanced designs; we will assume balance throughout the rest of this section.

Virtually every computer package will produce an ANOVA table for a two-factor experiment. The table consists of sums of squares for rows, columns, interaction, and error—in that order unless otherwise specified—the associated degrees of freedom (d.f.), and mean squares, defined as sums of squares divided by d.f. For example, consider an experiment to measure the heat loss through four different types of commercial thermal window glass. Five different levels of exterior temperature setting are used. Three panes of each type are tested at each temperature setting, and the heat loss is recorded for each pane. The data are shown here.

Exterior Temperature i	Pane Type j			
	A	**B**	**C**	**D**
60	3.2	7.5	10.3	12.4
	3.9	8.3	11.5	13.6
	4.3	8.0	10.9	12.9
50	5.7	10.6	12.9	15.0
	6.6	10.1	13.4	14.8
	6.1	9.7	13.0	15.5
40	7.5	11.0	13.4	15.5
	7.0	11.6	14.6	16.1
	6.5	10.7	14.0	16.2
30	8.0	12.0	14.6	17.5
	7.7	12.4	15.0	17.1
	8.2	11.7	15.3	16.4
20	10.1	13.6	17.1	18.8
	9.9	14.0	17.0	19.2
	10.0	14.5	16.8	18.8

The Minitab package produced the following ANOVA table:

```
Two-way ANOVA: HeatLoss versus Temp, PaneType

Source        DF        SS        MS          F        P
Temp           4   243.288    60.822    330.554    0.000
PaneType       3   689.244   229.748   1248.630    0.000
Interaction   12     0.074     0.006      0.034    1.000
Error         40     7.353     0.184
Total         59   939.960
```

A similar table could be obtained from most packages. The names for the sums of squares may vary; in particular, the error SS is sometimes called the *within-cell* SS or the *residual* SS. Interaction is often indicated by "multiplication" of factor names; for example, some packages might indicate the interaction of Temp and Panetype by Temp*Panetype or T*P. Don't treat this "multiplication" notation as literal multiplication; for our purposes, it's just conventional notation.

The first task in any two-factor experiment is to check for interaction. A profile plot is always a good idea; the profiles for the heat-loss data are very close to parallel, which indicates little or no interaction. The ANOVA tables allow for a formal F test of the null hypothesis of no interaction.

DEFINITION 10.5

Test for Interaction

1. H_0: No interaction

2. H_a: There is interaction

3. T.S.: $F = \text{MS(Interaction)}/\text{MS(Error)}$

4. R.R.: $F > F_\alpha$; the numerator d.f. are the indicated d.f. for interaction; the denominator d.f. are the error d.f.

For the heat-loss data, the computer output yields $F = .006/.184 = .03$, with 12 numerator d.f. and 40 denominator d.f. There's no need to even look this value up in the table; the expected value of an F statistic when H_0 is true is about 1.0, so $F = .03$ isn't even close to the expected value, let alone to the right-tail rejection region. (Note that all entries in the F table are greater than 1.0.) Thus we have no indication of more than random interaction, either by the formal F test or by the profile plot.

EXAMPLE 10.7

A consultant tested three different sets of materials for teaching basic statistical concepts. Three groups were the target audiences: college students, production workers, and staff managers. Randomly, 20 individuals from each group were taught with each set of materials. A score that measures ability to use statistical ideas in context was obtained for each individual. ANOVA output from Minitab and a table of mean scores by material and group follow:

```
Two-way ANOVA: Score versus Group, Material

Source          DF          SS          MS           F        P
Group            2     195.300      97.650       0.992    0.373
Material         2    1435.633     717.817       7.291    0.001
Interaction      4    6633.667    1658.417      16.845    0.000
Error          171   16835.200      98.451
Total          179   25099.800
```

		Material	
Group	**A**	**B**	**C**
Students	72.10	74.00	75.65
Workers	82.50	69.00	63.05
Managers	66.50	84.90	68.85

Is there evidence of interaction?

SOLUTION The F test for interaction, using the "multiplication" notation Group*Material, is shown as $F = 16.845$, with a p-value .000. Interaction is significant (detectable) at any reasonable α value. Just by looking at the means, we can see the interaction. As we go from A to B to C, the mean increases slightly for students, decreases sharply for workers, and first increases then decreases for managers. A profile plot would be thoroughly nonparallel. There is substantial, significant interaction.

Further analysis of two-factor experiments usually depends on the result of the interaction check. If interaction is not close to significant (perhaps with a *p*-value around .25 or higher), or if the profile plots are close enough to parallel that we consider interaction to be negligible, we can assume the additive model

$$Y_{ijk} = \mu + \text{row effect} + \text{column effect} + \text{error}$$

main effects

with the interaction term set to 0. In this case the **main effects** for rows and columns become relevant. These are differences between row (or column) averages and the grand mean. Thus, if the means for all levels of the row factor are equal—and therefore are equal to the grand mean—the row effects are 0. To say that the row factor means differ is to say that there are nonzero row effects. The ANOVA table also yields an *F* test for row effects and for column effects. Technically, these tests are

fixed factors

valid only for **fixed factors,** those for which the levels constitute the entire set of relevant levels. Most management experiments meet this condition; the exceptional

random factors

random factors, in which the levels are only a sample of the relevant levels (like a sample of teachers leading classes, or a sample of possible orderings of a report), must be handled by more advanced methods.

DEFINITION 10.6

Test for Row and Column Effects

1. H_0: No row effects

2. H_a: There are row effects

3. T.S.: $F = $ MS(Row factor)/MS(Error)

4. R.R.: Reject H_0 if $F > F_\alpha$, the tabled *F* value with numerator d.f. = d.f. for row factor and denominator d.f. = error d.f.

Note: To test column effects, replace "row" by "column."

In the example of four types of window panes, the relevant effect to test is Panetype; we don't need a statistical test to know that outside temperature has an effect on heat loss through windows. For Panetype, the output yields $F = 229.748/.184$ with 3 and 40 d.f.; this is a huge number, far beyond all table values. Therefore, we have conclusive evidence that there are real, more than random, differences in mean heat loss among types. Recall that in this example we found that there was no temperature–Panetype interaction. Therefore, we can also conclude that the Panetype differences are consistent across different temperatures.

When there is significant interaction, or when the profile plots are substantially nonparallel (whether significant or not), then the tests for row and column effects often don't mean much. Interaction means that the effect of varying levels of the row factor depends on which column we're talking about; the overall average obscures this fact. Occasionally, the test makes sense. For example, suppose we had found interaction between outside temperature and type of pane in our heat-loss example, and suppose that the temperatures used were representative of the range of temperatures that the windows will actually be exposed to. We can't change window panes every time the outside temperature changes, so the pane that is best on average is the one to use, even if its relative effectiveness depends on the temperature. Usually, though, when there is interaction, the main effects (averages) aren't very relevant.

EXAMPLE 10.8   In Example 10.7 what do the F tests for main Group and Material effects tell us?

SOLUTION   Not much. There is a large interaction. The materials that are most effective for one group are relatively ineffective for other groups. There is no need to use the same materials for all groups, so there's no reason to consider the overall average scores for each set of materials. Similarly, the performance of each group depends so heavily on the materials used that the average scores don't indicate much.

Even if interaction is present, Tukey comparisons of cell means are still possible and useful. In effect, we simply consider the IJ cell means as if they were means from a single factor.

DEFINITION 10.7

Confidence Intervals for Cell Means, Tukey Method   Treat the cell means as means from a single-factor experiment and carry out the Tukey procedure. Formally,

$$(\bar{y}_{ij} - \bar{y}_{i*j*}) - q_\alpha(IJ, \text{d.f.}_2)\sqrt{\text{MS(Within)}/n} \le \mu_{ij} - \mu_{i*j*}$$
$$\le (\bar{y}_{ij} - \bar{y}_{i*j*}) + q_\alpha(IJ, \text{d.f.}_2)\sqrt{\text{MS(Within)}/n}$$

where IJ is the number of cells, $\text{d.f.}_2 = IJ(n - 1)$ is the d.f. for MS(Within), $q_\alpha(IJ, \text{d.f.}_2)$ is given by Appendix Table 8, and $n =$ sample size per cell. n is the total sample size divided by the number of cells.

EXAMPLE 10.9   A state environmental agency tests two different methods of burning bituminous coal to generate electricity in connection with four different "scrubbers" to reduce the resulting air pollution. The primary concern is the emission of particulate matter. Four trials are run with each combination of scrubber and burning method. Particulate emission is measured for each trial. The data are

Method	*Scrubber* 1	2	3	4
A	18.9	8.8	23.7	23.6
	16.1	16.5	15.9	22.1
	14.7	11.7	16.2	16.7
	16.9	13.0	18.0	18.9

Method	*Scrubber* 1	2	3	4
B	24.3	24.0	9.3	18.4
	21.1	27.1	12.1	8.6
	18.0	22.6	15.6	15.1
	16.2	23.1	12.4	9.9

A portion of computer output (Minitab) is shown here.

```
Two-way ANOVA: Emission versus Method, Scrubber

Source          DF        SS        MS        F       P
Method           1     1.163     1.163     0.12    0.737
Scrubber         3    48.031    16.010     1.59    0.217
Interaction      3   475.472   158.490    15.78    0.000
Error           24   240.976    10.041
Total           31   765.644

Tabulated statistics: Method, Scrubber

Rows: Method    Columns: Scrubber

               1       2       3       4     All

A          16.65   12.50   18.45   20.33   16.98
B          19.90   24.20   12.35   13.00   17.36
All        18.28   18.35   15.40   16.66   17.17

Cell Contents:   Emission  :   Mean
```

Construct a profile plot. Does it indicate that interaction is present? Does the ANOVA table confirm your answer?

SOLUTION A profile plot is shown in Figure 10.16. The profiles aren't close to parallel, indicating that interaction is present. The ANOVA table in the output shows the interaction SS to be more than half the total variation and much larger than the effect for Sample or Columns. The output shows a large F value and a very small p-value, confirming that interaction is present.

FIGURE 10.16 **Profile Plots for Emission Means**

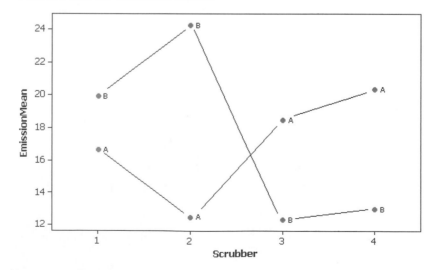

EXAMPLE 10.10   Because there is considerable interaction in the situation of Example 10.9, we would like to compare the performance of each method when mated with the best scrubber. Construct a 95% Tukey confidence interval for the difference in best-scrubber performance for each method.

SOLUTION   The best (lowest-emission) scrubber for Method A is scrubber 2, with $\bar{y}_{A2} = 12.50$. The best scrubber for Method B is scrubber 3, with $\bar{y}_{B3} = 12.35$. There are 8 means being compared, 2 methods times 4 scrubbers. For a 95% confidence interval with $IJ = 8$ means being compared, and error degrees of freedom $\text{d.f.}_2 = 24$, the value of $q_{.05}(8, 24)$ is 4.68. Substituting into the formula with $n = 4$ and $\text{MS(Within)} = 10.041$, we have

$$(12.50 - 12.35) - 4.68\sqrt{10.041/4} \leq \mu_{A2} - \mu_{B3} \leq (12.50 - 12.35)$$
$$+ 4.68\sqrt{10.041/4}$$

or

$$-7.265 \leq \mu_{A2} - \mu_{B3} \leq 7.565$$

When interaction is not substantial or significant or when a manager is willing to ignore it and compare equally weighted means, the Tukey method still applies. Take the row means and allow for random error with the usual plus-or-minus a table value times a standard error. The notation is different, but the idea is exactly the same as in a one-factor study.

DEFINITION 10.8

> **Confidence Intervals for Row Means, Tukey Method**   Treat the row means as though they came from a single-factor study.
>
> $$(\bar{y}_{i..} - \bar{y}_{i'..}) - q_\alpha(I, \text{d.f.}_2)\sqrt{\text{MS(Error)}/nJ} < \mu_{i..} - \mu_{i'..} < (\bar{y}_{i..} - \bar{y}_{i'..})$$
> $$+ q_\alpha(I, \text{d.f.}_2)\sqrt{\text{MS(Error)}/nJ}$$
>
> Note that nJ is the number of observations per row mean; it can also be calculated as the total sample size divided by the number of rows.

In this section we have relied on computer output for ANOVA tables and the resulting inferences. This is the way we usually analyze two-factor experiments; occasionally, the work must be done by hand. Therefore, for the record, we present methods for computing the ANOVA table by hand. Skip to the end of the section unless you need this for reference.

The formulas for these sums of squares use the following notation:

y_{ijk}: kth observation at the ith level (row) of factor 1

and the jth level (column) of factor 2

$$i = 1, 2, \ldots, I$$
$$j = 1, 2, \ldots, J$$
$$k = 1, 2, \ldots, n$$

Note that n is the number of observations per cell, not the overall sample size.

$\bar{y}_{ij.}$: sample mean response for the ith level of factor 1 and the jth level of factor 2

$$\bar{y}_{ij.} = \sum_{k} \frac{y_{ijk}}{n}$$

$\bar{y}_{i..}$: sample mean response for the ith level of factor 1

$$\bar{y}_{i..} = \sum_{j,k} \frac{y_{ijk}}{nJ}$$

$\bar{y}_{.j.}$: sample mean response for the jth level of factor 2

$$\bar{y}_{.j.} = \sum_{i,k} \frac{y_{ijk}}{nI}$$

$\bar{y}_{...}$: grand mean for all sample observations

$$\bar{y}_{...} = \sum_{i,j,k} \frac{y_{ijk}}{nIJ}$$

sums of squares for a two-factor ANOVA

With this notation, the **sums of squares for a two-factor ANOVA** are defined as follows:

Factor 1: $SS(\text{Rows}) = nJ \sum_{i} (\bar{y}_{i..} - \bar{y}_{...})^2$

Factor 2: $SS(\text{Columns}) = nI \sum_{j} (\bar{y}_{.j.} - \bar{y}_{...})^2$

Interaction: $SS(\text{Interaction}) = n \sum_{i,j} (\bar{y}_{ij.} - \bar{y}_{i..} - \bar{y}_{.j.} + \bar{y}_{...})^2$

$SS(\text{Within}) = \sum_{i,j,k} (y_{ijk} - \bar{y}_{ij.})^2$

EXAMPLE 10.11   Compute the sums of squares for an ANOVA of the heat-loss data.

SOLUTION   The following table of means can be used to compute these sums of squares. Entries in the body of the table are the $\bar{y}_{ij.}$'s. Note that $n = 3, I = 5$, and $J = 4$.

Exterior Temperature i	Pane Type j				
	A	B	C	D	$\bar{y}_{i..}$
60	3.800	7.933	10.900	12.967	8.900
50	6.133	10.133	13.100	15.100	11.117
40	7.000	11.100	14.000	15.933	12.008
30	7.967	12.033	14.967	17.000	12.992
20	10.000	14.033	16.967	18.933	14.983
$\bar{y}_{.j.}$	6.980	11.047	13.987	15.987	$\bar{y}_{...} = 12.000$

Substituting (unrounded) means from this table, we find

$$SS(Rows) = (3)(4)[(-3.100)^2 + (-.883)^2 + (.008)^2 + (.992)^2 + (2.983)^2]$$
$$= 243.288$$
$$SS(Columns) = (3)(5)[(-5.020)^2 + (-.953)^2 + (1.987)^2 + (3.987)^2]$$
$$= 689.244$$
$$SS(Interaction) = 3[(-.080)^2 + (-.014)^2 + \cdots + (-.037)^2] = .074$$

The within-cell sum of squares must be calculated from the original data. For this example,

$$SS(Within) = (3.2 - 3.800)^2 + (7.5 - 7.933)^2 + \cdots + (3.9 - 3.800)^2$$
$$+ (8.3 - 7.933)^2 + (4.3 - 3.800)^2 + (8.0 - 7.933)^2$$
$$+ \cdots + (18.8 - 18.933)^2$$
$$= 7.353$$

Exercises

10.21 Three products are tested in each of five geographic regions. A mean approval rating is found in each case. The sample sizes are large enough that the means can be regarded essentially as population means.

Region	*Product*		
	A	B	C
1	68	80	77
2	55	64	58
3	62	72	67
4	67	76	70
5	58	68	63

a. Calculate the grand mean. Interpret this value.
b. Calculate region effects and product effects.
c. What does the difference in effects of products A and B represent?
d. Calculate a table of interaction effects.
e. Construct a profile plot for the means. (Arbitrarily, put products along the horizontal axis.)
f. Is there interaction in the means?
g. Is there a consistent superiority of any one product over all regions?

10.22 A manufacturer of (snow) skis must bond the main assembly to the bottom of the ski (the part that makes contact with the snow). The bonding agent should be applied as uniformly as possible to obtain a good ski. Uniformity is indicated by low "wiggle" values. The manufacturer tested various temperatures for the application, bonding 20 skis at each of ten temperatures. The data were analyzed using JMP, with results shown in Figure 10.17. Is there clear evidence that temperature makes a difference in the average "wiggle" value?

10.23 The bonding agents for the data for the ski manufacturer of the preceding exercise were obtained from two different suppliers. The data were reanalyzed, taking into account the supplier factor. The results are shown in Figure 10.18. Is there clear evidence that temperature matters? Supplier? The interaction between them?

FIGURE 10.17 **One-Way ANOVA for Ski Bonding Data**

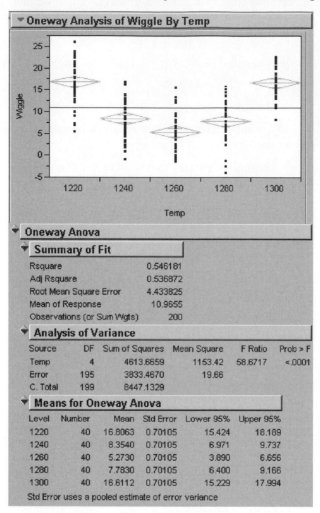

FIGURE 10.18 **Two-Way ANOVA with Interaction for Ski Bonding Data**

Summary of Fit

RSquare	0.557747
RSquare Adj	0.536799
Root Mean Square Error	4.434177
Mean of Response	10.9655
Observations (or Sum Wgts)	200

Analysis of Variance

Source	DF	Sum of Squares	Mean Square	F Ratio
Model	9	4711.3665	523.485	26.6243
Error	190	3735.7665	19.662	Prob > F
C. Total	199	8447.1329		<.0001

Parameter Estimates

Effect Tests

Source	Nparm	DF	Sum of Squares	F Ratio	Prob > F
Temp	4	4	4613.6659	58.6624	<.0001
Supplier	1	1	0.6986	0.0355	0.8507
Temp*Supplier	4	4	97.0020	1.2334	0.2981

10.24 A profile plot of the means for the ski bonding data is shown in Figure 10.19. Is there a clear indication that interaction is present? Is your answer consistent with the output shown in the previous exercise?

FIGURE 10.19 **Profile Plots for Ski Bonding Data**

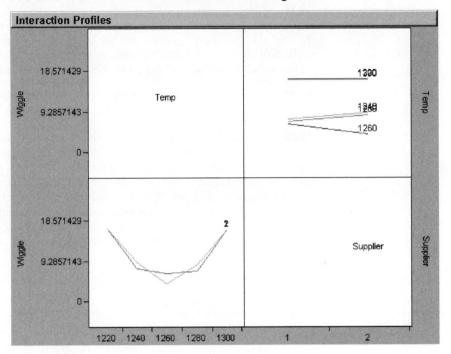

10.25 An experiment on workfare programs is undertaken by a state welfare agency. Three plans are tested. Plan A requires that all physically able welfare recipients work at assigned jobs for minimum wages. Plan B allows recipients to select or reject jobs, and welfare benefits are reduced by $1 for every $2 earned. Plan C is a "control": Welfare officials visit plan C recipients as often as subjects in plans A and B and encourage job searching, but they offer no special job-taking incentives. Each plan is used with 20 families in each of four geographic areas of the state. For each family, the one-year increase in income is found. The following means (in thousands of dollars) are observed:

	Area			
Plan	1	2	3	4
A	2.1	1.7	1.3	1.7
B	1.9	1.8	1.7	1.8
C	.8	.7	.6	.7

An ANOVA table follows:

Source	SS	d.f.	MS
Plan	59.20	2	29.60
Area	4.80	3	1.60
Interaction	2.40	6	.40
Error	273.60	228	1.20
Total	340.00	239	

a. Find the grand mean.

b. Find the row and column effects.

10.26 Refer to Exercise 10.25. Calculate F tests for the effects of (a) plan, (b) area, and (c) interaction. Use $\alpha = .05$ in each case. State a conclusion for each test.

10.27 Refer to Exercise 10.25.

a. Construct a profile plot for the data. Arrange plans along the horizontal axis.

b. Does this plot suggest the possibility that interaction is present?

c. Does the F test of Exercise 10.26 indicate that interaction is present? Is that a conflict between the plot and the test? If so, what is a possible explanation?

10.28 Refer to the data of Exercise 10.25. Use a Tukey test with $\alpha = .05$ to see if any of the plan mean differences can be declared statistically significant.

10.29 A maker of packaged cake mixes wants consistently good results from its mixes and therefore minimal variation in quality from one box to another. Standard procedure in testing any new mix is to prepare four versions of the mix. Six batches of each version are tested at each of three geographical altitudes. Typically, there is greater variability at higher altitudes. Most customers are at altitude 1, the lowest altitude, and most of the rest are at the middling altitude, 2. Altitude 3 is highest. A standard measure of variability is computed for the cakes baked from each batch. The variability measure reflects differences in the height and texture among cakes, which is ideally very small. The data were analyzed by Minitab to obtain the following averages of the variation measure:

```
Tabulated statistics: Altitude, Mixture

Rows: Altitude    Columns: Mixture

              1       2       3       4      All

1          64.67   59.23   54.08   66.32   61.08
2          69.90   53.20   73.63   92.63   72.34
3          36.97   90.45   88.23   94.70   77.59
All        57.18   67.63   71.98   84.55   70.33

Cell Contents:  Variation  :  Mean
```

a. Would it be sensible to say that mixture 1, which has the lowest average score, appears to be the most desirable mixture?

b. A profile plot of the mean variation score, constructed using Minitab, is shown in Figure 10.20. What does this plot say about your answer to part (a)?

10.30 The data for Exercise 10.29 also were analyzed to yield an ANOVA table. The Minitab output is as follows:

```
Two-way ANOVA: Variation versus Altitude, Mixture

Source       DF       SS       MS      F      P
Altitude      2    3417.0   1708.47   5.12   0.009
Mixture       3    6934.0   2311.34   6.92   0.000
Interaction   6   11666.5   1944.42   5.82   0.000
Error        60   20035.9    333.93
Total        71   42053.4
```

a. Show that there is a statistically detectable (significant) interaction at any reasonable α value.

b. Explain what interaction means in this context. In particular, how does interaction relate to your answers to Exercise 10.29?

c. How meaningful are the tests for the main effects in this case?

FIGURE 10.20   Profile Plot of Variation Score Means

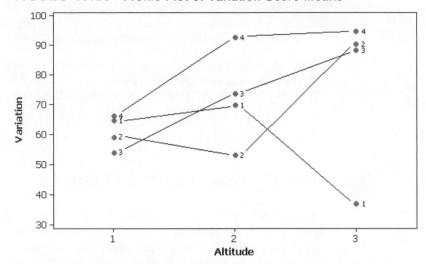

10.31   A supermarket chain wanted to select a new "house brand" of instant coffee. A taste test was arranged. Three different methods for preparing the coffee were used. Also, three different ages of coffee were tested. Age 1 was as fresh as the distribution system would allow, age 2 was the maximum age allowed for selling the coffee, and age 3 was basically "What's this stuff in the back of the cupboard?" The chain manager obtained six jars of each method of coffee at each age and prepared coffee from every jar. A consensus rating was obtained for each jar from a tasting panel; the ideal rating was 100. Mean ratings were obtained from Minitab output as follows:

```
Tabulated statistics: Age, Method

Rows: Age    Columns: Method

            1       2       3     All

1       63.00   55.00   57.17   58.39
2       50.67   43.67   40.17   44.83
3       46.33   37.00   27.67   37.00
All     53.33   45.22   41.67   46.74

Cell Contents:   Rating  :  Mean
```

a.   Which method seems to obtain the best ratings?

b.   Is there an evident effect of age? Does the pattern of changes in means make sense in this context?

c.   Are differences between methods reasonably consistent across different ages? What effect is being considered here?

10.32   The data underlying Exercise 10.31 were given to the Minitab package, which yields the following ANOVA output:

```
Two-way ANOVA: Rating versus Age, Method

Source       DF        SS        MS       F       P
Age           2    4215.6   2107.79   18.75   0.000
Method        2    1287.3    643.63    5.73   0.006
Interaction   4     306.5     76.63    0.68   0.608
Error        45    5059.0    112.42
Total        53   10868.3
```

a. Is there clear evidence that the effect of Method depends on which Age is considered? That is, is there clear evidence of an interaction effect?

b. What does the *p*-value for Age indicate about the main effect of Age?

c. Is there conclusive evidence of a more-than-random difference of Method averages?

10.33 Use the means from Exercise 10.31 and the output from Exercise 10.32 to test for significant differences of all pairs of Method means. You'll need to compute Method means by hand from the cell means. Do the results indicate a clear choice of the method to adopt?

10.5 Randomized Block Designs

The ANOVA methods we discussed in this chapter extend the basic methods of comparing two means to the more general problem of comparing several means. We applied the procedure in two experimental settings—one-factor ANOVA, which we described in Section 10.1, and two-factor ANOVA, which we described in Section 10.4. In this section we describe an experimental design that is a hybrid of these settings, the **randomized block design.**

randomized block design

A chain of personal computer stores wants to test three possible point-of-purchase displays of a new type of holder for compact discs (CDs). The chain managers propose to test-market the displays in three stores in each of three sales districts. One approach is to assign displays completely randomly to stores. The only factor is the type of display; the one-factor ANOVA methods of Section 10.1 can be used to analyze the resulting sales-volume data. One problem with this approach is that there is a chance of obtaining an assignment such as the following:

	Products Displayed		
District 1:	A	A	A
District 2:	B	B	B
District 3:	C	C	C

confounded effects

This would be a disastrous assignment. Because all the displays of a given type are in one district, there is no way to tell whether differences in sales volume are due to differences in displays or to differences in districts; that is, with this assignment, effect of display and effect of district are **confounded effects.** But even if the assignment of displays to stores does not turn out to be confounded, there is another objection to a one-factor experiment. By not controlling for district, this design implies that any district-to-district differences are part of random error. If there are, in fact, large district-to-district differences, MS(Error) is large; by failing to control for district, this design leads to very wide confidence intervals and to tests with very poor power.

The one-factor experimental design can be modified to control for differences among districts. The chain's managers can restrict the random assignment of displays to stores by requiring that each display be used once in each district. One such randomization is shown here. Note that each display is placed in one (randomly chosen) store in each district.

	Products Displayed		
District 1:	A	C	B
District 2:	B	A	C
District 3:	A	B	C

treatment factor

block factor

This experimental setting is referred to as a randomized block design. Characteristically, there is one factor, called the **treatment factor,** that is of primary interest; in this example, the treatment factor is type of display. In addition, there is another factor, called a **block factor,** that is of less interest in itself but should be controlled to avoid confounding and to reduce random error. In this example, districts would be considered block factors. Randomized block methods can be thought of as extensions of the paired-sample methods of Chapter 9; had the chain been considering only displays A and B, the sales-volume data could be regarded as paired by district. One reason for blocking is the same as the reason for pairing—to reduce the amount of random variation.

A randomized block is a two-factor (treatments and blocks) experiment with a one-factor focus; that is, the primary aim of the design is to compare means for the treatment factor. The block factor tends to be regarded as a "nuisance" factor; it is controlled, not so much to find out what its effects are as to avoid having those effects contaminate the analysis of the treatment factor.

There is another difference between a randomized block design and the two-factor designs we discussed in Section 10.4. There is typically only $n = 1$ observation per cell in a randomized block design. In the ANOVA table for a two-factor design, the d.f. for error is $IJ(n - 1)$; if we used two-factor methods for a randomized block design, we would have no d.f. for error, no MS(Error) number, and no way to do tests or confidence intervals. To avoid this problem, we assume that there is no interaction between treatments and blocks; the degrees of freedom that would have been used up in estimating interaction become available, given the assumption of no interaction, for estimating error.

The model for a randomized block design is

$$Y_{ij} = \text{grand mean} + \text{treatment effect} + \text{block effect} + \text{error}$$

Note that, by assumption, there is no interaction term in the model.

The ANOVA computations (again, easily done by computer) for a randomized block design are similar to those of a two-factor ANOVA, with the exception that there is, by assumption, no SS(Interaction).

DEFINITION 10.9

Sums of Squares for a Randomized Block Design

$$SS(\text{Treatment}) = J \sum (\bar{y}_{i.} - \bar{y}_{..})^2, \text{ with d.f.} = I - 1$$

$$SS(\text{Block}) = I \sum (\bar{y}_{.j} - \bar{y}_{..})^2, \text{ with d.f.} = J - 1$$

$$SS(\text{Error}) = \sum (y_{ij} - \bar{y}_{i.} - \bar{y}_{.j} + \bar{y}_{..})^2, \text{ with d.f.} = (I - 1)(J - 1)$$

$$SS(\text{Total}) = \sum (y_{ij} - \bar{y}_{..})^2$$

$$= SS(\text{Treatment}) + SS(\text{Block}) + SS(\text{Error}), \text{ with d.f.} = IJ - 1$$

In these formulas, $\bar{y}_{i.}$ is the mean for treatment i, $\bar{y}_{.j}$ is the mean for block j, and $\bar{y}_{..}$ is the grand mean; I is the number of treatments and J is the number of blocks. Usually, the easy way is to compute SS(Treatment), SS(Block), and SS(Total), and then find SS(Error) by subtraction.

Suppose that the sales-volume data for the three different displays in three different districts are as follows:

Display	District 1	2	3	Average
A	86	97	96	93.0
B	55	82	79	72.0
C	60	88	77	75.0
Average	67.0	89.0	84.0	80.0

Then

$$SS(\text{Treatment}) = SS(\text{Display})$$
$$= 3[(93.0 - 80.0)^2 + (72.0 - 80.0)^2 + (75.0 - 80.0)^2]$$
$$= 774.0$$
$$SS(\text{Block}) = SS(\text{District})$$
$$= 3[(67.0 - 80.0)^2 + (89.0 - 80.0)^2 + (84.0 - 80.0)^2]$$
$$= 798.0$$
$$SS(\text{Total}) = (86 - 80.0)^2 + (97 - 80.0)^2 + \cdots + (77 - 80.0)^2$$
$$= 1684.0$$
$$SS(\text{Error}) = SS(\text{Total}) - SS(\text{Treatment}) - SS(\text{Block})$$
$$= 1684.0 - 774.0 - 798.0$$
$$= 112.0$$

The ANOVA table and F tests are completed just as in previous sections. The results for the sales-volume data are as follows:

Source	SS	d.f.	MS	F
Treatment (display)	774.0	2	387.0	13.82
Block (district)	798.0	2	399.0	14.25
Error	112.0	4	28.0	
Total	1684.0	8		

The F statistics are obtained, as usual, by dividing the indicated MS by MS(Error); the degrees of freedom for the F statistic are those indicated by the ANOVA table. For the sales-volume data, both F statistics have $d.f._1 = 2$ and $d.f._2 = 4$; for these d.f., $F_{.025} = 10.65$ and $F_{.01} = 18.00$. For the display factor, the F statistic falls between 10.65 and 18.00; the p-value is therefore between .025 and .01. Thus, the chain's managers have fairly conclusive evidence that there are real, more than random, differences in mean sales volume by type of display. The F test for the district factor also shows that there are differences in mean volume by district; the managers knew that very well already. Note that the block factor does indeed account for a large fraction of SS(Total); had the managers not adopted a randomized block design, the SS(Error) would have been much larger, possibly concealing the effect of the display factor.

The Tukey method for comparing pairs of means works the same way as for other designs. The role of MS(Within) is taken by MS(Error) and the d.f. are those for error. In a randomized block design, the sample size per mean, n, is equal to the number of blocks; however, it can also be calculated as the total number of observations divided by the number of treatments. For example, suppose that there had been 4 levels of a treatment factor applied within each of 11 blocks; there would be a total of 44 observations (and 43 total d.f.). If an ANOVA table showed MS(Error) = 16.0 with 30 d.f., the Tukey plus-or-minus for $\alpha = .05$ (95% confidence) would be $q_{.05}(I = 4, \text{d.f.} = 30)\sqrt{\text{MS(Error)}/n} = 3.85\sqrt{16.0/11} = 4.64$. The Tukey procedure is the same for randomized block designs as for other designs, given the proper interpretation of the various entries.

Most computer packages can compute the ANOVA table for a randomized block design.

Exercises

10.34 An information systems manager tests four database management systems for possible use. A key variable is speed of execution of programs. The manager chooses six representative tasks and writes programs within each management system. The following times and Minitab output are recorded:

	Task					
System	1	2	3	4	5	6
I	58	324	206	94	39	418
II	47	331	163	75	30	397
III	73	355	224	106	59	449
IV	38	297	188	72	25	366

```
Two-way ANOVA: Time versus System, Task

Source   DF      SS        MS       F       P
System    3    7505    2501.8   18.41   0.000
Task      5  472214   94442.8  694.94   0.000
Error    15    2039     135.9
Total    23  481758

S = 11.66    R-Sq = 99.58%    R-Sq(adj) = 99.35%

                    Individual 95% CIs For Mean Based on
                    Pooled StDev
System    Mean    ---+---------+---------+---------+------
I       189.832                    (----*----)
II      173.832           (----*----)
III     210.999                          (-----*----)
IV      164.332   (----*----)
                  ---+---------+---------+---------+------
                   160       180       200       220
```

```
                    Individual 95% CIs For Mean Based on
                    Pooled StDev
Task     Mean    -------+---------+---------+---------+--
1        54.00   (*-)
2       326.75                                   (-*)
3       195.25                   (-*)
4        86.75      (-*)
5        38.25   (*)
6       407.50                                          (*)
                 -------+---------+---------+---------+--
                    100       200       300       400
```

Locate means for each system. Find the grand mean.

10.35 Is there a statistically detectable (significant) difference among system means? State the *p*-value.

10.36 An experiment compares four different mixtures of the components of a rocket propellant; the mixtures contain differing proportions of oxidizer, fuel, and binder. To compare the mixtures, five different samples of propellant are prepared for each mixture. Each of five investigators is randomly assigned one sample of each of the four mixtures and is asked to measure the propellant thrust. The data are shown here:

	Investigator				
Mixture	**1**	**2**	**3**	**4**	**5**
1	2340	2355	2362	2350	2348
2	2658	2650	2665	2640	2653
3	2449	2458	2432	2437	2445
4	2403	2410	2418	2397	2405

a. Identify the blocks and treatments for this design.
b. Why would one want to use this design, as opposed to assigning mixtures completely randomly to investigators?

10.37 Refer to Exercise 10.36.
a. Use the output from Minitab that is shown here to conduct an ANOVA. Use $\alpha = .05$.
b. Which mixture appears to have the best (highest) mean? Is its mean significantly ($\alpha = .05$) higher than each of the other three means?

```
Two-way ANOVA: Thrust versus Mixture, Investigator

Source          DF      SS       MS         F        P
Mixture          3   261260   87086.9  1264.72   0.000
Investigator     4      453     113.1     1.64   0.227
Error           12      826      68.9
Total           19   262539

S = 8.298    R-Sq = 99.69%    R-Sq(adj) = 99.50%

                    Individual 95% CIs For Mean Based on
                    Pooled StDev
Mixture    Mean   -------+---------+---------+---------+--
1        2351.0   (*)
2        2653.2                                     (*)
3        2444.2                 (*)
4        2406.6         (*)
                  -------+---------+---------+---------+--
                     2400      2480      2560      2640
```

```
                              Individual 95% CIs For Mean Based on Pooled StDev
Investigator    Mean           -+---------+---------+---------+--------
1              2462.49                      (----------*----------)
2              2468.24                            (----------*----------)
3              2469.24                            (----------*----------)
4              2455.99          (----------*----------)
5              2462.74                 (----------*----------)
                              -+---------+---------+---------+--------
                            2448.0    2456.0    2464.0    2472.0
```

10.38 Is there evidence of a significant investigator effect in the computer output of Exercise 10.37? What would such an effect indicate about the accuracy of the investigators?

10.39 As one part of a taste-testing experiment, three different formulations of a new frozen dinner product are tested. Samples of each formulation are given, in random order, to each of 12 testers. Each tester gives a score to each formulation. A Minitab analysis of the data is shown here:

```
Two-way ANOVA: Rating versus Form, Person

Source   DF       SS        MS      F      P
Form      2    767.39   383.693   5.51  0.012
Person   11   5301.21   481.928   6.92  0.000
Error    22   1532.60    69.664
Total    35   7601.21

S = 8.347   R-Sq = 79.84%   R-Sq(adj) = 67.92%

                       Individual 99% CIs For Mean Based on
                       Pooled StDev
Form     Mean     ---+---------+---------+---------+------
1      57.6666                     (--------*---------)
2      46.9166    (---------*---------)
3      49.2499       (--------*---------)
                  ---+---------+---------+---------+------
                  42.0      49.0      56.0      63.0

                       Individual 99% CIs For Mean Based on
                       Pooled StDev
Person   Mean     -----+---------+---------+---------+----
  1    63.3332                       (------*-----)
  2    60.6666                       (-----*------)
  3    56.3332                   (------*------)
  4    40.9999           (------*-----)
  5    34.3332       (------*------)
  6    52.9999                  (------*-----)
  7    23.3332    (------*-----)
  8    64.9999                         (------*-----)
  9    55.3332                  (------*-----)
 10    46.9999             (------*-----)
 11    60.9999                       (------*-----)
 12    54.9999                  (------*-----)
                  -----+---------+---------+---------+----
                     20        40        60        80
```

a. Perform an *F* test of the null hypothesis of equal score (rating) means by formulation (form). State bounds on the *p*-value.

b. Are there statistically significant ($\alpha = .01$) differences among taste-tester (person) means? What does the result of the test indicate about the people in the experiment?

c. Calculate 95% confidence intervals for all pairwise differences of score means for the three formulations. Note that each mean is an average of 12 scores.

d. According to these intervals, which pairwise differences, if any, are statistically significant at $\alpha = .05$?

10.40 A supermarket chain offered a private label product in competition with national labels. The package design had been a generic, boring one, and the product had not sold well at all. The chain decided to use an upgraded package design but needed to choose among three alternative designs. As a test, the chain manager had substantial numbers of packages made up in each of the three designs. Each store in the chain offered each type of package for one day. The order was randomized so that a few stores sold design 1, then 2, then 3; others sold 3, then 1, then 2; and still others 2, then 1, then 3; and so on. The sales in each market each day were recorded. JMP results follow:

```
Response: Sales
Effect Test
Source     Nparm          DF    Sum of Squares  F Ratio   Prob>F
Design         2           2    1476.722        4.3055    0.0172
Store         35          35    26525.667       4.4192    0.0000

Least Squares Means
Level     Least Sq Mean         Std Error      Mean
1         79.38888889           2.182598123    79.3889
2         84.08333333           2.182598123    84.0833
3         75.02777778           2.182598123    75.0278
```

a. Is there a clear indication that store makes a difference in sales? Defend your answer briefly.

b. Is there a clear indication that design 2 is better than design 3? You will need to do some calculations by hand. MS(Error) = 171.49.

c. Why was it important for each store to sell each design, rather than having some stores sell only design 1, others only design 2, and others only design 3?

d. Why was it desirable to randomize the order in which the designs were sold?

BUSINESS DECISION-MAKING IN ACTION

CHAPTER CASE

ANALYSIS

Checker's Pizza

High employee turnover rate is a key problem faced by the Checker's Pizza chain. Terri Chester, the new general manager, hired Dr. Shannon Train to find out why store employees were leaving. Based on his findings, Dr. Train recommended two possible ways to solve the employee retention problem: (1) a training program for new hires and (2) a bonus program that would reward store managers for improved retention.

While Terri liked both ideas, she wasn't ready to proceed with both on a company-wide basis, so Dr. Train suggested that Terri run an experiment to see if either, or both, approaches affected retention before she committed funds. He designed an experiment in which 40 store managers were randomly assigned in groups of 10 to one of four "experimental" conditions that reflected all combinations of the training and bonus conditions: (1) no training–no bonus, (2) no training–bonus, (3) training–no bonus, and (4) training–bonus.

All restaurant employees hired during the month the experiment began were included in the study. Their tenure was followed for 12 months and was recorded in days, from the date of hire until the date of termination or until the date the study ended. Thus, tenure could range from 1 day up to 365 days for those still employed when the study ended.

As a member of the retention task force, you were asked by Terri to examine the data collected. Based on your analysis of the data and other information presented, you are to recommend to Terri whether or not to use either, or both, of the training and bonus interventions to slow down turnover.

The collected data from Dr. Train's study are stored in the Checkers file on the CD that came with your book. We begin our analysis by partitioning the data set into subgroups that correspond to the cells of the 2×2 experimental design. Descriptive statistics for the tenure variable within each cell (n's, means and standard deviations) are given in the following Minitab output:

```
Tabulated statistics: Training, Bonus

Rows: Training    Columns: Bonus

            0       1      All

0         91.6   141.3   115.4
          56.64   54.18   60.56
             48      44      92

1        126.0   219.5   160.4
          60.15   74.25   79.47
             48      28      76

All      108.8   171.7   135.8
          60.63   73.13   73.08
             96      72     168

Cell Contents:   Tenure   :   Mean
                 Tenure   :   Standard deviation
                 Tenure   :   Nonmissing
```

These descriptive results provide a number of important pieces of information. First, the low tenure average of 91.6 days for the no training–no bonus (NT–NB) group shows that more employees needed to be replaced in that group than any of the other three groups. This, of course, represents the current way of doing business in the Checker's restaurants and therefore serves as a "control group" for interpreting results in the other three groups. Second, the mean retention times for the treatment conditions clearly suggest that the experimental factors have an impact on tenure. Employees in the no training–bonus (NT–B) and the training–no bonus (T–NB) groups have average retention times over a month longer than the control group, and employees in the training–bonus (T–B) condition have an average retention time over four months longer than the control group. Finally, while the variances within conditions are somewhat different, they are not so divergent (based on an F test) as to make ANOVA inappropriate. Box plots of tenure by the four groups are shown in Figure 10.21.

Note the range of scores is considerably lower for the control condition (NT–NB) than for either the training only (T–NB) or bonus only (NT–B) groups, and the same is true when comparing these two groups to the group that received both the training and bonus programs (T–B). Thus it appears that combining the training and bonus programs has the desired effect.

In order to verify this conclusion statistically, we would like to apply a two-way ANOVA procedure to the data. Unfortunately, Minitab's two-way ANOVA procedure requires an equal number of observations in each cell. Advanced statistical techniques not covered here can be used to show that the interaction effect is highly significant,

FIGURE 10.21

Box Plots of Tenure by Experimental Group

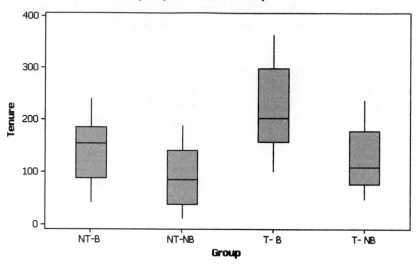

FIGURE 10.22

Profile Plot of Tenure Versus Training (and Bonus)

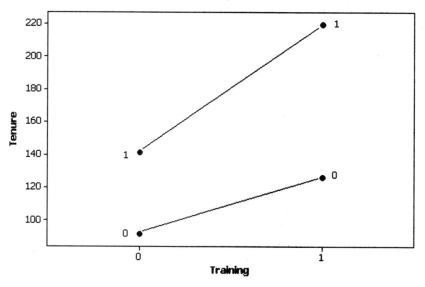

as we suspect, and that an additive model is not appropriate. The profile plot in Figure 10.22 further supports the conclusion of a significant interaction effect.

As an alternative, we can treat each cell of the 2×2 experimental design as a level of a single factor (with a total of four levels) and use one-way ANOVA and the Tukey multiple comparison technique discussed earlier in this chapter. Minitab output is shown next.

```
One-way ANOVA: Tenure versus Group

Source    DF       SS      MS      F      P
Group      3   296052   98684  27.16  0.000
Error    164   595878    3633
Total    167   891931

S = 60.28   R-Sq = 33.19%   R-Sq(adj) = 31.97%
```

```
                            Individual 95% CIs For Mean Based on
                            Pooled StDev
   Level   N     Mean   StDev   -----+---------+---------+---------+----
   NT-B   44   141.32   54.18                (--*---)
   NT-NB  48    91.60   56.64   (--*---)
   T-B    28   219.54   74.25                               (----*---)
   T-NB   48   125.98   60.15          (--*---)
                                -----+---------+---------+---------+----
                                   100       150       200       250
```

Pooled StDev = 60.28

Tukey 95% Simultaneous Confidence Intervals
All Pairwise Comparisons among Levels of Group

Individual confidence level = 98.97%

Group = NT-B subtracted from:

```
Group    Lower   Center    Upper   -------+---------+---------+---------+--
NT-NB   -82.36   -49.71   -17.07             (--*--)
T-B      40.40    78.22   116.03                       (---*---)
T-NB    -47.99   -15.34    17.31                (--*---)
                                   -------+---------+---------+---------+--
                                        -100        0       100       200
```

Group = NT-B subtracted from:

```
Group    Lower   Center    Upper   -------+---------+---------+---------+--
T-B      90.73   127.93   165.13                            (--*--)
T-NB      2.44    34.37    66.31                 (--*---)
                                   -------+---------+---------+---------+--
                                        -100        0       100       200
```

Group = T-B subtracted from:

```
Group    Lower   Center    Upper   -------+---------+---------+---------+--
T-NB   -130.75   -93.56   -56.36       (---*--)
                                   -------+---------+---------+---------+--
                                        -100        0       100       200
```

The F statistic of the one-way ANOVA ($F = 27.16$, $p = .000$) indicates that at least two of the four tenure means are different. The Tukey procedure shows that all pairwise differences are significant with the exception of the difference between the T–NB and NT–B groups. In particular, the T–B tenure mean for the combined training–bonus group is significantly higher than that of any of the other four groups.

Thus the data indicate that the combination of both training and bonus programs results in significantly longer retention times on average than either program alone, which, in turn, results in significantly longer retention times on average than the control condition.

SUMMARY

Here are some points to consider when dealing with designed experiments.

1. Before running any analyses, think carefully about all the experimental factors that are being varied. Make sure that all of them are considered together in the analysis.

2. The various F tests are intended to see if the overall pattern of means is a statistically detectable (significant) result (that is, at least one mean is different from

the others). It does not directly tell you which means differ, unless there are only two means and that's the only possible difference.

3. The Tukey procedure (along with other multiple comparison methods in some packages) is designed to make more specific comparisons of particular means.

4. When dealing with two or more factors, consider possible interactions first. When substantial interaction is present, the averages for any one factor usually aren't very interesting (or interpretable) and conceal the essential story told by the data.

5. The idea of blocking is a direct extension of the idea of paired samples. The reason for blocking is to control a major source of variability that is not of much interest. The typical randomized block experiment can be recognized by having only one observation per cell.

6. The key assumptions for analysis of variance are the same as those of the pooled-variance t method: no biases, independence, normality, and constant variance, basically in that order of importance.

In addition, you may want to reread the summary of key ideas in the Executive Overview at the beginning of this chapter.

Supplementary Exercises

10.41 Three different designs of video recording equipment are subjected to accelerated use testing, and the times to failure (in hours) of each unit are recorded:

					Time					
Design A:	226	400	462	489	510	541	547	563	581	603
Design B:	329	366	409	451	465	490	517	546	577	615
Design C:	421	484	506	566	589	605	619	634	651	600

The data were analyzed using Excel to obtain the results in Figure 10.23.
a. Locate means and variances for each design. Which design appears to be best?
b. Locate SS(Between) and SS(Within).
c. Explain why the d.f. shown are correct.

FIGURE 10.23 **One-Way ANOVA of Data in Exercise 10.41**

	A	B	C	D	E	F	G
1	Anova: Single Factor						
2							
3	SUMMARY						
4	*Groups*	*Count*	*Sum*	*Average*	*Variance*		
5	A	10	4922	492.2	12351.3		
6	B	10	4765	476.5	8360.06		
7	C	10	5735	573.5	6258.94		
8							
9							
10	ANOVA						
11	*Source of Variation*	*SS*	*df*	*MS*	*F*	*P-value*	*F crit*
12	Between Groups	54217.3	2	27108.6	3.01539	0.06577	3.35413
13	Within Groups	242733	27	8990.1			
14							
15	Total	296950	29				

10.42 Refer to Exercise 10.41. Is the research hypothesis of unequal means supported? First use $\alpha = .05$, then place bounds on the p-value.

10.43 Perform the Kruskal–Wallis test for the hypothesis of Exercise 10.42. Is the conclusion substantially different from that of Exercise 10.42?

10.44 Box plots of the data in Exercise 10.41 are shown in Figure 10.24. Do there appear to be any major violations of ANOVA assumptions?

FIGURE 10.24 **Box Plots of Failure Time Data**

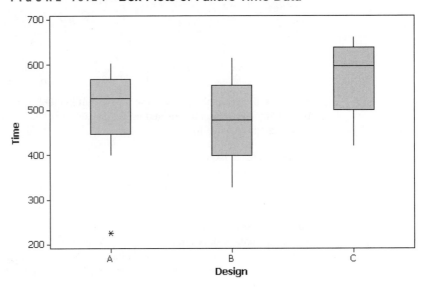

10.45 Use the Tukey procedure to calculate overall 95% confidence intervals for the pairwise differences among the means of Exercise 10.41.

10.46 In a study of the effects of television commercials on 7-year-old children, the attention span of children watching commercials for clothing, food products, and toys is measured. To reduce the effects of outliers, only the median attention span for each commercial is used.

Commercial	Median Attention Span (seconds)											
Clothes	21	30	23	37	21	18	30	42	36			
Food	32	51	46	30	25	41	38	50	45	53	57	41
Toys	48	59	51	47	58	56	49	55	52	49	60	

Minitab output follows.

```
One-way ANOVA: AttSpan versus Commercial

Source       DF      SS      MS      F      P
Commercial    2   2953.6  1476.8  23.10  0.000
Error        29   1853.8    63.9
Total        31   4807.5

S = 7.995   R-Sq = 61.44%   R-Sq(adj) = 58.78%
```

```
                                    Individual 95% CIs For Mean Based on
                                    Pooled StDev
Level     N    Mean    StDev    -------+---------+---------+---------+--
Clothes   9   28.667   8.426    (-----*----)
Food     12   42.417   9.839                  (---*----)
Toys     11   53.091   4.700                            (----*----)
                                 -------+---------+---------+---------+--
                                       30        40        50        60
Pooled StDev = 7.995
```

```
Kruskal-Wallis Test: AttSpan versus Commercial

Commercial   N   Median   Ave Rank      Z
Clothes      9    30.00       6.7    -3.71
Food        12    43.00      16.1    -0.18
Toys        11    52.00      25.0     3.69
Overall     32               16.5

H = 18.84   DF = 2   P = 0.000
H = 18.87   DF = 2   P = 0.000   (adjusted for ties)
```

a. Locate the value of the F statistic for the null hypothesis of equal means.
b. Can this hypothesis be rejected using $\alpha = .01$?
c. Locate the p-value for this test.

10.47 Refer to Exercise 10.46.
a. Find the value of the Kruskal–Wallis statistic.
b. Can the hypothesis of equal means (or more properly "locations") be rejected using $\alpha = .01$?

10.48 Refer to Exercise 10.46.
a. Plot the data of the exercise.
b. Do there appear to be serious violations of ANOVA assumptions?
c. Does it matter much whether an F test or a Kruskal–Wallis test is used?

10.49 Use a statistical package to find 99% Tukey confidence intervals for differences in means for the data of Exercise 10.46. Are any differences significant at $\alpha = .01$?

10.50 A township manager had four appraisers estimate the fair market value of 12 houses. The estimates, in thousands of dollars, are

Appraiser	1	2	3	4	5	6	7	8	9	10	11	12
A	86	76	93	110	73	55	96	74	96	140	88	72
B	81	75	95	105	70	53	91	75	95	120	75	68
C	90	76	96	108	78	63	99	77	99	135	94	75
D	90	76	96	108	78	63	99	77	99	135	94	75

Home

Output from the Minitab package follows:

```
Two-way ANOVA: Value versus Appraiser, Home

Source      DF        SS        MS        F       P
Appraiser    3     381.6    127.19    10.66   0.000
Home        11   16086.0   1462.36   122.58   0.000
Error       33     393.7     11.93
Total       47   16861.2
```

a. How relevant is the null hypothesis of equality of house prices? Is this hypothesis rejected?
b. Locate the value of the F statistic for testing the null hypothesis of the equality of appraiser effects.
c. Can the null hypothesis be rejected at typical α levels? What is the indicated p-value?

10.51 Use the Tukey method to test ($\alpha = .05$) the significance of pairwise differences in appraiser effects for the data of Exercise 10.50.

10.52 The data of Exercise 10.50 were also analyzed incorrectly as a one-way ANOVA experiment, with the following output:

```
One-way ANOVA: Value versus Appraiser

Source       DF      SS    MS     F      P
Appraiser     3     382   127  0.34  0.797
Error        44   16480   375
Total        47   16861
```

a. Would the null hypothesis of equal appraiser means be rejected at $\alpha = .05$?
b. How important is it to control for the effect of house differences in Exercise 10.50?

10.53 A paint manufacturer experimented with six possible formulations for a new economy-grade paint. Six samples of each formulation were tested in a high-stress laboratory environment. The time to paint failure was recorded for each sample. High scores are preferable and the company regarded 40 as a minimum acceptable score. The following results were obtained:

```
Tabulated statistics: Formulation

Rows: Formulation

        FailTime  FailTime
          Mean      StDev

1        42.00     6.542
2        51.83     7.139
3        48.83     4.956
4        45.00     4.733
5        55.33     3.615
6        49.50     5.167
All      48.75     6.720


One-way ANOVA: FailTime versus Formulation

Source         DF       SS     MS     F      P
Formulation     5    678.3  135.7  4.51  0.003
Error          30    902.5   30.1
Total          35   1580.8

S = 5.485    R-Sq = 42.91%    R-Sq(adj) = 33.39%

                          Individual 95% CIs For Mean Based on
                          Pooled StDev
Level  N    Mean   StDev   --------+---------+---------+---------+-
1      6  42.000   6.542   (-------*-------)
2      6  51.833   7.139                  (------*-------)
3      6  48.833   4.956            (------*-------)
4      6  45.000   4.733      (-------*-------)
5      6  55.333   3.615                      (------*-------)
6      6  49.500   5.167             (------*-------)
                          --------+---------+---------+---------+-
                             42.0      48.0      54.0      60.0


Pooled StDev = 5.485

Tukey 95% Simultaneous Confidence Intervals
All Pairwise Comparisons among Levels of Formulation

Individual confidence level = 99.51%
```

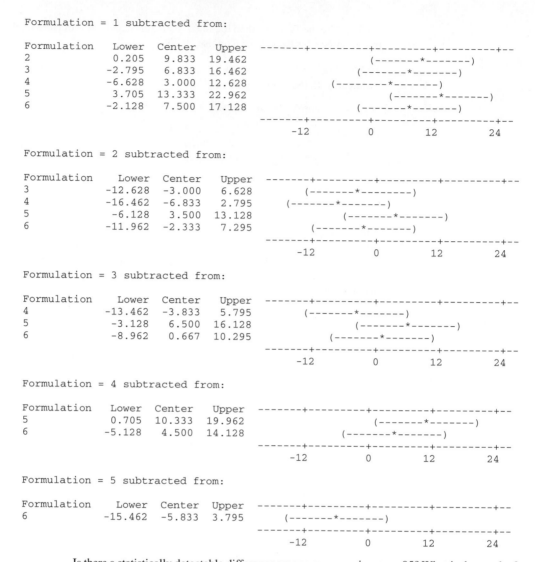

```
Formulation = 1 subtracted from:

Formulation    Lower   Center   Upper   -------+---------+---------+---------+--
2              0.205    9.833  19.462                  (-------*------)
3             -2.795    6.833  16.462             (-------*------)
4             -6.628    3.000  12.628         (--------*------)
5              3.705   13.333  22.962                   (-------*------)
6             -2.128    7.500  17.128              (-------*------)
                                               -------+---------+---------+---------+--
                                                    -12        0        12       24


Formulation = 2 subtracted from:

Formulation    Lower   Center   Upper   -------+---------+---------+---------+--
3            -12.628   -3.000   6.628            (-------*--------)
4            -16.462   -6.833   2.795        (-------*-------)
5             -6.128    3.500  13.128                 (-------*------)
6            -11.962   -2.333   7.295          (-------*------)
                                               -------+---------+---------+---------+--
                                                    -12        0        12       24


Formulation = 3 subtracted from:

Formulation    Lower   Center   Upper   -------+---------+---------+---------+--
4            -13.462   -3.833   5.795        (-------*-------)
5             -3.128    6.500  16.128              (-------*-------)
6             -8.962    0.667  10.295           (-------*-------)
                                               -------+---------+---------+---------+--
                                                    -12        0        12       24


Formulation = 4 subtracted from:

Formulation    Lower   Center   Upper   -------+---------+---------+---------+--
5              0.705   10.333  19.962                 (-------*-------)
6             -5.128    4.500  14.128             (-------*-------)
                                               -------+---------+---------+---------+--
                                                    -12        0        12       24


Formulation = 5 subtracted from:

Formulation    Lower   Center   Upper   -------+---------+---------+---------+--
6            -15.462   -5.833   3.795          (-------*------)
                                               -------+---------+---------+---------+--
                                                    -12        0        12       24
```

Is there a statistically detectable difference among means, using $\alpha = .05$? What is the p-value?

10.54 According to the Tukey method of paired comparisons, which pairs of means in Exercise 10.53 are detectably different, using $\alpha = .05$?

10.55 The 36 samples in Exercise 10.53 were collected and then tested in the lab in completely random order. Why is this method preferable to (for example) testing all of formulation 1 first, all of formulation 2 next, and so on?

10.56 The six paint formulations in Exercise 10.53 were in fact put together as all combinations of three bases and two coloring agents. If we wanted to separate the effect of different bases from the effect of different coloring agents, how should we reanalyze the data?

10.57 The data of Exercise 10.53 were treated as a two-factor ANOVA. The following computer output was obtained using Excel:

```
Anova: Two-Factor With Replication

SUMMARY                   Color1  Color2
            Base1
Count                        6       6
Average                     42      45

            Base2
Count                        6       6
Average                   51.833  55.333

            Base3
Count                        6       6
Average                   48.833   49.5

ANOVA
Source of Variation SS       df      MS       F     P-value  F crit
Sample              613.17    2    306.583  10.191  0.0004  3.315833
Columns             51.361    1     51.361   1.7073 0.2013  4.170886
Interaction         13.722    2      6.861   0.228  0.7974  3.315833
Within              902.5    30     30.083

Total              1580.75   35
```

a. Is there evidence of a statistically significant interaction between the factors?

b. Show that the effect of coloring is not statistically significant at usual α levels, but the effect of base is statistically significant.

10.58 Use the Tukey method to construct 95% confidence intervals for all differences of "base" means, using the computer output in Exercise 10.57. Are any of the differences of means significant at $\alpha = .05$?

10.59 A manufacturer of laser printers is trying to improve the design of the toner cartridge, which determines much of the perceived quality of the printer output. In particular, the manufacturer wants to increase the life of the cartridge as measured by the number of thousands of pages printed satisfactorily. Four cartridge designs are tested. Sixteen cartridges of each design are tested and the number of thousands of pages produced is obtained for each cartridge. A computer analysis of the data yields the following output:

```
One-way ANOVA: Copies versus Design

Source  DF      SS     MS      F       P
Design   3     7022   2341   17.08   0.000
Error   60     8222    137
Total   63    15244

S = 11.71    R-Sq = 46.06%    R-Sq(adj) = 43.36%

                              Individual 95% CIs For Mean Based on
                              Pooled StDev
Level   N    Mean   StDev   ------+---------+---------+---------+---
1      16   123.31  12.40                     (-----*-----)
2      16   109.44  12.59   (----*-----)
3      16   137.25  10.75                                   (-----*-----)
4      16   115.00  10.97        (-----*-----)
                              ------+---------+---------+---------+---
                                  110       120       130       140

Pooled StDev = 11.71

Tukey 95% Simultaneous Confidence Intervals
All Pairwise Comparisons among Levels of Design

Individual confidence level = 98.96%
```

```
Design = 1 subtracted from:

Design  Lower   Center   Upper    ---------+---------+---------+---------+
2       -24.82  -13.87   -2.93           (----*-----)
3         2.99   13.94   24.88                       (-----*----)
4       -19.26   -8.31    2.63             (-----*----)
                                  ---------+---------+---------+---------+
                                        -20         0        20        40
```

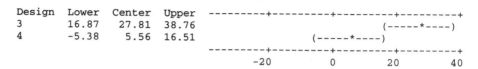

```
Design = 2 subtracted from:

Design  Lower   Center   Upper    ---------+---------+---------+---------+
3       16.87   27.81   38.76                           (-----*----)
4       -5.38    5.56   16.51                  (-----*----)
                                  ---------+---------+---------+---------+
                                        -20         0        20        40
```

```
Design = 3 subtracted from:

Design  Lower   Center   Upper    ---------+---------+---------+---------+
4       -33.20  -22.25  -11.30      (-----*----)
                                  ---------+---------+---------+---------+
                                        -20         0        20        40

Kruskal-Wallis Test: Copies versus Design

Design    N   Median   Ave Rank      Z
1        16    122.0       35.5    0.75
2        16    107.0       18.4   -3.50
3        16    138.5       51.2    4.63
4        16    116.5       24.9   -1.88
Overall  64                32.5

H = 28.32   DF = 3   P = 0.000
H = 28.35   DF = 3   P = 0.000   (adjusted for ties)
```

According to the ANOVA table, is there a statistically significant difference somewhere among the means, using $\alpha = .05$?

10.60 According to the Kruskal–Wallis output shown in Exercise 10.59, is there a significant difference among the cartridges in their average life? Again, use $\alpha = .05$. Does the result differ greatly from the result for the F test?

10.61 In the output for Exercise 10.59, which design seems to be best? (The first question is whether high or low scores are best.) Use the Tukey approach with $\alpha = .05$ to see if this design has a significantly better mean than each of the other designs.

10.62 As part of a market test of a new package design, a cereal manufacturer prepared boxes in each of two colors with each of two new type styles. Each color–type-style combination was tested in 12 randomly assigned supermarkets in the test area. Sales of the cereal over a three-day period were recorded. The data are recorded in the EX1062 file on the data disk. Load the data into your computer program. Sales are shown in column 1, color code (1 or 2) in column 2, and type-style code (1 or 2) in column 3.
a. Obtain mean sales for each combination of color code and type style code.
b. Does there appear to be a large interaction between color and type style, based on these means?

10.63 Refer to Exercise 10.62.
a. Obtain an analysis of variance (ANOVA) table for the data, with sales as the dependent variable. Is there a relatively large interaction sum of squares?
b. Are there statistically detectable (significant) effects of color and of type style? Obtain p-values if the program will do so; otherwise, try $\alpha = .05$ and $\alpha = .01$.

10.64   If the computer program will do so conveniently, obtain "residuals" (actual sales minus the mean for the color–type-style combination) for the data of Exercise 10.62. Obtain a histogram, stem-and-leaf display, or normal plot of the residuals. Is there any evidence of serious nonnormality in the data?

10.65   A furniture store targeted eight ZIP codes for promotional activity. The store's records for the past two months indicated all purchases by residents of each ZIP code. The data are stored in the EX1065 file on the data disk, which should be read into your computer package. Sales amounts are stored in column 1 of the file, and numbers 1–8 for the eight ZIP codes are stored in column 2.
a. Obtain box plots of the sales data separately for each ZIP code. Do these box plots indicate that the data are roughly normally distributed within each ZIP code?
b. Obtain an ANOVA table for testing the null hypothesis of equal means. Can this hypothesis be rejected at conventional α values?

10.66   Refer to Exercise 10.65.
a. Use the computer program to perform a Kruskal–Wallis test of the null hypothesis of equal distributions for the data. Can the null hypothesis be rejected at conventional α values?
b. Do the F and Kruskal–Wallis tests give similar conclusions? If not, what explains the difference in results?

10.67   A company wanted to select a long-distance telephone service on the basis of lowest cost. A clerk took 50 calls at random from the list of those made by the company in the last three months and determined what each call would cost using each service. The results are in the EX1067 file on the data disk. Cost of the calls is in column 1, call number is in column 2, and service company number is in column 3. Load the data into your statistical computer program.
a. Obtain an analysis of variance (ANOVA) table using call number and service number as factors.
b. Is there a statistically detectable (significant) effect of service number? If possible, obtain a p-value.
c. Explain why there shouldn't be an interaction term between the two factors in the ANOVA model.

10.68   If your computer program will do so conveniently, perform Tukey tests of significance for all pairwise differences among service company means in Exercise 10.67, using $\alpha = .05$. If the computer isn't programmed to do so, obtain the means for each service and do the tests by hand. Is there a clear-cut lowest-cost service among the four?

10.69   Refer to Exercise 10.67.
a. Reanalyze the data of the exercise, ignore the call number factor, and treat the service company number as the only factor. Obtain an ANOVA table.
b. Does the error mean square for this analysis differ much from the error mean square in the two-factor analysis? If so, what does that fact say about the wisdom of blocking, using call numbers (as opposed to allocating 200 calls completely at random, 50 to each of the four service companies)?

10.70   Refer to Exercise 10.67.
a. If possible, have the computer program find predicted values and residuals (actual − predicted) for the data of the exercise. Obtain a plot of residuals against predicted values. Does the variability around predicted values appear to be constant?
b. Have the computer program calculate the logarithms, either natural (base e) or common (base 10), of the costs. Obtain a new ANOVA table and use the logarithm of cost as the dependent variable, with call number and service company number as factors. Is there a statistically detectable (significant) service company effect?
c. Obtain a plot of residuals against predicted values for the logarithm model. Does the variability around predicted values appear constant?

BUSINESS CASES

Improving Worker Efficiency

A large insurance company employs many clerical workers for routine computer-based tasks. The flow of tasks is enormous and never ending, so worker efficiency is crucial to the company's smooth operation. The director of human resources feels that new working conditions could improve productivity by a few percentage points, more than enough to cover the cost of the changes. What isn't clear is *which* new conditions would have the best effect on productivity. An experiment was carried out to test the effects.

The director of human resources has written you a memo asking you to analyze the results. The relevant part of the memo says:

> We took three divisions: claims (1), data processing (2), and investments (3). The way it turned out, we could get 33 clerical people in each division to participate. We picked the people randomly from personnel lists and—even though there were a few refusals so we had to pick other people—we think that the groups are reasonably representative. Then we had everybody draw numbers from a hat. Number 1 meant that the person went to a flextime schedule, 2 meant a four-day work week, and 3 meant a regular week in an enhanced work environment. We ignored the data for the first two weeks while people were getting used to the new setup. Then we measured percentage efficiency gains for everybody over the next four weeks. The efficiency measures are good enough that we think they'll be accurate for our purposes. We think we did the study pretty well.
>
> We can't figure out the results. The averages for the three conditions are practically the same, so it seems like it didn't make much difference. But I've got some supervisors who think that one or another of the new conditions is doing great things for efficiency, and other supervisors who think some condition is actually hurting efficiency. Are they nuts, or is there something in the results that we haven't noticed?

Assignment: The data are contained in the file BusinessCase10 on the CD that came with your book. Reanalyze the data and see what you can find about average efficiency gains. Write a memo to the director and explain your findings. The director doesn't remember any statistical theory, so try to use ordinary language.

Devon College

Devon College had always had a great reputation for liberal arts education and was recently named one of the top 25 educational values in the country among private universities. Alumni often talked of their positive college experiences. Devon had in fact established a track record for graduating students who were in demand at some of the nation's best professional and graduate schools and in some of America's top companies.

Located in rural northern New England, Devon enrolls just over 2000 students, 80% from the New England area. Devon's faculty and administrators agree that diversity is an important part of a liberal education and encourage it in many ways, including geographical diversity. In fact, Devon's promotional literature proudly states that its students come from over 25 states and dozens of countries.

But like all four-year undergraduate colleges, Devon has increasingly fallen on hard times. The drop in college-age students, rising costs due to inflation, and fewer and smaller donations and other gifts due to the depressed economy have taken their toll. While disaster isn't at hand, the chancellor has asked each unit on campus to examine its expenditures and ensure that college monies are being spent wisely.

Angela Brock, director of admissions, is responsible for recruiting new students and then orienting entering freshmen once they arrive. The admission's office divides its staff time, and resources, among several key responsibilities—giving campus tours to prospective students, going on nationwide recruiting trips, manning Devon's "1–800" recruiting number, sending out information packets, and running the annual freshman orientation program.

A full 30% of Brock's budget goes to recruiting visits to high schools. Of this budget, approximately 50% is spent visiting high schools in the New England region. The rest goes to visits to major cities in the Midwest, West, Southwest, and South. Brock has called her staff together to discuss these visits.

She began the meeting by stating, "The chancellor has asked all units on campus to examine their expenditures and be sure that they actually contribute to the unit's mission. I've taken a look at our budget and think that we're OK on the orientation programs, information services, and campus tours, but I'm not so sure about our recruitment tour program. Given its cost, maybe it's time we take a look and decide about its effectiveness. Any thoughts?"

Bernie Shyna was the first to speak. "I think we need to cut out all trips to the West Coast, particularly LA and San Francisco. Those kids don't really seem to fit in here. I mean, they're over 2000 miles from home and in what has to be a strange part of the world to them. We can save over $10,000 a year just by cutting out those two cities alone!"

Mary Washington agreed, adding that kids from outside New England have a hard time adjusting not only socially but academically. She said her sister roomed with a girl from San Francisco who dropped out after the first semester and that she knew of two other girls from the West Coast who dropped out after the first year.

Kara Roberts didn't agree with this. "I think we might be jumping the gun here. I also know students we recruited from the West Coast and they did great! If we just depend on what we happen to hear, we might be making a big mistake in evaluating these recruiting trips. It seems to me that we can answer questions about whether it's useful to visit cities like LA by actually seeing what's happened to all the students, as a group, that we've recruited from these cities. Maybe Bernie and Mary are right—but maybe not. I'd be willing to look at the data and report back to the committee."

Mary quickly agreed with Kara, admitting she may not have thought through what she'd heard about some of the girls. Everybody at the table in fact thought that Kara had a good idea and several offered to help. That's when Kara asked, "Exactly what do we need to know to decide about going to a particular city or not?" This brought on another round of discussion, and a number of people made useful suggestions.

Angela Brock summed up. "We'll take a look at the recruiting efforts for certain cities in different parts of the country. I think we should focus on our most expensive recruiting trips. For the West, that would be Los Angeles and San Francisco; for the Southwest, Houston; Chicago in the Midwest, and Atlanta and Miami in the South. Each of these trips is budgeted for around $10,000. We'll look at data for all of the students from these cities who enrolled as freshmen in each of the past couple of years and create a data file of information from our admission and enrollment records. Kay and Bernie can put this together for us. We should be able to identify the freshmen who dropped out during their first year and the ones who completed their first year. Can you think of anything else?"

Bernie added that they also should look at the number of people who received admission offers but didn't come to Devon, which the group thought was a good idea. Kara suggested that they also look at the "demographics" of those who were successful. Everyone seemed to like this idea, too. She also thought that it would be interesting to see how many students graduated from those who started as freshmen, but that idea didn't go over as well. Angela didn't want to wait four to five years. She suggested instead an alternative, proxy measure. "We have pretty good results from other institutional research studies that can help us estimate eventual graduation rates. In fact, our own studies indicate that about 85% of the students who survive their first year with a GPA of 2.50 or higher will graduate within five years of entering Devon. About 60% of those who finish their first year with a lower GPA don't graduate. These data make it pretty clear that . . ."

"If that's the case," Kara jumped in, "then we might want to project graduation rates from the GPAs of students who finish their first year. I know that this won't be perfect, but maybe it'll help us decide whether it's a good idea, for Devon and for the students, to continue to recruit from a particular city."

Everyone agreed and Angela added GPA to the list. She then asked Kara if she needed any help in analyzing, interpreting, and writing up the results for each of the cities selected. Kara said that she would welcome your assignment to the task force because of your data analysis experience, and Angela agreed.

Assignment: The data collected by Kay and Bernie provide information on people recruited in each of six cities for the last two recruiting classes that had the opportunity to complete their freshman year. In total, data were collected for 209 entering freshmen. Data were also collected for a group of 87 prospective students who were offered admission but chose to go to school elsewhere. For everyone in the database, information was collected on race and gender. Since 96% of the students were between 18 and 19 years old, this information was not recorded. For those who actually enrolled at Devon, information concerning whether or not they completed their freshman year and the GPAs of those who did were also recorded.

To help Kara Roberts with this project, your analysis should examine the data in each of the six cities for each of the two yearly samples and, based on your findings, identify those cities for which recruiting should and should not be continued. Use important details from your analysis to support your recommendation.

The data for Devon College are contained in the file Devon on the CD that came with your book. The file contains information on 296 prospective students, 209 of whom actually enrolled as a freshman at Devon College. Data are grouped together by city. A partial listing of the data within Excel is shown in Figure 10.25.

FIGURE 10.25   **Partial Listing of the Devon College Data**

	A	B	C	D	E	F	G
1	Year	City	Enrolled	Gender	Minority	Stayed	GPA
2	1	LA	Yes	F	No	Yes	3.70
3	1	LA	Yes	F	No	Yes	2.42
4	1	LA	Yes	F	No	Yes	2.75
5	1	LA	Yes	M	No	Yes	1.90
6	1	LA	Yes	M	Yes	Yes	2.27
7	1	LA	Yes	F	No	Yes	3.23
8	1	LA	Yes	M	No	Yes	3.66
9	1	LA	Yes	M	No	Yes	3.17
10	1	LA	Yes	F	No	No	*
11	1	LA	Yes	M	No	Yes	2.51
12	1	LA	Yes	M	Yes	Yes	2.88
13	1	LA	Yes	M	Yes	Yes	2.82
14	1	LA	Yes	F	No	No	*
15	1	LA	Yes	F	No	Yes	3.44

In the Devon file, the variables are defined as follows:

Year: 1 = in first-year recruitment sample,
         2 = in second-year recruitment sample

City: LA, SF, Houston, Chicago, Miami, or Atlanta

Enrolled: Yes, if actually enrolled at Devon,
           No, if did not enroll at Devon

Gender: F (female) or M (male)

Minority: Yes, if minority; No, otherwise

Stayed: Yes, if completed freshman year,
         No, if did not complete freshman year

GPA: Grade point average at the end of the freshman year (4.0 scale)

Important Note: The symbol "*" (asterisk) is used in the Devon data file to denote nonresponse or missing data. Consult your statistical software documentation for a list of valid missing data codes. If your statistical software package does not accept "*" as a valid missing code, you have two options. Your statistical software package may allow you to specify another missing code. Otherwise, you will need to change each occurrence of "*" in the data file to a missing symbol that is acceptable to your particular statistics package. This can be done by editing the file within a word processing package. See your instructor if you need assistance.

Review Exercises—Chapters 9–10

10.71 A sample of 40 testers rates the thirst-quenching property of an old formulation of a soft drink and a new formulation. The drinks are scored on a 0–100 scale. The results are

Formulation	Mean	Standard Deviation
Old	41.15	14.7
New	45.55	17.8

a. Calculate a 95% confidence interval for the difference of the true (population) means using a pooled-variance procedure.

b. Based on this interval, can the null hypothesis of equal means be rejected, using $\alpha = .05$?

c. In fact, it's a very bad idea to use a pooled-variance procedure for these data. Why?

10.72   The differences between ratings of the new formulation and the old one are shown here:

```
  4   3  -1   9  -4   7  -6   4  -2   7   2   4  14   1
  2  12  -7  11  12   9   4  10  -5  -7  -2  -3  10
 -1  23   2   7   5  15   4   0   1   5  -4  16  15
```

Minitab output follows:

```
One-Sample T: Diffs

Test of mu = 0 vs not = 0

Variable    N     Mean     StDev  SE Mean        95% CI          T      P
Diffs      40  4.39999  7.04854  1.11446  (2.14575, 6.65423)  3.95  0.000

Stem-and-leaf of Diffs   N  = 40
Leaf Unit = 1.0

  3    -0  776
  6    -0  544
  9    -0  322
 11    -0  11
 14     0  011
 18     0  2223
 (7)    0  4444455
 15     0  777
 12     0  99
 10     1  001
  7     1  22
  5     1  455
  2     1  6
  1     1
  1     2
  1     2  3
```

a. Locate the 95% confidence interval for the population mean difference.

b. Based on this interval, can the null hypothesis that the mean difference is zero be rejected using $\alpha = .05$?

c. Show that the formal test and p-value give the same conclusion about the null hypothesis as the confidence interval.

d. Is there any evidence of a serious violation of assumptions for this procedure?

10.73   Minitab carried out a rank test for the difference data of Exercise 10.72, using $\alpha = .05$ (two-sided). Does this test lead to the same conclusion as the t test of that exercise?

```
Wilcoxon Signed Rank Test: Diffs

Test of median = 0.000000 versus median not = 0.000000

                    N
                  for   Wilcoxon            Estimated
            N    Test   Statistic     P      Median
Diffs      40     39      628.5    0.001     4.000
```

10.74   Are the t test and rank test p-values similar in the two preceding exercises?

10.75 Compare the widths of the confidence intervals for independent and for paired samples. What do the relative sizes of the intervals indicate about the effect of having the same tasters rate both formulations (as opposed to having different tasters rating each formulation)?

10.76 A large corporation has a pool of individuals responsible for most word-processing jobs. As a means of providing a pleasant and productive atmosphere, the company plays taped music during the workday. Some individuals complain that the music occasionally becomes distracting. As an experiment, the company provides varying degrees of control over the music's volume (ranging from 1 = no control to 4 = complete control) to samples of size 16 each of word-processing operators. An efficiency score is obtained for each person.

	Degree of Control			
Efficiency	**1**	**2**	**3**	**4**
	42	55	63	66
	57	50	57	63
	37	65	24	64
	52	22	55	57
	58	65	64	64
	58	56	56	60
	56	63	61	62
	57	58	60	62
	41	65	63	58
	49	57	64	54
	53	52	67	65
	55	61	66	60
	53	64	66	63
	42	57	52	64
	48	65	47	49
	48	66	65	61
$\bar{y}$	50.38	57.56	58.13	60.75
s	6.80	10.76	10.71	4.45

Minitab output follows:

```
One-way ANOVA: Efficiency versus Control

Source    DF      SS      MS     F      P
Control    3   946.9   315.6  4.26  0.009
Error     60  4448.4    74.1
Total     63  5395.4

S = 8.610   R-Sq = 17.55%   R-Sq(adj) = 13.43%

                          Individual 95% CIs For Mean Based on
                          Pooled StDev
Level  N    Mean   StDev  --------+---------+---------+---------+-
1      16  50.375  6.801  (--------*-------)
2      16  57.563  10.764              (-------*--------)
3      16  58.125  10.707              (-------*--------)
4      16  60.750   4.450                    (-------*--------)
                          --------+---------+---------+---------+-
                             50.0      55.0      60.0      65.0

Pooled StDev = 8.610

Tukey 95% Simultaneous Confidence Intervals
All Pairwise Comparisons among Levels of Control
```

```
Individual confidence level = 98.96%

Control = 1 subtracted from:

Control   Lower   Center   Upper    ----+---------+---------+---------+-----
2        -0.863   7.188   15.238                           (---------*---------)
3        -0.301   7.750   15.801                          (---------*---------)
4         2.324  10.375   18.426                              (---------*---------)
                                     ----+---------+---------+---------+-----
                                       -8.0       0.0       8.0      16.0

Control = 2 subtracted from:

Control   Lower   Center   Upper    ----+---------+---------+---------+-----
3        -7.488   0.563    8.613              (---------*---------)
4        -4.863   3.188   11.238                (---------*---------)
                                     ----+---------+---------+---------+-----
                                       -8.0       0.0       8.0      16.0

Control = 3 subtracted from:

Control   Lower   Center   Upper    ----+---------+---------+---------+-----
4        -5.426   2.625   10.676                (---------*---------)
                                     ----+---------+---------+---------+-----
                                       -8.0       0.0       8.0      16.0
```

a. Test the null hypothesis that the four population means are equal, using $\alpha = .01$. State the conclusion carefully.

b. Place bounds on the p-value.

c. Is there any indication that any of the formal mathematical assumptions have been violated? If so, do the violations make your answers to parts (a) and (b) seriously wrong?

10.77 Refer to Exercise 10.76.

a. Using the output of the exercise, calculate simultaneous 99% confidence intervals for the differences of all pairs of means.

b. Which pairs of means, if any, are significantly different at $\alpha = .05$?

10.78 Minitab also calculated the Kruskal–Wallis statistic for the efficiency and control data of Exercise 10.76.

```
Kruskal-Wallis Test: Efficiency versus Control

Control    N   Median   Ave Rank      Z
1         16   52.50      16.0      -4.10
2         16   59.50      36.2       0.92
3         16   62.00      37.7       1.29
4         16   62.00      40.1       1.89
Overall   64              32.5

H = 17.18   DF = 3   P = 0.001
```

a. Can the null hypothesis that the four groups' distributions are equal be rejected at $\alpha = .01$? Place bounds on the p-value of the statistic.

b. Does this test yield essentially the same conclusion as the F test?

10.79 In the efficiency study of Exercise 10.76, the participants who have some degree of control also rate that control as not useful, somewhat useful, or very useful. Minitab was used to analyze these results.

```
Tabulated statistics: Rating, Control

Rows: Rating   Columns: Control
```

```
                1       2       3      All

Not             7       3       2       12
             4.000   4.000   4.000   12.000
             2.2500  0.2500  1.0000     *

Somewhat        4       7       5       16
             5.333   5.333   5.333   16.000
             0.3333  0.5208  0.0208     *

Very            5       6       9       20
             6.667   6.667   6.667   20.000
             0.4167  0.0667  0.8167     *

All            16      16      16       48
            16.000  16.000  16.000   48.000
               *       *       *        *
```

```
Cell Contents:        Count
                      Expected count
                      Contribution to Chi-square
```

Pearson Chi-Square = 5.675, DF = 4, P-Value = 0.225
Likelihood Ratio Chi-Square = 5.457, DF = 4, P-Value = 0.244

* NOTE * 3 cells with expected counts less than 5

a. Is there a statistically significant relation between rating and degree of control, using $\alpha = .05$?

b. Locate the p-value for the test statistic used in part (a).

c. Is there any reason to be skeptical of the (approximate) p-value?

10.80   Do the frequencies of Exercise 10.79 indicate a moderately strong relation, whether or not the relation is statistically significant?

10.81   One person interprets the results of the χ^2 test in Exercise 10.79 as proving that there is no relation between rating and degree of control. Is this interpretation appropriate?

10.82   A real-estate firm in the headquarters city of a large corporation is contracted to find housing and mortgages for the corporation's newly arriving managers. One concern is the length of mortgage contracts. Samples are taken of managers arriving by transfer from other corporation offices and of newly hired managers. The data are taken over a time when mortgage availability and terms are stable. The following lengths (in months) of mortgage contracts are obtained:

Transfer: 180 240 300 360 240 180 144 300 240 240 360 180 180
             300 240   ($n = 15, \bar{y} = 245.6, s = 66.9$)

New hires: 360 360 360 240 270 300 360 360 300 360 360 300 300
             240 300 360 360 360 360 360 300 300 360 240 360 360
             360 360 300 360 360 300   ($n = 32, \bar{y} = 329.1, s = 41.4$)

The following results were obtained from Excel:

t-Test: Two-Sample Assuming Equal Variances

	Transfer	New Hire
Mean	245.6	329.1
Variance	4481.83	1712.00
Observations	15	32
Pooled Variance	2573.72	
Hypothesized Mean Difference	0	
df	45	

```
t Stat                      -5.2575
P(T<=t) one-tail             0.0000
t Critical one-tail          1.6794
P(T<=t) two-tail             0.0000
t Critical two-tail          2.0141
```

a. According to the output, is there strong evidence of a real difference in means?

b. Use pooled-variance methods to calculate a 95% confidence interval for the difference of population means. Based on this interval, can you conclude that there is a statistically significant difference?

10.83   The use of pooled-variance methods in the mortgage-length data of Exercise 10.82 is a poor idea for (at least) two reasons. Why?

10.84   Additional Excel output for the mortgage-length data of Exercise 10.82 follows:

t-Test: Two-Sample Assuming Unequal Variances

	Transfer	New Hire
Mean	245.6	329.1
Variance	4481.8	1712.0
Observations	15	32
Hypothesized Mean Difference	0	
df	19	
t Stat	-4.4467	
P(T<=t) one-tail	0.0001	
t Critical one-tail	1.7291	
P(T<=t) two-tail	0.0003	
t Critical two-tail	2.0930	

a. According to this test, is there strong evidence of a real difference of means?

b. Recalculate the confidence interval for the difference of means using a more appropriate method. Does the new interval lead to the same conclusion about the significance of the difference?

10.85   When the mortgage-length data of Exercise 10.82 are ranked, the sum of the ranks in the transfers sample is 198.0. Test the null hypothesis that the distribution of mortgage lengths is the same in the transfers and new-hires populations against a general research hypothesis. State a bound on the p-value.

10.86   An income-tax preparation service tests three computer programs designed to help its staff prepare state and federal tax returns. Random samples of 10 experienced and 10 inexperienced preparers are assigned to each of three programs. The time required to prepare a standard return is obtained for each of the 60 preparers. The following Minitab output was used to analyze the data:

Tabulated statistics: Program, Experience

Rows: Program   Columns: Experience

	0	1	All
1	36.80	36.20	36.50
	2.700	8.094	5.880
2	29.50	42.10	35.80
	2.550	5.896	7.831
3	34.30	40.40	37.35
	2.584	5.680	5.314
All	33.53	39.57	36.55
	3.980	6.892	6.355

```
Cell Contents:  Time  :  Mean
                Time  :  Standard deviation


Two-way ANOVA: Time versus Program, Experience

Source        DF       SS       MS       F      P
Program        2    24.10   12.050    0.47  0.626
Experience     1   546.02  546.016   21.41  0.000
Interaction    2   435.63  217.816    8.54  0.001
Error         54  1377.09   25.502
Total         59  2382.84
```

Is there a statistically significant difference among the program means, using $\alpha = .05$?

10.87 In Exercise 10.86, which pairs of program means, if any, are significantly different, using $\alpha = .05$?

10.88 Minitab was used to construct a profile plot for the data of Exercise 10.86, as shown in Figure 10.26. Is there any reason to think that the overall program means might not be a good indication of the relative merits of the programs? It might be relevant to know that the service has relatively low turnover among its preparers; only about 15% of the preparers are inexperienced.

FIGURE 10.26 **Profile Plot for Tax Preparation Data**

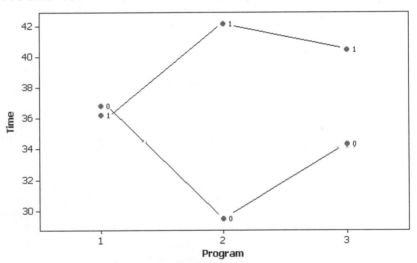

10.89 Data are collected on the price-to-earnings ratio (P/E) of common stocks of companies in two industries, electric utilities and computer services. Basic financial concepts suggest that the mean P/E should be lower for utilities than for the computer service industry. Do the data support this hypothesis? The following Minitab output will be helpful:

```
Two-Sample T-Test and CI: P/E Ratio, Industry

Industry   N   Mean  StDev  SE Mean
1         20  10.75   6.52      1.5
2         20  17.50   9.42      2.1


Difference = mu (1) - mu (2)
Estimate for difference:  -6.74999
95% CI for difference:  (-11.96294, -1.53705)
T-Test of difference = 0 (vs not =): T-Value = -2.63  P-Value = 0.013  DF = 33
```

```
Two-Sample T-Test and CI: P/E Ratio, Industry

Industry   N    Mean   StDev  SE Mean
1         20   10.75    6.52      1.5
2         20   17.50    9.42      2.1


Difference = mu (1) - mu (2)
Estimate for difference:  -6.74999
95% CI for difference:  (-11.93701, -1.56298)
T-Test of difference = 0 (vs not =): T-Value = -2.63  P-Value = 0.012  DF = 38
Both use Pooled StDev = 8.1025
```

10.90   Test the hypothesis in Exercise 10.89 about price/earnings ratios using the following Minitab rank sum test. Interpret the *p*-value.

```
Mann-Whitney Test and CI: Industry1, Industry2

            N   Median
Industry1  20    9.000
Industry2  20   13.000

Point estimate for ETA1-ETA2 is -5.000
95.0 Percent CI for ETA1-ETA2 is (-8.999,-2.001)
W = 291.0
Test of ETA1 = ETA2 vs ETA1 not = ETA2 is significant at 0.0013
The test is significant at 0.0013 (adjusted for ties)
```

10.91   From the two preceding exercises and the appearance of the price/earnings data in Figure 10.27, is a *t* test or a rank test more appropriate? How much difference does the choice of test make in the conclusion?

FIGURE 10.27   **Box Plots for Price/Earnings Ratios**

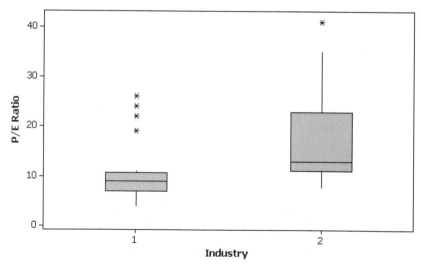

10.92   The P/E ratios of the preceding exercises should be more variable in the computer services stocks than in the utilities. Without doing any formal test, does this theory seem to be supported by the data?

10.93   What are the critical assumptions underlying your choice of method in analyzing the price/earnings ratio data of the preceding exercises? Do these assumptions appear reasonable?

10.94   A package delivery company tests its current dispatching procedure rule against a computerized rule. One of the methods is selected randomly for use on a given day; a key customer records the service as excellent, good, fair, or poor for each day. The following Minitab output is obtained:

```
Tabulated statistics: Method, Rating

Rows: Method    Columns: Rating

              Excellent    Fair    Good    Poor      All

Computerized         48       8      42       2      100
                  48.00    8.00   42.00    2.00   100.00

Current              36      15      39      10      100
                  36.00   15.00   39.00   10.00   100.00

All                  84      23      81      12      200
                  42.00   11.50   40.50    6.00   100.00

Cell Contents:     Count
                   % of Row

Pearson Chi-Square = 9.289, DF = 3, P-Value = 0.026
Likelihood Ratio Chi-Square = 9.818, DF = 3, P-Value = 0.020
```

a. Calculate a 95% confidence interval for the difference of proportions of excellent ratings between the current and computerized rules.
b. Use this interval to test the null hypothesis of equal proportions. What conclusion can be reached?

10.95   Perform a formal hypothesis test for the null hypothesis of equal proportions of excellent ratings in Exercise 10.94. Assume that $\alpha = .05$.

10.96   In gathering the service rating data of Exercise 10.94, it is noted that there may be carryover effects from one day to the next such that one poor day may tend to be followed by another poor day. If in fact there are carryover effects, does this violate any of the assumptions underlying the methods used in analyzing the data?

10.97   Using the ratings data and Minitab output of Exercise 10.94, test the null hypothesis that the distribution of opinion is the same for the current rule as for the computerized rule. State the p-value.

10.98   Other than the potential carryover problem cited in Exercise 10.96, are there any serious violations of assumptions for this test?

10.99   A law firm tests two models of printers for use in its office. A random sample of 20 documents is chosen; each document is printed out by each printer. The time required (in seconds) is recorded. The data are as follows:

									Document					
	1	2	3	4	5	6	7	8	9	10	11	12	13	14
Printer A	24	40	16	28	28	43	18	25	19	17	17	21	37	25
Printer B	22	36	29	21	20	36	16	27	15	13	11	13	30	20
$A - B$	2	4	−13	7	8	7	2	−2	4	4	6	8	7	5

Continues

	15	16	17	18	19	20	$\bar{y}$	s
Printer A	43	22	38	30	32	41	28.20	9.32
Printer B	36	23	29	24	25	30	23.80	7.83
$A - B$	7	−1	9	6	7	11	4.40	5.21

Minitab output for the data follows:

```
Paired T-Test and CI: Printer A, Printer B

Paired T for Printer A - Printer B

              N      Mean     StDev   SE Mean
Printer A    20   28.1999    9.3167    2.0833
Printer B    20   23.7999    7.8311    1.7511
Difference   20    4.39999   5.20525   1.16392

95% CI for mean difference: (1.96385, 6.83613)
T-Test of mean difference = 0 (vs not = 0): T-Value = 3.78   P-Value = 0.001
```

a. Is the paired-sample method an appropriate t test for the null hypothesis of equal means against a two-sided research hypothesis? What is the conclusion, using $\alpha = .05$?

b. State the p-value for the test in part (a). Can one safely come to a conclusion about the relative speed of the two printers?

10.100   Use the following Minitab signed-rank test output for the printer data in Exercise 10.99 to test the null hypothesis that the mean (or median) difference is zero. Does this test give the same conclusion as the t test?

```
Wilcoxon Signed Rank Test: A - B

Test of median = 0.000000 versus median not = 0.000000

                 N
               for   Wilcoxon              Estimated
         N    Test   Statistic      P       Median
A - B   20     20       186.0    0.003      5.500
```

10.101   Compare the standard deviation of the differences in Exercise 10.99 to the A and B standard deviations in the printer data from Exercise 10.100. What does this comparison indicate about the desirability of printing out the same 20 documents on both printers rather than using one set of 20 documents for one printer and a different set for the other printer?

10.102   As part of a performance review, junior managers are classified by college major and rated on a 50-point scale of managerial potential. The following results are obtained:

```
Anova: Single Factor

SUMMARY
      Groups     Count    Sum    Average   Variance
Business            12     254    21.167    68.152
Engineer             9     139    15.444    53.528
LibArts             18     493    27.389    66.369

ANOVA
Source of Variation    SS      df      MS       F     P-value   F crit
Between Groups      897.73      2    448.87   7.007   0.0027    3.259
Within Groups      2306.17     36     64.06

Total              3203.90     38
```

a. Verify the computation of the sums of squares.

b. Is there a statistically significant difference among the means, using $\alpha = .05$?

10.103   Examination of the managerial potential data from Exercise 10.102 shows a definite right-skewness in all three samples. What does this fact indicate about the relative appropriateness of the F and Kruskal–Wallis tests for these data?

10.104   The scale underlying the managerial potential data of Exercise 10.102 is interpreted such that a score under 20 indicates little potential, a score between 20 and 29 indicates some potential, and a score of 30 or above indicates high potential. Examination of the data gives the following frequencies:

		Potential		
Major	Little	Some	High	Total
Business	7	3	2	12
Engineering	8	0	1	9
Liberal Arts	2	9	7	18
Total	17	12	10	39

Test the null hypothesis that rated managerial potential is unrelated to type of education. Use $\alpha = .05$.

10.105   A fast-food chain has a continuing problem of training new employees. The director of human resources carried out an experiment on the relative effectiveness of three forms of training. Method 1 was based on videotape, method 2 was a combination tape/manual approach, and method 3 was based on the current employee manual. The director classified employees as teenagers (coded age = 1) and adults (age = 2). Store managers assigned the first new employees hired in a season to training method 1 until there were 20 people in each age category in this method. The next set of new employees went to method 2 until there were 20 in each age in this method, and then similarly for method 3. The employees were rated after one month on the job on a standard 100-point scale, where 60 is the minimum acceptable score. JMP output follows. The director has asked you to explain the results of the study clearly. What do the data indicate about the effects of training method and age? In addition, you should note any oddities in the data and make any suggestions about how to carry out a repetition of the same study.

```
Effect Test
Source          Nparm    DF    Sum of Squares  F Ratio   Prob>F
Training          2       2      2636.8667      4.6676    0.0113
Age               1       1      3979.0083     14.0866    0.0003
Training*Age      2       2       260.8667      0.4618    0.6313

Analysis of Variance
Source       DF    Sum of Squares  Mean Square   F Ratio
Model         5       6876.742      1375.35       4.8691
Error       114      32201.250       282.47       Prob>F
C Total     119      39077.992                    0.0004

Means for Training, then for Age
Least Squares Means
Level       Least Sq Mean       Std Error        Mean
1            60.92500000       2.657381725      60.9250
2            68.87500000       2.657381725      68.8750
3            57.72500000       2.657381725      57.7250

Least Squares Means
Level       Least Sq Mean       Std Error        Mean
1            56.75000000       2.169743093      56.7500
2            68.26666667       2.169743093      68.2667
```

```
Least Squares Means
Level            Least Sq Mean         Std Error
1,1              56.75000000           3.758105276
1,2              65.10000000           3.758105276
2,1              61.15000000           3.758105276
2,2              76.60000000           3.758105276
3,1              52.35000000           3.758105276
3,2              63.10000000           3.758105276
```

10.106 A gift company has the following sample data on dollar sales, separated according to how the order was paid for. Test the hypothesis that there is no difference in the dollar amount of orders paid for by cash, by check, or by credit card. Use a Kruskal–Wallis test with a 5% level of significance.

Credit card orders	78	64	75	45	82	69	60
Check orders	110	70	53	51	61	68	
Cash orders	90	68	70	54	74	65	59

10.107 The Environmental Protection Agency and certain state agencies have established rigid regulations on the output of polluting effluents from manufacturing plants. A wood products firm has four branch plants located in a certain western state. In a study of this issue, five samples of liquid waste were selected from each plant and the polluting effluents measured in each sample to see if the four plants differed in pollution output. The data are shown next.

Plant	Polluting Effluents (Pounds of Waste per Gallon)					Average	Std. Dev.
A	1.65	1.72	1.50	1.37	1.60	1.568	.1366
B	1.70	1.85	1.46	2.05	1.80	1.772	.2160
C	1.40	1.75	1.38	1.65	1.55	1.546	.1592
D	2.10	1.95	1.65	1.88	2.00	1.916	.1689

a. Perform the appropriate hypothesis test for this situation using a 5% level of significance. State the conclusion in the wording of the problem.
b. Use the Tukey multiple-comparisons procedure to identify statistically significant differences at a 5% overall level of significance.

10.108 In studying the effect of price and the number of product features on the sales of a certain product, a researcher collected data on three levels of product features (very few, some, many) and two levels of price (high, low). Three local test markets were randomly assigned to each combination of the two variables. The sales levels (in thousands of dollars) for each of the 18 test markets are given next:

Price	Number of Packaging Features			Totals
	Very Few	**Some**	**Many**	
High	22.8	20.9	23.1	
	21.4	22.9	21.9	200.6
	23.5	21.6	22.5	
Low	17.3	19.7	18.6	
	20.4	18.8	20.2	168.8
	18.2	17.9	17.7	
Totals	123.6	121.8	124.0	369.4

a. What term best classifies this particular experimental design?
b. Conduct an appropriate ANOVA using these data. Interpret the results of the ANOVA in terms of the problem. Use 5% as the level of significance wherever necessary.

Linear Regression
and Correlation Methods

This chapter introduces regression analysis. It is devoted to simple regression, using only one independent variable, x, to predict a quantitative dependent variable, y. The basic questions involve the nature of the relation (linear or curved), the amount of variability around the predicted value, whether that variability is constant over the range of prediction, how useful the independent variable is in predicting the dependent variable, and how much to allow for sampling error. The key concepts of the chapter include the following:

- The data should be plotted in a scatterplot. A smoother such as LOWESS is useful in deciding whether a relation is nearly linear or is clearly curved. Curved relations can often be made nearly linear by transforming either the independent variable or the dependent variable, or both.

- The coefficients of a linear regression are estimated by the least-squares method, which minimizes the sum of squared residuals (actual values minus predicted). Because squared error is involved, this method is sensitive to outliers.

- Observations which are extreme in the x (independent variable) direction have high leverage in fitting the line. If a high-leverage point also falls well off the line, it has high influence, in that removing the observation substantially changes the fitted line. A high-influence point should be omitted if it comes from a different population than the remainder. If it must be kept in the data, a fitting method other than least squares should be used.

- Variability around the line is measured by the standard deviation of the residuals. This standard deviation may be interpreted using the Empirical Rule. The standard deviation sometimes increases as the predicted value increases. In such a case, try transforming the dependent variable.

- Hypothesis tests and confidence intervals for the slope of the line (and, less interestingly, the intercept) are based on the t distribution. If there is no relation between x and y, the slope is 0. The line is estimated most accurately if there is a wide range of variation in the x variable.

- The fitted line may be used to forecast at a new x value, again using the t distribution. This forecasting is potentially inaccurate if the new x value is extrapolated far from the previous ones.

- A standard method of measuring the strength of relation is the coefficient of determination, the square of the correlation. This measure is diminished by nonlinearity or by an artificially limited range of x variation.

CHAPTER CASE

INTRODUCTION

Ryder Appraisal District

Ryder Appraisal District (RAD) is the county agency responsible for property taxation in Ryder County, South Carolina. RAD is charged with appraising property for tax purposes, determining the amount of tax owed, and collecting the taxes. There are approximately 12,000 residential properties in Ryder County.

James Bradford was elected three months ago to the position of Ryder County tax commissioner. For many years, taxpayers have complained about the inequities in residential property tax assessments. Bradford promised county residents that, if elected, he would do what he could to make the property taxing system more equitable. After the election, he appointed you as the new deputy tax commissioner for Ryder County to help him in improving the system.

The current residential property taxing system in Ryder County has evolved over several decades. Unimproved property—a residential lot without a house—is currently taxed at a flat amount of $150. Owners of improved residential property are charged a flat amount plus an additional amount based on the characteristics of the house built on the property, such as the total square footage of heated/cooled floor space, the number of bedrooms, the number of bathrooms, and so on. If the owner actually lives in the house, a homestead exemption is granted that reduces the property tax bill by a fixed 10%. If the owner of the property is retired, a retirement exemption reduces the property tax bill by 10%. A retired owner who lives on the property receives both exemptions for a total reduction of 20% in property taxes. While it would seem that the current system of taxing is fair, several factors have led to inequities.

Each year, new property assessments are mailed out to property owners that set the value of the property as determined by RAD for taxing purposes. The property owners have one month to contest their assessments before the County Review Board, which hears the appeals and makes any adjustments it deems necessary. In the past, the County Review Board has been judged "too responsive" in changing assessed values. Those homeowners who complain to the board are usually granted a reduction, unfortunately leading to many inconsistencies and discrepancies across the county.

RAD is supposed to reappraise each piece of residential property once every three years to keep its database up-to-date and include recent improvements to the property, such as swimming pools or other additions. Poor economic conditions however have reduced the state and federal funding to county governments. The appraisal staff at RAD has dwindled in the past few years to one full-time appraiser, and no funds are available for hiring professional appraisers on a part-time basis. Over time, the database has become outdated and inaccurate. This, of course, has led to further inequities in the taxing system.

With your assistance, James Bradford has proposed a simplified property tax assessment plan that should avoid the problems and inequities of the past and cost less to implement than the current system. The plan is to tax unimproved property using the current rate of $150. For improved properties, the new tax will consist of a flat tax plus an amount based on the square footage of heated/cooled space in the house. Both the flat tax and the variable tax components for improved properties are yet to be determined. Bradford wants to maintain the current 10% reductions for homestead exemptions and retired homeowners. The square footage measurement would be made once for each house, with an appraisal update occurring whenever an addition is made to the house. This will reduce the workload of RAD appraisers and the amount of record keeping. The simplified taxing system should also result in more consistency in property taxation and fewer complaints from homeowners about incorrect assessments.

Two major concerns about switching to the simplified tax assessment plan are, first, the importance of keeping individual taxes under the new plan as close as possible to what they are now; otherwise there will be problems. Everyone understands that some property owners will have higher taxes and others will have lower taxes, but the size of the changes should be minimized as much as possible. Second, the new tax plan must be revenue neutral, that is, the total amount of property taxes under the new structure should be roughly the same as before. James Bradford has said that attention to the first concern will largely mitigate this second concern.

The current database contains information on the square footage of each house in Ryder County. Bradford believes that these data may not be accurate. In most cases, the builder reports the square footage and it is never checked by RAD. Before launching a massive and costly effort to determine the actual square footage of each house in Ryder County, Bradford has decided to see whether or not the current data are sufficiently accurate.

In fact, Bradford believes that he can kill two birds with one stone. With your help, he has selected a random sample of 80 residential properties from around the county. Over the course of the past two months, the RAD staff appraiser has examined the houses on these properties and their blueprints to come up with an accurate estimate of the actual square footage of heated/cooled space of each house. Other information from the RAD database was also included in the sample data.

Bradford has asked you to do two things. First, he wants to know whether the square footage estimates in the current database for all 12,000 residential properties are sufficiently accurate (that is, close enough to the actual square footage values). Second, he wants you to use the sample data to come up with the flat tax and the tax rate per square foot that must be charged in order to minimize the changes from the current tax system for all property owners.

The collected data for the 80 sampled properties are contained in the file Ryder on the CD that came with your book. A partial listing of the data within Excel is shown in Figure 11.1.

FIGURE 11.1   **Partial Listing of Ryder Appraisal District Data**

	A Sub	B Block	C Lot	D Improved	E Homestead	F Retired	G Recorded Sqft	H Actual Sqft	I Current Tax
2	7	3	34	1	1	1	1595	1598	922.48
3	2	21	47	1	1	1	1855	1876	1047.90
4	11	8	52	1	1	0	1538	1528	967.03
5	9	21	8	1	1	0	1687	1713	985.22
6	2	21	51	1	1	0	1785	1764	1031.35
7	5	19	66	1	1	1	2084	2107	1093.42
8	11	15	5	1	1	1	2068	2021	1137.31
9	6	3	42	1	0	1	2020	1965	1215.69
10	7	23	45	1	1	0	2077	2011	1170.40
11	11	17	7	1	1	0	1702	1701	1087.31
12	5	20	45	1	1	0	1870	1867	1079.86
13	11	8	65	1	1	0	1723	1708	1111.80
14	7	8	55	1	0	0	1716	1697	1145.50
15	4	3	45	1	0	0	1759	1767	1202.17
16	8	10	9	1	0	0	1582	1597	1079.34
17	9	21	57	1	1	0	1851	1824	1043.86
18	4	11	44	1	1	0	1743	1723	1117.92
19	4	6	32	1	0	0	1831	1879	1196.84

In the Ryder file, the variables are defined as follows:

Sub: Subdivision in which the property is located

Block: Block in the subdivision in which the property is located

Lot: Lot number of the property (Sub, Block, and Lot together describe the location of the property.)

Improved: 1, if improved (that is, a house is built on the property) 0, if unimproved

Homestead: 1, if homestead exemption (that is, owner lives in house) 0, otherwise

Retired: 1, if owner retired; 0, otherwise

Recorded Sqft: Square footage recorded in the RAD database

Actual Sqft: Actual square footage as measured by the RAD appraiser

Current Tax: Current property tax under the existing taxing system

The material covered in this chapter and in the previous chapters will prove to be extremely helpful in your analysis and decision-making process. At the conclusion of this chapter, we will carry out the analysis and make recommendations for the new taxation system to James Bradford. ■

regression analysis

dependent and independent variables

ONE OF THE MOST important uses of statistics for managers is prediction. A manager may want to forecast the cost of a particular contracting job, given the size of that job; to forecast the sales of a particular product, given the current rate of growth of the gross national product; or to forecast the number of parts that will be produced, given a certain size workforce. The statistical method most widely used in making predictions is **regression analysis.**

In the regression approach, past data on the relevant variables are used to develop and evaluate a prediction equation. The variable that is being predicted by this equation is the **dependent variable.** A variable that is being used to make the prediction is an **independent variable.** In this chapter we discuss regression methods involving a single independent variable. In Chapter 12 we extend these methods to multiple regression, the case of several independent variables.

There are a number of tasks can be accomplished in a regression study.

1. The data can be used to obtain a prediction equation.

2. The data can be used to estimate the amount of variability or uncertainty around the equation.

3. The data can be used to identify unusual points far from the predicted value, which may represent unusual problems or opportunities.

4. Because the data are only a sample, inferences can be made about the true (population) values for the regression quantities.

5. The prediction equation can be used to predict a reasonable range of values for future values of the dependent variable.

6. The data can be used to estimate the degree of correlation between the dependent and independent variables, a measure that indicates how strong the relation is.

In this chapter these tasks are carried out for the case of one independent variable.

Like any statistical method, regression analysis is based on a model that incorporates some assumptions. We begin in Section 11.1 by describing the simplest regression model and its assumptions. Methods for estimating the prediction equation and estimating the variability around it are given in Section 11.2. In that section we consider how to identify and deal with outliers. We discuss basic inference methods for regression in Section 11.3. In Section 11.4 we deal with prediction of future values of the dependent variable. Section 11.5 contains methods for assessing correlation.

11.1 The Linear Regression Model

Predicting future values of a variable is a crucial management activity. Financial officers must predict future cash flows, production managers must predict needs for raw materials, and human resource managers must predict future personnel needs. Explanation of past variation is also important. Explaining the past variation in the number of clients of a social service agency can help its personnel to understand the demand for the agency's services. Finding the variables that explain deviations from an automobile component's specifications can help to improve the quality of that component. The basic idea of regression analysis is to use data on a *quantitative* independent variable to predict or explain variation in a *quantitative* dependent variable.

prediction versus explanation

We can distinguish between **prediction** (reference to future values) and **explanation** (reference to current or past values). The virtues of hindsight indicate that explanation is easier than prediction. However, it is often clearer to use "prediction" to include both cases. Therefore, in this book, we will sometimes blur the distinction between prediction and explanation.

unit of association

For prediction (or explanation) to make much sense, there must be some connection between the variable we're predicting (the dependent variable) and the variable we're using to make the prediction (the independent variable). No doubt, if you tried long enough, you could find 28 common stocks whose price changes over a year have been accurately predicted by the won–loss percentage of the 28 major league baseball teams on the Fourth of July. But such a prediction is absurd, because there is no connection between the two variables. Prediction requires a **unit of association.** There should be an entity that relates the two variables. With time series data, the unit of association may be simply time. The variables may be measured at the same time period or, for genuine prediction, the independent variable may be measured at a time period before the dependent variable. For cross-sectional data, there should be an economic or physical entity that connects the variables. If we're trying to predict the change in market share of various soft drinks, we should consider the promotional activity for those drinks, not the advertising for various brands of spaghetti sauce. The need for a unit of association seems obvious, but there are many, many attempts made at prediction in which no such unit is evident.

simple linear regression

In this chapter we consider **simple linear regression** analysis, in which there is a single independent variable, and the equation for predicting a dependent variable y is a linear function of a given independent variable x. Suppose, for example, that the director of a county highway department wants to predict the cost of a resurfacing contract that is up for bids. We could reasonably predict the costs to be a function of the road miles to be resurfaced. A reasonable first attempt is to use a linear prediction function. Let y = total cost of a project in thousands of dollars, x = number of miles to be resurfaced, and $\hat{y}$ = the predicted cost, also in thousands of dollars. A prediction equation, $\hat{y} = 2.0 + 3.0x$ (for example), is a linear equation. The constant term, such as the 2.0, is the **intercept** term and is interpreted as the predicted value of y when $x = 0$. In the road resurfacing example, we may interpret the intercept as the fixed cost of beginning the project. The coefficient of x, such as the 3.0, is the **slope** of the line, the predicted change in y when there is a one-unit change in x. In the road resurfacing example, if two projects differed by 1 mile in length, we would predict that the longer project cost 3.0 (thousand dollars) more than the shorter one. In general, we write the prediction equation as

intercept

slope

$$\hat{y} = \hat{\beta}_0 + \hat{\beta}_1 x$$

where $\hat{\beta}_0$ is the intercept and $\hat{\beta}_1$ is the slope (see Figure 11.2).

FIGURE 11.2

Linear Prediction Function

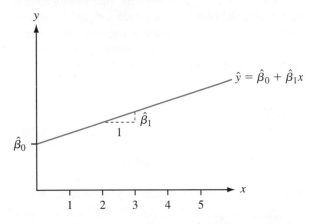

The basic idea of simple linear regression is to use data to fit a prediction line that relates a dependent variable y and a single independent variable x. The first assumption in simple regression is that the relation is, in fact, linear. According to the **linearity assumption,** the slope of the equation does not change as x changes.* In the road resurfacing example, we would assume that there were no (substantial) economies or diseconomies from projects of longer mileage. There is little point in using simple linear regression unless the linearity assumption makes sense (at least roughly).

linearity assumption

Linearity is not always a reasonable assumption, on its face. For example, if we tried to predict y = number of drivers that are aware of a car dealer's midsummer sale using x = number of repetitions of the dealer's radio commercial, the assumption of linearity means that the first broadcast of the commercial leads to no greater an increase in aware drivers than the thousand-and-first. (You've heard commercials like that.) We strongly doubt that such an assumption is valid over a wide range of x values. It makes far more sense to us that the effect of repetition would diminish as the number of repetitions got larger, so a straight-line prediction wouldn't work well.

*In terms of calculus, we assume the first derivative of the equation (of total cost with respect to mileage) to be constant.

random error term

Assuming linearity, we would like to write y as a linear function of x; $y = \beta_0 + \beta_1 x$. However, according to such an equation y is an exact linear function of x; no room is left for the inevitable errors (deviation of actual y values from their predicted values). Therefore, corresponding to each y we introduce a **random error term** ϵ_i and assume the model

$$Y = \beta_0 + \beta_1 x + \epsilon$$

We assume the random variable Y to be made up of a predictable part (a linear function of x) and an unpredictable part (the random error ϵ_i). The coefficients β_0 and β_1 are interpreted as the true, underlying intercept and slope. The error term ϵ includes the effects of all other factors, known or unknown. In the road resurfacing project, unpredictable factors such as strikes, weather conditions, and equipment breakdowns would contribute to ϵ; so would factors such as hilliness or prerepair condition of the road that might have been used in prediction but were not. The combined effects of unpredictable and ignored factors yield the random error term ϵ.

For example, one way to predict the gas mileage of various new cars (the dependent variable) based on their curb weight (the independent variable) would be to assign each car to a different driver for, say, a one-month period. What unpredictable and ignored factors might contribute to prediction error? Unpredictable (random) factors in this study would include the driving habits and skills of the drivers, the type of driving done (city or highway), and the number of stoplights encountered. Factors that would be ignored in a regression analysis of mileage and weight would include engine size and type of transmission (manual or automatic).

In regression studies, the values of the independent variable (the x_i values) are usually taken as predetermined constants, so the only source of randomness is the ϵ_i terms. While most economic and business applications have fixed x_i values, this is not always the case. For example, suppose that x_i is the score of an applicant on an aptitude test and Y_i is the productivity of the applicant. If the data are based on a random sample of applicants, X_i (as well as Y_i) is a random variable. The question of fixed versus random in regard to X is not crucial for regression studies. If the X_i's are random, we can simply regard all probability statements as conditional on the observed x_i's.

When we assume that the x_i's are constants, the only random portion of the model for Y_i is the random error term ϵ_i. We make the following formal assumptions:

DEFINITION 11.1

Formal Assumptions of Regression Analysis

1.   The relation is in fact linear, so the errors all have an expected value of zero; $E(\epsilon_i) = 0$ for all i.

2.   The errors all have the same variance; $\text{Var}(\epsilon_i) = \sigma_\epsilon^2$, for all i.

3.   The errors are independent of each other.

4.   The errors are all normally distributed; ϵ_i is normally distributed for all i.

scatterplot

These assumptions, illustrated in Figure 11.3, are made to derive the significance tests and prediction methods that follow. We can begin to check these assumptions by looking at a **scatterplot** of the data. This is a plot of each x, y point, with the independent variable value on the horizontal axis and the dependent variable value measured on the vertical axis. Look to see whether the points basically fall around a straight line or whether there is a definite curve in the pattern. Also look

FIGURE 11.3

Theoretical Distribution of *Y* in Regression

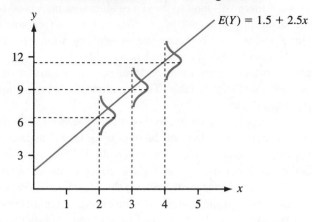

to see if there are any evident outliers falling far from the general pattern of the data. Figure 11.4 shows a scatterplot from Minitab.

smoothers   Recently, **smoothers** have been developed to sketch a curve through data without necessarily assuming any particular model. If such a smoother yields something close to a straight line, then linear regression is reasonable. One such method is called LOWESS (locally weighted scatterplot smoother). It is related to the smoothed histogram in Section 2.1. Roughly, a smoother takes a relatively narrow "slice" of data along the *x*-axis, calculates a line that fits the data in that slice, moves the slice slightly along the *x*-axis, recalculates the line, and so on. Then all the little lines are connected in a smooth curve. The width of the slice is called the *bandwidth* and may often be controlled in the computer program that does the smoothing. A LOWESS curve is shown in Figure 11.4. The scatterplot shows a curved relation. The LOWESS curve confirms that impression.

FIGURE 11.4   **Scatterplot with LOWESS Curve**

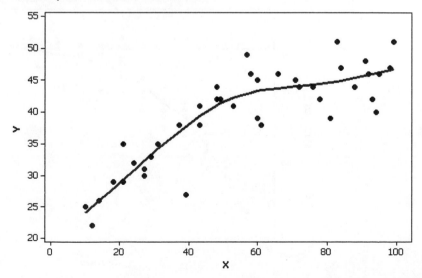

transformation

Many economic relations are not linear. For example, any "diminishing returns" pattern will tend to yield a relation that increases, but at a decreasing rate. If the scatterplot does not appear linear, by itself or when fitted with a LOWESS curve, it can often be "straightened out" by a **transformation** of either the independent variable or the dependent variable. A good statistical computer package or a spreadsheet program will compute such functions as the square root or logarithm of each value of a variable. The transformed variable should be thought of as simply another variable.

For example, a large city dispatches crews each spring to patch potholes in its streets. Records are kept of the number of crews dispatched each day and the number of potholes filled that day. Figure 11.5 shows a Minitab scatterplot of the number of potholes patched and the number of crews with a LOWESS curve. The relation is not linear. Even without the LOWESS curve, the decreasing slope is obvious. That's not surprising; as the city sends out more crews, they will be using less-effective workers, the crews will have to travel farther to find holes, and so on. All these reasons suggest that diminishing returns will occur.

We can try several transformations of the independent variable to find a more linear scatterplot. Three common transformations are square root, natural logarithm, and inverse (one divided by the variable). We applied each of these transformations to the pothole repair data in Minitab. The results are shown in Figure 11.6 with LOWESS curves. The square root and inverse transformations didn't really give us a straight line. The natural logarithm worked very well. Therefore, we would use LnCrew as our independent variable.

Finding a good transformation often requires some trial and error. Some suggestions follow for transformations to try. Notice that there are *two* key features to look for in a scatterplot. First, is the relation nonlinear? Second, is there a pattern of increasing variability along the Y (vertical) axis? If there is, the assumption of constant variance is questionable. These suggestions don't cover all the possibilities, but do include the most common problems.

FIGURE 11.5   **Scatterplot with LOWESS Curve for Pothole Data**

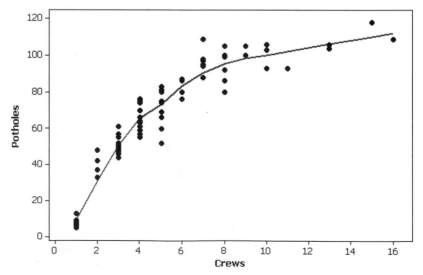

FIGURE 11.6 **Scatterplots with Transformed Predictor**

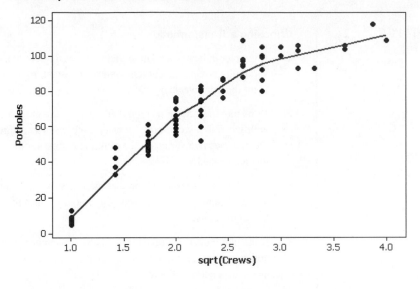

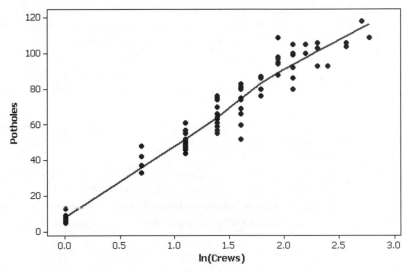

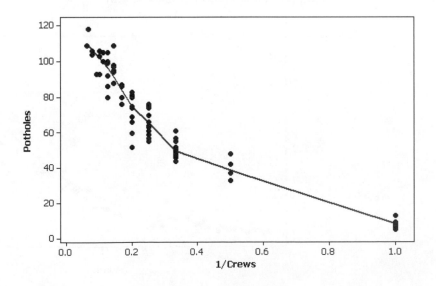

DEFINITION 11.2

Choosing a Transformation

1. If the plot indicates a relation that is increasing but at a decreasing rate, and if variability around the curve is roughly constant, transform x using square root, logarithm, or inverse transformations.

2. If the plot indicates a relation that is increasing at an increasing rate, and if variability is roughly constant, try using both x and x^2 as predictors. (Because this method uses two variables, the multiple regression methods of the next two chapters are needed.)

3. If the plot indicates a relation that increases to a maximum and then decreases, and if variability around the curve is roughly constant, again try using both x and x^2 as predictors.

4. If the plot indicates a relation that is increasing at a decreasing rate, and if variability around the curve increases as the predicted y value increases, try using y^2 as the dependent variable.

5. If the plot indicates a relation that is increasing at an increasing rate, and if variability around the curve increases as the predicted y value increases, try using $\ln(y)$ as the dependent variable. It sometimes may also be helpful to use $\ln(x)$ as the independent variable. Recall that a change in a natural logarithm corresponds quite closely to a percentage change in the original variable. Thus the slope of a transformed variable can be interpreted quite well as a percentage change.

EXAMPLE 11.1

An airline has seen a very large increase in the number of free flights used by participants in its frequent flyer program. To try to predict the trend in these flights in the near future, the director of the program assembled data for the last 72 months. The dependent variable y is the number of thousands of free flights; the independent variable x is month number. Figure 11.7 shows a scatterplot with a LOWESS smoother, done by Minitab. What transformation is suggested?

FIGURE 11.7

Frequent Flyer Free Flights by Month

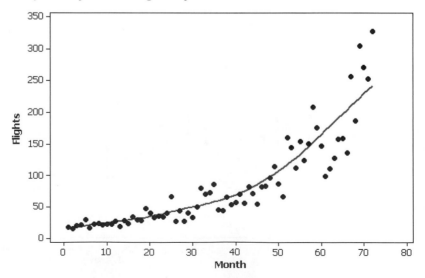

SOLUTION The pattern shows flights increasing at an increasing rate. The LOWESS curve is definitely turning upward. In addition, variation (up and down) around the curve is increasing as predicted values increase. The points around the high end of the curve (on the right, in this case) scatter much more than the ones around the low end of the curve. The increasing variability suggests transforming the y variable. A natural logarithm (ln) transformation often works well. Minitab computed the logarithms and replotted the data, as shown in Figure 11.8. The pattern is much closer to a straight line, and the scatter around the line is much closer to constant.

FIGURE 11.8

Result of Logarithm Transformation

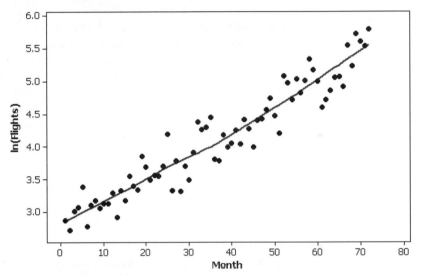

We have more to say about checking regression model assumptions in Chapter 13. For a simple regression, with a single predictor, careful checking of a scatterplot, ideally with a smooth curve fit through it, will help avoid serious blunders.

Once we have decided on any mathematical transformations, we must estimate the actual equation of the regression line. In practice, only sample data are available. The population intercept, slope, and error variance all have to be estimated from limited sample data. The assumptions we made in this section allow us to make inferences about the true parameter values from the sample data.

11.2 Estimating Model Parameters

The intercept β_0 and slope β_1 in the regression model

$$Y = \beta_0 + \beta_1 x + \epsilon$$

are population quantities. We must estimate these values from sample data. The error variance σ_ϵ^2 is another population parameter that must be estimated. The first regression problem is to obtain estimates of the slope, intercept, and variance; we discuss how to do so in this section.

The road resurfacing example of Section 11.1 is a convenient illustration. Suppose the following data for similar resurfacing projects in the recent past are available. Note that we do have a unit of association; the connection between a particular cost and mileage is that they're based on the same project.

Cost y_i (in thousands of dollars): 6.0   14.0   10.0   14.0   26.0
Mileage x_i (in miles):   1.0   3.0   4.0   5.0   7.0

A first step in examining the relation between y and x is to plot the data as a scatterplot. Remember that each point in such a plot represents the (x, y) coordinates of one data entry, as in Figure 11.9. The plot makes it clear that there is an imperfect but generally increasing relation between x and y. A straight-line relation appears plausible; there is no evident transformation with such limited data.

FIGURE 11.9

Minitab Scatterplot of Cost Versus Mileage

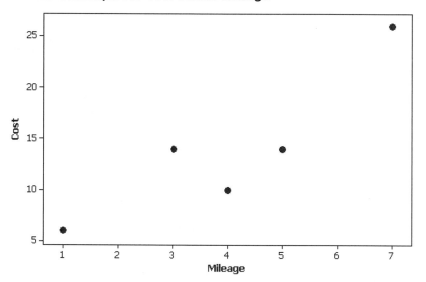

The regression analysis problem is to find the best straight-line prediction. The most common criterion for "best" is based on squared prediction error. We find the equation of the prediction line, that is, the slope $\hat{\beta}_1$ and intercept $\hat{\beta}_0$ that minimize the total squared prediction error. The method that accomplishes this goal is called the **least-squares** method, because it chooses $\hat{\beta}_0$ and $\hat{\beta}_1$ to minimize the quantity

least-squares

$$\sum_i (y_i - \hat{y}_i)^2 = \sum_i [y_i - (\hat{\beta}_0 + \hat{\beta}_1 x_i)]^2$$

The prediction errors are shown on the plot of Figure 11.10 as vertical deviations from the line. The deviations are taken as vertical distances because we're trying to predict y values and errors should be taken in the y direction. For these data the least-squares line can be shown to be $\hat{y} = 2.0 + 3.0x$; one of the deviations from it is indicated by the smaller brace. For comparison, the mean $\bar{y} = 14.0$ is also shown; the deviation from the mean is indicated by the larger brace. The least-squares principle leads to some fairly long computations for the slope and intercept. Usually, these computations are done by computer.

FIGURE 11.10   **Deviations from the Least-Squares Line and from the Mean**

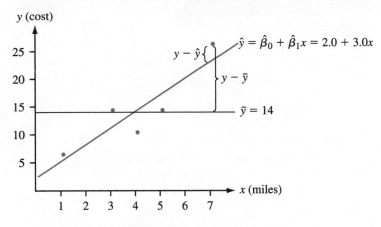

DEFINITION 11.3   **Least-Squares Estimates of Slope and Intercept** The least-squares estimates are obtained as follows:

$$\hat{\beta}_1 = \frac{S_{xy}}{S_{xx}} \qquad \text{and} \qquad \hat{\beta}_0 = \bar{y} - \hat{\beta}_1 \bar{x}$$

where

$$S_{xy} = \sum_i (x_i - \bar{x})(y_i - \bar{y})$$

and

$$S_{xx} = \sum_i (x_i - \bar{x})^2$$

Thus S_{xy} is the sum of x deviations times y deviations; S_{xx} is the sum of x deviations times x deviations, that is, the sum of x deviations squared.

For the road resurfacing data, $n = 5$ and

$$\sum x_i = 1.0 + \cdots + 7.0 = 20.0, \qquad \text{so } \bar{x} = \frac{20.0}{5} = 4.0$$

Similarly,

$$\sum y_i = 70.0, \qquad \bar{y} = \frac{70.0}{5} = 14.0$$

Also,

$$\begin{aligned}
S_{xx} &= \sum (x_i - \bar{x})^2 \\
&= (1.0 - 4.0)^2 + \cdots + (7.0 - 4.0)^2 \\
&= 20.00
\end{aligned}$$

and

$$\begin{aligned}
S_{xy} &= \sum (x_i - \bar{x})(y_i - \bar{y}) \\
&= (1.0 - 4.0)(6.0 - 14.0) + \cdots + (7.0 - 4.0)(26.0 - 14.0) \\
&= 60.0
\end{aligned}$$

So

$$\hat{\beta}_1 = \frac{60.0}{20.0} = 3.0$$

and

$$\hat{\beta}_0 = 14.0 - (3.0)(4.0) = 2.0$$

EXAMPLE 11.2   Data from a sample of 10 pharmacies are used to examine the relation between prescription sales volume and the percent of prescription ingredients purchased directly from the supplier. The sample data are shown here:

Pharmacy	Sales Volume, y (in $1000)	% of Ingredients Purchased Directly, x
1	25	10
2	55	18
3	50	25
4	75	40
5	110	50
6	138	63
7	90	42
8	60	30
9	10	5
10	100	55

a. Find the least-squares estimates for the regression line $\hat{y} = \hat{\beta}_0 + \hat{\beta}_1 x$.

b. Predict sales volume for a pharmacy that purchases 15% of its prescription ingredients directly from the supplier.

c. Plot the x, y data and the prediction equation, $\hat{y} = \hat{\beta}_0 + \hat{\beta}_1 x$.

SOLUTION

a. The equation can be calculated by virtually any statistical computer package; for example, here is abbreviated Minitab output.

```
Regression Analysis: Sales versus Directly

The regression equation is
Sales = 4.70 + 1.97 Directly

Predictor    Coef   SE Coef      T      P
Constant    4.698     5.952   0.79  0.453
Directly   1.9705    0.1545  12.75  0.000
```

Just to see how the computer does the calculations, the least-squares estimates can be obtained from the following table:

y	x	$y - \bar{y}$	$x - \bar{x}$	$(x - \bar{x})(y - \bar{y})$	$(x - \bar{x})^2$
25	10	−46.3	−23.8	1101.94	566.44
55	18	−16.3	−15.8	257.54	249.64
50	25	−21.3	−8.8	187.44	77.44
75	40	3.7	6.2	22.94	38.44
110	50	38.7	16.2	626.94	262.44
138	63	66.7	29.2	1947.64	852.64
90	42	18.7	8.2	153.34	67.24
60	30	−11.3	−3.8	42.94	14.44
10	5	−61.3	−28.8	1765.44	829.44
100	55	28.7	21.2	608.44	449.44

Totals	713	338	0	0	6714.60	3407.60
Means	71.3	33.8			

$$S_{xx} = \sum (x - \bar{x})^2 = 3407.6$$

$$S_{xy} = \sum (x - \bar{x})(y - \bar{y}) = 6714.6$$

Substituting into the formulas for $\hat{\beta}_0$ and $\hat{\beta}_1$,

$$\hat{\beta}_1 = \frac{S_{xy}}{S_{xx}} = \frac{6714.6}{3407.6} = 1.9704778, \text{ rounded to } 1.97$$

$$\hat{\beta}_0 = \bar{y} - \hat{\beta}_1 \bar{x} = 71.3 - 1.9704778(33.8) = 4.6978519, \text{ rounded to } 4.70$$

b. When $x = 15\%$, the predicted sales volume is $\hat{y} = 4.70 + 1.97(15) = 34.25$ (that is, \$34,250).

c. The prediction equation is shown in Figure 11.11 in a scatterplot of the data from Minitab.

FIGURE 11.11   **Sample Data and Least-Squares Prediction Equation for Example 11.2**

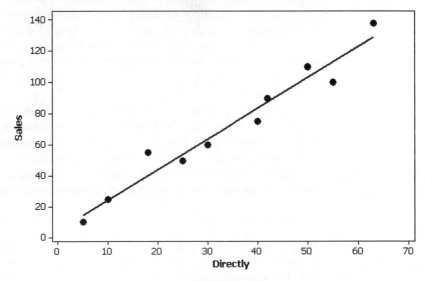

EXAMPLE 11.3   Use the Minitab output shown next to identify the least-squares estimates for the road resurfacing data:

```
Regression Analysis: Cost versus Mileage

The regression equation is
Cost = 2.00 + 3.00 Mileage

Predictor     Coef   SE Coef      T      P
Constant     2.000     3.830   0.52  0.638
Mileage     3.0000    0.8563   3.50  0.039

S = 3.82970   R-Sq = 80.4%   R-Sq(adj) = 73.8%

Analysis of Variance

Source           DF       SS       MS      F      P
Regression        1   180.00   180.00  12.27  0.039
Residual Error    3    44.00    14.67
Total             4   224.00
```

SOLUTION   The intercept is shown in the Coef column as $\hat{\beta}_0 = 2.000$. The slope (coefficient of x = miles) is $\hat{\beta}_1 = 3.0000$.

high leverage point

The estimate of the regression slope can potentially be greatly affected by **high leverage points.** These are points that have very high or very low values of the independent variable—outliers in the x direction. They carry great weight in the estimate of the slope. A high leverage point that also happens to correspond to a y outlier is a **high influence point.** It will alter the slope and twist the line badly.

high influence point

A point has high influence if omitting it from the data will cause the regression line to change substantially. To have high influence, a point must first have high leverage and in addition must fall outside the pattern of the remaining points. Consider the two scatterplots in Figure 11.12. In plot (a) the point in the upper left corner is far to the left of the other points; it has a much lower x value and therefore it has high leverage. If we drew a line through the other points, it would fall far below this point, so the point is an outlier in the y direction as well. Therefore, it also has high influence. Including this point would change the slope of the line greatly. In contrast, in plot (b) the y outlier point corresponds to an x value very near the mean, having low leverage. Including this point would pull the line upward, increasing the intercept, but it wouldn't increase or decrease the slope much at all. Therefore, it does not have great influence.

A high leverage point only indicates a *potential* distortion of the equation. Whether or not including the point will "twist" the equation depends on its influence (whether or not the point falls near the line through the remaining points). A point must have *both* high leverage and an outlying y value to qualify as a high influence point.

Mathematically, the effect of a point's leverage can be seen in the S_{xy} term that enters into the slope calculation. One of the many ways this term can be written is

$$S_{xy} = \sum (x_i - \bar{x})y_i$$

We can think of this equation as a weighted sum of y values. The weights are large positive or negative numbers when the x value is far from its mean and has high leverage. The weight is almost 0 when x is very close to its mean and has low leverage.

FIGURE 11.12   **(a) High Influence and (b) Low Influence Points**

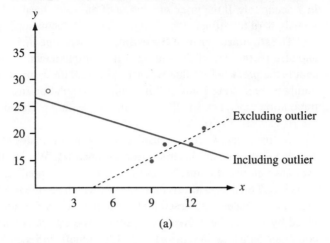

(a)

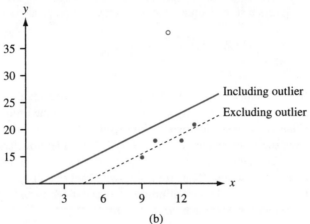

(b)

diagnostic measures

Most computer programs that perform regression analyses will calculate one or another of several **diagnostic measures** of leverage and influence. We won't try to summarize all of these measures. We only note that very large values of any of these measures correspond to very high leverage or influence points. The distinction between high leverage (x outlier) and high influence (x outlier and y outlier) points is not universally agreed upon yet. Check the program's documentation to see what definition is being used.

standard error of the estimated slope $\hat{\beta}_1$

The **standard error of the estimated slope $\hat{\beta}_1$** indicates how accurately one can estimate the correct population or process slope. The quality of estimation with $\hat{\beta}_1$ is influenced by two quantities, the error variance σ_ϵ^2 and the amount of variation in the independent variable S_{xx}.

$$\sigma_{\hat{\beta}_1} = \frac{\sigma_\epsilon}{\sqrt{S_{xx}}}$$

The greater the variability σ_ϵ of the y value for a given value of x, the larger $\sigma_{\hat{\beta}_1}$ is. Sensibly, if there is high variability around the regression line, it is difficult to estimate that line. Also, the smaller the variation in x values (as measured by S_{xx}), the larger $\sigma_{\hat{\beta}_1}$ is. The slope is the predicted change in Y per unit change in x; if x changes very little in the data, so that S_{xx} is small, it is difficult to estimate the rate of change in Y accurately. If the price of a brand of diet soda hasn't changed for years, it's obviously hard to estimate the change in quantity demanded when price changes.

standard error of the estimated intercept $\hat{\beta}_0$

The **standard error of the estimated intercept $\hat{\beta}_0$** is influenced by n, naturally, and also by the size of the square of the sample mean, $\bar{x}^2$, relative to S_{xx}. The intercept is the predicted y value when $x = 0$; if all the x_i are, for instance, large positive numbers, predicting Y at $x = 0$ is a huge extrapolation from the actual data. Such extrapolation magnifies small errors, and $\sigma_{\hat{\beta}_0}$ is large. The ideal situation for estimating $\hat{\beta}_0$ is when $\bar{x} = 0$.

To this point, we have considered only the estimates of intercept and slope. We also have to estimate the true error variance σ_ϵ^2. We can think of this quantity as "variance around the line," or as the mean squared prediction error. The estimate of

residuals

σ_ϵ^2 is based on the **residuals** $e_i = y_i - \hat{y}_i$, which are the prediction errors in the sample. The estimate of σ_ϵ^2 based on the sample data is the sum of squared residuals divided by $n - 2$, the degrees of freedom. The estimated variance is often shown in computer output as MS(Error) or MS(Residual). MS stands for "mean square" and is always a sum of squares divided by the appropriate degrees of freedom.

$$s_\epsilon^2 = \frac{\sum_i (y_i - \hat{y}_i)^2}{n - 2} = \frac{\text{SS(Residual)}}{n - 2}$$

In the computer output for Example 11.3, SS(Residual) is shown to be 44.0.

Just as we divide by $n - 1$ rather than n in the ordinary sample variance s^2 (in Chapter 2), we divide by $n - 2$ in s_ϵ^2, the estimated variance around the line. To see why, suppose our sample size is $n = 2$. No matter how large or small σ_ϵ^2 may be, the estimated regression line goes exactly through the two points, and the residuals are automatically zero. Thus for $n = 2$ we simply don't have enough information to estimate σ_ϵ^2 at all. In our definition, s_ϵ^2 is undefined for $n = 2$, as it should be. Another argument for dividing by $n - 2$ is that

$$E(s_\epsilon^2) = \sigma_\epsilon^2$$

Dividing by $n - 2$ makes s_ϵ^2 an unbiased estimator of σ_ϵ^2. In the computer output of Example 11.3, $n - 2 = 5 - 2 = 3$ is shown as DF (degrees of freedom) for Residual Error and $s_\epsilon^2 = 14.67$ is shown as MS for Residual Error.

residual standard deviation

The square root s_ϵ of the sample variance is called the **sample standard deviation around the regression line,** the **standard error of estimate,** or the **residual standard deviation.** Because s_ϵ estimates σ_ϵ, the standard deviation of Y_i, s_ϵ estimates the standard deviation of the population of y values associated with a given value of the independent variable x. The Minitab output in Example 11.3 labels s_ϵ as S; it shows that s_ϵ, rounded off, is 3.830.

Like any other standard deviation, the residual standard deviation may be interpreted by the Empirical Rule. About 95% of the prediction errors will fall within ± 2 standard deviations of the mean error; the mean error is always 0 in the least-squares regression model. Therefore, a residual standard deviation of 3.830 means that about 95% of prediction errors will be less than $|\pm 2(3.830)| = 7.660$.

The estimates $\hat{\beta}_0$, $\hat{\beta}_1$ and s_ϵ are basic in regression analysis. They specify the regression line and the probable degree of error associated with y values for a given value of x. The next step is to use these sample estimates to make inferences about the true parameters.

EXAMPLE 11.4   The human resources director of a chain of fast-food restaurants studied the absentee rate of employees. Whenever employees called in sick, or simply didn't appear, the restaurant manager had to find replacements in a hurry or else work short-handed. The director had data on the number of absences per 100 employees per week (y) and the average number of months experience at the restaurant (x) for 10 restaurants in the chain. The director expected that longer-term employees would be more reliable and absent less often. For the following data and Minitab output,

a. examine the scatterplot, and decide whether a straight line is a reasonable model;

b. identify the least-squares estimates for β_0 and β_1 in the model $Y = \beta_0 + \beta_1 x + \epsilon$;

c. predict y for $x = 19.5$;

d. identify s_ϵ, the sample standard deviation about the regression line.

y = Absence rate: 31.5 33.1 27.4 24.5 27.0 27.8 23.3 24.7 16.9 18.1
x = Tenure: 18.1 20.0 20.8 21.5 22.0 22.4 22.9 24.0 25.4 27.3

```
Regression Analysis: y versus x

The regression equation is
y = 64.7 - 1.75 x

Predictor      Coef   SE Coef       T      P
Constant     64.672     6.762    9.56  0.000
x           -1.7487    0.2995   -5.84  0.000


S = 2.38785   R-Sq = 81.0%   R-Sq(adj) = 78.6%

Analysis of Variance

Source          DF        SS       MS      F      P
Regression       1    194.45   194.45  34.10  0.000
Residual Error   8     45.61     5.70
Total            9    240.06
```

SOLUTION

a. A scatterplot drawn by the Minitab package is shown in Figure 11.13; the data appear to fall approximately along a downward-sloping line. There is no reason to use a more complicated model.

b. The output shows the coefficients twice, with differing numbers of digits. The intercept (constant) is 64.672 and the slope (coefficient of x) is -1.7487. Note that the negative slope corresponds to a downward-sloping line.

c. The least-squares prediction value when $x = 19.5$ is

$$\hat{y} = 64.672 - 1.7487\,(19.5) = 30.57$$

d. The standard deviation around the line (the residual standard deviation) is shown as $s = 2.388$. Therefore, about 95% of the prediction errors should be less than $|\pm 2(2.388)| = 4.776$.

FIGURE 11.13   **Scatterplot of Absences Versus Average Length of Employment**

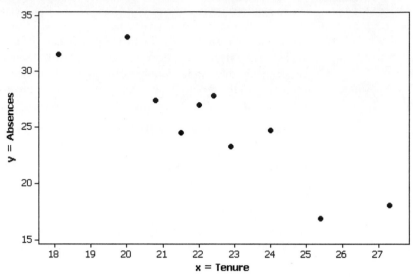

Exercises

11.1   A regression study yielded the following data and the Minitab plots shown in Figure 11.14.

x:	1	1	1	3	3	3
$x' = \log_{10} x$:	.000	.000	.000	.477	.477	.477
y:	13.5	15.4	16.1	18.3	19.9	20.9

x:	5	5	5	7	7	7
$x' = \log_{10} x$:	.699	.699	.699	.845	.845	.845
y:	20.8	23.1	22.1	22.8	24.9	24.5

a. In the plot of y versus x, approximate the slope as the difference between predicted values for $x = 7$ and for $x = 1$ divided by the difference in x values, namely, 6.
b. In the plot of y versus x', approximate the slope of the prediction line.
c. Which plot appears more nearly linear to you?

11.2   Refer to the data of Exercise 11.1, and the following Minitab output:

```
Regression Analysis: y versus x

The regression equation is
y = 14.3 + 1.47 x

Predictor      Coef  SE Coef       T       P
Constant    14.2916   0.7962   17.95   0.000
x            1.4750   0.1737    8.49   0.000

S = 1.34579    R-Sq = 87.8%    R-Sq(adj) = 86.6%
```

FIGURE 11.14   **Scatterplots for Exercise 11.1**

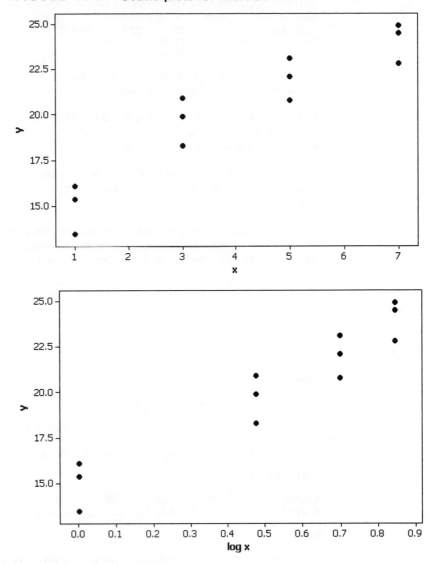

Analysis of Variance

```
Source          DF      SS      MS      F       P
Regression       1   130.54  130.54  72.07  0.000
Residual Error  10    18.11    1.81
Total           11   148.65

Regression Analysis: y versus log x

The regression equation is
y = 14.9 + 10.5 log x

Predictor     Coef   SE Coef     T      P
Constant   14.8754    0.6106  24.36  0.000
log x      10.522     1.021   10.30  0.000

S = 1.13118   R-Sq = 91.4%   R-Sq(adj) = 90.5%
```

Analysis of Variance

Source	DF	SS	MS	F	P
Regression	1	135.85	135.85	106.17	0.000
Residual Error	10	12.80	1.28		
Total	11	148.65			

a. Locate the least-squares equation $\hat{y} = \hat{\beta}_0 + \hat{\beta}_1 x$.
b. Locate the residual standard deviation.

11.3 Refer to the output for the data in Exercise 11.2.
a. Find the least-squares equation $\hat{y} = \hat{\beta}_0 + \hat{\beta}_1 x'$.
b. What is the residual standard deviation?

11.4 Compare the residual standard deviations s_ϵ in the two preceding exercises. Which is smaller? Does this confirm your opinion about the choice of model based on the plots of Exercise 11.1?

11.5 As one part of a study of commercial bank branches, data are obtained on the number of independent businesses (x) located in sample ZIP code areas and the number of bank branches (y) located in these areas. The commercial centers of cities are excluded.

x: 92 116 124 210 216 267 306 378 415 502 615 703
y: 3   2   3   5   4   5   5   6   7   7   9   9

Output (Minitab) for the analysis of the data follows:

Regression Analysis: Branches versus Business

The regression equation is
Branches = 1.77 + 0.0111 Business

Predictor	Coef	SE Coef	T	P
Constant	1.7668	0.3212	5.50	0.000
Business	0.0111049	0.0008453	13.14	0.000

S = 0.558299   R-Sq = 94.5%   R-Sq(adj) = 94.0%

Analysis of Variance

Source	DF	SS	MS	F	P
Regression	1	53.800	53.800	172.60	0.000
Residual Error	10	3.117	0.312		
Total	11	56.917			

a. Plot the data. Does a linear equation relating y to x appear plausible?
b. Locate the regression equation (with y as the dependent variable).
c. Locate the sample residual standard deviation s_ϵ.

11.6 Does it appear that variability of y increases with x in the data plot of Exercise 11.5? (This would violate the assumption of constant variance.)

11.7 A manufacturer of cases for sound equipment requires drilling holes for metal screws. The drill bits wear out and must be replaced. There is expense not only for the cost of the bits but also for lost production. Engineers varied the rotation speed of the drill and measured lifetime y (thousands of holes drilled) of four bits at each of five speeds x. The data were

x: 60   60   60   60   80   80   80   80   100 100
y: 4.6 3.8 4.9 4.5 4.7 5.8 5.5 5.4 5.0 4.5

x: 100 100 120 120 120 120 140 140 140 140
y: 3.2 4.8 4.1 4.5 4.0 3.8 3.6 3.0 3.5 3.4

a. Create a scatterplot of the data. Does there appear to be a relation? Does it appear to be linear?

b. Is there any evident outlier? If so, does it have high influence?

11.8 The data of Exercise 11.7 were analyzed using Excel's regression function. The following output was obtained:

```
SUMMARY OUTPUT

Regression Statistics
Multiple R              0.6254
R Square                0.3911
Adjusted R Square       0.3573
Standard Error          0.6324
Observations               20
```

ANOVA

	df	SS	MS	F	Significance F
Regression	1	4.624	4.624	11.563	0.0032
Residual	18	7.198	0.400		
Total	19	11.822			

	Coefficient	Standard Error	t Stat	P-value
Intercept	6.03	0.5195	11.606	8.617E-10
Speed	-0.017	0.0050	-3.400	3.188E-03

a. Locate the intercept and slope of the least-squares regression line.

b. What does the sign of the slope indicate about the relation between speed and bit lifetime?

c. Locate the residual standard deviation. Interpret the resulting number.

11.9 Again refer to Exercise 11.7.

a. Use the regression line of Exercise 11.8 to calculate predicted values for $x = 60, 80, 100, 120,$ and 140.

b. For which x values are most of the actual y values larger than the predicted values? For which x values are most y values lower than predicted? What does this pattern indicate about whether there is a linear relation?

11.10 A realtor studied the relation between $x =$ yearly income (in thousands of dollars per year) of home purchasers and $y =$ sale price of the house (in thousands of dollars). Data were obtained from mortgage applications for 24 sales in the realtor's basic sales area in one season. Minitab output was obtained, as shown after the data.

x:	25.0	28.5	29.2	30.0	31.0	31.5	31.9	32.0	33.0
y:	84.9	94.0	96.5	93.5	102.9	99.5	101.0	105.0	99.9

x:	33.5	34.0	35.9	36.0	39.0	39.0	40.5	40.9	42.5
y:	110.0	100.0	116.0	110.0	125.0	119.9	130.6	120.8	129.9

x:	44.0	45.0	50.0	54.6	65.0	70.0
y:	135.5	140.0	150.7	170.0	110.0	185.0

```
Regression Analysis: Price versus Income

The regression equation is
Price = 47.2 + 1.80 Income

Predictor    Coef   SE Coef      T      P
Constant    47.15     10.93   4.31  0.000
Income     1.8026    0.2681   6.72  0.000

S = 14.4452    R-Sq = 67.3%    R-Sq(adj) = 65.8%
```

Analysis of Variance

Source	DF	SS	MS	F	P
Regression	1	9432.6	9432.6	45.20	0.000
Residual Error	22	4590.7	208.7		
Total	23	14023.2			

Unusual Observations

Obs	Income	Price	Fit	SE Fit	Residual	St Resid
23	65.0	110.00	164.32	7.50	-54.32	-4.40RX
24	70.0	185.00	173.34	8.75	11.66	1.01 X

R denotes an observation with a large standardized residual.
X denotes an observation whose X value gives it large influence.

Regression Analysis: Price(w/o obs 23) versus Income(w/o obs 23)

The regression equation is
Price(w/o obs 23) = 24.4 + 2.46 Income(w/o obs 23)

Predictor	Coef	SE Coef	T	P
Constant	24.358	4.286	5.68	0.000
Income(w/o obs 23)	2.4620	0.1088	22.63	0.000

S = 5.11720   R-Sq = 96.1%   R-Sq(adj) = 95.9%

Analysis of Variance

Source	DF	SS	MS	F	P
Regression	1	13408	13408	512.02	0.000
Residual Error	21	550	26		
Total	22	13957			

Unusual Observations

Obs	Income (w/o obs 23)	Price (w/o obs 23)	Fit	SE Fit	Residual	St Resid
22	54.6	170.00	158.78	2.08	11.22	2.40R
23	70.0	185.00	196.70	3.63	-11.70	-3.24RX

R denotes an observation with a large standardized residual.
X denotes an observation whose X value gives it large influence.

FIGURE 11.15 **Scatterplot with LOWESS Smooth**

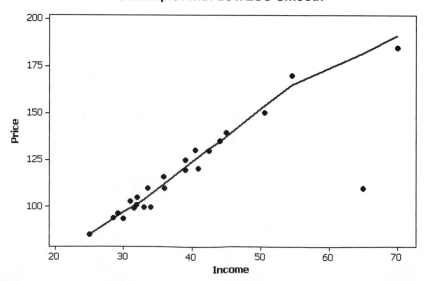

a. A scatterplot with a LOWESS smooth, drawn using Minitab, is shown in Figure 11.15. Does the relation appear to be basically linear?
b. Are there any high leverage points? If so, which ones seem to have high influence?
c. Locate the least-squares regression equation for the data.
d. Interpret the slope coefficient. Is the intercept meaningful?
e. Find the residual standard deviation.
f. The output also contains a regression line when we omit the point with $x = 65.0$ and $y = 110.0$. Does the slope change substantially? Why?

11.11 A mail-order retailer spends considerable effort in "picking" orders—selecting the ordered items and assembling them for shipment. A small study took a sample of 100 orders. An experienced picker carried out the entire process. The time in minutes needed was recorded for each order. A scatterplot and smoothing spline fit, created using JMP, are shown in Figure 11.16. What next step in the data analysis is suggested by the plot?

FIGURE 11.16 **Scatterplot and Smoothing Spline Fit for Order-Picking Data**

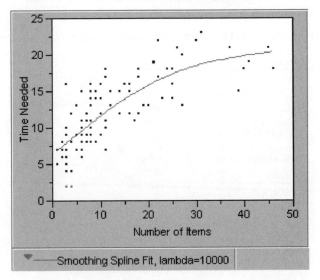

11.12 The order-picking time data in Exercise 11.11 were transformed by taking the square root of the number of items. A scatterplot from JMP of the result is shown in Figure 11.17 and JMP regression results are shown in Figure 11.18.
a. Does the transformed scatterplot appear reasonably linear?
b. Write out the prediction equation based on the transformed data.
c. In the JMP output of Figure 11.18, the residual standard deviation is called "Root Mean Square Error." Locate and interpret this number in the language of the problem.
d. Why is it possible to compare the residual standard deviation for the transformed data to the residual standard deviation for the original data in this situation?

FIGURE 11.17 **Scatterplot of Transformed Order-Picking Data**

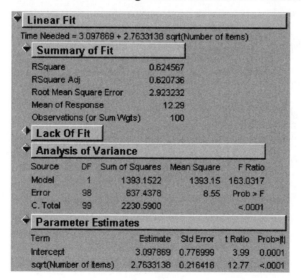

FIGURE 11.18 **Regression Results for Transformed Data**

Linear Fit

Time Needed = 3.097869 + 2.7633138 sqrt(Number of Items)

Summary of Fit

RSquare	0.624567
RSquare Adj	0.620736
Root Mean Square Error	2.923232
Mean of Response	12.29
Observations (or Sum Wgts)	100

Lack Of Fit

Analysis of Variance

Source	DF	Sum of Squares	Mean Square	F Ratio
Model	1	1393.1522	1393.15	163.0317
Error	98	837.4378	8.55	Prob > F
C. Total	99	2230.5900		<.0001

Parameter Estimates

Term	Estimate	Std Error	t Ratio	Prob>|t|
Intercept	3.097869	0.776999	3.99	0.0001
sqrt(Number of Items)	2.7633138	0.216418	12.77	<.0001

11.3 Inferences about Regression Parameters

The slope, intercept, and residual standard deviation in a simple regression model are all estimates based on limited data. Just like all other statistical quantities, they are affected by random error. In this section we consider how to allow for that random error. The concepts of hypothesis tests and confidence intervals that we have applied to means and proportions apply equally well to regression summary figures.

The t distribution can be used to make significance tests and confidence intervals for the true slope and intercept. One natural null hypothesis is that the true slope

t test for slope

$\beta_1 = 0$. If this H_0 is true, a change in x yields no predicted change in y, and it follows that x has no value in predicting y. We know from the previous section that the sample slope $\hat{\beta}_1$ has the expected value β_1 and standard error

$$\sigma_{\hat{\beta}_1} = \sigma_\epsilon \sqrt{\frac{1}{S_{xx}}}$$

In practice, σ_ϵ is not known and must be estimated by s_ϵ, the residual standard deviation. The estimated standard error of $\hat{\beta}_1$ is given by

$$s_{\hat{\beta}_1} = s_\epsilon \sqrt{\frac{1}{S_{xx}}}$$

In almost all regression analysis computer output, the estimated standard error is shown next to the coefficient. A t test for the slope is given by the t statistic

$$t = \frac{\hat{\beta}_1 - \beta_1}{s_{\hat{\beta}_1}} = \frac{\hat{\beta}_1 - \beta_1}{s_\epsilon \sqrt{\dfrac{1}{S_{xx}}}}$$

The most common use of this statistic is in testing H_0: $\beta_1 = 0$, as in the following summary.

DEFINITION 11.4

t Test of H_0: $\beta_1 = 0$

H_0: $\beta_1 = 0$

H_a: 1. $\beta_1 > 0$
  2. $\beta_1 < 0$
  3. $\beta_1 \neq 0$

T.S.: $t = \dfrac{\hat{\beta}_1 - 0}{s_{\hat{\beta}_1}}$

R.R.: For d.f. $= n - 2$ and Type I error α,
  1. reject H_0 if $t > t_\alpha$
  2. reject H_0 if $t < -t_\alpha$
  3. reject H_0 if $|t| > t_{\alpha/2}$

All statistical packages show this t value.

In most computer output, this test is indicated after the standard error and labeled as T, T TEST, or T STATISTIC. Often, a p-value is also given, which eliminates the need for looking up the t value in a table.

EXAMPLE 11.5

Use the Minitab output of Example 11.3 reproduced here to locate the value of the t statistic for testing H_0: $\beta_1 = 0$ in the road resurfacing example. Give the observed level of significance for the test.

```
Regression Analysis: Cost versus Mileage

The regression equation is
Cost = 2.00 + 3.00 Mileage
```

```
Predictor     Coef   SE Coef      T      P
Constant     2.000     3.830   0.52   0.638
Mileage      3.0000    0.8563   3.50   0.039

S = 3.82970   R-Sq = 80.4%   R-Sq(adj) = 73.8%

Analysis of Variance

Source            DF       SS       MS      F       P
Regression         1   180.00   180.00  12.27   0.039
Residual Error     3    44.00    14.67
Total              4   224.00
```

SOLUTION   It is clear from the output that the value of the test statistic in the column labeled T is $t = 3.50$. The p-value for the two-tailed alternative $H_a: \beta_1 \neq 0$, labeled as P, is .039. Because this value is fairly small, we can reject the hypothesis that mileage has no effect on predicting cost.

EXAMPLE 11.6

The following data show mean ages of executives of 15 firms in the food industry and the previous year's percentage increase in earnings per share of the firms. Use the Minitab output shown to test the hypothesis that executive age has no predictive value for change in earnings. Should a one-sided or two-sided alternative be used?

$$\text{Mean age, } x: \quad 38.2 \quad 40.0 \quad 42.5 \quad 43.4 \quad 44.6 \quad 44.9 \quad 45.0 \quad 45.4$$
$$\text{Change, earnings per share, } y: \quad 8.9 \quad 13.0 \quad 4.7 \quad -2.4 \quad 12.5 \quad 18.4 \quad 6.6 \quad 13.5$$
$$x: \quad 46.0 \quad 47.3 \quad 47.3 \quad 48.0 \quad 49.1 \quad 50.5 \quad 51.6$$
$$y: \quad 8.5 \quad 15.3 \quad 18.9 \quad 6.0 \quad 10.4 \quad 15.9 \quad 17.1$$

```
Regression Analysis: EPSChange versus MeanAge

The regression equation is
EPSChange = - 17.0 + 0.617 MeanAge

Predictor     Coef   SE Coef      T      P
Constant    -16.99     18.87   -0.90   0.384
MeanAge     0.6174    0.4126    1.50   0.158

S = 5.63370   R-Sq = 14.7%   R-Sq(adj) = 8.1%

Analysis of Variance

Source            DF       SS       MS      F       P
Regression         1    71.05    71.05   2.24   0.158
Residual Error    13   412.60    31.74
Total             14   483.66
```

SOLUTION   In the model $Y = \beta_0 + \beta_1 x + \epsilon$, the null hypothesis is $H_0: \beta_1 = 0$. The myth in American business is that younger managers tend to be more aggressive and harder driving, but it is also possible that the greater experience of the older executives leads to better decisions. Therefore, there is a good reason to choose a two-sided research hypothesis, $H_a: \beta_1 \neq 0$. The t statistic is shown in the output column marked T, reasonably enough. It shows $t = 1.50$, with a (two-sided) p-value of .158. There is not enough evidence to conclude that there is any relation between age and change in earnings.

In passing, note that the interpretation of $\hat{\beta}_0$ is rather interesting in this example; it would be the predicted change in earnings of a firm with mean age of its managers equal to 0. Hmm.

It is also possible to calculate a confidence interval for the true slope. This is an excellent way to communicate the likely degree of inaccuracy in the estimate of that slope. The confidence interval once again is simply the estimate $\pm$ a t table value times the standard error.

DEFINITION 11.5

Confidence Interval for Slope β_1

$$\hat{\beta}_1 - t_{\alpha/2}s_{\hat{\beta}_1} \le \beta_1 \le \hat{\beta}_1 + t_{\alpha/2}s_{\hat{\beta}_1}$$

The required degrees of freedom for the table value $t_{\alpha/2}$ is $n - 2$, the error d.f.

EXAMPLE 11.7

Compute a 95% confidence interval for the slope β_1 using the output from Example 11.3.

SOLUTION In the output, $\hat{\beta}_1 = 3.000$ and the estimated standard error of $\hat{\beta}_1$ is shown as .856, rounded off. Because n is 5, there are $5 - 2 = 3$ d.f. for error. The required table value for $\alpha/2 = .05/2 = .025$ is 3.182. The corresponding confidence interval for the true value of β_1 is then

$$3.00 \pm 3.182(.856) \qquad \text{or} \qquad .276 \text{ to } 5.724$$

The predicted cost per additional mile of resurfacing could be anywhere from \$276 to \$5724. The enormous width of this interval results largely from the small sample size.

There is an alternative test, an F test, for the null hypothesis of no predictive value. It was designed to test the null hypothesis that *all* predictors have no value in predicting y. This test gives the same result as a two-sided t test of $H_0: \beta_1 = 0$ in simple linear regression; to say that all predictors have no value is to say that the (only) slope is 0. The F test is summarized next.

DEFINITION 11.6

F Test for $H_0: \beta_1 = 0$

$H_0: \beta_1 = 0$

$H_a: \beta_1 \ne 0$

T.S.: $F = \dfrac{\text{SS(Regression)}/1}{\text{SS(Residual)}/(n-2)} = \dfrac{\text{MS(Regression)}}{\text{MS(Residual)}}$

R.R.: With d.f.$_1 = 1$ and d.f.$_2 = n - 2$, reject H_0 if $F > F_\alpha$.

SS(Regression) is the sum of squared deviations of predicted y values from the y mean. SS(Regression) $= \sum (\hat{y}_i - \bar{y})^2$. SS(Residual) is the sum of squared deviations of actual y values from predicted y values. SS(Residual) $= \sum (y_i - \hat{y}_i)^2$.

Virtually all computer packages calculate this F statistic. In the road resurfacing example, the output shows $F = 12.27$ with a p-value of .0394. Again, the hypothesis of no predictive value can be rejected. It is always true for simple linear regression problems that $F = t^2$; in the example, $12.27 = (3.50)^2$, to within round-off error. The F and two-sided t tests are equivalent in simple linear regression; they will serve different purposes in multiple regression.

EXAMPLE 11.8   For the output of Example 11.4, reproduced here, use the F test for H_0: $\beta_1 = 0$. Show that $t^2 = F$.

```
Regression Analysis: y versus x

The regression equation is
y = 64.7 - 1.75 x

Predictor       Coef   SE Coef        T      P
Constant      64.672     6.762     9.56  0.000
x            -1.7487     0.2995    -5.84  0.000

S = 2.38785    R-Sq = 81.0%    R-Sq(adj) = 78.6%

Analysis of Variance

Source          DF        SS       MS      F      P
Regression       1    194.45   194.45  34.10  0.000
Residual Error   8     45.61     5.70
Total            9    240.06
```

SOLUTION   The F statistic is shown in the output as 34.10, with a p-value of .000 (indicating that the actual p-value is something smaller than .0005). Note that the t statistic is -5.84 and that $t^2 = (-5.84)^2 = 34.11$, equal to F to within round-off error.

You should be able to work out comparable hypothesis-testing and confidence interval formulas for the intercept β_0 using the estimated standard error of $\hat{\beta}_0$ as

$$s_{\hat{\beta}_0} = s_\epsilon \sqrt{\frac{1}{n} + \frac{\bar{x}^2}{S_{xx}}}$$

In practice, this parameter is of less interest than the slope. In particular, there is often no reason to hypothesize that the true intercept is zero (or any other particular value). Computer packages almost always test the null hypothesis of zero slope, but some don't bother with a test on the intercept term.

Exercises

11.13   Refer to the data of Exercise 11.5.
a. Calculate a 90% confidence interval for β_1.
b. What is the interpretation of H_0: $\beta_1 = 0$ in Exercise 11.5?
c. What is the natural research hypothesis H_a for that problem?
d. Do the data support H_a at $\alpha = .05$?
e. Find the p-value of the test of H_0: $\beta_1 = 0$.

11.14 A real estate appraiser is interested in developing a technique for estimating the selling price of a house in his city. Given that the size of the home, measured as the square footage of heated/cooled area, is a very important factor in the price of a house, the appraiser decides to use a simple linear regression of selling price (y, in thousands of dollars) on square footage (x). A sample of 100 homes sold in a three-month period was collected to estimate the coefficients of the model. Partial Minitab output is shown here.

```
Regression Analysis: Price versus Sqft

The regression equation is
Price = 28.0 + 0.0735 Sqft

Predictor       Coef   SE Coef      T      P
Constant      27.989     8.075   3.47  0.001
Sqft        0.073537  0.003104    a    0.000

S = 17.2508   R-Sq = 85.1%   R-Sq(adj) = 85.0%

Analysis of Variance

Source          DF       SS      MS      F      P
Regression       1   167080  167080      e  0.000
Residual Error   b    29164      d
Total            c   196244
```

a. Fill in the missing values indicated by the five blanks (a through e) in the output.
b. For each of the three following values from the Minitab output, write the symbol for the statistic represented by the value and the symbol for the parameter that is estimated by the value: .073537, .003104, 17.2508.
c. Interpret the value of the estimated slope from the output in the language of the problem.
d. Construct a 95% confidence interval for the true slope parameter.
e. Based on this output, is the relationship between Price and Sqft statistically significant (detectable)? Explain why or why not.

11.15 A firm that prints automobile bumper stickers investigates the relation between the total direct cost of a lot of stickers and the number produced in the printing run. The data are analyzed by the Minitab computer package. The relevant output is shown here.

```
Regression Analysis: TotalCost versus RunSize

The regression equation is
TotalCost = 99.8 + 51.9 RunSize

Predictor      Coef   SE Coef      T      P
Constant     99.777     2.827  35.29  0.000
RunSize     51.9178    0.5865  88.53  0.000

S = 12.2064   R-Sq = 99.6%   R-Sq(adj) = 99.6%

Analysis of Variance

Source          DF        SS        MS        F      P
Regression       1   1167747   1167747  7837.25  0.000
Residual Error  28      4172       149
Total           29   1171919
```

a. Plot the data. Do you detect any difficulties with using a linear regression model? Can you see any blatant violations of assumptions? The raw data are

Runsize:	2.6	5.0	10.0	2.0	.8	4.0	2.5	.6	.8	1.0	2.0	
Total cost:	230	341	629	187	159	327	206	124	155	147	209	

Runsize:	3.0	.4	.5	5.0	20.0	5.0	2.0	1.0	1.5	.5	1.0	1.0
Total cost:	247	135	125	366	1146	339	208	150	179	128	155	143

Runsize:	.6	2.0	1.5	3.0	6.5	2.2	1.0
Total cost:	131	219	171	258	415	226	159

b. Write the estimated regression equation indicated in the output. Find the residual standard deviation.

c. Calculate a 95% confidence interval for the true slope. What are the interpretations of the intercept and slope in this problem?

d. Locate the value of the t statistic for testing $H_0: \beta_1 = 0$.

e. Locate the p-value for this test. Is the p-value one-tailed or two-tailed? If necessary, calculate the p-value for the appropriate number of tails.

f. Locate the value of the F statistic and the associated p-value.

g. How do the p-values for this F test and the t test compare? Why should this relation hold?

11.4 Predicting New Y Values Using Regression

In all the regression analyses we've done so far, we have been summarizing and making inferences about relations in data that have already been observed. Thus we've been predicting the past. One of the most important uses of regression is in trying to forecast the future. In the road resurfacing example, the county highway director wants to predict the cost of a new contract that is up for bids. In a regression predicting quantity sold given price, a manager will want to predict the demand at a new price. In this section we discuss how to make such regression forecasts and how to determine the plus-or-minus probable error factor.

There are two possible interpretations of a Y prediction based on a given x. Suppose that the highway director substitutes $x = 6$ miles in the regression equation $\hat{y} = 2.0 + 3.0x$ and gets $\hat{y} = 20$. This can be interpreted as either

"the average cost $E(Y)$ of *all* resurfacing contracts for 6 miles of road will be $20,000,"

or

"the cost Y of *this specific* resurfacing contract for 6 miles of road will be $20,000."

The best-guess prediction in either case is 20, but the plus-or-minus factor differs. It's easier to predict an average value $E(Y)$ than an individual Y value, so the plus-or-minus factor should be less for predicting an average. We discuss the plus-or-minus range for predicting an average first, with the understanding that this is an intermediate step toward solving the specific-value problem.

In the mean-value forecasting problem, suppose that the value of the predictor x is known. Because the previous values of x have been designated $x_1, \ldots, x_n$, call the new value x_{n+1}. Then $\hat{y}_{n+1} = \hat{\beta}_0 + \hat{\beta}_1 x_{n+1}$ is used to estimate $E(Y|X = x_{n+1})$. As $\hat{\beta}_0$ and $\hat{\beta}_1$ are unbiased, $\hat{y}_{n+1}$ is an unbiased predictor of $E(Y|X = x_{n+1})$. The standard error of $\hat{y}_{n+1}$ can be shown to be

$$\sigma_\epsilon \sqrt{\frac{1}{n} + \frac{(x_{n+1} - \bar{x})^2}{S_{xx}}}$$

Here S_{xx} is the sum of squared deviations of the original n values of x_i; it can be found from most computer output as

$$\left(\frac{s_\epsilon}{s_{\hat{\beta}_1}}\right)^2$$

Again, t tables with $n - 2$ d.f. (the error d.f.) must be used. The usual approach to forming a confidence interval, namely, estimate $\pm\, t$ (standard error) yields a confidence interval for $E(Y|X = x_{n+1})$. Some of the better statistical computer packages will calculate this confidence interval if a new x value is specified without specifying a corresponding y.

DEFINITION 11.7

Confidence Interval for $E(Y|X = x_{n+1})$

$$\hat{y}_{n+1} - t_{\alpha/2}s_\epsilon \sqrt{\frac{1}{n} + \frac{(x_{n+1} - \bar{x})^2}{S_{xx}}} \leq E(Y|X = x_{n+1})$$

$$\leq \hat{y}_{n+1} + t_{\alpha/2}s_\epsilon \sqrt{\frac{1}{n} + \frac{(x_{n+1} - \bar{x})^2}{S_{xx}}}$$

where $t_{\alpha/2}$ cuts off area $\alpha/2$ in the right tail of the t distribution with $n - 2$ d.f.

Note: S_{xx} may be calculated as

$$\left(\frac{s_\epsilon}{s_{\hat{\beta}_1}}\right)^2$$

For the resurfacing example, the computer output shows the estimated value of $E(Y|X = x_{n+1})$ to be 20 when $x = 6$. The corresponding 95% confidence interval on $E(Y|X = x_{n+1})$ is 12.29 to 27.71.

The forecasting plus-or-minus term in the confidence interval for $E(Y|X = x_{n+1})$ depends on the sample size n and the standard deviation around the regression line, as one might expect. It also depends on the squared distance of x_{n+1} from $\bar{x}$ (the mean of the previous x_i values) relative to S_{xx}. As x_{n+1} gets farther from $\bar{x}$, the term

$$\frac{(x_{n+1} - \bar{x})^2}{S_{xx}}$$

gets larger. When x_{n+1} is far away from the other x values, so that this term is large, the prediction is a considerable extrapolation from the data. Small errors in estimating the regression line are magnified by the extrapolation. The term $(x_{n+1} - \bar{x})^2/S_{xx}$ could be **extrapolation penalty** called an **extrapolation penalty** because it increases with the degree of extrapolation.

Extrapolation—predicting the results at independent variable values far from the data—is often tempting and always dangerous. To do so requires an assumption that the relation will continue to be linear far beyond the data. By definition, you have no data to check this assumption. For example, a firm might find a negative correlation between the number of employees (ranging between 1200 and 1400) in a quarter and the profitability in that quarter; the fewer the employees, the greater the profit. It would be spectacularly risky to conclude from this fact that cutting the number of employees to 600 would vastly improve profitability. (Do you suppose we could have a negative number of employees?) Sooner or later, the declining number of employees must adversely affect the business so that profitability turns downward. The extrapolation penalty term actually understates the risk of extrapolation. It is based on the assumption of a linear relation, and that assumption gets very shaky for large extrapolations.

EXAMPLE 11.9

For the data of Example 11.4, and the following Minitab output from that data, obtain a 95% confidence interval for $E(Y|X = x_{n+1})$ based on an assumed x_{n+1} of 22.4. Compare the width of the interval to one based on an assumed x_{n+1} of 30.4.

```
Regression Analysis: y versus x

The regression equation is
y = 64.7 - 1.75 x

Predictor      Coef   SE Coef       T      P
Constant     64.672     6.762    9.56  0.000
x           -1.7487     0.2995  -5.84  0.000


S = 2.38785   R-Sq = 81.0%   R-Sq(adj) = 78.6%

Analysis of Variance

Source           DF       SS       MS      F      P
Regression        1   194.45   194.45  34.10  0.000
Residual Error    8    45.61     5.70
Total             9   240.06

Predicted Values for New Observations

New
Obs     Fit   SE Fit        95% CI              95% PI
  1  25.500    0.755  (23.758, 27.241)  (19.725, 31.275)
  2  11.510    2.500  ( 5.744, 17.276)  ( 3.537, 19.483)XX

XX denotes a point that is an extreme outlier in the predictors.

Values of Predictors for New Observations

New
Obs     x
  1   22.4
  2   30.4
```

SOLUTION For $x_{n+1} = 22.4$, the first of the two "Fit" entries shows a predicted value equal to 25.5. The confidence interval is shown as 23.758 to 27.241. For $x_{n+1} = 30.4$, the predicted value is 11.51, with a confidence interval of 5.744 to 17.276. The second interval has a width of about 11.5, much larger than the first interval's width of about 3.5. The value $x_{n+1} = 30.4$ is far outside the range of x data; the extrapolation penalty makes the interval very wide.

Usually the more relevant forecasting problem is that of predicting an individual Y_{n+1} value rather than $E(Y|X = x_{n+1})$. In most computer packages, the interval for predicting an individual value is called a **prediction interval.** The same best-guess $\hat{y}_{n+1}$ is used, but the forecasting plus-or-minus term is larger when predicting Y_{n+1} rather than $E(Y|X = x_{n+1})$. In fact, it can be shown that the plus-or-minus forecasting error using $\hat{y}_{n+1}$ to predict Y_{n+1} is as follows.

prediction interval

DEFINITION 11.8

Prediction Interval for Y_{n+1}

$$\hat{y}_{n+1} - t_{\alpha/2}s_\epsilon \sqrt{1 + \frac{1}{n} + \frac{(x_{n+1} - \bar{x})^2}{S_{xx}}} \le Y_{n+1}$$

$$\le \hat{y}_{n+1} + t_{\alpha/2}s_\epsilon \sqrt{1 + \frac{1}{n} + \frac{(x_{n+1} - \bar{x})^2}{S_{xx}}}$$

where $t_{\alpha/2}$ cuts off area $\alpha/2$ in the right tail of the t distribution with $n - 2$ d.f.

In the road resurfacing example, the corresponding 95% prediction limits for Y_{n+1} when $x = 6$ are 5.58 to 34.42, as shown in the following Minitab output. The 95% intervals for $E(Y|X = x_{n+1})$, and for Y_{n+1} are shown in Figure 11.19; the inner curves are for $E(Y|X = x_{n+1})$, the outer ones for Y_{n+1}.

```
Regression Analysis: Cost versus Mileage

The regression equation is
Cost = 2.00 + 3.00 Mileage

Predictor     Coef   SE Coef      T      P
Constant     2.000     3.830   0.52  0.638
Mileage      3.0000    0.8563   3.50  0.039

S = 3.82970    R-Sq = 80.4%    R-Sq(adj) = 73.8%

Analysis of Variance

Source            DF       SS       MS      F      P
Regression         1   180.00   180.00  12.27  0.039
Residual Error     3    44.00    14.67
Total              4   224.00

Predicted Values for New Observations

New
Obs    Fit   SE Fit       95% CI            95% PI
  1  20.00     2.42  (12.29, 27.71)   (5.58, 34.42)

Values of Predictors for New Observations

New
Obs  Mileage
  1     6.00
```

FIGURE 11.19   **Scatterplot with Fitted Line and 95% Confidence and Prediction Limits**

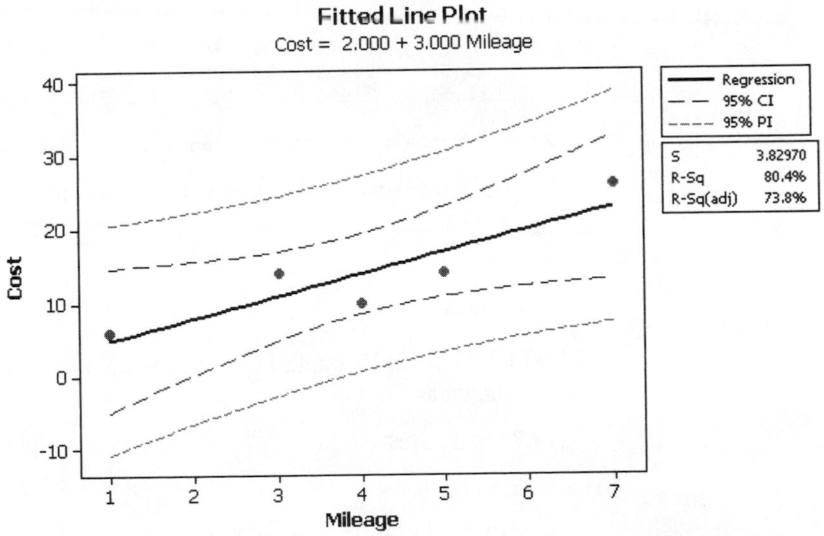

The only difference between prediction of a mean $E(Y|X = x_{n+1})$ and prediction of an individual Y_{n+1} is the term "1+" in the standard error formula. The presence of this extra term indicates that predictions of individual values are less accurate than predictions of means. The extrapolation penalty term still applies, as does the warning that it understates the risk of extrapolation. If n is large and the extrapolation term is small, the "1+" term dominates the square root factor in the prediction interval. In such cases the interval becomes, approximately, $\hat{y}_{n+1} - t_{\alpha/2}s_\epsilon \leq Y_{n+1} \leq \hat{y}_{n+1} + t_{\alpha/2}s_\epsilon$. Thus for large n, roughly 68% of the residuals (forecast errors) are less than $\pm 1s_\epsilon$ and 95% less than $\pm 2s_\epsilon$. There isn't much point in devising rules for when to ignore the other terms in the square root factor. They are normally calculated in computer output and it does no harm to include them.

EXAMPLE 11.10

Using the output of Example 11.9 reproduced here, find a 95% prediction interval for Y_{n+1} with $x_{n+1} = 22.4$, and find the interval with $x_{n+1} = 30.4$. Compare these to widths estimated by the preceding $\pm 2s_\epsilon$ rules.

```
Regression Analysis: y versus x

The regression equation is
y = 64.7 - 1.75 x

Predictor      Coef   SE Coef        T      P
Constant     64.672     6.762     9.56  0.000
x           -1.7487     0.2995    -5.84  0.000

S = 2.38785    R-Sq = 81.0%    R-Sq(adj) = 78.6%

Analysis of Variance

Source           DF       SS       MS       F      P
Regression        1   194.45   194.45   34.10  0.000
Residual Error    8    45.61     5.70
Total             9   240.06

Predicted Values for New Observations

New
Obs     Fit  SE Fit         95% CI             95% PI
  1  25.500   0.755  (23.758, 27.241)  (19.725, 31.275)
  2  11.510   2.500  ( 5.744, 17.276)  ( 3.537, 19.483)XX

XX denotes a point that is an extreme outlier in the predictors.

Values of Predictors for New Observations

New
Obs      x
  1   22.4
  2   30.4
```

SOLUTION As in Example 11.9, $\hat{y}_{n+1} = 25.5$ if $x_{n+1} = 22.4$. The prediction interval is shown as

$$19.73 \leq Y_{n+1} \leq 31.28$$

The $\pm 2s_\epsilon$ range is

$$25.5 - (2)(2.388) \leq Y_{n+1} \leq 25.5 + (2)(2.388) \qquad \text{or} \qquad 20.72 \leq Y_{n+1} \leq 30.28$$

The latter interval is a bit too narrow, mostly because the tabled t value with only 8 d.f. is quite a bit larger than 2.

For $x_{n+1} = 30.4$, $\hat{y}_{n+1} = 11.51$, the 95% prediction interval is

$$3.54 \leq Y_{n+1} \leq 19.48$$

The $\pm 2s_e$ range is

$$11.5 - (2)(2.388) \leq Y_{n+1} \leq 11.5 + (2)(2.388) \quad \text{or} \quad 6.72 \leq Y_{n+1} \leq 16.28$$

The latter is much too narrow. Not only is the tabled *t* value larger than 2 but also the large extrapolation penalty is not reflected. The output labels this prediction XX and notes that the *x* value used is far from the data. Be warned.

Exercises

11.16   A heating contractor sends a repairperson to homes in response to calls about heating problems. The contractor would like to have a way to estimate how long the customer will have to wait before the repairperson can begin work. Data on the number of minutes of waiting time (Wait Time) and the backlog of previous calls waiting for service (Backlog) were obtained. A scatterplot and a regression analysis of the data, obtained from JMP, are shown in Figure 11.20 (see next page).

a. Calculate the predicted value and an approximate 95% prediction interval for the time to respond to a call when the backlog is 6. Neglect the extrapolation penalty.

b. If we had calculated the extrapolation penalty, would it most likely be very small?

c. Is the calculated prediction interval likely to be too narrow or too wide?

11.17   Here is some Minitab output related to Exercise 11.16.

```
Regression Analysis: Wait Time versus Backlog

The regression equation is
Wait Time = 23.8 + 48.1 Backlog

Predictor    Coef   SE Coef     T      P
Constant    23.82    24.72   0.96  0.339
Backlog     48.13    11.02   4.37  0.000

S = 107.366   R-Sq = 24.1%   R-Sq(adj) = 22.9%

Analysis of Variance

Source          DF       SS      MS      F      P
Regression       1   220008  220008  19.09  0.000
Residual Error  60   691661   11528
Total           61   911670

Unusual Observations

Obs  Backlog  Wait Time    Fit  SE Fit  Residual  St Resid
  7     3.00      470.0  168.2    18.5     301.8     2.85R
  8     4.00      540.0  216.3    27.1     323.7     3.12R
 27     2.00      370.0  120.1    13.7     249.9     2.35R
 29     3.00      450.0  168.2    18.5     281.8     2.66R

R denotes an observation with a large standardized residual.
```

FIGURE 11.20 Analysis of Waiting Time Data

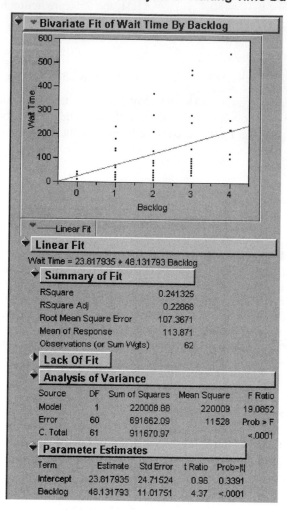

Predicted Values for New Observations

```
New Obs   Fit   SE Fit      95% CI            95% PI
   1     71.9   16.7   (38.6, 105.3)   (-145.4, 289.3)
```

Values of Predictors for New Observations

```
New Obs   Backlog
   1        1.00
```

Regression Analysis: log(Wait Time) versus Backlog

```
The regression equation is
log(Wait Time) = 1.47 + 0.194 Backlog

Predictor     Coef   SE Coef      T        P
Constant   1.47007   0.08999   16.34   0.000
Backlog    0.19399   0.04011    4.84   0.000

S = 0.390956   R-Sq = 28.0%   R-Sq(adj) = 26.8%
```

```
Analysis of Variance

Source           DF      SS      MS      F      P
Regression        1   3.5744  3.5744  23.39  0.000
Residual Error   60   9.1708  0.1528
Total            61  12.7451
```

```
Unusual Observations

               log(Wait
Obs  Backlog    Time)    Fit   SE Fit  Residual  St Resid
 21    2.00    1.0000  1.8581  0.0499   -0.8581    -2.21R
 54    2.00    1.0000  1.8581  0.0499   -0.8581    -2.21R
```

R denotes an observation with a large standardized residual.

```
Predicted Values for New Observations

New Obs    Fit   SE Fit      95% CI             95% PI
   1    1.6641  0.0607  (1.5426, 1.7855)  (0.8727, 2.4555)
```

```
Values of Predictors for New Observations

New Obs  Backlog
   1       1.00
```

a. If the model with Wait Time as a linear function of Backlog is adopted, what is the predicted Wait Time when the Backlog is 1?

b. If the model with the base-10 logarithm of Wait Time as a linear function of Backlog is adopted, what is the predicted Wait Time when the Backlog is 1?

c. Which of the two predictions seems more reasonable (or perhaps less unreasonable)? Explain why.

d. Give a 95% prediction interval (in minutes) for the prediction you selected in part (c).

11.18   Refer to the output of Exercise 11.15 reproduced here in part.

```
New Obs    Fit   SE Fit      95% CI             95% PI
   1    203.61   2.30  (198.90, 208.32)  (178.17, 229.06)
```

```
Values of Predictors for New Observations
New Obs  RunSize
   1       2.00
```

a. Predict the mean total direct cost for all bumper sticker orders with a print run of 2000 stickers (that is, with Runsize = 2.0).

b. Locate a 95% confidence interval for this mean.

11.19   Does the prediction in Exercise 11.18 represent a major extrapolation?

11.20   Refer to Exercise 11.18.

a. Predict the total direct cost for a particular bumper sticker order with a print run of 2000 stickers. Obtain a 95% prediction interval.

b. Would an actual total direct cost of $250 be surprising for this order?

11.21   Refer to the data of Exercise 11.2.

```
Regression Analysis: y versus x

The regression equation is
y = 14.3 + 1.47 x

Predictor     Coef   SE Coef      T      P
Constant   14.2916   0.7962   17.95  0.000
x           1.4750   0.1737    8.49  0.000

S = 1.34579   R-Sq = 87.8%   R-Sq(adj) = 86.6%
```

```
Predicted Values for New Observations
New Obs     Fit  SE Fit        95% CI              95% PI
   1     43.792   2.807   (37.538, 50.046)   (36.856, 50.727)XX

XX denotes a point that is an extreme outlier in the predictors.

Values of Predictors for New Observations
New Obs      x
   1      20.0
```

Regression Analysis: y versus log x

The regression equation is
y = 14.9 + 10.5 log x

```
Predictor      Coef  SE Coef       T      P
Constant    14.8754   0.6106   24.36  0.000
log x        10.522    1.021   10.30  0.000

S = 1.13118    R-Sq = 91.4%    R-Sq(adj) = 90.5%
```

```
Predicted Values for New Observations
New Obs       Fit  SE Fit        95% CI                95% PI
   1      225.310  19.910   (180.948, 269.672)   (180.877, 269.743)XX

XX denotes a point that is an extreme outlier in the predictors.

Values of Predictors for New Observations
New Obs   log x
   1       20.0
```

a. If the model with Y a linear function of x is adopted, what is the predicted Y when $x = 20$?
b. If the model with Y a linear function of $x' = \log_{10}x$ is adopted, what is the predicted value of Y when $x = 20$?
c. Which of the two predictions seems more reasonable (or perhaps less unreasonable)?
d. Explain how to correct the "unreasonable" prediction within Minitab.

11.22 Give a 95% prediction interval for the prediction you selected in the preceding exercise.

11.5 Correlation

Once we've found the prediction line, we need to measure how well it predicts actual values. One way to do so is to look at the size of the residual standard deviation in the context of the problem. About 95% of all errors will be within $\pm 2s_\epsilon$. For example, suppose we are trying to predict the yield of a chemical process, where yields range from .50 to .94. If a regression model had a residual standard deviation of $s_\epsilon = .01$, we could predict most yields within $\pm.02$, fairly accurate in context. But if the residual standard deviation were $s_\epsilon = .08$, we could predict most yields within $\pm.16$, which isn't very impressive given that the yield range is only $.94 - .50 = .44$. But this approach requires that we know the context of the study well; an alternative, more general approach is based on the idea of correlation.

Suppose that we compare the squared prediction error for two prediction methods—one using the regression model, the other ignoring the model and always predicting the mean y value. In the road resurfacing example, if we are given the mileage values x_i, we could use the prediction equation $\hat{y}_i = 2.0 + 3.0x_i$ to predict costs. The deviations of actual values from predicted values, the residuals, measure prediction errors. These errors are summarized by the sum of squared residuals SS(Residual) $= \sum (y_i - \hat{y}_i)^2$, which is 44 for these data. For comparison, if we were not given the x_i values, the best squared error predictor of y would be the mean value $\bar{y} = 14$, and the sum of squared prediction errors would, in this case, be $\sum_i (y_i - \bar{y}_i)^2 =$ SS(Total) $= 224$. The proportionate reduction in error would be

$$\frac{\text{SS(Total)} - \text{SS(Residual)}}{\text{SS(Total)}} = \frac{224 - 44}{224} = .804$$

In words, use of the regression model reduces squared prediction error by 80.4%, which indicates a fairly strong relation between the mileage to be resurfaced and the cost of resurfacing.

correlation coefficient   This proportionate reduction in error is closely related to the **correlation coefficient** of x and y. *A correlation measures the strength of the linear relation between x and y.* The stronger the correlation, the better x predicts y. The mathematical definition of the correlation coefficient, denoted r_{yx}, is

$$r_{yx} = \frac{S_{xy}}{\sqrt{S_{xx}S_{yy}}}$$

where S_{xy} and S_{xx} are defined as before and

$$S_{yy} = \sum_i (y_i - \bar{y})^2 = \text{SS(Total)}$$

In the example,

$$r_{yx} = \frac{60}{\sqrt{(20)(224)}} = .896$$

Generally, the correlation r_{yx} is a positive number if y tends to increase as x increases; r_{yx} is negative if y tends to decrease as x increases; and r_{yx} is zero if either there is no relation between changes in x and changes in y, or there is a nonlinear relation such that patterns of increase and decrease in y (as x increases) cancel each other.

EXAMPLE 11.11   Consider the following data:

$$y: \quad 25 \quad 41 \quad 47 \quad 59 \quad 54 \quad 56 \quad 49 \quad 43 \quad 30$$
$$x: \quad 10 \quad 20 \quad 20 \quad 30 \quad 30 \quad 30 \quad 40 \quad 40 \quad 50$$

a.   Should the correlation be positive or negative?

b.   Calculate the correlation.

SOLUTION

a.   Notice that as x increases from 10 to 50, y first increases, then decreases. Therefore, the correlation should be small. The y values don't decrease quite back to where they started, so the correlation should be positive.

b.   By easy calculation, the sample means are $\bar{x} = 30.0000$ and $\bar{y} = 44.8889$.

$$S_{xx} = (10 - 30.0000)^2 + \cdots + (50 - 30.0000)^2 = 1200$$
$$S_{yy} = (25 - 44.8889)^2 + \cdots + (30 - 44.8889)^2 = 1062.8889$$
$$S_{xy} = (10 - 30.0000)(25 - 44.8889)$$
$$+ \cdots + (50 - 30.0000)(30 - 44.8889) = 140$$

$$r_{yx} = \frac{140}{\sqrt{(1200)(1062.8889)}} = .1240$$

The correlation is indeed a small positive number.

**coefficient of
determination**

Correlation and regression predictability are closely related. The proportionate reduction in error for regression we defined earlier is called the **coefficient of determination.** The coefficient of determination is simply the square of the correlation coefficient,

$$r_{yx}^2 = \frac{\text{SS(Total)} - \text{SS(Residual)}}{\text{SS(Total)}}$$

which is the proportionate reduction in error. In the resurfacing example, $r_{yx} = .896$ and $r_{yx}^2 = .804$.

A correlation of zero indicates no predictive value in using the equation $y = \hat{\beta}_0 + \hat{\beta}_1 x$; that is, one can predict y as well without knowing x as one can knowing x. A correlation of 1 or -1 indicates perfect predictability—a 100% reduction in error attributable to knowledge of x. A correlation coefficient should routinely be interpreted in terms of its squared value, the coefficient of determination. Thus, a correlation of $-.3$, say, indicates only a 9% reduction in squared prediction error. Many books and most computer programs use the equation

$$\text{SS(Total)} = \text{SS(Residual)} + \text{SS(Regression)}$$

where

$$\text{SS(Regression)} = \sum_i (\hat{y}_i - \bar{y})^2$$

Because the equation can be expressed as $\text{SS(Residual)} = (1 - r_{yx}^2)\text{SS(Total)}$, it follows that $\text{SS(Regression)} = r_{yx}^2\text{SS(Total)}$, which again says that regression on x explains a proportion r_{yx}^2 of the total squared error of y.

EXAMPLE 11.12   Find SS(Total), SS(Regression), and SS(Residual) for the data of Example 11.11.

SOLUTION $\text{SS(Total)} = S_{yy}$, which we computed to be 1062.8889 in Example 11.11. We also found that $r_{yx} = .1240$, so $r_{yx}^2 = (.1240)^2 = .015376$. Using the fact that $\text{SS(Regression)} = r_{yx}^2 \, \text{SS(Total)}$, we have $\text{SS(Regression)} = (.015376)(1062.8889) = 16.3430$. Because $\text{SS(Residual)} = \text{SS(Total)} - \text{SS(Regression)}$, $\text{SS(Residual)} = 1062.8889 - 16.3430 = 1046.5459$.

Note that SS(Regression) and r_{yx}^2 are very small. This suggests that x is not a good predictor of y. The reality, though, is that the relation between x and y is extremely nonlinear. A *linear* equation in x does not predict y very well, but a nonlinear equation would do far better.

The sample correlation r_{yx} is the basis for estimation and significance testing of the population correlation ρ_{yx}. Statistical inferences are always based on assumptions. The assumptions of regression analysis—linear relation between x and y, and constant variance around the regression line, in particular—are also **assumptions for correlation inference.** In regression analysis, we regard the x values as predetermined constants. In correlation analysis, we regard the x values as randomly selected (and the regression inferences are conditional on the sampled x values). If the x's are not drawn randomly, it is possible that the correlation estimates are biased. In some texts, the additional assumption is made that the x values are drawn from a normal population. The inferences we make do not depend crucially on this normality assumption.

assumptions for correlation inference

The most basic inference problem is potential bias in estimation of ρ_{yx}. A problem arises when the x values are predetermined, as often happens in regression analysis. The choice of x values can systematically increase or decrease the sample correlation. In general, a wide range of x values tends to increase the magnitude of the correlation coefficient, and a small range to decrease it. This effect is shown in Figure 11.21. If all the points in this scatterplot are included, there is an obvious, strong correlation between x and y. But suppose we consider only x values in the range between the dashed vertical lines. By eliminating the outside parts of the scatter diagram, the sample correlation coefficient (and the coefficient of determination) are much smaller. Correlation coefficients can be affected by systematic choices of

FIGURE 11.21   **Effect of Limited *x* Range on Sample Correlation Coefficient**

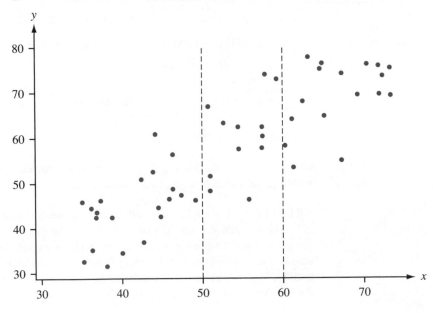

x values; the residual standard deviation is *not* affected systematically, though it may change randomly if part of the *x* range changes. Thus it's a good idea to consider the residual standard deviation s_ϵ and the magnitude of the slope when you decide how well a linear regression line predicts *y*.

EXAMPLE 11.13   Suppose that a company has the following data and Minitab output on productivity *y* and aptitude test score *x* for 12 data-entry operators:

y: 41   39   47   51   43   40   57   46   50   59   61   52
x: 24   30   33   35   36   36   37   37   38   40   43   49

```
Regression Analysis: y versus x

The regression equation is
y = 20.5 + 0.775 x

Predictor     Coef   SE Coef      T      P
Constant     20.54     10.73   1.92  0.084
x           0.7752    0.2900   2.67  0.023

S = 5.99235    R-Sq = 41.7%    R-Sq(adj) = 35.8%

Analysis of Variance
Source          DF       SS       MS      F      P
Regression       1   256.58   256.58   7.15  0.023
Residual Error  10   359.08    35.91
Total           11   615.67

Pearson correlation of y and x = 0.646

Regression Analysis: y(x>=37) versus x(x>=37)

The regression equation is
y(x>=37) = 44.7 + 0.232 x(x>=37)

Predictor     Coef   SE Coef      T      P
Constant     44.74     24.81   1.80  0.146
x(x>=37)    0.2317    0.6067   0.38  0.722

S = 6.34356    R-Sq = 3.5%    R-Sq(adj) = 0.0%

Analysis of Variance
Source          DF       SS       MS      F      P
Regression       1     5.87     5.87   0.15  0.722
Residual Error   4   160.96    40.24
Total            5   166.83

Pearson correlation of y(x>=37) and x(x>=37) = 0.188
```

Compare the correlation for all 12 scores to the correlation for the subset of scores with *x* greater than or equal to 37. Do the same for the residual standard deviations.

SOLUTION   For all 12 observations, the output shows a correlation coefficient of .646; the residual standard deviation is 5.992. For the six highest *x* scores, shown as the subset having *x* greater than or equal to 37, the correlation is .188 and the residual standard deviation is 6.344. In going from all 12 observations to the 6 observations with the highest *x* values, the correlation has decreased drastically but the residual standard deviation has hardly changed at all.

Just as it is possible to test the null hypothesis that a true slope is zero, we can also test H_0: $\rho_{yx} = 0$.

DEFINITION 11.9

Test of H_0: Correlation = 0

H_0: $\rho_{yx} = 0$

H_a: 1. $\rho_{yx} > 0$
     2. $\rho_{yx} < 0$
     3. $\rho_{yx} \neq 0$

T.S.: $t = r_{yx} \dfrac{\sqrt{n-2}}{\sqrt{1 - r_{yx}^2}}$

R.R.: With $n - 2$ d.f. and Type I error probability α,
     1. $t > t_\alpha$
     2. $t < -t_\alpha$
     3. $|t| > t_{\alpha/2}$

We tested the hypothesis that the true slope is zero (in predicting resurfacing cost from mileage) in Example 11.5; the resulting t statistic was 3.50. For that data, we can calculate r_{yx} as .896421 and r_{yx}^2 as .803571. Hence, the correlation t statistic is

$$\frac{.896\sqrt{3}}{\sqrt{1 - .803571}} = 3.50$$

In general, the t tests for a slope and for a correlation give identical results; it doesn't matter which form is used. It follows that the t test is valid for any choice of x values. The bias we mentioned previously does not affect the sign of the correlation.

EXAMPLE 11.14

Perform t tests for the null hypothesis of zero correlation and zero slope for the data of Example 11.13 (all observations). Use an appropriate one-sided alternative.

SOLUTION   First, the appropriate H_a ought to be $\rho_{yx} > 0$ (and therefore $\beta_1 > 0$). It would be nice if an aptitude test had a positive correlation with the productivity score it was predicting! In Example 11.13 $n = 12$, $r_{yx} = .646$, and

$$t = .\frac{646\sqrt{12 - 2}}{\sqrt{1 - (.646)^2}} = 2.68$$

Because this value falls between the tabled t values for d.f. = 10, $\alpha = .025$ (2.228) and for d.f. = 10, $\alpha = .01$ (2.764), the p-value lies between .010 and .025. Hence, H_0 may be rejected.

The t statistic for testing the slope β_1 is shown in the output of Example 11.13 as 2.67, which equals (to within round-off error) the correlation t statistic, 2.68.

The test for a correlation provides a neat illustration of the difference between statistical significance and statistical importance. Suppose that a psychologist has devised a skills test for production line workers and tests it on a huge sample of

40,000 workers. If the sample correlation between test score and actual productivity is .02, then

$$t = \frac{.02\sqrt{39,998}}{\sqrt{1 - (.02)^2}} = 4.0$$

We would reject the null hypothesis at any reasonable α level, so the correlation is "statistically significant." However, the test accounts for only $(.02)^2 = .0004$ of the squared error in skill scores, so it is *almost* worthless as a predictor. Remember, the rejection of the null hypothesis in a statistical test is the conclusion that the sample results cannot plausibly have occurred by chance if the null hypothesis is true. The test itself does not address the practical significance of the result. Clearly, for a sample size of 40,000, even a trivial sample correlation like .02 is not likely to occur by mere luck of the draw. There is no practically meaningful relationship between these test scores and productivity scores in this example.

Exercises

11.23   The output of Exercise 11.5 is reproduced here. Calculate the correlation coefficient r_{yx} from the R-square (r_{yx}^2) value. Should its sign be positive or negative?

```
Regression Analysis: Branches versus Business

The regression equation is
Branches = 1.77 + 0.0111 Business

Predictor        Coef     SE Coef        T       P
Constant       1.7668      0.3212     5.50   0.000
Business    0.0111049   0.0008453    13.14   0.000

S = 0.558299    R-Sq = 94.5%    R-Sq(adj) = 94.0%

Analysis of Variance

Source            DF      SS       MS       F        P
Regression         1   53.800   53.800   172.60   0.000
Residual Error    10    3.117    0.312
Total             11   56.917
```

11.24   Refer to the Minitab output in Exercise 11.23.
a. Test the hypothesis of no true correlation between x and y. Use a one-sided H_a and $\alpha = .05$.
b. Compare the result of this test to the t test of the slope found in the output.

11.25   Refer to the computer output of Exercise 11.15 as reproduced here.

```
Regression Analysis: TotalCost versus RunSize

The regression equation is
TotalCost = 99.8 + 51.9 RunSize

Predictor      Coef   SE Coef       T       P
Constant     99.777     2.827   35.29   0.000
RunSize     51.9178     0.5865   88.53   0.000

S = 12.2064    R-Sq = 99.6%    R-Sq(adj) = 99.6%
```

```
Analysis of Variance

Source            DF      SS       MS        F       P
Regression         1   1167747  1167747  7837.25  0.000
Residual Error    28      4172      149
Total             29   1171919
```

a. Locate r_{yx}^2. How is its very large value reflected in the sum of squares shown in the output?

b. The estimated slope $\hat{\beta}_1$ is positive; what must be the sign of the sample correlation coefficient?

c. Suppose that the study in Exercise 11.15 had been restricted to RunSize values less than 1.8. Would you anticipate a larger or smaller r_{yx} value?

11.26 Suppose that an advertising campaign for a new product is conducted in 10 test cities. The intensity of the advertising x, measured as the number of exposures per evening of prime time television, is varied across cities; the awareness percentage y is found by survey after the ad campaign.

x:	4.0	4.5	5.0	5.5	6.0	6.5	7.0	7.5	8.0	8.5
y:	10.1	10.3	10.4	21.7	36.7	51.5	67.0	68.5	68.2	69.3

```
Correlations: Intensity, Awareness
Pearson correlation of Intensity and Awareness = 0.956
```

a. Interpret the correlation coefficient r_{yx}.

b. Plot the data. Does the relation appear linear to you? Does it appear to be generally increasing?

11.27 A survey of recent M.B.A. graduates of a business school obtained data on first-year salary (in thousands of dollars) and years of prior work experience. Consider the data:

Case	Experience	Salary	Case	Experience	Salary
1	8	53.9	27	7	51.7
2	5	52.5	28	9	56.2
3	5	49.0	29	6	48.9
4	11	65.1	30	6	51.9
5	4	51.6	31	4	36.1
6	3	52.7	32	6	53.5
7	3	44.5	33	5	50.4
8	3	40.1	34	1	38.7
9	0	41.1	35	13	60.1
10	13	66.9	36	1	38.9
11	14	37.9	37	6	48.4
12	10	53.5	38	2	50.6
13	2	38.3	39	4	41.8
14	2	37.2	40	1	44.4
15	5	51.3	41	5	46.6
16	13	64.7	42	1	43.9
17	1	45.3	43	4	45.0
18	5	47.0	44	1	37.9
19	1	43.8	45	2	44.6
20	5	47.4	46	7	46.9
21	5	40.2	47	5	47.6
22	7	52.8	48	1	43.2
23	4	40.7	49	1	41.6
24	3	47.3	50	0	39.2
25	3	43.7	51	1	41.7
26	7	61.8			

a. By scanning the numbers, can you sense that there is a relationship between Experience and Salary? In particular, does it appear that those with less experience have smaller salaries?

b. Plot the data in a scatterplot. Can you notice any cases that seem to fall outside the pattern of the data?

11.28 Minitab computed a regression equation from the data in Exercise 11.27 with Salary as the dependent variable and Experience as the independent variable. A portion of the output is shown here.

```
Regression Analysis: Salary versus Experience

The regression equation is
Salary = 40.5 + 1.47 Experience

Predictor      Coef   SE Coef      T      P
Constant     40.507     1.257  32.22  0.000
Experience   1.4698    0.2125   6.92  0.000

S = 5.40193   R-Sq = 49.4%   R-Sq(adj) = 48.4%

Analysis of Variance

Source          DF       SS      MS      F      P
Regression       1   1396.0  1396.0  47.84  0.000
Residual Error  49   1429.9    29.2
Total           50   2825.8

Unusual Observations

Obs  Experience  Salary     Fit  SE Fit  Residual  St Resid
 10        13.0  66.900  59.615   1.914     7.285    1.44 X
 11        14.0  37.900  61.085   2.111   -23.185   -4.66RX
 16        13.0  64.700  59.615   1.914     5.085    1.01 X
 26         7.0  61.800  50.796   0.898    11.004    2.07R
 35        13.0  60.100  59.615   1.914     0.485    0.10 X

R denotes an observation with a large standardized residual.
X denotes an observation whose X value gives it large influence.
```

a. Write out the prediction equation. Interpret the coefficients. Is the constant term (intercept) meaningful in this context?

b. Locate the residual standard deviation. Interpret this value in the context and wording of the problem.

c. Is the apparent relationship statistically detectable (significant)?

d. How much of the variability in salaries is accounted for by variation in years of prior work experience?

11.29 The 11th person in the data of Exercise 11.27 went to work for a family business in return for a low salary but a large equity in the firm. This case was removed from the data and the results were reanalyzed in Minitab. A portion of the output follows:

```
Regression Analysis: Salary_11 versus Experience_11

The regression equation is
Salary_11 = 39.2 + 1.86 Experience_11

Predictor         Coef   SE Coef      T      P
Constant       39.1877    0.9711  40.35  0.000
Experience_11   1.8626    0.1723  10.81  0.000
```

```
S = 4.07080   R-Sq = 70.9%   R-Sq(adj) = 70.3%
```

Analysis of Variance

Source	DF	SS	MS	F	P
Regression	1	1937.3	1937.3	116.91	0.000
Residual Error	48	795.4	16.6		
Total	49	2732.7			

Unusual Observations

Obs	Experience_11	Salary_11	Fit	SE Fit	Residual	St Resid
10	13.0	66.900	63.402	1.567	3.498	0.93 X
15	13.0	64.700	63.402	1.567	1.298	0.35 X
20	5.0	40.200	48.501	0.581	-8.301	-2.06R
25	7.0	61.800	52.226	0.715	9.574	2.39R
30	4.0	36.100	46.638	0.583	-10.538	-2.62R
34	13.0	60.100	63.402	1.567	-3.302	-0.88 X

R denotes an observation with a large standardized residual.
X denotes an observation whose X value gives it large influence.

a. Should removing the high-influence point in the plot increase or decrease the slope? Did it?

b. In which direction (larger or smaller) should the removal of this point change the residual standard deviation? Did it? How large was the change?

c. How should the removal of this point change the correlation? How large was this change?

11.30 Quantum Computing, Inc. sells specialized computer hardware to certain high-tech businesses. Quantum's sales force is located in various areas around the country. Each salesperson is in charge of selling Quantum products in his or her individual territory. The director of marketing at Quantum is interested in analyzing sales performance in the territories, primarily for promotion, raise, and bonus decisions. To begin her analysis, she randomly selected 120 salespeople from the entire force and determined their annual sales (in millions of dollars) for last year. She also measured the potential of each territory by estimating the number of businesses in the territory that were current or potential customers of Quantum products. Some Minitab output from her analysis is shown here.

```
Regression Analysis: Sales versus Potential
```

The regression equation is
Sales = 18.0 + 0.236 Potential

Predictor	Coef	SE Coef	T	P
Constant	17.972	1.113	16.14	0.000
Potential	0.23571	0.01539	a	0.000

```
S = 4.019     R-sq = __b__ %    R-sq(adj) = 66.2%
```

Analysis of Variance

Source	DF	SS	MS	F	P
Regression	1	3787.6	3787.6	c	0.000
Error	118	1905.6	16.1		
Total	119	5693.2			

Unusual Observations

Obs	Potential	Sales	Fit	SE Fit	Residual	St Resid
6	136	46.200	d	1.105	e	-0.99X
10	48	37.800	29.286	0.482	8.514	2.13R
25	179	63.900	60.164	1.743	3.736	1.03 X
33	85	28.400	38.007	0.448	-9.607	-2.41R
50	67	42.600	33.764	0.367	8.836	2.21R

```
   79          62       40.700      32.586      0.379       8.114       2.03R
   97         122       44.600      46.728      0.904      -2.128      -0.54 X
  110         146       50.600      52.385      1.251      -1.785      -0.47 X
```

R denotes an observation with a large standardized residual.
X denotes an observation whose X value gives it large influence.

Use this output to answer the following questions:

a. Fill in the blanks for the five missing items in the output (a–e).

b. Provide a meaningful interpretation of the coefficient .236 in the regression equation in the language of the problem.

c. Construct a 95% confidence interval for the slope of the regression line. What conclusion can be drawn from this interval about sales and territory potential? Why?

d. Give an interpretation of the value of R-sq in the language of the problem.

e. Based on the output, which salesperson appears to be performing best? Worst? Explain your reasoning.

BUSINESS DECISION-MAKING IN ACTION

CHAPTER CASE

ANALYSIS

Ryder Appraisal District

James Bradford, the new tax commissioner of Ryder County, has decided to make property taxation more equitable and less costly to carry out by going to a simplified system, a flat amount plus an amount based on the square footage of heated/cooled floor space in houses on improved properties. Both the flat and variable tax rates are to be determined. Bradford has decided to maintain the current homestead and retirement exemptions: If the owner of the property lives there, a homestead exemption reduces the property tax bill by 10%; if the owner is retired, a retirement exemption reduces the property tax bill by 10%. There is a 20% reduction if both exemptions apply. For all unimproved residential properties, the tax rate will remain at the current $150 per lot.

In switching to the new system, the size of the changes in property taxes for individual owners should be as small as possible. The new tax plan must also be revenue neutral, that is, the total amount of property taxes under the new structure should be roughly the same as under the current system. A second issue concerns the square footage values recorded in the RAD database. In most cases, the builder reports square footage but the Ryder Appraisal District (RAD) never checks the figure. Bradford suspects that these data may not be accurate, but he does not want to undertake measuring every house until he has evidence that it is necessary.

As the first step in solving both problems, Bradford selected a random sample of 80 residential properties from around the county and had the staff appraiser accurately measure the square footage of these houses.

Bradford has asked you, his deputy commissioner, to do two things. First, he wants to know whether or not the square footage estimates in the current RAD database differ significantly from the actual square footage values. Second, he wants you to estimate the flat tax amount and the tax rate per square foot that must be charged under the new tax system.

The following Minitab output provides numerical summaries of the main quantitative and categorical variables in the data set:

```
Descriptive Statistics: Recorded Sqft, Actual Sqft, Current Tax

Variable        N    Mean   StDev  Minimum      Q1  Median      Q3  Maximum
Recorded Sqft  80  1788.7   405.9      0.0  1713.3  1817.5  2003.5   2376.0
Actual Sqft    80  1790.5   403.1      0.0  1704.3  1832.0  1985.8   2313.0
Current Tax    80  1083.3   217.5    150.0  1039.0  1105.7  1184.0   1587.3


Tally for Discrete Variables: Improved

Improved  Count
       0      3
       1     77
      N=     80


Tabulated Statistics: Homestead, Retired

Rows: Homestead   Columns: Retired

        0   1  All

0      14   1   15
1      56   9   65
All    70  10   80


Cell Contents:       Count
```

From the output, we note that the average recorded square footage for the 80 homes is not much different from the average actual square footage. Also note that there are 3 unimproved properties in the data set (properties with no houses built on them). Before proceeding, we should remove these 3 observations from the data because (1) we are primarily interested in improved properties and (2) we know that unimproved properties (empty lots) will continue to be assessed a flat tax of $150 per year. A scatterplot of Current Tax versus Recorded Sqft (not shown here) also reveals that the 3 empty lots do not follow the linear pattern of the rest of the properties and could dramatically influence the analysis for improved properties. For the remainder of our analysis, we will omit these 3 observations from the data.

We first consider the issue of the accuracy of the recorded square footage values in the RAD database of 12,000 properties. For the 77 improved properties in the sample, we can examine a scatterplot of Actual Sqft versus Recorded Sqft, as shown in Figure 11.22, to assess the accuracy of the Recorded Sqft values.

Another approach to seeing whether or not actual square footages differ significantly from recorded square footages in the RAD database is performing a paired-difference analysis of the actual and recorded square footage values for the 77 sampled properties, as shown in the Minitab output here and in Figure 11.23.

```
Paired T for Actual Sqft - Recorded Sqft

                N      Mean     StDev   SE Mean
Actual Sqft    77   1860.26    193.52     22.05
Recorded Sqft  77   1858.34    200.09     22.80
Difference     77   1.92207  37.31790   4.25276

95% CI for mean difference: (-6.54804, 10.39220)

T-Test of mean difference = 0 (vs not = 0): T-Value = 0.45   P-Value = 0.653
```

FIGURE 11.22   **Scatterplot of Actual Sqft Versus Recorded Sqft**

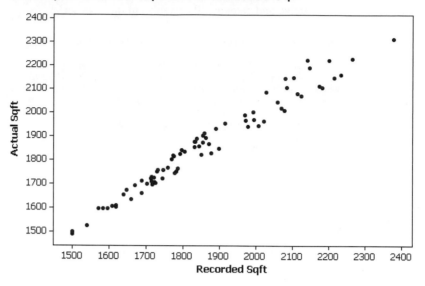

FIGURE 11.23   **Histogram of the Paired Differences in Actual and Recorded Square Footage**

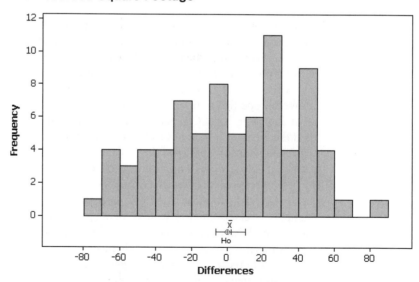

The paired-differences test shows that the average difference between actual and recorded square footage is not statistically significant ($p = .65$). The majority of recorded values appear to fall within 30 square feet of the actual values (1–2% error). A difference of 1–2% is relatively small and does not lead to a great difference in the actual tax assessed so it is probably not practically significant and the cost of a full-scale measurement of all 12,000 properties in the county can be avoided. The recorded square footage values should be accurate enough.

From the wording of the case, it is obvious that we want to find a property tax equation of the form

Tax = $a + b \cdot$ Sqft

where a is the flat tax amount and b is the tax rate based on square footage. A scatterplot of the data in Figure 11.24 suggests that there is indeed a strong linear relationship between current property taxes and recorded square footage.

FIGURE 11.24   **Scatterplot of Current Tax Versus Recorded Sqft**

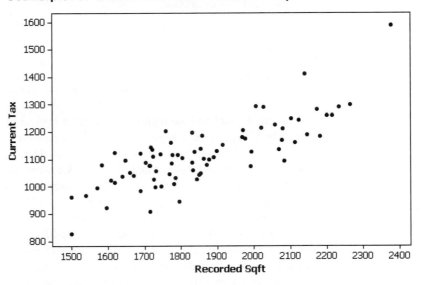

Before computing a regression, however, we should first adjust the property taxes for the 10% homestead and retirement exemptions to put the tax values on an equal footing. These adjustments are made *after* taxes have been computed from the tax equation. The adjusted tax computation in Minitab is shown next.

```
MTB > let 'Adjusted Tax'
         = 'Current Tax' / (1 - .1*('Homestead'=1) - .1*('Retired'=1))
```

Logical expressions in Minitab are used to produce the appropriate adjustment. If an owner has neither exemption (Homestead = 0, Retired = 0), Current Tax is divided by 1. If the owner has a homestead exemption only (Homestead = 1, Retired = 0) or a retired exemption only (Homestead = 0, Retired = 1), then Current Tax is divided by .9. Finally, if the owner has both exemptions (Homestead = 1, Retired = 1), then TAX is divided by .8. A scatterplot of Adjusted Tax versus Recorded Sqft with a fitted least-squares line, drawn in Minitab, is shown in Figure 11.25 and Minitab output for the simple linear regression is shown here.

```
Regression Analysis: Adjusted Tax versus Recorded Sqft

The regression equation is
Adjusted Tax = 208 + 0.557 Recorded Sqft
```

```
Predictor          Coef   SE Coef        T       P
Constant         208.03     75.03     2.77   0.007
Recorded Sqft   0.55649   0.04014    13.86   0.000

S = 70.0275    R-Sq = 71.9%    R-Sq(adj) = 71.6%

Analysis of Variance

Source           DF        SS        MS        F       P
Regression        1    942315    942315   192.16   0.000
Residual Error   75    367788      4904
Total            76   1310105

Unusual Observations

        Recorded  Adjusted
Obs        Sqft       Tax       Fit  SE Fit  Residual  St Resid
 52        2376   1984.16   1530.27   22.26    453.90    6.84RX

R denotes an observation with a large standardized residual.
X denotes an observation whose X value gives it large influence.
```

From the plot and the regression output, it is clear that one of the observations, property 52, is having a large impact on the regression results. Its current property taxes are much higher than we would expect based on the pattern of the other properties (large standardized residual of 6.80). The house on the property is also much larger than other houses in the data set (high leverage). The effect of this observation on the regression line can be observed in Figure 11.25. The plot shows that the presence of property 52 in the regression causes properties with small square footage values to tend to have lower predicted taxes (positive residuals) and properties with large square footage values to tend to have higher predicted taxes (negative residuals). This property may have special characteristics that caused it to have higher taxes under the existing taxation system. An argument is easily made for removing this house from the analysis in order for the regression to better represent the majority of houses in the data set. The reanalysis of the data after the removal of property 52 is shown in Minitab output here and in Figure 11.26.

FIGURE 11.25   **Scatterplot of Adjusted Tax Versus Recorded Sqft with Fitted Line**

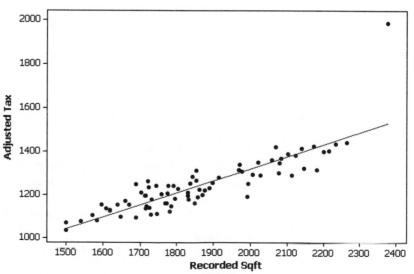

FIGURE 11.26   **Scatterplot and Fitted Line after Deleting the Influential Point**

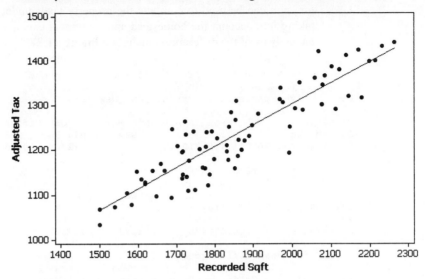

```
Regression Analysis: Adjusted Tax versus Recorded Sqft

The regression equation is
Adjusted Tax = 361 + 0.471 Recorded Sqft

Predictor          Coef  SE Coef      T      P
Constant         361.11    48.39   7.46  0.000
Recorded Sqft   0.47059  0.02599  18.10  0.000

S = 43.2790   R-Sq = 81.6%   R-Sq(adj) = 81.3%

Analysis of Variance

Source          DF       SS      MS       F      P
Regression       1   613734  613734  327.66  0.000
Residual Error  74   138607    1873
Total           75   752343

Unusual Observations

     Recorded  Adjusted
Obs      Sqft       Tax      Fit  SE Fit  Residual  St Resid
  7      2068   1421.63  1334.30    7.50     87.33      2.05R
 49      1721   1262.99  1171.00    6.01     91.99      2.15R
 61      1688   1246.53  1155.47    6.54     91.06      2.13R
 76      1992   1192.76  1298.53    6.16   -105.78     -2.47R

R denotes an observation with a large standardized residual.
```

Note that four observations are labeled as unusual in the Minitab output because their standardized residuals are greater than 2.0 in absolute value. This is really not so unusual, since we expect roughly 5% of our 76 standardized residuals to be this large. Analysis of residual plots and other residual diagnostics reveal no additional points of concern.

Based on the regression output, Bradford should set the flat tax amount at $361.11 and the variable tax rate at $.47059 per square foot. (Compare to $208.03

and $.55649 with property 52 included in the data set.) The fitted values from the regression can be used to compute the property taxes under the proposed system by taking into account the homestead and retirement exemptions, as shown here, with an analysis of the differences, including Figure 11.27.

```
MTB > let 'New Tax' = 'FITS1' * (1 - 0.1*'Homestead' - 0.1*'Retired')

Descriptive Statistics: Current Tax, New Tax

Variable       N     Mean  StDev  Minimum      Q1  Median      Q3  Maximum
Current Tax   76   1113.5  103.3    827.8  1044.3  1109.6  1184.0   1411.6
New Tax       76   1114.0  101.5    853.2  1052.0  1104.3  1194.2   1367.7

Paired T for Current Tax - New Tax

                N       Mean      StDev   SE Mean
Current Tax    76    1113.53     103.33     11.85
New Tax        76    1114.02     101.48     11.64
Difference     76  -0.490475  38.382292  4.402751

95% CI for mean difference: (-9.261205, 8.280254)

T-Test of mean difference = 0 (vs not = 0): T-Value = -0.11  P-Value = 0.912
```

FIGURE 11.27   **Histogram of Paired Differences Between Current Tax and New Tax**

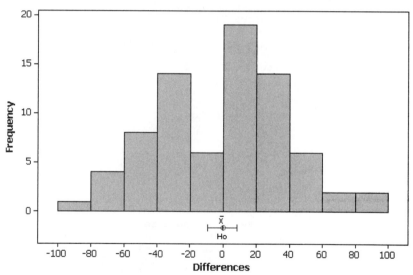

It appears that taxes under the proposed system will not be dramatically different from what they were under the current system. Also note that changing to the new system will be revenue neutral—the total tax collection under the new system ($84,675 for the 76 homes) will be very close to that under the old system ($84,629 for the 76 homes). This is due in large part to the fact that the sum of the fitted values (FITS1) is equal to the sum of the observed values (Adjusted Tax) in least-squares regression. (The slight difference in the totals is caused by the adjustments for exemptions.)

SUMMARY

Here are some considerations when doing simple regression—trying to predict or explain variation in one variable based on values of one other variable.

1. Before you even think about doing calculations, plot the data. (Yes, we have suggested this step once or twice before in other data analysis situations.) A scatterplot can reveal nonlinear relations, increasing variability, or potentially influential points.

2. A scatterplot smoother such as LOWESS, if available in your computer package, can help in identifying curved relationships. If there is a definite curve in the plot, consider a transformation such as a logarithm, square root, or reciprocal (inverse).

3. If the plot shows a pattern of increasing variability around a line or curve, try redefining the dependent variable, either by a transformation such as a logarithm or as a ratio to some other variable.

4. If the plot shows an outlier, determine the reason for its unusual value. If it is a typographical error, fix it. If it is a point that doesn't belong with the others in the data set, delete it. If there is no apparent reason why the point is odd, do the analysis both with and without the point to see what parts of the results can be trusted.

5. As always, statistical tests in regression only indicate whether an apparent relationship could have resulted from sheer random variation. A low p-value does not necessarily imply a strong relationship. Consideration of the correlation coefficient and the residual standard deviation will tell you more about how good the prediction is from a practical viewpoint.

6. The residual standard deviation is a beast with many names. It may be called the standard error of estimation, the root mean square error, or something else. If in doubt, it can be calculated as the square root of the mean squared error value shown in the analysis of variance table.

7. In planning a regression study, it's desirable to have a wide range of variation in the independent variable. Having a large range of X values also helps avoid extrapolation troubles when using the model to predict Y at a new X value.

In addition, you may want to reread the summary of key ideas in the Executive Overview at the beginning of this chapter.

Supplementary Exercises

11.31 Consider the data shown here:

x: 10 12 14 15 18 19 23
y: 25 30 36 37 42 50 55

a. Plot the data.
b. Using the data, find the least-squares estimates for the model $Y_i = \beta_0 + \beta_1 x_i + \epsilon_i$.
c. Predict Y when $x = 21$.

11.32   Refer to Exercise 11.31.

a. Calculate s_ϵ, the residual standard deviation.

b. Compute the residuals for these data. Do most lie within $\pm 2s_\epsilon$ of zero?

11.33   A government agency responsible for awarding contracts for much of its research work is under careful scrutiny by a number of private companies. One company examines the relationship between the amount of the contract ($\times\$10,000$) and the length of time between the submission of the contract proposal and contract approval:

Length (in months), y: 3   4   6   8   11   14   20
    Size ($\times\$10,000$), x: 1   5   10   50   100   500   1000

A plot of y versus x is in Figure 11.28; Minitab output follows.

FIGURE 11.28   Scatterplot of Length Versus Size

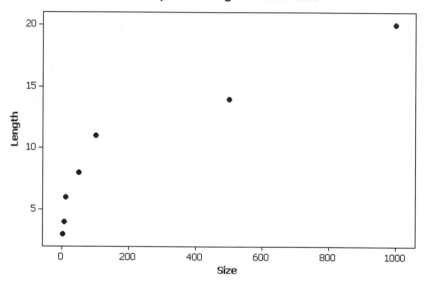

```
Regression Analysis: Length versus Size

The regression equation is
Length = 5.89 + 0.0149 Size

Predictor        Coef      SE Coef       T       P
Constant        5.891        1.086    5.42   0.003
Size         0.014865     0.002557    5.81   0.002

S = 2.38012    R-Sq = 87.1%    R-Sq(adj) = 84.5%

Analysis of Variance

Source          DF        SS        MS       F       P
Regression       1    191.39    191.39   33.78   0.002
Residual Error   5     28.33      5.67
Total            6    219.71
```

a. What is the least-squares line?

b. Conduct a test of the null hypothesis $H_0: \beta_1 = 0$. Give the p-value for your test, assuming $H_a: \beta_1 > 0$.

11.34   Refer to the data of Exercise 11.33. A plot of y versus the (natural) logarithm of x (Figure 11.29), plus more Minitab output, are given here.

FIGURE 11.29   **Scatterplot of Length Versus Logarithm of Size**

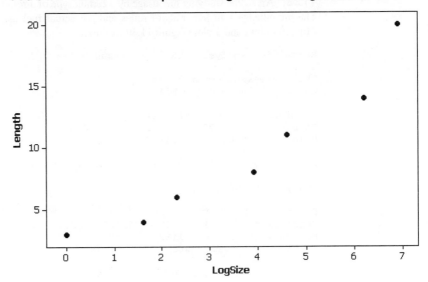

```
Regression Analysis: Length versus LogSize

The regression equation is
Length = 1.01 + 2.31 LogSize

Predictor    Coef   SE Coef     T      P
Constant    1.007    1.421   0.71   0.510
LogSize     2.3070   0.3289   7.01   0.001

S = 2.01346   R-Sq = 90.8%   R-Sq(adj) = 88.9%

Analysis of Variance

Source          DF      SS      MS      F      P
Regression       1   199.44  199.44  49.20  0.001
Residual Error   5    20.27    4.05
Total            6   219.71

Unusual Observations

Obs  LogSize  Length    Fit  SE Fit  Residual  St Resid
  7     6.91  20.000  16.944   1.314     3.056     2.00R

R denotes an observation with a large standardized residual.
```

a. What is the regression line using $\log x$ as the independent variable?
b. Conduct a test of H_0: $\beta_1 = 0$ and give the level of significance for a one-sided alternative, H_a: $\beta_1 > 0$.

11.35   Use the results of Exercises 11.33 and 11.34 to determine which regression model provides the better fit. Give reasons for your choice.

11.36   Refer to the output of the previous exercises.
a. Construct a 95% confidence interval for β_1, the slope of the linear regression line.
b. Construct a 95% confidence interval for the slope in the logarithm model.

11.37 Use the model you prefer for the data of Exercise 11.33 to predict the length of time in months before approval of a $750,000 contract. Give a rough estimate of a 95% prediction interval.

11.38 An airline studying fuel usage by a certain type of aircraft obtains data on 100 flights. The air mileage x in hundreds of miles and the actual fuel use y in gallons are recorded. Minitab output and a plot (Figure 11.30) follow:

```
Regression Analysis: Gallons versus Miles

The regression equation is
Gallons = 140 + 0.619 Miles

Predictor      Coef   SE Coef       T       P
Constant     140.07     44.13    3.17   0.010
Miles       0.61895   0.04855   12.75   0.000

S = 34.3852   R-Sq = 94.2%   R-Sq(adj) = 93.6%

Analysis of Variance

Source          DF       SS       MS        F       P
Regression       1   192107   192107   162.48   0.000
Residual Error  10    11823     1182
Total           11   203931

Predicted Values for New Observations

New Obs     Fit   SE Fit        95% CI               95% PI
      1  759.04    11.38   (733.69, 784.39)   (678.34, 839.74)

Values of Predictors for New Observations

New Obs   Miles
      1    1000
```

FIGURE 11.30 **Scatterplot of Gallons Used Versus Miles**

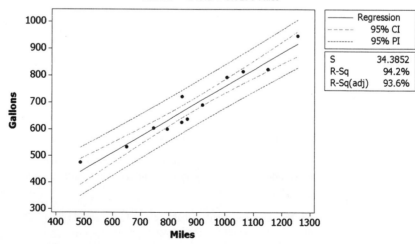

Fitted Line Plot
Gallons = 140.1 + 0.6190 Miles

a. Locate the regression equation.
b. What are the sample correlation coefficient and coefficient of determination? Interpret these numbers.
c. Is there any point in testing H_0: $\beta_1 = 0$?

11.39 Refer to the data and output of Exercise 11.38.

a. Predict the mean fuel usage of all 1000-mile flights. Give a 95% confidence interval.

b. Predict the fuel usage of a particular 1000-mile flight. Would a usage of 628 gallons be considered exceptionally low?

c. What is the interpretation of $\hat{\beta}_1$ in this situation? Is there a sensible interpretation of $\hat{\beta}_0$?

11.40 A large suburban motel derives income from room rentals and purchases in its restaurant and lounge. It seems very likely that there should be a relation between room occupancy and restaurant/lounge sales, but the manager of the motel does not have a sense of how close that relation is. Data were collected for 36 nonholiday weekdays (Monday through Thursday nights) on the number of rooms occupied and the restaurant/lounge sales. A scatterplot of the data and regression results from JMP are shown in Figure 11.31.

a. According to the output, is there a statistically significant relation between rooms occupied and revenue from the restaurant and lounge?

b. If the point at the upper left of the scatterplot is deleted, will the slope be increased or decreased? Do you expect a substantial change?

FIGURE 11.31   **Scatterplot and Analysis of Motel Data from JMP**

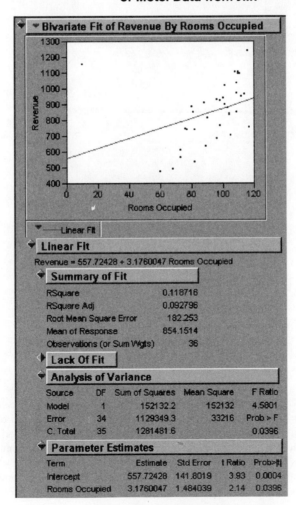

11.41   One point in the motel data was a data-entry error, with occupancy listed as 10 rather than 100. The error was corrected, leading to the output in Figure 11.32.

a. How has the slope changed as a result of the correction?

b. How has the intercept changed?

c. Did the outlier make the residual standard deviation (root mean square error) larger or smaller?

d. Did the outlier make the r^2 value larger or smaller?

FIGURE 11.32   JMP Results for Corrected Motel Data

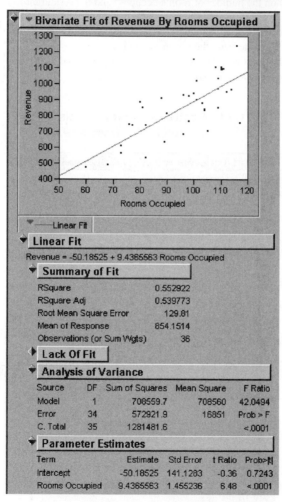

11.42   The management science staff of a grocery products manufacturer is developing a linear programming model for the production and distribution of its cereal products. The model requires transportation costs for a monstrous number of origins and destinations. It is impractical to do the detailed tariff analysis for every possible combination, so a sample of 50 routes is selected. For each route, the mileage x and shipping rate y (in dollars per 100 pounds) are found. A regression analysis is performed, yielding the scatterplot in Figure 11.33 and the following Excel output:

```
SUMMARY OUTPUT

Regression Statistics
Multiple R              0.9929
R Square                0.9859
Adjusted R Square       0.9856
Standard Error          2.2021
Observations            48

ANOVA
                    df          SS          MS          F       Significance F
Regression          1       15558.63    15558.63    3208.47         0.00
Residual           46         223.06        4.85
Total              47       15781.70

            Coefficients   Standard Error   t Stat    P-value   Lower 95%   Upper 95%
Intercept     9.7709           0.4740      20.6122    0.0000     8.8167     10.7251
Mileage       0.0501           0.0009      56.6434    0.0000     0.0483      0.0519
```

FIGURE 11.33   Scatterplot of Rate Versus Mileage

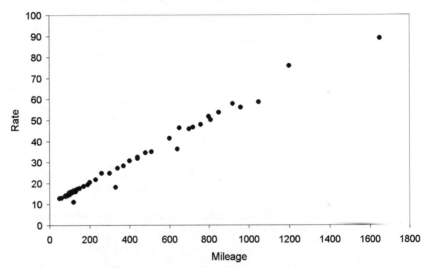

The data are as follows:

Mileage:	50	60	80	80	90	90	100	100	100	110	110	110
Rate:	12.7	13.0	13.7	14.1	14.6	14.1	15.6	14.9	14.5	15.3	15.5	15.9

Mileage:	120	120	120	120	130	130	140	150	170	190	200	230
Rate:	16.4	11.1	16.0	15.8	16.0	16.7	17.2	17.5	18.6	19.3	20.4	21.8

Mileage:	260	300	330	340	370	400	440	440	480	510	540	600
Rate:	24.7	24.7	18.0	27.1	28.2	30.6	31.8	32.4	34.5	35.0	36.3	41.4

Mileage:	650	700	720	760	800	810	850	920	960	1050	1200	1650
Rate:	46.4	45.8	46.6	48.0	51.7	50.2	53.6	57.9	56.1	58.7	75.8	89.0

a. Write the regression equation and give the value of the residual standard deviation.
b. Calculate a 90% confidence interval for the true slope.
c. In the plot of Figure 11.33, do you see any problems with the data?

11.43 Refer to Exercise 11.42. Predict the shipping rate for a 340-mile route. Obtain a 95% prediction interval. How serious is the extrapolation problem in this exercise?

11.44 Suburban towns often spend a large fraction of their municipal budgets on public safety (police, fire, and ambulance) services. A taxpayers' group felt that very small towns were likely to spend large amounts per person, just because they have such small financial bases. The group obtained data on the per capita expenditure for public safety of 29 suburban towns in a metropolitan area as well as the population of each town. The data were analyzed using the Minitab package. A regression model with dependent variable Expend and independent variable TownPop yields the following output:

```
Regression Analysis: Expend versus TownPop

The regression equation is
Expend = 119 + 0.000532 TownPop

Predictor        Coef     SE Coef      T      P
Constant       118.96       23.26   5.11  0.000
TownPop     0.0005324   0.0006181   0.86  0.397


S = 43.3125    R-Sq = 2.7%    R-Sq(adj) = 0.0%

Analysis of Variance

Source           DF      SS      MS      F      P
Regression        1    1392    1392   0.74  0.397
Residual Error   27   50651    1876
Total            28   52043


Unusual Observations

Obs   TownPop   Expend     Fit   SE Fit   Residual   St Resid
  8     74151   334.00  158.43    25.32     175.57       5.00RX

R denotes an observation with a large standardized residual.
X denotes an observation whose X value gives it large influence.
```

a. If the taxpayers' group is correct, what sign should the slope of the regression model have?
b. Does the slope in the output confirm the opinion of the group?

11.45 Minitab produced a scatterplot and LOWESS smooth of the data in Exercise 11.44, shown as Figure 11.34. Does this plot indicate that the regression line is misleading? Why?

FIGURE 11.34 **Scatterplot for Expenditure Data with LOWESS Curve**

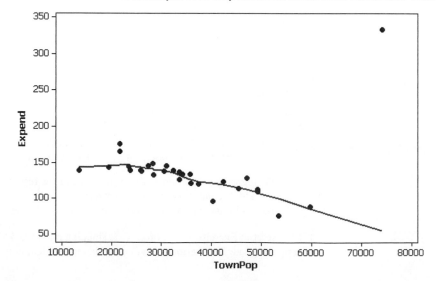

FIGURE 11.35 **Scatterplot with Unusual Town Data Removed**

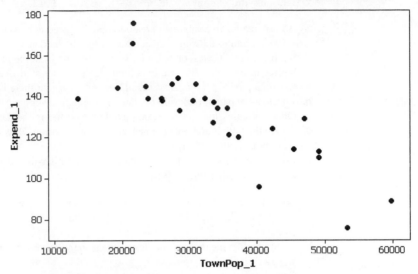

11.46 One town in the database of Exercise 11.44 is the home of an enormous regional shopping mall. A very large fraction of the town's expenditure on public safety is related to the mall; the mall management pays a yearly fee to the township that covers these expenditures. That town's data were removed from the database and the remaining data were reanalyzed by Minitab. A scatterplot is shown in Figure 11.35.

a. Explain why removing this one point from the data changed the regression line substantially.

b Does the revised regression line appear to conform to the opinion of the taxpayers' group in Exercise 11.44?

11.47 Regression output for the data of Exercise 11.44, excluding the one unusual town, is shown here. How has the slope changed from the one obtained previously?

```
Regression Analysis: Expend_1 versus TownPop_1

The regression equation is
Expend_1 = 184 - 0.00157 TownPop_1

Predictor        Coef     SE Coef       T      P
Constant      184.239       7.481   24.63  0.000
TownPop_1  -0.0015766   0.0002099   -7.51  0.000

S = 12.1441   R-Sq = 68.5%   R-Sq(adj) = 67.2%

Analysis of Variance

Source          DF       SS       MS       F      P
Regression       1   8322.7   8322.7   56.43  0.000
Residual Error  26   3834.5    147.5
Total           27  12157.2

Unusual Observations

Obs   TownPop_1   Expend_1      Fit  SE Fit   Residual  St Resid
  5       40307      96.00   120.69    2.66     -24.69     -2.08R
  6       13457     139.00   163.02    4.87     -24.02     -2.16R
 13       59779      89.00    89.99    5.89      -0.99     -0.09 X
 22       21701     176.00   150.03    3.44      25.97      2.23R
 27       53322      76.00   100.17    4.67     -24.17     -2.16R
```

```
R denotes an observation with a large standardized residual.
X denotes an observation whose X value gives it large influence.
```

11.48   A realtor in a suburban area attempted to predict house prices solely on the basis of size. From a multiple listing service, the realtor obtained size in thousands of square feet and asking price in thousands of dollars. The information is stored in the EX1148 file on the CD, with price in column 1 and size in column 2. Have your statistical program read this file.
a. Obtain a plot of price against size. Does it appear that there is an increasing relation?
b. Locate an apparent outlier in the data. Is it a high-leverage point?
c. Obtain a regression equation and include the outlier in the data.
d. Delete the outlier and obtain a new regression equation. How much does the slope change without the outlier? Why?
e. Locate the residual standard deviations for the outlier-included and outlier-excluded models. Do they differ much? Why?

11.49   Obtain the outlier-excluded regression model for the data of Exercise 11.48.
a. Interpret the intercept (constant) term. How much meaning does this number have in this context?
b. What would it mean in this context if the slope were zero? Can the null hypothesis of zero slope be emphatically rejected?
c. Calculate a 95% confidence interval for the true population value of the slope. The computer output should give you the estimated slope and its standard error, but you'll probably have to do the rest of the calculations by hand.

11.50   Refer to Exercise 11.48.
a. If possible, use your computer program to obtain a 95% prediction interval for the asking price of a home of 5000 square feet, based on the outlier-excluded data of the exercise. If you must do the computations by hand, obtain the mean and standard deviation of the size data from the computer and find $S_{xx} = (n - 1)s^2$ by hand. Would this be a wise prediction to make, based on the data?
b. Obtain a plot of the price against the size. Does the constant-variance assumption seem reasonable, or does variability increase as size increases?
c. What does your answer to part (b) say about the prediction interval obtained in part (a)?

11.51   A lawn-care company tried to predict the demand for its service by ZIP code, using the housing density in the ZIP code area as a predictor. The owners obtained the number of houses and the geographic size of each ZIP code and calculated their sales per thousand homes and number of homes per acre. The data are stored in the EX1151 file on the CD. Sales data are in column 1 and density (homes/acre) data are in column 2. Read the data into your computer package.
a. Obtain the correlation between the two variables. What does its sign mean?
b. Obtain a prediction equation with sales as the dependent variable and density as the independent variable. Interpret the intercept (yes, we know the interpretation will be a bit strange) and the slope numbers.
c. Obtain a value for the residual standard deviation. What does this number indicate about the accuracy of prediction?

11.52   Refer to Exercise 11.51.
a. Obtain a value of the t statistic for the regression model. Is there conclusive evidence that density is a predictor of sales?
b. Calculate a 95% confidence interval for the true value of the slope. The package should have calculated the standard error for you.

11.53   Obtain a plot of the data of Exercise 11.51, with sales plotted against density. Does it appear that straight-line prediction makes sense?

11.54   Have your computer program calculate a new variable as 1/density (the reciprocal of density).
a. What is the interpretation of the new variable? In particular, if the new variable equals .50, what does that mean about the particular ZIP code area?
b. Plot sales against the new variable. Does a straight-line prediction look reasonable here?
c. Obtain the correlation of sales and the new variable. Compare its magnitude to the correlation obtained in Exercise 11.51 between sales and density. What explains the difference?

11.55   A manufacturer of paint used for marking road surfaces developed a new formulation that needs to be tested for durability. One question concerns the concentration of pigment in the paint. If the concentration is too low, the paint will fade quickly; if the concentration is too high, the paint will not adhere well to the road surface. The manufacturer applies paint at various concentrations to sample road surfaces and obtains a durability measurement for each sample. The data are stored in the EX1155 file on the CD, with durability in column 1 and concentration in column 2.
a. Have your computer program calculate a regression equation with durability predicted by concentration. Interpret the slope coefficient.
b. Find the coefficient of determination. What does it indicate about the predictive value of concentration?

11.56   In the regression model of Exercise 11.55, is the slope coefficient significantly different from 0 at $\alpha = .01$?

11.57   Obtain a plot of the data of Exercise 11.55 with durability on the vertical axis and concentration on the horizontal axis.
a. What does this plot indicate about the wisdom of using straight-line prediction?
b. What does this plot indicate about the correlation found in Exercise 11.55?

BUSINESS CASES

Employer-Sponsored Life Insurance

In one of the Business Cases at the end of Chapter 7, the benefits manager of a large university obtained data from a sample of 61 employees on their intended use of a possible flexible benefits plan. Now the manager wants to analyze the data in more detail. In particular, the manager is interested in the relation between monthly life insurance cost and age of the employee. This relation is a matter of increasing concern because the age of the employee group has been rising and it will continue to rise. A work–study student took age and life insurance cost data from the sample and performed some basic Minitab analysis, as shown. A scatterplot is shown in Figure 11.36.

```
Data Display

Row   Employee   Age   Cost       Row   Employee   Age   Cost
 1           1    52    759         6           6    44    559
 2           2    28    424         7           7    46    651
 3           3    42    157         8           8    49    519
 4           4    51    616         9           9    51    358
 5           5    42    655        10          10    25    456
```

Row	Employee	Age	Cost	Row	Employee	Age	Cost
11	11	33	97	37	37	39	579
12	12	59	478	38	38	43	666
13	13	35	129	39	39	35	596
14	14	44	661	40	40	61	251
15	15	30	245	41	41	51	341
16	16	37	602	42	42	27	77
17	17	32	557	43	43	28	225
18	18	41	215	44	44	51	590
19	19	29	331	45	45	53	330
20	20	48	545	46	46	47	736
21	21	61	395	47	47	50	601
22	22	38	577	48	48	40	555
23	23	32	345	49	49	40	775
24	24	33	367	50	50	52	745
25	25	24	189	51	51	46	630
26	26	43	716	52	52	58	139
27	27	43	238	53	53	44	521
28	28	50	867	54	54	55	647
29	29	55	475	55	55	29	543
30	30	56	369	56	56	44	699
31	31	68	245	57	57	53	602
32	32	47	585	58	58	54	493
33	33	32	472	59	59	45	731
34	34	65	535	60	60	38	267
35	35	22	174	61	61	49	689
36	36	52	751				

```
Correlations: Age, Cost

Pearson correlation of Age and Cost = 0.271

Regression Analysis: Cost versus Age

The regression equation is
Cost = 259 + 5.07 Age

Predictor    Coef   SE Coef     T      P
Constant    258.9     105.7   2.45  0.017
Age         5.073     2.344   2.16  0.035

S = 195.314   R-Sq = 7.4%   R-Sq(adj) = 5.8%

Analysis of Variance

Source          DF        SS       MS      F      P
Regression       1    178623   178623   4.68  0.035
Residual Error  59   2250733    38148
Total           60   2429357

Unusual Observations

Obs   Age    Cost     Fit   SE Fit  Residual  St Resid
 31  68.0   245.0   603.9    62.0    -358.9     -1.94 X
 52  58.0   139.0   553.1    41.7    -414.1     -2.17R

R denotes an observation with a large standardized residual.
X denotes an observation whose X value gives it large influence.
```

In a cover note to you accompanying the output, the benefits manager said "I don't understand this very well. There doesn't seem to be a very good correlation, but the work–study student says that it is significant. Can you explain what's going on in the output for me?"

FIGURE 11.36   **Plot of Life Insurance Cost Versus Employee Age**

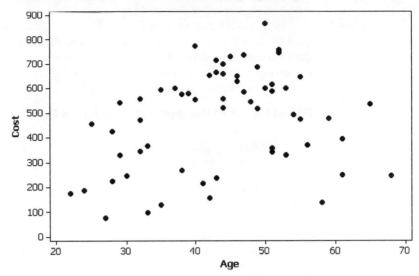

Assignment: Explain what you think are the most important conclusions to be obtained from the output, in language the manager can understand. You're welcome to suggest and carry out any further analysis that might help you interpret the data.

BackInTheBlack.com

Debt counseling services have been a booming business in recent years. The average credit card debt carried by U.S. households is estimated to be over $8000. Personal bankruptcies have risen to more than 1.5 million per year and account for over 98% of all bankruptcies filed. On average, Americans spend $1.22 for every $1.00 earned.

BackInTheBlack.com is an on-line debt counseling service started two years ago. As a first step in providing debt counseling to a client, the client's financial situation is assessed to determine if the consumer debt load could eventually lead to problems. Many guidelines, or rules of thumb, exist for determining the amount of consumer debt that a household can reasonably manage given its income level and other information. Given the rapidly changing environment, the management of BackInTheBlack.com believes that these guidelines are in need of revision.

In order to develop new guidelines for identifying consumer debt problems, BackInTheBlack.com has collected a random sample of 100 low- and middle-class households, none of which are clients, to examine the current relationship between the total consumer debt of a household and its income. The company estimates that 2–3% of all U.S. households carry more consumer debt than they can handle.

Assignment: You have been asked to examine the collected data and do two things: (1) provide a thorough analysis of the relationship between the total consumer debt and the income of low- to middle-income households, and (2) develop a rule of thumb, based on this relationship, for identifying the 2–3% of all households with serious consumer debt problems.

The data are contained in the file BackInTheBlack on the CD that came with your book. For each of the 100 households in the random sample, the file contains the total consumer debt (Debt) and total income (Income) of the household. A partial listing of the data within the Excel file is shown in Figure 11.37.

FIGURE 11.37

Partial Listing of the BackInTheBlack.com Data

	A	B
1	Debt	Income
2	15420	66440
3	12586	56526
4	14133	46259
5	6898	46215
6	17027	62168
7	7359	33886
8	15804	68061
9	13083	54460
10	5242	29519
11	14962	50099
12	18138	60843

Multiple Regression Methods

CHAPTER CONTENTS

This chapter introduces the technical aspects of multiple regression, using several independent variables. The chapter is devoted to estimation, testing, and forecasting methods. The next chapter deals with constructing a multiple regression model and checking underlying assumptions. The key methods discussed in this chapter are the following:

- The basic multiple regression model is a first-order model, containing each predictor but no nonlinear terms such as squared values. In this model, each slope should be interpreted as a partial slope, the predicted effect of a one-unit change in a variable, holding all other variables constant. The intercept is the predicted y value when all predictors equal 0; this condition may not mean much in context.

- The slope coefficients in multiple regression do not generally equal the slopes in a series of simple regressions. This occurs because of collinearity, correlation among the independent variables.

- The overall strength of predictability is often measured by R^2, the coefficient of determination. It measures how much of the variation (squared error) in y is accounted for or explained by variation in the independent variables. When there is substantial collinearity, it can be difficult to say which independent variables are responsible for most of R^2.

- There are three distinct hypothesis tests on the slope coefficients in multiple regression. A test of the overall predictive value of all of the predictors together is done by an F test similar to the analysis of variance. A test of the value of one predictor, given all others, is based on a t statistic. A test of the value of some—a subset—of the predictors, given the remaining ones is done by an incremental F test. The latter test may be based either on the increment to R^2 obtained by adding the subset of predictors to the others, or on the increment to SS(Regression).

- Forecasts using new x values in multiple regression are constructed in much the same way as in simple regression. It is important to consider whether the new x values are extrapolated far from the data, either individually or in combination.

CHAPTER CASE

Colvard Office Products

INTRODUCTION

Colvard Office Products, a national producer and supplier of a line of office furniture products, including desks, chairs, bookcases, and filing cabinets, currently employs a sales force of 240 scattered across the United States. Richard Garrett, the vice president of marketing, has the primary responsibility for Colvard's sales and product distribution.

Each year, Colvard hires approximately 20–40 new salespeople, who are put through the company's excellent one-week sales training program. At the conclusion of the training program, they take a four-hour written test that measures what the employee has learned and also contains a section on general knowledge and a section designed to capture information about the employee's personality and character traits. A total score is produced along with the three subscores.

After their first year of employment with Colvard, the new sales employees are evaluated by their regional sales managers, who submit performance ratings, based on a scale from 0 to 100, to Richard Garrett. Over the years, Garrett has noted that these performance ratings are highly correlated with the total score from the post-training test, and he has used the test results as an "early performance indicator" for new hires.

The personnel office at Colvard wants to cut costs by reducing the length of the four-hour sales training test. Garrett has been asked for his opinion about the value of the test and whether it would be reasonable to eliminate portions of it. His initial reaction was that the test was a proven indicator of future sales performance and that it should be continued as is, but he agreed to investigate whether a subset of the test might serve just as well.

Garrett had never before examined the relationship of the three individual subscores to sales performance. He was not sure how to predict sales performance from a subset of the three subscores or how to assess their predictive ability.

Garrett has provided you with a database containing total test scores and subscores for the most recent 120 salespeople hired along with their individual sales performance ratings after one year on the job. He wants you to determine which subscores, alone or in combination, provide the best prediction of sales performance at the end of the first year. Garrett also wants you to compare this approach to using just the total score and recommend how he should respond to the personnel office's request to shorten the test.

The personnel data for the last 120 salespeople hired by Colvard are contained in the file Colvard on the CD that came with your book. The recorded data include their test results and their sales performance ratings after one year. A partial listing of the data within Excel is shown in Figure 12.1.

In the Colvard file, the variables are defined as follows:

Rating: Sales performance rating for first year on the job
SubScore1:   Subscore on the first section of the test
SubScore2:   Subscore on the second section of the test
SubScore3:   Subscore on the third section of the test
TotalScore: Total of the three subscores of the test

The material covered in this chapter on multiple regression analysis and the material covered in earlier chapters will prove to be very helpful in analyzing this

FIGURE 12.1   **Partial Listing of the Colvard Office Products Data**

	A	B	C	D	E
1	Rating	SubScore1	SubScore2	SubScore3	TotalScore
2	75	50	51	54	155
3	56	40	34	45	119
4	86	48	56	64	168
5	63	46	43	51	140
6	80	50	57	56	163
7	63	45	46	49	140
8	61	44	59	56	159
9	66	48	49	53	150
10	61	43	38	42	123
11	45	30	29	41	100
12	43	43	37	31	111
13	50	55	46	45	146
14	56	40	50	43	133
15	68	47	50	48	145
16	47	39	47	40	126

situation and making your recommendation to Richard Garrett. A complete analysis of the data will be considered at the end of this chapter. ■

MULTIPLE REGRESSION USES MANY independent variables to predict or explain variation in a quantitative dependent variable. It's an extremely useful way to assess the explanatory value of many different, plausible predictors. In many management situations, there are several possible predictors of a result. We use multiple regression to try to sort out which of these plausible predictors really do explain variation in the dependent variable, and which others add little or no predictive value. It is probably the statistical technique most widely used by managers.

We'll devote two chapters to multiple regression. In this chapter we'll develop the basic theoretical concepts, the assumptions, and the methods. We'll consider what the multiple regression model is and how it's interpreted; how the coefficients can be estimated from data; how inferences can be made from the limited database of the model; and how to use the model in forecasting new cases. Then, in Chapter 13, we'll describe how all the concepts fit together in developing a multiple regression study.

12.1   The Multiple Regression Model

Every manager faces situations in which changes or variations in something need to be understood and predicted and in which there are many plausible indicators pointing (in possibly conflicting ways) to predicted changes. In every publicly held company, changes in the price of the company's common stock are of more than mild interest. There are both internal predictors of the price (such as earnings, growth rate, market share of primary products, and debt/equity ratio) and external predictors (such as interest rates, consumer confidence levels, and current unemployment). Variation in the cost of a print job depends on the number of pages, the number of graphic displays, the hours needed to set up, and the number of copies. Variation in the sales of a new product can be predicted by the size of the market, the rate of growth of that market, consumer satisfaction in tests of the product, and type of sales outlet for the product.

Multiple regression is a method for using data to sort out the predictive value of the competing predictors. Therefore, it is a very widely used statistical method for many types of managers.

Given the data, the first task in multiple regression is to specify a model, the mathematical form of the prediction equation. The simplest model takes each predictor, multiplies it by a numerical weight (coefficient), and adds the resulting quantities to an intercept term. For example, a multiple regression model for variation in price of a common stock over time might be

$$\text{price} = -12.72 + 5.21\text{earnings} + 3.34\text{growth} - 0.68\text{D/E}$$

where price = closing price of the stock at the end of each quarter; earnings = reported earnings per share in the quarter; growth = change in earnings from the same quarter of the previous year; and D/E = ratio of corporate debt to corporate equity. The intercept term, -12.72 in the example, is the predicted dependent variable value when all the independent variables equal 0. In many cases, the intercept has little meaning because the condition that all predictors are 0 is economically absurd. There can't be a stock with a price of -12.72 (even the ones we own), but the conditions of 0 earnings, 0 growth, and 0 debt-to-equity ratio are so far outside of reasonable economic values that we needn't worry about the impossible value.

partial slopes

The coefficients of the predictor variables are usually more relevant. They are the **partial slopes** and they measure the predicted change in the dependent variable for a one-unit change in the independent variable, *holding other independent variables constant*. In the stock price equation, if we compare two quarters when the company had the same growth and debt/equity ratio, we'd predict that the price would be $5.21 higher for the quarter in which the earnings per share were $1 higher. Similarly, if we had two quarters when earnings and growth were the same, but D/E was 1.0 higher in quarter A than in quarter B, we would predict that the price would be $.68 *lower* (because of the minus sign) in quarter A.

EXAMPLE 12.1

The manager of a copy center must estimate costs for jobs that differ in number of pages, number of copies, setup hours, and number of graphics. Data from past jobs were put into a computer multiple regression program and yielded a model:

$$\text{cost} = -160 + 7.43\text{pages} + 1.84\text{copies} + 4.44\text{setup} + 2.67\text{graphics}$$

Interpret each numerical value in the model.

SOLUTION The intercept, -160, refers to a job with no pages, no copies, no setup, and no graphics—in other words, to a nonjob! It is not interpretable. The partial slope for "pages," 7.43, is the predicted difference in cost between two jobs with the same number of copies, setup hours, and graphics, differing by one page. The partial slope for "copies," 1.84, is the predicted difference in cost between two jobs of equal number of pages, setup hours, and graphics, differing by one copy. Similar interpretations hold for the other slopes. Note that the total number of copied pages can be obtained by multiplying "pages" by "copies"; we'd expect such a product term to be a useful predictor.

Symbolically, we write the multiple regression model as

$$Y = \beta_0 + \beta_1 x_1 + \beta_2 x_2 + \cdots + \beta_k x_k + \epsilon$$

where Y is the dependent variable to be predicted, the x's are independent predictor values, and ϵ is the error term (in recognition of the fact that every prediction is in error to some degree). The intercept term is β_0; β_1 through β_k are the partial slopes. (For those who know some calculus, the partial slope β_j is exactly the partial derivative of predicted y with respect to x_j.)

first-order model

The simplest regression model is called a **first-order model.** It contains each predictor by itself without mathematical transformations such as squared terms or logarithms. It doesn't combine predictors in such forms as product terms. Using a first-order model implicitly makes assumptions about the nature of the relation between y and the predictors. First, it assumes that y changes at a consistent rate as x_j changes, over the entire range of x_j—as opposed to, say, increasing at a decreasing rate or increasing to a maximum and then decreasing. In our first-order stock price model, we're implicitly assuming that, holding growth and D/E constant, an increase of \$1 in earnings leads to a \$5.21 increase in price per share, whether the earnings dollar is the first or the 379th. That may not be a good assumption. In the stock price case, it might well be that the price is very sensitive to changes in earnings on the low end of the scale but less sensitive when earnings start out very high.

interaction

A first-order model also assumes that there is no **interaction** among predictors. We encountered the idea of interaction in Chapter 10: The effect of changing one experimental factor depends on the level of another factor. Interaction in regression means the same thing. Two independent variables interact in their effect on the dependent variable if the predicted effect of a change in one predictor, holding the other constant, depends on *where* that other variable is held constant. In our stock price example, it wouldn't be surprising to have earnings and debt/equity ratio interact. At low D/E levels, higher earnings might have little effect; at high D/E levels, the leveraging effect might make stock prices very sensitive to changes in earnings. We will consider some methods for incorporating interaction into multiple regression in Chapter 13.

EXAMPLE 12.2

A brand manager for a new food product took data on y = brand recognition (percent of potential consumers who can describe what the product is), x_1 = length in seconds of an introductory TV commercial, and x_2 = number of repetitions of the commercial over a two-week period. What does the brand manager assume if a first-order model

$$y = .31 + .042x_1 + 1.41x_2$$

is used to predict y?

SOLUTION First, there is an assumption of a straight-line, consistent rate of change. The manager assumes that a one-second increase in length of the commercial will lead to a .042 percentage point increase in recognition, whether the increase is from, say, 10 to 11 seconds or from 59 to 60 seconds. Also, every additional repetition of the commercial is assumed to give a 1.41 percentage point increase in recognition, whether it is the second repetition or the twenty-second.

Second, there is a no-interaction assumption. The first-order model assumes that the effect of an additional repetition (that is, an increase in x_2) of a given length commercial (that is, holding x_1 constant) doesn't depend on *where* that length is held constant (at 10 seconds, 27 seconds, 60 seconds, whatever).

A first-order model is often a good starting point. In many managerial situations, there is no obvious reason to expect curvature or interaction. In such situations, a first-order model is a natural first try. In the next chapter, we'll have more to say about other, more mathematically complicated models. Until then, we simply note that a first-order multiple regression model is a useful possibility, but not the only one.

The error term ϵ plays exactly the same role in multiple regression as in simple linear regression. It includes all the effects of unpredictable and ignored factors. (The basic hope of multiple regression is to make the ϵ_i values small by including all or most of the relevant predictive factors.) The assumptions on the random error terms are identical to those stated in Chapter 11.

DEFINITION 12.1

Assumptions for Multiple Regression

1. The mathematical form of relation is correct, so $E(\epsilon_i) = 0$ for all i.

2. $\text{Var}(\epsilon_i) = \sigma_\epsilon^2$ for all i.

3. The ϵ_i's are independent.

4. ϵ_i is normally distributed.

The effect of violations of these formal assumptions is discussed in Chapter 13.

We turn our attention now to the important problem of determining estimates for the coefficients (the intercept β_0 and the partial slopes $\beta_1, \ldots, \beta_k$) in the multiple regression model in order to obtain the multiple regression forecasting equation.

12.2 Estimating Multiple Regression Coefficients

The first task of a multiple regression analysis is to estimate the intercept, the partial slopes, and the error variance. The basic principle is least-squares estimation, just as in simple linear regression. The arithmetic involved in multiple regression gets heavy very quickly, so the work is almost always done by a computer.

In simple linear regression, the least-squares principle leads to two equations, which must be solved to obtain the estimated slope and intercept. In multiple regression using k independent variables, there are $k + 1$ equations to solve for the intercept and the k partial slopes. If you recall the time and effort required to solve four equations in four unknowns by hand, you can appreciate why multiple regression is virtually always done by a computer package. There is a pattern to the equations for any number of independent variables that can be programmed. Therefore, a single program can handle any number of independent variables, up to the limits of computer storage.

Literally thousands of computer programs have been written to perform the calculations needed in multiple regression. The output of such programs typically has a list of variable names, together with the estimated partial slopes, labeled COEFFICIENTS (or ESTIMATES or PARAMETERS). The intercept term $\hat{\beta}_0$ is usually called INTERCEPT (or CONSTANT); sometimes it is shown along with the slopes, but with no variable name.

EXAMPLE 12.3   The data for three variables (shown next) are analyzed with the Excel spreadsheet program. Identify the estimates of the partial slopes and the intercept.

$$
\begin{array}{lrrrrrrrrr}
y: & 25 & 34 & 28 & 40 & 36 & 42 & 44 & 53 & 49 \\
x_1: & -10 & -10 & -10 & 0 & 0 & 0 & 10 & 10 & 10 \\
x_2: & -5 & 0 & 5 & -5 & 0 & 5 & -5 & 0 & 5
\end{array}
$$

	Coefficients	Standard Error	t Stat	P-value
Intercept	39.0	1.256	31.055	7.4E-08
X1	0.983	0.154	6.393	0.0007
X2	0.333	0.308	1.084	0.3202

SOLUTION   The intercept value 39.0 is labeled as such. The estimated partial slopes .983 and .333 are associated with x_1 and x_2, respectively. Most programs label the coefficients similarly, in a column.

The coefficient of an independent variable x_j in a multiple regression equation does not, in general, equal the coefficient that would apply to that variable in a simple linear regression. In multiple regression, the coefficient refers to the effect of changing that x_j variable while other independent variables stay constant. In simple linear regression, all other potential independent variables are ignored. If other independent variables are correlated with x_j (and therefore don't tend to stay constant while x_j changes), simple linear regression with only x_j as an independent variable captures not only the direct effect of changing x_j but also the indirect effect of the associated changes in other x's. In multiple regression, by holding the other x's constant, we eliminate that indirect effect.

EXAMPLE 12.4   Compare the coefficients of x_1 in the multiple regression model and in the simple (one-predictor) regression model shown in the following partial Minitab output. Explain why the two coefficients differ.

```
Regression Analysis: y versus x1, x2

The regression equation is
y = 10.0 + 1.00 x1 + 3.00 x2

Predictor    Coef   SE Coef    T      P
Constant   10.000    1.183   8.45  0.014
x1          1.000    1.871   0.53  0.646
x2          3.000    4.183   0.72  0.548

Regression Analysis: y versus x1

The regression equation is
y = 10.0 + 2.20 x1

Predictor    Coef   SE Coef    T      P
Constant   10.000    1.083   9.23  0.003
x1          2.2000   0.7659   2.87  0.064

Correlations: y, x1, x2

          y       x1
x1    0.856
x2    0.870    0.894
```

SOLUTION In the multiple regression model, the coefficient is shown as 1, but in the simple regression model, it's 2.2. The difference occurs because the two x's are correlated (correlation .894 in the output). In the multiple regression model, we're thinking of varying x_1 while holding x_2 constant; in the simple regression model, we're thinking of varying x_1 and letting x_2 go wherever it goes.

residual standard deviation

In addition to estimating the intercept and partial slopes, it is important to estimate the **residual standard deviation,** s_ϵ, sometimes called the *standard error of estimation.* The residuals are defined as before, as the difference between the observed value and the predicted value of y:

$$y_i - \hat{y}_i = y_i - (\hat{\beta}_0 + \hat{\beta}_1 x_{i1} + \hat{\beta}_2 x_{i2} + \cdots + \hat{\beta}_k x_{ik})$$

The sum of squared residuals, SS(Residual), also called SS(Error), is defined exactly as it sounds. Square the prediction errors and sum the squares.

$$\begin{aligned} \text{SS(Residual)} &= \sum (y_i - \hat{y}_i)^2 \\ &= \sum [y_i - (\hat{\beta}_0 + \hat{\beta}_1 x_{i1} + \hat{\beta}_2 x_{i2} + \cdots + \hat{\beta}_k x_{ik})]^2 \end{aligned}$$

The d.f. for this sum of squares is $n - (k + 1)$. One d.f. is subtracted for the intercept and one d.f. is subtracted for each of the k partial slopes. The mean square residual MS(Residual), also called MS(Error), is the residual sum of squares divided by $n - (k + 1)$. Finally, the residual standard deviation s_ϵ is the square root of MS(Residual).

The residual standard deviation may be called "std dev," "standard error," or "root MSE." If the output's not clear, you can take the square root of MS(Residual) by hand. As always, interpret the standard deviation by the Empirical Rule. About 95% of the prediction errors will be within ± 2 standard deviations of the mean (and the mean error is automatically zero).

$$\begin{aligned} s_\epsilon &= \sqrt{\text{MS(Residual)}} \\ &= \sqrt{\frac{\text{SS(Residual)}}{n - (k + 1)}} \end{aligned}$$

EXAMPLE 12.5 Identify SS(Residual) and s_ϵ in the Minitab output shown here for the data of Example 12.3.

```
Regression Analysis: y versus x1, x2

The regression equation is
y = 39.0 + 0.983 x1 + 0.333 x2

Predictor     Coef    SE Coef        T       P
Constant    39.000      1.256    31.05   0.000
x1          0.9833     0.1538     6.39   0.001
x2          0.3333     0.3076     1.08   0.320

S = 3.768     R-Sq = 87.5%    R-Sq(adj) = 83.3%

Analysis of Variance

Source            DF       SS       MS       F       P
Regression         2   596.83   298.42   21.02   0.002
Residual Error     6    85.17    14.19
Total              8   682.00
```

SOLUTION   In the section of the output labeled Analysis of Variance, SS(Residual) is shown as SS(Residual Error) = 85.17, with 6 d.f. MS(Error) is 14.19. The residual standard deviation is indicated by S = 3.768. Note that $3.768 = \sqrt{14.19}$ to within round-off error.

The residual standard deviation is crucial in determining the probable error of a prediction using the regression equation. The precise standard error to be used in forecasting an individual y value is stated in Section 12.5. A rough approximation, ignoring extrapolation and d.f. effects, is that the probable error is $\pm 2s_\epsilon$. This approximation can be used as a rough indicator of the forecasting quality of a regression model.

EXAMPLE 12.6   The admissions office of a business school develops a regression model that uses aptitude test scores and class rank to predict the grade average (4.00 = straight A; 2.00 = C average, the minimum graduation average; 0.00 = straight F). The residual standard deviation is $s_\epsilon = .46$. Does this value suggest highly accurate prediction?

SOLUTION   A measure of the probable error of prediction is $2s_\epsilon = .92$. For example, if a predicted average is 2.80, then an individual's grade is roughly between $2.80 - .92 = 1.88$ (not good enough to graduate) and $2.80 + .92 = 3.72$ (good enough to graduate magna cum laude)! This is *not* an accurate forecast.

coefficient of determination   The **coefficient of determination,** R^2, is defined and interpreted very much like the r^2 value in Chapter 11. (The customary notation is R^2 for multiple regression and r^2 for simple linear regression.) As in Chapter 11, we define the coefficient of determination as the proportional reduction in the squared error of y, which we obtain by knowing the values of $x_1, \ldots, x_k$. For example, if we have the multiple regression model with three x values, and $R^2_{y \cdot x_1 x_2 x_3} = .736$, then we can account for 73.6% of the variability of the y values by variability in x_1, x_2, and x_3. Formally,

$$R^2_{y \cdot x_1 \cdots x_k} = \frac{SS(Total) - SS(Residual)}{SS(Total)}$$

where

$$SS(Total) = \sum (y_i - \bar{y})^2$$

EXAMPLE 12.7   Locate the value of $R^2_{y \cdot x_1 x_2}$ in the computer output of Example 12.5.

SOLUTION   We want R-Sq = 87.5%, not R-Sq(adj). Alternatively, SS(Total) = 682.00 and SS(Residual) = 85.17 are shown in the output, and we can compute $R^2_{y \cdot x_1 x_2} = (682.00 - 85.17)/682.00 = .875$.

There is no general relation between the multiple R^2 from a multiple regression equation and the individual coefficients of determination $r^2_{yx_1}, r^2_{yx_2}, \ldots, r^2_{yx_k}$ other than that multiple R^2 must be at least as big as any of the individual r^2 values. If all the independent variables are themselves perfectly uncorrelated with each other, then multiple R^2 is just the sum of the individual r^2 values. Equivalently, if all the x's are uncorrelated with each other, SS(Regression) for the all-predictors model is equal to the sum of SS(Regression) values for simple regressions using one x at a time. If the x's are correlated, it is much more difficult to take apart the overall predictive value of $x_1, x_2, \ldots, x_k$ as measured by $R^2_{y \cdot x_1 \cdots x_k}$, into separate pieces that can be attributable to x_1 alone, to x_2 alone, $\ldots$, and to x_k alone.

collinearity   When the independent variables are themselves correlated, **collinearity** (sometimes called *multicollinearity*) is present. In multiple regression, we are trying to separate out the predictive value of several predictors. When the predictors are highly correlated, this task is very difficult. For example, suppose that we try to explain variation in regional housing sales over time, using gross domestic product (GDP) and national disposable income (DI) as two of the predictors. DI has been almost exactly a fraction of GDP, so the correlation of these two predictors will be extremely high. Now, is variation in housing sales attributable more to variation in GDP or to variation in DI? Good luck taking those two apart! It's very likely that either predictor alone will explain variation in housing sales almost as well as both together.

Collinearity is usually present to some degree in a multiple regression study. It is a slight problem for slightly correlated x's but a more severe one for highly correlated x's. Thus, if collinearity occurs in a regression study, and it usually does to some degree, it is not easy to take apart the overall $R^2_{y \cdot x_1 x_2 \cdots x_k}$ into separate components associated with each x variable. The correlated x's often account for overlapping pieces of the variability in y, so that often, but not inevitably,

$$R^2_{y \cdot x_1 x_2 \cdots x_k} < r^2_{y x_1} + r^2_{y x_2} + \cdots + r^2_{y x_k}$$

sequential sums of squares   Many statistical computer programs will report **sequential sums of squares.** These SS are *incremental* contributions to SS(Regression), when the independent variables enter the regression model in the order you specify to the program. Sequential sums of squares depend heavily on the particular order in which the independent variables enter the model. Again, the trouble is collinearity. For example, if all variables in a regression study are strongly and positively correlated (as often happens in economic data), whichever independent variable happens to be entered first typically accounts for most of the explainable variation in y, and the remaining variables add little to the sequential SS. The explanatory power of any x, given all the other x's (which is sometimes called the *unique predictive value* of that x), is small. When the data exhibit severe collinearity, separating out the predictive value of the various independent variables is very difficult indeed.

EXAMPLE 12.8   Interpret the sequential sums of squares in the following Minitab output for the data of Example 12.3. If x_2 and x_1 were used as predictors (in that order), would we obtain the same sequential sums of squares numbers?

```
Correlations: y, x1, x2

           y        x1
x1    0.922
x2    0.156   0.000
```

```
Regression Analysis: y versus x1, x2

The regression equation is
y = 39.0 + 0.983 x1 + 0.333 x2

Predictor     Coef    SE Coef      T       P
Constant    39.000      1.256   31.05   0.000
x1           0.9833     0.1538    6.39   0.001
x2           0.3333     0.3076    1.08   0.320

S = 3.76754    R-Sq = 87.5%    R-Sq(adj) = 83.3%

Analysis of Variance

Source            DF      SS      MS      F       P
Regression         2   596.83  298.42  21.02   0.002
Residual Error     6    85.17   14.19
Total              8   682.00

Source   DF   Seq SS
x1        1   580.17
x2        1    16.67

Regression Analysis: y versus x2, x1

The regression equation is
y = 39.0 + 0.333 x2 + 0.983 x1

Predictor     Coef    SE Coef      T       P
Constant    39.000      1.256   31.05   0.000
x2           0.3333     0.3076    1.08   0.320
x1           0.9833     0.1538    6.39   0.001

S = 3.76754    R-Sq = 87.5%    R-Sq(adj) = 83.3%

Analysis of Variance

Source            DF      SS      MS      F       P
Regression         2   596.83  298.42  21.02   0.002
Residual Error     6    85.17   14.19
Total              8   682.00

Source   DF   Seq SS
x2        1    16.67
x1        1   580.17
```

SOLUTION The "SEQ SS" column shows that x_1 by itself accounts for 580.17 of the total variation in y and that adding x_2 after x_1 accounts for another 16.67 of the y variation. This example is a rarity in that the predictors are completely uncorrelated; in this unusual case, the order of adding predictors doesn't matter.

Exercises

12.1 A manufacturer of industrial chemicals investigates the effect on its sales of promotion activities (primarily direct contact and trade show), direct development expenditures, and short-range research effort. Data are assembled for 24 quarters (6 years) and analyzed by Minitab as shown (in $100,000 per quarter).

```
Regression Analysis: Sales versus Promotion, Development, Research

The regression equation is
Sales = 326 + 136 Promotion - 61.2 Development - 43.7 Research
```

```
Predictor      Coef   SE Coef     T       P
Constant      326.4    241.6    1.35   0.192
Promotion    136.10    28.11    4.84   0.000
Development  -61.18    50.94   -1.20   0.244
Research     -43.70    48.32   -0.90   0.377

S = 25.6282   R-Sq = 77.0%   R-Sq(adj) = 73.5%

Analysis of Variance

Source          DF      SS      MS      F       P
Regression       3   43902   14634   22.28   0.000
Residual Error  20   13136     657
Total           23   57038
```

a. Write the estimated regression equation.
b. Locate MS(Residual) and its square root, the residual standard deviation.
c. Locate SS(Residual) and the coefficient of determination R^2.

12.2 State the interpretation of $\hat{\beta}_1$, the estimated coefficient of promotion expenses, of Exercise 12.1.

12.3 The following artificial data are designed to illustrate the effect of correlated and uncorrelated independent variables:

$$
\begin{array}{lcccccccccccc}
y\colon & 17 & 21 & 26 & 22 & 27 & 25 & 28 & 34 & 29 & 37 & 38 & 38 \\
x\colon & 1 & 1 & 1 & 1 & 2 & 2 & 2 & 2 & 3 & 3 & 3 & 3 \\
w\colon & 1 & 2 & 3 & 4 & 1 & 2 & 3 & 4 & 1 & 2 & 3 & 4 \\
v\colon & 1 & 1 & 2 & 2 & 3 & 3 & 4 & 4 & 5 & 5 & 6 & 6 \\
\end{array}
$$

```
Regression Analysis: y versus x

The regression equation is
y = 14.5 + 7.00 x

Predictor      Coef   SE Coef     T       P
Constant     14.500    2.888    5.02   0.001
x             7.000    1.337    5.24   0.000

S = 3.78152   R-Sq = 73.3%   R-Sq(adj) = 70.6%

Analysis of Variance

Source          DF      SS      MS      F       P
Regression       1   392.00  392.00   27.41   0.000
Residual Error  10   143.00   14.30
Total           11   535.00

Regression Analysis: y versus x, w, v

The regression equation is
y = 10.0 + 5.00 x + 2.00 w + 1.00 v

Predictor      Coef   SE Coef     T       P
Constant     10.000    5.766    1.73   0.121
x             5.000    6.895    0.73   0.489
w             2.000    1.528    1.31   0.227
v             1.000    3.416    0.29   0.777

S = 2.64574   R-Sq = 89.5%   R-Sq(adj) = 85.6%
```

```
Analysis of Variance

Source              DF       SS      MS      F      P
Regression           3   479.00  159.67  22.81  0.000
Residual Error       8    56.00    7.00
Total               11   535.00

Source  DF  Seq SS
x        1  392.00
w        1   86.40
v        1    0.60

Correlations: y, x, w, v

        y       x       w
x   0.856
w   0.402   0.000
v   0.928   0.956   0.262
```

a. Plot x versus w, x versus v, and w versus v.
b. Which of these plots indicate zero correlations?

12.4 Use the Minitab output for the data of Exercise 12.3.
a. For both models, write the least-squares prediction equation. Locate the residual standard deviation s_ϵ.
b. Show that the multiple R^2 is larger than the r^2 of the simple regression. Is the residual standard deviation smaller?

12.5 A chemical firm tests the yield that results from the presence of varying amounts of two catalysts. Yields are measured for five different amounts of catalyst 1 paired with four different amounts of catalyst 2. A second-order model is fit to approximate the anticipated nonlinear relation. The variables are y = yield, x_1 = amount of catalyst 1, x_2 = amount of catalyst 2, $x_3 = x_1^2$, $x_4 = x_1 x_2$, and $x_5 = x_2^2$. The data are analyzed by Minitab. Selected output is shown next.

```
Regression Analysis: Yield versus Cat1, Cat2, Cat1Sq, Cat1*Cat2, Cat2Sq

The regression equation is
Yield = 50.0 + 6.64 Cat1 + 7.31 Cat2 - 1.23 Cat1Sq - 0.772 Cat1*Cat2
        - 1.18 Cat2Sq

Predictor      Coef  SE Coef      T      P
Constant     50.020    4.391  11.39  0.000
Cat1          6.644    2.012   3.30  0.005
Cat2          7.314    2.740   2.67  0.018
Cat1Sq      -1.2314   0.3020  -4.08  0.001
Cat1*Cat2   -0.7724   0.3196  -2.42  0.030
Cat2Sq      -1.1755   0.5053  -2.33  0.036

S = 2.25972   R-Sq = 86.2%   R-Sq(adj) = 81.3%

Analysis of Variance

Source              DF       SS      MS      F      P
Regression           5  448.192  89.639  17.55  0.000
Residual Error      14   71.489   5.106
Total               19  519.681

Source     DF  Seq SS
Cat1        1  286.438
Cat2        1   19.369
Cat1Sq      1   84.919
Cat1*Cat2   1   29.830
Cat2Sq      1   27.636
```

a. Write the estimated regression equation.
b. Locate SS(Residual) and the residual standard deviation.

12.6   Refer to Exercise 12.5.
a. Find the R^2 value for predicting yield using all five predictors.
b. According to the conditional (sequential) sum of squares, how much of the variability is accounted for by Cat1 and Cat2, without the other terms?

12.3   Inferences in Multiple Regression

The ideas of the preceding section involve point (best-guess) estimation of the regression coefficients, the standard deviation s_ϵ, and the coefficient of determination R^2. Because these estimates are based on sample data, they will be in error to some extent, and a manager should allow for that error in interpreting the model. In this section we discuss tests about the partial slope parameters in a multiple regression model.

First, we present a test of an overall null hypothesis about the partial slopes (β_1, $\beta_2, \ldots, \beta_k$) in the multiple regression model. According to this hypothesis, H_0: $\beta_1 = \beta_2 = \cdots = \beta_k = 0$, none of the variables included in the multiple regression has any predictive value at all. This is the "nullest" of null hypotheses; it says that all those carefully chosen predictors are absolutely useless. The research hypothesis is a very general one, namely, H_a: At least one $\beta_j \neq 0$. This merely says that there is some predictive value somewhere in the set of predictors.

The test statistic is the F statistic of Chapter 11. To state the test, we first define the sum of squares attributable to the regression of y on the variables $x_1, x_2, \ldots, x_k$. We designate this sum of squares as SS(Regression); it is also called SS(Model) or the *explained sum of squares*. It is the sum of squared differences between predicted values and the mean y value.

DEFINITION 12.2

SS(Regression)

$$\text{SS(Regression)} = \sum (\hat{y}_i - \bar{y})^2$$
$$\text{SS(Total)} = \sum (y_i - y)^2$$
$$= \text{SS(Regression)} + \text{SS(Residual)}$$

Unlike SS(Total) and SS(Residual), we don't interpret SS(Regression) in terms of prediction error. Rather, it measures the extent to which the predictions $\hat{y}_i$ vary as the x's vary. If SS(Regression) = 0, the predicted y values ($\hat{y}$) are all the same. In such a case, information about the x's is useless in predicting y. If SS(Regression) is large relative to SS(Residual), the indication is that there is real predictive value in the independent variables $x_1, x_2, \ldots, x_k$. We state the test statistic in terms of mean squares rather than sums of squares. As always, a mean square is a sum of squares divided by the appropriate d.f.

DEFINITION 12.3

F Test of H_0: $\beta_1 = \beta_2 = \cdots = \beta_k = 0$

H_0: $\beta_1 = \beta_2 = \cdots = \beta_k = 0$

H_a: At least one $\beta \neq 0$

T.S.: $F = \dfrac{\text{SS(Regression)}/k}{\text{SS(Residual)}/[n - (k + 1)]} = \dfrac{\text{MS(Regression)}}{\text{MS(Residual)}}$

R.R: With d.f.$_1 = k$ and d.f.$_2 = n - (k + 1)$, reject H_0 if $F > F_\alpha$

EXAMPLE 12.9

a. Locate SS(Regression) in the Minitab computer output of Example 12.5, reproduced here.

b. Locate the F statistic.

c. Can we safely conclude that the independent variables x_1 and x_2 together have at least some predictive power?

```
Regression Analysis: y versus x1, x2

The regression equation is
y = 39.0 + 0.983 x1 + 0.333 x2

Predictor     Coef   SE Coef       T       P
Constant    39.000     1.256   31.05   0.000
x1          0.9833    0.1538    6.39   0.001
x2          0.3333    0.3076    1.08   0.320

S = 3.768      R-Sq = 87.5%    R-Sq(adj) = 83.3%

Analysis of Variance

Source           DF       SS      MS       F       P
Regression        2   596.83  298.42   21.02   0.002
Residual Error    6    85.17   14.19
Total             8   682.00
```

SOLUTION

a. SS(Regression) is shown in the Analysis of Variance section of the output as 596.83.

b. The MS(Regression) and MS(Residual) values are also shown there. MS(Residual) is labeled as MS(Residual Error), a common alternative name.

$$F = \frac{\text{MS(Regression)}}{\text{MS(Residual)}} = \frac{298.42}{14.19} = 21.02$$

c. For d.f.$_1$ = 2, d.f.$_2$ = 6, and α = .01, the tabled F value is 10.92. Therefore, we have strong evidence (p-value well below .01 and shown as .002) to reject the null hypothesis and to conclude that the x's collectively have at least some predictive value.

This F test may also be stated in terms of R^2. Recall that $R^2_{y \cdot x_1 \cdots x_k}$ measures the reduction in squared error for y attributed to knowledge of all the x predictors. Because the regression of y on the x's accounts for a proportion $R^2_{y \cdot x_1 \cdots x_k}$ of the total squared error in y,

$$\text{SS(Regression)} = R^2_{y \cdot x_1 \cdots x_k}\text{SS(Total)}$$

The remaining fraction, $1 - R^2$, is incorporated in the residual squared error

$$\text{SS(Residual)} = (1 - R^2_{y \cdot x_1 \cdots x_k})\text{SS(Total)}$$

F and R^2

Showing the relationship of **F and R^2**, the overall F test statistic can be rewritten as

$$F = \frac{\text{MS(Regression)}}{\text{MS(Residual)}} = \frac{R^2_{y \cdot x_1 \cdots x_k}/k}{(1 - R^2_{y \cdot x_1 \cdots x_k})/[n - (k + 1)]}$$

This statistic is to be compared with tabulated F values for d.f.$_1$ = k and d.f.$_2$ = $n - (k + 1)$.

EXAMPLE 12.10   A large city bank studies the relation of average account size in each of its branches to per capita income in the corresponding ZIP code area, number of business accounts, and number of competitive bank branches. The data are analyzed by Minitab, as shown.

```
Regression Analysis: AvgAcctSize versus BusAccts, Competition, Income

The regression equation is
AvgAcctSize = 0.151 - 0.00288 BusAccts - 0.0076 Competition + 0.265 Income

Predictor          Coef     SE Coef       T      P
Constant         0.1509      0.7378    0.20   0.840
BusAccts      -0.0028856   0.0008894   -3.24   0.005
Competition     -0.00759     0.05809   -0.13   0.897
Income           0.2653      0.1013    2.62   0.018

S = 0.199207   R-Sq = 79.7%   R-Sq(adj) = 76.2%

Analysis of Variance

Source          DF        SS        MS       F      P
Regression       3   2.65375   0.88458   22.29  0.000
Residual Error  17   0.67461   0.03967
Total           20   3.32837

Source        DF    Seq SS
BusAccts       1   1.60032
Competition    1   0.78111
Income         1   0.27230
```

a. Identify the multiple regression prediction equation.

b. Use the R^2 value shown to test $H_0: \beta_1 = \beta_2 = \beta_3 = 0$. (*Note: n = 21.*)

SOLUTION

a. From the output, the multiple regression forecasting equation is

$$\hat{y} = 0.151 - 0.00288x_1 - 0.006x_2 + 0.265x_3$$

b. The test procedure based on R^2 is

$$H_0: \beta_1 = \beta_2 = \beta_3 = 0$$
$$H_a: \text{At least one } \beta_j \text{ differs from zero}$$

$$\text{T.S.: } F = \frac{R^2_{y \cdot x_1 x_2 x_3}/3}{(1 - R^2_{y \cdot x_1 x_2 x_3})/(21 - 4)}$$

$$= \frac{.797/3}{.203/17} = 22.29$$

R.R.: For d.f.$_1$ = 3 and d.f.$_2$ = 17, the critical .05 value of F is 3.20.

Because the computed F statistic, 22.29, is greater than 3.20, we reject H_0 and conclude that one or more of the x values has some predictive power. This also follows because the p-value, shown as .0000, is (much) less than .05. Note that the F value we compute is the same as that shown in the output.

Rejection of the null hypothesis of this F test is not an overwhelmingly impressive conclusion. This rejection merely indicates that there is good evidence of *some* degree of predictive value *somewhere* among the independent variables. It does not give any direct indication of how strong the relation is, nor any indication of which individual independent variables are useful. The next task, therefore, is to make inferences about the individual partial slopes.

To make these inferences, we need the estimated standard error of each partial slope. As always, the standard error for any estimate based on sample data indicates how accurate that estimate should be. These standard errors are computed and shown by most regression computer programs. They depend on three things: the residual standard deviation, the amount of variation in the predictor variable, and the degree of correlation between that predictor and the others. The expression that we present for the standard error is useful in considering the effect of collinearity (correlated independent variables), but it is *not* a particularly good way to do the computation. Let a computer program do the arithmetic.

DEFINITION 12.4

Estimated Standard Error of $\hat{\beta}_j$ in a Multiple Regression

$$s_{\hat{\beta}_j} = s_\epsilon \sqrt{\frac{1}{\sum (x_{ij} - \bar{x}_j)^2 (1 - R^2_{x_j \cdot x_1 \cdots x_{j-1} x_{j+1} \cdots x_k})}}$$

where $R^2_{x_j \cdot x_1 \cdots x_{j-1} x_{j+1} \cdots x_k}$ is the R^2 value obtained by letting x_j be the *dependent* variable in a multiple regression with all other x's as independent variables. Note that s_ϵ is the residual standard deviation for the multiple regression of y on the $x_1, x_2, \ldots, x_k$.

Just as in simple regression, the larger the residual standard deviation, the larger the uncertainty in estimating coefficients. Also, the less variability there is in the predictor, the larger is the standard error of the coefficient. The most important use of

effect of collinearity   the formula for estimated standard error is to illustrate the **effect of collinearity.** If the independent variable x_j is highly collinear with one or more other independent variables, $R^2_{x_j \cdot x_1 \cdots x_{j-1} x_{j+1} \cdots x_k}$ is by definition very large and $1 - R^2_{x_j \cdot x_1 \cdots x_{j-1} x_{j+1} \cdots x_k}$ is near zero. Division by a near-zero number yields a very large standard error. Thus one important effect of severe collinearity is that it results in very large standard errors of partial slopes and therefore very inaccurate estimates of those slopes.

variance inflation factor   The term $1/(1 - R^2_{x_j \cdot x_1 \cdots x_{j-1} x_{j+1} \cdots x_k})$ is called the **variance inflation factor** (VIF). It measures how much the variance (square of the standard error) of a coefficient is increased because of collinearity. This factor is printed out by some computer packages and is a good way to assess how serious the collinearity problem is. If the VIF is 1, there is no collinearity at all. If it is very large, like 10 or more, collinearity is a serious problem.

A large standard error for any estimated partial slope indicates a large probable error for the estimate. The partial slope $\hat{\beta}_j$ of x_j estimates the effect of increasing x_j by one unit while all other x's remain constant. If x_j is highly collinear with other x's, when x_j increases the other x's also vary rather than stay constant. Therefore, it is difficult to estimate β_j, and its probable error is large when x_j is severely collinear with other independent variables.

The standard error of each estimated partial slope $\hat{\beta}_j$ is used in a confidence interval and statistical test for β_j. The confidence interval follows the familiar format of estimate $\pm$ (table value)(estimated standard error). The table value is from the t table with the error d.f., $n - (k + 1)$.

DEFINITION 12.5

Confidence Interval for β_j

$$\hat{\beta}_j - t_{\alpha/2}s_{\hat{\beta}_j} \le \beta_j \le \hat{\beta}_j + t_{\alpha/2}s_{\hat{\beta}_j}$$

where $t_{\alpha/2}$ cuts off area $\alpha/2$ in the tail of a t distribution with d.f. $= n - (k + 1)$, the error d.f.

EXAMPLE 12.11

Calculate a 95% confidence interval for β_1 in the two-predictor model for the data of Example 12.4. Relevant Minitab output follows. The sample size was 5.

```
Regression Analysis: y versus x1, x2

The regression equation is
y = 10.0 + 1.00 x1 + 3.00 x2

Predictor     Coef   SE Coef      T      P
Constant    10.000     1.183   8.45  0.014
x1           1.000     1.871   0.53  0.646
x2           3.000     4.183   0.72  0.548

S = 2.64574   R-Sq = 78.8%   R-Sq(adj) = 57.6%
```

SOLUTION $\hat{\beta}_1$ is 1.00 and the standard error is shown as 1.871. The t value that cuts off an area of .025 in a t distribution with d.f. $= n - (k + 1) = 5 - (2 + 1) = 2$ is 4.303. The confidence interval is $1.00 - 4.303(1.871) \le \beta_1 \le 1.00 + 4.303(1.871)$, or $-7.050 \le \beta_1 \le 9.050$.

EXAMPLE 12.12

Locate the estimated partial slope for x_2 and its standard error in the Minitab output of Example 12.5. Calculate a 90% confidence interval for β_2.

```
Regression Analysis: y versus x1, x2

The regression equation is
y = 39.0 + 0.983 x1 + 0.333 x2

Predictor     Coef   SE Coef      T      P
Constant    39.000     1.256  31.05  0.000
x1          0.9833    0.1538   6.39  0.001
x2          0.3333    0.3076   1.08  0.320
```

SOLUTION $\hat{\beta}_2$ is .3333 with standard error (labeled SE Coef) .3076. The tabled t value is 1.943 [tail area .05, $9 - (2 + 1) = 6$ d.f.]. The desired interval is $.3333 - 1.943(.3076) \le \beta_2 \le .3333 + 1.943(.3076)$, or $-.2644 \le \beta_2 \le .9310$.

interpretation of
H_0: $\beta_j = 0$
last predictor in

The usual null hypothesis for inference about β_j is H_0: $\beta_j = 0$. This hypothesis does not assert that x_j has no predictive value by itself. It asserts that it has no *additional* predictive value over and above that contributed by the other independent variables; that is, if all other x's had already been used in a regression model and then x_j was added last, no improvement in prediction would result. Our **interpretation of** H_0: $\beta_j = 0$ means that x_j has no additional predictive value as the **"last predictor in."** The t test of this H_0 is summarized next.

DEFINITION 12.6

Summary for Testing H_0: $\beta_j = 0$

H_0: $\beta_j = 0$

H_a: 1. $\beta_j > 0$
 2. $\beta_j < 0$
 3. $\beta_j \neq 0$

T.S.: $t = \hat{\beta}_j / s_{\hat{\beta}_j}$

R.R.: 1. $t > t_\alpha$
 2. $t < -t_\alpha$
 3. $|t| > t_{\alpha/2}$

where t_a cuts off a right-tail area a in the t distribution with d.f. $= n - (k + 1)$.

This test statistic is shown by virtually all multiple regression programs.

EXAMPLE 12.13

a. Use the information given in Example 12.11 to test H_0: $\beta_1 = 0$ at $\alpha = .05$. Use a two-sided alternative.

b. Is the conclusion of the test compatible with the confidence interval?

SOLUTION

a. The test statistic for H_0: $\beta_1 = 0$ versus H_a: $\beta_1 \neq 0$ is $t = \hat{\beta}_1 / s_{\hat{\beta}_1} = 1.00/1.871 = .535$. Because the .025 point for the t distribution with $5 - (2 + 1) = 2$ d.f. is 4.303, H_0 must be retained; x_1 has not been shown to have any additional predictive power in the presence of the other independent variable, x_2.

b. The 95% confidence interval includes zero, which also indicates that H_0: $\beta_1 = 0$ must be retained at $\alpha = .05$, two-tailed.

EXAMPLE 12.14

Locate the t statistic for testing H_0: $\beta_2 = 0$ in the output of Example 12.12. Can H_a: $\beta_2 > 0$ be supported at any of the usual α levels?

SOLUTION The t statistics are shown under the heading T. For x_2 the t statistic is 1.08. The t table value for 6 d.f. and $\alpha = .10$ is 1.440, so H_0 cannot be rejected even at $\alpha = .10$. Alternatively, the one-tailed p-value is .320/2, larger than $\alpha = .10$, so again H_0 can't be rejected.

The multiple regression F and t tests that we discuss in this chapter test different null hypotheses. It sometimes happens that the F test results in the rejection of H_0: $\beta_1 = \beta_2 = \cdots = \beta_k = 0$, while no t test of H_0: $\beta_j = 0$ is significant. In such a case, we can conclude that there is predictive value in the equation as a whole, but we cannot identify the specific variables that have predictive value. Remember that each t test is testing "last predictor in" value. Does this variable add predictive value, given all the other predictors, wherever they are listed? When two or more predictor variables are highly correlated among themselves, it often happens that no x_j can be shown to have significant "last in" predictive value, even though the x's together have been shown to be useful. If we are trying to predict housing sales based on gross domestic product and disposable income, we probably can't prove that GDP adds value, given DI, or that DI adds value, given GDP. Whichever predictor we take last may not add more-than-random predictive value.

Exercises

12.7 Refer to the Minitab computer output of Exercise 12.1. Here it is again.

```
Regression Analysis: Sales versus Promotion, Development, Research

The regression equation is
Sales = 326 + 136 Promotion - 61.2 Development - 43.7 Research

Predictor        Coef   SE Coef       T      P
Constant        326.4     241.6    1.35  0.192
Promotion      136.10     28.11    4.84  0.000
Development     -61.18     50.94   -1.20  0.244
Research        -43.70     48.32   -0.90  0.377

S = 25.6282    R-Sq = 77.0%    R-Sq(adj) = 73.5%

Analysis of Variance

Source            DF      SS      MS      F      P
Regression         3   43902   14634  22.28  0.000
Residual Error    20   13136     657
Total             23   57038
```

a. Locate the F statistic.
b. Can the hypothesis of no overall predictive value be rejected at $\alpha = .01$?
c. Locate the t statistic for the coefficient of promotion $\hat{\beta}_1$.
d. Test the research hypothesis that $\beta_1 \neq 0$. Use $\alpha = .05$.
e. State the conclusion of the test in part (d).

12.8 Locate the p-value for the test of the previous exercise, part (d). Is it one-tailed or two-tailed?

12.9 Summarize the results of the t tests in Exercise 12.7. What null hypotheses are being tested?

12.10 Refer to the computer output of Exercise 12.3 or the following Minitab output:

```
Regression Analysis: y versus x, w, v

The regression equation is
y = 10.0 + 5.00 x + 2.00 w + 1.00 v

Predictor       Coef   SE Coef      T      P
Constant      10.000     5.766   1.73  0.121
x              5.000     6.895   0.73  0.489
w              2.000     1.528   1.31  0.227
v              1.000     3.416   0.29  0.777

S = 2.64574    R-Sq = 89.5%    R-Sq(adj) = 85.6%

Analysis of Variance

Source            DF      SS      MS      F      P
Regression         3  479.00  159.67  22.81  0.000
Residual Error     8   56.00    7.00
Total             11  535.00
```

```
Source   DF   Seq SS
x         1   392.00
w         1    86.40
v         1     0.60
```

a. Locate MS(Regression) and MS(Residual).
b. What is the value of the F statistic?
c. Determine the p-value for the F test.
d. What conclusion can be established from the F test?
e. Calculate a 95% confidence interval for the true coefficient of x.

12.11 A metalworking firm conducts an energy study using multiple regression methods. The dependent variable is y = energy consumption cost per day (in thousands of dollars), and the independent variables are x_1 = tons of metal processed in the day, x_2 = average external temperature $-60°F$ (a union contract requires cooling of the plant whenever outside temperatures reach $60°$), x_3 = rated wattage for machinery in use, and $x_4 = x_1 x_2$. The data are analyzed by Minitab. Selected output is shown here.

```
Correlations: Energy, Metal, MetalxTemp, Temp, Watts

            Energy    Metal   MetalxTemp    Temp
Metal        0.613
MetalxTemp   0.493    0.109
Temp         0.401   -0.061    0.983
Watts        0.577    0.224    0.363      0.353
```

```
Regression Analysis: Energy versus Metal, Temp, Watts, MetalxTemp

The regression equation is
Energy = 7.2 + 1.36 Metal + 0.31 Temp + 0.0102 Watts - 0.0028 MetalxTemp
```

```
Predictor        Coef    SE Coef      T      P      VIF
Constant         7.20      17.53   0.41  0.685
Metal          1.3629     0.9244   1.47  0.156      8.8
Temp            0.306      1.621   0.19  0.852    250.0
Watts        0.010242   0.004732   2.16  0.043      1.5
MetalxTemp   -0.00277    0.07722  -0.04  0.972    246.4
```

```
S = 2.55255   R-Sq = 66.4%   R-Sq(adj) = 59.6%
```

```
Analysis of Variance

Source          DF       SS       MS      F      P
Regression       4  257.048   64.262   9.86  0.000
Residual Error  20  130.310    6.516
Total           24  387.359
```

a. Write the estimated model.
b. Summarize the results of the various t tests.
c. Calculate a 95% confidence interval for the coefficient of MetalxTemp.
d. What does the VIF column of the output indicate about collinearity problems?

12.4 Testing a Subset of the Regression Coefficients

F test for several β_j's

In the last section we presented an F test for testing *all* the coefficients in a regression model and a t test for testing *one* coefficient. There is also another F test of the null hypothesis that *several* of the true coefficients are zero; that is, that several of the predictors have no value, given the others. For example, if we try to predict the prevailing wage rate in various geographical areas for clerical workers based on the national minimum wage, national inflation rate, population density in the area, and median apartment rental price in the area, we might well want to test if the variables related to area (density and apartment price) added anything, given the national variables.

A null hypothesis for this situation would say that the true coefficients of density and apartment price were zero. According to this null hypothesis, these two independent variables together have no predictive value once minimum wage and inflation are included as predictors. The *t* test of the preceding section tests a single coefficient on a "last predictor in" basis. Now we are testing predictors on a "last two predictors in" basis.

The idea is to compare the SS(Regression) or R^2 values when density and apartment price are excluded and when they are included in the prediction equation. When they are included, the R^2 is automatically at least as large as the R^2 when they are excluded, because we can predict at least as well with more information as with less. Similarly, SS(Regression) will be larger for the complete model. The *F* test for this null hypothesis tests whether the gain is more than could be expected by chance alone. In general, let *k* be the total number of predictors, and let *g* be the number of predictors with coefficients not hypothesized to be zero ($g < k$). Then $k - g$ represents the number of predictors with coefficients that are hypothesized to be zero.

complete and reduced models

The idea is to find SS(Regression) or R^2 values using all predictors (the **complete model**) and using only the *g* predictors that do not appear in the null hypothesis (the **reduced model**). Once these have been computed, the test proceeds as outlined in Definition 12.7. The notation is easier if we assume that the reduced model contains $\beta_1, \beta_2, \ldots, \beta_g$, so that the variables in the null hypothesis are listed last.

DEFINITION 12.7

F Test of a Subset of Predictors

H_0: $\beta_{g+1} = \beta_{g+2} = \cdots = \beta_k = 0$

H_a: H_0 is not true

T.S.: $F = \dfrac{(R^2_{\text{complete}} - R^2_{\text{reduced}})/(k - g)}{(1 - R^2_{\text{complete}})/[n - (k + 1)]}$

R.R.: $F > F_\alpha$, where F_α cuts off a right tail of area α of the *F* distribution with d.f.$_1 = (k - g)$ and d.f.$_2 = [n - (k + 1)]$

Note: This test may also be performed with SS(Regression, complete) − SS(Regression, reduced) replacing $(R^2_{\text{complete}} - R^2_{\text{reduced}})$ and SS(Residual, complete) replacing $(1 - R^2_{\text{complete}})$.

EXAMPLE 12.15

A state fisheries commission wants to estimate the number of bass caught in a given lake during a season in order to restock the lake with the appropriate number of young fish. The commission could get a fairly accurate assessment of the seasonal catch by extensive "netting sweeps" of the lake before and after a season, but this technique is much too expensive to be done routinely. Therefore, the commission samples a number of lakes and records *y*, the seasonal catch (thousands of bass per square mile of lake area); x_1, the number of lakeshore residences per square mile of lake area; x_2, the size of the lake in square miles; $x_3 = 1$ if the lake has public access, 0 if not; and x_4, a structure index. (Structures are weed beds, sunken trees, dropoffs, and other living places for bass.) The data are

y	x_1	x_2	x_3	x_4
3.6	92.2	.21	0	81
.8	86.7	.30	0	26
2.5	80.2	.31	0	52
2.9	87.2	.40	0	64
1.4	64.9	.44	0	40
.9	90.1	.56	0	22
3.2	60.7	.78	0	80
2.7	50.9	1.21	0	60
2.2	86.1	.34	1	30
5.9	90.0	.40	1	90
3.3	80.4	.52	1	74
2.9	75.0	.66	1	50
3.6	70.0	.78	1	61
2.4	64.6	.91	1	40
.9	50.0	1.10	1	22
2.0	50.0	1.24	1	50
1.9	51.2	1.47	1	37
3.1	40.1	2.21	1	61
2.6	45.0	2.46	1	39
3.4	50.0	2.80	1	53

The commission is convinced that x_1 and x_2 are important variables in predicting y because they both reflect how intensively the lake has been fished. There is some question as to whether x_3 and x_4 are useful as additional predictor variables. Therefore, regression models (with all x's entering linearly) are run with and without x_3 and x_4. Relevant portions of the Minitab output follow:

```
Regression Analysis: Catch versus Residences, Size, Access, Structure

The regression equation is
Catch = - 1.94 + 0.0193 Residences + 0.332 Size + 0.836 Access
        + 0.0477 Structure

Predictor       Coef    SE Coef      T      P   VIF
Constant     -1.9378     0.9081  -2.13  0.050
Residences   0.01928    0.01017   1.90  0.077   3.2
Size          0.3323     0.2458   1.35  0.196   3.5
Access        0.8355     0.2250   3.71  0.002   1.3
Structure   0.047714   0.005056   9.44  0.000   1.0

S = 0.433635   R-Sq = 88.2%   R-Sq(adj) = 85.0%

Analysis of Variance

Source          DF       SS      MS      F      P
Regression       4  21.0473  5.2619  27.98  0.000
Residual Error  15   2.8206  0.1880
Total           19  23.8679
```

```
Source         DF    Seq SS
Residences      1    0.2780
Size            1    1.5667
Access          1    2.4579
Structure       1   16.7447
```

Regression Analysis: Catch versus Residences, Size

```
The regression equation is
Catch = - 0.11 + 0.0310 Residences + 0.679 Size


Predictor       Coef   SE Coef      T      P   VIF
Constant      -0.107     2.336  -0.05  0.964
Residences   0.03101   0.02649   1.17  0.258   3.2
Size          0.6794    0.6178   1.10  0.287   3.2


S = 1.13819    R-Sq = 7.7%    R-Sq(adj) = 0.0%

Analysis of Variance

Source           DF      SS      MS     F      P
Regression        2   1.845   0.922  0.71  0.505
Residual Error   17  22.023   1.295
Total            19  23.868

Source         DF   Seq SS
Residences      1    0.278
Size            1    1.567
```

a. Write the complete and reduced models.

b. Write the null hypothesis for testing that the omitted variables have no (incremental) predictive value.

c. Perform an F test for this null hypothesis.

SOLUTION

a. The complete and reduced models are, respectively,

$$Y_i = \beta_0 + \beta_1 x_{i1} + \beta_2 x_{i2} + \beta_3 x_{i3} + \beta_4 x_{i4} + \epsilon_i$$

and

$$Y_i = \beta_0 + \beta_1 x_{i1} + \beta_2 x_{i2} + \epsilon_i$$

The corresponding multiple regression forecasting equations based on the sample data are

$$\text{Complete: } \hat{y} = -1.94 + .0193x_1 + .332x_2 + .836x_3 + .477x_4$$
$$\text{Reduced: } \hat{y} = -.11 + .0310x_1 + .679x_2$$

b. The appropriate null hypothesis of no predictive power for x_3 and x_4 is H_0: $\beta_3 = \beta_4 = 0$.

c. The test statistic for the H_0 of part (b) makes use of $R^2_{\text{complete}} = .882$, $R^2_{\text{reduced}} = .077$, $k = 4$, $g = 2$, and $n = 20$:

$$\text{T.S.: } F = \frac{(R^2_{\text{complete}} - R^2_{\text{reduced}})/(4 - 2)}{(1 - R^2_{\text{complete}})/(20 - 5)} = \frac{(.882 - .077)/2}{(1 - .882)/15} = 51.165$$

Alternatively, we can use the SS(Regression) values shown.

$$\text{T.S.: } F = \frac{\text{SS(Regression, complete)} - \text{SS(Regression, reduced))}/(4 - 2)}{\text{SS(Residual, complete)}/(20 - 5)}$$

$$= \frac{(21.0473 - 1.845)/2}{2.8206/15} = 51.059$$

which gives the same result except for round-off error. The tabled value $F_{.01}$ for 2 and 15 d.f. is 6.36. The actual value of roughly 51 is much larger than the tabled value, so we have conclusive evidence that the Access and Structure variables add predictive value.

Exercises

12.12   The Minitab output for Exercise 12.1 follows.
a. Locate the R^2 value. Use it to confirm the calculation of the F statistic.
b. Can we conclude that there is at least some more-than-random predictive value among the independent variables?

```
Regression Analysis: Sales versus Promotion, Development, Research

The regression equation is
Sales = 326 + 136 Promotion - 61.2 Development - 43.7 Research

Predictor       Coef   SE Coef       T       P
Constant       326.4     241.6    1.35   0.192
Promotion      136.10     28.11    4.84   0.000
Development    -61.18     50.94   -1.20   0.244
Research       -43.70     48.32   -0.90   0.377

S = 25.6282    R-Sq = 77.0%    R-Sq(adj) = 73.5%

Analysis of Variance

Source          DF      SS      MS       F      P
Regression       3   43902   14634   22.28  0.000
Residual Error  20   13136     657
Total           23   57038
```

12.13   Another regression analysis of the data of Exercise 12.12 used only promotion expenditures as an independent variable. The Minitab output follows:

```
Regression Analysis: Sales versus Promotion

The regression equation is
Sales = - 0.6 + 78.2 Promotion

Predictor    Coef   SE Coef       T       P
Constant    -0.65     44.59   -0.01   0.989
Promotion   78.25     10.98    7.13   0.000

S = 27.9912    R-Sq = 69.8%    R-Sq(adj) = 68.4%

Analysis of Variance

Source          DF      SS      MS       F      P
Regression       1   39801   39801   50.80  0.000
Residual Error  22   17237     784
Total           23   57038
```

a. Locate R^2 for this reduced model. Use this value and the R^2 for the complete model to calculate an F statistic to test the null hypothesis that the other slopes are zero.

b. Carry out the steps of an F test, using $\alpha = .01$.

c. Can we conclude that there is at least some more-than-random predictive value among the omitted independent variables?

12.14 Two models based on the data of Example (not Exercise) 12.10 were calculated in Minitab, with the following results:

```
Regression Analysis: AvgAcctSize versus BusAccts, Competition, Income

The regression equation is
AvgAcctSize = 0.151 - 0.00288 BusAccts - 0.0076 Competition + 0.265 Income

Predictor          Coef      SE Coef       T      P
Constant         0.1509       0.7378    0.20  0.840
BusAccts      -0.0028856    0.0008894   -3.24  0.005
Competition    -0.00759      0.05809   -0.13  0.897
Income          0.2653       0.1013     2.62  0.018

S = 0.199207    R-Sq = 79.7%    R-Sq(adj) = 76.2%

Analysis of Variance

Source          DF       SS       MS       F      P
Regression       3    2.65375  0.88458   22.29  0.000
Residual Error  17    0.67461  0.03967
Total           20    3.32837


Regression Analysis: AvgAcctSize versus Income

The regression equation is
AvgAcctSize = 0.124 + 0.202 Income

Predictor      Coef    SE Coef     T       P
Constant     0.1241    0.9677    0.13   0.899
Income       0.20190   0.09124   2.21   0.039

S = 0.373212    R-Sq = 20.5%    R-Sq(adj) = 16.3%

Analysis of Variance

Source          DF      SS       MS       F      P
Regression       1    0.6819   0.6819    4.90  0.039
Residual Error  19    2.6465   0.1393
Total           20    3.3284
```

a. Locate R^2 for the reduced model, with Income as the only predictor.

b. Locate R^2 for the complete model.

c. Calculate the F statistic based on the incremental R^2. State what null hypothesis is being tested, and state the conclusion.

12.15 An automobile financing company uses a rather complex credit rating system for car loans. The questionnaire requires substantial time to fill out, taking sales staff time and risking alienating the customer. The company decides to see if three variables (age, monthly family income, and debt payments as a fraction of income) will reproduce the credit score reasonably accurately. Data were obtained on a sample (with no evident biases) of 500 applications. The complicated credit rating score was calculated and served as the dependent variable in a multiple regression. Some results from JMP are shown in Figure 12.2.

a. How much of the variation in credit scores is accounted for by the model?
b. Use this number to verify the computation of the overall F statistic.
c. Does the F test clearly show that the three independent variables have predictive value for the credit rating score?
d. Give a rough estimate of the variation of credit scores around the predicted credit score from this regression model.

FIGURE 12.2 **Regression Results for Credit Score Data**

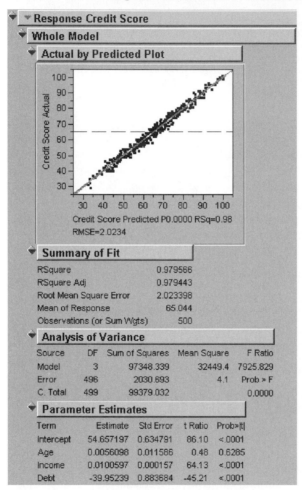

12.16 The credit score data were reanalyzed, using only the monthly income variable as a predictor. JMP results are shown in Figure 12.3.
a. By how much has the regression sum of squares been reduced by eliminating age and debt payment percentage as predictors?
b. Do these two variables add statistically significant predictive value (at normal α levels), given the presence of income in the model?

FIGURE 12.3 **Regression Results Using Income Only**

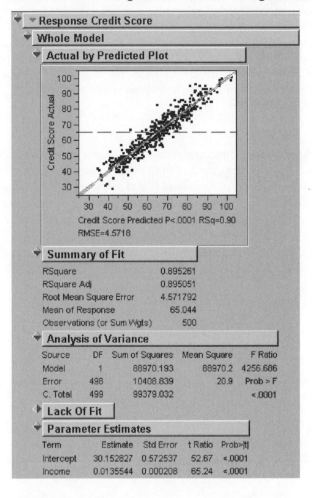

Summary of Fit	
RSquare	0.895261
RSquare Adj	0.895051
Root Mean Square Error	4.571792
Mean of Response	65.044
Observations (or Sum Wgts)	500

Analysis of Variance

Source	DF	Sum of Squares	Mean Square	F Ratio
Model	1	88970.193	88970.2	4256.686
Error	498	10408.839	20.9	Prob > F
C. Total	499	99379.032		<.0001

Lack Of Fit

Parameter Estimates

Term	Estimate	Std Error	t Ratio	Prob>|t|
Intercept	30.152827	0.572537	52.67	<.0001
Income	0.0135544	0.000208	65.24	<.0001

12.5 Forecasting Using Multiple Regression

One of the major uses for multiple regression models is in forecasting a y value given certain values of the independent x variables. The best-guess forecast is easy; just substitute the assumed x values into the estimated regression equation. In this section, we discuss the relevant standard errors.

As in simple regression, the forecast of y for given x values can be interpreted two ways. The resulting value can be thought of as the best guess for $E(Y)$, the long-run average y value that results from averaging infinitely many observations of y when the x's have the specified values. The alternative, and usually more interesting, interpretation is that this is the predicted y value for *one* individual case having the given x values. The standard errors for both interpretations require matrix algebra ideas that aren't required for this text.

Computer programs typically give a standard error for an individual y forecast. While this information can also be used to find a standard error for estimating $E(Y)$, the individual y forecast is usually more relevant. In most computer output, a forecast interval for the mean value is called a *confidence interval;* a forecast interval for an individual value is called a *prediction interval.* The appropriate plus-or-minus term for forecasting can be found by multiplying the standard error by a tabled t value with d.f. $= n - (k + 1)$. In fact, many computer programs give the plus-or-minus term directly. As a rough approximation, we can use $\pm 2s_\epsilon$ as an allowance for forecast error of an individual prediction.

EXAMPLE 12.16   An advertising manager for a manufacturer of prepared cereals wants to develop an equation to predict sales (y) based on advertising expenditures for children's television (c), daytime television (d), and newspapers (n). Data were collected monthly for the previous 30 months (and divided by a price index to control for inflation). A multiple linear regression is fit, yielding the following Minitab output:

```
Regression Analysis: y versus c, d, n

The regression equation is
y = 0.350 + 0.0649 c + 0.0063 d + 0.0579 n

Predictor      Coef    SE Coef      T       P
Constant     0.3495     0.5378    0.65    0.521
c            0.06487    0.01705   3.80    0.001
d            0.00628    0.02393   0.26    0.795
n            0.05784    0.02112   2.74    0.011

S = 0.181599    R-Sq = 67.5%    R-Sq(adj) = 63.7%

Analysis of Variance

Source           DF        SS        MS       F       P
Regression        3   1.77786   0.59261   17.97   0.000
Residual Error   26   0.85742   0.03297
Total            29   2.63529

Source   DF   Seq SS
c         1   1.12460
d         1   0.40612
n         1   0.24712

Predicted Values for New Observations

New Obs     Fit   SE Fit        95% CI               95% PI
   1     3.0866   0.1397   (2.7994, 3.3738)   (2.6156, 3.5576)X

X denotes a point that is an outlier in the predictors.

Values of Predictors for New Observations

New Obs      c      d      n
   1      31.0   5.00   12.0
```

a.   Write the regression equation.

b.   Locate the predicted y value ($\hat{y}$) when $c = 31$, $d = 5$, and $n = 12$. Locate the lower and upper limits for a 95% confidence interval for $E(Y)$ and the upper and lower 95% prediction limits for an individual y value.

SOLUTION

a. The column labeled Coef yields the equation

$$\hat{y} = 0.3495 + 0.06487c + 0.00628d + 0.05784n$$

b. The predicted y value is shown as Fit. As can be verified by substituting $c = 31$, $d = 5$, and $n = 12$ into the equation, the predicted y is 3.0866. The 95% confidence limits for the mean $E(Y)$ are shown in the 95% C.I. part of the output as 2.7994 to 3.3738, while the wider prediction limits for an individual y value are 2.6156 to 3.5576.

**extrapolation in
multiple regression**

The notion of **extrapolation** is more subtle in multiple regression than in simple linear regression. In simple regression, extrapolation occurred when we tried to predict Y using an x value that was well beyond the range of the data. In multiple regression, we must be concerned not only about the range of each individual predictor but also about the set of values of several predictors together. It might well be reasonable to use multiple regression to predict the salary of a 30-year-old middle manager, or the salary of a middle manager with 25 years of experience, but it would *not* be reasonable to use regression to predict the salary of a 30-year-old middle manager with 25 years of experience! Extrapolation depends not only on the range of each separate x_j predictor used to develop the regression equation but also on the correlations among the x_j values. In the salary prediction example, obviously age and experience will be positively correlated, so the combination of a low age and high amount of experience wouldn't occur in the data. When making forecasts using multiple regression, we must consider not only whether each independent variable value is reasonable by itself but also whether the chosen combination of predictor values is reasonable.

EXAMPLE 12.17   The state fisheries commission hoped to use the data of Example 12.15 to predict the catch at a lake with 8 residences per square mile, size .7 square mile, 1 public access, and structure index 55, and also for another lake with values 55, 1.0, 1, and 40. The following Minitab output was obtained:

```
Regression Analysis: Catch versus Residences, Size, Access, Structure

The regression equation is
Catch = - 1.94 + 0.0193 Residences + 0.332 Size + 0.836 Access
            + 0.0477 Structure

Predictor        Coef    SE Coef       T      P
Constant      -1.9378     0.9081   -2.13  0.050
Residences    0.01928    0.01017    1.90  0.077
Size           0.3323     0.2458    1.35  0.196
Access         0.8355     0.2250    3.71  0.002
Structure     0.047714   0.005056   9.44  0.000

S = 0.433635   R-Sq = 88.2%   R-Sq(adj) = 85.0%
```

```
Analysis of Variance

Source           DF       SS      MS      F      P
Regression        4   21.0473  5.2619  27.98  0.000
Residual Error   15    2.8206  0.1880
Total            19   23.8679

Source       DF   Seq SS
Residences    1   0.2780
Size          1   1.5667
Access        1   2.4579
Structure     1  16.7447

Predicted Values for New Observations

New Obs    Fit   SE Fit        95% CI            95% PI
   1    1.9090   0.6812  (0.4570, 3.3610)  (0.1878, 3.6302)XX
   2    2.1998   0.1850  (1.8055, 2.5940)  (1.1949, 3.2046)

XX denotes a point that is an extreme outlier in the predictors.

Values of Predictors for New Observations

New Obs  Residences  Size  Access  Structure
   1            8.0  0.70    1.00       55.0
   2           55.0  1.00    1.00       40.0
```

Locate the 95% prediction intervals for the two lakes. Why is the first interval so much wider than the second?

SOLUTION The prediction intervals are the respective 95% P.I. values, .1878 to 3.6302 for the first lake and 1.1949 to 3.2046 for the second. The first interval carries a warning that the x values are "extreme." If we check back with the data, we find that no lake was even close to 8 residences per square mile. Thus the prediction is a severe extrapolation, which makes the interval very wide. The problem is with one predictor; the remaining x values are well within the range of the data.

Exercises

12.17 A prediction was made based on the data of Exercise 12.3. Recall that x varied from 1 to 3, w from 1 to 4, and v from 1 to 6. Here is partial Minitab output:

```
Correlations: y, x, w, v

        y       x       w
x   0.856
w   0.402   0.000
v   0.928   0.956   0.262

Regression Analysis: y versus x, w, v

The regression equation is
y = 10.0 + 5.00 x + 2.00 w + 1.00 v

S = 2.64574   R-Sq = 89.5%   R-Sq(adj) = 85.6%

Predicted Values for New Observations
New Obs    Fit   SE Fit        95% CI            95% PI
   1     33.000   4.077  (23.598, 42.402)  (21.792, 44.208)XX
```

```
XX denotes a point that is an extreme outlier in the predictors.

Values of Predictors for New Observations
New Obs     x     w     v
  1       3.00  1.00  6.00
```

Locate the 95% prediction interval. Explain why Minitab gave the "extreme x values" warning.

12.18 Refer to the chemical firm data of Exercise 12.5. Predicted yields for $x_1 = 3.5$ and $x_2 = .35$ (observation 21) and also for $x_1 = 3.5$ and $x_2 = 2.5$ (observation 22) are calculated based on models with and without second-order terms. Minitab output follows:

```
Regression Analysis: Yield versus Cat1, Cat2, Cat1Sq, Cat1*Cat2, Cat2Sq

The regression equation is
Yield = 50.0 + 6.64 Cat1 + 7.31 Cat2 - 1.23 Cat1Sq - 0.772 Cat1*Cat2
        - 1.18 Cat2Sq

Predictor      Coef  SE Coef       T      P
Constant     50.020    4.391   11.39  0.000
Cat1          6.644    2.012    3.30  0.005
Cat2          7.314    2.740    2.67  0.018
Cat1Sq      -1.2314   0.3020   -4.08  0.001
Cat1*Cat2   -0.7724   0.3196   -2.42  0.030
Cat2Sq      -1.1755   0.5053   -2.33  0.036

S = 2.25972   R-Sq = 86.2%   R-Sq(adj) = 81.3%

Analysis of Variance

Source           DF       SS      MS      F      P
Regression        5  448.192  89.639  17.55  0.000
Residual Error   14   71.489   5.106
Total            19  519.681

Source      DF   Seq SS
Cat1         1  286.438
Cat2         1   19.369
Cat1Sq       1   84.919
Cat1*Cat2    1   29.830
Cat2Sq       1   27.636

Predicted Values for New Observations

New
Obs     Fit  SE Fit        95% CI              95% PI
  1  59.657   2.129  (55.091, 64.223)  (52.998, 66.316)
  2  62.368   0.983  (60.260, 64.475)  (57.083, 67.653)

Values of Predictors for New Observations

New
Obs  Cat1  Cat2  Cat1Sq  Cat1*Cat2  Cat2Sq
  1  3.50  0.35    12.2       1.22    0.12
  2  3.50  2.50    12.2       8.75    6.25

Regression Analysis: Yield versus Cat1, Cat2, Cat1Sq, Cat1*Cat2, Cat2Sq

The regression equation is
Yield = 50.0 + 6.64 Cat1 + 7.31 Cat2 - 1.23 Cat1Sq - 0.772 Cat1*Cat2
        - 1.18 Cat2Sq

Predictor      Coef  SE Coef       T      P
Constant     50.020    4.391   11.39  0.000
Cat1          6.644    2.012    3.30  0.005
```

```
Cat2          7.314    2.740    2.67   0.018
Cat1Sq       -1.2314   0.3020   -4.08  0.001
Cat1*Cat2    -0.7724   0.3196   -2.42  0.030
Cat2Sq       -1.1755   0.5053   -2.33  0.036

S = 2.25972   R-Sq = 86.2%   R-Sq(adj) = 81.3%

Analysis of Variance

Source          DF        SS       MS       F      P
Regression       5   448.192   89.639   17.55  0.000
Residual Error  14    71.489    5.106
Total           19   519.681

Source      DF    Seq SS
Cat1         1   286.438
Cat2         1    19.369
Cat1Sq       1    84.919
Cat1*Cat2    1    29.830
Cat2Sq       1    27.636

Predicted Values for New Observations

New
Obs    Fit   SE Fit      95% CI            95% PI
  1  59.657   2.129  (55.091, 64.223)  (52.998, 66.316)
  2  62.368   0.983  (60.260, 64.475)  (57.083, 67.653)

Values of Predictors for New Observations

New
Obs  Cat1  Cat2  Cat1Sq  Cat1*Cat2  Cat2Sq
  1  3.50  0.35   12.2      1.22      0.12
  2  3.50  2.50   12.2      8.75      6.25
```

a. Locate the 95% limits for individual prediction in the complete model for the two new observations.

b. Locate the 95% limits for individual prediction in the reduced model for the two observations.

c. Are the limits for the complete model much tighter than those for the reduced model?

BUSINESS DECISION-MAKING IN ACTION

CHAPTER CASE

ANALYSIS

Colvard Office Products

Richard Garrett, vice president of marketing for Colvard, has asked you to examine the relationship between sales performance of newly hired salespeople and the components of a post-training examination that has proven valuable in the past for predicting sales performance. The personnel director has indicated that he wants to reduce the length of the test by eliminating one or more portions. Garrett wants to know if this can be done without losing valuable information.

As a first step, we can compute correlations for all pairs of variables of interest, as shown next, and construct a matrix of scatterplots, as shown in Figure 12.4.

```
Correlations: Rating, TotalScore, SubScore1, SubScore2, SubScore3

                Rating   TotalScore    SubScore1    SubScore2
TotalScore      0.829
                0.000

SubScore1       0.600      0.853
                0.000      0.000

SubScore2       0.642      0.910        0.790
                0.000      0.000        0.000

SubScore3       0.807      0.689        0.297        0.421
                0.000      0.000        0.001        0.000

Cell Contents: Pearson correlation
               P-Value
```

FIGURE 12.4 **Scatterplot Matrix of Rating, Total Score, and Three Subscores**

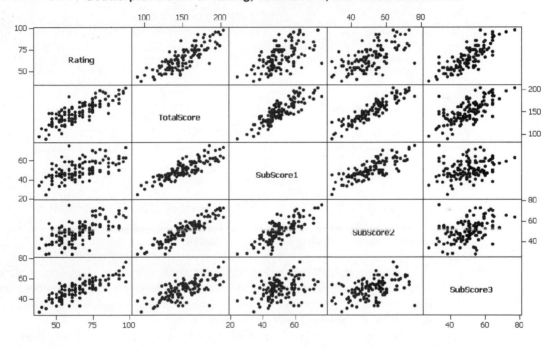

Several interesting findings emerge from this analysis. The correlation between Rating and TotalScore of .829 is larger than the correlation between Rating and any of the three subscores. TotalScore explains 68.7% of the total variation in Ratings, and no single subscore performs better as the single predictor in a simple linear regression model. Of the three subscores, SubScore2 is most strongly correlated with TotalScore (.910) and is the second most strongly correlated subscore with Rating, all of which suggests that it will be kept. SubScore3 has the weakest correlation with TotalScore (.689), which might suggest that it is the leading candidate for removal. The correlation matrix and the matrix plot show a strong relationship between SubScore1 and SubScore2, indicating the potential for collinearity if both are included in a regression model.

A regression model with Rating as the response variable and the three subscores as predictor variables was fit in Minitab and the resulting output is shown here.

```
Regression Analysis: Rating versus SubScore1, SubScore2, SubScore3

The regression equation is
Rating = - 14.9 + 0.457 SubScore1 + 0.156 SubScore2 + 0.997 SubScore3

Predictor      Coef   SE Coef       T      P   VIF
Constant    -14.895     3.923   -3.80  0.000
SubScore1    0.4572    0.1008    4.53  0.000   2.7
SubScore2   0.15619   0.09550    1.64  0.105   3.0
SubScore3   0.99654   0.06891   14.46  0.000   1.2

S = 6.45528   R-Sq = 79.8%   R-Sq(adj) = 79.3%

Analysis of Variance

Source            DF        SS       MS       F      P
Regression         3   19134.7   6378.3  153.06  0.000
Residual Error   116    4833.8     41.7
Total            119   23968.5

Source      DF  Seq SS
SubScore1    1  8626.2
SubScore2    1  1795.3
SubScore3    1  8713.3

Unusual Observations

Obs  SubScore1  Rating     Fit  SE Fit  Residual  St Resid
 21       47.0  86.000  68.589   0.800    17.411      2.72R
 40       76.0  59.000  64.609   2.445    -5.609     -0.94 X
 50       45.0  52.000  69.139   0.867   -17.139     -2.68R
 53       45.0  45.000  58.587   1.466   -13.587     -2.16R
 96       59.0  56.000  69.033   0.952   -13.033     -2.04R
101       47.0  54.000  68.158   0.999   -14.158     -2.22R

R denotes an observation with a large standardized residual.
X denotes an observation whose X value gives it large influence.
```

From the multiple regression output, we see that Richard Garrett has been underutilizing the information contained in the post-training test. The multiple regression on the three subscores explains 79.8% of the total variation in Ratings, while the TotalScore explained only 68.7% of the variation.

We also note that in this model the SubScore2 variable is not statistically significant (p-value $= .105$) given the presence of the other two subscores in the model. Recall that this variable had the strongest correlation with TotalScore and second-strongest correlation of the three subscores with Rating, yet the results of the multiple regression suggest removing this predictor variable from the model. Although the VIF values do not indicate any collinearity problems (none of the values are greater than 3.0), the strong relationship between SubScore1 and SubScore2 might explain the lack of need for SubScore2 given the presence of SubScore1 in the model. The following Minitab output shows the results after removing SubScore2 from the model:

```
Regression Analysis: Rating versus SubScore1, SubScore3

The regression equation is
Rating = - 15.2 + 0.584 SubScore1 + 1.03 SubScore3
```

```
Predictor      Coef   SE Coef       T      P   VIF
Constant    -15.180     3.947   -3.85  0.000
SubScore1   0.58387   0.06502    8.98  0.000   1.1
SubScore3   1.03231   0.06581   15.68  0.000   1.1

S = 6.50131   R-Sq = 79.4%   R-Sq(adj) = 79.0%
```

Analysis of Variance

```
Source            DF        SS       MS       F      P
Regression         2   19023.2   9511.7  225.04  0.000
Residual Error   117    4945.3     42.3
Total            119   23968.5
```

```
Source       DF   Seq SS
SubScore1     1   8626.2
SubScore3     1  10397.0
```

Unusual Observations

```
Obs  SubScore1  Rating       Fit  SE Fit  Residual  St Resid
 12       55.0  50.000    63.388   0.766   -13.388     -2.07R
 19       24.0  43.000    38.062   1.782     4.938      0.79 X
 21       47.0  86.000    69.040   0.757    16.960      2.63R
 31       63.0  98.000   101.092   1.824    -3.093     -0.50 X
 40       76.0  59.000    63.262   2.319    -4.262     -0.70 X
 50       45.0  52.000    68.905   0.861   -16.905     -2.62R
 96       59.0  56.000    69.853   0.815   -13.853     -2.15R
101       47.0  54.000    66.976   0.694   -12.976     -2.01R
111       50.0  93.000    80.083   1.115    12.917      2.02R
```

R denotes an observation with a large standardized residual.
X denotes an observation whose X value gives it large influence.

Deleting the SubScore2 variable resulted in a fit nearly as good as that when using all three variables. The R^2 value decreased slightly from 79.8% to 79.4%, and the residual standard deviation increased only slightly, from 6.455 to 6.501 Rating points. In addition, the VIF's indicate no collinearity problems.

Richard Garrett should be very pleased with these results. He can agree to eliminate the portion of the exam corresponding to SubScore2 and at the same time have a better predictor (with an $R^2 = 79.8\%$ from the regression fit based on the other two subscores) than he was using previously (with an $R^2 = 68.7\%$ based on the TotalScore only). If the personnel director insists on further eliminations, Garrett can offer to eliminate the portion of the test corresponding to SubScore1, leaving only SubScore3 (with an R^2 of 65.1%), which is not much worse than using the TotalScore only.

SUMMARY

Here are some reminders about multiple regression concepts.

1. Regression coefficients in a first-order model (one not containing transformed variables, such as squares of a variable or product terms) should be interpreted as partial slopes—the predicted change in a dependent variable when an independent variable is increased by one unit while the other independent variables are held constant.

2. Correlations are important, not only between the dependent variable and an independent variable but also between independent variables. Collinearity—correlation between independent variables—implies that regression coefficients will change as variables are added to or deleted from a regression model.

3. The effectiveness of a regression model can be indicated not only by the R^2 value but also by the residual standard deviation. It's often helpful to use that standard deviation to see roughly how much of a plus or minus must be allowed around a prediction.

4. As always, the various statistical tests in a regression model only indicate how strong the evidence is that the apparent pattern is more than random. They don't directly indicate how good a predictive model is. In particular, a large overall F statistic may merely indicate a weak prediction in a large sample.

5. A t test in a multiple regression assesses whether that independent variable adds predictive value as the last predictor included in the model. It is quite possible that several variables may not add a statistically detectable amount of predicted value when each is added last; yet, deleting all of them from the model causes a serious drop in predictive value. Especially when there is severe collinearity, being added second to last is quite different from being added last.

6. The variance inflation factor (VIF) is a useful indicator of the overall impact of collinearity in estimating the coefficient of an independent variable. The higher the VIF value, the more serious the impact of collinearity on the accuracy of a slope estimate.

7. Extrapolation in multiple regression can be subtle. A new set of x values may not be unreasonable when considered one by one, but the combination of values may be far outside the range of previous data.

In addition, you may want to reread the summary of key ideas in the Executive Overview at the beginning of this chapter.

Supplementary Exercises

12.19 A study of demand for imported subcompact cars consists of data from 12 metropolitan areas. The variables are

Demand: Imported subcompact car sales as a percentage of total sales

Educ: Average number of years of schooling completed by adults

Income: Per capita income

Popn: Area population

Famsize: Average size of intact families

Minitab output is shown next.

```
Regression Analysis: Demand versus Educ, Income, Popn, Famsize

The regression equation is
Demand = - 1.3 + 5.55 Educ + 0.89 Income + 1.92 Popn - 11.4 Famsize
```

```
Predictor        Coef SE Coef       T      P
Constant        -1.32   57.98   -0.02  0.982
Educ            5.550   2.702    2.05  0.079
Income          0.885   1.308    0.68  0.520
Popn            1.925   1.371    1.40  0.203
Famsize       -11.389   6.669   -1.71  0.131

S = 2.68627   R-Sq = 96.2%   R-Sq(adj) = 94.1%

Analysis of Variance

Source          DF          SS        MS       F       P
Regression       4     1295.69    323.93   44.89   0.000
Residual Error   7       50.51      7.22
Total           11     1346.21

Source    DF   Seq SS
Educ       1  1239.95
Income     1    32.85
Popn       1     1.86
Famsize    1    21.04

Unusual Observations

Obs  Educ  Demand    Fit  SE Fit  Residual  St Resid
  9   9.3  13.100  9.760   2.149     3.340     2.07R

R denotes an observation with a large standardized residual.
```

a. Write the regression equation. Place the standard error of each coefficient below the coefficient, perhaps in parentheses.
b. Locate R^2 and the residual standard deviation.
c. The "Unusual Observations" entry in the output indicates that observation 9 had a value 2.07 standard deviations away from the predicted, "Fit" value. Does this indicate that observation 9 is a very serious outlier?

12.20 Summarize the conclusions of the F test and the various t tests in the output of Exercise 12.19.

12.21 Another analysis of the data of Exercise 12.19 uses only Educ and Famsize to predict Demand. The Minitab output is shown next.

```
Regression Analysis: Demand versus Educ, Famsize

The regression equation is
Demand = - 19.2 + 7.79 Educ - 9.46 Famsize

Predictor     Coef  SE Coef       T      P
Constant    -19.17    45.87   -0.42  0.686
Educ         7.793    2.490    3.13  0.012
Famsize     -9.464    5.207   -1.82  0.103

S = 2.93888   R-Sq = 94.2%   R-Sq(adj) = 92.9%

Analysis of Variance

Source          DF       SS      MS       F      P
Regression       2  1268.47  634.24   73.43  0.000
Residual Error   9    77.73    8.64
Total           11  1346.21
```

a. Locate the R^2 value for this reduced model.
b. Test the null hypothesis that the true coefficients of Income and Popn are zero. Use $\alpha = .05$. What is the conclusion?

12.22 The manager of documentation for a computer software firm wants to forecast the time required to document moderate-size computer programs. Records are available for 26 programs. The variables are y = number of writer-days needed, x_1 = number of subprograms, x_2 = average number of lines per subprogram, $x_3 = x_1x_2$, $x_4 = x_2^2$, and $x_5 = x_1x_2^2$. A portion of the output from a Minitab regression analysis of the data is shown here.

```
Regression Analysis: Y versus X1, X2, X1X2, X2sq, X1X2sq

The regression equation is
Y = - 16.8 + 1.47 X1 + 0.995 X2 - 0.0240 X1X2 - 0.0103 X2sq
        + 0.000250 X1X2sq

Predictor       Coef     SE Coef       T      P
Constant      -16.82       11.63   -1.45  0.164
X1            1.4702      0.3659    4.02  0.001
X2            0.9948      0.6114    1.63  0.119
X1X2         -0.02400     0.02375  -1.01  0.324
X2Sq         -0.010310    0.007374 -1.40  0.177
X1X2Sq       0.0002496    0.0003518 0.71  0.486

S = 3.39010    R-Sq = 91.7%    R-Sq(adj) = 89.6%

Analysis of Variance

Source             DF        SS       MS       F      P
Regression          5   2546.02   509.21   44.31  0.000
Residual Error     20    229.86    11.49
Total              25   2775.87

Source   DF    Seq SS
X1        1   2502.84
X2        1     13.27
X1X2      1      0.30
X2sq      1     23.82
X1X2sq    1      5.78

Unusual Observations

Obs    X1        Y      Fit   SE Fit   Residual   St Resid
  2   24.0   21.000   28.604   1.280     -7.604     -2.42R

R denotes an observation with a large standardized residual.
```

a. Write the multiple regression model and locate the residual standard deviation.
b. Does x_1x_2 have a statistically significant predictive value as "last predictor in"?

12.23 The model $Y = \beta_0 + \beta_1x_1 + \beta_2x_2 + \epsilon$ is fit to the data of Exercise 12.22. Selected output is shown here.

```
Regression Analysis: Y versus X1, X2

The regression equation is
Y = 0.84 + 1.02 X1 + 0.0558 X2

Predictor       Coef     SE Coef       T      P
Constant       0.840       3.434    0.24  0.809
X1            1.01582     0.07928   12.81  0.000
X2            0.05582     0.05150    1.08  0.290

S = 3.36065    R-Sq = 90.6%    R-Sq(adj) = 89.8%
```

Analysis of Variance

```
Source          DF      SS      MS       F       P
Regression       2   2516.1  1258.1  111.39   0.000
Residual Error  23    259.8    11.3
Total           25   2775.9
```

```
Source  DF  Seq SS
X1       1  2502.9
X2       1    13.3
```

Unusual Observations

```
Obs    X1      Y      Fit  SE Fit  Residual  St Resid
  2  24.0  21.000  27.900   0.906    -6.900    -2.13R
 12  21.0  17.000  23.345   1.156    -6.345    -2.01R
```

R denotes an observation with a large standardized residual.

a. Write the complete and reduced-form estimated models.
b. Is the improvement in R^2 obtained by adding x_3, x_4, and x_5 statistically significant at $\alpha = .05$? Approximately, what is the p-value for this test?

12.24 A chain of small convenience food stores performs a regression analysis to explain variation in sales volume among 16 stores. The variables in the study are

Sales: Average daily sales volume of a store, in thousands of dollars

Size: Floor space in thousands of square feet

Parking: Number of free parking spaces adjacent to the store

Income: Estimated per household income of the ZIP code area of the store

Output from Minitab is shown here.

Regression Analysis: Sales versus Size, Parking, Income

```
The regression equation is
Sales = 0.87 + 2.55 Size + 0.220 Parking + 0.589 Income
```

```
Predictor    Coef   SE Coef      T      P   VIF
Constant    0.873    1.946    0.45  0.662
Size        2.548    1.201    2.12  0.055   1.9
Parking     0.2203   0.1554   1.42  0.182   1.8
Income      0.5893   0.1781   3.31  0.006   1.2
```

```
S = 0.772401    R-Sq = 79.1%    R-Sq(adj) = 73.9%
```

Analysis of Variance

```
Source          DF       SS      MS       F       P
Regression       3  27.1295  9.0432  15.16   0.000
Residual Error  12   7.1592  0.5966
Total           15  34.2887
```

a. Write down the regression equation. Indicate the standard errors of the coefficients.
b. Carefully interpret each coefficient.
c. Locate R^2 and the residual standard deviation.
d. Is there a severe collinearity problem in this study?

12.25 Summarize the results of the F and t tests for the output of Exercise 12.24.

12.26 A producer of various feed additives for cattle conducts a study of the number of days of feedlot time required to bring beef cattle to market weight. Eighteen steers of essentially identical age and weight are purchased and brought to a feedlot. Each steer is fed a diet with a specific combination of protein content, antibiotic concentration, and percentage of feed supplement. The data are

```
Steer:     1    2    3    4    5    6    7    8    9
Protein:  10   10   10   10   10   10   15   15   15
Antibio:   1    1    1    2    2    2    1    1    1
Supplem:   3    5    7    3    5    7    3    5    7
Time:     88   82   81   82   83   75   80   80   75

Steer:    10   11   12   13   14   15   16   17   18
Protein:  15   15   15   20   20   20   20   20   20
Antibio:   2    2    2    1    1    1    2    2    2
Supplem:   3    5    7    3    5    7    3    5    7
Time:     77   76   72   79   74   75   74   70   69
```

Computer output from a Minitab regression analysis follows:

```
Regression Analysis: Time versus Protein, Antibio, Supplem

The regression equation is
Time = 103 - 0.833 Protein - 4.00 Antibio - 1.38 Supplem

Predictor        Coef   SE Coef       T      P    VIF
Constant      102.707     2.310   44.46  0.000
Protein      -0.83332   0.09869   -8.44  0.000    1.0
Antibio       -4.0000    0.8059   -4.96  0.000    1.0
Supplem       -1.3750    0.2468   -5.57  0.000    1.0

S = 1.70956    R-Sq = 90.1%    R-Sq(adj) = 87.9%

Analysis of Variance

Source             DF        SS       MS       F      P
Regression          3    371.08   123.69   42.32  0.000
Residual Error     14     40.92     2.92
Total              17    412.00

Source    DF   Seq SS
Protein    1   208.33
Antibio    1    72.00
Supplem    1    90.75

Unusual Observations

Obs   Protein     Time      Fit   SE Fit   Residual   St Resid
  5      10.0   83.000   79.500    0.754      3.500      2.28R

R denotes an observation with a large standardized residual.

Predicted Values for New Observations

New Obs      Fit   SE Fit        95% CI                95% PI
      1   77.333    0.403   (76.469, 78.198)   (73.566, 81.100)

Values of Predictors for New Observations

New Obs   Protein   Antibio   Supplem
      1      15.0      1.50      5.00
```

a. Write the regression equation.
b. Find the standard deviation.
c. Find the R^2 value.
d. How much of a collinearity problem is there with these data?

12.27 Refer to Exercise 12.26.

a. Predict the feedlot time required for a steer fed 15% protein, 1.5% antibiotic concentration, and 5% supplement.

b. Do these values of the independent variables represent a major extrapolation from the data?

c. Give a 95% confidence interval for the mean time predicted in part (a).

12.28 The data of Exercise 12.26 are also analyzed by a regression model using only protein content as an independent variable, with the following Minitab output:

```
Regression Analysis: Time versus Protein

The regression equation is
Time = 89.8 - 0.833 Protein

Predictor      Coef   SE Coef      T      P
Constant     89.833     3.202  28.05  0.000
Protein     -0.8333    0.2060  -4.05  0.001

S = 3.56779   R-Sq = 50.6%   R-Sq(adj) = 47.5%

Analysis of Variance

Source          DF       SS      MS      F      P
Regression       1   208.33  208.33  16.37  0.001
Residual Error  16   203.67   12.73
Total           17   412.00
```

a. Write the regression equation.

b. Find the R^2 value.

c. Test the null hypothesis that the coefficients of Antibio and Supplem are zero at $\alpha = .05$.

12.29 A sex discrimination suit alleges that a small college discriminated in salaries against women. A regression study considers the following variables:

Salary: Base salary per year (thousands of dollars)

Senior: Seniority at the college (in years)

Sex: 1 for men, 0 for women

RankD1:   1 for full professors, 0 for others

RankD2:   1 for associate professors, 0 for others

RankD3:   1 for assistant professors, 0 for others

Doct: 1 for holders of doctorate, 0 for others

Note that lecturers and instructors have value 0 for all 3 RankD variables. Computer output (Excel) from the study is shown next.

```
Regression Statistics
Multiple R              0.9716
R Square                0.9440
Adjusted R Square       0.9294
Standard Error          2.3375
Observations                30

ANOVA
                 df         SS       MS         F   Significance F
Regression        6   2119.347  353.225    64.646           0.0000
Residual         23    125.672    5.464
Total            29   2245.019
```

	Coefficients	Standard Error	t Stat	P-value
Intercept	18.6784	1.3788	13.5470	0.0000
Senior	0.5420	0.0762	7.1176	0.0000
Sex	1.2074	1.0649	1.1339	0.2685
RankD1	8.7779	1.9380	4.5293	0.0002
RankD2	4.4211	1.7797	2.4842	0.0207
RankD3	2.7165	1.4239	1.9079	0.0690
Doct	0.9225	1.2589	0.7328	0.4711

a. Write down the regression equation.
b. What is the interpretation of the coefficient of Sex?
c. What is the interpretation of the coefficient of RankD1?

12.30 Refer to Exercise 12.29.
a. Test the hypothesis that the true coefficient of Sex is positive. Use $\alpha = .05$.
b. What does the conclusion of this test indicate about allegations of discrimination?

12.31 Refer once again to Exercise 12.29.
a. Locate the value of the F statistic.
b. What null hypothesis is being tested by this statistic?
c. Is this null hypothesis rejected at $\alpha = .01$? How plausible is this null hypothesis?

12.32 Another regression model of the data of Exercise 12.29 omits Sex and Doct from the list of independent variables. The output (Excel) is shown next.

```
Regression Statistics
Multiple R              0.9697
R Square                0.9403
Adjusted R Square       0.9307
Standard Error          2.3160
Observations                30
```

ANOVA

	df	SS	MS	F	Significance F
Regression	4	2110.925	527.731	98.389	0.0000
Residual	25	134.093	5.364		
Total	29	2245.019			

	Coefficients	Standard Error	t Stat	P-value
Intercept	19.7113	1.0776	18.2913	0.0000
Senior	0.5572	0.0744	7.4893	0.0000
RankD1	9.2414	1.8214	5.0738	0.0000
RankD2	5.1050	1.5875	3.2158	0.0036
RankD3	3.2243	1.3204	2.4418	0.0220

a. Locate R^2 for this reduced model.
b. Test the null hypothesis that the true coefficients of Sex and Doct are zero. Use $\alpha = .01$.

12.33 A survey of information systems managers was used to predict the yearly salary of beginning programmer/analysts in a metropolitan area. Managers specified their standard salary for a beginning programmer/analyst, the number of employees in the firm's information processing staff, the firm's gross profit margin in cents per dollar of sales, and the firm's information processing cost as a percentage of total administrative costs. The data are stored in the EX1233 file on the CD, with salary in column 1, number of employees in column 2, profit margin in column 3, and information processing cost in column 4.
a. Obtain a multiple regression equation with salary as the dependent variable and the other three variables as predictors. Interpret each of the (partial) slope coefficients.
b. Is there conclusive evidence that the three predictors together have at least some value in predicting salary? Locate a p-value for the appropriate test.
c. Which of the independent variables, if any, have statistically detectable ($\alpha = .05$) predictive value as the "last predictor in" the equation?

12.34   Refer to Exercise 12.33.

a. Locate the coefficient of determination (R^2) for the regression model.

b. Obtain another regression model with number of employees as the only independent variable. Find the coefficient of determination for this model.

c. By hand, test the null hypothesis that adding profit margin and information processing cost does not yield any additional predictive value, given the information about number of employees. Use $\alpha = .10$. What can you conclude from this test?

12.35   Obtain correlations for all pairs of predictor variables in Exercise 12.33. Does there seem to be a major collinearity problem in the data?

12.36   A government agency pays research contractors a fee to cover overhead costs, over and above the direct costs of a research project. Although the overhead cost varies considerably among contracts, it is usually a substantial share of the total contract cost. An agency task force obtained data on overhead cost as a fraction of direct costs, number of employees of the contractor, size of contract as a percentage of the contractor's yearly income, and personnel costs as a percentage of direct cost. These four variables are stored (in the order given) in the EX1236 file on the CD.

a. Obtain correlations of all pairs of variables. Is there a severe collinearity problem with the data?

b. Plot overhead cost against each of the other variables. Locate a possible high-influence outlier.

c. Obtain a regression equation (overhead cost as dependent variable) using all the data, including any potential outlier.

d. Delete the potential outlier and get a revised regression equation. How much did the slopes change?

12.37   Consider the outlier-deleted regression model of Exercise 12.36.

a. Locate the F statistic. What null hypothesis is being tested? What can we conclude based on the F statistic?

b. Locate the t statistic for each independent variable. What conclusions can we reach based on the t tests?

12.38   Use the outlier-deleted data of Exercise 12.36 to predict overhead cost of a contract when the contractor has 500 employees, the contract is 2.50% of the contractor's income, and personnel cost is 55% of the direct cost. Obtain a 95% prediction interval. Would an overhead cost equal to 88.9% of direct cost be unreasonable in this situation?

12.39   The owner of a rapidly growing computer store tried to explain the increase in biweekly sales of computer software using four explanatory variables: number of titles displayed, display footage, current customer base of IBM-compatible computers, and current customer base of Apple-compatible computers. The data are stored in time series order in the EX1239 file of the CD, with sales in column 1, titles in 2, footage in 3, IBM base in 4, and Apple base in 5.

a. Before doing the calculations, consider the economics of the situation and state what sign you would expect for each of the partial slopes.

b. Obtain a multiple regression equation with sales as the dependent variable and all other variables as independent. Does each partial slope have the sign you expected in part (a)?

c. Calculate a 95% confidence interval for the coefficient of the titles variable. The computer output should contain the calculated standard error for this coefficient. Does the interval include 0 as a plausible value?

12.40   Consider the regression model of Exercise 12.39.

a. Can the null hypothesis that none of the variables has predictive value be rejected at normal α levels?

b. According to t tests, which predictors, if any, add statistically detectable predictive value ($\alpha = .05$) given all the others?

12.41 Obtain correlation coefficients for all pairs of variables from the data of Exercise 12.39. How severe is the collinearity problem in the data?

12.42 Compare the coefficient of determination (R^2) for the regression model of Exercise 12.39 to the square of the correlation between sales and titles in Exercise 12.41. Compute the incremental F statistic for testing the null hypothesis that footage, IBM base, and Apple base add no predictive value, given titles. Can this hypothesis be rejected at $\alpha = .01$?

12.43 A function of bank branch offices is to arrange profitable loans to small businesses and individuals. As part of a study of the effectiveness of branch managers, a bank collected data from a sample of branches on current total loan volumes (the dependent variable, in millions of dollars), the total deposits (in millions of dollars) held in accounts opened at that branch, the number of such accounts, the average number of daily transactions, and the number of employees at the branch. Correlations and a scatterplot matrix (JMP output) are shown in Figure 12.5.
a. Which independent variable is the best predictor of loan volume?
b. Is there a substantial collinearity problem?
c. Do any points seem extremely influential?

FIGURE 12.5 **Correlations and Scatterplot Matrix for Bank Branch Data**

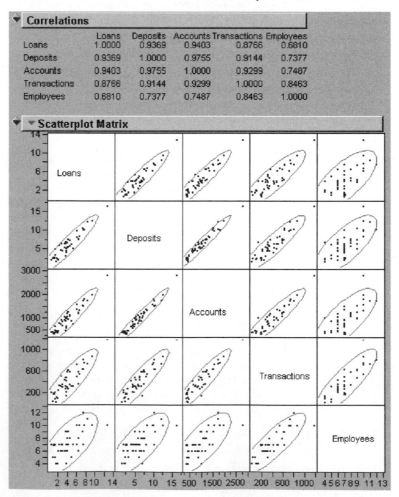

12.44   A regr   .on model was created for the bank branch office data using JMP. Some of the results ɛ ᵕ shown in Figure 12.6.

a. Use the R^2 value shown to compute an overall F statistic. Is there clear evidence that there is predictive value in the model, using $\alpha = .01$?

b. Which individual predictors have been shown to have "last-in" predictive value, again using $\alpha = .01$?

c. Explain the apparent contradiction between your answers to the first two parts.

F I G U R E   12.6   Regression Results for Bank Branch Data

Summary of Fit

RSquare	0.894477
RSquare Adj	0.883369
Root Mean Square Error	0.870612
Mean of Response	4.383395
Observations (or Sum Wgts)	43

Analysis of Variance

Source	DF	Sum of Squares	Mean Square	F Ratio
Model	4	244.14940	61.0374	00.5279
Error	38	28.80269	0.7580	Prob > F
C. Total	42	272.95209		<.0001

Parameter Estimates

Term	Estimate	Std Error	t Ratio	Prob>|t|
Intercept	0.2204301	0.6752	0.34	0.7370
Deposits	0.3222099	0.191048	1.69	0.0999
Accounts	0.0025812	0.001314	1.96	0.0569
Transactions	0.0010058	0.001878	0.54	0.5954
Employees	-0.119898	0.130721	-0.92	0.3648

12.45   Another multiple regression model used only deposit volume and number of accounts as independent variables, with results as shown in Figure 12.7.

a. Does omitting the transactions and employees variables seriously reduce R^2?

b. Use the R^2 values to test the null hypothesis that the coefficients of transactions and employees are both 0. What is your conclusion?

F I G U R E   12.7   Regression with Two Predictors for Bank Branch Data

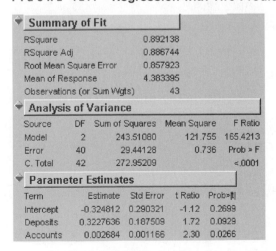

Summary of Fit

RSquare	0.892138
RSquare Adj	0.886744
Root Mean Square Error	0.857923
Mean of Response	4.383395
Observations (or Sum Wgts)	43

Analysis of Variance

Source	DF	Sum of Squares	Mean Square	F Ratio
Model	2	243.51080	121.755	165.4213
Error	40	29.44128	0.736	Prob > F
C. Total	42	272.95209		<.0001

Parameter Estimates

Term	Estimate	Std Error	t Ratio	Prob>|t|
Intercept	-0.324812	0.290321	-1.12	0.2699
Deposits	0.3227636	0.187509	1.72	0.0929
Accounts	0.002684	0.001166	2.30	0.0266

BUSINESS CASES

Product Design

Engineers for a manufacturer of power tools for home use were trying to design an electric drill that didn't heat up under strenuous use. The three key design factors are insulation thickness, quality of the wire used in the motor, and size of the vents in the body of the drill. The engineers had learned a little about off-line quality control, so they designed an experiment that varied these design factors. They created 10 drills using each combination of the three design factors, split them into two lots, and tested the lots under two (supposedly equivalent) "torture tests." The temperature of each drill was measured at the end of each test; for each lot, the mean temperature and the logarithm of the variance of temperatures were computed. The engineers wanted to minimize both the mean and (the logarithm of) the variance.

Assignment: The engineers have asked you to analyze the resulting data. They present you with the following data and explain that they included squared terms to try to capture any curves in the relation. Average temperature is "avtem," logarithm of variance is "logv," insulation thickness is IT, quality of wire is QW, vent size is VS, and the "2" variables are the respective squared terms. The squared terms are of the form

$$(predictor - mean\ of\ predictor)^2$$

They have asked you to try to figure out which of the predictors seem to affect the mean (and by how much), which affect the variance, which squared terms seem to matter, and finally whether the lot number (corresponding to the type of test) is relevant. They don't know any statistical jargon, so please write your report without it.

avtem	logv	IT	QW	VS	I2	Q2	V2	Lot	avtem	logv	IT	QW	VS	I2	Q2	V2	Lot
185	3.6	2	6	10	4	1	1	1	168	3.4	4	7	11	0	0	0	2
176	3.7	2	6	10	4	1	1	2	160	2.9	4	7	12	0	0	1	1
177	3.6	2	6	11	4	1	0	1	154	3.1	4	7	12	0	0	1	2
184	3.7	2	6	11	4	1	0	2	169	2.8	4	8	10	0	1	1	1
178	3.6	2	6	12	4	1	1	1	156	2.9	4	8	10	0	1	1	2
169	3.4	2	6	12	4	1	1	2	168	2.7	4	8	11	0	1	0	1
185	3.2	2	7	10	4	0	1	1	161	2.7	4	8	11	0	1	0	2
184	3.2	2	7	10	4	0	1	2	156	2.6	4	8	12	0	1	1	1
180	3.2	2	7	11	4	0	0	1	158	2.7	4	8	12	0	1	1	2
184	3.5	2	7	11	4	0	0	2	164	3.7	5	6	10	1	1	1	1
179	3.0	2	7	12	4	0	1	1	163	3.7	5	6	10	1	1	1	2
173	3.2	2	7	12	4	0	1	2	161	3.7	5	6	11	1	1	0	1
179	2.9	2	8	10	4	1	1	1	158	3.4	5	6	11	1	1	0	2
185	2.7	2	8	10	4	1	1	2	154	3.4	5	6	12	1	1	1	1
180	2.8	2	8	11	4	1	0	1	162	3.7	5	6	12	1	1	1	2
180	2.7	2	8	11	4	1	0	2	163	2.8	5	7	10	1	0	1	1
169	2.9	2	8	12	4	1	1	1	166	3.0	5	7	10	1	0	1	2
177	2.8	2	8	12	4	1	1	2	159	3.3	5	7	11	1	0	0	1
172	3.6	3	6	10	1	1	1	1	156	3.3	5	7	11	1	0	0	2
171	3.9	3	6	10	1	1	1	2	152	3.3	5	7	12	1	0	1	1
172	3.8	3	6	11	1	1	0	1	150	3.3	5	7	12	1	0	1	2
167	3.6	3	6	11	1	1	0	2	165	2.9	5	8	10	1	1	1	1
165	3.3	3	6	12	1	1	1	1	156	2.7	5	8	10	1	1	1	2
159	3.4	3	6	12	1	1	1	2	155	2.8	5	8	11	1	1	0	1
169	3.0	3	7	10	1	0	1	1	155	3.2	5	8	11	1	1	0	2
174	3.3	3	7	10	1	0	1	2	149	2.6	5	8	12	1	1	1	1

163	3.3	3	7	11	1	0	0	1		152	2.9	5	8	12	1	1	1	2
170	3.3	3	7	11	1	0	0	2		165	3.4	6	6	10	4	1	1	1
169	3.2	3	7	12	1	0	1	1		160	3.7	6	6	10	4	1	1	2
163	3.2	3	7	12	1	0	1	2		157	3.7	6	6	11	4	1	0	1
178	2.7	3	8	10	1	1	1	1		149	3.7	6	6	11	4	1	0	2
165	2.7	3	8	10	1	1	1	2		149	3.8	6	6	12	4	1	1	1
167	2.8	3	8	11	1	1	0	1		145	3.7	6	6	12	4	1	1	2
171	2.8	3	8	11	1	1	0	2		154	3.4	6	7	10	4	0	1	1
166	2.9	3	8	12	1	1	1	1		153	3.2	6	7	10	4	0	1	2
166	2.7	3	8	12	1	1	1	2		150	3.0	6	7	11	4	0	0	1
161	3.7	4	6	10	0	1	1	1		156	3.1	6	7	11	4	0	0	2
162	3.7	4	6	10	0	1	1	2		146	3.2	6	7	12	4	0	1	1
169	3.4	4	6	11	0	1	0	1		153	3.3	6	7	12	4	0	1	2
162	3.7	4	6	11	0	1	0	2		161	2.8	6	8	10	4	1	1	1
159	3.5	4	6	12	0	1	1	1		160	2.9	6	8	10	4	1	1	2
168	3.4	4	6	12	0	1	1	2		156	2.9	6	8	11	4	1	0	1
169	3.1	4	7	10	0	0	1	1		150	2.7	6	8	11	4	1	0	2
165	3.2	4	7	10	0	0	1	2		149	2.9	6	8	12	4	1	1	1
163	3.2	4	7	11	0	0	0	1		151	2.8	6	8	12	4	1	1	2

Southern Electric Cooperative

Southern Electric Cooperative (SEC) is a distribution cooperative that serves customers in a region covering 15 counties across three southern states. An electric cooperative is a private, independent electric utility business owned by the customers served by the company. Distribution cooperatives purchase power at wholesale from electricity-generating companies to distribute it, over their own distribution lines, to their individual residential and commercial customers.

Forecasting revenue from energy sales in future months is important to the financial planning efforts of Bill Kelly, CFO of Southern Electric Cooperative. For each of the past several years, Kelly has estimated monthly revenue for the coming year by taking the monthly revenue figures from the current year and factoring in any anticipated price increases in the wholesale price of electricity purchased from the various power suppliers used by SEC. These price increases have remained fairly steady at a rate of 4% per year over the past several years. Kelly's simple forecasting approach has worked reasonably well over the last few years, but he thinks that a more sophisticated approach might work better.

Weather, in particular temperatures, is a major determinant of SEC electricity sales. Kelly has access to a long-range weather forecast that predicts the average daily high temperature over each of the following 12 months. He believes that by working this variable into the forecasts, he will do a better job of predicting monthly sales. To test his theory, Kelly has collected data for the past 60 months on SEC monthly revenues and the average daily high temperatures.

Assignment: Kelly has assigned you the task of developing a model for predicting SEC's monthly revenue from electricity sales that takes into account the monthly average daily high temperature. He has asked you to determine whether the long-term weather forecast has any value in forecasting sales revenue over his current method and how much improvement is gained from the weather forecast. Kelly has also asked you to prepare some ideas for other data variables that might be collected to further improve the forecasts. Finally, he wants you to provide monthly forecasts from your final model for the next 12 months based on the long-range weather forecast shown here.

	Month											
	Jan	**Feb**	**Mar**	**Apr**	**May**	**Jun**	**Jul**	**Aug**	**Sep**	**Oct**	**Nov**	**Dec**
Forecast average daily high	47	40	52	64	78	80	85	87	76	65	56	52

Write a report to Bill Kelly providing your analysis of the data and final recommendation. The report should consist of two parts: (1) a one-page memo that briefly summarizes the results of your analysis and your recommendation, and (2) a detailed analysis of the data that describes your analysis and interpretations. Be sure to compare your forecasting method to that previously used by Kelly, commenting on the strengths and weaknesses of each approach. Incorporate important details, graphs, and tables from your analysis to support your recommendation.

The data are contained in the file Southern on the CD that came with your book. The file contains data for the past 60 months. For each month, the year, the average daily high temperature, and the sales revenue are given. A partial listing of the data within Excel is shown in Figure 12.8.

FIGURE 12.8   **Partial Listing of the Southern Electric Cooperative Data**

	A	B	C	D
1	Month	Year	AvgHighTemp	Revenue
2	1	1	42	176.789
3	2	1	40	197.775
4	3	1	46	144.296
5	4	1	52	137.207
6	5	1	73	125.046
7	6	1	80	133.868
8	7	1	87	177.739
9	8	1	86	163.441
10	9	1	78	133.143
11	10	1	68	109.002
12	11	1	59	103.280
13	12	1	51	128.341
14	1	2	46	147.643
15	2	2	41	195.133
16	3	2	48	161.623

In the Southern file, the variables are defined as follows:

Month: 1 = Jan, 2 = Feb, . . . , and 12 = Dec

Year: 1, 2, 3, 4, or 5 (where 5 = most recent year)

AvgHighTemp: Average daily high temperature for the month (in Farenheit)

Revenue: Total revenue from sales of electricity (in thousands of dollars)

CHAPTER 13

Constructing a Multiple
Regression Model

CHAPTER CONTENTS

This chapter describes the typical steps in constructing a multiple regression model. The important steps in this procedure are initial selection of possible predictors, creating nonlinear terms, selecting among the predictors, checking critical assumptions, and possibly validating the model using new or reserved data. The key ideas for this procedure are

- Predictor variables should be selected on the basis of understanding the management situation. Each predictor should be correlated with the dependent variable, but not severely collinear with other predictors.

- In the presence of collinearity, coefficients are sensitive to which variables are included in the model. In addition, the explanatory power of a variable depends strongly on the order in which predictors are listed in the model.

- Categorical predictors may be incorporated into the model by using dummy variables. Each dummy variable equals 1 if a specified category holds, 0 if not. Use one less dummy variable than there are categories. The "undummied" category serves as a baseline against which we compare the effects of other categories. The coefficient of a dummy variable is the difference in intercept as compared to the baseline category.

- Interaction effects may be incorporated by using product terms. When a product term is a dummy variable times a quantitative variable, its coefficient is the difference in slope as compared to the slope for the baseline category.

- In a time series regression, independent variables may be lagged by one or more time periods. This is a necessity if the model is to be used for forecasting and may improve predictive value in general.

- Stepwise regression is used to select predictors for the model. This method tends to overstate the predictive value of the resulting model. A check on the reasonableness of the chosen model can be done using the C_p statistic.

- Assumption checking is based on plots of residuals. A plot of residuals against an independent variable may reveal a nonlinear relation. A smoother such as LOWESS helps to see any nonlinearity. A plot of residuals against predicted values may reveal increasing variability. Data transformations are used to correct for these problems.

- In time series data, a plot of residuals against period number may reveal that the errors are autocorrelated. A value of the Durbin–Watson statistic much below 2.0 also indicates autocorrelation. This violation of the independence assumption results in some overstatement of the predictive value of the model and severe overstatement of the accuracy of the estimated coefficients. If autocorrelation is present, try using differences of all variables.

- Because of the possibility of overfitting the data, it is highly recommended to validate the selected model using new data whenever possible.

Easton Realty Company

Sam Easton started out as a real estate agent in Atlanta ten years ago. After working two years for a national real estate firm, he moved to Dallas, Texas. His friends and relatives convinced him that with his experience and knowledge of the real estate business, he should open his own agency. He eventually acquired his broker's license and before long started his own company, Easton Realty, in Fort Worth. Easton currently has eight real estate agents working for him. Before the real estate slump, the combined residential sales for Easton Realty amounted to approximately $15 million annually.

Two days ago, Easton received a special delivery letter from the president of the local board of realtors. The board had received complaints from two people who had listed and sold their homes through Easton Realty in the past month. The president of the board of realtors was informing Sam of these complaints and giving him the opportunity to respond. Both complaints were triggered by a recent article on home sales appearing in one of the local newspapers. The article contained the following table:

Typical Home Sale in the DFW Area

Average sales price	$154,250
Average size	1860 sq. ft.

Note: Includes all homes sold in Dallas, Fort Worth, Arlington, and the MidCities over the past 12 months.

The two sellers charged that Easton Realty had underpriced their homes in order to accelerate the sales. The first house, located in Arlington, is four years old, has 2190 square feet, and sold for $143,300. The second house, located in Fort Worth, is nine years old, has 1848 square feet, and sold for $125,700. Both houses are three-bedroom houses. Both sellers believe that they would have received more money for their houses if Easton Realty had priced them at their true market value.

Sam knew from experience that people selling their homes invariably overestimate the value, but Sam also knew that his agents would not intentionally underprice houses. However, in the recent slow housing market, many real estate companies, including Easton Realty, had large inventories of houses for sale and needed to make sales. One quick way to reduce the inventories is to price the houses under their market value. On a residential sale, an agent working under a real estate broker typically makes about 3% of the sales price if he or she originally listed the property. Dropping the sales price of a $100,000 home down to $90,000 would speed up the sale and the agent's commission would only fall from $3,000 to $2,700. Some real estate agents might consider sacrificing $300 in order to get their commission sooner, but it is unethical because the agent represents the seller and is supposed to be acting in the seller's best interests. Sam had to convince the two sellers and the board of realtors that there was no substance to the complaints. The question was, how was he going to do it?

First, he needed to obtain recent residential sales data. Unfortunately, the local MLS (multiple listing service) did not contain actual sales prices of homes. However, Pat McCloskey, a local real estate appraiser, did maintain a database that had the sales information Sam needed. Phoning Pat, Sam found that she would have to merge her personal database with data downloaded from the MLS in order to give Sam the necessary information—fortunately, a relatively simple task.

Sam asked Pat to give him the data she had on home sales that had taken place in the DFW area over the previous four months. Although Pat's database did not contain all home sales in the DFW metroplex over that period of time, the data she had were representative of the entire population. The data for each home sold included the sale month, the sale price, the size of the home (in square feet of heated floor space), the number of bedrooms, the age of the house, the area within the DFW metroplex where the house is located, and the real estate company that sold the home.

After several attempts at analyzing the data himself, Sam realized he was in over his head. Fortunately, he recalled that you, currently serving as legal counsel for Easton Realty, had earned a joint MBA–JD degree with a concentration in quantitative analysis. Sam has asked you to take a look at the data and give him your opinion of the situation. In particular, he wants you to determine whether or not the two houses in question were underpriced relative to the market, that is, relative to comparable houses sold by other realtors. Secondly, he wants you to determine whether or not Easton has been underpricing houses relative to its competitors.

The sales data from Pat McCloskey are contained in the file Easton on the CD that came with your book. A partial listing of the data within Excel is shown in Figure 13.1.

FIGURE 13.1

Partial Listing of the Easton Realty Company Data

	A	B	C	D	E	F	G
1	Month	Price	Size	Bedrooms	Age	Area	Agency
2	March	127.4	1800	3	3	2	0
3	March	106.9	1362	2	7	2	0
4	March	135.5	1819	3	6	2	1
5	March	107.5	1594	3	7	3	0
6	March	132.6	1605	3	6	1	0
7	March	212.3	2741	4	5	1	0
8	March	139.2	2190	3	8	3	0
9	March	190.3	2393	3	7	1	0
10	March	113.0	1654	2	7	2	0
11	March	178.3	2209	4	8	1	0
12	March	137.4	1544	3	7	1	0
13	March	111.6	1528	3	6	3	1
14	March	176.1	2088	3	5	1	0

In the Easton file, the variables are defined as follows:

Month: Month in which the sale took place (March, April, May, or June)

Price: Sale price of the house (in thousands of dollars)

Size: Square feet of heated floor space

Bedrooms: Number of bedrooms in the house

Age: Age of the house in years

Area: Area in the DFW metroplex in which the house is located
           1, if Dallas,
           2, if Fort Worth,
           3, if elsewhere in the metroplex

Agency: 1, if Easton Realty Company sold the house,
           0, otherwise

The material covered in this chapter on multiple regression model building and the material covered in earlier chapters will prove to be very helpful in analyzing this situation and making your recommendation to Sam Easton. A complete analysis of the data will be considered at the end of this chapter. ∎

THIS CHAPTER PRESENTS SOME suggestions for actually creating a useful multiple regression model. It is, we hope, a practical chapter that builds on and extends the material of Chapter 12.

four steps in a multiple regression study

A typical multiple regression study passes through at least four steps. First, we select potentially useful independent variables (Section 13.1). Qualitative variables can be incorporated by the "dummy variable" device that we discuss in Section 13.2. Additional variables may be created (in time series data) by lagging independent variables; we discuss this process in Section 13.3. The second step is tentative selection of plausible forms for the multiple regression model. This may require transformation or combination of either the dependent variable or the independent variables, as we discuss in Section 13.4. The third step, which usually requires fitting several candidate models, is the selection of a particular model that is appropriate and useful for the given situation. This step may be done simply by comparing the results of several models or, more elaborately, by the process of stepwise regression, which we discuss in Section 13.5. The fourth step is checking the selected model for potential violations of assumptions. At this step, the residuals (actual y values minus predicted y values) are examined for evidence of severe nonnormality, nonlinearity, or nonconstant variance, as we discuss in Section 13.6. If, in addition, the multiple regression model involves time series data, it is also necessary to check the residuals for nonindependence (autocorrelation), as we discuss in Section 13.7. With luck, a satisfactory multiple regression model can be found by one pass through this four-step process. Usually, several passes are necessary.

We should ideally take a fifth step before the model is put into use. This step is checking the results of the model on new data, which we discuss in Section 13.8. This check is to confirm that the selected model has the indicated predictive value and that it is not merely an artifact of too much "data massaging."

Obviously, a great deal of calculating is required in the process of selecting a model, and access to statistical software programs is a practical necessity. This chapter follows the basic steps in constructing a model; it should be of considerable practical use.

13.1 Selecting Possible Independent Variables (Step 1)

Perhaps the most critical decision in constructing a multiple regression model is the initial selection of independent variables. In later sections of this chapter we consider many methods for refining a multiple regression analysis, but first we must make a decision about which independent (x) variables to consider for inclusion and hence which data to gather. If we don't have useful data, we're unlikely to come up with a useful predictive model.

While initially it may appear that an optimum strategy might be to construct a monstrous multiple regression model with very many variables, these models are difficult to interpret and are much more costly from a data-gathering and computer-usage standpoint. How can a manager make a reasonable selection of initial variables to include in a regression analysis?

selection of the independent variables

Knowledge of the problem area is critically important in the initial **selection of the independent variables.** First, identify the dependent variable to be studied. Individuals who have had experience with this variable by observing it, trying to predict it, and trying to explain changes in it often have remarkably good insight as to what factors (independent variables) affect the variable. As a consequence, the first step involves consulting those who have the most experience with the dependent variable of interest. For example, suppose that the problem is to forecast the next quarter's sales volume of an inexpensive brand of computer printer for each of 40 districts. The dependent variable Y is, then, district sales volume. Certain independent variables, such as the advertising budget in each district and the number of sales outlets, are obvious candidates. A good district sales manager undoubtedly could suggest others.

collinearity

A major consideration in selecting predictor variables is the problem of **collinearity,** severely correlated independent variables (we discussed them in Sections 12.2 and 12.3). A partial slope in multiple regression estimates the predictive effect of changing one independent variable while holding all others constant. But when some or all of the predictors vary together, it can be almost impossible to separate out the predictive effects of each one. A common result when predictors are highly correlated is that the overall F test is highly significant but none of the individual t tests comes close to significance. The significant F result indicates only that there is detectable predictive value somewhere among the independent variables; the nonsignificant t values indicate that we can't detect *additional* predictive value for any variable, given all the others. The reason is that highly correlated predictors are surrogates for each other; any of them individually may be useful, but adding others will not be. When seriously collinear independent variables are all used in a multiple regression model, it can be virtually impossible to decide which predictors are in fact related to the dependent variable.

matrix of correlation coefficients

There are several ways to assess the amount of collinearity in a set of independent variables. The simplest method is to look at a **matrix of correlation coefficients,** which can be produced by almost all computer packages. The higher these correlations, the more severe the collinearity problem is. In most situations, any correlation over .9 or so definitely indicates a serious problem.

scatterplot matrix

Some computer packages can produce a **scatterplot matrix,** a set of scatterplots for each pair of variables. Collinearity appears in such a matrix as a close linear relation between two of the *independent* variables. For example, a sample of automotive writers rated a new compact car on 0 to 100 scales for performance, comfort, appearance, and overall quality. The promotion manager doing the study wanted to know which variables best predicted the writers' rating of overall quality. A Minitab scatterplot matrix is shown in Figure 13.2. There are clear linear relations among the performance, comfort, and appearance ratings, indicating substantial collinearity. The following matrix of correlations confirms that fact.

```
Correlations: Overall, Performance, Comfort, Appearance

               Overall   Performance     Comfort
Performance     0.583
Comfort         0.691        0.776
Appearance      0.534        0.328        0.593
```

FIGURE 13.2   **Scatterplot Matrix for Auto Writers Data**

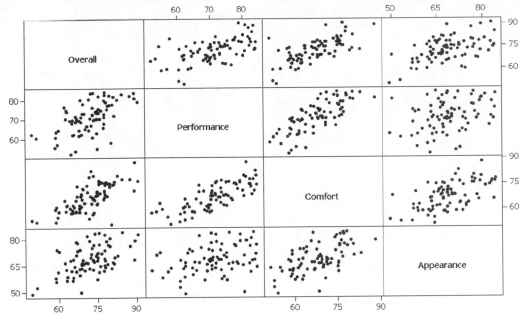

A scatterplot matrix can also be useful in detecting nonlinear relations or outliers. The matrix contains scatterplots of the dependent variable against each independent variable separately. Sometimes, a curve or a serious outlier will be clear in the matrix. Other times, the effect of other independent variables may conceal a problem. The analysis of residuals, discussed later in this chapter, is another good way to look for assumption violations.

The correlation matrix and scatterplot matrix may not reveal the full extent of a collinearity problem. Sometimes two predictors together predict a third all too well, even though either of the two by itself shows a more modest correlation with the third one. (Direct labor hours and indirect labor hours together predict total labor hours remarkably well, even if either one predicts the total imperfectly.) There are a number of more sophisticated ways of diagnosing collinearity built into various computer packages. One such diagnostic is the variance inflation factor (VIF) that we discussed in Chapter 12. It is $1/(1 - R^2)$, where this R^2 refers to how much of the variation in one *independent* variable is explained by the others. The VIF takes into account all relations among predictors, so it is more complete than simple correlations. The books by Cook and Weisberg (1982) and by Belsley, Kuh, and Welsch (1980) define several diagnostic measures for collinearity. The manuals for most statistical computer programs will indicate which of these can be computed and what the results indicate.

EXAMPLE 13.1   A supermarket chain staged a promotion for a "superpremium" brand of ice cream. Data on actual sales of the brand for the weekend of the promotion were obtained from scanner data gathered at the checkout stands. Three explanatory variables being considered were the size of the store, in thousands of square feet; the number of customers processed in the store, in hundreds; and the average size of purchase (also obtained from scanner data). A JMP scatterplot matrix is shown in Figure 13.3. What does it indicate about collinearity? Does it show any other problems?

SOLUTION Look at the six scatterplots in the upper right of the matrix. There is a clear increasing relation, but not extremely strong, between "SqFeet," the size of the store, and "NumCusts," the number of customers. There is little correlation between either of these independent variables and "AvgSize" of purchase. Thus there is a modest collinearity problem. There is no indication of a serious nonlinearity problem in the matrix. However, there is an outlier. In the plot of "Sales" against "SqFeet," one store has the largest size but nearly the smallest sales. This outlier has fairly high leverage; it is extreme on two of the independent variables (size and number of customers). It may well have substantial influence as well, because it falls well off the line for predicting sales from either of these predictors. Further checking showed that the ice cream display case at store 41 had lost power during the weekend, forcing the store manager to remove all the ice cream from the case. The store was omitted from the regression analysis.

FIGURE 13.3 **Scatterplot Matrix for Ice Cream Data**

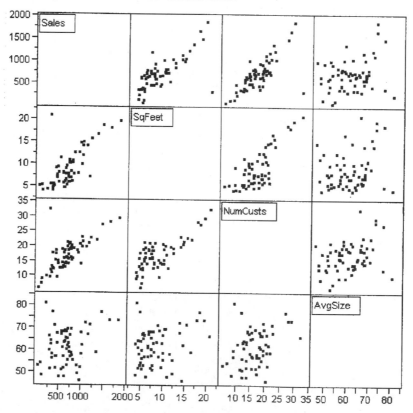

One of the best ways to avoid collinearity problems is to choose predictor variables intelligently right at the beginning of a regression study. Try to find independent variables that should correlate decently with the dependent variable but do not have obvious correlations with each other. If possible, try to find independent variables that reflect various components of the dependent variable. For example, suppose that we want to predict the sales of inexpensive printers for personal computers in each of 40 sales districts. Total sales are made up of several sectors of buyers. We might identify the important sectors as college students, home users, small businesses, and computer network workstations. Therefore, we might well try number of college freshmen, household income, small business starts, and new network installations as independent variables. Each one makes sense as a predictor of printer sales, and there is no screamingly obvious correlation among the predictors. People who are knowledgeable about the variable you want to predict can often identify components and suggest reasonable predictors for the different components.

EXAMPLE 13.2   A firm that sells and services computers is concerned about the volume of service calls. The firm maintains several district service branches within each sales region, and computer owners requiring service call the nearest branch. The branches are staffed by technicians trained at the main office. The key problem is whether technicians should be assigned to main-office duty or to service branches; assignment decisions have to be made monthly. The required number of service-branch technicians grows in almost exact proportion to the number of service calls. Discussion with the service manager indicates that the key variables in determining the volume of service calls seem to be the number of computers in use, the number of new installations, whether or not a model change has been introduced recently, and the average temperature. (High temperatures, or possibly the associated high humidity, lead to more frequent computer troubles, especially in imperfectly air-conditioned offices.) Which of these variables can be expected to be correlated with each other?

SOLUTION   It is hard to imagine why temperature should be correlated with any of the other variables. There should be some correlation between number of computers in use and number of new installations, if only because every new installation is a computer in use. Unless the firm has been growing at an increasing rate, we wouldn't expect a severe correlation (we would, however, like to see the data). The correlation of model change to number in use and new installations isn't at all obvious; surely data should be collected and correlations analyzed.

13.2 Using Qualitative Predictors: Dummy Variables (Step 1)

dummy variable

One special type of independent variable that could be included in the multiple regression model is the **dummy** or **indicator variable.** Such variables are used to represent qualitative (categorical) variables such as geographic region, type of incentive plan, or "protected-class" membership in a discrimination suit. The simplest dummy-variable situation occurs when the qualitative variable has only two categories, such as female–male or protected–not protected; then the dummy variable is defined by assigning one category of the qualitative variable the value 1 and the other the value 0. For example, suppose that y is the total production cost (in dollars) of a print run, x_1 is the number of items printed (in thousands of items), and x_2 is a dummy variable that equals 1 when the run is on a rush basis and 0 when it is on a regular basis. Assume that the multiple regression prediction equation is

$$\hat{y} = 86.2 + 5.1x_1 + 20.5x_2$$

The coefficient $\hat{\beta}_2 = 20.5$ of x_2 may be interpreted as the estimated difference in cost between a rush job ($x_2 = 1$) and a regular job ($x_2 = 0$) for any specified run size (x_1). By substituting $x_2 = 1$ into the multiple regression prediction equation, we get an equation relating y to x_1 for rush jobs. The corresponding equation relating y to x_1 for regular jobs is obtained by substituting $x_2 = 0$.

Rush jobs: $\hat{y} = 86.2 + 5.1x_1 + 20.5(1) = 106.7 + 5.1x_1$

Regular jobs: $\hat{y} = 86.2 + 5.1x_1 + 20.5(0) = 86.2 + 5.1x_1$

Note that the two prediction equations (corresponding to $x_2 = 0$ or $x_2 = 1$) are parallel lines with different intercepts. These equations are shown in Figure 13.4.

FIGURE 13.4

Effect of a Two-Value Dummy Variable

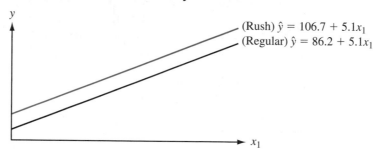

If a qualitative variable can take on more than two levels, definition of the dummy variable is a bit more complicated. We do not want to code residence as $0 =$ urban, $1 =$ suburban, and $2 =$ rural and then use the resulting x in a regression. A one-unit increase in this x could mean either a change from urban to suburban or a change from suburban to rural. There is no reason to assume that the two possible changes would predict the same change in any y; the coefficient of such a variable wouldn't mean much. Instead, we could use two dummy variables to define residence: Define $x_1 = 1$ if residence $=$ suburban and $x_1 = 0$ otherwise, and define $x_2 = 1$ if residence $=$ rural and $x_2 = 0$ otherwise. If both x_1 and x_2 are 0, it follows by elimination that residence $=$ urban. In general, with this scheme, a qualitative variable with k categories can be coded using $k - 1$ dummy variables. If all $k - 1$ dummies are 0 for an observation, the observation must fall into the kth category.

interpretation of regression coefficients

The **interpretation of regression coefficients** in the prediction equation requires some thought. Suppose that x_1 and x_2 are the dummy variables for the qualitative variable residence, x_3 is education in years, and y is income in thousands of dollars. An appropriate multiple regression model is

$$Y = \beta_0 + \beta_1 x_1 + \beta_2 x_2 + \beta_3 x_3 + \epsilon$$

where

$$x_1 = \begin{cases} 1 & \text{if suburban} \\ 0 & \text{otherwise} \end{cases} \qquad x_2 = \begin{cases} 1 & \text{if rural} \\ 0 & \text{otherwise} \end{cases}$$

The interpretations assigned to the β's for the dummy variables x_1 and x_2 can be seen by examining the corresponding expectations $E(Y)$.

$$\text{For urban residence } (x_1 = x_2 = 0): \quad E(Y) = \beta_0 + \beta_3 x_3$$
$$\text{For suburban residence } (x_1 = 1, x_2 = 0): \quad E(Y) = \beta_0 + \beta_1 + \beta_3 x_3$$
$$\text{For rural residence } (x_1 = 0, x_2 = 1): \quad E(Y) = \beta_0 + \beta_2 + \beta_3 x_3$$

It follows that the coefficient for the "suburban" dummy is the difference in expected income between suburban and urban residents for a fixed number of years of education, x_3. Similarly, the coefficient for the "rural" dummy is the difference in expected income between rural and urban residents for a fixed number of years of education, x_3. It follows, too, that the difference between the coefficients of the dummy variables is the difference in expected income between rural and suburban residents at a fixed education level.

Knowing the interpretations of the coefficients, one can make sense of a least-squares prediction equation. Suppose that the least-squares prediction equation based on sample data is

$$\hat{y} = 3.05 + 5.91x_1 - 1.84x_2 + .12x_3$$

The coefficient of x_1, the "suburban" dummy, is the estimated difference in incomes (in thousands of dollars) for suburban residents when compared to urban residents with the same years of education. Similarly, the coefficient of x_2, the "rural" dummy, is the predicted difference in average income between rural and urban residents with the same education. With years of education x_3 fixed, the regression equation tells us that suburban residents average \$5910 higher income than urban residents, while rural residents average \$1840 lower than urban residents. The "undummied" category (urban residents in the example) serves as the comparison standard. A comparison of rural and suburban residents can be made by comparing each to an urban resident. For education held constant, a suburban resident is predicted to earn $5.91 - (-1.84) = 7.75$ thousand dollars more than a rural resident.

Dummy variables are often used in product terms, typically a dummy variable multiplied by another independent variable. We will return to this topic when we consider nonlinear models later in this chapter.

EXAMPLE 13.3   A regression model relates Y = a person's percentage salary increase to seniority in years, gender, and location of the workplace (urban, suburban, or rural). The prediction equation is

$$\hat{y} = 1.31 + 0.09x_1 - 0.43x_2 + 1.02x_3 - 0.66x_4$$

where x_1 = seniority in years,

$$x_2 = \begin{cases} 1 & \text{if female} \\ 0 & \text{otherwise} \end{cases} \qquad x_3 = \begin{cases} 1 & \text{if suburban} \\ 0 & \text{otherwise} \end{cases} \qquad x_4 = \begin{cases} 1 & \text{if rural} \\ 0 & \text{otherwise} \end{cases}$$

Interpret the coefficients in the general linear model.

SOLUTION   Because there are several dummy variables and one quantitative independent variable, the easiest way to interpret the coefficients is to obtain expected values $E(Y)$ for each combination of settings of the dummy variables. These expected values are listed next.

Urban $(x_3 = 0, x_4 = 0)$	Suburban $(x_3 = 1, x_4 = 0)$	Rural $(x_3 = 0, x_4 = 1)$
Male: $\hat{y} = 1.31 + 0.09x_1$ $(x_2 = 0)$	$\hat{y} = 1.31 + 0.09x_1 + 1.02$	$\hat{y} = 1.31 + 0.09x_1 - 0.66$
Female: $\hat{y} = 1.31 + 0.09x_1 - 0.43$ $(x_2 = 1)$	$\hat{y} = 1.31 + 0.09x_1 - 0.43 + 1.02$	$\hat{y} = 1.31 + 0.09x_1 - 0.43 - 0.66$

From this table, it is clear that $\hat{\beta}_2 = -.043$ is the difference in mean salary increase $E(Y)$ between females and males, for a given level of seniority (x_1) and location of residence. For example, at a given level of x_1 in an urban district, the difference in mean salary increases between females and males is

$$(\hat{\beta}_0 + \hat{\beta}_1 x_1 + \hat{\beta}_2) - (\hat{\beta}_0 + \hat{\beta}_1 x_1) = \hat{\beta}_2 = -.043$$

This result also applies for any other fixed geographic location. Similarly, $\hat{\beta}_3$ is the difference in mean salary increase between suburban and urban residences for females (or males) at a given seniority level, and $\hat{\beta}_4$ is the difference in mean salary increase in the rural and urban districts for females (or males) at a given seniority level.

EXAMPLE 13.4

The computer firm of Example 13.2 is concerned with recent model changes as a source of service calls. The firm feels that most of the effects of model changes occur in the first two months. After that time, minor manufacturing changes eliminate any blatant problems. Discuss how dummy variables could be used in a regression model (based on monthly data) to treat the issue of model change.

SOLUTION   There are three possibilities in any given month: Model has changed that month, model has changed the previous month, or neither of these. Two dummies are needed, and one way to define them is

$$x_1 = \begin{cases} 1 & \text{if model has changed this month} \\ 0 & \text{if not} \end{cases}$$

$$x_2 = \begin{cases} 1 & \text{if model has changed the previous month} \\ 0 & \text{if not} \end{cases}$$

A problem with this approach is that it does not reflect the *number* of new installations in the model-change months.

13.3   Lagged Predictor Variables (Step 1)

lagged variables

In many time series regression problems, the independent variables in the equation should be **lagged variables.** A regional sales manager may try to forecast monthly sales (y) given the number of initial calls (c) and the number of sales presentations (p) by salespeople. For many types of products, the calls and presentations will result in sales some months later, rather than immediately. The sales manager does not want an equation of the form

$$\hat{y}_t = \hat{\beta}_0 + \hat{\beta}_1 c_t + \hat{\beta}_2 p_t$$

but rather an equation something like

$$\hat{y}_t = \hat{\beta}_0 + \hat{\beta}_1 c_{t-2} + \hat{\beta}_2 p_{t-1}$$

In this example initial calls are lagged two months behind sales, and presentations one month behind. The implicit idea is that initial calls in one month tend to generate presentations the next month, which in turn tend to generate sales a month later.

Lagging variables is often necessary when regression is to be used for forecasting. A sales forecasting equation like

$$\hat{y}_t = \hat{\beta}_0 + \hat{\beta}_1 c_t + \hat{\beta}_2 p_t$$

is most likely useless, because the values of c_t and p_t are not known when the forecast has to be made. To make regression useful in forecasting, the predictor variables must be lagged at least far enough so that their values can be known at forecast time.

The major problem with lagging variables is deciding the number of periods to lag. Should the sales manager lag the presentation variable by one month, two months, or what? It's tempting to include many lags in a single regression equation, such as

$$\hat{y}_t = \hat{\beta}_0 + \hat{\beta}_1 c_{t-1} + \hat{\beta}_2 c_{t-2} + \hat{\beta}_3 c_{t-3} + \hat{\beta}_4 c_{t-4} + \hat{\beta}_5 c_{t-5}$$
$$+ \hat{\beta}_6 p_{t-1} + \hat{\beta}_7 p_{t-2} + \hat{\beta}_8 p_{t-3} + \hat{\beta}_9 p_{t-4} + \hat{\beta}_{10} p_{t-5}$$

There are two problems with this strategy. First, the number of independent variables is large. Because one must have more observations than variables in a regression (the d.f. for error is number of observations − number of predictors − 1), this strategy requires a lot of data. Second, the lagged variables are likely to be severely correlated.

Econometricians have proposed several other strategies for deciding on lags (see Johnston, 1977, or any other econometrics text.). These strategies typically involve rather severe assumptions that are difficult to verify. If one has no inkling of plausible lag structures, these methods are worth a try.

Often it's possible to find reasonable lags by thoughtful trial and error. The sales manager may well try lagging presentations by one month in one regression equation and by both one and two in a second. If the second equation doesn't forecast much better than the first, and if most sales result within a month or so of presentations, there is no reason to try further lags. Knowledge of the basic process involved is almost always useful in choosing lags.

EXAMPLE 13.5   An automobile dealer offers a 12-month or 12,000-mile warranty on new cars and a 3-month or 3,000-mile warranty on used cars. As a consequence, the dealer's repair department handles a certain number of warranty-covered repair jobs each month. Data are collected on y_t, the number of warranty repair jobs in month t; x_{t1}, the number of new car sales in month t; and x_{t2}, the number of used car sales in month t. The data are analyzed by two regression models:

$$Y_t = \beta_0 + \beta_1 x_{t1} + \beta_2 x_{t2} + \epsilon_t$$

$$Y_t = \beta_0 + \beta_1 x_{t1} + \beta_2 x_{t-1,1} + \beta_3 x_{t-2,1} + \beta_4 x_{t2} + \beta_5 x_{t-1,2}$$
$$\quad + \beta_6 x_{t-2,2} + \epsilon_t$$

Partial computer output from Minitab is shown below.

```
Regression Analysis: Repairs versus NewCars, UsedCars

The regression equation is
Repairs = 0.33 + 0.312 NewCars + 0.171 UsedCars

Predictor    Coef   SE Coef      T      P
Constant    0.326     6.535   0.05  0.961
NewCars    0.3115    0.1412   2.21  0.035
UsedCars   0.1715    0.1857   0.92  0.363

S = 5.17354    R-Sq = 38.3%    R-Sq(adj) = 34.3%

Analysis of Variance

Source            DF        SS      MS      F      P
Regression         2    514.50  257.25   9.61  0.001
Residual Error    31    829.74   26.77
Total             33   1344.23

Regression Analysis: Repairs versus NewCars, NewLag1, ...

The regression equation is
Repairs = - 25.1 + 0.176 NewCars + 0.141 NewLag1 + 0.123 NewLag2
          + 0.264 UsedCars - 0.003 UsedLag1 + 0.259 UsedLag2

Predictor    Coef    SE Coef       T      P
Constant  -25.052      5.776   -4.34  0.000
NewCars    0.17642    0.08727   2.02  0.053
NewLag1    0.14054    0.09186   1.53  0.138
NewLag2    0.12296    0.08969   1.37  0.182
UsedCars   0.2644     0.1082    2.44  0.021
UsedLag1  -0.0030     0.1060   -0.03  0.977
UsedLag2   0.2590     0.1241    2.09  0.046

S = 2.90283    R-Sq = 83.1%    R-Sq(adj) = 79.3%

Analysis of Variance

Source            DF        SS      MS      F      P
Regression         6   1116.71  186.12  22.09  0.000
Residual Error    27    227.51    8.43
Total             33   1344.23
```

a. Write the regression equation for the nonlagged model, together with the residual standard deviation and R^2 values.

b. Do the same for the lagged model.

c. Is there reason to believe that the lagged variables are useful in prediction?

SOLUTION

a. For this model, the regression equation is

$$\hat{y}_t = .33 + .312 x_{t1} + .171 x_{t2}$$

The corresponding values of s_ϵ and R^2 are

$$s_\epsilon = 5.174 \quad \text{and} \quad R^2 = .383$$

b. The regression equation for the second model is

$$\hat{y}_t = -25.1 + .176x_{t1} + .141x_{t-1,1} + .123x_{t-2,1} + .264x_{t2}$$
$$- .003x_{t-1,2} + .259x_{t-2,2}$$

The values of s_ϵ and R^2 are

$$s_\epsilon = 2.903 \quad \text{and} \quad R^2 = .831$$

c. The inclusion of lagged variables has helped in the prediction of y. The value of R^2 has been increased considerably, and s_ϵ is much smaller. We could carry out the incremental F test of Chapter 12, but the result is clear.

EXAMPLE 13.6

In Example 13.2 new-model introduction affected service calls for two months. What lags should be used in a (monthly) database?

SOLUTION New installations reflect only the current month. To capture the two-month effect, the new-installations variable should also be lagged by a month. As a check on the belief that the new-model effect lasts only two months, it wouldn't be totally inappropriate to lag new installations by another month as well.

Exercises

13.1 A city probation office tries to use various reported crime rates to forecast the volume of new cases. The total number of nonviolent crimes reported in the city is determined for 12 quarters, as is the volume of new cases. The data are

Quarter, t:	1	2	3	4
Crimes (thousands), x_t:	6.4	5.6	5.8	6.6
New cases (hundreds), y_t:	13.1	13.5	12.7	12.9

5	6	7	8	9	10	11	12
7.0	6.7	6.5	7.1	7.2	6.9	6.8	6.7
14.3	14.8	14.4	13.9	15.0	15.5	15.1	14.6

Output from Minitab follows:

```
Correlations: NewCases, Crimes, LagCrimes

            NewCases    Crimes
Crimes        0.635
LagCrimes     0.974     0.597
```

```
Regression Analysis: NewCases versus LagCrimes

The regression equation is
NewCases = 2.82 + 1.73 LagCrimes

11 cases used, 1 cases contain missing values

Predictor     Coef   SE Coef      T       P
Constant     2.8224   0.8854    3.19   0.011
LagCrimes    1.7308   0.1338   12.94   0.000

S = 0.215719    R-Sq = 94.9%    R-Sq(adj) = 94.3%

Analysis of Variance

Source            DF     SS       MS       F       P
Regression         1   7.7885   7.7885  167.37  0.000
Residual Error     9   0.4188   0.0465
Total             10   8.2073
```

a. Locate the correlation between x_t and y_t.
b. Locate the "lag1" correlation—the correlation between x_{t-1} and y_t. Note that the effective sample size is 11, not 12.
c. Which of the correlations is stronger? Does this result seem sensible?

13.2   Refer to the output of Exercise 13.1.
a. Locate the regression equation $\hat{y}_t = \hat{\beta}_0 + \hat{\beta}_1 x_{t-1}$.
b. Find the residual standard deviation.

13.3   Refer to Exercise 13.1. What would happen if you tried to calculate lag 10 and lag 11 correlations? (What sample size would you have?)

13.4   A textbook publisher begins a sales forecasting system. The chief editors for each of three divisions forecast first-year sales for all new books published in a certain year. These forecasts are later compared to actual sales. Excel output from a regression study follows:

```
Regression Statistics
Multiple R               0.9613
R Square                 0.9240
Adjusted R Square        0.9156
Standard Error           1.6506
Observations                 31

ANOVA
                df        SS        MS         F      Significance F
Regression       3    894.745   298.248   109.468      3.178E-15
Residual        27     73.562     2.725
Total           30    968.307
```

	Coefficients	Standard Error	t Stat	P-value	Lower 95%	Upper 95%
Intercept	-1.8631	1.0017	-1.8599	0.0738	-3.9184	0.1923
Forecast	1.3542	0.0829	16.3292	0.0000	1.1840	1.5243
Div2	-4.0066	0.7068	-5.6688	0.0000	-5.4567	-2.5564
Div3	0.9158	0.7302	1.2541	0.2205	-0.5825	2.4141

a. Identify the dummy variables.
b. What is the interpretation of the coefficients of these dummy variables?
c. Do the t statistics suggest that the dummy variables separately have some predictive value?

13.5   For the data of Exercise 13.4, what additional computer output would you need to test the null hypothesis that the dummy variables collectively have no predictive value once the forecast value has been included in the regression equation?

13.6   Refer to Exercise 13.4.
a. What null hypothesis is being tested by the *F* statistic? What does this hypothesis say about the forecasting system?
b. Can this null hypothesis be rejected at $\alpha = .01$? Locate the *p*-value.

13.7   Refer to Exercise 13.4.
a. If the forecast sales had been exactly correct on the average within each division, what would the regression equation be? In particular, what would the coefficient of forecast equal?
b. Locate a 95% confidence interval for the forecast coefficient. Does it include the value you specified in part (a)?

13.4   Nonlinear Regression Models (Step 2)

In Section 12.1 we pointed out that use of a first-order regression model (one containing only linear terms in the *x*'s) assumes linearity in each variable separately and also assumes that there are no interactions among the independent variables. In this section we discuss how to modify a first-order model to handle curved relations and also interactions.

In some situations it is evident in advance that a model that is linear in all the independent variables will be inadequate. A regression model that predicts *y*, a taste-test preference score for a lime drink, as a linear function of x_1, lime concentration, and x_2, sweetness, is very dubious. Assuming both coefficients are positive, say, that would mean that the ideal drink would have the maximum concentration of lime flavor and maximum sweetness (syrup?). If, however, the range of variation in the independent variables is not large, a linear relation may be a good approximation *over that range*.

In other cases, scatterplots of the data may reveal nonlinearities. In linear regression, the ordinary plot of *y* versus *x* is adequate. In multiple regression, the effect of variation in other *x*'s can obscure the nonlinearity. For this reason, a standard strategy is to fit a first-order model and then plot the residuals from this model against each independent variable. If a more appropriate model should contain, for instance, a term in x_1^2, then the plot of residuals against x_1 shows a nonlinear pattern. Because the use of a first-order model removes the linear effect of the other independent variables, nonlinearities often show up more clearly in these **residual plots.**

residual plots

For example, in a regression analysis with three independent variables, a plot of *y* against x_1 is shown in Figure 13.5. The pattern of relation isn't too easy to see. A multiple regression run (with all three independent variables) yielded residuals, which are plotted against x_1 in Figure 13.6. Now the curve pattern is easier to see. Also, it appears that variability in the residuals may be increasing as x_1 increases. The up-and-down variation in Figure 13.6 is larger on the right side of the plot.

Once potential nonlinearity has been discovered, we can deal with it either by transforming existing variables or by adding additional, higher-order terms such as x^2 in the *x*'s. Often we use both of these strategies. Transformations may be suggested either by the nature of the problem or by the look of the data. Recall that we discussed transformations in Section 11.1 while looking at scatterplots of the data. The same principles work when examining residual plots. Some packages will fit a LOWESS smoother to residual plots. If a curve is evident in plotting residuals against an *x* variable (either by eye or using a smoother), transform that *x* or the

FIGURE 13.5

Plot of *y* Against x_1

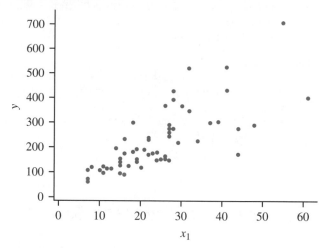

FIGURE 13.6

Plot of Residuals Against x_1

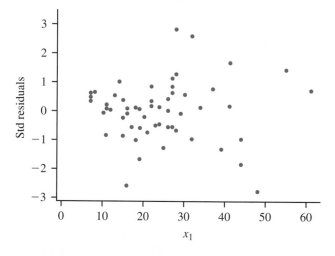

dependent variable, or both. If the residual plot looks like a parabola, try adding an x^2 term to the model. If the residual plot has an "elbow," with a clear curve followed by a straighter part, try replacing x by its square root, its logarithm, or its inverse. (When in doubt, it's often helpful to go back to the original scatterplot.) If several residual plots show both curvature and increasing variability from one side to the other, try replacing *y* by its logarithm.

Figure 13.6 seems to show both an "elbow" pattern and increasing variability. We transformed all the variables to natural logarithms and recalculated the regression. A plot of the residuals from this regression against the logarithm of x_1 is shown in Figure 13.7. Now the pattern appears quite random, indicating that we succeeded in removing the nonlinearity (and the increasing variability).

Some of the output from the original and logarithmic models is shown in the following output. Note that the R^2 and residual standard deviation values have changed. The standard deviation changed greatly. When we transform the dependent variable *y*, the results before and after transformation can't be compared directly. The dependent variable scales change, so the summary statistics refer to completely different scales.

FIGURE 13.7   **Plot of Residuals Against ln(x_1), Logarithmic Model**

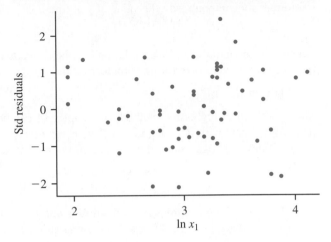

```
Regression Analysis

The regression equation is
Y = - 32.3 + 3.06 X1 + 5.22 X2 + 2.98 X3

Predictor        Coef        Stdev      t-ratio          p
Constant       -32.28       17.34        -1.86      0.068
X1             3.0646       0.8538         3.59      0.001
X2             5.2171       0.9513         5.48      0.000
X3             2.9844       0.5515         5.41      0.000

s = 53.30       R-sq = 83.8%     R-sq(adj) = 82.9%

Regression Analysis

The regression equation is
lnY = 2.09 + 0.357 lnX1 + 0.450 lnX2 + 0.257 lnX3

Predictor        Coef        Stdev      t-ratio          p
Constant       2.0870      0.1859        11.23      0.000
lnX1          0.35709     0.08994         3.97      0.000
lnX2           0.4499      0.1042         4.32      0.000
lnX3          0.25673     0.06096         4.21      0.000

s = 0.2087      R-sq = 85.2%     R-sq(adj) = 84.3%
```

With economic variables and time series data, growth often occurs at a roughly constant percentage rather than at an absolute rate. For instance, total sales of a large company may grow at the rate of 8% per year, as opposed to $8 million per year. Of course, if initial sales are $100 million, 8% growth in the first year is the same as $8 million growth. But in later years, constant percentage growth and constant additive growth differ. The following table shows the total sales for a company over a five-year period, based on each of the two types of growth:

	Year					
	0	**1**	**2**	**3**	**4**	**5**
8% growth	100.0	108.0	116.6	126.0	136.0	146.9
$8 million growth	100.0	108.0	116.0	124.0	132.0	140.0

Most basic finance books show that if a quantity y grows at a rate r per unit time (continuously compounded), the value of y at time t is

$$y_t = y_0 e^{rt}$$

where y_0 is the initial value. This relation may be converted into a linear relation between Y_t and t by a **logarithmic transformation.**

logarithmic transformation

$$\log y_t = (\log y_0) + rt$$

The simple linear regression methods of Chapter 11 can be used to fit data for this regression model with $\beta_0 = \log y_0$ and $\beta_1 = r$. When y is an economic variable such as total sales, the logarithmic transformation is often used in a multiple regression model:

$$\log Y_i = \beta_0 + \beta_1 x_{i1} + \beta_2 x_{i2} + \cdots + \beta_k x_{ik} + \epsilon_i$$

The Cobb–Douglas production function is another standard example of a nonlinear model that can be transformed into a regression equation:

$$y = cI^\alpha k^\beta$$

where y is production, I is labor input, k is capital input, and α and β are unknown constants. Again, to transform the dependent variable we take logarithms to obtain

$$\log y = (\log c) + \alpha(\log I) + \beta (\log k)$$
$$= \beta_0 + \beta_1(\log I) + \beta_2(\log k)$$

This suggests that a regression of log production on log labor and log capital is linear.

EXAMPLE 13.7

An important economic concept is the *price elasticity of demand,* defined as the negative of the percentage change in quantity demanded per percentage change in price. It can be shown that a price elasticity of 1 means that a (small) price change yields no change in total revenue. An inelastic demand (elasticity less than 1) means that a small price increase yields an increase in revenue; elastic demand is the opposite.

Data are obtained on y, daily demand for lettuce (in heads sold per hundred customers) for varying levels of price x (dollars per head). As much as possible, other conditions that might affect demand are held constant; all participating stores are located in middle-class suburbs, no competitors are running sales on lettuce, and so on. The data are

x:	.79	.79	.84	.84	.89
y:	40.2	37.1	37.4	34.9	32.8
xy:	31.758	29.309	31.416	29.316	29.192

x:	.89	.94	.94	.99	.99
y:	35.5	30.6	34.2	31.2	29.8
xy:	31.595	28.764	32.148	30.888	29.502

a. What economic quantity does xy represent?

b. Does there appear to be any trend in xy values as x increases?

c. If xy is constant, what is true of $\log x + \log y$?

d. If a product has price elasticity equal to 1, what does the regression equation of $\log y$ versus $\log x$ look like?

SOLUTION

a. The term xy is price per head times heads per hundred customers. Therefore, it represents revenue per hundred customers.

b. No trend is apparent in a plot of the data. Revenue, xy, appears constant.

c. Because $\log xy = \log$ constant $= \log x + \log y$, $\log x + \log y$ should be constant.

d. A price elasticity of 1 means that $\log y = $ constant $- \log x$. The regression equation with $\log y$ as dependent variable and $\log x$ independent should have a slope nearly equal to -1 (plus-or-minus random error). Thus a regression model in $\log y$ and $\log x$ is useful in elasticity studies.

A logarithmic transformation is only one possibility. It is, however, a particularly useful one, because logarithms convert a multiplicative relation to an additive one. A natural logarithm (base $e = 2.7182818$), often denoted $\ln(y)$, is especially useful, because the results are interpretable as percentage changes. For example, if a prediction of high school teachers' salaries yields predicted $\ln(\text{salary}) = $ constant $+ .042$ (years' experience) $+$ other terms, then an additional year's experience, other terms held constant, predicts a 4.2 *percent* increase in salary. This guideline isn't perfect, but very close for values less than .2 or so.

Another transformation that is sometimes useful is an inverse transformation, $1/y$. If, for instance, y is speed in meters per second, then $1/y$ is time required in seconds per meter. This transformation works well with very severe curvature; a logarithm works well with moderate curvature. Try them both; it's easy with a computer package. Another transformation that is particularly useful when a dependent variable increases to a maximum, then decreases, is a quadratic, x^2 term. In this transformation, do not replace x by x^2; use them both as predictors. The same use of both x and x^2 works well if a dependent variable decreases to a minimum, then increases. A fairly extensive discussion of possible transformations is found in Tukey (1977).

EXAMPLE 13.8

For the service-call situation of Example 13.2, the effect of temperature may not be linear. A regression model is calculated using the independent variables indicated in Example 13.2. Residuals are plotted against average temperature, as shown in Figure 13.8 on the next page. A LOWESS smooth is also shown in the figure. Does this plot suggest that a quadratic term would be a useful predictor?

SOLUTION There is certainly nothing blatant here. The LOWESS curve does not look at all like a parabola, which is the shape for a quadratic term. What curve there is seems to be caused by a few points at the right. We wouldn't expect any additional benefit to speak of using a quadratic term.

Interactions among variables can sometimes be detected in scatterplots of the original data or in residual plots. If x_1 and x_2 interact in determining y, three variables are involved; unfortunately, three-dimensional plots are hard to draw. Common sense is one approach to determining whether interactions are present. For the special case in which one of the independent variables is a qualitative variable

FIGURE 13.8   **Residual Plot for Example 13.8**

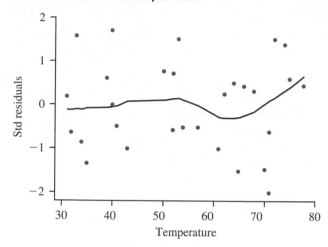

represented by one or more dummy variables, interaction may be detected in the original plot or by plotting residuals (from a first-order model) against the other independent variables. The better statistical packages have rotating (3-D) scatterplots or will allow you to identify each point by a value of a third variable.

For example, a department store is considering sending mail-order catalogs to cities in its region that are too small to support a branch store. As a test, it sends catalogs to a sample of ZIP (mail) code areas. A market research firm, using Census data, has classified ZIP codes into a number of types, depending on income, education, and lifestyle. The store selects three upscale (maybe even "yupscale") types and selects 15 areas of each type. They record the resulting sales volume in thousands of dollars, along with the population in thousands of each selected area. A plot of sales against population, identified by the three types of areas, is shown in Figure 13.9.

FIGURE 13.9   **Plot of Sales Volume Against Population, by Region**

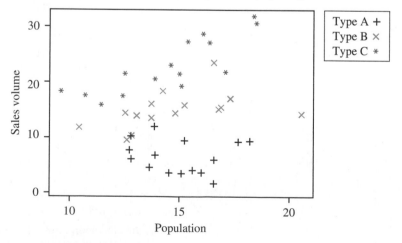

Think of drawing separate lines through each type of symbol. A line through the asterisks (shown in the legend at the upper right of the figure as type C) would clearly go up as population increases. A line through the plus signs (ZIP code type

A) would be flat or maybe even decrease. The third line, for type B, would be flat or increase slowly. The first-order, no-interaction model implies that these lines should be parallel. Because the separate lines are not close to parallel, the possibility of interaction should be considered. Exactly the same idea works for residual plots. Plot residuals against a quantitative variable. Identify each point in the plot by the value of a qualitative variable. Draw separate lines through each set of symbols. If these lines clearly aren't parallel, interaction is present.

EXAMPLE 13.9

In Example 13.4 we noted that the new-model dummy variables did not reflect the number of new installations in new-model months. Data for 29 months are collected on the following variables:

Variable	Description
7	Total number of service calls in the month
1	Number of computers in use, beginning of month
2	Number of new installations this month
3	Number of new installations, previous month
4	1, if model change in this month; 0 if not
5	1, if model change in previous month; 0 if not
6	Average temperature this month

A first-order model is fit to the data. Plots of residuals against NewInst and LagNewIn are shown in Figure 13.10 (see next page). To see if the effect of this month's installation depends on whether or not there was a model change this month, we plot residuals against NewInst and identify the cases where NewModel = 1 by a different symbol. Similarly, to see if the effect of installations in the previous month depends on whether or not there was a model change last month, we plot residuals against LagNewIn and identify the cases where LagNewMo = 1 specially. Is there evidence that interaction terms should be used?

SOLUTION There is some indication of interaction. There are only four points corresponding to new-model introductions, so the pattern isn't obvious. It appears that these four points slope upward in the plot of residuals against NewInst. If there were no interaction, the four points should appear random. The theoretical reasoning behind the idea is strong enough, and the plot suggestive enough, that we may well want to test for interaction.

Interaction terms may also be added to the multiple regression model to cure some forms of nonlinearity. Unfortunately, multiple regression was not designed to capture interaction effects. The experimental design, ANOVA approach (where every possible value of one predictor is combined with each possible value of every other predictor) yields a much more easily intelligible treatment of this form of nonlinearity. In practice, however, it may not be possible to plan the neatly balanced data-gathering schemes of the ANOVA approach. In such situations, the regression approach may be modified to yield some information about interaction effects.

cross-product terms   One device is to include **cross-product terms.** This method is very often used to test interaction of a qualitative variable and a quantitative one in predicting the

FIGURE 13.10   **Residual Plots for Example 13.9**

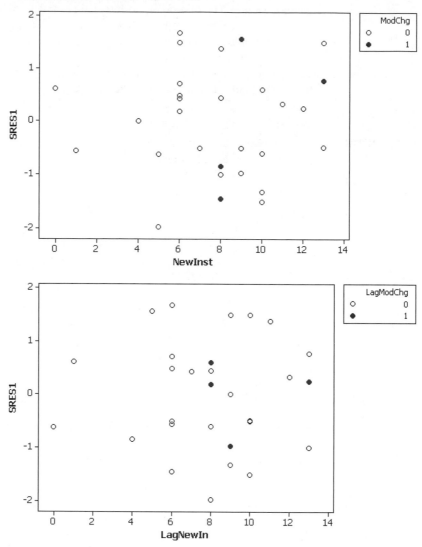

dependent variable. In the example of the department store testing types of ZIP code areas, there seemed to be an interaction of type of area with population in predicting sales volume. We used Minitab to create dummy variables for types B and C, and then created new, cross-product variables by multiplying each dummy by population. The following results were obtained; the product terms are "DumB_Pop" and "DumC_Pop".

```
Regression Analysis

The regression equation is
SalesVol = 9.60 - 0.199 Popn - 3.42 DummyB - 9.45 DummyC + 0.794 DumB_Pop
             + 1.77 DumC_Pop
```

A model involving dummy variables and product terms can be understood by plugging in appropriate 1s and 0s. In the department store example, the equations for the three types of zip codes are

Type A (both dummy variables equal 0):
SalesVol = 9.60 − .199Popn − 3.42(0) − 9.45(0) + .794(0)Popn
    + 1.77(0)Popn = 9.60 − .199 Popn

Type B (DummyB equal 1, DummyC equal 0):
SalesVol = 9.60 − .199Popn − 3.42(1) − 9.45(0) + .794(1)Popn
    + 1.77(0)Popn = 6.18 + .595Popn

Type C (DummyB equal 0, DummyC equal 1):
SalesVol = 9.60 − .199 Popn − 3.42(0) − 9.45(1) + .794(0)Popn
    + 1.77(1)Popn = .15 + 1.571Popn

The coefficients of the dummy variables change the intercept. For type B, the intercept decreased from 9.60 to 6.18, exactly because the coefficient of DummyB was −3.42. The coefficients of the product terms change the slope. For type B, the slope for Popn increased from −.199 to .595, exactly because the coefficient of DumB_Pop was .794.

If there is no interaction at all, the lines will be parallel and have the same slopes. Therefore, the product terms (which control the change in slope) will have 0 coefficients. If the coefficients of these product terms are very small compared to the coefficient of the quantitative predictor, the slopes will be nearly parallel and interaction will be small. In our department store example, the coefficients of the product terms are quite large, compared to the coefficient of Popn. Therefore, we have an indication of substantial interaction, just as we saw in looking at the scatterplot.

We can test product terms to see if the apparent nonzero value could reasonably have occurred by sheer randomness. If there is only one product term of interest, the t test shown on most outputs will indicate whether the coefficient is statistically detectable (significant). If there are several product terms, the incremental F test is useful. Take the complete model as including the product terms, and the reduced model as excluding them. Test the difference in R^2 values, or equivalently, the difference in SS(Regression) values, to see if we can reject the null hypothesis that the true coefficients are all 0. Although we don't show it here, the product terms in the department store, ZIP code type example yielded a very large, statistically significant value. Therefore, there is strong evidence that the apparent interaction is real, not just a fluke.

Product terms can also be used with two quantitative variables. A sales forecasting equation such as

$$\hat{y} = .40 + .04c + .01d + .005cd$$

allows for a certain type of interaction between d and c. If $c = 200$, the predicted change in y per unit change in d is $.01 + .005(200)$. If $c = 500$, the predicted change in sales y per unit change in d is $.01 + .005(500)$. In general, if

$$\hat{y} = \hat{\beta}_0 + \hat{\beta}_1c + \hat{\beta}_2d + \hat{\beta}_3cd$$

the predicted change in y per unit change in d is $\hat{\beta}_2 + \hat{\beta}_3c$ for a given value of c. Thus the effect of a change in d depends in a certain way on the level of c. This is one form of interaction, though by no means the only one. A cross-product term such as cd may be treated as just another predictor variable. Its coefficient may be tested for statistical significance by a t test, and its predictive value may be assessed by the increase in squared correlation. Therefore, this approach to the problem of interaction can be done routinely within the ordinary regression structure.

Note that interaction is *not* the same concept as collinearity. Collinearity refers to the degree of (linear) correlation between independent variables and says nothing about the dependent variable; interaction refers to an "it depends" combination effect of independent variables on the dependent variable.

EXAMPLE 13.10

Salary data for 427 teachers are examined for a seniority and unionization study. Product terms are created: $x_6 = x_1x_2$ and $x_7 = x_1x_3$. A Minitab summary is shown for the model $Y = \beta_0 + \beta_1x_1 + \beta_2x_2 + \cdots + \beta_7x_7 + \epsilon$. Test the hypotheses that x_6 and x_7 have no incremental predictive value.

Predictor	Coef	Std Error	t-statistic
Constant	10.243	---------	-----------
X1	2.070	7.912	0.262
X2	2.963	0.031	16.065
X3	1.475	0.203	7.249
X4	1.932	0.396	5.590
X5	0.808	0.301	2.686
X6	0.177	0.032	5.554
X7	0.093	0.011	8.183

SOLUTION It would be better to test both values, using an incremental F test. That way, we would be seeing if adding both variables together improved prediction by a detectable amount. However, the output doesn't give us the required information, so we'll have to settle for the second-best method of using two t tests. For these data, $n = 427$. The d.f. for the t test is $427 - (7 + 1) = 419$, so the relevant t table is effectively the normal table. The t statistics for x_6 and x_7 fall far beyond normal table values. Therefore, we may conclude that some degree of interaction between x_1 and x_2 and between x_1 and x_3 has been shown.

Insertion of cross-product terms into the regression equation is sometimes thought to be the only way to handle interaction in regression. Certainly this approach does not handle all possible kinds of interaction, but it does provide a useful approximation to solving the problem of interaction within regression. A manager who believes that interaction effects are crucial in predicting a dependent variable may well spend the extra money to gather data in the neatly balanced form of ANOVA methods.

Finally, thoughtful consideration of underlying economic relations may suggest other combinations of variables to address questions of nonlinearity. For example, suppose that a regression study is made of the total yearly expenditures of cities (y) on water supply systems. Natural independent variables are x_1, the population size; x_2, the total water consumption; and x_3, the number of miles of water lines (of course, there are other possibilities). A regression analysis based on these variables would be bedeviled by collinearity; every other variable would be strongly correlated with city size. A better analysis would take the dependent variable as y/x_1, the per capita expenditure. Natural independent variables would be x_2/x_1, x_3/x_1, and perhaps x_1 itself.

EXAMPLE 13.11

The data of Example 13.9 indicated (to no one's surprise) that variable 7, the number of service calls, increases as variable 1, the number of computers in use, increases. What would be the interpretation of a new variable, defined as variable 7 divided by variable 1? Why might the new variable be an appropriate dependent variable?

SOLUTION   The new variable represents the number of service calls per computer. For a growing business such as the computer firm, defining the variables as fractions of the number of computers in use might well reduce collinearity.

EXAMPLE 13.12   A manufacturer of feed for chickens faces a great deal of month-to-month variability in sales. A regression study attempts to forecast monthly sales volumes. The feed is used largely for chickens aged 20–50 days, so the number of chicken starts in the previous month is expected to be a critical predictor variable. Monthly data on starts are available. In addition, feed sales are expected to be quite sensitive to price. The prices of the manufacturer's feed and the primary competitor's feed, as well as the wholesale price of chickens, are very plausible predictor variables.

The working group charged with performing the regression study argues over the form of the regression equation. The following suggestions are made:

1. A linear (first-order) model in starts, price, competitor's price, and chicken price.

2. A first-order model in starts, difference in price (between manufacturer and competitor), and chicken price.

3. A first-order model in starts and the price difference as a fraction of chicken price.

Write the three suggested models. Is there a simple relation between one model and any other?

SOLUTION   Let

y = monthly sales of the manufacturer's feed

x_1 = starts in the previous month

x_2 = current price of the manufacturer's feed

x_3 = current price of competitor's feed

x_4 = current price of chickens

Model 1 is a first-order model in these variables:

$$Y = \beta_0 + \beta_1 x_1 + \beta_2 x_2 + \beta_3 x_3 + \beta_4 x_4 + \epsilon$$

Model 2 involves x_2 and x_3 only through their difference:

$$Y = \beta_0^* + \beta_1^* x_1 + \beta_2^* (x_2 - x_3) + \beta_3^* x_4 + \epsilon$$

Model 3 involves the difference as a fraction of chicken price x_4:

$$Y = \beta_0^{**} + \beta_1^{**} x_1 + \beta_2^{**} (x_2 - x_3)/x_4 + \epsilon$$

Model 2 is equal to model 1 if $\beta_2^* = \beta_2$ and $-\beta_2^* = \beta_3$.

Model 3 is not a first-order model in $x_1, \ldots, x_4$, so there is no simple relation between it and the others.

Exercises

13.8   A consultant who specializes in corporate gifts to charities, schools, cultural institutions, and the like is often asked to suggest an appropriate dollar amount. The consultant undertakes a regression study to try to predict the amount contributed by corporations to colleges and universities and is able to obtain information on the contributions of 38 companies. Financial information about these companies is available from their annual reports. Other information is obtained from such sources as business magazines. From experience, the consultant believes that the level of contributions is affected by the profitability of a firm, the size of the firm, whether the firm is in a high-education industry (such as data processing, electronics, or chemicals), the educational level of the firm's executives, and whether the firm matches the contributions of employees. Profitability can be measured by pretax or posttax income, size by number of employees or gross sales, and educational level by average number of years of education or by percentage of executives holding advanced degrees.

a. Would you expect pretax and posttax income to be highly correlated? How about number of employees and gross sales?

b. Discuss how to define profitability, size, and educational level so that the correlations among these variables are not automatically huge.

13.9   The consultant of Exercise 13.8 proposes to define an industry-type variable as follows:

$$\text{INDUSTRY} = \begin{cases} 3 & \text{if firm is primarily in the electronics industry} \\ 2 & \text{if firm is primarily in the data-processing industry} \\ 1 & \text{if firm is primarily in the chemical industry} \\ 0 & \text{otherwise} \end{cases}$$

a. Explain why this is not a good idea.

b. Suggest an alternative approach for indicating these industries.

c. How could the factor of whether or not the firm matches employee contributions be incorporated into a regression model?

13.10   The consultant of Exercise 13.8 collects data on the following variables:

CONTRIB:	Millions of dollars contributed
INCOME:	Pretax income, in millions of dollars
SIZE:	Number of employees, in thousands
DPDUMMY:	1, if firm is primarily in the data-processing industry, 0, if not
ELDUMMY:	1, if firm is primarily in the electronics industry, 0, if not
CHDUMMY:	1, if firm is primarily in the chemical industry, 0, if not
EDLEVEL:	Proportion of executives holding advanced degrees
MATCHING:	1, if firm matches employee contributions, 0, if not

a. Does it seem like a good idea to take CONTRIB as the dependent variable, with all other variables as independent variables? In particular, why would this method invite collinearity troubles?

b. What does the variable CONTRIB/INCOME represent?

13.11   Refer to Exercise 13.10. The consultant suspects that the effect of SIZE on CONTRIB/INCOME differs greatly among firms in the data-processing, electronics, chemical, and other industries. How can the regression model be modified to test this suspicion?

13.12   Refer to Exercise 13.10. The consultant suspects that the effect of increasing EDLEVEL is itself increasing; that is, all else being equal, there is little difference in CON-

TRIB/INCOME for firms with EDLEVEL = .2 versus .3, more for firms with EDLEVEL = .4 versus .5, and still more for firms with EDLEVEL = .6 versus .7.

a. How can a regression model be formulated to test this suspicion?

b. If the consultant's suspicion is correct, and if the residuals from a first-order regression model are plotted against EDLEVEL, what pattern of residuals would you expect to see?

13.13 A company that has developed a plastic film for use in wrapping food (such as crackers and cookies) has a problem with film stiffness. To be useful with modern packaging machines, stiffness (as given by an accepted measure) must be high. Stiffness is thought to be the result of certain variables of the production process. A regression study attempts to predict film stiffness for various combinations of these variables. A total of 32 pilot plant runs are made. Data are recorded on the following variables:

STIFF: Stiffness

MELT: Melt temperature (°F)

CHILL: Chill temperature (°F)

REPEL: Percentage of recycled pelletized material used

SPEED: Line production speed (feet per minute)

KNIFE: Setting of vacuum knife

There is considerable uncertainty among the firm's chemical engineers as to the mathematical form of the relation among these variables. The following Minitab output is obtained for a first-order model:

```
Correlation Matrix

              CHILL       KNIFE        MELT       REPEL       SPEED
CHILL         1.000
KNIFE        -0.000       1.000
 MELT        -0.000       0.000       1.000
REPEL         0.000       0.000       0.000       1.000
SPEED         0.000      -0.000      -0.000      -0.000       1.000
STIFF         0.138      -0.308       0.059      -0.886       0.030
```

a. How much collinearity is present in these data?

b. The 32 observations involved one measurement of each combination of MELT = 510, 530, 550, 570 with CHILL = 70, 80, 90, 100 and REPEL = 20, 30. How much correlation should there be between MELT and CHILL and between MELT and REPEL?

13.14 A first-order model is fit to the data of Exercise 13.13. The output below is obtained and plotted in Figure 13.11 (see next page). Is there any evidence, by eye, of nonlinearity?

```
Regression Analysis: STIFF versus MELT, CHILL, REPEL, SPEED, KNIFE

The regression equation is
STIFF = 171 + 0.0275 MELT + 0.127 CHILL - 1.84 REPEL + 0.0069 SPEED
        - 0.319 KNIFE

Predictor       Coef   SE Coef         T       P
Constant      170.96     20.51      8.34   0.000
MELT         0.02749   0.02822      0.97   0.339
CHILL        0.12749   0.05645      2.26   0.033
REPEL        -1.8375    0.1262    -14.56   0.000
SPEED        0.00687   0.01410      0.49   0.630
KNIFE       -0.31874   0.06311     -5.05   0.000

S = 3.57057   R-Sq = 90.4%   R-Sq(adj) = 88.5%

Analysis of Variance

Source           DF        SS       MS       F       P
Regression        5   3106.39   621.28   48.73   0.000
Residual Error   26    331.48    12.75
Total            31   3437.87
```

FIGURE 13.11 Residual Plots for Exercise 13.14

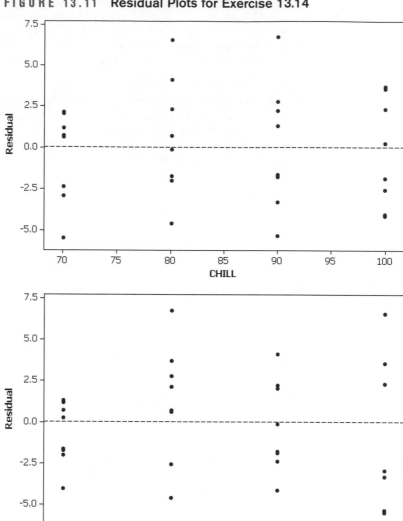

13.15 In an attempt to detect nonlinearity in the data of Exercise 13.13, a second-order model (containing squared MELT and CHILL terms) is run, and the following Minitab output is obtained:

```
Regression Analysis: STIFF versus MELT, CHILL, ...

The regression equation is
STIFF = - 308 + 1.38 MELT + 3.63 CHILL - 1.84 REPEL - 0.0344 SPEED
        - 0.319 KNIFE - 0.00124 MELT^2 - 0.0206 CHILL^2
```

Predictor	Coef	SE Coef	T	P
Constant	-308.0	459.0	-0.67	0.509
MELT	1.377	1.677	0.82	0.420
CHILL	3.634	2.362	1.54	0.137
REPEL	-1.8375	0.1242	-14.79	0.000
SPEED	-0.03437	0.03104	-1.11	0.279
KNIFE	-0.31874	0.06210	-5.13	0.000
MELT^2	-0.001250	0.001553	-0.81	0.429
CHILL^2	-0.02062	0.01388	-1.49	0.151

```
S = 3.51336   R-Sq = 91.4%   R-Sq(adj) = 88.9%

Analysis of Variance

Source           DF        SS       MS      F      P
Regression        7   3141.61   448.80   36.36   0.000
Residual Error   24    296.25    12.34
Total            31   3437.87
```

a. How much larger is the R^2 for this model than the R^2 for the first-order model of Exercise 13.14?

b. Use the F test for complete and reduced models to test the null hypothesis that the addition of the squared terms yields no additional predictive value. Use $\alpha = .05$.

c. Do the t statistics indicate that either squared term is a statistically significant ($\alpha = .05$) predictor as "last predictor in"?

13.16   A supermarket chain analyzed data on sales of a particular brand of snack cracker at 104 stores in the chain for a certain one-week period. The analyst tried to predict sales based on the total sales of all brands in the snack cracker category, the price charged for the particular brand in question, and whether or not there was a promotion for a competing brand at a given store (Promotion = 1 if there was such a promotion, 0 if not; there were no promotions for the brand in question). A portion of the JMP multiple regression output is shown in Figure 13.12.

FIGURE 13.12 **JMP Regression Results for Snack Cracker Data**

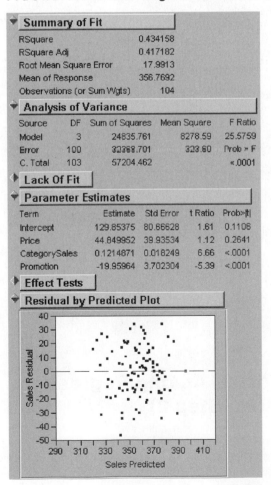

a. Interpret the coefficient of the Promotion variable.

b. Should a promotion by a competing product increase or decrease sales of the brand in question? According to the coefficient, does it?

c. Is the coefficient significantly different from 0 at usual α values?

d. How accurately can sales be predicted for one particular week, with 95% confidence?

13.17 An additional regression model for the snack cracker data is run, incorporating products of the promotion variable with price and with category sales. The JMP output for this model is given in Figure 13.13. What effects do the product term coefficients have in predicting sales when there is a promotion by a competing brand? In particular, do these coefficients affect the intercept of the model or the slopes?

FIGURE 13.13 **JMP Regression Results with Product Terms**

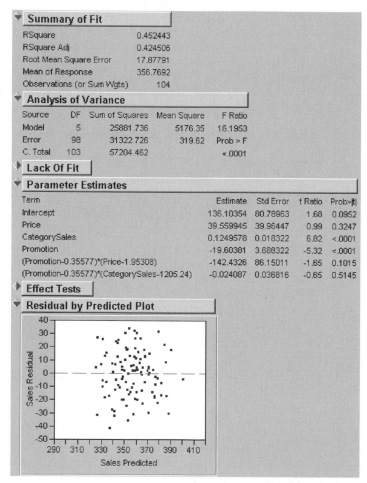

13.5 Choosing Among Regression Models (Step 3)

In the previous sections of this chapter, we have suggested many reasons to include variables in a regression study. The variables may be defined directly or they may be defined by using dummy variables, lagged variables, transformed variables, interaction cross-product variables, or some other combination. Most of these suggestions involve adding more independent variables to the study. A manager who begins a regression study may well suffer from the "kitchen-sink syndrome" and try to throw every possible variable into a regression model. Some sensible guidelines are needed for selecting the independent variables, from all candidates, to be used in the final regression model.

Stepwise regression is a rather mechanical device for computerized selection of the "best" independent variables. There are several types of stepwise regression procedure; we concentrate on the simplest one, **forward selection.**

forward selection

Forward-selection stepwise regression selects independent variables for inclusion in a regression model one at a time. The first variable included is the one that has the highest r^2 value for predicting y; assume that this variable is called x_1. The second variable included is the one that, when combined with x_1, yields the highest R^2 value; call the second variable x_2. If there is any degree of collinearity among the x's, x_2 may not have the second-largest r^2_{xy} value. In fact $R^2_{y \cdot x_1 x_2}$ may not even have the highest R^2 value of any two-x regression model.

The third variable included by forward selection yields the highest R^2 value when combined with x_1 and x_2. The process continues in this same manner. Obviously, a considerable amount of computation is necessary. That is why we would never attempt stepwise regression without access to a computer.

When should the selection process stop? There are several criteria, depending in part on which stepwise computer program is used. A common one uses the t test (or $F = t^2$) for the statistical significance of a single regression coefficient. When a variable is selected for possible inclusion, a t test is performed on the coefficient. If the null hypothesis, $H_0: \beta_j = 0$, can be rejected at an α level specified by the user, the variable x_j is included and stepwise selection continues. If the null hypothesis is retained, the variable is not included and selection stops. To avoid stopping too early, a relatively large α such as .10 or .20 is typically used. Of course, it is also possible to force the procedure to include all variables, one at a time, if the α value is very large.

EXAMPLE 13.13

A forward-selection stepwise regression analysis is performed in Minitab for the data of Example 13.9 (first-order model). The variables are as indicated in that example, and the row labeled R-Sq gives the value of R^2 at each step. Thus, InUse explains 64.19% of the variation in ServiceCalls, NewInst an additional 25.13% (for a total of 89.32%), and so on.

```
Stepwise Regression: ServiceCalls versus InUse, NewInst, ...

Forward selection.  F-to-Enter: 1

Response is ServiceCalls on 6 predictors, with N = 29
N(cases        missing observations) = 1 N(all cases) = 30

Step              1        2        3        4        5
Constant      72.39   -83.73  -101.94   -98.54   -97.08

InUse         1.137    1.527    1.484    1.467    1.450
T-Value        6.96    14.72    16.51    16.37    16.19
P-Value       0.000    0.000    0.000    0.000    0.000

NewInst                  9.0      8.3      8.0      7.5
T-Value                 7.82     8.25     7.82     7.06
P-Value                0.000    0.000    0.000    0.000
```

Temp			0.61	0.63	0.70
T-Value			3.23	3.39	3.65
P-Value			0.003	0.002	0.001
LagModChg				10.5	13.2
T-Value				1.31	1.60
P-Value				0.203	0.122
ModChg					10.7
T-Value					1.26
P-Value					0.219
S	30.8	17.1	14.7	14.5	14.3
R-Sq	64.19	89.32	92.46	92.97	93.42
R-Sq(adj)	62.86	88.50	91.56	91.79	91.99
Mallows C-p	94.8	12.7	4.2	4.5	5.0

a. Which variables are not statistically significant at $\alpha = .10$ as "last predictor in"?

b. How much higher an R^2 value does the five-variable model have than the model with only InUse and NewInst?

SOLUTION

a. The p-values for LagModChg and ModChg are both greater than $\alpha = .10$ when added last, so these variables are statistically insignificant.

b. The five-variable R^2 is 93.42% as compared to the R^2 of 89.32% given by the two-variable model. The F statistic for incremental R^2 could be computed; it is small.

backward elimination

There are many variations in stepwise procedures. Variables may be successively removed from the model in **backward elimination.** This process begins with all variables included in the model. Then, one at a time, variables that offer very little predictive value are deleted. Additionally, forward or backward selection can be modified to use various check-up procedures for retesting variables already included in, or excluded from, the model. For example, in forward selection a variable included at one step can be found at a later step to be of little use; a check-up procedure allows later elimination of the variable. There are sophisticated stepwise procedures that incorporate these and other checks. In fact, some packages will compute regression models based on all possible subsets of independent variables.

Stepwise regression can be helpful in suggesting reasonable models. Like any other statistical method, it requires thinking and judgment for proper use. One technical problem is that some **stepwise biases** are introduced by this type of regression. Because stepwise regression selects variables to yield a large R^2 value, it is quite likely that the resulting R^2 is an overestimation of the actual predictive value of the variables in the model. The magnitudes of the resulting coefficients and of the t and F tests also tend to be too large.

stepwise biases

Additionally, stepwise regression involves decisions that are based on differences of R^2 values. These differences contain an element of random error, which can be quite large. For example, suppose that in a forward selection based on 28 y values, the correlation between y and the first selected variable x_1 is $r_{yx_1} = .6$ (hence $r_{yx_1}^2 = .36$). A 95% confidence interval on $r_{yx_1}^2$, calculated by a method not shown in this text, ranges from .09 to .64. Because of this large sampling variation, one variable could be selected over another for inclusion in the regression model, even though the selected variable has less actual predictive value than others not selected.

Stepwise methods usually involve some form of hypothesis test to select among models. An alternative approach to model selection is based on Mallows' (1973) C_p statistic. If a model contains p coefficients—typically one intercept and $p - 1$ slopes corresponding to $p - 1$ independent variables—then

$$C_p = \frac{\text{SS(Residual, } p \text{ coefficients)}}{\text{MS(Residual, all coefficients)}} - (n - 2p)$$

$$= \frac{(n - p)\text{MS(Residual, } p \text{ coefficients)}}{\text{MS(Residual, all coefficients)}} - (n - 2p)$$

where the last step follows because the d.f. for MS(Residual, p coefficients) is $n - (k + 1) = n - (p - 1 + 1) = n - p$. If the p-coefficient model contains all the useful predictors, MS(Residual, p coefficients) is essentially the same as MS(Residual, all coefficients). In this case, C_p roughly equals $(n - p) - (n - 2p) = p$. But if the p-coefficient model is inadequate, C_p is substantially larger than p. One plausible model-selection strategy is to select the regression model with the fewest independent variables having C_p approximately equal to p.

EXAMPLE 13.14   Assume that data are collected for 20 independent pharmacies in an attempt to predict prescription volume (sales per month). The independent variables are total floor space, percentage of floor space allocated to the prescription department, number of available parking spaces, whether or not the pharmacy is in a shopping center, and per capita income for the surrounding community. The data and selected Minitab output follow, using a "best subsets" method that locates the best six models for each number of variables. What does the C_p statistic suggest as the most reasonable model?

```
Best Subsets Regression: VOLUME versus FLOOR_SP, PRESC_RX, ...

Response is VOLUME

                                             F P   S
                                             L R P H
                                             O E A O I
                                             O S R P N
                                             R C K C C
                                             _ _ I N O
                                  Mallows     S R N T M
     Vars  R-Sq  R-Sq(adj)   C-p        S    P X G R E
        1  43.9       40.8  10.2   4.8351    X
        1  14.8       10.1  23.8   5.9604            X
        1   4.1        0.0  28.8   6.3234        X
        1   3.4        0.0  29.1   6.3482    X
        1   0.5        0.0  30.5   6.4418          X
        2  66.6       62.6   1.6   3.8420    X X
        2  64.7       60.6   2.5   3.9474    X   X
        2  54.7       49.4   7.1   4.4697    X       X
        2  53.1       47.6   7.9   4.5484    X X
        2  49.6       43.6   9.5   4.7182          X X
        3  69.1       63.3   2.4   3.8089    X X   X
        3  67.9       61.9   3.0   3.8778    X X X
        3  66.6       60.4   3.6   3.9558    X X     X
        3  66.3       59.9   3.7   3.9784      X X X
        3  64.7       58.1   4.5   4.0686    X   X X
```

```
4   69.9      61.8      4.1   3.8825   X X X X
4   69.3      61.1      4.3   3.9176   X X    X X
4   68.1      59.5      4.9   3.9978   X X X    X
4   66.3      57.3      5.7   4.1063      X X X X
4   50.1      36.8     13.3   4.9954   X    X X X
5   70.0      59.3      6.0   4.0099   X X X X X
```

SOLUTION   Note that for k variables in the model, $p = k + 1$; there are k slopes and one intercept. For the one-variable models, no C_p is close to $p = 2$. The model using FLOOR_SP and PRESC_RX (shown as variables A and D) has $C_p = 1.6$, actually below p. On the C_p criterion, this model appears to be a good one. Note also that the R^2 value for this model is almost as large as the R^2 value for the model involving all variables.

EXAMPLE 13.15   Minitab also performed a stepwise regression for the data of the previous example. Did the stepwise procedure identify the same model as the "best subsets" procedure?

```
Stepwise Regression: VOLUME versus FLOOR_SP, PRESC_RX, ...

  F-to-Enter: 1  F-to-Remove: 1

Response is VOLUME on 5 predictors, with N = 20

Step              1        2        3
Constant      25.98    48.29    42.83

PRESC_RX     -0.321   -0.582   -0.529
T-Value       -3.76    -5.67    -4.74
P-Value       0.001    0.000    0.000

FLOOR_SP              -0.0038  -0.0025
T-Value               -3.39    -1.50
P-Value                0.003    0.152

SHOPCNTR                        -3.0
T-Value                         -1.14
P-Value                          0.272

S              4.84     3.84     3.81
R-Sq          43.93    66.57    69.07
R-Sq(adj)     40.82    62.63    63.27
Mallows C-p   10.2      1.6      2.4
```

SOLUTION   The stepwise procedure added SHOPCNTR as a third predictor, with only a modest increment to R^2 and very little change to MSE. The t value, -1.14, for this variable indicates there is little evidence that it adds any real predictive value; we would omit it. Effectively, the two procedures have given the same solution.

Mallows (1973) points out the C_p statistic is as susceptible to random variation as any other statistic; it is not an infallible guide. Neither is any other statistical method. In selecting a regression model, a manager should use experience and judgment as well as statistical results. If one model involves reasonable relations and variables, yet does somewhat less well than another, less plausible model on a purely statistical basis, a manager might well choose the first model anyway.

Exercises

13.18 A forward-selection stepwise regression is run using a first-order model for the data of Exercise 13.13. The following Minitab output is obtained:

```
Correlations: STIFF, MELT, CHILL, REPEL, SPEED, KNIFE

           STIFF    MELT   CHILL   REPEL   SPEED
MELT       0.059
CHILL      0.138   0.000
REPEL     -0.886   0.000   0.000
SPEED      0.030   0.000   0.000   0.000
KNIFE     -0.308   0.000   0.000   0.000   0.000


Stepwise Regression: STIFF versus MELT, CHILL, REPEL, SPEED, KNIFE

Forward selection.  F-to-Enter: 0.1

Response is STIFF on 5 predictors, with N = 32

Step              1       2       3       4       5
Constant      170.0   201.9   191.0   176.2   171.0

REPEL         -1.84   -1.84   -1.84   -1.84   -1.84
T-Value      -10.49  -13.79  -14.77  -14.77  -14.56
P-Value       0.000   0.000   0.000   0.000   0.000

KNIFE                -0.319  -0.319  -0.319  -0.319
T-Value               -4.79   -5.12   -5.12   -5.05
P-Value               0.000   0.000   0.000   0.000

CHILL                         0.128   0.128   0.128
T-Value                        2.29    2.29    2.26
P-Value                       0.030   0.030   0.033

MELT                                  0.028   0.028
T-Value                                0.99    0.97
P-Value                               0.332   0.339

SPEED                                         0.007
T-Value                                        0.49
P-Value                                       0.630

S              4.96    3.77    3.52    3.52    3.57
R-Sq          78.57   88.03   89.92   90.27   90.36
R-Sq(adj)     77.86   87.20   88.84   88.83   88.50
Mallows C-p    29.8     6.3     3.2     4.2     6.0
```

a. List the order in which the independent variables enter the regression model.
b. List the independent variables from largest (in absolute value) to smallest correlation with STIFF.
c. Compare the ordering of the variables given by the two lists.

13.19 Refer to Exercise 13.18. Use the F test for complete and reduced models described in Section 12.4 to test the hypothesis that the last two variables entered in the stepwise regression have no predictive value.

13.20 The consultant of Exercise 13.10 runs a Minitab regression model with CONTRIB/INCOME as the dependent variable.

```
Regression Analysis: CONT/INC versus INCOME, SIZE, ...

The regression equation is
CONT/INC = 0.0211 - 0.000093 INCOME + 0.00152 SIZE + 0.00167 DPDUMMY
           + 0.00712 ELDUMMY + 0.00280 CHDUMMY - 0.0144 EDLEVEL
           + 0.00137 MATCHING

Predictor         Coef     SE Coef      T      P
Constant       0.021085    0.003497    6.03   0.000
INCOME        -0.0000933   0.0001033  -0.90   0.372
SIZE           0.0015301   0.0006699   2.28   0.028
DPDUMMY        0.001684    0.004720    0.36   0.723
ELDUMMY        0.007132    0.006355    1.12   0.269
CHDUMMY        0.002808    0.003810    0.74   0.466
EDLEVEL       -0.01435     0.01596    -0.90   0.374
MATCHING       0.001381    0.002092    0.66   0.513


S = 0.00605713   R-Sq = 21.3%   R-Sq(adj) = 6.8%

Analysis of Variance
Source           DF          SS          MS       F      P
Regression        7    0.00037698   0.00005385   1.47   0.208
Residual Error   38    0.00139418   0.00003669
Total            45    0.00177115
```

a. Can the hypothesis that none of the independent variables has predictive value be rejected (using reasonable α values)?

b. Which variables have been shown to have statistically significant (say, $\alpha = .05$) predictive value as "last predictor in"?

13.21 A simpler regression model than that of Exercise 13.20 is obtained by regressing the dependent variable on the independent variables DPDUMMY, ELDUMMY, EDLEVEL, and MATCHING. The following Minitab output is obtained:

```
Regression Analysis: CONT/INC versus DPDUMMY, ELDUMMY, EDLEVEL, MATCHING

The regression equation is
CONT/INC = 0.0202 - 0.00377 DPDUMMY - 0.00098 ELDUMMY + 0.0097 EDLEVEL
           + 0.00196 MATCHING

Predictor         Coef     SE Coef      T      P
Constant       0.020233    0.002304    8.78   0.000
DPDUMMY       -0.003775    0.003912   -0.97   0.340
ELDUMMY       -0.000995    0.005131   -0.19   0.847
EDLEVEL        0.00968     0.01275     0.76   0.452
MATCHING       0.001974    0.001995    0.99   0.328

S = 0.00634282   R-Sq = 6.9%   R-Sq(adj) = 0.0%

Analysis of Variance
Source           DF          SS          MS       F      P
Regression        4    0.00012167   0.00003042   0.76   0.560
Residual Error   41    0.00164949   0.00004023
Total            45    0.00177115
```

a. What is the increment to R^2 for the model of Exercise 13.20, as opposed to the model considered here?

b. Is this increment statistically significant by an F test, at $\alpha = .05$?

c. Compute C_p for this model, treating the previous model as the "all-coefficients" model. Which of the two models do you think is more sensible, given the information you have?

13.6   Residuals Analysis (Step 4)

Once independent variables, including any polynomial or cross-product terms, have been defined and a tentative model selected, the next step in a careful regression analysis is to check for any gross violations of assumptions. The method for this check is analysis of the residuals from the model.

standardized residuals

Recall that residuals are differences between actual y values and predicted values using the regression model. In plotting residuals, we often use **standardized residuals.** A standardized residual is expressed in standard deviation units, so a standardized residual of -3.00 means that the point is 3 standard deviations from the regression line. Often, subtracting out the predictive part of the data reveals other structure more clearly. In particular, plotting the residuals from a first-order (linear terms only) model against each independent variable often reveals further structure in the data that can be used to improve the regression model.

One possibility is nonlinearity. We discussed nonlinearity and transformations earlier in the chapter. A noticeable curve in the residuals reflects a curved relation in the data, indicating that a different mathematical form for the regression equation would improve the predictive value of the model. A plot of residuals against each independent variable x often reveals this problem. A scatterplot smoother, such as LOWESS, can be useful in looking for curves in residual plots. For example, Figure 13.14 shows a scatterplot of y against x_2 and a residual plot against x_2. We think that the curved relation is more evident in the residual plot. The LOWESS curve helps considerably in either plot.

When nonlinearity is found, try transforming either independent or dependent variables. One standard method is to use (natural) logarithms of all variables except dummy variables. Such a model essentially estimates *percentage* changes in the dependent variable for a small percentage change in an independent variable, other independent variables held constant. Other useful transformations are logarithms of one or more independent variables only, square roots of independent variables, or inverses of the dependent variable or an independent variable. With a good computer package a number of these transformations can be tested easily.

skewness

A simple histogram of the residuals reveals severe **skewness** or wild outliers. Skewness is not a terribly serious problem for sample sizes of, say, 30 or more. The Central Limit Theorem effect works for normal-distribution methods for inferences about means, even if the population distribution is not normal. A more complicated version of the theorem allows us to make inferences about the coefficients and correlations if the distribution of errors isn't normal. In particular, the t and F tests of Chapter 12 are valid to a good approximation for even modestly large sample sizes. The guidelines given in discussing inferences about means also apply in regression.

Nonnormality arising from skewness may have some effect when predicting individual y values. Because the prediction is about one particular y value, there is no averaging involved and the Central Limit Theorem doesn't apply. If serious skewness is detected in a histogram of residuals, the "95%" of a 95% prediction interval must be taken with a grain of salt.

outlier

An **outlier** is a data point that falls far away from the rest of the data. Recall from Chapter 11 that we must be concerned with the leverage (x-outlier) and influence (both x- and y-outlier) properties of a point. A high-influence point may seriously distort the regression equation. In addition, some outliers may signal a need for management action. If a regression analysis indicates that the price of a particular parcel of land is very much lower than predicted, that parcel may be an excellent

FIGURE 13.14   **y and Residual Plots Showing Curvature**

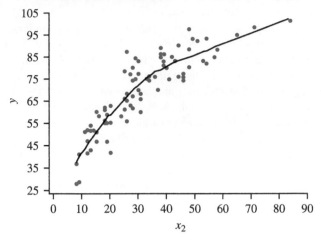

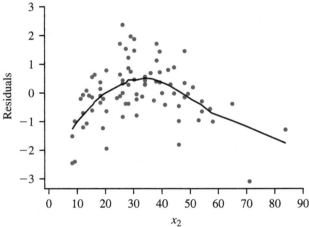

purchase. (It may also be useless because it's under water. Regression analysis can't cover everything.) A sales office that has far better results than a regression model predicts may indicate outstanding work that can be copied. Conversely, a sales office that has far poorer results than the model predicts may be an indication of problems. Sometimes it is possible to isolate the reason for the outlier; other times it is not. Such a point may arise because of an error in recording the data, or in entering it into a computer, or because the observation is obtained under different conditions than the other observations. If such a reason can be found, the data entry can be corrected or the point omitted from the analysis. If there is no identifiable reason to correct or omit the point, run the regression both with and without the point, to see which results are sensitive to that point. No matter what the source or reason for outliers, if they go undetected they can cause serious distortions in a regression equation.

EXAMPLE 13.16   Suppose the data for a regression study are as shown here.

x:	10	13	16	18	20	22	24	27	30
y:	31	35	42	45	51	53	59	31	70

Draw a scatterplot of the data, identify the outlier, and fit a simple regression model with and without the outlier point.

SOLUTION   A scatterplot of the data (Figure 13.15) shows that any line with slope about 2 and intercept about 10 fits all the data points fairly well, except for the $x = 27$, $y = 31$ point. If that point is included, the least-squares equation is

$$\hat{y} = 19.94 + 1.32x$$

If it is excluded, the equation is

$$\hat{y} = 9.93 + 2.00x$$

The scatterplot shows clearly that the observation (27, 31) is a high-influence outlier and that the regression equation is distorted by inclusion of this point.

FIGURE 13.15   **Effect of an Outlier**

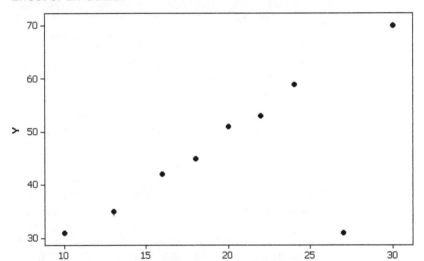

Outliers cause particularly serious distortions because regression is based on minimizing total squared error. Rather than fitting a line with many small errors and one or two large ones (which yield huge squared errors), the least-squares method accepts numerous moderate errors to avoid large ones. The effect is to twist the line in the direction of the outlier.

The first problem with outliers is detection. In simple linear regression, a scatterplot of y versus x reveals outliers very clearly. In multiple regression, because it is not possible to plot all variables at once, scatterplots of y against each x separately are sometimes helpful. However, examination of the residuals (prediction errors) often provides more information regarding outliers than the separate scatterplots. A large residual suggests that the data point may be an outlier, but the fact that the regression line is twisted toward outliers (as indicated in the simple linear regression situation) sometimes causes an outlier to have a modest residual while residuals for perfectly legitimate data points are larger.

EXAMPLE 13.17 Use the Minitab output shown here and the residual ($y - \hat{y}$) for each observation to identify potential outliers for the data of Example 13.16.

```
Row      y    Predicted   Residual
  1     31     33.1381    -2.1381
  2     35     37.0966    -2.0966
  3     42     41.0552     0.9448
  4     45     43.6943     1.3057
  5     51     46.3333     4.6667
  6     53     48.9724     4.0276
  7     59     51.6114     7.3886
  8     31     55.5700   -24.5700
  9     70     59.5286    10.4714
```

SOLUTION From the output, the residual for the data point $x = 27$, $y = 31$ is $31 - 55.57 = -24.57$. The next largest residual is 10.47 for the data point $x = 30$, $y = 70$. Most other residuals are quite a bit smaller. Note that the outlier data point $x = 27$, $y = 31$ twists the least-squares line down, making larger residuals for the data points near $x = 27$.

jackknife method

Another formal approach to detecting outliers is the **"jackknife" method.** This involves calculating a series of regression equations, each time excluding one data point. When an outlier is excluded, coefficients in the regression equation change substantially. In principle, one could try excluding two or three points at a time, but the number of equations to calculate and examine would become prohibitive. The one-at-a-time jackknife method may not always catch multiple outliers, but often it does.

In practice, it may be necessary to consider a combination of techniques for examining the sample data for outliers. First, simple x, y scatterplots may suggest that certain observations are outliers. An examination of the residuals may (or may not) confirm this suspicion. If neither the scatterplots nor residuals suggest the existence of one or more outliers, one can probably end the search. However, identification of possible outliers could require additional work with jackknife techniques to isolate specific outliers.

If you detect outliers, what should you do with them? Of course, recording or transcribing errors should simply be corrected. Sometimes an outlier obviously comes from a different population than the other data points. For example, a Fortune 500 conglomerate firm doesn't belong in a study of small manufacturers. In such situations, the outliers can reasonably be omitted from the data. Unless a compelling **robust regression** reason can be found, throwing out a data point seems like cheating. There are **"robust regression"** methods that retain possible outliers and try to minimize distortions caused by them. One such method minimizes the sum of absolute (rather than squared) deviations. These methods should be used if there appear to be outliers that cannot be justifiably excluded from the data.

EXAMPLE 13.18 Apply a jackknife procedure, eliminating one data point at a time, to the data of Example 13.16. Examine the estimated slopes and intercepts to locate possible outliers.

SOLUTION We ran repeated regression analyses by computer, each time omitting one of the points. The estimated slopes and intercepts are listed next. Note that the last two data points appear to be outliers, because omitting them caused a large change in the equation.

Data Point Excluded	Slope	Intercept
10,31	1.21286	22.47672
13,35	1.26116	21.42333
16,42	1.33281	19.55234
18,45	1.32834	19.60120
20,51	1.31953	19.35947
22,53	1.29235	19.97601
24,59	1.21563	21.04531
27,31	2.00354	9.93239
30,70	.79712	28.42905

Thus, while the scatterplot of Figure 13.15 identified one potential outlier (the point 27, 31), an examination of the residuals as well as the jackknife procedure detects a second potential outlier (the point 30, 70). An examination of residuals from the regression omitting the point 27, 31 indicates that the point 30, 70 is not in fact an outlier.

constant variance

Another formal assumption of regression analysis is that the (true, population) error variance σ_ϵ^2 is constant, regardless of the values of the x predictors. This assumption may also be violated in practice. In particular, it often occurs that combinations of x values leading to large predicted values of y also lead to relatively large variance around the predicted value. We here consider the consequences, detection, and possible cure of the problem of nonconstant error variance.

When the variance around the prediction equation is not constant, there are two basic consequences. Ordinary least-squares regression does not give the most accurate possible estimate of the regression equation, and the plus-or-minus error of prediction given in Chapters 11 and 12 may be seriously in error.

The estimation problem is less serious. If the error variance is not constant, the usual least-squares estimates are still valid in the sense of being unbiased. Furthermore, various studies have indicated that the F and t statistics may be slightly biased but still give about the same conclusions. The issue here is one of "opportunity cost"; **heteroscedasticity** if **heteroscedasticity** (nonconstant variance) is recognized, it is possible to improve the estimation of the regression equation and the various related statistics. The technique **weighted least squares** nique of **weighted least squares** yields somewhat more accurate estimates of the regression coefficients than does ordinary least-squares regression (more accurate estimates have smaller standard errors). The same technique makes the F and t statistics more powerful for testing the appropriate null hypotheses. Weighted least squares, in the presence of heteroscedasticity around the equation, makes more efficient use of the data.

The more serious problem arises in making forecasts. The best-guess forecast based on ordinary least-squares regression is still unbiased, but (given nonconstant error variance) the usual plus-or-minus formulas can be badly wrong. If the forecast

y value falls in a high-variance zone, the theoretical plus-or-minus term may be much too small.

Probably the best way to detect heteroscedasticity is by eye and by data plot. The most useful is actual y versus predicted y, or residual $y - \hat{y}$ versus predicted y. Most standard statistical computer programs can calculate predicted, actual, and residual values. Some have commands that produce the desired plots. In such plots, look for evidence that the variability of actual y values (or of residuals) increases as predicted y increases. There are several statistical significance tests for the research hypothesis of nonconstant variance, such as regressing the absolute value of the residuals against predicted values from the original regression. They generally tend to confirm the evidence of the "eyeball test."

EXAMPLE 13.19   A very crude model for predicting the price of common stocks might take price per share (y) as a linear function of the previous year's earnings per share (x_1), change in earnings per share (x_2), and asset value per share (x_3). A scatterplot of residuals versus predicted y values for a regression study of 26 stocks is shown in Figure 13.16. Is there evidence of a problem of heteroscedasticity?

SOLUTION   In the plot of residuals versus predicted values, there is a general tendency for the magnitude of the residuals to increase as $\hat{y}$ increases. All residuals on the left are small, but "the plot thickens" as we move to the right. Therefore, there seems to be a problem of nonconstant variance.

FIGURE 13.16   **Residuals Versus Predicted Values**

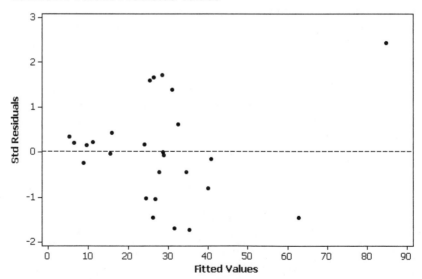

Once we detect the problem of nonconstant variance, there are two basic cures. One is weighted least squares. The other, which often turns out to be equivalent to weighted least squares, is appropriate reexpression of the dependent variable. For example, one may try to predict the number of airline tickets sold for a particular airport from the population of the relevant metropolitan area, the average disposable income in the area, the number of Fortune 500 companies in the area, and so on. Almost certainly, there will be larger variance in number of tickets sold at larger airports. If the dependent variable is redefined as number of tickets sold per capita, the problem of heteroscedasticity may well disappear. A little thought in defining the regression equation often goes a long way.

EXAMPLE 13.20   The dependent variable in Example 13.19 is redefined to be price per share divided by earnings per share (the P/E ratio). The Minitab output is shown here and the residuals from the revised model are plotted in Figure 13.17.

```
Regression Analysis: P/E Ratio versus ChangeInEPS, AssetValue

The regression equation is
P/E Ratio = 7.38 - 0.46 ChangeInEPS + 0.0089 AssetValue

Predictor        Coef  SE Coef      T      P
Constant       7.3755   0.3968  18.59  0.000
ChangeInEPS    -0.461    1.860  -0.25  0.806
AssetValue    0.00888  0.02395   0.37  0.714

S = 0.959258   R-Sq = 0.7%   R-Sq(adj) = 0.0%

Analysis of Variance

Source       DF       SS      MS     F      P
Regression    2   0.1500  0.0750  0.08  0.922
Residual Error 23  21.1640  0.9202
Total        25  21.3140

Source       DF  Seq SS
ChangeInEPS   1  0.0233
AssetValue    1  0.1267

Unusual Observations

Obs  ChangeInEPS  P/E Ratio    Fit  SE Fit  Residual  St Resid
 10         1.03      6.902  7.533   0.623    -0.631     -0.86 X
 13         0.62      8.455  7.746   0.725     0.709      1.13 X

X denotes an observation whose X value gives it large influence.
```

FIGURE 13.17   **Residuals Versus Predicted Values**

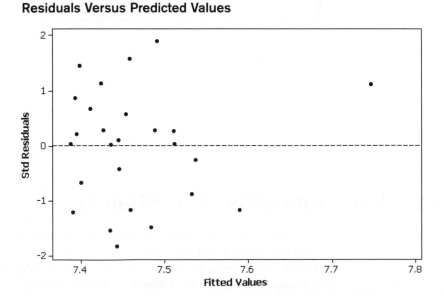

EXAMPLE 13.20
(continued)

a. Identify the estimated coefficients in the revised model.

b. Does there appear to be a problem of nonconstant variance with the revised model?

c. Use the revised model to predict the price of a stock with earnings 3.00, change in earnings .27, and assets 14.25.

SOLUTION

a. $\hat{\beta}_0 = 7.3755$, $\hat{\beta}_1 = -.461$, and $\hat{\beta}_2 = .00888$.

b. The residual plot is much better for the revised model.

c. Substituting ChangeInEPS $= .27$ and AssetValue $= 14.25$ into the ratio model, we have $\hat{y} = 7.3755 - .461(.27) + .00888(14.25) = 7.378$. This is the predicted value of price/earnings; multiply by earnings (3.00) and obtain a predicted price $= 22.13$.

EXAMPLE 13.21

A first-order model is developed for predicting feed sales using the independent variables defined in Example 13.12. A plot of residuals versus predicted values is shown in Figure 13.18. Is there evidence of nonconstant variance?

SOLUTION   No. The variation of the standardized residuals is roughly the same across the plot. There is no evidence of nonconstant variance.

FIGURE 13.18

Standardized Residuals Versus Predicted Values

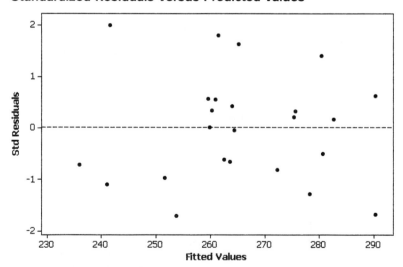

13.7 Autocorrelation (Step 4)

One of the crucial assumptions of regression analysis is that the error terms ϵ_i, which might be called the "true residuals," are independent. Much of the statistical theory of regression depends heavily on this assumption. In practice, the assumption may be wrong. Time series data, where the data points are measured at successive times, often show more-or-less cyclic behavior. If such behavior is shown by a dependent variable *y*, and if no *x* variable matches the apparent cycles, the sample residuals show evidence of dependence. This problem, which is largely restricted to time se-

autocorrelation

ries data, is called **autocorrelation.**

Autocorrelation occurs when there is a carryover from one observation to the next. If one *y* value is higher than predicted, the next one also tends to be higher than predicted. Similarly, if one *y* is lower than predicted, the next one also tends to be lower. Thus autocorrelation appears as a pattern in which positive residuals tend to be followed by other positive ones, negative residuals by more negative ones. In such a pattern, each residual is positively correlated with the succeeding one. If the errors were independent, there should be no pattern, simply random variation, in the residuals. In a plot of residuals versus time, autocorrelation yields a "snakelike" pattern that looks somewhat cyclical.

Note that autocorrelation is a different idea from collinearity. Collinearity is correlation among independent *variables;* autocorrelation is correlation of successive *residuals.*

effects of autocorrelation

What are the **effects of autocorrelation** on the results we obtain in regression? First, the least-squares prediction equation provides too good a fit to the sample data; that is, the least-squares line is closer to the *y* values than is the true regression line. Because of this, the residuals (the observed errors, $y - \hat{y}$) are smaller than the true errors (the ϵ's), and the residual standard deviation s_ϵ provides an underestimate of the population standard deviation σ_ϵ. Positive correlation of residuals leads to "delusions of predictability." We think that we can predict more accurately than we actually can.

Furthermore, when autocorrelation is present, the effective sample size is smaller than the number of measurements. Because there is a carryover from one residual to the next, a measurement reflects partly the previous measurement and only partly new information. Therefore, there is not as much information in the data as the apparent sample size indicates. At the extreme, where the errors are perfectly correlated, we would really have *one* observation on the errors, not the apparent sample size *n*. With a smaller "effective *n*," standard errors are underestimated, often quite badly. Therefore, when there is positive autocorrelation, confidence intervals will be too narrow. All *F* and *t* tests will be more significant (for example, have smaller *p*-values) than they really should be. Autocorrelation leads to "delusions of significance." We think that estimates are more accurate and tests more conclusive than they actually are.

Finally, if the residual standard deviation is somewhat too small in the presence of autocorrelation, the coefficient of determination is somewhat too large, another case of "delusions of predictability."

In practice, the detection of autocorrelation is based on the residuals, because the true errors (the ϵ's) are unknown. If a plot of the residuals versus time shows a cyclic, nonrandom pattern, it is likely that the true errors are dependent, and hence that autocorrelation is present.

EXAMPLE 13.22   Suppose that the data for a simple regression study of *y* = sales of a new product and *x* = week number are as follows:

y:	6.1	6.0	5.9	6.3	6.8	6.8	7.0	7.1
x:	1	2	3	4	5	6	7	8

y:	7.0	6.7	6.8	7.0	7.2	7.4	7.6
x:	9	10	11	12	13	14	15

Calculate and graph the least-squares regression line on a scatterplot of the data. Does there seem to be an autocorrelation problem?

SOLUTION   First, notice that we have time series data, so autocorrelation is a reasonable possibility. The regression line is $\hat{y} = 5.98 + .10x$. It is shown on a scatterplot of the data in Figure 13.19. The cyclic pattern (several negative residuals followed by several positive residuals, and so on) clearly indicates that autocorrelation is present.

FIGURE 13.19   **Autocorrelated Errors**

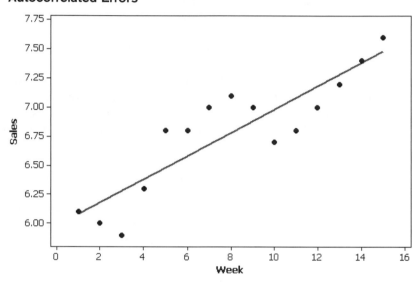

Durbin–Watson statistic

A formal test for autocorrelation uses the **Durbin–Watson statistic,** which is calculated by virtually all regression programs. This statistic is based on the idea that given (positive) autocorrelation, any one residual tends to be close to the following residual; a large positive residual tends to be followed by another large positive one, and so on. Therefore, the squared differences of successive residuals tend to be smaller under positive autocorrelation than they are when independent. The Durbin–Watson statistic is

$$ d = \frac{\sum_{t=1}^{n-1} (\hat{\epsilon}_{t+1} - \hat{\epsilon}_t)^2}{\sum_{t=1}^{n} \hat{\epsilon}_t^2} $$

where $\hat{\epsilon}_t$ is the residual at time t. If the true errors are in fact independent, the expected value of d is about 2.0. Positive autocorrelation tends to make $\hat{\epsilon}_{t+1}$ close to $\hat{\epsilon}_t$ and therefore to make d less than 2.0. Tables for a formal hypothesis test based on d are available (see Johnston, 1977). In practice, though, we would hope to accept the null hypothesis of zero autocorrelation. Because accepting any null hypothesis leads to the nasty question of Type II errors, we prefer to use the Durbin–Watson statistic as an index rather than as a formal test. Any value of d less than 1.5 or 1.6 leads us to suspect autocorrelation.

EXAMPLE 13.23 Calculate (just this once) the Durbin–Watson statistic for the data of Example 13.22. Does it indicate an autocorrelation problem?

SOLUTION

x_t	y_t	$\hat{y}_t = 5.98 + .10x_t$	$\hat{\epsilon}_t = y_t - \hat{y}_t$	$\hat{\epsilon}_{t+1} - \hat{\epsilon}_t$	$(\hat{\epsilon}_{t+1} - \hat{\epsilon}_t)^2$	$\hat{\epsilon}_t^2$
1	6.1	6.08	+.02	−.20	.04	.0004
2	6.0	6.18	−.18	.20	.04	.0324
3	5.9	6.28	−.38	+.30	.09	.1444
4	6.3	6.38	−.08	+.40	.16	.0064
5	6.8	6.48	+.32	−.10	.01	.1024
6	6.8	6.58	+.22	+.10	.01	.0484
7	7.0	6.68	+.32	.00	.00	.1024
8	7.1	6.78	+.32	−.20	.04	.1024
9	7.0	6.88	+.12	−.40	.16	.0144
10	6.7	6.98	−.28	.00	.00	.0784
11	6.8	7.08	−.28	+.10	.01	.0784
12	7.0	7.18	−.18	+.10	.01	.0324
13	7.2	7.28	−.08	+.10	.01	.0064
14	7.4	7.38	+.02	+.10	.01	.0004
15	7.6	7.48	+.12	—	—	.0144
					.59	.764

The Durbin–Watson statistic $d = .59/.764 = .772$. This value is far below the ideal value of 2.0 and the cutoff of 1.5. Autocorrelation is clearly a problem.

EXAMPLE 13.24 Data for 24 months for the feed manufacturer of Example 13.12 follow from Minitab. Starts is the number of starts in the previous month, Relpri is the manufacturer's feed price in the month (relative to an index), Chickp is the monthly average price of chickens, Comppr is the chief competitor's price (also relative to an index), and Sales is monthly feed sales by the manufacturer.

```
Month Starts  Relpri  Chickp  Comppr  Sales
    1   6.96   16.21   0.493   15.99    231
    2   7.20   16.19   0.517   16.31    264
    3   6.68   16.06   0.462   16.26    259
    4   7.01   15.97   0.490   16.12    258
    5   7.47   16.31   0.536   16.41    265
    6   7.68   16.58   0.594   16.49    255
    7   7.65   16.97   0.570   17.00    241
    8   7.49   17.21   0.538   17.01    233
    9   7.38   17.08   0.499   16.96    244
   10   7.46   17.00   0.486   17.21    268
   11   7.58   17.15   0.525   17.47    277
   12   7.56   17.31   0.490   17.22    260
   13   7.60   17.08   0.473   17.11    266
   14   7.31   17.11   0.431   17.01    277
   15   7.04   16.97   0.456   16.99    275
   16   7.03   16.90   0.464   17.16    278
   17   7.36   16.84   0.477   17.24    295
```

```
18    7.53   17.17   0.509   17.38   277
19    7.68   17.52   0.492   17.46   264
20    7.73   17.67   0.474   17.81   284
21    7.51   17.65   0.510   17.70   267
22    7.84   17.34   0.495   17.47   291
23    7.67   17.59   0.501   17.50   263
24    7.70   17.52   0.423   17.63   279
```

A first-order model is run with independent variables Starts, Relpri, Chickp, and Comppr (using Minitab). The following selected output is obtained. Is there evidence of autocorrelation?

```
Regression Analysis: Sales versus Starts, Relpri, Chickp, Comppr

The regression equation is
Sales = 181 + 24.3 Starts - 66.8 Relpri - 204 Chickp + 66.9 Comppr

Predictor      Coef   SE Coef       T       P
Constant     181.01     73.04    2.48   0.023
Starts        24.29     11.32    2.14   0.045
Relpri       -66.85     11.75   -5.69   0.000
Chickp      -203.80     61.16   -3.33   0.003
Comppr        66.91     11.23    5.96   0.000

S = 8.39106   R-Sq = 78.6%   R-Sq(adj) = 74.1%

Analysis of Variance

Source           DF       SS       MS       F       P
Regression        4   4918.2   1229.5   17.46   0.000
Residual Error   19   1337.8     70.4
Total            23   6256.0

Source   DF   Seq SS
Starts    1    303.7
Relpri    1    363.1
Chickp    1   1750.1
Comppr    1   2501.3

Unusual Observations

Obs   Starts   Sales      Fit   SE Fit   Residual   St Resid
  6     7.68  255.00   241.51     5.04      13.49       2.01R

R denotes an observation with a large standardized residual.

Durbin-Watson statistic = 1.45300
```

SOLUTION There is some suggestion of autocorrelation. The Durbin–Watson statistic is 1.45 and Figure 13.20 may show some cyclic behavior. In a previous example we had also seen an indication of nonconstant variance, so this model seems to have several assumption problems.

EXAMPLE 13.25   In an attempt to solve the problem of nonconstant variance detected in Example 13.24, a revised model is run. The dependent variable is Share = Sales/Starts. The independent variables are Relpri and Reldif = (Relpri − Comppr)/Chickp. Selected Minitab output is shown on page 668, and the residuals are plotted in Figure 13.21. Is there evidence of an autocorrelation problem?

FIGURE 13.20   **Sequence Plot of Standardized Residuals**

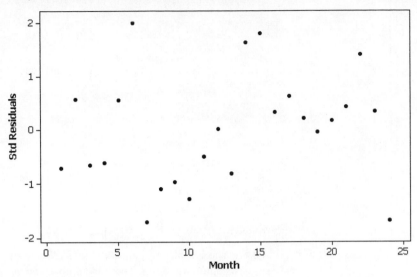

FIGURE 13.21   **Sequence Plot of Standardized Residuals**

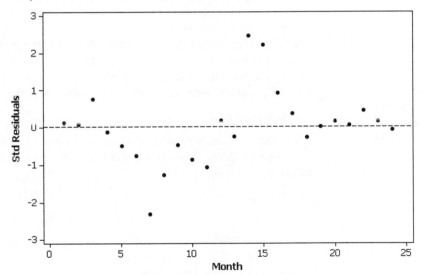

EXAMPLE 13.25
(continued)

```
Regression Analysis: Share versus Relpri, Reldif

The regression equation is
Share = 39.7 - 0.269 Relpri - 5.20 Reldif

Predictor      Coef   SE Coef      T       P
Constant      39.69     12.01    3.31   0.003
Relpri       -0.2692    0.7061  -0.38   0.707
Reldif       -5.196     1.094   -4.75   0.000

S = 1.71756    R-Sq = 52.7%    R-Sq(adj) = 48.2%

Analysis of Variance

Source          DF       SS      MS       F       P
Regression       2   69.004  34.502   11.70   0.000
Residual Error  21   61.951   2.950
Total           23  130.954

Durbin-Watson statistic = 0.777717
```

SOLUTION The Durbin–Watson statistic is .78 and the sequence plot of residuals clearly suggests autocorrelation. There is an up-down-up pattern to the residuals.

If autocorrelation is suspected, either because of a plot of residuals versus time or because of a Durbin–Watson statistic less than about 1.5 or 1.6, what should be done about the regression model? Ideally, we can find another predictor that accounts for the "snakelike" behavior of the data; we would try to find a predictor whose cycles matched the cycles of the residuals. If we found such a predictor, we would improve the predictive value of the model, as well as solve an assumption problem. Failing that, we could adopt an autocorrelation model for the error terms.

first-order autoregressive model

One simple error model is the **first-order autoregressive model**

$$\epsilon_t = u_t + \rho u_{t-1}$$

where the u_t values are independent and ρ is a model parameter; $\rho > 0$ yields positive autocorrelation. If this model is correct and if (miraculously) ρ is known, then it can be proven that

$$Y_t - \rho Y_{t-1} = \beta_0(1 - \rho) + \beta_1(x_{t1} - \rho x_{t-1,1})$$
$$+ \cdots + \beta_k(x_{tk} - \rho x_{t-1,k}) + (\epsilon_t - \rho \epsilon_{t-1})$$

is a model satisfying the assumption of independent error. In practice, the problem is to estimate the unknown error parameter ρ.

A quick approach to the problem is to assume $\rho = 1$. This leads to a regression of the differences $y_t - y_{t-1}$ on the differences $x_{t1} - x_{t-1,1}, \ldots, x_{tk} - x_{t-1,k}$. Often,

using differences

using differences eliminates any autocorrelation problems. This method also tends to reduce collinearity, which is often a major problem with time series data.

Regression of differences is a crude approach because it assumes that the autocorrelation parameter $\rho = 1$. A more sophisticated approach is the **Cochrane–Orcutt method.** In this method, we begin with a raw-data regression, estimate $\hat{\rho}$, calculate all differences $y_t - \hat{\rho}y_{t-1}$ and $x_t - \hat{\rho}x_{t-1}$, regress using these differences, reestimate $\hat{\rho}$, and so on to convergence. This is a technical chore for a special computer program, so we only mention the possibility. Alternatively, it is possible to search for the least-squares value of $\hat{\rho}$. For details, consult a time series specialist.

Cochrane–Orcutt method

EXAMPLE 13.26   First differences of the variables of Example 13.25 are calculated and a regression run. Selected Minitab output is shown here. Note that although there were 24 observations initially, we now have 23 first differences.

```
Regression Analysis: DShare versus DRelpri, DReldif

The regression equation is
DShare = 0.239 - 3.43 DRelpri - 2.89 DReldif

23 cases used, 1 cases contain missing values

Predictor      Coef   SE Coef        T       P
Constant     0.2388    0.2940     0.81   0.426
DRelpri      -3.429     1.633    -2.10   0.049
DReldif     -2.8934    0.8211    -3.52   0.002


S = 1.30961   R-Sq = 64.1%   R-Sq(adj) = 60.5%

Analysis of Variance

Source          DF       SS       MS       F       P
Regression       2   61.225   30.613   17.85   0.000
Residual Error  20   34.302    1.715
Total           22   95.527

Source     DF   Seq SS
DRelpri     1   39.929
DReldif     1   21.296

Unusual Observations

Obs  DRelpri  DShare      Fit  SE Fit  Residual  St Resid
 14    0.030   2.893   -0.719   0.401     3.612     2.90R

R denotes an observation with a large standardized residual.

Durbin-Watson statistic = 2.20068
```

The variables are DShare, DRelpri, and DReldif, where the initial D in the variable names indicates that the quantities are differences. Is there evidence of an autocorrelation problem or a problem of nonconstant variance? See Figure 13.22 on the next page.

SOLUTION   The Durbin–Watson statistic is 2.20, and the sequence plot of residuals (Figure 13.22a) shows no particular pattern. If anything, the differencing method has produced overkill; positive autocorrelation has been converted to apparent negative autocorrelation. Negative autocorrelation at least yields conservative results. A Cochrane–Orcutt or search method might make more efficient use of the data. The plot of residuals against predicted values shows no pattern, so there is no reason to think that nonconstant variance is a problem.

FIGURE 13.22 **(a) Sequence Plot of Standardized Residuals; (b) Plot of Standardized Residuals Versus Predicted Values**

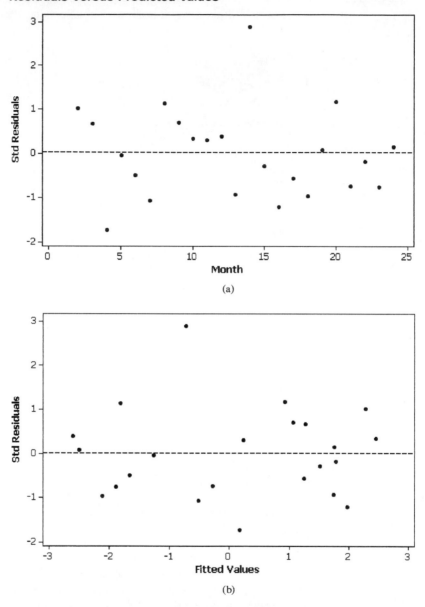

(a)

(b)

Exercises

13.22 Residual plots for the regression model of Exercise 13.21 are shown in Figure 13.23.
a. Is there any strong suggestion of nonlinearity?
b. Is there any strong suggestion of nonconstant variance?

13.23 The district sales office for a particular automobile is interested in predicting the sales of the "top of the line" luxury car in the district. It is obvious that sales are affected by the rated gasoline mileage of the car and by the car loan interest rate charged by the company's

FIGURE 13.23 **Residual Plots for Exercise 13.22**

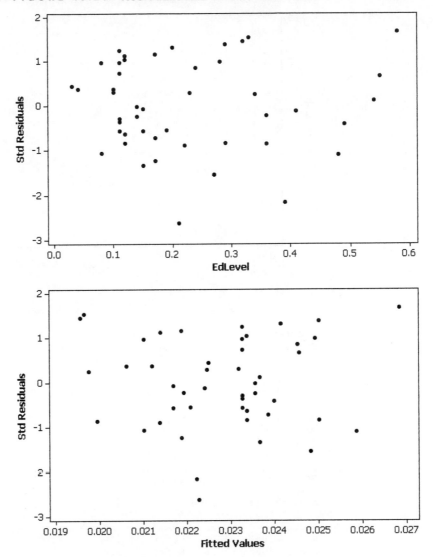

financing agency. It also seems plausible that sales are affected by gasoline prices and by the price of the car. Data are collected for 48 months; the last 6 months are reserved for model validation (to be discussed in Section 13.8). The variables are

Mileage: Rated gas mileage of the car

GasPrice: Average price per gallon (in cents) in the district

PreGas: Average gas price in the previous month

IntRate: Interest rate (percent per year)

CarPrice: Sticker price divided by the consumer price index

A first-order model is fit. Selected Minitab output is shown here. Figure 13.24 shows the sequence plot of residuals.

FIGURE 13.24 **Sequence Plot of Residuals for Exercise 13.23**

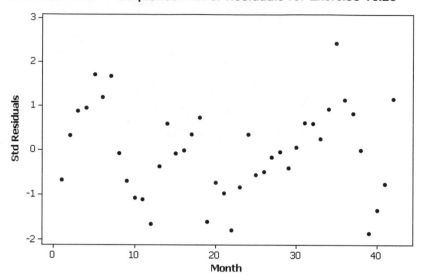

```
Regression Analysis: Sales versus Mileage, GasPrice, ...

The regression equation is
Sales = 5760 + 231 Mileage - 8.49 GasPrice - 14.5 PreGas - 252 IntRate
        - 56.4 CarPrice

Predictor      Coef  SE Coef      T      P
Constant       5760     2098   2.75  0.009
Mileage      230.79    53.91   4.28  0.000
GasPrice     -8.493    1.701  -4.99  0.000
PreGas      -14.538    1.637  -8.88  0.000
IntRate     -251.70    94.15  -2.67  0.011
CarPrice     -56.44    42.27  -1.34  0.190

S = 47.5433   R-Sq = 87.2%   R-Sq(adj) = 85.4%

Analysis of Variance

Source            DF       SS      MS      F      P
Regression         5   554701  110939  49.08  0.000
Residual Error    36    81373    2260
Total             41   636075

Source      DF   Seq SS
Mileage      1     3111
GasPrice     1   308872
PreGas       1   214165
IntRate      1    24523
CarPrice     1     4030

Unusual Observations

Obs  Mileage    Sales      Fit  SE Fit  Residual  St Resid
 35     13.9  3874.99  3764.93   14.76    110.06     2.44R

R denotes an observation with a large standardized residual.

Durbin-Watson statistic = 0.799894
```

a. In the estimated regression model, what do the positive and negative signs indicate about the effect of each independent variable?

b. Locate the residual standard deviation.

c. Does the Durbin–Watson statistic indicate that there is a problem of (positive) auto-correlation?

d. Does the sequence plot of residuals indicate that autocorrelation is a problem?

13.24 The auto-sales forecasting model of Exercise 13.23 is modified in two ways. First, the gas price variables are divided by the mileage figure to yield rated gas price per mile driven. The current month's price per mile is called PriMil, and the previous month's is Lag-PrM. Second, differences of the variables Sales, PriMil, LagPrM, IntRate, and CarPrice are calculated; the names are prefaced by a D. A regression model based on these differences is fit in Minitab, with the following results. The sequence plot of residuals is shown in Figure 13.25.

FIGURE 13.25 Sequence Plot of Residuals for Exercise 13.24

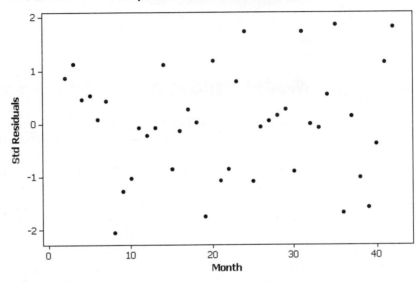

```
Regression Analysis: DSales versus DPriMil, DLagPrM, DIntRate, DCarPrice

The regression equation is
DSales = - 0.66 - 89.7 DPriMil - 222 DLagPrM - 110 DIntRate
            + 5.9 DCarPrice

41 cases used, 1 cases contain missing values

Predictor      Coef   SE Coef       T      P
Constant     -0.662     6.603   -0.10  0.921
DPriMil      -89.66     16.95   -5.29  0.000
DLagPrM     -221.95     15.78  -14.06  0.000
DIntRate    -109.50     85.13   -1.29  0.207
DCarPrice      5.90     39.18    0.15  0.881

S = 37.3388   R-Sq = 86.0%   R-Sq(adj) = 84.5%

Analysis of Variance

Source          DF      SS     MS      F      P
Regression       4  309523  77381  55.50  0.000
Residual Error  36   50191   1394
Total           40  359714

Source      DF   Seq SS
DPriMil      1    31566
DLagPrM      1   275646
DIntRate     1     2280
DCarPrice    1       32
```

```
Unusual Observations

Obs   DPriMil   DSales    Fit   SE Fit   Residual   St Resid
 8      0.164   -44.00   27.51   13.23    -71.51     -2.05R

R denotes an observation with a large standardized residual.

Durbin-Watson statistic = 1.88674
```

    a. In the regression equation, have any signs changed compared to the original model? How different are the coefficients?

    b. Locate the residual standard deviation.

    c. Is the residual standard deviation larger for the difference model than for the original? Why would this be a common result?

13.8 Model Validation

In this computer era, data can be "massaged" repeatedly at little cost. Regressions can be run with every conceivable combination of variables, transformations, and lags. It isn't unusual to have a hundred different regression equations run to try to predict a variable y. The statistical theory of regression analysis implicitly assumes that the choice of predictors x and dependent variable y has been made, once and for all, and that a single regression equation is found. The gap between theory and practice is wide.

The practice of calculating many regression equations and selecting the best one often leads to overoptimism. The apparent predictability decreases when the equation is used with new data—for two reasons. First, any regression equation is based on predicting the past; the equation is chosen to yield the best fit to available data. If the underlying economic structure changes, the predictive value of the model will decrease. Second, when one selects the best of many equations, one runs a risk of "capitalizing on chance." Even purely random phenomena can be explained after the fact by some combination of variables, if you search long enough.

A good practical approach to selecting an appropriate prediction equation is to validate the chosen regression equation with new data. In a time series study, we can withhold the most recent data from the original regression study. Then we can use the chosen regression equation to predict recent values. The resulting standard deviation gives a good indication of the future predictive value of the equation. We can use the same procedure with cross-section data. Select some subset of observations (perhaps 10% or 20%) at random, withhold them from the original study, and use them for validation. The chosen regression typically does not perform quite as well in the validation study. If it still works reasonably well, that's good grounds for believing that it will be useful in practice.

EXAMPLE 13.27 An additional 12 months' data are collected for the feed manufacturer of Example 13.12. The difference model of Example 13.26 is used with these data. The results are shown next.

	Actual DShare	Predicted DShare	Error
	.6243	1.4735	−.8492
	2.7931	1.7694	1.0237
	−1.4616	−1.6785	.2169
	−2.1039	−.4668	−1.6371
	1.0487	.2520	.7967
	3.4225	1.3979	2.0246
	.8994	1.9018	−1.0024
	−1.1583	−.7206	−.4377
	1.2767	.4526	.8241
	4.0023	4.2146	−.2123
	−2.9046	−3.9520	1.0474
	−.8726	−.5465	−.3261
Mean	.4638	.3414	.1224
Standard deviation	2.2153	2.0665	1.0520

a. Is there any flagrant bias in the predictions?

b. Is the error standard deviation grossly different?

SOLUTION

a. There's no obvious systematic error. The mean error is small (.1224) relative to the size of the actual values and to the error standard deviation. Exactly half of the errors are positive.

b. The error standard deviation (1.0520) is slightly smaller, in fact, than 1.310.

BUSINESS DECISION-MAKING IN ACTION

CHAPTER CASE

ANALYSIS

Easton Realty Company

Based on a local newspaper article suggesting that the average selling price of homes in the Dallas–Fort Worth area was $154,250 over the past 12 months, two people who had recently sold their homes through Easton Realty complained to the board of realtors that Easton had underpriced their homes in order to speed up the sales. Sam Easton does not believe his agents would do that, even given the current poor real estate market. The database that a local real estate appraiser gave him did not contain all home sales over the past 4 months, but it did represent the population of homes sold in the DFW area during that period. The data included the sale month, the sale price, the size of the home in square feet, the number of bedrooms, the age of the house, the location of the house within the DFW metroplex, and an indicator variable that tells whether Easton or another company sold the home.

Sam has asked you to give him your opinion of the situation. He especially wants you to take a look at whether the two houses in question were underpriced relative to comparable houses sold by other realtors. He also wants you to determine whether Easton has been generally underpricing houses relative to its competitors.

The following Minitab output summarizes the quantitative and categorical variables.

```
Descriptive Statistics: Price, Size, Age

Variable    N     Mean    StDev   Minimum      Q1   Median       Q3  Maximum
Price     518   140.22    24.73     85.50  123.00   137.60   156.77   220.80
Size      518   1870.1    339.2    1067.0  1638.0   1821.5   2092.3   2872.0
Age       518   6.1757   2.0848    1.0000  5.0000   6.0000   8.0000   13.000

Tally for Discrete Variables: Month, Bedrooms, Area, Agency

Month  Count  Percent    Bedrooms  Count  Percent    Area  Count  Percent
March    140    27.03           2     82    15.83       1    243    46.91
April    131    25.29           3    309    59.65       2    166    32.05
  May    127    24.52           4    127    24.52       3    109    21.04
 June    120    23.17          N=    518              N=    518
  N=     518

Agency  Count  Percent
     0    469    90.54
     1     49     9.46
    N=    518
```

Note that the average size of homes in the sample is close to that reported in the newspaper article, but the average selling price ($140,220) is less than that reported in the article ($154,250), a fact easily explained by the downward slide of the real estate market and inclusion of only the last 4 months of data as opposed to the past 12 months. Boxplots of Price by Month in Figure 13.26 shows the downward trend in home prices. The following Minitab analysis of variance output verifies that there are statistically detectable differences in the average selling prices for the 4 months.

FIGURE 13.26   **Box Plots of Price by Month**

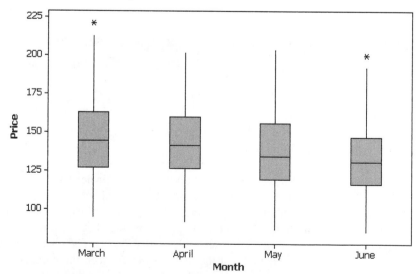

```
One-way ANOVA: Price versus Month

Source   DF      SS    MS      F      P
Month     3   13061  4354   7.38  0.000
Error   514  303018   590
Total   517  316079
```

```
        S = 24.28    R-Sq = 4.13%    R-Sq(adj) = 3.57%

                             Individual 95% CIs For Mean Based on
                             Pooled StDev
        Level    N    Mean   StDev  ------+---------+---------+---------+---
        March  140  146.18   25.39                        (------*-----)
        April  131  142.75   23.14                  (------*------)
        May    127  138.08   24.87            (------*------)
        June   120  132.77   23.52   (------*-------)
                             ------+---------+---------+---------+---
                                  132.0     138.0     144.0     150.0

        Pooled StDev = 24.28
```

As a first check on the underpricing claims, we use a one-sided, two-sample *t* test to see if Easton's average selling price is lower than that of other agencies. Based on the following Minitab output and the boxplots in Figure 13.27, we can conclude, at the 5% level of significance, that Easton's average selling price is lower. Could Easton's agents be underpricing houses or could there be another explanation?

```
Two-Sample T-Test and CI: Price, Agency

Two-sample T for Price

Agency    N    Mean   StDev   SE Mean
0        469   140.8   25.0     1.2
1         49   134.8   21.3     3.0

Difference = mu (0) - mu (1)
Estimate for difference:  5.97367
95% lower bound for difference:  0.53786
T-Test of difference = 0 (vs >): T-Value = 1.84   P-Value = 0.036   DF = 62
```

FIGURE 13.27   **Box Plots of Price by Agency**

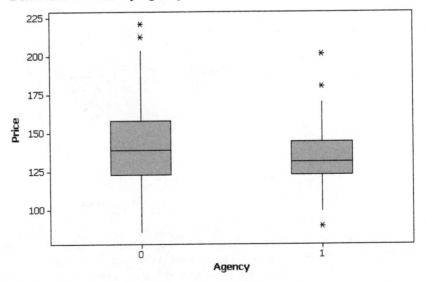

Obviously, the selling price of a house depends on many things. We begin by examining the pairwise relationships between selling price and its potential predictors. From Figure 13.26, we learned that the month in which a house sold affected the selling price. Boxplots of Price versus Bedrooms and Area in Figures 13.28 and 13.29 show that these are also important predictors of Price.

FIGURE 13.28

Box Plots of Price by Bedrooms

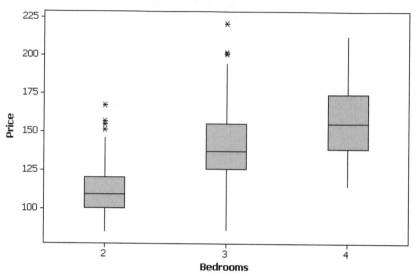

FIGURE 13.29

Box Plots of Price by Area

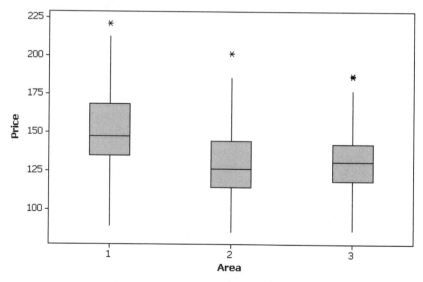

Figure 13.30 contains a scatterplot matrix for Price, Size, and Age. Price is clearly a useful predictor of Price, but Age is not.

There appear to be two parallel groups of points in the scatterplot of Price versus Size. If the two groups correspond to the two levels of the Agency variable (Easton and Other), there would be strong evidence for underpricing by Easton, but this is not the case. Figure 13.31 shows there are actually three roughly parallel groups of points in the plot that correspond to the three levels of Area.

FIGURE 13.30   **Scatterplot Matrix for Price, Size, and Age**

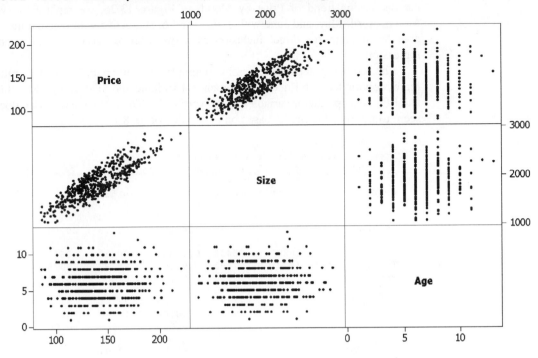

FIGURE 13.31   **Scatterplot of Price Versus Size with Symbols for Area**

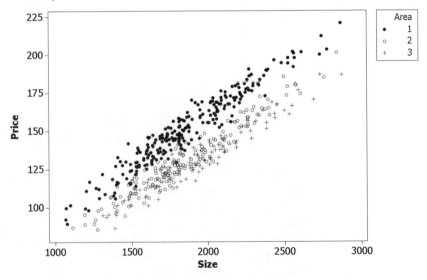

We now use stepwise regression in Minitab to help us identify a multiple regression model that explains the variation in selling prices of homes in the DFW area. Potential predictor variables for the stepwise regression include Size, Age, and Agency. (No transformations of Price, Size, and Age were indicated by the scatterplot matrix in Figure 13.30.) Other variables require recoding. Two indicator variables (3-Bed and 4-Bed) can be created from the Bedrooms variable. Two indicator variables (Dallas and FW) can also be created from the Area variable. Given the linear decreasing trend of Price by Month in Figure 13.26, we replace the values March, April, May, and June with 3, 4, 5, and 6, respectively, to create a new variable MonthNum for direct inclusion as a quantitative variable in the stepwise regression.

The following stepwise regression output from Minitab indicates that a multiple regression model with Price as the dependent variable and Size, Dallas, MonthNum, and FW as the predictor variables works very well. (The inclusion of 4-Bed does not seem to improve the model based on its p-value of .098.)

```
Stepwise Regression: Price versus Size, Age, ...
   Alpha-to-Enter: 0.15  Alpha-to-Remove: 0.15

Response is Price on 8 predictors, with N = 518

Step                1        2        3        4        5
Constant       22.955    9.567   24.206   20.073   20.948

Size          0.06270  0.06438  0.06381  0.06439  0.06380
T-Value         38.31    77.63    90.51    95.80    83.88
P-Value         0.000    0.000    0.000    0.000    0.000

Dallas                   21.81    21.52    24.51    24.60
T-Value                  38.73    44.98    41.10    41.16
P-Value                  0.000    0.000    0.000    0.000

MonthNum                          -3.03    -3.01    -3.02
T-Value                          -14.17   -14.88   -14.96
P-Value                           0.000    0.000    0.000

FW                                          4.92     4.93
T-Value                                     7.72     7.75
P-Value                                     0.000    0.000

4-Bed                                                0.99
T-Value                                              1.66
P-Value                                              0.098

S                12.6     6.39     5.42     5.14     5.13
R-Sq            73.99    93.35    95.22    95.72    95.74
R-Sq(adj)       73.94    93.33    95.19    95.68    95.70
Mallows C-p    2602.1    284.5     62.7      5.0      4.3
```

Note that the Agency variable was never included in the model. This tells us that after accounting for the effects of the other variables on Price, Agency is not a useful predictor. The following Minitab regression output shows the outcome from adding Agency to the model selected from stepwise regression. We fail to reject the null hypothesis H_0: $\beta_{Agency} = 0$ (given Size, Dallas, MonthNum, and FW in the model) based on the t-value of -0.61 (p-value $= .545$) and conclude that there is insufficient evidence of a difference in the average selling prices for Easton and all other real estate agencies, holding Size, Dallas, MonthNum, and FW fixed.

```
Regression Analysis: Price versus Size, Dallas, MonthNum, FW, Agency

The regression equation is
Price = 20.1 + 0.0644 Size + 24.5 Dallas - 3.01 MonthNum + 4.93 FW
        - 0.479 Agency
```

```
Predictor        Coef    SE Coef         T      P   VIF
Constant       20.090      1.711     11.74  0.000
Size        0.0644167  0.0006730     95.71  0.000   1.0
Dallas        24.4629     0.6025     40.60  0.000   1.8
MonthNum      -3.0067     0.2027    -14.83  0.000   1.0
FW             4.9342     0.6380      7.73  0.000   1.7
Agency        -0.4792     0.7910     -0.61  0.545   1.1


S = 5.13991    R-Sq = 95.7%    R-Sq(adj) = 95.7%

Analysis of Variance

Source           DF       SS      MS        F      P
Regression        5   302552   60511  2290.43  0.000
Residual Error  512    13526      26
Total           517   316079

Source       DF   Seq SS
Size          1   233863
Dallas        1    61201
MonthNum      1     5906
FW            1     1573
Agency        1       10
```

To test the customers' underpricing claims, we can construct 95% prediction intervals for the selling prices of those two houses from our regression model. Minitab results follow. In each case, the actual selling price of the house is very close to the predicted value and is contained in the prediction interval.

```
Predicted Values for New Observations

NewObs      Fit   SE Fit         95% CI               95% PI
     1  143.044    0.606  (141.853, 144.235)  (132.882, 153.206)
     2  125.938    0.504  (124.948, 126.929)  (115.798, 136.079)

Values of Predictors for New Observations

NewObs  Size    Dallas  MonthNum    FW
     1  2190  0.000000      6.00  0.00
     2  1848  0.000000      6.00  1.00
```

Of course, the final step in our multiple regression model building is to check residual plots for violations of model assumptions and any unusual data or patterns. We leave that step up to you.

So why are Easton's selling prices so much lower than those of other realtors in the DFW area (based on our earlier two-sample t test)? The two-way table of Area by Agency from Minitab shown here indicates that Easton's selling efforts across the three areas differ from those of the other agencies.

```
Tabulated statistics: Area, Agency

Rows: Area    Columns: Agency

              0       1      All

    1       236       7      243
          50.32   14.29    46.91


    2       139      27      166
          29.64   55.10    32.05
```

```
3              94      15     109
            20.04   30.61   21.04

All           469      49     518
           100.00  100.00  100.00

Cell Contents:        Count
                      % of Column
```

Since Easton Realty is located in Fort Worth, we would naturally expect it to do more business there. Furthermore, the following Minitab output shows that the average selling prices for Easton and other agencies are actually very similar within each of the three areas.

```
Tabulated statistics: Area, Agency

Rows: Area    Columns: Agency

             0      1     All

1        150.6   151.2   150.6
           236       7     243

2        130.0   132.1   130.3
           139      27     166

3        132.2   132.1   132.2
            94      15     109

All      140.8   134.8   140.2
           469      49     518

Cell Contents:  Price  :  Mean
                          Count
```

So, there is good news for Sam Easton. There is insufficient evidence that the two houses in question were underpriced, and there is insufficient evidence of underpricing in general by Easton after taking other important determinants of selling price into consideration.

SUMMARY

Here are some suggestions for the process of constructing a multiple regression model.

1. The most important step in obtaining a useful regression model is the choice of dependent and independent variables. Knowledge of the situation and any theoretical reasoning that's available should be used in selecting variables.

2. Possible lags in time series data and possible interactions should be identified by whatever knowledge and theory are available. The analyst must identify these possibilities to be able to test them. No computer package does this automatically.

3. In selecting predictor variables, try to avoid obvious collinearity. Very little can be gained by having predictor variables that are nearly the same.

4. Before starting the analysis, it's a useful practice to set aside a small fraction of the data for validating the final model.

5. A scatterplot matrix and a table of correlations are a good way to start the data analysis. They will indicate which predictors seem most effective, which predictors are collinear, and possibly the presence of outliers.

6. The goal of regression modeling is to obtain a relatively simple equation that captures almost all of the predictive ability in the data. Try to eliminate variables that add little to the overall value of the model.

7. Residual plots and (for time series) the Durbin–Watson statistic should be checked routinely for assumption violations.

8. If data are available for validation, check to see if the average error in the validation sample is near zero and if the standard deviation of the validation errors is reasonably close to the residual standard deviation of the model.

In addition, you may want to reread the Executive Overview at the beginning of this chapter.

Supplementary Exercises

13.25 A firm that manufactures and sells moderately sophisticated desktop publishing equipment budgets a certain dollar amount for postsale support activities. This support is provided by field representatives who train users initially and by home-office representatives who answer questions by telephone. Individuals shuttle between home- and field-representative positions frequently, so it is not very meaningful to separate the positions in the budget. A regression study is made in an attempt to forecast the required support budget.

Analysis of the support requirements suggests that the training aspect of postsales support typically involves users who have installed the equipment in the current and preceding months. For the next four months, there is substantial callback support as users forget aspects of training or add new equipment operators. After that period, support activity is mostly troubleshooting and new application work. Therefore, the installation data to be used as independent variables are broken down as

1. number of installations in budget month (known in previous month),
2. number of installations in previous month,
3. number of installations in preceding four months.

These data are collected separately for the two levels of sophistication (A and B) of equipment (the A class requires more sophisticated training). Thus, six independent variables are entered.

There is some question as to whether support costs increase in proportion to the number of installations. One opinion holds that the cost per installation decreases as installations increase because of improved users' manuals and more efficient training methods.
a. Identify any lagged variables.
b. Does the description of the situation indicate that any severe interaction can be expected?
c. Is there any indication of possible need for nonlinear terms in a regression model?

13.26 The firm of Exercise 13.25 collects data on the budgeted number of representatives (y) and the six independent variables described in that exercise. Data are available for 36 months, and the most recent 6 months' data are reserved for validation. A first-order regression model is fit to the remaining 30 months' data. A plot of the residuals against time is shown in Figure 13.32.

FIGURE 13.32 **Residuals Versus Time**

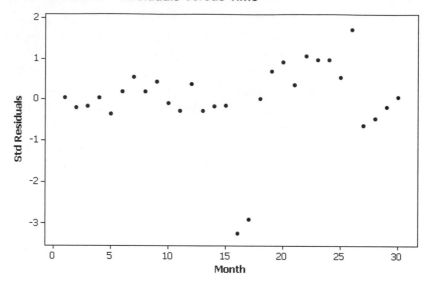

a. Is there any indication of possible outliers?
b. Is there any indication of autocorrelation?

13.27 Investigation of the data of Exercise 13.26 shows that the support budget in months 16 and 17 had been cut back drastically in a spasm of cost cutting. This action led to many user complaints, so the attempt was abandoned. The budget numbers of those months are changed in the database to the figures that had been planned before the cost-cutting attempt. A first-order model yields the plots of residuals versus predicted values shown in Figure 13.33. Is there any indication of possible heteroscedasticity (nonconstant variance)?

FIGURE 13.33 **Residuals Versus Predicted Values**

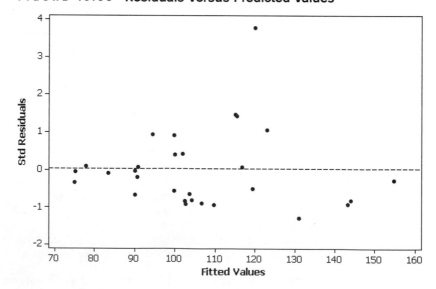

13.28 The squares of the current month's installations (both A and B types) are added as independent variables. A stepwise (forward-selection) regression analysis yields the following Minitab output:

```
Stepwise Regression: SUPP versus ACURR, APREV, ...

Forward selection.  F-to-Enter: 0.01

Response is SUPP on 8 predictors, with N = 30
```

Step	1	2	3	4	5	6
Constant	63.51	63.60	40.10	39.39	25.23	-13.82
BCURRSQ	0.0597	0.0401	0.0268	0.0253	0.0224	-0.0353
T-Value	8.11	5.66	4.75	5.37	6.00	-1.89
P-Value	0.000	0.000	0.000	0.000	0.000	0.071
ACURRSQ		0.0680	0.0655	0.0603	0.0507	0.0540
T-Value		4.56	6.17	6.74	6.91	8.48
P-Value		0.000	0.000	0.000	0.000	0.000
BPREV			1.30	0.95	0.65	0.63
T-Value			5.24	4.17	3.35	3.82
P-Value			0.000	0.000	0.003	0.001
APREV				0.91	0.92	0.96
T-Value				3.55	4.61	5.60
P-Value				0.002	0.000	0.000
BPREC4					0.263	0.262
T-Value					4.15	4.83
P-Value					0.000	0.000
BCURR						3.04
T-Value						3.14
P-Value						0.005
S	11.5	8.77	6.23	5.19	4.04	3.45
R-Sq	70.15	83.14	91.80	94.54	96.82	97.77
R-Sq(adj)	69.08	81.89	90.85	93.67	96.16	97.19
Mallows C-p	359.6	193.7	84.0	50.5	23.1	12.8

a. List the sequence in which the variables are added.

b. How much of an increment to R^2 is obtained by inclusion of the last four variables?

13.29 Additional output from the regression analysis of Exercise 13.28, for the model with all variables included, yields the residual plots shown in Figure 13.34 (see next page).

a. Is there evidence of serious autocorrelation?

b. Is there evidence of nonconstant variance?

13.30 Differences for all variables in the data of Exercise 13.28 are calculated, and a stepwise (forward-selection) regression is run. The Minitab output follows below and continues on pages 686 and 687. Is the sequence in which the variables are added similar to that found in Exercise 13.28?

```
Stepwise Regression: DSUPP versus DACURR, DAPREV, ...

Forward selection.  F-to-Enter: 0.01

Response is DSUPP on 8 predictors, with N = 29
N(cases with missing observations) = 1 N(all cases) = 30
```

Step	1	2	3	4	5	6
Constant	2.2719	1.4511	1.0583	0.9208	0.9090	0.6913
DACURR	1.46	1.92	1.60	1.53	1.54	1.59
T-Value	4.84	8.43	10.94	11.31	11.68	11.65
P-Value	0.000	0.000	0.000	0.000	0.000	0.000

FIGURE 13.34 **Residual Plots for Exercise 13.29: (a) Residuals Versus Predicted Values; (b) Residuals Versus Time**

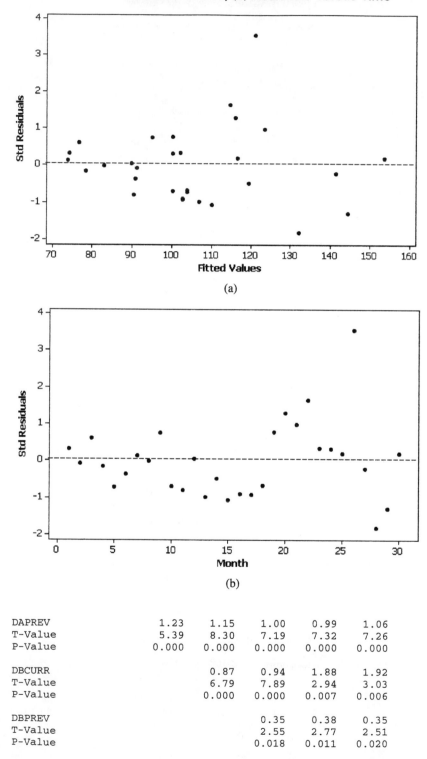

(a)

(b)

DAPREV	1.23	1.15	1.00	0.99	1.06
T-Value	5.39	8.30	7.19	7.32	7.26
P-Value	0.000	0.000	0.000	0.000	0.000
DBCURR		0.87	0.94	1.88	1.92
T-Value		6.79	7.89	2.94	3.03
P-Value		0.000	0.000	0.007	0.006
DBPREV			0.35	0.38	0.35
T-Value			2.55	2.77	2.51
P-Value			0.018	0.011	0.020

```
DBCURRSQ                                -0.017  -0.018
T-Value                                  -1.49   -1.57
P-Value                                  0.149   0.131

DAPREC4                                           0.13
T-Value                                           1.24
P-Value                                          0.230

S               8.73    6.11    3.70    3.35    3.26    3.23
R-Sq           46.41   74.69   91.09   92.99   93.61   94.03
R-Sq(adj)      44.42   72.74   90.03   91.82   92.22   92.40
Mallows C-p    157.6    63.2     9.3     4.9     4.8     5.4
```

13.31 Additional output from the all-variables model of Exercise 13.30 is shown in Figure 13.35 (see next page).
a. Is there an autocorrelation problem with the differenced data?
b. Is there evidence of heteroscedasticity?

13.32 Consider the output from the regression study of Exercise 13.30.
a. Write out the final regression model.
b. Can the null hypothesis that all partial slopes are zero be rejected at reasonable α levels?
c. Which variables have coefficients that differ significantly (at $\alpha = .05$) from zero as "last predictor in"?
d. Identify and interpret the R^2 value.
e. Identify the residual standard deviation.

13.33 In Exercise 13.26 the most recent six months' data were reserved for validation. These values, in difference form, are shown here along with the predicted values given by the model of Exercise 13.30.

ACURR	APREV	APREC4	BCURR	BPREV	BPREC4	ACURRSQ	BCURRSQ	Actual Support	Predicted Support
−2	−3	9	5	3	1	−80	−135	2	5.78
5	−2	3	−6	5	1	215	−80	−3	−.97
−4	5	−1	4	−6	3	−176	215	5	2.99
−4	−4	−7	−6	4	8	−144	−176	−5	−9.94
14	−4	−4	7	−6	6	644	−144	17	15.29
−2	14	−5	4	7	−3	−116	644	11	12.78

a. Calculate the residuals and their standard deviation.
b. Is this residual standard deviation much larger than the one found in Exercise 13.30?
c. Previous forecasts of the budget were often in error by as much as ± 20 units. Does it appear that the regression model will be useful in predicting the budget figure?

13.34 A wholesale hardware company fills orders at a large warehouse. The volume of orders fluctuates substantially from day to day, and the company has a policy of filling each order on the day of receipt. Orders are phoned or mailed, and they are received by 10 A.M. The warehouse supervisor estimates the total time required for each order and assigns the required number of workers to order filling. Excess workers, if any, are assigned to other tasks and cannot be recalled until the next day. The supervisor's estimates of time per order are often quite erroneous, so that sometimes workers are idle and other times substantial overtime must be paid. A regression study is attempted to improve the prediction of required time per order. The computer used for order processing and inventory control can easily calculate predicted times once a model is determined.

Items in the order are classified as frequently, moderately, or rarely ordered. The rarely ordered items are stored in the most distant parts of the warehouse and therefore require more

FIGURE 13.35 **Residual Plots for Exercise 13.31: (a) Residuals Versus Predicted Values; (b) Residuals Versus Time**

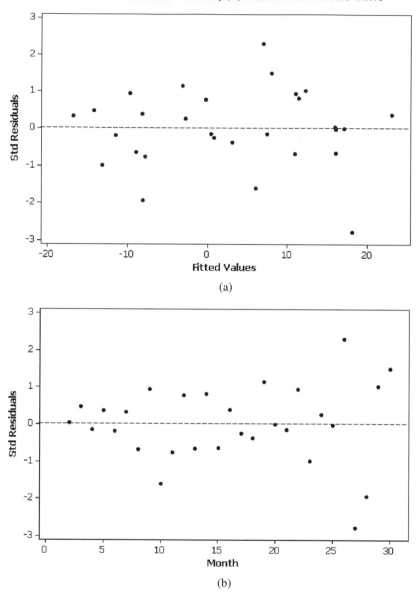

(a)

(b)

time to obtain. Both the number of items ordered in each category and the average size per item are thought to influence the order-filling time. Most items ordered are in carton units, and less-than-carton items (which are mostly rarely ordered) are filled as "loose-box" items. Certain orders require special packing to protect fragile items. The supervisor assigns each such order to either packing station A or B. All items are assembled at a central station and placed on skids. A forklift is used to move the skids from the assembly station to delivery trucks.

A sample of 50 orders is selected; care is taken to include relatively extreme types of order (small and large, mostly loose-box and mostly carton, mostly frequent and mostly rare). Values for each of the following variables are recorded:

Time:	Time (in worker-minutes) needed to fill order
NumFreq:	Number of frequently ordered items in the order
NumMod:	Number of moderately ordered items in the order
NumRare:	Number of rarely ordered items in the order
NumLoose:	Number of loose-box items
AvSzCar:	Average size of carton items (cartons/item)
AvSzLB:	Average size of loose-box items (pieces/item)
Special:	0, if no special packing need, 1, if special packing done at station A, 2, if special packing done at station B
Skids:	Number of skids needed

The supervisor thinks that the most important predictor variables are the NUM ones, because much of the order-filling time is taken up by workers moving to the appropriate locations. However, this travel time is not likely to be directly proportional to the number of items, because a worker can combine items found in the same general area of the warehouse. The order size of each item is also relevant, because some time is used in taking each item from the shelf. This time is expected to be in proportion to AvSz. The time spent moving skids is expected to be in proportion to Skids. The only other major time factor is assembly-station time, which is expected to depend on a combination of Num and AvSz variables.

a. Explain why the Special variable should be recoded as two variables:

SpecialA = 1, if special packing done at station A; 0 if not

SpecialB = 1, if special packing done at station B; 0 if not

b. Explain the interpretation of the coefficients of these two variables.
c. According to the information given by the supervisor, which independent variables might be transformed?
d. Is there any indication that interaction terms might be useful?

13.35 The data for the study of Exercise 13.34 are shown on the next page along with Minitab output from a first-order model fit. A residual plot is shown in Figure 13.36.

FIGURE 13.36 Residual Plot for Exercise 13.35

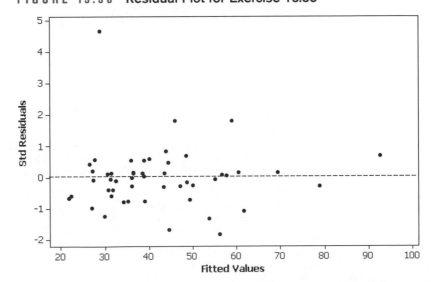

Time	NumFreq	NumMod	NumRare	NumLoose	AvSzCar	AvSzLB	SpecialA	SpecialB	Skids
27	16	6	3	4	1.6	3.5	1	0	2
57	70	25	2	2	3.2	2.7	0	0	18
39	25	6	8	4	2.4	3.3	0	0	8
20	10	2	1	1	6.2	4.0	0	0	4
55	50	30	6	7	2.6	3.0	0	0	12
95	85	43	16	10	4.7	6.2	0	1	25
19	12	3	1	1	2.4	3.0	0	0	3
35	10	12	13	3	5.0	6.0	0	0	5
61	87	12	4	6	3.0	4.0	1	0	16
44	50	22	8	2	4.0	1.5	0	0	9
23	12	8	8	2	1.4	3.5	0	0	2
47	27	6	12	14	1.6	7.2	0	0	4
53	64	8	1	2	3.0	2.5	0	0	14
70	71	34	7	10	2.1	4.6	0	0	16
32	25	1	2	2	2.8	5.0	0	0	10
39	16	10	3	8	2.0	4.7	1	0	6
32	25	12	4	2	1.8	6.0	0	0	4
30	40	6	1	1	2.6	3.0	0	0	7
38	72	21	8	3	2.0	2.7	0	0	6
78	64	37	21	6	3.0	4.3	0	1	20
30	23	6	2	1	4.2	2.0	0	0	6
38	35	13	7	1	1.4	8.0	0	0	5
25	16	4	2	4	1.6	9.3	0	0	3
47	19	17	10	6	3.2	2.7	1	0	8
42	31	12	16	3	1.4	2.3	0	1	4
46	46	8	11	2	4.0	2.5	0	0	13
48	12	6	1	5	2.0	6.2	0	0	3
28	16	4	4	2	6.1	1.5	0	0	5
28	37	8	2	1	2.2	2.0	1	0	3
32	21	9	6	4	1.8	6.5	0	0	3
51	58	4	3	6	4.0	8.3	0	0	11
48	24	15	1	8	3.0	9.1	0	1	10
49	36	12	9	2	4.0	6.0	0	0	15
42	51	18	3	5	1.8	2.8	0	0	8
58	77	30	15	12	1.2	1.2	1	0	6
37	24	6	2	2	4.0	6.0	0	0	10
37	16	8	5	1	6.0	10.0	0	0	9
46	36	12	4	6	2.6	5.1	0	1	8
58	74	15	16	4	1.8	1.5	0	0	13
49	51	10	3	8	3.7	4.5	0	0	16
41	24	6	8	3	4.1	3.3	1	0	9
31	36	8	1	1	2.7	5.0	0	0	6
31	21	4	5	6	1.6	1.3	0	0	3
49	42	10	2	2	4.0	8.5	0	1	18
29	16	3	4	2	2.7	3.5	0	0	7
29	28	15	2	1	3.0	6.0	0	0	5
66	73	18	15	5	1.9	4.2	0	0	12
31	15	8	8	6	1.2	2.3	0	0	4
36	23	4	10	4	1.5	2.8	0	0	6
36	44	9	2	1	4.0	5.0	1	0	10

Regression Analysis: Time versus NumFreq, NumMod, ...

The regression equation is
Time = 12.6 + 0.139 NumFreq + 0.234 NumMod + 0.542 NumRare
       + 1.17 NumLoose - 0.216 AvSzCar + 0.498 AvSzLB
       + 0.70 SpecialA + 1.82 SpecialB + 1.35 Skids

Predictor	Coef	SE Coef	T	P
Constant	12.584	2.695	4.67	0.000
NumFreq	0.13946	0.05318	2.62	0.012
NumMod	0.2344	0.1086	2.16	0.037
NumRare	0.5424	0.1551	3.50	0.001
NumLoose	1.1713	0.2539	4.61	0.000

```
AvSzCar    -0.2162    0.6220   -0.35   0.730
AvSzLB      0.4975    0.3188    1.56   0.126
SpecialA    0.701     1.784     0.39   0.696
SpecialB    1.820     2.301     0.79   0.434
Skids       1.3513    0.2312    5.85   0.000

S = 4.34091    R-Sq = 93.2%    R-Sq(adj) = 91.6%

Analysis of Variance

Source           DF        SS       MS       F       P
Regression        9   10273.3   1141.5   60.58   0.000
Residual Error   40     753.7     18.8
Total            49   11027.0

Durbin-Watson statistic = 2.12593
```

a. Is there any indication of outliers?

b. Is there any indication of nonconstant variance?

c. Is there any indication of autocorrelation? Would autocorrelation be expected in this study?

13.36 It was discovered that observation 27 of the data in Exercise 13.35 was taken during a brief strike. The order was filled by the president and vice president of the firm, who couldn't find most of the items. This observation is deleted from the data set. Regression runs are made using logarithms of the NumFreq, NumMod, and NumRare variables and using the square roots of these variables. The resulting residual standard deviations and R^2 values are

	Logarithms	Square Roots
s_ϵ	3.4804	3.0561
R^2	.9570	.9669

Which transformation appears more effective?

13.37 A forward-selection stepwise regression is run on the data resulting from Exercise 13.36. The square root transformation is used. The following output is obtained:

```
Stepwise Regression: Time versus NumLoose, AvSzCar, ...

Forward selection.  F-to-Enter: 4

Response is Time on 9 predictors, with N = 49

Step            1        2        3        4        5
Constant    20.913   15.387    8.691    5.818    1.803

Skids         2.43     2.17     1.75     1.80     1.55
T-Value      10.96    13.71    12.35    15.22    12.58
P-Value      0.000    0.000    0.000    0.000    0.000

NumLoose               1.93     1.45     1.23     1.19
T-Value                7.21     6.53     6.45     7.09
P-Value                0.000    0.000    0.000    0.000

sqrt(NumMod)                    3.77     2.74     1.85
T-Value                         5.79     4.67     3.24
P-Value                         0.000    0.000    0.002
```

```
sqrt(NumRare)                              2.89   3.00
T-Value                                    4.58   5.39
P-Value                                   0.000  0.000

sqrt(NumFreq)                                     1.53
T-Value                                           3.71
P-Value                                          0.001

S                    8.11   5.62   4.30   3.58   3.15
R-Sq                71.88  86.80  92.44  94.88  96.12
R-Sq(adj)           71.28  86.23  91.93  94.41  95.67
Mallows C-p         285.9  112.3   48.0   21.3    8.7
```

a. How much does inclusion of the last variable increase R^2?

b. Test the null hypothesis that the last two variables have no incremental predictive value.

13.38 The dependent variable in Exercise 13.37 is redefined to be the time *per item,* that is,

$$\frac{\text{Time}}{\text{NumFreq} + \text{NumMod} + \text{NumRare}}$$

All independent variables are divided by (NumFreq + NumMod + NumRare), including the dummy variables. The following Minitab output results from regression run on the transformed data.

```
Regression Analysis: TimePer versus sqtNFPer, sqtNMPer, ...

The regression equation is
TimePer = 0.0244 + 1.80 sqtNFPer + 1.63 sqtNMPer + 2.73 sqtNRPer
          + 1.15 NumLPer + 0.360 ASzCrPer + 0.210 ASzLBPer
          + 1.88 SpecAPer + 2.92 SpecBPer + 1.29 SkidsPer

Predictor    Coef    SE Coef      T      P
Constant   0.02435   0.04059    0.60   0.552
sqtNFPer    1.8013    0.3227    5.58   0.000
sqtNMPer    1.6311    0.5503    2.96   0.005
sqtNRPer    2.7348    0.4012    6.82   0.000
NumLPer     1.1491    0.1345    8.55   0.000
ASzCrPer    0.3600    0.1633    2.20   0.033
ASzLBPer    0.2104    0.1279    1.64   0.108
SpecAPer    1.8752    0.8549    2.19   0.034
SpecBPer    2.925     1.411     2.07   0.045
SkidsPer    1.2882    0.1234   10.44   0.000

S = 0.0492153   R-Sq = 97.1%   R-Sq(adj) = 96.4%

Analysis of Variance

Source           DF      SS       MS       F      P
Regression        9  3.16377  0.35152  145.13  0.000
Residual Error   39  0.09445  0.00241
Total            48  3.25824

Durbin-Watson statistic = 2.09396
```

a. Write the regression model and the residual standard deviation.

b. Is any violation of assumptions shown by the residual plots in Figures 13.37–13.40?

13.39 A validation study of the model obtained in Exercise 13.38 is based on an additional 10 orders. The results are shown on page 696 following Figure 13.40.

FIGURE 13.37   Residual Plots for Exercise 13.38

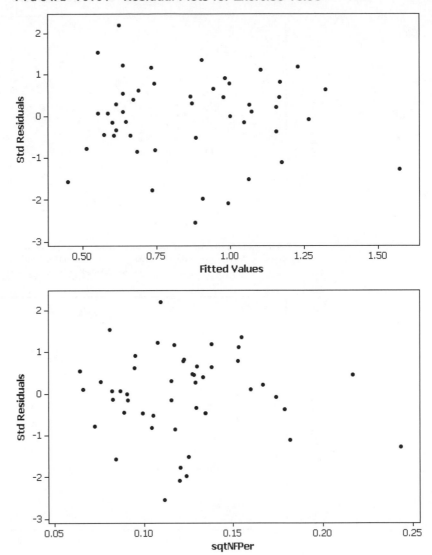

FIGURE 13.38 Residual Plots for Exercise 13.38

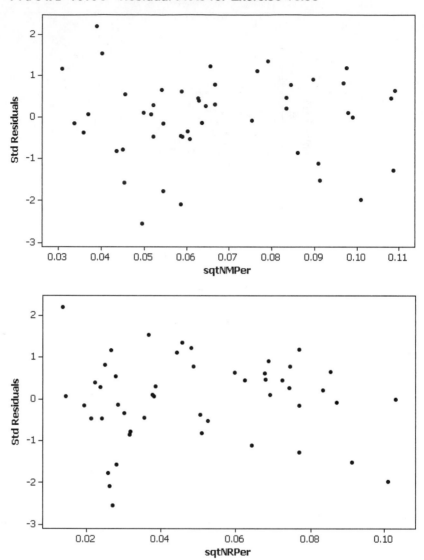

FIGURE 13.39   **Residual Plots for Exercise 13.38**

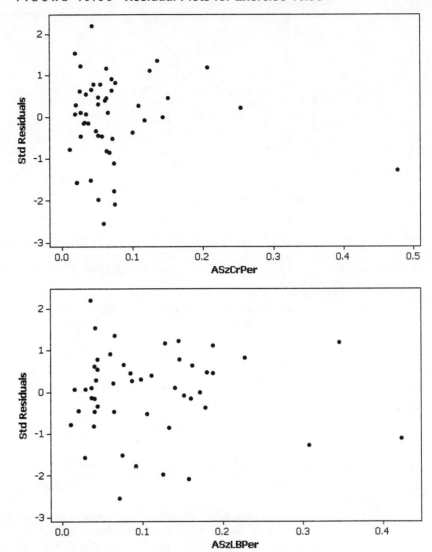

FIGURE 13.40 **Residual Plot for Exercise 13.38**

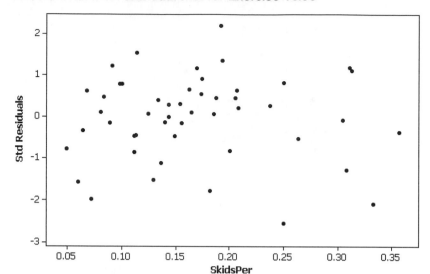

Actual Time	Time per Item	Regression Forecast	Superintendent's Forecast
36	.6316	.6691	.7895
24	1.0000	.9057	.8333
26	.7647	.8482	.7692
42	.7925	.6558	.9434
34	.5667	.5608	.8333
31	.9688	.9021	.7813
27	.8182	.9247	.9091
32	.6531	.7567	.8163
34	.8293	.9272	.7317
38	.7451	.7479	.7843

a. Compute the standard deviation of the regression prediction errors and the standard deviation of the superintendent's prediction errors.

b. Has the regression standard deviation increased from the standard deviation shown in Exercise 13.38?

c. Does the result of this study suggest that the regression model will yield better forecasts than the superintendent's forecasts?

13.40 An airline that is the major carrier at its airport hub analyzed its sales of full-fare seats on flights to various other cities. These sales are the most profitable for the airline, so it would like to reserve adequate space; full-fare passengers almost always reserve seats in the last few days before the flight. In addition, any exceptionally low sales figures may indicate a problem in scheduling or in operations at the destination city. For each of the airline's 315 weekly flights, the full-fare demand, averaged over 10 weeks, was determined; this demand included any requests for seats that couldn't be accommodated. In addition, the day of the flight (Sunday = 1 through Saturday = 7), the scheduled departure time (in military time, so 1700 = 5:00 P.M., for example), the airline's share of the gates at the destination airport, and the per capita income of the destination metropolitan area were recorded. The data are in the EX1340 file of the CD. Column 1 contains demand, column 2 has the day code, column 3 lists the departure time, column 4 is a dummy variable indicating the peak travel times (portions of Sunday afternoon, Monday morning, and Friday afternoon), column 5 contains the gate share, and column 6 has income.

a. Explain why it would not make sense to include day and departure time as independent variables in a first-order model for predicting demand.

b. Obtain a first-order regression equation using the peak-time dummy variable, gate share, and income as independent variables.

c. Have the computer program create two new variables by multiplying the dummy variable by gate share and by income. Obtain a regression equation including the previous three independent variables plus the two new ones.

d. Test the null hypothesis that the new product variables add no predictive value, given the previous three variables. Can this hypothesis be rejected at $\alpha = .05$? What does this test indicate about interaction in the data?

13.41 Obtain residuals from the regression equation without product terms found in Exercise 13.40.

a. Plot the residuals against predicted values. Is there a clear indication that variability increases as the predicted value increases?

b. Plot the residuals against gate share and against income. Is there a clear reason to incorporate nonlinear terms in these variables?

c. Plot the residuals against the dummy variable. Does this plot reveal anything?

d. Plot the residuals against observation number (time). Is there any evidence of a roughly cyclic pattern, which indicates autocorrelation?

e. Obtain the Durbin–Watson statistic for the model without product terms. Does this statistic indicate that there is a serious autocorrelation problem?

13.42 An auto-supply store had 60 months of data on variables that were thought to be relevant to sales. The data, stored in the EX1342 file of the CD, include monthly sales in thousands of dollars (column 1), average daily low temperature in degrees Fahrenheit (column 2), advertising expenditure for the month in thousands of dollars (column 3), used-car sales in the previous month (column 4), and month number (column 5).

a. Identify any variables that are already in lagged form.

b. Obtain a regression equation using temperature, current month's advertising, previous month's used-car sales, and month number as the independent variables.

c. Have your computer program create a one-month lagged variable for advertising expense. Use this lagged variable in place of the current month's advertising and obtain a new regression equation. Does this new model have a small residual standard deviation (and therefore a smaller mean square error) than the model in part (b)?

13.43 Consider the regression model using temperature, previous month's advertising, previous month's used-car sales, and month number, as in part (c) of Exercise 13.42.

a. Obtain correlations; is there a major collinearity problem?

b. Test to see if the four predictors together have at least some predictive value. Locate a p-value.

c. Test to see if each predictor adds statistically detectable predictive value, given the others. Locate p-values.

13.44 Obtain residuals for the model of Exercise 13.43.

a. Plot to see if there is evidence of nonconstant variance.

b. Plot to see if there is evidence of nonlinearity.

c. Plot to see if there is evidence of autocorrelation.

d. Obtain the Durbin–Watson statistic. What does it tell you?

13.45 Based on the results you obtained in the last three exercises, determine what changes, if any, you want to make in the regression model. Carry out these changes and see if the resulting regression model is more satisfactory.

13.46 A construction firm wanted to use regression methods to estimate the amount of concrete-block foundation that could be constructed in a day, using various combinations of workers and delivery vehicles. Data on a sample of recent projects are included in the EX1346 file on the CD. The variables are completion rate, the number of square feet of foundation wall constructed in a day (column 1), number of skilled workers (column 2), number of helpers (column 3), and number of delivery vehicles (column 4).

a. Obtain correlations. Is there an obvious collinearity problem?

b. Are there any variables that should be replaced by dummy variables? Would it make sense to have lagged variables?

c. Obtain a first-order regression model to predict completion rate and use the other variables as they are. Locate the coefficient of determination.

13.47 Obtain residuals from the regression model of Exercise 13.46.

a. Plot the residuals against the predicted values. Is there a "fan" shape characteristic of increasing variability? Is there any other evident problem?

b. Plot the residuals against each of the predictors. Is there any evidence of a high-influence outlier? Is there any other evident problem?

c. Why wouldn't the Durbin–Watson statistic be of much relevance in this problem?

13.48 Have your computer program calculate logarithms (natural, base e, if that's convenient) of all the variables from Exercise 13.46.

a. Obtain a regression equation using the logarithm of completion as the dependent variable and the other logarithm variables as independent variables.

b. Obtain residuals for this model and plot them against each independent variable. Is there an evident curve in any of the plots?

c. Convert (by hand) the logarithmic model back to a model in the original variables. Remember that the logarithm of a product is the sum of the logarithms of each component and that the logarithm of a variable raised to a power is the power times the logarithm of the variable.

BUSINESS CASES

Evaluating Sales Performance

The marketing managers of an office products company have some difficulty in evaluating the field sales representatives' performance. The representatives travel among the outlets for the company's products, create displays, try to increase volume, introduce new products, and discover any problems that the outlets are having with the company's products. The job involves a great deal of travel time. The marketing managers believe that one important factor in the representatives' performance is the motivation to spend a great deal of time on the road. Other variables also have an effect. Some sales districts have more potential than others, either because of differences in population or differences in the number of retail outlets. Large districts are difficult because of the extra travel time.

One important variable is compensation. Some of the representatives are paid a salary plus a commission on sales; others work entirely for a larger commission on sales. The marketing managers suspect that there is a difference between the two groups in their effectiveness, although some of them argue that the important factor is the combination of commission status and number of outlets. In particular, they suspect that commission-only representatives with many outlets to cover are highly productive. Also, the managers suspect that profit may be inflated for representatives with many outlets; they would prefer measuring profit per outlet.

Data are collected on 51 representatives. The data include DISTRICT number, PROFIT (net profit margin for all orders placed through the representative—the dependent variable of interest), AREA (of the district in thousands of square miles), POPN (millions of people in the district), OUTLETS (number of outlets in the district), and COMMIS, which is 1 for full-commission representatives and 0 for partially salaried representatives.

Assignment: Use the tabulated data to perform a multiple regression analysis. Find out if the variables suspected by the managers as having an effect on PROFIT actually do have an effect; in particular, try to discover if there is a combination effect of COMMIS and OUTLETS. Consider whether PROFIT itself or PROFIT divided by OUTLETS works better as a dependent variable. Omit variables that show little predictive value. Locate and, if possible, correct any serious violations of assumptions. Write a brief report to the marketing managers and explain your findings; the managers are not familiar with the technical language of statistics, although they do have an idea what a standard deviation is.

DIST	PROFIT	AREA	POPN	OUTLETS	COMMIS
1	1011	16.96	3.881	213	1
2	1318	7.31	3.141	158	1
3	1556	7.81	3.766	203	1
4	1521	7.31	4.587	170	1
5	979	19.84	3.648	142	1
6	1290	12.37	3.456	159	1
7	1596	6.15	3.695	178	1
8	1155	14.21	3.609	182	1
9	1412	7.45	3.801	181	1
10	1194	14.43	3.322	148	1
11	1054	6.12	5.124	227	0
12	1157	11.71	4.158	139	1
13	1001	9.36	3.887	179	0
14	831	19.14	2.230	124	1
15	857	11.75	4.468	205	0
16	188	40.34	.297	85	1
17	1030	7.16	4.224	211	0
18	1331	9.37	3.427	145	1
19	643	7.62	4.031	205	1
20	992	27.54	2.370	166	1
21	795	15.97	3.903	149	1
22	1340	12.97	3.423	186	1
23	689	17.36	2.390	141	0
24	1726	6.24	4.947	223	1
25	1056	11.20	4.166	176	0
26	989	18.09	4.063	187	1
27	895	13.32	3.105	131	1
28	1028	14.97	4.116	170	0
29	771	21.92	1.510	144	1

DIST	PROFIT	AREA	POPN	OUTLETS	COMMIS
30	484	34.91	.741	126	1
31	917	8.46	5.260	234	0
32	1786	7.52	5.744	210	0
33	1063	14.43	2.703	141	1
34	1001	15.37	3.583	158	0
35	1052	11.20	4.469	167	1
36	1610	7.20	4.951	174	1
37	1486	13.49	3.474	211	1
38	1576	6.56	4.637	172	1
39	1665	9.35	3.900	185	1
40	878	11.12	3.766	166	0
41	849	10.58	3.876	189	0
42	775	17.82	2.753	164	0
43	1012	10.03	4.449	193	0
44	1436	10.01	4.680	157	1
45	798	10.70	4.806	200	0
46	519	24.38	2.367	142	0
47	1701	6.57	5.563	199	0
48	1387	6.64	4.357	166	1
49	1717	9.24	4.670	221	1
50	1032	11.62	3.993	180	0
51	973	12.85	3.923	193	0

Westmore MBA Program

The MBA program at Westmore University has undergone several dramatic changes over the past five years. During that time, the goal of the business school was to recruit as many students as possible into the MBA program in order to build up its student base and credit-hour production. Five years ago the school launched a massive campaign to attract more applicants. Special brochures were printed and mailed to prospective students as well as to other colleges and universities likely to have undergraduates who might be interested in coming to Westmore. Mailings were also sent to students who indicated an interest in Westmore on their GMAT exam (a national standardized test used by most business schools in making graduate admissions decisions). Representatives from the Westmore School of Business began attending regional "MBA fairs" where they could meet with prospective MBA students and share information. In the beginning, the number of students applying to the Westmore MBA program was small, but eventually the advertising campaign began to work and the number of qualified applicants each year increased to the target value of 150 initially set by the dean and the director of the MBA program. The yield, that is, the number of admitted applicants who actually enroll and attend Westmore, is typically around 70%. Admitted students who do not enroll either attend other MBA programs or accept job offers. The following table shows the admissions and enrollment figures for the five years of the MBA student-base building plan at Westmore.

Year	Admissions	Enrollment
1	86	54
2	108	77
3	134	91
4	141	96
5	154	106

Wayne McDonald, the director of the program, is currently putting the second phase of the plan into action. He knows that in order for the MBA program at Westmore to attain national recognition the admissions process must become more selective. The number of applicants is now large enough to do this without falling below a critical mass of 60 enrolled students each year.

The major issue is how to go about selecting students. Wayne recently met with the MBA admissions committee, which consists of himself and two faculty members, Dr. Susan Thompson, who is a finance professor, and Dr. Hector Gonzalez, who is a marketing professor.

Wayne: Thanks for coming today. You both know our recruiting efforts over the past five years have been really successful, and last year we even exceeded our original enrollment goal. Many of our students have been outstanding and have given our program visibility in the business community, but we've had a number of weak performers. Professors have watered down their courses to keep these people afloat. If we're to have a nationally recognized, high-quality MBA program, we must get stricter in our admission policies. Fortunately, we're now at the point where we can be much more selective and still have our yearly minimum critical mass of 60 enrollees.

Susan: Wayne's right. Our current admission standards require a minimum score of 400 on the GMAT and a minimum undergraduate GPA of 2.0. This is obviously not much of a hurdle. Personally, I'd like to see the minimum requirements set at 580 on the GMAT and 2.75 for the GPA.

Wayne: Well, raising the minimums is one way of going about it, but many other factors determine a student's success and we should consider including these factors in our decision making.

Hector: Too bad we don't know in advance which students are going to excel. Wayne, do you know what other schools are doing?

Wayne: From conferences I've attended, I've found that many MBA programs put a lot of emphasis on the GMAT score and the undergraduate GPA. Some schools set minimum entrance requirements on each of these, as we do currently; others combine them into a single overall score. For instance, there's a "formula score" used by many schools that multiplies the undergraduate GPA by 200 and adds the result to the GMAT score. If the formula score is above a certain figure, say 1000, then the student is considered admittable.

Susan: But there are so many other factors. Surely we don't want our admissions decisions to be based solely on a formula. Many students attend colleges with a high level of grade inflation. They would have an unfair advantage with regard to GPA over applicants from stronger schools.

Hector: I agree. Studies have also indicated the GMAT is not a strong predictor of success in graduate school for many reasons, including cultural bias.

Wayne: I'm not suggesting we go to a strictly mathematical basis for making our decisions. But higher minimum standards than we currently have or some sort of formula involving GMAT and GPA might be useful for screening applicants.

Susan: I'm not opposed—we could use something like that to identify those with high potential for success. In a sense, many of these decisions could be automated.

Wayne: That would certainly be a great timesaver. Then we'd only have to meet to discuss those applicants with other strong characteristics or extenuating circumstances.

Susan: I'm in favor of that! Now, if we go with raising the minimum requirements for GMAT and GPA, how much should we raise them? Or if we go with a combined-score approach, what formula should we use and how should we set its cutoff values?

Wayne: We could go with your earlier suggestion of a 580/2.75 minimum requirement or with the formula score I just spoke of. I could talk with directors of other MBA programs to find out how they set their cutoff criteria. And after we get some experience we could adjust our cutoff.

Hector: Why wait? We have five years' worth of data already! We should be able to develop our own criteria based on our own past experience.

Susan: We might even consider developing our own formula.

Wayne: Great ideas! That's why I like working with the two of you on this committee. But I'd limit the data to the last two years because of the changes we made in the program a few years back. The data for the last two years are more reflective of our current program.

Hector: How are we going to measure the degree to which a student is successful? Whether they graduate or not?

Wayne: Well, fortunately or unfortunately, depending on how you look at it, practically all of our students have eventually graduated. One thing we're trying to accomplish is to make our program more rigorous and demanding, to raise the level of quality. If this is going to happen, we have to be more selective in admissions.

Susan: Why not consider the GPA at the end of the program?

Wayne: The major problem with that, don't forget, is not everyone takes the same set of courses in the second year because of different areas of concentration. Some go into marketing, some into finance, others into either accounting or management. There's a real lack of comparability in those final GPA figures. But what we might do is look at the first-year GPA. Those courses are essentially the same because they're required. What first-year GPA would the two of you, as faculty members, set as indicating a successful first year?

Hector: Given the breadth of those first-year core courses, their level of difficulty, and our mild degree of grade inflation, I'd say that any student in the past two years with at least a 3.2 average would be considered successful in the first year. Would you agree, Susan?

Susan: I believe most of the faculty would go along with that.

Wayne: Don't set your goals too high! Remember, we need at least 60 students per year to even have a program. We probably need to look at the data to see what's possible.

Hector: When can we get access to the past data? I'd really like to get started.

Wayne: I'll have someone on the staff write a database program to pull up the relevant information on all students who completed the first year of the program in the past two years and I'll get the data to you as soon as I can. Let's plan to meet again in two weeks to see what we've discovered by then. I look forward to hearing your ideas.

Assignment: Wayne McDonald's assistant gathered the data for the past two years on students in the Westmore MBA program. Using this data set and other information given in the case, help Wayne and the MBA admissions committee develop admissions guidelines. In particular, you should examine the usefulness of the suggested guidelines discussed by the committee and consider the possibility of modifying its proposals. Keep in mind that you want to set the guidelines in such a way that the best students are selected and the minimum enrollment of 60 students per year is reached. For each proposal you consider, check for any potential bias in the guidelines, that is, check to see if there were any unsuccessful students in the past two years who meet the proposed guidelines or any successful students in the past two years who would not meet them.

Write a report to Wayne and the committee providing your analysis of the data and final recommendation. The report should consist of two parts: (1) a one-page memo that briefly summarizes the results of your analysis and your recommendation, and (2) a detailed analysis of the data that describes your analysis and interpretations. Incorporate important details, graphs, and tables from your analysis into your report to support your recommendation.

The data are contained in the file Westmore on the CD that came with your book. The file contains data for 202 students who completed their first year in the MBA program over the past two years. A partial listing of the data within Excel is shown in Figure 13.41.

FIGURE 13.41   **Partial Listing of the Westmore MBA Program Data**

	A	B	C	D	E	F	G	H
1	ID	MBA GPA	GMAT	UGPA	Major	School	Age	Foreign
2	4001	3.201	540	2.974	1	3	25	0
3	4002	2.964	540	2.529	1	4	23	0
4	4003	3.745	510	3.727	3	4	25	0
5	4004	3.290	570	2.905	1	3	23	0
6	4005	3.028	640	2.641	1	5	23	0
7	4006	2.855	540	2.720	1	4	25	0
8	4007	2.847	470	2.600	1	3	25	0
9	4008	3.392	670	3.226	1	4	25	0
10	4009	3.035	560	2.991	3	3	23	0
11	4010	3.006	540	2.814	3	3	24	0
12	4011	2.902	570	2.814	2	3	24	0
13	4012	3.836	700	3.965	1	3	25	0
14	4013	3.275	640	3.221	1	5	23	0
15	4014	3.256	610	2.582	1	4	22	0
16	4015	3.283	640	2.459	2	4	22	0
17	4016	3.006	510	2.950	1	3	23	1
18	4017	3.633	650	3.541	2	5	23	0

In the Westmore file, the variables are defined as follows:

ID: Student identification number

MBA GPA: Grade point average for the first year of courses in the Westmore
                    MBA program

GMAT: Score on the GMAT test

UGPA: Undergraduate grade point average

Major: 1, if business undergraduate,
                    2, if science, engineering, or other technical,
                    3, otherwise

School: 5, if in the top 20% of undergraduate schools,
                    4, if in the second 20%,
                    3, if in the third 20%,
                    2, if in the fourth 20%,
                    1, if in the bottom 20%

Age: Age of the student in years

Foreign: 1, if foreign citizen,
                    0, if U.S. citizen

Review Exercises—Chapters 11–13

13.49   A contractor bids on many small jobs. The current process of preparing bids is expensive and time-consuming. An attempt is made to predict y, the total direct cost of a job, based on x, the direct labor hours required. Data are collected on 26 jobs:

x:	214	228	235	239	247	248	278	289	291
y:	7444	7223	10,509	8931	9674	8084	11,784	10,067	11,344

x:	298	306	314	319	333	353	364	464	495
y:	7355	14,946	15,088	7409	15,475	11,524	13,209	16,012	22,570

x:	505	607	625	651	738	771	796	840
y:	26,285	18,427	22,892	20,689	33,636	28,465	22,018	29,744

The following regression output was obtained using Minitab:

```
Regression Analysis: Cost versus Labor

The regression equation is
Cost = 1161 + 34.6 Labor

Predictor     Coef  SE Coef      T      P
Constant      1161     1677   0.69  0.496
Labor       34.562    3.524   9.81  0.000

S = 3462.08   R-Sq = 80.7%   R-Sq(adj) = 79.9%

Analysis of Variance

Source          DF          SS          MS      F      P
Regression       1  1152786655  1152786655  96.18  0.000
Residual Error  23   275679557    11986068
Total           24  1428466212
```

  a. Write out the least-squares regression equation.
  b. What is the economic interpretation of the slope coefficient?
  c. What is the economic interpretation of the intercept coefficient?
  d. Locate the residual standard deviation. Interpret its numerical value using the Empirical Rule.

13.50 Locate the correlation between x and y for the data of the preceding exercise. Interpret the resulting number.

13.51 Refer again to the regression of total cost on direct labor hours in Exercise 13.49.
  a. Locate the estimated standard error of the slope.
  b. Find a 95% confidence interval for the true value of the slope.

13.52 In the regression of cost on labor hours in the preceding exercises, is the null hypothesis that the slope is zero economically plausible? Can this hypothesis be rejected conclusively by the data?

13.53 Refer to Exercise 13.49.
  a. The contractor has a new job with $x = 890$ hours. Calculate the predicted y value for the actual cost.
  b. The contractor has another new job with $x = 436$ hours. Calculate the predicted y value for the actual cost.
  c. Which of the predictions calculated in parts (a) and (b) should be more accurate? Why?

13.54 A plot of the residuals from the regression analysis of the data of Exercise 13.49 shows that residuals corresponding to small x values are small positive or negative numbers, but that several of the residuals corresponding to large x values are relatively large in magnitude. What regression assumption is called into question by this finding? What are the consequences for the interpretation of the output?

13.55 A bank that offers charge cards to customers studies the yearly purchase amount on the card as related to the age, income, and years of education of the cardholder and whether the cardholder owns or rents a home. The following Minitab output is obtained; the variables are self-explanatory, except for Owner, which equals 1 if the cardholder owns a home and 0 if the cardholder rents a home.

```
Correlations: Purchase, Age, Income, Owner, Education

             Purchase       Age      Income     Owner
Age            0.932
Income         0.928      0.837
Owner          0.462      0.212      0.686
Education      0.222      0.057      0.310     0.476

Regression Analysis: Purchase versus Age, Income, Owner, Education

The regression equation is
Purchase = - 0.744 + 0.0329 Age + 0.00899 Income + 0.115 Owner
           + 0.00817 Education

Predictor       Coef    SE Coef        T      P    VIF
Constant     -0.74438    0.06977   -10.67  0.000
Age          0.032896   0.003809     8.64  0.000   20.4
Income       0.008999   0.005075     1.77  0.078   36.7
Owner         0.11501    0.04981     2.31  0.022   11.4
Education    0.008176   0.003611     2.26  0.025    1.3

S = 0.0926341   R-Sq = 94.6%   R-Sq(adj) = 94.4%
```

```
Analysis of Variance

Source                DF        SS       MS        F       P
Regression             4   23.1294   5.7824   673.85   0.000
Residual Error       155    1.3301   0.0086
Total                159   24.4595

Source       DF   Seq SS
Age           1   21.2585
Income        1    1.7745
Owner         1    0.0524
Education     1    0.0440
```

a. Locate the least-squares regression equation.
b. Explain what each slope coefficient means.
c. How meaningful is the intercept term?

13.56   Refer to the Minitab output of Exercise 13.55.
a. What would the hypothesis "all slopes are zero" mean about predictability in this context?
b. Show that this null hypothesis may be rejected emphatically.
c. What do the various t statistics indicate about the incremental predictive value of the variables?

13.57   Is there evidence of collinearity in the Minitab output of Exercise 13.55?

13.58   A stepwise regression of the purchase amount data of Exercise 13.55 was conducted using Minitab, yielding the following output:

```
Stepwise Regression: Purchase versus Age, Income, Owner, Education

   F-to-Enter: 0.01   F-to-Remove: 0.01

Response is Purchase on 4 predictors, with N = 160

Step                  1        2        3        4
Constant        -0.5865  -0.5672  -0.6789  -0.7444

Age             0.04200  0.03936  0.03946  0.03289
T-Value           32.39    44.58    45.34     8.64
P-Value           0.000    0.000    0.000    0.000

Owner                      0.218    0.198    0.115
T-Value                    14.13    11.47     2.31
P-Value                    0.000    0.000    0.022

Education                           0.0088   0.0082
T-Value                               2.44     2.26
P-Value                              0.016    0.025

Income                                       0.0090
T-Value                                        1.77
P-Value                                       0.078

S                 0.142   0.0947   0.0933   0.0926
R-Sq              86.91    94.24    94.45    94.56
R-Sq(adj)         86.83    94.17    94.35    94.42
Mallows C-p       217.0     10.2      6.1      5.0
```

a. Is the order in which the predictors enter the model the same as that indicated by the correlations of the predictors with Purchase?
b. Do the coefficients change a great deal as new predictors are entered?
c. Based on the stepwise output, what predictors would you use?
d. Calculate the C_p statistic for this model (relative to the all-predictors model). Does the value of this statistic indicate that your choice of predictors is sensible?

13.59   Additional predictor variables for the purchase amount problem of Exercise 13.55 are created by multiplying Owner by each of the other independent variables. Minitab output is shown here; the product terms are indicated as a product of *X* variables.

```
Regression Analysis: Purchase versus Age, Income, ...

The regression equation is
Purchase = - 0.916 + 0.0272 Age + 0.0204 Income + 0.247 Owner
           + 0.00535 Education + 0.00042 Own*Age - 0.0066 Own*Inc
           + 0.00509 Own*Ed

Predictor        Coef    SE Coef       T       P      VIF
Constant      -0.9156     0.1332   -6.87   0.000
Age          0.027249   0.005535    4.92   0.000     43.4
Income       0.020373   0.008714    2.34   0.021    109.3
Owner          0.2468     0.2083    1.18   0.238    201.7
Education    0.005361   0.005250    1.02   0.309      2.8
Own*Age      0.000432   0.009902    0.04   0.965   1036.1
Own*Inc      -0.00655    0.01311   -0.50   0.618   2180.8
Own*Ed       0.005105   0.007254    0.70   0.483     52.7

S = 0.0921737   R-Sq = 94.7%   R-Sq(adj) = 94.5%

Analysis of Variance

Source            DF        SS       MS        F       P
Regression         7   23.1681   3.3097   389.56   0.000
Residual Error   152    1.2914   0.0085
Total            159   24.4595

Source        DF    Seq SS
Age            1   21.2585
Income         1    1.7745
Owner          1    0.0524
Education      1    0.0440
Own*Age        1    0.0327
Own*Inc        1    0.0018
Own*Ed         1    0.0042
```

a. What is the reason for introducing the three product terms?
b. Test the null hypothesis that the coefficients of all the product terms are zero.

13.60   Residuals for the product terms model are plotted against predicted values, as shown in Figure 13.42 on the next page. Are there any obvious violations of regression assumptions?

13.61   Another regression model for the purchase amount data of Exercise 13.55 is attempted using the natural logarithm of Income, rather than Income itself, as an independent variable. The following output is from Minitab:

```
Regression Analysis: Purchase versus Age, LogIncome, Owner, Education

The regression equation is
Purchase = - 3.38 + 0.0247 Age + 0.913 LogIncome + 0.0118 Owner
           + 0.00783 Education

Predictor        Coef    SE Coef       T       P      VIF
Constant      -3.3834     0.6754   -5.01   0.000
Age          0.024719   0.003765    6.57   0.000     21.5
LogIncome      0.9134     0.2273    4.02   0.000     38.7
Owner         0.01182    0.04915    0.24   0.810     12.0
Education    0.007844   0.003462    2.27   0.025      1.3

S = 0.0890447   R-Sq = 95.0%   R-Sq(adj) = 94.8%
```

FIGURE 13.42   **Residuals Versus Predicted Values for Purchase Data**

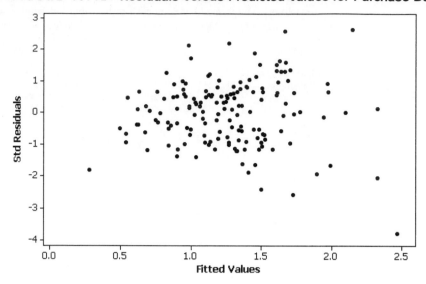

```
Analysis of Variance

Source            DF        SS        MS        F        P
Regression         4   23.2305    5.8076   732.46    0.000
Residual Error   155    1.2290    0.0079
Total            159   24.4595

Source       DF    Seq SS
Age           1   21.2585
LogIncome     1    1.9296
Owner         1    0.0016
Education     1    0.0407
```

a. As compared to the original model, has predictive value improved?

b. As compared to the original model, is the incremental predictive value of the LogIncome variable greater?

c. Is the LogIncome variable more statistically significant than the Income variable in the original model?

13.62   A regression model is constructed to predict the spread between interest rates of government bonds (risk-free) and corporate bonds rated BAA (somewhat risky). The independent variables are a privately constructed leading economic indicator (Leading), a measure of the relative supply of corporate and governmental bonds in a given month (Supply), the actual rate of government bonds in that month (Rate), and the month number (Month). Minitab output follows. A scatterplot matrix is shown in Figure 13.43. Is there evidence of collinearity in the data? Of a nonlinear relation? Of outliers?

```
Correlations: Spread, Leading, Supply, Rate, Month

           Spread   Leading   Supply    Rate
Leading    -0.848
Supply      0.678    -0.235
Rate        0.871    -0.982    0.265
Month      -0.860     0.997   -0.251   -0.986
```

13.63   A regression model is constructed using the bond spread data of Exercise 13.62, omitting Month. Minitab output is shown next.

FIGURE 13.43 **Scatterplot Matrix for Bond Spread Data**

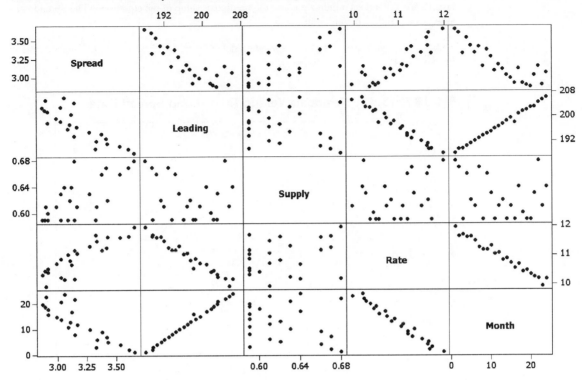

Regression Analysis: Spread versus Leading, Supply, Rate

The regression equation is
Spread = - 0.81 - 0.00524 Leading + 3.59 Supply + 0.255 Rate

Predictor	Coef	SE Coef	T	P	VIF
Constant	-0.807	2.373	-0.34	0.737	
Leading	-0.005253	0.007912	-0.66	0.514	28.4
Supply	3.5893	0.2721	13.19	0.000	1.1
Rate	0.25469	0.07724	3.30	0.004	28.8

S = 0.0395660   R-Sq = 97.5%   R-Sq(adj) = 97.2%

Analysis of Variance

Source	DF	SS	MS	F	P
Regression	3	1.23938	0.41312	263.90	0.000
Residual Error	20	0.03130	0.00156		
Total	23	1.27069			

Source	DF	Seq SS
Leading	1	0.91391
Supply	1	0.30844
Rate	1	0.01701

Durbin-Watson statistic = 1.05624

a. Show that the null hypothesis (all slopes are zero) can be rejected at any reasonable level of significance.

b. Do all the t tests of individual slopes lead to rejection of the null hypothesis?

13.64 Locate the residual standard deviation in the bond spread regression output of Exercise 13.63. What does it indicate about the predictive value of the equation? (The Spread variable has a standard deviation of about .2.)

13.65 The residuals for the bond spread model of Exercise 13.62 are plotted against time in Figure 13.44.

FIGURE 13.44   Residuals Versus Time—Bond Spread Data

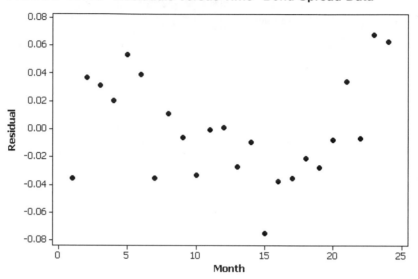

a. Does there appear to be a violation of regression assumptions?
b. Show that the regression output indicates a violation.
c. What are the consequences of this violation?

13.66 The bond spread data of Exercise 13.62 are converted to differences and the model is recalculated. Minitab output follows:

```
Regression Analysis: DSpread versus DLeading, DSupply, DRate

The regression equation is
DSpread = - 0.0001 - 0.0046 DLeading + 3.16 DSupply + 0.216 DRate

23 cases used, 1 cases contain missing values

Predictor      Coef   SE Coef        T      P   VIF
Constant    -0.00004   0.01211    -0.00  0.997
DLeading    -0.00458   0.01076    -0.43  0.675   1.1
DSupply       3.1579    0.1667    18.94  0.000   1.1
DRate        0.21557   0.04824     4.47  0.000   1.0

S = 0.0343691   R-Sq = 95.8%   R-Sq(adj) = 95.2%

Analysis of Variance

Source          DF        SS        MS       F      P
Regression       3   0.51769   0.17256  146.09  0.000
Residual Error  19   0.02243   0.00117
Total           22   0.54014
```

```
Source     DF   Seq SS
DLeading    1   0.03717
DSupply     1   0.45694
DRate       1   0.02357

Durbin-Watson statistic = 2.30355
```

a. How much have the coefficients changed as compared to those in the original model?

b. Have the results of F and t tests changed, as compared to the previous results? If so, which set of tests is more believable?

c. Does it appear that working with differences has cured the violation of assumptions found previously?

13.67   The residuals from the difference model of Exercise 13.66 are plotted against month number in Figure 13.45. Is there a clear pattern in this plot? Should there be, given the Durbin–Watson results?

FIGURE 13.45   Residuals Versus Time—Difference Model

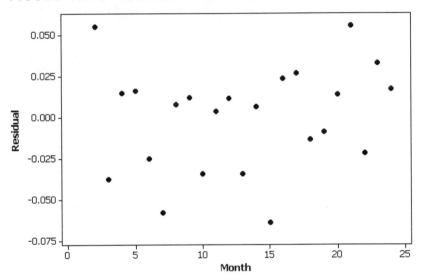

13.68   Correlations for the difference data of Exercise 13.67 are shown here. Has differencing decreased collinearity?

```
Correlations: DSpread, DLeading, DSupply, DRate

          DSpread   DLeading   DSupply
DLeading   0.262
DSupply    0.956     0.275
DRate      0.355     0.132      0.157
```

13.69   An oil company does a small study of the sale of kerosene at its service stations. The dependent variable is monthly sales (thousands of gallons) of kerosene. The independent variables are monthly sales of gasoline (thousands of gallons), average income in the census tract where the station is located, and a rough index of the amount of traffic past the station. The sample is of 21 company stations in a particular month. The data were analyzed using Excel.

```
Correlations
          Kero     Gas      Avginc   Traffic
Kero      1.0000
Gas       0.7559   1.0000
Avginc    0.3736   0.5321   1.0000
Traffic   0.5601   0.5659   0.3768   1.0000

Regression Statistics
Multiple R              0.7745
R Square               0.5999
Adjusted R Square      0.5293
Standard Error         4.3406
Observations               21
ANOVA
                df       SS       MS       F     Significance F
Regression       3   480.172  160.057   8.495          0.001
Residual        17   320.295   18.841
Total           20   800.467

             Coefficients  Standard Error   t Stat   P-value
Intercept        -3.333          8.682     -0.384     0.706
Gas               0.079          0.024      3.294     0.004
Avginc           -0.132          0.392     -0.336     0.741
Traffic           7.861          7.304      1.076     0.297
```

a. Locate the least-squares regression equation. Interpret each of the slopes.

b. Negative sales are impossible; should we be concerned about a negative intercept?

13.70 Refer to the Excel output of the kerosene sales model of Exercise 13.69.

a. Locate SS(Regression).

b. Do the results of t tests also suggest deleting one or more independent variables from the model?

13.71 Refer again to Exercise 13.69.

a. Does the Excel output for the kerosene sales data indicate a serious collinearity problem?

b. Would one expect autocorrelation in this study?

13.72 Refer to Exercise 13.69. A plot of residuals versus predicted values is shown in Figure 13.46. Is there evidence of nonconstant variance? Are there any potentially serious outliers?

FIGURE 13.46 **Residuals Versus Predicted for Kerosene Sales Data**

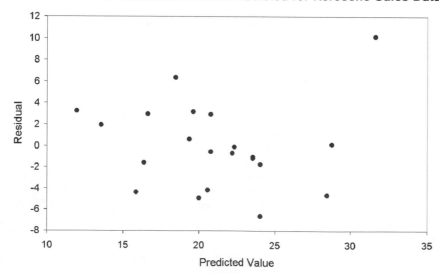

13.73 It is discovered that station number 9 in the kerosene sales data of Exercise 13.69 has a rather large contract to supply kerosene to a group of stores. No other station known to the company has a similar contract. Therefore, station 9 is deleted from the sample and the regression is recalculated. The variables are given an N (no-contracts) prefix. Excel output follows:

```
Regression Statistics
Multiple R          0.7165
R Square            0.5134
Adjusted R Sq       0.4221
Standard Error      3.2585
Observations            20
ANOVA
                df          SS        MS        F   Significance F
Regression       3   179.2128   59.7376   5.6260          0.0079
Residual        16   169.8892   10.6181
Total           19   349.1020
              Coefficients   Standard Error   t Stat   P-value
Intercept         7.8171          7.1591      1.0919    0.2910
NGas              0.0640          0.0185      3.4512    0.0033
NAvginc          -0.2793          0.2972     -0.9395    0.3614
NTraffic          2.9033          5.6394      0.5148    0.6137
```

a. Have the regression slopes changed because of the omission of station 9?
b. How has the residual standard deviation changed?
c. How has the coefficient of determination changed?

13.74 The kerosene sales data of Exercise 13.69, omitting station 9, were also modeled using only "NGas" as a predictor, yielding the following Excel output:

```
Regression Statistics
Multiple R          0.7587
R Square            0.5756
Adjusted R Sq       0.5520
Standard Error      4.2417
Observations            20
ANOVA
                df          SS         MS         F    Significance F
Regression       1   439.2271   439.2271   24.4122          0.0001
Residual        18   323.8584    17.9921
Total           19   763.0855
```

Test the null hypothesis that the coefficients of NAvginc and NTraffic are both zero. Can this hypothesis be rejected at the usual α values?

13.75 Data are collected on the yield of a chemical under various combinations of temperature and pressure. The data were as follows:

TEMP	PRES	YIELD	TEMP	PRES	YIELD	TEMP	PRES	YIELD
2200	3.8	75.50	2250	3.8	76.80	2300	3.8	78.50
2200	4.2	77.90	2250	4.2	79.20	2300	4.2	80.20
2200	3.8	75.90	2250	3.8	76.00	2300	3.8	78.80
2200	4.2	77.90	2250	4.2	78.90	2300	4.2	80.20

a. A plot of temperature versus pressure is shown in Figure 13.47. What must the value of $r_{\text{TEMP,PRES}}$ be?
b. How severe is the collinearity problem for these data?

FIGURE 13.47   **Plot of Temperature and Pressure for Yield Data**

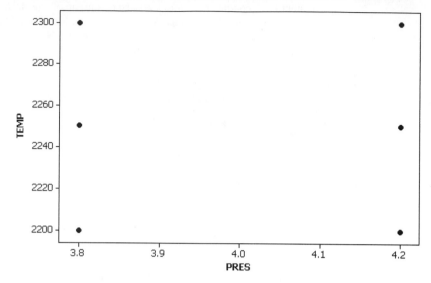

13.76   A regression model is fit to the yield data of Exercise 13.75. Minitab output follows:

```
Regression Analysis: YIELD versus TEMP, PRES

The regression equation is
YIELD = - 2.41 + 0.0262 TEMP + 5.33 PRES

Predictor       Coef    SE Coef      T       P   VIF
Constant      -2.412      6.915   -0.35   0.735
TEMP        0.026250   0.002889    9.09   0.000   1.0
PRES          5.3333     0.5897    9.04   0.000   1.0

S = 0.408532   R-Sq = 94.8%   R-Sq(adj) = 93.7%

Analysis of Variance

Source          DF      SS       MS       F       P
Regression       2   27.435   13.717   82.19   0.000
Residual Error   9    1.502    0.167
Total           11   28.937

Source   DF   Seq SS
TEMP      1   13.781
PRES      1   13.653

Unusual Observations

Obs   TEMP   YIELD     Fit   SE Fit   Residual   St Resid
  7   2250   76.000   76.917   0.167    -0.917      -2.46R

R denotes an observation with a large standardized residual.

Durbin-Watson statistic = 2.27796
```

a. Locate the prediction equation.
b. Roughly, what is the width of a 95% prediction interval for a value of YIELD? Assume that any extrapolation penalty can be neglected.

13.77   Summarize the results of overall F and t tests for the yield data of Exercise 13.75. What do the results indicate about the predictive value of TEMP and PRES?

13.78 A residual plot against values of TEMP for the yield model of Exercise 13.75 is shown in Figure 13.48. Is there any evidence of a problem shown by this plot?

FIGURE 13.48 **Residuals Versus Temperature—Yield Data**

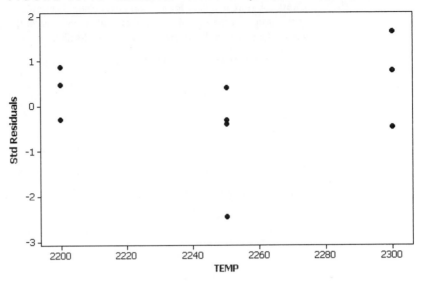

13.79 Based on the residual plot of Exercise 13.78, a new variable is created: TEMPSQ = $(TEMP - 2250)^2$. A new regression analysis is performed.

```
Regression Analysis: YIELD versus TEMP, PRES, TEMPSQ

The regression equation is
YIELD = - 2.67 + 0.0262 TEMP + 5.33 PRES + 0.000155 TEMPSQ

Predictor        Coef      SE Coef       T      P   VIF
Constant       -2.671        6.283   -0.43  0.682
TEMP         0.026250     0.002624   10.00  0.000   1.0
PRES           5.3333       0.5356    9.96  0.000   1.0
TEMPSQ     0.00015500   0.00009090    1.71  0.127   1.0

S = 0.371091   R-Sq = 96.2%   R-Sq(adj) = 94.8%

Analysis of Variance

Source            DF       SS       MS       F      P
Regression         3  27.8349   9.2783   67.38  0.000
Residual Error     8   1.1017   0.1377
Total             11  28.9366

Source   DF   Seq SS
TEMP      1  13.7811
PRES      1  13.6532
TEMPSQ    1   0.4004

Unusual Observations

Obs  TEMP   YIELD     Fit  SE Fit  Residual  St Resid
  7  2250  76.000  76.658   0.214    -0.658     -2.17R

R denotes an observation with a large standardized residual.

Durbin-Watson statistic = 2.88608
```

a. Have the coefficients of TEMP and PRES changed much?

b. Does adding TEMPSQ greatly improve the prediction of YIELD? Indicate the parts of the output that support your judgment.

c. Is there reason to be concerned about autocorrelation in this study?

13.80 A store manager for a supermarket chain does a regression study of the weekly sales of the store and the volume of promotional activity (advertising and coupons) the previous week. The resulting data were analyzed using Minitab.

```
Regression Analysis: Sales versus Promo

The regression equation is
Sales = - 7.8 + 5.31 Promo

Predictor    Coef   SE Coef      T      P
Constant    -7.79     24.95  -0.31  0.758
Promo      5.3129    0.6382   8.33  0.000

S = 12.9635   R-Sq = 75.9%   R-Sq(adj) = 74.8%

Analysis of Variance

Source           DF      SS     MS      F      P
Regression        1   11647  11647  69.31  0.000
Residual Error   22    3697    168
Total            23   15344

Unusual Observations

Obs   Promo    Sales     Fit  SE Fit  Residual  St Resid
  1    43.0   247.00  220.67    3.73     26.33      2.12R

R denotes an observation with a large standardized residual.

Durbin-Watson statistic = 0.433104
```

a. Is there evidence of a statistically significant predictive value of Promo for predicting Sales?

b. How much of the variability (squared error) of Sales is accounted for by Promo?

13.81 The Minitab output for the sales and promotion model in Exercise 13.80 indicates that there is a serious violation of at least one assumption. What is it, how do you know that this violation has occurred, and what are the consequences of the violation on your answers in the previous exercise?

13.82 Differences are calculated for the sales and promotion data of Exercise 13.80 and a new regression equation is found.

```
Regression Analysis: DSales versus DPromo

The regression equation is
DSales = - 1.70 + 5.02 DPromo

23 cases used, 1 cases contain missing values

Predictor    Coef  SE Coef      T      P
Constant   -1.696    1.737  -0.98  0.340
DPromo     5.0187   0.2764  18.16  0.000

S = 8.32823   R-Sq = 94.0%   R-Sq(adj) = 93.7%
```

Analysis of Variance

```
Source           DF      SS      MS       F      P
Regression        1   22870   22870  329.74  0.000
Residual Error   21    1457      69
Total            22   24327
```

Unusual Observations

```
Obs  DPromo  DSales    Fit  SE Fit  Residual  St Resid
 10     6.0   45.00  28.42    2.40     16.58     2.08R
```

R denotes an observation with a large standardized residual.

Durbin-Watson statistic = 1.43141

a. Is there a statistically significant predictive value of DPROMO for predicting DSALES?

b. How much of the variability of DSALES is accounted for by variation in DPROMO?

c. How do your answers here compare to the answers for the undifferenced model?

13.83 Did the use of differences in Exercise 13.82 reduce the violation of assumptions in the original model?

13.84 In a paper mill, a liquid slurry of wood fibers is forced through a screen. The yield of fibers is known to increase as the difference in pressure between the two sides of the screen increases. Data are collected and a regression equation is found.

Regression Analysis: Yield versus ChgPres

The regression equation is
Yield = 60.8 + 0.630 ChgPres

```
Predictor       Coef   SE Coef       T      P
Constant     60.7843    0.9604   63.29  0.000
ChgPres      0.63001   0.03095   20.35  0.000
```

S = 2.43493   R-Sq = 93.7%   R-Sq(adj) = 93.4%

Analysis of Variance

```
Source           DF      SS      MS       F      P
Regression        1  2456.0  2456.0  414.23  0.000
Residual Error   28   166.0     5.9
Total            29  2622.0
```

Unusual Observations

```
Obs  ChgPres   Yield     Fit  SE Fit  Residual  St Resid
 14     25.0  81.400  76.535   0.451     4.865     2.03R
```

R denotes an observation with a large standardized residual.

Durbin-Watson statistic = 1.34286

a. What should the null hypothesis that the true slope is zero mean in this situation?

b. Show that this hypothesis can be conclusively rejected.

13.85 Locate and interpret the residual standard deviation in the output of Exercise 13.84.

13.86 Consider the residual plot and LOWESS smooth in Figure 13.49 for the paper mill data.

a. Is there an indication that a nonlinear equation may give a better fit to the data?

b. Are there any severe outliers?

FIGURE 13.49 **Residual Plot with LOWESS Smooth for Paper Mill Data**

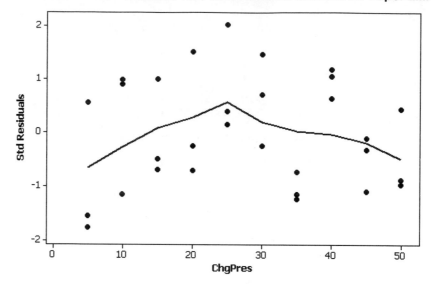

13.87 The square root of the pressure change is calculated for the data of Exercise 13.84 and a new regression is calculated. Has the square-root transformation improved the fit of the model?

```
Regression Analysis: Yield versus sqrt(ChgPres)

The regression equation is
Yield = 47.8 + 6.04 sqrt(ChgPres)

Predictor        Coef   SE Coef      T      P
Constant       47.752     1.463  32.64  0.000
sqrt(ChgPres)  6.0426    0.2790  21.66  0.000

S = 2.29663   R-Sq = 94.4%   R-Sq(adj) = 94.2%

Analysis of Variance

Source           DF      SS      MS      F      P
Regression        1  2474.3  2474.3  469.10  0.000
Residual Error   28   147.7     5.3
Total            29  2622.0

Durbin-Watson statistic = 1.51142
```

APPENDIX

Appendix

TABLE 1 Binomial Probabilities (*n* between 2 and 6)

n = 2

π

y↓	.05	.10	.15	.20	.25	.30	.35	.40	.45	.50	
0	.9025	.8100	.7225	.6400	.5625	.4900	.4225	.3600	.3025	.2500	2
1	.0950	.1800	.2550	.3200	.3750	.4200	.4550	.4800	.4950	.5000	1
2	.0025	.0100	.0225	.0400	.0625	.0900	.1225	.1600	.2025	.2500	0
	.95	.90	.85	.80	.75	.70	.65	.60	.55	.50	y↑

n = 3

π

y↓	.05	.10	.15	.20	.25	.30	.35	.40	.45	.50	
0	.8574	.7290	.6141	.5120	.4219	.3430	.2746	.2160	.1664	.1250	3
1	.1354	.2430	.3251	.3840	.4219	.4410	.4436	.4320	.4084	.3750	2
2	.0071	.0270	.0574	.0960	.1406	.1890	.2389	.2880	.3341	.3750	1
3	.0001	.0010	.0034	.0080	.0156	.0270	.0429	.0640	.0911	.1250	0
	.95	.90	.85	.80	.75	.70	.65	.60	.55	.50	y↑

n = 4

π

y↓	.05	.10	.15	.20	.25	.30	.35	.40	.45	.50	
0	.8145	.6561	.5220	.4096	.3164	.2401	.1785	.1296	.0915	.0625	4
1	.1715	.2916	.3685	.4096	.4219	.4116	.3845	.3456	.2995	.2500	3
2	.0135	.0486	.0975	.1536	.2109	.2646	.3105	.3456	.3675	.3750	2
3	.0005	.0036	.0115	.0256	.0469	.0756	.1115	.1536	.2005	.2500	1
4	.0000	.0001	.0005	.0016	.0039	.0081	.0150	.0256	.0410	.0625	0
	.95	.90	.85	.80	.75	.70	.65	.60	.55	.50	y↑

n = 5

π

y↓	.05	.10	.15	.20	.25	.30	.35	.40	.45	.50	
0	.7738	.5905	.4437	.3277	.2373	.1681	.1160	.0778	.0503	.0313	5
1	.2036	.3281	.3915	.4096	.3955	.3602	.3124	.2592	.2059	.1563	4
2	.0214	.0729	.1382	.2048	.2637	.3087	.3364	.3456	.3369	.3125	3
3	.0011	.0081	.0244	.0512	.0879	.1323	.1811	.2304	.2757	.3125	2
4	.0000	.0005	.0022	.0064	.0146	.0284	.0488	.0768	.1128	.1563	1
5	.0000	.0000	.0001	.0003	.0010	.0024	.0053	.0102	.0185	.0313	0
	.95	.90	.85	.80	.75	.70	.65	.60	.55	.50	y↑

n = 6

π

y↓	.05	.10	.15	.20	.25	.30	.35	.40	.45	.50	
0	.7351	.5314	.3771	.2621	.1780	.1176	.0754	.0467	.0277	.0156	6
1	.2321	.3543	.3993	.3932	.3560	.3025	.2437	.1866	.1359	.0938	5
2	.0305	.0984	.1762	.2458	.2966	.3241	.3280	.3110	.2780	.2344	4
3	.0021	.0146	.0415	.0819	.1318	.1852	.2355	.2765	.3032	.3125	3
4	.0001	.0012	.0055	.0154	.0330	.0595	.0951	.1382	.1861	.2344	2
5	.0000	.0001	.0004	.0015	.0044	.0102	.0205	.0369	.0609	.0938	1
6	.0000	.0000	.0000	.0001	.0002	.0007	.0018	.0041	.0083	.0156	0
	.95	.90	.85	.80	.75	.70	.65	.60	.55	.50	y↑

TABLE 1 (continued) Binomial Probabilities (*n* between 7 and 10)

n = 7 π

y↓	.05	.10	.15	.20	.25	.30	.35	.40	.45	.50	
0	.6983	.4783	.3206	.2097	.1335	.0824	.0490	.0280	.0152	.0078	7
1	.2573	.3720	.3960	.3670	.3115	.2471	.1848	.1306	.0872	.0547	6
2	.0406	.1240	.2097	.2753	.3115	.3177	.2985	.2613	.2140	.1641	5
3	.0036	.0230	.0617	.1147	.1730	.2269	.2679	.2903	.2918	.2734	4
4	.0002	.0026	.0109	.0287	.0577	.0972	.1442	.1935	.2388	.2734	3
5	.0000	.0002	.0012	.0043	.0115	.0250	.0466	.0774	.1172	.1641	2
6	.0000	.0000	.0001	.0004	.0013	.0036	.0084	.0172	.0320	.0547	1
7	.0000	.0000	.0000	.0000	.0001	.0002	.0006	.0016	.0037	.0078	0
	.95	.90	.85	.80	.75	.70	.65	.60	.55	.50	y↑

n = 8 π

y↓	.05	.10	.15	.20	.25	.30	.35	.40	.45	.50	
0	.6634	.4305	.2725	.1678	.1001	.0576	.0319	.0168	.0084	.0039	8
1	.2793	.3826	.3847	.3355	.2670	.1977	.1373	.0896	.0548	.0313	7
2	.0515	.1488	.2376	.2936	.3115	.2965	.2587	.2090	.1569	.1094	6
3	.0054	.0331	.0839	.1468	.2076	.2541	.2786	.2787	.2568	.2188	5
4	.0004	.0046	.0185	.0459	.0865	.1361	.1875	.2322	.2627	.2734	4
5	.0000	.0004	.0026	.0092	.0231	.0467	.0808	.1239	.1719	.2188	3
6	.0000	.0000	.0002	.0011	.0038	.0100	.0217	.0413	.0703	.1094	2
7	.0000	.0000	.0000	.0001	.0004	.0012	.0033	.0079	.0164	.0313	1
8	.0000	.0000	.0000	.0000	.0000	.0001	.0002	.0007	.0017	.0039	0
	.95	.90	.85	.80	.75	.70	.65	.60	.55	.50	y↑

n = 9 π

y↓	.05	.10	.15	.20	.25	.30	.35	.40	.45	.50	
0	.6302	.3874	.2316	.1342	.0751	.0404	.0207	.0101	.0046	.0020	9
1	.2985	.3874	.3679	.3020	.2253	.1556	.1004	.0605	.0339	.0176	8
2	.0629	.1722	.2597	.3020	.3003	.2668	.2162	.1612	.1110	.0703	7
3	.0077	.0446	.1069	.1762	.2336	.2668	.2716	.2508	.2119	.1641	6
4	.0006	.0074	.0283	.0661	.1168	.1715	.2194	.2508	.2600	.2461	5
5	.0000	.0008	.0050	.0165	.0389	.0735	.1181	.1672	.2128	.2461	4
6	.0000	.0001	.0006	.0028	.0087	.0210	.0424	.0743	.1160	.1641	3
7	.0000	.0000	.0000	.0003	.0012	.0039	.0098	.0212	.0407	.0703	2
8	.0000	.0000	.0000	.0000	.0001	.0004	.0013	.0035	.0083	.0176	1
9	.0000	.0000	.0000	.0000	.0000	.0000	.0001	.0003	.0008	.0020	0
	.95	.90	.85	.80	.75	.70	.65	.60	.55	.50	y↑

n = 10 π

y↓	.05	.10	.15	.20	.25	.30	.35	.40	.45	.50	
0	.5987	.3487	.1969	.1074	.0563	.0282	.0135	.0060	.0025	.0010	10
1	.3151	.3874	.3474	.2684	.1877	.1211	.0725	.0403	.0207	.0098	9
2	.0746	.1937	.2759	.3020	.2816	.2335	.1757	.1209	.0763	.0439	8
3	.0105	.0574	.1298	.2013	.2503	.2668	.2522	.2150	.1665	.1172	7
4	.0010	.0112	.0401	.0881	.1460	.2001	.2377	.2508	.2384	.2051	6
5	.0001	.0015	.0085	.0264	.0584	.1029	.1536	.2007	.2340	.2461	5
6	.0000	.0001	.0012	.0055	.0162	.0368	.0689	.1115	.1596	.2051	4
7	.0000	.0000	.0001	.0008	.0031	.0090	.0212	.0425	.0746	.1172	3
8	.0000	.0000	.0000	.0001	.0004	.0014	.0043	.0106	.0229	.0439	2
9	.0000	.0000	.0000	.0000	.0000	.0001	.0005	.0016	.0042	.0098	1
10	.0000	.0000	.0000	.0000	.0000	.0000	.0000	.0001	.0003	.0010	0
	.95	.90	.85	.80	.75	.70	.65	.60	.55	.50	y↑

Appendix

TABLE 1 (continued) Binomial Probabilities (*n* between 12 and 16)

n = 12
π

y↓	.05	.10	.15	.20	.25	.30	.35	.40	.45	.50	
0	.5404	.2824	.1422	.0687	.0317	.0138	.0057	.0022	.0008	.0002	12
1	.3413	.3766	.3012	.2062	.1267	.0712	.0368	.0174	.0075	.0029	11
2	.0988	.2301	.2924	.2835	.2323	.1678	.1088	.0639	.0339	.0161	10
3	.0173	.0852	.1720	.2362	.2581	.2397	.1954	.1419	.0923	.0537	9
4	.0021	.0213	.0683	.1329	.1936	.2311	.2367	.2128	.1700	.1208	8
5	.0002	.0038	.0193	.0532	.1032	.1585	.2039	.2270	.2225	.1934	7
6	.0000	.0005	.0040	.0155	.0401	.0792	.1281	.1766	.2124	.2256	6
7	.0000	.0000	.0006	.0033	.0115	.0291	.0591	.1009	.1489	.1934	5
8	.0000	.0000	.0001	.0005	.0024	.0078	.0199	.0420	.0762	.1208	4
9	.0000	.0000	.0000	.0001	.0004	.0015	.0048	.0125	.0277	.0537	3
10	.0000	.0000	.0000	.0000	.0000	.0002	.0008	.0025	.0068	.0161	2
11	.0000	.0000	.0000	.0000	.0000	.0000	.0001	.0003	.0010	.0029	1
12	.0000	.0000	.0000	.0000	.0000	.0000	.0000	.0000	.0001	.0002	0
	.95	.90	.85	.80	.75	.70	.65	.60	.55	.50	*y*↑

n = 14
π

y↓	.05	.10	.15	.20	.25	.30	.35	.40	.45	.50	
0	.4877	.2288	.1028	.0440	.0178	.0068	.0024	.0008	.0002	.0001	14
1	.3593	.3559	.2539	.1539	.0832	.0407	.0181	.0073	.0027	.0009	13
2	.1229	.2570	.2912	.2501	.1802	.1134	.0634	.0317	.0141	.0056	12
3	.0259	.1142	.2056	.2501	.2402	.1943	.1366	.0845	.0462	.0222	11
4	.0037	.0349	.0998	.1720	.2202	.2290	.2022	.1549	.1040	.0611	10
5	.0004	.0078	.0352	.0860	.1468	.1963	.2178	.2066	.1701	.1222	9
6	.0000	.0013	.0093	.0322	.0734	.1262	.1759	.2066	.2088	.1833	8
7	.0000	.0002	.0019	.0092	.0280	.0618	.1082	.1574	.1952	.2095	7
8	.0000	.0000	.0003	.0020	.0082	.0232	.0510	.0918	.1398	.1833	6
9	.0000	.0000	.0000	.0003	.0018	.0066	.0183	.0408	.0762	.1222	5
10	.0000	.0000	.0000	.0000	.0003	.0014	.0049	.0136	.0312	.0611	4
11	.0000	.0000	.0000	.0000	.0000	.0002	.0010	.0033	.0093	.0222	3
12	.0000	.0000	.0000	.0000	.0000	.0000	.0001	.0005	.0019	.0056	2
13	.0000	.0000	.0000	.0000	.0000	.0000	.0000	.0001	.0002	.0009	1
14	.0000	.0000	.0000	.0000	.0000	.0000	.0000	.0000	.0000	.0001	0
	.95	.90	.85	.80	.75	.70	.65	.60	.55	.50	*y*↑

n = 16
π

y↓	.05	.10	.15	.20	.25	.30	.35	.40	.45	.50	
0	.4401	.1853	.0743	.0281	.0100	.0033	.0010	.0003	.0001	.0000	16
1	.3706	.3294	.2097	.1126	.0535	.0228	.0087	.0030	.0009	.0002	15
2	.1463	.2745	.2775	.2111	.1336	.0732	.0353	.0150	.0056	.0018	14
3	.0359	.1423	.2285	.2463	.2079	.1465	.0888	.0468	.0215	.0085	13
4	.0061	.0514	.1311	.2001	.2252	.2040	.1553	.1014	.0572	.0278	12
5	.0008	.0137	.0555	.1201	.1802	.2099	.2008	.1623	.1123	.0667	11
6	.0001	.0028	.0180	.0550	.1101	.1649	.1982	.1983	.1684	.1222	10
7	.0000	.0004	.0045	.0197	.0524	.1010	.1524	.1889	.1969	.1746	9
8	.0000	.0001	.0009	.0055	.0197	.0487	.0923	.1417	.1812	.1964	8
9	.0000	.0000	.0001	.0012	.0058	.0185	.0442	.0840	.1318	.1746	7
10	.0000	.0000	.0000	.0002	.0014	.0056	.0167	.0392	.0755	.1222	6
11	.0000	.0000	.0000	.0000	.0002	.0013	.0049	.0142	.0337	.0667	5
12	.0000	.0000	.0000	.0000	.0000	.0002	.0011	.0040	.0115	.0278	4
13	.0000	.0000	.0000	.0000	.0000	.0000	.0002	.0008	.0029	.0085	3
14	.0000	.0000	.0000	.0000	.0000	.0000	.0000	.0001	.0005	.0018	2
15	.0000	.0000	.0000	.0000	.0000	.0000	.0000	.0000	.0001	.0002	1
	.95	.90	.85	.80	.75	.70	.65	.60	.55	.50	*y*↑

TABLE 1 (continued) **Binomial Probabilities (*n* between 18 and 20)**

n = 18   π

y↓	.05	.10	.15	.20	.25	.30	.35	.40	.45	.50	
0	.3972	.1501	.0536	.0180	.0056	.0016	.0004	.0001	.0000	.0000	18
1	.3763	.3002	.1704	.0811	.0338	.0126	.0042	.0012	.0003	.0001	17
2	.1683	.2835	.2556	.1723	.0958	.0458	.0190	.0069	.0022	.0006	16
3	.0473	.1680	.2406	.2297	.1704	.1046	.0547	.0246	.0095	.0031	15
4	.0093	.0700	.1592	.2153	.2130	.1681	.1104	.0614	.0291	.0117	14
5	.0014	.0218	.0787	.1507	.1988	.2017	.1664	.1146	.0666	.0327	13
6	.0002	.0052	.0301	.0816	.1436	.1873	.1941	.1655	.1181	.0708	12
7	.0000	.0010	.0091	.0350	.0820	.1376	.1792	.1892	.1657	.1214	11
8	.0000	.0002	.0022	.0120	.0376	.0811	.1327	.1734	.1864	.1669	10
9	.0000	.0000	.0004	.0033	.0139	.0386	.0794	.1284	.1694	.1855	9
10	.0000	.0000	.0001	.0008	.0042	.0149	.0385	.0771	.1248	.1669	8
11	.0000	.0000	.0000	.0001	.0010	.0046	.0151	.0374	.0742	.1214	7
12	.0000	.0000	.0000	.0000	.0002	.0012	.0047	.0145	.0354	.0708	6
13	.0000	.0000	.0000	.0000	.0000	.0002	.0012	.0045	.0134	.0327	5
14	.0000	.0000	.0000	.0000	.0000	.0000	.0002	.0011	.0039	.0117	4
15	.0000	.0000	.0000	.0000	.0000	.0000	.0000	.0002	.0009	.0031	3
16	.0000	.0000	.0000	.0000	.0000	.0000	.0000	.0000	.0001	.0006	2
17	.0000	.0000	.0000	.0000	.0000	.0000	.0000	.0000	.0000	.0001	1
	.95	.90	.85	.80	.75	.70	.65	.60	.55	.50	y↑

n = 20   π

y↓	.05	.10	.15	.20	.25	.30	.35	.40	.45	.50	
0	.3585	.1216	.0388	.0115	.0032	.0008	.0002	.0000	.0000	.0000	20
1	.3774	.2702	.1368	.0576	.0211	.0068	.0020	.0005	.0001	.0000	19
2	.1887	.2852	.2293	.1369	.0669	.0278	.0100	.0031	.0008	.0002	18
3	.0596	.1901	.2428	.2054	.1339	.0716	.0323	.0123	.0040	.0011	17
4	.0133	.0898	.1821	.2182	.1897	.1304	.0738	.0350	.0139	.0046	16
5	.0022	.0319	.1028	.1746	.2023	.1789	.1272	.0746	.0365	.0148	15
6	.0003	.0089	.0454	.1091	.1686	.1916	.1712	.1244	.0746	.0370	14
7	.0000	.0020	.0160	.0545	.1124	.1643	.1844	.1659	.1221	.0739	13
8	.0000	.0004	.0046	.0222	.0609	.1144	.1614	.1797	.1623	.1201	12
9	.0000	.0001	.0011	.0074	.0271	.0654	.1158	.1597	.1771	.1602	11
10	.0000	.0000	.0002	.0020	.0099	.0308	.0686	.1171	.1593	.1762	10
11	.0000	.0000	.0000	.0005	.0030	.0120	.0336	.0710	.1185	.1602	9
12	.0000	.0000	.0000	.0001	.0008	.0039	.0136	.0355	.0727	.1201	8
13	.0000	.0000	.0000	.0000	.0002	.0010	.0045	.0146	.0366	.0739	7
14	.0000	.0000	.0000	.0000	.0000	.0002	.0012	.0049	.0150	.0370	6
15	.0000	.0000	.0000	.0000	.0000	.0000	.0003	.0013	.0049	.0148	5
16	.0000	.0000	.0000	.0000	.0000	.0000	.0000	.0003	.0013	.0046	4
17	.0000	.0000	.0000	.0000	.0000	.0000	.0000	.0000	.0002	.0011	3
18	.0000	.0000	.0000	.0000	.0000	.0000	.0000	.0000	.0000	.0002	2
	.95	.90	.85	.80	.75	.70	.65	.60	.55	.50	y↑

Appendix

TABLE 1 (continued) Binomial Probabilities ($n = 50$ and 100)

$n = 50$ π

$y\downarrow$	.05	.10	.15	.20	.25	.30	.35	.40	.45	.50	
0	.0769	.0052	.0003	.0000	.0000	.0000	.0000	.0000	.0000	.0000	50
1	.2025	.0286	.0026	.0002	.0000	.0000	.0000	.0000	.0000	.0000	49
2	.2611	.0779	.0113	.0011	.0001	.0000	.0000	.0000	.0000	.0000	48
3	.2199	.1386	.0319	.0044	.0004	.0000	.0000	.0000	.0000	.0000	47
4	.1360	.1809	.0661	.0128	.0016	.0001	.0000	.0000	.0000	.0000	46
5	.0658	.1849	.1072	.0295	.0049	.0006	.0000	.0000	.0000	.0000	45
6	.0260	.1541	.1419	.0554	.0123	.0018	.0002	.0000	.0000	.0000	44
7	.0086	.1076	.1575	.0870	.0259	.0048	.0006	.0000	.0000	.0000	43
8	.0024	.0643	.1493	.1169	.0463	.0110	.0017	.0002	.0000	.0000	42
9	.0006	.0333	.1230	.1364	.0721	.0220	.0042	.0005	.0000	.0000	41
10	.0001	.0152	.0890	.1398	.0985	.0386	.0093	.0014	.0001	.0000	40
11	.0000	.0061	.0571	.1271	.1194	.0602	.0182	.0035	.0004	.0000	39
12	.0000	.0022	.0328	.1033	.1294	.0838	.0319	.0076	.0011	.0001	38
13	.0000	.0007	.0169	.0755	.1261	.1050	.0502	.0147	.0027	.0003	37
14	.0000	.0002	.0079	.0499	.1110	.1189	.0714	.0260	.0059	.0008	36
15	.0000	.0001	.0033	.0299	.0888	.1223	.0923	.0415	.0116	.0020	35
16	.0000	.0000	.0013	.0164	.0648	.1147	.1088	.0606	.0207	.0044	34
17	.0000	.0000	.0005	.0082	.0432	.0983	.1171	.0808	.0339	.0087	33
18	.0000	.0000	.0001	.0037	.0264	.0772	.1156	.0987	.0508	.0160	32
19	.0000	.0000	.0000	.0016	.0148	.0558	.1048	.1109	.0700	.0270	31
20	.0000	.0000	.0000	.0006	.0077	.0370	.0875	.1146	.0888	.0419	30
21	.0000	.0000	.0000	.0002	.0036	.0227	.0673	.1091	.1038	.0598	29
22	.0000	.0000	.0000	.0001	.0016	.0128	.0478	.0959	.1119	.0788	28
23	.0000	.0000	.0000	.0000	.0006	.0067	.0313	.0778	.1115	.0960	27
24	.0000	.0000	.0000	.0000	.0002	.0032	.0190	.0584	.1026	.1080	26
25	.0000	.0000	.0000	.0000	.0001	.0014	.0106	.0405	.0873	.1123	25
26	.0000	.0000	.0000	.0000	.0000	.0006	.0055	.0259	.0687	.1080	24
27	.0000	.0000	.0000	.0000	.0000	.0002	.0026	.0154	.0500	.0960	23
28	.0000	.0000	.0000	.0000	.0000	.0001	.0012	.0084	.0336	.0788	22
29	.0000	.0000	.0000	.0000	.0000	.0000	.0005	.0043	.0208	.0598	21
30	.0000	.0000	.0000	.0000	.0000	.0000	.0002	.0020	.0119	.0419	20
31	.0000	.0000	.0000	.0000	.0000	.0000	.0001	.0009	.0063	.0270	19
32	.0000	.0000	.0000	.0000	.0000	.0000	.0000	.0003	.0031	.0160	18
33	.0000	.0000	.0000	.0000	.0000	.0000	.0000	.0001	.0014	.0087	17
34	.0000	.0000	.0000	.0000	.0000	.0000	.0000	.0000	.0006	.0044	16
35	.0000	.0000	.0000	.0000	.0000	.0000	.0000	.0000	.0002	.0020	15
36	.0000	.0000	.0000	.0000	.0000	.0000	.0000	.0000	.0001	.0008	14
37	.0000	.0000	.0000	.0000	.0000	.0000	.0000	.0000	.0000	.0003	13
38	.0000	.0000	.0000	.0000	.0000	.0000	.0000	.0000	.0000	.0001	12
	.95	.90	.85	.80	.75	.70	.65	.60	.55	.50	$y\uparrow$

$n = 100$ π

$y\downarrow$	.05	.10	.15	.20	.25	.30	.35	.40	.45	.50	
0	.0059	.0000	.0000	.0000	.0000	.0000	.0000	.0000	.0000	.0000	100
1	.0312	.0003	.0000	.0000	.0000	.0000	.0000	.0000	.0000	.0000	99
2	.0812	.0016	.0000	.0000	.0000	.0000	.0000	.0000	.0000	.0000	98
3	.1396	.0059	.0001	.0000	.0000	.0000	.0000	.0000	.0000	.0000	97
4	.1781	.0159	.0003	.0000	.0000	.0000	.0000	.0000	.0000	.0000	96
5	.1800	.0339	.0011	.0000	.0000	.0000	.0000	.0000	.0000	.0000	95
6	.1500	.0596	.0031	.0001	.0000	.0000	.0000	.0000	.0000	.0000	94
7	.1060	.0889	.0075	.0002	.0000	.0000	.0000	.0000	.0000	.0000	93
8	.0649	.1148	.0153	.0006	.0000	.0000	.0000	.0000	.0000	.0000	92
9	.0349	.1304	.0276	.0015	.0000	.0000	.0000	.0000	.0000	.0000	91
10	.0167	.1319	.0444	.0034	.0001	.0000	.0000	.0000	.0000	.0000	90
11	.0072	.1199	.0640	.0069	.0003	.0000	.0000	.0000	.0000	.0000	89
12	.0028	.0988	.0838	.0128	.0006	.0000	.0000	.0000	.0000	.0000	88
13	.0010	.0743	.1001	.0216	.0014	.0000	.0000	.0000	.0000	.0000	87

($n = 100$ *continued on next page*)

TABLE 1 (continued)   Binomial Probabilities ($n = 100$)

$n = 100$ π

$y\downarrow$	.05	.10	.15	.20	.25	.30	.35	.40	.45	.50	
14	.0003	.0513	.1098	.0335	.0030	.0001	.0000	.0000	.0000	.0000	86
15	.0001	.0327	.1111	.0481	.0057	.0002	.0000	.0000	.0000	.0000	85
16	.0000	.0193	.1041	.0638	.0100	.0006	.0000	.0000	.0000	.0000	84
17	.0000	.0106	.0908	.0789	.0165	.0012	.0000	.0000	.0000	.0000	83
18	.0000	.0054	.0739	.0909	.0254	.0024	.0001	.0000	.0000	.0000	82
19	.0000	.0026	.0563	.0981	.0365	.0044	.0002	.0000	.0000	.0000	81
20	.0000	.0012	.0402	.0993	.0493	.0076	.0004	.0000	.0000	.0000	80
21	.0000	.0005	.0270	.0946	.0626	.0124	.0009	.0000	.0000	.0000	79
22	.0000	.0002	.0171	.0849	.0749	.0190	.0017	.0001	.0000	.0000	78
23	.0000	.0001	.0103	.0720	.0847	.0277	.0032	.0001	.0000	.0000	77
24	.0000	.0000	.0058	.0577	.0906	.0380	.0055	.0003	.0000	.0000	76
25	.0000	.0000	.0031	.0439	.0918	.0496	.0090	.0006	.0000	.0000	75
26	.0000	.0000	.0016	.0316	.0883	.0613	.0140	.0012	.0000	.0000	74
27	.0000	.0000	.0008	.0217	.0806	.0720	.0207	.0022	.0001	.0000	73
28	.0000	.0000	.0004	.0141	.0701	.0804	.0290	.0038	.0002	.0000	72
29	.0000	.0000	.0002	.0088	.0580	.0856	.0388	.0063	.0004	.0000	71
30	.0000	.0000	.0001	.0052	.0458	.0868	.0494	.0100	.0008	.0000	70
31	.0000	.0000	.0000	.0029	.0344	.0840	.0601	.0151	.0014	.0001	69
32	.0000	.0000	.0000	.0016	.0248	.0776	.0698	.0217	.0025	.0001	68
33	.0000	.0000	.0000	.0008	.0170	.0685	.0774	.0297	.0043	.0002	67
34	.0000	.0000	.0000	.0004	.0112	.0579	.0821	.0391	.0069	.0005	66
35	.0000	.0000	.0000	.0002	.0070	.0468	.0834	.0491	.0106	.0009	65
36	.0000	.0000	.0000	.0001	.0042	.0362	.0811	.0591	.0157	.0016	64
37	.0000	.0000	.0000	.0000	.0024	.0268	.0755	.0682	.0222	.0027	63
38	.0000	.0000	.0000	.0000	.0013	.0191	.0674	.0754	.0301	.0045	62
39	.0000	.0000	.0000	.0000	.0007	.0130	.0577	.0799	.0391	.0071	61
40	.0000	.0000	.0000	.0000	.0004	.0085	.0474	.0812	.0488	.0108	60
41	.0000	.0000	.0000	.0000	.0002	.0053	.0373	.0792	.0584	.0159	59
42	.0000	.0000	.0000	.0000	.0001	.0032	.0282	.0742	.0672	.0223	58
43	.0000	.0000	.0000	.0000	.0000	.0019	.0205	.0667	.0741	.0301	57
44	.0000	.0000	.0000	.0000	.0000	.0010	.0143	.0576	.0786	.0390	56
45	.0000	.0000	.0000	.0000	.0000	.0005	.0096	.0478	.0800	.0485	55
46	.0000	.0000	.0000	.0000	.0000	.0003	.0062	.0381	.0782	.0580	54
47	.0000	.0000	.0000	.0000	.0000	.0001	.0038	.0292	.0736	.0666	53
48	.0000	.0000	.0000	.0000	.0000	.0001	.0023	.0215	.0665	.0735	52
49	.0000	.0000	.0000	.0000	.0000	.0000	.0013	.0152	.0577	.0780	51
50	.0000	.0000	.0000	.0000	.0000	.0000	.0007	.0103	.0482	.0796	50
51	.0000	.0000	.0000	.0000	.0000	.0000	.0004	.0068	.0386	.0780	49
52	.0000	.0000	.0000	.0000	.0000	.0000	.0002	.0042	.0298	.0735	48
53	.0000	.0000	.0000	.0000	.0000	.0000	.0001	.0026	.0221	.0666	47
54	.0000	.0000	.0000	.0000	.0000	.0000	.0000	.0015	.0157	.0580	46
55	.0000	.0000	.0000	.0000	.0000	.0000	.0000	.0008	.0108	.0485	45
56	.0000	.0000	.0000	.0000	.0000	.0000	.0000	.0004	.0071	.0390	44
57	.0000	.0000	.0000	.0000	.0000	.0000	.0000	.0002	.0045	.0301	43
58	.0000	.0000	.0000	.0000	.0000	.0000	.0000	.0001	.0027	.0223	42
59	.0000	.0000	.0000	.0000	.0000	.0000	.0000	.0001	.0016	.0159	41
60	.0000	.0000	.0000	.0000	.0000	.0000	.0000	.0000	.0009	.0108	40
61	.0000	.0000	.0000	.0000	.0000	.0000	.0000	.0000	.0005	.0071	39
62	.0000	.0000	.0000	.0000	.0000	.0000	.0000	.0000	.0002	.0045	38
63	.0000	.0000	.0000	.0000	.0000	.0000	.0000	.0000	.0001	.0027	37
64	.0000	.0000	.0000	.0000	.0000	.0000	.0000	.0000	.0001	.0016	36
65	.0000	.0000	.0000	.0000	.0000	.0000	.0000	.0000	.0000	.0009	35
66	.0000	.0000	.0000	.0000	.0000	.0000	.0000	.0000	.0000	.0005	34
67	.0000	.0000	.0000	.0000	.0000	.0000	.0000	.0000	.0000	.0002	33
68	.0000	.0000	.0000	.0000	.0000	.0000	.0000	.0000	.0000	.0001	32
69	.0000	.0000	.0000	.0000	.0000	.0000	.0000	.0000	.0000	.0001	31
	.95	.90	.85	.80	.75	.70	.65	.60	.55	.50	$y\uparrow$

Source: Computed by D. K. Hildebrand

TABLE 2 Poisson Probabilities (μ between .1 and 5.0)

y	.1	.2	.3	.4	.5	.6	.7	.8	.9	1.0
					μ					
0	.9048	.8187	.7408	.6703	.6065	.5488	.4966	.4493	.4066	.3679
1	.0905	.1637	.2222	.2681	.3033	.3293	.3476	.3595	.3659	.3679
2	.0045	.0164	.0333	.0536	.0758	.0988	.1217	.1438	.1647	.1839
3	.0002	.0011	.0033	.0072	.0126	.0198	.0284	.0383	.0494	.0613
4	.0000	.0001	.0003	.0007	.0016	.0030	.0050	.0077	.0111	.0153
5	.0000	.0000	.0000	.0001	.0002	.0004	.0007	.0012	.0020	.0031
6	.0000	.0000	.0000	.0000	.0000	.0000	.0001	.0002	.0003	.0005

y	1.1	1.2	1.3	1.4	1.5	1.6	1.7	1.8	1.9	2.0
					μ					
0	.3329	.3012	.2725	.2466	.2231	.2019	.1827	.1653	.1496	.1353
1	.3662	.3614	.3543	.3452	.3347	.3230	.3106	.2975	.2842	.2707
2	.2014	.2169	.2303	.2417	.2510	.2584	.2640	.2678	.2700	.2707
3	.0738	.0867	.0998	.1128	.1255	.1378	.1496	.1607	.1710	.1804
4	.0203	.0260	.0324	.0395	.0471	.0551	.0636	.0723	.0812	.0902
5	.0045	.0062	.0084	.0111	.0141	.0176	.0216	.0260	.0309	.0361
6	.0008	.0012	.0018	.0026	.0035	.0047	.0061	.0078	.0098	.0120
7	.0001	.0002	.0003	.0005	.0008	.0011	.0015	.0020	.0027	.0034
8	.0000	.0000	.0001	.0001	.0001	.0002	.0003	.0005	.0006	.0009

y	2.1	2.2	2.3	2.4	2.5	2.6	2.7	2.8	2.9	3.0
					μ					
0	.1225	.1108	.1003	.0907	.0821	.0743	.0672	.0608	.0550	.0498
1	.2572	.2438	.2306	.2177	.2052	.1931	.1815	.1703	.1596	.1494
2	.2700	.2681	.2652	.2613	.2565	.2510	.2450	.2384	.2314	.2240
3	.1890	.1966	.2033	.2090	.2138	.2176	.2205	.2225	.2237	.2240
4	.0992	.1082	.1169	.1254	.1336	.1414	.1488	.1557	.1622	.1680
5	.0417	.0476	.0538	.0602	.0668	.0735	.0804	.0872	.0940	.1008
6	.0146	.0174	.0206	.0241	.0278	.0319	.0362	.0407	.0455	.0504
7	.0044	.0055	.0068	.0083	.0099	.0118	.0139	.0163	.0188	.0216
8	.0011	.0015	.0019	.0025	.0031	.0038	.0047	.0057	.0068	.0081
9	.0003	.0004	.0005	.0007	.0009	.0011	.0014	.0018	.0022	.0027
10	.0001	.0001	.0001	.0002	.0002	.0003	.0004	.0005	.0006	.0008
11	.0000	.0000	.0000	.0000	.0000	.0001	.0001	.0001	.0002	.0002

y	3.1	3.2	3.3	3.4	3.5	3.6	3.7	3.8	3.9	4.0
					μ					
0	.0450	.0408	.0369	.0334	.0302	.0273	.0247	.0224	.0202	.0183
1	.1397	.1304	.1217	.1135	.1057	.0984	.0915	.0850	.0789	.0733
2	.2165	.2087	.2008	.1929	.1850	.1771	.1692	.1615	.1539	.1465
3	.2237	.2226	.2209	.2186	.2158	.2125	.2087	.2046	.2001	.1954
4	.1733	.1781	.1823	.1858	.1888	.1912	.1931	.1944	.1951	.1954
5	.1075	.1140	.1203	.1264	.1322	.1377	.1429	.1477	.1522	.1563
6	.0555	.0608	.0662	.0716	.0771	.0826	.0881	.0936	.0989	.1042
7	.0246	.0278	.0312	.0348	.0385	.0425	.0466	.0508	.0551	.0595
8	.0095	.0111	.0129	.0148	.0169	.0191	.0215	.0241	.0269	.0298
9	.0033	.0040	.0047	.0056	.0066	.0076	.0089	.0102	.0116	.0132
10	.0010	.0013	.0016	.0019	.0023	.0028	.0033	.0039	.0045	.0053
11	.0003	.0004	.0005	.0006	.0007	.0009	.0011	.0013	.0016	.0019
12	.0001	.0001	.0001	.0002	.0002	.0003	.0003	.0004	.0005	.0006
13	.0000	.0000	.0000	.0000	.0001	.0001	.0001	.0001	.0002	.0002

y	4.1	4.2	4.3	4.4	4.5	4.6	4.7	4.8	4.9	5.0
					μ					
0	.0166	.0150	.0136	.0123	.0111	.0101	.0091	.0082	.0074	.0067
1	.0679	.0630	.0583	.0540	.0500	.0462	.0427	.0395	.0365	.0337
2	.1393	.1323	.1254	.1188	.1125	.1063	.1005	.0948	.0894	.0842
3	.1904	.1852	.1798	.1743	.1687	.1631	.1574	.1517	.1460	.1404
4	.1951	.1944	.1933	.1917	.1898	.1875	.1849	.1820	.1789	.1755
5	.1600	.1633	.1662	.1687	.1708	.1725	.1738	.1747	.1753	.1755
6	.1093	.1143	.1191	.1237	.1281	.1323	.1362	.1398	.1432	.1462
7	.0640	.0686	.0732	.0778	.0824	.0869	.0914	.0959	.1002	.1044
8	.0328	.0360	.0393	.0428	.0463	.0500	.0537	.0575	.0614	.0653
9	.0150	.0168	.0188	.0209	.0232	.0255	.0281	.0307	.0334	.0363
10	.0061	.0071	.0081	.0092	.0104	.0118	.0132	.0147	.0164	.0181

TABLE 2 (continued) Poisson Probabilities (μ between 4.1 and 20.0)

y	4.1	4.2	4.3	4.4	4.5	4.6	4.7	4.8	4.9	5.0
11	.0023	.0027	.0032	.0037	.0043	.0049	.0056	.0064	.0073	.0082
12	.0008	.0009	.0011	.0013	.0016	.0019	.0022	.0026	.0030	.0034
13	.0002	.0003	.0004	.0005	.0006	.0007	.0008	.0009	.0011	.0013
14	.0001	.0001	.0001	.0001	.0002	.0002	.0003	.0003	.0004	.0005
15	.0000	.0000	.0000	.0000	.0001	.0001	.0001	.0001	.0001	.0002

y	5.5	6.0	6.5	7.0	7.5	8.0	8.5	9.0	9.5	10.0
0	.0041	.0025	.0015	.0009	.0006	.0003	.0002	.0001	.0001	.0000
1	.0225	.0149	.0098	.0064	.0041	.0027	.0017	.0011	.0007	.0005
2	.0618	.0446	.0318	.0223	.0156	.0107	.0074	.0050	.0034	.0023
3	.1133	.0892	.0688	.0521	.0389	.0286	.0208	.0150	.0107	.0076
4	.1558	.1339	.1118	.0912	.0729	.0573	.0443	.0337	.0254	.0189
5	.1714	.1606	.1454	.1277	.1094	.0916	.0752	.0607	.0483	.0378
6	.1571	.1606	.1575	.1490	.1367	.1221	.1066	.0911	.0764	.0631
7	.1234	.1377	.1462	.1490	.1465	.1396	.1294	.1171	.1037	.0901
8	.0849	.1033	.1188	.1304	.1373	.1396	.1375	.1318	.1232	.1126
9	.0519	.0688	.0858	.1014	.1144	.1241	.1299	.1318	.1300	.1251
10	.0285	.0413	.0558	.0710	.0858	.0993	.1104	.1186	.1235	.1251
11	.0143	.0225	.0330	.0452	.0585	.0722	.0853	.0970	.1067	.1137
12	.0065	.0113	.0179	.0263	.0366	.0481	.0604	.0728	.0844	.0948
13	.0028	.0052	.0089	.0142	.0211	.0296	.0395	.0504	.0617	.0729
14	.0011	.0022	.0041	.0071	.0113	.0169	.0240	.0324	.0419	.0521
15	.0004	.0009	.0018	.0033	.0057	.0090	.0136	.0194	.0265	.0347
16	.0001	.0003	.0007	.0014	.0026	.0045	.0072	.0109	.0157	.0217
17	.0000	.0001	.0003	.0006	.0012	.0021	.0036	.0058	.0088	.0128
18	.0000	.0000	.0001	.0002	.0005	.0009	.0017	.0029	.0046	.0071
19	.0000	.0000	.0000	.0001	.0002	.0004	.0008	.0014	.0023	.0037
20	.0000	.0000	.0000	.0000	.0001	.0002	.0003	.0006	.0011	.0019
21	.0000	.0000	.0000	.0000	.0000	.0001	.0001	.0003	.0005	.0009
22	.0000	.0000	.0000	.0000	.0000	.0000	.0001	.0001	.0002	.0004
23	.0000	.0000	.0000	.0000	.0000	.0000	.0000	.0000	.0001	.0002

y	11.0	12.0	13.0	14.0	15.0	16.0	17.0	18.0	19.0	20.0
0	.0000	.0000	.0000	.0000	.0000	.0000	.0000	.0000	.0000	.0000
1	.0002	.0001	.0000	.0000	.0000	.0000	.0000	.0000	.0000	.0000
2	.0010	.0004	.0002	.0001	.0000	.0000	.0000	.0000	.0000	.0000
3	.0037	.0018	.0008	.0004	.0002	.0001	.0000	.0000	.0000	.0000
4	.0102	.0053	.0027	.0013	.0006	.0003	.0001	.0001	.0000	.0000
5	.0224	.0127	.0070	.0037	.0019	.0010	.0005	.0002	.0001	.0001
6	.0411	.0255	.0152	.0087	.0048	.0026	.0014	.0007	.0004	.0002
7	.0646	.0437	.0281	.0174	.0104	.0060	.0034	.0019	.0010	.0005
8	.0888	.0655	.0457	.0304	.0194	.0120	.0072	.0042	.0024	.0013
9	.1085	.0874	.0661	.0473	.0324	.0213	.0135	.0083	.0050	.0029
10	.1194	.1048	.0859	.0663	.0486	.0341	.0230	.0150	.0095	.0058
11	.1194	.1144	.1015	.0844	.0663	.0496	.0355	.0245	.0164	.0106
12	.1094	.1144	.1099	.0984	.0829	.0661	.0504	.0368	.0259	.0176
13	.0926	.1056	.1099	.1060	.0956	.0814	.0658	.0509	.0378	.0271
14	.0728	.0905	.1021	.1060	.1024	.0930	.0800	.0655	.0514	.0387
15	.0534	.0724	.0885	.0989	.1024	.0992	.0906	.0786	.0650	.0516
16	.0367	.0543	.0719	.0866	.0960	.0992	.0963	.0884	.0772	.0646
17	.0237	.0383	.0550	.0713	.0847	.0934	.0963	.0936	.0863	.0760
18	.0145	.0255	.0397	.0554	.0706	.0830	.0909	.0936	.0911	.0844
19	.0084	.0161	.0272	.0409	.0557	.0699	.0814	.0887	.0911	.0888
20	.0046	.0097	.0177	.0286	.0418	.0559	.0692	.0798	.0866	.0888
21	.0024	.0055	.0109	.0191	.0299	.0426	.0560	.0684	.0783	.0846
22	.0012	.0030	.0065	.0121	.0204	.0310	.0433	.0560	.0676	.0769
23	.0006	.0016	.0037	.0074	.0133	.0216	.0320	.0438	.0559	.0669
24	.0003	.0008	.0020	.0043	.0083	.0144	.0226	.0328	.0442	.0557
25	.0001	.0004	.0010	.0024	.0050	.0092	.0154	.0237	.0336	.0446
26	.0000	.0002	.0005	.0013	.0029	.0057	.0101	.0164	.0246	.0343
27	.0000	.0001	.0002	.0007	.0016	.0034	.0063	.0109	.0173	.0254
28	.0000	.0000	.0001	.0003	.0009	.0019	.0038	.0070	.0117	.0181
29	.0000	.0000	.0001	.0002	.0004	.0011	.0023	.0044	.0077	.0125
30	.0000	.0000	.0000	.0001	.0002	.0006	.0013	.0026	.0049	.0083
31	.0000	.0000	.0000	.0000	.0001	.0003	.0007	.0015	.0030	.0054
32	.0000	.0000	.0000	.0000	.0001	.0001	.0004	.0009	.0018	.0034
33	.0000	.0000	.0000	.0000	.0000	.0001	.0002	.0005	.0010	.0020

Source: Computed by D. K. Hildebrand.

TABLE 3 Normal Curve Areas

z	.00	.01	.02	.03	.04	.05	.06	.07	.08	.09
0.00	.0000	.0040	.0080	.0120	.0160	.0199	.0239	.0279	.0319	.0359
0.10	.0398	.0438	.0478	.0517	.0557	.0596	.0636	.0675	.0714	.0753
0.20	.0793	.0832	.0871	.0910	.0948	.0987	.1026	.1064	.1103	.1141
0.30	.1179	.1217	.1255	.1293	.1331	.1368	.1406	.1443	.1480	.1517
0.40	.1554	.1591	.1628	.1664	.1700	.1736	.1772	.1808	.1844	.1879
0.50	.1915	.1950	.1985	.2019	.2054	.2088	.2123	.2157	.2190	.2224
0.60	.2257	.2291	.2324	.2357	.2389	.2422	.2454	.2486	.2517	.2549
0.70	.2580	.2611	.2642	.2673	.2704	.2734	.2764	.2794	.2823	.2852
0.80	.2881	.2910	.2939	.2967	.2995	.3023	.3051	.3078	.3106	.3133
0.90	.3159	.3186	.3212	.3238	.3264	.3289	.3315	.3340	.3365	.3389
1.00	.3413	.3438	.3461	.3485	.3508	.3531	.3554	.3577	.3599	.3621
1.10	.3643	.3665	.3686	.3708	.3729	.3749	.3770	.3790	.3810	.3830
1.20	.3849	.3869	.3888	.3907	.3925	.3944	.3962	.3980	.3997	.4015
1.30	.4032	.4049	.4066	.4082	.4099	.4115	.4131	.4147	.4162	.4177
1.40	.4192	.4207	.4222	.4236	.4251	.4265	.4279	.4292	.4306	.4319
1.50	.4332	.4345	.4357	.4370	.4382	.4394	.4406	.4418	.4429	.4441
1.60	.4452	.4463	.4474	.4484	.4495	.4505	.4515	.4525	.4535	.4545
1.70	.4554	.4564	.4573	.4582	.4591	.4599	.4608	.4616	.4625	.4633
1.80	.4641	.4649	.4656	.4664	.4671	.4678	.4686	.4693	.4699	.4706
1.90	.4713	.4719	.4726	.4732	.4738	.4744	.4750	.4756	.4761	.4767
2.00	.4772	.4778	.4783	.4788	.4793	.4798	.4803	.4808	.4812	.4817
2.10	.4821	.4826	.4830	.4834	.4838	.4842	.4846	.4850	.4854	.4857
2.20	.4861	.4864	.4868	.4871	.4875	.4878	.4881	.4884	.4887	.4890
2.30	.4893	.4896	.4898	.4901	.4904	.4906	.4909	.4911	.4913	.4916
2.40	.4918	.4920	.4922	.4925	.4927	.4929	.4931	.4932	.4934	.4936
2.50	.4938	.4940	.4941	.4943	.4945	.4946	.4948	.4949	.4951	.4952
2.60	.4953	.4955	.4956	.4957	.4959	.4960	.4961	.4962	.4963	.4964
2.70	.4965	.4966	.4967	.4968	.4969	.4970	.4971	.4972	.4973	.4974
2.80	.4974	.4975	.4976	.4977	.4977	.4978	.4979	.4979	.4980	.4981
2.90	.4981	.4982	.4982	.4983	.4984	.4984	.4985	.4985	.4986	.4986
3.00	.4987	.4987	.4987	.4988	.4988	.4989	.4989	.4989	.4990	.4990

z	area
3.50	.49976737
4.00	.49996833
4.50	.49999660
5.00	.49999971

Source: Computed by P. J. Hildebrand.

TABLE 4   Percentage Points of the *t* Distribution

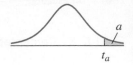

d.f.	a = .1	a = .05	a = .025	a = .01	a = .005	a = .001
1	3.078	6.314	12.706	31.821	63.657	318.309
2	1.886	2.920	4.303	6.965	9.925	22.327
3	1.638	2.353	3.182	4.541	5.841	10.215
4	1.533	2.132	2.776	3.747	4.604	7.173
5	1.476	2.015	2.571	3.365	4.032	5.893
6	1.440	1.943	2.447	3.143	3.707	5.208
7	1.415	1.895	2.365	2.998	3.499	4.785
8	1.397	1.860	2.306	2.896	3.355	4.501
9	1.383	1.833	2.262	2.821	3.250	4.297
10	1.372	1.812	2.228	2.764	3.169	4.144
11	1.363	1.796	2.201	2.718	3.106	4.025
12	1.356	1.782	2.179	2.681	3.055	3.930
13	1.350	1.771	2.160	2.650	3.012	3.852
14	1.345	1.761	2.145	2.624	2.977	3.787
15	1.341	1.753	2.131	2.602	2.947	3.733
16	1.337	1.746	2.120	2.583	2.921	3.686
17	1.333	1.740	2.110	2.567	2.898	3.646
18	1.330	1.734	2.101	2.552	2.878	3.610
19	1.328	1.729	2.093	2.539	2.861	3.579
20	1.325	1.725	2.086	2.528	2.845	3.552
21	1.323	1.721	2.080	2.518	2.831	3.527
22	1.321	1.717	2.074	2.508	2.819	3.505
23	1.319	1.714	2.069	2.500	2.807	3.485
24	1.318	1.711	2.064	2.492	2.797	3.467
25	1.316	1.708	2.060	2.485	2.787	3.450
26	1.315	1.706	2.056	2.479	2.779	3.435
27	1.314	1.703	2.052	2.473	2.771	3.421
28	1.313	1.701	2.048	2.467	2.763	3.408
29	1.311	1.699	2.045	2.462	2.756	3.396
30	1.310	1.697	2.042	2.457	2.750	3.385
40	1.303	1.684	2.021	2.423	2.704	3.307
60	1.296	1.671	2.000	2.390	2.660	3.232
120	1.289	1.658	1.980	2.358	2.617	3.160
240	1.285	1.651	1.970	2.342	2.596	3.125
∞	1.282	1.645	1.960	2.326	2.576	3.090

Source: Computed by P. J. Hildebrand.

TABLE 5   Percentage Points of the χ^2 Distribution ($a > .5$)

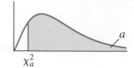

χ_a^2

d.f.	$a = .999$	$a = .995$	$a = .99$	$a = .975$	$a = .95$	$a = .9$
1	.000002	.000039	.000157	.000982	.003932	.01579
2	.002001	.01003	.02010	.05064	.1026	.2107
3	.02430	.07172	.1148	.2158	.3518	.5844
4	.09080	.2070	.2971	.4844	.7107	1.064
5	.2102	.4117	.5543	.8312	1.145	1.610
6	.3811	.6757	.8721	1.237	1.635	2.204
7	.5985	.9893	1.239	1.690	2.167	2.833
8	.8571	1.344	1.646	2.180	2.733	3.490
9	1.152	1.735	2.088	2.700	3.325	4.168
10	1.479	2.156	2.558	3.247	3.940	4.865
11	1.834	2.603	3.053	3.816	4.575	5.578
12	2.214	3.074	3.571	4.404	5.226	6.304
13	2.617	3.565	4.107	5.009	5.892	7.042
14	3.041	4.075	4.660	5.629	6.571	7.790
15	3.483	4.601	5.229	6.262	7.261	8.547
16	3.942	5.142	5.812	6.908	7.962	9.312
17	4.416	5.697	6.408	7.564	8.672	10.09
18	4.905	6.265	7.015	8.231	9.390	10.86
19	5.407	6.844	7.633	8.907	10.12	11.65
20	5.921	7.434	8.260	9.591	10.85	12.44
21	6.447	8.034	8.897	10.28	11.59	13.24
22	6.983	8.643	9.542	10.98	12.34	14.04
23	7.529	9.260	10.20	11.69	13.09	14.85
24	8.085	9.886	10.86	12.40	13.85	15.66
25	8.649	10.52	11.52	13.12	14.61	16.47
26	9.222	11.16	12.20	13.84	15.38	17.29
27	9.803	11.81	12.88	14.57	16.15	18.11
28	10.39	12.46	13.56	15.31	16.93	18.94
29	10.99	13.12	14.26	16.05	17.71	19.77
30	11.59	13.79	14.95	16.79	18.49	20.60
40	17.92	20.71	22.16	24.43	26.51	29.05
50	24.67	27.99	29.71	32.36	34.76	37.69
60	31.74	35.53	37.48	40.48	43.19	46.46
70	39.04	43.28	45.44	48.76	51.74	55.33
80	46.52	51.17	53.54	57.15	60.39	64.28
90	54.16	59.20	61.75	65.65	69.13	73.29
100	61.92	67.33	70.06	74.22	77.93	82.36
120	77.76	83.85	86.92	91.57	95.70	100.62
240	177.95	187.32	191.99	198.98	205.14	212.39

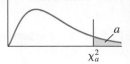

$a = .1$	$a = .05$	$a = .025$	$a = .01$	$a = .005$	$a = .001$	d.f.
2.706	3.841	5.024	6.635	7.879	10.83	1
4.605	5.991	7.378	9.210	10.60	13.82	2
6.251	7.815	9.348	11.34	12.84	16.27	3
7.779	9.488	11.14	13.28	14.86	18.47	4
9.236	11.07	12.83	15.09	16.75	20.52	5
10.64	12.59	14.45	16.81	18.55	22.46	6
12.02	14.07	16.01	18.48	20.28	24.32	7
13.36	15.51	17.53	20.09	21.95	26.12	8
14.68	16.92	19.02	21.67	23.59	27.88	9
15.99	18.31	20.48	23.21	25.19	29.59	10
17.28	19.68	21.92	24.72	26.76	31.27	11
18.55	21.03	23.34	26.22	28.30	32.91	12
19.81	22.36	24.74	27.69	29.82	34.53	13
21.06	23.68	26.12	29.14	31.32	36.12	14
22.31	25.00	27.49	30.58	32.80	37.70	15
23.54	26.30	28.85	32.00	34.27	39.25	16
24.77	27.59	30.19	33.41	35.72	40.79	17
25.99	28.87	31.53	34.81	37.16	42.31	18
27.20	30.14	32.85	36.19	38.58	43.82	19
28.41	31.41	34.17	37.57	40.00	45.31	20
29.62	32.67	35.48	38.93	41.40	46.80	21
30.81	33.92	36.78	40.29	42.80	48.27	22
32.01	35.17	38.08	41.64	44.18	49.73	23
33.20	36.42	39.36	42.98	45.56	51.18	24
34.38	37.65	40.65	44.31	46.93	52.62	25
35.56	38.89	41.92	45.64	48.29	54.05	26
36.74	40.11	43.19	46.96	49.65	55.48	27
37.92	41.34	44.46	48.28	50.99	56.89	28
39.09	42.56	45.72	49.59	52.34	58.30	29
40.26	43.77	46.98	50.89	53.67	59.70	30
51.81	55.76	59.34	63.69	66.77	73.40	40
63.17	67.50	71.42	76.15	79.49	86.66	50
74.40	79.08	83.30	88.38	91.95	99.61	60
85.53	90.53	95.02	100.43	104.21	112.32	70
96.58	101.88	106.63	112.33	116.32	124.84	80
107.57	113.15	118.14	124.12	128.30	137.21	90
118.50	124.34	129.56	135.81	140.17	149.45	100
140.23	146.57	152.21	158.95	163.65	173.62	120
268.47	277.14	284.80	293.89	300.18	313.44	240

Source: Computed by P. J. Hildebrand

TABLE 6 Percentage Points of the *F* Distribution (d.f.$_2$ between 1 and 6)

d.f.$_2$	a	\(d.f._1\) 1	2	3	4	5	6	7	8	9	10
1	.25	5.83	7.50	8.20	8.58	8.82	8.98	9.10	9.19	9.26	9.32
	.10	39.86	49.50	53.59	55.83	57.24	58.20	58.91	59.44	59.86	60.19
	.05	161.4	199.5	215.7	224.6	230.2	234.0	236.8	238.9	240.5	241.9
	.025	647.8	799.5	864.2	899.6	921.8	937.1	948.2	956.7	963.3	968.6
	.01	4052	5000	5403	5625	5764	5859	5928	5981	6022	6056
2	.25	2.57	3.00	3.15	3.23	3.28	3.31	3.34	3.35	3.37	3.38
	.10	8.53	9.00	9.16	9.24	9.29	9.33	9.35	9.37	9.38	9.39
	.05	18.51	19.00	19.16	19.25	19.30	19.33	19.35	19.37	19.38	19.40
	.025	38.51	39.00	39.17	39.25	39.30	39.33	39.36	39.37	39.39	39.40
	.01	98.50	99.00	99.17	99.25	99.30	99.33	99.36	99.37	99.39	99.40
	.005	198.5	199.0	199.2	199.2	199.3	199.3	199.4	199.4	199.4	199.4
	.001	998.5	999.0	999.2	999.2	999.3	999.3	999.4	999.4	999.4	999.4
3	.25	2.02	2.28	2.36	2.39	2.41	2.42	2.43	2.44	2.44	2.44
	.10	5.54	5.46	5.39	5.34	5.31	5.28	5.27	5.25	5.24	5.23
	.05	10.13	9.55	9.28	9.12	9.01	8.94	8.89	8.85	8.81	8.79
	.025	17.44	16.04	15.44	15.10	14.88	14.73	14.62	14.54	14.47	14.42
	.01	34.12	30.82	29.46	28.71	28.24	27.91	27.67	27.49	27.35	27.23
	.005	55.55	49.80	47.47	46.19	45.39	44.84	44.43	44.13	43.88	43.69
	.001	167.0	148.5	141.1	137.1	134.6	132.8	131.6	130.6	129.9	129.2
4	.25	1.81	2.00	2.05	2.06	2.07	2.08	2.08	2.08	2.08	2.08
	.10	4.54	4.32	4.19	4.11	4.05	4.01	3.98	3.95	3.94	3.92
	.05	7.71	6.94	6.59	6.39	6.26	6.16	6.09	6.04	6.00	5.96
	.025	12.22	10.65	9.98	9.60	9.36	9.20	9.07	8.98	8.90	8.84
	.01	21.20	18.00	16.69	15.98	15.52	15.21	14.98	14.80	14.66	14.55
	.005	31.33	26.28	24.26	23.15	22.46	21.97	21.62	21.35	21.14	20.97
	.001	74.14	61.25	56.18	53.44	51.71	50.53	49.66	49.00	48.47	48.05
5	.25	1.69	1.85	1.88	1.89	1.89	1.89	1.89	1.89	1.89	1.89
	.10	4.06	3.78	3.62	3.52	3.45	3.40	3.37	3.34	3.32	3.30
	.05	6.61	5.79	5.41	5.19	5.05	4.95	4.88	4.82	4.77	4.74
	.025	10.01	8.43	7.76	7.39	7.15	6.98	6.85	6.76	6.68	6.62
	.01	16.26	13.27	12.06	11.39	10.97	10.67	10.46	10.29	10.16	10.05
	.005	22.78	18.31	16.53	15.56	14.94	14.51	14.20	13.96	13.77	13.62
	.001	47.18	37.12	33.20	31.09	29.75	28.83	28.16	27.65	27.24	26.92
6	.25	1.62	1.76	1.78	1.79	1.79	1.78	1.78	1.78	1.77	1.77
	.10	3.78	3.46	3.29	3.18	3.11	3.05	3.01	2.98	2.96	2.94
	.05	5.99	5.14	4.76	4.53	4.39	4.28	4.21	4.15	4.10	4.06
	.025	8.81	7.26	6.60	6.23	5.99	5.82	5.70	5.60	5.52	5.46
	.01	13.75	10.92	9.78	9.15	8.75	8.47	8.26	8.10	7.98	7.87
	.005	18.63	14.54	12.92	12.03	11.46	11.07	10.79	10.57	10.39	10.25
	.001	35.51	27.00	23.70	21.92	20.80	20.03	19.46	19.03	18.69	18.41

Appendix

				d.f.$_1$								
12	**15**	**20**	**24**	**30**	**40**	**60**	**120**	**240**	**∞**	**a**	**d.f.$_2$**
9.41	9.49	9.58	9.63	9.67	9.71	9.76	9.80	9.83	9.85	.25	**1**
60.71	61.22	61.74	62.00	62.26	62.53	62.79	63.06	63.19	63.33	.10	
243.9	245.9	248.0	249.1	250.1	251.1	252.2	253.3	253.8	254.3	.05	
976.7	984.9	993.1	997.2	1001	1006	1010	1014	1016	1018	.025	
6106	6157	6209	6235	6261	6287	6313	6339	6353	6366	.01	
3.39	3.41	3.43	3.43	3.44	3.45	3.46	3.47	3.47	3.48	.25	**2**
9.41	9.42	9.44	9.45	9.46	9.47	9.47	9.48	9.49	9.49	.10	
19.41	19.43	19.45	19.45	19.46	19.47	19.48	19.49	19.49	19.50	.05	
39.41	39.43	39.45	39.46	39.46	39.47	39.48	39.49	39.49	39.50	.025	
99.42	99.43	99.45	99.46	99.47	99.47	99.48	99.49	99.49	99.50	.01	
199.4	199.4	199.4	199.5	199.5	199.5	199.5	199.5	199.5	199.5	.005	
999.4	999.4	999.4	999.5	999.5	999.5	999.5	999.5	999.5	999.5	.001	
2.45	2.46	2.46	2.46	2.47	2.47	2.47	2.47	2.47	2.47	.25	**3**
5.22	5.20	5.18	5.18	5.17	5.16	5.15	5.14	5.14	5.13	.10	
8.74	8.70	8.66	8.64	8.62	8.59	8.57	8.55	8.54	8.53	.05	
14.34	14.25	14.17	14.12	14.08	14.04	13.99	13.95	13.92	13.90	.025	
27.05	26.87	26.69	26.60	26.50	26.41	26.32	26.22	26.17	26.13	.01	
43.39	43.08	42.78	42.62	42.47	42.31	42.15	41.99	41.91	41.83	.005	
128.3	127.4	126.4	125.9	125.4	125.0	124.5	124.0	123.7	123.5	.001	
2.08	2.08	2.08	2.08	2.08	2.08	2.08	2.08	2.08	2.08	.25	**4**
3.90	3.87	3.84	3.83	3.82	3.80	3.79	3.78	3.77	3.76	.10	
5.91	5.86	5.80	5.77	5.75	5.72	5.69	5.66	5.64	5.63	.05	
8.75	8.66	8.56	8.51	8.46	8.41	8.36	8.31	8.28	8.26	.025	
14.37	14.20	14.02	13.93	13.84	13.75	13.65	13.56	13.51	13.46	.01	
20.70	20.44	20.17	20.03	19.89	19.75	19.61	19.47	19.40	19.32	.005	
47.41	46.76	46.10	45.77	45.43	45.09	44.75	44.40	44.23	44.05	.001	
1.89	1.89	1.88	1.88	1.88	1.88	1.87	1.87	1.87	1.87	.25	**5**
3.27	3.24	3.21	3.19	3.17	3.16	3.14	3.12	3.11	3.10	.10	
4.68	4.62	4.56	4.53	4.50	4.46	4.43	4.40	4.38	4.36	.05	
6.52	6.43	6.33	6.28	6.23	6.18	6.12	6.07	6.04	6.02	.025	
9.89	9.72	9.55	9.47	9.38	9.29	9.20	9.11	9.07	9.02	.01	
13.38	13.15	12.90	12.78	12.66	12.53	12.40	12.27	12.21	12.14	.005	
26.42	25.91	25.39	25.13	24.87	24.60	24.33	24.06	23.92	23.79	.001	
1.77	1.76	1.76	1.75	1.75	1.75	1.74	1.74	1.74	1.74	.25	**6**
2.90	2.87	2.84	2.82	2.80	2.78	2.76	2.74	2.73	2.72	.10	
4.00	3.94	3.87	3.84	3.81	3.77	3.74	3.70	3.69	3.67	.05	
5.37	5.27	5.17	5.12	5.07	5.01	4.96	4.90	4.88	4.85	.025	
7.72	7.56	7.40	7.31	7.23	7.14	7.06	6.97	6.92	6.88	.01	
10.03	9.81	9.59	9.47	9.36	9.24	9.12	9.00	8.94	8.88	.005	
17.99	17.56	17.12	16.90	16.67	16.44	16.21	15.98	15.86	15.75	.001	

TABLE 6 (continued) **Percentage Points of the *F* Distribution (d.f.$_2$ between 7 and 12)**

| d.f.$_2$ | a | \multicolumn{10}{c}{d.f.$_1$} | | | | | | | | | |
		1	2	3	4	5	6	7	8	9	10
7	.25	1.57	1.70	1.72	1.72	1.71	1.71	1.70	1.70	1.69	1.69
	.10	3.59	3.26	3.07	2.96	2.88	2.83	2.78	2.75	2.72	2.70
	.05	5.59	4.74	4.35	4.12	3.97	3.87	3.79	3.73	3.68	3.64
	.025	8.07	6.54	5.89	5.52	5.29	5.12	4.99	4.90	4.82	4.76
	.01	12.25	9.55	8.45	7.85	7.46	7.19	6.99	6.84	6.72	6.62
	.005	16.24	12.40	10.88	10.05	9.52	9.16	8.89	8.68	8.51	8.38
	.001	29.25	21.69	18.77	17.20	16.21	15.52	15.02	14.63	14.33	14.08
8	.25	1.54	1.66	1.67	1.66	1.66	1.65	1.64	1.64	1.63	1.63
	.10	3.46	3.11	2.92	2.81	2.73	2.67	2.62	2.59	2.56	2.54
	.05	5.32	4.46	4.07	3.84	3.69	3.58	3.50	3.44	3.39	3.35
	.025	7.57	6.06	5.42	5.05	4.82	4.65	4.53	4.43	4.36	4.30
	.01	11.26	8.65	7.59	7.01	6.63	6.37	6.18	6.03	5.91	5.81
	.005	14.69	11.04	9.60	8.81	8.30	7.95	7.69	7.50	7.34	7.21
	.001	25.41	18.49	15.83	14.39	13.48	12.86	12.40	12.05	11.77	11.54
9	.25	1.51	1.62	1.63	1.63	1.62	1.61	1.60	1.60	1.59	1.59
	.10	3.36	3.01	2.81	2.69	2.61	2.55	2.51	2.47	2.44	2.42
	.05	5.12	4.26	3.86	3.63	3.48	3.37	3.29	3.23	3.18	3.14
	.025	7.21	5.71	5.08	4.72	4.48	4.32	4.20	4.10	4.03	3.96
	.01	10.56	8.02	6.99	6.42	6.06	5.80	5.61	5.47	5.35	5.26
	.005	13.61	10.11	8.72	7.96	7.47	7.13	6.88	6.69	6.54	6.42
	.001	22.86	16.39	13.90	12.56	11.71	11.13	10.70	10.37	10.11	9.89
10	.25	1.49	1.60	1.60	1.59	1.59	1.58	1.57	1.56	1.56	1.55
	.10	3.29	2.92	2.73	2.61	2.52	2.46	2.41	2.38	2.35	2.32
	.05	4.96	4.10	3.71	3.48	3.33	3.22	3.14	3.07	3.02	2.98
	.025	6.94	5.46	4.83	4.47	4.24	4.07	3.95	3.85	3.78	3.72
	.01	10.04	7.56	6.55	5.99	5.64	5.39	5.20	5.06	4.94	4.85
	.005	12.83	9.43	8.08	7.34	6.87	6.54	6.30	6.12	5.97	5.85
	.001	21.04	14.91	12.55	11.28	10.48	9.93	9.52	9.20	8.96	8.75
11	.25	1.47	1.58	1.58	1.57	1.56	1.55	1.54	1.53	1.53	1.52
	.10	3.23	2.86	2.66	2.54	2.45	2.39	2.34	2.30	2.27	2.25
	.05	4.84	3.98	3.59	3.36	3.20	3.09	3.01	2.95	2.90	2.85
	.025	6.72	5.26	4.63	4.28	4.04	3.88	3.76	3.66	3.59	3.53
	.01	9.65	7.21	6.22	5.67	5.32	5.07	4.89	4.74	4.63	4.54
	.005	12.23	8.91	7.60	6.88	6.42	6.10	5.86	5.68	5.54	5.42
	.001	19.69	13.81	11.56	10.35	9.58	9.05	8.66	8.35	8.12	7.92
12	.25	1.46	1.56	1.56	1.55	1.54	1.53	1.52	1.51	1.51	1.50
	.10	3.18	2.81	2.61	2.48	2.39	2.33	2.28	2.24	2.21	2.19
	.05	4.75	3.89	3.49	3.26	3.11	3.00	2.91	2.85	2.80	2.75
	.025	6.55	5.10	4.47	4.12	3.89	3.73	3.61	3.51	3.44	3.37
	.01	9.33	6.93	5.95	5.41	5.06	4.82	4.64	4.50	4.39	4.30
	.005	11.75	8.51	7.23	6.52	6.07	5.76	5.52	5.35	5.20	5.09
	.001	18.64	12.97	10.80	9.63	8.89	8.38	8.00	7.71	7.48	7.29

Appendix

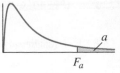

				d.f.₁							
12	**15**	**20**	**24**	**30**	**40**	**60**	**120**	**240**	**∞**	**a**	**d.f.₂**
1.68	1.68	1.67	1.67	1.66	1.66	1.65	1.65	1.65	1.65	**.25**	7
2.67	2.63	2.59	2.58	2.56	2.54	2.51	2.49	2.48	2.47	**.10**	
3.57	3.51	3.44	3.41	3.38	3.34	3.30	3.27	3.25	3.23	**.05**	
4.67	4.57	4.47	4.41	4.36	4.31	4.25	4.20	4.17	4.14	**.025**	
6.47	6.31	6.16	6.07	5.99	5.91	5.82	5.74	5.69	5.65	**.01**	
8.18	7.97	7.75	7.64	7.53	7.42	7.31	7.19	7.13	7.08	**.005**	
13.71	13.32	12.93	12.73	12.53	12.33	12.12	11.91	11.80	11.70	**.001**	
1.62	1.62	1.61	1.60	1.60	1.59	1.59	1.58	1.58	1.58	**.25**	8
2.50	2.46	2.42	2.40	2.38	2.36	2.34	2.32	2.30	2.29	**.10**	
3.28	3.22	3.15	3.12	3.08	3.04	3.01	2.97	2.95	2.93	**.05**	
4.20	4.10	4.00	3.95	3.89	3.84	3.78	3.73	3.70	3.67	**.025**	
5.67	5.52	5.36	5.28	5.20	5.12	5.03	4.95	4.90	4.86	**.01**	
7.01	6.81	6.61	6.50	6.40	6.29	6.18	6.06	6.01	5.95	**.005**	
11.19	10.84	10.48	10.30	10.11	9.92	9.73	9.53	9.43	9.33	**.001**	
1.58	1.57	1.56	1.56	1.55	1.54	1.54	1.53	1.53	1.53	**.25**	9
2.38	2.34	2.30	2.28	2.25	2.23	2.21	2.18	2.17	2.16	**.10**	
3.07	3.01	2.94	2.90	2.86	2.83	2.79	2.75	2.73	2.71	**.05**	
3.87	3.77	3.67	3.61	3.56	3.51	3.45	3.39	3.36	3.33	**.025**	
5.11	4.96	4.81	4.73	4.65	4.57	4.48	4.40	4.35	4.31	**.01**	
6.23	6.03	5.83	5.73	5.62	5.52	5.41	5.30	5.24	5.19	**.005**	
9.57	9.24	8.90	8.72	8.55	8.37	8.19	8.00	7.91	7.81	**.001**	
1.54	1.53	1.52	1.52	1.51	1.51	1.50	1.49	1.49	1.48	**.25**	10
2.28	2.24	2.20	2.18	2.16	2.13	2.11	2.08	2.07	2.06	**.10**	
2.91	2.85	2.77	2.74	2.70	2.66	2.62	2.58	2.56	2.54	**.05**	
3.62	3.52	3.42	3.37	3.31	3.26	3.20	3.14	3.11	3.08	**.025**	
4.71	4.56	4.41	4.33	4.25	4.17	4.08	4.00	3.95	3.91	**.01**	
5.66	5.47	5.27	5.17	5.07	4.97	4.86	4.75	4.69	4.64	**.005**	
8.45	8.13	7.80	7.64	7.47	7.30	7.12	6.94	6.85	6.76	**.001**	
1.51	1.50	1.49	1.49	1.48	1.47	1.47	1.46	1.45	1.45	**.25**	11
2.21	2.17	2.12	2.10	2.08	2.05	2.03	2.00	1.99	1.97	**.10**	
2.79	2.72	2.65	2.61	2.57	2.53	2.49	2.45	2.43	2.40	**.05**	
3.43	3.33	3.23	3.17	3.12	3.06	3.00	2.94	2.91	2.88	**.025**	
4.40	4.25	4.10	4.02	3.94	3.86	3.78	3.69	3.65	3.60	**.01**	
5.24	5.05	4.86	4.76	4.65	4.55	4.45	4.34	4.28	4.23	**.005**	
7.63	7.32	7.01	6.85	6.68	6.52	6.35	6.18	6.09	6.00	**.001**	
1.49	1.48	1.47	1.46	1.45	1.45	1.44	1.43	1.43	1.42	**.25**	12
2.15	2.10	2.06	2.04	2.01	1.99	1.96	1.93	1.92	1.90	**.10**	
2.69	2.62	2.54	2.51	2.47	2.43	2.38	2.34	2.32	2.30	**.05**	
3.28	3.18	3.07	3.02	2.96	2.91	2.85	2.79	2.76	2.72	**.025**	
4.16	4.01	3.86	3.78	3.70	3.62	3.54	3.45	3.41	3.36	**.01**	
4.91	4.72	4.53	4.43	4.33	4.23	4.12	4.01	3.96	3.90	**.005**	
7.00	6.71	6.40	6.25	6.09	5.93	5.76	5.59	5.51	5.42	**.001**	

TABLE 6 (continued) Percentage Points of the *F* Distribution (d.f.₂ between 13 and 18)

d.f.₂	*a*	1	2	3	4	5	6	7	8	9	10
13	.25	1.45	1.55	1.55	1.53	1.52	1.51	1.50	1.49	1.49	1.48
	.10	3.14	2.76	2.56	2.43	2.35	2.28	2.23	2.20	2.16	2.14
	.05	4.67	3.81	3.41	3.18	3.03	2.92	2.83	2.77	2.71	2.67
	.025	6.41	4.97	4.35	4.00	3.77	3.60	3.48	3.39	3.31	3.25
	.01	9.07	6.70	5.74	5.21	4.86	4.62	4.44	4.30	4.19	4.10
	.005	11.37	8.19	6.93	6.23	5.79	5.48	5.25	5.08	4.94	4.82
	.001	17.82	12.31	10.21	9.07	8.35	7.86	7.49	7.21	6.98	6.80
14	.25	1.44	1.53	1.53	1.52	1.51	1.50	1.49	1.48	1.47	1.46
	.10	3.10	2.73	2.52	2.39	2.31	2.24	2.19	2.15	2.12	2.10
	.05	4.60	3.74	3.34	3.11	2.96	2.85	2.76	2.70	2.65	2.60
	.025	6.30	4.86	4.24	3.89	3.66	3.50	3.38	3.29	3.21	3.15
	.01	8.86	6.51	5.56	5.04	4.69	4.46	4.28	4.14	4.03	3.94
	.005	11.06	7.92	6.68	6.00	5.56	5.26	5.03	4.86	4.72	4.60
	.001	17.14	11.78	9.73	8.62	7.92	7.44	7.08	6.80	6.58	6.40
15	.25	1.43	1.52	1.52	1.51	1.49	1.48	1.47	1.46	1.46	1.45
	.10	3.07	2.70	2.49	2.36	2.27	2.21	2.16	2.12	2.09	2.06
	.05	4.54	3.68	3.29	3.06	2.90	2.79	2.71	2.64	2.59	2.54
	.025	6.20	4.77	4.15	3.80	3.58	3.41	3.29	3.20	3.12	3.06
	.01	8.68	6.36	5.42	4.89	4.56	4.32	4.14	4.00	3.89	3.80
	.005	10.80	7.70	6.48	5.80	5.37	5.07	4.85	4.67	4.54	4.42
	.001	16.59	11.34	9.34	8.25	7.57	7.09	6.74	6.47	6.26	6.08
16	.25	1.42	1.51	1.51	1.50	1.48	1.47	1.46	1.45	1.44	1.44
	.10	3.05	2.67	2.46	2.33	2.24	2.18	2.13	2.09	2.06	2.03
	.05	4.49	3.63	3.24	3.01	2.85	2.74	2.66	2.59	2.54	2.49
	.025	6.12	4.69	4.08	3.73	3.50	3.34	3.22	3.12	3.05	2.99
	.01	8.53	6.23	5.29	4.77	4.44	4.20	4.03	3.89	3.78	3.69
	.005	10.58	7.51	6.30	5.64	5.21	4.91	4.69	4.52	4.38	4.27
	.001	16.12	10.97	9.01	7.94	7.27	6.80	6.46	6.19	5.98	5.81
17	.25	1.42	1.51	1.50	1.49	1.47	1.46	1.45	1.44	1.43	1.43
	.10	3.03	2.64	2.44	2.31	2.22	2.15	2.10	2.06	2.03	2.00
	.05	4.45	3.59	3.20	2.96	2.81	2.70	2.61	2.55	2.49	2.45
	.025	6.04	4.62	4.01	3.66	3.44	3.28	3.16	3.06	2.98	2.92
	.01	8.40	6.11	5.18	4.67	4.34	4.10	3.93	3.79	3.68	3.59
	.005	10.38	7.35	6.16	5.50	5.07	4.78	4.56	4.39	4.25	4.14
	.001	15.72	10.66	8.73	7.68	7.02	6.56	6.22	5.96	5.75	5.58
18	.25	1.41	1.50	1.49	1.48	1.46	1.45	1.44	1.43	1.42	1.42
	.10	3.01	2.62	2.42	2.29	2.20	2.13	2.08	2.04	2.00	1.98
	.05	4.41	3.55	3.16	2.93	2.77	2.66	2.58	2.51	2.46	2.41
	.025	5.98	4.56	3.95	3.61	3.38	3.22	3.10	3.01	2.93	2.87
	.01	8.29	6.01	5.09	4.58	4.25	4.01	3.84	3.71	3.60	3.51
	.005	10.22	7.21	6.03	5.37	4.96	4.66	4.44	4.28	4.14	4.03
	.001	15.38	10.39	8.49	7.46	6.81	6.35	6.02	5.76	5.56	5.39

Appendix

12	15	20	24	30	40	60	120	240	∞	a	d.f.$_2$
1.47	1.46	1.45	1.44	1.43	1.42	1.42	1.41	1.40	1.40	.25	13
2.10	2.05	2.01	1.98	1.96	1.93	1.90	1.88	1.86	1.85	.10	
2.60	2.53	2.46	2.42	2.38	2.34	2.30	2.25	2.23	2.21	.05	
3.15	3.05	2.95	2.89	2.84	2.78	2.72	2.66	2.63	2.60	.025	
3.96	3.82	3.66	3.59	3.51	3.43	3.34	3.25	3.21	3.17	.01	
4.64	4.46	4.27	4.17	4.07	3.97	3.87	3.76	3.70	3.65	.005	
6.52	6.23	5.93	5.78	5.63	5.47	5.30	5.14	5.05	4.97	.001	
1.45	1.44	1.43	1.42	1.41	1.41	1.40	1.39	1.38	1.38	.25	14
2.05	2.01	1.96	1.94	1.91	1.89	1.86	1.83	1.81	1.80	.10	
2.53	2.46	2.39	2.35	2.31	2.27	2.22	2.18	2.15	2.13	.05	
3.05	2.95	2.84	2.79	2.73	2.67	2.61	2.55	2.52	2.49	.025	
3.80	3.66	3.51	3.43	3.35	3.27	3.18	3.09	3.05	3.00	.01	
4.43	4.25	4.06	3.96	3.86	3.76	3.66	3.55	3.49	3.44	.005	
6.13	5.85	5.56	5.41	5.25	5.10	4.94	4.77	4.69	4.60	.001	
1.44	1.43	1.41	1.41	1.40	1.39	1.38	1.37	1.36	1.36	.25	15
2.02	1.97	1.92	1.90	1.87	1.85	1.82	1.79	1.77	1.76	.10	
2.48	2.40	2.33	2.29	2.25	2.20	2.16	2.11	2.09	2.07	.05	
2.96	2.86	2.76	2.70	2.64	2.59	2.52	2.46	2.43	2.40	.025	
3.67	3.52	3.37	3.29	3.21	3.13	3.05	2.96	2.91	2.87	.01	
4.25	4.07	3.88	3.79	3.69	3.58	3.48	3.37	3.32	3.26	.005	
5.81	5.54	5.25	5.10	4.95	4.80	4.64	4.47	4.39	4.31	.001	
1.43	1.41	1.40	1.39	1.38	1.37	1.36	1.35	1.35	1.34	.25	16
1.99	1.94	1.89	1.87	1.84	1.81	1.78	1.75	1.73	1.72	.10	
2.42	2.35	2.28	2.24	2.19	2.15	2.11	2.06	2.03	2.01	.05	
2.89	2.79	2.68	2.63	2.57	2.51	2.45	2.38	2.35	2.32	.025	
3.55	3.41	3.26	3.18	3.10	3.02	2.93	2.84	2.80	2.75	.01	
4.10	3.92	3.73	3.64	3.54	3.44	3.33	3.22	3.17	3.11	.005	
5.55	5.27	4.99	4.85	4.70	4.54	4.39	4.23	4.14	4.06	.001	
1.41	1.40	1.39	1.38	1.37	1.36	1.35	1.34	1.33	1.33	.25	17
1.96	1.91	1.86	1.84	1.81	1.78	1.75	1.72	1.70	1.69	.10	
2.38	2.31	2.23	2.19	2.15	2.10	2.06	2.01	1.99	1.96	.05	
2.82	2.72	2.62	2.56	2.50	2.44	2.38	2.32	2.28	2.25	.025	
3.46	3.31	3.16	3.08	3.00	2.92	2.83	2.75	2.70	2.65	.01	
3.97	3.79	3.61	3.51	3.41	3.31	3.21	3.10	3.04	2.98	.005	
5.32	5.05	4.78	4.63	4.48	4.33	4.18	4.02	3.93	3.85	.001	
1.40	1.39	1.38	1.37	1.36	1.35	1.34	1.33	1.32	1.32	.25	18
1.93	1.89	1.84	1.81	1.78	1.75	1.72	1.69	1.67	1.66	.10	
2.34	2.27	2.19	2.15	2.11	2.06	2.02	1.97	1.94	1.92	.05	
2.77	2.67	2.56	2.50	2.44	2.38	2.32	2.26	2.22	2.19	.025	
3.37	3.23	3.08	3.00	2.92	2.84	2.75	2.66	2.61	2.57	.01	
3.86	3.68	3.50	3.40	3.30	3.20	3.10	2.99	2.93	2.87	.005	
5.13	4.87	4.59	4.45	4.30	4.15	4.00	3.84	3.75	3.67	.001	

TABLE 6 (continued) Percentage Points of the *F* Distribution (d.f.₂ between 19 and 24)

d.f.₂	*a*	1	2	3	4	5	6	7	8	9	10
19	.25	1.41	1.49	1.49	1.47	1.46	1.44	1.43	1.42	1.41	1.41
	.10	2.99	2.61	2.40	2.27	2.18	2.11	2.06	2.02	1.98	1.96
	.05	4.38	3.52	3.13	2.90	2.74	2.63	2.54	2.48	2.42	2.38
	.025	5.92	4.51	3.90	3.56	3.33	3.17	3.05	2.96	2.88	2.82
	.01	8.18	5.93	5.01	4.50	4.17	3.94	3.77	3.63	3.52	3.43
	.005	10.07	7.09	5.92	5.27	4.85	4.56	4.34	4.18	4.04	3.93
	.001	15.08	10.16	8.28	7.27	6.62	6.18	5.85	5.59	5.39	5.22
20	.25	1.40	1.49	1.48	1.47	1.45	1.44	1.43	1.42	1.41	1.40
	.10	2.97	2.59	2.38	2.25	2.16	2.09	2.04	2.00	1.96	1.94
	.05	4.35	3.49	3.10	2.87	2.71	2.60	2.51	2.45	2.39	2.35
	.025	5.87	4.46	3.86	3.51	3.29	3.13	3.01	2.91	2.84	2.77
	.01	8.10	5.85	4.94	4.43	4.10	3.87	3.70	3.56	3.46	3.37
	.005	9.94	6.99	5.82	5.17	4.76	4.47	4.26	4.09	3.96	3.85
	.001	14.82	9.95	8.10	7.10	6.46	6.02	5.69	5.44	5.24	5.08
21	.25	1.40	1.48	1.48	1.46	1.44	1.43	1.42	1.41	1.40	1.39
	.10	2.96	2.57	2.36	2.23	2.14	2.08	2.02	1.98	1.95	1.92
	.05	4.32	3.47	3.07	2.84	2.68	2.57	2.49	2.42	2.37	2.32
	.025	5.83	4.42	3.82	3.48	3.25	3.09	2.97	2.87	2.80	2.73
	.01	8.02	5.78	4.87	4.37	4.04	3.81	3.64	3.51	3.40	3.31
	.005	9.83	6.89	5.73	5.09	4.68	4.39	4.18	4.01	3.88	3.77
	.001	14.59	9.77	7.94	6.95	6.32	5.88	5.56	5.31	5.11	4.95
22	.25	1.40	1.48	1.47	1.45	1.44	1.42	1.41	1.40	1.39	1.39
	.10	2.95	2.56	2.35	2.22	2.13	2.06	2.01	1.97	1.93	1.90
	.05	4.30	3.44	3.05	2.82	2.66	2.55	2.46	2.40	2.34	2.30
	.025	5.79	4.38	3.78	3.44	3.22	3.05	2.93	2.84	2.76	2.70
	.01	7.95	5.72	4.82	4.31	3.99	3.76	3.59	3.45	3.35	3.26
	.005	9.73	6.81	5.65	5.02	4.61	4.32	4.11	3.94	3.81	3.70
	.001	14.38	9.61	7.80	6.81	6.19	5.76	5.44	5.19	4.99	4.83
23	.25	1.39	1.47	1.47	1.45	1.43	1.42	1.41	1.40	1.39	1.38
	.10	2.94	2.55	2.34	2.21	2.11	2.05	1.99	1.95	1.92	1.89
	.05	4.28	3.42	3.03	2.80	2.64	2.53	2.44	2.37	2.32	2.27
	.025	5.75	4.35	3.75	3.41	3.18	3.02	2.90	2.81	2.73	2.67
	.01	7.88	5.66	4.76	4.26	3.94	3.71	3.54	3.41	3.30	3.21
	.005	9.63	6.73	5.58	4.95	4.54	4.26	4.05	3.88	3.75	3.64
	.001	14.20	9.47	7.67	6.70	6.08	5.65	5.33	5.09	4.89	4.73
24	.25	1.39	1.47	1.46	1.44	1.43	1.41	1.40	1.39	1.38	1.38
	.10	2.93	2.54	2.33	2.19	2.10	2.04	1.98	1.94	1.91	1.88
	.05	4.26	3.40	3.01	2.78	2.62	2.51	2.42	2.36	2.30	2.25
	.025	5.72	4.32	3.72	3.38	3.15	2.99	2.87	2.78	2.70	2.64
	.01	7.82	5.61	4.72	4.22	3.90	3.67	3.50	3.36	3.26	3.17
	.005	9.55	6.66	5.52	4.89	4.49	4.20	3.99	3.83	3.69	3.59
	.001	14.03	9.34	7.55	6.59	5.98	5.55	5.23	4.99	4.80	4.64

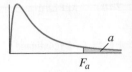

F_a

				d.f.$_1$								
12	**15**	**20**	**24**	**30**	**40**	**60**	**120**	**240**	**∞**	**a**	**d.f.$_2$**
1.40	1.38	1.37	1.36	1.35	1.34	1.33	1.32	1.31	1.30	**.25**	**19**
1.91	1.86	1.81	1.79	1.76	1.73	1.70	1.67	1.65	1.63	**.10**	
2.31	2.23	2.16	2.11	2.07	2.03	1.98	1.93	1.90	1.88	**.05**	
2.72	2.62	2.51	2.45	2.39	2.33	2.27	2.20	2.17	2.13	**.025**	
3.30	3.15	3.00	2.92	2.84	2.76	2.67	2.58	2.54	2.49	**.01**	
3.76	3.59	3.40	3.31	3.21	3.11	3.00	2.89	2.83	2.78	**.005**	
4.97	4.70	4.43	4.29	4.14	3.99	3.84	3.68	3.60	3.51	**.001**	
1.39	1.37	1.36	1.35	1.34	1.33	1.32	1.31	1.30	1.29	**.25**	**20**
1.89	1.84	1.79	1.77	1.74	1.71	1.68	1.64	1.63	1.61	**.10**	
2.28	2.20	2.12	2.08	2.04	1.99	1.95	1.90	1.87	1.84	**.05**	
2.68	2.57	2.46	2.41	2.35	2.29	2.22	2.16	2.12	2.09	**.025**	
3.23	3.09	2.94	2.86	2.78	2.69	2.61	2.52	2.47	2.42	**.01**	
3.68	3.50	3.32	3.22	3.12	3.02	2.92	2.81	2.75	2.69	**.005**	
4.82	4.56	4.29	4.15	4.00	3.86	3.70	3.54	3.46	3.38	**.001**	
1.38	1.37	1.35	1.34	1.33	1.32	1.31	1.30	1.29	1.28	**.25**	**21**
1.87	1.83	1.78	1.75	1.72	1.69	1.66	1.62	1.60	1.59	**.10**	
2.25	2.18	2.10	2.05	2.01	1.96	1.92	1.87	1.84	1.81	**.05**	
2.64	2.53	2.42	2.37	2.31	2.25	2.18	2.11	2.08	2.04	**.025**	
3.17	3.03	2.88	2.80	2.72	2.64	2.55	2.46	2.41	2.36	**.01**	
3.60	3.43	3.24	3.15	3.05	2.95	2.84	2.73	2.67	2.61	**.005**	
4.70	4.44	4.17	4.03	3.88	3.74	3.58	3.42	3.34	3.26	**.001**	
1.37	1.36	1.34	1.33	1.32	1.31	1.30	1.29	1.28	1.28	**.25**	**22**
1.86	1.81	1.76	1.73	1.70	1.67	1.64	1.60	1.59	1.57	**.10**	
2.23	2.15	2.07	2.03	1.98	1.94	1.89	1.84	1.81	1.78	**.05**	
2.60	2.50	2.39	2.33	2.27	2.21	2.14	2.08	2.04	2.00	**.025**	
3.12	2.98	2.83	2.75	2.67	2.58	2.50	2.40	2.35	2.31	**.01**	
3.54	3.36	3.18	3.08	2.98	2.88	2.77	2.66	2.60	2.55	**.005**	
4.58	4.33	4.06	3.92	3.78	3.63	3.48	3.32	3.23	3.15	**.001**	
1.37	1.35	1.34	1.33	1.32	1.31	1.30	1.28	1.28	1.27	**.25**	**23**
1.84	1.80	1.74	1.72	1.69	1.66	1.62	1.59	1.57	1.55	**.10**	
2.20	2.13	2.05	2.01	1.96	1.91	1.86	1.81	1.79	1.76	**.05**	
2.57	2.47	2.36	2.30	2.24	2.18	2.11	2.04	2.01	1.97	**.025**	
3.07	2.93	2.78	2.70	2.62	2.54	2.45	2.35	2.31	2.26	**.01**	
3.47	3.30	3.12	3.02	2.92	2.82	2.71	2.60	2.54	2.48	**.005**	
4.48	4.23	3.96	3.82	3.68	3.53	3.38	3.22	3.14	3.05	**.001**	
1.36	1.35	1.33	1.32	1.31	1.30	1.29	1.28	1.27	1.26	**.25**	**24**
1.83	1.78	1.73	1.70	1.67	1.64	1.61	1.57	1.55	1.53	**.10**	
2.18	2.11	2.03	1.98	1.94	1.89	1.84	1.79	1.76	1.73	**.05**	
2.54	2.44	2.33	2.27	2.21	2.15	2.08	2.01	1.97	1.94	**.025**	
3.03	2.89	2.74	2.66	2.58	2.49	2.40	2.31	2.26	2.21	**.01**	
3.42	3.25	3.06	2.97	2.87	2.77	2.66	2.55	2.49	2.43	**.005**	
4.39	4.14	3.87	3.74	3.59	3.45	3.29	3.14	3.05	2.97	**.001**	

TABLE 6 (continued)   Percentage Points of the *F* Distribution (d.f.$_2$ between 25 and 30)

d.f.$_2$	*a*	1	2	3	4	5	6	7	8	9	10
25	.25	1.39	1.47	1.46	1.44	1.42	1.41	1.40	1.39	1.38	1.37
	.10	2.92	2.53	2.32	2.18	2.09	2.02	1.97	1.93	1.89	1.87
	.05	4.24	3.39	2.99	2.76	2.60	2.49	2.40	2.34	2.28	2.24
	.025	5.69	4.29	3.69	3.35	3.13	2.97	2.85	2.75	2.68	2.61
	.01	7.77	5.57	4.68	4.18	3.85	3.63	3.46	3.32	3.22	3.13
	.005	9.48	6.60	5.46	4.84	4.43	4.15	3.94	3.78	3.64	3.54
	.001	13.88	9.22	7.45	6.49	5.89	5.46	5.15	4.91	4.71	4.56
26	.25	1.38	1.46	1.45	1.44	1.42	1.41	1.39	1.38	1.37	1.37
	.10	2.91	2.52	2.31	2.17	2.08	2.01	1.96	1.92	1.88	1.86
	.05	4.23	3.37	2.98	2.74	2.59	2.47	2.39	2.32	2.27	2.22
	.025	5.66	4.27	3.67	3.33	3.10	2.94	2.82	2.73	2.65	2.59
	.01	7.72	5.53	4.64	4.14	3.82	3.59	3.42	3.29	3.18	3.09
	.005	9.41	6.54	5.41	4.79	4.38	4.10	3.89	3.73	3.60	3.49
	.001	13.74	9.12	7.36	6.41	5.80	5.38	5.07	4.83	4.64	4.48
27	.25	1.38	1.46	1.45	1.43	1.42	1.40	1.39	1.38	1.37	1.36
	.10	2.90	2.51	2.30	2.17	2.07	2.00	1.95	1.91	1.87	1.85
	.05	4.21	3.35	2.96	2.73	2.57	2.46	2.37	2.31	2.25	2.20
	.025	5.63	4.24	3.65	3.31	3.08	2.92	2.80	2.71	2.63	2.57
	.01	7.68	5.49	4.60	4.11	3.78	3.56	3.39	3.26	3.15	3.06
	.005	9.34	6.49	5.36	4.74	4.34	4.06	3.85	3.69	3.56	3.45
	.001	13.61	9.02	7.27	6.33	5.73	5.31	5.00	4.76	4.57	4.41
28	.25	1.38	1.46	1.45	1.43	1.41	1.40	1.39	1.38	1.37	1.36
	.10	2.89	2.50	2.29	2.16	2.06	2.00	1.94	1.90	1.87	1.84
	.05	4.20	3.34	2.95	2.71	2.56	2.45	2.36	2.29	2.24	2.19
	.025	5.61	4.22	3.63	3.29	3.06	2.90	2.78	2.69	2.61	2.55
	.01	7.64	5.45	4.57	4.07	3.75	3.53	3.36	3.23	3.12	3.03
	.005	9.28	6.44	5.32	4.70	4.30	4.02	3.81	3.65	3.52	3.41
	.001	13.50	8.93	7.19	6.25	5.66	5.24	4.93	4.69	4.50	4.35
29	.25	1.38	1.45	1.45	1.43	1.41	1.40	1.38	1.37	1.36	1.35
	.10	2.89	2.50	2.28	2.15	2.06	1.99	1.93	1.89	1.86	1.83
	.05	4.18	3.33	2.93	2.70	2.55	2.43	2.35	2.28	2.22	2.18
	.025	5.59	4.20	3.61	3.27	3.04	2.88	2.76	2.67	2.59	2.53
	.01	7.60	5.42	4.54	4.04	3.73	3.50	3.33	3.20	3.09	3.00
	.005	9.23	6.40	5.28	4.66	4.26	3.98	3.77	3.61	3.48	3.38
	.001	13.39	8.85	7.12	6.19	5.59	5.18	4.87	4.64	4.45	4.29
30	.25	1.38	1.45	1.44	1.42	1.41	1.39	1.38	1.37	1.36	1.35
	.10	2.88	2.49	2.28	2.14	2.05	1.98	1.93	1.88	1.85	1.82
	.05	4.17	3.32	2.92	2.69	2.53	2.42	2.33	2.27	2.21	2.16
	.025	5.57	4.18	3.59	3.25	3.03	2.87	2.75	2.65	2.57	2.51
	.01	7.56	5.39	4.51	4.02	3.70	3.47	3.30	3.17	3.07	2.98
	.005	9.18	6.35	5.24	4.62	4.23	3.95	3.74	3.58	3.45	3.34
	.001	13.29	8.77	7.05	6.12	5.53	5.12	4.82	4.58	4.39	4.24

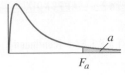

				d.f.₁								
12	**15**	**20**	**24**	**30**	**40**	**60**	**120**	**240**	**∞**	***a***	**d.f.₂**
1.36	1.34	1.33	1.32	1.31	1.29	1.28	1.27	1.26	1.25	.25	25
1.82	1.77	1.72	1.69	1.66	1.63	1.59	1.56	1.54	1.52	.10	
2.16	2.09	2.01	1.96	1.92	1.87	1.82	1.77	1.74	1.71	.05	
2.51	2.41	2.30	2.24	2.18	2.12	2.05	1.98	1.94	1.91	.025	
2.99	2.85	2.70	2.62	2.54	2.45	2.36	2.27	2.22	2.17	.01	
3.37	3.20	3.01	2.92	2.82	2.72	2.61	2.50	2.44	2.38	.005	
4.31	4.06	3.79	3.66	3.52	3.37	3.22	3.06	2.98	2.89	.001	
1.35	1.34	1.32	1.31	1.30	1.29	1.28	1.26	1.26	1.25	.25	26
1.81	1.76	1.71	1.68	1.65	1.61	1.58	1.54	1.52	1.50	.10	
2.15	2.07	1.99	1.95	1.90	1.85	1.80	1.75	1.72	1.69	.05	
2.49	2.39	2.28	2.22	2.16	2.09	2.03	1.95	1.92	1.88	.025	
2.96	2.81	2.66	2.58	2.50	2.42	2.33	2.23	2.18	2.13	.01	
3.33	3.15	2.97	2.87	2.77	2.67	2.56	2.45	2.39	2.33	.005	
4.24	3.99	3.72	3.59	3.44	3.30	3.15	2.99	2.90	2.82	.001	
1.35	1.33	1.32	1.31	1.30	1.28	1.27	1.26	1.25	1.24	.25	27
1.80	1.75	1.70	1.67	1.64	1.60	1.57	1.53	1.51	1.49	.10	
2.13	2.06	1.97	1.93	1.88	1.84	1.79	1.73	1.70	1.67	.05	
2.47	2.36	2.25	2.19	2.13	2.07	2.00	1.93	1.89	1.85	.025	
2.93	2.78	2.63	2.55	2.47	2.38	2.29	2.20	2.15	2.10	.01	
3.28	3.11	2.93	2.83	2.73	2.63	2.52	2.41	2.35	2.29	.005	
4.17	3.92	3.66	3.52	3.38	3.23	3.08	2.92	2.84	2.75	.001	
1.34	1.33	1.31	1.30	1.29	1.28	1.27	1.25	1.24	1.24	.25	28
1.79	1.74	1.69	1.66	1.63	1.59	1.56	1.52	1.50	1.48	.10	
2.12	2.04	1.96	1.91	1.87	1.82	1.77	1.71	1.68	1.65	.05	
2.45	2.34	2.23	2.17	2.11	2.05	1.98	1.91	1.87	1.83	.025	
2.90	2.75	2.60	2.52	2.44	2.35	2.26	2.17	2.12	2.06	.01	
3.25	3.07	2.89	2.79	2.69	2.59	2.48	2.37	2.31	2.25	.005	
4.11	3.86	3.60	3.46	3.32	3.18	3.02	2.86	2.78	2.69	.001	
1.34	1.32	1.31	1.30	1.29	1.27	1.26	1.25	1.24	1.23	.25	29
1.78	1.73	1.68	1.65	1.62	1.58	1.55	1.51	1.49	1.47	.10	
2.10	2.03	1.94	1.90	1.85	1.81	1.75	1.70	1.67	1.64	.05	
2.43	2.32	2.21	2.15	2.09	2.03	1.96	1.89	1.85	1.81	.025	
2.87	2.73	2.57	2.49	2.41	2.33	2.23	2.14	2.09	2.03	.01	
3.21	3.04	2.86	2.76	2.66	2.56	2.45	2.33	2.27	2.21	.005	
4.05	3.80	3.54	3.41	3.27	3.12	2.97	2.81	2.73	2.64	.001	
1.34	1.32	1.30	1.29	1.28	1.27	1.26	1.24	1.23	1.23	.25	30
1.77	1.72	1.67	1.64	1.61	1.57	1.54	1.50	1.48	1.46	.10	
2.09	2.01	1.93	1.89	1.84	1.79	1.74	1.68	1.65	1.62	.05	
2.41	2.31	2.20	2.14	2.07	2.01	1.94	1.87	1.83	1.79	.025	
2.84	2.70	2.55	2.47	2.39	2.30	2.21	2.11	2.06	2.01	.01	
3.18	3.01	2.82	2.73	2.63	2.52	2.42	2.30	2.24	2.18	.005	
4.00	3.75	3.49	3.36	3.22	3.07	2.92	2.76	2.68	2.59	.001	

TABLE 6 (continued) Percentage Points of the *F* Distribution (d.f.₂ at least 40)

d.f.₂	*a*	**1**	**2**	**3**	**4**	**5**	**6**	**7**	**8**	**9**	**10**
40	.25	1.36	1.44	1.42	1.40	1.39	1.37	1.36	1.35	1.34	1.33
	.10	2.84	2.44	2.23	2.09	2.00	1.93	1.87	1.83	1.79	1.76
	.05	4.08	3.23	2.84	2.61	2.45	2.34	2.25	2.18	2.12	2.08
	.025	5.42	4.05	3.46	3.13	2.90	2.74	2.62	2.53	2.45	2.39
	.01	7.31	5.18	4.31	3.83	3.51	3.29	3.12	2.99	2.89	2.80
	.005	8.83	6.07	4.98	4.37	3.99	3.71	3.51	3.35	3.22	3.12
	.001	12.61	8.25	6.59	5.70	5.13	4.73	4.44	4.21	4.02	3.87
60	.25	1.35	1.42	1.41	1.38	1.37	1.35	1.33	1.32	1.31	1.30
	.10	2.79	2.39	2.18	2.04	1.95	1.87	1.82	1.77	1.74	1.71
	.05	4.00	3.15	2.76	2.53	2.37	2.25	2.17	2.10	2.04	1.99
	.025	5.29	3.93	3.34	3.01	2.79	2.63	2.51	2.41	2.33	2.27
	.01	7.08	4.98	4.13	3.65	3.34	3.12	2.95	2.82	2.72	2.63
	.005	8.49	5.79	4.73	4.14	3.76	3.49	3.29	3.13	3.01	2.90
	.001	11.97	7.77	6.17	5.31	4.76	4.37	4.09	3.86	3.69	3.54
90	.25	1.34	1.41	1.39	1.37	1.35	1.33	1.32	1.31	1.30	1.29
	.10	2.76	2.36	2.15	2.01	1.91	1.84	1.78	1.74	1.70	1.67
	.05	3.95	3.10	2.71	2.47	2.32	2.20	2.11	2.04	1.99	1.94
	.025	5.20	3.84	3.26	2.93	2.71	2.55	2.43	2.34	2.26	2.19
	.01	6.93	4.85	4.01	3.53	3.23	3.01	2.84	2.72	2.61	2.52
	.005	8.28	5.62	4.57	3.99	3.62	3.35	3.15	3.00	2.87	2.77
	.001	11.57	7.47	5.91	5.06	4.53	4.15	3.87	3.65	3.48	3.34
120	.25	1.34	1.40	1.39	1.37	1.35	1.33	1.31	1.30	1.29	1.28
	.10	2.75	2.35	2.13	1.99	1.90	1.82	1.77	1.72	1.68	1.65
	.05	3.92	3.07	2.68	2.45	2.29	2.18	2.09	2.02	1.96	1.91
	.025	5.15	3.80	3.23	2.89	2.67	2.52	2.39	2.30	2.22	2.16
	.01	6.85	4.79	3.95	3.48	3.17	2.96	2.79	2.66	2.56	2.47
	.005	8.18	5.54	4.50	3.92	3.55	3.28	3.09	2.93	2.81	2.71
	.001	11.38	7.32	5.78	4.95	4.42	4.04	3.77	3.55	3.38	3.24
240	.25	1.33	1.39	1.38	1.36	1.34	1.32	1.30	1.29	1.27	1.27
	.10	2.73	2.32	2.10	1.97	1.87	1.80	1.74	1.70	1.65	1.63
	.05	3.88	3.03	2.64	2.41	2.25	2.14	2.04	1.98	1.92	1.87
	.025	5.09	3.75	3.17	2.84	2.62	2.46	2.34	2.25	2.17	2.10
	.01	6.74	4.69	3.86	3.40	3.09	2.88	2.71	2.59	2.48	2.40
	.005	8.03	5.42	4.38	3.82	3.45	3.19	2.99	2.84	2.71	2.61
	.001	11.10	7.11	5.60	4.78	4.25	3.89	3.62	3.41	3.24	3.09
∞	.25	1.32	1.39	1.37	1.35	1.33	1.31	1.29	1.28	1.27	1.25
	.10	2.71	2.30	2.08	1.94	1.85	1.77	1.72	1.67	1.63	1.60
	.05	3.84	3.00	2.60	2.37	2.21	2.10	2.01	1.94	1.88	1.83
	.025	5.02	3.69	3.12	2.79	2.57	2.41	2.29	2.19	2.11	2.05
	.01	6.63	4.61	3.78	3.32	3.02	2.80	2.64	2.51	2.41	2.32
	.005	7.88	5.30	4.28	3.72	3.35	3.09	2.90	2.74	2.62	2.52
	.001	10.83	6.91	5.42	4.62	4.10	3.74	3.47	3.27	3.10	2.96

Appendix

				d.f.$_1$							
12	**15**	**20**	**24**	**30**	**40**	**60**	**120**	**240**	**∞**	**a**	**d.f.$_2$**
1.31	1.30	1.28	1.26	1.25	1.24	1.22	1.21	1.20	1.19	**.25**	**40**
1.71	1.66	1.61	1.57	1.54	1.51	1.47	1.42	1.40	1.38	**.10**	
2.00	1.92	1.84	1.79	1.74	1.69	1.64	1.58	1.54	1.51	**.05**	
2.29	2.18	2.07	2.01	1.94	1.88	1.80	1.72	1.68	1.64	**.025**	
2.66	2.52	2.37	2.29	2.20	2.11	2.02	1.92	1.86	1.80	**.01**	
2.95	2.78	2.60	2.50	2.40	2.30	2.18	2.06	2.00	1.93	**.005**	
3.64	3.40	3.14	3.01	2.87	2.73	2.57	2.41	2.32	2.23	**.001**	
1.29	1.27	1.25	1.24	1.22	1.21	1.19	1.17	1.16	1.15	**.25**	**60**
1.66	1.60	1.54	1.51	1.48	1.44	1.40	1.35	1.32	1.29	**.10**	
1.92	1.84	1.75	1.70	1.65	1.59	1.53	1.47	1.43	1.39	**.05**	
2.17	2.06	1.94	1.88	1.82	1.74	1.67	1.58	1.53	1.48	**.025**	
2.50	2.35	2.20	2.12	2.03	1.94	1.84	1.73	1.67	1.60	**.01**	
2.74	2.57	2.39	2.29	2.19	2.08	1.96	1.83	1.76	1.69	**.005**	
3.32	3.08	2.83	2.69	2.55	2.41	2.25	2.08	1.99	1.89	**.001**	
1.27	1.25	1.23	1.22	1.20	1.19	1.17	1.15	1.13	1.12	**.25**	**90**
1.62	1.56	1.50	1.47	1.43	1.39	1.35	1.29	1.26	1.23	**.10**	
1.86	1.78	1.69	1.64	1.59	1.53	1.46	1.39	1.35	1.30	**.05**	
2.09	1.98	1.86	1.80	1.73	1.66	1.58	1.48	1.43	1.37	**.025**	
2.39	2.24	2.09	2.00	1.92	1.82	1.72	1.60	1.53	1.46	**.01**	
2.61	2.44	2.25	2.15	2.05	1.94	1.82	1.68	1.61	1.52	**.005**	
3.11	2.88	2.63	2.50	2.36	2.21	2.05	1.87	1.77	1.66	**.001**	
1.26	1.24	1.22	1.21	1.19	1.18	1.16	1.13	1.12	1.10	**.25**	**120**
1.60	1.55	1.48	1.45	1.41	1.37	1.32	1.26	1.23	1.19	**.10**	
1.83	1.75	1.66	1.61	1.55	1.50	1.43	1.35	1.31	1.25	**.05**	
2.05	1.94	1.82	1.76	1.69	1.61	1.53	1.43	1.38	1.31	**.025**	
2.34	2.19	2.03	1.95	1.86	1.76	1.66	1.53	1.46	1.38	**.01**	
2.54	2.37	2.19	2.09	1.98	1.87	1.75	1.61	1.52	1.43	**.005**	
3.02	2.78	2.53	2.40	2.26	2.11	1.95	1.77	1.66	1.54	**.001**	
1.25	1.23	1.21	1.19	1.18	1.16	1.14	1.11	1.09	1.07	**.25**	**240**
1.57	1.52	1.45	1.42	1.38	1.33	1.28	1.22	1.18	1.13	**.10**	
1.79	1.71	1.61	1.56	1.51	1.44	1.37	1.29	1.24	1.17	**.05**	
2.00	1.89	1.77	1.70	1.63	1.55	1.46	1.35	1.29	1.21	**.025**	
2.26	2.11	1.96	1.87	1.78	1.68	1.57	1.43	1.35	1.25	**.01**	
2.45	2.28	2.09	1.99	1.89	1.77	1.64	1.49	1.40	1.28	**.005**	
2.88	2.65	2.40	2.26	2.12	1.97	1.80	1.61	1.49	1.35	**.001**	
1.24	1.22	1.19	1.18	1.16	1.14	1.12	1.08	1.06	1.00	**.25**	**∞**
1.55	1.49	1.42	1.38	1.34	1.30	1.24	1.17	1.12	1.00	**.10**	
1.75	1.67	1.57	1.52	1.46	1.39	1.32	1.22	1.15	1.00	**.05**	
1.94	1.83	1.71	1.64	1.57	1.48	1.39	1.27	1.19	1.00	**.025**	
2.18	2.04	1.88	1.79	1.70	1.59	1.47	1.32	1.22	1.00	**.01**	
2.36	2.19	2.00	1.90	1.79	1.67	1.53	1.36	1.25	1.00	**.005**	
2.74	2.51	2.27	2.13	1.99	1.84	1.66	1.45	1.31	1.00	**.001**	

Source: Computed by P. J. Hildebrand.

Appendix

TABLE 7   Critical Values for the Wilcoxon Signed-rank Test ($n = 5(1)54$)

One-sided	Two-sided	$n = 5$	$n = 6$	$n = 7$	$n = 8$	$n = 9$	$n = 10$	$n = 11$	$n = 12$	$n = 13$	$n = 14$
$p = .1$	$p = .2$	2	3	5	8	10	14	17	21	26	31
$p = .05$	$p = .1$	0	2	3	5	8	10	13	17	21	25
$p = .025$	$p = .05$		0	2	3	5	8	10	13	17	21
$p = .01$	$p = .02$			0	1	3	5	7	9	12	15
$p = .005$	$p = .01$				0	1	3	5	7	9	12
$p = .0025$	$p = .005$					0	1	3	5	7	9
$p = .001$	$p = .002$						0	1	2	4	6

One-sided	Two-sided	$n = 15$	$n = 16$	$n = 17$	$n = 18$	$n = 19$	$n = 20$	$n = 21$	$n = 22$	$n = 23$	$n = 24$
$p = .1$	$p = .2$	36	42	48	55	62	69	77	86	94	104
$p = .05$	$p = .1$	30	35	41	47	53	60	67	75	83	91
$p = .025$	$p = .05$	25	29	34	40	46	52	58	65	73	81
$p = .01$	$p = .02$	19	23	27	32	37	43	49	55	62	69
$p = .005$	$p = .01$	15	19	23	27	32	37	42	48	54	61
$p = .0025$	$p = .005$	12	15	19	23	27	32	37	42	48	54
$p = .001$	$p = .002$	8	11	14	18	21	26	30	35	40	45

One-sided	Two-sided	$n = 25$	$n = 26$	$n = 27$	$n = 28$	$n = 29$	$n = 30$	$n = 31$	$n = 32$	$n = 33$	$n = 34$
$p = .1$	$p = .2$	113	124	134	145	157	169	181	194	207	221
$p = .05$	$p = .1$	100	110	119	130	140	151	163	175	187	200
$p = .025$	$p = .05$	89	98	107	116	126	137	147	159	170	182
$p = .01$	$p = .02$	76	84	92	101	110	120	130	140	151	162
$p = .005$	$p = .01$	68	75	83	91	100	109	118	128	138	148
$p = .0025$	$p = .005$	60	67	74	82	90	98	107	116	126	136
$p = .001$	$p = .002$	51	58	64	71	79	86	94	103	112	121

One-sided	Two-sided	$n = 35$	$n = 36$	$n = 37$	$n = 38$	$n = 39$	$n = 40$	$n = 41$	$n = 42$	$n = 43$	$n = 44$
$p = .1$	$p = .2$	235	250	265	281	297	313	330	348	365	384
$p = .05$	$p = .1$	213	227	241	256	271	286	302	319	336	353
$p = .025$	$p = .05$	195	208	221	235	249	264	279	294	310	327
$p = .01$	$p = .02$	173	185	198	211	224	238	252	266	281	296
$p = .005$	$p = .01$	159	171	182	194	207	220	233	247	261	276
$p = .0025$	$p = .005$	146	157	168	180	192	204	217	230	244	258
$p = .001$	$p = .002$	131	141	151	162	173	185	197	209	222	235

One-sided	Two-sided	$n = 45$	$n = 46$	$n = 47$	$n = 48$	$n = 49$	$n = 50$	$n = 51$	$n = 52$	$n = 53$	$n = 54$
$p = .1$	$p = .2$	402	422	441	462	482	503	525	547	569	592
$p = .05$	$p = .1$	371	389	407	426	446	466	486	507	529	550
$p = .025$	$p = .05$	343	361	378	396	415	434	453	473	494	514
$p = .01$	$p = .02$	312	328	345	362	379	397	416	434	454	473
$p = .005$	$p = .01$	219	307	322	339	355	373	390	408	427	445
$p = .0025$	$p = .005$	272	287	302	318	334	350	367	384	402	420
$p = .001$	$p = .002$	249	263	277	292	307	323	339	355	372	389

Source: Computed by P. J. Hildebrand.

TABLE 8 Percentage Points of the Studentized Range

t = number of treatment means

Error d.f.	α	2	3	4	5	6	7	8	9	10	11
5	.05	3.64	4.60	5.22	5.67	6.03	6.33	6.58	6.80	6.99	7.17
	.01	5.70	6.98	7.80	8.42	8.91	9.32	9.67	9.97	10.24	10.48
6	.05	3.46	4.34	4.90	5.30	5.63	5.90	6.12	6.32	6.49	6.65
	.01	5.24	6.33	7.03	7.56	7.97	8.32	8.61	8.87	9.10	9.30
7	.05	3.34	4.16	4.68	5.06	5.36	5.61	5.82	6.00	6.16	6.30
	.01	4.95	5.92	6.54	7.01	7.37	7.68	7.94	8.17	8.37	8.55
8	.05	3.26	4.04	4.53	4.89	5.17	5.40	5.60	5.77	5.92	6.05
	.01	4.75	5.64	6.20	6.62	6.96	7.24	7.47	7.68	7.86	8.03
9	.05	3.20	3.95	4.41	4.76	5.02	5.24	5.43	5.59	5.74	5.87
	.01	4.60	5.43	5.96	6.35	6.66	6.91	7.13	7.33	7.49	7.65
10	.05	3.15	3.88	4.33	4.65	4.91	5.12	5.30	5.46	5.60	5.72
	.01	4.48	5.27	5.77	6.14	6.43	6.67	6.87	7.05	7.21	7.36
11	.05	3.11	3.82	4.26	4.57	4.82	5.03	5.30	5.35	5.49	5.61
	.01	4.39	5.15	5.62	5.97	6.25	6.48	6.67	6.84	6.99	7.13
12	.05	3.08	3.77	4.20	4.52	4.75	4.95	5.12	5.27	5.39	5.51
	.01	4.32	5.05	5.50	5.84	6.10	6.32	6.51	6.67	6.81	6.94
13	.05	3.06	3.73	4.15	4.45	4.69	4.88	5.05	5.19	5.32	5.43
	.01	4.26	4.96	5.40	5.73	5.98	6.19	6.37	6.53	6.67	6.79
14	.05	3.03	3.70	4.11	4.41	4.64	4.83	4.99	5.13	5.25	5.36
	.01	4.21	4.89	5.32	5.63	5.88	6.08	6.26	6.41	6.54	6.66
15	.05	3.01	3.67	4.08	4.37	4.59	4.78	4.94	5.08	5.20	5.31
	.01	4.17	4.84	5.25	5.56	5.80	5.99	6.16	6.31	6.44	6.55
16	.05	3.00	3.65	4.05	4.33	4.56	4.74	4.90	5.03	5.15	5.26
	.01	4.13	4.79	5.19	5.49	5.72	5.92	6.08	6.22	6.35	6.46
17	.05	2.98	3.63	4.02	4.30	4.52	4.70	4.86	4.99	5.11	5.21
	.01	4.10	4.74	5.14	5.43	5.66	5.85	6.01	6.15	6.27	6.38
18	.05	2.97	3.61	4.00	4.28	4.49	4.67	4.82	4.96	5.07	5.17
	.01	4.07	4.70	5.09	5.38	5.60	5.79	5.94	6.08	6.20	6.31
19	.05	2.96	3.59	3.98	4.25	4.47	4.65	4.79	4.92	5.04	5.14
	.01	4.05	4.67	5.05	5.33	5.55	5.73	5.89	6.02	6.14	6.25
20	.05	2.95	3.58	3.96	4.23	4.45	4.62	4.77	4.90	5.01	5.11
	.01	4.02	4.64	5.02	5.29	5.51	5.69	5.84	5.97	6.09	6.19
24	.05	2.92	3.53	3.90	4.17	4.37	4.54	4.68	4.81	3.92	5.01
	.01	3.96	4.55	4.91	5.17	5.37	5.54	5.69	5.81	5.92	6.02
30	.05	2.89	3.49	3.85	4.10	4.30	4.46	4.60	4.72	4.82	4.92
	.01	3.89	4.45	4.80	5.05	5.24	5.40	5.54	5.65	5.76	5.85
40	.05	2.86	3.44	3.79	4.04	4.23	4.39	4.52	4.63	4.73	4.82
	.01	3.82	4.37	4.70	4.93	5.11	5.26	5.39	5.50	5.60	5.69
60	.05	2.83	3.40	3.74	3.98	4.16	4.31	4.44	4.55	4.65	4.73
	.01	3.76	4.28	4.59	4.82	4.99	5.13	5.25	5.36	5.45	5.53
120	.05	2.80	3.36	3.68	3.92	4.10	4.24	4.36	4.47	4.56	4.64
	.01	3.70	4.20	4.50	4.71	4.87	5.01	5.12	5.21	5.30	5.37
∞	.05	2.77	3.31	3.63	3.86	4.03	4.17	4.29	4.39	4.47	4.55
	.01	3.64	4.12	4.40	4.60	4.76	4.88	4.99	5.08	5.16	5.23

(continued on next page)

TABLE 8 (continued)   Percentage Points of the Studentized Range

t = number of treatment means

12	13	14	15	16	17	18	19	20	α	Error d.f.
7.32	7.47	7.60	7.72	7.83	7.93	8.03	8.12	8.21	.05	5
10.70	10.89	11.08	11.24	11.40	11.55	11.68	11.81	11.93	.01	
6.79	6.92	7.03	7.14	7.24	7.34	7.43	7.51	7.59	.05	6
9.48	9.65	9.81	9.95	10.08	10.21	10.32	10.43	10.54	.01	
6.43	6.55	6.66	6.76	6.85	6.94	7.02	7.10	7.17	.05	7
8.71	8.86	9.00	9.12	9.24	9.35	9.46	9.55	9.65	.01	
6.18	6.29	6.39	6.48	6.57	6.65	6.73	6.80	6.87	.05	8
8.18	8.31	8.44	8.55	8.66	8.76	8.85	8.94	9.03	.01	
5.98	6.09	6.19	6.28	6.36	6.44	6.51	6.58	6.64	.05	9
7.78	7.91	8.03	8.13	8.23	8.33	8.41	8.49	8.57	.01	
5.83	5.93	6.03	6.11	6.19	6.27	6.34	6.40	6.47	.05	10
7.49	7.60	7.71	7.81	7.91	7.99	8.08	8.15	8.23	.01	
5.71	5.81	5.90	5.98	6.06	6.13	6.20	6.27	6.33	.05	11
7.25	7.36	7.46	7.56	7.65	7.73	7.81	7.88	7.95	.01	
5.61	5.71	5.80	5.88	5.95	6.02	6.09	6.15	6.21	.05	12
7.06	7.17	7.26	7.36	7.44	7.52	7.59	7.66	7.73	.01	
5.53	5.63	5.71	5.79	5.86	5.93	5.99	6.05	6.11	.05	13
6.90	7.01	7.10	7.19	7.27	7.35	7.42	7.48	7.55	.01	
5.46	5.55	5.64	5.71	5.79	5.85	5.91	5.97	6.03	.05	14
6.77	6.87	6.96	7.05	7.13	7.20	7.27	7.33	7.39	.01	
5.40	5.49	5.57	5.65	5.72	5.78	5.85	5.90	5.96	.05	15
6.66	6.76	6.84	6.93	7.00	7.07	7.14	7.20	7.26	.01	
5.35	5.44	5.52	5.59	5.66	5.73	5.79	5.84	5.90	.05	16
6.56	6.66	6.74	6.82	6.90	6.97	7.03	7.09	7.15	.01	
5.31	5.39	5.47	5.54	5.61	5.67	5.73	5.79	5.84	.05	17
6.48	6.57	6.66	6.73	6.81	6.87	6.94	7.00	7.05	.01	
5.27	5.35	5.43	5.50	5.57	5.63	5.69	5.74	5.79	.05	18
6.41	6.50	6.58	6.65	6.73	6.79	6.85	6.91	6.97	.01	
5.23	5.31	5.39	5.46	5.53	5.59	5.65	5.70	5.75	.05	19
6.34	6.43	6.51	6.58	6.65	6.72	6.78	6.84	6.89	.01	
5.20	5.28	5.36	5.43	5.49	5.55	5.61	5.66	5.71	.05	20
6.28	6.37	6.45	6.52	6.59	6.65	6.71	6.77	6.82	.01	
5.10	5.18	5.25	5.32	5.38	5.44	5.49	5.55	5.59	.05	24
6.11	6.19	6.26	6.33	6.39	6.45	6.51	6.56	6.61	.01	
5.00	5.08	5.15	5.21	5.27	5.33	5.38	5.43	5.47	.05	30
5.93	6.01	6.08	6.14	6.20	6.26	6.31	6.36	6.41	.01	
4.90	4.98	5.04	5.11	5.16	5.22	5.27	5.31	5.36	.05	40
5.76	5.83	5.90	5.96	6.02	6.07	6.12	6.16	6.21	.01	
4.81	4.88	4.94	5.00	5.06	5.11	5.15	5.20	5.24	.05	60
5.60	5.67	5.73	5.78	5.84	5.89	5.93	5.97	6.01	.01	
4.71	4.78	4.84	4.90	4.95	5.00	5.04	5.09	5.13	.05	120
5.44	5.50	5.56	5.61	5.66	5.71	5.75	5.79	5.83	.01	
4.62	4.68	4.74	4.80	4.85	4.89	4.93	4.97	5.01	.05	∞
5.29	5.35	5.40	5.45	5.49	5.54	5.57	5.61	5.65	.01	

Source: This table is abridged from E. S. Pearson and H. O. Hartley, eds., *Biometrika Tables for Statisticians,* Vol. 1, 2nd ed. (New York: Cambridge University Press, 1958), Table 29. Reproduced with the kind permission of the editors and the trustees of *Biometrika.*

Books and Articles

Belsley, D. A., Kuh, E., and Welsch, R. E. (1980). *Regression Diagnostics: Identifying Influential Data and Sources of Collinearity.* New York: Wiley.

Cook, R. D., and Weisberg, S. (1982). *Residuals and Influence in Regression.* New York: Chapman and Hall.

Deming, W. E. (1986). *Out of the Crisis.* Cambridge, MA: MIT Center for Advanced Engineering Study.

Draper, N. R., and Smith, H. (1998). *Applied Regression Analysis,* 3rd ed. New York: Wiley.

Hollander, M., and Wolfe, D. (1999). *Nonparametric Statistical Methods,* 2nd ed. New York: Wiley.

Johnston, J. (1977). *Econometric Methods,* 2nd ed. New York: McGraw-Hill.

Mallows, C. L. (1973). "Some Comments on C_p." *Technometrics 15:* 661–675.

Ott, L., and Longnecker, M. (2001). *An Introduction to Statistical Methods and Data Analysis,* 5th ed. Pacific Grove, CA: Duxbury.

Peters, L. H., and Gray, J. B. (1994). *Business Cases in Statistical Decision-Making: Computer Based Applications.* Englewood Cliffs, NJ: Prentice-Hall.

Tukey, J. W. (1977). *Exploratory Data Analysis.* Reading, MA: Addison-Wesley.

Walton, M. (1986). *The Deming Management Method.* New York: Dodd, Mead.

Warner, S. L. (1965). "Randomized Response: A Survey Technique for Eliminating Evasive Answer Bias." *Journal of the American Statistical Association 60:* 63–69.

Welch, B. L. (1939). "The Significance of the Differences Between Two Means When the Population Variances Are Unequal." *Biometrika 29:* 350–362.

Statistical Program Packages

Excel

Microsoft Corporation (2003). *Microsoft Excel User's Guide.* Seattle WA: Microsoft Corporation.

Minitab

Minitab, Inc. (2004). *Minitab Reference Manual,* release 14 for Windows. State College, PA: Minitab, Inc.

JMP

Sall, J., Lehman, A., and Creighton, L. (2001). *JMP Start Statistics,* 2nd ed. Pacific Grove, CA: Duxbury.

References

ANSWERS TO SELECTED EXERCISES

Chapter 2

2.2 a. About 845, some variability, little skewness **b.** Suggests slightly skewed to the right **c.** Different width and midpoints; same shape

2.3 a. Right skew **b.** Histogram is also right-skewed

2.15 Right-skewed

2.19 a. Sample 1: 10, sample 2: 12 **b.** Sample 1: 4.16, sample 2: 2.92
c. Sample 1 has more variability.

2.22 Variation in operator skill and experience, in nature of calls, many other possibilities

2.23 a. 760 through 828 **b.** 85% rather than 68%; outliers or skewness may have inflated the standard deviation.

2.24 Outliers, including one extreme one, made the standard deviation large.

2.25 a. Increase the mean, decrease the standard deviation. **b.** Small increase in mean, large decrease in standard deviation

2.38 a. One possible result, using a class width of 5, is based on the following table:

Class	Midpoint	Frequency
7.5–12.4	10	10
12.5–17.4	15	0
17.5–22.4	20	5
22.5–27.4	25	0
27.5–32.4	30	10

The data are symmetric and trimodal (three-peaked).

b. Mean and median are both 20, by symmetry **c.** $s = 9.18$ **d.** 9 of 25 points, or 36%. Differs from 68% (Empirical Rule) because the data are not single-peaked.
e. 100%, compared to Empirical Rule 95%. Again, the data aren't mound-shaped.

2.44 In the last five days

2.45 In days 54 through 58

2.46 a. 0.60 to 2.40 **b.** Days 54 through 58

2.47 Also days 54 through 58

2.52 Nothing; qualitative data (mean and median are meaningless)

2.53 a. Codes 6, 7, and 9 **b.** Pay

2.54 Pay, clearly

2.60 **a.** About 50 or 60, we'd guess   **b.** About 1.0, we'd guess

2.61 **a.** Skewness makes it hard to guess MINPERBID; perhaps 50? BIDPERHR: a bit above 1.0, not 2.   **b.** No. BIDPERHR is much less skewed.

2.62 **a.** 62.462 and 1.432   **b.** No; 60/62.462 is less than 1.0, but the mean is 1.432.

Chapter 3

3.3 **a.** $P(C) = 541/723$ **b.** $P(\text{Serious}) = 453/723$
c. $P(\text{Dealer not fully reimbursed}) = 22/723$

3.4 **a.** $P(\text{Engine}|C) = 106/541$

b.

		Problem area				
		Engine	Transm.	Exhaust	Fit/finish	Other
Given brand	C	.196	.390	.124	.246	.044
	G	.115	.632	.088	.132	.033

The probabilities are not similar.

3.5 a. $P(\text{more than one problem}) = 92/609$ **b.** $P(\text{more than one problem}|C) = 71/453$

3.6

		Number of problems		
		1	2	3
Given brand	C	.843	.119	.038
	G	.865	.103	.032

The probabilities are nearly identical.

3.7 No; depends on how many sold

3.16 $P(\text{No substitute needed}) = (.6)(.6)(.5) = .18$

3.17 No; the reasons for absences (illness, bad weather) are common to all the schools.

3.21 Independence seems plausible. Form of order should not affect the chance of a return.

3.27 **a.** $P(\text{first-time bidder and satisfactory}) = .06$ by table or tree
b. $P(\text{satisfactory}) = .84$ **c.** $P(\text{first-time bidder}|\text{satisfactory}) = .071$

3.33 $P(\text{has disease}|\text{positive}) = .045$

3.38 **a.** $P(\text{MBA or undergrad degree}) = .45$ **b.** $P(\text{neither}) = .55$

3.39 $P(\text{exactly one degree}) = .37$

3.49 **a.** $P(F_1 \cap F_2) = .25$ **b.** $P(F_1 \cap F_2) = .25$ **c.** Independence of F_1 and F_2, reasonable for different customers, not for same customer

3.50 **a.** $P(F_1 \cap F_2) = .45$ **b.** $P(\text{not } F_1 \cap \text{not } F_2) = .45$ **c.** $P(\text{exactly one}) = .10$

3.51 $P(F_1|F_2) = .90$

3.56 $P(\text{equipment works}) \approx .610$

3.57 P(equipment works) = .605

3.58 P(equipment works) $\approx$ .604

3.61 P(decrease|not correct) = .160

3.62   **a.** mean 1.794, standard deviation 1.333. Empirical Rule doesn't work, because of skewness.   **b.** Hi outliers in each variable except TypeBank (qualitative)

3.65   **a.** mean 2.31, standard deviation 1.38   **b.** Meaningless; qualitative variable

3.66 P(bottom 1/3 $\cap$ not canceled) = .075

3.67   Not independent; independence would mean chance of cancellation is not affected by ratings.

3.68   **a.** P(excellent $\cap$ definite) = .0432   **b.** Independence; unreasonable. Probability is too low.

3.75   **a.** Separately, right-skewed. Together, bimodal.   **b.** means: 11.250, 12.972, and 32.138; medians: 10.75, 12.25, and 31. Each mean larger than median; right skew.

3.77   **a.** No obvious trend   **b.** No trend   **c.** Yes, except for one mean

3.78   Special cause, no real improvement

Chapter 4

4.4   **a.** The probability histogram has a mode at $y = 2$ and a long right tail.
b. $P(Y \leq 2) = .500$ **c.** $P(Y \geq 7) = .130$ **d.** $P(1 \leq Y \leq 5) = .71$

y:	0	1	2	3	4	5	6	7	8	9	10
$F_Y(y)$:	.10	.25	.50	.64	.73	.81	.87	.92	.96	.985	1.00

4.8   **a.** The histogram has a peak at $y = 3$ and a long tail to the right.   **b.** $E(Y) = 4.32$
c. The expected value is the balance point of the histogram. The right skew pulls it well above the mode, 3.

4.9   **a.** $\sigma_Y = 2.2798$ **b.** $\sigma_Y = \sqrt{23.86 - (4.32)^2} = 2.2798$

4.10 $P(2.04 \leq Y \leq 6.60) = .63$, differing from .68 because of skewness and discreteness of the histogram.

4.13   **a.** $\mu_Y = 3.97$ **b.** Var$(Y) = 7.0891$ **c.** Var$(Y) = 22.85 - (3.97)^2 = 7.0891$

4.14 $P(-1.35 \leq Y \leq 9.29) = .97$

4.18   **a.**

y:	0	1	2	3
$P_Y(y)$:	.343	.441	.189	.027

b. Same probability; independence. They seem reasonable.

4.19 $\mu_Y = 0.90$, Var$(Y) = 0.63$

4.20   Same expected value, higher variance

4.21   **a.** $P(X = 1, Y = 2) = P_{XY}(1, 2) = .055$ **b.** $P(X \leq 1, Y \leq 2) = .21$

c.

x:	1	2	3	4
$P_X(x)$:	.23	.27	.27	.23

y:	1	2	3	4
$P_Y(y)$:	.23	.27	.27	.23

d. No

4.27 **a.** $\mu_x = \mu_Y = 2$, by symmetry   **b.** $\sigma_X = 1.353$, $\sigma_Y = 1.285$

4.28 **a.** $\text{Cov}(X, Y) = -0.70$ **b.** $\rho_{XY} = -0.403$. Inverse relation, not independent.

4.29

x:	0	1	2	3	4
$E(Y|X = x)$:	2.778	2.359	2.000	1.641	1.222

The conditional expected value decreases as x increases.

4.30 **a.**

t:	0	1	2	3	4	5	6	7	8
$P_T(t)$:	.010	.035	.090	.205	.320	.205	.090	.035	.010

b. $\mu_T = 4$, $\sigma^2 = 2.08$

4.35 **a.**

y:	0	1	2	3
$P_Y(y)$:	.080	.314	.414	.192

b. $P(Y \geq 2) = .606$

c.

y:	0	1	2	3
$F_Y(y)$:	.080	.394	.808	1.000

4.36 $\mu_Y = 1.718$, $\sigma_Y = .8640$

4.37 **a.**

x:	0	100	150	200	250	300	350	450
$P_X(x)$:	.080	.020	.070	.224	.030	.096	.288	.192

b. $\mu_X = 280.8$, $\sigma_X = 128.69$

4.40 **a.**

x:	0	1	2	3	4	5	6
$F_Y(y)$:	.02	.15	.35	.65	.84	.99	1.00

b. $E(Y) = \mu_Y = 3.00$, $\sigma_Y = 1.33$
c. $P(\text{within 1 standard deviation of mean}) = .69$

Chapter 5

5.3 70 subsets

5.4 16 choices

5.5 **a.** $P_Y(3) = .2013$ **b.** $P_Y(2) = .3456$ **c.** $P_Y(12) = .2040$

5.7 **a.** $P(Y \geq 4) = .9840$ **b.** $P(Y > 4) = .9490$ **c.** $P(Y \leq 10) = .8723$
d. $P(Y > 16) = .0000$

5.8 $P(Y \leq 16) = .9840$, $P(Y < 16) = .9490$, same as previous exercise

5.12 **a.** Independence is questionable.   **b.** $P(Y \geq 85) = .9601$

5.13 $\mu_Y = 90$, $\sigma_Y = 3$

5.24 **a.** $P(Y \leq 10) = .7060$ **b.** $P(Y \geq 7) = .7933$ **c.** $P(7 \leq Y \leq 11) = .5963$
d. $\mu_Y = 9.0$, $\sigma_Y = 3.0$

5.25 Multihome fires, higher rate in winter?

5.31 **a.** $k = 2.33$ **b.** $k = 2.33$ **c.** $-k = -2.33$ **d.** $k = 1.00$ **e.** $k = 2.00$
f. $k = -1.645$

5.32 Same, to more decimal places

5.33 **a.** $(130 - 100)/15 = 2$ **b.** $z \geq -1.17$ **c.** $P(Y \leq 130) = .9772$,
$P(Y \geq 82.5) = .8790$ **d.** $P(Y > 106) = .3446$, $P(Y < 94) = .3446$,
$P(94 \leq Y \leq 104) = .3108$ **e.** $P(Y \leq 70) = .0228$, $P(Y \geq 130) = .0228$,
$P(70 < Y < 130) = .9544$

5.37 **a.** $P(Y > 7.40) = .2266$ **b.** $P(6.70 < Y < 7.50) = .6826$
c. $P(Y > 5.90) = .9987$

5.52 **a.** Binomial; $P(Y \leq 1) = .2794$ **b.** $P(Y \geq 4) = .2396$

5.53 **a.** $\binom{30}{14} = \dfrac{30!}{(14!)(16!)}$ **b.** $\binom{6}{5}\binom{24}{9}$ **c.** $P(Y \geq 5) = .059$

5.54 **a.** $P(Y = 1) = .3614$, $P(Y \leq 1) = .6626$ **b.** $E(Y) = 1.2$, $\sigma_Y = 1.095$

5.55 **a.** $P(Y \leq 72.8) = .6915$, $P(71.2 \leq Y \leq 72.8) = .3830$ **b.** $P(Y \geq 74.0) = .1056$
c. 75.7 cases

5.56 **a.** $P(Y > 73.0) = .2659$, "splitting the difference" of table values
b. $P(3 \text{ successes}) = .055$

5.59 **a.** $P(Y < 8) = .8666$ **b.** Possible dependence (noisy lines or the like)

5.60 $P(Y < 8) = .2203$

5.66 $P(\text{at least one}) = .3935$.

5.72 **a.** $E(Y) = 3.5$ **b.** $P(Y \geq 4) = .4634$ **c.** Nonclumping and independence;
independence wrong if a fire causes greater care

Chapter 6

6.2 Selection bias

6.5 Biased in favor of those holding many seats

6.7 $\mu_Y = 7$, $\sigma_Y = 3.5496$, $\mu_{\bar{Y}} = 7$, $\sigma_{\bar{Y}} = 1.2550$

6.10 **a.** $E(\bar{Y}) = 327$, $\sigma_{\bar{Y}} = 10.75$ **b.** $P(315 \leq \bar{Y} \leq 339) = .7372$

6.11 $k \approx 21$

6.16 **a.** $P(Y > 170) = .1469$ **b.** $P(\bar{Y} > 155 \text{ or } \bar{Y} < 135) = .1413$

6.17 **a.** Left-skewed **b.** No; Central Limit Theorem helps for sample mean.

6.20 **a.** $P(Y > 80) = .2743$ **b.** $P(\bar{Y} > 80) = .0287$

6.21 No; n isn't big enough for Central Limit Theorem to work well.

6.26 **a.** 20% or 10 beads **b.** Unbiased sampling

6.27 Small bias against red

6.32 **a.** $E(\overline{Y}) = 2.13$ **b.** $\sigma_{\overline{Y}} = 0.083$

6.33 Random sampling, including independence

6.34 Normal, by Central Limit Theorem

6.42 **a.** .8224, .8202, .7808, respectively **b.** Not good for $n = 2$ and 4, better for $n = 8$ **c.** .9224, .9024, .9334, respectively; fairly close to .95

6.43 **a.** Data right skewed **b.** mean = 3.623, standard deviation = 2.904. If data are regarded as a sample, divide by $n - 1$, not by n, with tiny effect. **c.** Result varies randomly. **d.** Much closer to normal, by Central Limit Theorem

6.44 Approximate standard error of the mean, should be about 0.65.

6.52 **a.**

x:	0	1	2	3	4	5	6	7	8	9	10
$P_X(x)$:	1/66	2/66	3/66	4/66	5/66	6/66	7/66	8/66	9/66	10/66	11/66

b. $E(X) = 6.667$, $\sigma_X = 2.687$ **c.** $P(X \geq 3) = 60/66 = .909$

6.53 **a.** $E(\overline{X}) = 6.667$, $\mathrm{Var}(\overline{X}) = 1.806$ **b.** Random sampling, specifically independence

6.54 $P(\overline{Y} > 7) = .0401$, good approximation by Central Limit Theorem

6.63 $P(Y \leq 3) = .0281$

6.64 Same probability of success for each (random) customer, independence, fixed number of customers

6.69 Poisson $P(Y \geq 10) = .2833$

6.70 No "clumps" of special handling orders, no dependence. Seems sensible to us.

Chapter 7

7.3 **a.** Unbiased **b.** Sample mean

7.6 **a.** Yes, by symmetry **b.** The mean

7.9 **a.** $22.23 \leq \mu \leq 25.74$ **b.** $21.68 \leq \mu \leq 26.29$

7.10 The interval is the result of a process that is correct 95% of the time.

7.11 Yes; data are near normal, so sampling distribution will be too.

7.13 $4.43 \leq \mu \leq 7.17$

7.14 Not too good, because of skewness and modest n

7.20 $.60 \leq \pi \leq .74$

7.21 Yes; $n\pi$ and $n(1 - \pi)$ are both large.

7.24 $n = 171$; $n = 96$

7.28 **a.** $n = 9604$ **b.** $n = 2827$

7.31 **a.** .05, .05, .80, .05, .05 **b.** Quite close

7.32   **a.** $39.841 \le \mu \le 73.898$ **b.** Right-skewed   **c.** Interval is very wide and unhelpful

7.33 $n = 252$

7.37   **a.** $1.071 \le \mu \le 1.189$ **b.** $1.074 \le \mu \le 1.186$ **c.** Almost identical

7.38   Slightly suspect for this n

7.49 $.516 \le \pi \le .604$, $.456 \le \pi \le .544$, $.416 \le \pi \le .504$, respectively

7.50   Confidence interval allows for sampling error. Bias is a valid concern.

7.58   **a.** $1.89 \le \mu \le 3.94$ **b.** A mean 2.5 per 500 feet is included. The goal *might* be being met.

7.59   Undercount; too low

7.60   **a.** Skewed right   **b.** Not obvious

7.63   **a.** $0.99371 \le \mu \le 1.00697$ **b.** No; the 95% refers to the chance that the true *mean* is included, not to individual values.

7.64   No indication of nonnormality

7.69   **a.** $n = 1692$ **b.** $n = 863$ **c.** The required n is just about cut in half.

7.70 $.030 \le \pi \le .057$, $.037 \le \pi \le .066$, $.076 \le \pi \le .114$, respectively

7.71   All *combinations* of meters don't have the same probability of being sampled; meters in the same sector are either not sampled or all sampled.

7.76   **a.** $n = 271$ **b.** No; would have to quadruple n

7.77   **a.** That only half its customers were satisfied!   **b.** $n = 174$

7.79   **a.** mean 5.52, standard deviation 2.60   **b.** $5.174 \le \mu \le 5.873$
c. Long run; 95% of such intervals will be correct.

7.80   **a.** Right-skewed, with outliers   **b.** No, by Central Limit Theorem

Chapter 8

8.1   **a.** The mean waiting time for the whole population of such patients

b. H_0: $\mu \le 30$, H_a: $\mu > 30$ **c.** $z = \dfrac{\bar{y} - 30}{10/\sqrt{22}} > 1.645$

8.2 $z = 3.7992$; reject H_0

8.3   For $\mu_a = 34$, $\beta = .4086$

8.4   Violates independence assumption

8.10   **a.** H_0: $\mu \ge 20,000$, H_a: $\mu < 20,000$ **b.** $z = -2.95$; $p = .0016$

8.11   Statistically significant, but small change

8.13   **a.** $t = 3.64 > 1.333$; support H_a **b.** $p < .005$; quite strongly supported

8.17   **a.** $\bar{d} = 1.8$, $s_d = 1.988858$ **b.** One-tailed $p = .00935$; support H_a

8.18 **a.** H_0: $\pi = .50$ **b.** Two-sided ("mu not = 0.5000") **c.** Yes; $p < \alpha$
d. No; p is an index of evidence, not importance.

8.20 Yes; expected frequencies far larger than 5

8.26 **a.** Retain H_0: $\mu = 4.62$; it's included in the interval. **b.** Not significant, but that doesn't prove it's exactly 4.62.

8.27 No, using Central Limit Theorem

8.31 **a.** $10,888.9 \leq \mu \leq 12,871.9$ **b.** The value 11,260 is well within the interval.

8.32 No; the interval is very wide.

8.33 Yes; increasing trend

8.37 Consumers would be misled only if ratings were too high.

8.38 $z = -2.02$; retain null hypothesis

8.39 $p = .0434$, two-tailed

8.40 No; retain that value, but that doesn't prove it's true. There's not enough evidence to reject it. In fact, we would reject that value at $\alpha = .05$.

8.41 $24.8 \leq \mu \leq 28.6$; retain $\mu = 28.2$, but we can only reliably assume that the mean is somewhere in this range.

8.45 **a.** H_a: $\mu < 20$; H_0: $\mu = 20$ or H_0: $\mu \geq 20$ **b.** z test, if σ is known
c. $z = -1.52$, which is not less than -1.645; retain null hypothesis

8.46 $p = .065$

8.47 Right-skewed; small n. Probabilities may be incorrect.

8.48 t test also retains H_0

8.53 **a.** H_0: $\pi = .50$ **b.** $z = -1.50$, which is not smaller than (more negative than) -1.645 **c.** No; we have not proved that the null hypothesis is true.

8.54 Yes; expected numbers of wins and losses are each 8, given H_0.

8.65 **a.** Mean 5.04, median 4, standard deviation 4.02; right-skewed data
b. Right skewed, in any plot

8.66 **a.** $t = -1.16$; retain null hypothesis **b.** One-tailed p-value $= .126$

8.67 **a.** $240.4 \leq \mu \leq 266.2$ **b.** No; the plot is a line, indicating the data came from a normal population.

8.68 Yes; not included in interval

8.69 $z = 4.62 > 2.58$; reject null hypothesis

8.70 $p = .0000$ to four decimal places

8.71 $239.6 \leq \mu \leq 267.0$; p-value .0000; reject null hypothesis

8.72 Yes; not in interval

8.73 Median interval is wider, so mean is more efficient. Data are normally distributed.

8.84 $.102 \le \pi \le .229$

8.85 **a.** $n = 590$ **b.** $n = 1068$

8.86 Yes; expected frequencies are much larger than needed for this purpose.

8.87 Biased in favor of large accounts

8.88 **a.** $5093 \le \mu \le 5669$ **b.** Biased sample; skewness is not crucial by Central Limit Theorem.

8.95 **a.** T, C, F, T **b.** False; quadruple the sample size

Chapter 9

9.1 **a.** $-1.26 \le \mu_1 - \mu_2 \le 0.56$ for the equal-variance analysis, $-1.28 \le \mu_1 - \mu_2 \le 0.58$ for the unequal-variance case. Negligible difference. **b.** No; 0 is contained in the 95% confidence interval.

9.2 Equal variance assumption is suspect, but it doesn't matter here.

9.4 **a.** Unequal variances and sample sizes; t' should be better in that the claimed α probability should be more accurate. **b.** Yes; the frequency for t_{pooled} is seriously wrong.

9.6 **a.** Pooled StDev = 9.38 **b.** $5.69 \le \mu_A - \mu_B \le 21.31$ **c.** Yes; 0.0 is not in the interval. **d.** $5.12 \le \mu_A - \mu_B \le 21.88$; yes; 0.0 is not in the interval.

9.14 **a.** $z = -1.66$; retain null hypothesis **b.** $p = .0970$

9.15 Yes; data (and presumably populations) are right-skewed.

9.16 **a.** $t = 4.05, p = .0012 < \alpha$; support the research hypothesis. **b.** $1.960 \le \mu_{diff} \le 4.974$; 0 not included **c.** Test statistic = 98.0; $p = .005$; reject H_0 **d.** Slightly less conclusive, but both reject H_0. **e.** Slight left-skewness, but not severe

9.17 **a.** $t = 0.75, p = .46$; can't come close to rejecting H_0 **b.** Yes; tests are much more conclusive.

9.18 $p = .0129 < \alpha = .10$; reject null hypothesis

9.27 **a.** $.0785 \le \pi_1 - \pi_2 \le .1467$ **b.** One-tailed test; $z = 6.47$, reject H_0

9.28 $p \approx .0000$; very conclusive evidence

9.29 $t = 2.31, p = .021$; support the research hypothesis. We have reasonably strong evidence of a real difference in population proportions.

9.30 $.014 \le \pi_1 - \pi_2 \le .167$ does not include .000.

9.33 **a.** $z = 1.64$; retain null hypothesis **b.** Not proved!

9.34 $-.039 \le \pi_1 - \pi_2 \le .439$; we are reasonably sure that supplier 1 produces somewhere between 3.9% fewer and 43.9% more passing motors(!)

9.37 **a.** 7.50, 11.25, and 6.25, respectively **b.** $\chi^2 = 4.493$; "good fit" but small n

9.38   **a.** $\chi^2 = 44.93$; "bad fit" with bigger n **b.** Larger n and lower probability of a false negative error

9.41   **a.**

	Under 30	30-39	40-49	50 or Over	Total
			Age		
Promoted	16.0	22.4	25.6	16.0	80
Not promoted	34.0	47.6	54.4	34.0	170
Total	50	70	80	50	250

b. $(r-1)(c-1) = 3$ **c.** $\chi^2 = 13.025 > 7.81$; there is evidence of a relation.

9.42 $.001 < p < .005$

9.43   **a.** No; χ^2 is very small.   **b.** Combining categories hid the relation.

9.48   **a.** $t = 0.80$, $p = .43$ (but two-tailed); can't support H_a **b.** Sum of ranks in first sample $= 162$, $z = 0.69$; can't support H_a

9.49   Little evidence; doesn't matter

9.50   For t, the one-tailed $p = .215$; for z, $p = .2451$.

9.51   **a.** $t = 3.15$; support research hypothesis   **b.** $p < .10$ whether one- or two-tailed; support H_a

9.52   Differences heavy-tailed, suggesting signed rank. Same conclusion either way.

9.53   One-tailed $p = .0046$ (t); $p = .0085$ (signed rank)

9.54   Controls for variability among plots. Choose plots for full variety of conditions.

9.65 $\chi^2 = 72.521 > 20.09$; clear evidence of some relation

9.67   **a.** $p = .936$; not detectable   **b.** No evidence that *means* differ, but other characteristics still may.

9.68   **a.** $p < .00005$ **b.** Source 1 is definitely lower in variability.

9.74   **a.** Plots slightly right-skewed
        b. 95% confidence intervals
               mu1 − mu2: $(-11.3385, -0.567797)$ assuming equal variances
               mu1 − mu2: $(-11.3501, -0.556203)$ not assuming equal variances
               In each case, reject the null hypothesis.
c. Virtually identical

9.75   **a.** $p = .031$ for both tests   **b.** $p = .0242$ **c.** Rank sum slightly more conclusive, all believable

Chapter 10

10.7   **a.** Right skew, not normal   **b.** Not too badly, by Central Limit Theorem

10.8   **a.** By hand or computer, no evident trend or cycles   **b.** Independence

10.9   **a.** Yes; $p = .0007$ **b.** Even more conclusive

10.13   **a.** No; F is much less than tabled values.   **b.** Virtually no such evidence

10.14   a. Right skew   **b.** Normality assumption   **c.** Still not conclusive, though better

10.17   Mean for policy 2 differs from means for policies 1 and 3

10.18   Potential for bias; use a random mechanism

10.25   a. Grand mean = 1.4   **b.** Row effects = .3, .4, −.7 respectively; column effects = .2, 0, −.2, 0 respectively

10.26 F = 24.67, 1.60, 0.33 respectively. Only the Plan effect is significant.

10.27   b. Some interaction; profiles aren't parallel.   **c.** Test says the interaction could have occurred by random variation.

10.28   Plans A and C are significantly different, as are plans B and C. A and B are not.

10.29   a. No; mixture 1 has a much higher score than mixture 3 at low altitudes, where most people live.   **b.** Major interaction

10.30   a. F = 5.82, $p < .001$; significant even for $\alpha = .001$ **b.** The relative quality of mixtures depends on the altitude.   **c.** Not very meaningful at all

10.36   a. Treatments: mixtures. Blocks: investigators.   **b.** Control for variation among investigators

10.37   a. Investigator effect not significant; mixture effect highly significant with tiny p-value   **b.** Mixture 2 appears to be best (highest); it is clearly different than any other mean, by Tukey's method.

10.38   Not significant. If present, it would indicate systematic differences among investigators, hence some lack of accuracy.

10.46   a. F = 23.10   **b.** Yes; $F > 5.42$ **c.** p = .0000 (less than .00005)

10.47   a. Chi-square = 18.84   **b.** Yes; p = .000 < .01.

10.48   a. No obvious skewness, no outliers (and unequal n's); but the result is very clear   **b.** Slight problem of unequal variability   **c.** No; same, clear result

10.49   Use a computer package, because of unbalanced sample sizes.

10.50   a. Irrelevant; we know they differ. F = 122.58, p = .000   **b.** F = 10.66   **c.** Yes; p = .000

10.51   The mean for appraiser 2 differs significantly from each of the other means. There are no other significant differences.

10.52   a. Not close; F = 0.34; p = .797   **b.** Crucial to control for variation in home prices, which would otherwise mask the appraiser differences

10.59   Yes; F = 17.08, p = .000(< .05)

10.60   Same result; H = 28.32; p = .000(< .05)

10.61   Design 3 appears highest, and is significantly different from each of the other means.

10.65   **a.** Right skewness, with several outliers   **b.** $F = 1.849$, $p = .085$

10.66   **a.** $H = 15.080$, $p = .035$ **b.** Kruskal–Wallis is more conclusive, because less sensitive to skewness and outliers

10.71   **a.** $-11.70 \le \mu_1 - \mu_2 \le 2.90$ **b.** No; 0 is included in the interval.
c. Samples are paired by tester; not independent.

10.72   **a.** $2.15 \le \mu_d \le 6.65$ **b.** Yes; 0 is not included in the interval.
c. $t = 3.95 > 2.0xx$, $p = .000$ **d.** No evident violation

10.73   Yes; $p = .001$

10.74   Similar; t slightly more conclusive.

10.75   Pairing helped greatly, by controlling for rater variability.

10.86 $F = 0.47 < 3.2$; not close to significant. (*Note:* Significant interaction renders this test meaningless.)

10.87   No significant differences

10.88   Serious interaction; program 1 seems best for experienced preparers.

10.94   **a.** $-.256 \le \pi_1 - \pi_2 \le .016$ **b.** Fail to reject H_0

10.95 $z = -1.73$; fail to reject H_0

10.96   Violates independence assumption

10.97 $\chi^2 = 9.29$, $p = .026$

10.98   No other evident violations

Chapter 11

11.1   **a.** slope $\approx (25 - 16)/6 = 1.5$ **b.** slope $\approx (24 - 15)/0.9 = 10$ **c.** vs. $\log x$

11.2   **a.** $\hat{y} = 14.3 + 1.47\,x$ **b.** $s = 1.346$

11.3   **a.** $\hat{y} = 14.9 + 10.5 \log x$ **b.** $s = 1.131$

11.4   Smaller in the $\log x$ model, indicating that model fits better

11.10   **a.** Linear with slight bend at the high end   **b.** Two highest-income points have high leverage; outlier from line has high influence   **c.** $\hat{y} = 47.15 + 1.8026x$
d. Comparing two purchasers, the one with one thousand dollars per year higher income is predicted to spend 1.80 thousand dollars more on a house. The intercept isn't meaningful; 0 income is not within the data.   **e.** $s = 14.445$ **f.** Large change; the omitted point was a high-influence outlier.

11.15   **a.** Relation linear, one extreme observation, no violations evident
b. $\hat{y} = 99.777 + 51.9178x$; $s_\epsilon = 12.2064$ **c.** $50.695 \le \beta_1 \le 53.141$ **d.** $t = 88.53$
e. $p = .000$, two-tailed. One-tailed will also be .000.   **f.** $F = 7837.25$, $p = .000$
g. Identical, because $F = t^2$ in simple regression

11.18   **a.** $\hat{y} = 203.613$ **b.** $198.902 \le E(Y_{n+1}) \le 208.323$

11.19 No; 2.0 is close to the average of the x data.

11.20 **a.** $178.169 \leq Y_{n+1} \leq 229.057$ **b.** Yes; 250 is far above the interval.

11.23 $r_{yx} = .9721$

11.24 **a.** $t = 13.134 > 1.812$; reject H_0 **b.** Identical

11.26 **a.** Variation in intensity accounts for $r_{yx}^2 = (.956)^2 = .914$, or 91.4% of the variation in awareness.   **b.** Increasing but not linear

11.31 **a.** Increasing, linear plot   **b.** $\hat{y} = 2.0252 + 2.3498x$ **c.** $\hat{y} = 51.37$

11.32 **a.** $s_{\epsilon} = 1.9583$ **b.** All within $\pm 2s_{\epsilon}$

11.38 **a.** Predicted Gallons $= 140.07 + 0.61895$ Miles   **b.** $r_{yx}^2 = .9420$, so $r_{yx} = .9706$; 94.2% reduction in prediction error by using Miles   **c.** No; longer flights obviously take more fuel.

11.39 **a.** $\hat{y} = 759.03$; $733.68 \leq E(Y_{n+1}) \leq 784.38$ **b.** $678.33 \leq Y_{n+1} \leq 839.73$; 628 is not in this interval and is exceptionally low.   **c.** $\hat{\beta}_1$ is the usage per mile; $\hat{\beta}_0$ is the initial usage for taking off.

11.44 **a.** Negative slope   **b.** No; slope is positive

11.45 One very high-influence outlier twists the line.

11.46 **a.** The point had very high influence.   **b.** Yes; slope is now negative.

11.47 Changed sign, larger in magnitude

11.51 **a.** $r_{yx} = -.7707$ **b.** $\hat{y} = 141.525 - 12.8926x$. The intercept is the predicted sales for a ZIP code with 0 density (no homes)! An area with 1 extra home per acre is predicted to have sales that are 12.8926 lower.   **c.** $s_{\epsilon} = 21.74$; about 95% of ZIP codes will be predicted within ± 43.5.

11.52 **a.** $t = -6.63$; highly conclusive   **b.** $-16.87 \leq \beta_1 \leq -8.92$

11.53 Evident curve in the plot

11.54 **a.** Typical lot size   **b.** Much nearer to linear   **c.** $r_{yx} = .9517$

Chapter 12

12.5 **a.** $\hat{y} = 50.020 + 6.644\text{Cat1} + 7.314\text{Cat2} - 1.2314\text{Cat1Sq} - .7724\text{Cat1Cat2} - 1.1755\text{Cat2Sq}$ **b.** SS(Residual) $= 71.489$, $s_{\epsilon} = 2.25972$

12.6 **a.** $R^2 = .862$ **b.** SS(Model) would be 305.807; R^2 would be .5885.

12.7 **a.** $F = 22.28$ **b.** $F > 4.94$, or $p = .000$; reject H_0 **c.** $t = 4.84$
d. $p = .000$; support the research hypothesis   **e.** Conclude that Promotion has additional predictive value, given the other variables.

12.8 As before, $p = .000$, two-tailed

12.9 Only Promotion has been shown to have "last predictor in" predictive value.

12.14 **a.** $R_{y.x_3}^2 = .205$ **b.** $R_{y.x_1x_2x_3}^2 = .797$ **c.** $F = 24.84$; reject H_0 that BUSIN and COMPET have no additional predictive value, once INCOME is used.

12.17 $21.792 \le Y_{n+1} \le 44.208$. Predicting when w is low but v is high violates the strong positive correlation between them, hence the extrapolation warning.

12.22 **a.** $\hat{y} = -16.82 + 1.4702X1 + 0.9948X2 - 0.02400X1X2 - 0.01030X2SQ + .0002496X1X2SQ$; $s_\epsilon = 3.3901$ **b.** $t = -1.01, p = .324$; not significant

12.23 **a.** Complete model as 12.22a, reduced model: $\hat{y} = .840 + 1.01582X1 + .05582X2$
b. Incremental $F = 0.867, p > .25$

12.29 **a.** $\hat{y} = 18.678 + .5420\text{Senior} + 1.2074\text{Sex} + 8.7779\text{RankD1} + 4.4211\text{RankD2} + 2.7165\text{RankD3} + 0.9225\text{Doct}$ **b.** All else equal, a male (Sex = 1) is predicted to have a salary 1.2074 thousand dollars higher than a female (Sex = 0).   **c.** All else equal, a full professor (RankD1 = 1) is predicted to have a salary 1.2074 thousand dollars higher than a lecturer (all Rank variables = 0).

12.30 **a.** $t = 1.1339, p = .1342$; not significant   **b.** Not proved, *if* men and women have the same seniority, rank, and doctorate levels

12.31 **a.** $F = 64.646$ **b.** Implausible; it says that none of the predictors matters to salary.   **c.** $F > 3.71; p \approx 0$; reject the implausible hypothesis

12.32 **a.** $R^2 = .9403$ **b.** $F = 0.760$; retain the null hypothesis

12.33 **a.** Predicted Salary = $25.5378 + 0.00389372\text{Employees} + 0.0957243\text{Margin} + 0.216348\text{IPCost}$ **b.** $F = 13.10, p \approx 0$. Yes, conclusive   **c.** All of them

12.34 **a.** $R^2 = .3842$ **b.** $R^2 = .0358$ **c.** $F = 17.82$; strong evidence that these predictors do add predictive value

12.35 Not bad; largest correlation of x values is .5315

Chapter 13

13.4 **a.** Div2 and Div3; we need two dummies to identify the three divisions.
b. -4.0066 is the difference in expected sales between division 1 and division 2 for a fixed forecast. 0.9158 is the difference in expected sales between division 1 and division 3 for a fixed forecast.   **c.** $t = 5.67$ for division 2; $t = 1.25$ for division 3. Division 2 dummy has been shown to have predictive value.

13.5 We need regression done without the dummy variables.

13.6 **a.** Forecast value and division are useless predictors.   **b.** $F = 109.468; p = 14$ zeros after the decimal; reject H_0

13.7 **a.** Should be Actual = $0.0000 + 1.0000$ Forecast. Slope should equal 1.0000.
b. $1.18 \le \beta_1 \le 1.52$ doesn't include 1.0000.

13.13 **a.** No collinearity at all   **b.** None; the values are completely balanced.

13.14 Nothing severe; perhaps slight nonlinearity vs. CHILL

13.15 **a.** By .01 (.914 vs. .904)   **b.** $F = 1.427$; retain the null hypothesis.
c. No; both p-values are greater than .05.

13.18 **a.** REPEL, KNIFE, CHILL, MELT, SPEED   **b.** REPEL, KNIFE, CHILL, MELT, SPEED   **c.** Same

13.19 $F = 3.113 < 3.35$; retain H_0

13.23 **a.** As Mileage increases, all else equal, Sales tend to increase. An increase in any of the other variables (holding the remaining ones constant) predicts a decrease in Sales. **b.** $s_\epsilon = 47.54$ **c.** Yes; the statistic equals 0.80, much lower than 1.50. **d.** Yes; there is a clear cyclic pattern.

13.24 **a.** The coefficient of interest rate is still negative but smaller in magnitude. The coefficient of car price became positive but small. (Note that autocorrelation disappeared.) **b.** $s_\epsilon = 37.34$ **c.** It actually decreased. Often it will increase because autocorrelation biases s_ϵ to be too low.

13.25 **a.** Installations in previous month, and installations in 4 preceding months **b.** No indication of an "it depends" situation **c.** Yes; support costs may increase at a decreasing rate as installations increase.

13.26 **a.** Yes, large negative ones at months 16 and 17 **b.** Yes, especially in the early months

13.27 Yes, there is some degree of fan shape.

13.28 **a.** BCURRSQ, ACURRSQ, BPREV, APREV, BPREC4, BCURR **b.** $.1463 = .9777 - .8314$

13.31 **a.** No; no evident cycles in the sequence plot **b.** No severe fan shape in the plot vs. fitted values

13.33 **a.** Standard deviation 3.25 **b.** A bit smaller **c.** Yes; most errors will be predicted with an error less than 7.

13.46 **a.** Serious collinearity; all X correlations are bigger than .8. **b.** All variables are quantitative; no dummies are needed. The data aren't a time series, so lags are not useful. **c.** $\hat{y} = 18.402 + 4.248$ skilled $+ 2.493$ helpers $+ 6.644$ vehicles; $R^2 = .838$.

13.47 **a.** Slight fan shape, no other problems **b.** At least one high-leverage, high-influence outlier. There is a suggestion of a curved relation. **c.** Data aren't a time series.

13.48 **a.** The regression equation predicts the natural logarithm of 'sqft' as $3.013 + 0.390$ log(skilled) $+ 0.206$ log(helpers) $+ 0.252$ log(vehicles). **b.** No evident curves **c.** Predicted sqft $= e^{3.013}(\text{skilled})^{.390}(\text{helpers})^{.206}(\text{vehicles})^{.252}$

13.49 **a.** $\hat{y} = 1,161 + 34.562x$ **b.** Variable direct cost per additional direct labor hour **c.** Fixed cost, but an extrapolation **d.** $s_\epsilon = 3462.08$

13.50 $r_{yx} = .898$; $r^2 = .807$

13.51 **a.** SE Coef $= 3.524$ **b.** $27.19 \le \beta_1 \le 41.74$

13.52 No; surely labor hours affect cost. Reject H_0; $t = 9.81$

13.53 **a.** $\hat{y} = 1,161 + 34.562(890) = 31,921$ **b.** $\hat{y} = 1,161 + 34.562(436) = 16,230$ **c.** The 436 prediction; 890 is an extrapolation

13.54 The constant-variance assumption is shaky. Prediction intervals will be wrong. Tests and intervals may be slightly off.

13.62 Severe collinearity among Leading, Rate, and Month. No evident nonlinearity or outliers.

13.63   **a.** $F = 263.90, p = .000$ **b.** Reject H_0 for Supply and Rate ($p < .01$) but retain for Leading (p large).

13.64 $s_\epsilon = 0.03957$ is much lower than the Spread standard deviation, indicating good predictive value.

13.65   **a.** Cyclic plot indicates autocorrelation   **b.** Durbin–Watson statistic is 0.81, much less than 1.50, indicating autocorrelation.   **c.** Overoptimism of tests and about predictability

13.66   **a.** Coefficients changed little   **b.** Tests similar; more believable in this model **c.** Yes; Durbin-Watson $= 2.30$. Also, the VIF numbers are much smaller, indicating elimination of the collinearity problem.

13.67   No evident cycles and no autocorrelation, agreeing with the Durbin–Watson results.

13.68   Correlations among independent variables are much lower, confirming the VIF results.

13.84   **a.** No (linear) relation, contradicting the exercise statement **b.** $t = 20.35, p = .000$

13.85 $s = 2.435$; about 95% of the prediction errors will be within 4.870 in magnitude.

13.86   **a.** Yes; there's a clear curve in the plot and LOWESS.   **b.** Nothing far from the pattern

13.87   Modestly; R^2 is larger, s_ϵ smaller.

Index